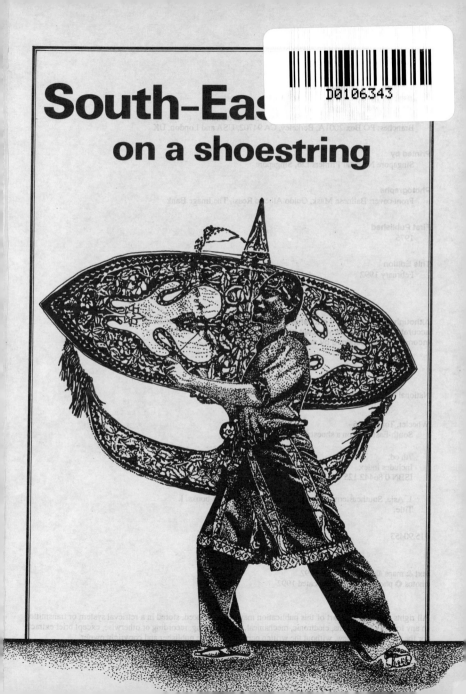

South-Eas[t]
on a shoestring

South-East Asia on a shoestring

7th edition

Published by
  Lonely Planet Publications
  Head Office: PO Box 617, Hawthorn, Vic 3122, Australia
  Branches: PO Box 2001A, Berkeley, CA 94702, USA and London, UK

Printed by
  Singapore National Printers Ltd, Singapore

Photographs
  Front cover: Balinese Mask, Guido Alberto Rossi, The Image Bank

First Published
  1975

This Edition
  February 1992

Although the authors and publisher have tried to make the information as accurate as possible, they accept no responsibility for any loss, injury or inconvenience sustained by any person using this book.

National Library of Australia Cataloguing in Publication Data

Wheeler, Tony, 1946–
  South-East Asia on a shoestring.

  7th ed.
  Includes index.
  ISBN 0 86442 125 7.

  1. Asia, Southeastern – Description and travel – Guide-books. I.
  Title.

915.90453

Tony Wheeler

Tony Wheeler was born in England but spent most of his youth overseas. He returned to England to do a university degree in engineering, worked as an automotive design engineer, returned to university to complete an MBA, and then dropped out on the Asian overland trail with his wife, Maureen. They've been travelling, writing and publishing guidebooks ever since, having set up Lonely Planet Publications in the mid-70s.

Joe Cummings

Joe has travelled extensively and frequently in Asia over the last 14 years. Before travel writing became a full-time job, he was a Peace Corps volunteer in Thailand, a translator/interpreter of Thai, a graduate student of South-East Asian Studies at UC Berkeley (MA 1981), a columnist for the *Asia Record*, a university lecturer in Malaysia and a Lao bilingual consultant for public schools in California. He is the author of LP's *Thailand – a travel survival kit*, co-author of *Vietnam, Laos & Cambodia – a travel survival kit* and contributor to several other of LP's guides to the South-East Asian region.

Daniel Robinson

Daniel was raised in the San Francisco Bay area and Glen Ellyn, Illinois. He has travelled extensively in the Middle East and South, South-East and East Asia. Daniel holds a BA in Near Eastern Studies from Princeton University; his major languages of study and research were Arabic and Hebrew. He is co-author of LP's *Vietnam, Laos & Cambodia – a travel survival kit*.

Robert Storey

Robert, an experienced budget traveller, has spent much of his life trekking all over the backwaters of the world pursuing his favourite hobby, mountain climbing. He has had a number of distinguished careers including taking care of monkeys and repairing slot machines. It was in Taiwan that Robert finally got a respectable job – teaching English. He also learned Chinese, became a computer hacker, wrote LP's *Taiwan – a*

travel survival kit, and co-wrote *Hong Kong, Macau & Canton – a travel survival kit* and *China – a travel survival kit*.

Hugh Finlay

After deciding there must be more to life than a career in civil engineering, Hugh first took off around Australia in the mid-70s working at all manner of jobs. He then spent three years travelling and working in three continents before joining LP in 1985. He has also written LP's *Jordan & Syria – a travel survival kit*, co-authored *Morocco, Algeria & Tunisia – a travel survival kit* and has contributed to other guides including *Africa on a shoestring*, *India – a travel survival kit* and *Malaysia, Singapore & Brunei – a travel survival kit*.

James Lyon

James is an Australian by birth, social scientist by training and a sceptic by nature. He first travelled in Asia on the overland trail in the '70s, and has returned a number of times, most recently with his wife Pauline and their two children. He joined LP as an editor in 1988 and has updated LP's *Bali & Lombok – a travel survival kit*.

Peter Turner

Peter was born in Melbourne and studied English, politics and Asian studies before setting off on the Asian trail. His long-held interest in South-East Asia has seen him make numerous trips to the region. He joined LP as an editor in 1986 and has also worked on *Australia – a travel survival kit, Malaysia, Singapore & Brunei – a travel survival kit* and the *Singapore – city guide*.

Richard Nebesky

Richard was born in Prague, Czechoslovakia. He left there after the Soviet-led invasion in 1968 and settled in Australia. He has a BA in politics and history, and has travelled and worked in Europe, Asia, North America and Africa. He joined LP in 1987 and has also worked on *Australia – a travel survival kit*.

This Edition

The comprehensive update of this book, the 7th edition of *South-East Asia on a shoestring*, required lots of people and lots of days on the road.

Hugh Finlay and Peter Turner covered Singapore, Brunei and both Peninsular and East Malaysia for the new edition of *Malaysia, Singapore & Brunei – a travel survival kit* and Hugh then wrote up the Malaysia and Brunei sections for this book. I made a last minute check on Singapore, and of major centres in Malaysia.

Indonesia, by virtue of its size, required a considerable effort to update. Joe Cummings researched Sumatra, Sulawesi, Kalimantan, Maluku and Irian Jaya for this chapter while I made two forays into the country covering the Riau Islands near Singapore, Java, part of Bali and the islands of Nusa Tenggara. My visit to recently reopened East Timor was the first time I had been there since 1974, when it was still Portuguese Timor. The rest of Bali and all of Lombok were updated by James

Lyon (researching the new *Bali & Lombok – a travel survival kit*), and parts of Sumatra were updated by Richard Nebesky as he researched Sumatra for a revision of *Indonesia – a travel survival kit*.

Joe Cummings also researched the Burma and Thailand chapters and contributed to the Philippines chapter which was updated from the new edition of Jens Peters' *Philippines – a travel survival kit*. Jens Peters also gave the Philippines chapter a valuable perusal, indicating a number of up-to-the-minute changes.

Robert Storey handled the chapters on Hong Kong and Macau, and I also made a brief visit to those two city states.

Finally, comprehensive new chapters on Vietnam and Cambodia were written by Daniel Robinson while Joe Cummings contributed the new chapter on Laos. In my third and final foray through the region for this edition, I continued on from Hong Kong to make a brief visit to Thailand followed by a fascinating journey from Saigon (Ho Chi Minh City) to Hanoi in Vietnam.

Tony Wheeler

From the Publisher

This 7th edition of *South-East Asia on a shoestring* was edited at the offices of Lonely Planet in Australia by Alan Tiller (who coordinated the project) and Jeff Williams. Vicki Beale was responsible for design and cover design, and coordinated the mapping with assistance from Sandra Smythe, Tamsin Wilson and Trudi Canavan. Thanks to Tamsin Wilson, Anne Jefree and Margaret Jung for additional illustrations.

Thanks must also go to Sharon Wertheim for indexing, Dan Levin for his help with computers and Tom Smallman for his proofing and invaluable advice.

See page 921 for a list of travellers who have written to us.

Warning & Request

Things change, prices go up, schedules change, good places go bad and bad ones go bankrupt – nothing stays the same. So if you find things better or worse, recently opened or long since closed, please write and tell us and help make the next edition better!

Your letters will be used to help update future editions and, where possible, important changes will also be included as a Stop Press section in reprints.

All information is greatly appreciated, and the best letters will receive a free copy of the next edition, or any other Lonely Planet book of your choice.

Contents

Map Legend

BOUNDARIES

— — — · — · — .... International Boundary
— — — — — .... Internal Boundary
————————— .... National Park or Reserve
- - - - - - - - - - .... The Equator
· · · · · · · · · · · · · · · · · .... The Tropics

SYMBOLS

◉ NEW DELHI .... National Capital
● BOMBAY .... Provincial or State Capital
● Pune .... Major Town
● Borsi .... Minor Town
■ .... Places to Stay
▼ .... Places to Eat
≜ .... Post Office
✈ .... Airport
ℹ .... Tourist Information
◉ .... Bus Station or Terminal
66 .... Highway Route Number
⚥ ⚨ ⚩ ...... Mosque, Church, Cathedral
∴ .... Temple or Ruin
✚ .... Hospital
✳ .... Lookout
⚘ .... Camping Area
⋈ .... Picnic Area
⌂ .... Hut or Chalet
▲ .... Mountain or Hill
.... Railway Station
.... Road Bridge
.... Railway Bridge
.... Road Tunnel
.... Railway Tunnel
.... Escarpment or Cliff
.... Pass
.... Ancient or Historic Wall

ROUTES

——————— .... Major Road or Highway
- - - - - - - - - .... Unsealed Major Road
——————— .... Sealed Road
- - - - - - - - - ..... Unsealed Road or Track
═══════ .... City Street
+++++++++ .... Railway
═══◉═══ .... Subway
· · · · · · · · · · · · · .... Walking Track
- - - - - - - - - .... Ferry Route
+++++++ .... Cable Car or Chair Lift

HYDROGRAPHIC FEATURES

.... River or Creek
- - - - - - .... Intermittent Stream
.... Lake, Intermittent Lake
.... Coast Line
.... Spring
.... Waterfall
.... Swamp
.... Salt Lake or Reef
.... Glacier

OTHER FEATURES

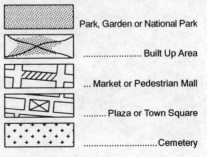

Park, Garden or National Park

.... Built Up Area

... Market or Pedestrian Mall

.... Plaza or Town Square

..............................Cemetery

Note: not all symbols displayed above appear in this book

Introduction

Facts about the Region

If I had to nominate one region of the world as my favourite for travelling, the one area I would choose if I had to quit travelling everywhere else, I would have no second thoughts – South-East Asia. There is simply more variety here than almost any other region of the world. In food, religion and culture, South-East Asia has everything you could possibly ask for.

If island hopping sounds like fun, then it's hard to top South-East Asia for the numerous opportunities available in that field. The Philippines, for example, claim to have over 7000 islands and there are countless ships ploughing back and forth between them. In lots of places, you can make island hopping even more adventurous – I'll never forget the time six of us chartered an Indonesian *perahu* (outrigger) to sail from Flores to Sumbawa via the island of Komodo to see the famous dragons. We spent four solid days pumping the bilge to keep that leaky bucket afloat.

Food is another great pleasure of South-East Asia. After my first long trip through the region, I became a complete addict for tropical fruit – thoughts of rambutans, salaks and mangosteens still make me glassy eyed! I must admit, I'm still working on developing a taste for durians though. Singapore just has to be one of the world's food capitals; every time I fly there I seem to spend the last half hour of the flight thinking over where I'm going to eat each and every meal for the next few days.

Of course, travelling and eating are not the only parts to exploring a region, but if you want memorable scenes and unforgettable moments, you'll certainly find those. The great Shwedagon Pagoda in Rangoon (Yangon) is still one of those 'magical' places where time seems to stand still, and each visit reveals something new. Early mornings in Bali have a pastoral beauty words and even pictures simply cannot capture. Or in Hong Kong, you can feel yourself at the cutting edge of world events and high technology, and experience that strange sensation that money is actually being created all around you!

Recently, Vietnam, Cambodia and Laos have become much easier to visit, and a whole new wealth of great sights have become accessible, including the magnificent monuments of Angkor in Cambodia.

South-East Asia also has a healthy share of the world's most interesting volcanoes. Over the years, I've stood on top of Mayon in the Philippines, the world's 'most perfect' volcano; gazed down on the three different-coloured crater-lakes of Keli Mutu in Flores, and watched the sun rise from the crater rim of Bromo in Java.

Even if simply lying on beaches is more your thing, South-East Asia has plenty to offer. You can spend a lot of time wrestling with momentous decisions about whether Tioman, Phuket or Ko Samui is the most beautiful tropical island. In fact, the more I think about it, the more enthusiastic I am to go back again!

Facts about the Region

PLANNING
When to Go?

Anytime for any amount of time might be the answer to this one. Although there are wet and dry seasons, the changes are not as distinct as they are on the subcontinent. Nor are there seasons when you can and cannot do things (as for trekking in Nepal). The Climate sections of the various countries and regions detail what to expect and when to expect it, but anytime is the right time somewhere or other!

What to Bring

As little as possible is the best policy – but not so little that you have to scrounge off other travellers, as some of the 'super lightweight' travellers do. It's very easy to find almost anything you need along the way, and since you'll inevitably buy things as you go, it's better to start with too little rather than too much.

A backpack is still the most popular method of carrying gear as it is commodious and the only way to go if you have to do any walking. On the debit side, a backpack is awkward to load on and off buses and trains, it doesn't offer too much protection for your valuables, the straps tend to get caught on things and some airlines may refuse to be responsible if the pack is damaged or broken into. Fortunately, backpacks no longer have the 'pack equals hippy' and 'hippy equals bad' connotation they used to have.

Recently, travelpacks, a combination of backpack and shoulder bag, have become very popular. The backpack straps zip away inside the pack when not needed so you almost have the best of both worlds. Although not really suitable for long hiking trips, they're much easier to carry than a bag. I use a travelpack for my travels these days. Another alternative is a large, soft zip bag with a wide shoulder strap so it can be carried with relative ease if necessary. Backpacks or travelpacks can be reasonably thief-proofed with small padlocks. Forget suitcases.

Once in the region, you will, no doubt, be buying local clothes along the way (Levi jeans are cheaper in Singapore or Hong Kong than back home, wherever that might be), so start light. My list of clothing to bring along would include:

underwear & swimming gear
a pair of jeans & a pair of shorts
a few T-shirts & shirts
a sweater for cold nights
a pair of runners or shoes
sandals or thongs
a lightweight jacket or raincoat
a dress-up set of clothes

Modesty is rated highly in Asian countries, especially for women. Wearing shorts away from the beach is often looked down upon as being rather 'low class'. Other items I'd consider bringing include:

washing gear
a medical & a sewing kit
sunglasses
a padlock
a sleeping bag
a Swiss Army knife
a sarong
an umbrella

Sleeping bags are only necessary if you're going to be roughing it, getting well off the beaten track, climbing mountains and the like. They can also double as a coat on cold days, a cushion on hard train-seats, a seat for long waits at bus or railway stations and a bed top-cover, since hotels rarely give you one. A sarong is equally useful since it can be everything from a bed sheet to a towel, a beach wrap or a dressing gown.

A padlock is useful to lock your bag to a train or bus luggage rack or to fortify your hotel room – which often locks with a latch. I've made trips with an umbrella and have been pleased to have it once or twice. I've also made trips without an umbrella and hardly missed it. Updating this edition, however, I had an umbrella with me and it came in useful nearly every day I was on the road! Soap, toothpaste and so on are readily obtainable but well off the beaten track, toilet paper can be impossible to find. Tampons are also difficult to find away from the big cities.

There are two final considerations. The secret of successful packing is plastic bags or 'stuff bags' – they not only keep things separate and clean but also dry.

Airlines do lose bags from time to time – you've got a much better chance of it not being yours if it is tagged with your name and address *inside* the bag as well as outside. Outside tags can always fall off or be removed.

Appearances & Conduct

If you want to have a smooth trip, attention to your appearance is most important. Throughout South-East Asia the official powers-that-be have a morbid hatred of 'hippies', 'freaks' and other similar low forms of life. When you arrive at embassies or consulates for visas, at the border to enter a country, or at docks or airports, you'll find life much more simple if you look neat and affluent. Particularly disliked are thongs, shorts, jeans (especially with patches on them), local attire, T-shirts – I could go on. It's advisable to have one set of conventional 'dress up' gear to wear for these types of formal occasions.

Encounters with Asian officialdom are made much smoother if you keep repeating 'I must retain my cool' the more they annoy you! Displays of temper usually have a counter-productive effect. They just want to show you who's boss – if you imply that you realise they are but that you still insist (calmly) on your rights you'll probably manage OK. Exaggerated politeness can go a long way in Asia.

VISAS

Visas remain my pet Asian hate. Visas are a stamp in your passport permitting you to enter the country in question and stay for a specified period of time. They're generally pure red tape and another means of gouging a few more dollars out of you. If you spend much time travelling around the region you'll waste a lot of time, money, effort and passport pages on them, although I'm pleased to say that over the years the visa situation in South-East Asia has become much better. This is not so for Burma (Myanmar), however.

Several steps can make obtaining visas a little easier. As far as possible, get your visas as you go rather than all at once before you leave home. Two reasons – one, they often expire after a certain number of days, and two, it is often easier and very often cheaper to get them in neighbouring countries than it is from far away. Shop around for your visas – you'll hear on the grapevine that city A is far better than city B for such and such a visa.

Finally, there is the dreaded ticket-out problem. For some reason, several countries have this phobia that if you don't arrive clutching a departure ticket in your hand, you'll never leave. This is a real hassle if you intend to depart by some unusual means for which the tickets can only be bought after you arrive!

There are two possible answers. One is to get an MCO, 'Miscellaneous Charges Order', which is like an airline ticket but with no destination. Some places will accept this. Alternatively, just get the cheapest ticket out and get a refund on it later – make sure it's the cheapest and safest as there are some airlines who part with refunds like Scrooge with his pennies.

Of course, if you really intend to depart as planned, you will not have any problems. Note that in places where renewing visas can be difficult, a confirmed ticket out from the place you're trying to renew in will be much more acceptable. If you're in Bali, a confirmed ticket out of Denpasar will stand you in much better stead than an undated one from Medan in north Sumatra.

If you hit a sticky visa problem, shop around. In some other city or country, the situation may be better. See the sections on Visas under the individual countries in this

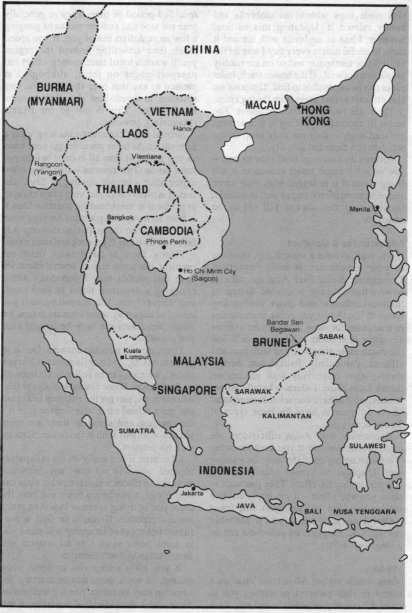

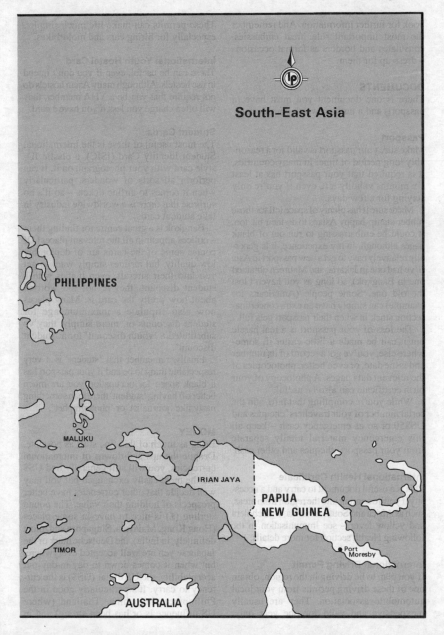

South-East Asia

PHILIPPINES

MALUKU

IRIAN JAYA

PAPUA NEW GUINEA

TIMOR

AUSTRALIA

Port Moresby

book for further information. And remember the most important rule: treat embassies, consulates and borders as formal occasions – dress up for them.

DOCUMENTS

There is one document you must have (a passport) and a number worth considering.

Passport

Make sure your passport is valid for a reasonably long period of time. In many countries, it is required that your passport has at least six months validity left, even if you're only staying for a few days.

Make sure it has plenty of space left for those rubber-stamp-happy Asians to do their bit, too. It could be embarrassing to run out of blank pages although, in my experience, it is generally relatively easy to get a new passport in Asia (I've had one in Jakarta, and Maureen obtained one in Bangkok), so long as you haven't lost the old one. Some people (Americans for example) can simply have an extra concertina-section stuck in when their passport gets full.

The loss of your passport is a real hassle but it can be made a little easier if, somewhere else, you've got a record of its number and issue date, or even better, photocopies of the relevant data pages. A photocopy of your birth certificate can also be useful.

While you're compiling that info, add the serial number of your travellers' cheques and US$50 or so as emergency cash – keep all this emergency material totally separate from your passport, cheques and other cash.

International Health Certificate

This is a useful document to carry and a necessity if you're coming into the region from areas, such as Africa and South America, with cholera and yellow fever – see Immunisation in the following Health section for more details.

International Driving Permit

If you plan to be driving in the region, obtain one of these driving permits from your local automobile association. They are usually inexpensive and valid for one year only. These permits can make life much simpler, especially for hiring cars and motorbikes.

International Youth Hostel Card

These can be useful, even if you don't intend to use hostels. Although many Asian hostels do not require that you be a YHA member, they will often charge you less if you have a card.

Student Cards

The most useful of these is the International Student Identity Card (ISIC), a plastic ID-style card with your photograph on it. It can perform all sorts of wonders, particularly when it comes to airline tickets – so it's no surprise that there is a worldwide industry in fake student cards.

Bangkok is a great centre for finding them – notices appear in all the relevant places! Of course some of the cards are of deplorably low quality, but airlines simply want to get you into their aircraft, even if it is with a student discount, they're not too worried about how pretty the card is. Many places now also stipulate a maximum age for student discounts or, more simply, they've substituted a 'youth discount' for a 'student discount'.

Finally, remember that 'student' is a very respectable thing to be and if your passport has a blank space for occupation you are much better off having 'student' there than something nasty like 'journalist' or 'photographer'.

MONEY

Bring as much of this fine stuff as possible. Despite the ups and downs of international currencies, you will still generally find US$ are the most easily exchanged but you may well decide that other currencies have better prospects of holding their value. The pound sterling (£) is nice to have in some places (Hong Kong, Malaysia, Singapore and, most definitely, in India), the Deutsche mark or the Japanese yen are well accepted everywhere, but when it comes down to day-in-day-out acceptability, the US dollar (US$) is the currency to carry. It's particularly good in the Philippines, Indochina, Thailand (where US influence is or has been strong) and in

Indonesia, where the US$ often seems to enjoy a strange premium over the other currencies.

American Express or Thomas Cook travellers' cheques are probably the best to carry because of their 'instant replacement' policies. The main idea of carrying cheques rather than cash is the protection they offer from theft, but it doesn't do a lot of good if you have to go back home first to get the refund. Amex have offices in most of the major cities but remember that 'instant replacement' may not be instantaneous, although overall most people seem to be pretty satisfied with the service.

Keeping a record of the cheque numbers and the initial purchase details is vitally important. Without this you may well find that 'instant' is a very long time indeed. If you're going to really out-of-the-way places, it may be worth taking a couple of different brands of travellers' cheques since banks may not always accept all varieties.

Take nearly all the cheques in large denominations, say US$100s. It's only at the very end of a stay that you may want to change a US$20 or US$10 cheque just to get you through the last day or two. A number of institutions charge a per-cheque service fee, so changing US$100 in 20s can end up five times as expensive as a single US$100 cheque. In most countries these days, the exchange rate for travellers' cheques is better than the exchange rate for cash.

It is a good idea to take some cash with you. Often, it is much easier to change just a few dollars (when leaving a country for example) in cash rather than cheques – and more economical. When banks are closed, cash is also better.

In countries where there is a black market, cash is what's wanted, not travellers' cheques, but note that big denominations get a much better rate than small ones. Nobody wants US$1 notes. Of course, the odd dollar laid in the right place (the right hand) can perform wonders.

If you run out of cash, due to simply having spent it all or from more disastrous events, and need more, instruct your bank back home to send a draft to you (always

assuming you've got some cash back home to send!). Specify the city and the bank – once I made the mistake of saying 'to your usual bank' and then spent a day trying to find out which was their 'usual bank'. If you don't know a bank to transfer money too, ask your bank to write and tell you where a suitable one is.

Money sent by telegraphic transfer should reach you in a couple of days but, by mail, allow at least two weeks. When it gets there, it will most likely be converted into local currency – you can take it as it is or buy travellers' cheques. Singapore and Hong Kong are easily the best countries referred to in this book to transfer money to. Malaysia and Thailand are not bad either but even Indonesia and the Philippines are far easier than countries further west like India and Pakistan where money transfers seem to drop into a bottomless pit sometimes never to be seen again.

If you're very sound financially, an ideal travelling companion is an American Express card. It always amuses me how many backpackers also have their credit cards! With one of these you can put a lot of things (like airline tickets) on your account and save carrying so much with you. If you run low, rather than have money transferred out to you from home base you can get an instant cash transfusion from any American Express office – very convenient!

There are other ways of carrying money or obtaining cash as well. In some places, you can cash Eurocheques or personal cheques with the appropriate identification. Some Dutch travellers I met on one circuit of the region explained how, with a Dutch post office account, they could conveniently obtain cash from Indonesian post offices. These *girobetaalkaarten* are very useful in the many Indonesian towns where there is no bank.

Your budget is dependent upon how you live and travel. If you're moving around fast, going to lots of places, spending time in the big cities, then your day-to-day living costs are going to be quite high. People who tell you they spent six months on a dollar a day

Cost Comparison Chart
All figures in $US

	Aus	HK	Indo	Mal	Phil	Sing	Thai	UK	USA
Exchange Rates	0.75	7.75	1964	2.75	26.7	1.70	25.6	0.58	1
GNP (per capita)	17000	12000	500	2500	700	13000	1418	17500	21500
Daily Paper	0.45	0.50	0.50	0.20	0.11	0.30	0.40	0.70	0.35
Kodachrome 64	11	8	9	9	7	10	7	13	7.5
Cheap Hotel	25	15	5	8	7.5	15	5	34	25
Hostel Bed	10	6.5	2	3	3	5	2	10	12
Cheap Meal	7	5	2	3	3.5	4	1.25	8	6
Glass of beer	2	2	1	0.90	0.60	2.50	1.50	2.50	2
Big Mac	1.76	1.15	1.80	1.10	2.43	1.60	1.80	3.10	1.90
Litre of petrol	0.50	0.85	0.25	0.40	0.60	0.70	0.40	0.84	0.30
Local phone call	0.23	0.13	0.03	0.07	0.05	0.06	0.04	0.17	0.20
Time Magazine	2.10	3.25	1.90	2.00	1.65	3.15	3.00	2.57	2.50

did it by sitting on the beach for five months and three weeks. The dollar-a-day places are fast fading! Remember, you're not on some sort of travelling economy run – being tight with your money can mean you lose the whole purpose of being there.

See the above table for a comparison of prices between Western and South-East Asian countries.

POST

Poste restante (at almost any post office) is the best way of getting mail. American Express have client mail services but it's not usually worth the effort. If you've got some definite contact point or know you will be at a certain hotel then use that. Nowadays, very few embassies will hold mail for their people – they'll just forward it on to poste restante. When getting people to write to you, ask them to leave plenty of time for mail to arrive and to print your name very clearly. Underlining the surname also helps. Remember, in some countries the surname comes first, so it's not surprising that many 'missing' letters are just misfiled.

When sending mail from the less affluent countries, it's often recommended that you have the stamps franked before your eyes, to prevent the stamps being stolen, but this doesn't seem to be such a problem anymore, not in affluent South-East Asia anyway.

Aerograms are quite safe of course. I am very distrustful of 'mail it home' packaging

services, however. I've sent parcels home from South-East Asia on a few occasions and (touch wood) they've always arrived – slightly battered and a long time later. If it's something you value, consider air freight. Enquire at the post office before you bring a parcel in as there may be special wrapping requirements or it may have to be inspected (as in Indonesia) before you wrap it.

BOOKS
Guide Books

In a guide book of this size and scope we can't possibly cover every conceivable aspect of travel in South-East Asia. If you'd like more detailed information on a specific area or country, Lonely Planet produces a range of travel survival kits which are updated regularly and provide useful maps and a wealth of information for travellers.

The titles to look for are:

Bali & Lombok – a travel survival kit
by Tony Wheeler et al
Burma – a travel survival kit
by Tony Wheeler et al
Hong Kong, Macau & Canton – a travel survival kit
by Robert Storey
Indonesia – a travel survival kit
by Joe Cummings et al
Malaysia, Singapore & Brunei – a travel survival kit
by Tony Wheeler et al
North-East Asia on a shoestring
by Tony Wheeler et al

Philippines – a travel survival kit
  by Jens Peters
Thailand – a travel survival kit
  by Joe Cummings
Vietnam, Laos & Cambodia – a travel survival kit
  by Joe Cummings & Daniel Robinson
West Asia on a shoestring
  by Tony Wheeler

Phrasebooks

Also of interest to travellers in South-East Asia are Lonely Planet's range of phrasebooks which includes:

Burmese Phrasebook
Indonesian Phrasebook
Pilipino Phrasebook
Thai Phrasebook
Thai Hill Tribes Phrasebook

FILM & PHOTOGRAPHY

You'll run through plenty of film in South-East Asia, and in Singapore and Hong Kong it's fairly cheap, particularly if you buy it in bulk – say a dozen at a time. Elsewhere, film is readily available (Malaysia or Thailand for example), but rather more expensive than in the West.

Cameras are also cheap in Singapore or Hong Kong where the choice of camera equipment is literally staggering. If you have any difficulties, these are also the places to have your camera attended to.

Particular points to note when taking photos in the region are to compensate for the intensity of the light – for a few hours before and after midday the height of the sun will tend to leave pictures very washed out. Try to photograph early or late in the day. There will also be plenty of occasions when you'll want a flash, either for indoor shots or in jungle locations where the amount of light that filters through can be surprisingly low. When taking photographs of people, make sure they don't mind. They generally don't but it's polite to check first.

HEALTH

Travel health depends on your predeparture preparations, your day-to-day health care while travelling and how you handle any medical problem or emergency that may

develop. While the list of potential dangers can seem quite frightening, with a little luck, some basic precautions and the right information, few travellers experience more than upset stomachs.

Travel Health Guides

There are a number of books on travel health, some include:

Staying Healthy in Asia, Africa & Latin America by Volunteers in Asia. Probably the best all-round guide to carry, as it's compact but very detailed and well organised.
Travellers' Health by Dr Richard Dawood, Oxford University Press. Comprehensive, easy to read, authoritative and also highly recommended, although it's rather large to lug around.
Where There is No Doctor by David Werner, Hesperian Foundation. A very detailed guide intended for someone, like a Peace Corps worker, going to work in undeveloped countries, rather than for the average traveller.
Travel with Children by Maureen Wheeler, Lonely Planet Publications. Includes basic advice on travel health for younger children.

Predeparture Preparations

Health Insurance A travel insurance policy to cover theft, loss and medical problems is a wise idea. There are a wide variety of policies and your travel agent will make specific recommendations. The international student travel policies handled by STA Travel or other student travel organisations are usually good value. South-East Asia is not a high medical cost area, so you don't need the very high payout policies particularly intended for travellers to North America. Check the small print:

1. Some policies specifically exclude 'dangerous activities' which can include scuba diving, motorcycling, climbing with ropes and even trekking. If such activities are on your agenda, you don't want that sort of policy.
2. You may prefer a policy which pays doctors or hospitals directly rather than you having to pay on the spot and claim later. If you have to claim later, make sure you keep all documentation. Some policies ask you to call back (reverse charges) to a centre in your home country where an immediate assessment of your problem is made.
3. Check if the policy provides for ambulances or an emergency flight home. If you have to stretch out you will need two seats and somebody has to pay for them!

Medical Kit It is wise to carry a small, straightforward medical kit. A possible kit list includes:

- Aspirin or Panadol – for pain or fever.
- Antihistamine (such as Benadryl) – useful as a decongestant for colds, allergies, to ease the itch from insect bites or stings, or to help prevent motion sickness.
- Antibiotics – useful if you're travelling well off the beaten track, but they must be prescribed and you should carry the prescription with you.
- Kaolin preparation (Pepto-Bismol), Imodium or Lomotil – for stomach upsets.
- Rehydration mixture – for treatment of severe diarrhoea, this is particularly important if travelling with children.
- Antiseptic, mercurochrome and antibiotic powder or similar 'dry' spray – for cuts and grazes.
- Calamine lotion – to ease irritation from bites or stings.
- Bandages and Band-aids – for minor injuries.
- Scissors, tweezers and a thermometer (note that mercury thermometers are prohibited by airlines).
- Insect repellent, sunscreen, suntan lotion, chap stick and water purification tablets.

Ideally, antibiotics should be administered only under medical supervision and should never be taken indiscriminately.

Overuse of antibiotics can weaken your body's ability to deal with infections naturally and can reduce the drug's efficacy on a future occasion. Take only the recommended dose at the prescribed intervals and continue using the antibiotic for the prescribed period, even if the illness seems to be cured earlier. Antibiotics are specific to the infections they can treat. Stop immediately if there are any serious reactions to the antibiotics, and don't use them at all if you are unsure if you have the correct one.

In many South-East Asian countries, if a medicine is available at all it will generally be available over the counter and the price will be much cheaper than in the West. However, be careful of buying drugs in developing countries, particularly where the expiry date may have passed or correct storage conditions may not have been observed. It's possible that drugs which are no longer recommended (or have even been banned) in the West may still be dispensed in the region.

Health Preparations Make sure you're healthy before you start travelling. If you are embarking on a long trip make sure your teeth are OK. There are lots of places where a visit to the dentist would be the last thing you'd want to do.

If you wear glasses, take a spare pair and your prescription. Losing your glasses can be a real problem, although in many places you can get new spectacles made up quickly, cheaply and competently.

If you require a particular medication take an adequate supply, as it may not be available locally. Take the prescription, with the generic rather than the brand name (which may not be locally available), as it will make getting replacements easier. It's a wise idea to have the prescription with you to show that you legally use the medication – it's surprising how often over-the-counter drugs from one place are illegal without a prescription, or even banned, in another.

Immunisations Vaccinations are given to provide protection against diseases you might be exposed to along the way. For some countries, such as Singapore and Hong Kong, no immunisations are necessary. However, the further off the beaten track you go, the more you need to take precautions. These days, vaccination as an entry requirement is usually only enforced when you are coming from an infected area – yellow fever and cholera are the two most likely requirements. Nevertheless, all vaccinations should be recorded on your International Health Certificate, which is available from your physician or government health department.

Plan ahead for getting your vaccinations – some of them require an initial shot followed by a booster, while some vaccinations should not be given together. Most travellers from Western countries will have been immunised against various diseases during childhood but your doctor may still recommend booster shots against measles or polio, diseases still prevalent in many developing countries. The period of protection offered by vaccinations differs widely and some are contraindicated if you are pregnant.

In some countries, immunisations are available from airport or government health centres. Travel agents or airline offices will tell you where. A possible list of vaccinations includes:

Cholera – Some countries require a cholera vaccination if you are coming from an infected area, but protection is not very effective, only lasts six months and is contraindicated for pregnancy.

Infectious Hepatitis – Gamma globulin is not a vaccination but a ready-made antibody which has proven very successful in reducing the chances of hepatitis infection. Because it may interfere with the development of immunity, it should not be given until at least 10 days after administration of the last vaccine needed; it should also be given as close as possible to departure because of its relatively short-lived protection period of six months.

Smallpox – Smallpox has now been wiped out worldwide, so immunisation is no longer necessary.

Tetanus & Diptheria – Boosters are necessary every 10 years and protection is highly recommended.

Typhoid – Protection lasts for three years and is useful if you are travelling for long in rural, tropical areas. You may get some side effects such as pain at the injection site, fever, headache and a general unwell feeling.

Yellow Fever – Protection lasts for 10 years and is recommended where the disease is endemic, chiefly in Africa and South America. You usually have to go to a special yellow fever vaccination centre. Vaccination is contraindicated during pregnancy but if you must travel to a high-risk area it is probably advisable.

Basic Rules

Care in what you eat and drink is the most important health rule; stomach upsets are the most likely travel health problem but the majority of these upsets will be relatively minor. Don't become paranoid, trying the local food is part of the experience of travel after all.

Water The number one rule is *don't drink the water* and that includes ice. If you don't know for certain that the water is safe always assume the worst – the water in Singapore and Honk Kong is generally OK. Reputable brands of bottled water or soft drinks are generally fine, although in some places bottles refilled with tap water are not unknown. Take care with fruit juice, particularly if water may have been added. Milk should be treated with suspicion, as it is often unpasteurised. Boiled milk is fine if it is kept hygienically and yoghurt is always good. Tea or coffee should also be OK, since the water should have been boiled.

Water Purification The simplest way to purify water is to boil it thoroughly. In order to do it thoroughly it requires boiling for 10 minutes, something which happens very rarely! Remember that at high altitude water boils at lower temperature, so germs are less likely to be killed.

Simple filtering doesn't remove all dangerous organisms, so if you cannot boil water it should be treated chemically. Chlorine tablets (Puritabs, Steritabs or other brand names) will kill many but not all pathogens. Iodine is very effective in purifying water and is available in tablet form (such as Potable Aqua), but follow the directions carefully and remember that too much iodine can be harmful.

If you can't find tablets, tincture of iodine (2%) or iodine crystals can be used. Two drops of tincture of iodine per litre or quart of clear water is the recommended dosage; the treated water should be left to stand for 30 minutes before drinking. Iodine crystals can also be used to purify water but this is a more complicated process, as you have to first prepare a saturated iodine solution. Iodine loses its effectiveness if exposed to air or damp, so keep it in a tightly sealed container. Flavoured powder will disguise the taste of treated water and is a good idea if you are travelling with children.

Food Salads and fruit should be washed with purified water or peeled where possible. Ice cream is usually OK if it is a reputable brand name, but be wary of some street vendors and of ice cream that has melted and been refrozen. Thoroughly cooked food is safest but not if it has been left to cool or if it has been reheated.

Take great care with shellfish or fish and avoid undercooked meat. If a place looks clean and well-run and if the vendor also looks clean and healthy, then the food is probably safe. In general, places that are packed with travellers or locals will be fine, while empty restaurants are questionable.

Nutrition If your food is poor or limited in availability, if you're travelling hard and fast and therefore missing meals, or if you simply lose your appetite, you can soon start to lose weight and place your health at risk.

Make sure your diet is well balanced. Eggs, tofu, beans and nuts are all safe ways to get protein. Fruit you can peel (bananas, oranges or mandarins, for example) is always safe and a good source of vitamins. Try to eat plenty of grains (rice) and bread. Remember that although food is generally safer if it is cooked well, overcooked food loses much of its nutritional value. If your diet isn't well balanced or if your food intake is insufficient, it's a good idea to take vitamin and iron pills.

In hot climates, make sure you drink enough – don't rely on feeling thirsty to indicate when you should drink. Not needing to urinate or very dark yellow urine is a danger sign. Always carry a water bottle with you on long trips. Excessive sweating can lead to loss of salt and, therefore, muscle cramping. Salt tablets are not a good idea as a preventative but in places where salt is not used much, adding salt to food can help.

Everyday Health Normal body temperature is 37°C, or 98.6°F; more than 2°C higher is a 'high' fever. A normal adult pulse rate is from 60 to 80 per minute (children 80 to 100 and babies 100 to 140). You should know how to take a temperature and a pulse rate. As a general rule the pulse increases about 20 beats per minute for each °C rise in fever.

Respiration (breathing) rate is also an indicator of illness. Count the number of breaths per minute: between 12 and 20 is normal for adults and older children (up to 30 for younger children and 40 for babies). People suffering a high fever or serious respiratory illness (like pneumonia) breathe more quickly than normal. More than 40 shallow breaths a minute usually means pneumonia.

Many health problems can be avoided by taking care of yourself. Wash your hands frequently – it's quite easy to contaminate your own food. Clean your teeth with purified water rather than water straight from the tap. Avoid climatic extremes: keep out of the sun when it's hot and dress warmly when it's cold.

You may avoid potential diseases by dressing sensibly. Worm infections can occur through your walking barefoot or from dangerous coral cuts caused by walking over coral without shoes. You can avoid insect bites by covering bare skin when insects are around, by screening windows or beds or by using insect repellents. Seek local advice: if you're told the water is unsafe due to jellyfish, crocodiles or bilharzia, don't go in. In situations where there is no information, discretion is the better part of valour.

Last but not least, don't be too concerned with your health. In 15 years of kicking around Asia I've had nothing more serious than a few stomach upsets. South-East Asia is generally a pleasantly healthy area to travel around, and even Bali Belly is less common and less serious than it's relative from Delhi!

Medical Problems & Treatment
Potential medical problems can be broken down into several areas. First there are the

climatic and geographical considerations – problems caused by temperature extremes, altitude or motion. Then there are diseases and illnesses caused by insanitation, insect bites or stings, and animal or human contact. Simple cuts, bites or scratches can also cause problems.

Self-diagnosis and treatment can be risky, so wherever possible seek qualified help. Although we do give treatment dosages in this section, they are for emergency use only. Medical advice should be sought before administering any drugs.

An embassy or consulate is usually able to recommend a good place to go for such advice. So can five-star hotels, although they often recommend doctors with five-star prices. (This is when that medical insurance really comes in useful!) In some countries, standards of medical attention are so low that for some ailments the best advice is to get on a plane and go somewhere else.

Climatic & Geographical Considerations
Sunburn In the tropics, the desert or at high altitude, you can get sunburnt surprisingly quickly, even through cloud. Use a sunscreen and take extra care to cover areas which don't normally see sun – eg, your feet. A hat provides added protection, and you should also use zinc cream or some other barrier cream for your nose and lips. Calamine lotion is good for mild sunburn.

Prickly Heat Prickly heat is an itchy rash caused by excessive perspiration trapped under the skin. It usually strikes people who have just arrived in a hot climate and whose pores have not yet opened sufficiently to cope with greater sweating. Keeping cool but bathing often, using a mild talcum powder or even resorting to air-conditioning may help until you acclimatise.

Heat Exhaustion Salt deficiency or dehydration can cause heat exhaustion. Take time to acclimatise to high temperatures and make sure you get sufficient liquids.

Salt deficiency is characterised by fatigue, lethargy, headaches, giddiness and muscle cramps and in this case salt tablets may help. Vomiting or diarrhoea can deplete your liquid and salt levels. Anhydrotic heat exhaustion, caused by an inability to sweat, is quite rare. Unlike the other forms of heat exhaustion, it is likely to strike people who have been in a hot climate for some time, rather than newcomers.

Heat Stroke This serious, sometimes fatal, condition can occur if the body's heat-regulating mechanism breaks down and the body temperature rises to dangerous levels. Long, continuous periods of exposure to high temperatures can leave you vulnerable to heat stroke. You should avoid excessive alcohol or strenuous activity when you first arrive in a hot climate.

The symptoms are feeling unwell, not sweating very much or at all and a high body temperature (39°C to 41°C). Where sweating has ceased, the skin becomes flushed and red. Severe, throbbing headaches and lack of coordination will also occur, and the sufferer may be confused or aggressive. Eventually, the victim will become delirious or convulse. Hospitalisation is essential, but meanwhile get patients out of the sun, remove their clothing, cover them with a wet sheet or towel and then fan continually.

Fungal Infections Hot weather fungal infections are most likely to occur on the scalp, between the toes or fingers (athlete's foot), in the groin (jock itch or crotch rot) and on the body (ringworm). You get ringworm (which is a fungal infection, not a worm) from infected animals or by walking on damp areas, like shower floors.

To prevent fungal infections, wear loose, comfortable clothes, avoid artificial fibres, wash frequently and dry carefully. If you do get an infection, wash the infected area daily with a disinfectant or medicated soap and water, and rinse and dry well. Apply an antifungal powder like the widely available Tinaderm. Try to expose the infected area to air or sunlight as much as possible and wash all towels and underwear in hot water as well as changing them often.

Cold Too much cold is just as dangerous as too much heat, particularly if it leads to hypothermia. If you are trekking at high altitudes or simply taking a long bus trip over mountains, particularly at night, be prepared.

If climbing one of the many volcanoes or mountains of South-East Asia, such as Bromo, Batur, Gunung Tahan, Mayon or Kinabalu, be prepared for extremes of hot and cold.

Motion Sickness Eating lightly before and during a trip will reduce the chances of motion sickness. If you are prone to motion sickness, try to find a place that minimises disturbance – near the wing on aircraft, close to midships on boats, near the centre on buses. Fresh air usually helps, reading or cigarette smoke doesn't. Commercial anti-motion-sickness preparations, which can cause drowsiness, have to be taken before the trip commences. When you're feeling sick it's too late. Ginger, a natural preventative, is available in capsule form.

Diseases of Insanitation

Diarrhoea A change of water, food or climate can all cause the runs. Diarrhoea caused by contaminated food or water is more serious. Despite all your precautions, you may still have a bout of mild travellers' diarrhoea but a few rushed toilet trips with no other symptoms is not indicative of a serious problem.

Moderate diarrhoea, involving half-a-dozen loose movements in a day, is more of a nuisance. Dehydration is the main danger with any diarrhoea, particularly for children, so fluid replenishment is the number one treatment. Weak black tea with a little sugar, soda water, or soft drinks allowed to go flat and diluted 50% with water are all good. In instances of severe diarrhoea, a rehydrating solution is necessary to replace minerals and salts. You should stick to a bland diet as you recover.

Lomotil or Imodium can be used to bring relief from the symptoms, although they do not actually cure the problem. Only use these drugs if absolutely necessary – eg, if you *must* travel. For children, Imodium is preferable, but do not use these drugs if the patient has a high fever or is severely dehydrated.

Antibiotics can be very successful in the treatment of severe diarrhoea especially if it is accompanied by nausea, vomiting, stomach cramps or mild fever. Ampicillin, a broad spectrum penicillin, is recommended. Two capsules of 250 mg each taken four times a day is the recommended dose for an adult. Children aged between eight and 12 years should have half the adult dose; younger children should have half a capsule four times a day. Note that if the patient is allergic to penicillin, ampicillin should not be administered.

Three days of treatment should be sufficient and an improvement should occur within 24 hours.

Giardia This intestinal parasite is present in contaminated water. The symptoms are stomach cramps, nausea, a bloated stomach, watery, foul-smelling diarrhoea and frequent gas. Giardia can appear several weeks after you have been exposed to the parasite. The symptoms may disappear for a few days and then return; this can go on for several weeks. Metronidazole, also known as Flagyl, is the recommended drug, but it should only be taken under medical supervision. Antibiotics are of no use.

Dysentery This serious illness is caused by contaminated food or water and is characterised by severe diarrhoea, often with blood or mucus in the stool. There are two kinds of dysentery. Bacillary dysentery is characterised by a high fever and rapid development; headache, vomiting and stomach pains are also symptoms. It usually does not last longer than a week, but it is highly contagious.

Amoebic dysentery is more gradual in developing, has no fever or vomiting but is a more serious illness. It is not a self-limiting disease: it will persist until treated and can recur and cause long term damage.

A stool test is necessary to diagnose which kind of dysentery you have, so you should seek medical help urgently. In case of an emergency, note that tetracycline is the prescribed treatment for bacillary dysentery, metronidazole for amoebic dysentery.

With tetracycline, the recommended adult dosage is one 250 mg capsule four times a day. Children aged between eight and 12 years should have half the adult dose; the dosage for younger children is a third the adult dose. It's important to remember that tetracycline should be given to young children only if it's absolutely necessary and only for a short period; pregnant women should not take it after the 4th month of pregnancy.

With metronidazole, the recommended adult dosage is one 750-mg to 800-mg capsule three times daily for five days. For children aged between eight and 12 years, half the adult dose is correct; the dosage for younger children is a third the adult dose.

Viral Gastroenteritis This is caused not by bacteria but, as the name suggests, by a virus. It is characterised by diarrhoea, stomach cramps and sometimes by vomiting and/or a slight fever. All you can do is rest and drink lots of fluids.

Hepatitis Hepatitis A is the more common form of this disease and is commonly spread by contaminated food or water. The first symptoms are fever, chills, headache, fatigue, feelings of weakness and aches and pains. This is followed by loss of appetite, nausea, vomiting, abdominal pain, dark urine, light-coloured faeces and jaundiced skin; the whites of the eyes may also turn yellow.

In some cases, there may just be a feeling of being unwell or tired, accompanied by loss of appetite, aches and pains and the jaundiced effect. You should seek medical advice, but in general there is not much you can do apart from rest, drink lots of fluids, eat lightly and avoid fatty foods. People who have had hepatitis must forego alcohol for six months after the illness, as hepatitis attacks the liver and it needs that amount of time to recover.

Hepatitis B, which used to be called serum hepatitis, is spread through sexual contact or through skin penetration – it can be transmitted via dirty needles or blood transfusions, for instance. Avoid having your ears pierced, tattoos done or injections where you have doubts about the sanitary conditions. The symptoms and treatment of type B are much the same as for type A, but gamma globulin as a prophylactic is effective against type A only.

Typhoid Typhoid fever is another gut infection that travels the faecal-oral route – ie, contaminated water and food are responsible. Vaccination against typhoid is not totally effective and it is one of the most dangerous infections, so medical help must be sought.

Worms These parasites are most common in rural, tropical areas and a stool test when you return home is not a bad idea. They can be present on unwashed vegetables or in undercooked meat, and you can pick them up through your skin by walking in bare feet. Infestations may not show up for some time, and although they are generally not serious, if left untreated, they can cause severe health problems. A stool test is necessary to pinpoint the problem and medication is often available over the counter.

Diseases Spread by People & Animals

Tetanus This potentially fatal disease is found in undeveloped tropical areas. It is difficult to treat but is preventable with immunisation. Tetanus occurs when a wound becomes infected by a germ which lives in the faeces of animals or people, so clean all cuts, punctures or animal bites. Tetanus is known as lockjaw, and the first symptom may be discomfort in swallowing, or stiffening of the jaw and neck; this is followed by painful convulsions of the jaw and whole body.

Rabies Rabies, found in many countries, is caused by a bite or scratch from an infected animal – dogs and monkeys are common carriers. Any bite, scratch or even lick from a mammal should be cleaned immediately and thoroughly. Scrub with soap and running water, and then clean the area with an alcohol solution. If there is any possibility that the animal is infected, medical help should be sought immediately.

Even if the animal is not rabid, all bites should be treated seriously as they can become infected or can result in tetanus. A rabies vaccination is now available and should be considered if you are in a high-risk category – eg, if you intend to explore caves (bat bites can be dangerous) or work with animals.

Meningococcal Meningitis This very serious disease – a problem in countries such as Vietnam – attacks the brain and can be fatal. A scattered, blotchy rash, fever, severe headache, sensitivity to light and neck stiffness which prevents forward bending of the head are the first symptoms. Death can occur within a few hours, so immediate treatment is important.

Treatment is large doses of penicillin given intravenously, or, if that is not possible, intramuscularly (such as in the buttocks).

Vaccination offers good protection for over a year, but you should also check for reports of current epidemics.

Tuberculosis Although this disease is wide-spread in many developing countries, it is not a serious risk to travellers. Young children are more susceptible to this disease than adults and vaccination is a recommended precaution for children under 12 travelling in endemic areas. TB is commonly spread by coughing or by unpasteurised dairy products from infected cows. Milk that has been boiled is safe to drink; the souring of milk to make yoghurt or cheese also kills the bacilli.

Sexually Transmitted Diseases The sexual attractions of Bangkok and Manila lead many unwary travellers (usually males) into these dangers. Sexual contact with an infected sexual partner spreads such diseases. While abstinence is the only 100%

preventative, the use of condoms is also effective.

Gonorrhoea and syphilis are the most common of these diseases; sores, blisters or rashes around the genitals, discharges or pain when urinating are common symptoms. Symptoms may be less marked or not observed at all in women. The symptoms of syphilis eventually disappear completely but the disease continues and can cause severe problems in later years. The treatment of gonorrhoea and syphilis is by antibiotics.

There are numerous other sexually transmitted diseases, for most of which effective treatment is available. However, there is no cure for herpes and there is also currently no cure for AIDS.

AIDS The AIDS virus has, of course, been widely publicised. It is common in parts of Africa and is becoming more widespread in South-East Asia, especially in Thailand and the Philippines.

AIDS can be sexually transmitted or spread through infected blood transfusions; most developing countries cannot afford to screen blood for transfusions. It can also be spread by dirty needles, and vaccinations, acupuncture and tattooing can potentially be as dangerous as intravenous drug use if the equipment is not clean. If you do need an injection it may be a good idea to buy a new syringe from a pharmacy and ask the doctor to use it.

Insect-Borne Diseases

Malaria Malarial mosquitoes are rife in much of South-East Asia including the more remote parts of Malaysia, Thailand and the Philippines, and much of Indochina and Indonesia. This serious disease is spread by mosquito bites. If you are travelling in endemic areas it is extremely important to take malarial prophylactics. Symptoms include headaches, fever, chills and sweating which may subside and recur. Without proper treatment, malaria can develop more serious, potentially fatal effects.

Antimalarial drugs do not actually prevent the disease but suppress its symptoms.

Chloroquine is the most usual malarial prophylactic; a tablet is taken once a week for two weeks prior to arrival in the infected area and six weeks after you leave it.

Unfortunately, there is now a strain of malaria which is resistant to Chloroquine; if you are travelling in an area infected with this strain an alternative drug will be necessary. In South-East Asia, Irian Jaya is the most dangerous area, but note that other places are not necessarily 100% safe: only in Central America, the Middle East and West Africa is Chloroquine completely effective. Where resistance is reported, you should continue to take Chloroquine but supplement it with a weekly dose of Maloprim or a daily dose of Proguanil.

Chloroquine is quite safe for general use, side effects are minimal and it can be taken by pregnant women. Maloprim can have rare but serious side effects if the weekly dose is exceeded and some doctors recommend a check-up after six months continuous use. Fansidar, once a Chloroquine alternative, is no longer recommended as a prophylactic, as it can have dangerous side effects, but it may still be recommended as a treatment for malaria. Chloroquine is also used for malaria treatment but in greater doses than for prophylaxis. Doxycycline is another antimalarial for use where chloroquine resistance is reported; it causes hypersensitivity to sunlight, so sunburn can be a problem.

Mosquitoes appear after dusk. Avoiding bites by covering bare skin and using an insect repellent will further reduce the risk of catching malaria. Insect screens on windows and mosquito nets on beds offer protection, as does burning a mosquito coil. Mosquitoes may be attracted by perfume, aftershave or certain colours. The risk of infection is higher in rural areas and during the wet season.

Dengue Fever There is no prophylactic available for this mosquito-spread disease; the main preventative measure is to avoid mosquito bites. A sudden onset of fever, headaches and severe joint and muscle pains are the first signs before a rash starts on the trunk of the body and spreads to the limbs and face. After a further few days, the fever will subside and recovery will begin. Serious complications are not common.

Typhus Typhus is spread by ticks, mites or lice. It begins as a bad cold, followed by a fever, chills, headache, muscle pains and a body rash. There is often a large painful sore at the site of the bite and nearby lymph nodes are swollen and painful.

Tick typhus is spread by ticks. Scrub typhus is spread by mites that feed on infected rodents and exists mainly in Asia and the Pacific Islands. Take precautions if walking in rural areas in South-East Asia. Seek local advice on areas where ticks pose a danger and always check yourself carefully for ticks after walking in a danger area. A strong insect repellent can help, and serious walkers in tick areas should consider having their boots and trousers impregnated with benzyl benzoate and dibutylphthalate.

Cuts, Bites & Stings
Cuts & Scratches Skin punctures can easily become infected in hot climates and may be difficult to heal. Treat any cut with an antiseptic solution and mercurochrome. Where possible avoid bandages and Band-aids, which can keep wounds wet. Coral cuts are notoriously slow to heal, as the coral injects a weak venom into the wound. Avoid coral cuts by wearing shoes when walking on reefs, and clean any cut thoroughly.

Bites & Stings Bee and wasp stings are often more painful rather than dangerous. Calamine lotion will give relief or ice packs will reduce the pain and swelling. There are some spiders with dangerous bites but antivenins are usually available.

There are various fish and other sea creatures which can sting or bite dangerously or which are dangerous to eat. Again, local advice is the best suggestion.

Snakes To minimise your chances of being bitten, always wear boots, socks and long trousers when walking through undergrowth where snakes may be present. Don't put your hands into holes and crevices, and be careful when collecting firewood.

Snake bites do not cause instantaneous death and antivenins are usually available. Keep the victim calm and still, wrap the bitten limb tightly, as you would for a sprained ankle, and then attach a splint to immobilise it. Then seek medical help, if possible with the dead snake for identification. Don't attempt to catch the snake if there is even a remote possibility of being bitten again. Tourniquets and the sucking out of the poison are comprehensively discredited as a means of treatment now.

Jellyfish Local advice is the best way of avoiding contact with these sea creatures with their stinging tentacles. Stings from most jellyfish are simply rather painful. Dousing in vinegar will de-activate any stingers which have not 'fired'. Calamine lotion, antihistamines and analgesics may reduce the reaction and relieve the pain.

Bedbugs & Lice Bedbugs live in various places, but particularly in dirty mattresses and bedding. Spots of blood on bedclothes or on the wall around the bed can be read as a suggestion to find another hotel. Bedbugs leave itchy bites in neat rows. Calamine lotion may help.

All lice cause itching and discomfort. They make themselves at home in your hair (head lice), your clothing (body lice) or in your pubic hair (crabs). You catch lice through direct contact with infected people or by sharing combs, clothing and the like. Powder or shampoo treatment will kill the lice and infected clothing should then be washed in very hot water.

Leeches & Ticks Leeches may be present in damp rainforest conditions; they attach themselves to your skin to suck your blood. Trekkers often get them on their legs or in their boots. Salt or a lighted cigarette end will make them fall off. Do not pull them off, as the bite is then more likely to become infected. An insect repellent may keep them

away. Vaseline, alcohol or oil will persuade a tick to let go. You should always check your body if you have been walking through a tick-infested area, as they can spread typhus.

Women's Health

Gynaecological Problems Lowered resistance due to the taking of antibiotics for stomach upsets, poor diet and even contraceptive pills can lead to vaginal infections when travelling in hot climates. Keeping the genital area clean, and wearing skirts or loose-fitting trousers and cotton underwear will help to prevent infections.

Yeast infections, characterised by a rash, itch and discharge, can be treated with a vinegar or even lemon-juice douche or with yoghurt. Nystatin suppositories are the usual medical prescription. Trichomonas is a more serious infection. The symptoms are a discharge and a burning sensation when urinating. Male sexual partners must also be treated, and if a vinegar-water douche is not effective medical attention should be sought. Flagyl is the prescribed drug.

Pregnancy Most miscarriages occur during the first three months of pregnancy, so this is the most risky time to travel. The last three months should also be spent within reasonable distance of good medical care, as quite serious problems can develop at this time. Pregnant women should avoid all unnecessary medication, but vaccinations and malarial prophylactics should still be taken where possible. Additional care should be taken to prevent illness and careful attention should be paid to diet and nutrition.

WOMEN TRAVELLERS

South-East Asia is generally a fairly straightforward region for women to travel in. In some places, the time honoured fixation that Western women are more easy-going (or of easy virtue) still exists but many parts of South-East Asia have really moved on from mere developing status to fully fledged developed, and people's ideas have also become more sophisticated.

Nevertheless, there are some places where

a little extra care is needed and women should take precautions. South-East Asia does not have any really fundamentalist Muslim regions, so Muslim attitudes towards women do not present a major problem, despite which women travellers do experience more difficulty in Sumatra, along the east coast of Malaysia and in the southern Philippines, and extra care should be taken there.

Respectful dressing is certainly necessary – beachwear should be reserved for the beach and basically the less skin you expose the better. South-East Asia is not the sort of place where veils are required, however.

Attitude can be as important as what you wear. Never respond to come ons or rude comments. Completely ignoring them is always best. A haughty attitude can work wonders, in India you might call it a hint of the *memsahib*!

Of course, a husband (which equals any male partner) or children also confers respectability but the husband doesn't have to be present. Some women travellers wear a wedding ring simply for the aura it confers. The imaginary husband doesn't even have to be left at home, who is to say you're not meeting him that very day?

Some precautions are simply the same for any traveller, male or female, but women should take extra care not to find themselves alone on empty beaches, down dark streets or in other situations where help might not be available.

Look upon any holes in the walls of cheap hotels with deep suspicion, especially in showers. In some parts of the region, cheap hotels often double as brothels. If you find yourself in one of these, turning the haughty attitude up a notch may help but as often as not it's no problem; some people may be there because it's a brothel, but it's recognised that you're there because it's a cheap hotel. Nevertheless, you should take care, especially at night, and if you're uncomfortable move to another hotel.

Solo women travellers, just like solo male ones, should be wary when strangers are unexpectedly friendly. See the note in the following Dangers & Annoyances section about theft.

Tampons and other such necessities are reasonably widely available in the region. If you're worried that you won't be able to find something while you're in the back blocks of Borneo for a month, then stock up in a place like Singapore before you start out.

DANGERS & ANNOYANCES
Theft
I've made several trips through South-East Asia and not lost a thing – and one trip where every time I turned round something went missing. Theft is a problem but it's probably no more endemic than in Western countries. As a traveller, however, you're often fairly vulnerable and when you do lose things it can be a real hassle. Most important things to guard are your passport, papers, tickets and money. It's best to always carry these next to your skin or in a sturdy leather pouch on your belt.

You can further lessen the risks by being careful of snatch thieves in certain cities. Cameras or shoulder bags are great for these people. Be careful on buses and trains and even in hotels. Don't leave valuables lying around in your room. A very useful antitheft item is a small padlock – you can use it to double lock your room (there's often a latch for this purpose) or to tie your bag down to a train luggage rack.

A few years back there were a spate of druggings, particularly in Thailand. A solo traveller would be befriended by a local who would buy him a tea or coffee, a day later the unfortunate traveller wakes up with a splitting headache and with all his possessions gone. Food or drink on buses can also be risky – one traveller wrote of being drugged and robbed on a long-distance tour bus in Thailand! This particular technique seems to have moved on from South-East Asia to the subcontinent these days but be wary of sudden friendships. Also be wary of your fellow travellers as not all of them are scrupulously honest.

There are a variety of other ways of losing things apart from straightforward theft. Over the years, we've had letters from unfortunate travellers who have been the victims of just about every scam imaginable.

Two favourites have been airline-ticket rackets and buy-here, sell-there operations. Often people lose money on these deals through sheer stupidity.

Ask yourself, would you give somebody whose 'office' is a table in a coffee bar US$1000 to get you an airline ticket? Will he be there again tomorrow? And before you lay out large amounts of money for amazing gemstones (or some other high value item) which you are assured you can sell at a huge profit back home just ask yourself if this is so easy why doesn't everybody do it? Gambling rackets, 'losing' travellers' cheques, guaranteeing loans, they're all scams which unfortunate or foolish travellers have lost their shirts on.

Drugs

Always treat drugs with a great deal of caution. There is, of course, lots of dope available in the region but these days even a little harmless grass can cause a great deal of trouble. Also, as soon as you start messing with heavier stuff or trying to export it they'll land on top of you. There are a hell of a lot of travellers languishing behind bars and more have found themselves inside looking out after they've tried to bring stuff back home with them. Don't.

The days of paying off a few cops and then making a speedy exit from the country have pretty much disappeared. Even easy-going Bali now has a jail just down the road from Kuta Beach where a number of travellers are spending much longer enjoying the tropical climate than at first intended. In Indonesia, you can actually end up behind bars because your travel companion had dope and you didn't report them.

Other places can be a whole lot worse. A spell in a Thai prison is nobody's idea of a pleasant way to pass the time, while in Malaysia and Singapore, a prison spell may be supplemented with a beating with the *rotan*. In those countries, simple possession can have you dangling from a rope, as two

Australians discovered in 1986. On a per capita basis, the Malaysians execute far more people for drug offences (and with far less publicity) than the Americans do for murder.

Don't bother bringing drugs home with you either. Back home in the West you may not get hung for possession but with the stamps you'll have on your passport you're guaranteed to be a subject of suspicion. I would have thought I had a fairly good reason for spending some time kicking around odd places, but for a couple of years every time I arrived home in Melbourne the customs guys always seemed glad to see me, to usher me off to a private room and to go through everything with a fine tooth comb.

ACCOMMODATION

In most of South-East Asia, accommodation is no problem. About the only time you might have difficulty is over Chinese New Year, when finding a room can be a hassle in some places. Also, peak holiday periods like Christmas, when there is a mass exodus from Australia, can be a problem.

In Indonesia, cheap hotels are usually known as *losmen* – they're small, often family-run places. Elsewhere hotels are often Chinese-run – spartan, noisy, but in general clean and well-kept. Costs are very variable but in most of the region, you can get a reasonable room for two from around US$5 to US$15 – more expensive in some of the big cities and sometimes less in remote areas.

If you arrive in a country by air, there is often an airport hotel booking desk, although they often do not cover the lower strata of hotels. Some airports (like Bangkok's) are better than others (like Singapore's) for this game. Otherwise, you'll generally find hotels clustered around the bus and train station areas – always good places to start hunting. Check your room and the bathroom before you agree to take it. If the sheets don't look clean, ask to have them changed right away.

If you think a hotel is too expensive, ask if they have anything cheaper. Often they may try to steer you into more expensive rooms, simply be trying it on a bit or even be open to a little bargaining. A very important point to remember in Chinese hotels is that a 'single' room usually has a double bed while a 'double' has two beds. A couple can always request a single room. Many cheaper hotels throughout the region only supply one sheet on the bed, if you want a top sheet (useful for keeping mosquitoes away) you have to supply your own. I've been carrying the same Indonesian sarong around for this purpose for over 10 years now.

FOOD

Eat what you like when you want to would be my first advice. In general, food in South-East Asia is pretty healthy. A good rule of thumb is to glance at the restaurant or food stall and its proprietor – if it looks clean and they look healthy then chances are the food will be OK too.

There are two main things to be careful about – water and fresh, uncooked food. Only in Singapore, Hong Kong and some other major cities can you drink water straight from the taps – elsewhere you should ensure that water is boiled or purified. It's no good avoiding the water if you then eat fruit or vegetables that have been washed in that unhealthy water. Ice can be a danger too as freezing things certainly doesn't kill all germs. Cooked food that has been allowed to go cold can also be dangerous.

In general, you should have few problems and, in places like Singapore, you can usually eat from street stalls with impunity. Of course, you'll also find Coke and other hygienically pure Western delights. McDonald's are spreading their tentacles through the region too and you'll find branches in Hong Kong, Macau, Malaysia, the Philippines, Singapore and Thailand. Kentucky Fried Chicken have spread their influence even more widely.

Despite the pleasures of the local cuisine, some travellers feel there are benefits to be had by preparing their own food. This requires carrying cooking gear and a Camping Gaz cooker (replacement cylinders are available in most places in the region) but

you can save money this way and also eat well.

Fruit

South-East Asian travel can be a special taste treat when it comes to fruit. Apart from all those mundane bananas, pineapples and coconuts, there is a host of fruits that will do wonderful things for your taste buds. Fruit stalls are on hand all over to sell iced slices or segments of these fruits in season.

Durian – the most infamous fruit of the region, the durian is a large green fruit with a hard spiny exterior. Crack it open to reveal the biggest stink imaginable! Drains blocked up? No, it's just the durian season.

If you can hold your nose you might actually learn to love them, although one traveller felt that I should come right out with it and admit that durians 'look like shit, smell like shit and taste like shit. On the other hand,' he went on, 'you can try durian in a milder form by having a durian ice cream – which also smells like shit and tastes like shit but looks like ice cream.' You can't satisfy everybody but as smelly as they are Durians are reputed to be a phenomenal aphrodisiac!

Jeruk – the all-purpose term for citrus fruit. There are many kinds available including the huge *jeruk muntis* or *jerunga*, known in the West as a *pomelo*. It's larger than a grapefruit, has a very thick skin, but tastes sweeter, more like an orange.

Mangosteen – the small purple-brown mangosteen cracks open to reveal tasty white segments with a very fine flavour. Queen Victoria once offered a reward to anyone able to transport a mangosteen back to England while still edible.

Nangcur – an enormous yellow-green fruit that can weigh over 20 kg. Inside are hundreds of individual bright yellow segments. Also called jackfruit, the taste is distinctive and the texture slightly rubbery.

Rambutan – a bright red fruit covered in soft, hairy spines, the name means 'hairy'. Break it open to reveal a delicious, white, lychee-like fruit inside.

Salak – found chiefly in Indonesia, the salak is immediately recognisable by its brown 'snakeskin' covering. Peel the skin off to reveal segments that taste like a cross between an apple and a walnut. Bali salaks are much nicer than any others.

Starfruit – called blimbing in Bali, the name is obvious when you see a slice – it's star shaped. It has a cool, crispy, watery taste.

Zurzat – also spelt sirsat, sometimes called a white mango and known in the West as custard apple or soursop, a warty green skin covers a thirst-quenching interior with a slight lemonish taste. They are ripe when they feel squishy.

Other – the *sawo* looks like a potato and tastes like a pear. *Jambu* is pear shaped but has a radish-like crispy texture and a pink, shiny colour. *Papaya,* or *paw paw,* has a sweet, yellow pulp. Bananas are *pisang* and pineapple are *nanas* in Indonesia.

BUYING & SELLING

Making money out of selling things isn't what it used to be – in most cases, people can find pretty much everything you have and cheaper to boot. Obvious exceptions are places like Burma (Myanmar) where almost everything has its demand and its price. Nor is there much opportunity for picking up casual work in the region. You have to get up to North-East Asia before you get into the lucrative 'English lessons' racket. In Hong Kong, for example, English teaching pays HK$50 an hour, but we've had warnings from people who have been ripped off by English-teaching schools.

Buying is a different game but don't get carried away with the idea of making your fortune with the goodies you bring back home with you. The people who buy art and handicrafts to profitably resell in the West are usually experts and the Asian clothes you see for sale in the West are usually brought in as a full-time business, not some one-off trip.

There are plenty of things you'll want to buy just for their own sake and it's worth having a few ground rules to follow. First of all, don't buy it unless you really want it.

Secondly, outside of the odd 'fixed price' store, where prices are really fixed, the name of the game is bargaining. Food in markets, handicrafts, even transport are things you may have to bargain for. The secrets of successful bargaining are to make a game of it, to make a first offer that is sufficiently low to allow both buyer and seller room to manoeuvre (but not so low as to be laughable) and to be good humoured about it. Accept that you're simply going to have to end up paying more money than the locals, and remember that it's not a matter of life and death or personal honour!

FINAL THOUGHTS

It's people that make travel – seeing things

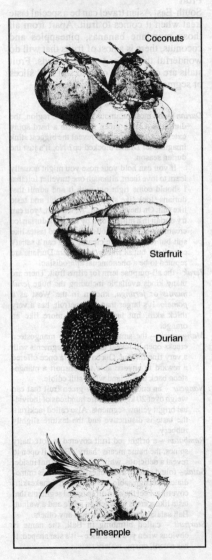

Coconuts

Starfruit

Durian

Pineapple

may be great, doing things may be exciting, but it's the people who'll stay in your memory. So make the most of them, go out of your way to meet people and to get to know them. It's the only way you'll really get to know the countries you visit.

The same consideration applies to your fellow travellers. For perhaps obvious reasons, a cross-section of travellers seems to be a whole lot more interesting than a similar slice of the general population. Apart from making friends, you'll run into time and again over the years, travel also provides a lot of immediate benefits through the friends you make. You rarely travel alone for long, it always seems that somebody else is going the same direction as you and you soon end up as part of a group heading to who knows where. Remember also, that your fellow travellers are the best source of information on what lies ahead.

Since the shoestring traveller seems to get a fair amount of flak from time to time, I'd better outline my philosophy of what he/she is not. They're not scroungers, penniless lay-abouts, permanently high or rip-off merchants. If I had to define my belief in travel it's that if you've been some place and stayed in the local Hilton, you've probably not been there (sorry Conrad). Tourists stay in Hiltons, travellers don't.

The traveller wants to see the country at ground level, to breathe it, experience it – live it. This usually requires two things the tourist can't provide – more time and less money. If you're going to really travel, it's going to take longer and on a day-to-day basis cost less. So blend in, enjoy yourself, but most important of all, make it easy for the travellers who are going to follow in your footsteps.

Getting There & Away

Step one is to get to Asia and, in these days of severe competition between the airlines, there are plenty of opportunities to find cheap tickets to a variety of 'gateway' cities. You virtually have no choice apart from flying though – boat services are now limited and apart from odd routes there are virtually no regular shipping services to South-East Asia from Australia or anywhere else.

The major Asian gateways for cheap flights are Singapore, Bangkok and Hong Kong. They are all good places to fly to and good places to fly from. Bangkok has long had a reputation as a bargain centre for cheap airline tickets, but first Singapore and then Penang (Malaysia) and Hong Kong joined the group.

Cheap tickets are available in two distinct categories – official and unofficial. Official ones are advance purchase tickets, budget-fares, Apex, super-Apex or whatever other brand name the airlines care to tack on them in order to put, as it is so succinctly expressed, 'bums on seats'.

Unofficial tickets are simply discounted tickets which the airlines release through selected travel agents. Don't go looking for discounted tickets straight from the airlines. They are only available through travel agents. Generally, you can find discounted tickets at prices as low or lower than the Apex or budget tickets, plus there is no advance-purchase requirement nor should there be any cancellation penalty, although individual travel agents may institute their own cancellation charges.

It is necessary to exercise a little caution with discounted tickets. Make sure 'OK' on the ticket really means you have a confirmed seat, for example. Phone the airline and reconfirm again, better to find out immediately if the agent has made a firm booking.

Air Travellers with Special Needs

If you have special needs of any sort - you've broken a leg, you're vegetarian, travelling in a wheelchair, taking the baby, terrified of flying – you should let the airline know as soon as possible so that they can make arrangements accordingly. You should remind them when you reconfirm your booking (at least 72 hours before departure) and again when you check in at the airport. It may also be worth ringing round the airlines before you make your booking to find out how they can handle your particular needs.

TO/FROM THE UK & EUROPE

Ticket discounting has been long established in the UK and it's wide open – the various agents advertise their fares and there's nothing under the counter about it at all.

Trailfinders (☎ 071-938 3366) in west London put out a lavish illustrated brochure which includes airfare details. STA Travel (☎ (071) 937 9962) also has branches in the UK. Look in the listings magazines *Time Out* and *City Limits* plus the Sunday papers and *Exchange & Mart* for ads. Also, look out for the free magazines widely available in London – start by looking outside the main railway stations.

Most British travel agents are registered with ABTA (Association of British Travel Agents). If you have paid for your flight to an ABTA-registered agent who then goes out of business, ABTA will guarantee a refund or an alternative.

Unregistered bucket shops are riskier but also sometimes cheaper. The danger with discounted tickets in the UK is that some of the 'bucket shops', as ticket discounters are known, are more than a little shonky. Back-stairs travel agents sometimes tend to fold up and disappear after you've handed over the money and before they hand over the tickets. Always make sure you have tickets in hand before you give them the folding stuff. Don't fear, there are plenty of highly reputable and efficient ticket discounters – such as Trailfinders and STA Travel.

The Globetrotters Club (BCM Roving, London WC1N 3XX) publishes a newsletter *Globe* which covers obscure destinations and can help in the finding of travelling companions.

On the Continent, Amsterdam and Antwerp are among the best places for buying airline tickets. WATS, Keyserlei 44, Antwerp, Belgium, has been recommended. In Amsterdam, NBBS is a popular travel agent.

Many of the cheapest fares from Europe to South-East Asia are offered by Eastern European carriers.

Quoted fares from London to South-East Asia (return in brackets) include Bangkok for £275 (£465), Singapore £275 (£460), Jakarta £330 (£630), Denpasar (Bali) £310 (£620), Manila £325 (£580) and Hong Kong from around £240 (£440). Flights from London to Australia or New Zealand with stopovers in South-East Asia are available from £400 one way.

TO/FROM AUSTRALIA & NZ

Ticket pricing in Australasia is now totally deregulated. Agents can charge what they like. Since there are far fewer airlines flying to and from Australia and New Zealand than there are to and from London, you won't find the same wide variety of fares, nevertheless bargains can still be found with a little shopping around. STA Travel and Flight Centres International are major dealers in cheap airfares. Check them for starters or simply scan the ads in newspaper travel sections.

Regular excursion return fares from New Zealand and Australia usually have a low and a high-season period. Often the high season only applies for a very limited time over the December-January school holiday period. There are also 'special fares' which are usually operated by airlines who are not regulars over that route (Alitalia or British Airways to Singapore for example) or by a more roundabout route (save money to Hong Kong by flying via Kuala Lumpur).

Melbourne and Sydney are often 'common rated' but fares from Sydney are sometimes slightly cheaper, and cheaper still from Brisbane, Perth or Darwin, if flights are available. Flights from New Zealand are a bit more expensive.

Return fares from Melbourne include Bangkok from around A$1150 to A$1400; Hong Kong from around A$1150 to A$1250; Kuala Lumpur from A$950 to A$1150; Manila from A$900 to A$1000; and Indonesia from A$950 to A$1050 (Denpasar is about A$50 cheaper than fares to Jakarta). You will also find special fares offered throughout the year that are cheaper than the prices mentioned here – check the travel sections in local newspapers or enquire at a travel agency that specialises in discounted tickets.

From Auckland, you can get return flights to Singapore for around NZ$1600 and to Bangkok for around NZ$1800.

Other possibilities out of Australia include flights from Darwin to Kupang (on the Indonesian island of Timor), an economical and interesting way out of the country, and from Melbourne to Nauru and on from there to the Philippines, Hong Kong or Japan. The tiny (but very rich) island nation of Nauru operates a small airline at a hefty loss and has interesting ticketing possibilities to the region – as well as to other Pacific nations.

TO/FROM NORTH AMERICA

You can pick up interesting tickets to South-East Asia, particularly from the US west coast and Vancouver. In fact, the intense competition between Asian airlines is resulting in ticket discounting operations very similar to the London bucket shops.

The *New York Times*, the *Chicago Tribune*, the *LA Times*, the *San Francisco Examiner*, the *Vancouver Sun* and the *Toronto Globe & Mail* all produce weekly travel sections in which you'll find any number of travel agents' ads. Council Travel and STA Travel have offices in major US cities, while Travel CUTS have outlets throughout Canada.

The magazine *Travel Unlimited* (PO Box 1058, Allston, Mass 02134) publishes details of the cheapest airfares and courier possibilities for destinations all over the world from the USA.

Typical fares from the US west coast include Singapore for US$1100 return,

Bangkok US$1125 return or Hong Kong US$990 return. One-way fares are a bit more than half the return fares.

ROUND-THE-WORLD TICKETS & CIRCLE PACIFIC FARES

Round-the-World (RTW) tickets have become very popular in the last few years.

The airline RTW tickets are often real bargains, and can work out no more expensive or even cheaper than an ordinary return ticket. Prices start from about £850, A$1900 or US$1400.

The official airline RTW tickets are usually put together by a combination of two airlines and permit you to fly anywhere you

---

Air Travel Glossary

Apex Apex, or 'advance purchase excursion', is a discounted ticket which must be paid for in advance. There are penalties if you wish to change it.

Baggage Allowance This will be written on your ticket: usually one 20 kg item to go in the hold, plus one item of hand luggage.

Bucket Shop An unbonded travel agency specialising in discounted airline tickets.

Bumped Just because you have a confirmed seat doesn't mean you're going to get on the plane – see Overbooking.

Cancellation Penalties If you have to cancel or change an Apex ticket, there are often heavy penalties involved – insurance can sometimes be taken out against these penalties. Some airlines impose penalties on regular tickets as well, particularly against 'no show' passengers.

Check In Airlines ask you to check in a certain time ahead of the flight departure (usually 1½ hours on international flights). If you fail to check in on time and the flight is overbooked, the airline can cancel your booking and give your seat to somebody else.

Confirmation Having a ticket written out with the flight and date you want doesn't mean you have a seat until the agent has checked with the airline that your status is 'OK', or confirmed. Meanwhile you could just be 'on request'.

Discounted Tickets There are two main types of discounted fares – officially discounted (see Promotional Fares) and unofficially discounted. The lowest prices often impose drawbacks like flying with unpopular airlines, inconvenient schedules, or unpleasant routes and connections.

A discounted ticket can save you things other than money – you may be able to pay Apex prices without the associated Apex advance booking and other requirements. Discounted tickets only exist where there is fierce competition.

Full Fares Airlines traditionally offer first class (coded F), business-class (coded J) and economy-class (coded Y) tickets. These days there are so many promotional and discounted fares available from the regular economy class that few passengers pay full economy fare.

Lost Tickets If you lose your airline ticket, an airline will usually treat it like a travellers' cheque and, after inquiries, issue you with another one. Legally, however, an airline is entitled to treat it like cash and if you lose it then it's gone forever. Take good care of your tickets.

No Shows No shows are passengers who fail to show up for their flight, sometimes due to unexpected delays or disasters, sometimes due to simply forgetting, and sometimes because they made more than one booking and didn't bother to cancel the one they didn't want. Full fare passengers who fail to turn up are sometimes entitled to travel on a later flight. The rest of us are penalised (see Cancellation Penalties).

On Request An unconfirmed booking for a flight, see Confirmation.

---

want on their route systems, so long as you do not backtrack. Other restrictions are that you (usually) must book the first sector in advance and cancellation penalties then apply. There may be restrictions on how many stops you are permitted and usually the tickets are valid for 90 days and up to a year. An alternative type of RTW ticket is one where a travel agency combines a number of discounted tickets.

Circle Pacific tickets use a combination of airlines to circle the Pacific – combining Australia, New Zealand, North America and Asia. As with RTW tickets, there are advance purchase restrictions and limits to how many stopovers you can make. These fares are

---

Open Jaws A return ticket where you fly out to one place but return from another. If available, this can save you backtracking to your arrival point.

Overbooking Airlines hate to fly empty seats and since every flight has some passengers who fail to show up (see No Shows) airlines often book more passengers than they have seats. Usually the excess passengers balance those who fail to show up but occasionally somebody gets bumped. If this happens, guess who it is most likely to be? The passengers who check in late.

Promotional Fares Officially discounted fares like Apex fares which are available from travel agents or direct from the airline.

Reconfirmation At least 72 hours prior to departure time of an onward or return flight, you must contact the airline and 'reconfirm' that you intend to be on the flight. If you don't do this, the airline can delete your name from the passenger list and you could lose your seat. You don't have to reconfirm the first flight on your itinerary or if your stopover is less than 72 hours. It doesn't hurt to reconfirm more than once.

Restrictions Discounted tickets often have various restrictions on them – advance purchase is the most usual one (see Apex). Others are restrictions on the minimum and maximum period you must be away, such as a minimum of 14 days or a maximum of one year. For more information see Cancellation Penalties.

Standby A discounted ticket where you only fly if there is a seat free at the last moment. Standby fares are usually only available on domestic routes.

Tickets Out An entry requirement for many countries is that you have an onward or return ticket – in other words, a ticket out of the country. If you're not sure what you intend to do next, the easiest solution is to buy the cheapest onward ticket to a neighbouring country or a ticket from a reliable airline which can later be refunded if you do not use it.

Transferred Tickets Airline tickets cannot be transferred from one person to another. Travellers sometimes try to sell the return half of their ticket, but officials can ask you to prove that you are the person named on the ticket. This is unlikely to happen on domestic flights, on an international flight, however, tickets may be compared with passports.

Travel Agencies Travel agencies vary widely and you should ensure you use one that suits your needs. Some simply handle tours while full-service agencies handle everything from tours and tickets to car rental and hotel bookings. A good one will do all these things and can save you a lot of money but if all you want is a ticket at the lowest possible price, then you really need an agency specialising in discounted tickets. A discounted ticket agency, however, may not be useful for other things, like hotel bookings.

Travel Periods Some officially discounted fares, Apex fares in particular, vary with the time of year. There is often a low (off-peak) season and a high (peak) season. Sometimes there's an intermediate or shoulder season as well. At peak times, when everyone wants to fly, not only will the officially discounted fares be higher but so will unofficially discounted fares, or there may simply be no discounted tickets available. Usually the fare depends on your outward flight – if you depart in the high season and return in the low season, you pay the high-season fare. ■

likely to be around 15% cheaper than Round-the-World tickets.

BUYING A PLANE TICKET

Plane tickets will probably be the most expensive items in your budget, and buying them can be an intimidating business. There is likely to be a multitude of airlines and travel agents hoping to separate you from your money, and it is always worth putting aside a few hours to research the current state of the market.

Start early: some of the cheapest tickets have to be bought months in advance, and some popular flights sell out early. Talk to other recent travellers – they may be able to stop you making some of the same old mistakes. Look at the ads in newspapers and magazines (not forgetting the press of the ethnic group whose country you plan to visit), consult reference books and watch for special offers.

Then phone round travel agents for bargains. (Airlines can supply information on routes and timetables; however, except at times of inter-airline war they do not supply the cheapest tickets.) Find out the fare, the route, the duration of the journey and any restrictions on the ticket. (See Restrictions in the Air Travel Glossary in this chapter.) Then sit back and decide which is best for you.

You may discover that those impossibly cheap flights are 'fully booked, but we have another one that costs a bit more...' Or, the flight is on an airline notorious for its poor safety standards and leaves you in the world's least favourite airport in mid-journey for 14 hours. Or, they claim only to have the last two seats available for that country for the whole of July, which they will hold for you for a maximum of two hours. Don't panic – keep ringing around.

Use the fares quoted in this book as a guide

only. They are approximate and based on the rates advertised by travel agents at the time of going to press. Quoted airfares do not necessarily constitute a recommendation for the carrier.

If you are travelling from UK or the USA, you will probably find that the cheapest flights are being advertised by obscure bucket shops whose names haven't yet reached the telephone directory. Many such firms are honest and solvent, but there are a few rogues who will take your money and disappear, to reopen elsewhere a month or two later under a new name.

If you feel suspicious about a firm, don't give them all the money at once – leave a deposit of 20% or so and pay the balance when you get the ticket. If they insist on cash in advance, go somewhere else. And once you have the ticket, ring the airline to confirm that you are actually booked onto the flight.

You may decide to pay more than the rock-bottom fare by opting for the safety of a better-known travel agent. Firms such as STA Travel, who have offices worldwide, Council Travel in the USA or Travel CUTS in Canada are not going to disappear overnight, leaving you clutching a receipt for a nonexistent ticket, but they do offer good prices to most destinations.

Once you have your ticket, write its number down together with the flight number and other details, and keep this information somewhere separate and safe. If the ticket is lost or stolen, this will help you get a replacement.

It's sensible to buy travel insurance as early as possible. If you buy it the week before you fly, you may find, for example, that you're not covered for delays to your flight caused by industrial action.

Getting Around

AIR

There are all sorts of ticket bargains around the region available to you once you arrive in South-East Asia. These inter-Asia fares are widely available, although Bangkok, Singapore, Penang and Hong Kong are the major ticket discounting centres.

In Australia, you can buy inter-Asia tickets as add-on fares to Apex tickets. These cost much the same as you would pay through agents in Asia.

A little caution is necessary when looking for tickets in Asia. First of all, shop around – a wise move anywhere, of course. Secondly, don't believe everything you are told – ticket agents in Penang (Malaysia) are very fond of telling people that tickets there are cheaper than in Bangkok or Singapore or wherever.

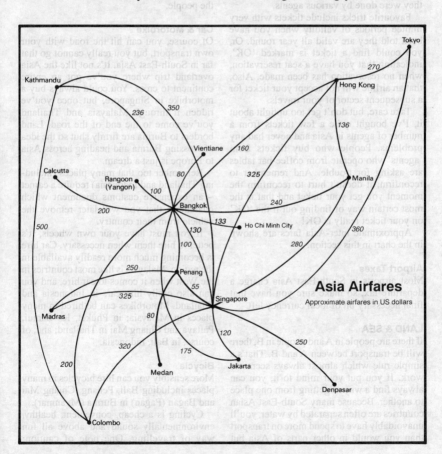

Asia Airfares

Approximate airfares in US dollars

In actual fact, they are often much the same price anywhere; if there is any difference it's likely to be in the favour of the originating city. For example, you're unlikely to find a Bangkok to Kathmandu ticket cheaper in Penang than in Bangkok. Or a Penang to Hong Kong ticket cheaper in Singapore than in Penang.

Most important of all, be very careful that you get what you want before handing over money and that the ticket is precisely what you pay for. Over the years, we have had many letters from people complaining that they were done by various agents.

Favourite tricks include tickets with very limited periods of validity when you have been told they are valid all year round. Or, you could find a ticket is marked 'OK', indicating that you have a seat reservation, when no reservation has been made. Also, that an airline will not accept your ticket for a subsequent sector of your travels.

Take care, but don't get too uptight about it, I've bought quite a few tickets from a number of agents in Asia and never had any problems. People who buy tickets from 'agents' who operate from coffee-bar tables are asking for trouble. And remember to reconfirm, it doesn't hurt to reconfirm the moment you get your ticket and that is the most certain way of finding out if the 'OK' on your ticket really is OK!

Approximate inter-Asia fares are shown in the chart in this section.

Airport Taxes
Most airports in South-East Asia charge a departure tax, so make sure you have that final necessary bit of local currency left.

LAND & SEA
If there are people in A and people in B, there will be transport between A and B. That's a simple rule which almost always seems to work. If you put your mind to it, you can always find a way of getting from one place to another. Because many South-East Asian countries are often separated by water, you'll unavoidably have to spend more on transport than you would in other parts of Asia but

some of these trips can be great experiences. There are not a lot of intercountry shipping services, although those that are available are often very interesting.

Land transport in the region is generally great value. In Malaysia and Thailand, for example, trains and buses are both reasonably cheap and, certainly by the standards further west in Asia, absurdly comfortable. Usually public transport is far more convenient and frequent than in the West simply because far more people use it. Remember that it's by travelling that you actually meet the people.

Car & Motorbike
Of course, you can hit the road with your own transport, but you really cannot go that far in South-East Asia. It's not like the Asia overland trip where you've got an entire continent to cross. You could always buy a motorbike in Singapore, but once you've ridden it through Malaysia and Thailand you've come to the end of the road. Land borders to Burma are firmly shut so the idea of crossing Burma and heading across Asia to Europe is just a dream.

Remember too that many places (including Thailand and Indonesia) require a carnet – an expensive customs document which guarantees that you will later remove the vehicle from their country.

If you must have your own wheels, it's better to hire them when necessary. Car hire is becoming much more readily available in the region. Malaysia is like most countries in the West when it comes to car hire, and you can also easily hire cars in Indonesia and Thailand. Motorbikes can be hired in many places in Malaysia; in Phuket, Ko Samui, Pattaya and Chiang Mai in Thailand; and, of course, in Bali, Indonesia.

Bicycle
More sensibly you can hire bicycles in many places including Bali, Penang, Chiang Mai and Bagan (Pagan) in Burma (Myanmar).

Cycling is a cheap, convenient, healthy, environmentally sound and above all fun way of travelling. One note of caution:

before you leave home, go over your bike with a fine-toothed comb and fill your repair kit with every imaginable spare. As with cars and motorbikes, you won't necessarily be able to buy that crucial gizmo for your machine when it breaks down somewhere in the back of beyond as the sun sets.

Bicycles can travel by air. You can take them to pieces and put them in a bike bag or box, but it's much easier simply to wheel your bike to the check in desk, where it should be treated as a piece of baggage. You may have to remove the pedals and turn the handlebars sideways so that it takes up less space in the aircraft's hold; check all this with the airline well in advance, preferably before you pay for your ticket.

Yachts

With a little effort, it's often possible to get yacht rides from various places in the region. Very often, yacht owners are just travellers too and they often need another crew member or two. Willingness to give it a try is often more important than experience and often all it costs you is a contribution to the food kitty. Check out anywhere that yachts pass through or in towns with Western-style yacht clubs.

Maureen and I managed a yacht ride from Bali to Exmouth in Western Australia once. Over the years we've had letters from people who've managed to get rides from Singapore, Penang, Phuket and (like us) Benoa in Bali.

Tony Wheeler

OVERLANDING IN SOUTH-EAST ASIA

With all the water in the way 'overlanding' through South-East Asia seems a misnomer. However, if by the term overlanding you mean travelling from place to place by local transport with the minimum use of aircraft then South-East Asia offers enormous scope.

Indonesia

If you want to trek right through Indonesia from the Australian end, the logical starting point is Kupang in Timor. There are now regular flights from Darwin in Australia's Northern Territory to Kupang. From Kupang, you could work your way through the amazing and varied islands of Nusa Tenggara. Along the way you could climb to see the multicoloured lakes of Keli Mutu in Flores, see the dragons of Komodo and pause at the wonderful Gili Islands off Lombok.

From Bali, after you've explored that magical island, the next stage is to hop on a bus to Surabaya, usually an overnight trip. On the way to Surabaya, it's worth stopping off to climb the extraordinary Mt Bromo in Java. From Surabaya, you can continue to Yogyakarta, the cultural heartland of Java and Indonesia. Yogya is also the second of Indonesia's three major travellers' centres. The first is, of course, Bali and the third is Lake Toba in Sumatra.

On from Yogya, you can catch a train or bus to Jakarta, although if you have time, there are interesting stops en route at, for example, the Dieng Plateau, Pangandaran, Bandung and Bogor.

At Jakarta, you may be forced to make a decision. If your visa is running short, and unfortunately present Indonesian visa limitations make it virtually impossible to really explore the country in one bite, you have to leave. If you're in that situation, then head to Singapore from where you can then re-enter Indonesia and start again. There's no need to go right back to Jakarta though.

You can fly to Padang or Pakanbaru in Sumatra or even to Bintan and Batam islands in the Riau Archipelago, the Indonesian islands south of Singapore, and go on from there to Sumatra. If you're not embroiled in visa problems back in Jakarta, you could continue to Sumatra either by bus or train, and then by ferry.

Travel in southern Sumatra is the hardest in Indonesia, so many people opt instead for the regular ship or flight from Jakarta to Padang. After Padang, the roads through Sumatra aren't so bad and you continue north through delightful Bukittinggi, perhaps make a side trip to Nias Island and then take a well-earned rest at relaxing Lake Toba.

Finally, you exit Sumatra by flying from Medan to Penang in Malaysia. An alternative to this route would be to go from Singapore up to Penang and enter Sumatra at Medan then do the trip back down through Sumatra in reverse, finally exiting to Jakarta or to the Riau Archipelago and/or Singapore.

And of course, there are other Indonesian islands to the north and east, including Kalimantan (the southern half or Borneo), wonderful Sulawesi, the Maluku islands and Irian Jaya.

Malaysia & Thailand

Assuming you've followed the traditional path up through Indonesia, you're now in Penang and after enjoying yourself there you can head south to the hill stations like the Cameron Highlands, to Pulau Pangkor, to modern Kuala Lumpur, to historic Melaka and, finally, arrive at Singapore. Then you can head up the east coast and sample Malaysia's beaches and offshore islands. Travel in Malaysia is just about the most hassle-free of anywhere in Asia. There are excellent train and bus services, and very economical share-taxis; even the hitching is easy.

The northern Borneo states – Malaysia's Sabah and Sarawak and the independent kingdom of Brunei – are most easily visited from Singapore or Peninsular Malaysia since connections between north Borneo and Kalimantan are very tenuous; but it can be done. You can sometimes, and only with some effort, cross from Sabah to Mindanao, the southernmost island of the Philippines, but it's easier to fly from Sabah direct to Manila or Hong Kong.

There are a variety of ways of crossing to Thailand from Malaysia, but the usual routes are to take a taxi or train from Penang to Hat Yai if you're on the west coast, or to simply walk across the border from Rantau Panjang to Sungai Golok on the east coast.

From Hat Yai, the major city in the south of Thailand, you can continue by bus to Phuket, a resort island with superb beaches. Then continue north to Surat Thani and the equally beautiful island of Ko Samui, where you can wrestle with the important question of whether Phuket or Ko Samui is the better

place to get away from it all. Finally, you reach hyperactive Bangkok and decide where to head next.

For most travellers, that decision will be to continue north to Chiang Mai, the second city of Thailand and another great travellers' centre. On the way, you could pause to explore the ancient cities of Ayuthaya and Sukhothai. From Chiang Mai, you can make treks into the colourful hill-tribe areas or you can loop back to Bangkok through the north-east region. Bangkok is more than just the sin city of South-East Asia, it's also a centre for cheap airline tickets, so the next question is where to fly to – east or west.

Burma (Myanmar) & West

Since you can still only get 14-day visas for Burma (Myanmar), it's generally a well orchestrated rush around the attractions of that unusual country. Rangoon (Yangon) is the only entry point and you can either make a Burma visit as an out-and-back foray from Bangkok or use Burma as a stepping stone between South-East Asia and West Asia. If the latter is your intention, then it's time to pack *South-East Asia on a shoestring* away and pick up Lonely Planet's *West Asia on a shoestring* for details on Bangladesh, India, Nepal and beyond.

Vietnam, Laos & Cambodia

This area of South-East Asia, often referred to as Indochina, has just recently opened its doors to foreign travellers.

Really, the only practicable way into or out of Vietnam is by air. There are a number of flights to and from Ho Chi Minh City's Tan Son Nhut or Hanoi's Noi Bai airports. From Vietnam, it is possible to overland into Cambodia but not Laos.

The usual way into Cambodia is by air and the choices here are limited: Aeroflot, Lao Aviation, Kampuchean Airlines and Vietnam Airlines.

Laos has only one travel option – by air to Vientiane and by air out, and the choices of carrier are limited. Bangkok is the best point of departure for Vietnam and Laos, whereas

Ho Chi Minh City, Hanoi and Vientiane are the best places to depart for Cambodia.

Hong Kong & East

From Hong Kong, the frenetic city state and gateway to China, you've got a choice of heading further east or west (in which case you need Lonely Planet's *North-East Asia on a shoestring* for China, Japan, Korea and Taiwan) or turning south for the Philippines. Travelling across China to the far west and then down into Pakistan via the Karakoram Highway from Kashgar or, if Tibet is open, into Nepal via Lhasa are adventurous routes.

The Philippines

Manila is overwhelmingly the gateway city to the Philippines, but from there you can head north to the rice terraces and beaches of north Luzon, and south to the Mayon volcano and other attractions of south Luzon. Or, island hop off into the tightly clustered islands of the Visayas.

Eventually, you can hop back to Manila and decide where to next – on to Australia or further afield. A good loop through the region includes travelling from Australia to Indonesia, Singapore, Malaysia, Thailand, Indochina, Hong Kong, Philippines and, finally, back to Australia. But, of course, there are lots of other possibilities.

STUDENT TRAVEL

There are student travel offices in most South-East Asian capitals, most of them associated in some way with STA Travel –

the major force in student travel in the region. They're most useful for discounted airfares and are generally worth checking out if you want to fly somewhere.

Other services they can provide include local tours and accommodation bookings. Usually the hotels they deal with are somewhat up-market and even with discounts they're outside the usual budget travellers' range. If you're a real student, they can also provide student cards. Major student travel offices and agents in the region include:

Hong Kong
> Hong Kong Student Travel Bureau, 10th Floor, 1021 Star House, Tsimshatsui, Kowloon (☎ 3-721 3269)

Indonesia
> Carefree Bali Holidays, Kuta Beach Club, Kuta Beach, Bali (☎ 51 261)
> Indo Shangrila Travel, 219G Jalan Gajah Mada, Jakarta (☎ 63 2703)

Malaysia
> STA Travel, UBN Tower, 6th Floor, 10 Jalan P Ramlee, Kuala Lumpur (☎ 2305720)
> MSL Travel, 1st Floor, South-East Asia Hotel, 69 Jalan Haji Hussein, Kuala Lumpur (☎ 298 4132)

Philippines
> Ystaphil (Youth Student Travel Association of the Philippines), 4227 Tomas Claudio St, Paranque, Manila (☎ 832 0680; fax 818 7948)

Singapore
> STA Travel, 2/17 Orchard Parade Hotel, cnr Orchard and Tanglin Rds, Singapore (☎ 734 5681)

Thailand
> STA Wall Street Tower Building, 14th Floor (Rm 1405), 33 Surawong Rd, Bangrak, Bangkok, 10500 (☎ 233 2582/2626; fax 234 0732)

Brunei

A comic-book little country, Brunei is blessed with a supply of that most prized commodity – oil. It shows from the grandiose public buildings of the capital, Bandar Seri Begawan (commonly called Bandar), and the airport terminal, large enough for a country 10 times Brunei's size, to the Sultan's fleet of exotic Italian cars.

Brunei has a population of about 230,000 in an area of 5700 sq km. The people are Malays, Chinese, Indians, and around 25,000 are Iban, Dusan and other tribespeople of the interior. Brunei is strictly Islamic. Apart from the capital and the oil town of Seria, the country is mainly jungle. A little rubber is exported along with oil. It's also a fiendishly expensive place. It's cheaper to fly between Sabah and Sarawak than it is to pass through Brunei!

Facts about the Country

HISTORY

At one time, Brunei was a considerable power in these parts. Under the fifth sultan, Bolkiah (known as the 'singing admiral' for his love of music), Brunei's power extended throughout Borneo and into the Philippines. The arrival of the British, in the guise of Rajah Brooke, and their intention to wipe out piracy (a favourite Bruneian occupation) along the Borneo coast spelt the end of its power.

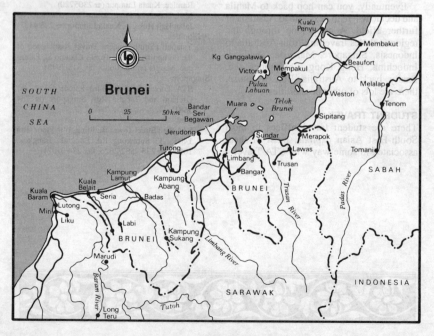

46

Gradually, the country was whittled away. The final absurdity was when it was forced to cede Limbang to Sarawak, splitting the country into two halves. Then, in 1929, oil was discovered on the tiny bit of land left.

That windfall allows Brunei to flourish with no income tax, pensions for all, magnificent and rather redundant public buildings and what must be the highest per capita consumption of cars in South-East Asia. Car importers appear to be plentiful but repairers are in very short supply, so the slightest dent is a ticket to one of Brunei's many scrapyards.

The current Sultan is 29th in line. His father pragmatically kept the country out of the Malaysian confederation before abdicating and now matches his son's sports cars with his own London taxi.

Rather reluctantly, in 1984, Brunei gained independence from Britain. The Sultan celebrated by building himself a new US$350 million palace and renaming the country Brunei Darussalam, or 'Haven of Peace'. The *Guinness Book of Records* rates the Sultan among the richest men in the world, and his spending habits at exclusive London stores make great stories for the tabloids.

He also had enough loose cash around the palace to chip in US$10 million for Ronald Reagan's Nicaraguan 'contra' fund but, unfortunately, the money ended up in the wrong Swiss bank account.

CLIMATE
It's uniformly warm year-round with quite heavy rainfall that peaks from October to February.

Facts for the Visitor

VISAS & EMBASSIES
For visits of up to 14 days, visas are not necessary for citizens of Switzerland, France, Canada, Thailand, Philippines, Japan, Indonesia, the Netherlands, Belgium, Luxembourg, Germany and the Republic of Korea. British, Malaysian and Singaporean citizens do not require a visa for visits of 30 days or less.

All other nationalities, including British overseas citizens and citizens of British dependencies, must have visas to visit Brunei.

If entering from Sarawak or Sabah, there's no fuss on arrival – no money showing, no requirement for an onward ticket and it's unlikely your bags will even be looked at. A one-week stay permit is more or less automatic but, if you ask, you can usually get two weeks. It might be useful, you never know.

Two-day transit visas are reportedly available on the land borders if you don't have a visa but this is not official. It seems to depend largely on the whim of immigration officials at the time – some people get them whereas others are knocked back.

Brunei Embassies
Brunei Darussalam has diplomatic offices in countries including:

Indonesia
    Bank Central Asia Building, Jalan Jenderal Sudirman, Jakarta (☎ 021-578 2180)
Malaysia
    Plaza MBF, Jalan Ampang, Kuala Lumpur (☎ 03-457 4149)
Singapore
    7A Tanglin Hill, Singapore (☎ 474 3393)
Thailand
    Orakarn Building, 26/50 Soi Chitlon, Ploenchit Rd, Bangkok 10500 (☎ 02-51 5766)

MONEY
Currency
The official currency is the Brunei dollar (B$), which is worth exactly the same as the Singapore dollar (which can be used in Brunei). The B$ is worth much more than the Malaysian ringgit. Banks give around 10% less for cash than they do for travellers' cheques.

Costs
Brunei is fiercely expensive, mainly because the cheap accommodation options are limited and unreliable. For budget travellers, Brunei is a bit of a disaster and many people

travelling overland between Sabah and Sarawak find it more economical to take one of the MAS flights between Miri and Labuan or Lawas and jump right over the country.

Transport and food within the country are comparable with prices in the rest of East Malaysia – more expensive than Peninsular Malaysia but not outrageously expensive.

Getting There & Away

AIR

Airline offices in Bandar include:

MAS
   144 Jalan Pemancha (☎ 02-24141)
Royal Brunei Airlines
   RBA Plaza, Jalan Sultan (☎ 02-42222)
Singapore Airlines
   Jalan Sultan (☎ 02-44901)
Thai International
   51 Jalan Sultan (☎ 02-42991)

Royal Brunei Airlines (RBA) connects Bandar with Singapore, Hong Kong, Manila, Darwin and other destinations. The standard economy fare to Singapore is B$320 one way. To Kuching, the airfare is B$192, Kota Kinabalu B$65 and Kuala Lumpur B$372.

When coming *from* any of these cities, the fare is in Malaysian ringgit not Brunei dollars, so it is much cheaper. The fare to Bangkok is about B$500 and it is B$450 to Manila.

LAND
To/From Sarawak

From Bandar, many buses leave every day for Seria (B$4; 1½ hours). From Seria to Kuala Belait, there are frequent buses (B$1; 30 minutes). If you want to reach Miri in one day from Bandar, start out early in the day.

There are four or five buses daily from Kuala Belait to Miri (B$11; 2½ hours). After going through Brunei customs, a Malaysian bus takes you to the Malaysian immigration checkpoint and then on to Miri.

BOAT

Unless you are going to fly to Labuan or Kota Kinabalu, the only way to get from Brunei to Sabah or the isolated eastern Sarawak outposts of Limbang or Lawas is to use launches or launch/taxi combinations.

All international boats leave from the dock at the end of Jalan Roberts, where Brunei immigration formalities are taken care of.

To/From Sabah
Via Limbang There are several private *expres* boats which do this run at various times of the day – departure times depend on demand. The fare is B$7 and the trip takes about 30 minutes; ask around at the dock.

You can either stay at Limbang overnight, take another boat to Punang (further up the coast) or choose to fly to Miri, Lawas or Kota Kinabalu.

Via Labuan Labuan is a duty-free island off Brunei from where you can get ferries to Sabah and then a bus into Kota Kinabalu, ferries direct to Kota Kinabalu, or flights to Sabah, Sarawak or Peninsular Malaysia.

From Bandar, there are two daily services to Labuan at 8 am (B$18; 80 minutes) and 3 pm (B$15). Tickets should be bought a day or so in advance. The ticketing agent is Borneo Leisure Travel (☎ 02-23407) on the ground floor of Brittania House, on the corner of Jalan Sungai Kianggeh and Jalan Cator.

Via Lawas There are usually one or two launches daily between Bandar and Lawas (in Sarawak) which cost B$25 (or M$25 from Lawas) and take about two hours. Runners will accost you as you enter the wharf area at the end of Jalan Roberts so there is no problem finding a boat.

From Lawas, you can continue on to Sabah by minibus.

Around the Country

BANDAR SERI BEGAWAN

The capital, Bandar Seri Begawan (often abbreviated to Bandar), is the only town of any size and really one of the few places to go in the country. It's a neat, very clean and modern city with some fine, overstated buildings. It's also incredibly dull.

Things to See

Omar Ali Saifuddin Mosque Named after the 28th Sultan of Brunei, this mosque was built in 1958 at a cost of about US$5 million. Designed by an Italian architect, the golden-domed structure stands close to the Brunei River in its own artificial lagoon and is the tallest building in Bandar. It's one of the most impressive structures in the East.

Brunei Museum At Kota Batu, six km from the centre of Bandar, this museum is housed in a beautifully constructed building on the banks of the Brunei River. When combined with a visit to the Malay Technology Museum on the riverbank below, it's well worth the short trip out of town.

City buses depart from the downtown depot and the fare is 50 sen, but buses are not that frequent. Taxis cost B$6, but you can hitch quite easily. After visiting the museum, you can continue in the same direction to the bottom of the hill and the turn-off to the Malay Technology Museum.

Malay Technology Museum This new and very impressive museum is built right on the edge of the river directly below the National Museum. It's a 15-minute walk as you have to go well past the Brunei Museum to get to the road leading to this museum. There are three galleries with various exhibits.

Kampung Ayer This collection of 28 water villages, built on stilts out in the Brunei River, has been there for centuries and at present houses a population of around 30,000 people. It's a strange mixture of ancient and modern – old traditions and ways of life are juxtaposed with electricity, modern plumbing and colour TVs.

A visit to one of the villages is probably the most rewarding experience you'll have in Brunei but the garbage floating around has to be seen to be believed. The villages are at their best at high tide.

To get there, go down to any of the wharfs either by the path to the west of the mosque, near the end of the Limbang and Lawas boat wharf, or by the food stalls on the other side of the canal from the information office. Hail one of the many outboard launches which act as water taxis and shuttle people back and forth between early morning and late evening. The fare across the river should be no more than B$1.

Places to Stay

Pusat Belia (☎ 02-23936), the youth centre on Jalan Sungai Kianggeh, is a short walk from the town centre. It's the only cheap place to stay in town and definitely the place to head for when you arrive. The drawback is that it seems to be more or less fully booked with national football teams, athletes and youth groups.

If it's not booked out, there's usually no problem in a traveller with a student card or Youth Hostel card getting a bed, but it's very much at the discretion of the manager. Don't expect a bed as your God-given right as they're doing you a favour letting you stay. Without a student card, you will probably have to do some lengthy talking.

The price is only B$10 for up to three nights and then B$5 for each subsequent night.

The next cheapest place in Bandar is the *Capital Hostel* (☎ 02-23561), off Jalan Tasik Lama just behind the Pusat Belia. It's the only other real budget choice if you can't get into the youth centre. Rooms cost a hefty B$70/85 for singles/doubles and all have air-con, TV and fridge.

Places to Eat

All the hotels and the youth centre have their own restaurants. The meals at the *Capital*

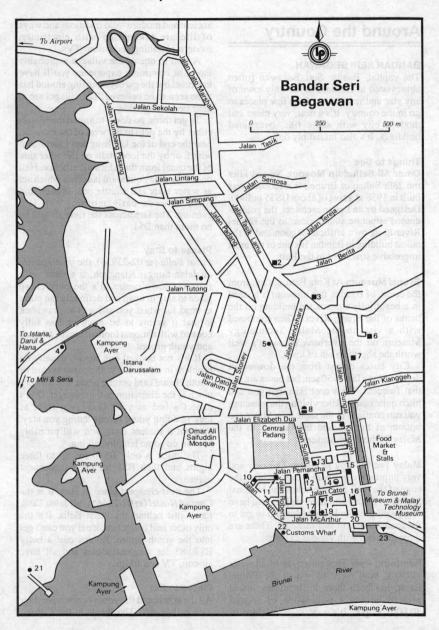

Bandar Seri Begawan

To Airport

Jalan Dato Marshall

Jalan Sekolah

Jalan Kumbang Pasang

Jalan Tasik

Jalan Lintang

Jalan Sentosa

Jalan Simpang

Jalan Tereja

Jalan Tasik Lama

Jalan Padang

Jalan Berita

1●

Jalan Tutong

2■

3■

To Istana, Darul & Hana

4●

Kampung Ayer

Jalan Bendehara

6■

7■

Istana Darussalam

5●

Jalan Stoney

To Miri & Seria

Jalan Dato Ibrahim

Jalan Kianggeh

Jalan Sungai Kianggeh

Omar Ali Saifuddin Mosque

8■

Jalan Elizabeth Dua

9

Jalan Sultan

Kampung Ayer

Central Padang

Food Market & Stalls

Jalan Pemancha

J3

15

10●

12

14●

16

Jalan Roberts

Jalan Cator

To Brunei Museum & Malay Technology Museum

11

17▼

18▼

19▼

20

Kampung Ayer

Jalan McArthur

Jalan Pretty

22●

Customs Wharf

23▼

21●

Kampung Ayer

Brunei River

Kampung Ayer

0   250   500 m

■	PLACES TO STAY
2	Ang's Hotel
3	Sheraton Hotel
6	Capital Hostel
7	Pusat Belia
15	Brunei Hotel

▼	PLACES TO EAT
18	Express Fast Food
23	Food Centre

	OTHER
1	Immigration
4	High Court
5	Churchill Museum
8	Post Office
9	Chinese Temple
10	MAS
11	Malayan Bank
12	Oriental Travel
13	Hong Kong & Shanghai Bank
14	Bus Station
16	Borneo Leisure Travel
17	Teck Guan Complex
19	Darussalam Complex
20	Harrisons
21	Makam Di-Raja (Mausoleum)
22	Boats to Labuan, Limbang, Lawas

Hostel are pretty good and quite cheap. You can get tasty Hokkien noodles and other noodle dishes for B$4.50. The food centre on the riverfront, just over the canal from the Customs Wharf, is not a bad place to eat. As is the case all over Bandar, there's not much going on in the evenings.

Another place to try are the food stalls by the river, across the footbridge near the intersection of Jalan Sungai Kianggeh and Jalan Pemancha. In the evenings, another group of stalls springs up in the car park behind the Chinese temple, opposite the post office.

Express Fast-Food, on the corner of Jalan Sultan and Jalan Cator, is an American-style fast-food place with typically bland food. Of the other restaurants, two which stand out, if only because they are open in the evenings, are the *Hua Hua* and *Al Hilal* which serve

basic Chinese and Malay food respectively. On Jalan McArthur, the *Sri Indah Restoran* has decent roti (unleavened bread) and martabak (paper-thin dough folded around an egg and mutton filling), good for grabbing a quick breakfast before catching a boat.

There are very few bars in town and only Chinese restaurants have a liquor licence. Although Muslims are not allowed to drink, beer, wine and spirits are *much* cheaper in Brunei than in Sarawak or Sabah.

Getting Around

To/From the Airport Although the taxi drivers would have you believe otherwise, there are minibuses between the city bus station and the airport. Look for the minibuses with the words 'Lapangan Terbang Antarabangsa' (International Airport) painted on the side.

Taxis charge a hefty B$20 – welcome to Brunei! The big, modern airport is only eight km from the city.

Bus Local buses around Bandar are few and far between and only leave when full. The bus station is beneath the central market, behind the Brunei Hotel.

To get to the museums, take a Muara or Kota Batu bus (50 sen). There are also regular buses to Seria.

AROUND BRUNEI

Muara

This is a small town north of Bandar at the top of the peninsula. It's a new oil centre with not much of interest to see but there is a decent beach.

The *World Wide Club*, basically for expats, is a good place to have a beer and to meet someone who lives in the country.

Bangar

Bangar is another small town, but it is reached only by boat. You can get launches there from Bandar. Bangar, the district centre, is on the Temburong River south-east of the capital. The town has a couple of shops and a market.

Places to Stay There is a *Government Rest House* which travellers can use at a cost of B$8 per night.

There are several Iban longhouses along the upper reaches of the river. While there are basic cafes in Bangar, take food with you if you're going upstream. You can get one of the three taxis in town or a private car to take you to longhouses. The fare should be no more than B$1 per km.

Getting There & Away There's one road going inland from Bangar to Limbang, and another follows the river upstream for a distance to the village of Batang Duri.

Between 7 am and 3 pm daily, you can get launches to Bangar from Bandar.

Seria

Seria, the main town on the north coast, is situated between Tutong and Kuala Belait, quite close to the Malaysian border. There are at least three banks in town and a few interesting cafes and cake shops.

Places to Stay The *Hotel Seria* has fan-cooled singles/doubles for B$35/40.

Kuala Belait

The last town before Malaysia, Kuala Belait is where you get buses for Miri in Sarawak. There are two banks in town and an efficient post office.

Places to Stay & Eat At the cheap end of the scale, there's a *Government Rest House* where, if you're permitted to stay, rooms are about B$12.

Otherwise, there's the *Sentosa Hotel* at 92 Jalan McKerron which is all air-con and has single rooms from B$100 and a Chinese restaurant downstairs which serves excellent seafood. The *Seaview Hotel* by the beach has rooms for well over B$100.

Getting There & Away For Malaysia, there are quite a few buses daily (mostly in the morning), and the fare is just under B$11 for the 30-minute trip.

Burma (Myanmar)

Burma, now officially called Myanmar, is one of the world's least Western-influenced countries – even China has Coca-Cola today. For the visitor Burma (Myanmar) is a fascinating glimpse of a culturally unique country which exists in a social, political and economic time warp. It is virtually sealed off from the outside world save for a steady stream of black-market commodities and a trickle of visitors.

Although a visit to Burma (Myanmar) involves a fair bit of red tape and initial expense, the good news is that 14-day tourist visas are now being issued. For many, the effort is well worthwhile; this is a country with which nearly every visitor becomes enthralled.

Should You Visit Burma (Myanmar)?

Anyone contemplating visiting Burma (Myanmar) should bear in mind any small contribution they make to the nation's economy may allow Burma's (Myanmar's) repressive, inept government to stay in power that little bit longer.

If you'd like to find out more about what's really happening in Burma (Myanmar), write to the Burmese Relief Centre, PO Box 48, Chiang Mai University, Chiang Mai, Thailand.

On the other hand, keeping the Burmese isolated from international witnesses to the internal oppression may also help to cement government control over the Burmese people. This is why the Ne Win government restricted tourism in the first place. It's your choice!

Facts about the Country

HISTORY

The Mons were the first people known to have lived in the area and their influence extended into what is now Thailand. The Mons were pushed back when the Burmese, who now comprise two-thirds of the total population, arrived from the north.

King Anawrahta came to the throne of Pagan (now called Bagan) in 1044, and, with his conquest of the kingdom of Thaton in 1057, inaugurated the golden age of Burmese history. The spoils he brought back developed Pagan to fabled heights and he also introduced Buddhism and the Burmese alphabet. Today, Burma (Myanmar) is 90% Buddhist, although belief in *nats*, or animal spirits, still persists.

Despite Anawrahta's efforts, Burma (Myanmar) had entered a period of decline by the 13th century, helped on its way by the vast amounts of money and effort squandered on making Pagan such an incredible monument to man's vanity. Kublai Khan hastened the decline by ransacking Pagan in 1287, at that time said to contain 13,000 pagodas. In the following centuries, the pattern of Burmese history was basically one of conflicts with kingdoms in neighbouring Siam and a series of petty tribal wars.

The coming of Europeans to the East had little influence on the Burmese, who were too busy fighting to be interested in trade. Unfortunately for the Burmese, their squabbles eventually encroached on the Raj in neighbouring Bengal and the British moved in to keep their borders quiet. In three moves in 1824, 1852 and 1883, the British took over all of Burma (Myanmar). They built railroads, made Burma (Myanmar) the world's greatest rice exporter and developed large teak markets. Less commendably, they brought in large numbers of Chinese and Indians who exploited the less commercially minded Burmese.

As in other South-East Asian countries, WW II was at first seen as a chance of liberation. An idea which the Japanese, as in Indonesia, soon dispelled. The wartime group of 'Thirty Comrades' was able to form a government after the war, with Aung San as their leader. In 1947 he was assassinated with most of his cabinet. Independence came in 1948 but the uniting of Burma (Myanmar) proved difficult and ongoing confrontation with breakaway tribes and Communist rebels take place to this day.

U Nu led the country during the early years of independence, attempting to establish a Buddhist socialism whose objective was 'Social Nibbana'. In 1962, General Ne Win led that most unusual event, a left-wing army takeover. After throwing out U Nu's government and imprisoning U Nu for four years, Ne Win set the country on the 'Burmese Way to Socialism'. The path was all downhill. He nationalised everything in sight, including retail shops, and quickly crippled the country. The Burmese saw their naturally well-endowed economy stumble as exports of everything plummeted.

It was said that the three major Burmese industries were rice, teak and smuggling but for a few years, in the early '80s, the economy did improve slightly. Then world commodity prices slumped and Burma's (Myanmar's) already crumbling economy slid even faster downhill.

Finally, in 1987 and 1988, after a long period of suffering, the Burmese people had had enough of their incompetent, arrogant government. They packed the streets in huge demonstrations, insisting that Ne Win had to go. He finally did go in July 1988 but in the following month massive confrontations between prodemocracy demonstrators and the military contributed to an estimated 3000 deaths over a six-week period.

Ne Win's National Unity Party (formerly the Burmese Socialist Programme Party) was far from ready to give up control and the public protests continued as two wholly unacceptable Ne Win stooges followed him. The third Ne Win successor came to power after a military coup in September 1988 which, it is generally believed, was organised by Ne Win.

The new State Law & Order Restoration Council (SLORC) established martial law under the leadership of General Saw Maung, Commander-in-Chief of the armed forces,

and promised to hold democratic National Assembly elections in May 1989.

The opposition quickly formed a coalition party and called it the National League for Democracy (NLD) and in the following months it campaigned tirelessly.

The long-suppressed Burmese population rallied around the charismatic NLD spokesperson Aung San Suu Kyi, daughter of national hero Aung San. Nervous, the SLORC tried to appease the masses with new roads and paint jobs in Rangoon (Yangon), and then attempted to interfere in the electoral process by shifting villages from one part of the country to another.

In spite of all preventive measures, the National Unity Party lost the May National Assembly election to the NLD. The military, however, has refused to allow the opposition to assume their parliamentary seats and have arrested most of the party leadership, including Aung San Suu Kyi who was awarded the Nobel Prize in 1991.

Martial law continues and all signs indicate that the current government will never hand over the reins of power peacefully. Whether or not the majority of Burmese can mount an effective opposition to their military rulers remains to be seen.

GEOGRAPHY

Burma (Myanmar) covers an area of 671,000 sq km; it is sandwiched between Thailand and Bangladesh with India and China bordering to the north. The centre of the country is marked by wide rivers and expansive plains, and mountains rise to the east along the Thai border and to the north, where you find the easternmost end of the Himalaya.

Burma (Myanmar) possesses huge stands of teak and other hardwoods but, if timber smuggling to Thailand and other countries continues at current rates, mass deforestation will be inevitable. Even if the central government had the means to curb the illegal timber trade (they don't, since most of the forests lie in ethnic rebel territory), they would probably sell it off quickly to increase or maintain the *Tatmadaw*, or military strength, as they are doing with oil and other resources.

One of the cursory changes instituted by the government since the 1988 uprising has been a long list of geographic name changes in an effort to further purge the country of its colonial past. The official name of the country has been changed from the 'Socialist Republic of the Union of Burma' to the 'Union of Myanmar'.

According to the government, 'Myanmar' doesn't identify the nation with the Burmese ethnic group. 'Burma' is said to be an English corruption of the Burmese term for that ethnic group (Bamar). Inexplicably,

'Burma Airways' is now 'Myanma Airways' with no 'r'. In all other cases, the new Romanised versions are phonetically closer to the everyday Burmese pronunciation.

Old Name	New Name
Akyab	Sittwe
Burma	Myanmar
Bassein	Pathein
Irrawaddy River	Ayeyarwady River
Mandalay	no change
Maymyo	Pyin Oo Lwin
Moulmein	Mawlamyine
Pagan	Bagan

Pegu	Bago
Prome	Pyi
Rangoon	Yangon
Salween River	Thanlwin River
Sittang River	Sittoung River

CLIMATE

The rainy season lasts from mid-May until mid-October. For the next few months, the weather is quite reasonable. In fact, it is actually cool in Mandalay at night and near freezing in Kalaw. From February, it gets very hot until the rains arrive once more. The Burmese New Year in April, at the peak of the hot season, means much fun and throwing water at all concerned. November to February are the best months to visit. In late December it can be quite difficult to travel as the number of visitors to the country can exceed the transport and accommodation capacity.

GOVERNMENT

The armed forces (Tatmadaw) and their political junta, the SLORC, currently rule Burma (Myanmar) with an iron fist. The only political party with any actual power is Ne Win's National Unity Party (originally the Burmese Socialist Programme Party), now headed by his successor General Saw Maung, a borderline lunatic who has been known to ramble on in his political speeches about Jesus Christ's sojourn in Tibet, as well as other tangential utterances.

Burmese citizens have relative economic freedom in all but state-owned trade spheres (naturally these are the big ones, like timber and oil), but their political freedom is strictly curtailed by continued martial law.

Peaceful political assembly is now banned and citizens are forbidden to discuss politics with foreigners. All government workers in Burma (Myanmar), regardless of level and status of their occupation, must sign a pledge not to discuss the government among themselves or risk losing their jobs. Rangoon (Yangon) has an 11 pm curfew.

The opposition movement that began in 1988 appears to be quelled now, with all leaders and spokespersons under arrest and the SLORC firmly in control. Amnesty International's November 1990 report on Burma (Myanmar), 72 pages long, states that the junta has effectively silenced the democracy movement through the systematic use of terror and torture.

The streets in Rangoon (Yangon) are festooned with huge red bilingual banners bearing slogans: 'Crush All Destructive Elements', 'The Strength of the Nation Lies Only Within', 'Only When There Is Discipline Will There Be Progress' and 'Down With Minions of Colonialism'.

Cynics say that the opposition never stood a chance and that the 1989 election was simply a small tactical error on the part of the military. Some even contend that had the opposition taken over, Burma (Myanmar) would now be in a state of anarchy. Many younger Burmese, however, still harbour hopes that they will, one day, wrest control of their homeland from the feared and hated Tatmadaw.

ECONOMY

Military rule has done nothing for Burma's (Myanmar's) sorry economy, or at least for the official economy but the secondary economy, the black economy, continues to boom. For years, things have just fallen apart, gone out of stock or simply become unusable. Apart from ineffectual moves, like changing to driving on the right despite the fact that most cars are right-hand drive and that neighbouring countries all drive on the left, constructive development seems but a dream.

The weakness of the Burmese economy is ridiculous when it is considered that Burma (Myanmar) has enormous potential both in the areas of agriculture and minerals, and that neighbouring countries in the South-East Asia region are undergoing rapid economic development.

Currently, approximately two-thirds of the population is employed in agriculture and only 7.5% in processing or manufacturing. Gross domestic product (GDP) and per capita income have dropped steadily since 1985. Inflation is running at around 75% – a basket of rice that cost K73 in 1987 cost K400 in 1990. According to UN standards, Burma (Myanmar) is one of the 10 poorest countries in the world.

An open-door economic policy, launched in 1989 to attract foreign investment, has had little success, since few investors are willing to risk their cash while the political situation remains so volatile. What few profits the nation takes in are absorbed by the Tatmadaw military junta, which directs all foreign trade in timber, gems, fisheries and oil – the only moneymakers. The Tatmadaw officers live in colonial-style villas in Rangoon's (Yangon's) best suburbs and are chauffeured about in the latest model Japanese cars. Most conduct multiple business affairs that will ensure their comfortable retirement.

Tourism, the most obvious source of hard currency, was brought to a halt following the 1988 uprising but it is slowly building up again with the new visa regulations.

POPULATION & PEOPLE

No accurate census has been taken for years but the official population estimate for 1990 was 40.7 million, with an annual growth rate of 1.9%. The population is made up of several racial groupings indigenous to Burma (Myanmar), including the Burmese, Mon, Kachin, Shan, Kayah, Kayin (Karen), Chin and Rakhine (Arakanese). There are still quite a few Indians and Chinese in Burma (Myanmar), but not many other foreigners or immigrants.

RELIGION

Burma (Myanmar) is Theravada Buddhist from top to bottom, but there is also strong belief in nats, the animist spirits of the land. Many of the hill tribes are Christian.

Barefooting It

Burma (Myanmar) is a land of temples, and your two-week visit can begin to feel like a procession from one of them to another. The

Burmese are very insistent that you barefoot it in the temple precincts, and that includes the steps from the very bottom of Mandalay Hill, the whole shop-lined arcade to the Shwedagon and even the ruins of Bagan. Carry your shoes with you.

LANGUAGE

There is a wide variety of languages spoken in Burma (Myanmar) and, fortunately, English is also widely spoken. The Burmese alphabet is most unusual, it looks like a collection of interlocked circles. If you'd like to tackle Burmese, look for Lonely Planet's handy *Burmese Phrasebook*.

The following words are in Burmese, the main language.

Greetings & Civilities
excuse me
kwin pyu baa
good morning/afternoon/evening
min ga la baa
goodbye (I'm going)
pyan dor mai (may)
How are you?
mah yeh laa
I'm well
maa bah day
please
chay-zoo tin-baa day
thank you
kyai (chay) *zoo tin baa dai* (day)

Useful Words & Phrases
Do you understand?
kin byar har lai tha laa
How much?
bah lout lai (lay)?
Too much
myar dai (day)
I do not understand
chun note nar ma lai boo
Where is...?
...beh mah lai (lay)?
no
ma hoke boo
yes
hoke ket

Numbers

1	tit	၁
2	nit	၂
3	thone	၃
4	lay	၄
5	ngar	၅
6	chowk	၆
7	kun nit	၇
8	sit	၈
9	co	၉
10	ta sei	၁၀
11	sair tit	၁၁
12	sair nit	၁၂
20	na sei	၂၀
30	thone sei	၃၀
100	ta yar	၁၀၀

Facts for the Visitor

VISAS

The tourist visa situation in Burma (Myanmar) has been in a state of flux since the upheavals in mid-1988 when the country was briefly closed to all visitors, then reopened under more strict regulations.

By the end of 1990, 14-day tourist visas were being issued with regularity but they could only be obtained through authorised agents of state-owned Myanmar Tours & Travel (MTT) – formerly Tourist Burma. Any attempt to apply for a tourist visa at the Myanmar Embassy in Bangkok is met with a referral to one of the Bangkok agencies. There are only a handful of such authorised agencies in Bangkok, but they in turn have other representatives who deal in visas. Several have set up shop in the city's Khao San Rd (Banglamphu) area.

This new 14-day tourist visa is a vast improvement over the old seven-day visa which compelled many travellers to rush around Burma (Myanmar) in a frenzy. Unfortunately, the new fly in the ointment is that in order to obtain this visa, you must purchase a package 'tour' through the agencies (this is very similar to current policies in Cambodia, Laos and Vietnam). Some

of these agencies, such as the infamous Deithelm Travel, charge thousands of dollars for a five to 10-day trip through the country that includes air travel, accommodation, meals, guided tours and all ground transport.

A few agencies, however, specialise in the minimum two-day, accommodation-only packages for individuals who want to arrange their own travel in Burma (Myanmar). You get the 14-day visa with the purchase of the package.

Once in Rangoon (Yangon), you're free to plan your own itinerary and go where you like – within the confines of the officially designated tourist destinations, as in previous years. No extension of the visa is necessary after the two days paid accommodation has been used – the visa is automatically valid for the entire 14-day period.

The cost of the visa itself is only 400B. The minimum cost, however, for processing the visa plus two nights of accommodation only (at the Strand Hotel in Rangoon) is usually around US$100 to US$200, a steep entrance fee. Basically, this policy is a way of ensuring that the government gets a stash of your hard currency at the official rate (see the following Money section) before you arrive. It's a case of 'same carnival, higher admission'.

Before you can be issued a tourist visa, you must sign a pledge that your are not a 'journalist, newspaperman or freelance correspondent'. If you're any of the aforementioned, you'd best conjure up a new occupation for all visa paperwork. If you're feeling paranoid (we did), you'd best leave behind all name cards, press passes, microcassette recorders or other evidence that might suggest that you're a 'minion of colonialism'.

Visa Extensions

The government currently allows no routine extensions of the 14-day visa. If you show up at the Rangoon (Yangon) Airport a day or two late due to unavoidable transport difficulties, there's usually little hassle if immigration authorities can verify your story. If not, be prepared to part with some baksheesh (a tip).

Foreign Embassies in Burma (Myanmar)
Rangoon (Yangon) is usually a good place to get visas for other countries. You can pay for them with your whisky kyats (see the following Money section) so they're very cheap and because the embassy officials know your time is limited they issue them very quickly. You may be able to get Nepalese visas here in as little as 15 minutes.

TRAVEL RESTRICTIONS
The xenophobic government does try to keep tabs on you while you are in Burma (Myanmar), more so since the events of August 1988. They don't want you wandering off into touchy regions and that's part of the reason for the 14-day visa. Also, with so much difference between the official exchange rate and the real one, the government obviously wants to stop you from spending 'black' money. The farther you get from MTT-approved destinations, the less likely you'll have to pay official rates.

With so little time to spare, however, visitors have little incentive to get off the beaten track. Most visitors don't wander off the Rangoon (Yangon)-Mandalay-Bagan-Inle Lake circuit apart from short detours to Bago, Syriam, Pyin Oo Lwin or the deserted cities around Mandalay. If you ask about going to other places, you'll probably receive a firm 'no'. But if you simply set out to go there it's quite possible you'll manage it.

Of course, there are really touchy areas (the north-east towards the Golden Triangle and north of Mandalay towards the China border) which are absolutely no go. Lots of people manage, however, to get to Kyaikto to see the balancing pagoda (of Kyaiktiyo) and even further to Thaton. A few have even managed Myohaung, while Pathein and Pyi are quite easy to get to. If only we all had more time!

MONEY
Currency
The *kyat* (say 'chat') is divided into 100 *pyas* with a collection of confusing coins which are now rarely seen since the tremendous decrease in the value of the kyat over the last few years. Generally, it's easier to change money at Myanmar Tours & Travel (MTT) offices which have longer opening hours than the banks.

The government has a nasty habit of demonetising large denomination notes from time to time. The theory is that anybody who has some large denomination notes sitting around must have obtained them by less than legal means. So the government simply declares that (say) all even-numbered denominations are no longer legal tender.

This does not tend to inspire much confidence in the currency, particularly if you happened to have a stash of now worthless kyat notes under the mattress. You can be sure that government officials get advance notice of which denominations are going to be invalidated so that they can cash in before it's too late.

In 1991, only these paper denominations were in use: K1, K5, K10, K15, K45, K90 and K200. Don't accept any other denominations (say 50s or 100s) when changing money since you won't be able to use them in any transactions.

Official Exchange Rates
A$1	=	K5.0
C$1	=	K5.6
NZ$1	=	K3.7
UK£1	=	K10.8
US$1	=	K6.3

The official exchange rates for travellers' cheques and cash (travellers' cheques are worth more than cash) bear little relation to reality. Unofficially, cash is worth far more than the official rates above. You can buy kyats in Singapore, Penang or Bangkok and illegally bring them in with you. Or you can illegally change $US on the black market – Rangoon (Yangon) is the best place and you can expect to get around K80 to US$1. Larger denomination $US notes are preferred. There is also a good market for Thai baht and Singapore dollars, at their equivalent rates.

Either of these procedures has some element of risk but it's part of Burma's (Myanmar's) often benevolent incompetence that there is a delightfully simple way round this. At the airport, when you depart for Rangoon (Yangon), invest in some duty-free goods. A couple of cartons of 555 cigarettes and two bottles of Johnny Walker Red Label whisky (that's the current duty-free limit) will cost you around US$15. If you can't get the preferred brands move down-market rather than up.

No sooner have you left customs at Rangoon (Yangon) Airport than people will leap forward offering to take them off your hands. It's better to wait until you're in town for a day or two before you sell them, however, so you can find out from other foreigners what the going rate is.

For one carton of 555s and one 750 ml bottle of whiskey, around K1200 (K800 for the whisky, K400 for the cigarettes) seems to be the norm although the price varies from week to week. You've now changed your US$15 at a rate of K80 for US$1. If you sell two of each, the K2400 will be more than enough for two weeks' spending money (a university professor in Burma (Myanmar) earns a monthly salary of about half that).

If you run low, there's a place in Rangoon (Yangon) called the Tourist Department Stores (formerly the Diplomatic Store) just north of Sule Pagoda where the Burmese government has set up further opportunities for visitors to indulge in small-scale capitalism, supply and demand, etc. It's a good practice to carry a few packets of 555s with you through Burma (Myanmar) as payment for the occasional bureaucratic favour.

There is no longer a requirement that you change a minimum amount of money at the official rate (the new visa arrangement is the obvious substitute). However, you'll most likely not be able to get through two weeks in Burma (Myanmar) without paying for at least some hotels at the official rate, which means having your currency declaration form stamped.

Here's how the currency form works: on arrival you must fill in a complicated form accounting for all your cash and travellers' cheques. Each time you change money it must be entered on the form and each time you pay for accommodation or travel, which must be bought through MTT offices, it must be entered on the form. At the end of the week, the figures should match up. That is, you should have cashed enough money 'officially' to cover everything you've paid for officially and the amount of money you brought in, minus what you exchanged, should equal what you take out.

The best way to minimise form-stamping is to travel with other people – one person can have their form stamped and the others can claim that this person generously took care of all travel expenses. Of course, there's practically zero chance of your form being laboriously checked out at the end of the two weeks – by which time it is crumpled, dirty, crossed out, rewritten and totally confused anyway. Plus, you'll find that accommodation or transport costs don't always get entered on your form – MTT is not everywhere.

If you simply purchase a railway ticket at a station outside the MTT field of view, you can be certain nobody is going to want to see your currency form. It's that benevolent incompetence at work again.

The main drag about all this is not the money, but the sheer amount of time you have to waste chasing MTT to their often out-of-the-way offices to pay for hotels and transport which could more conveniently be paid for at the source.

Costs

Whether or not you think Burma (Myanmar) is cheap or expensive depends on how you look at it. Using the official exchange rate with money changed through MTT make it appear to be quite expensive. With whisky kyats it is a great deal cheaper, but that initial 'entry fee' (minimum US$200 for the visa and two-nights accommodation) removes it from the traveller's list of dirt-cheap places.

Tours booked in Bangkok generally cost a minimum of US$40 a day. San Express on Khao San Rd, for example, charges US$670 for a nine-day tour that includes a round-trip airfare from Bangkok, a visa, airport taxes, all accommodation and ground transport for visits to Rangoon (Yangon), Mandalay and Bagan.

If you exclude the fixed rates for visas (400B), airport taxes (200B out of Bangkok, US$6 out of Rangoon) and the round-trip airfare (around US$200), this means that MTT ground charges in this example average around US$40 a day for the nine days. It pays to shop around. In 1991, the same tour could be booked at Vista Travel on Khao San for about US$100 less.

Cheapest of all, of course, is to find an agent that will sell the basic two-night accommodation-and-visa-only tour for US$100 to US$200. Even then, you will have to contend with the official rates set for MTT-designated hotels throughout the country, which now average around US$20 to US$25 per night.

When it's possible to pay these rates with unofficial kyats, this works out to only US$1.50 to US$1.80 a night, cheap by any standards. In order to get around paying with officially exchanged kyats, you'll have to either convince the hotel staff not to stamp your currency form (this may require throwing in an extra wad of kyats or a packet of 555s, or using the group approach described earlier in the Money section).

Certain kinds of transport also officially require the the purchaser's currency form to be stamped, ie the Rangoon (Yangon) to Mandalay Express train, the Mandalay to Bagan boat and Myanma Airways flights. Here again, you'll have to deal with MTT – usually directly. Other train, bus and boat fares can be paid with unofficial kyats, however, as can all meals (even at the official tourist hotels), drinks, souvenirs and so on. Those so inclined might even consider it a moral duty to divert as much of their spend-ing money away from the government as they possibly can.

Tipping

There is no tradition of tipping in Burma (Myanmar), even in the tourist hotels – unless the common practice of bribery is viewed as a form of tipping. MTT guides will usually ask for 'something for the driver' at the end of a guided tour – this actually means something for both the guide *and* the driver, so giving is left to your discretion.

Bargaining

Prices are always negotiable, except for in government establishments (MTT craft shops, hotels, etc).

TOURIST OFFICES

The main tourist information office is on Sule Pagoda Rd in Rangoon (Yangon), close to the central Sule Pagoda. The information it has to hand out is sparse and uninteresting, but they're friendly and helpful. Anything to do with timetables and costs in places you are 'officially' permitted to visit they will have right on hand. There are MTT offices in all the main centres, but they sometimes give the feeling that their purpose is to hinder rather than to be useful.

In Bangkok, the official representative for MTT is Skyline Travel Service (☎ 233 1864/3440, 234 1240), 491/39-40 Silom Plaza, 2nd Floor, Silom Rd.

POST & TELECOMMUNICATIONS

Consider yourself incommunicado while in Burma (Myanmar), as post and telephone services are notoriously unreliable.

Aerogrammes have a better chance of getting through than either letters or post-cards. Parcels – forget it, unless you have a friend at your embassy or foreign office in Rangoon (Yangon).

TIME

Burma (Myanmar) is seven hours ahead of GMT, half an hour behind Bangkok time and half an hour ahead of Dacca time. When it is 12 noon in Rangoon (Yangon), it is 4 pm in

Sydney, 6 am in London, 1 am in New York and 10 pm the previous day in San Francisco.

BOOKS & MAPS

For more information about travelling in Burma (Myanmar) look for Lonely Planet's *Burma – a travel survival kit*. Apa Productions have the informative *Insight Guide Burma* in their series of glossy coffee-table guidebooks. In Rangoon (Yangon), before you head upcountry, or in Bagan itself, get a copy of *Pictorial Guide to Pagan*, an invaluable introduction to the many temples, pagodas and ruins.

The most comprehensive socio-political account of pre-1988 Burma is *Burma: A Socialist Nation of Southeast Asia* by David Steinberg (Westview Press, Boulder, Colorado, 1982).

George Orwell's *Burmese Days* is the book to read in order to get a feel for Burma under the British Raj. *Golden Earth* by Norman Lewis (Eland Books) is a reprint of a classic account of a visit to Burma soon after WW II.

Rangoon (Yangon) has quite a few bookshops, most along Bogyoke Aung San St opposite the Bogyoke Market, where you can find some really interesting books. Also check the Pagan Bookshop at 100 37th St, quite close to the Strand Hotel. You never know what will turn up in this little shop that specialises in English-language material – much of it is vintage stuff.

The Tourist Department Stores on Sule Pagoda Rd has a selection of tourist-oriented books on Burma (Myanmar) as well as recent political treatises like *The Conspiracy of the Treasonous Minions within the Myanmar Naing-Ngan (Nation) and Traitorous Cohorts Abroad.*

Photographic evidence of collusion between foreign powers and the Burmese 'minions' includes pictures of ordinary Burmese citizens walking in and out of foreign embassies or the local residences of foreigners. In xenophobic Burma (Myanmar), even walking into a foreign enclave is an act of treason.

MEDIA
Newspapers & Magazines

The only English-language newspaper readily available in Burma (Myanmar) is the unintentionally humourous *Working People's Daily*, a thin state-owned daily that's chock full of Orwellian propaganda of the 'War is Peace' or 'Freedom is Slavery' nature.

Recent issues of international magazines like *Time*, *Newsweek* or the *Economist* are often available at the Strand Hotel in Rangoon (Yangon). Whenever a feature about Burma (Myanmar) appears in one of these magazines, however, that issue mysteriously fails to appear. Older issues are sold on the street by sidewalk vendors.

Radio & TV

All legal radio and television broadcasts are state-controlled. Voice of Myanmar radio broadcasts only 2½ hours a day.

A typical daily radio schedule (unedited) follows:

Time	Programme
0830	News
0840	Slogans & Music
0900	Close Down
1330	News
1340	Slogans & Music
1400	Close Down
2100	World of Music
2110	Editorial
2115	News
2130	Slogans & Music
2200	Portfolio for Easy Listening
2230	Close Down

TV Myanmar broadcasts nightly from 7 to 9.35 pm. Regular features include military songs and marching performances, 'Songs of Yesteryear', locally produced news and weather reports and a sports presentation. One drama, aired for part of the rousing 1990-91 season, was the soap opera *Rich Man, Poor Man*.

Educated Burmese generally listen to shortwave BBC and VOA broadcasts for news from the world outside. On Friday evenings, the American Center on Merchant

St packs them in for the 4.30 pm broadcast of the *ABC World News*.

FILM & PHOTOGRAPHY

Bring a sufficient film supply with you to Burma (Myanmar) as brand-name film is unavailable. The Burmese don't seem to mind having their photos taken, but you should always ask first as a gesture of courtesy.

Photographing airports, train stations, bridges or military installations is prohibited by law. If anything political starts happening, you will risk having your camera confiscated if you try to take photos. Government observers (or their informers) may also accuse you of being a foreign journalist and arrange for your immediate detention. Saw Maung and his cronies are at war with foreign journalists, including photographers.

If you're a professional photographer and generally carry a lot of gear, you might streamline it to avoid giving the impression that you're a photojournalist – they're not permitted entry on a tourist visa, whether on vacation or not.

HEALTH

Burma (Myanmar) doesn't have the highest of sanitation standards, but then you can't expect very much from one of the world's 10 poorest countries. Frankly, it pays to be very careful with food and drink throughout this country. Eat only food that is cooked, or if eating raw fruits or vegetables, ensure they are of the peelable type and peel them yourself. All water should be boiled or otherwise treated before consumption, and safe bottled water is available at most tourist destinations.

Dysentery of various types is quite common and you should stock up on appropriate medicines for the prevention and treatment of both the bacillic and amoebic forms (consult a doctor in advance). A supply of diarrhoeal suppressants like Lomotil or Imodium is a must unless you're unusually stoic. If you eat only in the hotels, you'll probably be OK but you'll have to put up with bland, uninspired cooking (the Strand Hotel is one exception).

Malaria is not a problem in the areas most frequented by foreign travellers.

DANGERS & ANNOYANCES

Tourist theft seems quite rare in Burma (Myanmar), but don't tempt fate by leaving valuables lying around. The common presence of Tatmadaw troops, especially in Rangoon (Yangon) and Mandalay, can be unsettling but unless you get caught up in a prodemocracy demonstration, you have little to worry about.

Beggars are common in Rangoon (Yangon) and Mandalay, less common elsewhere. They are not particularly persistent. Buddhist monks or novices (usually the latter) will occasionally approach foreign visitors to plead for money.

ACCOMMODATION

Hotel rooms in Burma (Myanmar) are very poor value at the official exchange rate, or bargains at the free market rate. Facilities are often in a state of disrepair, but otherwise they're quite adequate as places to sleep and shower.

The official selection is quite slim: six hotels in Rangoon (Yangon), three each in Mandalay and Bagan, and one each in Bago, Kalaw, Taunggyi, Pindaya, Ngapali Beach (Sandoway) and Chaungtha Beach. They range in price from a low of US$10 for a single at the YMCA in Rangoon (Yangon) to a high of US$76 for a bungalow at Chaungtha Beach.

These are official rates at the exchange rate of K6.3 to the US$. If you can manage to pay for accommodation with free market kyat, these same rates range from US$0.75 to US$5.70. In reality, if you travel all over Burma (Myanmar), you'll probably find that you'll have to pay official kyats about half the time, free market kyats the other half.

FOOD & DRINK

Food in Burma (Myanmar) is basically curry and rice. You normally get two kinds of rather mild curry and a side plate of salad.

Unlimited quantities of soup and Chinese tea will be included in the price. It's straightforward, unexciting but quite good food. You will probably also see some less appetising Burmese cuisine. A popular favourite on the trains are crunchy grasshopper kebabs! Indian and Chinese food are also generally available. In fact, you're far more likely to find restaurants run by Indians or Chinese than by Burmese.

Burmese soft drinks, usually around K10, are fairly safe and not too bad, particularly if you dilute them with soda water or ice.

One traveller wrote: 'You are amazingly kind about Burmese soft drinks. I encountered nobody who found them anything but appalling. The honourable exception is Vimto, a strange relic of British rule and usually obtainable only in the north of England'. His opinion was seriously devalued after I sought out and tried a bottle of Vimto and found it disgusting! It may not be around anymore – the latest rage is 'Sparkling Lemon' which is quite drinkable.

Tony Wheeler

A bottle of Mandalay Beer from the People's Brewery & Distillery will cost around K40. It's a bit watery but not bad beer – cheap at the free market rate of exchange. In 1987, there were a couple of months when none of the people's beer was brewed because Burma (Myanmar) ran out of bottle caps. It is not hard to see why it is considered a ramshackle economy?

Burmese tea is usually mixed with other herbs and stains your tongue a lurid orange colour, though some people grow to like it. Ice cream, in the more hygienic-looking ice cream parlours in Rangoon (Yangon) and Mandalay, seems to be OK and I managed to drink a lot of crushed sugar cane during one hot-season visit without any ill effects, but be careful. You cannot afford to be ill when you face the 14-day Burmese sprint.

Some useful words relating to food and drink include:

bread
  pow mohn
butter
  taw but
chicken
  kyet (chet) tar
coffee
  kaw pee
drinking water
  tao ye
egg (boiled)
  kyet (chet), u byok
egg (fried)
  kyet (chet), u chor
fish
  ngar
hot
  ah poo
mutton
  seik tar
noodles
  kaw swe
restaurant
  sar tao syne
rice (cooked)
  ta min
soup
  hin jo
sugar
  ta jar
tea
  la bet ye
tea shop
  la bet yea syne
toast
  pow moh gin

THINGS TO BUY

There is nice lacquerware available, particularly at Bagan. The black and gold items probably aren't as good quality as in Chiang Mai in Thailand, but coloured items are much more alive. Look for flexibility in bowls or dishes and clarity of design. Opium weights are cheaper than in Thailand. Beautiful shoulder bags are made by the Shan tribes. *Kalagas*, tapestries embroidered with silver thread, sequins and colourful glass beads, are a good buy.

Be very careful if you decide to buy gems. Many foolish travellers buy fake gemstones. It's another of those fields to dabble in only if you really know what is and what isn't.

However, I must admit I bought a 'ruby' on one trip and it turned out to actually be one.

If you want to sell things, virtually any Western goods from radio batteries to cheap make-up are in amazing demand in Burma (Myanmar) but they have to be name brands, not any old rubbish.

Getting There & Away

Burma (Myanmar) is purely fly in, fly out. Tourists are not permitted to arrive by ship and all roads are closed at the borders – except, of course, to smugglers. Myanma Airways' (MAC's) F-28s fly to and from Bangkok every day of the week and also connect to Calcutta and Kathmandu. They also have two weekly flights to and from Singapore.

Thai International also fly from Bangkok to Rangoon (Yangon) three times weekly. Bangladesh Biman fly Bangkok-Rangoon (Yangon)-Dhaka (once a week) and Air China (the old CAAC) fly from Rangoon (Yangon) to Kunming (once a week). Singapore International's offshoot Tradewinds, a subsidiary of Singapore Airlines, recently started flying between Singapore and Rangoon (Yangon) twice a week for around US$125 one way.

Fares are a bit of a mix-up due to the keen fare-cutting in Bangkok. Shopping around, with your student card handy, should enable you to fly Bangkok-Rangoon (Yangon)-Bangkok for around US$180 on Myanma Airways or $215 on Thai International. Bangkok-Rangoon (Yangon)-Calcutta or Bangkok-Rangoon (Yangon)-Kathmandu costs around US$220. Some travel agents in Bangkok will do an all-in deal getting you your tickets and your visa.

Aeroflot fly twice a week from Vietnam and Laos to Rangoon (Yangon), then on to Bombay and Moscow. Not many travellers are likely to use that route but some people have been entering Burma (Myanmar) from Kunming in China with Air China (one flight per week). If you're travelling around China, this makes a very interesting way of continuing on to South-East Asia, rather than going back to Hong Kong and flying on from there.

If you're counting on getting out on the last day that your visa is valid, be sure to reconfirm your departure before leaving the airport when you first arrive – all the airlines tend to overbook flights leaving Burma (Myanmar), especially from December to February.

Getting Around

Travel in Burma (Myanmar) is not that easy – its uncertain and often uncomfortable by whatever means of travel you choose.

AIR
Because of the short visa period, travellers to Burma (Myanmar) sometimes fly where normally they would be quite happy to travel by land, although with the new 14-day visa things are slightly more relaxed. Flying can save a lot of time and effort but all tickets must be bought through MTT with 'official' kyats. Once in a long while we hear of

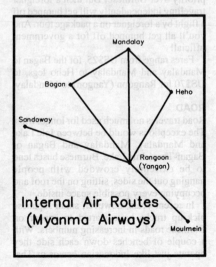

Internal Air Routes
(Myanma Airways)

someone buying an air ticket on the black market, but this seems to be rare.

The problem with flying MAC, apart from the airline's terrible safety record on internal flights, is that you never know if flights will leave or not. Schedules are fixed from day to day and you'll find it virtually impossible to be certain of any reservation. The officials tell you to arrive at the airport at 12 noon for a 2 pm flight which may not leave until 4, 5 pm or who knows when – very frustrating when time is limited.

There are only four planes currently in operation, all Fokker F-27 props. They fly only one daily, clockwise route Rangoon (Yangon)-Bagan-Mandalay-Heho (Inle Lake). You can't, therefore, fly from Bagan to Rangoon (Yangon), for example, without going through the rest of the loop.

For a while, there was a 'tourists only' service around the loop but this still wasted a lot of time and involved a lot of uncertainty before you actually got up in the air. The shortage of aircraft, due to the lack of foreign exchange to buy spare parts (and because of all the crashes), has made flight schedules even worse. If it's any consolation, when it comes to a fight for seats, foreigners have priority over Burmese! But then a foreigner travelling independently will get bumped off a flight by a foreigner on a package tour. And you'll all get bumped off for a government official!

Fares range from US$25, for the Bagan to Mandalay and Mandalay to Heho legs, to US$70 for Rangoon (Yangon) to Mandalay.

ROAD

Road travel is not much used for longer trips. The exceptions would be between Inle Lake and Mandalay, Mandalay and Bagan or Bagan-Thazi-Inle Lake. Burmese buses tend to be extremely crowded with people hanging out the sides, sitting on the roof and occupying every possible space inside.

In recent years, however, small Japanese pick-up trucks have started to appear on Burmese roads in increasing numbers. With a couple of benches down each side they operate just like Indonesian *bemos* or Thai *songthaews*. They can be uncomfortable when crowded but groups of people can sometimes charter them through MTT – such as between Bagan and Inle Lake or even further afield.

In the mid-1980s, this could be done through private arrangement but this method of transport became so popular that the government clamped down on it (of course). It has been further complicated by the fuel shortage – yes, the country has oil reserves but this is Burma (Myanmar), remember! The 'official' price of petrol is only about US$1 a gallon but it's rationed (only four gallons per month per vehicle) and it's said that black-market fuel can cost as much as US$20 a gallon.

TRAIN

Apart from the daily Rangoon (Yangon) to Mandalay special express, the ordinary-class trains are better forgotten – dirty, slow, unreliable and very dark at night due to a national shortage of light bulbs! Upper-class (equivalent to 1st class) and 1st-class (equivalent to 2nd class) travel are generally better.

Apart from the main tourist routes, you may find it impossible to buy railway tickets through MTT and the station is not supposed to sell tickets to foreigners, who should get them from MTT!

The answer is to ask somebody at the station to buy tickets for you although I've bought tickets at several points not watched over by MTT and had no trouble whatsoever.

BOAT

The boat trip downriver from Mandalay to Bagan is popular and you can also make other shorter trips from Mandalay or Rangoon (Yangon). If you had the time you could continue the boat trip from Bagan right down the river to Rangoon (Yangon) – on your two-week visa you'd be devoting an entire week to just that one trip!

LOCAL TRANSPORT

The impossibly crowded and delightfully ancient buses in Rangoon (Yangon) and Mandalay are very cheap and convenient although you may well end up hanging out the side or off the back. Trishaws, in which the passengers sit back to back, are also economic but always negotiate the fare beforehand.

Taxi-trucks are becoming more readily available throughout Burma (Myanmar). Some of them operate fixed routes, others can be hired like a taxi. There are also taxis in Rangoon (Yangon) and smaller three-wheelers like an Indian *autorickshaw* or Thai *samlor*. Mandalay also has horse carts (tongas) which are somewhat more expensive than trishaws. You can hire bicycles in Bagan.

BURMA IN 14 DAYS

With the nonextendable 14-day visa, it is possible to do the entire Rangoon (Yangon)-Inle Lake-Mandalay-Bagan-Rangoon (Yangon) loop by land. With allowances for arrival and departure times on day 1 and 15, a reasonable schedule would be:

Day 1
    Arrive, book train tickets to Thazi, see Rangoon (Yangon)
Day 2
    Train all day to Thazi
Day 3
    Bus to Taunggyi or Inle Lake
Day 4 & 5
    See Taunggyi and Inle Lake
Day 6
    Bus to Mandalay
Day 7 & 8
    See Mandalay area
Day 9
    Boat to Bagan
Day 10-12
    See Bagan
Day 13
    Back to Rangoon (Yangon) via Thazi, arrive at night or travel overnight
Day 14
    See Rangoon (Yangon), possible day trip to Bago
Day 15
    Depart

There are all sorts of alternative ways of spending your two weeks. Some possibilities include:

Alternative 1
    Cut something out. Some people miss Mandalay to have longer in Bagan, some cut out the Taunggyi-Inle Lake area and some deluded souls actually miss Bagan. Or, you could perhaps consider staying the first two nights in Rangoon (Yangon).
Alternative 2
    Fly a sector. If you've already taken the train from Rangoon (Yangon) to Thazi or Mandalay, the Bagan to Rangoon (Yangon) flight will save you a lot of time and effort.
Alternative 3
    If you get into Rangoon (Yangon) early enough, get the overnight train up to Mandalay and have an extra day to spare.
Alternative 4
    Do it all backwards – Bagan first and Mandalay second.
Alternative 5
    Try to fit in other things – Pyin Oo Lwin (Maymyo) for example. Kalaw makes a great stopover between Thazi and Taunggyi-Inle Lake.

Whichever alternative you choose it is recommended that you leave Rangoon (Yangon) till the end. It is best to arrive and get upcountry as quickly as possible. Ten to one you'll have plenty of time to see Rangoon (Yangon) at the end, even on the day you depart. If you're going to run into hassles getting back to the capital, it's better to have time in hand. If you fly to Burma (Myanmar) on a weekend, the tourist office closes earlier. Unless you're on an early flight, you have little chance of getting on the night train or even getting tickets for the train next morning.

In the days of seven-day visas, a popular way to see more of the country was for a small group of travellers to hire a Japanese pick-up truck with a driver and do it all by road. It was all quite unofficial at first, but now MTT is offering a charter service for US$350 a week and has apparently shut down the private operators.

At any rate, with the 14-day allowance, it's really not necessary to rush quite so much. Although you undoubtedly cover a lot of territory by chartered truck, most of your money goes toward the long road trip between Rangoon (Yangon) and Upper Burma (Myanmar). It is really more cost-

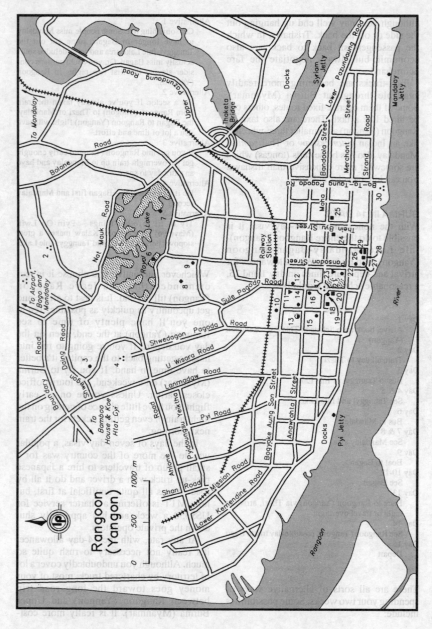

Rangoon
(Yangon)

efficient to fly or take a train north and then to charter trucks out of Mandalay, Bagan or Kalaw for local sightseeing. Also, if you travel by public transport you're more likely to get to know the locals, in spite of the current ban on political discussions.

Around the Country

RANGOON (Yangon)

The capital of Burma (Myanmar) for less than 100 years, Rangoon (now officially called Yangon) is 30 km upriver from the sea and has an air of seedy decay along with a great pagoda that is one of the real wonders of South-East Asia. A city of wide streets and spacious architecture, it looks run-down, worn-out and thoroughly neglected, although with the roadwork and new coats

1	Kyauk Htat Gyi Pagoda
2	Nga Htat Gyi Pagoda
3	Martyr's Mausoleum
4	Shwedagon Pagoda
5	Bogyoke Aungsan Park
6	Kandawagyi Hotel
7	Karaweik
8	Zoological Garden
9	Horticultural Garden
10	Bogyoke Market
11	Burma Patisserie
12	Dagon Hotel
13	Bus to Bagan
14	Indian Area
15	Chinatown
16	Tourist Department Store
17	Sule Pagoda
18	Thai International
19	Myanmar Tours & Travel
20	Garden Hotel
21	Maha Bandoola Park
22	Bank
23	Nan Yu Restaurant
24	YWCA
25	YMCA
26	Museum
27	MAC Office
28	Strand Hotel
29	GPO
30	Bo-Ta-Taung Pagoda

of paint ordered by the SLORC, your initial impression will probably be favourable. The streets are lively at night with hordes of stalls selling delicious-looking food, piles of huge cigars and those Western cigarettes you've just unloaded. Look for the tape-recorder studios where young Burmese entertain themselves by adding Burmese words to Western pop music. Recently, electronic games have also become a Rangoon (Yangon) craze. Watch out for rats late at night!

Orientation & Information

The MTT office is right by the Sule Pagoda at the junction of Sule Pagoda Rd and Maha Bandoola St. In central Rangoon (Yangon), it's relatively easy to find your way around. The centre is quite compact, the streets are laid out in a grid pattern and walking is no problem. The GPO is a short stroll east of the Strand Hotel on Strand Road.

Things to See

Shwedagon Pagoda Dominating the entire city from its hilltop site, this is the most sacred Buddhist temple in Burma (Myanmar). Nearly 100 metres high, it is clearly visible from the air as you fly in or out of Rangoon (Yangon). I saw it once as a tiny golden dot while flying over Burma (Myanmar) to Kathmandu – magic! Visit it in the early morning or evening when the gold spire gleams in the sun and the temperature is cooler. Or see its shimmering reflection from across the Royal Lake at night. In 1587, a European visitor wrote of its 'wonderful bignesse and all gilded from foote to the toppe'.

Facts and figures – the site is over 2500 years old (the current stupa dates to the 18th century); there are over 8000 gold plates covering the pagoda; the top of the spire is encrusted with more than 5000 diamonds and 2000 other precious or semiprecious stones; and the compound around the pagoda has 82 other buildings. It is this sheer mass of buildings that gives the place its awesome appeal.

In the pagoda's north-west corner is a

huge bell which the butter-fingered British managed to drop into the Rangoon River while carrying it off. Unable to recover it, they gave the bell back to the Burmese who refloated it by tying a vast number of bamboo lengths to it. The Shwedagon has an equally impressive appearance at night when it glows gold against a velvet backdrop.

The official admission fee for the pagoda is now US$5, which includes an elevator ride to the raised platform of the stupa. There are separate elevators for Burmese and foreigners. If you come before 7 am, you can get in for free.

Sule Pagoda Also over 2000 years old and right in the centre of town, the Sule Pagoda makes a fine spectacle at night and the inside of the complex is all lit by pulsating neon.

National Museum The museum, which is on Pansodan (Phayre) St (around the corner from the Strand Hotel), houses nothing spectacular, but if you have time to kill in Rangoon (Yangon) you could do worse.

There are three floors – the stairs to the upper floors are a bit difficult to find. The bottom floor contains jewellery and royal relics and the upper floors feature art and archaeology. Admission is US$4 (purchase tickets at the MTT office). It's open Tuesday to Friday from 10.30 am to 3 pm.

Other There's a mirror maze in the stupa of **Bo-Ta-Taung Temple**. Rangoon (Yangon) has a fine **open-air market** and the extensive **Bogyoke Market** is always worth a wander. It's a pleasant stroll around **Royal Lake** where you can visit the huge Karaweik non-floating restaurant. Rangoon (Yangon) has a **zoo** with a collection of Burmese animals, and on Sunday there is an elephant and a snake charmer performance.

The **Kaba Aye**, or World Peace, pagoda is about 11 km north of the city, and was built in the mid-1950s for the 2500th anniversary of Buddhism. The **Martyrs' Mausoleum** to Aung San and his comrades is close to the Shwedagon Pagoda. The huge reclining Buddha at **Chauk Htat Gyi Pagoda** is also

close by and there are a couple of other gigantic Buddha figures in Rangoon (Yangon).

An interesting excursion from Rangoon (Yangon) can be made across the river to Syriam, where you can take a bus to **Kyauktan** with its small island pagoda or take a longer river trip to **Twante**, two or three hours away.

About 45 minutes from Rangoon (Yangon) on the road to Pyi is the recently established **Hlawa Park** on the banks of a large reservoir. A joint operation of the ministries of forestry and agriculture, the park features an impressive animal reserve, boat rides, elephant rides and picnic areas.

Places to Stay
Upon arrival in Rangoon (Yangon), most visitors holding tourist visas will be staying at the hotel already paid for in the mandatory visa and accommodation package. This will be either the Strand or Inya Lake Hotels, the only ones permitted by MTT for tours booked overseas.

All of the MTT-approved hotels are well overpriced by Burmese or Asian standards at the official exchange rate, and it's unlikely than any will allow you to pay without stamping your currency form. For shoestringers, the only solution is to spend as few days as possible in Rangoon (Yangon) in the hope that you'll have better luck upcountry.

The *Strand Hotel*, the less expensive of the two, is a rare experience in itself. It's Rangoon's (Yangon's) 'name hotel' and has bags of old colonial charm to make up for the fact that it's a bit run-down. The cheapest fan-cooled economy singles/doubles start from US$25/35 and they're quite acceptable. Standard rooms with air-con are US$35/45.

The Strand will, unfortunately, only remain in its perfect old-world condition for about another two years. A Hong Kong company that specialises in exclusive 'exotic' lodgings (eg Amanpuri in Phuket and Amandari in Bali) has purchased a half interest in the hotel and plans to remodel the entire building after the fashion of

Bangkok's Oriental or Singapore's Raffles. This means that of the old South-East Asian colonials, only the E&O in Penang remains to exude anything like its original colonial charm.

The *Inya Lake Hotel* on the road to the Rangoon (Yangon) Airport should be avoided if at all possible. It's more expensive (US$45 up), the Russian-built facilities lack any charm whatsoever and the staff are a bit on the frosty side. It's also far from the city centre.

Once your paid-for accommodation has been utilised there are a few less expensive options. Least expensive is the *YMCA* which is relatively central, has reasonably good food and is tatty but bearable. The dormitory no longer exists, or if it does it's not open to foreigners. Rooms are now K70 for doubles with communal bath and K100 with private bath. Both sexes may stay at this Y.

On our first visit to Burma (Myanmar), we were plagued by mosquitoes here. They subsequently installed mosquito nets, then took them out again and put wire mesh on the windows – which keeps the air out and lets the insects in once the inevitable holes appear. They do have fans, however, and the toilets work.

Tony Wheeler

The *YWCA* is open to women only – unlike the YMCA which is open to either sex, although couples are supposed to be married if they share double rooms, a quaint custom for Asia. It's at 119 Brooking St and has just two singles and two doubles. Rates are approximately the same as for the YMCA.

If the Ys are full, as they occasionally are, there are a number of alternatives. Right next door to the MTT office on Sule Pagoda Rd is the *Garden Hotel*. It's a slightly more modern establishment than the Y and is kept fairly clean. Quoted rates for economy rooms are US$10/15 for singles/doubles with shared facilities. It seems the dorm here has also become unavailable to foreigners. The rooms with bath are clean but very plain and cost US$15/20 – they're small, spartan and not especially good value. You can leave bags at the Garden Hotel for K2 per day.

The old Orient Hotel at 256/260 Sule Pagoda Rd is now named the *Dagon* and is a fairly pleasant place to stay except that the rooms at the front are very noisy. There are nice views from the balcony, good food in the restaurant downstairs (upstairs from the street) and it's a fine place for a beer. Rooms are similar in cost to the Garden Hotel.

Rangoon (Yangon) has a dozen or more guest houses in the central district, such as the old travellers' standby *Pyin Oo Lwin* at 183 Barr St, two blocks east of the MTT office and Sule Pagoda. Doubles here are now K75 but all English signs have been removed and they say they're 'full'. In actuality, none of these fine little guest houses are permitted to accept foreigners these days.

If you're catching the 6 am express train to Mandalay, you might consider the *Sakantha*, a colonial period hotel reminiscent of the Strand (but several degrees more decrepit), which is located right at the Rangoon (Yangon) railway station. Here, the rooms are US$36/42 for singles/doubles and the restaurant downstairs isn't bad.

Places to Eat

With only a couple of days at the most in Rangoon (Yangon), you have little opportunity to explore the gourmet delights of socialist dining, Burmese-style. The *YMCA* has a pretty reasonable cafe where a number of separate food stalls engage in spirited but most un-Burmese competition.

There are numerous Indian restaurants around – particularly along Anawrahta St going west from Sule Pagoda Rd. The *New Delhi Restaurant* between 29th St and Shwebontha Rd serves a wide selection of north and south Indian dishes and is quite good. Some of the smaller Indian places specialise in biryani, spiced rice with chicken. Try the *Nila Briyane Shop* between 31st and 32nd Sts. It's crowded but the service is snappy.

The fancier restaurants sprinkled throughout Rangoon (Yangon) are mostly Chinese. At 84 37th St, the *Palace* has a well-deserved reputation for serving the best Chinese food

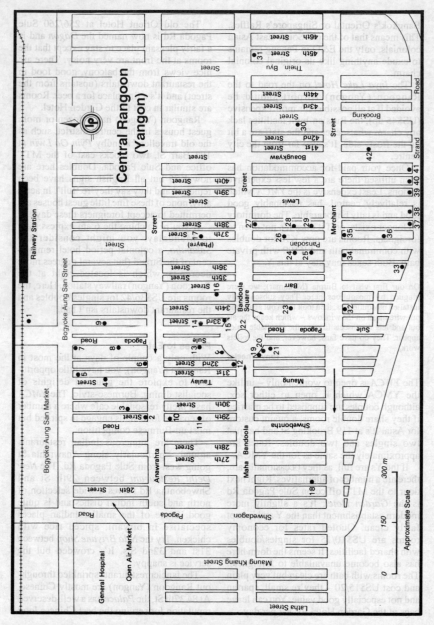

Central Rangoon (Yangon)

Approximate Scale

0   150   300 m

1	Sakartha Hotel
2	New Delhi Restaurant
3	Burmese Restaurants
4	Meiktila Buses (Road & Transport Co)
5	Bookstalls
6	Nila Briyane Shop
7	Burma Patisserie
8	Gold Cup Cafe
9	Dagon Hotel
10	Mawlamyine Buses
11	Pyi Buses
12	Yatha Tea Shop
13	Tourist Department Stores
14	Lombani Tea House
15	City Hall & Library
16	Pyin Oo Lwin Guest House
17	Great Wall Restaurant
18	Synagogue
19	Thai International
20	Myanmar Tours & Travel (MTT)
21	Garden Hotel
22	Sule Pagoda
23	Independence Monument
24	Nan Yu Restaurant
25	Mya Sabe Cafe
26	Bangladesh Biman Airways
27	Nilarwin Cold Drink Shop
28	Pagan Bookshop
29	Palace Restaurant
30	YWCA
31	YMCA
32	US Embassy
33	Customs House
34	Indian Embassy
35	Sarpay Beikman Library
36	National Museum
37	Myanma Airways
38	Strand Hotel
39	Australian Embassy
40	British Embassy
41	Post Office
42	Cheap Burmese Restaurants

in Rangoon (Yangon). It's a bit pricey but worth it.

There are lots of places for tea, a quick snack or a cold beer. The *Lombani Tea House* on Sule Pagoda Rd is a good place to try Burmese tea and the snacks served along with it. The large *Burma Patisserie* at the north end of Sule Pagoda Rd near the Bogyoke Market is a government-run tea house with low, subsidised prices. You can get yoghurt or *lassi* (a delicious yoghurt drink) at the *Nilarwin Cold Drink Shop* at 377 Maha Bandoola St about midway between the YMCA and the Sule Pagoda. Before 1988, it was quite a travellers' meeting spot and the proprietors have been keeping the premises well scrubbed in preparation for the travellers' return. *Yatha*, a white-fronted building within sight of the tourist office, is a good place for drinks and ice cream as well as tea and snacks. The friendly owner speaks excellent English.

In the evening a beer in the lounge of the *Strand Hotel* is a time-honoured pursuit. There's always a friendly crowd of people here to talk with. When the bar closes down, the reception desk still has a cache of cold bottles behind the counter!

If you decide to dine at the *Strand* then make it lobster – it's an incredible bargain even at the official exchange rate. Using free-market kyats, anything on the menu is cheap.

Try the genuine Burmese food in the *Hla Myanma Rice House* at 27 5th St, behind the Shwedagon Pagoda. It's popularly called the 'Shwe Ba' because the famous Burmese actor of the same name had his house nearby. It's a plain and straightforward restaurant, but the food is very good and they also have Chinese and Indian dishes. Prices are quite reasonable – count on around K60 per person. There are also dozens of Burmese food stalls along 41st St between Strand Rd and Merchant St.

One of the places to get a burger in Rangoon (Yangon) is at *Maggi*, 20 Inyin Rd, really just a stall tucked into the garden of a house facing Rangoon (Yangon) University. The students run the place and even make milkshakes.

Getting There & Away

See the Burma (Myanmar) Getting There & Away section or the relevant destinations for transport details to and from Rangoon (Yangon).

Getting Around

To/From the Airport The fixed fare for a taxi

between the airport and Rangoon (Yangon) is K85 (K65 to the Inya Lake Hotel, which is near the airport). You pay the fare at the MTT counter in the airport and four passengers may share one vehicle. You can also take local bus No 9, although that entails getting out to the main road, about a km away, first. On departure, MAC, provides a bus for its passengers but it departs so long before flight time that you may prefer to sleep in and get a taxi for an early morning departure. All international departures are levied a US$6 airport tax.

Local Transport You can get around Rangoon (Yangon) on the fairly comprehensive bus service or by trishaws, taxis or the small Mazda taxi-trucks. Some of these operate just like taxis (though they're cheaper) while others seem to run their own little bus routes with fares of a few kyats or so. A trishaw ride within the city centre should be around K10.

An interesting way of seeing the city, suburbs and surrounding countryside is to take the 'circle line' train from Rangoon (Yangon) station. It's crowded with commuters on weekdays but on Saturday morning you can make a 2½ hour loop, allowing you to see the outskirts of the city and surrounding villages.

BAGO (Pegu)
Bago is 80 km north-east from Rangoon (Yangon) on the Mandalay line. This city used to be a major seaport until the river changed course. This event, coupled with Bago's destruction by a rival Burmese king in 1757, was the city's downfall.

Things to See
Shwemawdaw Pagoda The 'Great Golden God Pagoda' was rebuilt after an earthquake in 1930 and is nearly as high as the Shwedagon Pagoda in Rangoon (Yangon). Murals tell the sad story of the quake. Note the large chunk of the *hti* (the umbrella or decorated top of a pagoda), toppled by an earlier 1917 quake, embedded in the north-east corner of the pagoda.

Shwethalyaung This huge reclining Buddha image is over five metres longer than the one in Bangkok and claimed to be extremely life-like. A terrific signboard gives the dimensions of the figure's big toe and other vital statistics.

Other Bago has other attractions. Beyond the Shwemawdaw is the **Hintha Gone**, a hilltop shrine guarded by mythical swans. On the Rangoon (Yangon) side of town, the **Kyaik Pun** has three back-to-back sitting Buddhas – the fourth one has fallen down. Just before the Shwethalyaung is the **Kalyani Sima**, or Hall of Ordination, and a curious quartet of standing Buddha figures.

Carry on beyond the Shwethalyaung and you soon come to the **Mahazedi Pagoda**, where you can climb to the top for a fine view over the surrounding country. The **Shwegugale Pagoda**, with 64 seated Buddha images, is a little beyond the Mahazedi.

Places to Stay & Eat
The official MTT-approved hotel is the *Shwewatan* with single/double rooms for US$25/35. There are a number of food stalls around the market place and some snack bars and restaurants near the railway station. A traveller recommended the *Three Five Zero Hotel* between the railway bridge and the river (left side as you walk from the station) for good, cheap Chinese food.

Getting There & Away
There are plenty of buses and trains between Rangoon (Yangon) and Bago. If you plan to disembark at Bago from the Mandalay to Rangoon (Yangon) special express, you can only officially do so on the day train.

On one trip to Burma (Myanmar), however, I took the night train from Thazi and it went through the station so slowly that I simply hopped off the moving train.

Don't try to visit Bago on the way north to Mandalay; you may have trouble getting a seat on another northbound train. Coming south, it's only another hour or two into Rangoon (Yangon) by train or bus. In

Rangoon (Yangon), train tickets to Bago must be purchased from MTT for US$8 one way. Coming back, you may be able to buy a ticket at the Bago station with free-market kyats.

Buses to Bago cost around K15 from Rangoon (Yangon); they start from Rangoon (Yangon) as early as 5 or 6 am. Avoid Bago on weekends when it is very crowded with Burmese – the excursion there from Rangoon (Yangon) is a popular one. If you want to splash out a bit, get a group together and hire a huge old American taxi from near the Strand and ride there like Al Capone. Count on around US$15 to US$20 for the whole day.

Getting Around

The easiest way to explore Bago is to hire a trishaw by the station and negotiate a rate to visit all the Bago attractions.

MANDALAY

Mandalay was the last capital of Burma (Myanmar) to fall before the British took over, and for this reason it still has great importance as a cultural centre. It is Burma's (Mynamar's) second city with a population around 330,000 and was founded, comparatively recently, in 1857. Dry and dusty in the hot season, Mandalay is a sprawling town of dirt streets, trishaws and horse carts.

In 1981, a disastrous fire destroyed a great number of buildings along the riverside but did not affect any of Mandalay's sights. Although Mandalay is of some interest in itself the 'deserted cities' around Mandalay are probably even more worthwhile.

Orientation & Information

The MTT office is in the Mandalay Hotel, a very long walk from the main part of town where most of the cheap hotels are located. Mandalay is laid out on an extremely straightforward grid pattern but it is very sprawling – distances in Mandalay are quite vast.

Things to See

Royal Palace Once within the enormous palace walls and moat, this amazing example of wooden architecture was completely burnt out during the closing days of WW II. Some foundations and a model can be seen. You must get permission to enter from the sentry at the south gate.

Mandalay Hill An easy half-hour's barefoot climb up the sheltered steps brings you to a wide view over the palace, Mandalay and the pagoda-studded countryside.

Kuthodaw Pagoda This pagoda's 729 small temples each shelter a marble slab inscribed with Buddhist scriptures. The central pagoda makes it 730. Built by King Mindon around 1860, it is the world's biggest book. Don't confuse it with the Sandamuni Pagoda which is right in front of it and also has a large collection of inscribed slabs. The ruins of the **Atumashi Kyaung**, or 'incomparable monastery', are also close to the foot of Mandalay Hill.

Shwenandaw Kyaung Once a part of King Mindon's palace, this wooden building was moved to its present site and converted into a monastery after his death. This is the finest remaining example of traditional wooden Burmese architecture since all the other palace buildings were destroyed during the WW II. Admission is US$3.

Kyauktawgyi The pagoda at the base of Mandalay Hill was another King Mindon construction. The marble Buddha is said to have taken 10,000 men 13 days to install in the temple.

Mahamuni Pagoda The 'Arakan Pagoda' stands to the south of town. It's noted for its venerated Buddha image which is thickly covered in goldleaf. Around the main pagoda are rooms containing a huge five tonne gong and statues of legendary warriors.

Rubbing parts of their bodies is supposed to cure afflictions on corresponding parts of your own. Outside the pagoda are streets of Buddha image makers. Admission is US$4.

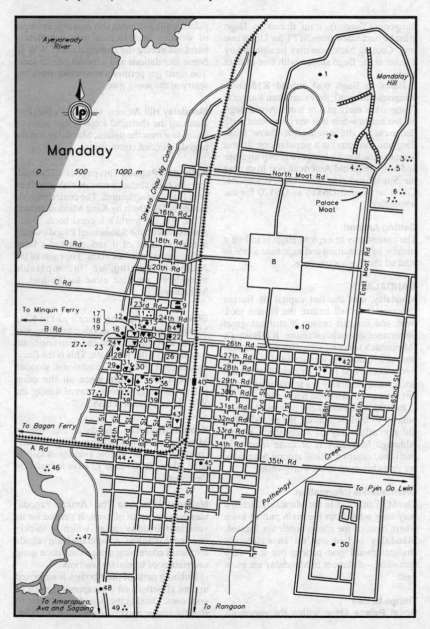

Mandalay

1	Golf Course
2	Military Cemetary
3	Kuthodaw (730 Pagodas)
4	Kyauktawgyi
5	Sandamuni Pagoda
6	Shwenandaw Kyaung
7	Atumashi Kyaung
8	Royal Palace Model & Museum
9	GPO
10	Independence Monument
11	Shwekyimyint Pagoda
12	Bagan Minibuses
13	Number 8 Amarapura Bus
14	National Museum & Library
15	HMV Pyin Oo Lwin Jeeps
16	Bank & Rangoon Newspaper
17	Nylon Ice-cream
18	Olympia Cafe
19	Orient Restaurant
20	Mann Restaurant
21	Bank
22	MAC Office
23	Clocktower
24	Food Stalls
25	Min Min Restaurant
26	Chiddy's
27	Eindawya Pagoda
28	Legyo Market
29	Bus to Pagan
30	Mosque
31	Golden Pearl Restaurant
32	Burmese Restaurant
33	Popular Restaurant Area
34	Pyin Oo Lwin Jeeps
35	Sagaing Taxi Trucks
36	Fire Lookout Tower
37	Setkyathika Pagoda
38	Small Pagoda
39	Bus to Bagan
40	Railway Station
41	Mya Mandala Hotel
42	Mandalay Hotel
43	Shwe Wah Restaurant
44	Shwegon Pagoda
45	Goldleaf Workshop
46	Shwe Ein Bin Monastery
47	Kin Wun Monastery
48	Buddha Image Makers
49	Mahamuni Pagoda
50	Royal Garden

Other The **Zegyo Market** in the centre of town comes alive at night. The **Eindawya Pagoda** and the **Shwekyimyint Pagoda** are also centrally located. The latter is older than Mandalay itself. Several of the town's pagodas have amusing clockwork coin-in-the-slot displays. Mandalay's **museum** is tatty and costs US$4 per entry.

Places to Stay

Mandalay has a lot of hotels and rest houses in the bottom-end bracket but, unfortunately, they've all been closed to foreigners since the 1988 rebellions. The shoestring hotels are all around the town centre (see map), south-west of the palace. The government may decide to reopen these places to non-Burmese (they're still in use by Burmese residents) – if so, head for this area.

Of the three MTT-sanctioned hotels, the *Mya Mandala* (formerly the Tun Hla), behind the more expensive Mandalay Hotel, has the most character. There are only 10 rooms, six of which cost US$25 for singles or doubles and the other four are US$31 each with bath. There is a restaurant and a swimming pool here.

The *Mandalay Hotel*, where the MTT is situated, has rooms with official rates of US$44/56 for singles/doubles. The *Inwa* costs about the same as the Mandalay.

Places to Eat

The grubby-looking little *Shwe Wah*, on 80th St between 32nd and 33rd Rds, is very popular for food – the quality of the food certainly outshines the surroundings.

On 83rd St, between 25th and 26th Rds (close to the Zegyo Market), there is a cluster of good places – try the *Mann Restaurant* for quite reasonable food and don't miss a delicious ice cream in the extremely popular *Nylon Ice Cream Bar*. Next door is the *Olympia Cafe* which is good for light snacks at any time of day. Next door again is the equally popular *Orient Restaurant*, while not far away on 83rd St, between 26th and 27th Rds, the *Min Min* does good Chinese Muslim food.

There are a number of very economical food stalls beside the Zegyo Market along 26th Rd. On 29th Rd, particularly between 83rd and 84th Sts, you'll find a number of Chinese restaurants. The *Golden Pearl* has been recommended for its 'excellent Chinese food'. For *Shan* food, which is similar to northern Thai cuisine, try *Kyaukmei* on 80th St between 38th and 39th Rds. For Indian, *Chiddy's* on the corner of 81st St and 27th Rd is a good choice. Mandalay's many sugar cane crushers provide a thirst-quenching (and seemingly reasonably healthy) drink for just one kyat. Watch out for strawberries on sale near the market in season.

Getting There & Away

Air The Rangoon (Yangon) to Mandalay flight (three times a week) is now by K1010 (F-27 prop) or K1144 (F-28 jet) and includes airport transport at each end. More than likely you'll have to pay the MTT set fare of US$70 for either flight. It takes about an hour by F-28 jet and 1½ hours by F-27. From Bagan, it's about US$25 and a 30-minute flight.

Train The daily express trains from Rangoon (Yangon) to Mandalay depart from both ends at around 6 am, 5 and 6.30 pm, arriving 12 hours later. The first two departures cost US$30 from MTT, the third is the 'special express' which has better seats and costs US$38. This tourist service is fairly uncrowded and admirably punctual, but reserve your seat as early as possible. If you can get away with using free-market kyats (impossible in Rangoon), the fare will be much less exorbitant.

If you're going straight to Mandalay from Rangoon (Yangon), I'd advise heading immediately for MTT from the airport and getting a ticket for the next morning or even that night if you arrive early. Get an excellent chicken biryani for lunch at one of the stations on the way – it will be neatly wrapped in a banana leaf.

Getting Around

To/From the Airport Recently, MAC has included airport transport in their ticket price for tourists.

Local Transport Around town, horse-drawn

tongas and Burma's (Myanmar's) familiar back-to-back trishaws are the usual transport. A couple of people could hire a trishaw for the day to get around Mandalay for about US$2, and tongas are about US$3. Hiring a Japanese pick-up with a guide for a day-trip to Amarapura and Sagaing would cost US$10 to US$15 for up to eight people. Count on K8 or K10 for a trishaw from the Mandalay Hotel (tourist office) to the town centre and K15 or K20 for a tonga from the centre down to the Ayeyarwady River.

Travel around Mandalay in the city's impossibly crowded buses (worse during rush hour) is actually quite fun and certainly very friendly. Take bus No 1 to the Mahamuni Pagoda, No 2 to the river end of B Rd (Mingun ferry departure point) or to the railway and airport in the other direction, No 4 to Mandalay Hill from the clocktower or the No 5 to Mandalay Hill via the Mandalay Hotel. Bus No 8 via the Mahamuni and Amarapura to Ava starts from the corner of 27th Rd and 84th St.

Don't start walking around Mandalay without giving it some thought as distances are great.

AROUND MANDALAY

Close to Mandalay are four 'deserted cities', which make interesting day trips. You can also visit Pyin Oo Lwin, further to the north-east, and probably requiring an overnight stop.

Amarapura

Situated 11 km south of Mandalay, this was the capital of upper Burma for a brief period before the establishment of Mandalay. Amongst the most interesting sights is the rickety **U Bein's Bridge** leading to the **Kyauktawgyi Pagoda**.

Sagaing

If you continue a little further beyond Amarapura, you'll reach the Ava Bridge, the only bridge across the Ayeyarwady River. Built by the British, it was put out of action during WW II and not repaired until 1954. Crossing the bridge will bring you to

Sagaing with its temple-studded hill. Sagaing's best-known pagoda is not on Sagaing Hill – you must continue 10 km beyond Sagaing to reach the **Kaungh-mudaw Pagoda** which is said to have been modelled on a well-endowed queen's perfect breast.

Ava

The ancient city of Ava, for a long time a capital of upper Burma after the fall of Bagan, is on the Mandalay side of the Ayeyarwady River close to the Ava Bridge. To get to it, take a bus No 8 which runs right down to the Myitnge River which you must cross by a ferry or canoe. Or, get off the Sagaing minibus at the Ava Bridge and stroll across the fields to the Myitnge River. There is very little left of Ava today apart from the **Maha Aungmye Bonzan** monastery and a crumbling 27-metre-high watchtower.

Mingun

The fourth of the old cities is Mingun, on the opposite bank from Mandalay, a pleasant 11-km trip upriver. Get a riverboat from the bottom of 26th St. The cost is around K10 and the trip takes anything from 45 minutes to two hours. The trip to Mingun is very pleasant and makes a very good introduction to Burmese river travel, particularly if you do not take the boat to Bagan.

Principal sights at Mingun are the huge ruined base of the **Mingun Pagoda** and the equally grandiose **Mingun Bell**. The pagoda would have been the largest in the world if it had been completed. The bell is said to be the largest uncracked bell in the world – there is a bigger one in Russia but it is badly cracked.

Monywa

The **Thanboddhay Pagoda** here is one of the largest in Burma (Myanmar) and there are said to be 582,357 Buddha images ensconced thereon. The town of Monywa, a trade centre for the Chindwin Valley, is 135 km north-west of Mandalay. Buses leave for Monywa regularly from the corner of 84th and 30th Sts, cost around K45 and take about three hours. You can also take a Ye-U train

from Mandalay for only K15, but this trip takes four to five hours.

Pyin Oo Lwin (Maymyo)

If you haven't time to head downriver to Bagan, then Pyin Oo Lwin may make an interesting substitute. It's an old British hill station, formerly called Maymyo after the British Colonel May. It's just 60 km north of Mandalay and about 800 metres higher. Get there in a jeep (frequent departures from the market) or rather cheaper, but much slower, by train – it zig-zags its way up the hills.

The chief pleasure of Pyin Oo Lwin is a stay at the old British bachelor's quarters Candacraig. You can read a delightful description of it in Paul Theroux's *Great Railway Bazaar*.

Places to Stay & Eat *Candacraig*, officially known as the *Pyin Oo Lwin Government Rest House*, was once the bachelor quarters of the Bombay Burma Trading Company. It was run by the late Mr Bernard until around his 90th birthday and maintained in exactly the state it was during the British era.

It has lost some of its colonial splendour but it is still pleasant, with rooms at US$25/31 (official rate) for singles/doubles. A roaring fire, a cold bottle of Mandalay beer and the English dinner all add to the atmosphere. You can hire bicycles here to explore Pyin Oo Lwin. You might inquire first at MTT in Mandalay to make sure the rest house is open as in recent times it has occasionally been closed for repairs.

Other places to stay in town include the *Thin Sabai, Shwe Yema, Ububahan* and the *Nann Myaing* at the beginning of town but, presently, they are closed to foreigners – but who knows what the future will hold. The *YMCA* might allow foreigners in for US$10 a room.

There are a variety of restaurants around the town centre, including a couple of Chinese places reputed to have some of the best Chinese food in Burma (Myanmar).

Getting There & Away From Mandalay, you can take a jeep from K55 to K70 if you wish to go all the way to the Rest House. Jeeps depart from near the Zegyo Market and the trip takes about two to 2½ hours up, one to 1½ down. Chartering a whole jeep costs around K500. There is also a daily train but it's more for railway enthusiasts than as straightforward transport as it takes four to five hours to negotiate the many switchbacks.

BAGAN (Pagan)

One of the true wonders of Asia, Bagan (formerly Pagan) is a bewildering, deserted city of fabulous pagodas and temples on the banks of the Ayeyarwady, to the south of Mandalay. Bagan's period of grandeur started in 1057 when King Anawrahta conquered Thaton and brought back artists, craftsmen, monks and 30 elephant-loads of Buddhist scriptures.

Over the next two centuries, an enormous number of magnificent buildings were erected but after Kublai Khan sacked the city in 1287 it was never rebuilt. A major earthquake in 1975 caused enormous damage but everything of importance has now been restored or reconstructed. Unhappily, the plunderers who visit places like Bagan to scavenge for Western art collectors have also done damage but it is definitely the place in Burma (Myanmar) not to be missed.

Information & Orientation

As a place of human habitation, Bagan is once again as deserted as it was after Kublai Khan passed through centuries ago. Following the 1988 uprising, the government forced the tiny village to move some four km away, supposedly to undertake archaeological digs (which so far haven't occurred). Actually, this typically ruthless move was an attempt to disrupt the May 1989 elections. The numerous shops, houses, small guest houses and restaurants that once lined the dirt road have all been demolished.

The largest nearby settlement to Bagan is Nyaung-Oo. Buses depart from the latter and the Mandalay ferry docks there. Bagan Airport is also near Nyaung-Oo. MTT has an office in the main street of Bagan. Without

fail, you should get a copy of the *Guide to Pagan* as an aid to exploring the ruins. A newer photographic guide entitled simply *Pagan* is also quite good but very expensive.

Things to See

The following section describes just a handful of the more interesting of Bagan's 5000 plus temples. The entry fee into the 'Archaeological Zone' is US$10 per day for the first two days, US$3 per day thereafter.

Ananda This huge white temple was built in 1091 and houses four standing Buddhas and two sacred Buddha footprints. It's close to the Bagan village and is one of the most important temples. In 1989 the tower was regilded and the niches filled with Buddha images.

Thatbyinnyu This is the highest temple in Bagan, with Buddha images in the upper storey and magnificent views from the top. Bagan has to be seen from above for proper appreciation.

Gawdawpalin Also close to the village of Bagan, the Gawdawpalin looks like a slightly smaller Thatbyinnyu. Built between 1174 and 1211, this is the best place to watch the sunset over the Ayeyarwady. This temple was probably the most extensively damaged in the '75 quake but has been completely restored.

Mingalazedi One of the last temples completed before Kublai Khan sacked the city. Fine terracotta tiles can be seen around the base of the huge bell-shaped stupa.

Shwesandaw A cylindrical stupa on top of five ultra-steep terraces with good views from the top. In the shed beside the stupa is a 20-metre reclining Buddha.

Shwezigon This traditionally shaped gold pagoda was started by King Anawrahta and stands close to the village of Nyaung-Oo. The view of the magnificent lions guarding

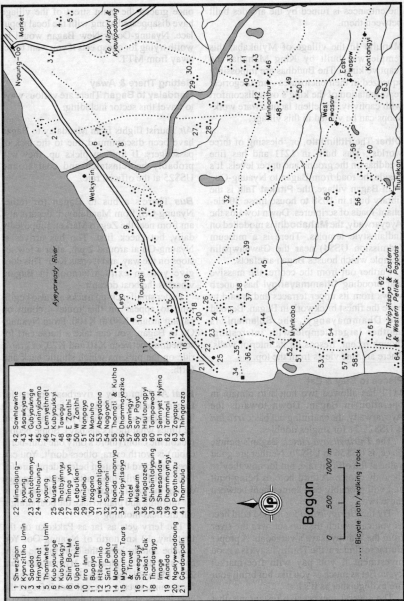

Bagan

0   500   1000 m

...... Bicycle path/walking track

1 Shwezigon
2 Kyanzittha Umin
3 Sapada
4 Hmyathat
5 Thamiwhet Umin
6 Kubyaukge
7 Kubyaukgyi
8 Shin Bo-Me
9 Upali Thein
10 Irra Inn
11 Bupaya
12 Htilominlo
13 Sint Pahto
14 Mahabodhi
15 Myanmar Tours
   & Travel
16 Shwegugyi
17 Pitakat Taik
18 Thandawgya
19 Image
20 Ngakywenadaung
21 Gawdawpalin

22 Mimalaung-
   kyaung
23 Pahtothamya
24 Nathloung-
   kyaung
25 Museum
26 Thatbyinnyu
27 Thinga yon
28 E Zanthi
29 Winidho
30 Izagona
31 Lawkahtipan
32 Sulamani
33 Nanda mannya
34 Thiripyitsaya
35 Museum
36 Mingalazedi
37 Shinbintalyaung
38 Shwesandaw
39 Dhammayangyi
40 Payathonzu
41 Thambula

42 Sawhlawine
43 Asawkyawn
44 Gubyauknge
45 Guninyiohma
46 Lemyethnat
47 Kubyaukkyi
48 Tawagu
49 E Zanthi
50 W Zanthi
51 Nanpaya
52 Manuha
53 Abeyadana
54 Nagayon
55 Thamoti & Kutha
56 Thiripyitsaya
57 Samingyi
58 Say Paya
59 Hsutoungpyi
60 Tampawadi
61 Seinnyet Nyima
62 Tarmani
63 Zayaput
64 Thingaroza

the entrances is ruined by the arcades built between them.

Manuha In the village of Myinkaba, this temple was built by King Manuha, the 'captive king'. The Buddhas are impossibly squeezed in their enclosures – an allegorical representation of the king's own discomfort with captivity. Excellent lacquerware workshops can be visited in this village.

Other The **Htiliminlo**, or 'blessing of three worlds', was built in 1211 and has fine Buddhas on the ground and upper levels. It's beside the road from Bagan to Nyaung-Oo.

In Bagan village, the **Pitakat Taik** is the library built in 1058 to house those 30 elephant-loads of scriptures. Down towards the Ayeyarwady, the **Mahabodhi** is modelled on Indian-style temples. There is a museum (admission US$4) near the Gawdawpalin Temple which houses Bagan artefacts.

Further out from the centre, the massive and brooding **Dhammayangyi** has superb views from its upper terraces and is said to have the finest brickwork in Bagan. Beyond the Dhammayangyi, the **Sulamani** is another larger temple with interesting, though recent, frescos on its interior walls. There are fine views from the top.

Places to Stay & Eat

MTT has allowed two hotels to remain in operation in Bagan. Down towards the Ayeyarwady, the charming but basic *Irra Inn* is US$25/31 for singles/doubles.

The *Thiripyitsaya Hotel*, Bagan's deluxe place, is US$56 to US$70. Neither are good value at the official rate, but for now they're the only choice. A third hotel is being built and will probably cost somewhere between these two.

Try the *Thiripyitsaya* for a good cold beer as you can watch the sun set over the river from the Thiripyitsaya's verandah. A proper Burmese dinner at the Thiripyitsaya is a good investment if you pay with free-market kyats. Eat as much as you like but bring your fire extinguisher as it's hot.

The several inexpensive restaurants that once graced the main street of the village have disappeared along with the local populace. Nyaung-Oo or New Bagan would be worth trying for cheap eats if you want to get away from MTT.

Getting There & Away

Mandalay to Bagan There are various ways to travel this sector including:

Air Tourist flights from Mandalay to Bagan have been discontinued due to the lack of passengers. If tourism picks up, they will probably be reinstated and cost around US$25 at the official rate.

Bus There's a bus to Bagan (or rather Nyaung-Oo) from Mandalay. It departs at 4 am from near the Zegyo Market, supposedly daily, but check first. The bus arrives at Nyaung-Oo at around 2 pm, after a few tea stops on the way, and it costs K45. This does give you an extra afternoon in Bagan, whereas the boat doesn't.

Faster small pick-up trucks are also beginning to appear on this route – count on paying around K80 to K100. From Nyaung-Oo to Bagan, you can take a horse cart for something between K10 and K20, or grab a ride on the pickups which shuttle back and forth.

Boat At 5 am daily a riverboat departs for Bagan. The fare is US$18 on deck or US$30 in the cabins at the official MTT rate (about 12 times what the locals pay). Some people reckon the cabin (there's only one four-berth cabin) is worth extra, others don't. You can sleep on board the night before departure for free. MTT will look after your baggage during the day if you arrive in Mandalay in the morning and plan to take the boat straight out the next morning.

The ferry gets as far as Pakkoku on the first day, 13 km north of Nyaung-Oo. You may be able to leave the boat for the night and stay in the pleasant *Myayatanar Inn*, 2288 Main Rd. Pakkoku also has some good restaurants, even a cinema! Don't forget the boat leaves at 5 am, but don't worry if you miss it, there are other boats later in the morning. The 5 am boat arrives in Bagan at 6.30 or 7 am – if on schedule. Travelling upriver from Bagan to Mandalay takes two days.

Apart from the mosquitoes, the main problem with the ferry is that it sometimes gets stuck on sandbanks. These can delay you for hours, sometimes days. Such delays are more likely to occur in March and April, towards the end of the dry season. The Ayeyarwady is wide and flat so you don't see all that much of the countryside but there is always plenty of activity on the riverbanks or on the river itself.

Most people have a thoroughly interesting time on the Mandalay to Bagan riverboat. Continuing on down to Rangoon (Yangon) is now more feasible with the two-week visa but we don't know anyone who has done it yet.

Bagan to Rangoon (Yangon) Transport for this sector includes:

Air To fly to Rangoon (Yangon) you must fly the full Bagan-Mandalay-Heho-Rangoon (Yangon) route. The fare is a sum of the fare for each sector – quite expensive. These days most visitors either fly back to Mandalay and then take the train to Rangoon (Yangon) or take the bus to Thazi and train on to Rangoon (Yangon). Another possibility, of course, is to continue east to Inle Lake, then fly to Rangoon (Yangon) from Heho.

Bus & Train There are a number of bus and train alternatives for getting from Bagan back to Rangoon (Yangon). One of them rates as the most miserable train trip I've ever made.

The simplest and most comfortable route is the one MTT organises. They run you from Bagan to Thazi, the railway town south of Mandalay, in a minibus (which means a Datsun pickup with a bench seat down each side!) which departs at 2 pm. You should arrive in Thazi between 7 and 8 pm, in plenty of time to catch the night express from Mandalay which leaves that town at 6.15 pm and

arrives in Thazi about 9.15 pm. MTT guarantee you a seat on the train if you take their truck, but you must book ahead in Bagan or Mandalay. If there are enough to fill a truck, the cost is only around US$10 per person. If not, the fare is prorated upward for the number of passengers.

Thazi has a small, grubby rest house where you may be able to stay, unofficially. On the main road, just before the railway line, there's the *Wonderful* restaurant with good Chinese food and the *Red Star* with excellent Indian food. The Thazi to Rangoon (Yangon) train fare is K154 in upper (tourist) class.

Another bus and train alternative is a do-it-yourself version of the above. First of all, get into Nyaung-Oo from Bagan, then take a bus-truck (ie a truck with benches in the back) to Kyauk Padaung, a couple of hours' ride. Follow this with another bus to Meiktila about three hours away, then a short half-hour ride to Thazi. Total fare will be about K45 but there is no way you can do this in time for the morning train. There's a catch to this method too. It's quite possible that when the comfortable Mandalay to Rangoon (Yangon) train rolls in it will be completely full and the alternative will be a dirty, slow, crowded, miserable local train that rolls in many hours later (and many hours late).

There are two solutions to this problem – one is to book a Mandalay to Rangoon (Yangon) ticket before you leave Mandalay. The fare from Thazi is only a few kyats less than from Mandalay so it's not very wasteful and much more comfortable. The other solution is just to ignore the fact that the fast train is full and you're not allowed on. Just get on anyway, you'll find the floor of the deluxe train much more comfortable than that of the slow train and you'll get there faster.

The final bus-train alternative is the one to be avoided at all costs. Stage one is to take the same bus-truck to Kyauk Padaung, which is the rail head nearest Bagan. At somewhere between 2 and 5 pm an absolute horror of a train crawls off to Rangoon (Yangon), arriving in something like over 24 hours later. The fare is virtually the same as from Thazi and it's a dirty, uncomfortable, unlit, slow, crowded, tedious and unpleasant train. Avoid it.

Getting Around

The ruins are fairly widespread, and this is particularly a problem when you want to get to some of the more remote ones. You can hire a horse cart for around K20 to K30 an hour or a jeep for around K60 an hour. Both are less by the day or half-day of course. You can also hire bicycles from MTT for around K50 for a day. They're a very pleasant way of getting around Bagan but check that the brakes and other vital equipment are operating.

AROUND BAGAN
Mt Popa

Near Kyauk Padaung, the monastery-topped hill of Mt Popa can be visited as a day trip from Bagan. If you get a group together to charter a taxi-truck to Thazi or Inle Lake, a detour can also be made to visit it. It takes 20 minutes or so to make the stiff climb to the top of the hill. This is a centre for worship of the *nats*.

INLE LAKE

Inle Lake and nearby Taunggyi are the only other destinations in the Shan states, besides Pyin Oo Lwin, that are open to foreigners. The lake itself is extraordinarily beautiful and famous for its leg rowers. Taunggyi is the centre for official and black-market trade in the region.

To get out on the lake, you must charter an MTT boat – K90 to K100 per person or K800 to K1000 for an entire boat with a mandatory guide. The boat tour takes about half a day and includes visits to the floating village of **Ywama, Phaungdaw Oo Pagoda,** a floating market (best on Ywama market days, otherwise just souvenir-oriented) and to the MTT souvenir shop.

You are not allowed to take ordinary water taxis around the lake like the Burmese do. MTT has, however, in the past tolerated a few entrepreneurs who arrange canoe rides along the canals that run off the lake in the town of Yaunghwe – check around. In

Yaunghwe, the **Yatamamanaung Temple** is worth a quick visit.

Orientation & Information

There are four place names to remember in the lake area. First, there's Heho, where the airport is located. Continue east from there and you reach Shwenyaung where the railway terminates and where you turn off the road, south to the lake. Continue further east and Taunggyi is the main town in the area. At the northern end of the lake is Yaunghwe. Since the guest houses at the lake have been closed to foreigners, visitors must stay overnight in Taunggyi.

Places to Stay

At Yaunghwe, right by the lake, the *Inle Inn* has been closed down but MTT says is may be reopened in the future following renovations. The nearby *Bamboo Lodge* has suffered the same, perhaps temporary, fate.

The *Taunggyi Hotel* now costs US$38 to US$50. The rooms are modern with bathrooms and it's very pleasant, if overpriced at the official exchange rate.

Places to Eat

Close to the lake in Yaunghwe, the *Friendship Restaurant* is a popular little hang-out with fair food. The *Sunflower* next door is a bit cleaner, however, and more popular with locals. *Shwe Inlay*, near the town entrance, is good for breakfast. The impecunious can find cheaper food in the market. Best for Chinese food is the clean *Hu Pin*.

There's excellent food at the *Lyan You*, in the hotel of the same name on the main street of Taunggyi. You can't stay here, however, as it's not on the approved list. The *Academy Cafe*, close to the San Pya, is a friendly place for breakfast. *Shan You Ma*, in the open market at the north end of town, is renowned for good Shan and Chinese food. The best tea house in town is the government-run *Shwe Kai Nai Yi* on the main street, featuring favourite Burmese snacks like nam-bya (flatbread) and palata with pots of free tea.

Getting There & Away

You can reach Inle Lake from Rangoon (Yangon), Mandalay or Bagan.

Air The Mandalay to Heho airfare is US$25 and Bagan to Heho is K50. The Bagan flight goes via Mandalay. MAC provides free transport from Heho to Taunggyi. Heho to Rangoon (Yangon) is US$60 and all Rangoon (Yangon) to Heho flights entail stops in Bagan and Mandalay and the total fare is the sum of each sector.

Bus You can reach Taunggyi by bus from all three centres. From Rangoon (Yangon), you have to make a 16-hour bus trip, leaving at 3.30 am and arriving at 7.30 pm. The fare for this exhausting trip is about K150. To and from Mandalay, there are buses and taxi-trucks every morning. The buses leave around 4.30 or 5 am – the trip takes 10 to 12 hours. The Datsun taxi-trucks depart around 6 am and are rather faster. Costs range from around K100 to K150.

It is now fairly feasible to combine Inle Lake with Bagan because the MTT bus which operates from Nyaung-Oo (Bagan) to Thazi continues right on to Taunggyi for the same K110 fare as Bagan to Thazi. From Taunggyi, it departs at 5.30 am and reaches Bagan at around 5.30 pm. With a group you can charter a pick-up truck for around K1200 to K1500. It's a long and fairly gruelling one-day trip from Bagan to the lake.

Train From Rangoon (Yangon), you may take the regular Mandalay train and disembark at Thazi, only an hour or so before Mandalay. From there, you can take another train to Shwenyaung, near the lake. This is rather time-consuming though and it's better to take a jeep from Thazi for K75, which only takes six to eight hours, or a bus (Japanese pick-up), which costs considerably less than a jeep but takes longer. If you're heading back to Rangoon (Yangon) by this method note the possible problems in getting a seat on the train from Thazi if you haven't pre-booked it.

KALAW & PINDAYA

There are several excursions you can make en route to the lake. The Thazi to Taunggyi road passes through Kalaw, once a popular British hill station. There is only one MTT-operated rest house in Kalaw, the rambling *Kalaw Hotel*, where rooms cost US$31/38 for singles/doubles.

At Aungban, you can turn off the main road and travel north to Pindaya where the **Pindaya Caves** are packed with countless Buddha images, gathered there over the centuries. The *Pindaya Hotel*, the only official choice here, has singles/doubles for US$25/31.

OTHER PLACES

For a while, it seemed to be getting easier to visit some of the supposedly 'off-limits' places. Following the crackdown of 1989, however, the government has become more xenophobic about foreigners travelling around without permission.

The **Sandoway Beach Resort** on the Bay of Bengal is now officially open and a room at the *Ngapali Hotel* costs US$31. A plane from Rangoon (Yangon) is US$35 in an F-27 or US$40 on an F-28 jet.

It may still be possible to make it to the **balancing pagoda** at Kyaikto, beyond Bago. Buses depart regularly from Bago since this is a popular pilgrimage spot. However, having got there you have a 10-km walk where you ascend about 1000 metres. It's not possible to get back to Bago (or Rangoon) in the same day so come prepared to camp out.

A sleeping bag is a wise thing to bring with you when travelling anywhere in the back blocks of Burma (Myanmar).

You can probably also visit **Pyi** (formerly Prome) without too much trouble. The scattered ruins of the ancient city of **Sri-Kshetra** are nearby and definitely worth exploring. **Pathein** (formerly Bassein) is also fairly easily visited. For all these places, ignore MTT and simply go!

Cambodia

Modern-day Cambodia is the successor-state of the mighty Khmer Empire, which during the Angkorian period (9th to 14th centuries) ruled much of what is now Vietnam, Laos and Thailand. Among the accomplishments of the Khmer civilisation are the fabled temples of Angkor, one of humanity's most magnificent architectural achievements, now open to foreign visitors for the first time in two decades. These stunning monuments, surrounded by dense jungle, are only 152 km from the Thai border, which is expected to open to tourists once the civil war ends.

Cambodia is just emerging from two decades of continual warfare and violence, including almost four years (1975-79) of rule by the genocidal Khmer Rouge, who killed at least one million of Cambodia's seven million people. Even today, all around the country you see mass graves and ruined structures. The latter result, not from neglect, but from a conscious, coordinated campaign by the Khmer Rouge to obliterate the country's prerevolutionary culture.

What to Call Cambodia

Khmers have called their country Kampuchea since at least the 16th century. The name is adapted from *kambu-ja* meaning those born of Kambu, a figure of Indian mythology. After gaining independence in 1953, the country was known as the Kingdom of Cambodia and then the Khmer Republic, but it was the Khmer Rouge who insisted that the outside world use the name Kampuchea. Changing the country's official English name back to Cambodia in 1989 was intended to distance the present government in Phnom Penh from the bitter connotations of the name Kampuchea, which Westerners and Khmers living overseas both associate with the murderous Khmer Rouge regime.

Facts about the Country

HISTORY

From the 1st to the 6th centuries, much of present-day Cambodia was part of the kingdom of Funan, whose prosperity was due in large part to its position on the great trade route between China and India. Funan played a vital role in South-East Asian history as a recipient of Indian culture, which shaped the political institutions, culture and art of later Khmer states (and that of their neighbours).

The Angkorian era, known for its brilliant achievements in architecture and sculpture, was begun by Jayavarman II around the year 800. During his rule, a new state religion establishing the Khmer ruler as a *devaraja* (god-king) was instituted. Jayavarman II's successors constructed a vast irrigation system that facilitated intensive cultivation of the land around Angkor and allowed the Khmers to maintain a densely populated, highly centralised state.

In 1863, French gunboats intimidated King Norodom (reigned 1860 to 1904), whose kingdom had been under Thai and Vietnamese suzerainty for several centuries, into signing a treaty of protectorate. For the next 90 years, French control of Cambodia developed as an adjunct to France's colonial interests in Vietnam.

Independence was declared in 1953, and during the next 15 years, King (later Prince, Prime Minister and Chief-of-State) Norodom Sihanouk dominated Cambodian politics. However, he managed to alienate both the left and the right with his erratic and repressive policies. Sihanouk was overthrown by the army in 1970 and fled to China.

In 1969, the USA secretly commenced to carpet bomb suspected Communist base camps in Cambodia and, during the next four years, thousands of civilians were killed.

Shortly after the 1970 coup, American and South Vietnamese troops invaded the country to root out Vietnamese Communist forces. In this they largely failed, but the invasion did manage to push Cambodia's indigenous leftist guerrillas, the Khmer Rouge ('Red Khmer' in French), into the country's interior. Savage fighting soon engulfed the entire country, ending only when Phnom Penh fell to the Khmer Rouge on 17 April 1975, two weeks before the fall of Saigon.

Upon taking Phnom Penh, the Khmer Rouge, under leader Pol Pot, implemented one of the most radical, brutal restructurings of a society ever attempted. Its goal was the transformation of Cambodia into a Maoist, peasant-dominated, agrarian cooperative.

Within two weeks of coming to power, the entire populations of the capital and provincial towns were forcibly marched out to the countryside and placed in mobile work teams to do slave labour for 12 to 15 hours a day. Disobedience of any sort often meant immediate execution.

During the next four years, hundreds of

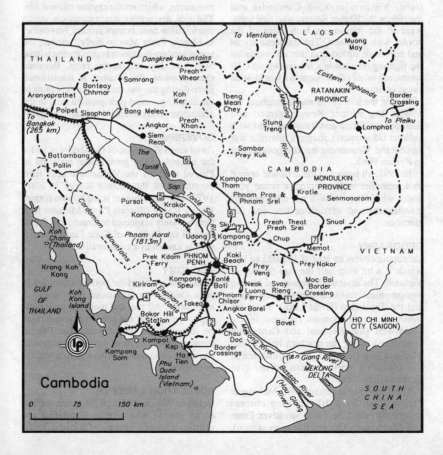

Cambodia

thousands of Cambodians, including the vast majority of the country's educated people, were tortured to death or executed. Thousands of people were branded as 'parasites' and systematically killed solely because they spoke a foreign language or wore spectacles. Hundreds of thousands more died of mistreatment, malnourishment and disease. At least one million Cambodians died between 1975 and 1979 as the result of the policies of the Khmer Rouge government.

At the end of 1978, in response to Khmer Rouge incursions into southern Vietnam in which hundreds of civilians had been slaughtered, Vietnam invaded Cambodia and overthrew the Khmer Rouge, who fled westward to the jungles on both sides of the border with Thailand. The immense social and economic dislocation that accompanied the fighting resulted in a famine whose UN-sponsored relief effort became a world-wide cause célèbre.

During the late 1970s and throughout the 1980s, the Khmer Rouge, armed and financed by China and Thailand (and with indirect US support), fought a guerrilla war against the Vietnamese-backed government in Phnom Penh.

In 1991, all parties to the civil war agreed to a ceasefire and accepted a peace plan under which the UN will run a transitional government and administer free and fair elections.

GEOGRAPHY
Cambodia covers an area of 181,035 sq km, which is a bit over half the size of Italy or Vietnam. The country is dominated by two topographical features, the Mekong River and the Tonlé Sap (Great Lake). There are three main mountainous regions: in the south-west (the Elephant and Cardamom mountains), along the northern border with Thailand (the Dangkrek Mountains) and in the country's north-eastern corner (the Eastern Highlands).

The Tonlé Sap is linked to the Mekong at Phnom Penh by a 100-km-long channel sometimes called the Tonlé Sap River. From mid-May to early October (the rainy season), the level of the Mekong rises, backing up the Tonlé Sap River and causing it to flow north-westward into the Tonlé Sap Lake. During this period, the Tonlé Sap swells from 3000 sq km to over 7500 sq km. As the water level of the Mekong falls during the dry season, the Tonlé Sap River reverses its flow, and the waters of the lake drain back into the Mekong. This extraordinary process makes the Tonlé Sap one of the world's richest sources of freshwater fish.

CLIMATE
The climate of Cambodia is governed by two monsoons, which set the rhythm of rural life. The cool, dry, north-eastern monsoon, which carries little rain, occurs around November to March. From May to early October, the south-western monsoon brings strong winds, high humidity and heavy rains. Between these seasons, the weather is transitional. Even during the wet season, it rarely rains in the morning – most precipitation falls in the afternoons, and even then, only sporadically.

GOVERNMENT
As of late 1991, most of Cambodia is under the control of the government installed in Phnom Penh by the Vietnamese after their overthrow of the Khmer Rouge in early 1979. That government is led by two former Khmer Rouge officers: Prime Minister Hun Sen, a widely respected reformer, and President of the Council of State Heng Samrin, who is known as a conservative.

ECONOMY
Cambodia is one of the poorest countries in Asia – 80% of the population is employed in agriculture. All fuel and most raw materials, capital equipment and consumer goods must be imported. In recent years, the Phnom Penh government have discarded dogmatic socialist economics in favour of free-market principles.

POPULATION & PEOPLE
Between 90% and 95% of the seven million or so people who live in Cambodia are ethnic-Khmers (ethnic-Cambodians),

making the country the most homogeneous in South-East Asia. Only about 10% of Cambodia's population resides in the cities or towns.

The most important minority group in Cambodia is the ethnic-Chinese, who until 1975 controlled the country's economy. There is a great deal of mutual dislike and distrust between the Khmers and the country's ethnic-Vietnamese. Cambodia's Cham Muslims (Khmer Islam) currently number some 190,000. They suffered vicious persecution between 1975 and 1979 and a large part of their community was exterminated.

Cambodia's diverse ethno-linguistic minorities (hill tribes), who live in the country's mountainous regions, numbered approximately 90,000 in 1975.

ARTS & CULTURE

Khmer architecture reached its zenith during the Angkorian era (the 9th to 14th centuries). Some of the finest examples of architecture from this period are Angkor Wat and the structures of Angkor Thom. Many of the finest works of Khmer sculpture are on display at the National Museum in Phnom Penh. Cambodia's highly stylised classic dance, adapted from Angkor dances (and similar to Thai dances derived from the same source), is performed to the accompaniment of an orchestra and choral narration.

Between the 15th century, when Angkor fell to the Thais and was abandoned, and the advent of the French protectorate, foreign invasions, civil war and political instability, left little opportunity and few resources to keep Cambodia's artistic traditions alive.

Avoiding Offence

Proper etiquette in wats (pagodas) is mostly a matter of common sense. A few tips:

• Don't wear shorts or tank tops.
• Take off your hat when entering the grounds of the wat.
• Take off your shoes before going into the *vihara* (sanctuary).
• If you sit down in front of the dais (the platform on which the Buddhas are placed), sit with your feet to the side rather than in the lotus position.
• Never point your finger – or, heaven forbid, the soles of your feet! – towards a figure of the Buddha (or human beings either).

RELIGION

Hinayana Buddhism is the dominant religion in Cambodia and was the state religion until 1975. It was reinstated as the state religion in the late 1980s. Between 1975 and 1979, the vast majority of Cambodia's Buddhist monks were murdered by the Khmer Rouge, who also destroyed virtually all of the country's 3000 wats.

LANGUAGE

Cambodia's official language is Khmer. For most Westerners, writing and pronouncing this language proves confusing and difficult. For over a century, the second language of choice among educated Cambodians was French, which is still spoken by many people who grew up before the 1970s. English has recently surged in popularity.

Greetings & Civilities

excuse me
suom tous
good night
rear trei suor sdei
goodbye
lear heouy
hello
joom reab suor/suor sdei
How are you?
tau neak sok sapbaiy jea te?
very well
sok touk jea thomada te
please
suom

Accommodation

I want a...
khjoom joung ban...
single room
bantuop kre samrap mouy neak
double room
bantuop kre samrap pee neak

room with a bathtub
bantuop deil meen thlang gnout teouk
bed
kre mouy
How much is a room?
chnoul mouy bantuop tleiy ponmaan?

Getting Around
I want a ticket to...
khjoom junh ban suombuot teou...
When does it depart?
tau ke jeng domneur moung ponmann?
When does it arrive here/there?
tau ke teou/mouk doul moung ponmaan?
Where is a/the...?
tau...nouv eir na?
railway station
sathani rout phleoung
bus station
ben lan
airport
veal youn huos
ticket office
kanleng luok suombuot
tourist office
kariyaleiy samrap puok tesajor
boat
kopal/tuok
bus
lan thom deouk monuos
train
rout phleoung

Emergencies
Please call...
suom jouy hao...
an ambulance
lan peit
a doctor
krou peit
the police
police
a dentist
peit thmenh
It's an emergency
nees jea pheap ason
I'm allergic to penicillin
khjoom min trouv theat neoung thanam peneecilleen

Some Useful Words & Phrases
no
te
thank you
ar kun
yes (used by men)
bat
yes (used by women)
jas

Numbers

1	*mouy*	១
2	*pee*	២
3	*bei*	៣
4	*boun*	៤
5	*bram*	៥
6	*bram-mouy*	៦
7	*bram-pee*	៧
8	*bram-bei*	៨
9	*bran-boun*	៩
10	*duop*	១០
11	*duop-mouy*	១១
12	*duop-pee*	១២
20	*maphei*	២០
21	*maphei-mouy*	២១
30	*samseb*	៣០
40	*sairseb*	៤០
100	*mouy-rouy*	១០០
500	*bram-rouy*	៥០០
1000	*mouy-paun*	១០០០
10,000	*mouy-meoun*	១០,០០០

Facts for the Visitor

VISAS & EMBASSIES
Vietnam is the transport and paperwork gateway to Cambodia, mostly because the Phnom Penh government, originally set up by the Vietnamese, has diplomatic relations with less than a dozen countries. With the changes in 1991 the level of world contact may be increased.

Lately, several travellers have requested Cambodian visas in Hanoi and, after a few weeks spent lazily working their way southward, have picked up their visas at the Cambodian Consulate in Saigon.

Alternatively, you can apply for the visa

in Saigon – it takes seven days, costs US$8 and requires three photos, three forms and a letter requesting the visa. Cambodian visas may also be issued in Vientiane, Laos and Moscow. Away from Vietnam, ordinary tourist visas are rarely granted to people not on an organised tour, but it never hurts to ask – so ask around.

When you apply, you may be asked to write a letter to Cambodia's foreign minister stating the purpose of your trip. Having a letter of reference from your own embassy may help. Although some people have obtained a visa in three days, seven is the usual and, sometimes, people have waited up to a month for approval.

Cambodian Embassies Cambodia's most useful consular sections are those in Laos and Vietnam:

Laos
>   Thanon Saphan Thong Neua, Vientiane (☎ 2750, 4527)

Vietnam
>   71 Tran Hung Dao St, Hanoi (☎ 53788/9). The embassy is open Monday to Saturday from 8 to 11 am and from 2 to 4.30 pm.
>   41 Phung Khac Khoan St, Saigon (☎ 92751/2, 92744). The consulate is open Monday to Saturday from 8 to 11 am and from 2 to 5 pm.

Visa Extensions
Visa extensions are granted by the Foreign Ministry (☎ 2.4641, 2.3241, 2.4441) in Phnom Penh, which is on the western side of Quai Karl Marx, at 240 St (opposite the Motel Cambodiana). The process may take three or more days. There is an unofficial charge of US$10 to help grease the wheels of the bureaucracy.

Internal Travel Permits Permits to travel outside Phnom Penh are issued by the Ministry of the Interior, which is known for its hard-line policies. The ministry offices are in Phnom Penh, on the south-eastern corner of Tou Samouth Blvd and 214 St.

MONEY
Currency
Cambodia's currency is the riel, abbreviated here by a lower-case 'r' written after the sum.

By far the most useful foreign currency in Cambodia is US$ cash. Travellers' cheques in US$ can be changed at the official rate from the Foreign Trade Bank in Phnom Penh. Credit cards are not practical yet.

Exchange Rates
A$1	=	635r
C$1	=	707r
NZ$1	=	467r
UK£1	=	1376r
US$1	=	800r

Black Market Cambodia's black market in hard currency is illegal but conducted quite openly, at least at the time this book was written. The black market rate for US$ is substantially above the official rate. To find someone interested in purchasing US$, ask around among foreigners who've been in town for a while or at shops that cater for foreigners.

Costs
Meals generally cost only a few US$, except in the fanciest restaurants. Hotel accommodation in Phnom Penh and Siem Reap costs between US$12 and US$20 per night. Public transport is cheap, but off-limits to foreigners. Hiring a car will set you back at least US$20 per day. All this will be included if you book a tour, for which you'll pay at least US$200 per day!

Tipping
Tipping is not expected but is very much appreciated. A person's monthly government salary may only total US$4 or less.

BUSINESS HOURS & CURFEW
Government offices are open Monday to Saturday from about 7.30 am to 4.30 pm with a siesta from 11 or 11.30 am to 2 or 2.30 pm. At last report, there was a 9 pm curfew in

Phnom Penh but check to see if this has changed.

POST & TELECOMMUNICATIONS
Postal Rates
Cambodia's postal rates are cheaper than those in Vietnam (an aerogramme costs US$0.30) but service is excruciatingly slow because most international mail is routed via Moscow. Letters sent to Cambodia from abroad take two to three months to arrive.

Telephone
Charges for international phone calls placed in Phnom Penh are high (US$4.75 per minute in US$ to most countries) but thanks to Phnom Penh's Intersputnik satellite link with Moscow, the wait is sometimes only a matter of minutes.

TIME
Cambodia, like Vietnam, Thailand and Laos, is seven hours ahead of GMT. So, when it is 12 noon in Cambodia, it is 3 pm in Sydney, 5 am in London and 1 am in New York.

BOOKS
A number of superb works on Angkor have been published over the years. *Angkor: An Introduction* (Oxford University Press, Hong Kong, 1963; reissued in paperback by Oxford University Press, Singapore, 1986) by George Coedes gives excellent background on the Angkorian Khmer civilisation. The 3rd edition of *Angkor, Guide Henri Parmentier* (EKLIP/Albert Portail, Phnom Penh, 1959/1960) by Henri Parmentier, probably the best guidebook to Angkor ever written, was published under the same title in both English and French.

MEDIA
Restrictions on the domestic press have been recently relaxed.

Foreign radio services – Radio Australia, the BBC World Service and Voice of America – can be picked up on short-wave frequencies.

FILM & PHOTOGRAPHY
Do not put film of any speed or type through the ancient X-ray machines at the airports in Phnom Penh, Saigon or Hanoi!

HEALTH
Hospitals
Cambodia's hospitals suffer from chronic shortages of almost everything. If you require emergency surgery in Cambodia, the surgeons in Phnom Penh are probably OK, although anaesthesia may not be handled properly. If at all possible, people requiring even minor surgery should be evacuated to Bangkok or at least Saigon.

Infusions
Most intravenous (IV) solution used in Cambodian hospitals is *not* sterile. According to foreign aid workers, people often die from septicaemia (blood poisoning) caused by bacteria introduced into their blood during infusions. Visitors should not *under any circumstances* receive infusions. Be aware, also, that injections are routinely carried out using unsterilised equipment.

DANGERS & ANNOYANCES
Security
Until the civil war definitely ends, travel outside areas under firm government control (of which there are few) will carry with it a certain degree of risk, especially in the evening and after dark.

While it is true that since 1979 not a single Western journalist or aid worker has been wounded or killed in the fighting, maintenance of that perfect record depends on continued good judgement on the part of many illiterate, nervous and heavily armed teenagers fighting on both sides.

Undetonated Mines, Mortars & Bombs
Never, ever touch any rockets, artillery shells, mortars, mines, bombs or other war materiel you may come across. In Vietnam, most of this sort of stuff is 15 or more years old, but in Cambodia it may have landed there or been laid as recently as last night.

In fact, a favourite tactic of the Khmer

Rouge has been to lay mines along roads and in rice fields in an effort to maim and kill civilians. Their demented logic concludes that this will further the rebel cause by demoralising the government. The only real result of this policy is the many limbless people you see all over Cambodia.

In short: *do not* stray from well-marked paths under any circumstances, even around the monuments of Angkor.

Snakes

Visitors to Angkor, and other overgrown archaeological sites, should beware of snakes, especially the small but deadly light green Hanuman snake.

ACCOMMODATION

Phnom Penh and Siam Reap (near Angkor) have a very limited number of one or two-star hotel rooms; when tourism picks up, prices are likely to rise as shortages develop. Most provincial capitals have some sort of very basic hotel or official guest house.

FOOD & DRINKS

In Phnom Penh, there is a growing number of decent restaurants. Both in the capital and in most towns there are food stalls, often clustered in the marketplace.

Soda water with lemon is called *soda kroch chhmar* and the custom here seems to be to let the customer squeeze their own lemons. In Phnom Penh, ice *(tuk kak)* is produced by a factory that apparently uses treated water of some sort. Drinking tap water is to be avoided, especially in the provinces. Beware, some of the flavoured soda sold in bottles by kerbside vendors has been made cheaply by a process that renders the result toxic enough to cause headaches and stomach upset.

Some useful words include:

Is there any...?
    tau ke mean...deir reou te?
meat
    saach
fish
    trei

chicken
    maan
soup
    suop
noodles
    mee/kuy teav/noum banjuok

Getting There & Away

AIR

Because of its diplomatic isolation, Phnom Penh is served by only four airlines: Kampuchean Airlines (the national carrier), Aeroflot, Lao Aviation and Vietnam Airlines. These carriers offer services linking Phnom Penh with Saigon, Hanoi, Vientiane (via Pakse, Laos) and Moscow (via Bombay). Short flights usually depart from the carrier's country of origin in the morning and make the return flight in the afternoon. Checked baggage is weighed carefully. The limit on international flights is 20 kg.

Most flights into and out of Cambodia are booked up well in advance. However, at 4 pm on the afternoon before departure, seats will often be allocated to people who have no reservation. Check with the Kampuchean Airlines booking office (☎ 2.5887) at 62 Tou Samouth Blvd in Phnom Penh for details.

A new possibility for getting to Cambodia is a daily charter flight which is reportedly operating from Bangkok. Check with Transindo (☎ 287 3241), 9th Floor, Thasos Building, 1675 Chan Rd, Bangkok. Using an aircraft chartered from Bangkok Airways, the flight costs US$250 one way plus US$50 for the visa.

LAND

To/From Vietnam

Buses from Saigon to Phnom Penh, via the Moc Bai border crossing, leave early each morning from Boi Xe 1A (☎ 93754) at 155 Nguyen Hue Blvd in Saigon. The trip, which costs about US$3, takes eight to 10 hours.

It's possible to rent a car and driver in Vietnam for trips into Cambodia. With

Saigon Tourist the cost is around US$200 but may be cheaper with independent agencies.

To/From Thailand

The Cambodians have plans to open their frontier with Thailand to travellers as soon as the Thais agree (and the border region is under government control). Before the war, there was a regular train service between Bangkok and Phnom Penh via Poipet (Poay Pet) and Aranyaprathet. The road between Bangkok and Phnom Penh also crosses the Thai-Cambodian border at Poipet.

SEA

Passenger ferries link the Vietnamese port of Phu Chau (Tan Chau) in the Mekong Delta with Phnom Penh. For more information, see Getting There & Away in the Phnom Penh section.

Getting Around

AIR

At present, the only two regularly scheduled domestic air routes link the capital with Angkor (Siem Reap) and the northern town of Stung Treng. Flights are usually booked up so reservations, especially to and from Siem Reap, should be made as far in advance as possible. The baggage weight limit for domestic flights is only 10 kg per passenger.

BUS

At last report, it is forbidden, and not without reason given the security situation, for foreign visitors to travel around Cambodia by bus. The various permits necessary to undertake any travel outside of Phnom Penh will not be issued for bus travel.

TRAIN

Cambodia's rail system consists of about 645 km of single-track, metre-gauge lines. The 382 km north-western line, built prior to WW II, links Phnom Penh with Pursat, Battambang and, in peacetime, Poipet on the Thai border. The 263 km south-western line,

completed in 1969, connects the capital with Takeo, Kep, Kampot and the port of Kompong Som.

Fares are calculated at the rate of about US$0.01 for each four km you travel. Recently, the country's rail system has often suffered from rebel sabotage.

ROAD

The French colonials designed Cambodia's 15,000 km of roads to link the agricultural hinterlands of Cambodia with the port of Saigon. Even the small part of the network that was at one time surfaced (some 2500 km) has seriously deteriorated during the last two decades. Today, it is only marginally serviceable, and virtually impassable to passenger cars.

Phnom Penh

Phnom Penh, capital of Cambodia for much of the period since the mid-15th century (when Angkor was abandoned), is situated at Quatre Bras (literally, 'four arms' in French) – the confluence of the Mekong, the Bassac and the Tonlé Sap rivers. Once considered the loveliest of the French-built cities of Indochina, Phnom Penh's charm is still evident despite the last three tumultuous and violent decades.

Orientation

Phnom Penh's most important north-south arteries are (from west to east): Achar Mean Blvd (where most of the hotels are), Tou Samouth Blvd, Lenin Blvd (in front of the Royal Palace) and, along the riverfront (which is also oriented roughly north to south), Quai Karl Marx. Forming two rough semi-circles in the quadrant south-west of the Central Market are Sivutha Blvd (which intersects Tou Samouth Blvd at the Victory Monument) and Keo Mony Blvd (which intersects Tou Samouth Blvd at the former US Embassy).

The most important east-west thorough-fares of the city are USSR Blvd, which intersects Achar Mean Blvd near the railway station, and Kampuchea-Vietnam Blvd (128 St), which heads due west from the Central Market.

All of Phnom Penh's streets were renamed after 1979. Major thoroughfares got real names whereas smaller streets were rather haphazardly assigned numbers. In most cases, odd-numbered streets run more or less north to south (usually parallel to Achar Mean Blvd), with the numbers rising semi-sequentially as you move from east to west. Even-numbered streets run in an east-west direction and their numbers rise semi-sequentially as you move from north to south.

Information

Tourist Office The head office of Phnom Penh Tourism (☎ 2.3949, 2.5349, 2.4059) is across from Wat Ounalom at the oblique intersection of Lenin Blvd and Quai Karl Marx. Its two entrances are at 313 Quai Karl Marx and next to 2 Lenin Blvd. Phnom Penh Tourism, which belongs to the Phnom Penh Municipality, at present restricts its activities to running three-day package tours.

General Directorate of Tourism Cambodia's newly established General Directorate of Tourism (in French, Direction Générale du Tourisme; ☎ 2.2107), at times referred to as Cambodia Tourism, is in a white, two-storey building across 232 St from 447 Achar Mean Blvd. The directorate rents cars with or without air-con for US$20/30 per day. Guides can also be hired.

Money The Foreign Trade Bank (in French, Banque du Commerce Extérieur du Cambodge; ☎ 2.4863) is at 26 Soeung Ngoc Ming St, on the corner of Achar Mean Blvd. The exchange window (bureau de change) is open Monday to Saturday from 7.30 to 11 am and from 2.30 to 5 pm.

Post & Telecommunications There is a Post & Telephone Office (PTT; ☎ 2.3324, 2.3509, 2.2909) across from the Hotel Monorom at the corner of Achar Mean Blvd

and 126 St. International telephone services, which must be paid for in US$ cash, are available from 7 am to 12 noon and from 1 to 11 pm. The postal desk is open from 7 to 11.30 am and from 2 to 7.30 pm.

The GPO (☎ 2.4511), which is on the western side of 13 St between 98 and 102 Sts, is open from 6.30 am to 9 pm daily. It offers postal services as well as domestic and international telegraph and telephone links.

Foreign Embassies The most useful embassies in Phnom Penh include:

Laos
    245 St, midway between Achar Mean and Tou Samouth Blvds (☎ 2.5181/2)
USSR
    Lenin Blvd, midway between 312 and 394 Sts (☎ 2.2081/2)
Vietnam
    Achar Mean Blvd at 436 St, which is blocked off (☎ 2.5481/2, 2.5681). The consular section (☎ 2.3142) is on the eastern side of Achar Mean Blvd opposite number 749 (between 422 St and Keo Mony Blvd). It is open weekdays (and on Saturday mornings) from 7.30 to 11 am and from 2 to 5 pm. Two photos are required for a visa, which takes at least two days to issue.

Emergency The best hospital in Phnom Penh is probably the Khmer-Soviet Hospital (Hôpital de l'Amitié Khmer-Sovietique), which is staffed by Soviet physicians and has a limited supply of medicines.

Things to See

Wat Phnom Set on top of a 27-metre-high, tree-covered knoll, Wat Phnom is visible from all over the city. According to legend, the first pagoda on this site, which is at the intersection of Tou Samouth Blvd and 96 St, was erected in 1373 to house four statues of the Buddha deposited here by the waters of the Mekong and discovered by a woman named Penh (thus the name Phnom Penh, 'the hill of Penh').

At the bottom of the hill on the north-western side is a small zoo, though Wat Phnom's most endearing animal residents, its monkeys, live free in the trees, feasting on people's banana offerings. Elephant rides

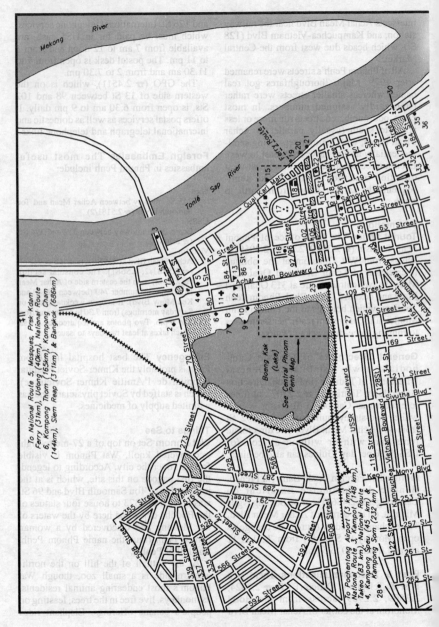

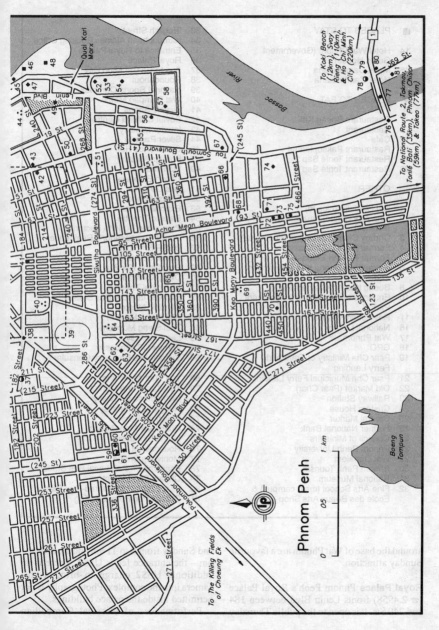

Phnom Penh

■ PLACES TO STAY

14 Hotel Wat Phnom (Government Guest House)
46 Motel Cambodiana
48 Hotel Cambodiana

▼ PLACES TO EAT

7 Restaurant Boeng Kak
9 Restaurant
12 Cafe
13 Restaurant Paksupieabal
15 Restaurant Tonlé Sap 2
20 Restaurant Tonlé Sap 1

OTHER

1 Old Stadium (closed)
2 Fine Arts School (music & dance faculties)
3 Chruoy Changvar Bridge (destroyed)
4 Former French Embassy
5 Former Korean Embassy
6 Entrance to Boeng Kak Amusement Park
8 Boeng Kak Amusement Park
10 Entrance to Boeng Kak Amusement Park
11 Revolution Hospital
16 National Library
17 Wat Phnom
18 GPO
19 Psar Cha Ministry of Transport Ferry Landing
21 Psar Cha Municipal Ferry Landing
22 Old Market (Psar Char)
23 Railway Station
24 Custom House
25 Central Market
26 Former National Bank
27 Council of Ministers
28 Phnom Penh University
29 Wat Ounalom
30 Phnom Penh Tourism
31 National Museum
32 Fine Arts School (main campus) & École des Beaux Arts Shop
33 'English Street'
34 Kampuchean Airlines Booking Office
35 Entrance to Royal Palace
36 Royal Palace
37 Bus to Ho Chi Minh City
38 Roundabout
39 National Sports Complex
40 Wat Sampao Meas
41 Bicycle Shops
42 Soviet Cultural Centre
43 Interior Ministry
44 Silver Pagoda
45 Conference Hall
47 Foreign Ministry
49 Monument
50 Czech Embassy
51 Wat Lang Ka
52 Circus School
53 Exposition Hall
54 Bassac Theatre
55 Prayuvong Buddha Factories
56 Soviet Ambassador's Residence
57 USSR Embassy
58 Soviet Compound
59 Psar Dang Kor Bus Station
60 Dang Kor Market
61 Municipal Theatre
62 Olympic Intercity Bus Station
63 Olympic Market
64 Wat Moha Montrei
65 Tuol Sleng Museum
66 Lao Embassy
67 Former US Embassy
68 Vietnamese Embassy Consular Section
69 Wat Tuol Tom Pong
70 Tuol Tom Pong Market
71 Vietnamese Embassy
72 Hungarian Embassy
73 Polish Embassy
74 Cham Kar Mon Palace
75 Indian Embassy
76 Roundabout
77 Monivong Bridge
78 Psar Chbam Pao Local Bus Station
79 Chbam Pao Market
80 Psar Cham Pao Shared-Taxi Station
81 Chbam Pao Ferry Landing

around the base of Wat Phnom are a favourite Sunday attraction.

Royal Palace Phnom Penh's Royal Palace (☎ 2.4958) fronts Lenin Blvd between 184 and 240 Sts. It is open to the public Thursday and Sunday from 8 to 11 am and from 2 to 5 pm – the entrance fee is US$2. There is an additional US$2 charge to bring a still camera into the complex. Photography is not permitted inside the palace buildings.

Performances of classical Cambodian

dance were staged in Chan Chaya Pavilion, through which guests gain entry to the grounds of the Royal Palace. The Throne Hall (Palais du Trône), topped by a 59-metre-high tower inspired by the Bayon Temple at Angkor, was inaugurated in 1919 by King Sisowath. It was used for coronations and ceremonies such as the presentation of credentials by diplomats. There are murals depicting the *Ramayana* epic on the walls and ceiling.

Silver Pagoda The spectacular Silver Pagoda is so named because the floor is covered with over 5000 silver tiles weighing one kg each. It is also known as Wat Preah Keo (Pagoda of the Emerald Buddha). The Emerald Buddha, which is presumably made of Baccarat crystal, sits on a gilt pedestal high atop the dais. In front of the dais stands a life-size Buddha made of solid gold and decorated with 9584 diamonds, the largest of which weighs 25 carats.

The pagoda and its contents were 'saved' by the Khmer Rouge in order to demonstrate to the outside world their 'concern' for the conservation of Cambodia's cultural riches.

Both foreigners and Cambodians must have special authorisation from the Ministry of Information & Culture (☎ 2.4769) at 395 Achar Mean Blvd to visit the Silver Pagoda, which is only open on Tuesday, Thursday and Saturday. Officially, the pagoda receives visitors from 7 to 11 am and from 2 to 5 pm, but don't count on it being open at 4.30 pm or 7.30 am. Photography inside the pagoda is forbidden for reasons of security.

National Museum The National Museum of Khmer Art & Archaeology (also known as the Musée des Beaux-Arts; ☎ 2.4369) is housed in an impressive red structure of traditional design (built 1917-20) on the western side of 13 St between 178 and 184 Sts, (just north of the Royal Palace). It is open Tuesday to Sunday, from 8 to 11 am and from 2 to 5 pm. The entry fee for foreigners is US$2, and English and French-speaking guides are available. Photography is prohibited inside. The Fine Arts School (École des

Beaux-Arts) is in a structure behind the main building.

The National Museum exhibits numerous masterpieces of Khmer art, artisanship and sculpture dating from the pre-Angkor period of Funan and Chenla (4th to 9th centuries AD), the Indravarman period (9th and 10th centuries), the classical Angkor period (10th to 14th centuries) and the post-Angkor period (after the 14th century).

Tuol Sleng Museum In 1975, Tuol Svay Prey High School was taken over by Pol Pot's security forces and turned into a prison known as Security Prison 21 (S-21). It soon became the largest such centre of detention and torture in the country. Almost all the people held at S-21 were later taken to the extermination camp at Choeung Ek to be executed. Detainees who died during torture were buried in mass graves on the prison grounds. During the first part of 1977, S-21 claimed an average of 100 victims per day.

S-21 has been turned into the Tuol Sleng Museum (☎ 2.4569), which is a testament to the crimes of the Khmer Rouge. The museum, whose entrance is on the western side of 113 St just north of 350 St, is open daily from 7 to 11.30 am and 2 to 5.30 pm.

Wat Ounalom Wat Ounalom, headquarters of the Cambodian Buddhist patriarchate, is on the south-western corner of the Lenin Blvd and 154 St intersection (across from Phnom Penh Tourism).

Under Pol Pot, the complex, which was founded in 1443 and includes 44 structures, was heavily damaged and its extensive library destroyed. Wat Ounalom was once home to over 500 monks. Now there are only 30, including all of the Buddhist hierarchy.

Other Wats Other wats in Phnom Penh worth visiting include **Wat Lang Ka**, which is on the southern side of Sivutha Blvd just west of Victory Monument; **Wat Koh**, which is on the eastern side of Achar Mean Blvd between 174 and 178 Sts; and **Wat Moha Montrei**, which is one block east of the

Olympic Market on the southern side of Sivutha Blvd between 163 and 173 Sts.

Chrouy Changvar Bridge The 700-metre Chrouy Changvar Bridge over the Tonlé Sap River, just off Achar Mean Blvd at 74 St, was the country's longest until it was blown up in 1975. It has since become something of a meeting place for young lovers. Refreshments are on sale near the unfenced drop-off.

Boeng Kak Amusement Park Lakeside Boeng Kak Amusement Park has a small zoo, paddleboats for hire and two restaurants. Its two entrances are 200 metres west of Achar Mean Blvd on 80 and 86 Sts.

English St This is a cluster of private language schools that teach English (and some French). It is one block west of the National Museum on 184 St between Tou Samouth Blvd and the back part of the Royal Palace compound. Between 5 and 7 pm, the whole area is filled with students who see learning English as the key to making it in postwar Cambodia. This is a good place to meet local young people.

Victory Monument Victory Monument, which is at the intersection of Tou Samouth and Sivutha Blvds, was built in 1958 as Independence Monument. It is now a memorial to Cambodia's war dead (or at least those the present government considers worthy of remembering).

Nur ul-Ihsan Mosque This mosque, seven km north of downtown Phnom Penh on National Route 5 and in Khet Chraing Chamres, was founded in 1813. According to local people, it was used by the Khmer Rouge as a pigsty and reconsecrated in 1979. It now serves a community of 360 Cham and ethnic-Malay Muslims. Next to the mosque is a *madrasa* (religious school). Shoes must be removed before entering the mosque.

To get to Nur ul-Ihsan Mosque, take a bus, Lambretta or *remorque-moto* (a trailer pulled by motorbike) heading towards Khet Prek Phnou from O Russei Market. Newly rebuilt

An-Nur An-Na'im Mosque is about one km north of Nur ul-Ihsan Mosque.

The Killing Fields of Choeung Ek Between 1975 and December 1978, about 17,000 men, women and children (including nine Westerners), detained and tortured at S-21 prison (now Tuol Sleng Museum), were transported to the extermination camp of Choeung Ek to be executed. They were bludgeoned to death to avoid wasting precious bullets.

The remains of 8985 people, many of whom were found bound and blindfolded, were exhumed in 1980 from mass graves in this one-time longan orchard. Some 43 of the 129 communal graves here have been left untouched. Fragments of human bone and bits of cloth are scattered around the disinterred pits. Over 8000 skulls, arranged by sex and age, are visible behind the clear glass panels of the Memorial Stupa, which was erected in 1988.

The Killing Fields of Choeung Ek are 15 km from downtown Phnom Penh. To get there, take Pokambor Blvd south-westward out of the city. The site is 8½ km from the bridge near 271 St.

Markets The dark-yellow, Art Deco **Central Market** has four wings filled with shops selling gold and silver jewellery, antique coins, fake name-brand watches and other such items. Around the main building are stalls offering *kramas* (checked scarves), household items, cloth for sarongs, etc.

'Luxury' foodstuffs, costume jewellery and imported toiletries are sold in hundreds of stalls at **O Russei Market**, which is on 182 St between 111 and 141 Sts. **Tuol Tom Pong Market**, bounded by 155 St on the east, 163 St on the west, 440 St on the north and 450 St on the south, is the city's best source of real and fake antiquities.

A great deal of wholesaling is done at the **Olympic Market** (Marché Olympique), which is near the National Sports complex and Wat Moha Montrei, between 193, 199, 286 and 283 Sts. **Dang Kor Market** is just north of the intersection of Keo Mony and

Pokambor Blvds, where the Municipal Theatre building stands.

Household goods, clothes and jewellery are on sale in and around the **Old Market** (Psar Cha), which is bounded by 13, 15, 108 and 110 Sts. Small restaurants, food vendors and jewellery stalls are scattered throughout the area.

Festivals

The Festival of the Reversing Current (Bon Om Touk or Sampeas Prea Khe in Khmer) is also known as the Water Festival (Fête des Eaux). It corresponds with the moment in late October or early November when the Tonlé Sap River (which since July has been filling the Tonlé Sap Lake with the waters of the flood-swollen Mekong) reverses its flow and begins to empty the Tonlé Sap back into the Mekong. *Pirogue* (long canoe) races are held in Phnom Penh.

Ethnic-Chinese and Vietnamese living in Cambodia celebrate New Year in late January or early February.

Places to Stay

All of Phnom Penh's hotels are run by assorted organs of the national or municipal governments, which compete with each other for valuable tourist and expat dollars.

Central Market Area In this area, you'll find the *Hotel Samaki* (☎ 2.4151, 2.3051). Run by the Ministry of Commerce, it is at the corner of Achar Mean Blvd and 92 St (Blvd Pologne), next to the National Library. Part of the film *The Killing Fields* was set here, although it was filmed in Thailand. Rooms with air-con and refrigerators (in the main building) cost from US$12 to US$17.

The *Hotel Monorom* (☎ 2.4549, 2.4951), run by Phnom Penh Tourism, is on the corner of Achar Mean Blvd and 118 St. Here, singles/doubles cost US$14/17 for 2nd class accommodation. The cheaper rooms are on the upper floors (usually the elevator isn't working). There is a great view of the city from the terrace of the 6th-floor restaurant.

The *Hotel Sukhalay* (the name means 'good health'; ☎ 2.2403) at the intersection of Achar Mean Blvd and 126 St belongs to the Cabinet du Conseil des Ministres. Until the elevator is repaired (which may be a very long time), the higher off the ground you are the cheaper the room. A single/double on the 7th floor costs only US$12/14. Adding a third person to a double costs an additional US$7 to US$10.

The *White Hotel* (Hotel Blanc; ☎ 2.2475) is on the south-western corner of the intersection of Achar Mean and Achar Hemcheay Blvds (at 219 Achar Mean Blvd). Run by the Ministry of Foreign Affairs, this place charges US$17 for a single or double with air-con and hot water. The elevator (again!) is usually out of order. Reception is up one flight of stairs from a street entrance opposite 214 Achar Mean Blvd.

The *Hotel Santépheap* (the name means 'peace'; ☎ 2.3227), run by the Commerce Directorate of the Phnom Penh Municipality, is on the corner of Achar Mean Blvd and 136 St (across the street from 169 Achar Mean Blvd). Singles/doubles with air-con and a fridge cost US$15/20.

The *Blue Hotel*, which is administered by the Ministry of National Defence, is across 136 St from the Hotel Santépheap. It is now used mostly by Soviet pilots but may become a regular hotel in the near future.

The *Ministry of Transport Hotel* is upstairs from the Post & Telephone Office on the corner of Achar Mean Blvd and 126 St. The Phnom Penh Municipality's 50-room *Hotel d'Asie*, on the corner of Achar Mean Blvd and 128 St (next to the Hotel Sukhalay), is being renovated.

Along the River Here, you'll find the *Motel Cambodiana* (☎ 2.5059), on Quai Karl Marx near the foot of 240 St. It's a collection of bungalows in the grounds of the huge *Hotel Cambodiana*, under construction since about 1967. At present, singles/doubles in the Motel Cambodiana, which belongs to Phnom Penh Tourism, cost US$18/22.

A couple of cheap guest houses have recently popped up around the intersection of Sivutha Blvd and 51 St. Prices start at US$3 per bed.

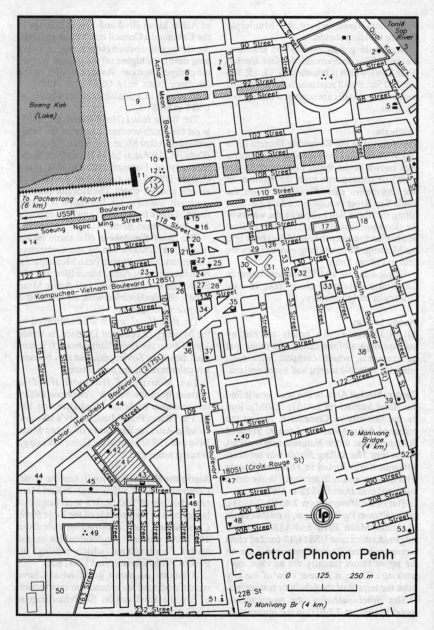

Central Phnom Penh

0   125   250 m

■ PLACES TO STAY		OTHER	
1	Hotel Wat Phnom	2	Entrance to Hotel Wat Phnom
8	Hotel Samaki	4	Wat Phnom
16	Hotel of the National People's	5	GPO
	Bank	6	Old Market
19	Hotel Monorom	7	National Library
21	Post/Telephone Office & Ministry of	9	Interspoutnik Satellite Ground Station
	Transport Hotel	11	Railway Station
22	Hotel Sukhalay	12	Stupa containing Buddha Relic
24	Hotel d'Asie	13	Night Market
27	Hotel Santépheap & Restaurant	14	Council of Ministers
	Santépheap	15	Foreign Trade Bank
34	Blue Hotel	17	Customs House
36	White Hotel & International Restaurant	18	Former National Bank Site
		31	Central Market
▼ PLACES TO EAT		35	Psar Thmei Local Bus Terminal
		37	Night Market
3	Restaurant Tonlé Sap 2	38	Military Museum (closed)
10	Faculty of Medicine Restaurant	39	Kampuchean Airlines Booking Office
20	'Restaurant'	40	Wat Koh
23	Small Restaurants	41	O Russei Market
25	Restaurant Samapheap & the	43	O Russei Local Bus Station
	'Cafeteria'	44	Motorbike Parts Shops
26	Restaurant Sereipheap	45	Bicycle Shops
28	Dancing Restaurant	46	Bicycle Shops
29	Restaurant Phsathu Thmei	47	Ministry of Information & Culture
30	Food Stalls	49	Wat Sampao Meas
32	Restaurant Sobhamongkol	50	National Sports Complex
33	Small Restaurants	51	General Directorate of Tourism
42	Food Stalls	52	'English Street'
48	Soup Restaurant	53	Soviet Cultural Centre

Places to Eat

Food Stalls Food stalls can be found in and around the Central Market (on the western side, which faces Kampuchea-Vietnam Blvd), O Russei Market (along 141 St, midway between 182 and 166 Sts), Tuol Tom Pong Market, the Olympic Market (along 286 St), Dang Kor Market (in the middle), the Old Market (Psar Cha) and near the Psar Cha Ministry of Transport ferry landing.

In the evening and at night, food stalls pop up between the railway station and USSR Blvd. There is a small night market on the corner of Achar Mean Blvd and 154 St (next to 232 Achar Mean Blvd).

Restaurants – Central Market Area The eatery across the street from the Hotel Monorom (opposite 103 Achar Mean Blvd),

signposted in Latin characters simply as 'Restaurant', has good food and decent service. Main dishes start at US$1.

The *Faculty of Medicine Restaurant*, which is on the grounds of the Faculty of Medicine of Phnom Penh University, is on the north-west corner of the Achar Mean Blvd and 106 St intersection (adjacent to the square in front of the railway station). This open-air place, which serves 'Asian' and French food, is open from 5 am to 9 pm.

Restaurant Sereipheap (the name means 'freedom'; ☎ 2.5837) at 76 Achar Mean Blvd has the usual selection of Khmer, French and Vietnamese dishes.

Restaurant Santépheap (☎ 2.2227), which is open from 5 am to 9 pm, is on the corner of Achar Mean Blvd and 136 St. A bilingual (Khmer and French) menu lists European,

Asian (they mean Vietnamese) and local Cambodian dishes – for some reason, the latter are listed only in Khmer. Main dishes cost between US$0.80 and US$1.20. In the evenings, locals drop by to watch Hong Kong gangster videos and similar fare. The *International Restaurant* is a quiet (no band or video!), well-lit place on the ground floor of the White Hotel.

Restaurant Samapheap (the name means 'equality') at 39 128 St (Kampuchea-Vietnam Blvd) is 100 metres west of the Central Market. Main dishes cost from US$0.85 to US$2. Next door at 37 128 St is the *Cafeteria* (open from 6 am to 9 pm), which offers Khmer and European food. The foreign-language menu (in French and Russian) lists only the European fare. Across the street at 26 128 St is the *Soup & Sweets Shop*.

Restaurant Phsathu Thmei is a proper sit-down restaurant at the northern edge of the Central Market complex (opposite the intersection of 126 and 61 Sts). *Restaurant Sobhamongkol*, which has a blue and white awning, is east of the Central Market on the south-eastern corner of the 53 and 130 Sts intersection. Two blocks away, on 136 St between 49 and 51 Sts, there are several other places to eat. There is a cluster of small restaurants across the street from the western side of the Central Market. There are also a number of small eateries and pastry shops along 128 St between Achar Mean Blvd and 109 St.

On the north-eastern corner of the Achar Mean Blvd and 208 St intersection there's a restaurant known by locals for Vietnamese beef soup made with white vermicelli.

Restaurants – Boeng Kak Area There are two restaurants in the lakeside Boeng Kak Amusement Park, whose two entrances are one long block west of Achar Mean Blvd at 80 St and 86 St. A delicious meal at the more expensive of the two, *Restaurant Boeng Kak*, costs about US$3.30 per person. The frogs' legs and lobster are excellent.

Restaurant Paksupieabal is at 40 Achar Mean Blvd, on the corner of 84 St. This relaxing place has a nice atmosphere and some of the best food in town, including great pancakes flambé. Diners sit alfresco under a thatched roof.

Restaurants – on the Riverfront *Restaurant Tonlé Sap 1* (also known as Restaurant Tespheap Tonlé Sap) is on Quai Karl Marx at the foot of 106 St. The prices are very reasonable. *Restaurant Tonlé Sap 2* (Restaurant Ti Pi Tonlé Sap) is at the intersection of Quai Karl Marx and 94 St. There are quite a few small places to eat along Quai Karl Marx between 154 and 178 Sts (near the Royal Palace and Wat Ounalom).

Things to Buy

Antiques, silver items and jewellery are available from shops at 163, 139, 105 and 99 Achar Mean Blvd and on the street that links the Hotel Monorom with the Central Market. There are also a number of jewellery shops, specialising in gold and silver, in the Central, Tuol Tom Pong and Old Markets.

The École des Beaux Arts shop on the corner of 19 and 184 Sts (at the back of the National Museum complex) is open daily (except Sunday afternoons) from 7 to 11.30 am and from 2 to 5.30 pm. The shop, which belongs to the Fine Arts School, sells traditional-style works made by the school's students, who share in the proceeds.

The checked cotton scarves everyone wears on their heads, around their necks or, if bathing, around their midriffs, are known as *kramas*. Fancier coloured versions are made of silk or a silk-cotton blend. Some of the finest cotton kramas come from the Kompong Cham area. They can be purchased at the Central Market (in the eaves of the main building), at other marketplaces and from the Hotel Monorom gift shop. You can request that unhemmed silk kramas be hemmed on the spot.

Bolts of colourful cloth for sarongs and *hols* (variegated silk shirts) are on sale at Nay Eng, a shop at 108 136 St (opposite the southern side of the Central Market). It is open from 7 am to 9 pm.

There are a number of photo stores selling

Kodak and ORWO print film. These are found along Achar Mean Blvd (try numbers 149 and 203 and around the White Hotel) and on 110 St near the Old Market. One-hour colour print processing is available from a store (☎ 2.3137) at 121-123 Achar Mean Blvd (across from the Hotel Sukhalay).

Getting There & Away

Air The Kampuchean Airlines booking office (signposted as both the Département de l'Aviation Civil du Cambodge and the Direction of Kampuchea Civil Aviation; ☎ 2.5887) is at 62 Tou Samouth Blvd. Official hours are from 7 to 11 am and from 2 to 5 pm Monday to Saturday. The office represents Aeroflot, Lao Aviation and Vietnam Airlines and is the only place in town where airline tickets can be purchased.

Bus Buses to points north, east and west of Phnom Penh depart from Olympic Intercity bus station (☎ 2.4613), which is on 199 St next to the Olympic Market (Marché Olympique).

Most buses to destinations south and south-west of Phnom Penh depart from Psar Dang Kor bus station, which is on Keo Mony Blvd next to Dang Kor Market (between 336 St and Pokambor Blvd).

At both stations, you would be wise to purchase tickets a day before departure. Intercity bus transport is in a state of flux and departure stations may be changed. Bus travel by foreigners is forbidden at present.

To Saigon Daily buses leave for Saigon at 6 am from an office (☎ 2.3139) on the south-western corner of 211 and Ok Nga Sou Sts (182 St). The office is open from 7 to 11 am and from 2 to 7 pm. One-way passage costs the equivalent of US$1.65. But, as of last reports, bus transit between Saigon and Phnom Penh is not looked upon with favour by officialdom.

Train The Phnom Penh railway station is on the western side of Achar Mean Blvd between 106 and 108 Sts (☎ 2.3115). Tickets can be purchased the day before departure,

between 3 and 5 pm, and on the morning you intend to travel from 5.55 am. The trip to Battambang is supposed to take 12 hours but, because of frequent attacks, rarely does.

Service Taxis Service taxis (mostly white Peugeot 404 station wagons) can be hired at Psar Chbam Pao shared-taxi station, which is on National Route 1 near Chbam Pao Market (between 367 and 369 Sts). To get there from the city, go south on Tou Samouth Blvd and turn left (eastward) across Monivong Bridge. It may be possible to rent a taxi here; the cost should be about US$25 per day for short distances.

River Transport Large government-run ferries to Kompong Cham, Kratie, Stung Treng, Kompong Chhnang and Phnom Krom (11 km south of Siem Reap) depart from the Psar Cha Ministry of Transport ferry landing (☎ 2.5619), which is on Quai Karl Marx between 102 and 104 Sts.

Passenger ferries to Kompong Cham (and ports along the way) depart from the Psar Cha Municipal ferry landing which is on Quai Karl Marx between 106 and 108 Sts (next to Tonlé Sap 1 Restaurant).

Passenger and goods ferries to Vietnam leave from the Chbam Pao ferry landing. To get there, walk a few hundred metres south from Chbam Pao Market on 369 St and turn right, down an unmarked alleyway, opposite number 210 369 St.

Getting Around

To/ From the Airport Pochentong International Airport is seven km west of central Phnom Penh via USSR or Kampuchea-Vietnam Blvds. Passenger vehicles departing from O Russei Market to Pochentong pass by the gate to the airport terminal.

Bus Buses and small passenger trucks serving Phnom Penh's suburbs (including Chbam Pao Market, which is across the river, the mosques of Chraing Chamres and Pochentong Airport) depart from a parking lot on 182 St next to O Russei Market. The station operates from about 5.30 am until sundown.

The Psar Thmei local bus terminal is 100 metres south-west of the Central Market at the intersection of Achar Hemcheay Blvd and 136 St. Buses leave for Chbam Pao, Chraing Chamres and Takmao from about 5.30 am to 5 pm.

Buses from the lot in front of Chbam Pao Market go to O Russei Market and the Central Market.

Bicycle Until rental bicycles are available, you might want to consider buying a cheap Vietnamese two-wheeler. Prices start from around US$20. There are two clusters of bicycle shops near O Russei Market: one is on 182 St across the street from number 23 (between Achar Mean Blvd and O Russei Market) and the other is on 182 St between 141 St and 163 St (between O Russei Market and Achar Hemcheay Blvd).

Cyclo Cyclos (samlors), which can be found cruising around town and at marketplaces, are a great way to see the city. Some of the drivers who hang out near major hotels speak a bit of English or French.

Around Phnom Penh

UDONG

Phnom Udong, 40 km north of the capital, consists of two parallel ridges, both of which offer great views of the Cambodian country-side and its innumerable sugar palm trees. The larger, uneven ridge, Phnom Preah Reach Throap (Hill of the Royal Fortune), is so named because a 16th century Khmer monarch is said to have hidden the national treasury here during a war with the Thais.

The most impressive structure on Phnom Preah Reach Throap is **Vihear Preah Ath Roes**, or 'Vihara of the 18 Cubit (nine metre) Buddha'. The vihara and the Buddha, dedicated in 1911 by King Sisowath, were blown up by the Khmer Rouge in 1977.

At the north-west extremity of the ridge stand **three large stupas.** The first one you come to is the final resting place of King Monivong (ruled 1927-41). Nearby, a stair-case leads down the hill to the access road and a **pavilion** decorated with graphic murals of Khmer Rouge atrocities. Across the street is a **memorial** containing the bones of some of the people who were buried in approximately 100 mass graves found on the other side of the hill.

Getting There & Away

To get to Udong, head north out of Phnom Penh on National Route 5. Continue on past Prek Kdam ferry for 4½ km and turn left (southward) at the roadblock and bunker. Udong is 3½ km south of the turnoff. By bus, take any vehicle heading from Phnom Penh towards Kompong Chhnang or Battambang and get off at the roadblock and bunker.

TONLÉ BATI

South of Phnom Penh, the laterite **Ta Prohm Temple** was built by King Jayavarman VII (ruled 1181 to 1201) on the site of a 6th century Khmer shrine. The main sanctuary consists of five chambers. In each is a statue or linga (or what is left of them after the destruction wrought by the Khmer Rouge). The site is open all day, every day. A Khmer-speaking guide can be hired for US$0.30 to US$0.60.

About 300 metres north-west of Ta Prohm Temple, a long, narrow peninsula juts into the Bati River. On Sunday, it is packed with picnickers and vendors selling food, drink and fruit.

Getting There & Away

The access road to Ta Prohm Temple, which is in Tonlé Bati district of Takeo Province, intersects National Route 2 at a point 33 km south of Phnom Penh, 21 km north of the access road to Phnom Chisor and 44 km north of Takeo. The temple is 2½ km from the highway. Any bus linking Phnom Penh with the town of Takeo by way of National Route 2 will pass by the access road.

PHNOM CHISOR

There is a spectacular view of the surrounding countryside from the top of Phnom Chisor. The main temple, which stands at the eastern side of the hilltop, was constructed in the 11th century of laterite and brick. The carved lintels are made of sandstone. On the plain to the east of Phnom Chisor are two other Khmer temples, **Sen Thmol** (at the bottom of Phnom Chisor) and **Sen Ravang** (farther east), and the former sacred pond of **Tonlé Om**. All three form a straight line with Phnom Chisor.

Getting There & Away

The intersection of National Route 2 with the eastward-bound access road to Phnom Chisor is marked by the two brick towers of Prasat Neang Khmau (Temple of the Black Virgin), which may have once served as a sanctuary to Kali, the dark goddess of destruction.

Prasat Neang Khmau is on National Route 2 at a point 55 km south of central Phnom Penh, 21 km south of the turnoff to Tonlé Bati and 23 km north of Takeo. The distance from the highway to the base of the hill is a bit over four km.

There are two paths up the 100-metre-high ridge, which takes about 15 minutes to climb. A good way to see the view in all directions is to go up the northern path and to come down the southern stairway.

Angkor

The world-famous temples of Angkor, built between seven and 11 centuries ago when Khmer civilisation was at the height of its extraordinary creativity, constitute one of humanity's most magnificent architectural achievements. From Angkor, the kings of the Khmer Empire ruled over a vast territory that extended from the tip of what is now southern Vietnam northward to Yunnan in China and from Vietnam westward to the Bay of Bengal.

The 100 or so temples constitute the sacred skeleton of a much larger, spectacular administrative and religious centre whose houses, public buildings and palaces were constructed of wood – now long decayed – because the right to dwell in structures of brick or stone was reserved for the gods.

SIEM REAP

The town of Siem Reap is only a few km from the temples of Angkor and serves as a base for visits to the monuments. The name Siem Reap (pronounced see-EM ree-EP) means 'Siamese Defeated'.

Orientation & Information

Siem Reap is 6.4 km south of Angkor Wat and 9.7 km south of the Bayon.

The offices of Angkor Tourism, the government tourism authority in the Angkor area, are in a small building next to the Villa Princière, the structure just east (towards the Siem Reap River) of the Grand Hotel d'Angkor.

Angkor Conservation (also referred to as Angkor Conservancy; ☎ 82), which has official responsibility for the study, preservation and upkeep of the Angkor monuments, is in a large compound between Siem Reap and Angkor Wat. Over 5000 statues, lingas and inscribed steles found in the vicinity of Angkor are stored here for safekeeping.

Fees Each visitor to Angkor is charged a fee of US$120, which theoretically consists of a US$60 charge to visit Angkor Wat and an identical fee to visit the Bayon. It is not clear how much of this money, if any, goes to help preserve the monuments.

Dangers Some areas in and around the temple complexes have been mined. Visitors should *not* stray from clearly marked paths. Don't worry about the troops deployed around the Grand Hotel d'Angkor each night as they're there to protect you!

Places to Stay

The venerable and old *Grand Hotel d'Angkor* (☎ 15), built in 1928, charges US$13/21 for singles/doubles including breakfast. There are plans to renovate this place for the hordes of better off tourists who are expected here when there is peace. The dilapidated *Hotel de la Paix* (☎ 41) is now a provincial government guest house. The *Villa Princière*, which is just east of the Grand Hotel d'Angkor, is slated to undergo repairs and become a hotel.

Places to Eat

The restaurant of the *Grand Hotel d'Angkor* charges foreigners US$6 for meals which, though decent, cost one-sixth that in riels. There are a number of other places to eat around town, including the *Bayon Chinese Restaurant* on National Route 6 about 200 metres east of the Siem Reap River. There are several refreshment stands near the Hotel de la Paix.

Getting There & Away

Air At present, the only way into or out of Siem Reap is by air from Phnom Penh – there are round trips on Wednesday and Saturday (or at least there are supposed to be). A round-trip costs US$91. By propeller-driven Antonov An-24, the flight takes 40 minutes.

Siem Reap Airport is seven km north-west of town and four km due west of Angkor Wat.

Road It should be relatively easy to go overland from Thailand to Angkor once the civil war ends. Angkor is only 418 km from Bangkok via the border crossing between Poipet, in Cambodia and Aranyaprathet, in Thailand.

Because the road from Phnom Penh to Angkor is in a state of extreme dilapidation, the 311 km drive takes two days.

Ferry Ferries from Phnom Penh to Phnom Krom, 11 km south of Siem Reap, depart from the capital's Psar Cha Ministry of Transport ferry landing, which is on Quai Karl Marx between 102 and 104 Sts. The trip takes two days, with an overnight stop at Kompong Chhnang.

Getting Around

The US$120 fee to visit the monuments includes transport by automobile for the first day of your visit. For subsequent days, Angkor Tourism hires out cars with drivers for US$40 per day.

THE TEMPLES OF ANGKOR

Between the 9th and the 13th centuries, a succession of Khmer kings who ruled from Angkor utilised the vast wealth and huge labour force of their empire to carry out a series of monumental construction projects. Intended to glorify both themselves and their capitals, a number were built in the vicinity of Siem Reap.

In this period, the evolution of Khmer architecture paralleled a change in religious focus from the Hindu cult of the god Shiva to that of Vishnu and then to a form of Mahayana Buddhism centred on Avalokitesvara.

The successive cities at Angkor were centred on a temple mountain identified with Mt Meru, home of the gods in Hindu cosmology, which served as both the centre of the earthly kingdom over which the king ruled and the symbolic centre of the universe within which the kingdom existed.

Many of the other temples around Angkor were built to serve as foci for cults through which various important personages were identified with one of the gods of the Indian pantheon and thus assured immortality. The grandest such structure was Angkor Wat.

Angkor's huge system of reservoirs, canals and moats was built to provide water for irrigation, allowing intensive cultivation of areas surrounding the capital.

The 'lost city' of Angkor became the centre of intense European popular and scholarly interest after the publication in the 1860s of *Le Tour du Monde*, an account by the French naturalist Henri Mouhot of his voyages. A group of talented and dedicated archaeologists and philologists, mostly French, soon undertook a comprehensive programme of research.

Under the aegis of the École Française d'Extrême Orient, they began an arduous effort – begun in 1908 and interrupted at the beginning of the 1970s by the war – to clear away the jungle vegetation that was breaking apart the monuments and to rebuild the damaged structures, restoring them to something approaching their original grandeur.

Things to See

The three most magnificent temples at Angkor are the Bayon, which faces east and is best visited in the early morning; Ta Prohm, which is overgrown by the jungle; and Angkor Wat, the only monument here facing westward and at its finest in the late afternoon.

If you've got the time, all these monuments are well worth several visits each. Angkor's major sites can be seen without undue pressure in three full days of touring.

Angkor Thom The fortified city of Angkor Thom, some 10 sq km in extent, was built in its present form by Angkor's greatest builder, Jayavarman VII (reigned 1181 to 1201), who came to power just after the disastrous sacking of the previous Khmer capital, centred around the Baphuon, by the Chams.

Angkor Thom, which may have had a million inhabitants (more than any European city of the period), is enclosed by a square wall eight metres high and 12 km in length. It is also encircled by a moat 100 metres wide said to have been guarded by a number of fierce crocodiles.

The city has five monumental gates, one each in the north, west and south walls and two in the east wall.

The Bayon The most outstanding feature of the Bayon, which was built by Jayavarman VII in the exact centre of the city of Angkor Thom, is the eerie and unsettling 3rd level, with its 49 towers projecting 172 icily smiling, gargantuan faces of Avalokitesvara.

Almost as extraordinary are the Bayon's 1200 metres of bas-reliefs, incorporating over 11,000 figures. The famous carvings on the outer wall of the first level depict vivid scenes of life in 12th century Cambodia.

The Baphuon The Baphuon, a pyramidal representation of Mt Meru, is 200 metres

north-west of the Bayon. It was constructed by Udayadityavarman II (reigned 1050 to 1066) at the centre of his city, the third built at Angkor.

The decor of the Baphuon, including the door frames, lintels and octagonal columns, is particularly fine. On the west side of the temple, the retaining wall of the second level was fashioned – apparently in the 15th century – into a reclining Buddha 40 metres in length.

The Terrace of Elephants The 350 metre long Terrace of Elephants was used as a giant reviewing stand for public ceremonies and served as a base for the king's grand audience hall. The middle section of the retaining wall is decorated with human-size *Garudas* (mythical human-birds) and lions. Towards either end are the two parts of the famous Parade of Elephants.

The Terrace of the Leper King The Terrace of the Leper King, just north of the Terrace of Elephants, is a platform seven metres in height on top of which stands a nude (though sexless) statue (actually a copy). The figure, possibly of Shiva, is believed by the locals to be of Yasovarman, a Khmer ruler whom legend says died of leprosy.

The front retaining walls are decorated with five or so tiers of meticulously executed carvings of seated *apsaras* (shapely dancing women).

On the south side of the Terrace of the Leper King (facing the Terrace of Elephants) is the entry to a long, narrow trench excavated by archaeologists. This passageway follows the front wall of an earlier terrace that was covered up when the present structure was built. The figures look as fresh as if they had been carved yesterday.

Angkor Wat Angkor Wat, with its soaring towers and extraordinary bas-reliefs, is considered by many to be one of the most inspired and spectacular monuments ever conceived by the human mind. It was built by Suryavarman II (reigned 1112 to 1152) to honour Vishnu (with whom he, as god-king, was identified) and for use as his funerary temple.

The central temple complex consists of three stories, each of which encloses a square surrounded by intricately interlinked galleries. Rising 31 metres above the third level and 55 metres above the ground is the central tower, which gives the whole ensemble its sublime unity.

At one time, the central sanctuary of Angkor Wat held a gold statue of Vishnu mounted on a winged Garuda representing the deified god-king Suryavarman II.

Stretching around the outside of the central temple complex is an 800-metre-long series of extraordinary bas-reliefs. The most famous scene, the Churning of the Ocean of Milk, is along the south section of the east gallery. This brilliantly executed carving depicts 88 *asuras* (devils) on the left and 92 *devas* (gods) with crested helmets on the right, churning up the sea in order to extract the elixir of immortality, which both groups covet.

The extraction is being accomplished by rotating the immense serpent Vasuki, who is entwined around Mt Mandara (in the centre, resting on a turtle). Vishnu, on the side of the mountain, is assisting the whole process. On top stands Indra, surveying the proceedings.

Other figures watching the churning include Shiva, Brahma, the monkey-god Hanuman and many agitated fish and sea monsters. Above, apsaras gracefully dance in the heavens.

Ta Prohm The 17th century Buddhist temple of Ta Prohm is one of the largest Khmer edifices of the Angkorian period. It has been left just as it looked when the first French explorers set eyes on it over a century ago. Whereas the other major monuments of Angkor have been preserved and made suitable for scholarly research by a massive programme to clear away the all-devouring jungle, this Buddhist temple has been left to its fate of inexorable, arboreous ruination.

Ta Prohm, its friezes enmeshed in tendrilous nets, its stones slowly being pried asunder by the roots of the huge trees rising from its galleries and towers, stands as a monument to the awesome fecundity and power of the jungle. It is not to be missed.

THE ROLUOS GROUP
The monuments of Roluos, which served as the capital of Indravarman I (reigned 877 to 889), are among the earliest large, permanent temples built by the Khmers and mark the beginning of Khmer classical art.

Preah Ko
Preah Ko was erected by Indravarman I in the late 9th century. The six brick *prasats* (towers), aligned in two rows and decorated with carved sandstone and plaster reliefs, face eastward. Sanskrit inscriptions appear on the doorposts of each temple.

Bakong
Bakong, constructed by Indravarman I and dedicated to Shiva, was intended to represent Mt Meru. The eastward-facing complex consists of a five-tier central pyramid of sandstone flanked by eight towers of brick and sandstone (or their remains) and other minor sanctuaries.

Getting There & Away
The Roluos Group is 13 km east of Siem Reap along National Route 6. Preah Ko is 600 metres south of National Route 6 (to the right as you head away from Siem Reap). Bakong is about a km further south.

The South Coast

KAMPOT
The pretty riverine town of Kampot (population 14,000) is on the Tuk Chhou River (also called the Prek Thom River), five km from the sea. Although many buildings in town were damaged by the Khmer Rouge, Kampot retains much of its charm. The **To Chu Falls** are north of Kampot towards the hills.

Places to Stay & Eat

Hotels include the *Phnom Kamchai Hotel* and the *Phnom Khieu Hotel* (Blue Mountain Hotel) near the central plaza and the *Kampot Province Hotel* on the river.

There are food stalls in the main market and elsewhere around town.

Getting There & Away

Because of the road's dilapidated state, the 148-km drive from Phnom Penh to Kampot along National Route 3 takes five hours.

BOKOR HILL STATION

The now-ruined mountain-top hill station of Bokor (elevation 1080 metres), 41 km west from Kampot and 190 km south-west from Phnom Penh, is known for its pleasant climate, rushing streams, forested vistas and stunning panoramas of the sea.

The best time of year to visit Bokor, which is in the Elephant Mountains, is said to be between November and May. The **two waterfalls** of Popokvil, 14 and 18 metres high, are not far from the access road to Bokor Hill Station.

KEP

The seaside resort of Kep (Kep-sur-Mer), with its six-km palm-shaded corniche, was once a favourite vacation spot for Cambodia's Frenchified elite.

Under the Khmer Rouge, the town (founded in 1908) and its many villas were completely destroyed – not neglected and left to dilapidate, but intentionally turned into utter ruins. The Khmer Rouge also turned the underground petrol tank of the old

Shell station into a mass grave. By 1979, not a single building remained intact in Kep.

Although there are plans to rebuild Kep and re-establish it as a beach resort, at present it is a ghost town with no hotels or other tourist facilities.

Getting There & Away

If you take the train, get off at the Damnak Chang Aeu railway station, which is a few km from Kep. By road, Kep is 24 km south-east of Kampot and 49 km from the Vietnamese town of Ha Tien. There is a border crossing eight km north of Ha Tien but it is not presently open to foreigners.

KIRIROM

The hill station of Kirirom, set amidst pine forests and 675 metres above sea level, is 112 km south-west of Phnom Penh. It is in the Elephant Mountains to the west of National Route 4.

KOMPONG SOM

Kompong Som (formerly Sihanoukville), Cambodia's only maritime port, once had a population of 16,000 in the mid-1960s and probably has the same population now. Near town, there are **superb beaches** and, for diving enthusiasts, shoals and reefs teeming with multicoloured fish.

Getting There & Away

Kompong Som is 232 km south-west from Phnom Penh via one of the best roads in the country, National Route 4. When the railway line is open, Kompong Som can also be reached from the capital by train.

Hong Kong

Precariously perched on the edge of China, Hong Kong is a curious anomaly. It's an energetic paragon of the virtues of capitalism but nevertheless gets the unofficial blessing of the largest Communist country in the world – on which it is dependent for its very existence. The countdown to 1997, when Hong Kong is due to be handed back to the People's Republic, has made it an even more volatile and interesting enigma.

For most visitors, its reputation as a centre for shopping eclipses almost everything else, but it's also a fascinating city-state where you can see glimpses of rural China in the New Territories and on some of the relatively untouched islands. These days, it is also the major jumping-off point for travel to China.

Facts about the Country

HISTORY

Hong Kong must stand as one of the more successful results of dope running. The dope was opium and the runners were backed by the British government. European trade with China goes back over 400 years. As the trade mushroomed during the 18th century and European demand for Chinese tea and silk grew, the balance of trade became more and more unfavourable to the Europeans – until they started to run opium into the country. The opium was grown in Bengal under the control of the British East India Company.

The Middle Kingdom finally grew tired of the barbarians and their 'foreign mud', as opium was known, and attempted to throw the chief offenders, the British, out – but not too far out, as their money if not their opium was still wanted. Unfortunately, the war of words ended when, in true British fashion, the gunboats were sent in. There were only two of them, but they managed to demolish a Chinese fleet of 29 ships. The ensuing First Opium War went much the same way and, at

its close in 1842, the island of Hong Kong was ceded to the British.

Following the Second Opium War in 1860, Britain took possession of the Kowloon Peninsula, adding another 11 sq km to the 78 sq km of the island. Finally, in 1898, a 99-year lease was granted for the 948 sq km of the New Territories. What would happen after the lease ended on 1 July 1997 was the subject of considerable speculation. Although Britain supposedly had possession of Hong Kong Island and the Kowloon Peninsula for all eternity, it was pretty clear that if they handed back the New Territories, China would want the rest as well. In any case, the PRC does not recognise any of the pre-1949 agreements.

In late 1984, an agreement was finally reached that China would take over the entire colony lock, stock and barrel, but that Hong Kong's unique free enterprise economy would be maintained for at least 50 years. It would be a tiny enclave of all-out capitalism within the Chinese sphere. China has issued an invitation to Taiwan to return to the motherland under similar conditions. However, many of Hong Kong's population – well aware of China's broken promises and erratic policies of the past – aren't buying it. The emigration queues at the embassies of Australia, Canada, New Zealand and the USA grow longer all the time.

The reality of the situation has always been, of course, that China could reclaim not only the New Territories, but all the rest of Hong Kong any time it wanted to. Hong Kong has survived so long already simply because it's useful. Conveniently situated, it acts as a funnel for Chinese goods to the West and for Western goods into China. Also, it is a valuable source of both foreign exchange and information, without the need for China to let corrupting foreign influences across the borders.

The upheavals of the Cultural Revolution, the China-inspired riots that had the colony in turmoil, and the subsequent relaxation of border controls that allowed a flood of Chinese into Hong Kong, all probably served as a flexing of the mainland muscles...just to show where true power lay.

Acting as an intermediary hasn't been Hong Kong's only function. During the Korean War, the USA placed an embargo on Chinese goods, which threatened to strangle the colony economically. To ensure survival, it vigorously developed manufacturing, banking and insurance industries instead.

Part of the reason for the boundless energy of Hong Kong is that it is a capitalist's dream; it has lax controls and a maximum tax rate of 18%. Fortunes could be made with haste because of the uncertainty of the future. Even with less than six years to go until the handover, fortunes are still being made, new skyscrapers are still being hurled up, and new BMWs and Mercedes are still pouring out of the showrooms. You can smell wealth in the air.

Buildings & Fung Shui

Some of the new office buildings and hotels in Kowloon and Hong Kong are very spectacular. The Bond Building, between Central and Wanchai, is all lumps and bumps and ominously mirrored glass. Nearby is the wonderful Hong Kong & Shanghai Bank which looks like one of those clear plastic models built so you can see how everything works inside. You can see the lifts go up and down, the chains wind round under the escalators, even the fire escape stairways are all on view.

The very tall building in Central with the spikes on top is the Bank of China and it's reputed to have terrible *fung shui*. Before any building can be put up in Hong Kong a fung shui expert has to be called in to ensure the design, position and alignment don't bring bad luck, or even worse. Well, the Bank of China's fung shui is bad news – not for the Bank of China but for the buildings around it. Reportedly, the Bank of China positively radiates bad vibes (all those sharp corners, of course) and some neighbouring buildings have had to actually seal up windows or cover them over in order to keep the harmful influence out. With China, the lease, 1997 and all that, it's hardly surprising say the local cynics.

GEOGRAPHY

Hong Kong's 1070 sq km is divided into four main areas – Kowloon, Hong Kong Island, the New Territories and the Outer Islands.

Hong Kong Island is the heart of the colony, but covers only 78 sq km or just 7% of Hong Kong's land area. Kowloon is the densely populated peninsula to the north. The New Territories, which include the Outer Islands, occupy 980 sq km, or 91% of Hong Kong's land area. Much of it is rural but tourists seldom visit this scenic part of Hong Kong.

Hong Kong Island is the original part of the colony on which Hong Kong Central, the 'city' of Hong Kong, stands. A short ferry ride across the harbour from the island is the Kowloon Peninsula which is also totally 'city'. These are the two parts which were originally conceded to the British and were not due to be handed back to China in 1997.

The southern tip of the peninsula is Tsimshatsui, the tourist heart of Kowloon. Most of Hong Kong's hotels are in Central or Tsimshatsui. People speak of 'Hong Kong side' and 'Kowloon side'. Hong Kong Island can be further subdivided into the 'northside' (also called 'harbourside') and 'southside'.

Kai Tak Airport is also in Kowloon, although its runway juts out into the harbour. Beyond Kowloon you move into the New Territories, the rural area that runs up to the Chinese border. The New Territories get progressively less rural each year as Kowloon sprawls further and further out.

The islands that dot the area to the west of Hong Kong Island, the fourth part of the colony, are really just more of the New Territories (except for tiny Stonecutter's Island) since they are also part of the 99-year lease package. Largest of the islands is sparsely populated Lantau, which is much larger than Hong Kong Island itself. The islands are relatively undeveloped and in some ways the most surprising and enjoyable part of Hong Kong.

CLIMATE

Although it never gets really cold, even in the middle of winter (January and February),

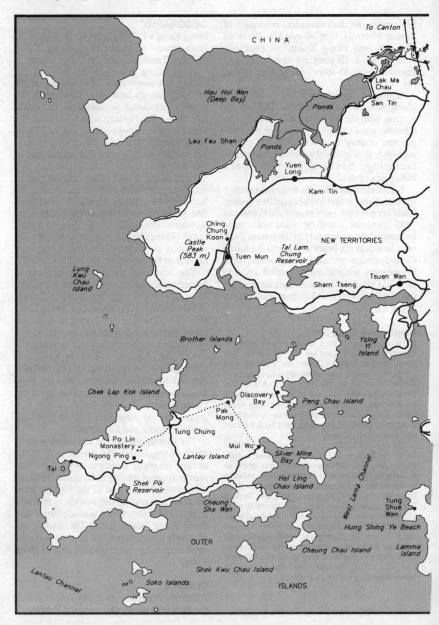

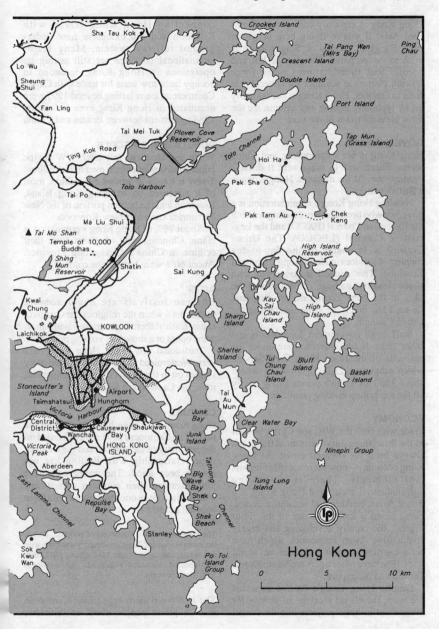

Hong Kong

0   5   10 km

Hong Kong is certainly colder than South-East Asia. If you're flying here in winter from Bangkok, Manila or Singapore, it is wise to be prepared. Summer is hot and humid, and thunderstorms often force unwary visitors to scamper for cover. From June to October, Hong Kong is occasionally hit by typhoons. Spring and autumn are the most pleasant times of the year.

GOVERNMENT

Hong Kong is not a democracy, and China seems determined to make sure it doesn't become one. At the moment, Hong Kong is a British colony.

Heading Hong Kong's administration is a governor who presides over meetings of both the Executive Council (EXCO) and the Legislative Council (LEGCO). The Urban Council is in charge of the day-to-day running of services in Hong Kong Island and Kowloon. This council is concerned with street cleaning, garbage collection and the like. In the New Territories, the Regional Council has much the same function as the Urban Council.

Staff in all government departments and other areas of administration are under the umbrella of the Hong Kong Civil Service which employs 173,000 people, of whom about 3500 are British expats filling nearly all the top policy-making positions.

ECONOMY

Trade with both the West and China, as well as the flourishing duty-free tourist trade, has always been the cornerstone of the Hong Kong economy – now there are other important elements. There is a thriving light-industrial sector and Hong Kong is a major Asian banking and insurance centre. Hong Kong is known as one of the 'Four Tigers', the rapidly developing and highly competitive Asian economies which have been exerting a great influence on world trade. The three other tigers are South Korea, Taiwan and Singapore.

Despite Hong Kong's limited expected life span, there's no shortage of money for investment in huge projects like the tunnel connecting Hong Kong Island with Kowloon and the extensive new underground railway system. Many major international concerns are still setting up operations in Hong .Kong, intended to occupy front row seats for trade with China. Commercial loans lasting beyond 1997 were negotiated in Hong Kong even before the 1984 agreement between Britain and China.

POPULATION & PEOPLE

When the Japanese left after WW II, the population was not much over half a million. Today it stands at around 5.8 million, most of it squeezed on to Hong Kong Island, Kowloon and the bottom portion of the New Territories known as New Kowloon.

About 98% of Hong Kong's population is ethnic Chinese, most of whom have their origins in China's Guangdong Province. About 60% were born in the colony.

ARTS

Chinese festivals are never sombre occasions – when the religious rites are over at any festival there is generally a lion dance, some opera or a show by a visiting puppeteer.

Traditional arts aside, Hong Kong is a very Westernised place which immediately latches on to the latest crazes in disco, punk, rock, the Lambada or whatever.

CULTURE

Hong Kong is Chinese, but with a Cantonese twist. The Cantonese have always existed on the periphery of the empire, and the status of their relationship with Beijing has not always been good. The northerners have long regarded their southern compatriots with disdain, or as one 19th-century northern account put it:

The Cantonese...are a coarse set of people... Before the times of Han and Tang, this country was quite wild and waste, and these people have sprung forth from unconnected, unsettled vagabonds that wandered here from the north.

The traditional stereotype of the Cantonese is of a proud people, frank in criticism, lacking in restraint, oriented to defending their own interests and hot-tempered. They are also regarded as shrewd in business and as quick, lively and clever in catching on to new skills, which for the most part are those of small traders and craftspeople. They also have the reputation of being willing to eat anything, including dog, cat, rat, snake and monkey's brain.

Of all the Chinese, the Cantonese have probably been the most influenced by the rest of the world.

RELIGION

In Chinese religion as it's now practised, Taoism, Confucianism and Buddhism have become inextricably entwined. Ancestor worship and ancient animist beliefs have also been incorporated into the religious milieu. Foreign influence has been heavy in Hong Kong, which explains the presence of more than 500,000 Christians (about 9% of the population). The cosmopolitan population also incorporates a smattering of Muslims, Jews, Sikhs and Hindus.

LANGUAGE

Cantonese is the most common Chinese dialect spoken in Hong Kong. Mandarin Chinese, or putonghua, is the official language in China, and about half the people in Hong Kong can also understand it.

Although English is widely spoken in Hong Kong and you are unlikely to have difficulty making yourself understood, it is not as widely used as in Singapore. A foreign devil, or *gwailo*, will find Cantonese difficult because it's tonal – the meaning varies with the tone but here are a few to have a go with.

Civilities

good morning
  jo san
goodbye
  joi gin
How are you?
  nei ho ma?
thank you
  m goi

Some Useful Phrases

How much?
  gay doa cheen?
Too expensive
  tie goo-why
Waiter, the bill
  fo-kay, my don
Go away!
  jaaw hoy!

Facts for the Visitor

VISAS & EMBASSIES

For most non-Communist nationalities there are no visa requirements. British passport holders are permitted to stay for 12 months, citizens of all the Commonwealth countries and British territories can stay for three months, citizens of the USA and certain Western European and South American nations can stay for one month.

China is now wide open and visas for individual travel in China are freely available in Hong Kong. Once in the Middle Kingdom, you can go almost anywhere you please.

The cheapest visas (HK$90) are available from the visa office of the Ministry of Foreign Affairs of the PRC (☎ 835 3657), 5th Floor, Low Block, China Resources Building, 26 Harbour Rd, Wanchai, Hong Kong Island. They require two days to process the application. Travel agencies can more quickly and coveniently obtain visas, but at a higher cost. Most single-entry visas are valid for 90 days. More expensive are the two-entry visas.

Multiple-entry visas are not only expensive, but you can stay for just 30 days at a time (no extensions permitted) but the visa remains valid for six months. Multiple-entry visas are only issued if you've already been to China at least once and have stamps in your passport to prove it.

Visa Extensions

For visa extensions, you should enquire at the Immigration Department (☎ 824 6111),

2nd Floor, Wanchai Tower Two, 7 Gloucester Rd, Wanchai. In general, they do not like to grant extensions unless there are special circumstances – cancelled flights, illness, registration in a legitimate course of study, legal employment, marriage to a local, etc.

DOCUMENTS
It is advisable to carry some identification on you at all times in Hong Kong. Anything with a photo on it will do.

MONEY
Currency
Hong Kong's unit of currency is the HK$, divided into 100 cents. There are different banknote designs in circulation, although the notes are interchangeable.

Bills are issued in denominations of HK$10 (green), HK$50 (blue), HK$100 (red), HK$500 (brown) and HK$1000 (yellow). Coins are issued in denominations of HK$5, HK$2, HK$1, 50 cents, 20 cents and 10 cents.

Changing Money
Hong Kong is a dream come true for money changing. Any major trading currency, and even many insignificant currencies, can be exchanged. All major international credit cards are accepted.

Banks give the best exchange rates by far, but it varies from bank to bank. One of the best is Wing Lung Bank, 4 Carnarvon Rd, Tsimshatsui, next to the New Astor Hotel. Another good bank for changing money is Hang Seng Bank which has numerous branches all over the city. The main Tsimshatsui branch is at 18 Carnarvon Rd. The small branches in the MTR stations do not change money.

The Hongkong Bank gives relatively poor rates for a bank, and in addition tacks on a HK$20 service charge for each transaction.

Licensed moneychangers in the tourist districts operate 24 hours a day, but give relatively poor exchange rates which are clearly posted. However, you can almost always get a much better rate by bargaining!

Moneychangers are no longer allowed to charge commissions.

Try not to change any money at the airport as the exchange rate there is pathetic; you can try bargaining.

Bank hours are from 9 am to 4 pm Monday to Friday, and from 9 am to 12 noon or 1 pm on Saturday.

Exchange Rates
A$1	=	HK$6.15
C$1	=	HK$6.85
NZ$1	=	HK$4.55
UK£1	=	HK$13.40
US$1	=	HK$7.75
Y100	=	HK$5.75

Costs
Hong Kong is certainly not cheap – it's a result of the continuing economic boom and the ever-increasing cost of land. You can still find dorm beds for around HK$40 but it takes some effort to find a double room for less than HK$100 these days.

On the other hand, food is reasonably priced, transport is cheap and efficient, and Hong Kong is still a great place to shop. Keep on your toes though, plenty of people in Hong Kong are after the faster dollar, and 'never give a sucker an even break' is often the motto of the day.

The main way to cut costs is to control yourself – shopping in Hong Kong can be addictive – Many people find all those cameras and electronic goodies on sale to be irresistible and suddenly decide they need to buy all sorts of things they don't need at all!

Tipping
A 10% service charge is usually added to restaurant bills so, if you're not sure if it's included, ask. In taxis you should round the fare up to the nearest HK$0.50 or dollar.

Bargaining
If you shop for cameras, Walkmans, and other big ticket items in the tourist ghetto of Tsimshatsui, bargaining is essential. However, bargaining is *not* the norm in Hong

Kong. It's only normal in places where the tourists congregate. Out in the shopping malls like Cityplaza where the Chinese shop, everything has a price tag and there is little or no scope for bargaining.

TOURIST OFFICES
Local Tourist Offices
The enterprising Hong Kong Tourist Association (HKTA) has desks at the airport, on the Kowloon side of the Star Ferry run, and in Central, Hong Kong Island. The one at the Kowloon Star Ferry Terminal is open from 8 am to 6 pm Monday to Friday, and from 9 am to 5 pm weekends and holidays.

The office on Hong Kong Island is in Shop 8, Basement, Jardine House, 1 Connaught Place, Central – it's open from 8 am to 6 pm weekdays, and from 8 am to 1 pm on Saturday but is closed on Sunday and holidays. The desks at Kai Tak Airport are open from 8 am to 10.30 pm daily but only provide information for arriving passengers.

You can call the HKTA hotline (☎ 801 7177) from 8 am to 6 pm daily. Shopping advice and enquiries on HKTA members can be obtained (☎ 801 7278) from 9 am to 5 pm Monday to Friday and from 9 am to 12.45 pm on Saturday.

USEFUL ORGANISATIONS
Since the likelihood of getting ripped off by shopkeepers is high, it's good to know about the Hong Kong Consumer Council (☎ 736 3322). The main office is in China Hong Kong City, Canton Rd, Tsimshatsui, Kowloon. It has a complaints and advice hot line (☎ 736 3636) and there is also an Advice Centre (☎ 541 1422) at 38 Pier Rd, Central, near the Outer Islands Ferry Pier.

BUSINESS HOURS & HOLIDAYS
Office hours are Monday to Friday from 9 am to 5 pm, and on Saturday from 9 am to 12 noon. Lunch hour is from 1 to 2 pm and many offices simply shut down and lock the door at this time.

Stores and restaurants that cater to the tourist trade keep longer hours, but almost nothing opens before 9 am. Even tourist-related businesses shut down by 9 or 10 pm, and many will close for major holidays, especially Chinese New Year.

Western and Chinese culture combine to create an interesting mix of holidays. The first day of the first moon (late January or early February) is Chinese New Year. Only the first three days of this are a public holiday, but everything pretty much shuts down for a week and all flights out of Hong Kong are booked solid for nearly three weeks.

The other big public holiday to avoid is Ching Ming (visits to ancestors' graves) which falls around Easter time. Transport at this time is also a problem.

The mid-year Dragon Boat (Tuen Ng) Festival is a dramatic sight culminating in the international races. The time to enjoy moon cakes is during the Mid-Autumn Festival (15th night of the eighth moon).

The last public holidays are Christmas (25 December) and Boxing Day (26 December), when the lights of Hong Kong are bright and the streets are packed.

Some colourful nonpublic holidays include the birthdays of Tin Hau (the goddess of fisherfolk), Tam Kung (another patron saint of boat people) and Lord Buddha. The Cheung Chau Bun Festival features raucous fun on the island of Cheung Chau. Then there's the Yue Lan Festival of Hungry Ghosts (late August or September) which is a great time to visit Taoist temples.

CULTURAL EVENTS
There are literally hundreds of cultural events throughout the year, but the exact dates vary. The HKTA publishes a complete schedule every month. If you want to time your visit to Hong Kong to coincide with a particular event, it would be wise to contact the HKTA beforehand. A brief rundown of important annual events includes:

HK Arts Festival – an assortment of exhibitions and shows usually held in January.

HK Festival Fringe – the Fringe Club supports upcoming artists and performers from Hong Kong and elsewhere. This three-week festival occurs from late January to February.

HK International Marathon – organised by the Hong Kong Amateur Athletic Association, this major event is held in Shatin, usually in March.

HK Food Festival – sponsored by the HKTA and usually held in March.

HK International Film Festival – organised by the Urban Council, this event usually occurs in March or April.

HK International Handball Invitation Tournament – organised by the Hong Kong Amateur Handball Association, this event is in March or April.

International Dragon Boat Festival – usually falling in June, the international festival is usually held the week after the Chinese dragon boat races.

International Arts Carnival – this unusual summer festival promotes performances by children's groups. The carnival usually falls in July or August.

Asian Regatta – organised by the Hong Kong Yachting Association, this event usually occurs in October.

Festival of Asian Arts – this is one of Asia's major international events, attracting performers from as far as Australia in addition to nearby countries. This festival usually occurs in October or November.

Cultural Centres

The main venue for cultural events is the shiny modern Hong Kong Cultural Centre (☎ 734 2009), 10 Salisbury Rd, Tsimshatsui, Kowloon. The Philharmonic Orchestra and Chinese Orchestra, among others, have regular performances here. Big events like rock concerts are held at the Hong Kong Coliseum (☎ 765 9234), 9 Cheoung Wan Rd, Hunghom, Kowloon, a 12,500-seat indoor facility next to the KCR station.

On Hong Kong Island, the main centre for cultural events is the Hong Kong Academy for the Performing Arts (☎ 823 1505), 1 Gloucester Rd, Wanchai. Just across the street is the Hong Kong Arts Centre (☎ 823 0230), 2 Harbour Rd, Wanchai.

Some groups book performances at City Hall Theatre (☎ 523 3800), beside the Star Ferry Terminal in Central. Queen Elizabeth Stadium (☎ 575 6793), 18 Oi Kwan Rd, Wanchai, is the site for both sporting events and concerts.

There are three big cultural centres in the New Territories: Shatin Town Hall (☎ 694 2503), 1 Yuen Ho Rd, Shatin; Tuen Mun Town Hall (☎ 452 7308), 3 Tuen Hi Rd, Tuen

Mun; and Tsuen Wan Town Hall (☎ 493 9143), 72 Tai Ho Rd, Tsuen Wan.

POST & TELECOMMUNICATIONS

All post offices are open Monday to Saturday from 8 am to 6 pm, and are closed on Sunday and public holidays. On the Kowloon side, one of the most convenient post offices is at 10 Middle Rd, east of Nathan Rd, Tsimshatsui.

Telephone

If you want to phone overseas, it's cheapest to use an IDD (International Direct Dialling) telephone. You can place an IDD call from most phone boxes, but you'll need a stack of HK$5 coins handy if your call is going to be anything but very brief. An alternative is to buy a 'Phonecard', which comes in denominations of HK$50, HK$100 or HK$150. You can find these phones in shops, on the street or at a Hong Kong Telecom office. There's a HK Telecom at 10 Middle Rd in Tsimshatsui and another at Exchange Square No 1 Building, next to the post office in Central.

For calls to countries that do not have IDD service, you can call from a HK Telecom office – first pay a deposit and they will hook you up (minimum three minutes) and give you your change after the call is completed.

TIME

The time in Hong Kong is GMT plus eight hours. When it is 12 noon in Hong Kong, it is also 12 noon in Singapore and Perth; 2 pm in Sydney; 8 pm in Los Angeles; 11 pm in New York; and 4 am in London. Daylight savings time is not observed.

BOOKS & MAPS

The Government's annual report is entitled *Hong Kong 1990, Hong Kong 1991*, etc. In addition to the excellent photographs, the text is a gold mine of information about the government, politics, economy, history, arts and just about any other topic relevant to Hong Kong.

A good antidote to the government's upbeat version of history is *The Other Hong*

Kong Report (Chinese University Press). It's a fascinating and somewhat cynical rebuttal.

Maurice Collin's *Foreign Mud* (Faber & Faber, UK, 1946) tells the sordid story of the Opium Wars.

Borrowed Place, Borrowed Time is the book to read on Hong Kong's birth and development. It was written by the late Richard Hughes, one of the real 'old China hands'. Novels to dip into include the readable (and highly dramatic) *Tai-pan* by James Clavell, which is (very) loosely based on the Jardine-Matheson organisation in its early days. Richard Mason's *The World of Suzie Wong* is also interesting – after all she was Hong Kong's best known citizen.

If you want more information on Hong Kong and the surrounding area, look for the Lonely Planet guidebook *Hong Kong, Macau & Canton – a travel survival kit*.

The giveaway maps provided by the HKTA are adequate for finding your way around most places in Kowloon or the city part of Hong Kong Island.

Bookshops

There are several excellent bookshops in Hong Kong. One of the biggest and best is Swindon Books, 13 Lock Rd, Tsimshatsui.

Times Books gives its address as Shop C, 96 Nathan Rd, but the entrance is around the corner on Granville Rd in Tsimshatsui. It's also large and has another branch (☎ 722 6583) in the Houston Centre, Lower Ground Floor, Shop No LG-23, Tsimshatsui East. Another Times Books (☎ 525 8797) is at Hutchison House, Shop G-31, Central, Hong Kong Island. Hutchison House is at the corner of Murray Rd and Lambeth Walk.

Wanderlust Books, 30 Hollywood Rd, Central, Hong Kong Island, is well worth visiting for its collections of travel books, maps and books about Hong Kong. The staff is extremely helpful and friendly, a rarity in Hong Kong bookshops.

There is a South China Morning Post Bookshop at the Star Ferry Terminal on Hong Kong Island. They have another branch on the 3rd floor, Ocean terminal in Tsimshatsui.

Peace Book Company, 35 Kimberly Rd, Tsimshatsui, is an excellent store and has many books about China.

Not to be overlooked is the Government Publications Centre in the GPO building next to the Star Ferry Terminal.

MEDIA

Newspapers & Magazines

The two main newspapers produced in Hong Kong are the *South China Morning Post* and the *Hong Kong Standard*.

Hong Kong is the home of the *Far Eastern Economic Review*, one of the most authoritative magazines covering Asian events.

Radio & TV

Radio Television Hong Kong (RTHK) has three stations: Radio 3 at AM 567 and 1584 kHz, and FM 97.9 and 106.8 mHz; Radio 4 at FM 97.6 and 98.9 mHz; and Radio 6, with the BBC World Service relay, at AM 675 kHz. Commercial Radio (CR) is at AM 864 kHz. The British Forces Broadcasting Service (BFBS) is at FM 93.1, 96.6, 102 and 104.8 mHz.

Hong Kong's TV stations are run by two companies, Television Broadcasts Ltd (TVB) and Asia Television Ltd (ATV). Each company operates one English-language and one Cantonese-language channel. The two English stations are TVB Pearl (channel 3) and ATV World (channel 4).

The programme schedules for radio & TV are listed in the English-language daily newspapers.

FILM & PHOTOGRAPHY

Everything you need in the way of film, camera and photographic accessories is available in Hong Kong. It is usually cheaper than at home.

HEALTH

Hong Kong is a very healthy place. You can drink water straight from the tap, and even the street markets are reasonably clean despite their dubious appearance.

Public hospitals charge low fees, but Hong Kong residents pay less than foreign visitors.

Hong Kong's public hospitals include: *Queen Elizabeth Hospital* (☎ 710 2111), Wylie Rd, Yaumati, Kowloon; *Princess Margaret Hospital* (☎ 742 7111), Laichikok, Kowloon; *Queen Mary Hospital* (☎ 817 9463), Pokfulam Rd.

Private doctors usually charge reasonable fees, but it pays to make some enquiries first. Most large hotels have resident doctors.

Hong Kong has a shortage of dentists and fees are consequently very high. If the next stop on your itinerary is Taiwan, you might want to wait because the cost for dental treatment is much lower there.

Most pharmacies in Hong Kong are open from 9 am to 6 pm, with some until 8 pm.

DANGERS & ANNOYANCES

In a form of poetic Chinese justice, the colony's initial opium-based founding has rebounded and Hong Kong has a serious dope problem. Like elsewhere, addicts turn to crime to finance their habit. For the most part, it's nonviolent crime: pickpocketing, burglaries and (in the case of women addicts) prostitution.

However, muggings do occasionally occur, though seldom in tourist areas since these are heavily patrolled by the police.

More visitors would have been ripped off by their fellow travellers than by Hong Kong residents. If you're staying in a dormitory, be careful with your valuables.

The biggest annoyance of life in Hong Kong is the appalling rudeness of shopkeepers. The HKTA is aware of the problem, and has attempted to educate sales clerks not to bite the tourists. They've tried all sorts of catchy slogans: 'Smile at our foreign friends', etc. Unfortunately, most of the shopkeepers prefer the motto 'Give us your money and get the hell out!'

HIGHLIGHTS

The trip on the Peak Tram to Victoria Peak has been practically mandatory for visitors since it opened in 1888. A 30-minute ride on a sampan through Aberdeen Harbour is equally exciting. Lunch at a good dim sum restaurant is one of the great pleasures of the

Orient, and of course, shopping is what Hong Kong is all about. For those who prefer a less frantic pace, a pleasant time can be spent exploring quiet backwaters in the Outlying Islands such as Lantau's Po Lin Monastery.

ACCOMMODATION & FOOD

For information on where to stay and eat in Hong Kong, see Places to Stay and Places to Eat in the following Around the Country section.

DRINKS

You can drink as much tea as you like usually free of charge in any Chinese restaurant. On the other hand, coffee is seldom available except in Western restaurants or coffee shops, and is never free.

There are three main types of tea: green or unfermented; *bolay* fermented, also known as black tea; and oolong, which is semi-fermented. There are many varieties of tea. Jasmine tea *(heung ping)* is a blend of tea and flowers which is always drunk straight, without milk or sugar.

Beer is extremely popular among the Chinese. The brands made in China are excellent, the most popular being Tsingtao, now a major export. It's actually a German beer – the town where it is made, Tsingtao (Qingdao), was once a German concession. The Chinese inherited the brewery when the Germans were kicked out.

THINGS TO BUY

Oh yeah, shopping – some people do come to Hong Kong for that. Well, a lot of the same things apply as in Singapore: shop around, try and find out what the 'real' retail price is before you believe the discounts, make sure guarantees are international and, most important, don't go on a buying binge. It's very easy in Hong Kong to decide suddenly that you need all sorts of consumer goods you don't really need at all.

It's hard to say just how Hong Kong and Singapore really compare in price or choice – they're probably pretty similar. The HKTA has a shopping guide booklet which lists approved shops but that old story, *caveat emptor* (buyer beware) applies as strongly as ever.

The worst neighbourhood for shopping happens to be the place where most tourists shop. Tsimshatsui, the tourist ghetto of Kowloon, is the most likely place to be cheated. Notice that none of the cameras or other big ticket items have price tags. This is *not* common practice elsewhere in Hong Kong. If you go out to the Chinese neighbourhoods where the locals shop, you'll find price tags on everything. Furthermore, the non-touristy shops seldom bargain.

If you're staying in Kowloon, Mongkok is a much better neighbourhood for shopping. On Hong Kong Island, Central and Causeway Bay are the tourist trap zones. You'll often do better by heading out to Cityplaza, a shopping mall in Quarry Bay. Take the MTR to the Tai Koo station.

If possible, try not to be in a hurry. Shop around a little bit and be sure you understand the prices. Of course, shops realise that the tourists do this, so they have other clever methods for cheating you. The most common trick is to offer you a good price on a camera and then rip you off on accessories such as filters, neckstrap, camera case and batteries.

More diabolical tricks include selling second-hand equipment as new, selling goods without proper guarantees, selling grey-market equipment (ie imported by somebody other than the official local agent), passing off superseded models as new ones, persuading you that standard equipment actually costs extra, and on and on! Yet another ploy is to deliberately sell you electronic equipment of the wrong voltage. When you discover the mistake later and bring it back, they refuse to exchange unless you pay more.

You should be especially wary if they want to take the goods into the back room to 'box it up'. This provides ample opportunity to remove essential items that you have already paid for.

There is really no reason to put a deposit on anything unless it is being custom-made

for you, like a fitted suit or a pair of eyeglasses.

If buying film you get a better price buying in bulk, say 10 or 12 rolls at a time.

Hong Kong's reputation for made-to-measure clothes is not what it was – prices have escalated so they're no longer really cheap. You'd do better to check out some of the places that sell ready-made clothes as Hong Kong is becoming fashion conscious. It's a good cheap place to buy jeans and other denim clothes. There are lots of T-shirt copies such as 'Erspit'!

Buying jade or antiques is more for the knowledgeable purchaser, and authenticity depends on buying from reputable dealers. Antique shops on Hollywood Rd (up from Central) are interesting to wander around. If you're into 'instant oil paintings' they're available very cheaply around Kowloon. Glasses and contact lenses are cheap and well made.

Check out the People's Republic Chinese Arts & Crafts emporiums where you'll find many unusual items, often of good quality and (sometimes) low prices. An excellent emporium is Yue Hwa Chinese Products at the corner of Nathan and Jordan Rds.

Getting There & Away

AIR

For most travellers, the normal arrival point will be Kai Tak Airport – with its runway sticking out from Kowloon into the harbour it makes a pretty dramatic entrance.

If you are going anywhere in the North-East Asian region (Japan, Korea, Taiwan or China), to the Philippines or to Sabah in Borneo, then Hong Kong is one of the best gateways to the region.

Hong Kong is a popular place for shopping for discounted airline tickets. Typical one-way fares include:

Destination	Fare
Auckland	HK$3350
Bangkok	HK$ 950

Beijing	HK$1450
Canton	HK$ 300
Honolulu	HK$2150
Jakarta	HK$2150
Kathmandu	HK$1900
Kuala Lumpur	HK$2250
London	HK$2500
Manila	HK$1030
New York	HK$2850
Perth	HK$2500
San Francisco	HK$2480
Seoul	HK$1900
Singapore	HK$1500
Sydney	HK$3200
Taipei	HK$1050
Tokyo	HK$1250
Toronto	HK$3500
Vancouver	HK$3150

These are special fares and will have various restrictions upon their use.

Travel Agencies

A major contender in the budget ticket business is Shoestring Travel (☎ 723 2306), Flat A, 4th Floor, Alpha House, 27-33 Nathan Rd, Tsimshatsui.

Traveller Services (☎ 367 4127), Room 704, Metropole Building, 57 Peking Rd, Tsimshatsui, is fast, cheap and reliable.

Equally good is Phoenix Services (☎ 722 7378) in Room B, 6th Floor, Milton Mansion, 96 Nathan Rd, Tsimshatsui. Many travellers have spoken very highly of this place.

Hong Kong Student Travel Bureau (☎ 730 3269) is in Room 1021, 10th Floor, Star House, Tsimshatsui.

Departure Tax

Airport departure tax is now a hefty HK$150, but you don't have to pay if you're aged under 12. If departing by ship to Macau or China, departure tax is included in the price of the ticket.

LAND

If you just want a brief guided visit to the People's Republic of China, you can do that quite easily. There are plenty of one-day cross-the-border jaunts available from Hong Kong or Macau, and slightly longer Canton

Quickies which give you a few days in the neighbouring city.

A train to Lo Wu at the border will cost you just HK$35. You walk across the border to the city of Shenzhen, and from there you can take a local train to Canton (Guangzhou) and beyond.

Alternatively, you can take an express train straight through from Hunghom station in Kowloon to Canton (Guangzhou) for HK$180.

SEA

Hong Kong has one of the most spectacular harbours in the world, so it's kind of a shame that there's not much of a chance of arriving by boat – unless you're rich and on a cruise liner. It may still be possible though for budget travellers, if you want to take a boat from China. The Shanghai to Hong Kong ferry is very popular with travellers, and it's a great way to leave China.

You can go to China by hovercraft from the China Hong Kong City Ferry Terminal in Tsimshatsui. Perhaps cheapest (HK$120) and most pleasant is to take the overnight ferry from Kowloon to Canton. You are able to sleep in dorm beds and save a night's accommodation charge at a hotel.

Getting Around

Hong Kong has a varied and frequent public transport system, but there are two advance words of warning. Before setting out to travel anywhere by bus, ensure you have a good pocketful of small change – the exact fare normally must be deposited in a cash box and nobody has change.

The second warning is that on weekends everybody, plus his/her brother, sister and boy/girlfriend, sets out to go somewhere. On Sunday in particular, you must be prepared for it to take much longer to get anywhere. You'll pay more on certain ferries, and even miss the odd full bus. Plus, everybody will be taking photographs of everybody else, so take care you don't appear in too many family portraits.

TO/FROM THE AIRPORT

There's a variety of ways of getting to and from the airport, the easiest of which is by taxi (fares to most hotels are listed at the airport). To most places in the Tsimshatsui area, it should cost from around HK$35 to HK$40.

It'll cost rather more to places on Hong Kong Island since taxis are entitled to charge an additional HK$20 to cover the toll for the Cross-Harbour Tunnel going both ways. During rush hour, the tunnel can get very clogged up – so allow sufficient time and be prepared for a higher fare at those times. Usually the fare from the airport should be from HK$55 to HK$60 to Causeway Bay, or from HK$65 to HK$75 to Central. The only other addition to the fare should be a charge of HK$2 per bag.

The Airbus (airport bus) services are very convenient and are significantly cheaper than taxis. There are three services – the A1 to Tsimshatsui (HK$8); the A2 to Wanchai, Central and the Macau Ferry Terminal (HK$12); and the A3 to Causeway Bay (also

HK$12). The buses operate every 15 minutes, from 7 am to midnight, and depart from right outside the arrival area. There's plenty of luggage space on board and they go past most of the major hotels.

The A1 service to Tsimshatsui in Kowloon goes down Nathan Rd right in front of Chungking Mansions, then turns around at the Star Ferry Terminal and heads back. There is an Airbus brochure at the departure area with a map showing the bus route. The Airbuses also stop at regular signposted bus stops.

BUS

There are plenty of buses with fares starting from HK$1.80 and going up to HK$9 for the longest ride you can take in the New Territories. You pay the fare as you enter the bus so make sure you have the exact change ready. The double-decker buses are blue and cream on Hong Kong Island (operated by China Motor Bus) or red and cream in Kowloon (operated by Kowloon Motor Bus).

Most services stop around 11 pm or midnight but the bus Nos 121 and 122 are 'Cross Harbour Recreation Routes' which operate through the Cross-Harbour Tunnel every 15

Hong Kong Island Buses

Bus No	From	To	Every (mins)	Trip (mins)	Costs
tram	Central	Sai Wan Ho	2-7	40	HK$1.00
6	Central	Stanley	10-20	40	HK$4.50
7	Aberdeen	Central	6-10	30	HK$3.00
14	Sai Wan Ho	Stanley	20-30	40	HK$4.50
70	Central	Aberdeen	4-10	25	HK$2.80
73	Stanley	Aberdeen	15-30	30	HK$4.50

New Territories Buses

Bus No	From	To	Every (mins)	Trip (mins)	Costs
51	Tsuen Wan	Kam Tin	15-25	50	HK$3.60
54	Yuen Long	Kam Tin	7-12	20	HK$1.40
60M	Tsuen Wan	Tuen Mun	7-15	36	HK$3.60
75K	Tai Po	Tai Mei Tuk	12-30	26	HK$2.40
77K	Kam Tin	Sheung Shui	12-20	25	HK$3.00
92	Choi Hung	Sai Kung	6-15	38	HK$2.60

minutes from 12.45 to 5 am. Bus No 121 runs from Macau Ferry Terminal on Hong Kong Island, then through the tunnel to Chatham Rd in Tsimshatsui East before continuing on to Choi Hung on the east side of the airport.

Bus No 122 runs from North Point on Hong Kong Island, through the Cross-Harbour Tunnel, to Chatham Rd in Tsimshatsui East, the northern part of Nathan Rd and on to Laichikok in the north-west part of Kowloon.

Minibus

Small red and yellow minibuses supplement the regular bus services. They are a little more expensive (generally HK$2 to HK$6) and the prices often go up during the rush hour or in rainy weather! They generally don't run such regular routes but you can get on or off almost anywhere. If you know where you are going and where they are going, you may well find them both fast and convenient.

Maxicabs are just like minibuses except they are green and yellow and they do run regular routes. Two popular ones are from the carpark in front of the Star Ferry in Central to Ocean Park or from HMS Tamar (east of the Star Ferry) to the Peak. Fares are around HK$1 to HK$5.

TRAIN

The Kowloon-Canton Railway (KCR) runs right up to the border where visitors to China once had to walk across the bridge and change trains. There are also four express trains daily which run right through to Canton. Apart from being one of the best ways of entering China, it's also an excellent alternative to buses for getting into the New Territories. The last stop before China is Lo Wu but you can only go there if you have a visa for China.

The trains operate every 10 to 15 minutes. There are two classes, first and ordinary. It's a scenic and interesting trip out to the New Territories. Tai Po Market and Fanling are interesting places to stop for a look around.

Mass Transit Railway

Opened in 1979-80, the Mass Transit Railway (MTR) operates from Central across the harbour and up along Kowloon Peninsula. This ultramodern, high-speed subway system has been quite a hit with office commuters but the price for the system's convenience is fairly high. Fares vary from HK$3 to HK$7 one way. The ticket machines do not give change and the tickets are valid only for the day they are purchased. Once you go past the turnstile, you must complete the journey within 90 minutes or the ticket becomes invalid. The harbour crossing costs HK$5. The MTR operates from 6 am to 1 am.

If you use the MTR frequently, it's very useful to buy a Common Stored Value Ticket for either HK$50 or HK$100. These can also be used on the KCR except for the Lo Wu station on the China border. The MTR Tourist Ticket is a rip-off at HK$25 because it gives you only HK$20 worth of fares!

Smoking, eating or drinking are not allowed in the MTR stations or on the trains (makes you wonder about all those Maxim Cake Shops in the stations!). The fine for eating or drinking is HK$1000, while smoking will set you back HK$2000. Busking, selling and soliciting are forbidden. There are no toilets in the MTR stations.

TRAM

There is just one tram line, but it is a long one – all the way from Kennedy Town (to the west of Central) to Shaukiwan (at the eastern end of the island); it also runs right through the middle of Central. As well as being ridiculously picturesque and fun to travel on the tram is quite a bargain at HK$1 for any distance and you pay as you get off.

Some of the trams diverge off the regular route to go to Happy Valley and some of them don't run all the way to the end of the line but basically you can just get on any tram that comes by. They pass frequently and there always seem to be half a dozen trams actually in sight.

TAXI

The minimum charge is HK$8 and then it's HK$0.90 for each 250 metres. There's an additional charge of HK$2 for each bag carried. In the New Territories, or on Lantau Island, the charges are lower. If you're taking a taxi through the harbour tunnel, taxi drivers are entitled to charge an additional HK$20 to cover return toll costs.

Taxi drivers can cover Kowloon or Hong Kong Island but in practice they tend to stick to one side or the other. It can be difficult to get taxis around shift change time (4 pm), and just like anywhere else in the world, taxis disappear when the rain pours. Saturday afternoon or Wednesday evening are also bad times to find taxis because that's when the horse races are held!

If you have a complaint about a taxi driver, get the licence number and call the police hotline (☎ 527 7177).

BOAT

Star Ferries

The Star Ferries shuttle back and forth across the harbour every few minutes for a mere HK$1 (lower class) or HK$1.20 (upper class) – a real travel bargain. It's often said that this is one of the most picturesque public transport journeys in the world. The crossing takes less than 10 minutes and the ferries operate from 6.30 am to 11.30 pm.

Once, you had to rent a sampan (*walla walla*) for after-hours crossings but these days there are all-night buses and taxis through the tunnel. The Star Ferry terminals are right at the end of Tsimshatsui on the Kowloon Peninsula and right in the middle of Central on Hong Kong Island.

There is a second Star Ferry service which operates between Wanchai and Tsimshatsui. Yet another boat operates from the Star Ferry Terminal in Central to Hunghom on the Kowloon side. If you're on your way to China by train this is a good way of getting to the railway station.

Other Harbour Ferries

There are other ferries making longer trips across the harbour – from Wanchai to Tsimshatsui for example. The Central to Tuen Mun (New Territories) hoverferry takes 30 minutes and is one of the longest rides you can take through the harbour. You can also get a ferry to or from Hunghom (the other side of the railway station in Kowloon) to North Point on Hong Kong Island (an interesting trip back through Causeway Bay and Wanchai). Out on the harbour, there seems to be a nonstop procession of ferries ploughing back and forth.

Island Ferries

The HKTA can supply you with a schedule for these ferries. There are more services on Sunday and holidays when the fares also go up and the boats are very crowded. From Central, most ferries go from the Outer Island terminal between the Star Ferry and Macau Ferry terminals. Fares range from about HK$6 on weekdays but can jump as much as 50% on weekends.

Lantau
    Most services go via Peng Chau Island to Silver Mine Bay (Mui Wo). There are approximately 19 services a day. There are two boats daily on Saturday, Sunday and on holidays to Tai O at the other end of the island.
Cheung Chau
    There are about 19 services a day, each taking just over an hour.
Lamma
    There are separate services to Sok Kwu Wan (seven per day) and Yung Shue Wan (12 per day).
Tolo Harbour
    There are just two ferries per day running out from Ma Liu Shui to Tap Mun (Grass Island) with lots of stops en route.
Peng Chau
    This isolated island gets only one ferry each weekend, departing on Saturday and returning on Sunday.

BICYCLE

Bicycling in Kowloon or Central would be suicidal, but in quiet areas of the islands or the New Territories a bike can be quite a nice way of getting around. The bike rental places tend to run out early on weekends.

RICKSHAW

These are really only for photographs –

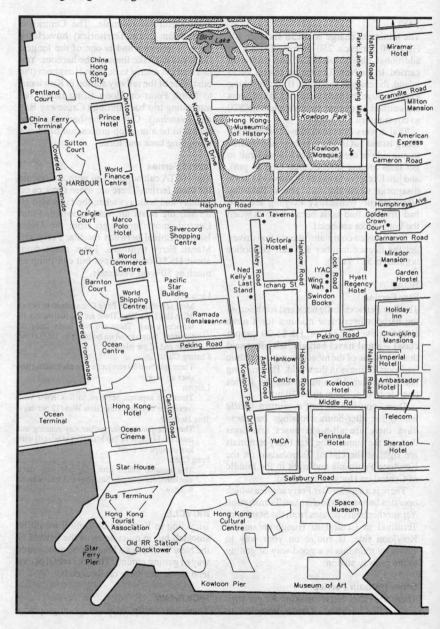

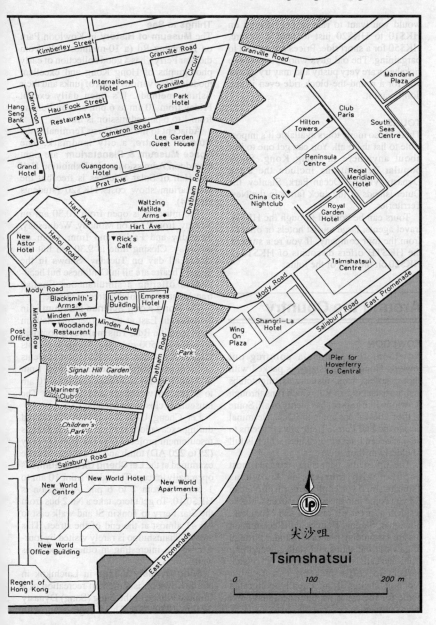

Kimberley Street

Granville Road

Granville Road

Mandarin Plaza

Granville Circuit

Granville

International Hotel

Park Hotel

Club Paris

Hang Seng Bank

Hau Fook Street

Restaurants

Carnarvon Road

Cameron Road

Hilton Towers

South Seas Centre

Lee Garden Guest House

Peninsula Centre

Grand Hotel

Guangdong Hotel

Prat Ave

Chatham Road

Regal Meridian Hotel

Waltzing Matilda Arms

China City Nightclub

Royal Garden Hotel

Hart Ave

Hart Ave

New Astor Hotel

Hanoi Road

Rick's Café

Tsimshatsui Centre

Mody Road

Blacksmith's Arms

Lyton Building

Empress Hotel

Minden Row

Minden Ave

Minden Ave

Woodlands Restaurant

Shangri-La Hotel

Post Office

Chatham Road

Park

Wing On Plaza

Salisbury Road

East Promenade

Signal Hill Garden

Pier for Hoverferry to Central

Mariners' Club

Children's Park

Salisbury Road

New World Hotel

New World Centre

New World Apartments

尖沙咀

Tsimshatsui

New World Office Building

East Promenade

0   100   200 m

Regent of Hong Kong

would you want to ride in one? Count on HK$10 to HK$20 just to take a picture, HK$50 for a short ride. Prices are subject to bargaining. The old guys who operate these rickshaws are very pushy and may try to take you for a round-the-block ride even if you don't want it.

TOURS

There are so many tours available it's impossible to list them all. You can get one to just about anywhere in Hong Kong. Some popular destinations include the Sung Dynasty Village, Ocean Park, Stanley, the Outer Islands or the duck farms in the New Territories.

Tours can be booked through the HKTA, travel agents, large tourist hotels or directly from the tour company. If you're a student, the HKSTB offers discounts of HK$10 or HK$20 on the cost of the tours.

Around the Country

KOWLOON

Kowloon, the peninsula pointing out towards Hong Kong Island, is packed with shops, hotels, bars, restaurants, nightclubs and tourists. Nathan Rd, which runs through Kowloon like a spine, has plenty of all. Some of the ritziest shops are in the Ocean terminal beside the Star Ferry. There always seems to be one ocean liner moored here which is full of elderly millionaires.

The tip of the peninsula, the area most popular with tourists, is known as Tsimshatsui. If you continue north up Nathan Rd you come into the tightly packed Chinese residential areas of Yaumati and Mongkok. Shanghai, Saigon, Battery and Reclamation Sts are fascinating places to wander through to gawk at the shops and stalls...everything from herbalists, snake dealers, streetside barbers to coffin makers. The Yaumati typhoon shelter is an equally congested home for the water people (the Tanka) and their sampans.

Things to See

The **Museum of History** in Kowloon Park on Haiphong Rd (a 10-minutes-walk from the Star Ferry), has a good collection of early photographs of Hong Kong and excellent models of the various types of junks and their fishing methods. It's open daily except Friday from 10 am to 6 pm, and on Sunday from 1 to 6 pm; admission is free.

Adjacent to the Star Ferry Terminal is the **Cultural Centre**, a city landmark. The **Space Museum & Planetarium** are right next door. Admission to the Exhibition Hall and Hall of Solar Sciences is free but the planetarium show costs HK$20 (students HK$14).

The museum is open from 10.30 am on Sunday, from 2 pm on Monday, Wednesday, Thursday and Friday and from 1 pm on Saturday. Closing time is 9.30 pm but it's closed all day on Tuesday. Shows in the Space Theatre are all in Cantonese but headphones offering a simultaneous English translation are available free of charge.

The **Hong Kong Science Museum** is in Tsimshatsui East at the corner of Chatham and Granville Rds. This multilevel complex houses over 500 exhibits. Admission costs HK$25 for adults and HK$15 for students and seniors. Operating hours are from 1 pm to 9 pm Tuesday to Friday, and from 10 am to 9 pm on weekends and holidays. The museum is closed on Monday.

Lei Cheng Uk's Tomb was discovered during excavations for one of Hong Kong's resettlement projects. The late Han Dynasty (25 to 220 AD) tomb and its contents can be examined at the **Lei Cheng Uk Museum**. It's open daily, except Thursday, from 10 am to 1 pm and from 2 to 6 pm. Admission is HK$0.10. To get there, take a No 2 bus from the Star Ferry to Tonkin St and walk east to No 41 almost at the end of the street. This area of Shamshuipo is rarely visited by tourists, so it's interesting in other respects as well.

Sung Dynasty Village in Laichikok in North Kowloon is a modern recreation of a Chinese village of the Sung (Song) Dynasty (960 to 1279 AD). The village is big with tour groups, but individuals are admitted from 10 am to 8.30 pm daily. Admission costs HK$95. It drops to HK$75 on weekends and public holidays between 12.30 pm and 5 pm. Take a No 6A bus from the Kowloon Star Ferry Terminal or a tunnel bus No 105 from Hong Kong Island.

The **Kowloon Mosque** stands on Nathan Rd at the corner of Kowloon Park. It was opened in 1984 on the site of an earlier mosque originally constructed in 1896.

HONG KONG ISLAND, NORTHSIDE

Hong Kong Central is only a small part of Hong Kong Island, crowded close to the harbour looking across to Kowloon. The island is steep and rugged which gives it much of its appeal – buildings cling to the hillsides and you start climbing steeply uphill only a block back from the middle of Central.

Central is the banking and business centre of Hong Kong. Des Voeux Rd is the main street and down it runs the tram line. A long ride on Hong Kong's delightfully ancient double-decker trams can be one of the best introductions to the city. Moving east from Central you come to Wanchai and Causeway Bay, both virtually continuous with Central.

Things to See

If you walk west up Des Voeux Rd you'll soon find one of the most interesting and colourful areas of Hong Kong. There are markets and streets for almost every kind of goods – the HKTA's walking tour of this area is an excellent introduction.

As the streets head up the hills, many of them become too steep for cars and famous Ladder St is aptly named! Unfortunately, Cat St (Upper and Lower Lascar Row to which Ladder St leads) has been redeveloped and much of its picturesque quality has been ploughed under.

At the junction of Ladder St and Hollywood Rd is **Man Mo Temple**, the oldest temple in Hong Kong. Next door is the building used as Suzie Wong's hotel in the film.

Hollywood Rd is a wonderful street for window shopping as it's packed with antique shops. The further up the road you go, the more bizarre the odds and ends you see. The high quality stuff is further down towards Central.

The **Tiger Balm Gardens** were constructed by the Haw Par brothers with a few of the millions gleaned from the Tiger Balm medicament. It is two hectares of Chinese imagination run wild. Admission is free and it's open from 9 am to 4 pm daily. A No 11 bus will get you there from Central.

Causeway Bay, east of Hong Kong Central, is another touristy shopping and amusement centre, though not as ridiculous as Tsimshatsui. Wander Jardine's Bazaar and Jardine's Crescent – busy shopping streets today but reminders that in the past this was the area where the Jardine-Matheson company operated in its early days. The noonday gun, by the waterfront across from the Excelsior Hotel, is a daily reminder of those pioneering days in Hong Kong's history.

Between Causeway Bay and Hong Kong Central is the girlie bar centre, **Wanchai** – full of topless bars but now a pale shadow of its peak of activity during the Vietnam War and not very exciting to wander around.

Take the famous Peak Tram from Garden Rd, up behind the Hilton Hotel, to the top of **Victoria Peak**. As you climb higher up the hill, the houses and apartment blocks get steadily flashier and more expensive. Don't just admire the view from the top – wander up Mt Austin Rd to the old **Governor's Lodge** (demolished by the Japanese during WW II) or take the more leisurely stroll around Lugard and Harlech Rds – together they make a complete circuit of the peak. You can walk right down to Aberdeen on the south side of the island or you can try the Old Peak Rd for a couple of km return trip to Hong Kong Central.

The Peak Tram costs HK$8 (return HK$14) to the top, but you can also get there by bus No 15 (HK$3.80) or the Peak minibus No 1 from HMS *Tamar*. The peak is very crowded on weekends. It's worth repeating the peak trip at night – the illuminated view is something else.

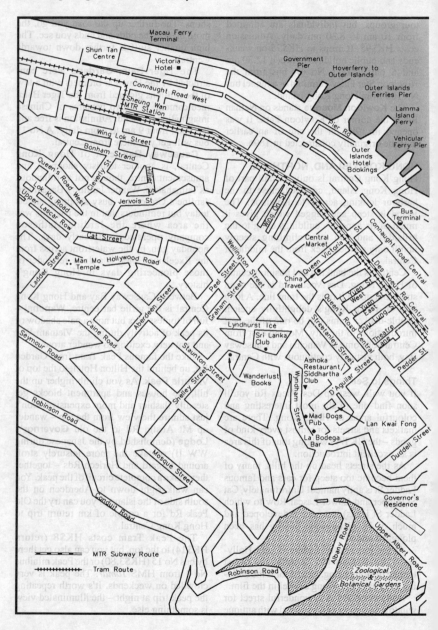

MTR Subway Route

+++++++ Tram Route

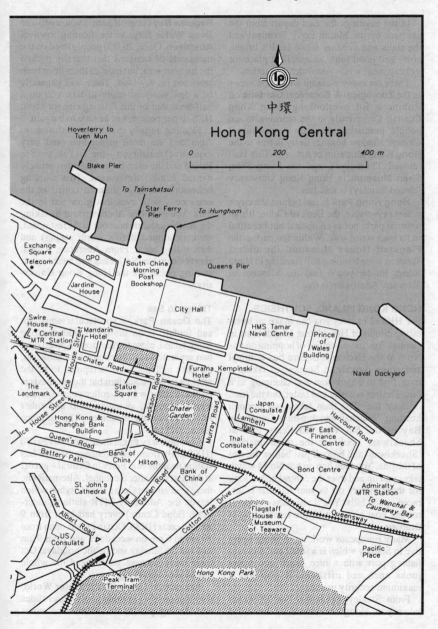

中環

Hong Kong Central

0   200   400 m

Hoverferry to Tuen Mun

Blake Pier

To Tsimshatsui

Star Ferry Pier

To Hunghom

Exchange Square
Telecom

GPO

South China Morning Post Bookshop

Queens Pier

Jardine House

City Hall

HMS Tamar Naval Centre

Prince of Wales Building

Swire House

Central MTR Station

Mandarin Hotel

Ice House Street

Chater Road

Furama Kempinski Hotel

Naval Dockyard

The Landmark

Statue Square

Chater Garden

Jackson Road

Japan Consulate

Lambeth Walk

Harcourt Road

Hong Kong & Shanghai Bank Building

Queen's Road

Battery Path

Bank of China

Hilton

Thai Consulate

Far East Finance Centre

St John's Cathedral

Garden Road

Bank of China

Murray Road

Bond Centre

Admiralty MTR Station

Lower Albert Road

Cotton Tree Drive

Flagstaff House & Museum of Teaware

Queensway

To Wanchai & Causeway Bay

US Consulate

Hong Kong Park

Pacific Place

Peak Tram Terminal

In the evenings the cars depart from the car park by the Macau Ferry Terminal and the stalls and vendors move in. It's bright, noisy and good fun – an excellent place for a cheap meal while you watch the action.

There are many pleasant walks and views in the **Zoological & Botanical Gardens** on Robinson Rd overlooking Hong Kong Central. Come early in the morning to see people practising *taijiquan* – traditional Chinese shadow boxing. Entry is free to the **Hong Kong Museum of Art** in the City Hall (closed Thursdays), and the **Fung Ping Shan Museum** in Hong Kong University (closed Sunday) is also free.

Hong Kong Park is just behind the city's tallest skyscraper, the Bank of China. It's an unusual park, not at all natural but beautiful in its own weird way. Within the park is the **Flagstaff House Museum**, the oldest Western-style building still standing in Hong Kong. Inside, you'll find the Museum of Teaware. Admission is free.

HONG KONG ISLAND, SOUTHSIDE

For HK$12 in fares you can make an interesting circuit of Hong Kong Island. Start in Central. You have a choice of hopping on bus No 6 at the Exchange Square bus terminal and going directly to Stanley, or taking a tram first to Shaukiwan and changing to a bus. The bus is easier and faster, but the tram is more fun. The tram takes you through hustling Wanchai and bustling Causeway Bay to the Sai Wan Ho Ferry Pier at Shaukiwan. Look for the trams marked 'Shaukiwan' and hop off just before the end of the line. You then hop on bus No 14 which takes you up and over the central hills – look for the cemetery off to your left that is terraced up the hills. You'll also pass a popular rowing boat hire spot before terminating at **Stanley**.

Many Europeans working in Hong Kong live in Stanley which is a small and pleasant fishing port with a nice beach and many junks anchored offshore. It also has a maximum security prison.

From Stanley, catch bus No 73 which takes you along the coast, by beautiful **Repulse Bay** (stop off here if you wish) and **Deep Water Bay**, to the floating town of **Aberdeen**. Once, 20,000 people lived on the thousands of sampans that literally packed the harbour area, but most of them have been rehoused on dry land. There will generally be a few sampans ready to take you on a half-hour tour of this floating city for about HK$40 per person, but be sure to bargain.

Floating regally amid the confusion in Aberdeen are three palace-like (and very expensive) restaurants – the Tai Pak, the Sea Palace and the even larger and appropriately named Jumbo Restaurant. This floating behemoth has huge dragons coiled at the entrance – with eyes that glow red in the dark. You get a free Aberdeen tour by taking the Jumbo's shuttle boat out to the restaurant, walking around it (it's worth seeing) and then riding back. From Aberdeen, a final short ride on bus No 7 takes you back to your starting point, via the Hong Kong University.

Things to See

The **Ocean Park**, a spectacular aquarium and funfair, is on the south side of Hong Kong Island, close to Aberdeen. Spread over two separate sites, connected by a cable car, the park includes what is reputed to be the world's largest aquarium but the emphasis is on the funfair with its roller coaster, space wheel, octopus, swinging ship and other astronaut-training machines. The entrance fee is HK$140.

Cheapest way to get there is on bus No 70 (HK$2.80) from the Exchange Square bus station near the Star Ferry in Central – get off at the first stop after the tunnel. Alternatively, there's an air-con Ocean Park Citybus which leaves the Admiralty MTR station (underneath Bond Centre) every half-hour from 9 am and costs HK$8. Ocean Park is open from 10 am to 6 pm on weekdays, and from 9 am to 6 pm on Sunday and public holidays. Get there early because you'll need the whole day to see everything.

Just next to Ocean Park is **Water World**, a collection of swimming pools, water slides and diving platforms. Admission costs

HK$60. Take bus No 70 and get off at the first stop after the tunnel. If you take the Ocean Park Citybus, be sure to get off at the first stop.

At the back side of Ocean Park is the **Middle Kingdom**, a modern-day version of ancient China. Admission is HK$140, half price for children aged six to 17. Operating hours are from 10 am to 6 pm daily. Take the Ocean Park Citybus and get off at the second stop.

NEW TERRITORIES

You can explore the New Territories by bus and train for around HK$20 – allow a full day for this interesting trip. You start out by taking the MTR to the last stop at **Tsuen Wan**.

The main attraction in Tsuen Wan is the **Yuen Yuen Institute**, a Taoist temple complex, and the adjacent Buddhist **Western Monastery**. You reach the institute by taking minibus No 81 from Shiu Wo St which is two blocks south of the MTR station. Alternatively, take a taxi, which is not expensive. The monastery is about 1½ km to the north-east of the MTR station.

From Tsuen Wan, take bus No 60M to the bustling city of **Tuen Mun**. Here you can visit Hong Kong's largest shopping mall, the Tuen Mun Town Centre. From here, hop on the Light Rail Transit (LRT) system to reach **Ching Chung Koon**, a huge temple complex on the north side of Tuen Mun.

You then get back on the LRT and head to Yuen Long. From here, it's only a short trip on bus No 54 to the nearby **Kam Tin walled villages**. These walled villages with their single stout entrances are said to date from the 16th century – long before the arrival of the British in Hong Kong. There are six walled villages around Kam Tin but you usually visit **Kut Hing Wei**. Once you've paid your entry charge you can wander the narrow little lanes, but it's very touristy with old crones in traditional gear who require payment before they can be photographed.

The town of Sheung Shui is about another eight km and is easily reached by bus No 77K. Here you can hop on the KCR and go

one stop south to **Fan Ling**. The main attraction in this town is the **Fung Ying Sin Kwun Temple**, a Taoist temple for the dead.

Get back on the KCR and head to Tai Po Market station. From here, you can walk 10 to 15 minutes to the **Hong Kong Railway Museum**. You can get back on the KCR and go south to the Chinese University where there's the Art Gallery at the **Institute of Chinese Studies**. Admission is free.

The KCR will bring you to Shatin, a lively, bustling city where you can visit the huge **Shatin Town Centre**, one of Hong Kong's biggest shopping malls. Also, from here you begin the climb up to the **Temple of 10,000 Buddhas** (which actually has over 12,000).

There are countless other places to visit in the New Territories, some of them far less developed. The **Sai Kung Peninsula** is probably the least spoilt area in the New Territories – great for hiking and you can get from village to village on boats in the Tolo Harbour.

THE OUTER ISLANDS

There are over 200 islands dotting the waters around Hong Kong, and if you have the time several are definitely worth visiting. Because they are part of the leased land, development has been slower than the frantic pace of Hong Kong Island and Kowloon, although some of them are almost commuter suburbs. There are frequent ferries to the islands but they're very crowded on weekends.

Cheung Chau

This dumbbell-shaped island has become very popular for Western residents who can't afford Hong Kong's sky-high rentals. It's a pleasant little place with a Mediterranean air to it. Were it not for the Chinese signs and people, you might think you were in some Greek island village.

The town sprawls across the narrow bar connecting the two ends of the island. You'll see junks being built on slips up from the beach, and, at the north end of the town, the old **Pak Tai Temple**, built in 1783. At the southern tip of the island is the hideaway cave of notorious pirate Cheung Po Tsai.

There are some pleasant beaches, and each May there is the frantic Bun Festival, when seekers of good fortune scramble up a 20-metre-high tower of sugar buns to get the topmost (and luckiest) one.

Cheung Chau has one expensive hotel, the *Cheung Chau Warwick Hotel* (☎ 981 0081) where doubles cost a mere HK$805 on a weekday and HK$1127 on a weekend, plus a 10% service charge and 5% tax. The best cheap place to stay is the *Star House Motel* (☎ 981 2186) at 149 Tai Sun Bak St. Double rooms start at HK$120 on weekdays and cost between HK$600 and HK$700 a night on weekends.

The big gwailo nightlife spot is the *Garden Cafe/Pub* (☎ 981 4610) at 84 Tung Wan Rd, in the centre of the island.

Peng Chau

This is another small island with a similarly Mediterranean-looking town and an **old temple** (Tin Hau, 1792). If you're going to Lantau it's worth stopping for a look around.

Lantau

This is the largest of the islands and the most sparsely populated – it's almost twice the size of Hong Kong Island but the population is only 20,000. It's definitely worth spending a couple of days here as there are some excellent walking trails and you can get a bit of a feel for rural Chinese life in relatively untouched parts of the island.

Mui Wo (Silver Mine Bay) is the normal arrival point for ferries, but there's a more interesting way of getting there. Take a ferry from HK Central bound for Mui Wo, but get off at Peng Chau. A small sampan (it meets every ferry) will shuttle you across the narrow stretch of water to Lantau Island, and if you follow the trail up the hill you'll find yourself at a Trappist Monastery.

Keep walking up and over the hill (fine views from the top), and you'll soon see Silver Mine Bay down below. On the descent, you pass a deserted building that looks like it would make a fine little hotel – Balinese losmen style. There are some good cheap eating places just before you reach

Mui Wo and you can get a cold drink right at the bottom of the hill when you arrive at the beach.

From Mui Wo, if you have the time, you can take a long (four to five-hour) walk right across the island to **Tung Chung**. The trail passes through a whole series of relatively unspoilt settlements including **Pak Mong**, a very fine example of an old walled village. At Tung Chung there is a fort and ferries run from here to Castle Peak, from where you can bus into Kowloon.

From Tung Chung, follow a paved footpath up an interminable hill for a couple of hours, finally pass through a tea plantation and you'll arrive at the ornate, spectacular **Po Lin (Precious Lotus) Monastery**.

It's a relatively recent construction and almost as much a tourist attraction as a religious centre. Just outside the monastery is the world's largest outdoor statue of Buddha, built at a total cost of HK$60 million. It's possible to have a vegetarian lunch at the monastery dining hall or even spend the night in the dormitories for HK$150 which includes three meals – lights are put out early and the beds are distinctly hard.

For HK$25 you can stay at the *S G Davis Youth Hostel* (YHA card required). Next day you can take a bus back to Mui Wo and thus complete a fairly in-depth look at the island.

It's a lot of walking to do in one day, so if you intend to do the whole circuit it might be better to start off by going straight from Central to Mui Wo and leave the Trappist monastery and Peng Chau until day two, catching the ferry back from Peng Chau to Hong Kong Central. You can also catch a bus straight from Mui Wo to Po Lin if you're not keen on walking.

Alternatively you can continue right down to the end of the island at Tai O, from where ferries also operate back to Central.

Apart from the monastery you can stay in Silver Mine Bay (Mui Wo) at the *Silver Mine Bay Beach Hotel* (☎ 984 8295) or the cheaper *Sea House* (☎ 984 7757).

Lamma

Another fairly large island, Lamma has good beaches and a very relaxed pace on weekdays, but on weekends it's mobbed like anywhere else. Ferries run to Yung Shue Wan or Sok Kwu Wan on the island.

There are several places to stay on Lamma and the cheapest is *Wing Yuen Hostel* (☎ 982 0222) at Hung Shing Ye beach where rooms are HK$160 on weekdays, or HK$330 on weekends. Right by the ferry pier in Yung Shue Wan is the *Man Lai Wah Hotel* (☎ 982 0220), where rooms on weekdays cost HK$250. There's a solid row of good seafood restaurants in Yung Shue Wan and Sok Kwu Wan. The *Corner Bar* is a lively place for nightlife, starting about 6 pm.

BEACHES

Hong Kong has many beaches both on the south side of Hong Kong Island and in the New Territories and on the outer islands. Sadly, in recent times these have become somewhat polluted. On Hong Kong Island, **Repulse Bay** is the best known beach, but others worth checking out in the summer include **Big Wave Bay** and **Shek O**.

Best beaches in the New Territories are in the east around the Sai Kung Peninsula, including **Clear Water Bay**. The 2-km long **Cheung Sha Wan** on Lantau Island is Hong Kong's longest beach, but Cheung Chau and Lamma Island also have good but small beaches.

PLACES TO STAY

The cost of accommodation is the major expense in visiting Hong Kong, although you can still get by reasonably cheaply with a little effort. There is a number of youth hostels and similarly oriented places with dormitory accommodation – many head for the guest houses which are clustered in Chungking Mansions.

The prices at guest houses are variable with supply and demand and also with the length of your stay. If you're in Hong Kong during a low-season period, or you plan to stay for an extended time, it's definitely worth bargaining over the price.

The majority of cheap accommodation is on the Kowloon side. With a few exceptions, the places on Hong Kong Island are the expensive 'international' hotels. You can, however, find some interesting cheap accommodation out on the islands or in the New Territories, at least on weekdays. At weekends, prices on the islands escalate dramatically, though you can often get cheap deals if you rent by the week or month. At the airport, there is a hotel reservation desk, but they generally only deal with the more expensive hotels.

You can get as much as a 40% discount at mid-range and luxury hotels if you book through certain travel agents. One agency which offers this service, Traveller Services (☎ 367 4127, fax 311 0387), is on the 7th Floor, 57 Peking Rd, Tsimshatsui.

Hostels

Many of the guest houses have dorm beds as well as rooms, particularly the ones that go out of their way to cater for backpackers. The *Travellers' Hostel* in Chungking Mansions is a particularly popular example but there are a couple of other popular hostels in Kowloon and a number of youth hostels which are members of the IYHF.

Victoria Hostel (☎ 312 0621), 1st Floor, 33 Hankow Rd, Tsimshatsui, is one of the nicest hostels in Hong Kong. There are several dorms. The cheaper ones have no air-con and cost HK$40; the air-con dorms are HK$51. On the 3rd floor of the same building is *Lucky Guest House* (☎ 367 0342), a very popular place with travellers. Dorm beds cost HK$38 a night.

The *International Youth Accommodation Centre* (☎ 366 3419) is on the 6th floor at 21A Lock Rd in Tsimshatsui. It's a little bit anonymous but quite easy to find, directly behind the Hyatt Hotel. It's another good information source, and beds in the air-con dorm costs HK$40.

Around the corner and not far from Chungking Mansions is the *Garden Hostel* (☎ 721 8567). It's in Mirador Mansion, 58 Nathan Rd, but it's easier to find if you enter from Mody Rd. Turn right as you come out of the main entrance to Chungking and then right at the first street (Mody Rd). On the left side of the street there is an obvious sign. Enter the stairwell and go to the 3rd floor. Accommodation costs HK$38 a night in an air-con dorm. This place is getting a bit tatty but it is certainly popular.

The *STB Hostel* (☎ 332 1073), operated by the Hong Kong Student Travel Bureau, costs HK$50 in the dorm, HK$250 to HK$300 for twins. Clean and well-managed, it's on the 2nd floor at Great Eastern Mansion, 255-261 Reclamation St, Mongkok, on the corner of Reclamation and Dundas Sts, just to the west of the Yaumati MTR station. Its chief disadvantage is that it's some distance from the Tsimshatsui area of Kowloon. From the airport, bus Nos 1A, 9 or 13 will get you there.

YHA Hostels Apart from these independent youth hostels, there is also a number of YHA places. The YHA representative is the Hong Kong Youth Hostels Association (☎ 788 1638), Room 225, Block 19, Shek Kip Mei Estate, Kowloon. The hostels are closed between 10 am and 4 pm, you must be a IYHA member to use them and lights-out is at 11 pm. If you're not already a member, the annual subscription is HK$60 in Hong Kong. The hostels are usually in remote areas and it's generally a good idea (or even required at some of the hostels) to book in advance. At some of the hostels, it's possible to camp.

Ma Wui Hall (☎ 817 5715) on top of Mt Davis on Hong Kong Island is beautifully situated, very popular and the most central of the YHA hostels. To get there, take a No 5B bus to the end of the line, walk back 100 metres and look for the YHA sign. You've then got a 20 to 30-minute climb up the hill! There are 112 beds here and the nightly cost is HK$25.

There are four other YHA hostels, but they are in remote areas of the New Territories or Outer Islands.

Sze Lok Yuen (☎ 488 8188) is on Tai Mo Shan Rd. Beds cost HK$25 and tent camping is permitted. Take the No 51 bus (Tsuen Wan

Ferry Pier-Kam Tin) at Tsuen Wan MTR station and alight at Tai Mo Shan Rd. Follow Tai Mo Shan Rd for about 45 minutes, then turn on to a small concrete path on the right-hand side which leads directly to the hostel. This is a good place from which to climb Tai Mo Shan, Hong Kong's highest peak. Because of the high elevation, it can get amazingly cold at night, so be prepared.

Wayfoong Hall is another YHA hostel. It was being rebuilt at the time this book was being researched, and didn't as yet have a telephone number. The name might also be changed in the future. The hostel is at the base of Plover Cove Reservoir on Ting Kok Rd, just a few hundred metres south of Tai Mei Tuk. Take the Kowloon-Canton Railway (KCR) train to Tai Po railway station, then take bus No 75K to Tai Mei Tuk and follow the access road (with the sea on your right side).

Pak Sha O Hostel (☎ 328 2327) charges HK$25 a bed and also permits camping. A YHA card is needed. Take bus No 92 from the Choi Hung Estate bus terminal and get off at the Sai Kung terminal. From Sai Kung, take bus No 94 towards Wong Shek Pier, but get off at Ko Tong village. From there, find Hoi Ha Rd and a road sign 30 metres ahead showing the way to Pak Sha O.

Also on the Sai Kung Peninsula is *Bradbury Hall* (☎ 328 2458), in Chek Keng. From Choi Hung Estate bus terminal, take bus No 92 to the Sai Kung terminal. From Sai Kung, take bus No 94 to Yellow Stone Pier, but get off at Pak Tam Au. There's a footpath at the side of the road leading to Chek Keng village. The hostel is right on the harbour just facing the Chek Keng Ferry Pier.

An alternative route is to take the ferry from Ma Liu Shui (adjacent to the Chinese University railway station) to Chek Keng Pier.

For more help in finding these hostels, contact the YHA.

Guest Houses
Chungking Mansions Next door to the Holiday Inn and across the road from the Hyatt on Nathan Rd, right in the centre of the

Tsimshatsui area of Kowloon, is Chungking Mansions – the magic word for cheap accommodation in Hong Kong. Down at the bottom of this multistorey block is the Chungking Arcade, a rather dumpy shopping arcade. If you wander around, you'll find a number of lifts labelled A to E and over the elevator doors are name plates for guest houses. There are lots of them and the standards vary widely. The best policy is to pick a block and try a few.

There's some concern in Hong Kong that Chungking Mansions is a potential fire risk.

In winter, they'll be less crowded than in summer and at any time of year it's worth haggling over the price, particularly if you plan a longer stay. With effort you can find a double room for less than HK$100. You pay a little more for rooms with extras such as bathrooms. Several of the guest houses specialise in catering for backpackers and have dormitories with beds for about HK$40.

Some of the places are the 'short-time' specialists – if you get an odd response it's likely that the place generally rents rooms by the hour. Others specialise in catering for visitors from India or Pakistan. If a place doesn't seem to want you, just try another! The lifts can be a real problem since there are only two of them for all 16 floors of each block. At peak times, you can have a long wait.

Walking down the steps of Chungking Mansions can be very depressing since they're extremely dirty and dismal. In between the guest houses are offices, private apartments, Indian 'club messes' (actually open to anyone and with excellent Indian food), and lots of cottage industries (such as clothes making and semi-precious-stone grinding) – it's a regular hotbed of Hong Kong enterprise.

There are far too many guest houses in Chungking Mansions to make any special recommendations. Although Chungking Mansions has a rough and ready reputation, in actual fact many of the guest houses are pleasant, friendly, well-run and spotlessly clean. The rooms may be minute but that's a reflection of the price of real estate in Hong Kong. Many places operate on several floors

or in different blocks or the same people may operate several different guest houses. The names that follow are just a few ideas to begin with.

Block A, at the front, is the block with the heaviest concentration of guest houses and here you'll find the *Travellers' Hostel* (☎ 368 7710) on the 16th floor. It's a reasonably clean and well-run place. Equally important, the noticeboard is an an excellent information source. Dorm beds cost from HK$38 while rooms range from HK$80 to HK$130. The same management also operates a cheap beach-side hostel at Ting Kau in the New Territories – enquire if interested.

Park Guest House (☎ 368 1689), 15th floor, has singles from HK$80 to HK$100 and doubles from HK$100 to HK$120. Doubles cost from HK$160 to HK$180 with bath. It's clean, has air-con and is friendly.

Moving down, there's the *New Grand* on the 14th floor and the *Ashoka Guest Houses* on the 13th. The 12th floor has the *Peking*. On the 11th floor, there's the *Lucky* with clean but small singles for HK$130. On the same floor is the *New International* which has singles with shared/private bath for HK$90/160.

Singles are HK$80 to HK$110 in the *New Asia* on the 8th floor, where you'll also find *Tom's*. The 7th floor has *Double Seven* and the popular *Welcome Guest House* which is clean and well-kept and has a variety of rooms and prices. For HK$120, you can get a tiny single room with an even tinier bathroom – you sort of stand on the toilet to shower!

The *London Guest House* (☎ 724 5000) on the 6th floor is friendly, clean and has singles from HK$85 to HK$180 with TV and air-con.

On the 4th and 5th floor, *Chungking House* (☎ 366 5362) is one of the biggest and fanciest places in Chungking Mansions. Rooms here are HK$230 per single or HK$320 per double, all with bathrooms. The single rooms are really doubles since they have a double bed. Rooms at the front have a view of the Hyatt Hotel, across the road, which is often 'better than television'!

Sky Guest House, A Block, 3rd floor, won't win any contests for cleanliness but it's one of the cheapest places in Hong Kong with dorm beds for HK$35.

That's just one of the blocks at Chungking Mansions although admittedly it's the block with the most guest houses. In B Block, the cheapest place to stay is *Friendship Travellers House* on the 6th floor, where beds are HK$35 a night. Moving slightly up-market, there's the *New Washington* on the 13th floor where clean doubles range from HK$100 to HK$160. *Harbour* on the 4th floor is clean, bright, friendly and has doubles for HK$150 with bath. Many people have good things to say about the *New Regent* on the 16th floor, where singles cost HK$110, and large, bright double rooms are HK$160.

C Block doesn't have as many places, but the big advantage is that there are seldom any queues for the lifts. It's also cleaner than the other blocks. *Tom's* on the 16th floor is clean and quiet and has singles for HK$80 and doubles for HK$120 to HK$130. *Berlin*, 14th floor, is small, comfortable and has singles/doubles for HK$70/110.

The *Garden* on the 7th floor is new and clean and charges HK$150 for a room with bath. *New Brother's*, 6th floor, is very clean and has singles for HK$120. *Centre Point Inn*, 3rd floor, is a Chungking Mansions classic with singles/doubles for HK$120/140 with shared bath.

There are some interconnecting walkways between C or E blocks and D Block. In D Block, there's the *Four Seas Guest House* on the 15th floor, the *Broadway Inn* on the 10th, *New Shanghai* on the 8th, and the friendly *Princess* on the 3rd.

E Block is another quiet backwater and seldom has queues for the lifts. Here you'll find, on the 17th floor, the *Shan-E-Punjab*. There's the *Far East Guest House* on the 14th and the up-market *Hometown* on the 10th. On the 3rd floor, you'll find a *Sheraton* – no relation to another larger Sheraton establishment further down Nathan Rd.

Take a look down the lightwells off the D block stairs for a vision of hell, Chungking Mansions at its worst.

They're dark, dirty, festooned with pipes and wires and covered in what looks like the debris of half a century. Why bother to put rubbish in the bin when it's so much easier to throw it out the window? Discarded plastic bags fall only halfway down before lodging on a ledge or drainpipe. Soon they're joined by old newspapers, used toilet paper, clothes fallen off lines, half-eaten apples, an expired rat (was it too dirty for him too?).

All manner of garbage drapes and hangs down from above. It's a horrible sight. Occasionally you're forced onto the stairs when the wait for the lift becomes too interminable. A buzzer sounds when one too many people have clambered aboard the lifts and in one of them I spotted a sign which announced, 'The Irresponsible for Accident due to Overloading'.

Other Guest Houses Guest houses aren't restricted to Chungking Mansions, although there are so many of them there. If you wander down the streets off Nathan Rd in Tsimshatsui, you'll see signs for many other guest houses. They will often be similar in character to the Chungking Mansions choices but simply not being in Chungking Mansions can be a major advantage.

A short way up Nathan Rd, at No 58, is Mirador Mansion, somewhat like a smaller and cleaner version of Chungking Mansions. The *First Class Guest House* on the 16th floor has singles starting from HK$100. The best deal seems to be the *Man Hing Lung Guest House* on the 14th, where singles with bath cost HK$90. You can also try the *Mini Hotel* on the 7th floor.

At 66-70 Nathan Rd there's Golden Crown Court with the *London, Golden Crown* and *Wah Tat* guest houses, all on the 5th floor. The Golden Crown has dorm beds for HK$40 as well as more expensive private rooms.

The very friendly *Lee Garden Guest House* (☎ 367 2284) is on the 8th Floor, D Block, 36 Cameron Rd, close to Chatham Rd. Doubles with shared/private bath cost HK$150/250.

The *Lyton Building*, 32-40 Mody Rd, has several good guest houses. *Lyton House Inn* on the ground floor is very quiet and has small but clean rooms with bath. Doubles are HK$150 but with air-con cost HK$200. On the 6th floor of the north-east block is *Tourist*

House, which has rooms with baths for HK$180.

A definitely up-market but great place to stay is the *Star Guest House* (☎ 723 8951), 6th Floor, 21 Cameron Rd. Immaculately clean rooms with bath and TV cost HK$250. The manager, Charlie Chan, is extremely helpful and friendly.

The Ys & Other Possibilities

The *YMCA International House* (☎ 771 9111), 23 Waterloo Rd, Yaumati, has some cheap rooms with shared baths for HK$125 for men only. The majority of their rooms are rented to both men and women, but these are expensive at HK$420 to HK$560. Get there on bus Nos 1A or 9 from the airport or bus Nos 7 or 7A from the Star Ferry. The Y has a Western and Chinese restaurant and the latter does very good dim sum.

The *YWCA* (☎ 713 9211) is inconveniently located near Pui Ching and Waterloo Rds in Mongkok. It's actually on Man Fuk Rd, up a hill behind a Caltex petrol station. Relatively cheap rooms for women only are HK$190. Other single rooms are HK$300, and twins cost from HK$380 to HK$410.

The Salvation Army runs a place called *Booth Lodge* (☎ 771 9266), 11 Wing Sing Lane, Yaumati, where doubles/twins are HK$374/462. Just around the corner is *Caritas Bianchi Lodge* (☎ 388 1111), 4 Cliff Rd, Yaumati, where doubles range from HK$405 to HK$465.

Hong Kong Island Guest Houses

Leishun Court, 116 Leighton Rd, Causeway Bay, is Hong Kong Island's answer to Chungking Mansions. The building houses a number of cheap guest houses, mostly on the lower floors. *Fuji House* on the 1st floor charges HK$150 for a room with bath. On the same floor is the *Villa Lisboa Hotel* and *Cannes House*.

An up-market guest house is *Noble Hostel* (☎ 576 6148) at Flat C1, 7th Floor, 37 Paterson St, Paterson Building, Causeway Bay, just above Daimaru department store. It's very clean and safe – they have locked metal gates and a security guard in the lobby.

Singles/doubles are HK$190/240 with shared bath, and HK$290 with bath – highly recommended.

A rather interesting place is the *Phoenix Apartments*, at 70 Lee Garden Hill Rd, Causeway Bay. This place houses a number of elegant and reasonably priced guest houses, but most are short-time hotels where rooms are rented by the hour. One hotel here proudly advertises 'Avoidance of Publicity & Reasonable Rates'. Nevertheless, as long as they've changed the sheets recently, it's not a bad place to stay.

The *Sunrise Inn* on the 1st floor charges HK$128 for overnight or HK$58 for two hours. Moving up-market, the *Hoi Wan Guest House*, 1st floor, Flat C has plush rooms for HK$280, but you might be able to negotiate a cheaper rate for a longer term (or shorter term).

Mid-Range Hotels

Kowloon In Hong Kong, the appellation 'mid-range' certainly doesn't mean cheap – you can pay HK$100 in a Chungking Mansions guest house or HK$250 in an up-market guest house, whereas a mid-range hotel will cost you HK$350 to HK$600. Which is still a lot cheaper than the HK$1500 a night some of the five-star places ask. Count on another 15% for service and tax, however.

You can get as much as a 40% discount at mid-range and luxury hotels if you book through certain travel agencies. An agent which offers this is *Traveller Services* (☎ 367 4127, fax 311 0387), 7th floor, 57 Peking Rd, Tsimshatsui. The *Mariner's Club* offers big discounts to sailors, in case you qualify.

Places in the mid-range category include the following:

Bangkok Royal, 2-12 Pilkem St, Yaumati (take MTR to Jordan station) has singles for HK$350, and twins from HK$410 to HK$580 (☎ 735 9181; fax 730 2209)

Imperial, 30-34 Nathan Rd, Tsimshatsui has singles from HK$500 to HK$620, and doubles/twins for HK$580/880 (☎ 366 2201; fax 311 2360)

International, 33 Cameron Rd, Tsimshatsui has singles from HK$380 to HK$680, and twins from HK$500 to HK$880 (☎ 366 3381; fax 369 5381)

King's, 473-473A Nathan Rd, Yaumati has singles for HK$340, and doubles/twins for HK$400/430 (☎ 780 1281, fax 782 1833)

Mariner's Club, 11 Middle Rd, Tsimshatsui has singles/doubles for HK$330/390 (☎ 368 8261)

Nathan, 378 Nathan Rd, Yaumati has singles for HK$550, and doubles/twins for HK$600/700 (☎ 388 5141; fax 770 4262)

Shamrock, 223 Nathan Rd, Yaumati has singles from HK$450 to HK$480, and twins from HK$520 to HK$700 (☎ 735 2271; fax 736 7354)

YMCA, 41 Salisbury Rd, Tsimshatsui has twins for HK$560 (☎ 369 2211; fax 739 9315)

Hong Kong Island In terms of mid-range hotels, there's even less available on Hong Kong Island than in Kowloon. Figure on HK$450 at the minimum. Again, check with the Student Travel Bureau or other travel agents for discounts. Some places to check out include:

Bonham, 50-54 Bonham Strand East, Sheung Wan has twins for HK$400 (☎ 544 2882; fax 544 3922)

China Merchants, 160-161 Connaught Rd West, Sheung Wan has singles from HK$560 to HK$800, and twins from HK$620 to HK$850 (☎ 559 6888; fax 559 0038)

Emerald, 152 Connaught Rd West, Sheung Wan has singles for HK$470, and doubles/twins for HK$570/690 (☎ 546 8111; fax 559 0255)

Garden View International House, 1 MacDonnell Rd, Central has twins from HK$480 to HK$580 (☎ 877 3737; fax 845 6263)

Harbour, 116-122 Gloucester Rd, Wanchai has singles from HK$460 to HK$620, and twins from HK$600 to HK$900 (☎ 574 8211; fax 572 2185)

Harbour View International, 4 Harbour Rd, Wanchai has doubles/twins for HK$560/700 (☎ 520 1111; fax 865 6063)

PLACES TO EAT

Hong Kong has just about every dining choice you can think of from McDonald's to Mexican or Sichuan to spaghetti. It's not a fantastically cheap food trip like Singapore but you can still eat well at a fairly low cost. If you're really economising, however, you might find yourself eating more Big Macs than you might have expected.

Breakfast

Starting the day with dim sum is customary with Hong Kongers, but it's easy to get a Western-style breakfast as well. There are handy little bakeries, and at breakfast time an apple or orange and a fresh bread roll or pastry makes an appetising and economical start to the day. Fruit stall prices vary but even in touristy Tsimshatsui, an apple will only cost around HK$3.

St Honore is a chain of excellent bakeries around Hong Kong with the name written only in Chinese, but you'll soon recognise their ideogram. There's one at 221 Nathan Rd, Yaumati, and a much smaller one at 1A Hanoi Rd, Tsimshatsui.

The window of the *Wing Wah Restaurant* in Tsimshatsui is always filled with great-looking cakes and pastries. It's at 21A Lock Rd, near Swindon Books and the Hyatt Regency. Either take it away or sit down with some coffee. A very similar place is the nearby *Kam Fat Restaurant* at 11 Ashley Rd.

Oliver's has two stores in Tsimshatsui: one in Ocean Centre and another at China Hong Kong City on Canton Rd, the same place where you catch the ferries to China. It's a great place for breakfast – HK$10 for bacon, eggs and toast. The sandwiches are equally excellent, though it gets crowded at lunch time.

Deep in the bowels of the MTR stations you can find *Maxim's Cake Shops*, but don't sink your teeth into the creamy delights until you're back on the street as it is prohibited to eat or drink anything in the MTR stations or on the trains – there's a HK$1000 fine if you do.

Fast fooders can head for *McDonald's* and have hot cakes or the 'big' breakfast special at HK$10.70.

Night Markets

Authentically Chinese fast food can be found at the *dai pai dongs* (street stalls) which set up at night from about 8 to 11 pm. You can get very good noodles for a couple of dollars and there's no language barrier – just point to whatever looks good. The largest night market is at the northern end of Temple St in Kowloon. A smaller night market called the *Poor Man's Nightclub*, sets up in the car park on the west side of the Macau Ferry Terminal.

Fast food

McDonald's has had quite an impact on Hong Kong and outlets have sprung up just about everywhere, so you're never too far from a burger, French fries and a shake. They're just like back home (wherever that might be), probably in part because many of the components are imported anyway. A Big Mac will set you back HK$8.90 – one of the cheapest you'll find anywhere in the world.

Burger King, Kentucky Fried Chicken, Pizza Hut and other international chains also operate in Hong Kong. The local *Maxim's* chain has a number of outlets around town – it sells burgers and similar snacks, and is not a bad place for a cheap breakfast.

Fairwood Fast Food is a Hong Kong chain, and if you don't throw up looking at the big plastic clown face on the door, it's a fine place to catch a quick meal. Prices are low and they do mixed Western and Chinese food. They have a branch at 6 Ashley Rd, Tsimshatsui.

Spaghetti House is a local restaurant chain with branches in a number of locations. In Tsimshatsui, there's one at 3B Cameron Rd, over in Wanchai there's one on the corner of Hennessy and Luard Rds, and in Central there's one at 10-12 Stanley St. They have sandwiches, pizza, spaghetti and beer at low prices.

Dim Sum

One of the most popular ways of lunching (or even breakfasting) in Hong Kong is to *yum cha*, or 'drink tea'. The name comes from the Chinese tea which is always consumed when eating dim sum. These restaurants are generally huge places with ladies circulating with trays or trolleys of dim sums.

You take your chances – pick plates of anything that looks appetising. You're issued a card which is stamped each time you choose a dish, and when you've had enough the bill is toted up from the number of

Some popular dim sum include:

har kau	淡水鲜虾饺	shrimp dumpling
shiu mai	蟹黄干蒸卖	meat dumpling
pai kwat	豉汁蒸排骨	steamed spare ribs
ngau yuk mai	干蒸牛肉卖	steamed beef balls
tsing fun kuen	鸡丝蒸粉卷	steamed shredded chicken
kai bao tsai	香菰鸡饱仔	steamed chicken bun
cha siu bau	蚝油叉烧饱	steamed barbeque pork bun
tsing ngau yuk	荷叶蒸牛肉	steamed beef ball in lotus leaf
cha chun kuen	炸鸡丝春卷	fried spring roll
wook kok	蜂巢香芋角	fried taro vegetable puff
ham sui kok	软滑咸水角	fried dumplings
fun gwor	凤城蒸粉果	steamed dumplings filled with vegetables and shrimps
daan tart	千层鸡蛋挞	custard tart
ma tai go	炸马蹄糕条	fried water chestnut sticks
ma lai go	榄仁马拉糕	steamed sponge cake
ma yung bau	蛋黄麻蓉饱	sesame sesame bun
yeh chup go	鲜奶椰汁糕	coconut pudding
shui tsung kau	雪耳水晶饺	white fungus sweet dumpling
chien tsang go	蛋黄千层糕	1000 layer sweet cake with egg yolk filling
tse chup go	爽滑蔗汁糕	sugar cane juice roll

stamps. This is a pretty economical way of eating, and it is often very crowded at lunch time when the office workers pack in. So arrive early if you want a seat and if you want the full variety of dim sum. Flip the lid over when you want the teapot refilled.

Dim sum restaurants can be difficult to locate as signs are rarely in English and will probably say something like 'Chinese Restaurant' or 'Seafood Restaurant'. This is because the same place which serves cheap dim sum by day is transformed at night into an expensive Cantonese restaurant.

Try along Nathan Rd in Kowloon or Queens Rd in Central. There are also many in Causeway Bay. On Hong Kong Island, you could try *Asiania*, 1st Floor, Asian House, 1 Hennessy Rd, Wanchai; *Diamond Restaurant* at 265-75 Des Voeux Rd, Central; or *Broadway Seafood Restaurant*, Hay Wah Building, 73-85B Hennessy Rd, Wanchai.

Dim sum is also served at the *Jade Garden Restaurant*, which has premises on the 1st Floor, Swire House, 9-25 Chater Rd, Central; and at Shop 5, Lower Ground Floor, Jardine House, 1 Connaught Place, Central.

Other Hong Kong Island dim sum places include:

Ruby, 1st Floor, Hong Kong Mansions, 1 Yee Wo St, Causeway Bay
Tai Woo, 15-19 Wellington St, Central
Tsui Hang Village, 2nd Floor, New World Tower, 16-18 Queen's Rd, Central
Tung Yuen Seafood, 3rd Floor, Tai Yau Building, 181 Johnston Rd, Wanchai
Victoria City Seafood, 2D, Sun Hung Kai Centre, 30 Harbour Rd, Wanchai.

In Kowloon, dim sum is served at:

Canton Court, Guangdong Hotel, 18 Prat Ave, Tsimshatsui
Dragon Feast Seafood, 5th Floor, Lifung Tower, China Hong Kong City, 33 Canton Rd, Tsimshatsui
Fook Follow, UG2, Chinachem Golden Plaza, 77 Mody Rd, Tsimshatsui East
Harbour View Seafood, 3rd Floor, Tsimshatsui Centre, 66 Mody Rd, Tsimshatsui East
Heichinrou Restaurant, 2nd Floor, Sun Plaza, 28 Canton Rd, Tsimshatsui

International, 3rd Floor, Good Hope Building, 612 Nathan Rd, Mongkok
Jade Garden, 4th Floor, Star House, 3 Salisbury Rd, Tsimshatsui.

Dim sum is also a popular way of having a long, leisurely Sunday brunch.

Other Chinese Restaurants

In the evening, the dim sum disappears and the same restaurants roll out more expensive Cantonese fare such as pigeon, snake and shark's fin soup. But Cantonese cuisine is not the only Chinese food around. If you like lots of dumplings, steamed bread, duck and noodles, try Beijing (Peking) food. Some Beijing-style restaurants include: *Beijing Restaurant*, 34-36 Granville Rd, Tsimshatsui; and the *Peking Garden*, 3rd Floor, Star House, 3 Salisbury Rd.

In Causeway Bay, *Food Street* is an artificial restaurant centre with a variety of places to eat. It may be a bit plastic but some of the restaurants are quite good.

The heavier and oilier cuisine of Shanghai can be sampled in Kowloon at *Great Shanghai*, 26 Prat Ave, Tsimshatsui.

Lotus Pond (☎ 730 8688), Shop 007, Ground Floor, Phase IV, Harbour City, 15 Canton Rd, Tsimshatsui, serves the type of spicy Sichuan (Szechuan) dish which brings tears to the eyes.

Vegetarian Restaurants

There are some good vegetarian places around like the traditional *Wishful Cottage* at 336 Lockhart Rd in Causeway Bay. There are several *Bodhi* vegetarian restaurants including one at 56 Cameron Rd in Tsimshatsui on the Kowloon side and one at 388 Lockhart Rd in Causeway Bay on Hong Kong side.

Another vegetarian restaurant in Kowloon is the *Pak Bo Vegetarian Kitchen* at 106 Austin Rd, Yaumati. Over in Causeway Bay, on Hong Kong side, *Vegi Food Restaurant* is at 8 Cleveland St, next to Food St.

Other Asian Cuisines

For good cheap subcontinent curries,

Chungking Mansions has some excellent Indian and Pakistani 'messes' between floors and a couple of bargain-priced ground floor places. At *Kashmir Fast Food* or *Lahore Fast Food* in the arcade, you can get curried mutton or chicken with rice and chapattis for HK$20, and they start serving it out from early in the morning...if curry for breakfast is your ticket.

Upstairs in Chungking Mansions are many other places with better food and a more pleasant atmosphere. Prices are still low, with set meals from HK$28 to HK$35. Highly rated by travellers is *Kashmir Club* (☎ 311 6308), 3rd Floor, A Block. The *Taj Mahal Club Mess* (☎ 722 5454), 3rd Floor, B Block is pleasantly air-con and comfortable, plus the food is superb. On the 6th floor of B Block is the highly recommended *Centre Point Club* (☎ 366 1086). Yet another cheap, good place is the *Delhi Club Mess* (☎ 368 1682) on the 3rd floor of C Block.

Behind Chungking Mansions, at 8 Minden Ave, is *Woodlands*, a name which is synonymous with south Indian vegetarian food on the subcontinent. Go there to get your fingers into a good thali.

Over in Central, *Club Sri Lanka* in the basement of 17 Hollywood Rd (almost at the Wyndham St end) has great Sri Lankan curries and their fixed price all-you-can-eat deal is a wonderful bargain. *Siddhartha Club* at 57 Wyndham St has good Indian food, as does the *Ashoka* next door.

There are a number of good Indonesian places like *Indonesia Padang Restaurant*, 85 Percival St, Causeway Bay.

With the Philippines so near, it's hardly surprising there are some good Filipino places around like the *Mabuhay Restaurant*, 11 Minden Ave, Tsimshatsui.

Vietnamese immigrants flooded into Hong Kong after the end of the Vietnam War and brought their cuisine with them. There are several good places on Hillwood Rd in Kowloon. On the Hong Kong side, you could try the small *Saigon Beach Restaurant* at 66 Lockhart Rd in Wanchai.

Korean, Singaporean, Malaysian, Japanese, Burmese and other regional cooking styles are also well represented in Hong Kong but Thai food has become the cuisine of the moment with some good places to try both in Kowloon and on Hong Kong Island. A reasonably priced, good Thai restaurant is *Royal Pattaya*, 9 Minden Ave, Tsimshatsui. Also good is *Sawadee*, 1 Hillwood Rd, Tsimshatsui.

Some of the most authentic and cheapest Thai food can be found out at the airport. If you're flying out at night, it's worth checking in early and eating here before you depart. That is so long as you like your Thai food hot – at *Thai Wah* they spell HOT with capital letters. To get there, take the footbridge from the terminal over the highway to the Regal Meridien Airport Hotel. Go through the hotel and out the back, turn left and at the corner take Kai Tak Rd, which bends back. Thai Wah, at No 24, is so popular it often spills out onto the pavement where you can sit and watch the 747s whistle in just overhead.

Set Meals & Western Food

Numerous places offer set meals at lunch time or in the evening where you can get a soup, main course, dessert and coffee at a knock-down price. *Singapore Restaurant*, 23 Ashley Rd, Tsimshatsui, is a great bargain: excellent Malaysian, Chinese and Western food costs about HK$45 for a set dinner. You might have to queue to get in.

In Tsimshatsui, *Rick's Cafe*, downstairs at 4 Hart Ave, has oddly named sandwiches and Mexican snacks.

At 7B Hanoi Rd, the *New Marseille* is good value with French and Chinese food and an inexpensive set dinner.

At the big hotels, the buffets on offer at breakfast and lunch time can be a good deal if you're very hungry. The *Holiday Inn* on Nathan Rd in Tsimshatsui is pretty good, and the *Hilton* on the Hong Kong side, just below the bottom station for the Peak Tram, has a highly regarded buffet. You could try the rotating restaurant atop the *Furama Kempinski Hotel* for a real splurge – it has terrific views and a not-too-expensive buffet.

Apart from the chain of *Spaghetti House* restaurants (see Fast Food) there are also several good Italian restaurants. On Kowloon side, you could try *La Taverna*, at 36-38 Ashley Rd in Tsimshatsui, or on Hong Kong side there's the pleasantly relaxed *Rigoletto's* at 16 Fenwick St in Wanchai.

Pubs

A number of the bars and pubs mentioned in the following Entertainment section have good food. They can be excellent places for a quiet break at lunch time. *Mad Dogs* at 33 Wyndham St in Central has good British-style pub food including pies and pasties for around HK$45 or sandwiches with salad and French fries. The *Jockey Pub*, Swire House, 11 Chater Rd, also has excellent sandwiches for HK$30 or so.

The *White Stag*, at 72 Canton Rd in Tsimshatsui, and the various Aussie pubs also have pretty reasonable food.

Down the block from the Siddhartha Club, at No 31C Wyndham St, Central, is a tapas bar called *La Bodega*.

ENTERTAINMENT
Pubs & Bars

Apart from a scattering of girlie bars, topless bars, hostess bars and god-knows-what-else bars around Tsimshatsui and Wanchai, Hong Kong also has lots of straightforward places where you can get a reasonably priced beer in pleasant surroundings. Many of them are English or Australian in flavour.

A beer typically costs HK$25 in these bars but in the early evening 'happy hours' you can get drinks at half price or two for the price of one. At some big hotels not only are the drinks cheap but there are lots of snacks and nibbles on offer under the heading of 'small chow'.

Try the very popular *Ned Kelly's Last Stand* at 11A Ashley Rd in Kowloon. There's live jazz there most nights of the week and the food is pretty good. Other places for a cold Fosters in Kowloon include *Kangaroo Pub* at 11A Chatham Rd, and *Harry's Bar* at 6-8A Prat Ave.

British-style pubs on the Kowloon side include the *Blacksmith's Arms* at 16 Minden Ave, and the *White Stag* at 72 Canton Rd.

Fancy a German beer? Then head to the *Biergarten* at 8 Hanoi Rd in the same area. A friendly atmosphere can be found at *Friar Tuck*, Room 053, World Shipping Centre, Harbour City, 7 Canton Rd, Tsimshatsui.

Over on Hong Kong Island there are dozens of great places. For good beer, visit *Schnurrbart* in the Winner Building on D'Aguilar St, Central. *Joe Bananas*, 23 Luard Rd, Wanchai, has become a trendy nightspot and has no admission charge – you may have to queue to get in. Happy hour is from 11.30 am until 9 pm when the disco party gets started. *DD II*, 38-44 D'Aguilar St, Central, is a trendy disco which is open from 10 pm to 4 am.

Wanchai also has lots of bars, although many of them are of the topless variety. That still leaves plenty of straightforward pubs. Also in Wanchai at 54 Jaffe Rd, just west of Fenwick Rd, is the *Wanchai Folk Club* (also called *The Wanch*), a very pleasant little folk-music pub with beer and wine at regular prices.

If you want to spend more – well, you can lay out twice as much for a beer in the big hotel bars, or head for the topless bars around Wanchai or Tsimshatsui East. Or, you can simply go up the Peak for a free view of the nightlife down below. And don't forget you can always head for a cinema.

Chinese Zodiac

If you want to know your sign in the Chinese Zodiac, look up your year of birth in the chart. Remember Chinese New Year usually falls in February, so January will be included in the year before.

snake	1929	1941	1953	1965	1977	1989
horse	1930	1942	1954	1966	1978	1990
sheep	1931	1943	1955	1967	1979	1991
monkey	1932	1944	1956	1968	1980	1992
cock	1933	1945	1957	1969	1981	1993
dog	1934	1946	1958	1970	1982	1994
pig	1935	1947	1959	1971	1983	1995
rat	1936	1948	1960	1972	1984	1996
ox	1937	1949	1961	1973	1985	1997
tiger	1938	1950	1962	1974	1986	1998
rabbit	1939	1951	1963	1975	1987	1999
dragon	1940	1952	1964	1976	1988	2000

Indonesia

Indonesia is a long chain of tropical islands offering a mixture of cultures, people, scenery, prospects, problems and aspirations unmatched in South-East Asia. For the budget traveller, Indonesia is a kaleidoscope of cheap food, adventurous travel and every sort of attraction – the tropical paradise of Bali, the untouched wilderness of Sumatra, the historical monuments of Yogyakarta, with the unbelievable squalor of Jakarta thrown in to leaven the mix.

Facts about the Country

HISTORY

It is generally believed that the earliest inhabitants of the Indonesian Archipelago came from India or Burma (Myanmar), while later migrants, known as 'Malays', came from southern China and Indochina. This second group is believed to have populated the archipelago gradually over several thousand years.

Powerful kingdoms began to appear in Java and Sumatra towards the end of the 7th century. The Buddhist Srivijaya Empire ruled south Sumatra and much of the Malay Peninsula for six centuries, whilst the Hindu Mataram Kingdom presided over Java. The two developed side by side as both rivals and partners and, between them, raised inspiring monuments like Borobudur.

The last important kingdom to remain Hindu was the Java-based Majapahit, founded in the 13th century. It reached its peak under the Prime Minister Gajah Mada, and although it is reputed to have ruled over a vast area of the archipelago, it probably controlled only Java, Bali and the island of Madura, off Java's north coast.

The spread of Islam into the archipelago spelt the end of the Majapahits – satellite kingdoms took on the new religion and declared themselves independent of the Majapahits. But unlike the fanatical brand exported initially by the Arabs, the Islamic religion was considerably mellowed by the time of its arrival in Java. The Majapahits retreated to Bali in the 15th century to found a flourishing culture while Java split into separate sultanates.

By the 15th century, a strong Muslim empire had developed with its centre at Melaka (Malacca) on the Malay Peninsula, but in 1511 it fell to the Portuguese and the period of European influence in the archipelago began. The Portuguese were soon displaced by the Dutch who began to take over Indonesia in the early 1600s. A British attempt to oust the Dutch in 1619 failed – Melaka fell to the Dutch in 1641 and by 1700 they dominated most of Indonesia by virtue of their supremacy at sea and control of the trade routes and some important ports. By the middle of the 18th century, all of Java was under their control.

The Napoleonic Wars led to a temporary British takeover between 1811 and 1816 in response to the French occupation of Holland, and Java came under the command of Sir Stamford Raffles.

Indonesia was eventually handed back to the Dutch after the cessation of the wars in Europe, and an agreement made whereby the English evacuated their settlements in Indonesia in return for the Dutch leaving India and the Malay Peninsula.

But whilst the Europeans may have settled their differences, the Indonesians were of a different mind – for five years from 1825 onwards the Dutch had to put down a revolt led by the Javanese Prince Diponegoro. It was not until the early 20th century that the Dutch brought the whole of the archipelago – including Aceh and Bali – under control.

Although Dutch rule was softened during this century, dissatisfaction still simmered and a strong nationalist movement – whose foremost leader was Sukarno – developed despite Dutch attempts to suppress it. The

Japanese occupied the archipelago during WW II and, after their defeat, the Dutch returned and tried to take back control of their old territories. For four bitter years, from 1945 until 1949, the Indonesians fought an intermittent war with the Dutch and, in the end, the Dutch were forced to recognise Indonesia's independence.

Weakened by the prolonged struggle and without the government structure bequeathed to British colonies, the transition to independence did not come easily. The first 10 years of independence saw the Indonesian politicians preoccupied with their own political games until, in 1957, President Sukarno put an end to the impasse by declaring 'Guided Democracy' and investing more power in himself. Sukarno proved to be less adept as a nation-builder than as a revolutionary leader. Grandiose building projects, the planned 'socialisation' of the economy and a senseless confrontation with Malaysia, led to internal dissension and a steady deterioration in the national economy.

As events came to a head, there was an attempted coup in 1965 led by an officer of Sukarno's palace guard, and several of Indonesia's top army generals were killed. The coup was suppressed by the Indonesian army under the leadership of General Suharto. The reasons for the coup are unclear but it was passed off as an attempt by the Communists to seize power and thousands of Communists, suspected Communists and sympathisers were killed or imprisoned.

Suharto eventually pushed Sukarno out of power and took over the presidency himself. In stark contrast to the turbulent Sukarno years, things have, on the whole, been more stable under Suharto.

The invasion of Portuguese Timor, in 1975, stands as much to Australia's discredit as Indonesia's, and it's surely no coincidence that Henry Kissinger left Jakarta the day before the invasion. Recently, Indonesia has shown signs of coming to grips with its internal economic problems and some of the worse excesses have been curbed.

Large oil exports and other substantial natural resources seem to offer the promise of better days but graft and corruption are still very much a way of life. While some people get very rich, the lot of the average Indonesian, particularly in parts of over-crowded Java, is very hard.

GEOGRAPHY

Indonesia has an area of 1,475,000 sq km scattered over about 13,700 islands. It is a far less compact mass of islands than the nearby Philippines, the other island nation of the region. Indonesia stretches far north of the equator in Sumatra, Sulawesi and Kalimantan – all of which straddle it. Parts of Indonesia are still vast, barely explored regions of dense jungle and many islands have extinct, active or dormant volcanoes.

CLIMATE

Draped over the equator, Indonesia is hot year round – hot and wet during the wet

season, and hot and dry during the dry season. Coastal areas are often pleasantly cool, however, and it can get extremely cold in the mountains. Generally, the wet season starts later the further south-east you go. In north Sumatra, the rain begins to fall in September but in Timor, it doesn't fall until November. Sumatran seasons have been fairly described as the wet and the wetter. The wet seasons are roughly: Sumatra, September to March; Java, October to April; and Bali & south, November to May.

In January and February, it can rain often, and an umbrella is an excellent item to have stuffed in your backpack. The odd islands out are Maluku (the Moluccas) where seasons are the reverse. The dry season in Maluku is September to March; the wet season is from the beginning of April to the end of August.

GOVERNMENT

Executive power rests with the president, who is head of state and holds power for a period of five years. Officially, the highest authority lies with the People's Consultative Congress (MPR) which sits at least every five years and is responsible for electing the president. The congress is made up of all members of the House of Representatives (which sits once a year) along with those appointed by the president to represent various groups and regions. Technically, the president is responsible only to the MPR, which elects him and his vice-president. The president appoints ministers to his cabinet and they are responsible only to him.

Party politics, what there is of it, continues under the one group and two-party system devised by Suharto in the early 1970s. This involves the government-run Golkar, which is technically not a political party, the Muslim United Development Party (PPP) and the Indonesian Democratic Party (PDI). Distinctions between the parties are deliberately being blurred.

The enforced acceptance of the Pancalisa (Five Principles) Democracy as the sole philosophical base for all political, social and religious organisations is also aimed partly at diffusing and suppressing dissent. The five principles are: Faith in God, Humanity, Nationalism, Representative Government and Social Justice.

ECONOMY

Indonesia still has a basically rural subsistence economy but it has large mineral resources which it is only now starting to tap. It has good oil reserves, although a unique combination of corruption and inefficiency allowed the huge Pertamina conglomerate to go bankrupt in the 1970s!

The fortunate combination of fertility and rainfall allows Indonesia to approach self-sufficiency in food production but, often, the food potential isn't where the population is, and every year the population increases.

POPULATION & PEOPLE

Indonesia is the fifth most populous country in the world. The population is around 160 million and fully 60% are crammed into just 7% of the nation's land area – the island of Java. The people are of the Malay race, although there are many different groupings and a vast number of local dialects.

RELIGION

Nominally a Muslim nation, there is actually an amazing diversity of religions and a commendable degree of religious tolerance. From the time of the Dutch, pockets of Christianity have continued to exist – in the islands of Timor and Flores, the Lake Toba region of north Sumatra and the Tanatoraja area of Sulawesi for example. At one time, Sumatra was predominantly Buddhist and Java predominantly Hindu – this was before the spread of Islam and its eventual dominance in the region. The last remnants of Hinduism are found in Bali.

LANGUAGE

Although there are a vast number of local languages and dialects in the country, Bahasa Indonesia, which is all but identical to Malay, is actively promoted as the one national language.

Like most languages, Indonesian has its

simplified colloquial form and its more developed literate language. For the visitor who wants to pick up enough to get by in the common language, *pasar*, or market Indonesian, is very easy to learn. It's rated as one of the simplest languages in the world as there are no tenses, no genders and often one word can convey the meaning of a whole sentence. There are often no plurals or it is only necessary to say the word twice – child is *anak*, children are *anak anak* or *anak 2*. Book is *buku*, and books are *buku 2*.

With other words, the context makes it clear that it's plural. It can also be a delightfully poetic language with words like *mata hari*, or 'sun', derived from *mata* (eye) and *hari* (day), so the sun is literally the eye of the day.

Lonely Planet's *Indonesian Phrasebook* is a pocket-size introduction to the language intended to make getting by in Bahasa as easy as possible.

Greetings & Civilities

excuse me
  permisi
good morning
  selamat pagi
good day
  selamat siang
good afternoon/evening
  selamat sore
good night
  selamat malam
goodbye (to person staying)
  selamat tinggal
goodbye (to person going)
  selamat jalan
How are you?
  apa kabar?
I'm fine
  kabar baik
please
  silakan
sorry
  ma'af
thank you
  terima kasih
    (very much)
      (banyak)

What is your name?
  siapa nama anda?
My name is....
  nama saya....

Getting Around

How many km?
  berapa kilometres?
I want to go to....
  saya mau ke....
Where is?
  dimana ada?
bus
  bis
ship
  kapal
ticket
  karcis
train
  kereta-api

Useful Words & Phrases

How much (money)?
  berapa (harga)?
I don't understand
  saya tidak mengerti
What is this?
  apa ini?
bank
  bank
expensive
  mahal
post office
  Kantor Pos
street
  jalan
toilet
  WC ('way say') or kamar kecil

Days of the Week

Monday	*Hari Senen*
Tuesday	*Hari Selasa*
Wednesday	*Hari Rabu*
Thursday	*Hari Kamis*
Friday	*Hari Jumat*
Saturday	*Hari Sabtu*
Sunday	*Hari Minggu*

Numbers

½	*setengah*
	(say 'stenger')
1	*satu*
2	*dua*
3	*tiga*
4	*empat*
5	*lima*
6	*enam*
7	*tujuh*
8	*delapan*
9	*sembilan*
10	*sepuluh*
12	*duabelas*
20	*duapuluh*
21	*duapuluh satu*
30	*tigapuluh*
50	*limapuluh*
100	*seratus*
1000	*seribu*

Facts for the Visitor

VISAS & EMBASSIES

Visitors from most Western countries can enter Indonesia without a visa, for a stay of up to two months, so long as they enter and exit through certain recognised airports or seaports. Officially (but not always in practice), you must have a ticket out of the country when you arrive. Officially (and almost certainly), you cannot extend your visa beyond two months. If you're really intending to explore Indonesia in some depth, then two months is inadequate and you will have to exit the country and re-enter.

One possibility is to start from north Sumatra and travel down to Palembang, then exit to Tanjung Pinang and Singapore for rest and refreshment. From there, you can start with a fresh two months and continue to Java and Bali. Which still leaves Nusa Tenggara and the outer islands to worry about!

The 'ticket out' requirements seem to be less strictly enforced these days. If you fly in to Kupang from Darwin, or take the ferry to Batam from Singapore, it's unlikely that any great fuss will be made. In Kupang, they may

ask to see a wad of travellers' cheques but Batam is a breeze. In the more 'normal' entry points, like Bali or Jakarta, they may still ask to see a ticket but most Bali visitors are on short-stay package trips, so you're unlikely to be troubled.

If you want a simple solution, the Malaysian Airline System (MAS) flight between Medan and Penang is straightforward, reasonably cheap and able to be refunded if you don't use it. The various flights between Jakarta and Singapore are also safe bets.

The real problem with the visa-free entry system is for that tiny minority of travellers who plan to arrive or depart through an unrecognised 'gateway'. Jayapura, for travellers to or from Papua New Guinea, is the most likely trouble spot. If you fall into that category then you have to get an Indonesian visa before arriving and visas are only valid for one month, not two months as for visa-free entry. Extending a one-month visa involves paying the expensive old 'landing tax' which currently seems to cost around 50,000 rp.

The recognised 'no visa' entry and exit points are:

Bali
Ngurah Rai Airport, Denpasar
Benoa & Padangbai Seaports
Irian Jaya
Frans Kaisiepo Airport, Biak
Java
Soekarno-Hatta Airport & Tanjung Priok Seaport, Jakarta
Juanda Airport & Tanjung Perak Seaport, Surabaya
Tanjung Emas Seaport, Semarang
Kalimantan
Sepinggan Airport, Balikpapan
Soepadio Airport, Pontianak
Maluku
Pattimura Airport & Yos Sudarso Seaport, Ambon
Nusa Tenggara
El Tari Airport, Kupang, Timor
Riau Archipelago
Tanjung Pinang Seaport, Bintan Island
Simpang Tiga Airport, Pakanbaru
Tabing Airport, Padang
Sulawesi
Sam Ratulangi Airport & Bitung Seaport, Manado

Sumatra
   Polonia Airport & Belawan Seaport, Medan
   Batu Besar Airport, Sekupang Seaport & Batu
   Ampar Seaport, Batam Island

The list of approved gateways changes with some frequency, so if you're planning an odd entry or exit find out the latest story. Finally, check your passport expiry date. Indonesia requires that your passport has six months life left in it on your date of arrival.

Indonesian Embassies

Countries with diplomatic relations with Indonesia will generally have their consular offices in Jakarta, the capital. Indonesian embassies, consulates and diplomatic offices in the region include:

Hong Kong
   Consulate-General, 127-129 Leighton Rd,
   Causeway Bay, Hong Kong (☎ 5 7904421/8)
Malaysia
   Embassy, Jalan Pekeliling 233, Kuala Lumpur
   (☎ 421011, 421141, 421228)
   Consulate, 37 Northam Rd, Penang (☎ 25162/
   3/4/8)
   Consulate, Jalan Sagunting 1, Kota Kinabalu,
   Sabah (☎ 54100, 54245, 55110)
Philippines
   Embassy, 185/187 Salcedo St, Legaspi Village,
   Makati, Manila (☎ 285 5061 to 68, 88 0301 to
   07)
Singapore
   Embassy, Wisma Indonesia, 435 Orchard Rd,
   Singapore (☎ 737 7422)
Thailand
   Embassy, 600-602 Petchburi Rd, Bangkok
   (☎ 252 3135/40)

Visit Indonesia Year & Longer Visas

Visit Indonesia Year took place in 1991 and it was regularly rumoured throughout the year that one of the promotional features would be an extension of the entry period from two months to three.

Lots of travellers, fed up with the expense of exiting Indonesia and coming back for more (I met one visitor who flew out from Kupang to Darwin and came back on the same flight!), were certain a three-month stay would finally happen. It didn't. Painting 'Visit Indonesia Year' on the side of Garuda aircraft, closing many museums for much of the year to refurbish them and generally putting up prices seemed to be the limit of Visit Indonesia Year ideas.

MONEY
Currency

The Indonesian *rupiah* is characterised by periods of stability punctuated by sudden devaluations. Afterwards, prices for visitors are initially much lower but they soon drift back towards predevaluation levels. In areas with many tourists, like Bali, even quite modest places quote prices in US$ these days. Or, alternatively, they simply decide, 'this is a US$5 hotel room so if the rate is 2000 rp to the dollar then it costs 10,000 rp but if the rate slips towards 2500 rp then we'll make it 12,500 rp'.

Reflecting this attitude many prices in this edition are also quoted in US$. If there should be another sudden devaluation, the dollar price may be closer to reality than the rupiah price.

US dollars are easily the most widely accepted foreign currency and often have a better exchange rate than other currencies – this is especially so outside of Jakarta. If you're going to be in really remote regions, carry sufficient cash with you as banks may be scarce. Even those you do come across may only accept certain varieties of travellers' cheques – stick to the major companies.

On the whole, changing money and travellers' cheques is a lot easier than it was a few years ago – notably in the islands of Nusa Tenggara where there are now more banks changing more varieties of cash and cheques. Dutch travellers can cash their giros (*girobetaalkaarten*) at all major post offices for up to 75,000 rp.

Exchange rates tend to vary a bit from bank to bank – shop around. Bank Bumi Daya gives the best rates all over Java according to one amateur banking expert. The rates also tend to vary between cities – Jakarta and Yogya seem to have better rates than Surabaya for example. In some remote regions, the rate can be terrible – or there may be no banks at all!

There are moneychangers in many locales and they're open longer hours and change money (cash or cheques) much faster than in the banks. In places like Bali, they offer extremely competitive rates.

Once you get well off the beaten track you'll discover, as in many other Asian countries, that there is a permanent shortage of small change and torn or dirty bank notes are not wanted! If you get stuck with any, don't cause hassles by complaining, just wait until you get to a big city or bank.

Exchange Rates

A$1	=	1558 rp
C$1	=	1738 rp
NZ$1	=	1148 rp
US$1	=	1964 rp
UK£1	=	3378 rp

Costs

Indonesian costs are very variable – similar places to stay can be four times as expensive in some places (like Irian Jaya) than in others (like Bali). So what it costs you depends on where you go. If you follow the well-beaten tourist track through Bali, Java and Sumatra, you may well find Indonesia one of the cheapest places in the region. Travellers' centres like Bali, Yogyakarta and Lake Toba are superb value for accommodation and food.

Indonesia has the cheapest fuel prices in the region, indeed it's cheap by any standards at around 450 rp a litre (about US$0.25 a US gallon), so transport costs are also pleasantly low, particularly if you've got your own motorbike to travel around on. Fuel prices are pretty much the same right throughout Indonesia, and only in really remote places (like the interior of Irian Jaya) do prices skyrocket.

TOURIST OFFICES

The Indonesian tourist office is the poorest in South-East Asia in terms of the utility of the information it offers to visitors. They have nothing apart from the odd brochure and not even many offices around the country.

The Indonesia National Tourist Organization does produce a *Calendar of Events* for the entire country and a useful *Indonesia Tourist Map* booklet which includes some good maps and helpful travel information. They're available from the Directorate General of Tourism office at Jalan Kramat Raya 81, Jakarta, where you should be able to get brochures on all tourist destinations.

Some of the regional offices produce local information or useful items such as the festival calendar available from the office in Denpasar, Bali. The Jakarta office, in the Jakarta Theatre Building on Jalan Thamrin (next to the Sarinah department store) is fairly helpful. There are other regional offices, as in north Sumatra or Yogyakarta, plus an excellent independent tourist office in Ubud, Bali. The usefulness of individual tourist offices in Indonesia often depends on who works there.

BUSINESS HOURS & HOLIDAYS

Most government offices are open Monday to Thursday from 8 am to 3 pm, Friday from 8 to 11.30 am, and Saturday from 8 am to 2 pm. Private business offices have staggered hours; Monday to Friday from 8 am to 4 pm or 9 am to 5 pm, with a break in the middle of the day. Some offices are also open on Saturday mornings till 12 noon. Banks are open Monday to Friday from 8 am to 12 noon (sometimes until 2 pm), and on Saturday mornings.

Shops tend to open about 8 am and stay open until around 9 pm. Sunday is a public holiday but some shops and many airline offices open for at least part of the day.

As most Indonesians are Muslims, many holidays and festivals are associated with the Islamic religion.

Ramadan (Bulan Puasa) – The traditional Muslim month of daily fasting from sunrise to sunset. Many restaurants shut down during the day.

Lebaran (Idul Fitri) – This marks the end of Ramadan and is a noisy celebration at the end of a month of gastric austerity. It is a national public holiday of two days in duration.

Kartini Day – This falls on 21 April and commemorates the birthday of Raden Ajeng Kartini. She was an early nationalist and Indonesia's first woman emancipationist.

Independence Day (Hari Proklamasi Kemerdekaan) – On 17 August 1945, Sukarno proclaimed Indonesian independence in Jakarta. It is a national public holiday.

Christmas Day & New Year's Day – These are national public holidays.

POST & TELECOMMUNICATIONS

Post

The postal service in Indonesia is generally good and the poste restantes at Indonesian *kantor pos* (post offices) – at least in the major travellers' centres like Jakarta, Yogya, Bali, Medan and Lake Toba – are efficiently run. Expected mail always seems to arrive.

Overseas parcels can be posted, insured and registered *(tercatat)* from a main post office but they'll usually want to have a look at the contents first so there's not much point in making up a tidy parcel before you get there. If you are going on to Singapore, postage is cheaper from there.

Telephone

The phone system has become much more efficient in recent years. International calls are easy to make from Wartel (Warung Telekomunikasi) offices which have sprung up all over the country. Many Wartels have card phones where you can directly dial overseas calls.

Direct Home Phones (press one button to get through to your home country operator) can be found in the Hotel Indonesia, President Hotel and Mid Plaza in Jakarta; at the international terminal in Denpasar Airport and at the Hotel Putri Bali and Hotel Bali Beach in Bali; and at the airport at Yogyakarta.

TIME

There are three time zones in Indonesia. Sumatra, Java, west and central Kalimantan are on West Indonesian Time which is seven hours ahead of GMT. Bali, Nusa Tenggara, south and east Kalimantan and Sulawesi are on Central Indonesian Time which is eight hours ahead of GMT. Irian Jaya and Maluku are on East Indonesian Time which is nine hours ahead of GMT.

Allowing for variations due to daylight saving, when it is 12 noon in Jakarta, it is 1 pm in Ujung Pandang, 2 pm in Jayapura, 5 am in London, 3 pm in Melbourne or Sydney, midnight in New York and 9 pm the previous day in Los Angeles.

BOOKS & MAPS

For more detailed information on the whole archipelago or just on Bali and neighbouring Lombok, look for the Lonely Planet guidebooks *Indonesia – a travel survival kit* and *Bali & Lombok – a travel survival kit*. For an introduction to the country, read *Indonesia* by Bruce Grant, *Indonesia since Sukarno* by Peter Polomka and *Suharto's Indonesia* by Hamish McDonald. The first two are available in Penguin paperbacks; the third was published by Fontana in 1980. *Sukarno – An Autobiography*, as related to Cindy Adams, captures the charisma and ego of the man.

The award-winning Australian novel *The Year of Living Dangerously* by Christopher Koch is an evocative reconstruction of life in Jakarta during the final chaotic months of the Sukarno period.

Twilight in Jakarta by the Indonesian journalist Mochtar Lubis is an outspoken condemnation of political corruption and one of the best documents of life in the capital, particularly of Jakarta's lower depths – the prostitutes, becak drivers and rural immigrants. Lubis has twice been imprisoned for his political convictions and the book goes on and off the ban list – at present the Oxford in Asia paperback is on sale in Jakarta.

Oxford in Asia have a number of other books on Indonesian subjects. *Indonesia, Between Myth & Reality* by Lee Khoon Choy is an excellent compilation of some of the intriguing religious, social and mystical customs of Indonesia; it is published by Federal Publications, Singapore.

Locally produced maps are often surprisingly inaccurate. The Nelles Verlag map series covers most of Indonesia in a number of separate sheets, and they're usually quite good.

MEDIA

Daily English-language newspapers are the *Indonesian Observer*, the *Jakarta Post*, the *Indonesian Times* (published in Jakarta) and the *Surabaya Post*. While these are subject to the same 'self-censorship' as Indonesian-language publications, they do, however, manage to tell you quite a lot about Indonesia − and the rest of the world − in a roundabout way.

Time and *Newsweek* are readily available in Indonesia but are sometimes bizarrely censored.

FILM & PHOTOGRAPHY

Indonesia is an incredible country to photograph, and you can whip through large quantities of film. All brands of film commonly used in the West, such as Kodak, Fuji and Agfa, are available in Indonesia but their cost is usually higher. If you're entering from Singapore, stock up on film there as it's much cheaper.

Shoot early or late. From 10 am to 1 or 2 pm, the sun is uncomfortably hot and high overhead, and you're likely to get a bluish washed-out look to your pictures. Those lush-green rice paddies come up best if back-lit by the sun.

Be careful of what you photograph in Indonesia − they're touchy about places of military importance and this can include airports (like the one at Malang in Java which is an air-force base that also handles civilian flights).

HEALTH

If you do need a doctor or other medical help, your embassy or consulate should be able to recommend someone, as should offices of foreign companies in places where large expatriate communities work − Balikpapan for instance. In the towns and cities, there seems to be a fair supply of doctors and dentists to choose from. A doctor in Bahasa is *dokter* and a dentist is *dokter gigi*. In the outback places like Irian Jaya, there are clinics set up by the missionaries. There are also public hospitals *(rumah sakit)* in the cities and towns.

Indonesia is hot! It's easy to dehydrate if you don't keep up your fluid intake, which is why it's a good idea to carry a water bottle with you. The Indonesian sun is bright and good sunglasses are a must. Sunburn is also a problem (particularly with people just off the plane in Denpasar who can't wait to hit the beach). Bring something to cover your head.

DANGERS & ANNOYANCES

Having valuables like your passport and/or travellers' cheques stolen in Indonesia is a problem because it often means a long trek back to Jakarta to get them replaced. There is, however, an Australian Consulate and also a US consular agent in Bali. Some travellers' cheque companies also have an office in Bali.

A money belt is the safest way to carry your valuables, particularly when travelling on the crowded buses and trains. One precaution you can take, which will help you if you do lose your valuables, is to leave a small stash of money (say US$100) in your hotel room, with a record of the travellers' cheque serial numbers and your passport number; you'll need the money if you have got a long trip to the replacement office.

If you get stuck, try ringing your embassy or consulate.

ACCOMMODATION

Look for *losmen* or *penginapan* or just say you want to *tidur*, or 'sleep'. The word *wisma*, akin to guest house, is also worth watching for and in some places you'll simply see the word *kosong* posted up; it means 'available'.

Losmen are usually very basic, rarely more than a bed and a small table. In compensation, tea or coffee is usually provided gratis a couple of times a day. Traditional washing facilities consist of a *mandi*, a large water tank from which you scoop water with a dipper. Climbing in the tank is very bad form! Toilets may also be the traditional hole in the floor variety but in places like Bali, showers and Western sit-up toilets are now common. Don't expect hot water in budget-priced places, though.

Prices in Indonesia vary considerably − Yogya, Bali and Lake Toba are much cheaper than other places in the country. In Bali, the austerity of the rooms is often balanced by pleasant gardens and courtyards. There are some really nice places around and finding rooms for US$2 to US$4 a night is often quite possible, particularly in Bali and Yogya.

FOOD & DRINK

A *rumah makan*, literally 'house to eat', is the equivalent of a restaurant, whereas a *warung*, or food stall, is a supposedly less grand eating place – the dividing line is hazy. In Bali, where food is cheap, the cost difference is minimal. In more expensive Java, food is often much cheaper in warungs. *Pasars* (markets) are good food sources, especially the *pasar malam* (night market).

As in the rest of Asia, Indonesian food is heavily based on rice. *Nasi goreng* is the national dish – fried rice, with an egg on top in deluxe *(istemiwa)* versions. *Nasi campur*, rice with whatever is available, is a warung favourite, often served cold. The two other real Indonesian dishes are *gado gado* and *satay*. Gado gado is a fresh salad with prawn crackers and peanut sauce. It tends to vary a lot, so if your first one isn't so special try again somewhere else. Satay are tiny kebabs served with a spicy peanut dip.

The Dutch feast, *rijsttafel*, or rice table, consists of rice served with everything imaginable – for gargantuan appetites only. Some big hotels still do a passable imitation. Indonesians are keen snackers, so you'll get plenty of *pisang goreng* (banana fritters), peanuts in palm sugar or shredded coconut cookies.

Popular throughout Indonesia, although it originated in Padang (Sumatra) is Padang food. In a Padang restaurant, a bowl of rice is plonked in front of you, followed by a whole collection of small bowls of vegetables, meat, fish and eggs. Eat what you want and your bill is added up from the number of empty bowls. In Sumatra, food can be hot enough to burn your fingers. Spicy hot that is. Did you expect knives and forks?

Drinking unboiled water is not recommended in Indonesia – the iced juice drinks can be good, but take care! Indonesian tea is fine and coffee is also good. Soft drinks are quite expensive compared to those in other Asian countries. Local beer is good – Bintang Baru is Heineken supervised, but moderately expensive. Bali Brem rice wine is really potent, and the more you drink the nicer it tastes. *Es buah* or *es campur* is a strange concoction of fruit salad, jelly cubes, syrup, crushed rice and condensed milk. Tastes absolutely *enak* (delicious).

Warning

This is the country in the region where the most travellers get the most stomach upsets, in some cases pretty serious ones. A lot of this is due to poor hygiene and contaminated drinking water. Take extra care with cold drinks – the drink itself may be made from boiled water but how about the ice?

The same warning applies to seafood, which is really susceptible to contamination. If you aren't positive it is safe and, equally important, fresh, then leave it alone. Don't be overly worried though, apart from my own trips to Indonesia, my children have also notched up numerous visits without an upset stomach between them.

Food *(makan)*

beef
  daging
chicken
  ayam
crab
  kepiting
egg
  telur
sweet & sour omelette
  fu yung hai
fish
  ikan
frog
  kodok
noodle soup
  mee kuah
fried noodles
  mee goreng
with crispy noodles
  tami

pork
  babi
potatoes
  kentang
prawns
  udang
rice with odds & ends
  nasi campur
fried rice
  nasi goreng
white rice
  nasi putih
soup
  soto
vegetables
  sayur
fried vegetables
  cap cai

Drink (minum)
beer
  bir
coffee
  kopi
cordial
  stroop
drinking water
  air minum
milk
  susu
orange juice
  air jeruk
tea with sugar
  teh manis
plain tea
  teh pahit

THINGS TO BUY

There are so many regional arts and crafts in Indonesia that they're dealt with under the separate regional sections. For an overview of the whole gamut of Indonesian crafts, pay a visit to the Sarinah department store or Ancol's Pasar Seni in Jakarta. They've got items from all over the archipelago. While you may not find all the most interesting products, you'll certainly see enough for a good introduction as to what is available.

Getting There & Away

AIR

Indonesia's two main international gateways are Denpasar in Bali and Jakarta in Java. Although Bali is by far Indonesia's major tourist attraction, the Indonesian's strictly limit the number of flights into Bali, so from many destinations arriving passengers have to arrive in Jakarta and transfer there. Airport tax for international departures from the country is around 11,000 rp.

To/From Australia

Qantas and Garuda both fly to Bali and Jakarta. One-way fares from the east coast of Australia to Bali range from A$630 to A$750 depending on the season; return fares are A$900 to A$1070. Fares are less from Perth or Darwin and slightly more to Jakarta. The high season is essentially just the Christmas-January summer school holiday period in Australia.

A very interesting way of entering Indonesia from Australia is the twice weekly flight from Darwin to Kupang in Timor, which costs A$200 one way or A$330 return. Darwin to Denpasar is about A$340 one way or A$620 return. From Kupang, you can fly on to Denpasar for 174,000 rp (A$115), so it's cheaper to fly only as far as Kupang and buy another ticket there. The Merpati agent in Darwin is Natrabu (☎ 81 3695) at 12 Westlane Arcade off Smith St Mall. You do not need a visa to enter or leave Indonesia through Kupang.

To/From Europe

From London, fares to Bali or Jakarta are from around £300 one way or £600 return. You can get a London-Australia return ticket with a stopover in Jakarta or Bali, Singapore or Bangkok for around £950. Good London agents to check with for cheap tickets include STA Travel on Old Brompton Rd and Trail Finders on Earls Court Rd or Kensington High St.

To/From North America

From the US west coast, the cheapest fares would probably be through Hong Kong, Bangkok or Singapore (US$900 to US$1200 return) with a flight on from there. These days, there are plenty of competitive fares offered to Indonesia from the USA.

Garuda has a Los Angeles-Honolulu-Biak-Denpasar route. If you get off at Biak, this can be a very interesting back-door route into the country, and Biak is a no-visa entry point so that's no problem. The discount return fare from Los Angeles to Bali is US$1500.

For discounted fares and ticketing, contact CIEE or STA Travel offices in the USA or check the Sunday newspaper travel sections for agents.

To/From Other Places

There are also a number of other lesser known international gateways to Indonesia from neighbouring Asian nations. From Papua New Guinea, there is a once-weekly flight that hops across the border from Vanimo to Jayapura.

There is no land or sea crossing permitted between the two countries, although it would be quite easy to do.

Between north Borneo (the Malaysian states of Sabah and Sarawak) a weekly flight with Merpati between Pontianak and Kuching is available. Bouraq also fly between Tarakan and Tawau.

From Singapore, the usual route into Indonesia is Singapore to Jakarta. There are all sorts of flights with all sorts of fares quoted at around S$200. Singapore to Denpasar costs from about S$380.

Also from Singapore, you can take the short ferry trip from Singapore to Batam Island and then fly on to Jakarta for less (but not an enormous amount less) than a regular Singapore to Jakarta flight.

Probably the most popular of all the 'local hops' into Indonesia is the 20-minute leap over the Melaka Straits from Penang to Medan in Sumatra – the fare is about US$80. Unfortunately, there is no short-hop between the Philippines and Indonesia, even though Sulawesi and Mindanao look temptingly close.

LAND

Only two countries – Malaysia and Papua New Guinea – have land borders with Indonesia. The land route between the Malaysian city of Kuching in Sarawak and the Indonesian city of Pontianak in Kalimantan is finally being opened up but a visa is required. It is physically possible to cross from Papua New Guinea to Irian Jaya by land but, officially, it certainly isn't possible at the moment.

SEA

Surprisingly, for an island country, opportunities to arrive there by sea are rather limited. There are now rather more of them than a few years ago. The possibilities include taking a regular ferry from Singapore to the island of Batam in Indonesia's Riau Archipelago. From there, several routes to Sumatra or Java are possible, most of them time consuming and hard work. Once having arrived in Riau, it is easier to continue by air.

Other alternatives are the regular ferry services between Penang (Malaysia) and Medan (Sumatra) or Melaka (Malaysia) and Dumai (Sumatra). The Penang to Medan ferry costs M$100 and no visa is required.

Getting Around

AIR

Indonesia has a surprising number of airlines although the equally amazing variety of aircraft has, unfortunately, been considerably rationalised of late. They still fly to some pretty amazing places, however. Fares vary between airlines so, if costs are all important, check the alternatives. Garuda, the national flag carrier, and its associate airline Merpati are the most expensive.

Garuda, named after the mythical man-bird vehicle of the Hindu god Vishnu and a hero of the *Ramayana*, operates all the long-distance international connections and has an extensive domestic network using jet aircraft. Their smaller jets are being transferred to Merpati, who operate the lesser domestic routes and the Darwin-Kupang international connection.

Garuda and Merpati provide three Visit Indonesia Air Passes available. They allow you to visit four cities in 20 days for US$350, eight cities in 30 days for US$500 or 12 cities in 60 days for US$600. If your travel was restricted to Java and Sumatra, you might not save any money with these passes but if you're going to fly way out to Irian Jaya, Maluku or Sulawesi, they can soon start to look very attractive. The route must start and finish at one of the eight Garuda or Merpati 'gateway' cities, and you can buy the pass overseas or on arrival at one of the gateway cities.

Other airlines include Sempati which has recently purchased a fleet of new jet aircraft. Bouraq have some useful flights to Kalimantan, Sulawesi and Nusa Tenggara; their slogan is 'fly to the most unreachable destinations'. It sounds distinctly dangerous! Mandala has an interesting fleet of vintage prop aircraft, most of which seem to spend most of the time stationary at Jakarta Airport.

Airport tax on domestic flights varies with the airport – at most airports, it's from 3300 or 5500 rp. It should be included on your ticket but check carefully to see if it has been when you buy tickets. It's not unusual to be told to go pay the airport tax when you check-in, when close inspection of the *small* print on your ticket would indicate that you've already paid it. Airfares in Indonesia are much cheaper in rupiah than in US$ fares quoted overseas.

BUS

There is an extensive bus network in Java – they're not very fast on the crowded daytime roads but at night the drivers really put their foot down. Safety – what's that? On certain routes, where there is no rail competition, or for shorter runs, the bus services are very useful. These include Denpasar to Surabaya and Bandung to Jakarta.

In Sumatra, the bus is just about all there is as the rail line only runs to Palembang.

Travelling through Sumatra in brightly painted and amazingly uncomfortable buses is one of those experiences which ends with you thinking, 'My God, I've done it, but never again'. Even here, there's progress – the roads are being improved and more modern buses are being introduced.

TRAIN

There is a pretty good railway service running from end to end of Java. In the east, it connects with the ferry to Bali, and in the west with the ferry to Sumatra. Otherwise, there's just a bit of rail into Sumatra but most of that vast island is reserved for buses. Trains vary – there are slow, miserable, cheap ones and fast, comfortable, expensive ones, and some in-between. So check out what you're getting before you pay.

Some major towns (eg Surabaya and Jakarta) also have several stations, so check where you'll be going to and from as well. Student discounts are generally available but tend to vary from about 10% to 25%.

BOAT

Indonesia is an island nation, so ships are important. If you're going to really explore you'll have to use them. Pelni are the biggest shipper with services almost everywhere; these days their ships operate to a regular schedule and are surprisingly comfortable. They have six modern, all air-con ships which operate regular two-weekly routes around the islands. The ships usually stop for four hours in each port, so there's time for a quick look around. The ships and routes are:

KM *Kerinci* – This ship operates from Jakarta to Surabaya, then on to Ujung Pandang in Sulawesi, to several Kalimantan ports and then back in the opposite direction to Jakarta, on to Padang and Sibolga in Sumatra and back again to Jakarta. The Jakarta to Padang route is very popular so book well ahead.

KM *Kambuna* – Starts from Jakarta and operates a generally similar route to the KM *Kerinci* but then continues from Kalimantan to Bitung at the north-eastern tip of Sulawesi. Then it sails back the opposite direction to Jakarta and up the other (eastern) coast of Sumatra to Belawan, the port for Medan.

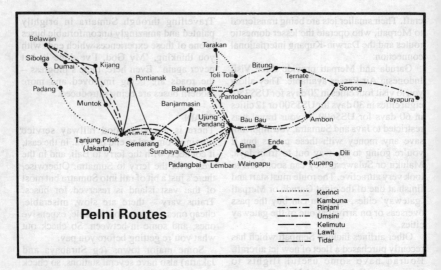

Pelni Routes

Routes legend:
- Kerinci
- Kambuna
- Rinjani
- Umsini
- Kelimutu
- Lawit
- Tidar

KM *Rinjani* – Like the KM *Kerinci* and KM *Kambuna*, it operates Jakarta-Surabaya-Ujung Pandang but then heads off east to Ambon in Maluku and Sorong in Irian Jaya. After returning to Jakarta, it continues to Belawan in Sumatra and back.

KM *Umsini* – Also starts with the standard Jakarta-Surabaya-Ujung Pandang route then heads off to Bitung in North Sulawesi, Ternate in Maluku and Sorong and Jayapura in Irian Jaya before returning on the reverse route to Jakarta.

KM *Kelimutu* – Starts from Semarang in Java and loops up to Banjarmasin in Kalimantan then back to Surabaya and Padangbai in Bali before making five stops in the Nusa Tenggara islands and another loop across to Ujung Pandang. Again the route is reversed back to Semarang.

KM *Lawit* – Starts from Jakarta and hops up the east coast of Sumatra then back to Jakarta, across to Pontianak in Kalimantan and back to Jakarta again.

KM *Tidar* – Starts from Tarakan in Kalimantan and goes onto Sulawesi and Maluku.

Opinions about Pelni are often coloured by the way they were 15 years ago but, today, they're modern and reliable. There are four cabin classes, the difference mainly being the number of people in a cabin, followed by Kelas Ekonomi which is the modern version

of the old deck class. There you are packed in a large room with a space to sleep but, even in Ekonomi, it's air-con and can get pretty cool at night, so bring warm clothes or a sleeping bag.

Class I and II have a dining room while in Ekonomi you queue up to collect a meal on a tray and then sit down wherever you can to eat it.

There are no locker facilities in Ekonomi, so you have to keep an eye on your gear. Shoestring travellers reckon Ekonomi is fine for short trips but Class IV is the best value for longer hauls. You can book tickets up to 10-days ahead and it's best to book at least a few days in advance. Pelni is not a tourist operation, so don't expect any special service although there is usually somebody hidden away in the ticket offices who can help foreigners.

See the table on the following page for Pelni fares from Jakarta.

Many smaller islands are now connected by fairly regular shipping – like the three-times weekly Sumbawa to Flores ferry which also drops in at Komodo Island once a week. There are also regular services between Kupang on Timor and Larantuka on Flores. Ships between Tanjung Pinang in the Riau and Pontianak in Sumatra do not run to a regular schedule but they are frequent.

The good ship *Ratu Rosari*, which I took from Timor to Flores way back in 1974, still wends its way between the islands of Nusa Tenggara on the Surabaya-Ende-Kupang-Atapupu-Larantuka-Maumere-Reo-Surabaya route.

Getting a boat in the outer islands is often a matter of hanging loose until something comes by. Check with shipping companies, the harbour office or anyone else you can think of. On these inter-island services, when the ship arrives it's usually better to negotiate your fare on board rather than buy tickets from the office in advance (apart from big centres like Jakarta and Surabaya.

If you're travelling deck class, unroll your sleeping bag on the deck and make yourself comfortable. Travelling deck class during the wet season can prove to be extremely uncomfortable. Either get one person in your party to take a cabin or discuss renting a cabin from one of the crew (it's a popular way for the crew to make a little extra). Bring some food of your own.

It's also possible to make some more unusual sea trips. Old Makassar schooners still sail the Indonesian waters and it's often possible to travel on them – from Sulawesi to other islands, particularly Java and Nusa Tenggara.

Some general advice from other travellers regarding ship travel through the archipelago includes: 'Unless it's really wet, I reckon deck class is as good as cabin but get as high in the ship as possible. Privacy and security are major considerations. If you want fresh air in your cabin, you get a lot of Indonesian faces too. If you keep your ultravaluables on you, an official will give you somewhere to stick your pack. Cabins get very hot, windows often don't help. Rats and cock-roaches do not abound on the higher decks'.

And a final thought about travelling on the old fashioned ships: 'Definitely a once-only experience!'

Approximate Pelni Fares (in 1000 rp) from Tanjung Priok (Jakarta)

Port	I	II	III	IV	Ekonomi
Medan	200	145	111	88	65
Padang	132	86	66	52	40
Ujung Pandang	196	144	110	88	65
Balikpapan	214	158	122	99	79
Ambon	306	223	171	133	104
Sorong	389	286	220	175	137
Ternate	380	279	214	171	128
Jayapura	509	373	286	227	179
Pontianak	126	99	–	–	50

LOCAL TRANSPORT

There's a great variety of local transport in Indonesia. This includes the ubiquitous Balinese *bemo* – a pick-up truck with two rows of seats down the sides or else a small minibus. Bemos usually run standard routes like buses and depart when full but can also be chartered like a taxi. A step up from the bemo is the small minibus known either as an *oplet, microlet* or a *colt* – since they are often Mitsubishi Colts. In some towns bemos are now known as *angkots*, from *angkutan* (transport) and *kota* (city).

Then there's the *becak*, or bicycle-rick-shaw – they're just the same as in so many other Asian countries, but are only found in towns and cities. Increasingly, they are being banned from the central areas of major cities. There are none in Bali. The *bajaj*, a three-wheeler powered by a noisy two-stroke engine, is only found in Jakarta. They're identical to what is known in India as an autorickshaw. In quieter towns, you may find *andongs* and *dokars* – horse or pony carts with two (dokars) or four (andongs) wheels.

In Bali, Yogya and some other centres you can hire bicycles or motorbikes. You can also hire drive-yourself cars in Jakarta and Bali. Then there are all sorts of oddities: you can hire horses in some places and many towns, of course, have taxis (they even use their meters these days in the big cities in Java).

Java

Indonesia's most populous island presents vivid contrasts of wealth and squalor, majestic open country and crowded filthy cities, quiet rural scenes and bustling modern traffic. For the traveller, it has everything from live volcanoes to inspiring 1000-year-old monuments.

Java is a long, narrow island that can be conveniently divided into three sections – west, central, and east Java. The western region, also known as Sunda, is predominantly Islamic, and it is here that you will find the capital, Jakarta.

Other important historic centres of the Sunda region were Banten, Bandung and Cirebon. Today, the most visited places, other than Jakarta, are Bogor, Bandung and the relaxing beach centre of Pangandaran.

This is an area noted for its wooden *wayang golek* puppets.

Central Java is the most 'Indonesian' part of Indonesia and the centre for much of the island's early culture. Here, the two great Buddhist and Hindu dynasties were centred and they constructed the immense Borobudur Temple and the complex of temples at Prambanan. Later, the rise of Islam carried sultans to power and the palaces, or *kratons,* at Yogyakarta and Solo (Surakarta) can be visited. This is a region for dance drama, or *wayang orang*, *gamelan* orchestras and *wayang kulit* shadow puppet performances.

Finally, there is east Java or Java Timur, the area most likely to be rushed through by travellers in their haste to get to Bali. The major city here is the important port of Surabaya and, although east Java's attractions include the ruins at Trowulan and around

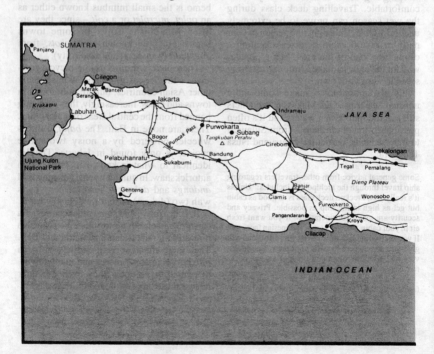

Malang, the main interest in the region is natural rather than man made – the many hill stations and the superb Mt Bromo volcano.

Most travellers travelling through Java follow the well-worn route of Jakarta-Bogor-Bandung-Pangandaran-Yogyakarta-Solo-Surabaya-Bali with short diversions or day trips from points along that route. Many only stop at Jakarta and Yogya! There are also a number of major towns along the north coast, but they attract few visitors.

Things to Buy

Yogya is the place in Java where your money deserves to be spent, but it's worth checking out the Sarinah department store in Jakarta. The 3rd floor of Sarinah on Jalan Thamrin is devoted to handicrafts from all over the country. It can be a little variable – you might not be able to find certain items that really interest you or you might find one area badly represented – but, overall, it's a great place for an overview of Indonesian crafts. The art market, Pasar Seni, at Ancol in Jakarta, is also worth a visit.

Batik The art of batik making is one of Indonesia's best known crafts, and it has been a Yogya speciality since who knows when. In my opinion Yogya is still the best place to look for batik. Batik is the craft of producing designs on material by covering part of it with wax then dyeing it. When the wax is scraped or melted off, an undyed patch is left. Repeated waxing and dyeing can produce colourful and complex designs. Batik pieces can be made by a hand-blocked process known as *batik cap* in which a copper stamp is used to apply the wax – or they can be hand drawn, *batik tulis*, using a wax-filled pen known as a *canting*.

Batik can be bought as pieces of material,

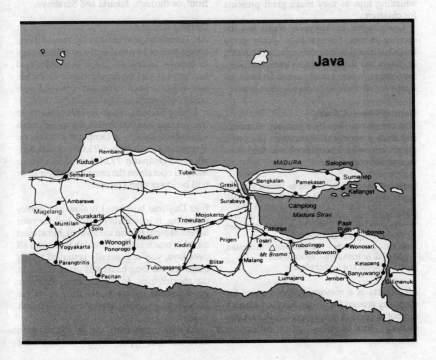

cushion covers, T-shirts, dresses, dinner sets and as batik paintings. An easy check for quality is to simply turn it over to ensure the design is of equal colour strength on both sides of the material – that makes it batik and not just printed material. In Yogya, you can buy batik in shops, in the market or from the many galleries. See Yogyakarta later in the Java section for more information on batik available there.

Other Crafts In Yogyakarta, silverwork can be found in the Kota Gede area. Wayang puppets can be found all over Yogya but wayang golek puppets are more frequently found in the west Java area around Bandung and Bogor. *Kebayas*, those flimsy lace jackets, are now outdated as a fashion but you can find lots of them in Yogya along with other popular Western clothing. At Prambanan and Borobudur, look for bamboo whistling tops as they make great presents for children.

Leatherwork in Yogya is cheap but the quality is not always high. Very good lampshades and other cane craft can be found in Yogya but they're hard to transport. Solo, near Yogya, is also a major centre for batik – it is also less touristy so prices are often lower.

Getting There & Away

You can get to Java by a number of means and from a variety of directions. The basic places from which people come to Java from around the region are:

Sumatra – either by the Padang to Jakarta shipping service or the short trip across the Sunda Strait from Bakauheni in Sumatra to Merak in Java.

Bali – at the eastern end of the island, take the very short ferry trip to or from Bali, between Banyuwangi and Gilimanuk.

From the outer islands – like Sulawesi, Kalimantan, Maluku or Irian Jaya – by air or sea.

From Singapore and further afield.

Air Jakarta is a reasonably good place for shopping around for airline tickets, although it is not as good as Singapore. See the Jakarta Getting There & Away section for further information.

From Australia, fares go pretty much by the book, principally because Bali is such a popular holiday destination for Australians. From Europe, on the other hand, Garuda are active fare cutters and you can find all sorts of interesting routes – simply to Jakarta or all the way to Australia – with stopovers in Indonesia. The other popular entry point to Jakarta is from Singapore, and here you'll find a variety of ticket prices.

Sea There are, of course, shipping services from other Indonesian islands, but there are no international connections to Java. The closest approach would be to travel to or from Singapore via the Riau Archipelago, just south of Singapore. See the Riau section in Sumatra for more details. See the introductory Indonesia Getting Around section for more information on the regular Pelni shipping services, most of which operate from, or through, Jakarta and Surabaya.

Getting Around

Air There's no real need to fly around Java, unless you're in a real hurry or have money to burn – there's so much available road transport. If you do decide to take to the air, you will get some spectacular views of Java's many mountains and volcanoes.

Flying Garuda, fares include Jakarta to Yogyakarta 100,000 rp, Jakarta to Surabaya 140,000 rp, Jakarta to Denpasar 170,000 rp, Yogyakarta to Denpasar 93,000 rp and Surabaya to Denpasar 72,000 rp. If Bouraq or Merpati operate on the same route, their fares will be lower than Garuda.

Bus Daytime bus travel is slow and nerve-wracking. It is probably just as bad for your nerves at night (if you are awake), but at least travel is much faster. Although buses run all over Java, you're generally better off taking trains for the long hauls and using buses on the shorter trips. In some places, there are good reasons for taking the bus, as on the Jakarta to Bandung trip over the Puncak Pass.

As with trains, there can be variations in fares and bus types. Where the fare isn't ticketed or fixed, it's wise to check the fare with other passengers − colt and oplet drivers are the worst culprits for jacking up fares for foreigners. Beware of the practice of taking your money and not giving you your change until later. It's OK, usually, but sometimes you find yourself bundled into the bus when it arrives at your stop and, only later, you remember you hadn't been given change.

The cheapest buses are the big public buses. There are also private bus companies, some which run air-con deluxe services on important routes. Colts are small minibuses which run the shorter routes more frequently and more comfortably than the big public buses. Oplet and microlets are very similar. There are also share-taxi services from Jakarta to Bogor, Bandung, Cirebon and a few other destinations.

Train Choose your trains for comfort, speed and destination. There is a wide variety ranging from cheap slow trains to reasonably cheap fast trains, very expensive expresses and squalid all-3rd-class cattle trains. The schedules change frequently and although departures may be punctual, arrivals will be late for most services and very late for others.

In Jakarta and Surabaya in particular, there are several stations, some of them far more convenient than others. Bear this in mind when choosing your trains. Student discounts are generally available, but not for the expensive Bima and Mutiara night expresses. Try going straight to the station master for speedier ticketing and to get tickets even when, officially, the train is booked out. Remember, once again, that fares for the same journey and in the same class will vary widely from train to train.

Local Transport Around towns in Java, there are buses, taxis, colts, becaks (bicycle rickshaws) and some very peculiar and purely local ways of getting from A to B.

JAKARTA
Jakarta, once a squalid and dirty city that most travellers tried to leave behind as quickly as possible, has become a much more attractive destination for visitors. For residents, particularly those recent arrivals from the country, it can still be a tough proposition − this is the biggest city in Indonesia, the vortex that sucks in the poor, often providing little more than the hope of hard work at low pay.

Behind it's hard facade, Jakarta actually has a lot to offer. Apart from a few interesting museums and a collection of terrible public monuments, Jakarta has some fine old Dutch architecture and at the old schooner dock you can see the most impressive reminder of the age of sailing ships to be found anywhere in the world. The Dutch took Jakarta and renamed it Batavia back in 1619, the name reverted to Jakarta after independence. You may still occasionally see it spelt Djakarta.

Orientation & Information
Sukarno's towering monument in Merdeka Square (Monas) is as an excellent landmark for Jakarta. You can always get your bearings from it. North of the monument is the older part of Jakarta, including the Chinatown area of Glodok, the old Dutch area of Kota, then the waterfront and the old harbour area known as Sunda Kelapa. The modern harbour, Tanjung Priok, is several km along the coast to the east. The more modern part of Jakarta is to the south of the monument.

Jalan Thamrin, which runs to the west of the monument, is the main north-south street of the new city and it is along this wide boulevard that you'll find the big hotels, big banks and the Sarinah department store. The Qantas airline office is at the intersection of Jalan Kebon Sirih and Jalan Thamrin, and a couple of blocks east along Kebon Sirih you'll find Jalan Jaksa, the cheap accommodation centre of Jakarta. Jakarta is very sprawling; it's 25 km from the docks to the suburb of Kebayoran.

Districts of Jakarta include the old Dutch town Kota and the adjoining Chinatown, Glodok. Menteng is the foreigners' enclave and Kebayoran is the new suburban area. Most visitors to Jakarta spend most of their time in the tourist enclave immediately south of Monas and east of Jalan Thamrin.

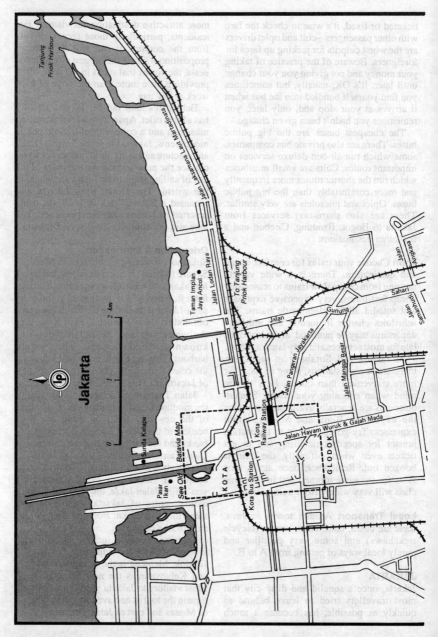

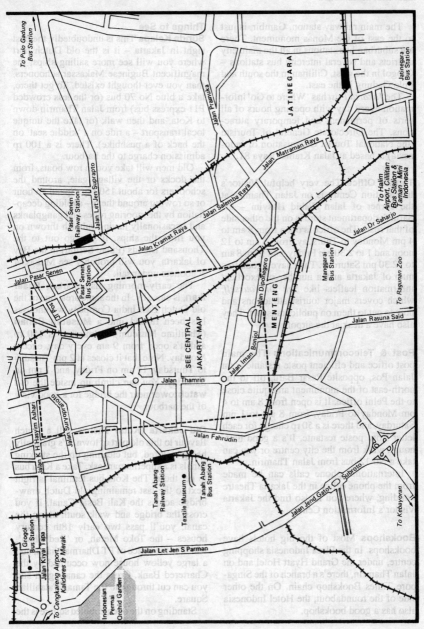

SEE CENTRAL JAKARTA MAP

The main railway station, Gambir, is just to the east of the Monas monument. There are suburban bus stations in all the main city districts and several intercity bus stations – Grogol in the west, Cililitan in the south and Pulo Gadung in the east.

The *Jakarta Post* has 'Where to Go' information every day with opening hours of all sorts of permanent and temporary attractions. The Directorate General of Tourism (the National Tourist Organisation of Indonesia) is based at Jalan Kramat Raya 81.

Tourist Office The very helpful Visitor's Information Centre is on Jalan Thamrin at the corner of Jalan Wahid Hasyim – the Sarinah department store is on the other side of that road. The office is open from 8 am to 4 pm Monday to Thursday, from 8 am to 12 noon and 1 to 2.30 pm Friday, and from 8 am to 12.30 pm Saturday. They have a good free map of Jakarta and a number of excellent information leaflets like *See for Yourself*, which covers major tourist attractions and how to get to them on public transport. They also have a desk at the airport.

Post & Telecommunications The main post office and efficient poste restante is on Jalan Pos, opposite Pasar Baru, off to the north-east of the monument and quite close to the Pelni office. It is open from 8 am to 4 pm Monday to Friday, from 8 am to 1 pm Saturday, and there is a 50 rp charge for each letter from poste restante. It's a good half-hour's walk from the city centre or you can take a No 12 bus from Jalan Thamrin.

International phone calls can be made from the phone office in the Jakarta Theatre building, where you'll also find the Jakarta Visitor's Information Centre.

Bookshops Most of the big hotels have bookshops. In the Plaza Indonesia shopping centre, under the Grand Hyatt Hotel and on Jalan Thamrin, there's a branch of the Singapore Times Bookshop chain. On the other side of the roundabout, the Hotel Indonesia also has a good bookshop.

Things to See

Sunda Kelapa This is undoubtedly the best sight in Jakarta – it is the old Dutch port where you will see more sailing ships, the magnificent Buginese Makassar schooners, than you ever thought existed. To get there, take a blue No 70 bus (or the less crowded P11 express bus) from Jalan Thamrin down to Kota, and then walk (or take the unique local transport – a ride on a 'kiddie seat' on the back of a pushbike). There is a 100 rp admission charge to the harbour.

Old men will take you in row boats, from the docks or the village gate, around the schooners for about 1500 rp. Spend an hour or so rowing around them – avoiding decapitation by the mooring ropes and gangplanks and occasionally having rubbish thrown on you from the ships. If you go out to the Thousand Islands (Pulau Seribu) in the Bay of Jakarta, you will probably see Makassar schooners under sail.

The early-morning fish market, **Pasar Ikan**, is close by. In the same area, one of the old Dutch East India Company warehouses has been turned into a **Museum Bahari** (Maritime Museum). Admission is 150 rp and it's open from 9 am every day, except Monday. Note that it closes at 2 pm Tuesday to Thursday, 11 am on Friday, and 1 pm on Saturday. You can climb up inside the **old watchtower** near the bridge for a good view of the harbour.

Old Jakarta (Kota) There's still a Dutch flavour to this old part of town. It's gradually being restored, but cleaning up the stinking canals is a superhuman task. Take a Kota bus to get there. The Kota bus terminal is right next to the last remaining old Dutch drawbridge across the Kali Besar Canal. If you cross the bridge and walk south along the canal, you'll pass two early 18th century houses – the Toko Merah, or 'Red Shop', which is the office of PT Dharma Niaga, and a large yellow house now occupied by the Chartered Bank. Cross the canal again and you can cut through to the Taman Fatahillah Square.

Standing on the open cobbled square is the

old City Hall which houses the **Old Batavia Museum** (also known as the Sejarah Jakarta Museum). In here, you'll find interesting exhibits of Dutch colonial life and the building itself, dating from 1710, is impressive.

The **City Hall** was also the main prison compound of Batavia – in the basement there are cells and 'water prisons' where often more than 300 people were kept. Admission to the museum is 150 rp. It opens at 9 am every day except Monday, and closes at 2 pm from Tuesday to Thursday, 11 am on Friday, 1 pm on Saturday, and 2 pm on Sunday.

The old Portuguese cannon, **Si Jagur**, or 'Mr Fertility', opposite the museum, was believed by women to be a cure for barrenness because of its strange clenched fist (a symbol of fertility on Java) and Latin inscription ('Ex me ipsa renata sum' – 'Out of myself I was reborn'). Women used to offer flowers to the cannon and sit on top of it before it was moved to the safety of a

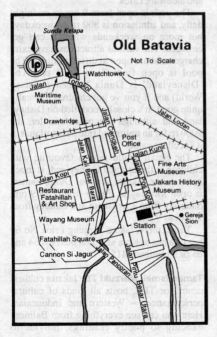

Old Batavia

museum for a few years to bring an end to this ritual.

Across the square on Jalan Pintu Besar Utara, the **Wayang Museum** has a good display of puppets not only from Indonesia but also China, Malaysia, India and Kampuchea. Wayang golek or wayang kulit performances are put on every Sunday between 10 am and 1.30 pm. The museum is open Thursday to Sunday from 9 am; until 11 am on Friday and until 1 pm on other days.

In the **Balai Seni Rupa** (Fine Art Museum) on the east side of the square, there's a small gallery of modern Indonesian paintings and a collection of ceramics. (Opening hours are as for the Bahari Museum.)

Nearby, at Jalan Pangeran Jayakarta 1, is the 1695 **Gereja Sion**, the oldest remaining church in Jakarta. It was built outside the old city walls for the 'black Portuguese' who were brought to Batavia as slaves and given their freedom if they joined the Dutch Reformed Church.

Glodok was the old Chinatown of Batavia. It is now a centre of trade, banking and entertainment but, behind the new Glodok shopping plazas, the lanes off Jalan Pancoran are still crammed with narrow crooked houses, small shops, temples and market stalls.

Monuments Inspired tastelessness best describes the plentiful supply of monuments Sukarno left to Jakarta – all in the Russian 'heroes of socialism' style. **Monas** (Monumen Nasional), the giant column in Merdeka Square is, according to a tourist brochure, 'constructed entirely of Italian marbles'. It's open from 9 am to 4.30 pm and admission is 300 rp to the **National History Museum** in the base, or 1500 rp for both the museum and ride to the top of the monument. The museum tells the whole history of Indonesia in 48 dramatic dioramas. 'So atrocious it shouldn't be missed,' according to one traveller, but they're quite interesting and kids would love them. A lift zips you up to the top where the views across Jakarta are superb. There are usually long queues to get up the monument but sometimes it will be nearly deserted.

Monas has been dubbed 'Sukarno's last erection' and all the other monuments have also acquired descriptive nicknames. The gentleman holding the flaming dish is 'the mad waiter' and the two children at the roundabout in front of the Indonesia Hotel are 'Hansel & Gretel'.

Around Merdeka Square To the north of Merdeka Square you'll see the gleaming white **Presidential Palace**. To the northeast is the vast **Istiqlal Mosque**, the largest mosque in South-East Asia.

Indonesian National Museum Situated on the west side of Merdeka Square, this is one of the most interesting museums in South-East Asia. There are excellent displays of pottery and porcelain, a huge ethnic map of Indonesia and an equally big relief map on which you can pick out all those volcanoes you have climbed.

Admission to the museum is 200 rp and it's open daily (except Monday) from 8.30 to 2 pm Tuesday to Thursday, to 11 am on Friday, to 1.30 pm on Saturday and to 3 pm on Sunday. On Sunday, the treasure room is also open. There are worthwhile free guided tours in English on Tuesday, Wednesday and Thursday at 9.30 am. Gamelan performances are held between 9.30 and 10.30 am, every Sunday.

Textile Museum This excellent museum is in an old Dutch colonial house at Jalan Satsuit Tubun 4, west of the National Museum past a huge daily market. It has a large collection of fabrics from all over Indonesia plus looms, batik-making tools and so on. Opening hours are as for the other Jakarta museums and admission is also 150 rp.

Taman Mini-Indonesia This is one more of those 'whole country in one park' collections which every South-East Asian country seems to have acquired. It's near the Halim Airport – take bus Nos 40, 41 or 401 from Banteng to Cililitan and then a metro-mini

T55 (marked 'Mini-Indonesia') to the park entrance. It's open from 9 am to 5 pm daily (the houses close at 4 pm). Admission is 600 rp and the exhibits include 27 traditional houses for the 27 provinces of Indonesia and a lagoon 'map' where you can row around the islands of Indonesia.

Allow 1½ hours to get there and three hours to look around. It's pretty good value. On Sunday morning there are free cultural performances in most regional houses and a monthly calendar of various events is available at the Visitor's Information Centre.

Taman Impian Jaya Ancol 'Dreamland' is on the bayfront between Kota and Tanjung Priok Harbour. This huge amusement complex has an oceanarium, an amazing swimming pool complex with wave making facilities, an Indonesian Disneyland and the excellent Pasar Seni Art Market with its numerous small shops, an exhibition gallery and sidewalk cafes.

The park is open from 9 am to midnight daily, and admission is 800 rp on weekdays but more on weekends when it can get crowded. The various attractions have extra charges and are open at different times. The pool is open from 7 am to 9 pm. The 'Disneyland' is Dunia Fantasi (Fantasy World) and if you've got children it's really quite good. It's closely modelled on Disneyland and although it's much smaller, the 9000 rp for an unlimited ride passport makes it excellent value.

The Small World ride, a favourite with children at the original Disneyland, is much better in the Jakarta version! Dunia Fantasi is open Monday to Friday from 2 to 9 pm, Saturday from 2 to 10 pm and Sunday from 10 am to 9 pm.

To get there, take a Tanjung Priok No 60 bus or a bus to Kota and then bus Nos 64 and 65 or a minibus M15.

Taman Ismail Marzuki The Jakarta cultural centre, or TIM, hosts all kinds of cultural performances – Western and Indonesian. Here you can see everything from Balinese dancing to poetry readings, movies to

Indonesia – Java 171

gamelan concerts, a batik exhibition or the planetarium. Events are listed in the TIM monthly programme and in the daily *Jakarta Post*. Bus No 34 from Jalan Thamrin for Megaria/Rawamangun will get you to TIM at Jalan Cikini Raya 73.

Thousand Islands The Pulau Seribu, or Thursday Islands, start only a few km out in the Bay of Jakarta. Some of them are virtually deserted and have fine beaches but others can be very crowded, particularly on weekends. From Sunda Kelapa, it's four hours to Pulau Panggang, and you can reach other islands from there.

There are also daily boats to some islands, or boats can be hired, from the Marina at Ancol. You can also reach some of the islands by light aircraft. It's a one-hour boat trip (15 km) from the Marina to Pulau Bidadari, and you can reach other islands from there. A boat leaves at 10.30 am and returns 3 or 4 pm.

The Pulau Putri islands, 75 km from Jakarta, are being developed as the city's 'tropical paradise' resort. You can obtain information about the Pulau Seribu Paradise resort from their office in the Jakarta Theatre on Jalan Wahid Hasyim.

Other The **Jakarta Ragunan Zoo**, in the Pasar Minggu district south of the city, has Komodo dragons, orang-utans and other interesting Indonesian wildlife. The **Sarinah department store**, with its fine handicrafts section, is always worth a browse. There are **antique market stalls** on Jalan Surabaya, and at Jalan Pramuka there is a **bird market**.

At 8.15 pm every evening, except Monday and Thursday, wayang orang can be seen at the **Bharata Theatre**, Jalan Kalilio 15 near Pasar Senen. *Ketoprak* (Javanese folk theatre) performances take place here on Monday and Thursday evenings.

The Ganesha Society has weekly films or lectures about Indonesia at Erasmus Huis by the Dutch Embassy, south of the centre. The National Museum has their schedule, or ask the volunteer guides there as they are another Ganesha Society project.

If you want to get away from Jakarta for a few days, try **Carita Beach** on the west coast of Java. It's a three to four-hour bus trip to Labuhan for Carita and buses go regularly from the Grogol station – see the following West Coast section for more information.

Places to Stay
There's a hotel booking counter at Soekarno-Hatta Airport but the Djody Hotel on Jalan Jaksa is about the cheapest place they handle.

Jalan Jaksa Jakarta's cheap accommodation is almost all centred around Jalan Jaksa, a small street very centrally located in the newer part of Jakarta. It runs between Jalan Kebon Sirih and Jalan Wahid Hasyim, a few blocks over from Jakarta's main drag – Jalan Thamrin.

Once, *Wisma Delima*, at Jalan Jaksa 5, was all there was when it came to cheap places to stay. In fact No 5 would actually be referred to as 'Jalan Jaksa' and as a consequence it was often hopelessly crowded and totally chaotic. Now, there are lots of alternatives and Wisma Delima is just one of many. Dorm beds are 2500 rp (2250 rp if you're a YHA member), or there are singles/doubles at 4500/6600 rp. You can also get food and cold drinks here, the meals are excellent value for Jakarta.

Moving down Jalan Jaksa from No 5, the *Norbek (Noordwijk) Hostel* (☎ 33 0392) is across the street at No 14 and has rooms at 7000/9000 rp up to 10,000/20,000 rp. It's very popular despite being one of those places which likes to have lists of rules posted on every vertical surface, including the front gate.

Continue down the street to the *Djody Hostel* at Jalan Jaksa 27. This is another old and popular standby with dorm beds for 7500 rp, and double rooms from 15,000 to 18,000 rp. A few doors further up is the related *Djody Hotel & Hostel* (☎ 33 2368, 34 6600) at No 35. This popular and well-run place has rooms ranging in price from 12,000 rp for a single up to 24,000 rp for a double with bath. Rooms with bath and air-con cost up to 30,000 rp.

Next is the *International Tator Hostel*

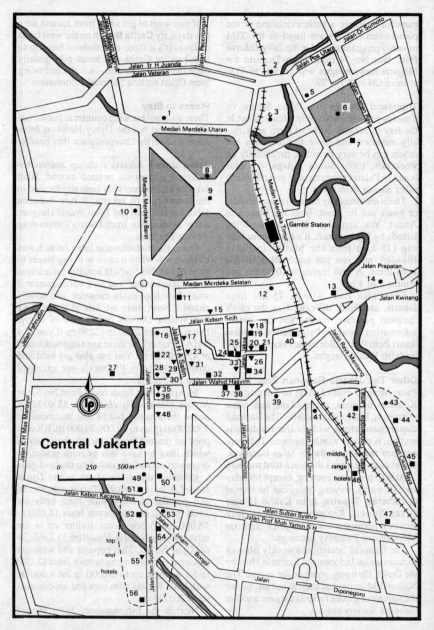

Central Jakarta

0   250   500 m

■ **PLACES TO STAY**

7	Borobudur Hotel
11	Hotel Sabang Metropolitan
13	Bumi Hyatt Hotel
19	Wisma Delima (Jalan Jaksa)
21	Bloem Steen & Kresna Homestays
22	Hotel Sari Pacific
24	Borneo Hostel
25	Norbek Hostel
27	Wisma Ise Guest House
32	Bali International Hotel
34	Djody Hostel & Hotel & International Tator Hostel
37	Hotel Indra International
38	Cipta Hotel
40	Celebes House
42	Hotel Menteng I
44	Hotel Cikini Sofyan
45	Hotel Menteng II
46	Losmen Luhandydan
47	Hotel Marcopolo
50	President Hotel
51	Grand Hyatt Hotel
52	Hotel Indonesia
54	Mandarin Oriental Hotel
56	Kartika Plaza Hotel

▼ **PLACES TO EAT**

15	Shalimar & Ikan Bakar Kebon Sirih Restaurants
17	Sakura Anpan Bakery
18	Senayan Satay House

20	Angie's Cafe
23	Natrabu Padang Restaurant
26	Memories Cafe
29	A & W Hamburgers
30	Pizza Hut
31	Budi Bundo Restaurant
33	Bagus Restaurant
35	MacDonald's
48	Studio 21 & Bakmi Gajah Manda
55	George & Dragon Pub

OTHER

1	Presidential Palace
2	Pelni Office
3	Istiqlal Mosque
4	Post Office
5	Cathedral
6	Unchained Statue
8	Entrance To Monas
9	Merdeka Monument (Monas)
10	National Museum
12	US Embassy
14	4848 Taxis
16	Qantas & Thai International
28	Jakarta Theatre Building & Tourist Office
36	Sarinah Department Store
39	Media Taxis
41	Immigration Office
43	TIM Cultural Centre
49	Australian Embassy
53	British Embassy

(☎ 32 5124, 32 3940) at Jalan Jaksa 37, where rooms are 12,000 rp, 15,000 rp with bath and 25,000 to 27,000 rp with air-con. *Hotel Karya* (☎ 32 0484) at Jalan Jaksa 32-34 is pricier with air-con rooms from 29,000 to 35,000 rp but they're rather dismal.

More places can be found in the small streets running off Jalan Jaksa. Gang 1 is a small alley connecting Jalan Jaksa to Jalan Kebon Sirih Timur Dalam (running east off Jalan Jaksa). A short distance down are two small places, the *Kresna* at No 175 and the *Bloem Steen* right next door at No 173. They're OK, although quite basic and spartan. Rooms at these quiet places are in the 10,000 to 12,000 rp bracket at the Kresna but less in the Bloem Steen.

At Kebon Sirih Barat Dalam 35, running west off Jalan Jaksa, *Borneo Hostel* (☎ 32 0095) has dorm beds at 3000 rp and rooms from 10,000 to 12,500 rp. There are more places dotted along this lane, such as the similarly priced *Bintang Kejora* across the road at No 52 or the *Tiara* at No 33. Further down, there's the *Pondok Wisata* at No 16 and the *Pondok Wisata Jaya* at No 10. After a couple of twists and turns the lane meets Jalan Kebon Sirih.

To the north-east of Jalan Jaksa, on a small lane parallel to Jalan Kebon Sirih and just before the Gambir railway lines, is *Celebes House* at Jalan Menteng 35. It's away from the heart of Jalan Jaksa and has rooms from 7000 to 14,000 rp (most at 10,000 rp) with fan or 22,000 with air-con.

Other Central Jakarta Places There are a couple of cheaper mid-range hotels close to Jalan Jaksa. Jalan Kebon Sirih is at one end of Jalan Jaksa, and Jalan Wahid Hasyim is at the other. Walk back towards Jalan Thamrin for a short distance and on the other side of the road is *Hotel Indra Internasional* (☎ 33 4556) at Jalan Wahid Hasyim 63. It's a bit worn and shabby but this is a pretty good mid-range place with air-con and bath for US$24/28 which includes breakfast, service and tax – good value for Jakarta.

Closer to Jalan H A Salim is the largish and rather ugly *Bali International Hotel* at Jalan Wahid Hasyim 116. In price, it's at the top of the cheap or bottom of the mid-price bracket but it's pretty evident that sleeping is not intended to be the main activity for guests at this hotel.

Keep walking along Jalan Wahid Hasyim and, across Jalan Thamrin at No 168, you'll come to the *Wisma Ise Guest House* (☎ 33 3463). The sign outside may say 'Mess Ise'. There are single/double rooms at 8000/ 12,000 rp and some fancier new rooms with air-con and bath from 25,000 to 30,000 rp. The basic rooms are fairly spartan but it's a clean and friendly place, and there's a pleasant balcony bar at the back where you can look out over Jakarta.

Mid-Range Hotels Looking for a pool and air-con close to the centre of things? Then try the *Sabang Metropolitan Hotel* (☎ 37 3933) at Jalan H A Salim 11. Singles are from US$33 to US$55, doubles US$43 to US$58 and there is a 15% tax and service.

There's an enclave of mid-range hotels just south-east of the city centre, along Jalan Cikini Raya and Jalan Gondangdia Lama. There are three Hotel Mentengs – *Menteng I* (☎ 35 7635/5208) is at Jalan Gondangdia Lama 28, *Menteng II* (☎ 32 5543) is at Jalan Cikini Raya 105 and the newest, *Menteng III* (☎ 88 1863), is at Jalan Matraman Raya 21. Singles are around 90,000 rp and doubles around 110,000 rp. *Marco Polo Hotel* (☎ 32 5409) at Jalan Cik Ditiro 19 is slightly cheaper. These places all have a pool and other amenities.

Also in the Menteng area is the family run *Losmen Luhandydan* (☎ 37 1865) at Jalan Sawo 15. It's a pleasant private home with spacious rooms from 17,500 to 25,000 rp, including breakfast.

Airport The new Soekarno-Hatta Airport at Cengkareng is a long way from central Jakarta. The terminal buildings seem to be shut up at night so there's probably no chance of sleeping there overnight.

The other option is the *Cengkareng Transit Hotel* (☎ 61 1964/4194) at Jalan Jurumudi Km 2.5, Cengkareng. There's nothing fancy about it – air-con rooms with bath are US$22/30 and there's a 24-hour coffee shop. It's very close to the airport in a straight line but since it's on the other side of the runways from the terminal it's a long distance by road. They operate a free minibus service which takes about 20 to 30 minutes – travelling at high speed. Their representative will be scouting round the terminals in the evening looking for clients.

Places to Eat

There's no shortage of eating places in Jakarta. They range from the cheap travellers' centres along Jalan Jaksa to a diverse collection of Western fast-food purveyors and some fancy local restaurants.

Popular places along Jalan Jaksa, all dishing out the standard travellers' menu, include *Angie's Cafe, Memories Cafe, Anedja KPPD Cafe* and, probably topping popularity polls, the *Bagus Restaurant*.

There are some interesting possibilities at the top end of Jalan Jaksa, on Jalan Kebon Sirih. At Jalan Kebon Sirih 31A is the *Senayan Satay House* which is comfortable, air-con and more expensive but the food is good. Head west towards Jalan H A Salim, and on the other side of the street at Jalan Kebon Sirih 40 is the *Shalimar* Indian restaurant. Above it in the same building, the *Ikan Bakar Kebon Sirih* specialises in that popular Sulawesi dish Makassar-style roast fish *(ikan bakar)*. Count on 4000 to 6000 rp for a meal.

Jalan H A Salim is probably the food centre of Jakarta and boasts many types of restaurants. There are some good places here for Padang food including *Budi Bundo* and the more expensive, but still moderately priced, *Natrabu*, where the Padang food is excellent. If you only try Padang food once in your whole stay in Indonesia, then this is an excellent place to do it.

Sakura Anpan, the Japanese bakery at Jalan H A Salim 25/27, has a truly mind-blowing selection of cakes, pastries and ice creams. It's good for a snack or cold drink in hygienic looking surroundings. *Sakura Fast Food* at Jalan H A Salim 37 serves good cafeteria-style Indonesian, Chinese and European food; it's OK for a quick meal. *Lim Thiam Kie* at No 53 serves excellent and economical Chinese food.

There's a *Kentucky Fried Chicken* next to the Natrabu and an *A&W* hamburger joint (burgers 2000 to 4000 rp) across the road with *Kim's Hamburgers* beside it. Western fast-food fanatics can also find a *Jakarta Ayam Goreng* at the top of Jalan H A Salim, and a *Mister Donut* (donuts 750 rp) at the bottom. There is also fast food, a *Pizza Hut* and *California Fried Chicken*, around the corner in the Djakarta Theatre building. The pizzas cost from 4000 to 6000 rp for small ones and 8000 rp and up for large ones. They make a good attempt to add some local flavour so you can even get a squid pizza!

The Djakarta Theatre building has the *Cafe A&A* upstairs for fast food or the very popular *Green Pub* with Mexican food (mainly around 10,000 rp). There's live music at night in this popular expat hang-out – Indonesians dressed in the outfits of Mexican wranglers seem a bit odd at first but you soon get used to it. Draught beer is 5000 rp but there's a happy hour.

Not to be missed, at the front of the Sarinah department store on Jalan Thamrin, is Indonesia's first *McDonalds*. It's huge, and a big Mac will set you back 3500 rp. The Sarinah department store has a supermarket, several snack bar areas and an excellent bakery on the car park side of the building.

Continue down Jalan Thamrin to the very popular, neat and clean *Bakmi Gajah Madah*

with its extensive menu of noodle and rice dishes from around 4000 rp. There's more Western fast food further down Jalan Thamrin, where the shopping centre under the Grand Hyatt has a *Burger King*, *Texas Fried Chicken*, *Kentucky Fried Chicken*, *Swensen's Ice Cream* and a *Del Taco*.

For real Indonesian food at a rock bottom price, there are lots of night stalls along Jalan Kebon Sirih and Jalan Wahid Hasyim. Some of them are of dubious cleanliness, so inspect them first.

Some of these stalls sell *pisang baka* (roast banana), and I've always liked *pisang goreng* (fried bananas), so one night I thought I'd try one. First they sliced and grilled the bananas, added grated cheese on top and sprinkled chocolate on top of the cheese. Then, they poured condensed milk on top of the bananas, cheese and chocolate, and my stomach decided it would rather have something else!

Tony Wheeler

You'll find plenty of Chinese restaurants in the Glodok area, numerous places along Jalan Gajah Mada, and the Blok M shopping centre, way down Jalan Thamrin, also has a wide variety of places to eat. On Jalan Thamrin, between the Hotel Indonesia and the Kartika Plaza, the *George & Dragon Pub* looks as properly British as suggested by its name. It's a good place for a beer and they also do some of the best Indian food in Jakarta.

Cross Jalan Thamrin and go down Jalan Blora, beside Jalan Thamrin to the railway line, turn left along Jalan Kendal (which runs beside the line) and you'll come to a string of interesting food stalls. Further east, close to the group of mid-range hotels (see the Jakarta Places to Stay section), there are a number of restaurants and fast-food places. The large international hotels have big, hearty buffets and mind-blowing breakfast spreads for around 20,000 rp.

Getting There & Away

Jakarta is the main travel hub for Indonesia. From here, ships depart for ports on the other islands, flights fan out all over the archipelago, trains come and go for other parts of Java and buses depart for destinations not only throughout Java but also for Bali and the towns in Sumatra.

Air The domestic airline offices are dotted around the city. Garuda has several offices around town including one in the Wisma Nusantara building (☎ 33 4425) on Jalan Thamrin, and another across the road in the Hotel Indonesia (☎ 310 0568/70). Mandala (☎ 36 8107) is at Jalan Veteran I No 34, en route to the Pelni office; Merpati (☎ 41 3608) is at Jalan Angkasa 2; and Bouraq (☎ 629 5150) is at Jalan Angkasa 1-3 – both are near Kemayoran Airport.

In the Pasar Baru district, there are travel agents who will discount domestic airline tickets, particularly those of Merpati and Mandala. For flights to Sulawesi, Sumatra, Nusa Tenggara or Bali you can get as much as 25% discount. There are plenty of agents around – try Mitra Kercana Tour & Travel Service (☎ 34 9699, 36 1366) at Jalan Pintu Air 20A, near the Pelni office.

For international flights, Kaliman Travel, in the Indonesia Plaza under the Hyatt Hotel on Jalan Thamrin, is a good place for cheap tickets, and they offer a discount on some airline tickets if you pay in cash. They're open from 8 am to 6 pm daily, but close at 2 pm on Sunday. Other agents worth checking are Vayatour (☎ 33 6640) next door to Kaliman, and Pacto Ltd (☎ 32 0309) at Jalan Cikini Raya 24.

The agent for STA Travel is Indo Shangrila Travel (☎ 63 2703), Jalan Gajah Mada 219G. Fares being quoted here include Singapore for US$110, when the regular fare on Singapore Airlines or Garuda is about US$160.

Within Indonesia, fares from Jakarta include Biak 510,000 rp, Batam 178,000 rp, Denpasar 170,000 rp, Jayapura 563,000 rp, Kupang 337,000 rp, Medan 259,000 rp, Padang 187,000 rp, Pontianak 153,000 rp, Surabaya 141,000 rp, Ujung Pandang 253,000 rp and Yogyakarta 100,000 rp.

Bus There are city bus stations in all main districts of Jakarta and buses radiate out from them to the suburban intercity stations.

Buses to towns around Jakarta go from the Cililitan suburban station out towards Halim Airport. Buses from here include Bogor (700 rp), Puncak, Sukabumi, Pelabuhan Ratu and Bandung (2500 rp). Buses to the east operate from the Pulo Gadung station; the bus to Cirebon costs 3000 rp.

To Yogyakarta, public buses cost from 6500 rp for economy service and air-con public buses are 9500 to 13,500 rp. The deluxe, private air-con services cost 17,000 or 18,000 rp and take about 14 hours. Buses for Merak depart every 10 minutes or so and go from the Grogol bus station in the northwest. They cost from 1500 rp.

Train Jakarta has a number of train stations, the most convenient of which is Gambir, beside the Merdeka Square. Jatinegara is further south, Pasar Senen is to the east, Tanah Abang is to the west, while Kota is in the old city area in the north. Check which station you will be departing from. During rush hour, it can take a long time to get to the Kota station from the Jalan Thamrin area of Jakarta.

To Merak For Merak, from where the ferry crosses to Sumatra, trains depart from Kota station and go via Tanah Abang station or directly from Tanah Abang. It takes about three to four hours to Merak and the fare is 1300 rp.

To Bogor Buses to Bogor are so fast and so frequent it makes little sense to take the train which can be very slow. The one advantage the train has is that the Cililitan bus station is some distance from central Jakarta.

To Bandung There are eight Parahyangan departures daily, taking about three hours between the two cities. Most services start or finish at Kota station and make stops at Gambir and Jatinegara but a few start from Gambir. Fares on the Parahyangan service are 6000 rp in 2nd class and 8000 rp in 1st. There is also a slower Cepat service which costs 2200 rp.

To Cirebon Cirebon trains take three to four hours and cost 3100 rp in 3rd class or 4000 rp in 2nd on the Gunung Jati service. It is 5000 rp in the all 3rd-class Cirebon Express. There are also services continuing to Semarang, Yogyakarta and/or Surabaya which go via Cirebon. The fares for these services are 6000 to 9500 rp in 2nd class and 10,500 rp in 1st.

To Yogyakarta Jakarta to Yogyakarta takes nine to 12 hours and most departures are from Gambir station. Fares vary from 4500 rp in 3rd class, from 7000 rp in 2nd class and from 10,500 rp in 1st. The deluxe Bima Express costs 17,000 rp in 1st class or 21,000 rp for a sleeper. At the other end of the luxury scale is the all 3rd-class Gaya Baru Malam Selatan which, like the Bima Express, continues through to Surabaya.

To Surabaya Trains between Jakarta and Surabaya either take the shorter northern route via Semarang or the longer southern route via Yogyakarta. The trip takes 15 to 20 hours although, in practice, the slower 3rd-class trains can take even longer. Fares vary from 5800 rp in 3rd class, from 9500 rp in 2nd and from 13,500 in 3rd.

The best services are with the deluxe Bima Express via Yogya (22,500 rp in 1st class or 27,000 rp with a sleeper) or the Mutiara Utara via Semarang (25,000 rp in 1st). The cheapest are the all 3rd-class services like the Senja Ekonomi or the Gaya Baru Malam Utara on the northern route, or the Selatan version on the southern route.

Taxis There are fast and convenient, but rather more expensive, intercity taxis and minibuses to Bandung. Fares start from 9000 rp and they depart as soon as they have five passengers. You can book ahead and they will pick you up from your hotel as well as drop you off at your hotel when you get there. Media Taxis are at Jalan Johar, near Jalan Jaksa. The 4848 Taxis (☎ 36 4488) are at Jalan Prapatan 34, just beyond the Aryaduta Hyatt Hotel.

Boat See the Indonesia Getting Around section for information on the Pelni shipping services which operate on a regular two-week schedule to ports all over the archipelago. Most of them go through Jakarta (Tanjung Priok). The Pelni ticketing office (☎ 35 8398) is at Jalan Pintu Air 1, behind the Istiqlal Mosque. The office is open from 8.30 am to 12 noon and 1 pm to 2 pm Monday to Friday but from 8.30 am to 12 noon on Saturday.

Getting Around

To/From the Airport Airport tax is 11,000 rp on international flights and is payable at the airport. A 5500 rp tax on domestic flights is levied although this is usually included in the ticket price. Most flights go from the newer Soekarno-Hatta International Airport although some domestic flights use the more centrally located Halim Airport.

Soekarno-Hatta is a long way out to the west of the city at Cengkareng. Allow at least an hour to cover the 35 km although you can do it in half an hour when it is quiet, eg Sunday morning. Getting into and out of Jakarta is the problem; once you're on the toll highway it's plain sailing.

There's a Damri bus service every 30 minutes between the airport and Gambir station (close to the Jalan Jaksa cheap-accommodation area) in central Jakarta. This quick and convenient service costs 3000 rp. Alternatively, a taxi costs about 15,000 to 20,000 rp plus the 3000 rp toll-road charge. Coming from the airport, there's an additional airport surcharge. Some of the larger hotels operate airport minibus services.

See the Airport section under Jakarta Places to Stay for accommodation near the airport. The airport restaurant facilities are fairly reasonable.

To/From Tanjung Priok Harbour The Pelni ships all use Pelabuhan (dock) No 1. The Tanjung Priok bus station is two km from the dock, past the harbour Pelni office. From Tanjung Priok, take bus No 64 or pale blue minibus M15 to Kota, and from there bus

Nos 70 or P1 to the Sarinah department store on Jalan Thamrin.

A P22 express bus will take you from Tanjung Priok to Grogol, or a P14 to Tanah Abang, both reasonably close the city centre. Tanjung Priok is quite a distance from the centre of the city, so allow at least an hour to get there. A taxi will cost around 6000 rp.

Bus The regular big city buses charge a fixed 200 rp, and the express Patas buses, which are usually less crowded, charge 450 rp. The Pasar Senen bus station, off to the east side of Merdeka Square, is the most central bus terminal. There are also a number of other stations for suburban and intercity buses, like the Cililitan suburban station or the Grogol and Pulo Gadung bus stations. The regular bus service is supplemented by orange metro-minis (minibuses) and, in a few areas, pale blue microlet buses.

Jakarta's crowded buses are notorious for their pickpockets and bag slashers. They will gang up on you, the driver or conductor may be in cohorts and the buses will often be so crowded you can't do anything anyway. Bus No 70 between Kota railway or Kota bus stations and the Jalan Thamrin area is particularly bad and many guest houses have signs recommending that you completely avoid this bus and take a taxi, despite the cost. Bus Nos 700, P1 and P11 are also risky. The air-con Damri bus to Kota costs 750 rp but 'that's all you lose'.

The *Jakarta See for Yourself* brochure has useful information on getting to Jakarta's main attractions by public transport. Buses all have their ultimate destination on the front. The Sarinah department store on Jalan Thamrin is a popular landmark and within easy walking distance of Jalan Jaksa. Some of the useful buses which will drop you off there include:

Bus No	Route
408 & P11	Chilitan bus station to Jalan Thamrin
59	Pulo Gadung bus station to Jalan Thamrin
16	Kalideres bus station to Jalan Thamrin
70, P1 & P11	Kota railway station to Jalan Thamrin
10	Pasar Senen bus & railway stations to Jalan Thamrin
34	Jalan Thamrin to 'TIM' on Jalan Cikini Raya
10, 12 & 16	Jalan Thamrin to Blok M, Kebayoran
507	Jalan Kebon Sirih to Pulo Gadung bus station

P is for 'Patas' or express
Bus Nos 10, 12 & 110 go by the post office

Railway Stations There are several railway stations in Jakarta. Most convenient is the Gambir station, right beside the Merdeka Square and on its east side. It's within walking distance of Jalan Jaksa (staggering if your gear is heavy). The bajaj drivers who come here are a mercenary lot so it might be better to take a metered taxi.

Kota station, for the Bima and Mutiara night trains, is in the old part of town. Allow plenty of time to get there during the rush hour – a metered taxi is about 2500 rp from Jalan Jaksa. Other stations are Pasar Senen, to the north-east of Jalan Jaksa, and Tanah Abang, directly to the west of Merdeka Square. Trains for Merak and Sumatra depart from Tanah Abang station.

Taxi These days the taxis in Jakarta are modern, well-kept, and have air-con and working meters which are used without argument. Flagfall is 800 rp then 40 rp more for each additional 100 metres. The Bluebird Taxis have a good reputation. President Taxis seem to get a fair number of complaints and need to be watched, although not all drivers are untrustworthy.

Other Transport Bajajs are nothing less than Indian auto-rickshaws – three wheelers that carry two passengers (three at a squeeze) and are powered by noisy two-stroke engines. You can get most places for less than 1000 rp but bajajs are not allowed along Jalan Thamrin.

Becaks (bicycle rickshaws) are meant to be banned from Jakarta and the authorities have seized thousands of them and dumped them in the sea, creating a becak reef. Nevertheless, there are still some around in the side roads and back streets of the city. Late at night, you still might see one hovering near Jalan Thamrin. Around Sunda Kelapa, the old port area north of Kota, you can get around on bicycles with padded 'kiddy carriers' on the back. A rider will *dink* you from Sunda Kelapa to Taman Fatahillah for 400 rp!

MERAK

This is the port at the western end of Java, from where the ferry crosses to Sumatra. It's a small place and the bus and train stations are within easy walking distance of each other.

Places to Stay

If you have to spend the night in Merak, there are a couple of reasonable losmen just across the railway line and opposite the bus station, on Jalan Florida. The *Hotel Anda* has rooms from 9000 rp, and the *Hotel Robinson* is right next door.

Getting There & Away

Buses for Merak depart roughly every 10 minutes – between 3 am and midnight – from the Kalideres bus station in Jakarta; they take about 3½ hours and cost from 2500 rp. Trains leave twice daily from the Tanah Abang railway station (the afternoon service starts from Kota). The day train is faster.

From Merak, it's a short trip to Carita Beach (Pantai Carita), just north of Labuhan on the west coast. Take the Jakarta bus to Cilegon and from there a colt along the coast road to Carita. Ferries to Bakauheni depart every hour from the dock near the bus station, the trip takes 1½ hours and costs from 1100 rp. Refer to the Sumatra Getting There & Away section for more details.

BANTEN

En route to Merak from Jakarta, you pass through Serang, the turn off for the historic town of Banten where the first bedraggled Dutch set foot on Java in 1596. In the 16th and 17th centuries, the town was the centre of a great and wealthy sultanate but it's hardly splendid now.

There's not a lot to see around this small coastal village but Banten has an interesting mosque, the **Mesjid Agung**, and a great white lighthouse of a minaret which was designed by a Chinese Muslim in the early 17th century. The old palaces are now in ruins and the Dutch **Speelwijk Fortress**, built in 1682, is equally decayed.

WEST COAST

There are good beaches along the west coast south of Merak at **Anyer**, **Karang Bolong** and **Carita**.

This is a good base for visits to the **Krakatau Islands** in the Sunda Strait, about 50 km from Carita and Labuhan, and to the **Ujong Kulon National Park**. Boat hire is expensive and difficult to find during the wet season. If you're interested in either place ask to view the Carita Hotel's documentary video about Krakatau's explosion and its effects on the west coast – it's free!

Places to Stay

Anyer has a luxury beach motel, and the rustic *Carita Krakatau Beach Hotel*, further south near Labuan, has rooms from as low as US$10, rather more on weekends. The hotel's information sheet, available from the Visitor's Information Centre in Jakarta, is good for a 25% discount on your first night (10% on weekends). The hotel restaurant is not cheap but there are a couple of very simple warungs close by. The associated *Hostel Rakata* has rooms from US$5.

Getting There & Away

Carita is a pleasant place if you want to escape from Jakarta for a few days but it's close enough to the capital for it to get crowded at weekends. Buses go hourly from the Kalideres bus station, near the Grogol station, so look for signs 'Jakarta-Labuhan'. The trip takes about three to four hours and the fare is 3500 rp.

From Labuhan, a colt will take you the seven km to the hotel at Carita Beach (Pantai Carita) for 500 rp. Alternatively, the hotel operates its own bus from the Wisata Hotel in Jakarta for US$15.

BOGOR

The **Kebun Raya** are huge botanical gardens in the centre of Bogor, just 60 km from Jakarta. Sir Stamford Raffles founded them in 1817, during the British interregnum, and they have a huge collection of tropical plants. A monument to Raffles' wife, Olivia, is near the main entrance to the gardens.

The **Presidential Palace**, built by the Dutch and much favoured by Sukarno (Suharto has ignored it), stands beside the gardens and deer graze on its lawns. The gardens are a popular place on the weekends for young flirting couples from Jakarta, as they can be safe from parental eyes.

Admission to the gardens is a hefty 1000 rp – its only 500 rp on Saturday but on the weekend the crowds are packed in. The gardens are open from 8 am to 4 pm daily.

Near the garden entrance there is a good **zoological museum** which exhibits a blue whale skeleton and other interesting items. If you ever heard about the island of Flores having a rat problem, one glance at the stuffed Flores version in the showcase of Indonesian rats will explain why. Admission to the museum is 300 rp and it's open from 8 am to 2 pm daily, except on Friday when it closes at 11 am.

Information

Bogor's Visitor's Information Centre is at Jalan Ir H Juanda 38, west of the gardens. At No 9 on the same street and next to the garden gates is the headquarters of the PPA (Perlindungan dan Pengawetan Alam) – the administrative body for all of Indonesia's wildlife reserves.

Places to Stay

Accommodation in Bogor has been revolutionised – the dreadful old places which made staying in Bogor uncomfortable have disappeared in favour of a selection of better new family-run places which make staying in Bogor a real pleasure.

Abu Pensione (☎ 32 2893), near the

1	Wisma Mirah
2	Wisma Teladan
3	Bogor Permai Coffee House
4	Elsana Transit Hotel
5	Lautan Restaurant
6	Wisma Karunia
7	Sempur Kencana Guest House
8	Abu Pensione
9	Food Court
10	Singapore Bakery
11	Hotel Salak
12	Presidential Palace
13	Hidangan Trio Masakan Padang & Hidangan Puti Bungsu
14	Pizza Hut
15	Orchid House
16	Wisma Permata
17	Visitor's Information Centre
18	Post Office
19	Homestay Puri Bali & Pensione Firman
20	Wisma Ramayana
21	Zoological Museum
22	Botanical Gardens Entrance
23	Kentucky Fried Chicken
24	Bus Station
25	Wisma Duta
26	Gong Factory

railway station at Jalan Mayor Oking 28, is clean, attractive and pleasantly situated. It overlooks the river, has a nice garden and the food is excellent. All in all, it's no wonder it's so popular. Dorm beds are 4000 rp, singles/doubles are US$6/10 or a double with hot water is US$12. Breakfast costs 2000 rp.

Just across from the gardens at Jalan Ir H Juanda 44 is the *Wisma Ramayana* with a variety of rooms from 12,000 rp for pleasant rooms to 22,000 rp for very nice rooms with fan and bath. Breakfast is included and there's a good laundry service.

Round the corner at Jalan Paledang 50 is the *Homestay Puri Bali* with rooms – all doubles and including breakfast – at 12,000, 15,000 and 20,000 rp. Next door at No 48 is the *Pensione Firman* with dorm beds at 5000 rp, single rooms from 6000 to 8000 rp and doubles from 10,000 to 18,000 rp. There's been some street number changes in Bogor recently so the number here may still say 28.

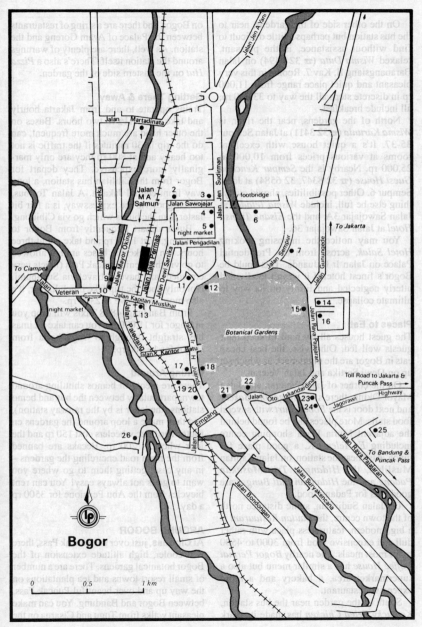

Jalan A Yani

Jalan Martadinata

Jalan MA Salmun

Merdeka

Jalan Sawojajar

Jalan Jen Sudirman

footbridge

night market

Jalan Pengadilan

Jalan Mayor Oking

To Jakarta

Jalan Dewi Sartika

Jalan Sempur

Jalan Gunungede

Jalan Raya Permas

Veteran

Jalan Kapitan Muslihat

night market

Jalan Paledang

Jalan X Kantor Batu

Botanical Gardens

Jalan Raya Pajajaran

Ir H Juanda

Jalan Oto Iskandardinata

Jalan Empang

Toll Road to Jakarta & Puncak Pass Highway

To Bandung & Puncak Pass

Jalan Raya Pajajaran

Jagorawi

Jalan Suryakencana

Jalan Bondongan

To Ciampes

To Bogor

Bogor

0 0.5 1 km

On the other side of the gardens, near to the bus station but perhaps a little difficult to find without assistance, is the pleasant, relaxed *Wisma Duta* (☎ 32 8494) on Jalan Baranangsiang II, Kav 7. Rooms in this very pleasant and quiet place range from 11,000 rp in discrete steps all the way to 33,000 rp; all include breakfast.

North of the gardens, near the river, is *Wisma Karunia* (☎ 32 3411) at Jalan Sempur 35-37. It's a quiet house with excellent rooms at various prices from 10,000 to 25,000 rp. Nearby is the *Sempur Kencana Guest House* (☎ 32 8347, 32 6584) at Jalan Sempur 6. Other possibilities, should everything else be full, include *Wisma Teladan* at Jalan Sawojajar 3A, and the *Elsana Transit Hotel* at Jalan Sawojajar 36.

You may notice the imposing looking *Hotel Salak*, across from the Presidential Palace on Jalan Ir H Juanda. This could be Bogor's finest hotel if it wasn't totally and utterly neglected and firmly on its way to ultimate collapse.

Places to Eat

The guest houses all try hard to keep their guests well fed. Otherwise, the best cheap eats in Bogor are the night markets which set up on Dewi Sartika and Jalan Veteran.

On the corner of Jalan Veteran and Jalan Mayor Oking, there's the *Singapore Bakery* and next door is the *Food Court* with several food stalls. More places can be found behind the adjacent Muria Plaza shopping centre including *Es Teler KK*, a good place for lunch. Also near the station, on Jalan Kapitan Muslihat, the *Hidangan Trio Masakan Padang* and the *Hidangan Puti Bungsu* are good bets for Padang food.

Up Jalan Sudirman, some distance north of the town centre, the *Lautan Restaurant* is a big, modern, featureless place with rather dull and expensive food from 3000 to 4500 rp for most meals. The nearby *Bogor Permai Coffee House* has a similar menu but also a supermarket area, a bakery and a more expensive restaurant.

South of the garden near the bus station, *Kentucky Fried Chicken* has made its mark on Bogor, and there are a string of restaurants between the Palace of Ayam Goreng and the station. As well, there are plenty of warungs around the station itself. There's also a *Pizza Hut* on the eastern side of the garden.

Getting There & Away

Trains operate to and from Jakarta hourly and take about 1½ to two hours. Buses on the other hand are much more frequent, can do the trip in 30 minutes if the traffic is not too heavy and at 800 rp they are only marginally more expensive. They depart for Bogor from the Cililitan bus station, a long way from central Jakarta. A Jalan Tol bus, which goes via the expressway, is a fair bit faster than the buses which go via Cibinong.

Buses depart frequently from Bogor to Bandung, cost 1750 rp and take about three hours. On weekends, buses are not allowed to go via the scenic Puncak Pass (it gets very crowded) and have to travel via Sukabumi. Not only does the trip take much longer, it's also more expensive at 2300 rp.

From Bandung, 4848 Taxis will drop you in Bogor for 11,000 rp. You can take a Limas bus straight through to Yogyakarta from Bogor for 16,000 rp.

Getting Around

There are plenty of bemos shuttling around town, particularly between the bus and bemo stations (the latter is by the railway station), and they make a loop around the gardens en route. The three wheelers cost 150 rp and the four wheelers 200 rp. Becaks are banned from the main road encircling the gardens – in any case, getting them to go where you want to go is not always easy! You can rent bicycles from the Abu Pensione for 3500 rp a day.

AROUND BOGOR

At **Cibodas**, just over the Puncak Pass, there is a cooler, high altitude extension of the Bogor botanical gardens. There are a number of small resort towns and tea plantations on the way up and over beautiful Puncak Pass, between Bogor and Bandung. You can make pleasant walks from Tugu and Cisarua on the

Bogor side of the pass, or from Cibodas and Cipanas on the other side.

On the way up to the Puncak summit from Bogor, you can stop at the **Gunung Mas Tea Plantation** and tour the tea factory or visit the pleasant lake of **Telaga Warna** (just before the summit).

The Cibodas gardens are four km off the main road and only a short distance from Cipanas. From here, you can climb **Gunung Gede**, a volcano peak offering fine views of the surrounding area. You have to obtain permission first from the PPA office at the entrance to the gardens, and they provide good maps of the route. The walk takes all day, so start as early as possible.

You can get up to the towns on the pass by taking a colt or any Bandung bus from Bogor.

Places to Stay

The small *Kopo Hostel* (☎ 0251-4296) at Jalan Raya Puncak 557 in Cisarua is on the the main Bogor to Bandung road. It has its own garden, dorm beds for 2500 rp and rooms from 7500 rp; blankets are provided. Cold drinks and breakfast are available, as is a wealth of good information on the area. The hostel is open from 7 am to 10 pm and it's about 45 minutes by bus or colt from Bogor. Ask for the Cisarua petrol station (*pompa bensin Cisarua*) – the hostel is next door.

Also in Cisarua, *Chalet Bali International* is affiliated with the Bali International in Jakarta and has dorm beds and rooms but is more expensive than the Kopo Hostel.

In Cibulan, the *Hotel Cibulan* is an old-world Dutch hotel – run-down but friendly. Rooms cost from around 7500 rp – they're more expensive on weekends when people from Jakarta flock up here to escape the heat.

The new *Pondok Pemuda Cibodas*, near the Cibodas PPA office, is comfortable, friendly and has dorm beds and rooms. In the village, 500 metres down the hill, you can stay with Mohammed Saleh Abdullah (also known as Freddy) for rock-bottom prices.

PELABUHANRATU

From Bogor, you can continue south-west of the small town of Sukabumi to Pelabuhanratu, a popular coastal resort where swimming and walking are possible. There are rocky cliffs, caves and gorges to explore and a fine beach but the sea here is treacherous and signs warn swimmers away. You're best off in the hotel pool.

Places to Stay

Pelabuhanratu is very crowded on weekends and it's expensive. There are a number of beach bungalows to rent along the four km between the big Samudra Beach Hotel and Pelabuhanratu's fish market – but prices are likely to be over 10,000 rp. The *Bayu Armta* (also known as the Fish Restaurant or Hoffman's), at the edge of a cliff, has doubles from 10,000 to 25,000 rp and there is a restaurant known for its good seafood.

Getting There & Away

Take a bus or train from Bogor to Cibadak or Sukabumi, then take a colt.

BANDUNG

The capital of west Java and the third largest city in Indonesia, Bandung's chief claim to fame is that it was the site for the first (and so far only) Afro-Asian conference back in 1955. Third World leaders from a variety of countries converged on Bandung but not much seems to have happened since. The city's 750-metre altitude makes the climate cool and comfortable. Treat it as a short stop between Yogya and Jakarta.

It's worth a brief pause to visit the nearby volcano, Tangkuban Perahu, and there are several interesting museums. If you travel between Bandung and Bogor take the bus so you can see the beautiful Puncak Pass. Bandung is a big university town which is surprisingly go ahead and affluent.

Information

There's a helpful Visitor's Information Centre on the corner of Alun Alun Square, the main square on Jalan Asia-Afrika, and the west Java regional tourist office is on

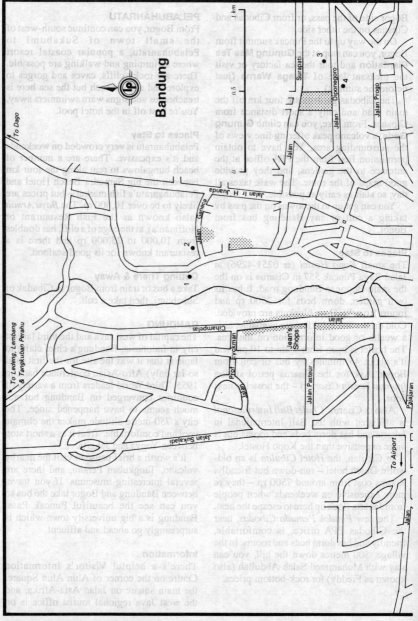

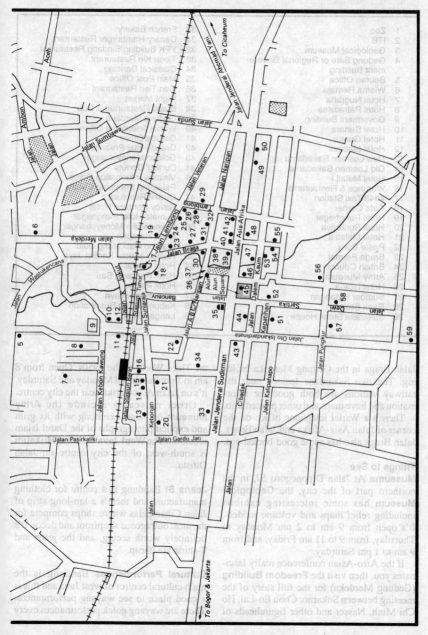

1	Zoo	30	French Bakery
2	ITB	31	Canary Hamburger Restaurant
3	Geological Museum	32	YPK Building/Sindang Restaurant
4	Gedung Sate or Regional Government Building	33	Tjoen Kie Restaurant
		34	Classical Dancing
5	Bouraq Office	35	Main Post Office
6	Wisma Remaja	36	Tien Tien Restaurant
7	Hotel Nugraha	37	Night Market
8	Hotel Patradissa	38	Braga Restaurant & Pub
9	Goverment Building	39	Gedung Merdeka
10	Hotel Sahara	40	Wartel Telephone Office
11	Hotel Guntur	41	Garuda Office
12	Hotel Malabar	42	Grand Hotel Preanger
13	New Losmen Sakadarna	43	Golden Moneychanger
14	Old Losmen Sakadarna	44	Dunkin' Donuts
15	Hotel Melati I	45	Visitor's Information Office
16	Warungs & Restaurants	46	Palaguna Shopping Centre
17	4848 Taxi Station	47	Queen Restaurant
18	Cafe Corner	48	Savoy Homann Hotel
19	Hotel Panghegar	49	Kumala Hotel Panghegar
20	Hotel Surabaya	50	Dwipa Mulia Moneychanger
21	Hotel Melati II	51	Hotel Harapan
22	Pasar Baru	52	Warung Nasi Mang Udju
23	Braga Permai	53	Rumah Makan Kartika Jaya
24	British Council	54	Hotel Mawar
25	Army Museum	55	Hotel Pangang Sari
26	Hotel Istana	56	Hotel Pacific
27	Sumber Hidangan	57	Hotel Brajawijaya
28	Rasa Bakery	58	Kebun Kelaba Bus Station
29	Sukarasa Steak House	59	Langen Setra

Jalan Braga in the Gedung Merdeka building. The two Sakardana losmen near the railway stations are both good for information and have maps and other printed info.

There's a Wartel telephone office on the corner of Jalan Asia-Afrika and Jalan Braga. Jalan Braga also has some good bookshops.

Things to See

Museums At Jalan Diponegoro 57, in the northern part of the city, the **Geological Museum** has some interesting exhibits including relief maps and volcano models. It's open from 9 am to 2 pm Monday to Thursday, from 9 to 11 am Friday, and from 9 am to 1 pm Saturday.

If the Afro-Asian conference really fascinates you, then visit the **Freedom Building** (Gedung Merdeka) for the full story of the meeting between Sukarno, Chou En-Lai, Ho Chi Minh, Nasser and other figureheads of the Third World of the 1950s. Open from 8 am to 1 pm but closed Monday and Saturday, it's on Jalan Asia-Afrika near the city centre.

Other museums include the **Army Museum** on Jalan Lembong with its grim and explicit photographs of the Darul Islam rebellion. The **West Java Cultural Museum** is south-west of the city centre on Jalan Ottista.

Jeans St Bandung is a centre for clothing manufacture and there's a km-long strip of Jalan Cihampelas where shops compete for the most outrageous shopfront and decor. It's definitely worth seeing, and the jeans and T-shirts are cheap.

Cultural Performances Bandung is the main cultural centres of west Java and this is a good place to see wayang performances. There are wayang golek performances every

Saturday night at Gedung Rumentangsiang on Baranangsiang St from 1000 to 2000 rp. The whole performance runs from 9 pm to 5 am, finishing just in time to catch an early morning train out! Performances also take place on Sunday night in the YPK Building/ Sindang Restaurant.

Sundanese dance performances are held on Wednesday and Saturday night from 7.30 to 10.30 pm at the Panghegar Hotel. In this five-star hotel, the performance costs 15,000 rp and you're also supposed to buy a drink. Angklung performances take place at Saung Angklung on Jalan Padasuka; they cost 5000 rp. Take a Damri city bus for Cicaheum and ask for Padasuka. From there, it's a 350-metre walk – ask for Saung Angklung or Pak Ujo. There are a number of other places around the city to see wayang, Sundanese dance, gamelan playing and *pencak silat*, an Indonesian martial art.

You can buy wayang golek puppets and masks and see them being made at a small cottage industry close to the main square. Ask for Pak Roehiyat, which is down a small alley behind Jalan Pangarang 22. Jalan Pangarang runs south off Jalan Dalem Kaum, and the Mawar and Pangarang Sari hotels are both on it.

Other Bandung is noted for its fine Dutch art-deco architecture. The expensive **Savoy Homann Hotel** and the recently restored **Grand Hotel Preanger** are worth a look. Also take a look at the magnificent **Regional Government Building** near the Geology Museum. It's known as Gedung Sate, or the Satay Building, because it's topped by what looks a satay stick.

Bandung's ITB or Institute of Technology is one of the most important universities in Indonesia – it's on the north side of the city. On Jalan Taman Sari, close to the ITB, Bandung's **zoo** has Komodo dragons, open park space and a wide variety of Indonesian bird life. Once a fortnight, on Sunday morning, traditional ram-butting fights are held at Ranca Buni, near Ledeng to the north of the city

Tangkuban Perahu

The 'overturned perahu' volcano crater stands 30 km north of Bandung. Legend tells of a god challenged to build a huge boat during a single night. His opponent, on seeing that he would probably complete this impossible task, brought the sun up early and the boat builder turned his nearly completed boat over in a fit of anger.

Tangkuban Perahu isn't really that special. If you've seen Bromo or other volcanoes, and feel satiated, then give it a miss. It's very commercial up at the crater – car parks, restaurants and an admission fee. To get there, take a Subang minibus from Bandung's train station which goes via Lembang to the park entrance.

At weekends, there is a minibus from the gate up to the main crater but on other days you'll have to hitch or walk. It's four km by road, or there is a more interesting short cut of two km through the jungle. Start up the road and take the first turning on the right – the path leads through the jungle to an active area of steaming and bubbling geysers and another steep path cuts up to the main crater.

It's best to go early, before 12 noon, as the main crater mists over about then. You can hire a minibus or taxi to take a group to the volcano and other local attractions for around 30,000 rp. Get it to drop you at the top and you can walk downhill past the active area and back to the road.

In Lembang, and on the road up to the crater, there are stalls selling hot corn on the cob, a delicious snack. **Ciater**, a few km beyond the crater entrance point, has hot springs as does **Maribaya**, five km beyond Lembang. Ciater is the better hot springs for a swim on a cold, rainy day but both are commercialised.

You can extend your Tangkuban Perahu trip by walking from the bottom end of the gardens at Maribaya down through a brilliant river gorge (there's a good track) to **Dago** – here, you can eat at the *Dago Tea House* at sunset. Allow about two hours for the walk to Dago. It's a good spot to watch the city light up. After a nasi goreng, you can then get back into the city on the local bemos which are known as angkots. You can also travel straight out to the tea house by taking a Dago angkot from the train station in Bandung.

Places to Stay

Bandung is not a great place for cheap hotels but there are a few possibilities around. Near the railway station and the city centre, on Jalan Kebonjati, there are two *Losmen Sakadarnas*. The original Sakardana (☎ 43 9897) is down a little alley beside the large Hotel Melati at No 50/7B. It's basic, well-kept and very popular with rooms from 5000/8000 rp.

At Jalan Kebonjati 34, the new Sakardana, run by the outgoing Rusty Muchfree, is a wonderful information source and has a good restaurant downstairs. It's neat and clean with dorm beds at 3500 rp or singles/doubles at 7000/8000 rp.

As well as the two Sakardanas, Jalan Kebonjati also has two Melati Hotels. *Melati I* is right by the old Sakardana and is noisy and poorly kept. Across the road, the *Melati II* (☎ 56409) is better with singles at 18,000 rp and doubles from 27,500 to 31,000 rp. A little further down the road at Jalan Kebonjati 71, *Surabaya Hotel* (☎ 51133) is a rambling, old-fashioned sort of place with grubby rooms at 5500/11,000 rp.

Across the railway tracks, the *Hotel Melati-2 Dunia* at Jalan Kebun Jukut 13 has simple rooms for 10,000 rp. Also across the tracks at Jalan Oto Iskandardinata 20, the *Hotel Guntur* (☎ 50763) is good value for a mid-range hotel with comfortable, if slightly tatty, rooms with bath and hot water for 25,000/28,000 rp including breakfast.

At Jalan Oto Iskandardinata 3, the *Hotel Sahara* (☎ 51684) is a rather old-fashioned losmen with clean, spartan rooms at 10,000/15,000 rp, or doubles with mandi and toilet for 24,000 to 30,000 rp. You even get a prayer mat and an arrow aligned to Mecca.

Turn left at the top of the road, in front of the imposing Government House, and there are two good places near the railway station, in roads leading off Jalan Kebon Kawung. *Hotel Nugraha* (☎ 43 6146) at Jalan H Mesri

11 has pleasant rooms around a garden from 16,500 to 33,000 rp including breakfast. A block back, there's the new *Patradissa Hotel* (☎ 56680) at Jalan H Moch Iskat 8 with clean, modern rooms with bath at 17,500, 25,000 and 30,000 rp.

There are two more budget hotels close to the city centre – they are on Jalan Pangarang which runs off Jalan Dalem Kaum and is within walking distance of the Kebun Kelapa bus station. At No 3, the *Pangarang Sari Hotel* (☎ 51205) has rooms with mandi for 15,000 rp including breakfast. Across the road at No 14, the *Hotel Mawar* is cheaper with rooms at 7500/8500 rp.

Other places include *Wisma Remaja* which is in a government youth centre at Jalan Merdeka 64. It has dormitory beds at 3500 rp rooms from 8000 to 15,000 rp and a good cafe. It's a 20-minute walk from the railway station or take a Dago minibus and ask for the youth centre, Gelanggang Generasi Muda Bandung.

Places to Eat

Accommodation may not be too hot in Bandung but there are plenty of tempting restaurants including an appetising night market which sets up on Jalan Cikapundung Barat, directly across Jalan Asia-Afrika from the Visitor's Information Centre. Sweet-toothed travellers can end the evening with a pisang goreng (fried banana), a putu dan lupis or go all the way with a martabak manis, a sort of pancake featuring susu, coklat, keju and kacang.

A second good area for cheap eats is the road where minibuses stop, directly in front of the railway station, through to Jalan Kebonjati. Good spots in this enclave of restaurants and warungs include the popular *Rumah Makan Hadori Satay House, Rumah Makan Gahaya Minang* (for Padang food) and *Warung Gizi*. Across the road at Jalan Kebonjati 5 is *La Resa* while down towards Jalan Oto Iskandardinata, Jalan Kebonjati changes to Jalan Suniaraja and you'll find the *Roti Lux* bakery near the junction.

There are all sorts of interesting places

along Jalan Braga, the fancy shopping street of Bandung. Centrepiece is the *Braga Permai* with its open-air cafe at No 74. Even cheaper meals are 3500 to 5000 rp but the ice cream at 1500 to 3500 rp is superb. Skip the mediocre *Braga Coffee Shop* in front of the Braga Hotel. Across the road at Jalan Braga 17 is the *Braga Restaurant & Pub* where you can get Indian curries from 3000 to 4000 rp. Indonesia and Western dishes also featured.

On the corner of Jalan Braga and Jalan ABC/Naripan is the *Canary Hamburger Restaurant* for fast food. Continue to the *Sumber Hidangan* bakery or across the road there's the *French Bakery*, all good places for a snack or light meal with croissants and Danish pastries available!

Turn the corner to the left to find the *Corner Cafe* at Jalan Suniaraja 9. It's a fresh, clean little place with pretty good Indonesian food and good interpretations of Italian pasta dishes. On Jalan ABC at the Banceung Permai centre and right by the night market, *Tien Tien* is a neat little Chinese restaurant with good if slightly more expensive food. Apart from the Westernised places along Jalan Braga, Bandung has various others including a *Kentucky Fried Chicken*, some distance out towards the Cicaheum bus station.

In the city centre, the Palaguna shopping centre, beside the Alun Alun Square, has an *Istana Peters* ice-cream parlour on the ground floor. Here you can choose from a range of interesting flavours including durian, jackfruit and zurzat for 800 rp. Upstairs, there's a *Home Bakery, Hero Fast Food, California Fried Chicken* (in the fashion of Kentucky Fried) and a stand selling pizza by the slice. On Jalan Dalem Kaum, on the southern side of the square, there's a *Dunkin' Donuts* (750 rp each) with what seems like at least 1000 varieties.

Just south of the Alun Alun Square, at Jalan Dewi Sartika 7A, there's the *Warung Nasi Mang Udju* which cooks Sundanese food which is eaten with the fingers like nasi padang. It's also known as M-Udju. A few steps down the alley from the square nearest the tourist office, there's the *Coffee Bego*

stall with excellent and very strong coffee, a local speciality.

Jalan Dalem Kaum, which runs east of Alun Alun Square, has several interesting restaurants, including the popular *Queen* Chinese restaurant at No 79. Further along, there's good nasi padang at *Rumah Makan Kartika Jaya*, Jalan Dalem Kaum 84, and *Ruma Makan Sari Bundo* at No 75. There's also *Pangkap 33* which offers Makassar-style ikan bakar.

On Jalan Tamblong, the *Rasa Bakery* sells very good ice cream and a wild assortment of expensive but irresistible cakes. At Jalan Jenderal Sudirman 64, the road towards Bogor and Jakarta, the *Tjoen Kie Restaurant* is another good local Chinese specialist. Or you could invest in a coffee, a drink or the fancy rijstaffel (a selection of rice dishes) at the genteel Savoy Homann on Jalan Asia-Afrika.

Getting There & Away

Air Garuda, Bouraq and Merpati fly from Bandung to Jakarta for around 48,000 rp. You can also fly to Yogyakarta with Bouraq for 71,000 rp.

Bus Buses to Bogor cost around 2000 rp and take 3½ hours but note that they are not allowed to take the Puncak Pass route on weekends when the trip is slower and costs more. The fare is about 2500 rp to the Cililitan station in Jakarta and by the Jagorawi Highway it only takes about 3½ hours.

The bus station for Jakarta, Kebun Kelapa on Jalan Dewi Sartika, is quite central but for Yogya and other places to the east it's a lengthy bus ride or bemo trip to the Cicaheum station east of the city. It costs from 9000 rp to Yogya.

Train The Bandung to Jakarta express takes just three hours and you can travel Bisnis class for 7500 rp, Eksekutif B for 10,000 rp or Eksekutif A for 15,000 rp. Regular trains are slower and cheaper with fares from 3000 rp in 3rd class.

Several daily trains also operate between

Yogya and Bandung and the fare varies from around 6000 rp in 3rd class, from 7000 rp in 2nd and from 18,000 rp in 1st. Trains to Surabaya costs from 8500 rp in 3rd class, from 12,000 rp in 2nd and around 25,000 rp in 1st.

A Bandung to Jakarta taxi costs 9000 rp per person.

Getting Around

Bandung's airport is only four km north-west of the city centre, about 3000 rp by taxi. There's a fairly good Damri city bus service costing a standard 150 rp. Bus No 1 runs from east to west right down Jalan Asia-Afrika to Cicaheum.

In Bandung, bemos are known as angkots; they cost a standard 200 rp. For most of the destinations they depart from the terminal outside the railway station or from the bus stations. Metered taxis are becoming increasingly common in Bandung and cost 750 rp for the first km then 350 rp for each subsequent km. As in other cities, the becaks are being relegated to the back streets and are no longer seen in such great numbers.

BANDUNG TO PANGANDARAN

Garut

This pleasant town is between Bandung and Banjar. There are popular **hot springs** *(air panas)* just five km north of Garut at Cipanas village, Tarogong. From Garut, you can climb **Gunung Papandayan** while east, towards Banjar is **Gunung Galunggung**. This volcano exploded dramatically a few years ago. You can get to Galunggung by motorbike from Tasikmalaya, although the locals will think you're nuts for wanting to climb it.

Places to Stay *Hotel Mulia* at Jalan Kenanga 17 is probably better than the *Hotel Nasional* nearby. There are more places at Tarogong.

Tasikmalaya & Cipatujah

Tasikmalaya is midway between Bandung and Pangandaran; you can stay at the *Santosa Hotel*. The beach at Cipatujah is 74

km south of Tasik and you can stay at the *Pantai Indah Losmen*. There's a **coral beach** at Sindangkerta, 14 km away, and minibuses run there from Cipatujah. Buses run from Bandung to Tasikmalaya, where you get another bus to Cipatujah.

PANGANDARAN

This coastal resort is one of the few places on the south Java coast where it is safe to swim – a coral reef cuts down the surf and dangerous undertows. It's centrally located between Yogyakarta and Bandung – Banjar, on the Yogya to Bandung road, is where you turn off. When coming from Yogya, many travellers take the interesting backwater trip from Cilacap to Kalipucang.

Orientation & Information

The main town part of Pangandaran with the bus terminal is at the head of the peninsula, over a km north of the area where all the accommodation is concentrated. Local maps tend to exaggerate the scale making it look much closer than it actually is. Hotels and restaurants are clumped together at the narrowest part of the peninsula and beyond there it widens out into the national park and nature reserve.

There's a large, useless tourist office in Pangandaran and another information centre, also with little information, at the national park visitor's centre. You're charged a once-only 300 rp when you enter the accommodation area from the bus station area. To enter the national park, however, you must pay another 300 rp each day. There's no bank at Pangandaran but you can change cash or travellers' cheques at the Restaurant Cilacap. Their rate is not as good as a bank, of course, but it's not too bad.

Avoid weekends and holidays – Christmas and after Ramadan, in particular – when it gets very crowded. At other times, this is a very peaceful and relaxing place to take a break from travel.

Things to See

Pangandaran has beaches on both sides of the peninsula, right by the town. The west

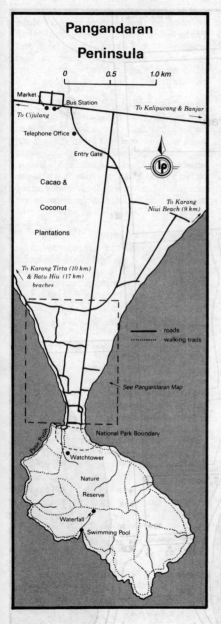

Pangandaran Peninsula

0   0.5   1.0 km

Market
Bus Station
To Cijulang
To Kalipucang & Banjar
Telephone Office
Entry Gate
Cacao & Coconut Plantations
To Karang Niui Beach (9 km)
To Karang Tirta (10 km) & Batu Hiu (17 km) beaches

— roads
⋯⋯ walking trails

See Pangandaran Map

National Park Boundary
Pasir Putih
Watchtower
Nature Reserve
Waterfall
Swimming Pool

beach is wide but dirty and overused but there are better beaches in the national park. **Pasir Putih**, the beach on the western side of the peninsula about a half-km walk from town, has good sand and snorkelling. The beaches on the eastern side are pleasant but the water is very shallow.

Continue through the park and there's a headland **reserve** cloaked in thick jungle, home to many monkeys and buffalo. There's a watchtower where you can see wildlife. Pangandaran also has good little **aquarium** on the west beach.

Places to Stay

Pangandaran has many places to stay in all price categories. It's a popular weekend escape for Indonesians and for expats working in Bandung and further afield. For this reason, it can be very crowded on weekends, and surprisingly empty mid-week. Simply wander around and look in a few places. With the great variety, this can be the best way of finding a good room. Look for the sign *kosong*, which means 'rooms available'.

Popular cheaper places include the two Losmen Minis. *Mini I* is on the main road across from the Sympathy Cafe and is clean, convenient, popular and the rooms cost from 7500 rp; this price also includes a good breakfast. Turn off the main road and towards the west beach, and then turn again to the north to find *Mini II* which is a more basic place with rooms at 4000/4500 rp.

Just beyond the Sympathy Cafe, on the main road, is the friendly *Losmen Laut Biru* with a variety of rooms from 7500 rp, including breakfast and tea or coffee anytime. There are some cheaper rooms in the main building. Also on the main road, there's the *Hotel Samudra*, a pleasant and clean place with rooms at 10,000 rp.

Just around the corner from the Cilicap Restaurant, almost on the east beach, is the now dirty and dilapidated *Penginapan Adem Ayem* with cheaper rooms at 5000 rp or better ones at 10,000 rp. Near is *Hotel Panorama*, which is right on the beach with rooms for 10,000 rp looking out over the sea. The

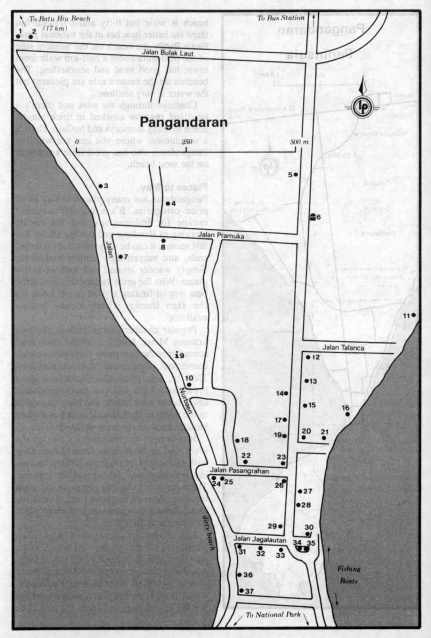

To Batu Hiu Beach
(17 km)

To Bus Station

Jalan Bulak Laut

Pangandaran

0   250   500 m

Jalan Pramuka

Jalan Talanca

Jalan Pasangrahan

Jalan Jagalautan

Fishing
Boats

dirty beach

To National Park

1	Bulah Laut
2	Pantai Sari
3	Pondok Percontohan
4	Penginapan Bahtera Jaya
5	Penginapan Bahagia
6	Post Office
7	Souvenir Market
8	Anggia Motel
9	Tourist Office
10	Hotel Bumi Nusantara
11	Hotel Bumi Pananjung
12	Penginapan Pantai Indah
13	Hotel Pamordian
14	Hotel Flamboyan
15	Losmen Srihana
16	Hotel Panorama
17	Rumah Makan Budi Jaya
18	Losmen Mini II
19	Hotel Samudra
20	Restaurant Cilicap
21	Penginapan Adem Ayem
22	Rumah Makan Sari Harum
23	Penginapan Damai
24	Rumah Makan Nanjung
25	Wisma Pelangi
26	Penginapan Rawamangun
27	Penginapan Setia Famili
28	Losmen Mini I
29	Sympathy Cafe
30	Gatul's Restaurant
31	Hotel Mangkabumi
32	Rumah Makan Mambo
33	Losmen Laut Biru
34	Warungs
35	Fish Auction
36	Aquarium
37	Pangandaran Beach Hotel

Sunrise Homestay, at Jalan Kidang Pananjung 175 on the east beach, is similar in price and pleasant.

Pondok Wisata Bulak Laut on Jalan Pamugaran has very nice bungalows for 10,000 rp including breakfast, tea and coffee. Each bungalow has a living room, open-air bathroom and a bedroom with a large double bed. *Pondok Wisata Pantai Sari* is next door and has similarly priced bungalows and a small Chinese restaurant.

More expensive places include the *Anggia Motel* at Jalan Pramuka 15 with standard doubles and some bigger bungalows. The *Penginapan Pantai Indah* is closer to the

town centre and has doubles at 20,000 rp. There's also the government run *Pondok Percontohan* with doubles and separate living rooms for 30,000 rp. *Pondok Pelangi*, also known as Wisma Pelangi, is close to the west beach and has comfortable individual bungalows each with toilet, mandi, kitchen, living room, two or three bedrooms and a veranda. They're great for families.

Some of the more expensive places are architecturally interesting. *Hotel Bumi Pananjung* on the east beach is like a Tyrolean-style chalet of timber and thatch with all the rooms off a gallery surrounding a large central sitting area. It's expensive for what it offers. On the west beach, the *Bumi Nusantara* is Indonesian in inspiration but equally imposing. Or there's the *Pangandaran Beach Hotel*, on the west beach near the park entrance. It looks exotic and fancy but the rooms are actually quite plain and simple at 25,000 rp with air-con.

Places to Eat
Restaurants are also in plentiful supply in Pangandaran, and the fish here is often superb. Usually, when you order fish you're invited back to the kitchen to see what's available and the price is dependent on weight. A larger fish will often feed two or more. Pangandaran is enough of a travellers' centre to feature all the regulars on the menus from fruit salad to banana pancakes.

On the main road, *Restaurant Cilicap* is a very popular and busy place with fairly standard prices and excellent fresh fish. In fact, all their food is very good, particularly the pancakes, but add your bill up carefully. Further down the road, the *Sympathy Cafe* is a basic and somewhat grotty little place with surprisingly good food at pleasing prices. I wish it looked a little cleaner but this doesn't seem to worry people as it's often crowded out at night.

There is a cluster of popular small warungs just beyond the Sympathy, opposite the Losmen Laut Biru. Round the corner, by the east beach, *Gatul's* is another popular small warung. Turn the opposite way towards the west beach and you come to the

Rumah Makan Mambo which is as clean and neat as the Sympathy is run-down and grubby!

Looking out on the west beach, at the end of Jalan Pasangrahan, is *Rumah Makan Nanjung* with a pleasant open-air dining area and excellent food including great barbecued fish. There are numerous other restaurants around and plenty of food carts and late night warungs along the beaches. There are even food carts where croissants are for sale!

Getting There & Away
Bus or Train From Jakarta, you can get a bus directly from Cililitan station to Banjar, via Bogor and Bandung. From Bandung, you can also approach Banjar by rail – it takes about five hours from Bandung. There's a pleasant losmen across the railway line from the Banjar station, and cheap restaurants near the bus station.

Bandung to Banjar takes four hours and costs about 2500 rp. The final stretch from Banjar, by bus or colt, takes two hours and costs about 2000 rp. Banjar to Yogya takes six to eight hours by train and nine hours by bus.

The 4848 taxi company have a direct minibus between Bandung and Pangandaran for 9000 rp.

Ferry An interesting route from Yogya is the backwater trip between Cilacap and Kalipucang. From Yogya, you can take an early morning train to Kroya. The trip takes about four to six hours and costs around 3700 rp. From there, take a colt to Cilacap. The ferry port is some distance out of town – a colt ride along the main road and then a 300 rp becak ride to the terminal. You can get the 7 am minibus from the Kartika Travel Agent on Jalan Sosrowijayan in Yogya. It costs 6000 rp and you will be dropped right at the terminal in time for the last ferry of the day.

You can also approach Cilacap from Dieng by taking a bus from Wonosobo, but early in the morning you may well have to change buses at Purwokerto. The trip takes about six hours and, with luck, you may get to Cilacap on time.

From Cilacap, the ferry winds down the river towards the sea, along the waterway sheltered by the island of Nusa Kambangan and across the wide expanse of Segara Anakan before going upriver to Kalipucang. It's a fascinating trip from village to village with numerous stops. The ferry is a rickety 25-metre wooden boat. There's usually plenty of room for people and baggage but it's a popular service with plenty of local use. Departures from Cilacap are at 7 am, 8 am, 12 noon and 1 pm, and the trip takes about 3½ to 4½ hours. The fare is 1200 rp.

Kalipucang is 17 km from Pangandaran. You can walk the few hundred metres from the ferry terminal to the main road or take one of the waiting becaks. Colts also run frequently between Kalipucang and Pangandaran for 300 rp.

From Yogya all the way to Pangandaran is a long day of travel. If you arrive in Cilacap too late to continue the same day, there is a variety of hotels around town. *Losmen Bahagia* is on Jalan Sudirman and rather basic. *Losmen Tiga* at Jalan Mayor Sutoyo 61 is central and of rather better standard; there are also a number of more expensive hotels. CV Luta in Yogya does a hotel to hotel bus-boat-bus service from Yogya to Pangandaran for 12,000 rp. In Pangandaran, they're next to the post office.

Getting Around
Arrivals at Pangandaran tend to be frantic as the becak mobs assault the bus in a screaming, shouting horde. Hang on to your gear if you want to evade them and watch out for the colt conductor who will try to disappear without giving you your change at this point in the proceedings. It's over a km from the bus stop to the beach, so you'll probably need a becak. The fare seems to depend on the time of day and the mood.

You can rent bicycles from Toha, opposite the Rumah Makan Mambo – they organise jungle walking tours as well. Aep, contacted through the Cilacap Restaurant, also does jungle walks and has been recommended. It's so easy to get lost in the jungle reserve that a local guide is a wise idea.

In the Hotel Bahtera Jaya on Jalan Sumardi, there's a travel agent in room 4. They sell bus tickets, rent bicycles and motorbikes and operate tours to Nusa Kambangan.

CIREBON

Cirebon, midway between Jakarta and Semarang, gets few visitors. The town has Javanese and Sundanese influences and is an important port with a busy fishing fleet. It is also a major centre for batik.

Things to See

In the south of the city, the **Kraton Kanoman** dates from 1588 but is sadly neglected. It's approached through the colourful Pasar Kanoman outdoor market. The more recent **Kraton Kesepuhan** is still in use but parts of it can be visited. There's an interesting, if somewhat run-down, museum.

Four km south-west of town is the **Gua Sunyaragi**, a bizarre 'cave' honeycombed with chambers, doors and staircases leading nowhere. The **Tomb of Sunan Gunungjati** is another of the town's claims to fame – he was one of the nine 'walis' who spread Islam through Java.

The harbour area is always an interesting place to visit, and Cirebon is famed for its distinctive batik, particularly from the nearby village of Trusmi (try the House of Masera) or from Indramayu, which is further out.

Places to Stay

Hotel Asia (☎ 2183) at Jalan Kalibaru Selatan 15 is good value with a variety of rooms with and without mandi from around 10,000 rp. It's about a 15-minute walk from the railway station alongside the quiet tree-lined canal near Pasar Pagi.

Cirebon's other low-budget places are along Jalan Siliwangi between the railway station and the canal. Walking from the station towards Jalan Siliwangi, the *Palapa Hotel* looks rather dreary but it's actually a pretty good place from 6000 rp. On the corner of the same street, at Jalan Siliwangi 66, the *Hotel Famili* has adequate rooms from 4000 rp.

Slightly more expensive places include the *Hotel Slamet* at Jalan Siliwangi 66, the *Hotel Cordova* at No 77, the *Hotel Langensari* at No 117 and the *Hotel Priangan* at No 108. At Jalan Siliwangi 98, next to the town square, the *Grand Hotel Cirebon* (☎ 2014/5) is an old-fashioned but pleasant upper mid-range hotel with rooms from around 18,000 rp up – a long way up!

Places to Eat

Nasi lengko, a rice dish with bean sprouts, tahu, tempe, fried onion and cucumber, is a local speciality. *Rumah Makan Jatibarang*, on the corner of Jalan Karanggetas and Jalan Kalibaru Selatan, is a good place for this dish. Nearby on Jalan Karanggetas is the clean and reasonable *Kopyor Restaurant*. The *Hong Kong Restaurant* at Jalan Karanggetas 20 has decent Chinese food.

Seafood restaurants along Jalan Bahagia, towards Jalan Pasekutan, include the well-known *Maxim's* at No 45-47. The Chinese seafood market, in the small square at the south end of Jalan Bahagia, has great food although not at rock-bottom prices. The *Pasar Pagi Market* has good fruit and food stalls. Nearby is *Toko Famili* at Jalan Siliwangi 96 with good baked snacks. Other Jalan Siliwangi bakeries include *La Palma*.

Getting There & Away

The bus station is a 15-minute minibus trip south-west of the town centre, and buses from Jakarta take about five hours, or 3½ hours from Bandung.

Cirebon is on the railway line from Jakarta for both Surabaya in the north and Yogyakarta in the south, so there are frequent trains. From Jakarta, it takes three to four hours and costs from 3100 rp in 3rd class and from 4000 rp in 2nd.

Getting Around

The minibus or taxi kota service costs a flat 200 rp, and there are also plenty of becaks.

YOGYAKARTA

The most popular city in Indonesia, Yogya is easy-going, economical and offers plenty for the budget traveller. Long a centre of power, the Mataram Kingdom extended control as far as Sumatra and Bali over 1000 years ago. The final Hindu-Buddhist kingdom of the Majapahits also controlled this area until the arrival of Islam and the second kingdom of Mataram drove them to Bali.

The coming of the Dutch resulted in the kingdom being split into sultanates. From 1825 to 1830, the great Indonesian hero, Prince Diponegoro, led a bitter revolt against the Dutch. This was finally resolved when he was captured by a rather nasty trick. After being invited to discuss truce negotiations, the unsuspecting Diponegoro was captured and exiled to Sulawesi. In this century, Yogya was again a centre of resistance to the Dutch and after WW II was the capital of the revolution until independence from Holland was eventually won. Today, Yogya is the cultural and artistic centre of Java.

Although Yogyakarta is now spelt with a Y (not Jogjakarta), it's still pronounced with a J. Asking for Yogya will get you blank stares.

Orientation & Information

It is easy to find your way around Yogya. Jalan Malioboro, named after the Duke of Marlborough, is the main road and runs straight down from the railway station to the Kraton at the far end. Most of the restaurants and shops are along this street and most of the cheap-accommodation places are just off it, in the enclave known as Sosro, near the railway line.

The Kraton, or Palace, is the centre of the intriguing area of old Yogya where you will also find the Water Palace and numerous batik galleries. There's a second enclave, principally of mid-range places, a couple of km south of the Kraton area around Jalan Prawirotaman.

Tourist Office There's a tourist information office at Jalan Malioboro 16, open from 8 am to 8 pm, Monday to Saturday. They give out free maps of the city and can give you all the latest information on cultural performances in Yogya.

1	Bus Stop For Borobudur
2	Monument
3	Hotel Santika
4	Army Museum
5	Holland Bakery
6	Affandi Museum
7	Ambarrukmo Palace Hotel
8	Yogyakarta Craft Centre
9	Diponegoro Museum
10	Garuda Airways
11	Gramedia Bookshop
12	Telephone Exchange Office
13	Tourist Office
14	ASRI
15	Pasar Beringharjo
16	Museum Bekas Benteng Vredeburg
17	Senopati Shopping Centre & Colt Station
18	Paku Alam Kraton
19	Batik Research Centre
20	Nitour
21	Sono-Budoyo Museum
22	Post Office
23	Taxi Stand
24	Wartel Telephone Office
25	Masjid Besar Mosque
26	Museum Kareta Kraton
27	Yogya Kraton
28	Zoo
29	Pasar Ngasem Bird Market
30	Taman Sari
31	Sasono Hinggil
32	THR
33	Batik Galleries
34	Dalem Pujokusuman Theatre
35	Agastya
36	Bus Station

Post & Telecommunications The main post office is at the bottom of Jalan Achmad Yani, the extension of Jalan Malioboro, in front of Kraton Square. Behind the post office is a Wartel telephone office where you can make international calls. There's another Wartel on Jalan Pasar Kembang in the Sosro cheap-accommodation enclave.

Other Information On Jalan Prawirotaman, the Prawirotaman International Bookshop has an excellent range of books in English. If the heat in Yogya gets too much you can, for a fee, use the swimming pool at the

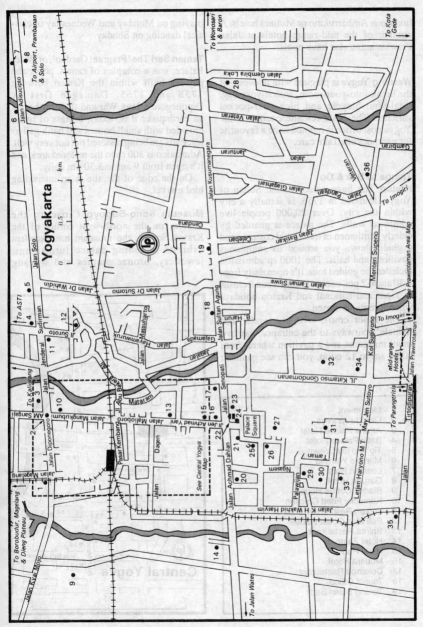

Yogyakarta

luxurious Ambarrukmo or Mutiara hotels. A number of the mid-range hotels at Jalan Prawirotaman also have pools.

Warning Yogya is plagued with thieves – of the break-into-your-room, snatch-your-bag, steal-your-bicycle and pick-your-pocket varieties. The poste restante counter in the Yogya post office is reputed to be a favourite for pickpockets. Take care.

Things to See & Do

Kraton The huge palace of the Sultan of Yogya, founded in 1756, is actually a city within the city. Over 20,000 people live within its walls. The palace is guarded by elderly gentlemen in traditional costume and a guide shows you around its sumptuous pavilions and halls. The 1000 rp admission includes the guided tour. It's open daily from 8.30 am to 2 pm, except Friday when it closes at 1 pm and national and Kraton holidays when it remains closed.

The inner court, with its 'male' and 'female' stairways to the entrance, has two small museums and a pavilion where, from 10.30 am to 12 noon, you can see gamelan playing on Monday and Wednesday or classical dancing on Sunday.

Taman Sari The 'Fragrant Garden', or Water Palace, was a complex of canals, pools and palaces built within the Kraton between 1758 and 1765. Damaged first by Diponegoro's Java War and then further by an earthquake it is, today, a mass of ruins, crowded with small houses and batik galleries. Parts are being restored but not very well. Admission is 300 rp to the restored area, and it's open from 9 am to 3.30 pm daily.

On the edge of the site is an interesting bird market.

Museum Sono-Budoyo Close to the Kraton, on the north-west corner of the Kraton Square, the museum has excellent exhibits including palace furnishings, jewellery, bronze statues and wayang

1	Monument
2	Garuda Airways
3	Arjuna Palace Hotel
4	Batik Palace Hotel
5	Tip Top Ice Cream
6	Mama's Warung
7	Losmen Kota
8	Garuda Hotel
9	Bladok Coffee House
10	Kentucky Fried Chicken
11	Legian Restaurant
12	Peti Mas Guest House
13	Shinta Restaurant
14	Hotel Zamrud
15	Hotel Puri
16	Mutiara Hotel
17	Colombo Restaurant
18	Tourist Office
19	Terang Bulan Batik

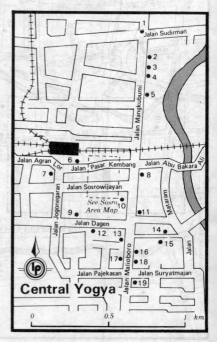

Central Yogya

puppets. It is open from 8 am to 1.30 pm Tuesday to Thursday, to 11.15 am Friday and to 12 noon on weekends. Entry is 200 rp and it's well worth a visit.

Other Museums On the side of the Kraton Square, between the Kraton entrance and the Sono-Budoyo Museum, the **Museum Kareta Kraton** has a collection of palace carriages, some of them are extravagantly ornate, and hearses are displayed. The museum is open from 8 am to 4 pm daily, and entry is 250 rp.

At the bottom of Jalan Achmad Yani, across from the post office, the **Museum Bekas Benteng Vredeburg** is built in the old Dutch fort and has interesting displays about the history of Yogya and it's role in Indonesia's struggle for independence. The museum is open from 8.30 am to 1.30 pm Tuesday to Thursday, to 11 am Friday, and to 12 noon on weekends. Entry is 250 rp.

Monumen Diponegoro This reconstruction is of Prince Diponegoro's residence, destroyed by the Dutch in 1825. The hole in the wall through which the prince escaped is still there. The site is open from 7.30 am to 4 pm, daily. It's four km out of Yogya – bus No 2 along Jalan Mataram will get you there, and bus No 1 will get you back to Jalan Malioboro.

Performances There are an enormous number of cultural performances in Yogyakarta. The tourist information office can advise you of what's on, or check in the tourist newspapers. There are classical dancing and gamelan rehearsals in the Kraton. See the Yogya Places to Eat section for information on the wayang golek, wayang kulit and other perfomances at Hanoman's Garden Restaurant. Performances also take place in hotels, restaurants and a variety of performing arts centres.

Wayang kulit (leather shadow puppets) can be seen at several places around Yogya on virtually every night of the week. The Agastya Art Institute has performances every afternoon, except Saturday. The

Yogyakarta Craft Centre puts on evening performances on Monday, Wednesday and Saturday. The Museum Sono-Budoyo has performances every day except Monday.

Wayang golek (wooden puppet) plays are also performed frequently. The Agastya Art Institute has performances on Saturday afternoon and there is a daily Nitour performance, except on holidays. Nitour also has a useful hand-out explaining the history of the wayang and the *Ramayana*. Wayang orang or wayang wong are Javanese dance dramas, and these can also be seen at a variety of venues.

The great Ramayana ballet performance at Prambanan takes place over the full moon nights from May to October, but there are also regular performances in the city. At the Trimurti Theatre, the Ramayana Ballet is performed on Tuesday, Wednesday and Thursday nights from 7.30 to 9.30 pm.

Batik & Batik Classes See the Java Things to Buy section for more information on batik. Batik cloth is sold all over Yogya but the Terang Bulan shop, before the market as you walk south on Jalan Malioboro, will give you a good idea of what is available. The prices are fixed but reasonable, and the quality is reliable.

For batik art in Yogya, there are a great number of galleries to visit. Top of the scale is Amri Yahya's flash gallery at Jalan Gampingan 67 – his beautiful modern batiks can cost over US$1000 and there are a number of beautiful, and more expensive, oil paintings on display. Nearby, on the same street, is ASRI (Academy of Fine Arts) which is open to visitors in the mornings from Monday to Saturday.

Carry on up Jalan Wates (the extension of Jalan Achmad Dahlan) and you'll come to other interesting – but more reasonably priced – places. Another good place for top-quality, but expensive, batik is Kuswadji's, in the north square near the Kraton. Or, there's Bambang Utoro to the east of town off Jalan Kusumanegara, the continuation of Jalan Sultan Agung and Jalan Senopati. There are also a number of batik workshops and galleries along Jalan Tirtodipuran and Jalan Prawirotaman in the south of Yogya.

Affandi, Indonesia's internationally renowned painter, has an interesting modern gallery about five km out of Yogya on the Solo road, a short distance before the Ambarrukmo Palace Hotel. Paintings are for sale but the gallery is also a permanent museum displaying the works of Affandi, his daughter Kartika and other artists. It's open from 9 am to 4 pm.

The Water Palace is the site for most of the cheaper galleries but the great percentage of them are very poor quality and very 'me-too' in their style. Look carefully and be very selective if you're buying there as original work can always be found. Some batik artists only draw the outline and then have teams of women fill in the intricate details. This certainly enables them to churn out pictures in great numbers!

When shopping around in the Water Palace, take great care not to be led into the galleries by the teams of touts who follow you – you'll end up paying commission on anything you buy. Yogya is literally crawling with would-be batik salesmen and many scams are tried. Don't believe the tales about huge ASEAN exhibitions in Singapore which empty the city of batik and that today is your last chance to buy!

If you want to have a go at batik yourself, there are lots of batik courses and classes in Yogya. Many teachers are self-proclaimed 'experts' out to make some easy money so, before investing time and money, it's a good idea to ask other travellers who may have just completed a course. The Intensive Batik Course of Hadjir Digdodarmojo seems to get a generally high approval rating although some people have also reported it as being rather mechanical and dull. It's on the left of the Water Palace main entrance, at Taman Kp 3/177, and there are three or five-day courses from 2 to 6 pm daily.

Cheaper and shorter courses can be found around the Sosro cheap-accommodation area. You can do a one-day course for 8000 rp; three days costs 22,500 rp.

The Yogya government-run Batik Research Centre at Jalan Kusumanegara 2 is an interesting place to visit – they explain the batik process in detail and have some unusual batiks on display and for sale. It's expensive but the quality is high. The centre has conducted comprehensive month long batik-making course for foreigners and may do so again.

Other At **Kota Gede** is the silverwork centre of Yogya, and the grave of Senopati, the first king of Mataram, can also be seen here. The **Ambarrukmo Palace** is in the grounds of the Ambarrukmo Palace Hotel, 11 km out of Yogya on the Solo road. It's another interesting example of Javanese palace architecture.

The Yogyakarta Craft Centre, opposite the Ambarrukmo Palace Hotel, is promoted by the government and has a good display of high-quality crafts which are reasonable in price.

Places to Stay

Accommodation in Yogya is remarkably good value and there is a superb choice. It's certainly the best city in Java for places to stay and places to eat. There are two particularly popular enclaves – the central Sosro area for the really cheap places and the Prawirotaman area, a couple of km south of the Kraton, for mid-range places. Recently, most of the development has taken place in the Prawirotaman area which has increased in popularity.

Sosro Area The real cheapies are almost all in the Sosro area, defined by Jalan Pasar Kembang (parallel to and immediately south of the railway line) and Jalan Sosrowijayan (a block south again). Connecting the two, and just a couple of doors down from the main street of Yogya (Jalan Malioboro), is the narrow alleyway known as Gang Sosrowijayan I (gang means alley) and a maze of other little alleys including Gang Sosrowijayan II. Numerous small guest houses and restaurants are dotted around these alleys.

At the end of Jalan Pasar Kembang, the road changes names to Jalan Gandekan Lor

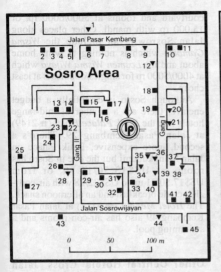

Jalan Pasar Kembang

Sosro Area

Jalan Sosrowijayan

0   50   100 m

and, at No 79, you'll find the spotlessly clean and highly efficient *Losmen Kota*. There are pleasant open lounges and the only real drawback to its corner location is that the front rooms are noisy. Rooms are 6000/10,000 rp for singles/doubles and there are some more rooms at 12,000 rp.

Although the general consensus is that it's a well-run and pleasant place, we also get infrequent (but regular) complaints that it's can be over-officious and even too security conscious. If you don't mind the rules (including a 20,000 rp security deposit on arrival), it's probably fine but if you do mind them, go somewhere else.

Back along Jalan Pasar Kembang, towards Jalan Malioboro, are numerous cheapies – some are rather grubby and others excellent value. They include the none too exciting *Mataram* at No 61 and *Nusantara* at No 59, both with rooms at 6000 rp. Further along there's the *Shinta*.

The *Asia-Afrika* (☎ 4489) at No 21 Jalan Pasar Kembang has a variety of rooms from 12,500/15,000 rp or from 25,000/30,500 rp with air-con. There's a pool and an attractive garden at the back. At No 11, there's a second *Asia-Afrika*. Between them, at 17A, the

Ratna is a pleasantly quiet place set back from the road. Rooms start at 8000 rp, or 14,000 rp with mandi and toilet.

Gang Sosrowijayan I, a little connecting alley, has some very low-cost places but make sure your room is secure as Yogyakarta is notorious for theft. *Losmen Beta* is basic, clean, small, noisy, popular and dirt cheap at 2500/4000 rp. *Losmen Sastrowihadi* is about the same price. A bit further along this gang are the *Rama* and *Jogja*, two adjoining losmen with rooms from 4000 rp. There are a number of small places close to Gang I including the *Lima Losmen* with rooms at 2000/3000 rp. It's clean and quiet, although dark and spartan.

On Gang Sosrowijayan II, the next alley back, is the clean, good-value and very popular *Hotel Bagus*. It's built around a central courtyard, run by a veritable classroom of children and rooms with fan cost 3500/4000 rp. There are a host of small losmen around Gang II and the small alleys off it, most of them in a similar rock-bottom price range.

The *Losmen Setia* ('setia' means nice) has very basic rooms at 3500 rp. The *Setia Kawan* ('nice friend') is nothing special at 7500 rp. The *Supriyanto Inn* is good value with bright rooms at 3500/4000 rp, as is the identically priced *Utar Pension Inn*. The *Jaya Losmen* at 4000/5000 rp is again pretty basic.

Between Gang I and Gang II, the *Dewi Homestay* is a brighter and glossier place with rooms at 6500 rp, or from 8000 to 9000 rp with bath. Across the road is the new *Losmen Happy Inn* with rooms with bath at 16,000 rp. This place is a definite notch up from Sosro's regular places.

On Jalan Sosrowijayan, between Gang I and Malioboro, is the security conscious *Aziatic* – at night the doors are locked and there are stout bars on the windows. 'As secure as Pentridge,' (Pentridge is a major Australian jail!) wrote one obviously impressed Australian visitor. It's also clean, cool and comfortable and has rooms at 8000 to 15,000 rp. There's a wide central hallway, liberally hung with batik art, where you can sit and chat. They also rent bicycles and have a good restaurant out the back.

Across the road, the *Indonesia* has a nice courtyard and rooms at 5000/6000 rp, or 15,000 rp with mandi. Other places along Jalan Sosrowijayan include the *Wisma Gambira* which is nothing to write home about and the *Losmen Wisma Wijaya* which at 4000/5000 rp for singles/doubles is at least cheap.

Although Sosro is essentially a budget enclave, there are a number of mid-range hotels like the *Batik Palace Hotel* (☎ 2149) at Jalan Pasar Kembang 29. There's a second, more expensive, Batik Palace on Jalan Mangkubumi but the one in Sosro has rooms at US$13.50/16.50, or from US$17.50/21 up to US$22/28 with air-con – all include breakfast and an afternoon snack. The *Hotel Mendut* (☎ 3114) at Jalan Pasar Kembang 49 also has air-con rooms and a swimming pool.

Other Central Hotels Cross Jalan Malioboro and follow the alley further down from the Legian Restaurant. You'll soon come to the extremely well-kept and very quiet *Hotel Puri* (☎ 4107) at No 22, with rooms at 5500/6500 rp and free tea or coffee in the morning and evening. A personal favourite, this one.

The nearby *Hotel WHW* (Wisma Hasta Wisata) at No 16 is similarly priced but not so good. *Intan* has rooms at 3500/5000 rp or with fan for an extra 250 rp. Or there's the the *Prambanan Guest House* at No 18-20, also in the same price bracket. Further down, is the *Hotel Zamrud* at No 47, an expensive place at 10,000/15,000 rp but it includes breakfast.

The *Peti Mas* (☎ 2896) is a mid-range hotel at Jalan Dagen 39, off Jalan Malioboro. Fan-cooled rooms range from US$8/10, and air-con ones from US$20/22. There's a pool and a pleasant garden with a restaurant area in this centrally located and attractive hotel.

North of the railway tracks at Jalan Mangkubumi 46, the pleasant *Batik Palace Hotel* (☎ 62229) has well-equipped rooms at US$22/28 which includes breakfast and an afternoon snack. There's also a pleasant swimming pool here.

Jalan Prawirotaman This street, a couple of km south of the city centre, has developed into a second travellers' enclave, but somewhat up-market from the places in Sosro. Where average rooms in the Sosro area might be in the 4000 to 8000 rp bracket, you're probably looking at 10,000 to 20,000 rp in the Prawirotaman area. The places here are definitely a step up from Sosro, many of them have swimming pools and the rooms may be built around pleasant gardens. There are also a number of restaurants and other places to eat, so it's quite self-sufficient.

A becak from the central Jalan Malioboro area is likely to cost you a standard 1000 rp, depending on the time of day and passenger load. Alternatively, an orange bus No 2 will take you to Jalan Mataram for 200 rp. You can return on a blue or white bus No 14 going down Jalan Malioboro.

This area does have some cheaper places like the neat and clean *Vagabond Youth Hostel* (☎ 71207) at Jalan Prawirotaman MG III/589, where dorm beds are 5000 rp, singles range from 5500 to 9000 rp and doubles from 11,000 to 13,500 rp. Student and YHA card holders can get a discount.

The popular and spacious *Sumaryo Guest*

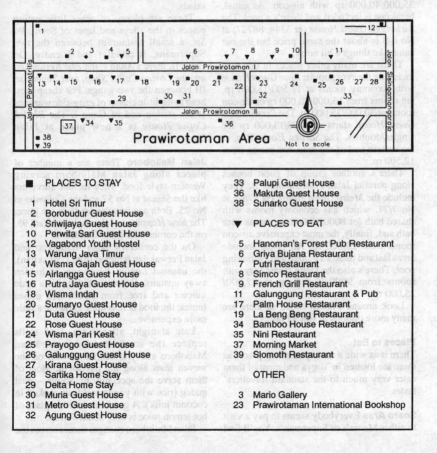

■ PLACES TO STAY

1 Hotel Sri Timur
2 Borobudur Guest House
4 Sriwijaya Guest House
10 Perwita Sari Guest House
12 Vagabond Youth Hostel
13 Warung Java Timur
14 Wisma Gajah Guest House
15 Airlangga Guest House
16 Putra Jaya Guest House
18 Wisma Indah
20 Sumaryo Guest House
21 Duta Guest House
22 Rose Guest House
24 Wisma Pari Kesit
25 Prayogo Guest House
26 Galunggung Guest House
27 Kirana Guest House
28 Sartika Home Stay
29 Delta Home Stay
30 Muria Guest House
31 Metro Guest House
32 Agung Guest House
33 Palupi Guest House
36 Makuta Guest House
38 Sunarko Guest House

▼ PLACES TO EAT

5 Hanoman's Forest Pub Restaurant
6 Griya Bujana Restaurant
7 Putri Restaurant
8 Simco Restaurant
9 French Grill Restaurant
11 Galunggung Restaurant & Pub
17 Palm House Restaurant
19 La Beng Beng Restaurant
34 Bamboo House Restaurant
35 Nini Restaurant
37 Morning Market
39 Slomoth Restaurant

OTHER

3 Mario Gallery
23 Prawirotaman International Bookshop

House (☎ 2852) at Jalan Prawirotaman 18A is comfortable and even has a swimming pool. Singles/doubles with bath cost 15,000/25,000 and include a good breakfast. The *Duta Guest House* (☎ 5219) at Jalan Prawirotaman 20 is similar in price but it has cheaper rooms without bath and expensive ones with air-con. Again, they have a pool and breakfast is included.

At the Jalan Parangtritis end of the street are a couple of the most expensive places in the enclave. The *Wisma Gaja Guest House* (☎ 2479) at Jalan Prawirotaman 4 has singles/doubles at 25,000/35,000 rp, or 35,000/40,000 rp with air-con. As usual, breakfast is included and there's a pool. The *Airlangga Guest House* (☎ 3344, 88727) at No 6-8 is about the same price but the bar can make things a bit noisy.

There are many other places in this area including the ever popular *Rose Guest House* with economy rooms at 12,500/15,000 rp, fan rooms from 15,000/20,000 rp or air-con rooms at 30,000/35,000 rp. The *Perwita Sari Guest House* starts at 8000/13,000 rp for singles/doubles. The *Sartika Home Stay*, at the eastern end of the road, has rooms from 12,500 rp.

There's another group of guest houses along parallel Jalan Prawirotaman II. They include the *Metro Guest House* (☎ 3982) at No 7/71, which has economy rooms with shared bath for 8000/10,000 rp, rooms with bath and, finally, the most expensive air-con rooms from 25,000 rp. All prices include breakfast and there's a garden and swimming pool. There's also the *Delta Home Stay* with rooms from 9000/13,000 rp to 17,000/25,000 rp.

Look around Prawirotaman as there are many more options to suit all tastes.

Places to Eat

There is as wide a variety of eating places as there are losmen in Yogya and most of them cater very much to the standard travellers' tastes.

Sosro Area Everybody seems to pay a visit to either Mama's or Superman's. You'll find both the original *Superman's* and its new larger offshoot on Gang Sosrowijayan I. They're both very popular and trendy but the food is good and reasonable in price. All the regular travellers' specials appear on the long menu, ranging from fruit salad to banana pancakes. Recently, a *Superman III* has been added to I and II; this one is slightly more expensive with a Japanese menu. It's also known as *Restaurant Marikho*.

On Jalan Pasar Kembang, beside the railway line, *Mama's* is definitely the number-one warung. Evening time is when it comes into full swing with good food and salads.

There are plenty of other little eating places in the alleys and lanes of Sosro. *Bu Sis*, a small restaurant between the two Supermans, is popular and friendly. On Gang II, there's *Anna's*, the *Eko Restaurant* and the *Lovina Coffee Shop*, near Superman III between the two gangs. For cheap eats, head to the little cluster of gang-side warungs at the station end of Gang I. The *Bladok Coffee House* is a new place at Jalan Sosrowijayan 76.

Jalan Malioboro There are a number of places along Jalan Malioboro serving Western-style food. They include survivors like the *Shinta* at No 57 and the *Colombo* at No 25. Both are popular for their ice juice. The *New Happy* is at Jalan Achmad Yani 95, on the corner with Jalan Gandekan.

On the corner of Jalan Malioboro and Jalan Perwakilan (entered from Perwakilan), the unusual *Legian Restaurant* is hidden away upstairs. Because of this, it's a little quieter and free from petrol and diesel fumes; the food here is quite good but a little more expensive.

Late at night, after 9 pm, food stalls replace the souvenir stands on Jalan Malioboro and you can take a seat on the woven mats along the pavement. Most of them serve the speciality of Yogya – nasi gudeg (rice with young jackfruit cooked in coconut milk). A good meal with a glass of hot lemon juice is only about 500 rp.

Jalan Malioboro changes names across the

railway line and becomes Jalan Mangkubumi. At No 28, you'll find the *Tip Top* with excellent ice cream and cakes.

Jalan Prawirotaman Restaurants are popping up to complement the guest houses on Jalan Prawirotaman. On the corner with Jalan Parangtritis, the *Warung Java Timur* (or Restaurant Tante Lies) is simple and deservedly popular. Most dishes are 1500 to 2000 rp or less.

Other restaurants along the street include *Galunggung Restaurant & Pub, Griya Bujana*, the *Prambanan Restaurant* and the popular *La Beng Beng Restaurant*. The bigger restaurants here are glossy affairs, more akin to restaurants at Kuta Beach in Bali.

One Prawirotaman restaurant, for which it's worth making a special excursion, is the excellent *Hanoman's Forest Pub* at No 9B. The restaurant is fine with good food at reasonable prices. Each night there's an excellent show in the back part of the restaurant – wayang kulit, wayang golek or classical dances for 2000 rp. Children under 130 cm are half price! You can find out at the tourist office about scheduled performances.

Getting There & Away

Air There are air connections between Yogyakarta and Jakarta (100,000 rp), Surabaya (51,000 rp), Denpasar (93,000 rp) and many other centres.

Bus The bus station is four km south-east from the city centre, beyond the Jalan Prawirotaman area. There are a number of ticket agents along Jalan Sosrowijayan who sell tickets for the various bus companies and, in some cases, their own services. Bus company offices are also found along Jalan Mangkubumi, the northern extension of Jalan Malioboro across the railway line.

Colts for Solo can be caught as they run up Jalan Mataram, a block east from Jalan Malioboro. Regular buses are 900 rp, or there's a door-to-door minibus service for 2000 rp. Other fares in the locality include Prambanan 400 rp, Parangtritis 900 rp,

Muntilan (for Borobudur) 600 rp and Kaliurang 800 rp. The bus for Borobudur runs along Jalan Magelang to the north; a city bus No 5 will drop you there.

Further afield, fares from Yogya include Jakarta from 6500 rp for the economy service, whilst air-con public buses are 9500 to 13,500 rp. The deluxe, private air-con services cost around 18,000 rp and take about 14 hours. Buses to Bandung cost from 6000 rp or from 8000 rp with air-con, to Surabaya cost from 6000 rp by day or 9000 rp by night, and buses to Malang will cost 9500 rp. It takes about 16 hours to Denpasar – 8000 rp by public bus or from 14,000 to 25,000 rp, depending on the bus and the company, for the better private buses.

Train Unlike Jakarta and Surabaya, there is only one station in Yogya and it is very conveniently located in the centre of town. Solo is on the main Yogya to Surabaya railway line, only about an hour out of Yogya. Trains to Jakarta take nine to 12 hours and cost from 6000 rp in 3rd class, from 10,000 rp in 2nd and from 14,000 rp in 1st.

The deluxe Bima Express costs 17,000 rp in 1st class or 21,000 rp for a sleeper. At the other end of the luxury scale is the all 3rd-class Gaya Baru Malam Selatan which, like the Bima Express, comes through Surabaya.

Trains to or from Surabaya take six to eight hours and cost from 3800 rp in 3rd class, from 5000 rp in 2nd and from 13,500 in 1st.

Getting Around

To/From the Airport Taxis from the airport to Yogya, about 10 km, cost a standard 5500 rp (6000 rp to Jalan Prawirotaman). You can walk out to the main road and turn left, only 200 metres from the terminal, and catch any colt or minibus into town for about 250 rp. The airport is on the main road to Prambanan and Solo, so they come by in a steady stream.

Local Transport Bis Kotas are bright orange minibuses operating on eight set routes around the city for a flat 200 rp fare. There are route maps for reference in the Visitor's

Information Centre. From the bus station, a No 2 bus will drop you on Jalan Mataram, a block over from Malioboro. Bus No 1 from Jalan Malioboro will get you out to the bus station, about 20 minutes from the city centre.

You can hire bicycles (1500 rp a day) and motorbikes (around 10,000 rp a day from the places along Jalan Pasar Kembang) but lock them up very securely. Theft is big business in Yogya. There's an enormous supply of becaks for around 1000 rp an hour but fares are dependent on the time of day, difficulty of the trip, weight of the passengers and assorted other factors. There are also horse-drawn andongs around town. Local colts and oplets go from the bus station next to the shopping centre on Jalan Senopati.

Tours to Prambanan, Borobudur and the Dieng Plateau are run by numerous agents around the Sosro hotels. You can visit both ancient sites and see Yogya city for US$7.50. Trips to climb Merapi for the sunrise are also organised. A taxi to Borobudur and back can be negotiated for less than 25,000 rp.

AROUND YOGYAKARTA
There are a whole series of places to visit around Yogyakarta. Best known, of course, are the great temple complex of Prambanan and the huge Buddhist centre at Borobudur, but there are a number of others worth a visit. Although most of them are day trips from Yogya, there are some places in which you can also stay.

Prambanan
The biggest Hindu temple complex in Java, Prambanan is 17 km east from Yogya on the Solo road. Of the original group, the outer compound contains the ruins of 224 temples, only two of which have been restored. Eight minor and eight main temples stand in the central court. The largest of these, the Shiva temple, has been restored and others are being reconstructed. The 50-metre-high temple bears 42 scenes from the *Ramayana*.

The statue of Shiva stands in the central chamber and statues of the goddess Durga, Shiva's elephant-headed son Ganesh and Agastya the teacher stand in the other chapels of the upper part of the temple. The Shiva temple is flanked by the Vishnu and Brahma temples, the latter carrying further scenes from the *Ramayana*. In the small central temple, opposite the Shiva temple, stands a fine statue of the bull Nandi, Shiva's mount.

Built in the 9th century AD, possibly 50 years after Borobudur, the complex at Prambanan was abandoned soon after its completion when its builders moved east. Many of the temples had collapsed by the last century and not until 1937 was any form of reconstruction attempted. Other temple ruins can be found close to Prambanan and on the road back to Yogya. If you are here at the right time don't miss the Ramayana dance which is performed on the full moon nights from May to October each year.

Getting There & Away To get to Prambanan, take a Solo bus or colt from Yogya for 400 rp. There's a bicycle roadway all the way to Prambanan from Yogya, so this can be an interesting place to visit by hired bicycle. There is a 500 rp admission charge to the temple complex plus a camera charge. It's open from 6 am to 6 pm and the temples are at their best in the early evening light or in the early morning when it's quiet.

Borobudur
Ranking with Bagan and Angkor Wat as one of the greatest South-East Asian Buddhist monuments, Borobudur is an enormous construction covering a hill, 40 km from Yogya. With the decline of Buddhism, Borobudur was abandoned and only rediscovered in 1814 when Raffles governed Java.

The temple consists of six square bases topped by three circular ones and it was constructed contemporaneously with Prambanan in the early part of the 9th century AD.

Over the centuries, the supporting hill became waterlogged and the whole immense stone mass started to subside at a variety of angles. A US$12 million restoration project has now been completed.

Nearly 1500 panels on the terraces illustrate Buddhist teachings and tales while over 400 Buddha images sit in chambers on the terraces. On the upper circular terraces there are latticed stupas which contain 72 more Buddha images.

The **Mendut Temple**, three km east of Borobudur, has a magnificent statue of Buddha seated with two disciples. He is three metres high and sits with both feet on the ground, rather than in the usual lotus position. It has been suggested that this image

was originally intended to top Borobudur but proved impossible to raise to the summit.

Places to Stay & Eat *Losmen Citra Rasa* is cheap with rooms from 6000 rp with mandi. *Losmen Saraswati* is good with rooms from 10,000 rp or there's the straightforward and similarly priced *Villa Rosita* to the west of the monument. There are many warungs near the temple and in the village. *Mamy's Warung* (look for the sign 'Rice Stall 2M') is at the temple end of the road from the bus terminal.

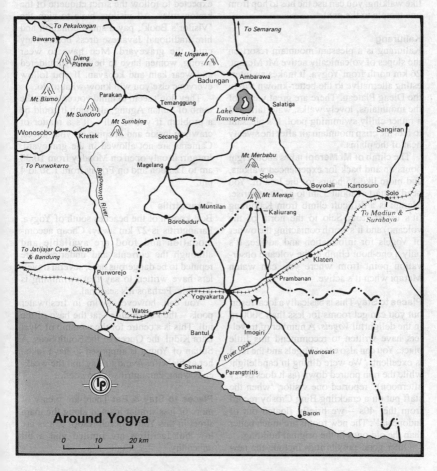

Around Yogya

0   10   20 km

Getting There & Away To get to Borobudur, take a bus to Muntilan (500 rp) and another on to the site (300 rp). There is a 500 rp admission charge to the site. If you stop off at Borobudur en route to somewhere else, you must leave your bags in a hut at the entrance where they will be looked after – it's free. There's an additional fee to the Mendut Temple.

The bus from Muntilan passes first Mendut and then the smaller Pawon Temple en route to Borobudur. So, if you don't feel like walking, you can use the bus to hop from one temple to the next.

Kaliurang

Kaliurang is a pleasant mountain resort on the slopes of volcanically active Mt Merapi, 26 km north from Yogya. It makes an interesting alternative to the better-known trip to the Dieng Plateau. There are great views of the mountains, lovely walks, waterfalls and a rather chilly swimming pool. It's pleasant to feel the crisp mountain air after the sweaty heat of the plains.

The climb of **Mt Merapi** takes about eight hours up and back for experienced walkers, and more like 15 hours for the less fit. You need to start at about 3 am to get the sunrise. Merapi is a difficult climb from Kaliurang (it's easier from Selo to the north of the volcano) and it's worth contacting the owner of Vogels for information and advice. It's only a one-hour climb to the volcano observation point from where you can watch Merapi when it's active.

Places to Stay This is basically a local resort but you can get rooms for less than 5000 rp in the delightful *Vogels*. A number of travellers have written to recommend this little place. You can also eat at Vogels and the food is excellent. 'We were dining in candlelight while the rain poured down (as it does every afternoon),' reported one visitor, 'when the staff put on a crackling Bing Crosby record from the '40s – we briefly floated out of Indonesia!'. The new rooms are much better than the old ones in the original building.

Other good possibilities include the new *Christian Hostel* with a dorm at 2000 rp, good rooms from 6000 rp and a great bar and restaurant.

Imogiri

The **Royal Cemetery of the Sultans of Mataram**, 20 km south-east from Yogya, sits high on a hillside at the top of 345 steps. Imogiri is a sacred site and many local people visit to pay their respects at the royal graves, especially that of the great Sultan Agung.

It's an interesting place to visit but you are expected to follow the strict etiquette of the kraton rules. All visitors have to sign the 'Visitor's Book', pay a small donation and hire traditional Javanese dress before they enter the graveyard. Men have to wear sarong, women have to be bare shouldered and wear kain and kebayan. If you follow everyone else you will know what to do.

They don't seem to mind you entering the tomb of Sultan Agung, although it could be a problem if you're tall – it's a matter of crawling inside and keeping on your knees. Cameras are not allowed in the graveyard. Imogiri is only open on Monday from 10.30 am to 12 noon and on Friday from 1.30 to 4 pm.

Parangtritis

Best known of the beaches south of Yogya, Parangtritis is 27 km away. Cheap accommodation and food are available and although the currents and undertows are reputed to be dangerous here, several travellers have written to say that swimming is possible. Perhaps it's seasonal.

You can, however, swim in freshwater pools – the *Pemandian* – at the base of the hill. This is a centre for the worship of Nyai Lara Kidul, the Queen of the South Seas. A Sultan of Yogya is supposed to have taken her as his wife. Avoid Friday and the weekends when Parangtritis is crowded.

Places to Stay & Eat There are plenty of more or less similar losmen along the main street in this Yogya beach resort. Prices are low but facilities are limited and a bit unhealthy.

Away from the main street, *Penginapan Parang Endong* has simple rooms for 3000 rp and a good swimming pool. *Losmen Widodo* is in the middle price bracket with rooms from around 10,000 rp. The *Agung Hotel & Garden Restaurant* is similarly priced. There are cheap warungs along the promenade.

Getting There & Away From Yogya, it's 600 rp from the bus station on Jalan Senopati. A bumpy one-hour trip over one of the worst roads in Java brings you to Parangtritis! The last bus back to Yogya leaves at 6 pm.

Badungan & Ambarawa

Between Solo or Yogya and Semarang, you can stop at Bandungan to see the **Gedung Songo** ('nine buildings' in Javanese), which are a collection of small but beautifully sited Hindu temples on the slopes of Mt Ungaran.

The town of Ambarawa, on the main central route, is the turn-off point for Bandungan and anyone who's fascinated by railway engines will enjoy the **Ambarawa Railway Museum**. The collection of 20 or so railway engines at the old depot includes a 1902 cog locomotive which is still in working order.

Places to Stay Places to stay in Bandungan include the cheap *Losmen Riani I* from 6000 rp and *Wisma Kereta Api* with comfortable bungalows which are similar in price. The modern *Madya Hillview Inn* is economical but watch out for the cockroaches. Other places include the pleasant *Losmen Pojok Sari* and the more expensive *Rawa Pening Hotel*. Avoid weekends when Bandungan gets very crowded.

Getting There & Away From Ambarawa to Bandungan, it's half an hour by colt, and from the market place (also worth a visit) in Bandungan you have to get another colt about six km to the actual site. To visit all of the temples could take up to six hours – you can go on horseback.

Other

Magelang was formerly a Dutch military garrison and it was here that the Javanese hero, Prince Diponegoro, was tricked into captivity in 1829. There's a small museum in the house where he was captured.

The **Jatijajar Cave** is 20 km south of Gombang, which is 130 km west of Yogya on the main road and railway line to Bandung or Cilicap. There are remarkable life-sized statues around the sides of the cave. Near the caves is the coastal resort of **Karang Bolong** where swallows nests are collected for that famous Chinese delicacy, bird's nest soup. Gombang has lots of losmen.

WONOSOBO

This is a pleasant place en route to the Dieng Plateau or as a break between Bandung and Yogya. The Wonosobo bus station is about a km out of town.

Places to Stay

Losmen Jawa Tengah, on Jalan Achmad Yani next to the market and colt terminal for Dieng, is a good, clean place with rooms from 5000 rp. Others include the *Losmen Petra*, 200 metres down from the Jawa Tengah at Jalan Achmad Yani 81, with rooms with mandi from 4000 rp and cheaper rooms without. The *Losmen Famili* at Jalan Sumbing 6 is clean, comfortable and priced about the same.

Places to Eat

Restaurant Asia and the *Dieng Restaurant*, on Jalan Kawedanan near the Jawa Tengah, both have good food. At the Dieng, Mr Agus has maps and photographs and lots of interesting tales about the plateau. You can also eat well and cheaply at the *Rumah Makan Klenyer*, in the small grocery shop next to Losmen Petra.

Getting There & Away

It's a short bus or colt trip from Yogya to Magelang and then a much longer one from there to Wonosobo. Allow at least three hours from Magelang to Wonosobo – it can take longer and there's inevitably some hanging around waiting for a full passenger load to assemble.

If you intend to visit Borobudur on the way, you need to start out as early as possible to make all the connections. Direct buses from Wonosobo to Cilicap don't arrive early enough to catch the last ferry to Kalipucang (for Pangandaran), but by departing at the crack of dawn you can get to Cilicap in time via Purwokerto.

DIENG PLATEAU

About 130 km from Yogya, this 2000-metre high plateau has a number of interesting temples, some beautiful scenery, good walks and (at night) freezing temperatures. Come prepared for the night-time cold, Dieng's basic losmen and unexciting food, and you'll probably find it interesting.

Dieng is the collapsed remnant of an ancient crater. In the centre, where it is very swampy, there are five Hindu-Buddhist temples. These temples are thought to be the oldest in Java, pre-dating Borobudur and Prambanan. There are a number of other temples scattered around. **Candi Bima**, to the south, is particularly fine but, like all too many places in Indonesia, has been defaced by graffitists.

The road forks at Bima. The right fork goes on to an area which smells of sulphur because of the frantically bubbling **mud ponds**. The left fork goes to placid **Lake Warna** with Semar Cave, an old meditation spot. The energetic can walk to many other places around the area, including the highest village in Java.

The kiosk next to Losmen Bu Jono, as you enter Dieng, sells hand-drawn maps of the area but you can ignore them and get a free map at the tourist office, almost next door.

Places to Stay & Eat

Bring a sleeping bag or be prepared to shiver. The *Losmen Bu Jono* is the only reasonable place in town. It has small, airy rooms from around 3000 to 6000 rp, blankets and really cold mandi water. It's good value in Dieng. The very unspecial *Hotel Dieng Plateau*, on the main road beside the tourist office, costs about the same and supplies blankets.

Food is available at Bu Jono's, or there's the very friendly *Warung Sederhana*, close by on the road to the mushroom factory. It's OK for a cheap and spicy nasi goreng or noodles.

Getting There & Away

From Yogya, take a bus or colt to Magelang and another to Wonosobo. Yogya to Wonosobo takes at least three hours. From the Wonosobo market place, it's a colt up the winding road to the plateau for around 1000 rp. The trip takes 1½ hours uphill, only an hour downhill.

Total fare from Yogya will be less than 3500 rp and it is possible to visit Borobudur on the way, although you need to start out very early to complete the trip by night. You've got to travel Yogya-Muntilan-Borobudur-Magelang-Wonosobo-Dieng Plateau, so there are a lot of connections to make.

If you're feeling fit, you can walk out to Bawang and continue from there by bemo to Pekalongan on the north coast. It's downhill nearly all the way and takes about four hours. If it has been raining, this route can be very slippery but if you start early from Dieng you can be in Pekalongan in the afternoon. It's a quiet, friendly, hassle-free town where you can buy interesting and colourful batik.

SOLO (Surakarta or Sala)

Situated between Yogya and Surabaya, Solo was for a time the capital of the Mataram Kingdom. The sultanate had shifted its capital several times from Kota Gede to Plered and then to Kartasura. The court of Kartasura was devastated by fighting in 1742 and the capital was moved east to the small village of Sala on the Bengawan Solo river.

It's a relatively quiet, easy-going and hassle-free town with two royal palaces where you are allowed to visit the pavilions and museums. Solo is also a good source of high-quality batik.

Information

The helpful tourist office at Jalan Slamet Riyadi 235 has a useful Solo guide map and a great many leaflets, including free booklets on Candi Sukuh and Sangiran. You can use the swimming pool at the Kusuma Sahid Prince Hotel for a fee.

Things to See

Kratons The Susuhunan of Mataram, Pakubuwono II, finally moved from Kartasura into his new palace, the **Kraton Surakarta**, in 1745. The museum here is particularly interesting, especially with one of the English-speaking guides, and exhibits include three Dutch carriages which have been used for weddings.

The oldest, named Kiyai Grudo, was used by the Susuhunan for his stately entry into the new capital. The giant pop-eyed figurehead with hairy whiskers once graced the royal perahu (outrigger boat) which, at one time, was able to navigate the Solo River all the way to the north coast. Admission is 600 rp (cheaper for students) and it's open every day, except Friday, from 9 am to 12.30 pm.

Puro Mangkunegaran, the minor kraton, was founded in 1757 by a dissident prince Raden Mas Said. The museum, in the main hall of the palace behind the pavilion, has some unusual exhibits, including an extraordinary gold genital cover. It's also worth having a look at the wayang kulit puppets in the palace shop. They're made at the kraton by the resident dalang and prices are reasonable for some very fine work.

The palace is open for the same hours as the Surakarta, but it closes at 11.30 am on Friday and it is closed on Sunday. At the pavilion, you can see dance practice sessions on Wednesday morning from 9.30 am or gamelan on Saturday morning.

Radya Pustaka Museum This small museum, next to the tourist office on Jalan Slamet Riyadi, has good exhibits of gamelan instruments and wayang puppets. Admission to the museum is 300 rp and it is open from 8 am to 12.15 pm but closed on Monday.

Performances You can see wayang orang performances every evening, except Sunday, at the Sriwedari amusement park theatres on Slamet Riyadi. The costumes are stunning and the seats are cheap, starting from around 450 rp.

Other cultural performances are sometimes held at the RRI, the local radio broadcasting station – the tourist office will have details. Dance and gamelan rehearsals can be seen at the Sasono Mulyo building, near the Kraton Surakarta, every afternoon, except Sunday, between 2 and 4 pm.

Batik Solo, a batik centre rivalling Yogya, has its own individual style. Many people find it better value for batik and handicrafts than Yogya, quite possibly because it attracts far fewer tourists. There are hundreds of stalls at Pasar Klewer with cheap batik, or try the numerous shops for more sophisticated work. Batik Semar is one good place and you can see the batik being made. The Trisne Batik and Artshop has some fine traditional batik tulis and other crafts.

There is also a good antiques market on Jalan Diponegoro. Look for old batik 'cap' stamps here. They're much cheaper than in Yogya but check that they are not damaged.

Places to Stay

Pak Mawardi's Homestay (☎ 3106) at Kemlayan Kidul 11, a small alley near Jalan Yos Sudarso and Jalan Secoyudan, is friendly and probably the best value going in Solo with singles at 5000 rp, and pleasant airy doubles at 6000, 7500 and 9000 rp. There is a quiet courtyard with tables and chairs, free tea and drinking water. Breakfast is available and you can buy coffee and soft drinks. It's also known as 'The Westerners'.

Since it's often full, there's an overflow *Westerners II*, booked through No I. It costs the same and is friendly but not that special. This is the only place I've ever seen with goldfish swimming in the mandi! Count on about 1000 rp for a becak from the bus station.

The long-running *Hotel Kota* is at Jalan Slamet Riyadi 125, very close to the centre

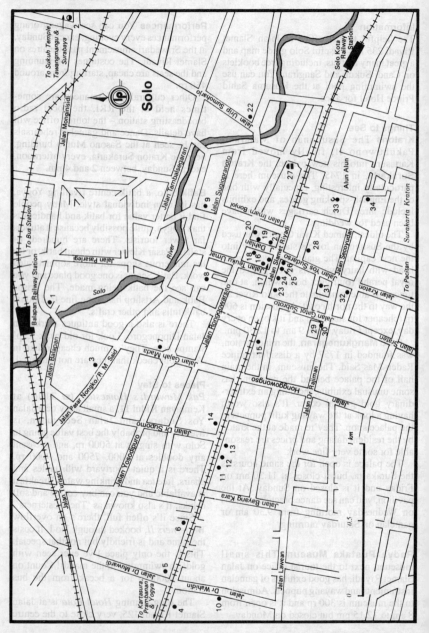

Solo

1	RRI
2	Bus Stop
3	Kondang Asri
4	Hotel Putri Ayu
5	Solo Inn
6	Adem Ayam Restaurant
7	Sahid Solo Hotel
8	Mangkunegaran Kraton
9	Kusuma Sahid Prince Hotel & Garuda Office
10	Ramayana Guest House
11	Sriwedari Park
12	Tourist Office
13	Radya Pustaka Museum
14	Hotel Dana
15	Hotel Cakra
16	Jalan Tenku Umar Night Market
17	American Donut Bakery
18	Warung Baru
19	Hotel Central
20	Losmen Nirwana
21	Superman's Restaurant
22	Pasar Gede
23	New Holland Bakery
24	Wartel Telephone Office
25	Hotel Kota
26	Kasuma Sari Restaurant
27	Post Office
28	Westerners II
29	Singosaren Plaza
30	Taxi Stand
31	Westerners (Pak Mawardi's Homestay)
32	Vihara Rahayu Chinese Temple
33	Mosque
34	Pasar Klewer

of town. Despite higher prices and reports of sliding standards, it's still popular. It's a double-storey place built around a large open courtyard. Rooms cost from 7000 rp for singles and from 10,000/12,500 for singles/doubles with mandi, It's at Jalan Slamet Riyadi 125, only a 100 metres from the town centre.

On the other side of Jalan Slamet Riyadi, at Jalan Achmad Dahlan 32, is the open and airy *Hotel Central*. It's clean and pleasant. With its very fine art deco woodwork, a thorough restoration would turn this hotel into a real showpiece. Meanwhile the rooms, all without bath, are just 4500 rp. Street rooms can be a bit noisy but you have a great view of the town, the sunset and Merapi volcano.

On this same street, you'll also find the *Islam, Moro Seneng* and *Hotel Keprabon*. The *Losmen Timur*, down a small alley alongside the Hotel Central, is cheap at just 3500 rp but it's also pretty dismal. Keep going down the alley to *Losmen Srigati*, pretty basic at 5000 rp.

A block over at Jalan Imam Bonjol 54, the *Hotel Mawar Melati* (☎ 6434) is clean and has rooms ranging from 5000 to 12,500 rp, including tea twice a day. Between the Central and the Mawar Melati is *Losmen Nirwana* at Jalan Ronggowarsito 59 with rooms at 5000 rp. Losmen near the railway station, Solo Balapan, include the really basic *Kondang Asri* at Jalan R M Said 86 at 6000 rp.

The *Hotel Dana* (☎ 3891) at Jalan Slamet Riyadi 286 is a pleasant place with peaceful grounds and rooms from 10,000 rp without bath up to 28,000 rp with bath and air-con. Further west from the town centre, the more expensive *Ramayana Guest House* (☎ 2184) is a very pleasant and quiet place at Jalan Dr Wahidin 15. Rooms cost from 20,000 rp or more with air-con.

Places to Eat

There are countless warungs and rumah makans including several serving Padang food. Since the last edition, the excellent Jalan Teuku Umar night market was moved, under local government orders, to the museum/tourist office area west of the town centre. This new location was too far from the centre of town and most of the stalls soon went broke and are now reappearing on Jalan Teuku Umar.

Unfortunately, it's still nothing like it was but you can get fresh milk, known as susu sagar or minuman sehat (healthy drink), from some of the warungs – hot or cold or with honey. Nasi gudeg is popular but the speciality of Solo is nasi liwet, rice with chicken and coconut milk. Other local specialities to try at night are the small rice puddings served up on a crispy pancake with banana, chocolate or jackfruit on top – best eaten when they're piping hot.

Jalan Achmad Dahlan is becoming quite a travellers' centre and *Superman's/Yant Favourite* is a popular little cafe at No 22. They do a superb nasi liwet. Across the road is the extremely popular *Warung Baru*, turning out all the travellers' favourites. *Rumah Makan Laris* is another place on this street.

Places along Jalan Slamet Riyadi include the *American Donut Bakery* and the *New Holland Bakery*. The latter has a bewildering array of baked goods and delicious savoury martabak rolls. At Jalan Slamet Riyadi 111, on the corner with Jalan Yos Sudarso, the *Kusama Sari* has seductive air-con and good food. Other possibilities include the *Adem Ayam*, west from the town centre at Jalan Slamet Riyadi 336.

Getting There & Away

There are air connections with a number of cities including Surabaya, less than an hour away.

Solo is on the main Yogya to Surabaya rail and road route. It's around 5000 rp for a public bus from Surabaya to Solo and takes six to seven hours by day but half that time by night. The better air-con buses are more like 8000 to 10,000 rp. It takes about the same time by train.

Yogya is two hours away by bus and costs 900 rp. There are deluxe door-to-door minibuses which cost 2000 rp. To Blitar, it's 3500 rp and takes about six hours. To Malang takes nine hours and costs around 5000 rp by bus. They leave frequently in the morning between 7 and 9 am.

Getting Around

To/From the Airport The airport is 14 km from town – an 8000 rp fixed fare by taxi.

Local Transport The main bus station is about three km from the town centre, 1000 rp by becak. For buses to Semarang, Prambanan and Yogya, it's cheaper to take the double decker to Kartasura (west of the centre) and catch a bus from there. A becak from the railway station

into the town centre is around 500 rp. The minibus station is by the kraton on the opposite side to the batik market.

The city double-decker bus runs between Kartasura in the west and Palur in the east, directly along Jalan Slamet Riyadi, and costs a flat fare of 150 rp. Bicycles can be hired from the Westerners for 1500 rp a day.

Solo has metered taxis – the main taxi stand is at the corner of the Singosaren Plaza shopping centre – ☎ 45678 to book a taxi.

Bicycle Rides All day bicycle rides around Solo and the surrounding country are organised from the Warung Baru or Yant Favourite restaurants. You cover about 15 km and the 7500 rp cost includes breakfast, bike rental and the guide – great value.

AROUND SOLO
Sangiran

Prehistoric 'Java Man' was discovered at Sangiran, 15 km north of Solo, and there is a small museum with fossil exhibits including some amazing 'mammoth' bones and tusks.

They are still finding things and if you wander up the road past the museum and have a look in some of the exposed banks you may find shells or fossil bones and crabs. To get there continue beyond Kalioso a km towards Sangiran turn-off. It's three km from there, saving you a km walk.

Candi Sukuh & Tawangmangu

Candi Sukuh is a primitive-style temple on the slopes of Mt Lawu, 36 km east of Solo. It dates from the 15th or 16th century and has a curious Inca-like look. The tourist office in Solo has a leaflet about the place.

To get there, take the double-decker to Tertomoyo, then a Tawangmangu bus to Karangpandan for 600 rp. From Karangpandan, catch a minibus to Candi Sukuh for 450 rp. On market days, the minibus stops right beside the temple but on other days, it's a couple of km uphill walk to the site. It is about 1½ hours travelling by bus in total but it's worth it for the superb views and atmosphere.

Tawangmangu, a mountain resort about a 1½ hour ride out of Solo, has an impressive waterfall (the Grojogan Sewu) where you can take a dip in the very chilly pool. You can catch a bus from Karangpandan but it's possible to walk to Tawangmangu from Candi Sukuh. It's a very pleasant 2½ hour stroll along well-worn cobble-stoned paths, and from Tawangmangu, you can bus back to Solo for around 750 rp. Some people find the walk more interesting than Tawangmangu or Candi Sukuh.

Places to Stay & Eat In Tawangmangu, you can stay at the *Pak Amat Losmen* which has a garden. The rooms, from 8000 rp, are each individual little houses with bathrooms and verandah. Further up the hill, the *Losmen Pondok Garuda*, next to the mosque, has a variety of rooms with and without bathroom at similar prices, some with a good view over the valley. On the main street, Jalan Lawu, about a km up from the bus station, *Hotel Lawu* has doubles at around 15,000 rp. There's good food in the warungs further up the hill.

SEMARANG

This north coast port is the capital of central Java. It's about 120 km north of Yogya and about two-thirds of the way from Jakarta to Surabaya. Although it's an important port, there are no deep-water berthing facilities and boats have to anchor out in the mouth of the Kali Baru River and transfer their cargo to shore by lighter.

Information

There is a Semarang tourist office in the Wisma Pancasila building on Simpang Lima, the town square. The office is open from 8 am to 2 pm Monday to Thursday, to 11 am Friday, and 1 pm Saturday. There is also a central Java tourist office, Kantor Dinas Pariwisata, at Jalan Pemuda 171. It's open the same hours as the Semarang tourist office but closes an hour earlier Monday to Thursday and Saturday.

Things to See

The **Sam Po Kong Temple** in the southwest of the city is dedicated to Admiral Cheng Ho – the famous Muslim eunuch of the Ming dynasty who led many expeditions from China to Java and other parts of South-East Asia in the early 15th century. He is particularly revered in Melaka (Malaysia), and the Chinese temple in Semarang is the largest in Indonesia, honoured by both Chinese Buddhists and Muslims.

It's better known as Gedong Batu (stone building) and is in the form of a huge cave. To get there, take a Daihatsu from Terminal Baru in the centre of town to Karang Ayu and another, from there, to Gedong Batu. The temple is about half an hour from the city centre.

There isn't a great deal to do or see in Semarang itself except for a sprinkling of old buildings from the Dutch colonial era. On Jalan Let Jen Suprapto, south of Tawang railway station, there's the 1753 **Gereja Blenduk** church with its huge dome and baroque organ. Behind Poncol railway station there is the ruin of an old **Dutch East India Company fort** and there are numerous old warehouses around Tawang. The **Thay Kak Sie Temple** is on Gang Lombok, off Jalan Pekojan in Semarang's old Chinatown. Semarang also has an interesting day market, **Pasar Johar**, on the square at the top of Jalan Pemuda.

Every evening there are wayang orang performances in the **Ngesti Pandowo Theatre** at Jalan Pemuda 116. Performances start at 7 pm. Or, take a city bus out to **Gombel**, the 'new town' on the hills to the south, and have a drink at the Sky Garden Hotel from where there is a fine view of the city and ships at sea. To get there, take a bus down Jalan Pemuda bound for Jatingalen and ask for Bukit Gombel, which is just past the hotel.

Places to Stay

Some of the bottom-end places at Semarang are extremely so, and standards can be very low. Most places are in the centre of town, near Pasar Johar, and the old bus terminal, now a shopping centre.

The *Losmen Jaya* at Jalan M T Haryono 85-87, about a km south of the bus station, has rooms with fan from 9000 rp, more with mandi but breakfast is included. *Losmen Agung*, in the same area at Jalan Petolongan 32-34, is a colonial relic with rooms from 6000 rp; it gets decidedly mixed reports. *Losmen Djelita* at Jalan M T Haryono 34-38 is better although similarly priced.

Other cheap hotels are scattered along or just off Jalan Imam Bonjol. Try and get a room back from the street. The *Losmen Singapore* at Imam Bonjol 12 is reasonably central, near Pasar Johar, and has rooms from 9000 rp. The nearby *Hotel Oewa-Asia* at Jalan Kol Sugiono 12 is a former colonial hotel. It's a friendly, comfortable place with rooms from 12,000 rp including breakfast. There are more expensive rooms with bathroom and fan or air-con.

Further west, near the Poncol railway station, is the fairly comfortable and friendly *Losmen Ardjuna* at Jalan Imam Bonjol 51, and the *Losmen Rahayu* at No 35. Much further out at Jalan Imam Bonjol 144 is the *Bali* with clean if somewhat overpriced rooms from 15,000 rp. Becak riders may try to steer you here for the commission.

The *Dibya Puri* (☎ 27821) at Jalan Pemuda 11 is a rambling old place with a pleasant courtyard with trees. They have a restaurant, bar and laundry service, and large, airy rooms start from around 20,000 rp with shared bathrooms. Prices rise towards 50,000 rp for fancier rooms with private bathroom and air-con; all prices include breakfast.

Places to Eat

The *Toko Oen* at Jalan Pemuda 52, a short walk from the Pasar, is a wonderfully genteel old place. It's not cheap but well worth a visit – the food is good and they have a terrific selection of exotic ice creams.

Restaurants along Jalan Gajah Mada include the reasonably priced *Gajah Mada* at No 43 with good Chinese food and seafood. On Gang Lombok, off Jalan Pekojan in Chinatown, there are good Chinese eating places. At Pasar Ya'ik, the night market next to Pasar Johar, there are plenty of cheap food stalls.

The *Hotel Dibya Puri* restaurant on Jalan Pemuda serves European and Indonesian food and their set Indonesian meal, complete with fruit and coffee, is good value. The *Ritzeky Pub* on Jalan Sinabung Buntu is an expat hang-out.

Getting There & Away

Semarang is on the main north coast Jakarta to Surabaya train route and can also be reached from those towns by bus. Surabaya trains are not that frequent and tend to go in the middle of the night. Tawang is the main railway station in Semarang.

The Jurnatan bus station on Jalan M T Haryono is close to Tawang and fairly central. Most bus ticket agents are near the bus station along the same street. From Yogya, it takes about 3½ hours by bus for around 1500 rp for the cheapest public buses. There are also regular bus services from Solo and door-to-door minibus services.

An air-con 4848 Taxis' minibus operates from Cirebon to Semarang, again door-to-door. Semarang to Surabaya costs about 4000 rp by public bus, from 8000 rp by night bus and takes about eight hours. Buses to Jakarta cost from around 6000 rp for the cheapest public buses but it's better to take the train. The night buses arrive at ungodly hours at the remote Pulo Gadung bus station.

Getting Around

You can get around town by fixed-price city bus or by Daihatsu minivan at a fixed cost of 150 rp. Daihatsus depart from Terminal Baru on Jalan H A Salim behind Pasar Johar.

OTHER NORTH COAST CENTRES
Pekalongan

The small town of Pekalongan is on the north coast between Semarang and Cirebon. Few travellers pause here but there's some fine local batik and a **batik museum**.

Places to Stay Directly opposite the railway station, at Jalan Gajah Mada 11A, the *Hotel*

Gajah Mada (☎ 41185) is clean, basic and good value. Nearby, you'll find the *Losmen Ramayana* and the *Losmen Damai*.

The *Hotel Istana* (☎ 61581) at Jalan Gaja Mada 23 is a more expensive hotel with rooms from around 20,000 rp.

Places to Eat Near the railway station, the *Rumah Makan Saiyo* has reasonable Padang food. Try the *Buana Restaurant* at Jalan Mansyur 5 for seafood or the *Purima* on Jalan Hayam Wuruk for snacks and ice cream.

Kudus

An important Islamic centre, Kudus is between Semarang and Surabaya on the north coast. The **Al-Manar Mosque** in the centre of the old town dates from 1549. Kudus is also noted for its *kretek*, clove-flavoured cigarette, manufacturing.

Near Kudus, the town of **Mayong** was the home of Raden Ajeng Kartini, a noted Indonesian writer who died in 1904. **Japara** is the centre for Java's best traditional wood-carvers. **Rembang**, further east from Kudus, has a good beach.

Places to Stay Within walking distance of the bus station, the *Hotel Notasari* (☎ 21245) at Jalan Kepodang 12 has rooms with mandi from 15,000 rp. The cheaper and more spartan *Losmen Slamet* is in the town centre at Jalan Sudirman 63.

Places to Eat The *Hotel Notasari* has a good restaurant with excellent gado-gado, or try the *Garuda* on Jalan Sudirman 1 for Chinese, Indonesian or Western food. The *Rumah Makan Hijau*, near the bus station at Jalan Achmad Yani 1, is cheap and has good food and fruit juices.

MALANG

Malang is a big country town on the alternative 'back route' between Yogyakarta and Banyuwangi. The countryside on this run is particularly beautiful and Malang is a nice city with just enough altitude to take the edge off the heat. It gets few Western visitors, although it has good parks and trees and a large central market. For an interesting trip in this area take a train from Solo to Jombang, then colts to Blimbing, Kandangan, Batu and, finally, Malang. There is also a bus which goes direct from Malang to Probolinggo.

There are a number of high mountains around Malang including **Gunung Semeru**, the highest point in Java at 3678 metres. It takes three or four days to climb to the top and back; it is a real climb, not an easy walk. Selecta (see Around Surabaya), a hill resort, is just 16 km north-west of Malang – take a colt to Batu and from there another colt will drop you right at the Selecta swimming pool.

Malang has some excellent ruins. A good, roughly circular day trip is to go 12 km north of Malang to **Candi Singosari** (the temple is to the right in Singosari, 500 metres from the main Malang to Surabaya road). A *candi* is a temple. Return to the village of Blimbang, north of Malang, and then travel east to **Candi Jago** at Tumpang, and then to **Candi Kidal** in the small village of Kidal. Finally, you can complete the circle back south to Malang via Tajinan. For transport, first take a bemo to the colt terminal at Blimbing, and from Blimbing you can take colts all the way.

Places to Stay

There are lots of places to stay and some excellent cheap places to eat. Surabaya's *Bamboe Denn* has a branch hostel (☎ 24859) at Jalan Semeru 35 which is only a 10-minute walk from the bus or railway station. Ignore the becak jockeys who say it's three km away. It's very cheap and has dorm beds for 2000 rp – you'll probably get roped into more English conversation lessons too! If it seems to be locked up, ring the bell inside the gate.

Only two minutes from the bus station, the excellent *Hotel Helios* on Jalan Pattimura has a very pleasant garden ('fantastic,' reported one guest) and rooms for 10,000 rp including breakfast.

The *Hotel Santosa* is central at Jalan H A Salim 24, just off the main square, and has basic but clean rooms with a private mandi from around 8000 rp. The *Hotel Malang* on Jalan Zainul Arifin, off Jalan H A Salim, is also central but rather noisy. The doubles have huge beds. Better value is the pleasantly old-fashioned *Hotel Malinda*, also on Jalan Zainul Arifin, with rooms with private mandi from 10,000 rp and up – and ceilings that must be seven metres high!

Hotel Aloha (☎ 26950) at Jalan Gajah Mada 7 is nice but expensive. Rooms with bath cost around 20,000 rp and include breakfast. *Hotel Pelangi*, a very large yellow building right on the town square, is good but expensive.

Places to Eat

One of the good places to eat is the anachronistically colonial *Toko Oen* on the town square, but it's rather expensive. *Rumah Makan Padang Minang Jaya* at Jalan Basuki Rachmat 111 has terrific Padang food, or try *Depot Pangsit Mie Gadjah Mada* on Jalan Pasar Besar for good cheap noodles. Malang also has an excellent cheap night market, *Pasar Senggol*, along Jalan Majapahit by the river.

Getting There & Away

Buses to or from Yogyakarta or Solo take about nine hours and cost 6000 rp, or around 12,000 rp by night bus. Buses leave regularly to and from Surabaya, take around 2½ hours and cost 1250 rp. The 3rd-class only train from Surabaya takes about three hours and is similarly priced. The bus to Probolinggo takes about two hours.

Buses to or from Banyuwangi cost 5000 rp and take about nine hours. Night buses to Bali cost around 10,000 rp. Bali Indah has an office on Jalan Pattimura, and Pemuda Express at Jalan Basuki Rachmat 1 operates night buses to Bali and other destinations.

SURABAYA

A big, busy and not particularly interesting place, the capital of east Java is a major port and the second largest city in Indonesia. For most people, it's just a short stop between central Java and Bali, although it is probably the most 'Indonesian' of all the large cities. People who do find Surabaya interesting, and to be fair quite a few people do, generally enjoy the Indonesian atmosphere of the place.

Information

The east Java regional tourist office is at Jalan Pemuda 118, across from the Surabaya Delta Plaza and near Gubeng railway station. The small office is open from 7 am daily, except Sunday, and closes at 2 pm Monday to Thursday, 11 am Friday, and 1 pm on Saturday.

There are plenty of banks around including a huge and flashy Bank Ekspor Impor office on Jalan Pemuda. Empress Money Changer is on Jalan Taman Nasution, at the junction with Jalan Sudirman. The post office is on Jalan Pemuda and if you continue along Jalan Pemuda, across Jalan Basuki Rachmat, you'll come to the telephone office, somewhat tucked away off the main road. There are swimming pools at the Garden Hotel and the Hotel Simpang.

We've had a couple of reports from people who have been befriended in Surabaya, have then been given drugged coffee and woken up later to find their valuables gone – so take care.

Things to See

Zoo The Surabaya zoo is reputed to be the largest in South-East Asia. It is well organised and has a couple of big Komodo dragons – who seem to spend half the time fast asleep. Admission is 600 rp and it costs 200 rp more for the aquarium (worth it) or the nocturama. The zoo is only a short ride by city bus No 2 or bemo V from Jalan Sudirman in the centre of town.

Other Close to the town centre is the **THR amusement park**, open in the evenings. Plenty of Makassar schooners can be seen at the **Kali Mas wharf**. The small **MPU Tantular Museum** has interesting archaeological exhibits and is across the road from the zoo.

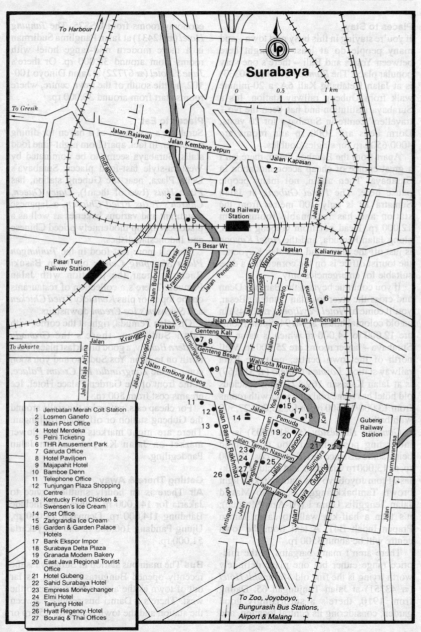

Surabaya

0   0.5   1 km

To Harbour

To Gresik

To Jakarta

To Zoo, Joyoboyo,
Bungurasih Bus Stations,
Airport & Malang

1 Jembatan Merah Colt Station
2 Losmen Ganefo
3 Main Post Office
4 Hotel Merdeka
5 Pelni Ticketing
6 THR Amusement Park
7 Garuda Office
8 Hotel Paviljoen
9 Majapahit Hotel
10 Bamboe Denn
11 Telephone Office
12 Tunjungan Plaza Shopping
    Centre
13 Kentucky Fried Chicken &
    Swensen's Ice Cream
14 Post Office
15 Zangrandia Ice Cream
16 Garden & Garden Palace
    Hotels
17 Bank Ekspor Impor
18 Surabaya Delta Plaza
19 Granada Modern Bakery
20 East Java Regional Tourist
    Office
21 Hotel Gubeng
22 Sahid Surabaya Hotel
23 Empress Moneychanger
24 Elmi Hotel
25 Tanjung Hotel
26 Hyatt Regency Hotel
27 Bouraq & Thai Offices

Jalan Rajawali
Jalan Kembang Jepun
Jalan Kapasan
Indrapura
Jalan Kapasari
Kota Railway Station
Ps Besar Wt
Pasar Turi Raliway Station
Jalan Peneleh
Jagalan
Kalianyar
Bangsa
Jalan Bubutan
Pasar Besar
Kramat Gantung
Jalan Undaan Kulon
Jalan Undaan Wetan
Gunsari
Jalan Akhmad Jais
Jalan Ag Soeprapto
Jalan Ambengan
Praban
Genteng Kali
Jalan Kedungdoro
Jalan Tunjungan
Genteng Besar
Jalan Krangan
Jalan Raja Arjuna
Jalan Embong Malang
Walikota Mustajab
Mas
Jalan Yos Sudarso
Jalan Basuki Rakhmad
Jalan Pemuda
Jalan Sudirman
Jalan Taman Nasution
Jalan Panglima Sudirman
Jalan Raya Gubeng
Jalan Sumatra
Jalan Kayoon
Jalan Jawa
Jalan Darmawangsa
Gubeng Railway Station
Antique Shops

Places to Stay
If you're staying in this busy port town – and many people do at least overnight here between Yogya and Bali – there's one very popular place. The *Bamboe Denn* (☎ 40333) is at Jalan Ketabang Kali 6A, a 20-minute walk from Gubeng railway station. It's a Surabaya institution and has been the No 1 travellers' centre in Surabaya for 20 years. Dorm beds are 3000 rp and rooms are 4000/6500 rp for singles/doubles.

Apart from the Bamboe Denn, there isn't a great choice of cheap accommodation in Surabaya. Then again, not many people pause here. The *Hotel Gubeng* at Jalan Sumatra 18 is only 100 metres from the station and has reasonable rooms from 12,000 rp. Head out from Gubeng station, along Jalan Pemuda, and the *Hotel Kayoon* is just off the main road on Jalan Kayoon – the tourist office is on the corner. It's a dive suitable for emergencies only.

If you continue beyond the Bamboe Denn and cross the river to Jalan Genteng Besar, you'll come to *Hotel Paviljoen* (☎ 43449) in an old colonial house at No 94. Small rooms are 12,000 to 14,000 rp which is value for Surabaya – larger rooms are 25,000 rp. Well north of the town centre, near the Kota railway station, *Losmen Ganefo* (☎ 311169) is at Jalan Kapasan 169-171. This spacious old hotel has some real character with rooms from 13,000/15,500 rp, or for 25,000/27,500 with bath.

Ganesha Homestay (☎ 81 8705) is an interesting possibility if you don't mind being some distance out. Rooms cost 10,000 rp, or 13,000 rp with bath, and include breakfast. From Joyoboyo bus station, take a light brown Tambakklanggri bemo to Masjid Jalan Tenggilis Utara I (Al-Azis Mosque); it's then a half-km walk to Jalan Taman Prapen Indah B41. A taxi from the town centre will be about 3500 rp.

There aren't many bargains in the mid-price range either but one place definitely worth trying is the fine old *Majapahit Hotel* (☎ 43351) at Jalan Tunjungan 65. Dating from 1910, there's a surprisingly good garden, considering its central location, and economy rooms from US$25. The *Tanjung Hotel* (☎ 42431) at Jalan Panglima Sudirman is a more modern mid-range hotel with rooms from around 35,000 rp. Or there's *Jane's Hotel* (☎ 67722) at Jalan Dinoyo 100-102, a little south of the town centre, where rooms start from around 30,000 rp.

Places to Eat
Surabaya's not much of a haven for dining out either. In fact, apart from night-time food stalls, Surabaya seems to be dominated by Western-style fast-food places. Surabaya's Delta Plaza, near the Gubeng station, has *Pizza Huts* (two of them!), *Dairy Queen, Church's Texas Fried Chicken,* a Japanese restaurant and various bakeries as well as a place serving up moderately priced Chinese and Indonesian dishes.

There's more fast food in the *Tunjungan Plaza Shopping Centre* on Jalan Basuki Rachmat, near the junction with Jalan Pemuda. There's a collection of restaurants on the top floor plus *Kentucky Fried Chicken* and *Swensen's Ice Cream* downstairs.

On Jalan Pemuda, right at the corner with Jalan Sudirman, there's the *Granada Modern Bakery,* a good breakfast place. Turn north on to Jalan Yos Sudarso and you soon come to the *Zangrandia Ice Cream Palace,* at the front of the Garden Palace Hotel. Ice creams cost from 500 rp.

For cheap eats, patronise the stalls around the Gubeng station or off Jalan Tunjungan. There are night markets near the flower market on Jalan Kayoon and on Jalan Pandegiling.

Getting There & Away
Air There is an hourly shuttle service to Jakarta for 141,000 rp. Other fares include Bandung 114,000 rp, Denpasar 72,000 rp, Ujung Pandang 160,000 rp and Yogyakarta 51,000 rp.

Bus The main bus station in Surabaya is the recently opened Bungurasih station, as far out of town as the airport but further to the west. There's a Damri bus service between the station and the town centre for 150 rp or a taxi would cost about 5000 rp. The old Joyoboyo bus station is now mainly for local bemo services.

There's are many bus company offices at the station for public and private buses. Eastbound fares include Probolinggo 1350 rp (2½ hours), Banyuwangi 4100 rp, Jember 2800 rp and Situbondo 2700 rp. Southbound, there are buses to Pandaan for 650 rp or Malang 1250 rp (2½ hours). Westbound, there are frequent buses to Towulan via Mojokerta, to Solo for 4000 to 8500 rp (anything from 3½ to seven hours) and to Yogya 5000 to 10,000 rp (from 4½ to nine hours).

For longer trips to Solo, Yogya or Denpasar, the night buses are faster since traffic is lighter. Day buses to Yogya cost from 6000 rp, night buses from 9000 rp. Night buses to Denpasar cost from around 10,000 to 15,000 rp. There are buses going straight through to Bandung and even Jakarta but that's a long trip by bus (859 km; 15 hours). It's better to take a train if you want to go there directly.

If you're heading to the north coast of Java, buses and colts depart from the Jembatan Merah station, north of the Kota railway station. Buses to Semarang cost 5500 to 11,000 rp. Buses run direct from Surabaya to various towns on Madura.

Train Trains from Jakarta, taking the northern route via Semarang, arrive at the Pasar Turi station. Trains taking the southern route via Yogya, and trains from Banyuwangi and Malang, arrive at Gubeng and carry on to Kota. The Gubeng station is much more convenient for central places than Kota or Pasar Turi.

The trip from Jakarta takes 15 to 20 hours although in practice, the slower 3rd-class trains can take even longer. Fares vary from 5800 rp in 3rd class, from 9500 rp in 2nd and from 13,500 in 1st. The best services are with the deluxe Bima Express via Yogya (22,500 rp in 1st class or 27,000 rp with a sleeper) or the Mutiara Utara via Semarang (25,000 rp in 1st class). The cheapest are the all 3rd-class services like the Senja Ekonomi or the Gaya Baru Malam Utara on the northern

route or the Selatan version on the southern route.

Trains to or from Yogyakarta take six to eight hours and cost from 3800 rp in 3rd class, from 5000 rp in 2nd, and from 13,500 in 1st.

Apart from services to the main cities, there is a 3rd-class evening train to Malang; from Malang, the train leaves at the crack of dawn. There's a morning and night train to Banyuwangi for the ferry to Bali. The fare to Banyuwangi costs from 2800 rp in 3rd class and from 3500 rp in 2nd. Through to Denpasar, the fare is around 7000 rp inclusive of the ferry to Bali and a bus to Denpasar.

Boat Surabaya is an important port and most of the regular Pelni services operate through here. See the Indonesia Getting Around section for more details. Connections to Kalimantan and Sulawesi are particularly popular.

The Pelni ticket office (☎ 21694) at Jalan Pahlawan 20 is open from 8 am to 4 pm (closed over lunch – 12 noon to 1 pm) Monday to Friday, and from 8 am to 1 pm Saturday. The front ticket counter is chaotic but you can go round to the back office where the staff are more helpful. For information on cargo boats, try the harbourmaster at Kalimas Baru 194, Tanjung Perak. PT Raptim (☎ 65506) at Jalan Mojopahit 36, Surabaya, can also be helpful.

The mission boat *Ratu Rosari* operates a regular service through the islands of Nusa Tenggara, sailing Surabaya-Reo-Maumere-Larantuka-Atapupu-Kupang-Ende and reverse. The islands of Flores and Timor are predominantly Christian.

Getting Around
To/From the Airport Juanda Airport is 18 km south of the city centre, and an air-con taxi costs a fixed 7500 rp. The air-con Damri bus service is 2000 rp.

Local Transport Surabaya has plenty of air-con metered taxis and flagfall is 700 rp. Becaks are useful for local transport and there are plenty of them around town. Bemos are labelled A, B, C, etc and all charge a standard 250 rp. City buses charge a fixed 200 rp fare. Gubeng station is within easy walking distance of the Bamboe Denn and other central accommodation.

The ferry to Madura is 400 rp and you take a city bus or K bemo to the harbour. Buses also go directly from Surabaya to towns on Madura, like Sumenep.

AROUND SURABAYA
Gresik
The **tomb** of the Muslim saint, Sunan Giri, credited with introducing the religion of Islam to Java in the 13th century, is in this town. It is 25 km north-west of Surabaya.

Trowulan
Scattered around Trowulan, near Mojokerto, 60 km south-west from Surabaya on the Surabaya to Solo road, are the remains of the ancient Majapahit Kingdom. The Majapahits were the final Hindu kingdom to rule on Java until the Muslims drove them out to Bali in the early 1500s.

The **Trowulan Museum** has a large map indicating the locations of the candis, tombs and graves. The museum is open from 7 am daily (except Monday) and closes at 2 pm Tuesday to Thursday and Sunday, at 11 am on Friday and 12.30 pm on Saturday.

Some of the temple remains are very impressive in their shattered grandeur and a few of the sites are within walking distance of the museum. If you're going somewhere else, you can leave your gear at the office. Or hire a becak – a three to four-hour trip costs about 7000 rp and the ride along the country lanes is easily as good as the temples themselves. A bus from Surabaya (800 rp) will drop you right at the museum on the main road, and it's another 1200 rp on to Madiun.

Pandaan
The open-air **Candra Wilwatikta Theatre** at Pandaan, 40 km south of Surabaya on the road to Malang, is the site of the east Java classical ballet festival held during the dry season on the first and third Saturday nights of the months of May to October.

Mountain Resorts
Tretes and **Prigen** have a network of footpaths and trails and many waterfalls. I wouldn't recommend it for a special trip but if you have to kill time in Surabaya, this is a good escape. On the other side of the same mountain, the similar resorts of **Selecta** and **Batu** are easily accessible from Malang. Selecta has an excellent swimming pool and **Songgoriti**, near Batu, is a spa town with relaxing hot sulphur baths. Others are **Tosari** and **Wendit** which has a lake where you can swim and lots of monkeys.

Places to Stay There are lots of cottages or individual rooms available in Tretes and Prigen, just below Tretes – somebody will find you a place although this is principally a local resort where few foreigners are seen. Prices are not cheap and go sky high. There are some good and cheap places to eat around the market. The situation is similar in Batu and Selecta.

Pasir Putih
Some distance east of Probolinggo on the Surabaya to Banyuwangi road, Pasir Putih is east Java's main coastal resort and it can be mobbed at weekends. The name means 'white beach' but the sand is more grey-black than white! No matter – there's clear water, pleasant swimming and lots of picturesque outrigger boats – but compared to Lovina Beach, only a few hours away on Bali, it's no big deal. Scuba diving at Pasir Putih can be organised from Surabaya.

Places to Stay There are a number of hotels jammed between the highway and the beach. Next door to the Oriental Restaurant, the *Hotel Bhayangkara Beach* has rooms facing the highway from 5000 rp as well as better rooms rooms facing the beach and with private mandi. The *Pasir Putih Inn* is better but more expensive, with rooms from around 7500 rp (including breakfast).

Situbondo

Only a short distance on the Banyuwangi side of Pasir Putih, there are several places to stay in this reasonably large town.

Places to Stay & Eat The *Hotel Asia* is on the main road and quite pleasant. The *Losmen Asita* is near the railway station, or there's the *Hotel Situbondo*. The *Restaurant Malang* has good seafood.

MADURA

Only half an hour from Surabaya by ferry, the relatively untouristed island of Madura has fine beaches and picturesque remote countryside. Coming up from Bali, Madura is also accessible by daily ferry from Panarukan, a few km north of Situbondo, to Kalianget on the island's eastern tip – you could make a trip through Madura and exit from Kamal to Surabaya.

Madura is a flat and rugged island, much of it dry and sometimes barren, and it's a contrast to Java in both landscape and lifestyle. Cattle raising is important rather than rice growing. The production of salt is another major industry – much of Indonesia's supply comes from the vast salt tracts around Kalianget in the east.

During the dry season, particularly in August and September, Madura is famed for its colourful bull races, the *kerapan sapi*, which climax with the finals held at Pamekasan. The bulls are harnessed in pairs, two teams compete at a time and they're raced along a 120-metre course in a special stadium. Races don't last long – the best time recorded is nine seconds over 100 metres, which is faster than the men's world track record. Bull races for tourists are sometimes staged at the Bangkalan Stadium. The east Java tourist board can supply details of where and when the bull races will be held.

Apart from beaches and the bull races, there are a number of interesting places to visit dotted around the island. Near the village of Arasbaya, on the west coast, is **Air Mata** ('Water of the Eye' or 'Tears') where the old royal cemetery of the Cakraningrat family is perched on the edge of a small ravine, with beautiful views along the river valley and across the terraced hills. To get there from Kamal, take a colt for Arasbaya (28 km north) and ask for the turn off to Air Mata. From there, it's a four km walk inland.

Along the south coast road to Pamekasan, 100 km east of Kamal, there are fields of immaculately-groomed cattle, small fishing villages and a sea of rainbow-coloured perahus. **Camplong**, about 15 km short of Pamekasan, has a fine sweeping beach and calm water. From **Pamekasan**, the capital of Madura, you can visit the strange natural fire resources of Api Abadi (Eternal Fire), where 'fire spouts out of the earth'. **Sumenep** is an old and attractive town, 53 km north-east of Pamekasan in the more isolated hills of the interior. You can see Sumenep's 18th century mosque, the kraton and its small, interesting museum of royal family possessions. **Asta Tinggi**, the royal cemetery, is only about three km from the town centre.

At **Salopeng**, 21 km from Sumenep and near the fishing village of Ambunten on the north coast, there are great yellow sand dunes, palm trees and rough seas. The beach at **Lombang**, 30 km from Sumenep, is reputed to be even more beautiful but less easily accessible – there are no roads and the local people ride their bicycles along the sands.

Places to Stay

In Pamekasan, you could try the *Hotel Garuda*, on Jalan Masigit near the town square, with rooms at around 5000 rp. Or there's the similarly priced *Hotel Trunojoyo*, round the corner and down a small alley off Jalan Trunojoyo. The cheaper *Losmen Bahagia* is further down Jalan Trunojoyo. They're all in the centre of town and a 300 rp becak ride from the bus station.

Sumenep, to the east of Pamekasan, is more interesting than Pamekasan and a good base for visiting remoter parts of the island. *Losmen Wijaya I* and *II*, both near the main bus station, are good with rooms from around 10,000 rp. Or try the cheaper *Losmen Damai* or *Losmen Matahari* near the town square on Jalan Sudirman.

Getting There & Away

It's only half an hour by ferry from Surabaya to Kamal, the harbour town in Madura, and from there you can take a bus or colt to other main towns. From Kamal, it's a bumpy two or three-hour bus trip to Pamekasan, the island's capital. Bangkalan is only about half an hour from the ferry terminal. There is a ferry from Panarukan to Kalianget at 1 pm and from Kalianget to Panarukan at 7 am.

MT BROMO

A visit to this fantastic, and still far from extinct, volcano is easy to fit in between Bali and Surabaya. The usual jumping-off point for Bromo is the town of Probolinggo on the main Surabaya to Banyuwangi road. From there, you have to get to Ngadisari, high on the slopes of an ancient volcano.

At Ngadisari, you sign the visitors' book (they may try to get you to pay a 'fee' as well) and think about a place to stay. You can stay with one of the villagers in Ngadisari or you can continue up the very steep final three km to Cemoro Lawang at the rim of the crater – bemos now go regularly for 1000 rp.

There's a slightly expensive hotel at Cemoro Lawang but the advantage of staying up here is that you've got a shorter and easier walk in the morning. On Bromo, as at so many other mountains, it's being there for the sunrise which is all-important!

As at Mt Batur in Bali, Bromo is a crater within a crater. The outer one is vast and across to Bromo and nearby Mt Batok is a scene of utter desolation. Get up at 4 am, or earlier for an easy stroll across, if you're staying at the top (the hotel will wake you up) and just follow the path down into the crater and the white markers across the lava sand to Bromo. Take a torch (flashlight) or the descent in the dark can be fairly dodgy. There is no need for a guide or horses although, if you want to, you can ride across for about 5000 rp.

By the time you've crossed the lava plain and started to climb up Bromo (246 steps, one traveller reported) it should be fairly light. From the top you'll get an unreal view of the sun sailing up over the outer crater.

Bromo continuously pours out some very smelly white smoke – New Zealanders will find it familiar!

A number of travellers have sent in more suggestions about the Bromo trip – almost all noting that it's definitely worthwhile and that it's worth staying a day or two and doing more walking. In the wet season, the dawn and the clouds often arrive simultaneously so at that time of year you might just as well stay in bed and stroll across later in the day when it's much warmer.

In January or February, there's a big annual festival and at that time of year getting up the mountain involves fighting your way through the crowds. One visitor even suggested that if you're really crazy, you could climb right down inside the crater. Another nutcase suggested climbing it at night while it's erupting, adding that it 'scares the shit out of you'!

As an alternative to the usual return to Probolinggo, you can walk right around Bromo across the lava plain and climb up over the opposite edge to Ngadas. You can walk down from village to village until you eventually get a ride into Malang. It entails six or seven hours of walking, so start early in order to get to Malang by evening.

Places to Stay

Mt Bromo There are plenty of places to stay in Ngadisari, although the quality varies a lot and security is not always so great. Prices vary from around 3500 rp, less for really basic rooms and much higher if you arrive too late to hunt around.

At Cemoro Lawang, right on the rim of the Tengger crater, the *Hotel Bromo Permai* has comfortable dorm beds for 5000 rp (cheaper for students or YHA members) and rooms from 10,000 up to 24,000 rp. The hotel has a bar and restaurant – food here is also pricey but they're quite substantial meals. It's warm and a good place for an early breakfast before setting out for Bromo. At night, it's very cold at the top (it is in Ngadisari too) but staying up here does save an hour or so of walking before dawn!

Only a couple of hundred metres down the

road, towards the village, there's the small *Losmen Lawa* with cheap rooms and simple meals. At the village of Lawang Sair, 300 metres below the hotel, you can stay with Mbuk Artini who provides good food. *Bromo Home Stay* at Jalan Wonokerto 5 in Ngadisari is another possibility.

Probolinggo This town is a useful mid-point between Surabaya and Banyuwangi as well as being the jumping-off point for Mt Bromo. There are hotels and some cheap restaurants along the main street, Jalan Raja P Sudirman, less than a 10-minute walk from the bus station. The *Hotel Bromo Permai II*, opposite the bus station, is a good source of information on Bromo and transport for Bali. It's open all hours – nice if your bus arrives in the middle of the night – and has dorm beds at 2500 rp and rooms from 4000 rp.

At the other end of the street, on a corner, you'll find the imposing *Hotel Victoria* with a variety of rooms from 5000 rp all the way to 20,000 rp and more. Tea on arrival and breakfast are thrown in too. There is also 'a never-ending cassette tape playing *Auld Lang Syne* in Indonesian,' warned one visitor!

Hotel Tampiar to Plaza at Jalan Suroyo 16, just round the corner from Jalan Raja P Sudirman, is a pleasant place and good value with rooms from 4000 rp. *Hotel Ratna* at Jalan Raja P Sudirman 94 is also good with rooms from 6000 rp up to 15,000 rp with bath and fan; the tariff includes breakfast. The *Hotel Kamayoran*, almost opposite the Victoria, is cheap but also rather dirty.

Getting There & Away

Probolinggo is a 1600 rp and two to 2½-hour trip by bus from Surabaya's Joyoboyo bus station. There are several departures an hour. If coming from Bali, there are now direct buses from Denpasar. It takes around nine hours to Probolinggo and the fare is 6000 rp. It's around 3000 rp to Probolinggo from Banyuwangi and takes six hours. The bus from Malang costs 1750 rp and takes two hours.

Colts from Probolinggo to Ngadisari, for Bromo, run roughly from 7 am to 7 pm. The colt station is only about 300 metres from the bus station and from there it's a 1250 rp, 1½ to two hour colt ride to Ngadisari. From Probolinggo, it's 28 km to Sukapura and another 14 km from there to Ngadisari.

If you're continuing from Probolinggo to Yogya without stopping in Surabaya, you might save time by taking a bus to Surabaya and then another from there rather than a 'direct' bus. The 'direct' buses often stop for a couple of hours in Surabaya and, therefore, actually take longer.

OTHER PLACES IN EAST JAVA

Although there are no particular attractions to drag you there, schedules or just the urge to be somewhere different might take you to Banyuwangi, the ferry departure point for Bali, or to Madiun, a small town between Surabaya and Solo.

Another interesting trip is to take a bus from Malang to Bondowoso and on from there to Gempol, a tiny village in a coffee growing area. You can spend the night there and climb the nearby small but beautiful volcano Ijen in the morning. There's a house near the top where you can leave your gear, retrieve it on the way down and continue walking until you reach the road leading to Banyuwangi.

Madiun

There is a group of cheap hotels clustered on the Surabaya side of town. The *Hotel Madiun* and *Hotel Sarangan* are similarly priced from 8000 rp, and the *Hotel Matahari* is a little cheaper.

Blitar

Blitar is a small town on the Malang to Kediri road. The very beautiful **Panataran Temple** complex is 10 km north of Blitar and can be reached by motorbike or an expensive and infrequent colt service. On the way out to Panataran, you can visit Sukarno's elaborate grave.

Places to Stay The *Hotel Sri Lestari*, a 10-minute walk from the bus station at Jalan

Merdeka 173, has rooms for 7000 rp and more expensive rooms with bath. The cheaper rooms tend to be noisy, and the more expensive ones are usually full. Still, it's a friendly place. Cheap meals are available at the family kitchen and the owner will arrange a motorbike for the trip to Panataran. They also have a pretty garden and a pond with an absolute orchestra of frogs.

Penginapan Aman at Jalan Merdeka 130 also has rooms from 6000 rp. There are others places in town but Sri Lestari is easily the best.

Banyuwangi

Banyuwangi is the ferry port for Bali but the actual ferry departure point is a few km from the town at Ketapang, where the railway station is also located. Colts run between the ferry terminal in Ketapang and the Blambangan bus terminal in Banyuwangi for 450 rp and take 20 to 30 minutes.

Places to Stay & Eat *Hotel Baru* (☎ 21369) at Jalan Pattimura 82-84 is friendly and good value with big airy rooms with and without bath from around 4500 rp to 10,000 rp (which includes breakfast). Next door, there's an excellent warung run by the same family. *Hotel Slamet* also has a good restaurant.

In the centre of town, the *Hotel Baru Raya* at Jalan Dr Sutomo 32 has reasonable and very cheap rooms from 2500 rp for a single. The *Hotel Anda* at Jalan Basuki Rachmat 36, a five-minutes walk from the bus terminal for Ketapang, is adequate with rooms from about 4000 rp.

Bali

Bali is a tropical island, so picturesque and immaculate it could easily be a painted backdrop. It's a combination of pleasant beaches lapped by warm blue waters, rice terraced country which looks like a vision of a rural paradise, and a friendly people who don't just have a culture but actually live it.

In Bali, every night is a festival and even a funeral is a joyous occasion. The main drawback is the horrible mangy dogs, an eyesore by day and a howling assault on the ears by night. They're there to remind you that it's not really paradise – the Balinese believe that there can be no good without something bad.

A curious mixture of position and events accounts for the vitality of Bali and the island's relative isolation from Indonesian history and religion. Gajah Mada, prime minister of the Majapahit Kingdom, ruled Bali from 1343 and his capital was based at Gelgel, near Klungkung. At that time, Muslim power was on the rise in Java and the final flight of the Majapahit rulers to Bali in 1478, with their entourage of scholars, intelligentsia and artists, was the impetus for Bali's extraordinary cultural activity.

Arts

Balinese Dances These days, dances are performed as often for tourists as for temple festivals, so you will have many chances to see them. The best known and most 'touristed' are the Kechak, or monkey dance, the Ramayana, the Barong-Rangda, or kris dance, and the Legong. They are performed regularly at Kuta Beach, Ubud and other centres at around 5000 rp per ticket.

Unfortunately, there's been a trend of late to present shortened tourist versions of the dances and convenient little combinations of the most popular dances. The Balinese dancing and buffet dinners, offered as a fixed-price evening by some restaurants, are good value for food but offer no more than a taste of Balinese culture. Half a Kechak and

a bit of a kris dance is not the way they should be seen.

Fortunately, if you're in Bali for long (and away from Kuta) there's a very good chance that you'll get to see a good performance and not one put on exclusively for tourists.

Ramayana This is one of the best known and best loved legends in Asia. A Hindu epic comparable to *The Odyssey* or *The Iliad*, it is the inspiration behind many carvings, wayangs and dances. The dance begins many years after Prince Rama, his wife Sita and brother Laksamana have been banished, unjustly, to the forest. Rawana, King of the Demons, devises a scheme to kidnap the beautiful Sita. He succeeds in luring Rama and his brother away, leaving Sita alone, and then carries her off.

After a long, weary search, Rama enlists the help of Hanuman, the white monkey general. Hanuman finds Sita and then helps Rama defeat the Demon King and rescue his wife. The Kechak is another version of the Ramayana.

Kechak The most exciting and visually spectacular of the dances, the Kechak tells a tale from the *Ramayana* of the capture of Sita by Rawana and her subsequent rescue by the monkey army. The excitement is provided by the circle of men who provide fantastically coordinated movements and the hypnotic 'Chak Chak Chak' noise which imitates monkeys.

Barong-Rangda, or Kris Dance This well-known trance dance tells a tale of good, in the shape of the lion-like Barong, in conflict with evil, the witch Rangda. The high point of the dance comes when the Barong's supporters attack Rangda, but her magic turns their knives – the famous *kris* – against themselves. The Barong in turn applies his magic to prevent their krises from wounding them. The 'every morning at 10 am' performances tend to be a little artificial, but when the dancers really do go into a trance, it's hard not to believe it!

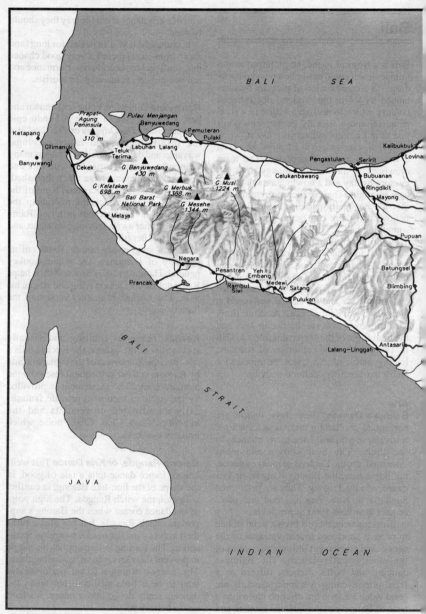

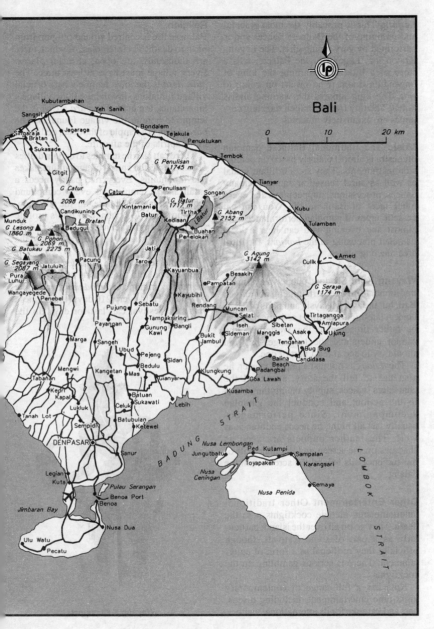

Legong This is probably the most graceful and feminine of the Balinese dances and is performed by very young girls. The Legong Kraton, or 'Legong of the Palace', tells a story of a little bird warning the king of impending doom if he insists on going to war. The king ignores the warning and is killed. The tiny figures in their dazzling costumes are exquisitely graceful.

Music The traditional Balinese gamelan orchestra is almost entirely based on percussion instruments. They are a brilliant visual as well as aural sensation and accompany dances, processions, puppet plays and every other facet of Balinese life. You can get cassette tapes of gamelan performances and almost any evening you can hear a local gamelan practising in the *banjars*, the local area meeting places.

Wayang Kulit Shadow puppet plays are a traditional form of entertainment, not only in Bali, but in Java, Malaysia and parts of Thailand. A late-night, all-night activity, they can be rather tiresome to the Westerner who cannot understand the language, but you should try to see at least part of one.

The *dalang* is not just a puppet master, he also has to tell the story, speak all the characters' voices, supply the rhythmic beat to the action, and conduct the gamelan accompaniment. Since performances usually last all night, he needs endurance as well. The leather puppets are seen as shadows on the screen and the male part of the audience sits behind the screen with the dalang.

Other Entertainment Other traditional entertainments include cockfights – to the death. They go on all over the island, particularly as a part of some festivals, though officially they're illegal as a form of entertainment. There is serious gambling on the cockfights.

Kuta has a full range of contemporary night-time entertainment, including discos, bars and karaoke for its international visitors.

Religion

Balinese life is centred around religion from birth to death. Their temples, of which there are thousands, are open, cheerful places. Every village must have at least three. The *pura desa* is the town temple where official village functions, involving all the village's inhabitants, are held. The *pura puseh* is the temple to honour the village founders. The *pura dalem* is a temple of the dead, dedicated to the spirits of the afterlife.

There can also be temples to certain deities or temples to the spirits of agriculture, lakes and mountains. Every rice paddy needs a small *subak* temple and every compound requires a family temple. In the morning, offerings have to be made to Bali's prolific spirits – on high shelves for the good ones and casually placed on the ground for the baddies.

Temple festivals are splashes of colour. They can be held for all sorts of reasons but the most common are the *odalans*, or temple birthdays. Held every 210 days (the Balinese year) the festival can last for days. In the

Wayang Kulit puppet

daytime there are cockfights, processions and offerings. The temples are decorated with flowers, umbrellas, streamers and a feast of food offerings. The gods can stuff themselves on the spirit and essence of the food but sensibly, the mere substance is taken home and eaten afterwards.

At night, it is like a country fair with food stalls, gambling and things for sale. Later there are dances, wayang kulits and fun till dawn. There is always a temple birthday on somewhere, so don't miss it.

Funerals are fun in Bali, with crowds of people and brilliantly decorated towers. A cremation is a release of the soul so that it can go to its afterlife, and therefore is a cause for celebration. To confuse the soul, the funeral tower containing the body is bounced, shaken, spun, twirled, splashed and run all the way from the deceased's home to the cremation field – guests and spectators sprint along behind. If the soul has not been sufficiently confused it might find its way back home, which would be annoying.

A funeral is an expensive business so bodies are often buried for months or even years until the cremation can be afforded. Alternatively, people will wait for a big funeral that they can join in.

Temple Behaviour Religion is an important part of Balinese life so please be respectful in the temples. Dress neatly and always wear a temple scarf around the waist – you can pick one up in the market quite cheaply. Also remember, it is very bad manners to put yourself on a higher level than the village elders, so don't stand on walls to get a better view or take photographs. Women are not supposed to enter temples during their periods.

Information

There are a variety of tourist offices and desks at the airport, at Kuta Beach, Denpasar and Ubud – see the relevant sections for details.

The American Express office is in the Bali Beach Hotel in Sanur, and they can arrange money transfers. The Bank Ekspor Impor at Jalan Gajah Mada 87 in Denpasar is probably the best bank for arranging money transfers to Bali.

The Kantor Imigrasi (immigration office) is in the Renon district, just around the corner from the main Denpasar post office.

Costs One of the delights of Bali is that it caters for visitors on almost any budget. You can travel for as little as US$5 to US$6 per day, or spend hundreds staying in luxury resorts. The cheapest accommodation is usually family-run and, therefore, friendlier and more personal. Cheap food from street stalls and warungs is often much tastier than the meals prepared in tourist restaurants for Western tastes.

Almost every tourist attraction in Bali takes an entrance charge now, and lots of them chase you for 'donations' too. One writer noted that donation books at temples indicated that most people seemed to make donations of 500, 1000 or even 2000 rp! More likely, you can read that as 50, 100 or even 200 rp – with an extra zero added later.

Most government-run attractions add a charge for insurance too, so if you've broken your leg in the museum and you want to sue them, you'll be pleased to know that they have a public liability cover.

Post Poste restante mail to Denpasar goes to the main post office which is inconveniently situated in the Renon district, south-east of the city centre. It's much more convenient to have mail sent to the post offices in Kuta or in Ubud, or to American Express if you're a customer.

Dangers & Annoyances

Drugs There's no drug scene on Bali. Guys on the street in Kuta will offer to sell you various substances, but it's usually a rip-off and they may turn you in to the police. You may be able to find a magic mushroom (oong) omelette, but the effects, both psychological and legal, are so unpredictable that it can't be recommended. Indonesian drug laws are severe these days, and drugs are just not a part of Balinese culture.

There's a large jail off in the rice paddies just east of Legian, and it's a sign of the times that there are now fewer than 20 Westerners in there for drug offences.

Theft There has been a resurgence of theft in Bali. Violent crime is relatively uncommon, but there is a fair amount of bag snatching, pickpocketing and theft from losmen rooms, particularly in tourist areas. Some years ago, there were mugging incidents down some of Kuta's less frequented *gangs* (alleys) at night, but that activity rapidly diminished when the local Kuta banjars organised vigilante groups to patrol at night.

Snatchers often work in pairs from a motorbike – they pull up next to someone in a busy area, the guy on the back grabs the bag and slashes the strap, and they're gone within half a second. The bulky money belts which many travellers now wear *outside* their clothes are particularly vulnerable.

Pickpockets on bemos are also prevalent. The usual routine is for somebody to start a conversation to distract you while their accomplice steals your wallet, purse or whatever. Bemos tend to be pretty tightly packed, and a painting, large parcel, basket or the like can serve as a cover.

Losmen rooms are often not at all secure, particularly at Kuta and other tourist areas. Don't leave valuables in your room and beware of people who wander in and out of losmen – keep your room locked if you're not actually in it. Many foolish people lose things by simply leaving them on the beach while they go swimming.

Many travellers leave their airline tickets or other valuables in safe deposit boxes which can be found at many moneychangers and other such places around Kuta.

Things to Buy
Don't buy anything in Bali until you've had a chance to look around. Get a feel for what's available, what the prices should be and what is good quality and what isn't. There are so many things to buy that it's easy to be tempted into a foolish purchase on day one. The trouble with Bali's handicrafts is that

there are just too many of them. A wood carving that looks very fine on your first day at Kuta looks pretty awful by the time you've seen another thousand of them. A lot of junk is churned out for the undiscerning tourists.

Do your little bit to preserve the good things by avoiding the mundane and the overpriced. Look around and develop a feel for quality before you consider making any purchase. Apart from the mass production of Balinese 'art' for tourists, there is an even worse trend to mass produce tacky imitations of Western art. It's a sad sight to see Balinese painters turning out imitation-Woolworths oil paintings. They only do it because some silly tourists buy it.

Having complained about the bad side let me add that many of the handicrafts are really nice. We've got a few things from Bali around the house which we like today every bit as much as we did on the day we bought them. One of the constant surprises about Bali is that there is always something new, every visit a new artistic trend has been started, and is being furiously followed by every imitator on the block! The government art centre, Sanggraha Kriya Asta (closed Sunday) is just outside of Denpasar towards Ubud and has a representative selection from which you can get an idea of prices. Look for:

Woodcarving Mas and Ubud are the centres of woodcarving, and shops there have a good selection of the good, the bad and the ugly. Birds, ducks, frogs, fish, owls and countless other creatures, real and mythical, are carved and painted. There are wonderful replicas of tropical fruit, delightful carved wooden flowers, beautiful painted mirror frames, lovely storage boxes or strange Balinese cherubs and angels who can sail majestically across your ceiling.

Balinese masks can be very good but there are an awful lot of churned out, run-of-the-mill Rangdas (widow-witch). The mask-dance *(topeng)* masks are excellent and often very cheap. Wooden bells are nice too. Look around a lot before buying anything and always keep an eye open for the odd exciting piece which seems to pop up without warning.

Paintings Look around the Neka Museum in Ubud or the Sanggraha Kriya Asta art centre to get a feel of what is available. Compare their 'young artist' paintings, the technicoloured, primitive, rural scenes, with the churned-out junk around Ubud to see what is good and bad. The four styles you see most often are: 'young artist'; the older, less bright rural and legendary scenes; 'Klungkung' style pictorial paintings; and the Balinese calendars. Just as with the woodwork there's a lot of garbage, but every now and then you come across a painting that stands out from all the rest.

Silver & Goldwork Lots of workshops at Celuk and Kuta produce a great deal of interesting work. Balinese jewellery has become so popular that in centres like Kuta or Ubud there are quite large fixed-price jewellery shops.

Clothes Clothes have become a major Balinese export industry and Kuta, in particular, is packed with little shops selling the same things which end up overseas with price tags 10 times as high. Interestingly, there are many styles which are purely Balinese, not imitations of clothes from the West at all. Traditional woven sarongs are also very good, but the batik is probably better and certainly a wider choice is available in Yogya.

Stone Statues Want to transport a stone Balinese statue home? It'll scare hell out of the neighbours' gnomes! This is one art form that hasn't been corrupted because it's too heavy for the tourists to buy. Or at least it looks too heavy – actually Balinese stone is surprisingly light (and somewhat fragile). Between a couple of people, if you've come to Bali without too much gear, it's quite possible to bring a stone statue home in your baggage! We've brought back a few pieces of Balinese stonework over the years. You could pick up a temple door guardian for as little as US$30.

Other You'll find carved coconut shells and bone work around Tampaksiring. Temple umbrellas are found all over the place but particularly at Klungkung. Kites and model perahus (sampans) are good buys for kids. Little rice paper umbrellas are also a useful buy. How about musical instruments? Wayang kulit shadow puppets?

At Kuta, in particular, there are many cassette shops selling all the latest recordings at pleasantly low prices. These days, they're all 100% legal after the pirate cassette business was clamped down on. On Kuta Beach, where being driven mad by the constant hustle of the beach sellers is part of the programme, hair braiding, beading and massages are popular ways to spend one's money.

Getting There & Away

Air See the Indonesia Getting There & Away section for details of flights to Bali. Reconfirming tickets in Bali is important because flights out of Bali are very often full. You can contact the airline yourself – Qantas is in the Bali Beach Hotel in Sanur, and Garuda has offices in Denpasar, Kuta, Sanur and Nusa Dua. Travel agents who offer to reconfirm flights may charge for the service, but sometimes they don't actually make the reconfirmation. Make sure you get the little bit of computer printout with your flight details on it.

To/From Java You can fly from Denpasar to Surabaya (72,000 rp), Yogyakarta (93,000 rp) or Jakarta (170,000 rp) in Java.

To/From Nusa Tenggara There are flights east to the various islands of Nusa Tenggara with Merpati and Bouraq. Merpati shuttle over to Lombok with bemo-like regularity; the short hop takes 20 minutes and costs about 42,000 rp. Further afield there are flights to Labuhanbajo on Flores (close to Komodo Island) for 168,000 rp or to Kupang on Timor for 174,000 rp. See the Nusa Tenggara section for more details.

To/From Sulawesi The Merpati flight to Ujung Pandang from Denpasar is cheaper (120,000 rp) than from Surabaya or other towns in Java.

Bus There are morning and evening departures for the trip to Surabaya in Java – with better roads and new buses it is now a fast, comfortable trip. If you're doing it overnight, look for a later evening departure or you'll get into Surabaya at a ridiculously early hour in the morning.

You can get buses from various depots in Denpasar and Kuta beach – there are a lot of companies making the trip so just shop around for a convenient departure time. Buses cost from around 16,000 to 19,000 rp. Buses to Surabaya also run from Singaraja, on the north coast, for a little less than the Denpasar buses.

You can also get a bus straight through to Yogya for between 21,000 to 29,000 rp, or even to Jakarta for about 43,000 rp. You would have to have amazing endurance! The

Bali to Java ferry is included in all the ticket prices.

Do-it-Yourself You can forget the straight-through bus and do it in stages if you want to stop at Mt Bromo on the way to Surabaya. Straight-through buses will drop you off in Probolinggo, or you can take a local bus to Gilimanuk (3500 rp), a bemo to the ferry terminal, then the ferry (2000 rp) across to Java and bus or train from there.

The crossing only takes about 15 minutes, but the town of Banyuwangi, to which the ferry supposedly runs, is actually a couple of km south of the ferry dock. Buses, however, go straight from the ferry terminal so you don't need to go into town.

Train There are no railways on Bali but there's a rail ticket office in Denpasar, and various agents, who sell train tickets to Surabaya and Yogya. They're a bit cheaper than the buses. The fare includes a minibus from Denpasar to Gilimanuk, a ferry across to Java and transport to the station at Banyuwangi.

Boat That overlander's dream of a cheap and regular ship service to Darwin in north Australia remains a dream, but you can island-hop through Nusa Tenggara and then take one of the twice weekly Merpati flights between Kupang (Timor) and Darwin. The first step is to Lembar Harbour on Lombok, by hydrofoil from Benoa (35,000 rp) or ferry from Padangbai (about 5000 rp). See Lombok in the following Nusa Tenggara section for the next stage.

The Pelni ship KM *Kelimutu* makes a loop from Java every two weeks, via Padangbai and through the Nusa Tenggara islands as far as Kupang.

Getting Around

Travelling without any definite plan is probably the nicest way to see Bali, but if time's short, you can make an interesting round-the-island circuit in about a week by car, motorbike or public transport. A possible route from Kuta would be:

Day 1 – to Candidasa (115 km)
Day 2 – via Amlapura to Penelokan (135 km)
Day 3 – on Lake Batur
Day 4 – Penelokan to Singaraja & Lovina (90 km)
Day 5 – Lovina Beaches
Day 6 – return to Kuta via Singaraja and Bedugul (140 km)

That's rushing it and your starting and finishing point could just as well be Singaraja as Kuta.

To/From the Airport There's a taxi counter at the airport where you can buy a fixed-price ticket – 4500 rp to the south end of Kuta; 6500 rp to the north end of Kuta or the south end of Legian; 9000 rp to northern Legian or to Denpasar; 12,000 rp to Sanur; and 34,000 rp direct to Ubud.

You can walk out beyond the exit and look for a public bemo, but it's much easier to take a taxi to Kuta's 'bemo corner', from where you can easily arrange transport to other places around the island. Real shoestring travellers have been known to walk the couple of km along the beach to Kuta.

There are separate terminals for domestic and international flights. You can change money at the international terminal though rates may be better in town, and there are tourist counters and shops in both arrival areas. The airport bar has expensive beer and soft drinks, and there are very expensive duty free stores.

If you're going out to the airport, it's usually easy to charter a bemo for a bit less than the taxi fare. Getting a public bemo to the airport is virtually impossible.

Bus Buses go from the same stations as the bemos, and for all practical purposes they operate the same way. Go to the appropriate bemo/bus station and get whatever vehicle is going your way. The bigger, older buses tend to be less frequent, more crowded and a little cheaper than the smaller minibuses/ bemos.

Shuttle Buses Perama operates a system of direct shuttle buses between the main tourist areas on Bali, with connections to Java,

Lombok and Sumbawa. This company's service is considerably more expensive than public transport, but is cheaper than a bemo charter.

There may be other tourist bus companies, but Perama is the most established and their services are efficient, comfortable and more convenient. They have offices in Kuta, Candidasa, Lovina and Ubud. Typical fares from Kuta are: Padangbai and Candidasa 7500 rp; Ubud 4000 rp; and to Lovina Beaches 10,000 rp.

Car Bali has developed a surprisingly large rent-a-car business, independently run just like the motorbike rentals, although there are some big-time rent-a-car people charging much higher prices. The most popular vehicles are the little Suzuki mini-jeeps which typically cost from around 35,000 rp a day or 210,000 rp per week, including insurance.

As for motorbike rentals – the longer you hire the lower the daily cost and the better the condition the higher the daily cost. Most places want to see an international driving permit, so get one before you leave home.

There are some drawbacks. A rental car may cost more than the charter of a bemo for the day and you have to drive it yourself. You are even more remote from the people and the countryside when inside a car, and you won't want to stop too long in one place if you're paying 30,000 rp a day for a rental car. Rental cars have to be returned to the place from which they were hired – you can't do a one-way rental. Lastly, there is the impact on Bali's road system and parking facilities – what would happen if every tourist wanted to drive round Bali in their own car?

Motorbike Driving yourself around Bali on a motorbike is a pleasant and convenient way of seeing the island – but there are several big *buts*. The biggest drawback is the danger of an accident – motorbikes are risky at the best of times and when you add in all the unique Asian hazards as well, Bali is no place for a beginner. They'll let you out on the road even though you have never ridden a bike before – but don't do it unless you're a reasonably experienced rider.

Drawback number two is that bikes are a miniature ecological disaster for Bali – there are thousands of them and they're horribly noisy as well as unsafe.

On the plus side, getting around Bali is often a matter of moving along until you see something happening, then stopping – there's always a procession, festival, funeral or something else going on. A bike is ideal for this sort of travel. You can stop whenever and wherever you choose. So if you can ride and you decide to bike it, here are the rules of the game:

First, get an international driving permit, endorsed for motorbikes, before you depart. Otherwise you'll have to get a Balinese licence, which involves an easy written test and riding round a car park without falling off. It's comparatively pricey (25,000 rp; valid for one week) and rather time-consuming (allow at least four hours). The police do occasional roadside licence checks, especially between Kuta and Denpasar. Virtually every tourist attraction in Bali also has a motorbike parking charge.

Before accepting a rental bike, make sure it's in good shape – there is a lot of old junk about. If you're hiring for longer periods expect to pay less than on a day or short-term rate. Shop around as there are no real rental agencies – it's all small scale private enterprise and the local members of the Kuta Hell's Angels chapter (100 cc division) will often be cheaper than the more established places.

Bike rental is usually just an individual hiring out his bike for a few days to help pay for it, and the condition is likely to depend upon how new it is. Typically you can expect to pay from 7500 rp – a really good new bike might cost you twice that, and they are often very reluctant to rent out bikes for just one or two days.

Most important of all, ride sensibly. You don't want to come home from Bali in a box. A 100 cc bike is really all you need to explore Bali as, after all, there's no hurry. Try to preserve a little of Bali and a lot of yourself.

Bicycle There are also plenty of places that hire bicycles, and if you can stand the traffic (or get off the main roads and avoid it) this can be a really peaceful way of seeing the island. On long trips, the uphill bits can be real killers – put your bike on a bus in those situations. Rental costs are typically 3000 rp a day.

Bemo Bemos are the basis of Bali's public transport system. They're cheap and fun, but can be inconvenient. Every town has a bemo station, or at least a bemo stop, and the bigger towns can have several. Denpasar is the hub of the system, and it has five main bus/bemo stations. In many cases, you will have to transfer from one station to another if you're making a trip through Denpasar.

The little three-wheeled bemos are still used for transport within towns, though more conventional, four-wheeled minibuses are taking over for longer trips. On some routes, they have quite large 'mini' buses, so it's hard to know when a bemo becomes a bus. Fares can vary with the type of vehicle – the smaller minibuses are more expensive than the larger old buses.

Bemo drivers are always ready to overcharge the unwary, but they're usually good-humoured about it. If they ask 400 rp but you know full well it should be 200 rp, they'll accept the correct fare with a grin.

Equally, if they make a huge protest that the fare you thought was 250 rp is actually 350 rp they're probably right. They often charge extra if you have a large bag. Ask your fellow passengers what the *harga biasa* (standard price) should be.

Make sure you know where you're going, and accept that they may take a roundabout route to collect/deliver as many passengers as possible. Don't make it a hassle for them to carry a tourist or they may become even more reluctant to do so. Beware of empty bemos – unscrupulous drivers will inform you at the end of the trip that they're not really working the route and that you've just chartered the whole bemo!

The Denpasar stations and some of their destinations and fares are:

Tegal This is the station for Bali's southern peninsula.

Destination	Fare
Kuta	400rp
Legian	500 rp
Airport	500 rp
Nusa Dua	1000 rp
Sanur (blue bemo)	500 rp
Ulu Watu (before 10 am)	1500 rp
Ubung station	300 rp
Suci station	300 rp
Kereneng station	500 rp
Batubulan station	500 rp

Ubung This is the station for the north and west of Bali. It's also the main station for buses to Surabaya, Yogyakarta and other destinations in Java.

Destination	Fare
Kediri	800 rp
Mengwi	900 rp
Negara	3000 rp
Gilimanuk	3500 rp
Bedugul	1700 rp
Singaraja	2500 rp
Tegal station	500 rp
Kereneng station	500 rp
Batubulan station	600 rp
Surabaya	19,000 rp
Yogyakarta	25,000 rp
air-con	32,000 rp
Jakarta	48,000 rp

Batubulan The new station for the east and central area of Bali.

Destination	Fare
Ubud	700 rp
Gianyar	700 rp
Tampaksiring	900 rp
Klungkung	1000 rp
Bangli	1000 rp
Padangbai	1500 rp
Candidasa	1500 rp
Amlapura	2500 rp
Kintamani	1700 rp

Kereneng Formerly the main station for the north and east, but since Batubulan opened it's just an urban transfer station.

Destination	Fare
Tegal station	500 rp
Ubung station	500 rp
Suci station	500 rp
Batubulan station	500 rp

Suci Mainly just the bemo stop for Benoa (500 rp), but the offices of many of the Surabaya bus lines and agents for shipping lines are also here.

Bemo Warning Bemos are favourite haunts for pickpockets. Be extra careful on crowded bemos and on the popular Kuta to Denpasar and Denpasar to Ubud trips.

Chartering Bemos It is always possible to charter bemos. It's much more convenient and, between a few people, the cost might not be much more than the regular fares. Bemos can be chartered by the day. The cost depends on how far you want to go, but around 35,000 to 60,000 rp is a good figure to work on. This is about the same as hiring a car by the day, but it's easier to arrange and the convenience of having a driver who knows the way around is a real plus.

As a rule of thumb for chartering bemos, count on around 12 times the regular fare – since a bemo will customarily carry about 12 passengers.

Tours If time is short, there are some good tours available from agents in Kuta. They can be especially good value for getting to places like Besakih where public transport is a problem. Standard day tours cost from around 10,000 rp but ask around for opinions on good operators. Some tours tend to be nothing more than shopping trips, made in the hope of earning commissions from your purchases.

DENPASAR
The capital of both Bali and the Badung District, Denpasar (population 250,000) has been the focus of a lot of the growth and wealth in Bali over the last 15 or 20 years. It now has all the bustle, noise and confusion which one associates with the fast-growing cities of Asia, though it still has some tree-lined streets and pleasant gardens.

The city also has an interesting **museum** (open from 8 am to 5 pm weekdays, and from 8 am to 3.30 pm Friday – closed Monday), an **art centre**, lots of shops, and the **Pasar**

Badung Market, said to be the biggest and busiest in Bali.

Orientation
The main street of Denpasar is Jalan Gajah Mada, which becomes Jalan Surapati in the centre, then Jalan Hayam Wuruk in the east, and finally Jalan Raya Sanur. There are a number of confusing one-way traffic restrictions, and it can be tricky to find your way around. Parking can also be difficult, so avoid driving here – take taxis, bemos or walk. The Renon district, south-east of the town centre, is the area of government offices, many of which are impressive structures on large landscaped grounds.

Information
The Badung District tourist office is on the main street at Jalan Surapati 7. They've got a useful calendar of festivals and events in Bali and a pretty good map. The office is open Monday to Thursday from 7 am to 2 pm, Friday from 7 to 11 am and Saturday from 7 am to 12.30 pm. All the major Indonesian banks have their main Bali offices in Denpasar, principally along Jalan Gajah Mada.

The main Denpasar post office, with the poste restante service, is inconveniently situated in the Renon district – have mail sent to offices in Kuta or Ubud. Permuntei, the telecommunications authority, has an office at Jalan Teuku Umar 6, near the intersection with Jalan Diponegoro, where you can make international phone calls and send telegrams and faxes.

The Kantor Imigrasi, or immigration office (☎ 27828), is at Jalan Panjaitan 4 in the Renon district, just around the corner from the main post office. It's open Monday to Thursday from 7 am to 2 pm, Friday from 7 to 11 am and Saturday from 7 am to 12.30 pm.

The main hospital in Denpasar, RSUP Sanglah, is in the south part of town, a couple of blocks west of Jalan Diponegoro. The hospital has a new casualty department and intensive care unit, and is probably the best

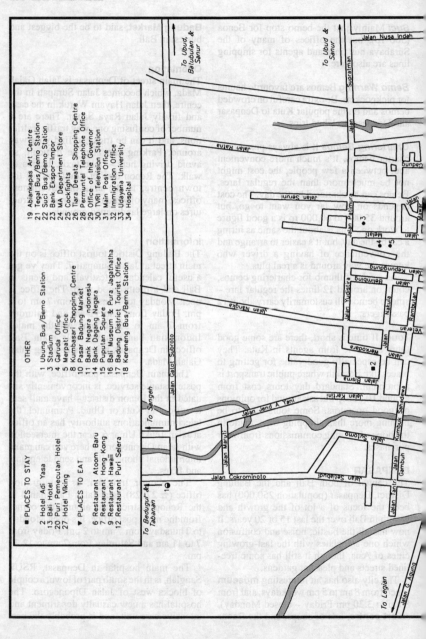

■ PLACES TO STAY

2 Hotel Adi Yasa
13 Bali Hotel
20 Puri Pemecutan Hotel
27 Hotel Viking

▼ PLACES TO EAT

6 Restaurant Atoom Baru
7 Restaurant Hong Kong
9 Restaurant Hawaii
12 Restaurant Puri Selera

OTHER

1 Ubung Bus/Bemo Station
3 Stadium
4 Garuda Office
5 Merpati Office
8 Kumbasari Shopping Centre
10 Pasar Badung Market
11 Bank Negara Indonesia
14 Bank Dagang Negara
15 Puputan Square
16 Bali Museum & Pura Jagatnatha
17 Badung District Tourist Office
18 Kereneng Bus/Bemo Station
19 Abiankapas Art Centre
21 Tegal Bus/Bemo Station
22 Suci Bus/Bemo Station
23 Bank Ekspor-Impor
24 MA Department Store
25 Cockfights
26 Tiara Dewata Shopping Centre
28 Permutel Telephone Office
29 Office of the Governor
30 TVRI Television Station
31 Main Post Office
32 Immigration Office
33 Udayana University
34 Hospital

To Ubud & Sanur
Jalan Nusa Indah
To Ubud, Batubulan & Sanur
Jalan Supratman
Jalan Kalya
Jalan Seruni
Jalan Patimura
Jalan Melati
Jalan Yudistira
Jalan Nangka
Jalan Kepundung
Belimbing
Rambutan
Natura
Jalan Markoesra
Jalan Bisma
Jalan Veteran
Jalan Kartini
Jalan Jend A Yani
Jalan Sulomo
Jalan Kumbuk Sahadewa
Jalan Gatot Subroto
To Sangeh
Jalan Maruti
Jalan Setiapudi
Jalan Selingjah
Jalan Cokrominoto
Jalan Tantri
Jalan Gembun
To Bedugul & Tabanan
To Legian
Jalan G Agung

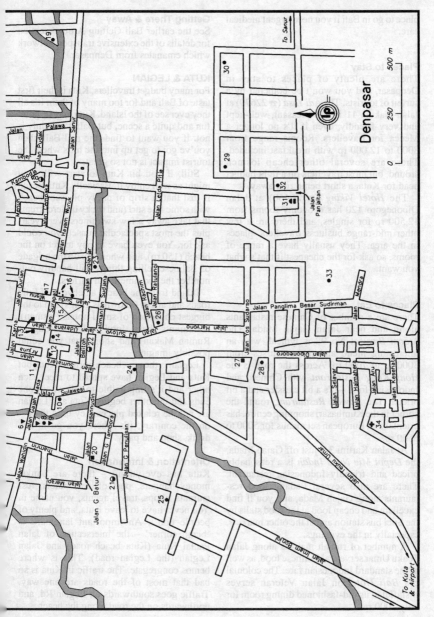

place to go in Bali if you need urgent medical care.

Places to Stay

There are plenty of places to stay in Denpasar, and you won't be bothered by a surfeit of tourists. The *Adi Yasa* (☎ 22679) at Jalan Nakula 11 is still pleasant, well-kept and very friendly, even if it's no longer a Mecca for travellers. Rooms range from 8000 to 12,000 rp with breakfast included. There are several other cheap losmen around, but most travellers on a tight budget head for Kuta, a short bemo ride away.

The *Hotel Viking* (☎ 26460) at Jalan Diponegoro 120 has economy rooms from 12,500 rp for singles, and there are a few other mid-range business travellers' places in the area. They usually have a range of rooms, so ask for the cheapest if that's what you want.

Places to Eat

There are a number of Chinese restaurants along and near Jalan Gajah Mada. The *Atoom Baru* at No 98 is typical, with an interesting menu and main courses from 3000 rp to 7000 rp. Across the road is the *Hong Kong Restaurant* with Chinese and Indonesian food – it's a bit classier and a bit pricier. The *Hawaii Restaurant*, round the corner in the Kumbasari shopping centre, has oriental and European set menus for 5000 to 6500 rp.

At Jalan Kartini 34, just off Gajah Mada, the *Depot Mie Nusa Indah* is a reasonably priced and friendly Indonesian restaurant. There are also several Padang food restaurants along Gajah Mada, and you'll find excellent and cheap food at the food stalls by the Suci bus station and at the other markets, especially in the evenings.

A number of rumah makans along Jalan Teuku Umar serve real Balinese food, as well as the standard Indonesian fare. The colonial era *Bali Hotel* on Jalan Veteran serves rijstaffel in its old-fashioned dining room for only 7000 rp.

Getting There & Away

See the earlier Bali Getting Around section for details of the extensive transport network which emanates from Denpasar.

KUTA & LEGIAN

For many budget travellers, Kuta is their first taste of Bali and for too many of them it's all they ever see of the island. Kuta may be good fun and quite a scene, but Bali it certainly is not. If you want to find 'the real Bali' then you've got to get up into the hills where the tourist impact is not so great.

Still, if you hit Kuta to start with, you might as well enjoy it. Basically Kuta Beach is just that, a strip of pretty pleasant beach with some fine surf (and tricky undercurrents that take away a few swimmers every year) plus the most spectacular sunsets you could ask for. You even have to pay to get on the beach (150 rp), and when you do the brigade of Balinese selling things will handily outnumber the swimmers and surfers.

Inland from the beach, a network of little roads and alleys (known as gangs) run to the biggest collection of small hotels (losmen), restaurants, bars, food stalls (warung or Rumah Makan) and shops that you could possibly imagine.

Legian is the next beach north of Kuta, but Kuta and Legian have spread to meet each other and it's impossible to tell where one ends and the other begins. Kuta and Legian are not the relaxed places they used to be – on the contrary, it's where you go to eat, drink, shop and party.

Orientation & Information

Kuta has everything – there are banks, moneychangers, post offices, hotels, restaurants, shops, travel agents, you name it. You never have to leave Kuta, and plenty of people don't. An important landmark is 'bemo corner' – the intersection of Jalan Pantai Kuta (Kuta beach road) and Jalan Legian (the Legian road). This is where bemos congregate. The traffic in Kuta is so bad that most of the roads are one way. Traffic goes southwards on Legian Rd, and northwards on the road along the beach.

Tourist Office On the corner of Jalan Bakung Sari and the airport road, there's a large building with tourist information counters for Bali and also for several other regions of Indonesia. The Bali counter has some brochures and copies of a Bali tourist newspaper.

Money There are now several banks around Kuta but for most people the numerous moneychangers are faster, more efficient, open longer hours and give just as good a rate. The only reason to use a real bank is for some complicated money transfer or other bank-like activity.

A number of the moneychangers have safety deposit boxes where you can leave airline tickets or other valuables and not have to worry about them during your stay in Bali.

Post There's a post office near the cinema and night market, off the airport road. It's small, efficient and has a sort-it-yourself poste restante service. The post office is open Monday to Saturday from 8 am, closing at 11 am on Friday and at 2 pm on other days of the week.

There is also a postal agent on the Legian road, about half a km along from bemo corner. If you want mail sent there, have it addressed to 'Kuta Postal Agent, Jalan Legian, Kuta'. These Kuta post offices are much more convenient than the main Denpasar post office. The tourist information office, on the corner of Jalan Bakung Sari and the airport road, also has a small post office counter.

Telephones There are Wartels (Warung Telekomunikasi) offices on Jalan Legian and on Jalan Bakung Sari in Kuta. You cannot yet dial international calls yourself, and there are very few of the card phones which are becoming more common in other parts of Indonesia. You can, however, make international calls quite quickly if you pay in cash. Reverse charge calls are much more time-consuming.

Outside the international airport terminal there is a 'Direct Home' phone, where one button gets you through to your home country operator. There are card phones at several other locations at the airport, including the domestic departure lounge. There's a phone office across the car park from the terminals.

Travel Agencies If you're flying Garuda, there's a small Garuda office (☎ 24764) in the Kuta Beach Hotel at the beach end of Jalan Pantai Kuta where you can make both reservations or reconfirmations. The office sometimes gets hopelessly crowded so it's an idea to arrive before opening time or during the lunch break and be at the head of the queue. It's open Monday to Friday from 7.30 am to 4 pm and Saturday and Sunday from 9 am to 1 pm.

The Bali Qantas office is at the Bali Beach Hotel at Sanur where there is also another Garuda office.

Books & Bookshops If you develop a real interest in Kuta, read Hugh Mabbett's *In Praise of Kuta* (January Books, Wellington, New Zealand, 1987). Kuta and Legian have lots of bookshops selling new and second-hand books. The Krishna Bookshop on Jalan Legian is the best place to look for new English-language books.

Places to Stay

Kuta and Legian have hundreds of places to stay, but it's surprisingly uncrowded apart from in the heart of Kuta or around Jalan Padma and Jalan Melasti in Legian. Even there, you only have to walk a couple of steps back from the main street to find palm trees and open fields.

Nowadays, Kuta has numerous middle and upper-bracket hotels, many catering for international package-tour visitors, but there are still many low-priced bargains. Their standards have risen over the years and, although you can still find a few of the old rock-bottom places, even cheap losmen have baths these days.

Once, even the cheapest Kuta losmen was an attractive and relaxed place built around a lush and well-kept garden. Today, there are

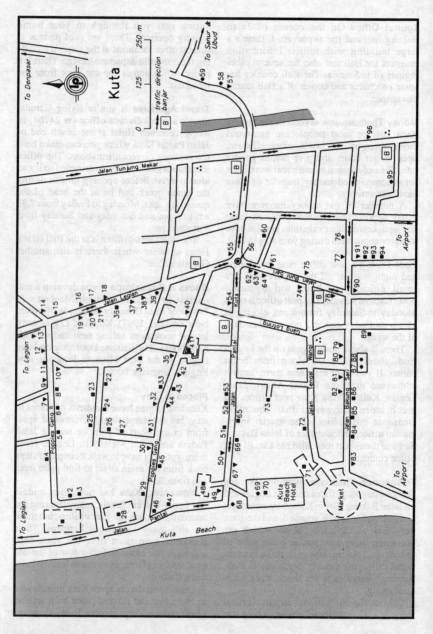

Kuta

To Denpasar

To Sanur & Ubud

To Airport

To Airport

To Legian

To Legian

To Legian

traffic direction

banjar

0   125   250 m

Jalan Tunjung Mekar

Jalan Legian

Poppies Gang I

Poppies Gang II

Poppies Gang

Jalan Pantai

Jalan Pantai

Kuta Beach

Jalan Bunut Sari

Jalan Kuta

Gang Lotring

Jalan Pantai

Jalan Wangi

Jalan Tengah

Jalan Bakung

Jalan Sari

Jalan Tengah

Market

Kuta Beach Hotel

Kuta Beach

■ PLACES TO STAY

1 Sahid Bali Seaside Hotel
2 Puri Beach Inn
3 Indah Beach Hotel
4 The Bounty Hotel
5 Poppies Cottages II
6 Palm Garden Homestay
8 Barong Cottages
11 Taman Sari Cottages
22 Puri Ayodia Inn
23 Sari Bali Bungalows
24 Suji Bungalows
25 Sorga Cottages
26 Mimpi Bungalows
27 Berlian Inn
28 Kuta Seaview Cottages
29 Kuta Puri Bungalows
33 Mutiara Bungalows
34 Kempu Taman Ayu
36 Viking Beach Inn
41 Poppies Cottages I
43 La Walon Bungalows
45 Cempeka
46 Sari Yasa Samudra Bungalows
47 Aneka Beach Bungalows
48 Yasa Samudra Bungalows
51 Kodja Beach Inn
52 Bali Summer Hotel
53 Budi Beach Inn
60 Anom Dewi Youth Hostel
65 Suci Bungalows
66 Yulia Beach Inn
70 Kuta Beach Hotel
71 Kuta Cottages
72 Asana Santhi (Willy) Homestay
73 Ida Beach Inn
84 Ramayana Seaside Cottages
85 Kuta Beach Club
86 Agung Beach Bungalows
89 Flora Beach Hotel
92 Bamboo Inn
93 Zet Inn
94 Jesen's Inn II

▼ PLACES TO EAT

7 Bali Corner Restaurant
9 Twice Pub Restaurant
10 Tubes Bar
12 Batu Bulong Restaurant
13 SC (Sari Club)
14 George & Dragon

16 Burger King
17 Peanuts Disco, Koala Blu Pub &
   Other Bars
18 Indah Sari Seafood
19 SC Restaurant
20 Twice Bar
21 Mini Restaurant
30 Tree House Restaurant
31 Warung Transformer
32 Nusa Indah Bar
35 TJs
37 Prawita Garden Restaurant
38 Aleang's
40 Poppies
42 Fat Yogi's Restaurant
44 Kempu Cafe
49 Made's Juice Shop
50 Melasti Restaurant
54 Made's Warung
55 Quick Snack Bar
57 Kentucky Fried Chicken
61 Casablanca Bar
62 Dayu II
63 Wayan's Tavern
64 Bali Indah
67 Green House Restaurant
74 Bagus Pub
75 Serrina Japanese Restaurant
77 Gantino Baru Padang Restaurant
78 The Pub
79 Bali Blessing Restaurant
80 Bali Bagus Restaurant
81 Nagasari Restaurant
82 Dayu I
83 Rama Bridge Restaurant
90 Gemini Chinese Restaurant
91 Kuta Plaza Restaurant
96 Night Market

OTHER

15 Kuta Postal Agency
39 Perama
56 Bemo Corner
58 Supermarket
59 Petrol Station
68 Kuta Lifesaving Club
69 Garuda Office
76 Tourist Information Office
87 Supermarket
88 Wartel Telephone Office
95 Post Office

lots of places which have obviously been thrown together as quickly and cheaply as possible to try and turn over as many rupiah with as little effort as they can manage.

What to look for in a losmen? You can start with that well known advice from real estate agents – location, location, location. Many places are close to busy roads where the traffic noise and exhaust fumes can make you think you're in the centre of a busy Western city. On the other hand, there are places so isolated that getting to restaurants for a meal is a major trek. Where do you want to be – close to the action or away in the peace and quiet? It's often possible to find a good combination of both factors – a place far enough off the main road to be quiet but close enough so that getting to the shops and restaurants is no problem.

Then look at what the rooms are like and how pleasant and generally well-kept the losmen is. My ideal losmen would be fairly small and as much like a traditional Balinese home as possible. That is, it should be enclosed by an outer wall and built around a central courtyard-garden. It should be an attractive and peaceful place to sit around and read or talk. It should be clean and well-kept. Many cheaper losmen still offer breakfast, even if it's only a couple of bananas and a cup of tea. It's a pleasant little extra that disappears as you move up the price scale.

With so many losmen to choose from, it's quite easy to wander from one to another until you find one that suits. If it's late, you're not in a wandering mood or you've hit one of those rare occasions when everything seems to be full, you can be certain someone will ask if you 'want a room?'. You'll have no trouble finding a place. The main secret to losmen hunting is to remember that there are lots more of them – if you find you don't like your first choice it's very easy to move somewhere else.

Don't commit yourself to more than one night at first, particularly with the accommodation touts who will promise all sorts of wonders if you will stay for a week. You can still find basic losmen for around 10,000 rp

a double, although Kuta is not as good value as other parts of Bali.

With so many places to choose from and so many of them so similar in what they offer, it's almost foolish to make specific recommendations. The 17 places that follow offer a wide variety of standards at an equally wide variety of locations from the centre of busy Kuta to the outer reaches of Legian. The location key number on the Kuta or Legian map is indicated after the name:

Anom Dewi Youth Hostel (Kuta No 60) – right in central Kuta, this youth hostel-associated losmen offers standard rooms at 10,000 and 12,000 rp.

Baleka Beach Inn (Legian No 12) – at the north end of Legian, this place has bottom-end prices from 12,000 to 25,000 rp and a swimming pool.

Bamboo Inn (Kuta No 92) – this traditional little losmen in central Kuta is some distance from the beach but close to the restaurants and bars. Good rooms cost from 10,000 to 15,000 rp including breakfast.

Berlian Inn (Kuta No 27) – a good central location, just off Poppies Gang, with rooms from 15,000 to 25,000 rp make this place value.

Budi Beach Inn (Kuta No 53) – this old-style losmen is in a busy location on Jalan Pantai Kuta (Kuta Beach Rd) and has rooms from 10,000/12,000 rp up to 20,000/25,000 rp.

Jesen's Inn II (Kuta No 94; ☎ 52647) – this inn is a pleasant little two storey block with a garden. Close to the centre of Kuta, it is in a reasonably quiet location and is some distance from the beach but good value from 10,000 to 15,000 rp.

Kempu Taman Ayu (Kuta No 34) – just round the corner from TJ's and Poppies this long-running and friendly little place has fairly standard cheap rooms from 9000 to 12,000 rp.

La Walon Bungalows (Kuta No 43) – in Poppies Gang, handy to the beach and the Kuta 'scene' there are pleasant little rooms with verandah and open-air bathrooms. It's good value at 20,000 rp for a double room including breakfast.

Legian Beach Bungalows (Legian No 34) – right in the centre of Legian, on busy Jalan Padma, this place has singles from US$10 to US$15 and doubles from US$12 to US$18.

Palm Garden Homestay (Kuta No 6) – a neat and clean place, the rooms are good value from 15,000 to 20,000 rp and the location is quiet.

Puri Ayodia Inn (Kuta No 22) – this small and very standard losmen is in a quiet but convenient location and has rooms for just 10,000 rp.

Sari Yasai Beach Inn (Legian No 7) – on Jalan Purana Bagus Taruna, at the north end of Legian, this small losmen has rooms at 12,000 rp.

Sinar Beach Cottages (Legian No 16) – towards the north end of Legian, this pleasant little place has a garden and rooms at 15,000/17,000 rp.

Sinar Indah (Legian No 22) – also at the midpoint between Jalan Padma, in central Legian, and Jalan Purana Bagus Taruna, at the north end of Legian, this standard-style losmen has rooms from 8000 to 20,000 rp plus bigger rooms with kitchen facilities.

Sorga Cottages (Kuta No 25) – there's a pool, the location is quiet and the rooms are from 12,500 to 21,000 rp with fan or from 21,000 to 31,500 rp with air-con.

Three Sisters (Legian No 37) – one of Legian's original losmen still offers straightforward rooms at low prices and a central location. Rooms are 12,000 rp.

Yulia Beach Inn (Kuta No 66) – this standard small hotel on Kuta Beach Rd has been going for years and offers standard rooms in a very central location from US$10 to US$22 for singles or from US$12 to US$25 for doubles.

There are a great many mid-range hotels, which at Kuta means something like US$15 to US$60. A 15½% tax and service charge is usually tacked on as well. The majority of these places cater to visitors on one or two-week package tours and many of them are utterly featureless and dull. They seem to have a checklist of amenities which must be supplied, and so long as these 'essentials' (like air-con and a swimming pool) are in place, nothing else matters.

Balinese style is unlikely to make an appearance, and monotonous rectangular blocks or places with the maximum number of rooms crammed into the minimum space are all too familiar. Worthwhile possibilities for the independent traveller include:

Bruna Beach Inn (Legian No 53) – this simple place has a good central location near the beach. The rooms are nothing special but they're cheap with prices from the top of the bottom-end category from US$12 to US$25 for singles, and from US$17 to US$30 for doubles.

Mutiara Bungalows (Kuta No 30) – conveniently located on Poppies Gang, the Mutiara is also excellent value with a spacious lush garden and straightforward, if slightly tatty, fan-cooled rooms with verandah at US$17.

Poppies Cottages I (Kuta No 41) – still setting the standard for what a good Bali hotel should be, Poppies has an exotically lush garden with cleverly designed and beautifully built rooms. It's right in the centre of things on Poppies Gang and has a swimming pool every bit as stunning as the overall design. At US$51/56 for singles/doubles, it's right at the top of the mid-range category.

Poppies Cottages II (Kuta No 5) – the earlier Poppies is neither as stunning in its design or setting nor as central. There is no pool but guests can use the one at Poppies I. It is cheaper at US$23/28.

Places to Eat

There are countless places to eat around Kuta and Legian; they range from tiny hawker's carts to fancy restaurants, from cheap warungs to bars and pubs, and from steak houses to juice bars. Like so much else about Kuta, there's not much which is straightforward Indonesian or Balinese – you could stay in Kuta for a month, eat in a different place every meal and never have to confront so much as a humble nasi goreng. In Kuta, the food is pseudo-Western top to bottom, although it's always going through some transient craze whether it's a spate of Mexican restaurants or the discovery of pizzas.

Prices in Kuta's fancier restaurants are no longer rock bottom, so if you want to eat cheaply try places like *Depot Viva* on Jalan Legian, the food carts which cater to local workers or the night market near the post office. Many of the fancier places have Australian wine for around 3500 rp a glass.

Around Kuta Places may come and go but *Poppies* remains one of the most popular restaurants ever, although the food is very straightforward and the prices (from 6000 to 9000 rp for main courses) are quite high. It's on Poppies Gang, close to the heart of things, with a beautiful and quite romantic garden and attentive service. A few steps west beyond Poppies is *TJ's*, the place in Kuta for Mexican food. In this deservedly popular restaurant, main courses are 5000 to 8000 rp.

Further down Poppies Gang, towards the beach, there are several popular places for light meals. *Fat Yogi's* turns out good pizzas from their genuine wood-fired pizza oven and their croissants aren't bad at breakfast time. Further down the gang, there's *Warung*

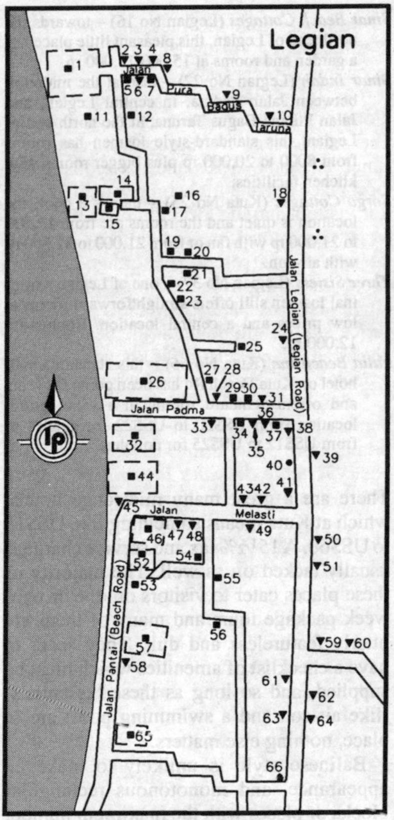

■ PLACES TO STAY

1   Kuta Palace Hotel
5   Orchid Garden Cottages
7   Sari Yasai Beach Inn
11 Mabisa Beach Inn
12 Baleka Beach Inn
13 Bali Niksoma Inn
14 Bali Coconut Hotel
15 Maharta Beach Inn
16 Sinar Beach Cottages
17 Adika Sari Bungalows
19 Bhvana Beach Cottages
20 Abdi Beach Inn
21 Surya Dewata Beach Cottages
22 Sinar Indah
23 Bali Sari Homestay
25 Sri Ratu Cottages
26 Bali Padma Hotel
27 Garden View Cottages
29 Legian Village Hotel
30 Puspasari Hotel
32 Bali Mandira Cottages
34 Legian Beach Bungalows
37 Three Sisters
44 Legian Beach Hotel
46 Bali Intan Cottages
52 Kul Kul Hotel
53 Bruna Beach Inn
54 Camplung Mas
55 Legian Mas Beach Inn
56 Sayang Beach Lodging
57 Kuta Jaya Cottage
65 Bali Anggrek Hotel

▼ PLACES TO EAT

2   Topi Koki Restaurant
3   Swiss Restaurant
4   Arak Bar
6   Sawasdee Thai Restaurant
8   Rum Jungle Road
9   Bamboo Palace Restaurant
10 Benny's Cafe
18 Restaurant Glory
24 Warung Kopi
28 Legian Snacks
31 Restaurant Happy
33 Padma Club Restaurant
35 Rama Garden Restaurant
36 Norman Garden Restaurant
38 MS Restaurant
39 Ned's Place
41 Do Drop Inn
42 Gosha Restaurant
43 Bali Waltzing Matilda Too
45 Karang Mas Restaurant
47 Restaurant Puri Bali Indah

48 Legian Garden Restaurant
49 Orchid Garden Restaurant
50 Manhattan Restaurant & Bar
51 Made's Restaurant
58 Southern Cross Restaurant
59 Yanies
60 Il Pirata
61 The Bounty
62 Depot Viva
63 Za's Bakery & Restaurant
64 Mama's German Restaurant

OTHER

40 Wartel Telephone Office
66 Krishna Bookshop

Legian

Transformer and the pleasant *Tree House Restaurant*, a good place for an excellent and economical breakfast.

On Jalan Pantai Kuta, quite close to Poppies, is *Made's Warung*. Like Poppies, this simple open-front place has been going since the early 1970s and it's probably the best place in Kuta for people watching, both for visitors and the local glitterati. The food is getting a touch expensive these days but there's always somebody strange to watch from first thing in the morning until late at night. Bali has lots of Made's so *Made's Juice Shop*, right down at the beach end of the road, is no relation, although it's also popular.

Jalan Buni Sari, which connects Jalan Pantai Kuta with Jalan Bakung Sari, has some more long-term survivors including the *Bali Indah*, *Wayan's Tavern* and *Dayu II*. Further along this short street are some popular pubs including *The Pub* itself, the original Kuta pub. See the following Kuta & Legian Entertainment section for more details. On Jalan Bakung Sari, the *Gemini Restaurant* is a popular choice for Chinese dishes. Across the road from it is the *Gantino Baru*, a nasi padang specialist. Down Jalan Bakung Sari, towards the beach, there are several restaurants including *Dayu I* and a supermarket which has many Western supermarket-style goods.

Along Jalan Legian There are lots of possibilities along Jalan Legian. Most of the time the road is an almost continuous traffic jam and a table near the road can mean you have to shout to be heard. Right on bemo corner is the *Quick Snack Bar*, a good place for a snack or breakfast and the yoghurt is particularly good. A little further along is *Aleang's*, another popular snack bar with good yoghurt, cakes and ice cream, plus lots of traffic noise.

Continue north, towards Legian, and you reach the *Mini Restaurant*, a big, open, busy place serving straightforward food at low prices. Across the road is the disco and bar centre, with the extremely popular *Koala Blu Pub* and *Peanuts Disco*. In the same vicinity,

there are several Western fast-food outlets. Slightly hidden off the east side of Jalan Legian is *George & Dragon*, reputed to have the best Indian curries in Bali. On the other side of the road is the *LG Club*, a big, bright restaurant where you choose your seafood at the front and it's cooked in the frenetic open kitchen area to one side.

Continue north to *Depot Viva* (see the Legian map), an open-roofed place with surprisingly good Indonesian and Chinese food despite its bare, basic and grubby appearance. The prices are pleasantly basic too, which accounts for its steady popularity. Across the road is *Za's Bakery & Restaurant*, a good spot for breakfast which also has a menu featuring everything from pasta dishes to curries.

Just off Jalan Legian is *Yanies* with excellent burgers from 3500 to 6000 rp. A little further along this same road is *Il Pirata*, noted both for its very good pizzas at 5000 to 7000 rp and for its late opening hours. Return to Jalan Legian and you're soon in the heart of Legian with numerous restaurants on Jalan Melasti, Jalan Padma and the other Legian roads. Further along Jalan Legian, you'll come to the ever popular *Do Drop Inn* and *Restaurant Glory*.

Around Legian Jalan Melasti has several good restaurants including the big *Orchid Garden Restaurant*, the *Legian Garden Restaurant* and the *Restaurant Puri Bali Indah* with excellent Chinese food. Jalan Padma also has restaurants but some of the most interesting places in Legian are further north on Jalan Purana Bagus Taruna, the somewhat twisting road leading to the big Kuta Palace Hotel.

Right by the hotel entrance is the *Topi Koki Restaurant* which has a pretty good go at la cuisine Français. A little further back from the beach is the *Swiss Restaurant*, popular with homesick Deutschlanders. Other restaurant's along this street include the *Sawasdee Thai Restaurant*, *Yudi Pizza* and, nearer to Jalan Legian, the big and very popular *Bamboo Palace Restaurant* and the small, but also popular, *Benny's Café*.

Entertainment

Nightspots are scattered around Kuta and Legian, many along Jalan Legian. Some of the wilder drunken excesses of Kuta have been cleaned up. Pub crawls, where bus loads of noisy, drunken revellers were hauled from one venue to another, have been cut back considerably. Many pubs and discos have been closed down and others have been concentrated into a sort of 'combat zone' on Jalan Legian. There everybody can get as drunk as they like without bothering other people.

The centrepiece of the Jalan Legian entertainment complex is the large *Peanuts* disco – it's rather like an Australian barnyard-pub venue, which might explain its popularity. Admission is usually around 5000 rp which includes a couple of drinks. There's a series of open bars flanking the entrance road into Peanuts. These places kick off earlier than the main disco, and continue even after it's in full flight. For some reason, *Koala Blu* has been the firm favourite for some time and Koala Blu T-shirts seem to pop up all over Asia. After midnight, it's quite a scene with music blasting out from every bar, hordes of people, mostly upright but some decidedly horizontal, and out in the parking lot lines of bemos and dokars waiting to haul the semiconscious back to their hotels.

You can make a fairly clean division between the bars you go to for a drink and the ones you go to for entertainment, music and pick-ups. It's generally immediately clear which category they fall into. The *Casablanca* on Jalan Buni Sari is definitely in the noise and activity category; ideal if you can handle beer drinking contests, cheese and vegemite sandwich eating contests, ladies' arm wrestling contests and other scenes of depravity. Also on Jalan Buni Sari is the *Pub Bagus* and *The Pub,* one of Kuta's original bars. The Pub is still a popular place for a beer without the associated noise and confusion.

Down Poppies Gang, the *Nusa Indah Bar* is a straightforward and pleasant little open-air place with about the cheapest beer prices around. Head further north to Poppies Gang

II, and just off Jalan Legian is the *Tubes Bar* with video movies every night and a giant concrete wave complete with an embedded surfboard where you can stand for heroic surfing snapshots! Continue a little further up Jalan Legian to the *Sari Club* (SC for short), a big, noisy, crowded, open-air bar. There are numerous other bars of all sorts along Jalan Legian.

Getting There & Away

Kuta has lots of travel agencies if you want to fly out from nearby Ngurah Rai Airport, but there are no real bargains here. Wait until Singapore or Malaysia for cheap tickets. If you're continuing to Java by land, there are agencies for buses to Surabaya and Yogyakarta; there's no need to go into Denpasar. Perama, on Jalan Legian, have direct tourist bus services to other centres in Bali, Lombok and Java.

Getting Around

See the Bali Getting Around section for information on airport transport, bemos, and car, motorbike or bicycle rental.

SANUR

Sanur is an up-market alternative to Kuta for those coming to Bali for sea, sand and sun. It has a pleasant beach with a reef which makes for more sheltered water (and provides a big surf break when it's working). Sanur is more peaceful than Kuta – the traffic isn't horrendous and you're not constantly badgered to buy things – badgered yes, but not constantly.

Sanur stretches for about three km along the coast, with the landscaped grounds and restaurants of expensive hotels fronting right onto the beach. The main road, Jalan Danau Toba/Jalan Danau Tamblingan, runs parallel to the beach, and has travel agencies, moneychangers and other facilities.

American Express and a number of airlines have offices in the big Bali Beach Hotel at the north end of town.

Sanur was a place favoured by Western artists during their prewar discovery of Bali. The former home of the Belgian artist Le

Mayeur is now a museum, squeezed in beside the Bali Beach Hotel.

Places to Stay

There are no rock-bottom Kuta-style places at Sanur, but some of the medium-price places are as good value as their equivalents in Kuta. The cheapest places are away from the beach at the northern end of town. On Jalan Segara, west of the main road, there are three lower-priced places side by side. The *Hotel Sanur-Indah*, closest to Denpasar, is the most basic and the cheapest at about 12,000/12,500 rp for single/double rooms. The *Hotel Taman Sari*, in the middle, has doubles from 15,000 rp, and the *Hotel Rani* has singles/doubles for 12,500/15,000 rp.

At the northern end of Sanur Beach, the *Ananda Hotel* (☎ 88327) is neat and clean with rooms from 25,000/30,000 rp. The *Watering Hole* (☎ 88289), opposite the Bali Beach Hotel entrance, is a friendly, well-run place with good food, a bar, and comfortable rooms at 20,000/25,000 rp.

Made Pub & Homestay, on the west side of the main drag, has some small rooms downstairs from 15,000 rp for singles, and some bigger rooms upstairs for 30,000 rp a double. The *Kalpataru Homestay & Restaurant* (☎ 88457), a little further south, is a pleasant place with a garden, swimming pool and budget rooms from 20,000/25,000 rp.

Further south again, on a side road to the beach, is the *Werdha Pura*. It's a government-run 'beach cottage prototype', with the type of service that will make you believe in private enterprise. It's cheap, however, at 25,000/50,000 rp for a single/double room or 60,000 rp for family rooms, and its in a good location.

Places to Eat

There are a number of reasonably priced places, very much from the Kuta restaurant mould. *Warung Aditya*, *Carlo's*, and the *Watering Hole* are three good mid-range places, but there are plenty of others.

You can get cheap meals at the rumah makans on the bypass road, where there is also a Kentucky Ayam Goreng and a *Swen-sen's Ice Cream* place. But the cheapest, and possibly the tastiest, food is from the food carts and warungs at the north end of the beach, near where the boats go to Nusa Lembongan.

SOUTH BALI – THE BUKIT PENINSULA

The southern peninsula is known as Bukit, or 'hill' in Indonesian. It's dry and quite sparsely populated, but it has the two extremes of Bali tourism – the luxury resort at Nusa Dua and the surfies' Mecca at Ulu Watu.

Jimbaran Bay

Just south of the airport, Jimbaran Bay is a superb crescent of white sand and blue sea. Jimbaran is a fishing village which has recently acquired some luxury hotels, but there are a couple of cheaper places within walking distance of the beautiful bay. *Puri Bambu Bungalows* is a basic losmen on the west side of the road. Further south, on the east side of the road, is the *Puri Indra Prasta* bungalows, with a restaurant, bar and comfortable rooms from 20,000 rp to 25,000 rp, including breakfast.

Ulu Watu

A sealed road goes south from Jimbaran village right down to Ulu Watu at the end of the peninsula. The important temple of **Pura Luhur Ulu Watu** perches at the southwestern tip of the peninsula, where sheer cliffs drop precipitously into the clear blue sea.

Just before the temple car park, there's a sign to **Pantai Suluban** (Suluban Beach), famous for its great surf. There will be a crowd of guys on motorbikes here, waiting to take you two km down the narrow track to the beach. Half a dozen warungs are perched on the cliffs with great views of the various surf breaks. The warungs have basic Indonesian tourist food, and surfers sometimes crash in them to get an early start on the morning waves. One tiny losmen, the *Gobleg Inn*, is off the motorbike track to the beach.

Benoa

Labuhan Benoa, the wide but shallow bay east of the airport, is one of Bali's main harbours. Benoa is actually in two parts. Benoa Port, with a wharf and some offices, is on the north side, with a two-km long causeway connecting it to the main Kuta to Sanur road. Benoa village is on a point at the south side of the bay, just north of Nusa Dua.

Nusa Dua

Nusa Dua is Bali's most expensive beach resort – a luxury tourist enclave, planned to ensure that the mistakes of Kuta would not be repeated! The beach here is very pleasant, the surf is often good on the reef and there's a host of water sports and other resort activities on offer. But really, it's a place for people who want to experience Bali in very small, controlled and sanitised doses, if at all. The nearest thing to budget accommodation here is the *Lancun Guesthouse* (☎ 71983/5), adjacent to the Club Bualu, which is run by the Hotel & Tourism Training School, and has rooms for about US$25 a double. You might find something cheaper in Benoa village.

UBUD

In the hills north of Denpasar, Ubud is the calm and peaceful cultural centre of Bali. In recent years, Ubud has been developing nearly as fast as the beach resorts and it's showing distinct signs of becoming a glossy culture resort. In the early 1970s, Ubud didn't even have electricity, but now there are dozens of hotels with swimming pools and some of the trendiest restaurants in Bali.

Orientation & Information

Ubud has engulfed the neighbouring villages of Campuan, Penestanan, Padangtegal, Peliatan and Pengosekan – the crossroads where the bemos stop marks the centre of all of sprawling Ubud. On the north *(kaja)* side is the Ubud Palace, on the south *(kelod)* side is the market. Monkey Forest Rd is the road beside the market and runs south to, of course, the Monkey Forest and Ubud's Pura Dalem, or Temple of the Dead.

Information Ubud is just high enough up to be noticeably cooler than the coast. It's also noticeably wetter. The town has a very friendly and helpful tourist office on the main street, known as Jalan Bima. They make a real effort to preserve 'the real Bali' in Ubud.

Ubud has numerous moneychangers offering competitive rates. The small post office has a good poste restante service and there's a telephone office near the market where you can make international calls. The excellent Ubud Bookshop is on the main road right next to Ary's Warung in the centre of Ubud. You can also find a small but fine selection of books in Murni's Warung and the Museum Neka. The Book Shop on the Monkey Forest Rd is a book exchange place. Ubud's colourful produce market operates every third day.

Things to See & Do

Museums, Galleries & Artists The **Museum Puri Lukisan**, in the middle of town, displays fine examples of all schools of Balinese art. It's open from 8 am to 4 pm daily and admission is 500 rp. Paintings are also sold in an adjacent building.

A km or so beyond the Campuan suspension bridge is the superb **Museum Neka** with displays of modern Balinese art and fine pieces by Western artists who have resided or worked in Bali. Admission is 500 rp.

There are a great many galleries in and around Ubud including the **Neka Gallery**, operated by Suteja Neka who also runs the Museum Neka. It's just past the post office turn-off on the main road out of Ubud. The other important commercial gallery is the **Agung Rai Gallery** at Peliatan, on the way out of Ubud to Denpasar.

The home of the late I Gusti Nyoman Lempad, a pioneering Balinese artist, is right across from the market. Walter Spies, the German artist who played a key role in the revival of Balinese art in the 1930s used to live near the Campuan river junction and his home is now one of the rooms at the Campuan Hotel.

Across the road from the hotel is the home

of the bizarre Antonio Blanco, entry is 500 rp and it's well worth seeing. Han Snel's work can be seen in his restaurant and hotel, just off the main road through Ubud.

Around Ubud Walk down Monkey Forest Rd to the **Monkey Forest** itself. The handsome troop of monkeys who live here always provide entertainment, but they can get decidedly aggressive if they think you've got a supply of peanuts and aren't handing them over. At the other side of the forest is Ubud's **Pura Dalem**, or Temple of the Dead.

Whatever else you do in Ubud, make sure you walk, walk, walk. It's a wonderful place for walking, and every stroll will take you somewhere picturesque and interesting. The cross-country stroll to Pejeng or the loop walk to Petulu where herons come to roost every night are particularly good. Ubud is also a very good centre for visiting many attractions in the vicinity. There's far more to see around Ubud than around Kuta.

Places to Stay
Even in the mid-70s, when the tourist boom had definitely arrived down on the coast, Ubud only had limited accommodation. The construction boom which reached here in the '80s, however, is still continuing and today Ubud not only has a great many budget hotels but also a wide choice of medium range and expensive places.

You'll find places fairly widely scattered in and around Ubud. In particular, the Monkey Forest Rd has become a real accommodation centre with places all the way down to the forest. If you are staying in one of the budget-priced 'remote' losmen – and they can be very relaxing, peaceful places to stay – it's probably wise to have a torch (flashlight) with you if you want to avoid actually falling in to the rice paddies on some starry, starry night.

Since Ubud is full of artists and dancers, you can often find a losmen run by someone involved with the arts – where you can pick up some information of Balinese art. At most cheaper and mid-price places, breakfast is included in the price. You can still find cheaper doubles with toilet and mandi for 10,000 rp and less. In the off season, you can still find a double room for 6000 rp.

In Ubud There are lots of places off the main road and down the Monkey Forest Rd. The small lanes and alleys between the Monkey Forest football field and the market have many of Ubud's lowest priced possibilities. There's nothing to choose between these numerous losmen, just wander down the narrow lanes, have a look in a few, compare the prices and facilities and make your choice. Prices depend on the demand at the time but you should be able to find doubles with breakfast at 10,000 rp or less with little difficulty.

Close to the top of Monkey Forest Rd, near the market, is one of Ubud's really long runners – *Canderi's* (also Candri's or Tjanderi's depending on which sign or spelling style you choose). It's a fairly straightforward losmen-style place with singles from 8000 to 10,000 rp and doubles at 15,000 rp. Canderi's has been going almost as long as travellers have been staying in Ubud.

There are lots of other places along the Monkey Forest Rd or amongst the nearby rice paddies, reached by narrow paths. *Warsi's House* and *Karyawan Accommodation* are simple, friendly and quite typical places. The very clean and well-kept *Frog Pond Inn* is becoming surrounded by the encroaching development along the road but there's still a sign at the entrance suggesting that if there's nobody around you can simply select a vacant room and make yourself at home. With breakfast included, single/double rooms are 7000/10,000 rp.

Further down is *Ibunda*, a pleasant place with rooms at 15,000 rp or 25,000 rp with hot water. There are many other places along Monkey Forest Rd but right at the bottom (southern end), almost in the forest, is the secluded and pleasant *Monkey Forest Hideaway* (☎ 0361-95354). Doubles cost around 20,000 rp and some of the rooms with their balconies looking out over the forest are quite romantic.

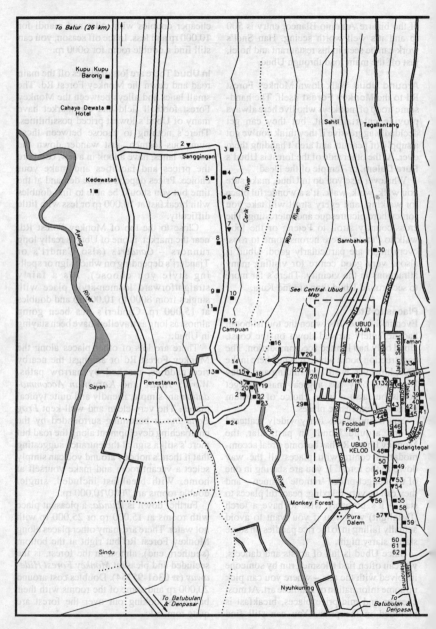

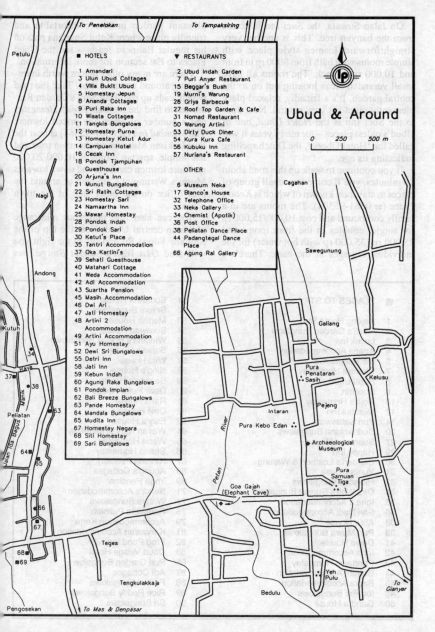

Ubud & Around

0   250   500 m

■ HOTELS

1 Amandari
3 Ulun Ubud Cottages
4 Villa Bukit Ubud
5 Homestay Jepun
8 Ananda Cottages
9 Puri Raka Inn
10 Wisata Cottages
11 Tangkis Bungalows
12 Homestay Purna
13 Homestay Ketut Adur
14 Campuan Hotel
16 Cecak Inn
18 Pondok Tjampuhan
    Guesthouse
20 Arjuna's Inn
21 Munut Bungalows
22 Sri Ratih Cottages
23 Homestay Sari
24 Namaartha Inn
25 Mawar Homestay
28 Pondok Indah
29 Pondok Sari
30 Ketut's Place
35 Tantri Accommodation
37 Oka Kartini's
39 Sehati Guesthouse
40 Matahari Cottage
41 Weda Accommodation
42 Adi Accommodation
43 Suartha Pension
45 Masih Accommodation
46 Dwi Ari
47 Jati Homestay
48 Artini 2
    Accommodation
49 Artini Accommodation
51 Ayu Homestay
52 Dewi Sri Bungalows
55 Detri Inn
58 Jati Inn
59 Kebun Indah
60 Agung Raka Bungalows
61 Pondok Impian
62 Bali Breeze Bungalows
63 Pande Homestay
64 Mandala Bungalows
65 Mudita Inn
67 Homestay Negara
68 Siti Homestay
69 Sari Bungalows

▼ RESTAURANTS

2 Ubud Indah Garden
7 Puri Anyar Restaurant
15 Beggar's Bush
19 Murni's Warung
26 Griya Barbecue
27 Roof Top Garden & Cafe
31 Nomad Restaurant
50 Warung Artini
53 Dirty Duck Diner
54 Kura Kura Cafe
56 Kubuku Inn
57 Nuriana's Restaurant

OTHER

6 Museum Neka
17 Blanco's House
32 Telephone Office
33 Neka Gallery
34 Chemist (Apotik)
36 Post Office
38 Peliatan Dance Place
44 Padangtegal Dance
   Place
66 Agung Rai Gallery

To Penelokan

To Tampaksiring

To Mas & Denpasar

To Gianyar

Petulu

Nagi

Andong

Kutuh

Raya

Manik

Peliatan

Jalan Ida Bagus

Teges

Tengkulakkaja

Pengosekan

Cagahan

Sawegunung

Galiang

Pura
Penataran
Sasih

Kelusu

Pejeng

Intaran

Pura Kebo Edan

Archaeological
Museum

Pura
Samuan
Tiga

River

Petan

Goa Gajah
(Elephant Cave)

Yeh
Pulu

Bedulu

On Jalan Suwata, the *Suci Inn* is across from the banyan tree. This is another very straightforward losmen-style place with simple rooms with bath from 8000 rp in front and 10,000 rp in back. The rooms all have small verandah areas looking out on to the central garden. It's a friendly, relaxed place pleasantly quiet yet very central. Next door to the Suci Inn is the *Hotel Ubud*, one of Ubud's oldest places – for many years it was called the 'Hotel Oboed', the Dutch spelling indicating its age.

If you continue to walk up this road about 10 minutes, you'll come to a small group of places to stay, best known of which is *Ketut's Place* (☎ 0361-95304). The rooms are in a family compound and cost 10,000/15,000 rp for singles/doubles in the front rooms and 25,000 rp (35,000 rp with hot water) for the individual cottages at the back. There's a pleasant garden in this comfortable and friendly place where Ketut Suartana puts on his regular Balinese feasts – see the Ubud Places to Eat section for more information.

There are many other places worth investigating around central Ubud. Take the road which leads up past Han Snel's Garden Restaurant to find the pleasant *Roja's Homestay* and a number of other low-priced losmen. The *Mumbul Inn* (☎ 0361-95364) is near the Puri Lukisan Museum on the main road and has simple, spartan rooms at 10,000/20,000 rp. More losmen can be found down towards Murni's Warung at Campuan or around the post office on the other side of the town centre.

You can also find numerous mid-range places in central Ubud. Near the top of the Monkey Forest Rd and off to the right you will find *Oka Wati's Sunset Bungalows*

■ PLACES TO STAY

1 Kajeng Home Stay	51 Sudartha House
2 Gusti's Garden Bungalow	52 Seroni Bungalows
3 Lecuk Inn	53 Mertha House
4 Arjana Accommodation	54 Surawan House
5 Siti Bungalows	55 Widiana's House Bungalows
7 Shanti's Homestay	56 Sania's House
8 Hotel Ubud	57 Wija House
9 Suci Inn	58 Ning's House
10 Roja's Homestay	59 Sayong's House
12 Mumbul Inn	60 Dewi Putra House
14 Puri Saraswati	61 Raka House
20 Sudharsana Bungalows	62 Devi House
27 Suarsena House	63 Esty's House
29 Happy Inn	64 Wayan Karya Homestay
30 Canderi's Losmen & Warung	65 Wena Homestay
31 Yuni's House	66 Shana Homestay
32 Hibiscus Bungalows	67 Nirvana Pension
34 Oka Wati's Sunset Bungalows	68 Agung's Cottages
35 Igna 2 Accommodation	69 Yoga Pension
36 Sari Nadi Accommodation	71 Bendi's Accommodation
38 Alit's House	74 Wahyu Bungalows
39 Puri Muwa Bungalows	76 Ramasita Pension
41 Dewa House	79 Accommodation Kerta
42 Igna Accommodation	81 Karyawan Accommodation
43 Pandawa Homestay	82 Frog Pond Inn
44 Gayatri Accommodation	83 Ubud Village Hotel
46 Badra Accommodation	85 Puri Garden Bungalow
48 Ibu Rai Bungalows	87 Adi Cottages
50 Gandra House	88 Pertiwi Bungalows
	89 Rice Paddy Bungalows
	90 Sri Bungalows

91	Villa Rasa Sayang
92	Nani House (Karsi Homestay)
93	Jati 3 Bungalows & Putih Accommodation
95	Jaya Accommodation
97	Ibunda Inn
98	Ubud Bungalows
99	Warsi's House
100	Dewi Ayu Accommodation
103	Ubud Tenau Bungalows
104	Fibra Inn
105	Ubud Inn
106	Lempung Accommodation
108	Pande Permai Bungalows
109	Monkey Forest Hideaway
110	Hotel Champlung Sari

▼ PLACES TO EAT

6	Han Snel's Garden Restaurant
13	Mumbul's Cafe
15	Lotus Cafe
16	Coconut's Cafe
21	Restaurant Puri Pusaka
23	Menara Restaurant
24	Ary's Warung
28	Satri's Warung
33	Oka Wati's Warung
37	Ayu's Kitchen
45	Enny's Restaurant
47	Restaurant Dennis
49	Lilies Restaurant
70	Beji's Cafe
72	Bendi's Restaurant
73	Harry Chew's Restoran
75	Ubud Dancer Restaurant
77	Ibu Rai Restaurant
78	Cafe Bali
80	Dian Restaurant
84	Coco Restaurant
86	Cafe Wayan
94	Jaya Cafe
96	Yudit Restaurant & Bakery
101	Warsa's Cafe
102	Ubud Restaurant
107	Fruit Bat Restaurant

OTHER

11	Museum Puri Lukisan
17	Cinema
18	Bemo Stop
19	Palace & Hotel Puri Saren Agung
22	Home of I Gusti Nyoman Lempad
25	Ubud Bookshop
26	Tourist Office (Bina Wisata)
40	Bookshop

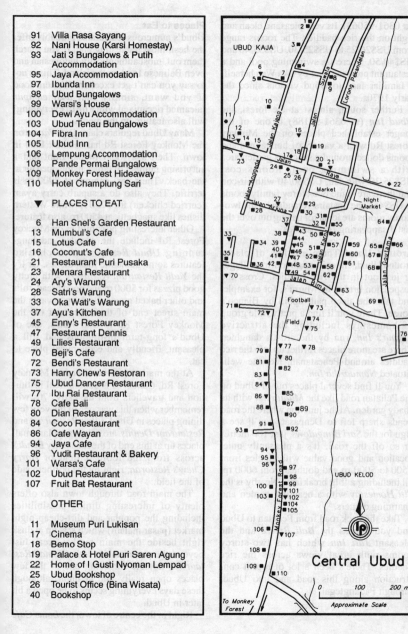

Central Ubud

0   100   200 m

Approximate Scale

(☎ 0361-95063). Its very pleasant, clean and right on the rice paddies. The rooms range from US$20/25 to US$25/30, US$35/40 and US$40/50. There's a swimming pool and a restaurant presided over by Oka Wati herself, a familiar face to Ubud visitors since the early 1970s.

Further south, almost at the forest, the *Ubud Inn* (☎ 0361-95188) is one of the longer established places on the Monkey Forest Rd with a variety of bungalows and rooms dotted around a spacious garden area with a swimming pool. Rooms cost US$25/30 with fan, US$30/40 with air-con and there are some two-storey family rooms at US$45. The upstairs verandah on the two-storey rooms are ideal for gazing out over the fast disappearing rice paddies.

Around Ubud There are lots of places around Ubud, either in neighbouring villages or just out in the rice paddies. Cross the suspension bridge by Murni's, for example, and take the steep path uphill by Blanco's house. There you'll find a pretty little group of homestays including the attractive *Arjuna's Inn*, run by the artist's daughter. There are more places further up into the rice paddies around Penestanan, like the well-situated *Namaartha Inn*.

You'll find several places out of Ubud on the Peliatan road like the *Mudita Inn* with its shady garden. At the junction where the road bends sharp left to Denpasar, you'll see a sign for the *Sari Bungalows*, just 100 metres or so off the road. It's a pleasantly quiet location and good value with singles from 3500 to 5000 rp and doubles from 6000 rp, all including a 'big breakfast'. Nearby is the *Siti Homestay* with a beautiful garden and charming owners.

Take the back road from Peliatan to Ubud and you'll pass the *Bali Breeze* and the pleasant *Jati Inn* which has two-storey rooms with great views across the rice paddies. There's been a lot of recent construction along this road and into Ubud, through Padangtegal.

Places to Eat

Ubud's numerous restaurants probably offer the best, most interesting and, if you search them out, most authentically Indonesian and even Balinese food on the island. This is not to say you can't get excellent Western food if you want, simply that *nasi campur* (steamed rice mixed with a bit of everything) will also feature on the menu.

Many Ubud regulars claim *Cafe Wayan* on the Monkey Forest Rd has the best food in town. There's a room in the front and a surprising number of tables in the open air at the back. Their nasi campur at 2900 rp is terrific. They also do a superb curry ayam (curried chicken) for 5250 rp while Western dishes like spaghetti, at 4500 rp, also feature.

Other interesting possibilities on Monkey Forest Rd include the popular and long-running *Ubud Restaurant* which also features some authentic local dishes. Or try the *Yudit Restaurant & Bakery* with pretty good pizzas for 5000 rp and good bread, rolls and other baked goods. Back up towards the main street end of the road, turn off the Monkey Forest Rd to *Oka Wati's*, one of Ubud's long-term institutions and still a pleasant, friendly and economical place to eat.

At the market (northern) end of Monkey Forest Rd, *Canderi's* is another real institution and travellers from the early '70s will remember when this was one of the very few dining places in Ubud. *Lilies Restaurant* and *Restaurant Dennis* are other popular small places up at this end of the road or try *Bendi's* across from the football field or *Harry Chew's Restoran*, right by the northern side of the field.

The main road through town also offers plenty of interesting dining possibilities including the popular and dirt-cheap night market (pasar malam) which sets up at dusk right beside the main market area. Just beyond the pasar malam is the *Nomad Restaurant*, notable for being one of the few places open really late at night, although these days everything seems to be open a bit later in Ubud.

Right in the centre of town, the *Lotus Cafe*

is a relaxed place for a light lunch or a snack any time. It's pricey but the Lotus is still the place to see and be seen in Ubud. The Lotus is closed on Monday. Across the road, *Ary's Warung* is just as glossy as the Lotus but somewhat cheaper, and a nasi campur is 2700 rp. Continue a few steps beyond the Lotus, on the same side of the road, to *Mumbul's Cafe*, a small place with friendly service and excellent food. They even have a children's menu.

Also on the main road, towards Campuan, you'll find the *Menara Restaurant* opposite the Lotus, the *Rumah Makan Cacik* (which is popular even with local people), the *Griya Barbecue* for barbecued food and the *Roof Top Garden & Cafe* with good views from it's elevated position.

Ubud has something of a reputation as an international jet setters hang-out, and if they aren't at the Lotus then Murni's is where you're likely to find them. *Murni's Warung* is right beside the Campuan suspension bridge and offers excellent food in a beautiful setting. Their satay is served in a personal charcoal holder for 3900 rp, the nasi campur for 3400 rp is fantastic and they do an excellent hamburgers for the same price. To top it all, the cakes are simply superb. It's closed on Wednesday.

A final Ubud dining possibility is *Ketut's Place*, up beyond the palace on the north side of the town centre, for one of Ketut Suartana's Balinese feasts. You can book at Ketut's Place or at the Suci Inn, and for 10,000 rp per person you get a delicious and very comprehensive Balinese meal. It is served in his family compound and you receive an excellent introduction to Balinese life and customs.

Entertainment

Entertainment in Ubud means watching Balinese dances. Head down to Kuta if you want discotheques and Western music. If you're in the right place at the right time, you can still see dances conducted as part of temple ceremonies. At these, there is an essentially local audience but even the strictly tourist dances are conducted with a high degree of skill and commitment.

Indeed the competition between the various Ubud dance troupes is so intense that local connoisseurs even whisper the unthinkable these days and suggest that the Peliatan troupe is no longer necessarily the best!

The usual entry price for the dances is 5000 rp – this even includes transport to performances further out from central Ubud, particularly at Bona Village, 12 km away. You can buy tickets at the performance place but it's hard to escape the entreaties of the commission ticket sellers around Ubud Market and down Monkey Forest Rd. Ubud's tourist office has information on current performance nights.

Getting There & Away

Bemos from the Batubulan bus station, outside Denpasar, are 700 rp. They arrive and depart from Ubud from right beside the cinema in the middle of town. Ubud is off the main routes to towns in the mountains, to the east and to the north coast so, in most cases, you will have to go down to Batubulan or Gianyar to travel elsewhere.

There are, however, direct tourist buses from Ubud to other important tourist sites around the island. Fares from Ubud include Sanur, Kuta or the airport for 4000 rp; Padangbai, Candidasa or Kintamani for 5000 rp; and Singaraja or Lovina Beaches for 10,000 rp.

Getting Around

To places around Ubud, bemos generally cost from around 250 rp. There are plenty of bicycle hire places in Ubud (3000 rp a day); it's also easy to hire motorbikes or cars here.

AROUND UBUD

On the road up to Tampaksiring from the main Denpasar to Klungkung road is **Bedula**, the centre of a powerful dynasty for two centuries. A short stroll through the rice paddies from the Ubud turn-off at Bedulu takes you to **Yeh Pulu** with its carved bas relief discovered in 1925. A km along the main road, towards Ubud, is **Goa Gajah**, or the elephant cave, discovered at much the same time as Yeh Pulu and believed to have been a Buddhist hermitage. The bathing place with the female-shaped fountains, which is out front, was only unearthed in 1954.

A km north of the turn-off at Pejeng, the **Pura Penataran Sasih** has a huge bronze drum said to be 2000 years old. A legend tells of it falling to earth as the 'moon of Pejeng'.

Tampaksiring

The **Gunung Kawi**, a group of burial towers, stands in the rice paddies to the right of the road shortly before Tampaksiring. They're one of the best sights in Bali, impressive both for their sheer size and their setting.

In the shadow of Sukarno's palace at Tampaksiring is the holy spring of **Tirta Empul**. An inscription dates the spring from 926 AD. There are fine carvings and Garudas on the courtyard buildings. As at Gunung Kawi, there is an admission charge and you will have to wear a temple scarf to enter the temple.

Getting Around

From Ubud, you can cover these places by bemo and on foot. Take a bemo right up to Tampaksiring as any walking from there on will be downhill. It's only a km or two back downhill to Gunung Kawi. You can follow the path beside the river and come out right in Gunung Kawi.

From there, you can take bemos back down to Pejeng, Bedulu, Goa Gajah and on to Ubud. Pejeng to the Bedulu turn-off is only about a km and from there it's a half km or so to Yeh Pulu and a similar distance to Goa Gajah. Alternatively, from Pejeng you can cut across country directly to Ubud. This is a pleasant walk with fine views along the way.

DENPASAR TO UBUD

The first few km out of Denpasar on the Ubud and Klungkung road is gallery alley. Stop at the government-run fixed-price store, **Sanggraha Kriya Asta**, for a window shop. First village reached is **Batubulan**, the

stone carving centre, where there are lots of apprentices chipping away at blocks of stone.

Next up is **Celuk**, the silverwork centre where again you're welcome to stop and explore the workshops. The main turn-off to Ubud is soon after Celuk, although there is also a back-road route from Batubulan. Before Ubud, you pass through **Mas**, which means 'gold' in Indonesian but it is actually the wood-carving centre.

EAST BALI

Continuing beyond the turn-off to Ubud, the Denpasar to Klungkung road takes you to **Kutri** where there is a temple dominated by a large banyan tree in the courtyard. A long flight of steps leads to a hilltop statue.

Gianyar is a weaving centre. Visit the workshop to the right just as you enter town. There are literally hundreds of children weaving and preparing the threads for dyeing. The traffic is heavy from Denpasar all the way to Klungkung, but beyond that point it immediately becomes much lighter.

Klungkung

Once the centre of an important Balinese kingdom, Klungkung is chiefly notable for the **Kherta Ghosa**, or hall of justice, and its connecting water palace. Disputes that could not be settled locally were brought here. The accused could study lurid paintings on the roof, of wrongdoers suffering in the afterlife.

Places to Stay & Eat The *Ramayana Palace Hotel*, on the Candidasa side of town, is a pleasant place and set far enough back from the busy main road to be quiet. There's a restaurant and the fairly spartan rooms cost 8000/12,000 rp for singles/doubles.

Less attractive alternatives include the *Losmen Wisnu* near the bus station in the town centre. The upstairs rooms are much brighter than those downstairs. The very basic *Hotel Sudihati* is between the town centre and the Ramayana Palace.

Apart from the Ramayana Palace, there are several eating establishments around town including the neat and clean Chinese *Restaurant Bali Indah* and *Restaurant Sumber Rasa*, both across from the market.

Klungkung to Padangbai

Lava flows from the 1963 eruption of Gunung Agung covered the road between Klungkung and Kusamba but vegetation is slowly obscuring the lava. Initially, 1500 people were killed. Two months later, a further 100 perished in a subsequent eruption. Shortly after Kusamba, to the left of the road, is **Goa Lawah**, or the Bat Cave. Bats spill out from the cave behind the temple. Along the beach, opposite the cave, smoothed-out piles of sand and wooden troughs indicate the local production of salt by an age-old method using wet sand.

Padangbai

The small fishing village of Padangbai is two km off the main road, perched on a perfectly shaped bay. The daily Lombok ferries run from here and cruise ships visiting Bali anchor offshore. The bay itself has a fine sweep of sand with colourful outrigger fishing boats drawn up on it.

There are some beautiful beaches outside the main bay. South of here is the infrequently visited island of Nusa Penida, and its more popular neighbour Nusa Lembongan with its big surf breaks.

Places to Stay There are several pleasant beach-front places starting with the *Rai Beach Inn's* collection of thatched two-storey cottages which cost 20,000 rp. There are also straightforward single-storey rooms with bath at 15,000 rp.

Next along the beach is the *Sedani Kerthi Beach Bungalows* with simple rooms at 8000 rp and also double-storey thatched cottages, very similar in style to the Rai Beach Inn. The third of the central beach-front cluster is

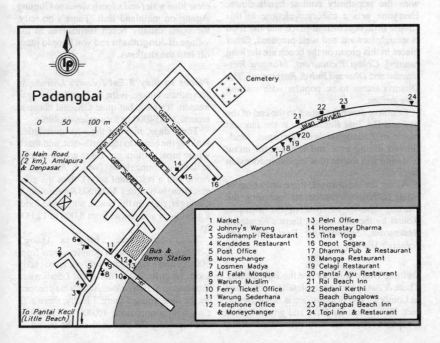

Padangbai

0   50   100 m

To Main Road
(2 km), Amlapura
& Denpasar

Cemetery

Jalan Silayukti

Gang Segara II
Gang Segara III
Gang Segara

Jalan Silayukti

Bus &
Bemo Station

Pier

To Pantai Kecil
(Little Beach)

1 Market	13 Pelni Office
2 Johnny's Warung	14 Homestay Dharma
3 Sudimampir Restaurant	15 Tinta Yoga
4 Kendedes Restaurant	16 Depot Segara
5 Post Office	17 Dharma Pub & Restaurant
6 Moneychanger	18 Mangga Restaurant
7 Losmen Madya	19 Celagi Restaurant
8 Al Falah Mosque	20 Pantai Ayu Restaurant
9 Warung Muslim	21 Rai Beach Inn
10 Ferry Ticket Office	22 Sedani Kerthi
11 Warung Sederhana	Beach Bungalows
12 Telephone Office	23 Padangbai Beach Inn
& Moneychanger	24 Topi Inn & Restaurant

the *Padangbai Beach Inn* where rooms are 12,000/15,000 rp for singles/doubles. The rooms are of the standard losmen design but they all face the sea.

At the far end of the bay, *Topi Restaurant & Inn* is a new addition to the Padangbai beach scene with rooms upstairs at 7000/10,000 rp. Nearer to the centre of the small town, the *Homestay Dharma* is a plain family compound with very neat and tidy rooms at 8000 rp for a double.

Losmen Madya, on the main street, was the town's original place to stay and has rooms at around 10,000 rp, although there's no real reason to stay here in preference to the more pleasantly situated places on the beach. *Johnny's Warung*, behind the post office, also has accommodation.

Places to Eat The simple beach-front warungs near the Rai Beach Inn include the *Pantai Ayu Restaurant*. Here, Ibu Komang wins the popularity contest hands down. Everyone gets a cheery welcome to this simple little beach-front place and the food is straightforward and well-prepared. Other places in this group on the beach are the long running *Celagi Restaurant*, *Mangga Restaurant* and *Dharma Pub & Restaurant*. The Dharma seems to be popular with visiting dive groups.

Continue down the beach to the end of the bay and the *Topi Restaurant* is the fanciest place in Padangbai with an open sand-floored dining area and a colourful menu featuring fish dishes plus regular Indonesian fare.

Along the main street, there are a host of small Indonesian restaurants including the *Warung Muslim* in front of the mosque. Round by the post office, there's *Kendedes Restaurant*, *Sudimampir Restaurant* and *Johnny's Warung*.

Getting There & Away See the Bali Getting There & Away section for details on the ferry to Lombok. The ticket office is down by the pier. Buses meet the ferry and go straight to Denpasar. There are also connections from Padangbai right through to Surabaya and Yogya in Java.

The fast, fibre-glass boats to Nusa Penida (about 3000 rp) leave from the beach near the eastern corner of the carpark next to the pier.

Around Nusa Penida

Nusa Penida is an administrative area within the Klungklung District, and it actually comprises three islands – Nusa Penida itself, the smaller Nusa Lembongan to the north-west, and tiny Nusa Ceningan in between. Nusa Lembongan attracts quite a number of visitors for its surf, seclusion and snorkelling. The island of Nusa Penida has few visitors and few facilities, while Nusa Ceningan is virtually uninhabited.

Nusa Lembongan The offshore coral reef is where the surf breaks, and it protects the beach, a perfect crescent of white sand with clear blue water and superb views to Gunung Agung on mainland Bali. There's no jetty, the boats usually beach themselves at the village of **Jungutbatu** and you have to jump off into the shallows.

Places to Stay & Eat *Johnny's Losmen*, in Jungutbatu village, is the original Lembongan losmen. It's basic but quite OK, and cheap at around 3000/4000 rp for singles/doubles.

These days, most of the accommodation is along the beach to the north-east, and that's where most visitors go. There are some miscellaneous bungalows (which may get a name and a restaurant soon), then the conspicuous, two-storey *Main Ski Restaurant & Cottages*, right on the beach, with good food, a great view and rooms from 8,000 to 12,000 rp.

The next place along is *Agung's Lembongan Lodge* with double rooms from 5000 rp and a restaurant with cheap but tasty food. Next to that is the *Nusa Lembongan Restaurant & Bungalows*, which may reopen by the time you get there. Finally, there's *Ta Chi*, with rooms from 10,000 to 12,000 rp and reputedly the best cook on the island.

Getting There & Away Boats leave from the north end of Sanur Beach, in front of the Ananda Hotel. The boat captains have fixed the tourist price to Lembongan at 15,000 rp, and that's what you'll have to pay. The boats leave before 9 am and the trip takes at least 1½ hours. Some of the agents in Kuta sell a ticket through to Lembongan via Sanur for 15,000 rp – in effect, you get free transport to Sanur.

There are boats which take the local people between Jungutbatu and Toyapakeh on Nusa Penida, particularly on market days. You'll have to ask around to find when they leave, and discuss the price. They will be chock full of people, produce and livestock.

Nusa Penida Clearly visible from Bali's south-east coast, the hilly island of Nusa Penida has a population of around 40,000 and was once used as a place of banishment for criminals from the Kingdom of Klungkung.

Nusa Penida is also the legendary home of the demon Jero Gede Macaling, and there is a shrine to him at the important **Pura Dalem Penetaran** at Ped. Foreigners rarely visit here, but thousands of Balinese come every year for religious observances aimed at placating the evil spirits.

The main town, **Sampalan**, is pleasant enough with a market, warungs, schools and shops strung out along the coast road. Buyuk Harbour, where the boats go to Padangbai, is a few hundred metres west of the market. The town's only losmen is opposite the police station, a couple of hundred metres to the east.

If you come by boat from Nusa Lembongan, you'll probably be dropped at the beach at **Toyapakeh**. It's quite a pretty town with lots of shady trees. The beach has clean white sand, clear blue water, a neat line of perahus, and Bali's Gunung Agung as a backdrop. The *Losmen Terang* has rooms from about 5000 rp.

Getting There & Away There are fast, twin-engined fibreglass boats now operating between Padangbai and Nusa Penida. The trip takes less than an hour and is 3000 rp.

Balina Beach

It's only 11 km from the Padangbai main road turn-off to Candidasa. Between the two, about seven km from the turn-off and four km from Candidasa, is the pretty and uncrowded Balina Beach. It is one of the major scuba diving centres on Bali.

The Balina Beach bungalows rent diving equipment and organise snorkelling and diving trips all around Bali (including to Nusa Penida or the north coast). Diving trips, including transport and a full air tank, range from US$25 to US$35 on the trips closer to Balina, US$45 for Nusa Penida or US$60 for Menjangan Island on the north coast.

Places to Stay & Eat *Balina Beach Bungalows* (☎ 0361-88451) have rooms at a host of prices from as low as US$15/18 up to US$40/45 for fancier rooms or US$55 for a large family unit. All prices include breakfast but the 15½% service and tax charge are extra.

Directly opposite the Balina Beach is *Puri Buitan* (☎ 0361-87182), a new development with fan-cooled rooms at US$30/35 plus tax and service. The *Sunrise Homestay* and the *Cangrin Beach Homestays* are about 200 metres to the east – you have to walk along the beach to find them. They cost about 15,000/20,000 rp for a bungalow.

Tenganan

Slightly inland from the main road and just before Candidasa, Tenganan is a Bali Aga village, reputed to be the oldest on the island. The Bali Aga remained relatively isolated from the Hindu-Javanese influence, and to this day retain traditions not found elsewhere in Bali. Tenganan is a typical example with its walled homes. This is also one of the few places where double *ikat* cloth is still woven.

Ikat cloth is woven with threads pre-dyed to a pattern – the pattern is determined before it is woven. Double ikat is simply twice as complicated – the warp and the weft are both dyed in the predetermined pattern.

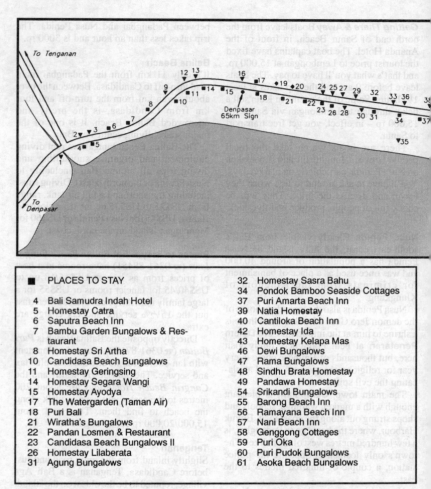

The village has become a bit commercialised with a few souvenir shops but it is still a fascinating place. Try to visit here if you hear of a festival. Local boys will ferry you to the village from the main road turn-off on their motorbikes. Candidasa is only a short stroll beyond the Tenganan turn-off and some of the Candidasa losmen are even beyond the turn-off towards Padangbai.

Candidasa

Candidasa became *the* new Bali beach resort with astonishing speed during the '80s and now looks rather burnt out in the '90s. Overdevelopment and the gouging out of the fringing coral reef has managed to totally wreck the beach. Attempts to save what little sand is left has resulted in the construction of monumentally ugly concrete piers.

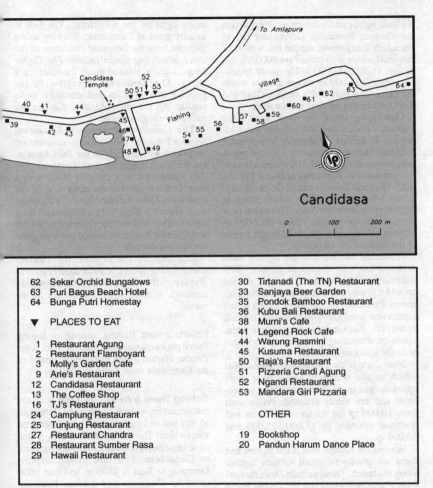

62	Sekar Orchid Bungalows		30	Tirtanadi (The TN) Restaurant
63	Puri Bagus Beach Hotel		33	Sanjaya Beer Garden
64	Bunga Putri Homestay		35	Pondok Bamboo Restaurant
			36	Kubu Bali Restaurant
▼	PLACES TO EAT		38	Murni's Cafe
			41	Legend Rock Cafe
1	Restaurant Agung		44	Warung Rasmini
2	Restaurant Flamboyant		45	Kusuma Restaurant
3	Molly's Garden Cafe		50	Raja's Restaurant
9	Arie's Restaurant		51	Pizzeria Candi Agung
12	Candidasa Restaurant		52	Ngandi Restaurant
13	The Coffee Shop		53	Mandara Giri Pizzaria
16	TJ's Restaurant			
24	Camplung Restaurant			OTHER
25	Tunjung Restaurant			
27	Restaurant Chandra		19	Bookshop
28	Restaurant Sumber Rasa		20	Pandun Harum Dance Place
29	Hawaii Restaurant			

Places to Stay When places first popped up at Candidasa they were almost all standard losmen – simple rooms with bath and a small verandah area out front. Now mass tourism has arrived and there are a number of larger and more luxurious places with air-con, swimming pools and the other accoutrements of the modern travel industry. There are still plenty of low-cost places

to choose from with prices from less than 10,000rp.

Look into a few places before making a decision about where to stay. Starting at the Denpasar (western) side don't confuse the *Candidasa Beach Bungalows* with the larger, more expensive Candidasa Beach Bungalows II in the centre of the village strip. At the original, the rooms are pleasant if a little tightly packed together. Next to it is the cheaper *Homestay Geringsing* or, at *Wiratha's Bungalows*, simple but well-kept singles/doubles with mandi are 8000/10,000 rp and 11,000/13,000 rp. The more expensive 20,000/22,000 rp rooms are not worth the extra. The *Puri Bali's* simple, clean and well-kept rooms are also good value.

Continuing along the road, there's the *Pandan Losmen* and the popular but rock bottom *Homestay Lilaberata*. The *Pondok Bamboo Seaside Cottages* is a fancier place with rooms at 25,600/31,500 rp and a beachfront restaurant. *Puri Amarta Beach Inn* has 6000 rp rooms straight out of the usual construct-a-losmen box plus larger ones at 10,000 rp as does the *Natia Homestay* next door, where the smaller rooms are 6000 rp although there are a couple of larger rooms at the seafront for 18,000 rp.

Homestay Ida, close to the lagoon, definitely doesn't fit the usual pattern, with pleasantly airy, bamboo cottages dotted around a grassy coconut plantation. Smaller rooms are 20,000 rp, the larger rooms with a mezzanine level are 40,000 rp – all include breakfast. Fortunately, they don't seem intent on cramming more and more rooms onto the spacious site.

Next door is the *Homestay Kelapa Mas* which is also well-kept and a little more spacious than usual. The rooms face the seafront and are nicely situated. Prices start from 10,000 rp for the smallest rooms and continue upwards to 15,000, 25,000 and 30,000 rp.

Beyond the Kelapa Mas is the lagoon and there are plenty of small losmen further along the beach. These include *Dewi Bungalows*, *Rama Homestay* and the *Sindhu Brata Homestay*, three fairly standard losmen right beside the lagoon. Further along the beach, the *Puri Oka* offers standard rooms at 25,000 rp and there's a swimming pool. Right at the end of the beach, the *Bunga Putri (Princess Flower) Homestay* is picturesquely situated with a view back down the coast.

Places to Eat Restaurants are dotted along the road, although curiously there are not many right on the waterfront. The fish is usually good at Candidasa. Working along the road from the Denpasar end, some of the more interesting places include *The Coffee Shop*, a quiet, relaxed place for lunch or a snack. *TJ's Restaurant* is related to the popular TJ's in Kuta and certainly looks similar but the only Mexican dish on the menu here is guacamole.

The *Camplung Restaurant*, *Restaurant Sumber Rasa* and the *Hawaii Restaurant* are long-term survivors, as is the *Puri Amarta*. On the beach side of the road, *Tirtanadi (The TN) Restaurant* is a cheerful place with a long cocktail list. On the other side of the road is the *Kubu Bali Restaurant*, a big place built around a pond with a bright and busy open kitchen area out front where Indonesian and Chinese dishes are turned out with great energy and panache.

Just beyond the lagoon, the *Pizzeria Candi Agung* and the *Mandara Giri Pizzaria* display different approaches to spelling although, at both, pizza is definitely on the menu!

Entertainment Barong, topeng or legong dance performances take place at 9 pm at the Pandan Harum dance place in the centre of the Candidasa strip. Entry is 4000 rp.

Getting There & Away Candidasa is on the main route between Amlapura and Denpasar, so any bus or bemo coming by will get you somewhere! The tourist shuttle buses, which have become so popular of late, also operate to Candidasa. The fare to the airport, Denpasar or Kuta is 7500 rp, to Ubud 5000 rp or to Singaraja and Lovina Beaches, 15,000 rp.

Amlapura

Amlapura (or Karangasem as it is sometimes called) is an attractive little town with a fine old **palace** – interesting for its tooth filing pavilion. The area around the temple in Amlapura is very soothing – plain little houses with courtyards, fountains and small gardens. The old Raja of Karangasem was

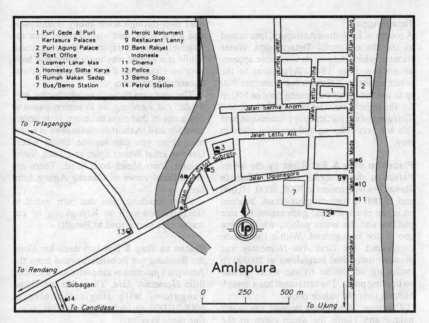

1 Puri Gede & Puri Kertasura Palaces	8 Heroic Monument
2 Puri Agung Palace	9 Restaurant Lenny
3 Post Office	10 Bank Rakyat Indonesia
4 Losmen Lahar Mas	11 Cinema
5 Homestay Sidha Karya	12 Police
6 Rumah Makan Sedap	13 Bemo Stop
7 Bus/Bemo Station	14 Petrol Station

Amlapura

very fond of water and all of his buildings made use of it.

Tirtagangga, near Amlapura, was one of his palaces and if you continue through Amlapura, down towards the seashore, you'll come to the ruins of his **Ujung Palace**. This palace was built in 1921 and for some reason has suffered much additional damage since the mid-70s. It's about three or four km out of town.

Over the bridge to the right, just beyond Ujung, a road leads down to the sea and a fishing village. You can get out to Ujung by bemo and there is an admission charge to the palace gardens. The town's name was changed from Karangasem after the 1963 eruption, to get rid of any influences which might provoke a similar occurrence in the future.

Places to Stay & Eat Candidasa and Tirtagangga are the better places to stay but in Amlapura, the *Losmen Lahar Mas* has rooms with toilet and shower at 10,000 rp, including breakfast. They're around a large common room area and quite comfortable.

On the other side of the road, a short distance in towards the town centre, *Homestay Sidha Karya* has slightly cheaper rooms. A third possibility is the *Losmen Kembang Ramaja*, just out of Amlapura on the Rendang road.

There's the usual collection of rumah makans and warungs around the bus station plus the *Restaurant Lenny* and the *Rumah Makan Sedap* on the main street. Amlapura tends to shut down early, so don't leave your evening meal until too late.

Getting There & Away Amlapura is the end of the road at the eastern end of the island. There are regular buses to and from Denpasar and less frequent connections around the east coast to Singaraja.

Tirtagangga

A couple of km before Amlapura, turn inland to see the delightful **Tirtagangga Water Palace**, which despite its venerable appearance dates from 1947. Admission to the water palace is 200 rp; it costs another 300 rp to use the lower swimming pool or 500 rp for the upper one. The rice terraces around Tirtagangga are particularly picturesque, and this is a very relaxing and peaceful place to stay.

Places to Stay & Eat Right by the Water Palace is the peaceful *Losmen Dhangin Taman Inn* with rooms at 7000, 8000, 10,000 and 15,000 rp including breakfast. You can sit in the courtyard and gaze across the rice paddies and the water palace, while doves coo in the background. Within the palace compound, the *Tirta Ayu Homestay* has pleasant individual bungalows at 20,000 rp including admission to the water palace swimming pools. The restaurant has a superb outlook over the palace pools.

Continue 300 metres beyond the water palace and climb the steep steps to the *Kusuma Jaya Inn*. The 'Homestay on the Hill' has a fine view over the rice paddies and rooms from 8000 to 15,000 rp including breakfast and tea. Across the road from the palace, the *Rijasa Homestay* is a small and simple place with extremely neat and clean single/double rooms at 5000/7000, 6000/8000 and 10,000/15,000 rp, all including breakfast and tea. A few steps back towards Amlapura, the *Taman Sari Inn* has rooms at 7000 and 8000 rp, but it looks rather derelict.

Getting There & Away Tirtagangga is about five or six km from the Amlapura turn-off on the road that runs around the eastern end of Bali. Bemos from Amlapura cost 250 rp. Buses continue around this way to Singaraja.

Amlapura to Rendang

At Amlapura, you can either head north around the coast to Singaraja or double back towards Denpasar. Doubling back, you can take an alternative route to **Klungkung**, higher up the slopes of Gunung Agung. This road runs through some pretty countryside and it's a quiet, less visited route than the relatively busy Amlapura to Denpasar road. While it is a good way to go when you have your own transport, it can be extremely time-consuming by bemo.

The road runs through *salak* country, particularly at Rendang, so in season pause to buy some of that most delicious fruit from a roadside stall. A short detour to **Iseh** is worth making so you can see the house where German artist Walter Spies and, later, Swiss painter Theo Meier both lived. There are magnificent views of Gunung Agung from here.

From Rendang, you can turn uphill to Besakih, downhill to Klungkung or cut across on a minor road to Bangli.

Places to Stay & Eat Just three km along the Rendang (or Bebandem) road from the Amlapura junction is the pretty and secluded little *Homestay Lila*. There are individual bungalows with singles/doubles at 6000/10,000 rp including breakfast. It's a fine place to relax.

Further along, 11 km beyond Bebandem, you can turn off to the *Putung Bungalows* right at the top of the ridge. From here, the land drops clear away to the coast, far below. You can see ships anchored off Padangbai and across to Nusa Penida. There are rooms from 20,000 rp.

Bangli

Bangli is halfway up the slope to Penelokan. You can reach it from the main Denpasar to Amlapura road near Gianyar; from Ubud via Tampaksiring (although this means going a considerable distance further uphill and then doubling back); or by a very pretty small road that cuts across just below Rendang.

Bangli has the fine **Pura Kehen** with a massive banyan tree in the first courtyard. Look for the old Chinese plates set into the inner courtyard walls. Just down from the temple is a little-used art centre – admire the fine gate inside. Just below Bangli, on the Gianyar road, there's a fine temple of the dead, **Pura Dalem Penunggekan**, with

some gruesome sculpture panels along the front.

Places to Stay & Eat The *Artha Sastra Inn* is a former palace residence and still run by the grandson of the last king of Bangli. Rooms, some with bathrooms, cost from 10,000 to 20,000 rp and it's pleasant, friendly and centrally located.

The Bangli alternative is the youth-hostel connected *Losmen Dharmaputra*, a short distance up the road towards Kintamani. It's cheaper but also fairly basic. Rather drab singles/doubles cost 6000/8000 rp and you can also get food here.

Bangli has a good night market in the square opposite the Artha Sastra, and there are some great warungs but they all close early. One catch in Bangli – 'the dogs are even worse than in Ubud'.

Besakih

Nearly 1000 metres up the side of mighty Gunung Agung, this is Bali's most important temple. It's big, majestically located and very well-kept. You contribute through charges to park, enter and rent a temple scarf. After braving all the souvenir sellers, you may well find most of the temple closed for the day!

Places to Stay About five km below Besakih is the *Arca Valley Inn* with rooms and a restaurant. It would be a good place to stay if you wanted to climb Gunung Agung from Besakih and would like to make an early-morning start.

Getting There & Away There are regular bemos from Klungkung to the temple. If you go with your own wheels, take the left fork about a km before the temple. This brings you to a car park close to the entrance. The right fork leaves you with a long walk up the main entrance road from the car park.

WEST BALI

There are a number of places to the west of Denpasar which make interesting day trips, but travellers on their way to or from Gilimanuk and Java rarely pause on the south-west coast.

Tanah Lot

Spectacularly balanced on a rocky islet which is connected to shore at low tide, Tanah Lot is probably the best known and most photographed temple in Bali, particularly at sunset. It's also horrifically touristy. If you come by public bemo, don't miss the last one back or you'll have to do a costly charter.

Mengwi

In Mengwi there's a beautiful royal water palace and temple, **Pura Taman Ayun**. Near Mengwi, at **Marga**, is a memorial to Ngurah Rai and the Balinese forces which tried to gain control of the island from the Dutch in 1946, after the Japanese had left.

Sangeh

Continue on from Mengwi to the monkey forest of Sangeh, but watch out as the monkeys are greedy little devils who don't take no for an answer. They'll tear a bag of peanuts right out of your hands, and snatch your sunglasses and camera for good measure. Sangeh can be reached from Denpasar or Ubud.

Tabanan

Tabanan is in the heart of the south Bali rice-belt, the most fertile and prosperous rice-growing area in the island. It's also the capital of Tabanan District and a centre for dancing and gamelan playing.

South-West Coast

The main road runs close to the south-west coast, though not actually along it. Numerous side roads lead to coastal villages with black-sand beaches, some beautiful scenery and very little tourist development.

Lalang-Linggah A get-away-from-it-all beach place, you can stay here at the *Balian Beach Club*, overlooking the Balian River and surrounded by coconut plantations. There are cheap bunk beds available, as well as more expensive accommodation.

Medewi The turn-off to Medewi surfing point is just west of Pulukan village – there's a large but faded sign on the main road. There is a cheap, basic losmen on the main road, while the *Hotel Nirwana*, on the west side of the beach road, has a restaurant and good rooms from 15,000 to 20,000 rp. The new *Medewi Beach Cottages*, opposite, cost much more.

Rambut Siwi Just south of the main road, Rambut Siwi is a beautiful temple perched high on a cliff top overlooking the sea.

Negara Bullock races are held here between July and October each year, but otherwise it's very quiet. There's a few losmen on the main street – try the *Hotel Ana* with rooms at around 3000, 5000 and 7000 rp. The *Hotel Ijo Gading*, on the main road which bypasses the town centre, has singles/doubles from 7500/10,000 rp.

Cekek The road to the north coast branches off here, and there's an information centre for the Bali Barat National Park, but it may be closed.

Gilimanuk

Right at the western end of the island, Gilimanuk is the port for ferries to and from Java. There's a bus station and a market on the main street about a km from the dock. Most people zip straight through Gilimanuk, but if you get stuck here there are several places to stay along the main road, including *Homestay Gili Sari*, *Homestay Surya* and *Lestari Homestay*.

GUNUNG BATUR AREA

The volcanic cone of Gunung Batur, and Lake Batur which fills half of the huge surrounding caldera, form a spectacular landscape which is one of Bali's natural wonders. Unfortunately, it is also an area where visitors can experience a lot of hassles, from very persistent hawkers to downright rip-offs.

The road around the caldera's western rim is on one of the main routes from the south to the north coast, and offers superb views across the caldera. You can descend into the caldera itself, stay in villages around the lake, explore the lava fields and climb to the top of Gunung Batur.

Climbing Gunung Batur There are several routes up Gunung Batur (1717 metres) – from Tirta, Kedisan or even Kintamani on the caldera rim. You can take one route up and another down, then get a bemo back to your starting point. Start very early in the morning, before mist and clouds obscure the view. Ideally, you should get to the top for sunrise – a magnificent sight.

The most straightforward route is from Tirtha (four or five hours round trip), where lots of locals will offer to be your guide. You don't really need one, but 4000 to 5000 rp would be a fair price if you're not confident about going it alone. The best source of information is Jero Wijaya, who can be found near Awangga Bungalows.

Penelokan
If you're coming up from Bangli or Tampaksiring in the south, Penelokan is the first place you'll come to on the rim of the caldera. Be prepared for wet, cold and cloudy conditions – it's often like that up here. Be prepared to face some aggressive souvenir selling too.

Places to Stay & Eat If you could sell views, the losmen here would be five-star. If you arrive from the south, the first place you'll come to is the *Caldera Batur*, which has a great view and may even rent rooms if you can find any staff.

A little further along from here, *Lakeview Restaurant & Homestay* (☎ 32023) clings to the crater rim and asks US$7.50 for very small 'economy' rooms. Again, not too far north, past the road down into the crater, you come to *Losmen & Restaurant Gunawan*. Again the rooms are tiny – they cost about 10,000 rp – but the views are spectacular!

The bigger restaurants along the road towards Kintamani are all geared to the tour groups which arrive by the bus-load. They all have fine views and do buffet-style lunches at international tourist prices. There are also some cheap warungs along the main road, like the *Warung Makan Ani Asih* or the *Warung Makan Sederhana*.

Kintamani & Batur
Further north is the town of Batur, which merges into Kintamani, the main town on the rim of the caldera. The original town of Batur, down in the crater, was engulfed in the 1926 eruption. Batur was rebuilt up on the caldera rim, and its temple was relocated to the impressive site it now occupies.

Places to Stay There are a number of losmen along the main street, but most of them are rather drab and dismal with unspectacular locations. Starting from the Penelokan end, there's the basic *Losmen Superman's* at 4000 rp, then the *Hotel Miranda* from 5000 to 6000 rp, where you can get information about treks into the caldera.

Further north again is a side road road going towards the crater, with a sign pointing to the *Hotel Puri Astini*, about a km off the main drag. It has great views and reasonably comfortable rooms starting at 12,000 rp. It is a good starting point for climbing Gunung Batur from the outer rim and the hotel can arrange a guide.

Penulisan
Just beyond Kintamani is Penulisan, site of the **Pura Tegeh Koripan**, the highest temple in Bali. It's a steep climb up from the road and offers a fine view right down to the north coast. A temple to the new gods has also been established here: the Bali TV relay station towers over Tegen Koripan.

Around Lake Batur
After you've seen the view from the rim, you can descend into the caldera itself, winding down the road from Penelokan to Kedisan on the shore of the lake. From there, you can take a boat across to the Bali Aga village of Trunyan, or follow the quaint little road across the lava fields to the hot springs at Tirtha.

The road continues to Sonam, under the north-east rim of the crater, and a side road goes around to the north side of Gunung Batur until it is stopped by a huge 'flow' of solidified black lava. You can climb to the

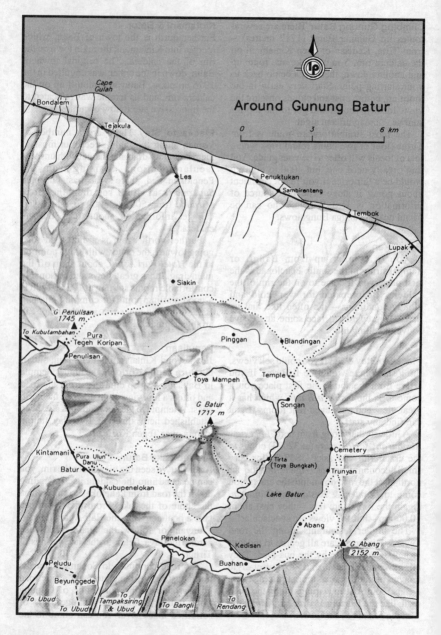

Around Gunung Batur

summit of **Gunung Batur** in just a few hours from either Kedisan or Tirtha, or make longer treks over and around the central volcano and up to the caldera rim.

Kedisan Turning left as you enter Kedisan, you come first to the *Segara Bungalows*, with basic singles/doubles from 6000/8000 rp, including breakfast. A bit further on is the *Surya Homestay & Restaurant* with adequate rooms from 8000 rp to 12,000 rp. Turning right as you come into town will bring you to the *Segara Homestay* which has the same owner as the Segara Bungalows, and similar prices.

A little south-east of Kedisan is **Buahan**, a small place with market gardens right down to the lake shore. You can stay here at the very peaceful and pleasant *Baruna Cottages*, which have a restaurant and single/double rooms with mandi for 5000/8000 rp.

Trunyan This village is inhabited by descendants of the original Balinese, the Bali Aga people who predate the Majapahit arrival. It's famous for its four-metre-high statue of the village's guardian spirit, Ratu Gede Pancering Jagat – but you're unlikely to be allowed to see it. About all you do get to do at Trunyan is sign the visitors' book, make a donation and be told you can't visit the temple. Trunyan is not a friendly place.

A little beyond Trunyan, accessible only by the lake, is the village cemetery where bodies are laid out in bamboo cages to decompose. You're welcome to visit the cemetery for a price, but unless you're a serious anthropologist or a ghoul, it's just a morbid tourist trap.

Tirta (Toyah Bungkah) This small settlement is famous for its hot springs (Tirtha and Toyah both mean 'holy water'). For 500 rp you can join half the village for a hot bath – women on one side and men on the other. Many travellers stay here rather than up at Penelokan. It's more convenient if you want to climb Gunung Batur in the early morning,

and you can soak your aching muscles in the hot springs afterwards.

There are quite a few places to stay in Tirtha and they seem to be building more. None of them are anything special, and the going price is about 5000/8000 rp for a basic single/double – it's worth bargaining. There are a number of warungs and restaurants, mostly with similar menus, food and prices. Fresh fish from the lake is a local speciality, usually barbecued with onion and garlic. They're tiny but tasty.

Getting Around the Lake Crossing the lake from Kedisan was once Bali's greatest rip-off. Boatman would try to renegotiate the price halfway across the lake, while back at Kedisan your motorbike was being stripped to the frame. It got so bad that the government stepped in, and now everything is at set prices, though they're still expensive.

The boats leave from a jetty near the middle of Kedisan, where there is a boat office, a fenced car park and the usual assortment of rumah makans and warungs. Your car or motorbike will be safe here! Don't try to hire a canoe and paddle yourself – the lake is much bigger than it looks from the shore and it can get very choppy if a wind blows up.

A better alternative is to walk around the lakeside to Trunyan, about two hours from Kedisan, then try to negotiate a cheaper boat ride to the cemetery and hot springs.

LAKE BRATAN AREA

The town of **Bedugul** is next to the serene Lake Bratan, on the most direct north-south route between Denpasar and the north coast. Three km north at **Candikuning** is the picturesque temple of Pura Ulu Danau, partly on an island near the lake's western shore. There are some pleasant hikes around the lake, which is also good for swimming.

Up-market water sports, such as water skiing and parasailing, are available in the **Taman Rekreasi** (Leisure Park) at the southern end of the lake – entry costs 200 rp. There's a big flower market near the temple on Sunday, and the **Botanical Gardens** are on the slopes of Gunung Pohen.

Places to Stay

There are several places along the road up to Bedugul from the south. The *Hadi Raharjo*, opposite the turn-off to the Taman Rekreasi, is a basic losmen with rooms at about 10,000 rp. The *Bedugul Hotel*, inside the park area and next to the lake, has rooms which range upwards from 21,500 rp.

Continuing north, the road climbs higher up the hillside to the turn-off for the new and expensive *Bukit Mungsu Indah Hotel*. Dropping down towards the lake again, you'll pass the turn-off to the botanical gardens – look for the phallic sweet corn cob statue. Just up this road you'll find the ugly *Losmen Mawa Indah* which asks 10,000 rp but should take less.

Back on the lakeside road you come to the well-located *Lila Graha*, up a steep drive on the left, with singles/doubles from 25,000/30,000 rp. Then there's the *Hotel Ashram*, right by the lake, with rooms from 15,000 rp.

OTHER MOUNTAIN ROUTES

West of the road down from Bedugul to Mengwi is Gunung Batukau with the remote **Pura Luhur** perched on its slopes. Still further west, there's a scenic but little-used road which winds up from the south, through Blimbing and Pupuan, to the north coast. Another route starts from near Pulukan on the south coast and climbs through spice growing country and picturesque paddy fields until it joins the other road at Pupuan.

SINGARAJA

Singaraja is Bali's principal north coast town, and the capital of Buleleng District. Until the advent of air travel this was the usual arrival point for Bali's infrequent international visitors. Singaraja's importance as a port has diminished in favour of more sheltered harbours, but it is pleasant and one of the few places in Bali where you can see old Dutch buildings.

Places to Stay

There are plenty of places to stay and eat in Singaraja but few people bother – the attractions of the Lovina area, only 10 km to the west, are too great. You'll find a string of hotels along the main street, Jalan Achmad Yani, starting in the east with the *Hotel Sentral*, with basic singles/doubles at 6500/9000 rp.

The *Hotel Garuda* (☎ 41191), further west at No 76, has rooms from 7500 to 12,500 rp, including breakfast, while the *Hotel Duta Karya*, across the road, costs 7500/10,000 rp or 35,000 rp with air-con. Further west again, and handy to the bus station, are the *Hotel Saku Bindu* and the *Hotel Gelar Sari*. On Jalan Imam Bonjol, the street that continues south to Bedugul and Denpasar, you'll find the pleasant *Hotel Segara Yoga*, with clean, fan-cooled rooms from 8000/12,000 rp and the friendly, funky *Tresna Homestay* which is a bit cheaper and doubles as a junk shop.

Places to Eat

There is a batch of places to eat in the small Mumbul Market on Jalan Achmad Yani, including the *Restaurant Gandhi*, a popular Chinese place. Another good Chinese place is the *Restaurant Segar II*, across the road. There are also a few restaurants along Jalan Imam Bonjol, and warungs near the two bus stations.

Getting There & Away

Singaraja has two bus stations, one on the east and one on the west side of town. Minibuses to Denpasar (Ubung station) via Bedugul leave every half hour from the west station, and cost around 2500 rp. Full-sized buses are typically more crowded, less frequent, and about 500 rp cheaper. There are also direct buses to Surabaya on Java.

LOVINA BEACHES

To the west of Singaraja is a string of coastal villages which have become popular beach resorts; they are collectively known as Lovina. Going along the main road, it's hard to know where one village ends and the next

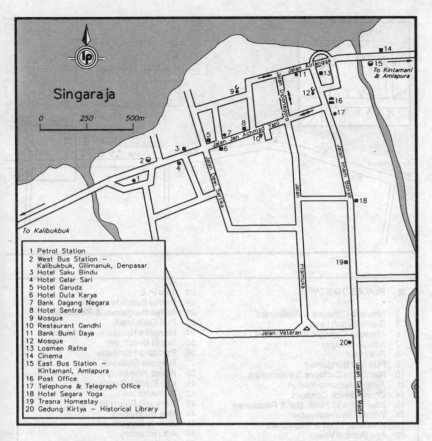

Singaraja

0   250   500m

To Kalibukbuk

1 Petrol Station
2 West Bus Station –
  Kalibukbuk, Gilimanuk, Denpasar
3 Hotel Saku Bindu
4 Hotel Gelar Sari
5 Hotel Garuda
6 Hotel Duta Karya
7 Bank Dagang Negara
8 Hotel Sentral
9 Mosque
10 Restaurant Gandhi
11 Bank Bumi Daya
12 Mosque
13 Losmen Ratna
14 Cinema
15 East Bus Station –
   Kintamani, Amlapura
16 Post Office
17 Telephone & Telegraph Office
18 Hotel Segara Yoga
19 Tresna Homestay
20 Gedung Kirtya – Historical Library

Jalan Airlangga
Jalan Diponegoro
Jalan Jen Achmad Yani
Jalan Dewi Sartika
Jalan Imam Bonjol
Jalan Veteran
Pramuka
Jalan Gajah Mada

To Kintamani
& Amlapura

one starts, so note the km posts which show distance from Singaraja.

The tourist area stretches out over seven or eight km, but the main focus is at Kalibukbuk, 10½ km from Singaraja. There are some shops, bars and other tourist facilities but they don't dominate the place as they do at Sanur and Kuta.

It's a popular stop for travellers who have come overland through Java and beyond, and want to take it easy for a few days. There's a relaxed atmosphere and quite a social scene here.

The beaches are black volcanic sand, not the white stuff you find in the south. It doesn't look as appealing but it's perfectly clean and fine to walk along. Nor is there any surf, a reef keeps it almost flat calm most of the time. There's good snorkelling on the reef, and beyond the reef you can see dolphins cavorting in the sea at sunrise. You will be overwhelmed with offers to arrange snorkelling and dolphin trips.

Places to Stay

There are now so many places to stay along the Lovina beach strip that it's impossible to

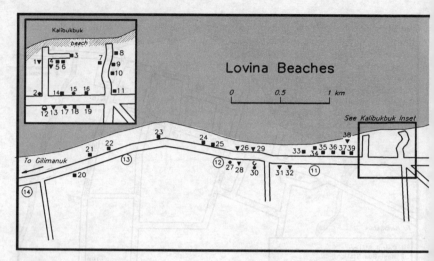

PLACES TO STAY

3	Nirwana Cottages & Restaurant
5	Susila Beach Inn 2
6	Angsoka Cottages & Restaurant
7	Astina Cottages
8	Rini Hotel
9	Puri Bali Bungalows
10	Rambutan Cottages & Restaurant
11	Ayodya Accommodation
14	Chono Beach Cottages
16	New Srikandi Hotel, Bar & Restaurant
18	Wisata Jaya Homestay
19	Khie Khie Hotel & Restaurant
20	Ayu Pondok Wisita
21	Krishna Beach Inn
22	Samudra Cottages
23	Toto Pub
24	Parma Beach Homestay
25	Aditya Bungalows & Restaurant
33	Puri Tasik Madu
34	Mangalla Homestay & Restaurant
35	Susila Beach Inn
36	Purnama Homestay
37	Permata Cottages
39	Arjuna Homestay
41	Kali Bukbuk Beach Inn
42	Yudhistra Inn
43	Banyualit Beach Inn
44	Mas Bungalows
45	Janur's Dive Inn
46	Adi Homestay
47	Lila Cita
48	Celuk Agung Cottages

list them all. During the peak times, from mid-July to the end of August and from mid-December to mid-January, accommodation can be tight and prices are a bit higher. At other times, prices may be more negotiable, particularly if there are a lot of empty rooms around. Generally, the cheapest places are away from the beach, some on the south side of the main road. Upstairs rooms are cooler and a bit more expensive, especially if they have a view. There's a 5% tax on accommodation.

Singaraja to Anturan Starting from the Singaraja end are the higher-priced *Baruna Beach Cottages* and the new, expensive *Bali Taman Beach Hotel*. On the side road, between these two places and close to the beach, are the comfortable *Jati Reef Bungalows*, with double rooms at around 15,000 rp.

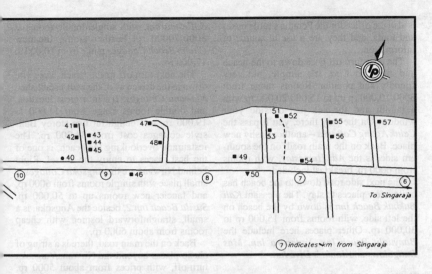

To Singaraja

⑦ indicates km from Singaraja

49	Hotel Perama & Postal Agency	
51	Simon's Seaside Cottages	
52	Homestay Agung & Restaurant	
53	Mandhara Cottages	
54	Bali Taman Beach Hotel	
55	Jati Reef Bungalows	
56	Permai Beach Bungalows	
57	Baruna Beach Cottages	

▼ PLACES TO EAT

1	Bali Bintang Restaurant
4	Kakatua Bar & Restaurant
13	Badai Restaurant
26	Johni's Restaurant
28	Restaurant Adi Rama

29	Marta's Warung
31	Superman Restaurant
32	Singa Pizza Restaurant
38	Bali Ayu Restaurant
50	Harmoni Restaurant

OTHER

2	Benny Tantra's Shop
12	Bus Stop
15	Tourist Office & Police Station
17	Moneychanger
27	Spice Dive
30	Mosque
40	Radio Mast

A little inland are the new *Permai Beach Bungalows,* with rooms from 10,000 rp.

Anturan There are three places in this little fishing village. *Mandhara Cottages,* on the right side of the road to the beach, have singles/doubles with bathrooms at 8000/10,000 rp, including breakfast. Walk a short distance east along the beach to the refurbished *Simon's Seaside Cottages,* with

a pool and comfortable rooms for US$20. Next door to Simon's is the very neat and clean little *Homestay Agung,* with rooms from 7000 to 10,000 rp, and good food in the restaurant.

Anturan to Kalibukbuk Continuing west you reach the *Hotel Perama* (☎ 21161) on the north side of the main road, with a restaurant, and rooms for about 10,000 rp. This is also the office for the Perama shuttle buses and tours, and they are a useful source of information.

The next turn-off goes down to the beach and the *Lila Cita*. It's simple, but very friendly and popular. Rooms range from 8000/10,000 rp up to 15,000/20,000 rp with a mandi and the sea just outside your window. On the way there, you'll pass the *Celuk Agung Cottages* – another flashy new place. Back on the main road, on the southern side, is the *Adi Homestay*, with rooms from 6000 rp, breakfast included.

The next side road down to the beach has quite a few places to stay. The pleasant *Kali Bukbuk Beach Inn* is down by the beach on the left side, with rooms from 15,000 rp to 30,000 rp. Other places here include the *Banyualit Beach Inn*, *Yudhistra Inn*, *Mas Bungalows* and *Janur's Dive Inn*.

Kalibukbuk This village, just past the 10 km marker, is the 'centre' of Lovina. Here you'll find *Ayodya Accommodation*, a traditional place in a big old Balinese house – clean, friendly and extremely well-run, with simple rooms from 4000 to 8000 rp.

Follow the track beside Ayodya down towards the beach and you come to the new and delightful *Rambutan Cottages*, with beautifully finished rooms from 15,000 to 20,000 rp, but 5000 rp more in peak seasons. Next along are the *Puri Bali Bungalows* which are good value for this location at 8000/10,000 rp for singles/doubles.

Closest to the beach is another nice new place, the *Rini Hotel*. It's very clean and well-run, with a good restaurant and rooms from 15,000 to 30,000 rp. Opposite Rini are the *Astina Cottages*, in a pretty garden setting with a variety of rooms and bungalows from 7000 to 10,000 rp.

Along the main road west of Ayodya, you'll find the *Khie Khie Hotel & Restaurant* on the south side, with a pool and rooms from 12,500 to 15,000 rp. A bit further along is the small *Wisata Jaya Homestay*, one of the cheapest around, with basic but satisfactory rooms for 5000 rp. On the other side of the road you'll find the *New Srikandi Hotel Bar*

& Restaurant, with single/double rooms at 5000/70000 rp. Further along, the new *Chono Beach Cottages* range from 10,000 to 17,000 rp.

The next turn-off to the beach takes you down to the driveway of the well-established *Nirwana Cottages*. It's in a great location, and double rooms range from 11,000 to 19,000 rp, and delightful two-storey Bali-style cottages cost from 34,000 rp. The restaurant, overlooking the beach, is one of the best places to enjoy the sunset. Right behind Nirwana are the *Angsoka Cottages*, a small place with simple rooms from 6000 rp, and fancier new rooms up to 50,000 rp. *Susila Beach Inn 2*, beside the Angsoka, is a small, straightforward losmen with cheap rooms from about 6000 rp.

Back on the main road, there is a string of cheap places beyond the Nirwana/Angsoka turn-off, with prices from about 5000 rp. They include the *Arjuna Homestay, Permata Cottages* (☎ 41653), *Purnama Homestay* and *Susila Beach Inn* which are all grouped together on the north side the road. Some of the places here extend through to the beach so you can get away from the road noise. Further along is the slightly more expensive *Mangalla Homestay*, then the *Puri Tasik Madu*.

Beyond Kalibukbuk Continuing further west along the road, there's the top-end *Aditya Bungalows & Restaurant*, with beach frontage, pool, shops, TV etc, then the friendly *Parma Beach Homestay* with its cottages from 5000 rp, which are in a garden extending down to the beach. The *Toto Pub* is another bottom-end place with a top location, at the end of town but right on the beach. Spartan rooms are 7000 rp a double.

The *Samudra Cottages*, with a secluded location further along the road, are more expensive. The *Krisna Beach Inn*, with rooms from 5000 rp, is the next one, and there are now even more places extending west of here.

Places to Eat

Most of the places to stay have restaurants

and snack bars. You're always welcome to visit other losmen for a meal – you don't have to be staying there. Many restaurants are also bars, depending on the time of night, and you can stop at any of them just for a drink. With all these places, plus a handful of warungs, there are dozens of places to eat. You'll do well just looking around and eating anywhere that takes your fancy.

Getting There & Away

To get to Lovina from the south of Bali, you first have to get to Singaraja, then take a bemo out from there (about 400 rp). The direct buses between Singaraja and Surabaya stop at Lovina – you don't have to go into Singaraja first. The Perama office (☎ 21161) is at the Perama Hotel in Anturan, and this is the stop for their shuttle buses, though they will also pick you up from your losmen if you book ahead.

THE NORTH COAST TO GILIMANUK

The road from Singaraja to Lovina continues along the north coast to the Bali Barat National Park, then swings south to connect with Gilimanuk at Bali's western tip. There are a number of sights along the way, and the route is quite scenic in places.

Singsing Air Terjun

'Daybreak Waterfalls' are about one km south of the main road – there's a sign about five km from Lovina.

Buddhist Monastery

Bali's only Buddhist monastery is about a half km beyond the village of Banjar Tega, which is about three km up a steep track south of the main coast road.

Hot Springs

The hot springs, or air panas, are only a couple of km from the monastery if you can cut across directly. There are a number of pools with water that is slightly sulphurous and pleasantly hot. There's a good restaurant and the area is beautifully landscaped – entry is 400 rp.

Seririt/Pengastulan

The junction for the road to Pulukan and the south is here. There's a petrol station, some shops and a market. The *Hotel Singarasari*, near the bus and bemo stop, has singles/doubles from 5000/7000. Although Seririt is on the beach and Pengastulan is inland, the area is usually just referred to as Seririt.

Celukanbawang

This picturesque place is now the main port for the north coast of Bali. You may see Bugis schooners anchored here, and there's also a small beach. The *Hotel Drupadi Indah*, a combination losmen, cinema, bar and restaurant, is the only place to stay.

Pulaki

The coastal temple here has been rebuilt but there are still lots of monkeys. One km past Pulaki are the **Pemuteran Hot Springs**, a few hundred metres north of the road.

Bali Barat National Park

The Bali Barat (West Bali) National Park, the park extension and the adjacent coral reef and coastal waters cover nearly 80,000 hectares of western Bali. Information and facilities for visitors are quite limited, but this may improve as the area becomes better known. You pay separately (about 450 rp) to visit the places of interest – they're called 'visitor objects' – but you don't have to pay any entrance fees just to drive through.

Banyuwedang Hot Springs There is a Balinese temple here and the hot springs will 'strengthen the endurance of your body against the attack of skin disease'.

Labuhan Lalang & Pulau Menjangan The office at the entrance to this national park has some information and a good relief model of the area. It's 450 rp to enter the foreshore area where there's a pleasant white-sand beach, a warung and some basic bungalows (about 7500 rp). There's also a jetty for boats to Pulau Menjangan (Deer Island), an unspoilt and uninhabited island reputed to offer the best diving in Bali. Excursions start at 35,000 rp.

Teluk Terima This is the site of Jayaprana's grave, a 10-minute walk up some stone stairs from the south side of the road. Jayaprana and his girlfriend, Layonsari, are Bali's answer to Romeo and Juliet. The *Pulau Menjangan Inn*, on the north side of the road and 13 km from Gilimanuk, has a small restaurant and clean rooms with good showers for 15,000 rp.

Jungle Treks Guided treks can be arranged through the national park office office at Labuhan Lalang (from 5000 rp). A 25-km walking track skirts round the Prapat Agung Peninsula, north of the Terima to Gilimanuk road.

EAST OF SINGARAJA

There are a number of places of interest just to the east of Singaraja. The local sandstone used in temple construction is very soft and easily carved. It has allowed sculptors to produce some extravagantly whimsical scenes. **Pura Beji** at Sangsit, on the coast side of the main road, has a whole Disneyland of demons and snakes on its front panels.

Continue east and turn inland to Jagaraga where the small **temple** to the left of the road has a vintage car, a steamship and even an aerial dogfight between early aircraft. A few km beyond Jagaraga is **Sawan**, a centre for the manufacture of gamelan gongs and full instruments.

About a km beyond the Kintamani turn-off, the **Pura Maduwe Karang** is on the coast side of the road. Its sculptured panels include the famous one of a gentleman riding a bicycle with flower-petal wheels.

Yeh Sanih

Yeh Sanih (also called Air Sanih) is 15 km east of Singaraja and here freshwater springs are channelled into a fine **swimming pool** (entry 150 rp). It's right by the sea set in attractive gardens, and the water is cool and very refreshing.

Places to Stay & Eat The *Bungalow Puri Sanih* is actually in the springs complex. It's got a very pretty garden and doubles from 10,000 to 20,000 rp. Just beyond the springs are the *Yeh Sanih Seaside Cottages* with pleasant single/double rooms at 25,000/30,000 rp. The Puri Sanih has a restaurant overlooking the gardens, and there are a number of warungs and a restaurant across the road.

East Coast Road

Beyond Yeh Sanih the road continues east round the coast to **Tulamben**, known for interesting diving around a shipwreck. The road then goes south to Tirtagangga and Amlapura (see the previous East Bali section).

Sumatra

Sumatra is one of Indonesia's 'new frontiers'. It has vast wealth in natural resources but is comparatively unpopulated and undeveloped. Today, major resettlement projects, or 'transmigration', from Java is occurring. Sumatra offers wild jungle scenery, the Bukit Barisan, or 'marching mountains', do just that – right down the west coast – and there are a diverse collection of highly individual cultures and peoples. In 1958, Sumatra tried to break away from the rest of Indonesia in an abortive rebellion.

Getting There & Away
You can approach Sumatra by a number of directions and means. The most conventional way is to fly or take the ferry from Penang to Medan, then travel down through the island on those famous Sumatran buses. Then, either take the ship from Padang to Jakarta or continue down via Palembang to the southern tip of Sumatra and take the ferry across to Merak in Java. This trip can be done in reverse.

There are other variations, such as arrival or departure via the islands in the Riau Archipelago, flying to or from various cities in Sumatra or taking the ferry service between Melaka (Malaysia) and Dumai.

Penang to Medan This is the easiest way into or out of Sumatra and since most of Sumatra's attractions are up at the northern end of the island, many people arrive and depart Sumatra via this route. Penang to Medan flights are operated by MAS, cost US$60 and the short hop across the Melaka Straits takes just 20 minutes. Sempati Air apparently do the same trip for US$45. This is a very popular flight to satisfy the 'ticket out' requirement of Indonesian visas.

The new Pelni hydrofoil service has replaced the old ship service and takes only six hours to reach Medan from Penang. It runs twice weekly, on Wednesday and Friday at 2.30 pm, and costs M$107 for general seating or M$135 for VIP seating, including all the additional charges. From Medan, the cost is 76,000 rp (general seating) and 96,000 rp (VIP seating) respectively, including various administrative charges, embarkation and insurance fees.

Additionally, there's a 4000 rp charge for the tourist bus to Belawan which has become something of a minor issue amongst budget travellers. You can opt out and take the public bus for 600 rp plus the 200 rp port entrance charge. Coming from Malaysia, however, you are charged M$5 for this bus with no option for declining. Since M$5 is about 3500 rp, there have been some complaints.

Melaka to Dumai There is a twice weekly ferry service operating between Melaka (Malaysia) and Dumai for M$80. Dumai is a small port where the only thing to do is get on a bus and head south 158 km to Pakanbaru. From Pakanbaru, buses depart regularly for Bukittinggi. This is not a 'no visa' entry point to Indonesia, so you need a visa to enter or leave Indonesia through Dumai.

Singapore or Kuala Lumpur to Sumatra Garuda have flights from Singapore to cities in Sumatra – there is a daily flight to Medan, three flights a week to Padang and daily flights to Pakanbaru (sometimes via Padang). Twice a week there are flights between KL and Medan.

Singapore to Sumatra via the Riau The Riau Archipelago is the scattering of Indonesian islands immediately south of Singapore – they can make an interesting and convenient stepping stone to Sumatra or to other destinations in Indonesia.

There are at least three ways of taking the first step from Singapore. The longest and least expensive route is to take a regular ferry service to Sekupang on Batam Island where you go through Indonesian immigration. The fare is S$18 (19,500 rp from Sekupang).

From there, you take a bus for 600 rp to Nagoya and a share taxi for 2000 rp to Kabil. From Kabil, a ferry crosses to Tanjung Uban, on Bintan Island, for 3000 rp. A bus runs from there to Tanjung Pinang, the biggest town in the archipelago, for 3000 rp. The total cost of this expedition is about 26,000 rp and it takes quite a time.

A faster alternative is to take a direct hydrofoil from Singapore to Tanjung Pinang. The cost is S$45 (50,000 rp in the reverse direction). There are two morning departures and one afternoon departure daily. The trip takes about 2½ hours via Batam, where you clear immigration. Departures are from Finger Pier on Prince Edward Rd, Singapore (☎ 336 0528 for details).

From Tanjung Pinang, the weekly Pelni boat service to Jakarta has been restored. Fares begin at 34,500 rp for economy class. The easiest way is to fly with Garuda as they have a variety of regular flights to and from Batu Besar on Batam, including two daily flights to Jakarta and a daily flight to Pakanbaru, continuing on to Medan. The Jakarta to Batam fare is about 178,000 rp which makes it a very economical way to travel to or from Singapore (about US$70 less than the regular Jakarta to Singapore fares).

A huge globe by the roadside north of Bukittinggi marks the equator. Spend 5 minutes hopping back and forth across the line and you'll be able to say, 'The equator? Oh, I've crossed it dozens of times.'

Merpati and Sempati also have flights between Tanjung Pinang (Bintan) or Batu Besar (Batam) and a variety of cities in Sumatra, Java and Kalimantan. The Tanjung Pinang Airport can only take smaller aircraft so the flights tend to be more heavily booked than from Batam. You can fly from Batam to Palembang with Merpati for around 116,000 rp, or from Batam to Padang with Sempati for 117,100 rp.

A more time-consuming route is to take a boat between Tanjung Pinang and Pakanbaru, a trip costing 16,000 to 21,000 rp depending on the class. There are two boats – a fast one that takes 24 to 28 hours and a slow one that takes 40 to 48 hours. The fare is the same for either so it's worth waiting around for the faster one. Tickets are sold on the quay and boats feature cramped conditions and abysmal food, although the scenery on the journey upriver to Pakanbaru is superb.

Also, there is another boat which goes from Pakanbaru to Batam Island three times a week. It takes 15 hours and costs 27,500 rp for deck class and 32,500 rp for a cabin.

The fastest way to go from Pakanbaru to Batam Island is to take a boat to Selatpanjang for 15,000 rp and it takes three hours. From Selatpanjang there is a connecting ferry to Batam – also for 15,000 rp and it takes three hours. From Batam there is a connecting ferry to Singapore which takes 25 minutes. Thus the whole trip, Pakanbaru to Singapore, takes about seven hours.

There are numerous stops at small ports along the way and there is plenty of time to visit the markets and buy fresh food – a necessity as the food on these boats is little more than boiled rice with a tiny portion of dried fish in chilli sauce and a cup of coffee if you're lucky.

There are other possibilities if you're willing to wait, including irregular ships to various ports in Sumatra or Java.

Jakarta to Sumatra Garuda have flights from Jakarta to all sorts of destinations in Sumatra including flights to Banda Aceh (daily; 398,700 rp), Bengkulu (twice daily;

115,500 rp), Jambi (twice daily; 133,000 rp), Medan (daily; 259,000 rp), Padang (three times daily; 187,000 rp) and Pakanbaru (twice daily; 189,000 rp).

Alternatively, Pelni have four ships which operate between Jakarta and ports in Sumatra on a regular two-weekly schedule. See the Indonesia Getting Around section for more details of the ships and routes.

The KM *Kerinci's* Jakarta-Padang-Sibolga service is the one most used by travellers. It departs Jakarta (Tanjung Priok Harbour) on alternate Fridays at 1 pm and arrives in Padang at 4 pm the following day. Fares vary from 40,200 rp ekonomi to 132,700 rp 1st class. The KM *Kerinci* is a modern ship, all air-con with hot and cold showers and other luxuries.

Merak to Bakauheni Ferries shuttle across the narrow Sunda Strait between Java and Sumatra. Car ferries take the shortest route from Merak to Bakauheni; they depart every hour, take about 1½ hours and cost from 1,100 to 2,200 rp. If you travel by bus between Jakarta and destinations in Sumatra, the price of the ferry is included in your ticket.

To get to Merak from Jakarta, you can travel by train or bus. Buses depart from the Kalideres bus station every 10 minutes and take about 3½ hours. Trains leave from the Tanah Abang railway station. The morning train is faster and connects with the daytime ferry service.

Other There are various interesting and/or easy possibilities for getting to or from Sumatra. From Pakanbaru, you can fly to Singapore for US$87. Pakanbaru is a bit of a hole, but it is easily accessible to or from Bukittinggi. You can also fly from Pakanbaru to Tanjung Pinang for 98,400 rp or from Palembang to Tanjung Pinang for 117,100 rp.

Getting Around
Air Of course, it's possible to fly around Sumatra and save a lot of time and trouble compared to travelling at surface level. Since

most of the interest in Sumatra is in the north, many visitors fly from Jakarta to Padang for 187,000 rp and skip the southern part of Sumatra completely.

Other Garuda fares include Bengkulu to Palembang 61,900 rp, Palembang to Padang 126,400 rp, Padang to Medan 136,350 rp or Palembang to Medan 237,050 rp. Merpati, Sempati, SMAC & Mandala also have flights through Sumatra.

Bus Travelling through Sumatra by bus is the most popular method. It's hard going and distances are long but the Trans-Sumatran Highway has made a huge improvement in speed and pleasure. Another improvement has been the introduction of more modern buses and minibuses. Nonetheless, travelling around Sumatra by bus can sometimes be grindingly slow, diabolically uncomfortable and thoroughly exhausting, particularly during the wet season when bridges are washed away and the roads develop huge potholes.

From major towns there are normally many bus companies covering popular routes and bus prices can vary greatly – so can the quality and comfort of the bus.

From Palembang to Padang, the road runs through as good a jungle as you're likely to find – you always expect to see those elusive Sumatran tigers, although wild boars and monkeys are probably the nearest you'll get to them. Rivers are muddy, wide, winding facsimiles of the Amazon. Construction of the Trans-Sumatran Highway, sealing dirt roads and rebuilding of bridges destroyed during the Sumatran rebellion of 1958 have all contributed to making travel easier.

Modern Mercedes buses also help (although it's unlikely that Mercedes ever imagined they could contain so many seats) but don't think that simply sealing the roads will take all the adventure out of Sumatran travel – as one traveller experienced it:

We took the new Mercedes bus from Bukittinggi to Parapat. If they are really better than the old ones (hard seats, no legroom, nonwaterproof windows) then I must come from a new generation of softies.

One window across the aisle from us was simply not there and since the pane could not be slid across to cover a window space twice its size, we had the comical situation, when the rain came down, of two Sumatrans shouting blue murder at each other, tugging the window in opposite directions in an attempt to keep dry. After this, a landslide, three breakdowns and a collapsed bridge, the 18-hour journey took 26.

Another madman travelled through Sumatra during the wet season and told how rain could turn hard work into real torture:

The trip involves sheer physical hardship and you need to be mentally prepared. Buses were taking five to seven days to reach Bukittinggi (from Palembang). Very little rest is possible when moving and also when stopped as the bus and other vehicles have to be pushed and the ground is wet and muddy. None of the new buses appear to have winches which means plenty of hold ups. Anyone doing Sumatra in the wet without unlimited time should fly from Palembang to Padang.

So, if travelling through Sumatra by bus be prepared. It's tough work and if you haven't got the endurance of a marathon runner, you need to give yourself time off to recover. Don't expect to be able to cover the whole island by bus if you are pressed for time. Avoid seats at the very back where the bouncing is multiplied. And in rough weather look for a bus with a winch!

Java to Palembang You can take a bus from Jakarta to Palembang (18,900 rp), Jambi (24,150 rp) or Padang (33,600 rp), which includes the ferry crossing from Java to Sumatra. This is for a basic service without air-con. For air-con and reclining seats, figure on a 40% increase in fares. See the Palembang section in this chapter for more fare details. The stretch of road from Jakarta to Palembang takes about 20 hours and there are frequent departures. ANS is one of the best of the various Sumatra bus companies.

Palembang to Padang This sector takes 24 hours if the going is easy and *jam karet,* or rubber time, during the wet season. Fares are typically around 18,100 or 21,000 rp with air-con. The road from Lubuklinggau – the end of the railway line north – to Padang, which runs along the eastern side of the mountains, is now one of the best and most scenic in Sumatra.

The Bengkulu to Lubuklinggau road is fairly good but slow going, it's all sealed but with some potholes. Lubuklinggau to Maurarupit is sealed but there are a few potholes and it can be slow going. Maurarupit to Bangko is generally good and the last 75 km is excellent. Bangko to Muarabungo is generally good apart from a few bad patches, and Muarabungo to Bukittinggi and beyond is excellent.

Apart from these 'usual' routes, there are also some unusual ones. From Jambi, if you are willing to hang around, you might get a river boat up to Sungaidareh. This is a good possibility for the wet season but it is better, of course, for the downstream trip.

Padang to Parapat Most people make one or more stops on this sector – usually Bukittinggi and/or Sibolga. The roads are sealed on this sector and travel is now much more reliable although it can still be a long, tough trip.

The Padang to Bukittinggi road is excellent and this scenic sector is no trouble at all. From Bukittinggi and further north, the going can be more difficult, although the trip is now generally much shorter than the 20 hours it used to take – ANS do it in 15 hours these days. There's a special tourist minibus operating once a week which claims to make the trip in 12 to 13 hours, and includes stops at the equator marker, hot springs and other attractions. See the Padang and Bukittinggi sections for more details.

Parapat to Medan Buses between Parapat (jumping-off point for Samosir Island and Lake Toba) and Medan operate frequently and take about four hours. Buses also operate frequently between Medan and Berastagi but the trip on from Berastagi to Parapat is time-consuming and involves changes at Kabanjahe and Siantar.

Train It is also possible to take a train through parts of Sumatra

Java to Palembang The rail choice involves the longer ferry crossing from Merak to Bakauheni. Trains operate from Tanjungkarang to Palembang and even further to Lubuklinggau, from where you can continue by bus to Bengkulu or Padang. See the Palembang section in this chapter for fare details.

Riau Archipelago

Immediately south of Singapore are the islands of the Riau Archipelago. There are hundreds of islands but only a few of them are inhabited. They can be divided roughly into three groups – one is bunched close to the coast of Sumatra, the second nearer to Singapore, the third further south.

The main islands in the group close to the Sumatran coast include Rupat, Bengkalis, Padang, Tebingtinggi, Rangsang, Mendol, Kundur and Karimun Besar. The group near Singapore includes Batam, Bintan, Rempang and Galang islands, all in the main Riau Archipelago. Further south are the Sebangka, Bakung, Lingga and Singkep islands in the Lingga Archipelago. Other islands are scattered east between Peninsular Malaysia and Borneo.

Much of the Riau is still explorer territory, unexploited and unspoilt, but it's also one of the richest areas in Indonesia due to its oil and tin exports. Islands which are closest to Singapore are also becoming economic development zones and weekend retreats for residents of that increasingly wealthy city state. A variety of industrial and resort developments are springing up on Batam and Bintan islands. For the traveller the Riau Archipelago can make a most interesting stepping stone to other parts of Indonesia.

Warning

Mosquitoes are rife in these islands and

chloroquine resistance has been reported. Take repellent, insect coils and antimalarials.

Visas

Sekupang on Batam Island and Tanjung Pinang on Bintan Island are immigration clearance points to and from Singapore. You do not need a visa to enter or leave Indonesia through these ports. Furthermore, you do not have to show an onward or return ticket on entry. If they ask for one, you could always buy a ferry ticket back to Singapore for less than US$10.

Getting There & Away

Batam and Bintan are the two major islands close to Singapore. There are very frequent ferry services to Batam from Singapore but less frequent services to Bintan. From Batam, there are regular flights to Jakarta and other parts of Indonesia.

Flights are not so frequent from the smaller airport on Bintan but the port of Tanjung Pinang does have frequent shipping services to other ports in the archipelago. See the following Batam and Bintan sections for more details.

BATAM

Batam is being heavily developed to become a virtual industrial suburb of Singapore. Already, there are resorts on the north coast and there will soon be factories, warehouses and even a huge reservoir to supply water to the nearby city state. Meanwhile, there's a distinct frontier town atmosphere to the place, with high prices, ugly construction sites and no reason to pause longer than you have to.

Sekupang is the arrival port and, after you clear immigration, there are counters for money exchange, taxis and hotels. **Nagoya**, the main town, looks and feels like some sort of gold-rush place, complete with bars and

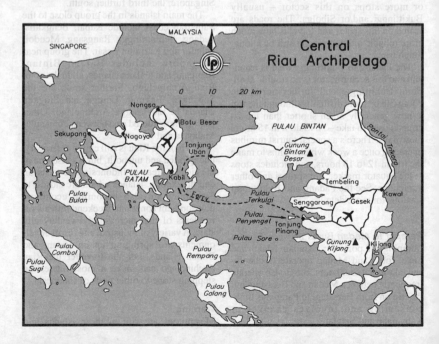

prostitutes. It's sometimes referred to as Batu Ampar. **Kabil** is the tiny port from where boats cross to Tanjung Uban and Tanjung Pinang on Bintan. **Batu Besar** is a small fishing village on the east coast from which the airport takes its name. **Nongsa** is the centre for the Singapore beach resort hotels on the north-east corner of the island.

Information

Singapore dollars are easier to spend than Indonesian rupiah on Batam. There's a money exchange counter at the Sekupang ferry building and a bank outside which will probably be closed. You can change money in Nagoya. There's an efficient phone office on Jalan Teuku Umar, out of town towards the cluster of cheap hotels.

Places to Stay

There is no pressing reason to stay on Batam but if you must there are a variety of places in Nagoya and a number of beach resorts on the north-east coast at Nongsa.

There are no accommodation bargains in Nagoya. About a km out of town at Blok C, Jalan Teuku Umar, there's a line-up of utterly rock bottom and extremely basic losmen or penginapan – the latter term is more widely used in Riau. Included are *Penginapan Minang Jaya* (☎ 57964), *Penginapan Purnama* (☎ 57816), *Losmen Sederhana*, *Penginapan Koto Sima* and the *Mutiara Batam Inn* (☎ 56446).

They'll ask you for 15,000 rp for a bare, partitioned-off single room and although they will reduce it a little, it's still absurdly expensive compared to almost anywhere else in Indonesia, including neighbouring Bintan.

In the town centre, there's the *Holiday Hotel* (☎ 58616) at Blok B, Jalan Imam Bonjol, with rooms at S$87. The big *Batamjaya Hotel* (☎ 58707) on Jalan Raja Ali Haji is better value with rooms from S$75. Better still is *Horisona Hotel* (☎ 45 7111) at Blok E, Kompleks Lumbung Rezeki, with rooms from S$50 and up. The pick of the bunch is probably the pleasant *Bukit Nagoya Hotel* (☎ 52871) at Jalan

Sultan Abdul Rahman 1 with rooms without bath at S$30 or more expensive rooms from S$40 to S$70.

The beach resorts around Nongsa are mainly for visitors from Singapore. The fancy *Batam View* and *Turi Beach Resort* both cost from about US$100 a night for a double. The *Nongsa Beach Cottages* are plain, cost from S$80 and include breakfast.

Places to Eat

The best eating in Nagoya is found at the night food stalls which are set up along Jalan Raja Ali Haji or at the big, raucous and noisy *Pujasera Nagoya* food centre. There are some good nasi padang places like *Mak Ateh Nasi Padang*.

There are a number of waterfront seafood places dotted around the coast of the island, particularly around the Singapore resorts at Nongsa. They include *Setia Budi* and *Sederhana* near the Nongsa Beach Cottages and *Selera Wisata* at Batu Besar.

Getting There & Away

To/From Singapore Ferries to Batam and Bintan depart from Finger Pier, just south of Singapore's Central Business District. There are about a dozen companies operating an assortment of fast ferries and catamarans; they all have counters in one large room. Don't believe claims that their boat is 'the next departure' until independently verified! Avoid Auto Batam who are particularly bad at keeping to schedules.

A one-way fare to Sekupang, the Batam port, is S$18 and a return ranges from S$27 to S$34. The trip takes less than half an hour. From Sekupang, the fare is 19,500 rp.

To/From Bintan Island Many travellers continue straight on from Batam to Bintan. Some Tanjung Pinang (Bintan) services from Singapore stop at Sekupang (Batam) on their way but the tiny port of Kabil, on the south-east coast, is the main departure point. From here, an assortment of boats shuttle across taking 30 minutes for the fastest boats (12,500 rp), 75 minutes for the medium-speed boats (8800 rp) and three to four hours for the slow boats (5000 rp).

The alternative is the shorter route between Kabil and Tanjung Uban, on Bintan's north-west coast. Operated by the slow boats, this trip takes 45 minutes and costs just 3000 rp. From Tanjung Uban, there's a bus to Tanjung Pinang, taking two hours and costing 3000 rp. Share taxis also sometimes do this trip at 5000 rp per person.

The slow boats from Kabil to Tanjung Pinang only go in the morning, and it makes more sense to take the ferry-bus combination via Tanjung Uban. It's slightly cheaper, slightly faster and a whole lot more comfortable.

To/From Elsewhere in Indonesia There are a variety of flights from Bintan's Batu Besar Airport to other places in Indonesia. Typical fares include Jakarta 178,000 rp, Pakanbaru 89,100 rp, Medan 172,100 rp, Padang 117,100 rp, Pontianak 151,200 rp and Balikpapan 304,100 rp. There are flights with SMAC and PT Deraya Air Taxi to Dabo on Singkep Island. Batam's airport terminal is a scruffy and stuffy little place.

Getting Around

There is a hard to find bus service from Sekupang to Nagoya for 600 rp but otherwise the only transport around Batam is taxi and you have to bargain hard. Between Sekupang and Nagoya or between Nagoya and Kabil, you should be able to get a share taxi at around 1500 to 2000 rp per person, otherwise pay 5000 rp for the whole taxi. From Nagoya to the airport should be a bit less. Don't believe cards showing 'official' fares.

BINTAN

Bintan is larger than Batam and much more interesting. Singapore development is, at present, on a much lower key on Bintan but a mega-resort is on the drawing boards for the north coast.

For visitors, the island has three areas of interest – the town of Tanjung Pinang and nearby Penyenget Island; the relatively

untouched beaches along the east coast; and Tanjung Pinang's useful role as a departure point for ships bound to other parts of the country.

Tanjung Pinang

Tanjung Pinang is the biggest town in the Riau Archipelago and there is a constant stream of boats arriving and departing. These vary from large freighters to tiny sampans. An old and quite picturesque wooden section of the town juts out over the sea on stilts but there are also some lush parks and gardens on dry land.

The town is famed for its two red-light villages – Batu Duabelas and Batu Enambelas – no prizes for guessing that they are respectively 12 (duabelas) km and 16 (enambelas) km out of town.

Orientation & Information PT Info Travel, one of the shipping agents at the main wharf, is used to dealing with visitors and has all the shipping information. They also rent motorbikes. The post office is on Jalan Merdeka, near the harbour.

Tanjung Pinang is not a good place to change money, the banks are either choosey about what currencies they accept or offer bad rates. The Bank Dagang Negara actually requires that you show the original purchase receipt for travellers' cheques. The PT Dasa Moneychanger rates are not so good.

Tanjung Pinang has a reputation for shady deals and theft so take notice of the *awas copet*, or beware of pickpockets, signs.

Around Town The piers and market are colourful places to explore. There is a **Chinese temple** right in town. Not far from the city centre is the small **Riau Kandil Museum** with its curious collection of old bits and pieces, some dating from the Riau Kingdom.

Penyenget Island Tiny Penyenget Island is in the harbour across from Tanjung Pinang. It was once capital of the kingdom and the whole place is steeped in history. After 1721, the island played an important political and

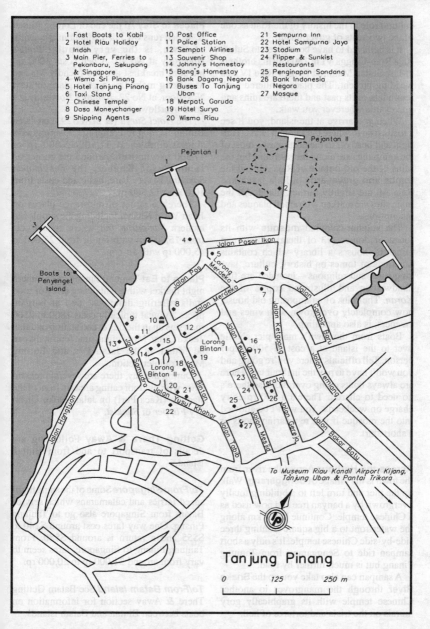

Tanjung Pinang

1 Fast Boats to Kabil
2 Hotel Riau Holiday Indah
3 Main Pier, Ferries to Pekanbaru, Sekupang & Singapore
4 Wisma Sri Pinang
5 Hotel Tanjung Pinang
6 Taxi Stand
7 Chinese Temple
8 Dasa Moneychanger
9 Shipping Agents
10 Post Office
11 Police Station
12 Sempati Airlines
13 Souvenir Shop
14 Johnny's Homestay
15 Bong's Homestay
16 Bank Dagang Negara
17 Buses To Tanjung Uban
18 Merpati, Garuda
19 Hotel Surya
20 Wisma Riau
21 Sempurna Inn
22 Hotel Sampurna Jaya
23 Stadium
24 Flipper & Sunkist Restaurants
25 Penginapan Sondang
26 Bank Indonesia Negara
27 Mosque

Pejantan I
Pejantan II

Boats to Penyenget Island

Jalan Pasar Ikan
Lorong Merdeka
Jalan Pos
Jalan Merdeka
Jalan Gambir Baru
Jalan Kelapong
Lorong Bintan I
Jalan Teuku Umar
Lorong Bintan II
Jalan Bintan
Jalan Samudra
Jalan Yusuf Khahar
Jalan Teratai
Jalan Temiang
Jalan Merdeka
Jalan Hangtuah
Jalan Tabib
Jalan Masjid
Jalan Geerja
Jalan Bakar Batu

To Museum Riau Kandil Airport Kijang, Tanjung Uban & Pantai Trikora

0   125   250 m

cultural role in the history of the Riau as one of the two seats of government.

It is believed to have been given to Sultan Raja Riau-Lingga VI in 1805 by his brother-in-law Sultan Mahmud Lingga-Riau IV as a wedding present. The place is littered with reminders of its past and there are ruins and graveyards wherever you walk.

When you arrive at the island, you'll see a road close to where the sampan lands. Turn right and head off to the north-east – most of the kampungs are along the shoreline but the ruins of the **old palace** of Raja Ali and the **tombs and graveyards** of Raja Jaafar and Raja Ali are slightly further inland. All the main sites are marked with small plaques and inscriptions.

The sulphur-coloured **mosque** with its forest of domes (13 of them), pillars and minarets, houses a library which contains hundreds of tomes on history, culture, law, languages and religions – included are five handwritten and illustrated copies of the *Koran*. The ruins of an imposing old house, now completely overgrown with vines and creepers, is also appealing.

Boats from the town's main pier shuttle over to the island at a cost of 500 rp per person. Tell officials where you're going and you won't have to pay the harbour tax. There are always boats going over there, so there's no need to charter. There's a 500 rp entry charge on weekends. You won't be allowed into the mosque if you're wearing shorts or a short skirt.

Across the Harbour Across the river from the town is the village of **Senggarang**. Walk up the pier and turn left to a building totally overgrown by a banyan tree and now used as a Chinese temple. Continue half a km along the waterfront to a big square fronting three side-by-side Chinese temple. It's only a short sampan ride to Senggarang from Tanjung Pinang but is much further by road.

A sampan can also take you up the **Snake River** through the mangroves to another Chinese temple with its graphically gory murals on the trials and tortures of hell.

Places to Stay At the end of Lorong Bintan II, which runs off Jalan Bintan in the centre of town, is the very popular *Bong's Homestay* at No 20. A bed costs 3000 rp, includes breakfast and the friendly Mr and Mrs Bong make this a great place to stay. Next door, at No 22, *Johnny's Homestay* is a good overflow.

The *Hotel Surya* (☎ 21811/293) on Jalan Bintan is a good average losmen with singles/doubles at 11,500/15,000 rp or 17,500 rp with bath. Around the corner on Jalan Yusuf Khahar, the *Penginapan Sondang* is very bare, basic and costs from 10,000 to 12,500 rp.

There's a string of mid-range places on Jalan Yusuf Khahar including the simple but modern *Sampurna Inn* where rooms cost from 15,000 rp with fan or from 25,000 to 45,000 rp with air-con.

Places to Eat Tanjung Pinang has a superb night market with a tantalising array of food stalls offering delicious food at bargain prices. A meal typically costs 1800 to 2500 rp. It sets up in the bus & taxi station on Jalan Teuku Umar. More night-time food stalls can be found at the Jalan Pos and Lorong Merdeka intersection.

During the day, there are several pleasant cafes with outdoor eating areas in front of the stadium (Kaca Puri) on Jalan Teuku Umar. Try *Flipper* or *Sunkist*.

Getting There & Away Following are details of transport to and from Bintan Island.

To/From Singapore Some of the same high-speed ferries and catamarans which service Batam from Singapore also go to Tanjung Pinang. One way fares cost around S\$40 to S\$55 and a return is around S\$80. From Tanjung Pinang to Singapore, fares seem to vary from around 31,000 rp to 50,000 rp.

To/From Batam Island See Batam Getting There & Away section for information on boats between Bintan and Batam islands.

To/From Java & Sumatra Bintan's airport is much smaller than Batam's, there are fewer flights and they operate with smaller aircraft. The Jakarta flight (177,450 rp with Sempati and 198,500 rp with Merpati) is often booked up a week ahead. In that case, the easiest alternative is to backtrack to Batam. You can easily get from Tanjung Pinang to Kabil by ferry and on to the airport by taxi in less than two hours. Despite modern phone connections Garuda charge 5000 rp to make a flight booking for Bintan and they need a day to do it!

For the journey from Tanjung Pinang to Pakanbaru in Sumatra see Singapore to Sumatra via the Riau in the Sumatra Getting There & Away section.

Boats also operate west to Tanjung Balai (16,500 rp) and south to Dabo, Singkep Island (15,500 rp).

Pelni has resumed its service through Tanjung Pinang with the ship KM *Lawit*. Ekonomi class (the old deck class) costs 32,000 rp to Jakarta and 31,000 rp to Belawan (Medan). Sailings are from Kijang, the port at the south-eastern corner of the island.

Getting Around Buses to other parts of Bintan, including Tanjung Uban for the cheap boat to Kabil, operate from the bus-cum-taxi station on Jalan Teuku Umar. The Tanjung Uban bus costs 3000 rp and takes two hours. The Kijang bus costs about 1100 rp.

Public motorbikes, known as *ojeks*, are the favourite form of local transport. You can recognise them by the yellow construction worker helmets worn by their riders. Around town a ride costs about 250 rp. There are also some local oplets around town, they also cost from 250 rp.

You can rent motorbikes from PT Info Travel on the main wharf for 25,000 rp a day. Other places may be cheaper, particularly by the day rather than 24 hours.

AROUND THE ISLAND
Beaches
Bintan's beaches are relatively untouched apart from the inevitable overlay of bottles

and other driftplastic. There's a fine 30-km-long beach strip along the east coast, although getting there can be a problem. **Pantai Trikora** is the main east coast beach with some accommodation. Snorkelling is fine most of the year except during the November to March monsoon period.

Off the north-east end of the island, a sunken 1754 Dutch VOC (Vereenigde Oost-Indische Compagnie) vessel was, to the considerable consternation of the Indonesian authorities, discovered and salvaged in the mid-80s by a team of scuba divers.

Places to Stay *Yasin's Guest House*, at the Km 46 marker, has simple wooden huts with a bed, mosquito nets, verandah and not much else. It's situated on a beach cum trash heap and costs 15,000 rp per day including three meals. At the Km 38 marker, the flashier *Trikora Country Club* at Pantai Trikora has singles from S\$50 to S\$70 and doubles from S\$60 to S\$80.

Getting There & Away The main beach stretch is 40 to 50 km from Tanjung Pinang. Getting there costs 4000 rp per person by the share taxis which mainly operate in the morning.

Other Attractions
Bintan is fairly flat except for the peaks Gunung Bintan Besar and Gunung Kijang. You can climb 348-metre **Gunung Bintan Besar**, although getting there and getting permission is not easy. Other nearby islands include **Pulau Mapor** and the tiny **Pulau Terkulai**, where the lighthouse keeper lives in solitary splendour – the trip out takes about 20 minutes.

OTHER RIAU ISLANDS
Galang
Not far from Bintan, this island is a detention centre for Vietnamese and Cambodian boat people.

Singkep
Well to the south of Tanjung Pinang, Singkep is the third largest island in the archipelago. It has a big Chinese population and is the

headquarters of Riau Tin and Timah mining companies. Few outsiders visit here, but it's fairly easy to get to and has most of the services of a much larger place.

Dabo, the main town, is shaded by lush trees and gardens and is clustered around a central park. Nearby, and on the road to Sungeibuluh, there is a big **mosque** which dominates the skyline. **Batu Bedua**, not far out of town, is a white sand beach fringed with palms. It's a good place to spend a relaxing few hours and there are a couple of others nearby called **Sergang** and **Jago**. You get fine views if you walk to the top of the hill just past the residential district of Bukit Asem.

Information Bank Dagang Negara changes money at quite good rates. The post office is on Jalan Pahlawan and there is also an overseas telephone office about three km out of town on the road to Sungeibuluh.

The fish and vegetable markets down near the harbour are interesting and among the best places in town to buy fresh, cheap food. Jalan Pasar Lamar is a good browsing and shopping area – if you need any snorkelling equipment, try Toko Aneka Tekni on Jalan Merdeka.

Every Saturday night at Taman Seni, classical Malay theatre is performed. The acting is very stylised and ritualistic and the costumes are elaborate and ornate.

Places to Stay & Eat *Penginapan Sri Indah* on Jalan Perusahaan has rooms from 10,000 rp. It's spotlessly clean and has a comfortable sitting-room. On the opposite side of the street and a bit north is *Penginapan Garupa Singkep* with rooms from 7000 rp. Also, there's the more expensive *Wisma Timah* on Jalan Penuba.

Eat at the markets behind Penginapan Sri Indah or try any of the warungs on Jalan Pasar Lama and Jalan Merdeka. Food stalls and warungs pop up all over the place at night. Try the *Wisma Timah* if you want a drink.

Getting There & Away The boat trip from Tanjung Pinang takes about 11 hours, costs 15,500 rp, crosses the equator and passes several shimmering islands on the way. For 17,500 rp you can take the faster MV *Sinar* which takes four hours. Singkep has an airport five km out of town.

Getting Around There are plenty of microbuses or becaks for getting around, but they're expensive and you can walk to most places.

South Sumatra

Bakauheni is now the arrival port when coming from Java. Panjang, formerly the main arrival port, has been closed. Trains arrive and depart from Tanjungkarang while Rajabasa has the main bus depot. Both of these are in the city of Bandarlampung.

PALEMBANG
Standing on the Musi River, only 50 km upstream from the sea, Palembang made an abrupt leap into the 20th century when oil was discovered in Sumatra earlier this century. Palembang quickly became the main export outlet for south Sumatra, and today it is a heavily industrialised city with tin mining operations and a petrochemical refinery. It's also the capital of south Sumatra but as it's a rather dull place to visit it attracts few travellers.

A thousand years ago, Palembang was the centre of the highly developed Srivijaya civilisation but, unfortunately, few relics remain from this period. There are a number of sculptures to be seen and no monuments or architecture of note – nor is there much of interest from the early 18th century when Palembang was an Islamic kingdom. Most of the buildings of the latter era were destroyed in battles with the Dutch – the last battle was in 1811.

Coming into Palembang from the south, you pass plantations of rubber, coffee, pepper and pineapples. In complete contrast are the smokestacks of the Sungai Gerong refinery and the petrochemical complex at Plaju, which impart a kind of futuristic look to the landscape, particularly at night.

Orientation & Information
The city is split in half by the Musi River and sprawls along both banks. The two halves of the city are connected by the Ampera Bridge, only built in the mid-60s. A hotchpotch of wooden houses on stilts crowd both banks, but the south side, known as Ulu, is where the majority of people live.

The 'better half', Ilir, is on the north bank and there you find most of the government offices, shops, hotels and the wealthy residential districts. Jalan Sudirman is the main street of town, running right on to the bridge.

Tourist Office The Palembang city tourist office (☎ 28450) is at the Museum Sultan Machmud Badaruddin II on Jalan Sudirman.

Money There are various bank branches including the Bank Bumi Daya on Jalan Sudirman and the Bank Ekspor Impor on Jalan T P Rustam Effendy. Dharma Perdana, a moneychanger at Jalan Kol Atmo 446, is open from 8 am to 5 pm Monday to Saturday.

Post The post office is close to the river and the Grand Mosque.

Things to See
There is very little reason to hang around in Palembang. It's not an interesting city to wander around and there's very little to see.

Museum The Museum Sumatera Selatan is about five km out from the town centre, off the airport and Jambi road. Take a Km 5 oplet and look for the signs just beyond the Jambi bus depots. The museum is several hundred metres off the road to the left, on Jalan Srivijaya, and is open Tuesday to Thursday from 8 am to 2 pm, Friday from 8 to 11 am, Saturday from 8 am to 12 noon and Sunday from 9 am to 3 pm.

It really doesn't have much of interest apart from the traditional Sumatran house, or Rumah Bari.

Around Town In town, there's a floating market which operates like an extension of the main market **Pasar Ilir**. There's usually lots of activity on the river and you can overlook it from the **Ampera Bridge**. Near the bridge and the Ampera oplet station is the **Museum Sultan Machmud Badaruddin II**. There are three rooms, each showing a different traditional room of Palembang royalty. They are in the process of upgrading the museum and the exhibits. Behind it is a curious monument and then the large and imposing **Grand Mosque**, built by Sultan Machmud Badaruddin in the 18th century.

Further Afield You can hire a boat and take a look at the **Chinese temple** on Kemaro Island. It's near the junction of the Musi, Oghan and Komering rivers. About 100 years old, its architectural design and ornamentation could only be Chinese, and statues of dragons and monkeys guard the entrance. You can also take a boat up to the refinery, **Sungai Gerong**, if you're interested. Or, cross the river and take an oplet to **Kayuagung** on the banks of the Komering to see the local pottery manufacture. Boats go from right by the bridge.

Places to Stay
Cheap hotels in Palembang are nothing special. At Jalan Sudirman 45E, close to the intersection with Jalan Diponegoro, the *Hotel Asiana* is bare and basic with single/double rooms at 6000/9000 rp. It's clean and not as noisy as it might be as it's elevated.

When heading north-east, turn left off Jalan Iskandar into Jalan Kol Atmo and then right into Jalan Dempo (opposite the big King's Hotel), and you'll find *Penginapan Riau* (☎ 22011) at Jalan Dempo 409C. Rooms here are 7500 rp.

Continue along Jalan Dempo (the name changes to Jalan Lematang) which bends back to cross Jalan Iskandar, and where it joins Jalan Segaran is the *Hotel Segaran* at Jalan Segaran 207C. It is another decidedly bottom-end hotel with rooms from around

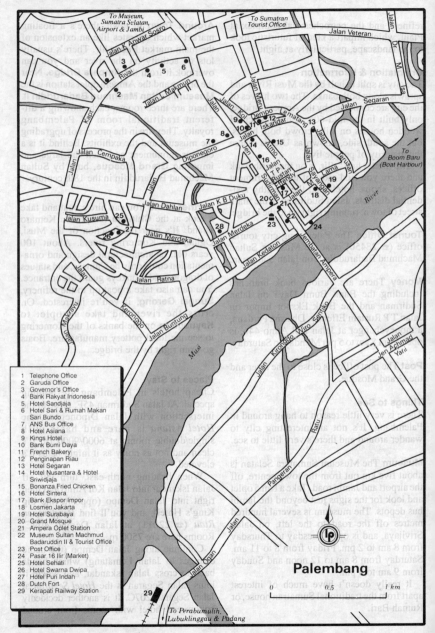

1   Telephone Office
2   Garuda Office
3   Governor's Office
4   Bank Rakyat Indonesia
5   Hotel Sandjaja
6   Hotel Sari & Rumah Makan
    Sari Bundo
7   ANS Bus Office
8   Hotel Asiana
9   Kings Hotel
10 Bank Bumi Daya
11 French Bakery
12 Penginapan Riau
13 Hotel Segaran
14 Hotel Nusantara & Hotel
    Sriwidjaja
15 Bonanza Fried Chicken
16 Hotel Sintera
17 Bank Ekspor Impor
18 Losmen Jakarta
19 Hotel Surabaya
20 Grand Mosque
21 Ampera Oplet Station
22 Museum Sultan Machmud
    Badaruddin II & Tourist Office
23 Post Office
24 Pasar 16 Ilir (Market)
25 Hotel Sehati
26 Hotel Swarna Dwipa
27 Hotel Puri Indah
28 Dutch Fort
29 Kerapati Railway Station

Palembang

0   0.5   1 km

6000 rp. The street numbers of Jalan Segaran follow no discernible pattern.

Almost down to the river at Jalan Sayangan 769, *Losmen Jakarta* is also cheap at 5000/9000 rp but this is a real rock-bottom, survival-only place. Across the road at No 669, *Hotel Surabaya* (☎ 26874) has rooms at 17,500 rp with fan or 25,000 rp with air-con.

There are numerous mid-range hotels including the Surabaya, already mentioned. At Jalan Iskandar 31/48, close to the inter-section with Jalan Sudirman, *Hotel Sriwidjaja* (☎ 24193) has rooms from 13,000 to 14,470 rp with fan, from 25,410 to 36,900 rp with air-con and all include breakfast. At Jalan Iskandar 17, in the same little alley off the main road, *Hotel Nusantara* (☎ 23306) has rooms at 14,000 rp with fan or 25,000 rp with air-con.

Places to Eat

At night, Jalan Sajangan, parallel to Jalan Sudirman, is crowded with Chinese food stands and satay places. This is a great area to eat with some excellent food. Round the corner on Jalan T P Rustam Effendy, there are fruit stalls and stands selling pisang goreng (fried bananas) and other snacks.

On Jalan Iskandar, near Jalan Sudirman, there are a cluster of places including *Yohan Bakery & Fried Chicken* and the *Warna Warni* ice-cream parlour next door. There are a number of bakeries around the centre which also do mee, or noodle, dishes and other simple meals. You'll find them along Jalan Sudirman. Or, try the *French Bakery* at Jalan Kol Atmo 481B, opposite King's Hotel.

Nasi padang restaurants can be found all over town, the *Rumah Makan Sari Bundo* on the corner of Jalan Sudirman and Jalan Kapitan Rivai is good, but more expensive. Finally, *Bonanza Fried Chicken* is Palem-bang's closest thing to a Western fast-food joint. It's upstairs at Jalan Kol Atmo 425, in the 'Yuppies Centre'!

Getting There & Away

Few travellers bother with Palembang as it's off the Trans-Sumatran Highway; you can skip right by it on a direct Jakarta to Padang bus; fly right over it; or, take the Jakarta to Padang ship and sail right around it.

Air If you do want to fly to Palembang there are regular flights with Garuda/Merpati. Merpati have two offices on Jalan Kapitan Rivai, in the Sandjaja Hotel and a little further along the road.

Bus ANS is at Jalan Iskandar 903C, just off Jalan Sudirman. Other bus companies are in the same area. There are frequent departures for Jakarta and the 20-hour trip costs 18,000 rp, or 30,000 rp with air-con. ANS have a bus to Padang at 1 pm daily – it takes 24 hours and costs 17,500 rp, or 21,000 rp with air-con. Jambi buses run from around the Km 4½ to Km 5 marker north of town towards the airport and cost 6000 rp.

Train The Kertapati railway station is on the south side of the river, eight km from the town centre.

Boat A regular daily boat operates from Palembang to Muntok, Bangka Island. The air-con boat takes 2½ hours and is 20,000 rp.

Getting Around

To/From the Airport The Talang Betutu Airport is 12 km north of town and a taxi costs a standard 10,000 rp from here to town. The road runs right in front of the terminal and you can get into town on a Talang Betutu-Ampera oplet for 400 rp.

Local Transport Oplets around town cost a standard 150 rp. Most routes start or finish at Amerapa, the oplet stop at the northern end of the Ampera Bridge. Take a Kertapati oplet for the railway station or a Km 5 oplet for the Jambi buses and the nearby museum.

JAMBI

There's nothing much to be said for this unexciting riverine town – it's just there. The surrounding province, however, is populated by a polyglot mix of Chinese, Arabs, Malays,

Minangkabaus, Bataks and the original inhabitants of Jambi, the forest-dwelling Kubus.

The tourist office (☎ 25330) is on Jalan Basuki Rachmat in Kota Bharu.

The **Museum of Jambi** is on the corner Jalan Urip Sumobaryo & Jalan Dr Sri Sudewi. It is small but interesting museum which exhibits tools, costumes and handicrafts from Jambi Province and some Hindu sculptures.

The **Muara Jambi Temples** are 25 km from Jambi and can easily be visited in one day. The easiest way to see them is by boat – on Sunday there are public boats for 5000 rp for a return trip, otherwise it costs 25,000 rp to charter a boat.

Places to Stay & Eat

The cheaper places are generally drab and unpleasant and the more expensive ones are...more expensive. The *Mustika* on the Padang and Palembang side of town has dirty rooms for 10,000 rp. Try also the *Mutiara*, slightly closer to the town centre. In the centre itself, the *Sumatera* at Jalan Kartini 73 and the *Jelita* are cheaper at 7500 rp. *Hotel Pinang*, Jalan Dr Sutomo, has basic but more pleasant rooms for 16,500 rp and *Hotel Merpati Inn* (☎ 24861), Jalan Y Leimena 71, has rooms for 5000 rp or 6000 rp with mandi.

Of course, nasi padang is what you'll find to eat, and there are two branches of the *Simpang Raya* restaurants at Jalan Wahidin 11 and Jalan Thamrin 22. There are also lots of stalls selling slices of chilled fruit, including delicious pineapple. *Safari* at Jalan Veteran 29 is also worth a try.

Getting There & Away

Like Palembang, the Trans-Sumatran Highway does not run through Jambi so it requires a definite decision to go there. Garuda flies to Jambi regularly, connecting directly with Jakarta and to other centres via Palembang. Buses to and from Palembang cost 6000 rp. From Jambi, you can continue on to Padang.

BENGKULU (Bencoolen)

Bengkulu was Raffles' foot in the door to Indonesia but this British attempt to displace the Dutch was half-hearted and never really successful. The British actually first established themselves here in 1685. Raffles didn't arrive until 1818 but, in 1824, Bengkulu was traded for Melaka on the Malay coast. From then on the British and Dutch stared at each other across the Melaka Straits.

There are still some reminders of the British presence in Bengkulu but overall the town is of little interest and, like Palembang and Jambi, getting there requires a detour off the Trans-Sumatran Highway.

Orientation & Information

Although Bengkulu is right by the sea, it only really touches it near Fort Marlborough. Otherwise, the town is set back from the coast. Jalan Suprapto and the nearby Pasar Minggu Besar are the modern 'town centre', separated from the old town area around Fort Marlborough by the long, straight Jalan Achmad Yani. The coast is surprisingly quiet, rural and only a km or so from the centre.

The post office and telephone office are opposite Pasar Barukoto, near the fort. There's another telephone office on Jalan Suprapto near the modern town centre but it's open shorter hours.

Things to See

Fort Marlborough Raffles' fort, Benteng Marlborough, was originally built between 1714 and 1719. It was restored in 1983 and reopened to the public in 1984 after a long period of use by the army. There's a few small and uninteresting exhibits about the restoration, together with a pile of cannonballs and a couple of old British gravestones; admission is 100 rp.

Bengkulu has a few other British reminders including the **Thomas Parr Monument** in front of the Pasar Barukoto and a couple of 'Monumen Inggris'. The one near the beach is to Captain Robert Hamilton who died in 1793, 'in command of the troops'.

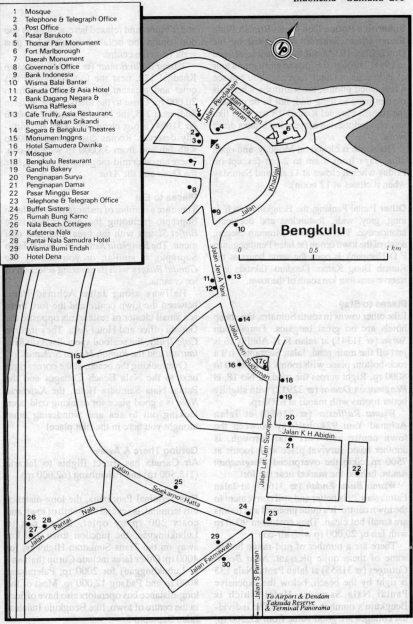

1	Mosque
2	Telephone & Telegraph Office
3	Post Office
4	Pasar Barukoto
5	Thomar Parr Monument
6	Fort Marlborough
7	Daerah Monument
8	Governor's Office
9	Bank Indonesia
10	Wisma Balai Bantar
11	Garuda Office & Asia Hotel
12	Bank Dagang Negara & Wisma Rafflesia
13	Cafe Trully, Asia Restaurant, Rumah Makan Srikandi
14	Segara & Bengkulu Theatres
15	Monumen Inggris
16	Hotel Samudera Dwinka
17	Mosque
18	Bengkulu Restaurant
19	Gandhi Bakery
20	Penginapan Surya
21	Penginapan Damai
22	Pasar Minggu Besar
23	Telephone & Telegraph Office
24	Buffet Sisters
25	Rumah Bung Karno
26	Nala Beach Cottages
27	Kafeteria Nala
28	Pantai Nala Samudra Hotel
29	Wisma Bumi Endah
30	Hotel Dena

Bengkulu

0   0.5   1 km

To Airport & Dendam
Taksuda Reserve
& Terminal Panorama

Sukarno's House Don't miss Rumah Bung Karno where Sukarno was exiled by the Dutch from 1938 until the Japanese arrived in 1941. Through the '30s he had a grand tour of Indonesia at Dutch expense. You can see a few faded photos, the wardrobe where his clothes used to hang and, not to be missed, the Bung's bicycle! Rusted it's true, but like any real Indonesian bicycle the brakes don't work.

His house is closed on Monday, and open other days from 8 am to 2 pm (except on Friday when it closes at 11 am and Saturday when it closes at 12 noon).

Other Pantai Panjang, the Bengkulu beach, is long, grey, wide, featureless and decidedly unattractive. The Bengkulu Museum Negeri, south of the town centre (at Jalan Pembangunan P D Harapan), is open the same hours as the Rumah Bung Karno. Dendam Taksuda is a reserve area four km south of the town.

Places to Stay
Like other towns in south Sumatra, the cheap hotels are no great bargains. *Penginapan Surya* (☎ 31341) at Jalan K H Abidin 26 is just off the main road, Jalan Suprapto. It's a rock-bottom place with rooms from 4500 to 8000 rp. Right across the road, at No 18, is *Penginapan Damai* (☎ 32912) with slightly better rooms with mandi at 6500 rp.

Wisma Rafflesia (☎ 31650) at Jalan Achmad Yani 924, halfway between the town centre and Fort Marlborough, is another basic survival place with rooms at 7500 rp. Skip the overpriced *Penginapan Aman*, behind the market near the fort.

Wisma Bumi Endah (☎ 31665) at Jalan Fatmawati 29 is better and still convenient to the town centre. It's quite pleasant and rooms are small but clean. They cost from 9000 rp with fan or 20,000 rp with air-con.

There are a number of mid-range hotels, some of them quite pleasant. *Nala Beach Cottages* (☎ 31855) at Jalan Pantai Nala 133 is right by the beach, below the expensive Pantai Nala Samudra Hotel which is Bengkulu's number-one hotel. The individual cottages are good value from 22,500 rp,

and it's quiet and relaxed here, so long as you don't mind the isolation as it's a km plus walk from the centre.

Wisma Balai Bantar (☎ 31254) is at Jalan Khadijal 122, near the fort. Rooms at this quiet and pleasant guest house cost from 20,000 rp. Close to the town centre, at Jalan Sudirman 245, the *Hotel Samudera Dwinka* (☎ 31604) is big, clean, well-kept and virtually deserted. Rooms cost from 18,000 rp with fan and from 33,000 rp with air-con. There are other mid-range hotels around, like the *Dena* and the *Asia*.

Places to Eat
There are a number of restaurants along Jalan Suprapto including the neat, clean little *Buffet Sisters* with the usual mee and nasi menu. The *Bengkulu Restoran*, also on Jalan Suprapto, is similar, or you can try the *Gandhi Bakery* with its amazing selection of ice creams.

Halfway along Jalan Achmad Yani, between the town centre and the fort, there is a small cluster of restaurants opposite the Garuda office and Hotel Asia. They include *Cafe Trully*, the seafood specialist *Asia Restaurant* and the *Rumah Makan Srikandi*.

Overlooking the beach, at the corner right next to the Nala Beach Cottages and the Pantai Nala Samudra Hotel, the *Kafeteria Nala* is a good place for drinking cold beer, looking out to sea and wondering what brought you here in the first place!

Getting There & Away
Air Garuda has direct flights to Jakarta (115,500 rp) and Palembang (62,000 rp).

Bus Terminal Panorama, the long-distance bus terminal, is several km south of town and costs 200 rp by oplet. Buses run to Lubuklinggau, the junction town 110 km away on the Trans-Sumatran Highway, for 4000 rp. Other fares include Curup (halfway to Lubuklinggau) for 2000 rp, Palembang 8000 rp and Padang 12,000 rp. Most of the long-distance bus operators also have offices in the centre of town, like Bengkulu Indah at Jalan Suprapto 5.

Boat The harbour below Fort Marlborough is just for small boats and fishing boats, the main harbour is 15 or so km south, beyond the airport. Sometimes you can catch ships going to Padang.

Getting Around

To/From the Airport The airport is 14 km south of town and the standard taxi fare is 6000 rp. You can walk 100 metres out to the road from where you should be able to get a bemo or bus into Bengkulu. The 200 rp microlets run out as far as Km 8 but make sure any vehicle that picks you up from there doesn't decide it's a chartered taxi.

Local Transport There are countless tiny microlets shuttling around town at a standard fare of 100 rp.

KERINCI

Kerinci is a mountain valley accessible by bus from either Jambi or Padang – the road from Padang is more beautiful and also a better road. It's a rich, green area with two very dominating features – **Gunung Kerinci**, the highest mountain in the Sumatra-Sunda island chain and **Danau Kerinci**, a lake at the other end of the valley. **Sungai Penuh** is the largest town with some 200 small villages in the area. Its matrilineal social structure is similar to that found in west Sumatra.

Things to See & Do

In Sungai Penuh there is a large, pagoda-style **mosque** with carved beams and old Dutch tiles. It is said to be over 400 years old but you need permission to go inside. **Dusun Sungai Tetung** is nationally renowned for its basket weaving. All over the area there are stone carvings which have not really been carefully investigated. Locals have a legend of a great kingdom here a long time ago. The carvings are very different from those of the Majapahit or Srivijaya areas. It's easy to find a cheap guide for day trips from Sungai Penuh.

Tours around the lake are good and the best starting points are at **Jujun** or **Keluru**

(20 km from Sungai Penuh and half a km apart). Make sure to ask to see **Batu Gong**. About 40 km out of Sungai Penuh, on the way to Gunung Kerinci, there is a tea plantation called **Kayo Aro**, worth going to see if you've never been over one before. There are hot springs nearby – too hot for swimming in the main pool, but you can get a private room with a hot mandi.

Watch for tigers as there are said to be many still around. If you are lucky you might be able to catch a magic dance or a pencak silat performance.

This was the last area to fall to the Dutch in 1902, the Japanese had a hard time here and, in Sukarno's time, it was a Communist stronghold – and we know what happened then.

Places to Stay & Eat

In Gunung Kerinci National Park, there is a family living at the base of Gunung Kerinci which takes in guests.

In town, the *Mata Hari Losmen* in Sungai Penuh is cheap and clean. One of the best restaurants in Sungai Penuh is the *Minang Soto*, which has good Padang food and is cheap and clean. For a taste treat, try dendeng batokok, a speciality of the region – these are strips of beef smoked and grilled over a fire and which, someone reported, taste like charcoal.

West Sumatra

PADANG

This is the centre of the matrilineal Minangkabau area where the eldest female is the boss and property is inherited through the female line. Beautiful examples of the high-peaked Minangkabau houses can be seen on the pastoral, tranquil road down to Padang from Solok. As you start the final descent down to Padang there are spectacular sweeping views along the coast.

Orientation & Information

It is easy to find your way around Padang;

the central area is quite compact. Jalan Prof M Yamin – from the bus terminal corner at Jalan Pemuda to Jalan Azizcham – is the main street of town. The main bus terminal and the oplet terminal across from the market are both very centrally located. It's a fairly easy-going town with Chinese making up about 15% of the population.

Tourist Office The tourist information office (☎ 28231) at Jalan Khatib Sulaiman is open from 8 am to 2 pm Monday to Thursday and Saturday, and from 8 to 11 am on Friday. It's a fair way out of the city centre so take an oplet going up Jalan Sudirman and tell them where you're going, or look for a No 269 microlet at the oplet station. The staff are very helpful and several can speak fairly good English.

Money Padang has a phenomenal number of extremely large and imposing banks. Building huge new bank buildings seems to be a current Indonesian craze but it's taken to extremes in Padang. Moneychangers include C V Eka Jasa Utama at Jalan Niaga 241.

Post & Telecommunications You'll find the post office at Jalan Azizcham 7, close to the junction with Jalan Prof M Yamin. Perumtel's telephone office is at Jalan Veteran 47.

Things to See & Do
Padang itself does not have much to offer apart from Padang food, although in the harbour you can see the rusting remains of Dutch ships, sunk by the Japanese when they entered WW II.

Museum In the centre of town, just down the road from the bus station, is the museum on Jalan Diponegoro, built in the Minangkabau tradition with two rice barns out front. It has a small but excellent collection of antiques and other objects of historical and cultural interest from all over west Sumatra – there is a good textile room.

Next door, in the **Cultural Centre**, local, regional, national, traditional and modern music and dances are performed regularly. They also hold poetry readings, plays and exhibitions of paintings and carvings. The museum is open daily (except Monday) from 9 am to 6 pm, and admission is 200 rp.

Beaches At **Bungus**, 22 km south of Padang, is a good beach, palm-fringed and, at one time, postcard pretty – there is now a big Korean timber mill on the beach. Oplets run there and you can hire a perahu and paddle out to a nearby island. The last oplet back to Padang leaves at dusk. Here you can

1	Perumtel Telephone Office
2	New Hotel Tiga Tiga
3	Taman Sari Restaurant
4	Tanpa Nama Restaurant
5	Wisma Mayang Sari
6	Merpati Office
7	Old Tiga Tiga Hotel
8	Mandala Office
9	Cendrawasih Hotel
10	Hang Tuah Hotel
11	Restoran Kubang
12	Oplet Station (Pasar Raya)
13	Roda Baru Restaurant
14	Taxi Stand
15	Hotel Benyamin
16	Bank Dagang Negara
17	Wisma Femina
18	Post Office
19	Police
20	Bank Rakyat Indonesia
21	Hotel Padang
22	Simpang Raya Restaurant
23	Mosque
24	Machudum's Hotel
25	Sriwijaya Hotel
26	Bank Negara Indonesia
27	Pangeran's Hotel
28	Mariani International Hotel
29	Museum
30	Art Centre
31	Hotel Muara
32	New Kartika Hotel
33	Octavia Restaurant
34	Pagi Sore Restaurant
35	Chan's Restaurant
36	Mie Yap Ki
37	Aromey Bakery
38	Chinese Temple

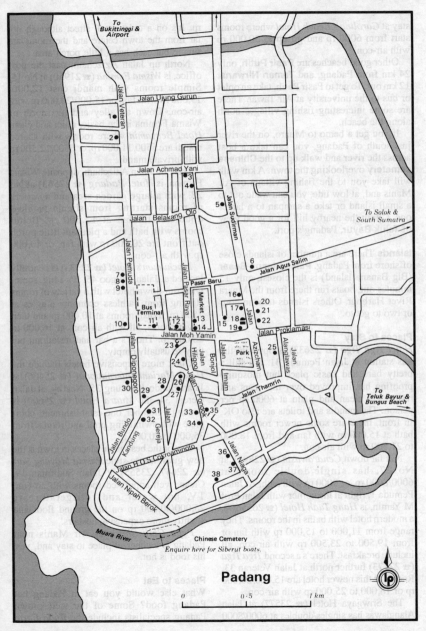

Jalan Ujung Gurun

Jalan Achmad Yani

Jalan Belakang Olo

Jalan Pemuda

Jalan Pasar Raya

Pasar Baru

Market

Jalan Sudirman

Jalan Agus Salim

Jalan Moh Yamin

Jalan Proklamasi

Jalan Diponegoro

Jalan Hiligoo

Jalan Bonjol

Jalan Pondok

Jalan Imam

Park

Azrcham

Jalan Alanglawas

Jalan Thamrin

Jalan Bundo

Jalan Kandung

Jalan Gereja

Jalan H O S Tokroaminoto

Jalan Nipah Berok

Jalan Niaga

To Bukittinggi & Airport

To Solok & South Sumatra

To Teluk Bayur & Bungus Beach

Bus Terminal

Muara River

Chinese Cemetery
Enquire here for Siberut boats.

Padang

0   0·5   1 km

stay at *Carolina's Beach Hotel* where rooms start from 6000 rp and go up to 30,000 rp with air-con.

Other good beaches are **Pasir Putih**, only 24 km from Padang, and **Taman Nirwana**, 12 km out. To get to Pasir Putih, take an oplet or bus to the university at Air Tawar. There are some interesting fishing villages north along the beach.

If you get a bemo to Muaro, on the river just south of Padang, you can take a boat across the river and walk up to the **Chinese cemetery** overlooking the town. A km walk will take you to the fishing village of Air Manis and, at low tide, you can wade out to a small island or take a sampan to a larger one. Climb the nearby hill for a good view of **Teluk Bayur**, Padang's port.

Islands There are a number of islands close offshore from Padang. **Palau Pisang Besar** (Big Banana Island) is the closest, only 15 minutes out; boats run there from the Muara River Harbour. Others islands take an hour or two to get to.

Places to Stay

Hotel Tiga Tiga (☎ 22633) is opposite the bus station at Jalan Pemuda 31. It's still a pretty bare and basic place but mosquito proofing has improved over the years and rooms are clean and plain at 6000 rp per person. The mandis and toilets are also OK. In front, there are some newer rooms with bath at 15,000 rp with fan and from 18,000 to 21,500 rp with air-con.

Not far down, *Cendrawasih* (☎ 22894), at No 27, has single/double rooms at 6000/8000 rp, or 9000 rp with bath. At Jalan Pemuda 1, right at the corner with Jalan Prof M Yamin, is *Hang Tuah Hotel* (☎ 26556/7), a modern hotel with baths in the rooms. They range from 11,000 to 15,000 rp with fan or from 19,500 to 23,500 rp with air-con, all include breakfast. There's a second *Tiga Tiga* (☎ 22173) further north at Jalan Veteran 33. Rooms at this newer hotel are 15,000/20,000 rp or 18,000 to 25,000 rp with air-con.

The Sriwijaya Hotel (☎ 23577) at Jalan Alanglawas has singles/doubles at 6000/8000

rp. It's on a quiet small street although not far from the town centre and the rooms are simple but each has a little porch area.

North up Jalan Azizcham, past the post office, is *Wisma Femina* (☎ 21950) at No 15. Simple rooms with mandi cost 12,000/15,000 rp with fan, or 15,000/20,000 rp with air-con. Down an alley and just north of Wisma Femina is the basic, quiet and clean *Hotel Benyamin* where rooms with shared mandi are 5500/11,000 rp, or 6500/12,500 rp with private mandi.

Back on Jalan Azizcham, opposite Wisma Femina, is *Hotel Padang* (☎ 22563) at No 28, with a large garden area and a variety of rooms starting from simple bathless doubles with fan at 12,500 rp. Better rooms with bath and a pleasant little porch out front are 20,000 rp with fan, or 40,000 rp with air-con.

Machudum's Hotel (☎ 22333) is centrally located at Jalan Hiligoo 45. It's a big, somewhat run-down hotel with a variety of rooms starting from bathless economy singles at 7500 rp, transit rooms at 10,000 rp and then larger rooms, all with air-con, at 16,000 to 28,000 rp. There's a bar and restaurant but they're usually empty.

Other more expensive hotels include the *Hotel Mariani International* (☎ 25466) at Jalan Bundo Kandung 35. Nearby, at Jalan Gereja 34, the *Muara Hotel* (☎ 25600) is Padang's number one-establishment, complete with swimming pool and rooms from 35,000 to 70,000 rp.

One of the best value places in town is the new guest house-style *Wisma Mayang Sari* (☎ 22647, 23555) at Jalan Sudirman 19. Clean, well-appointed rooms with air-con, TV, hot water and refrigerator are 25,000/30,000 rp on the ground floor and slightly more expensive upstairs.

Papa Chili-Chili's at Air Manis near Padang is a cheerful place to stay and, yes, his food is hot.

Places to Eat

What else would you eat in Padang but Padang food? Some of the well-known Padang specialists include the *Roda Baru*, upstairs at Jalan Pasar Raya 6 in the market buildings. *Simpang Raya*, for nasi padang, is at Jalan Azizcham 24, opposite the post office. *Pagi Sore* ('Morning Evening') is down towards the end of Jalan Pondok at No 143.

There are also some Chinese-Indonesian restaurants, particularly along Jalan Pondok and Jalan Niaga. *Restaurant Octavia* at Jalan Pondok 137 is a simple little place with the standard nasi goreng and mee goreng menu. Across the road is *Chan's* at No 94 with ice cream and live music at night and the similar *Ri & Ri* at No 86A. Also, *Mie Yap Ki* on Jalan Niaga has cheap, tasty Chinese noodles.

Towards the end of Jalan Niaga is the *Aromey Bakery* with good baked goods. Or try the *Restoran Kubang* at Jalan Prof M Yamin 138, near the bus terminal. They really turn out the martabaks here and it's a busy scene with tables set up across the pavement and lots of satisfied customers.

There are many small snack stalls operating around the microlet/oplet station in the morning. Or at the opposite extreme, there are several big and fancy restaurants along Jalan Achmad Yani, north of the town centre – like the *Taman Sari* and *Tanpa Nama*.

Getting There & Away

Air Garuda/Merpati and Mandala have flights to and from Padang, you can even arrive in Indonesia at Padang since there is a Garuda connection to Singapore.

The Merpati office (☎ 32010) is at Jalan Sudirman 2. Once a week, they fly from Padang to Rokot on Siberut Island. Mandala (☎ 21979) is at Jalan Pemuda 29A, also opposite the bus station.

Bus Padang bus terminal is conveniently central and there are frequent departures for buses north and south. There are frequent buses to Bukittinggi, the prime destination for travellers passing through Padang. The fare is 1300 rp (1600 rp air-con) and the trip takes two to 2½ hours along a fine road with wonderful scenery. If you arrive in Padang by air there's no need to go into town – the main road, with buses bound for Bukittinggi, is only 100 metres from the terminal.

From the city terminal, buses include Jambi for 7500 rp (12 hours) and Palembang for 18,000 rp (24 hours). To Pakanbaru is 5100 rp, or 7200 rp with air-con, but you go via Bukittinggi. Parapat, again via Bukittinggi is 12,000 rp and Medan is 15,000 rp. All the way to Jakarta costs 21,000 rp, or 33,000 rp with air-con. You can also take long-distance taxis from Padang, check with Natrabu at Jalan Pemuda 29B.

Train The railway line from Padang to Bukittinggi used to be quite an attraction for railway enthusiasts, but now the line is only used as far as Padangpanjang and only for freight trains. You can see some old steam engines parked at Padangpanjang and the line beyond here is spectacular, crossing and recrossing the road, but derelict and overgrown. Tourist groups often charter trains for trips.

Boat The Pelni ship KM *Kerinci* operates a regular Jakarta-Padang-Sibolga service. This is probably the shipping route most frequently used by travellers visiting Indonesia. See the Indonesia Getting Around section or the Sumatra Getting There & Away section for details. The KM *Kerinci* does the Jakarta to Padang trip every two weeks; it takes about 27 hours and costs from 40,200 to 132,700 rp. The Pelni office (☎ 22109) is on Jalan Tanjung Priok, Teluk Bayur.

There are occasional ships from Padang to Bengkulu, Nias or, more regularly, to Siberut Island.

Getting Around

To/From the Airport Padang's Tabing Airport is nine km north of the town centre on the Bukittinggi road. The standard taxi fare into town is 8000 rp but you can walk 100 metres out to the road and catch any oplet heading into town for 150 rp. You may wish to head north straight to Bukittinggi. A taxi to Bukittinggi will cost from 25,000 rp to 30,000 rp.

Local Transport There are numerous oplets and microlets around town. The standard fare is 150 rp in the light and dark blue microlets. A new fleet of metered Asindo taxis ply the streets of Padang for 400 rp flagfall and 400 rp per km. *Bendis* (horsecarts) cost around 750 rp per trip to anywhere in town.

SIBERUT ISLAND

The Mentawai Islands are a chain of islands off the coast of Sumatra from Padang. Further north, in this same chain, is the well-known Nias Island. Siberut is slowly attracting greater numbers of adventurous travellers. There are few facilities for visitors but the island has outstanding beaches, big surf along the long west coast beach and some fine diving opportunities.

The island's isolation has led to a unique culture and some unusual endemic wildlife, including several species of monkey. Unfortunately, despite its scientific interest the wildlife is not easily seen.

Information & Tours

The tourist office in Padang has some limited information about the island. Officially, you need a permit to visit Siberut and the tourist office can issue it in half an hour. *Saving Siberut* is a booklet on this interesting island by the World Wildlife Fund. There is no formal accommodation on the island and travel, once you get there, is difficult.

Most travellers opt for one of the 10-day, US$100 tours on the island offered by various guides in Bukittinggi. The tour price includes guide service and accommodation (in village huts), food (usually prepared by the guide) and transport to and from the island.

Tours usually don't go during the months of June and July when the seas are too rough for safe sailing. May is generally the best month for suitable weather. At anytime of the year you can expect heavy rains on Siberut. The treks usually include plenty of mud-slogging, river crossings and battles with indigenous insects, so it's definitely not a casual hiking experience.

The return on your suffering is the chance to experience unspoiled rainforest and the local culture of Siberut.

Getting There & Away

If you want to try and reach Siberut on your own, there's a boat from Padang to the island, a distance of approximately 150 km, about three times a week. Enquire around the harbour area on the Muara River or at the office of PT Rusco Lines (☎ 21941) at Jalan Bt Arau 31.

The fare is 8000 rp per person for deck class or 11,500 rp for a cabin and the journey takes about 10 hours. Sometimes people get groups together to charter a boat across and back, giving them transport around the coast as well.

PADANG TO BUKITTINGGI

It's a beautiful 90-km trip from Padang to Bukittinggi. There are rice paddies, mountains, Minangkabau houses and plenty of other scenery along the road as well as numerous possible diversions if you're in the mood. **Padangpanjang** is the main town through which the road passes and it has a conservatorium of Minangkabau culture. The Padangpanjang Monday market is worth visiting – it's not as big as Bukittinggi but just as interesting and there are lots of good taste treats.

Around Padangpanjang, at Air Agnat, **bullfights** are held every Tuesday afternoon around 4 pm. In the village of Kota Baru, there's a bullfight on Saturday at 4 pm – they're nothing like those in Spain as there's no bloodshed and the bulls don't get hurt. The fight is known as *adu sapi* and involves two water buffaloes, of roughly the same size and weight, locking horns under the keen eyes of their respective owners.

Most of the fun is in watching the locals make their bets. Once the fight starts it continues until one of the bulls breaks away and runs out of the ring. This usually results in two bulls chasing each other around and the on-lookers running in every direction.

About 45 km south-east of Bukittinggi, turning off the Padangpanjang-Solok road, is the village of Batu Sangkar. Turn off the road towards the village of Pagaruyung (four km distance) and you'll see many **Minangkabau houses**. Along the roadside are **stone tablets** inscribed in Sanskrit.

BUKITTINGGI
This cool, easy-going mountain town is a one of the most popular travellers' centres in Sumatra. Often called Kota Jam Gadang, the Big Ben Town, because of the clocktower that overlooks the large market square, Bukittinggi is also known as Tri Arga or the 'town of three mountains'. It stands at 930 metres above sea level and is encircled by the three majestic mountains – Merapi, Singgalang and Sago. Bukittinggi is a centre for Minangkabau culture and has a small university.

Orientation & Information
The centre of town is compact, and the rusty iron roofs make it look remarkably like hill station towns in India. Like them, the changes in level, connected by steps, initially makes it a little confusing.

Tourist Office The tourist office is beside the market car park, overlooked by the clocktower. They have a few leaflets and brochures on west Sumatra and they are open Monday to Thursday from 8 am to 2 pm, Friday from 8 to 11 am and Saturday from 8 am to 12.30 pm.

Money There's a Bank Negara Indonesia branch in the Pasar Atas Market building and you can also change money at P T Enzet, Jalan Minangkabau 51, by the market. The rate is only a couple of per cent down on the banks.

Things to See & Do
Market Bukittinggi's large and colourful market is crammed with stalls of fruit and vegetables, clothing and handicrafts. Market days are Wednesday and Saturday. There are several interesting antique shops and craft shops in the market streets near the clocktower.

Museum & Zoo On a hilltop site, right in the centre of town, is Taman Bundokanduag, a museum and zoo. The museum, which was built in 1934 by the Dutch 'Controleur' of the district, is a superb example of Minangkabau architecture with its two rice barns (added in 1956) out front. It is the oldest museum in the province and has a good collection of Minangkabau historical and cultural exhibits. There is a 350 rp entry fee to the gardens and zoo and a further 200 rp to the museum.

In contrast to the museum, the zoo is a disgrace. It's a depressing Third World zoo at its appalling worst with sadly neglected, moth-eaten looking animals kept captive in miserable conditions. The accompanying display of disintegrating stuffed animals sums the whole place up.

Fort de Kock Except for the defence moat and a few cannons, not much remains of Bukittinggi's old Fort de Kock. Built during the Padri Wars (1821-37) by the Dutch, it provides fine views out across the town and surrounding countryside from its hilltop position.

Panorama Park & Japanese Caves On the southern edge of the town, Panorama Park overlooks the deep Sianok Canyon that cuts right into Bukittinggi. In the park is the entry to the extensive grid of caves which the Japanese tunnelled out during WW II. Many of the tunnels look out from the cliff faces over the canyon. Entry to the caves, or Lobang Jepang, is 250 rp. At the entrance there's a bas relief showing the Japanese herding the helpless Indonesians inside.

Traditional Performing Arts At least two Minangkabau performance troupes hold local exhibitions of music, dance, folk theatre and *silek*, the Minangkabau martial arts technique (similar to Javanese *silat*). Minangkabau musical arts are unique among Indonesian traditions in the use of polyphony and chordal harmonies – a refreshing change from the linear gamelan sounds of Java and Bali.

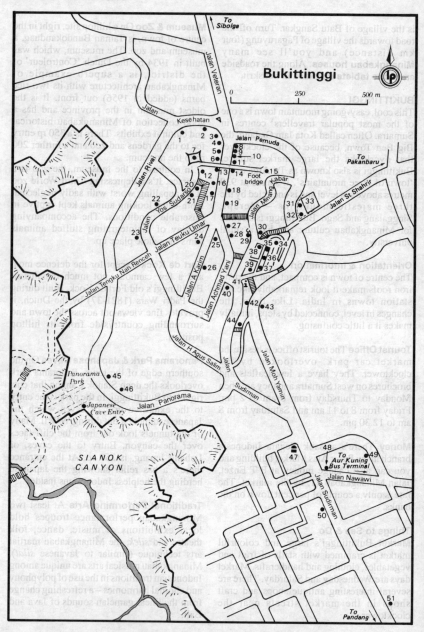

Bukittinggi

0   250   500 m

1	Denai Hotel	27	Gangga Hotel
2	Lima's Hotel	28	Mona Lisa Restaurant
3	Sri Kandi Hotel	29	Mosque
4	Murni's Hotel	30	Gloria Cinema
5	Hotel Nirwana	31	Roda Barn
6	The Coffe Shop	32	Pasar Bawar (Market)
7	Fort de Kock	33	Bemo & Oplet Station
8	Rendezvous Coffee Shop	34	Pasar Wisata
9	Three Tables Coffee House	35	Roda Group Restaurant
10	Mexican Coffee Shop	36	Pasar Atas
11	Singgalang Hotel	37	Bank Negara Indonesia
12	Famili Restaurant	38	Simpang Raya Restaurant
13	Hotel Yany	39	Simpang Raya Restaurant
14	Bukittinggi Coffee Shop	40	Clocktower
15	Zoo & Museum	41	Tourist Office
16	Grand Hotel & 24-hour Telephone Office	42	Jogja Hotel
		43	Hotel Antokan
17	Jazz & Blues Coffee Shop	44	Medan Nan Balituduang (Saliguri Dance Group)
18	Golden Leaf Restaurant		
19	Tigo Balai Hotel	45	Military Museum
20	Benteng Hotel	46	Minang Hotel
21	Suwarni Guest House	47	Post Office
22	Mountain Veiw Guest House	48	Dymens Hotel
23	Wisma Bukittinggi	49	Telephone Office
24	Surya Hotel	50	Bagindo Hotel
25	Singgalang Coffee Shop	51	Police
26	ASEAN Restaurant		

The most professional Bukittinggi troupe is the Saliguri Group, which has its own theatre on Jalan Khatib Sulaiman No 1, close to Hotel Yogya and below the clocktower. Weekly performances begin at 8.30 pm on Sunday, Tuesday and Friday. The show lasts 100 minutes and costs 5000 rp.

There's also a second group, the Saayutu Salangkah, that has performances on Monday, Wednesday, Thursday and Saturday from 8.30 pm, outside the tourist office.

Anyone who is interested in studying Minangkabau arts can write to the Saliguri Group, PO Box 70, Bukittinggi, West Sumatra.

Other Right across the road from Panorama Park is the **Army Museum** with weapons and pictures of the struggle against the Dutch in the 1940s. It's open from 8 am to 4 pm, daily, except on Friday. It closes from 11 am to 1 pm and they ask for a donation.

Places to Stay

Bukittinggi's cheap hotels are a pretty plain, dull and charmless lot, although they're cheap. Most of them are concentrated along Jalan Achmad Yani, right in the centre of town. Working down that street from the top, there's *Murni's* at No 115 which has plain but clean singles/doubles at 3500/5000 rp and a nice sitting area upstairs. The similar *Hotel Nirwana* (☎ 21292) is right next door at No 113. Then across the road, there's the *Singgalang Hotel* (☎ 21576) at Jalan Achmad Yani 130 which is a light and airy place with rooms at 5000 rp.

The *Hotel Yany* (☎ 22740) at No 101 has tiny closet size rooms for 3000 rp and larger rooms with bathrooms (of tiny closet size!) for 6000 rp. The *Grand Hotel* (☎ 2133) at No 99 has rooms in the old building for 3000/5000 rp and in the more modern building for 7500/10,000 rp with private mandi.

Wisma Tigo Balai (☎ 21824) at Jalan Achmad Yani 100 is out of the same rock-bottom mould with rooms at 3500/4000 rp.

The *Gangga Hotel* (☎ 22967) at No 70 costs 2500/4000 rp for basic rooms, better rooms are 5000 rp or 7000 rp with shower. A few steps off Jalan Jen Achmad Yani at Jalan Teuku Umar 7, the *Surya Hotel* (☎ 22587) has rooms from 7500 rp, or from 10,000 rp with bathroom.

There are some other places at lower and higher levels. *Hotel Jogja* (☎ 21142) is directly below the market and clocktower, at Jalan Prof M Yamin 17. There are straightforward rooms upstairs for 7500 rp per person (poor value for two people), downstairs rooms with mandi from 15,000 rp and deluxe rooms from 25,000 rp. Jalan Prof M Yamin is also known as Jalan Perintis Kemerdekaan.

There are several places on the way up to Fort de Kock. The *Mountain View Guest House* (☎ 21621) at Jalan Yos Sudarso 3 is a pleasant place with rooms at 15,000 rp with mandi. Further up the road, next to the Benteng Hotel, is the quiet *Suwarni Guest House* with dorm beds or rooms at 7500 rp.

The *Benteng Hotel*, up towards the top of Fort de Kock hill, is a very pleasant mid-range place with some old-fashioned charm. Economy rooms are 18,000 rp, standard rooms cost from 30,000 rp or deluxe rooms are from 50,000 rp. There's a restaurant and bar and great views over the town. After the Benteng, other mid-range hotels are somewhat overshadowed but *Lima's Hotel* (☎ 22641/763) at Jalan Kesehatan 34 has fairly nice rooms for 17,500 rp. Nearby, *Denai Hotel* is expensive.

Places to Eat

In amongst the cheap hotels along Jalan Achmad Yani are two very popular restaurants with menus which feature all those familiar travellers' specials from fruit salad to banana pancakes. The *Coffee House* at No 103 has a pleasant outdoor area overlooking the street. The newer *Three Tables Coffee House* at No 142 is a bit bigger (there are more than three tables) and equally popular.

They're both travellers' hang-outs but the food is good. They're also useful information sources, if you don't mind dealing with all the guides that stop by to offer their services (once they've talked to you they generally leave you alone).

Off by itself, on Jalan Teuku Umar, is the delightful *Canyon Coffee Shop* with lots of posted info on jungle treks, pig hunts, Pelni travel and the like. The food is also quite good here and you don't see as many would-be guides. Further down at Jalan Achmad Yani 58 is the *Mona Lisa*, a tiny place with a Chinese-influenced menu. The *ASEAN Restaurant* on Jalan A Karim 12A has better Chinese food.

Of course, Padang food is important in Bukittinggi and the *Roda Group Restaurant*, in the Pasar Atas Market building, has good food and a menu, so you know what you're paying for. In the Pasar Wisata building, right next to the Pasar Atas building, there are more restaurants and warungs including a branch of the *Simpang Raya* nasi padang restaurants at each end of the block. They also have a menu, unusual in Padang restaurants. Up on the Fort de Kock hill, right at the top of the road, the *Family Restaurant* (or *Famili*) also does pretty good Padang food.

A number of places in Bukittinggi, including the Western-oriented coffee houses, do the local speciality *dadiah campur*, a tasty mixture of oats, coconut, fruit, molasses and buffalo yoghurt.

Getting There & Away

Padang is only two to 2½ hours south of Bukittinggi, a pleasant trip costing 1300 to 1600 rp. The road north to Sibolga and Parapat is not so easy, although it has improved over the years. These days, regular buses can make the trip to Parapat in 15 hours, although heavy rain (and when it rains in Sumatra it can really rain) may still cause big problems.

The Aur Kuning bus station is some distance from the town centre but you can get there easily on the local oplets. Fares from Bukittinggi include Medan 16,000 rp, Parapat 15,000 rp, Sibolga 9000 rp, Pakanbaru 6000 rp and Dumai 7000 rp. You can get buses through to Bengkulu (10,000 to 15,000 rp), Palembang (15,000 to 18,000 rp) and Jambi (15,000 rp) but most people travel via Padang. Get tickets yourself as there have been various horror stories from people who let Bukittinggi agents get the tickets for them and ended up paying high prices for poor buses.

ANS have an office (☎ 21679) at the terminal. Also reliable is Parindo (☎ 21133) at Jalan Achmad Yani 99. A special tourist minibus operates to Parapat from the Hotel Benteng every Friday. It takes about 20 people, costs 20,000 rp and takes 12 to 13 hours including stops at hot springs and the Equator. Tickets can be booked at a number of places in town. The bus picks up people from travel agents who sell the tickets or from some hotels.

If you're arriving in Bukittinggi from the north (Parapat) or east (Pakanbaru) get off the bus near the town centre, saving the 150 rp oplet ride back from the bus terminal south of the centre.

Getting Around
Oplets around Bukittinggi cost a flat 150 rp. Bendis (horsecarts) cost from 500 to 750 rp depending on the distance.

AROUND BUKITTINGGI
There is a path through the Sianok Canyon to the other side and on to the village of **Koto Gadang**. Turn left at the bottom of the road just before the canyon and keep going. Don't cross the bridge there because if you do its a 12-km walk (instead of a relatively short five-km one). Koto Gadang is noted for its silverwork which, though exquisite, is limited in range. It is about 12 km from Bukittinggi.

There are several other villages around Bukittinggi which are still producing traditional crafts, one of the more interesting being **Pandai Sikat**, 13 km away, a centre for weaving and wood carving.

Ngalau Kamanga, 15 km to the east of Bukittinggi, was the scene of armed resistance against the Dutch in the 19th and early 20th centuries. Apparently, the villagers used a 1500-metre-long local cave as a hideout from the Dutch and conducted effective

guerrilla attacks in the surrounding country from this base. The cave is dripping with stalactites and stalagmites and has a small, clear lake.

There is a **Rafflesia sanctuary** about 15 km north of town and a sign at the village of Batang Palupuh indicates the path. Rafflesia are giant, cabbage-sized flowers named after Sir Stamford Raffles. The Rafflesia bloom between August and December. Further north, on the way to Sibolga, a large globe which indicates the position of the equator stands in a rice paddy beside the road.

Lake Maninjau
About 30 km south-west of Bukittinggi is Lawang Top and, directly below it, Lake Maninjau. Lake Maninjau is warmer than Toba and is an extremely beautiful crater lake. You can zip around it by speedboat or water scooter if you wish. The final 12 km descent to the lake twists and turns through 44 numbered hairpin bends.

You can catch a bus there directly from Bukittinggi or get off at Matur, climb to Lawang for the view and then walk down to the lake, which takes a couple of hours if you're fit but is much longer if you're not. If you miss the last bus, you either have to charter a bemo back – which can be expensive – or spend the night there.

Places to Stay & Eat Most guest houses are basic but good, with friendly owners. One of the best is *Beach Guest House* with rooms for 3000 rp per person and bungalows, on the edge of the lake, for 6000 rp. *Amai Guest House* in the centre of the village is an old teak house with large rooms from 3000/4000 and 5000 rp.

Pasir Panjang Permai is about one km from the centre of town but better value with rooms starting from 35,000/45,000 rp. All rooms overlook the lake and there are hot/cold showers and TV. *Palantha Guest House*, which is past the Pasir Panjang Permai Hotel, is a popular place to stay with rooms from 3000/4000 rp. The *Maninjau Indah* is another up-market hotel but it is starting to look a bit run-down. The *Coffee*

House Losmen and *Pilli Guest House* are far cheaper with rooms from 4000 to 6000 rp.

The *Three Tables Coffee House* and *Sri Kandi* are the best places to eat.

PAKANBARU

Pakanbaru is a grubby oil town with a sleazy port. There's no particular attraction to the place and it's simply somewhere to pass through on the way to or from Singapore via the Riau Archipelago. Catch a boat down river the day you arrive in Pakanbaru if you're on your way by boat to the Riau or get a bus straight out if you're heading for Bukittinggi.

Information

There is no tourist office as such – the local government department in the Governor's office (☎ 25301) on the corner of Jalan Gajah Mada 200 and Diponegoro handles this service. You can change money at the airport, in Bank Negara Indonesia at Jalan Sudirman 63 or in Toko Firmas at Jalan Sudirman 27.

Places to Stay

If you have to stay overnight, there are numerous losmen around the bus terminal on Jalan Nangka. *Penginapan Linda*, with clean rooms from 7500 rp, is one of the better places in this area. If you're departing by boat, there are a couple of run-down and depressing hotels with little to recommend them except for their proximity to the port. The *Nirmala* at Jalan Yatim 11 is typical with rooms from 4000 rp.

A better possibility is *Tommy's Place* (Rustami's), half a km from the bus station on Gang Nantongga at Jalan Nangka 41D. Rooms cost 2500 rp per person and include breakfast. From the bus station, turn right and Gang Nantongga is the second gang on your right side. Walk down it and keep asking for Tommy's until you get to it.

Other places to try in Pakanbaru are the *Hotel Cempaka* on Jalan H Wahid Hasyim, the *Hotel Dharma Utama* on Jalan Sisingamangaraja, or the *Hotel Tunteja II* on the same road. The *Asia Hotel*, in the town centre, has rooms at 4000 rp and is small, clean, dark and old!

Getting There & Away

To Singapore, you have a choice of flying directly with Garuda, flying to Tanjung Pinang (Merpati) or Batam (Garuda), or making the same trip by boat. See the Sumatra Getting There & Away section for details. Buses to Bukittinggi take about six hours and cost 4500 rp.

DUMAI

On the coast, 158 km north from Pakanbaru, Dumai is of interest only for the ferry service between here and Melaka in Malaysia. Dumai is strictly a one-street town and once you arrive the only thing to do is catch a bus to Pakanbaru. When you get to Pakanbaru there's not much to do either! You need a visa to arrive or depart Indonesia through Dumai.

North Sumatra & Lake Toba

SIBOLGA

There's no attraction to bring you to this rather dirty and drab little port, except as an overnight stop between Bukittinggi and Parapat or a jumping-off point to Nias. Sibolga is north of Bukittinggi, where the road turns inland to Parapat and Lake Toba. The descent into Sibolga – approaching from Parapat – is very beautiful, particularly at sunset. The harbour itself is attractive and there are some good beaches nearby.

Places to Stay

The losmen in the central area are generally dirty and/or unfriendly. They include the *Hotel Sudi Mampir* and the *Subur*, with rooms from around 5000 rp. *Hotel Indah Sari*, Jalan Achmad Yani 29, is slightly more expensive with rooms from 7000 rp but at least it's reasonable – they also have rooms with air-con and bathrooms from 15,000 rp. The *Maturi*, opposite the Indah, is dirt cheap.

Off to the north of town, *Hotel Tapian Nauli* is much nicer – rooms from 18,000 rp have bathrooms and a balcony. *Hotel Hidup Baru* (☎ 21957) at Jalan Suprapto 123 has rooms from 8000 to 13,000 rp with bath or at 22,000 rp with air-con – all prices include breakfast.

Places to Eat

To compensate for Sibolga's other drawbacks, there are some good restaurants and an ice-cream place on the corner across from the cinema. The *Telok Indah* at Jalan Achmad Yani 63-65 is an expensive but good Chinese restaurant.

Getting There & Away

Sibolga is on the Bukittinggi-Parapat-Medan route, so all the buses pass through here.

NIAS ISLAND

Off the west coast of north Sumatra, Nias is interesting for its traditional villages, unique customs and fine beaches. There are various good, easy jungle treks in the south, most of which follow stone tracks. Try to get hold of a map or copy the one in the Teluk Dalam police office. Surfers have discovered some of the best breaks in Indonesia here along the southern shore.

Orientation & Information

The roads on Nias are really shocking although, fortunately, the two most interesting towns in the south of the island are fairly close together. Teluk Dalam is the port and main town in the south. Gunung Sitoli is the main town in the north and the only place on the island where you can cash travellers' cheques, even then at a poor rate. Chloroquine-resistant malaria has been reported on Nias so take appropriate precautions.

Gunung Sitoli has a tourist information office (☎ 21545) on Jalan Sukarno 6.

Things to See

Bawomataluo This village has high-roofed traditional houses and the fine 'palace' of the tribal chief. In front of this building are stone tables where dead bodies were once left to decay. Traditional war dances may be performed by young, single males, who decorate themselves with feathers.

Although it's still well worth exploring, Bawomataluo is now very touristed and prices for statues, or for watching the dances, are exorbitant. Many of the villagers will pose for photographs – annoying in itself – then aggressively demand money for doing so. It's 14 km from Teluk Dalam to Bawomataluo, finishing with a climb up 480 stone steps!

Hilisimaetano There are 140 traditional houses in this larger but newer village, 16 km north-west from Teluk Dalam. Stone jumping is performed here most Saturdays – once a form of war training, the jumpers had to leap over a two-metre-high wall of stones surmounted by pointed sticks. These days the sticks are left off.

Lagundi With its perfect horseshoe bay, about 12 km from the harbour, Lagundi is a much more attractive place to stay than Teluk Dalam. A popular hang-out for surfies, Lagundi has plenty of losmen, all very similar in price and style. Most are clustered together at the far end of the horseshoe where the waves roll in across the reef.

There's not much to do here except surf, swim, walk and bask in the sun so bring books, cards and games to keep yourself amused when you get tired of the beach. The turn-off to Lagundi is about six km along the road to Hilisimaetano.

Gunung Sitoli The main town in the north is superficially a dump, but it's not as bad as it first seems. There are several nice walks near town and some *rumah adat* (traditional houses) uphill from Hilimbawodesolo, about 14 km from Gunung Sitoli. You can get there by bus but you need to walk two km from the main road to the village most of the time.

Places to Stay & Eat

Teluk Dalam *Wisma Jamburae* is on the waterfront with basic and clean rooms for

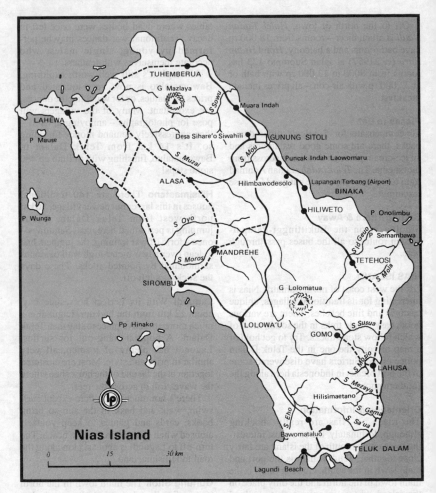

Nias Island

TUHEMBERUA

G Mazlaya

Muara Indah

LAHEWA

P Mause

Desa Sihare'o Siwahili

GUNUNG SITOLI

Puncak Indah Laowomaru

ALASA

S Muzai

S Mou

Hilimbawodesolo

Lapangan Terbang (Airport)

BINAKA

HILIWETO

P Onolimbu

P Wunga

S Oyo

S Id Gavo

Semambawa

S Moros

MANDREHE

TETEHOSI

S Mola

G Lolomatua

SIROMBU

Pp Hinako

LOLOWA'U

S Susua

GOMO

S Mozio

LAHUSA

S Mezaya

Hilisimaetano

S Gema

S Eho

S Sa'ua

Bawomataluo

TELUK DALAM

Lagundi Beach

0   15   30 km

7500 rp. The more expensive *Hotel Ampera* on Jalan Pasar has clean rooms with mandi for 15,000 rp.

Lagundi There are numerous places to stay at Lagundi, most cost from around 500 rp for a room and 2000 rp per person for one of the bungalows. All the losmen provide food, the

menu in most being exactly the same – mee goreng, omelettes, fried rice and vegetables, gado gado, pancakes, French fries and so on. They include the *Damai, Ama Sady, Friendly, Rufas, Happy Beach, Jamburae, Sea Breeze, Purba, Ama Gumi, Manuel* and *Tolong Menolong.*

There are more losmen, including the

Risky, Magdalena and the *Yanti,* near the centre of the horseshoe. If you're not into surfing, all three are good places to stay as they're cheap and the losmen owners are friendly, knowledgeable and helpful.

Some losmen expect their lodgers to have breakfast and dinner there and not somewhere else, otherwise they get nasty.

Gunung Sitoli Cheap accommodation in this town is expensive, dirty and depressing. Far and away the best place to stay is the *Wisma Soliga,* although it's two km from the town centre on the main road into the township. It's clean, spacious and the food, Chinese, is tasty, and there's lots of it. Rooms cost from around 10,000 rp, even less with bargaining.

In the centre of town at Jalan Gomo 148 is the *Hotel Gomo,* which has cheap rooms for 7500 rp. These are upstairs and are bright and airy whereas the air-con rooms downstairs with TV and mandi cost 15,000 rp and are dark. *Hotel Wisata* on Jalan Sirao 2 is a better alternative to Hotel Gomo with rooms for 7500 and 10,000 rp but none of them are air-con.

The cell-like *Hotel Beringin* on Jalan Beringin has rooms for 4000 rp. Cheaper and even sadder is the *Penginapan Banuada* on Jalan Kopri. Tiny rooms are 1500 rp per person, but you'd have to be really hard up to stay here.

Getting There & Away
Air SMAC, the north Sumatra airline, flies from Medan to Nias daily for 96,000 rp. The airport is 19 km from Gunung Sitoli and the taxi costs 3500 rp. There is talk of building a second airport at Teluk Dalam.

Boat Boats run daily except Sunday from Sibolga to Gunung Sitoli; they take about eight to 10 hours and cost 7500 rp in deck class and 11,500 rp for a cabin.

There are also three boats a week from Sibolga to Teluk Dalam for 8000 rp. This trip takes about 12 hours. The deck is not recommended for this boat as it gets fumes from

the motor and it is hot and noisy. A bunk in a four-berth cabin is 13,000 rp.

Most of the places of interest are down in the south so, from Gunung Sitoli, you have to take a bus to Lagundi for 5000 rp. The trip takes about six hours, or all day if you're unlucky. That leaves you six km from the beach. There are sometimes special 'tourist' buses which cost an extra 500 rp, or you can continue there by motorbike for 1000 rp.

Getting Around
To get around, you can rent bicycles, catch buses, walk or the locals will give you pillion rides on their motorbikes for a price.

PARAPAT
On the shores of Lake Toba, this is the arrival and departure point for ferries to Samosir Island. Buses for Medan to the north and Bukittinggi to the south also depart from here. There's nothing wrong with Parapat – in fact it's quite a pleasant place – but there's simply no reason to stay here, unless you arrive at an inconvenient time for getting across to the island.

Look in at the expensive Parapat Hotel, they sometimes put on performances of Batak singing or other local culture for tour groups. Parapat is also a good place to get Batak handicrafts like lime containers, leather, batik or wood carvings. Twenty-five km from Parapat is the village of **Labuhan Garaga** which is well worth a visit if you are interested in buying Batak blankets. They're not cheap as they range from 30,000 rp to 60,000 rp or more for good quality samples, but they are attractive and practical buys.

Orientation & Information
Parapat is essentially in two parts, the line of restaurants and shops on the Trans-Sumatran Highway, where buses to or from Medan or Bukittinggi pass by, and the area down by the lake from where ferries to Samosir Island depart. It's about a km between these two sections of town. Just where Jalan Pulau Samosir turns off from the Trans-Sumatran Highway, there's a small tourist office with

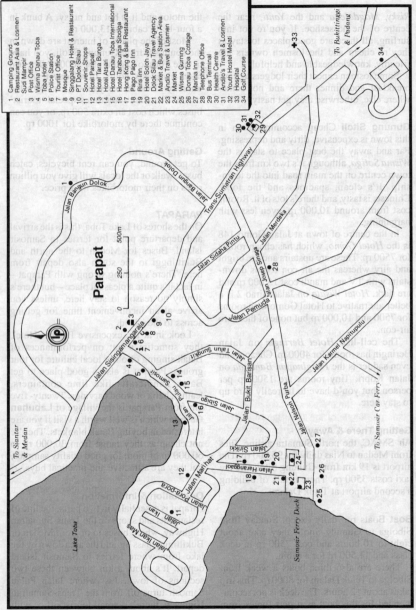

some limited information about Parapat and the lake.

Parapat travel agents are notorious for bungling bus bookings, neglecting to make flight reservations from Medan for which you have paid and other problems. Bonanza Holiday at the Pago Pago Inn generally seem to be quite good, and they will also change money, albeit at 5% less than bank rate.

Places to Stay

Parapat has plenty of places to stay, some of them quite pleasant, but the places over on Samosir Island are such a bargain that Parapat ends up looking very expensive. You've can either stay up on the main road through Parapat – handy for buses when you arrive or leave but otherwise rather noisy – or down by the lake, which is handy for the Samosir ferry. The expensive hotels, popular with weekend visitors from Medan or local holidaymakers, are mainly along the road from the Trans-Sumatran Highway to the ferry dock.

At Jalan Sisingamangaraja 56, the main road and the Trans-Sumatran Highway, *PT Dolok Silau* have a small losmen behind their travel agency with rooms for 2500 rp per person. This is where the air-con minibus from Bukittinggi arrives at night so most passengers end up staying here before crossing to Samosir Island in the morning. Rooms are basic but clean.

There are three places to stay at the bus station a couple of km from the ferry dock along the Trans-Sumatran Highway. Andilo Travel has moved there and they still have rooms for 5000/7000 rp and plenty of good information.

At No 84, directly opposite the lakeside turn-off, is the small and rather basic *Sudi Mampir* with rooms at 4000 rp. Continue further along and, at No 109, the *Singgalang Hotel* has rooms at 5000 rp.

Down at the lakeside, there are several places along Jalan Haranggaol including the popular *Pago Pago Inn*, close to the harbour, at No 50. It's airy, has clean but simple rooms with shared toilet facilities at 5000/10,000 rp and there are fine views across the lake.

Opposite, there's the *Riris Inn* (☎ 41392) at No 39, a modern place with simple, well-kept rooms with mandis at from 15,000 rp. Just down from it, at Jalan Haranggaol 47, is the *Hotel Soloh Jaya*, also a modern place but some of the rooms are just little boxes, even windowless, from 7500 rp. Better rooms with mandi cost from 15,500 rp.

Go right down to the ferry dock at the end of the road, turn the corner and *Wisma Gurning* is right by the lakeside, a simple place with rooms with two beds and a mandi for 10,000 rp. The big hotels in Parapat are often more expensive and rooms at the *Hotel Parapat* range from 85,000 to 125,000 rp.

Places to Eat

Parapat has plenty of place to eat including a host of nasi padang specialists along the main road. At No 80/82, right by the Sudi Mampir, the *Asia Restaurant* does good Chinese food as does the clean, neat and modern *Singgalang Restaurant* underneath the Singgalang Hotel.

Down towards the lake, there are several restaurants along Jalan Haranggaol including the side-by-side *Restaurant Hong Kong* at Nos 9 and 11, and the *Restaurant Bali* at No 13. They have very similar Chinese menus which are not cheap but chicken with lychees at the Bali is delicious.

Getting There & Away

See the warning under the Parapat Information section about making bookings from Parapat.

To/From Medan Buses to or from Medan run very regularly, cost 3500 rp and the trip takes about four hours. If you book them through a travel agent, the tickets are 3500 rp. To avoid the surcharge, buy the ticket on the bus at Parapat's bus terminal or board the bus directly at the pier where it meets incoming ferries from Samosir Island. The best Medan buses are run by the PMH company.

To/From Bukittinggi Buses going on to Bukittinggi take about 15 hours (although it can take much longer) and cost 15,000 to

18,000 rp. The ALS bus company has the most reliable service and best buses. There's a twice weekly tourist minibus which costs 20,000 rp and is supposed to make the trip in 12 or 13 hours, but the bus is sometimes overbooked and isn't always air-con as advertised.

To/From Berastagi If you want to travel via Berastagi, you have to change buses at Siantar and Kabanjahe, and it takes quite a time. See the Berastagi section for details and for information on the weekly tourist bus.

Other Fares to other destinations include Sibolga 6000 rp, Padang 10,100 rp, Pakanbaru 12,500 rp and Jakarta 65,000 rp (air-con). See the following Lake Toba section for details of ferry transport to Samosir Island.

Getting Around

Oplets around Parapat, including from the main road down to the harbour, cost 200 rp.

LAKE TOBA

Samosir Island in beautiful Lake Toba has become much more commercial and pushy over the years but it's still a relaxed, easy-going place. The lake, 174 km south of Medan, is high up (800 metres), big (1707 sq km) and deep (450 metres).

Parapat, on the shore of the lake, is the principal town of the area and a popular resort for Medan with its many restaurants, hotels, beaches and amusements. The real interest, however, starts nine km from Parapat on Samosir Island. The island is a centre for the likeable Batak people and you can see plenty of their high-peaked Batak houses in the villages around the island. Greet people with a hearty 'horas'!

The island is very beautiful and simple (no electricity in many parts), and the deep green lake invites swimming. Christian tombs (the Bataks are mainly Christian) are scattered in the fields and a high plateau rises up behind the narrow lakeside strip.

Orientation & Information

Most of the accommodation is concentrated around the Tuk Tuk Peninsula and nearby Ambarita. There are also places scattered north of Tuk Tuk and beyond plus a few places at Tomok, the main village a couple of km south of Tuk Tuk. Essentially, however, everything happens at Tuk Tuk.

You can pick up a map with information on island hiking at Gokhon Bookshop in Tuk Tuk. The small shop also has a selection of paperback books in English, French and German, including used travel guides.

Change money before you get to Lake Toba, as there are no banks and exchange rates are poor at Parapat or Samosir. Samosir does, however, have paved roads, electricity and some vehicles these days.

Things to See

Tomok If you follow the road away from the lakefront and the souvenir stalls in the village you will come to the **Tomb of King Sidabatu**, one of the last animist kings before the arrival of Christianity. Although Tomok is the main village and has several places to stay, Tuk Tuk, a few km away, is where all the action is.

Tuk Tuk This place is no longer as friendly and nice as it used to be as many locals are now concerned only with making money. There are quite often problems over rented motorbikes that have breakdowns and the owner wants the renter to pay for the fault. A road runs around the edge of the peninsula and there are losmen scattered all along it, just above the lake's inviting waters.

Ambarita A couple of km north of the Tuk Tuk Peninsula, Ambarita has a group of **stone chairs** where important matters and disputes were once settled. Until the arrival of Christianity about 250 years ago, serious wrongdoers were led to a further group of stone furnishings in an adjoining courtyard and despatched from this world by application of an axe to the back of the neck. The villagers will tell you they were then

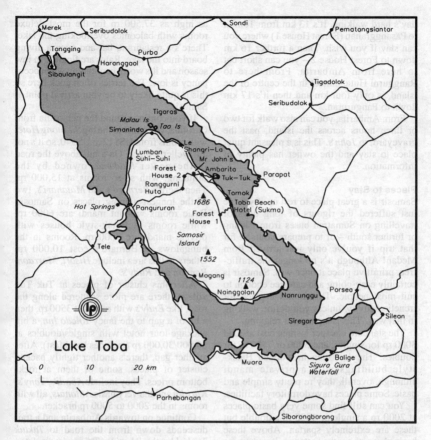

Lake Toba

0   10   20 km

chopped up and consumed, but it's probably just stories for the tourists.

If you climb the mountain from Ambarita, take the path to the right as the other is very difficult. When you reach the top, watch out for wild buffaloes as they are aggressive and dangerous. From here, there is a path that leads down to Simanindo, but it's hard going at the end. After following the plantation as far as it goes, the path cuts off at right angles and forces its way through tall undergrowth to the lakeside. Once you get there, the water is crystal clear, refreshing and ideal for swimming.

Simanindo & Pangururan On the northern tip of the island, Simanindo has a fine old **adat house** once used by a Batak king. The road around the island is slowly improving and there are occasional boats. At Pangururan, the island is only divided from the mainland by a canal. You can travel by bus from here to Berastagi but the road to Sidikalang is extremely bad. There are hot springs to relax in five km beyond Pangururan.

Across the Island The hardy can walk right on up and over the island from Tomok in a day's hard walking. It's 13 km from Tomok to Pasanggrahan (Forest House 1) where you can stay if you wish. Then a further 16 km down to Forest House 2 – you can short cut to here from Ambarita. From here to Ranggurni Huta, almost in the centre of the island, is only four km and then it's 17 km down to Pangururan.

From Ambarita, you can also walk for two or three hours across the island, past the graveyard, to *John's*. This is a pleasant quiet place to stay and the owner has plenty of information.

Places to Stay

Samosir is a great place to rest up if you've just suffered the rigours of long days of travelling on Sumatran buses from Padang or further south – or to prepare yourself for that trip if you've only just arrived from Medan! Although it's no longer the traffic-free, primitive place it once was, Samosir is certainly easy-going and carefree enough to suit most people. This is not a place for frenetic activity, unless you define walking in that way. This is a place for relaxing.

The standard cheaper losmen cost around 3000 rp for singles, and 5000 or 7500 rp for doubles. They're often in wooden Batak-style buildings with a private mandi although, overall, they're pretty simple and basic. Some places have dormitory facilities.

You can still find some very basic places at 2000 rp a single or 4000 rp a double but these are extremely spartan. Above these basic cheapies are the better equipped rooms in Batak-style houses, typically around 6000 rp and usually with a verandah. There is such a choice of places that the best advice is to wander around until you find something that suits. Some places are off by themselves, 'quiet' if you like that and 'isolated' if you don't. Nearly all of them are right by the lake.

There are a few larger hotels on Samosir, appealing to wealthy north Sumatrans or tourists from Singapore, but *Carolina* is still the longest-running and most popular 'up-market' place. They have a wide variety of rooms starting from the simplest ones at 10,000 to 15,000 rp with private mandi and

as high as 37,500 rp for the most deluxe rooms with balconies overlooking the lake. There's a restaurant, bar and even a diving board into the lake. Rates are flexible in low season and it's worth negotiating when occupancy is low. The ferries often dock here so this is quite likely to be your arrival point at Samosir.

If you continue round the peninsula from Carolina, you come to the big *Silintong Hotel* with rooms from US$12 to US$40, so it's not a traveller's place. On a hill above the road is the newer *Maduma*, owned by the Silintong, with so-so rooms at 15,000 rp. Then there's *Bernard's* and *Matahari's*, two of the longest-running places on Samosir. Basic rooms without mandi are 6000 rp, while rooms in Batak-style houses with private mandi are 7000 rp. Rooms in the bungalows at Bernard's cost 10,000 rp. Others in this area include *Hisari, Marraon, Romlan* and *Rudy's*.

After this cluster of places at Tuk Tuk village, there are more scattered along the road, like *Endy's* with rooms at 3500 rp, then a bit of a gap to the fancy *Toledo Inn*, a big package-tour hotel with singles/doubles at 20,000/30,000 rp (includes breakfast). After another gap, there's another tightly packed cluster of places, some of them at rock-bottom prices. They include *Abadi's, Tony's, Karidin* and the very basic *Antonius*, all with rooms in the 2000 to 5000 rp bracket.

Continue on towards Ambarita and a trail descends down from the road to *Tuktuk Timbul* by the lakeside. This quiet, isolated place has rooms at 4000 rp or nicer ones at 5000 rp. They're fine if you want to get away from it all.

Gordon's, a couple of km beyond Ambarita on the way to Simanindo, seems to be OK now although we had a number of complaints about it a few years ago. Right next to it is the flashy *Sopotoba* with rooms at 45,000 and 50,000 rp; it is surrounded by copious quantities of barbed wire.

Few people stay back at Tomok these days, although there are plenty of restaurants and warungs here for day-trippers. *Roy's Restaurant & Losmen* has singles/doubles

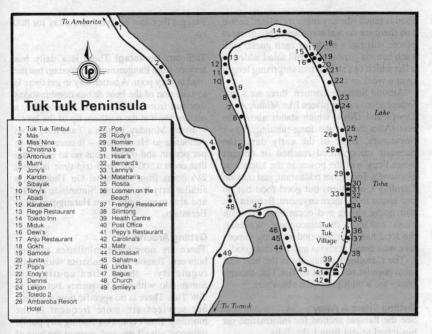

Tuk Tuk Peninsula

1	Tuk Tuk Timbul	27	Pos
2	Mas	28	Rudy's
3	Miss Nina	29	Romlan
4	Christina's	30	Marraon
5	Antonius	31	Hisar's
6	Murni	32	Bernard's
7	Jony's	33	Lenny's
8	Karidin	34	Matahari's
9	Sibayak	35	Rosita
10	Tony's	36	Losmen on the
11	Abadi		Beach
12	Karabien	37	Frengky Restaurant
13	Rege Restaurant	38	Silintong
14	Toledo Inn	39	Health Centre
15	Miduk	40	Post Office
16	Dewi's	41	Pepy's Restaurant
17	Anju Restaurant	42	Carolina's
18	Gokhi	43	Mafir
19	Samosir	44	Dumasari
20	Junita	45	Sahatma
21	Popi's	46	Linda's
22	Endy's	47	Bagus
23	Dennis	48	Church
24	Lekjon	49	Smiley's
25	Toledo 2		
26	Ambaroba Resort		
	Hotel		

for 3000/5000 rp. There are also three large Batak houses for up to ten people to stay in. Roy is friendly and provides plenty of good information. Ferries arrive roughly every day from Parapat. There are also regular bemos departing from Tomok to other parts of Samosir Island. There are two other basic places to stay in – *Mongoloi's* and *Tomok Shoganda Penginapan*.

Between Ambarita and Simanindo, near the village of Martahan, is the secluded *Le Shangri-La*. Spacious, clean Batak-style bungalows front a sandy beach and cost only 3000/4000 rp, plus there's dorm accommodation for 1500 rp. A pipe-smoking, somewhat eccentric Indian from Medan runs Le Shangri-La. He speaks great English and is quite forthcoming with knowledge about north Sumatra travel, including which scams to avoid. To get here, hop on a Simanindo-bound bus and get off when you see the Shangri-La sign on the right side of the road near Martahan, about 11 kms from Tomok.

There are always daily irregular oplets running from Ambarita to Simanindo that can drop people off at Le Shangri-La. Don't believe locals who might try and tell you that there is no bus as they only want you to charter their motorbike.

Round at Pangururan, on the other side of the island, Mr Richard Barat's *Kedai Kopi (Accommodation Barat)* is close to the wharf at Jalan Singamangaraja 2/4; 'he's a friendly guy with a maniac laugh'. The rooms are 3000 rp.

Wherever you stay, beware of theft. There have been a number of reports of thieves quietly sneaking into rooms at night and stealing cash or cameras.

Places to Eat
Once, dining out at Samosir was quite an occasion. 'Smorgasbords' were laid out for everybody at the place in which you were staying and these communal dinners were a nightly Samosir highlight. These days, the

food is much like any other travellers' centre and there are no real surprises although most places still run a book for each guest, with each banana pancake or fruit salad added to a list which can stretch to a surprising length over a week or two.

Around Samosir Losmen, there are a few independent eating places like *Miduk, Anju, Dewi's* and *Gokhi* which stands above the rest. Also there's the long-running *Pepy's Restaurant*. Back in the early days, the Samosir smorgasbord reached its heights when Pepy was the power in the kitchen at *Bernard's*. Today, her restaurant, just outside Carolina's, still turns out good food but no one seems to eat there anymore. Bernard's is still going strong and occasional live folk music enhances the atmosphere, however, the food has been reported as being expensive with small portions and not that good.

The *Carolina's* restaurant is the best and most popular restaurant in Tuk Tuk, though prices are a bit higher than elsewhere.

Getting There & Away
See the Parapat section for information on bus travel to and from Lake Toba.

Ferry There are a number of ferry services to/from Samosir Island

Tuk Tuk The ferries between Parapat and Samosir operate on an irregular, although frequent, schedule. There are always a host of colourful boats down at the Parapat harbourside but most of them are tour boats and the actual ferry is a simpler thing.

The trip over costs 800 rp and takes about half an hour if the weather is reasonable – it is 500 rp to return to Parapat. On Saturday, which is market day, the fare is only 800 rp. The ferry will usually drop off travellers at Carolina, but it picks up passengers from other losmen when you want to leave.

Tomok There's a car ferry which runs about five times daily from Ajibata, about two km from Parapat, to Tomok; the fare is 500 rp.

Ambarita Direct boats to Ambarita leave the

Parapat Pier four or five times a day for 800 rp.

To/From Berastagi There is a daily bus service from Pangururan to Berastagi but the road is very poor. A better way to get there is to take one of the boat & bus combinations that run from the island via Haranggaol, a market town at the northern tip of the lake.

Every Monday, there's a 7 am ferry from Ambarita to Haranggaol – it costs 1000 rp per person and meets a bus on to Berastagi that costs 1500 rp. Total trip time is about 2½ hours from Ambarita. On Thursday, a similar ferry leaves from Simanindo at 9 am and also meets a bus from Haranggaol on to Berastagi.

Getting Around
There are now some minibuses running between Tomok and Ambarita with some regularity – these often continue to Simanindo with less frequency but not to Tuk Tuk. There is no specific time schedule but services are more frequent in the morning. Don't count on finding any public transport after 3 pm and, even at the best of times, you can wait a long time between minibuses. It's a pleasant one-hour, five-km stroll from Tomok to Tuk Tuk.

Buses run several times a week from Ranggurni Huta to Pangururan and continue to Simanindo. You can rent motorbikes in Tuk Tuk for around 10,000 rp a day but they may ask more – rates are negotiable.

BERASTAGI (Brastagi)
On the back road from Medan to Lake Toba is Berastagi, a centre of the Karo tribes. Their traditional 'horned' roof houses can be seen in surrounding villages. On the way there from Lake Toba, near the northern end of the lake, are the impressive Si Piso-Piso Falls. The marquisha, a passionfruit variety, is grown only here and in Sulawesi; it makes a very popular drink.

Orientation & Information
Berastagi is essentially one main road, Jalan Veteran, with two popular places to stay at

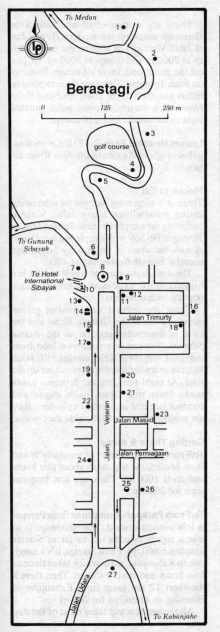

Berastagi

To Medan

To Gunung Sibayak

To Hotel International Sibayak

golf course

Jalan Trimurty

Jalan Maslid

Jalan Perniagaan

Jalan Udara

To Kabanjahe

1	Peceren Traditional Longhouse
2	Rose Garden Hotel
3	Rudang Hotel
4	Bukit Kubu Hotel
5	Power Station
6	Petrol Station
7	Fruit Market
8	Memorial
9	Ginsata Hotel
10	Tourist Office
11	Losmen Timur
12	Hotel Anda
13	Telephone Office
14	Post Office
15	Torong Inn
16	Losmen Trimurty
17	Asia Restaurant
18	Merpati Inn
19	Public Health Centre
20	Losmen Sibayak
21	Rumah Makan Terang
22	Eropah Restaurant
23	Ria Cinema
24	Restaurant Ora et Labora
25	Bus & Oplet Station
26	Market
27	Wisma Sibayak

opposite ends – Wisma Sibayak and the Hotel Ginsata, both good sources of information. There are a number of interesting antique and souvenir shops along Jalan Veteran and Crispo Antiques has interesting items for sale.

One place not to change money is at Wisma Sibayak as it offers a very bad rate. It is better to change at one of the large hotels like the Bukit Kuba Hotel or Hotel International Sibayak that have better exchange rates than the Bank BNI 1946 in Kabanjahe, the closest to Berastagi.

Things to See

Gunung Sibayak From Berastagi, you can climb Gunung Sibayak, a 2094-metre-high volcano and have a soak in the hot springs on the way back. Wear good walking boots because the path is wet and slippery all year round. Also, start early as the walk takes all day. Bring food and water and a torch (flashlight), just in case it takes more than all day.

The guest books at Wisma Sibayak have a

lot of useful information about this climb and various other walks in the area.

Around Berastagi There is a great deal of interesting Karo Batak architecture in and around Berastagi. Included is the **Peceren traditional longhouse** which is within walking distance north of the town centre. Go to Kabanjahe and, from there, walk four km to the primitive village of **Lingga**. The design of these houses, with their horn-shaped roofs, has remained unchanged for centuries. Most of the ones in Lingga are reputed to be well over 250 years old and no nails were used in their construction. You'll also find Karo Batak houses in nearby **Barusjahe**.

Ketambe and the **Leuser National Park** is good orang-utan country. It's beyond Kutacane, which is 106 km from Kabanjahe and takes about three hours to get to by jeep. **Gunung Sinabung**, a 2451-metre-high volcano, is also reached from Kabanjahe. Twenty-four km from Kabanjahe, and only about 300 metres from the road, are the **Si Piso-Piso Falls**.

A bus takes six to seven hours (3200 rp) via Kutacane where you take an oplet to Ketambe (800 rp).

Places to Stay
Berastagi Berastagi has a very popular travellers' centre and some other good backups. *Wisma Sibayak*, at the Kabanjahe end of the main street, has dorm beds at 2500 rp and double rooms at 5000 rp, all with shared toilet facilities. It's always packed with travellers and has a popular restaurant area. A lot of people seem to make lengthy stays here, and their guest books are packed with useful and amusing information about sightseeing, festivals, transport, walks, climbs and other things to do in the area.

At the other end of the main street is the *Ginsata Hotel* at Jalan Veteran 79. This is a normal hotel but clean and quite OK with rooms with mandi for 6000/8000 rp and a nasi padang restaurant downstairs. The manager here, Mr Ginting, is also helpful and informative.

There are a number of alternatives in Berastagi including the modern *Torong Inn* at Jalan Veteran 128 with rooms from 5000 rp to 7000 rp and dorms at 3000 rp. Or just off the main road, there's *Losmen Trimurty* on Jalan Trimurty. There are three expensive hotels just north of the town, the *Bukit Kubu Hotel* is an interesting older place situated right in the middle of a golf course.

Leuser National Park The PHPA rents bungalows right at the side of the Alas River for around 5000 rp.

Places to Eat
There is a surprising number of interesting eating possibilities along Jalan Veteran including the simple Chinese *Rumah Makan Terang* at No 369 with simple but tasty food. Across the street is the equally bright and cheerful *Eropah Restaurant* at 48G.

The *Asia Restaurant*, at Nos 9 and 10, is a bigger, more expensive Chinese place popular with travellers.

There are several nasi padang places including one at the *Ginsata Hotel* and the food is deservedly popular at the *Wisma Sibayak*. You can buy your own food from the fruit and vegetable market off Jalan Veteran or try the local market further up the road. At night-time, try the delicious cakes made from rice flour, palm sugar and coconut steamed in bamboo cylinders; they are available from a stall outside the cinema.

Getting There & Away
To/From Medan Buses run regularly to and from Medan, the trip takes about two hours and costs 1000 rp. There are less frequent taxis for 3000 rp.

To/From Parapat Getting to or from Parapat is less straightforward. The first stage is to take a regular Medan bus as far as Siantar (one hour; 600 rp). From Siantar, it's a rough ride to Kabanjahe, a trip which takes three to four hours and costs 1400 rp. Then there's the short 12 km jaunt from Kabanjahe to Berastagi in a minibus for 200 rp. Altogether, this trip takes most of the day so an early start from Lake Toba will get you to Berastagi by late afternoon.

To/From Samosir Island The fastest way to Berastagi from the Lake Toba area is by a boat and bus combination from Ambarita or Simanindo via Haranggaol on Monday or Thursday. See the Lake Toba Getting There & Away section for details.

Getting Around
Oplets around town are 150 rp. To get to Kutacane, take a bus to Kabanjahe and another bus from there (3200 rp). It's a further 800 rp from there to Ketambe in the Leuser National Park.

SIANTAR
Siantar, or Pematangsiantar to give it its full name, is basically just a pause between Medan and Lake Toba, or a place to change buses between Berastagi and the lake. If you have to stop overnight for some reason, you could try the *Hotel Delima* at Jalan Thamrin 131.

BINJEI
North of Berastagi, on the road from Medan to Bukit Lawang, Binjei is handy for all three locations.

Places to Stay
Stay at *Cafe de Malioboro Garden Restaurant & Guest House* (great name!), an old Dutch house at Jalan Ksatria 1. It's friendly, relaxing and economical but you need plenty of insect repellent and mosquito coils.

Getting There & Away
You can get to Binjei from Medan, just 22 km away, by minibus or share taxi from the Juwita shopping centre on Jalan Surabaya.

BUKIT LAWANG
Eighty km from Medan, near Bukit Lawang, is an **orang-utan rehabilitation centre** where these extraordinary and fascinating creatures are retrained to survive in the wild after a period of captivity. Apart from the wildlife, the country around here is wild and

enchanting with dense jungle, a clear, fast-flowing river and cascading waterfalls.

The number of visitors to the reserve is limited so avoid Sunday when there are lots of day-trippers from Medan. If you go in the morning you also avoid possible conflict with afternoon tour groups. Permits to visit the reserves cost 3000 rp and are valid for three days. There have been problems in the past with the park guides insisting that you could not visit the reserve without paying each time, insisting that you hire a guide and charging you each time you took the boat that shuttles across the river.

The Medan tourist office is supposed to have clamped down on this profiteering at the expense of foreign visitors but it still appears that as well as the real park rangers, there are some local imposters who will charge you for whatever you're willing to pay! 'There are only five real rangers,' reported one visitor.

It's a steep half-hour walk to the reserve along the Bohorok River, where you then cross by boat. The trail in the reserve is easy to pick-up and follow. Permits for the reserve are available from the PHPA Rest House in Bukit Lawang, from both Dinas PHPA (Kantor Kehutanan) and the tourist office in Medan. The orang-utan feeding times are posted in the rest house. At present, they are from 8 to 9 am and from 3 to 4 pm. Maximum viewing time is 50 minutes. Please do not play, feed or touch orang-utans as you are there to observe and not to play with them.

Another activity in the area is **tube rafting** down the Bohorok River. Wisma Leuser Sibayak rents tubes for 1000 rp a day. Be sure to ask about the water level first – tubing can be quite dangerous here when the river is swollen by rains. While you're in this district ask around to see whether you can find someone to show you the nearby **rubber processing plant**.

Places to Stay
Now there are nine guest houses that offer a place to stay and eat. These are spread out along the river from Bukit Lawang to the

river crossing where you'll find the orang-utan rehabilitation centre.

Wisma Leuser Sibayak and *Wisma Bukit Lawang* are the two long-established places and more expensive. Wisma Leuser Sibayak has dorm beds at 2000 rp, rooms from 5000 rp and cottages for 10,000 rp. Wisma Bukit Lawang has similar prices but it has several nicer bungalows further down the river in an isolated location.

The other places are further up the river, very similar in style and cheaper than the abovementioned two places. These are *Yusman, Wisma Bukit Lawang Indah, Selayang Inda, Queen Paradise Jungle* and *Bohorok River* are also much smaller than Sibayak or Bukit Lawang and friendlier. Even though some places have mandi most people wash in the river.

Getting There & Away

The road to Bukit Lawang, shown as Bohorok on some maps, is terrible. It takes four to five hours by bus from the Sei Wampa bus station via Binjei. The fare is 300 rp to Binjei and then another 1750 rp to Bukit Lawang. There's one daily direct bus from Berastagi, which costs 2000 rp but it goes via Medan and takes five to six hours.

From Bukit Lawang, there is one daily departure around 5.30 am.

MEDAN

Although it's the capital of Sumatra and a major entry or exit point for the country, for many travellers Medan conjures up images of belching becaks belting towards you and the pungent attack of their noxious fumes on the nostrils. It's actually not a bad city but apart from some good antique shops, a mosque, a museum, a palace, air-con malls and lots of people, it has little to offer beyond the remnants of a Dutch planter aristocracy.

Notice the forest of television aerials that rise high above Medan? They're not because of poor local reception but to pick up TV Tiga (Channel 3) from Malaysia. It's a reminder of how close you are to that country.

1	PT Indosat
2	Taman Budaya
3	Deli Plaza Shopping Centre
4	Medan Fair
5	Bohorok & Banda Aceh Bus Station
6	Bus Station for Brastagi
7	Westin Fried Chicken
8	Parisada Hindu Dharma Temple
9	Deli Dharama Hotel, Garuda
10	Bank Negara Indonesia
11	Post Office
12	Railway Station
13	Police Office
14	Krishen's Yoghurt House
15	Tapian Nabaru Hotel
16	Hotel Polonia
17	Tiara Medan Hotel, Garuda
18	Rumah Makan Gembira
19	Rumah Makan Famali
20	Dhaksina Hotel & Garuda Plaza Hotel
21	Sumatera Hotel
22	Merpati Office, Eka Sukma Wisata Tour & Mandala Office
23	Inda Taxi & Penang Ferry Office
24	Istana Maimoon
25	Great Mosque
26	Hotel Garuda
27	Padang Bus Station & Melati Hotel
28	Wisma Sibayak
29	Polonia Airport
30	Medan Zoo
31	Sarah's Guest House
32	Parapat Bus Station
33	Dirga Surya Hotel
34	Losmen Irama
35	Military Museum
36	Hotel Danau Toba International, MAS
37	Tip Top Restaurant
38	Tourist Office
39	Bank Dagang Negara
40	Pelni Office
41	Sigura Gura
42	Old Central Bus Station
43	Chinese Food Street

Orientation & Information

Finding your way around Medan is no problem, although it's sprawling and the traffic can be horrendous – a good map is essential. Street names can be confusing: one of the main city-centre arterial roads is Jalan Achmad Yani, which changes to Jalan Pemuda and, finally, Jalan Katamso as it stretches south-east from the city centre.

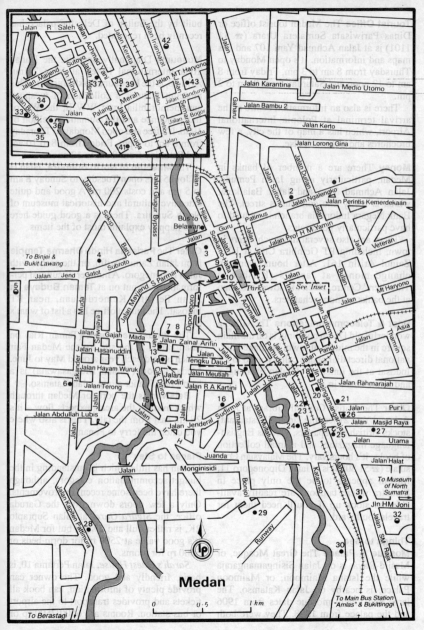

Medan

0   0.5   1 km

Tourist Office The Medan tourist office or Dinas Pariwisata Sumatera Utara (☎ 51 1101) is at Jalan Achmad Yani 107 and has maps and information. It's open Monday to Thursday from 8 am to 3 pm, Friday from 8 am to 12 noon and Saturday from 8 am to 2 pm.

There is also an information centre at the arrival terminal at Polonia International Airport, which has a map of the city, a few brochures and not much else.

Money There are a number of banks in Medan, particularly along Jalan Pemuda, Jalan Achmad Yani and Jalan Balaikota, which is really one continuous street. The Bank Negara Indonesia branch is reputed to have particularly good rates.

There are also several moneychangers in town, including PT Gembira City at Jalan Zainul Arifin 161. After hours, you can change money at Jacky's (Krishen's) Travellers' Centre, albeit at a lower rate than at the banks or moneychangers.

Post & Telecommunications The GPO, a wonderful old Dutch building, is on the main square in the middle of town. To make international direct dial phone calls, you go to PT Indosat at the junction of Jalan Ngalengko and Jalan Thamrin.

Other The British Council Library at Jalan Achmad Yani 2 (near the Tip Top Restaurant) stocks British newspapers, various English-language magazines and a small collection of books; it's hours vary. The Malaysian Consulate (☎ 51 8053) is at Jalan Diponegoro 11. Medan appears to be the only place in Sumatra where tampons are readily available, so stock up if you'll need them for travels southward.

Things to See
Mosque & Palace The Great Mosque, or Masjid Raya, is on Jalan Sisingamangaraja while the Istana Maimoon, or Maimoon Palace, is nearby on Jalan Katamso. The large and lovely mosque dates from 1906 and the palace from 1888. They were both built by the Sultan of Deli; the palace has recently been renovated.

Museums Diagonally opposite the Danau Toba International Hotel, at Jalan Zainul Arifin 8, is the **Museum Bukit Barisan**. This museum features a collection of weapons and memorabilia from WW II, the War of Independence and the Sumatra rebellion of 1958. It's free and open Monday to Thursday from 8 am to 1 pm, Friday from 8 to 10 am and Saturday from 8 am to 12 noon.

The **Museum of North Sumatra**, Jalan H M Joni 51, is open Tuesday to Sunday 8 am to 5 pm and costs 200 rp. A good and quite extensive cultural and historical museum of North Sumatra. There is a good guide here who happily explains most of the items.

Other The **Parisada Hindu Dharma Temple** is on Jalan Zainul Arifin, on the corner with Jalan Diponegoro. A number of cultural performances are put on at **Taman Budaya** on Jalan Perintis Kemerdekaan, near PT Indosat. The tourist office has a list of what's on.

The **amusement park** (Taman Ria) on Jalan Binjai is the site for the Medan Fair which is held each year around May to June. Medan's **zoo** (Taman Margasawata) is a bemo ride further along Jalan Katamso.

Belawan is the port for Medan through which most of the area's exports flow – it's 28 km east from the city. This is also where you catch the ferry to Penang.

Places to Stay
Medan has little which is outstanding in the budget-accommodation category, although there have been some recent improvements. Only a few doors down from the Garuda office, the *Sigura Gura*, at Jalan Suprapto 2K, is rather dull and dismal but for Medan it's good value at 2500 rp for dorm beds or 5000 rp for rooms.

Sarah's Guest House, Jalan Pertama 10, is basic, friendly and good. The owner can provide plenty of information, can book all tickets and provides transport to the airport or bus station. Rooms are 6000/7500 rp or

10,000 rp with mandi and the dorm is a donation.

The *Losmen Irama*, in a little alley at Jalan Palang Merah 1125 (by the junction of Jalan Listrik and very close to the big Hotel Danau Toba International), is brighter and much more popular. Some of the rooms are rather small and you should avoid rooms near the mandis which have thin walls. The rooms at the other end are much more solid. It's a convenient, friendly and well-kept place with dorm beds for 2500 rp or doubles/triples for 5000/7500 rp.

The *Tapian Nabaru Hotel* (☎ 51 2155), at Jalan Hang Tuah 6 and right by the river, has dorms for 2500 rp or rooms at only 5000 rp per person. It's quiet and somewhat off the beaten track – Medan's best bargain.

There are a couple of other cheapies in town, like the *Hotel Melati* (☎ 51 6021) at Jalan Amaluin 6, close to the bus station on Jalan Sisingamangaraja. It's a larger hotel with rooms from 7500 to 20,500 rp. *Hotel Waringin*, right across the road, is for emergencies only.

Krishen's Yoghurt House (☎ 51 6864) at Jalan Kediri 96 offers dorm beds for 3500 rp or doubles for 10,000 rp. Krishen (formerly Jacky) will also let impecunious travellers sleep on the floor of his Indian restaurant for 1000 rp per night. Be warned, however, that Jacky renamed both himself and the place Krishen's in an attempt to improve his tarnished image with Western women.

Krishen also provides free travel information and can book ferry, bus and airline tickets – although several travellers have reported that tickets have been overpriced and that transport arranged by Krishen didn't arrive.

There are a string of middle and upper-range hotels along Jalan Sisingamangaraja. The *Hotel Sumatera* (☎ 24973) at Jalan Sisingamangaraja 21 has rooms from 20,000 with mandi and from 26,000 rp with air-con. The *Hotel Garuda* (☎ 20213) at No 18 on the same street has rooms from 15,000 to 22,500 rp. Or try the *Dhaksina Hotel* (☎ 32 4561) at No 20 with economy doubles at 22,000 rp and other rooms from 40,000 to 48,000 rp.

Places to Eat

One of Medan's saving graces is Jalan Semarang which in the evening becomes a traffic jam of Chinese food. During the daytime, it's just a dirty back alley but come nightfall food stalls set up along the street across Jalan Bogor between Jalan Pandu and Jalan Bandung. Jalan Semarang is the third block beyond the railway line.

Kampung Keling on Jalan Zainul Arifin is an area with lots of small gangs and numerous warungs specialising in different kinds of food – Chinese, Indian, Indonesian and European.

The *Tip Top Restaurant* at Jalan Achmad Yani 92 has a large verandah outside which is, surprisingly, not too noisy despite the passing traffic. The food is consistently good and cheap and they also do breakfasts, baked goods and ice cream. A few doors down at No 98 is *Lyn's Cafe & Restaurant*, a gathering place for Medan businesspeople and expats. It's dim and cool, and the menu is predominantly Western. They actually ask how you like your steak done.

Medan Bakery at Jalan Zainul Arifin 148, just beyond the temple, has excellent baked goods. A few doors up the *Westin Bakery & Fried Chicken*, at No 166, is a very glossy looking fast-food specialist. Turn right at Jalan Taruma and you'll find three excellent bakeries – *Suan's, Royal Holland* and *Tahiti*. The Royal Holland offers tasty and inexpensive Indonesian dishes as well as pastries.

Off Jalan Cik Ditiro at Jalan Kediri 96 (two blocks south of Jalan Zainul Arifin) is *Krishen's Yoghurt House* (formerly Jacky's). They have a variety of north Indian dishes including biryanis as well as great yoghurt and lassis. Beer is half price from 7 pm until closing.

There are all sorts of eating possibilities in the big *Deli Plaza* shopping centre on the corner of Jalan Balaikota and Jalan Getah. *Enako*, on the ground floor, is a neat little place with light snacks and fruit juices. The *President Bakery* is also on the ground floor while on the 3rd floor there's a whole range of fast-food specialists including places offering Chinese, Indonesian, nasi padang and European food. Also, there's a *Kentucky Fried Chicken* and an excellent fruit juice and fruit-salad stand.

Things to Buy

The city has a number of interesting arts and crafts shops, particularly along Jalan Achmad Yani. Try Toko Asli at No 62, Toko Rufino at No 64, and Toko Bali Arts at No 68. There is a good selection of antique weaving, Dutch pottery, Batak carvings, and other interesting pieces in all of these shops.

Getting There & Away

Medan is the major travel centre in Sumatra and an important arrival or departure point from overseas.

Air Internationally, you can fly from Medan to Penang (Malaysia), Singapore, Kuala Lumpur or Amsterdam. See the Sumatra Getting There & Away section for details. Airport tax for international departures is 10,000 rp. Medan is also a major domestic air-travel centre with flights by Garuda, Mandala, Merpati and SMAC (Sabang Merauke Air Charter).

Reconfirm Garuda flights out of Medan by calling 51 5277 or 51 6680 between 8 am and 9 pm daily. For the location of other airline offices see the Medan street map.

Bus & Taxi Medan is the major crossroads for bus travel in north Sumatra. Parapat is the main destination from Medan; buses depart very regularly, take about four hours and cost 3000 rp. Touts may besiege you for this bus but you can safely ignore them. The buses depart along Jalan Sisingamangaraja.

There are a number of bus stations in Medan for various destinations. See the Medan map for locations. There is a new bus terminal 'Amplas' in South Medan on Jalan Pertahanan off Jalan S M Raja. A yellow oplet costs 250 rp to the centre of Medan. Buses from here depart to all destinations. The trip to Berastagi takes less than two hours and costs 1000 rp. Other fares include

Bukittinggi or Padang from 11,000 to 14,000 rp or Banda Aceh for 19,000 rp.

There are a number of long-distance taxi operators from Medan. At Jalan Katamso 60, near the Merpati office, you'll find Indah Taxi (☎ 516615). They have taxis to Parapat for 9500 rp, to Sibolga for 12,000 rp and to Pakanbaru for 25,500 rp. Two other companies with similar routes and fares are Cantik (☎ 32 7532) and Sumatera (☎ 29137), both on Jalan Semarang.

Boat A new Pelni high-speed ferry service to Penang has replaced the much slower overnight ferry. See the Sumatra Getting There & Away section for information on the boat.

Pelni ships connect Medan (actually nearby Belawan) with Jakarta and on to other ports in Indonesia, or the KM *Lawit* operates a service from port to port along the Sumatran east coast. The Pelni office in Medan is at Jalan Sugiono, a block back from Jalan Pemuda and close to the tourist office and Garuda office. For information on transport to the Belawan Harbour, see the following Medan Getting Around section.

Getting Around

To/From the Airport The metered taxi fare from the airport depends on your destination in the city but count on around 2000 rp.

The domestic terminal, much better than its international counterpart, has a restaurant, snack bar and magazine stand. There's a tourist office just outside the international terminal.

To/From Belawan The Belawan Harbour (for the Penang hydrofoil or other Pelni boat departures) is 27 km north of Medan. To get there cheaply, take a Damri Patas bus from Medan Plaza to Belawan (500 rp) and then walk or take an oplet (200 rp) for the last 1½ kms to the harbour. A taxi would cost around 15,000 rp one way. A tourist bus is 4000 rp.

Local Transport There are plenty of oplets around town at a standard 200 rp.

Medan also has plenty of motorised and human-powered becaks. Just as inexpensive (often much more inexpensive for foreigners) are the metered taxis that ply the streets in large numbers. Four different companies run metered taxis but the fare is always the same, 700 rp at flagfall and 300 per km thereafter.

BANDA ACEH

The capital of Aceh, Banda Aceh is right at the northern tip of Sumatra. Fiercely independent and devoutly Islamic, Aceh was once a powerful state in its own right and later held out against the Dutch longer than almost anywhere else in the archipelago. In recognition of this, it is now designated as a Special Territory by the Indonesian government, which gives it the freedom to pursue its own religious, cultural and educational policies.

Still the most staunchly Muslim part of the country, Aceh is run under Islamic law but despite their rigid religious conservatism, the Acehnese are friendly and helpful people, particularly the students, and many have a good grasp of English, which they're anxious to use.

You can make trips from Banda Aceh to the seaside at Lhok Nga, 12 km from the city, or take a ferry to Sabang, on Pulau We off the coast.

Orientation & Information

The centre of town is marked by an imposing five-domed mosque. Across the Krueng Aceh River is Jalan Achmad Yani, where most of the hotels are.

The tourist office (☎ 21377) is on Jalan T Nyak Arief 92. The Bank Negara Indonesia is on Jalan Merduati and the post office on Jalan Kuta Alam, one block from Simpang Tiga.

Things to See

Mosque With its stark white walls and licorice-black domes, the stunning Mesjid Raya Baiturrahman is like an oasis in the dust and fumes of central Banda Aceh. Ask the keeper to let you climb the staircase to one of the minarets so you can get a good view over the city.

Gunongan For a contrast in architectural styles, go and see Gunongan on Jalan Teuku Umar, near the clocktower. This 'stately pleasure dome' was apparently built for the wife of a 17th century sultan – a Malayan princess – as a private playground and bathing place.

The building itself is a series of frosty peaks with narrow stairways and a walkway leading to hummocks which are supposed to represent the hills of her native land so she could take an evening stroll – a liberty not permitted in Banda Aceh in that era.

Directly across from the Gunongan is a low vaulted-gate in the traditional Pintu Aceh style, which gave access to the sultan's palace and was supposed to have been used by royalty only. Nearby, is the cemetery for more than 2000 Dutch soldiers who fell in battle against the Acehnese. The entrance is about 250 metres from the clocktower on the road to Uleh-leh.

Museum Banda Aceh has a large museum which exhibits weapons, household furnishings, ceremonial costumes, everyday clothing, gold jewellery and books. At Jalan Alauddin Mahmudsyah 12, it's open, Tuesday to Sunday from 8.30 am to 6 pm.

In the same compound is the **Rumah Aceh**, a fine example of traditional architecture, which is built without nails and held together with cord or pegs. It's open Tuesday to Sunday from 8 am to 6 pm and contains more Acehnese artefacts and war memorabilia. In front of the Rumah Aceh is a large cast-iron bell, which was given to the Acehnese by a Chinese emperor in the 1st century AD.

Places to Stay

Accommodation in Banda Aceh is relatively expensive and not that good. The decent *Losmen International* on Jalan Achmad Yani, opposite the night market, has small rooms for 5000 rp and larger rooms with mandi for 7500 rp. Ask for one of the quieter rooms at the rear. There are a number of other hotels along this road including the *Hotel Medan* at No 9 with rooms with mandi from 13,500 rp, or the *Wisma Parapat* at No 11 with rooms from 13,500 to 20,000 rp with air-con.

On nearby Jalan Khairil Anwar are the *Losmen Palembang* at No 8 and the *Losmen Aceh Barat* with rooms in the 8000 to 15,000 rp range. Other places to try include the clean *Wisma Lading* at Jalan Cut Meutia 9 with accommodation from 5000 to 10,000 rp, and in the same range, the *Rasa Sayang* (not to be confused with the upscale Hotel Rasa Sayang Ayu on another street) at Jalan Cut Meutia 34E.

The colonial *Losmen Aceh*, opposite the mosque on Jalan Muhammed Jam, has basic rooms for 4000 rp and 8000 rp, or 12,100 rp with private bath and air-con. Near the market, at Jalan Muhammad Jam 1, is the *Losmen Yusri*, which is fairly dreary and has musty rooms with air-con and mandis from 12,500 rp and basic rooms from 7500 rp.

Places to Eat

Jalan Achmad Yani is a good place to start looking for food. If you take a stroll down it during the day, you'll come across the *Gembira* at 36, the *Happy* at 40, *Dian* at 44 and the *Restoran Tropicana* at 90-92. At night, this street and several off it are hopping with food stalls and warungs. It's a busy, noisy and colourful scene and the food is cheap, fresh, delicious – if you choose carefully – and has lots of variety.

At 3 Khairil Anwar is the *Satyva Modern Bakery*, which not only has lots of different kinds of mouth-watering cakes and breads but also more substantial dishes. For Padang food, try the *Sinar Surya* at Jalan Sri Ratu Safiatuddin 10, or there's the *Aroma* on Jalan Cut Nyak Dien which has an excellent Chinese menu. There is lots of different kinds of cheap food available around the Pasar Aceh or market area.

Getting There & Away

Air It takes less than an hour to fly between Medan and Banda Aceh with Garuda (☎ 21983, Hotel Rasay Sayang Aya, Jalan Teuku Umar) or SMAC (☎ 21626, Jalan Cut Nyak Dien 93), the north Sumatran airline.

Bus If the road is dry, the same trip from Medan takes 12 to 15 hours by bus. Fares vary around 19,000 rp – try Kurnia. The road is in good condition and takes you through numerous villages, mountains, rice fields and rolling country. The Setui bus terminal, on Jalan Teuku Umar is where buses depart for Medan, Meulaboh or Tapaktuan.

You can get smaller buses from the mosque area next to the old railroad station, if you want to stop off at places like Sigli and Lhokseumawe along the Medan road. Also, near the mosque in front of the Bank Dagang Negara on Jalan Diponegoro, large and fairly modern Damri buses depart for Darussalam, Lhok Nga and Blang Bintang.

PULAU WE

This small island north of Banda Aceh has lots of attractive, palm-fringed beaches.

There is some very good snorkelling on Pulau We, especially at a place called the Sea Garden near Rubiah Island. You have to organise a boat from one of the losmen to get there. Stingray Dive Centre, at the Losmen Pulau Jaya, rents out diving and snorkelling equipment and can organise transport. Remember that June to October is the wet season and not the best time to go.

Places to Stay

In Sabang there are a number of losmen. *Losmen Pulau Jaya* at Jalan Teuku Umar 17 has basic, good clean rooms for 2500 rp (no windows), 5000 rp with windows, 10,000 rp including mandi and 15,000 rp with air-con. Note that the common mandi have peepholes. The place is friendly, they have plenty of information about hiking as well as snorkelling around the island. It is possible to stay at their deserted beach, Tupin Gapang, (18 km from Sabang) for 5000 rp plus meals.

Losmen Irma is also on the same street at No 3 and it has rooms at similar prices, but they charge a single rate if only one person is staying in a double room. They also have bungalows on two different beaches, Iboih and Balik Gunung (closed June to October because of high winds) for 1500 rp per person with no mattress or 2000 rp with one.

Holiday Losmen is tucked away in a side lane down Jalan Perdagangan so it is quieter than the above two but also more expensive with singles/doubles at 6000/10,000 rp and air-con rooms for 25,000 rp. Mr Amin, a regular in the hotel, is a guide who can also organise hiking, snorkelling and diving trips.

Two other cheap losmen are *Raja Wali* and *Sabang Merauke*.

Places to Eat
There are numerous coffee places in Sabang but one of the best is *Rilzky Restaurant* on Jalan Teuku Umar and Perkapalan. It has good seafood, Chinese and Indonesian meals. *Café Ban* has a travellers type of menu at higher prices.

Getting There & Away
Boats leave every afternoon from the old Banda Aceh port of Pelabuhan Malahayati at Kreung Raya and arrive at Pulau We (Sabang) about two hours later. The port is 35 km from the centre of Banda Aceh (catch a bemo for 1200 rp for a 45-minute trip from Jalan Diponegoro) and the cost over to the island is 3400 rp or 4500 rp in 1st class, one way. The boat returns from Pulau We at 9 am.

You can also fly to Sabang from Banda Aceh.

Getting Around
Sabang town is 12 km from the harbour – you can get there by oplet (1000 rp) or taxi. The taxi station is in front of Toko Sahabar on Jalan Perdagangan. Ask there about renting motorbikes for 15,000 rp per day and boats for 50,000 rp per day.

Nusa Tenggara

Nusa Tenggara refers to the string of islands which starts to the east of Bali and ends with Timor. At one time they were governed as a group but now they are divided into three *propinsi*, or provinces, including Bali (capital Denpasar); Lombok and Sumbawa (capital Mataram); and Flores, Sumba and Timor (capital Kupang).

Some of the most spectacular attractions of Indonesia can be found in this string of islands – Mt Rinjani on Lombok, the dragons of Komodo, the immense stone tombs of Sumba and the coloured volcanic lakes of Keli Mutu on Flores.

Each island is distinctive culturally, although the cultures are not as accessible as those of Bali or Tanatoraja in Sulawesi.

The further you get from Bali, the less developed the islands are from every point of view, including that of the tourist. Whilst a steady stream of people pass through the islands, there's nothing like the tourist hordes you find in Bali or Java. In one way, this is an advantage because the reaction of the local people is generally more natural, but it does create one headache – you can be a constant centre of attraction. It's easy to generate an entourage of over 100 children in small, remote villages.

If you don't mind this, then travelling in Nusa Tenggara is fairly easy-going. People are very friendly, and there's been a great deal of improvement in recent years – there are more surfaced roads, losmen, flights and regular road transport. Also, there are now regular ferries between most of the islands.

Previously a lot of travel in Nusa Tenggara was just plain awful – you'd end up spending a lot of time hanging around in dreary ports waiting for boats, or shaking your bones loose in trucks that were trying to negotiate roads constructed out of large trenches. Parts of Nusa Tenggara are still like that, but on the whole the main attractions are now fairly easy to get to.

Just stick to the main routes, avoid travel in the wet season when some of the roads turn to slush, and you shouldn't have any trouble. You need at least a month to get a reasonable look around the whole chain.

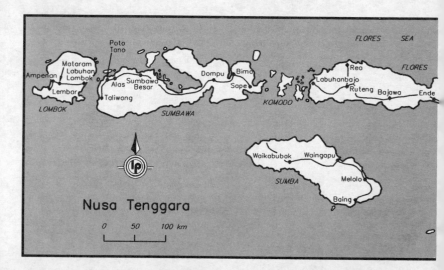

Language

It's absolutely essential to learn some Indonesian if you're going to travel through Nusa Tenggara. A lot of people here know a few phrases of English, but most don't know enough to have a conversation – those who speak reasonable English are few and very far between. Bahasa Indonesia is a simple language and learning sufficient to get by on is akin to learning to eat with chopsticks – if there's no other alternative you just have to.

Information

Money & Costs Nusa Tenggara's islands are marginally more expensive for food, accommodation and transport than Bali and Java, and you don't get such good value for money. However, by any standards, costs are still low. It's probably wise to allow for a couple of flights; one for getting back to Bali or Java, rather than backtracking all the way through the islands by road and ferry, and another if you want to go to Timor and/or Sumba.

There are fewer places in Nusa Tenggara to change money than in Bali and Java – but even this has improved of late. There will generally be at least one bank in each of the main towns that will change foreign cash and travellers' cheques: Cakranegara in Lombok; Sumbawa Besar and Bima in Sumbawa; Ruteng and Ende in Flores; Kupang and Dilli in Timor; and Waingapu in Sumba. Stick to the major brands of travellers' cheques, take US and Australian dollars, Deutsche marks, pounds sterling or Netherlands florin and you should be OK. If in doubt, take US$ – it's the most widely accepted foreign currency in Indonesia.

Getting There & Away

Denpasar is the usual jumping-off point for the islands of Nusa Tenggara – from Denpasar you can go by ferry, hydrofoil or plane across to Lombok, or fly to one of the other islands. You can also fly directly to some destinations in Nusa Tenggara from Java or Sulawesi.

Merpati have a twice-weekly connection between Kupang in Timor and Darwin in Australia's Northern Territory. This is an excellent way to travel to Indonesia from Australia. You can then island hop through Nusa Tenggara to Bali without having to

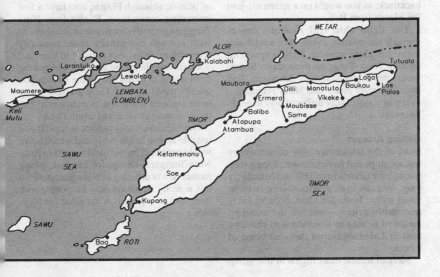

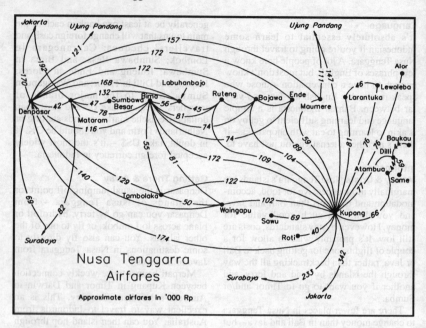

Nusa Tenggarra
Airfares

Approximate airfares in '000 Rp

backtrack, as you would on a return trip into the islands from Bali.

The Pelni ship KM *Kelimutu* comes through the islands every two weeks and there are more regular ferries operating through Nusa Tenggara these days. Sometimes, the Bugis Makassar schooners find their way right down into Nusa Tenggara – so if you want a really different way to get to Sulawesi...!

Getting Around

Most of the islands are now connected by regular ships and ferries, thus making a loop through the islands from Bali and back fairly easy. You can even charter sailing boats or small motor boats for short hops at fairly reasonable prices – one of the standard means of getting to Komodo is to charter a boat in Labuhanbajo on the west coast of Flores.

Merpati handle most flights in this group

of islands, although Bouraq also have a few interesting connections. Flights from Nusa Tenggara generally terminate in Surabaya or Bali, but you can usually make same-day connections on to other parts of Indonesia.

Boats and planes are the means of getting from island to island but on the islands you usually travel by bus. There are now many more surfaced roads and, consequently, bus travel is more reliable and comfortable.

Nevertheless, buses are not as regular and reliable as you might wish, and a motorbike would probably be the ideal way to explore Nusa Tenggara. Except for Lombok, hiring motorbikes is not easy in Nusa Tenggara, so this is really an option only for people with their own transport. It is the same for bicycles.

Lombok

Lombok combines the lushness of Bali with the starkness of outback Australia. Parts of the island drip with water while pockets are chronically dry. Droughts can last for months, and not so long ago people would starve to death if the rice crops failed. The people too reflect these extremes – many of the islanders are outgoing and friendly, whilst others are shy and withdrawn.

About 10% of the population is Balinese and the rest are mainly Sasaks. Balinese influence dates from a series of battles with the King of Sumbawa from 1723 to 1750. The Balinese aided the Lombok overlord Datu Selaparang. As a reward, they were allowed to settle on Lombok. The luckless Datu was killed in battle and his Balinese allies took over. A series of local squabbles in the 19th century ended with the Kingdom of Mataram dominant, but Balinese power eventually collapsed when the Dutch took over in 1894.

Lombok society is intricately woven around the three religions – Islam, Balinese Hinduism and the indigenous Wektu Telu – which predominate on the island. Wektu Telu is a complex mixture of Balinese Hinduism, Islam and animism. It originated in the north of Lombok in a village called Bayan, and does not exist outside the island. Almost 30% of the population of Lombok belongs to this faith, although the numbers are slowly diminishing as more young people turn to Islam.

Getting There & Away

Air Connections between Lombok and nearby islands include:

To/From Java Merpati has regular flights between Mataram and Surabaya (81,900 rp), Yogyakarta (134,450 rp) and Jakarta (192,400 rp). There should be at least one flight per day but schedules vary.

To/From Bali There are about eight flights per day with Merpati between Denpasar and Mataram; the fare costs about 42,000 rp. It's a very short flight with fine views of Nusa Penida, the south-east coast of Bali and the Gili Islands. The ferry is much cheaper but many budget travellers still fly to save the time and expense of getting to and from the ports of Padangbai and Lembar.

To/From Sumbawa There is one Merpati flight a day between Mataram and Sumbawa Besar (47,000 rp). Flights also go to Bima.

Shuttle Bus The Perama company runs an efficient and convenient transport service directly between various tourist destinations on Bali and Lombok, and has connections to Java and Sumbawa. For example, they can sell you a ticket from Ubud in Bali through to the Gili Islands for 17,500 rp, including the ferry to Lombok, a boat to the island and all the connections in between.

On public transport, you could probably do this trip for about 10,000 rp (if you weren't overcharged) but it would involve four bemo connections, the ferry and a boat. It would probably take longer and, if you missed a connection, you might have to spend a night somewhere in between.

Perama has offices in Mataram, Senggigi and Bangsal on Lombok, and in Kuta, Ubud, Lovina and Candidasa on Bali. You usually have to book the day before.

Boat Ferries to/from Lombok and other destinations in Indonesia include:

To/From Bali There are at least two ferries a day between Padangbai (Bali) and Lembar (Lombok), and up to four services at busy times such as Ramadan. Scheduled times of departure from Padangbai are 8 and 11 am, 2 and 5 pm, and from Lembar at 8 and 10 am, 2 and 5 pm. The schedules vary, so check first. Ekonomi costs around 4000 rp, 1st class 5700 rp and a bicycle is 600 rp.

Food and drinks are available on board or from the numerous hawkers who hang around the wharf until the ferry leaves. The trip takes at least four hours, sometimes up

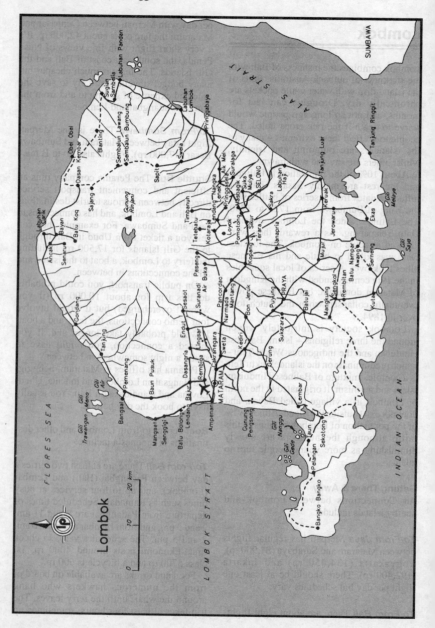

Lombok

to seven, and the afternoon ferries seem to be slower than the morning ones.

To/From Sumbawa
Passenger ferries leave Labuhan Lombok (in eastern Lombok) for Poto Tano (Sumbawa) at 8 and 9.30 am, 12 noon, 3 and 5 pm. In the other direction, boats depart Poto Tano at 7 and 9 am, 12 noon, 2.30 and 5 pm. Departure times may change, depending on demand and goodness knows what other local considerations. The trip takes about 1½ hours and costs around 2500 rp in Ekonomi A, 1500 rp in Ekonomi B and 500 rp for a bicycle.

To/From Other Islands
The Pelni ship KM *Kelimutu* makes a loop through the islands every two weeks, travelling from Padangbai to Lembar, Ujung Pandang (Sulawesi), Bima (Sumbawa), Waingapu (Sumba), Ende (Flores), Kupang (Timor), and back.

Hydrofoil
A new hydrofoil service operates between Bali's Benoa Port and Lembar Harbour on Lombok. Scheduled departure times from Benoa are 8.45 am and 3.30 pm, and from Lembar at 10.45 am and 3.30 pm. The trip takes about two hours, costs 35,000 rp to Lombok and 32,000 rp the other way. There are reports that they've lowered the fare to make it more competitive.

At the moment it's not much cheaper than the airfare, but it's a fun trip and it may be more reliable than Merpati's service. It is certainly quicker, more comfortable and more convenient than the ferry.

Getting Around
Shuttle Bus Perama has services between Mataram, Senggigi and the Gili Islands. They also go to Lembar and Labuhan Lombok for connections to Bali and Sumbawa.

Motorbike & Car Rental Motorbike rental is usually a pretty informal arrangement, but it's still relatively easy to do. At the Cakranegara end of Mataram, go to Jalan Gelantik, off Jalan Selaparang close to the junction with Jalan Sultan Hasanuddin.

There are a bunch of motorbike owners hanging around there with bikes to rent from 8000 to 10,000 rp a day. Some hotels will also arrange motorbike hire. As usual, the more you pay the better you get, and it's wise to check a bike over carefully before saying yes. If you suffer a breakdown or puncture in the boondocks of Lombok, you might be a long way from help.

Car hire is also less formal than on Bali – basically you arrange to borrow a car from a private owner. They rarely insist on a licence and sometimes want you to leave a passport for security. There is usually an insurance cover for damage to other people or property, but the car itself is often uninsured and you drive it at your own risk.

It costs about 35,000 to 50,000 rp per day for a Suzuki Jimny-type vehicle, depending on where you get it and how you bargain. If you take it for a few days or a week you should get a discount. Spread between four people it can be quite a cheap way of getting around.

Hotels in town, or at Senggigi, can often organise cars, or try Metro Photo (☎ 22146), Jalan Yos Sudarso 79 in Ampenan, where they have cheap rental cars. There are some 'official' car-rental companies, such as Rinjani Rent Car (☎ 21400) and Yoga Rent Car (☎ 21127), both in Mataram, but they tend to be more expensive.

Bemos There are several bemo terminals on Lombok. The main station is at Sweta, a couple of km out of Cakranegara. Here buses, minibuses and bemos depart for points all over the island. Other terminals are at Praya and Kopang, and you may have to go via one or more of these transport hubs to get from one part of Lombok to another. Bemos will pick up and put down passengers anywhere on their route. If you get on a bemo on the road make it clear that you don't want to charter the whole vehicle, especially if there are no other passengers on board.

Public transport is generally restricted to main routes, and away from these you can take a horse cart (*dokar* or *cidomo*) or walk. If you want to explore out-of-the-way places you must charter a bemo, or hire a motorbike or car.

Chartering It is easy to charter a bemo on Lombok. Count on about 35,000 rp a day, more if you're making a long trip. Check the vehicle first – you don't want to finish up driving through a rainstorm at night with bald tyres, faulty lights and no wipers. They're getting better, but many of the Lombok bemos would be ordered off the road in the West.

AMPENAN-MATARAM-CAKRANEGARA -SWETA

Ampenan-Mataram-Cakranegara-Sweta is the four-part capital, port and main town of Lombok. The four townships are continuous – you really can't tell where one ends and the next begins. These days, many visitors don't bother with the town at all, preferring to stay on the beach at nearby Senggigi.

Ampenan is the western end of the group, and while it isn't much to look at, there are plenty of budget places to stay, a couple of places of interest nearby, various tourist facilities and good transport connections. Once the main port of Lombok, Ampenan is now not much more than a small, dirty, dusty fishing harbour.

Mataram is the administrative capital of Nusa Tenggara Barat (West Nusa Tenggara) which covers all of Lombok and Sumbawa. There are some quite impressive public buildings such as the banks, the new post office and the governor's office. The main square, Lampangan Mataram, is on Jalan Pejanggik. Art exhibitions, theatre, dance and wayang kulit performances are held in the square.

Cakranegara (or just Cakra for short) is the old capital and now the main commercial centre of Lombok. It has a thriving Chinese community and many Balinese live here. It's also a centre for handicrafts and is well-known for its basketware and weaving. Check out the bazaar (Pusaka) and watch the silver and goldsmiths at work.

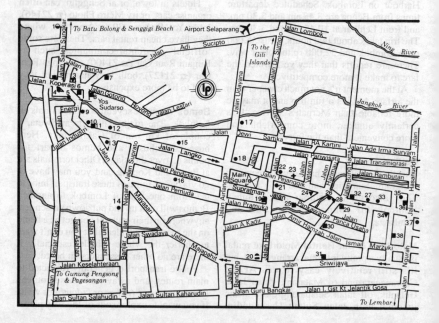

East of Cakra is Sweta, the fourth part of this strip-like development and the central transport terminal of Lombok. Sweta also has the largest market on the island, including a bird market.

Orientation

Ampenan-Mataram-Cakra-Sweta is spread out along one main road. This road has a variety of names – Jalan Yos Sudarso, Jalan Langko, Jalan Pejanggik and Jalan Selaparang – and it's one way, from west to east, for most of its length. A parallel road, Jalan Sriwi Jaya/Jalan Majapahit, brings traffic back towards the coast. The road names seem to overlap, so it can be difficult to find your way around, particularly if you're after a specific street address.

The central part of Ampenan is close to the coast, although the road fades out completely just before it hits the old port area and the grubby looking beach. Mataram has a small 'centre' near the river, and a larger shopping area and a market near the intersection of Jalan Selaparang and Jalan Hasanuddin, at the Cakra end. Ampenan-Mataram-Cakra-Sweta extends over nearly 10 km, so don't plan to walk from place to place.

■	PLACES TO STAY
2	Losmen Pabean
6	Zahir Hotel
7	Losmen Wisma Triguna
8	Losmen Horas & Latimojong
11	Wisma Melati
19	Hotel Kambodja
25	Losmen Rinjani
29	Mataram Hotel
30	Hotel Granada
31	Puri Indah Hotel
32	Selaparang Hotel
36	Hotel Pusaka
38	Hotel Shanti Puri

▼	PLACES TO EAT
3	Timur Tengah
4	Cirebon & Pabean
24	Garden House Restaurant
28	Rumah Makan Flamboyan
34	Sekawan Depot Es

	OTHER
1	Ampenan Bemo Stop
5	Ampenan Market
9	Merpati Office
10	Merpati Office
12	Tourist Office
13	Telephone Office
14	Museum Negeri
15	Bank Negara Indonesia
16	Mataram University
17	Immigration Office
18	Bank Indonesia
20	Main Post Office
21	Governor's House
22	Governor's Office
23	Hospital
26	Bali Ferry Office
27	Perama Office
33	Bank Eskpor-Impor
35	Motorbike Rental
37	Cakra Market
39	Mayura Water Palace
40	Selamat Riady
41	Pura Meru
42	Sweta Bemo/Bus Station
43	Sweta Market

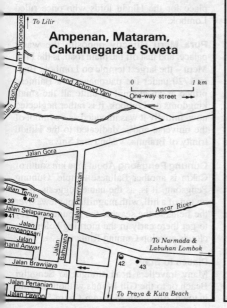

Ampenan, Mataram, Cakranegara & Sweta

To Lilir

To Diponegoro

Jalan Jend Achmad Yani

0   1 km

One-way street ⟶

Jalan Gora

Jalan Tenun

Jalan Selaparang

Jalan Lumpangsari

Jalan Jhanil Anwar

Jalan Brawijaya

Jalan Pertanian

Jalan Pawon

Jalan Peternakan

Jalan Bathvana

Ancar River

To Narmada & Labuhan Lombok

To Praya & Kuta Beach

Information

Tourist Office The Nusa Tenggara Barat government tourist office, the Kantor Dinas Pariwisata Daerah (☎ 21866/730), is in Mataram, on the north side of Jalan Langko 70, almost diagonally opposite the telephone office. They have a good map of Lombok with Ampenan-Mataram-Cakranegara-Sweta on the reverse, as well as a couple of pamphlets in English with information on sights, customs, addresses and so on. They're friendly and they welcome visitors.

The Perama office (☎ 22764, 23368) is at Jalan Penjanggik 66. They are very helpful, provide good information, organise their shuttle-bus connections, change money and arrange comparatively expensive day tours around Lombok.

Immigration Office Lombok's Kantor Imigrasi (immigration office) is on Jalan Udayana, the road out to the airport.

Money There are a number of banks along the main road, all of them large, impressive buildings. Most will change travellers' cheques though it can take some time. The Bank Ekspor Impor seems to be open longer than the others – weekdays from 7.30 am to 12 noon and 1 to 2 pm, and Saturday from 7.30 to 11.30 am.

The moneychanger in the Kompleks APHM in the Mataram shopping centre, on the south side of Jalan Pejanggik, is efficient, opens longer and has rates a little less than at the banks. You can also change travellers' cheques at the airport and at the Perama office.

Post & Telecommunications The Mataram GPO on Jalan Majapahit is the main post office and the place for poste restante mail.

The Permuntel telephone office is at the Ampenan end of Mataram, on Jalan Langko. It's very efficient, and you can get through an overseas call in minutes.

Books & Maps Toko Buku Titian in Ampenan has some English magazines and maps. The bookshop in the Kompleks APHM in the Mataram shopping centre, on the south side of Jalan Pejanggik, is also good.

Things to See

Around Ampenan There's an interesting **museum** on Jalan Banjar Tiler Negara in Ampenan with exhibits on the geology, history and culture of Lombok and Sumbawa. It's open Tuesday to Thursday from 8 am to 2 pm, from 8 to 11 am Friday and from 8 am to 12 noon on weekends.

On the beach, a few km north of Ampenan, is the Balinese temple complex of **Pura Segara**. Nearby, is a Chinese cemetery and the remnants of a Muslim cemetery.

Mayura Water Palace In Cakra, the water palace is dominated by a large artificial lake. It was built in 1744 and was once part of the Royal Court of the former Balinese Kingdom in Lombok. In the centre of the lake is an open-sided hall connected to the shoreline by a raised footpath. The hall was used both as a court of justice and a meeting place for the Hindu lords who once ruled Lombok.

Pura Meru Directly opposite the water palace, and just off the main road, is the Pura Meru – the largest temple on Lombok. Built in 1720 under the patronage of a Balinese prince as an attempt to unite all the small kingdoms on Lombok, it is rather neglected now. Initially it was intended as a symbol of the universe and is dedicated to the Hindu trinity of Brahma, Vishnu and Shiva.

Gunung Pengsong About nine km south of Cakra is another Balinese temple, Gunung Pengsong. It is, as the name suggests, built on top of a hill, with magnificent views over the fields to the sea and the mountains. Try to get there early in the morning before the clouds envelop Gunung Rinjani.

Places to Stay

Many travellers head straight to Senggigi Beach or to the Gili Islands without staying in town. Ampenan-Mataram-Cakra-Sweta is mainly a place to do business, and from Senggigi it's quite easy to zip into town for the morning or afternoon. If you do want to stay, there are plenty of hotels and losmen, with most of the cheapies in Ampenan.

Ampenan Only a short stroll from the centre of Ampenan is the *Zahir Hotel* (☎ 22403) at Jalan Koperasi 12, off Jalan Yos Sudarso. It's a simple place with singles/doubles at 4000/5000 rp, or 5000/6000 rp with bathroom. The price includes breakfast and tea or coffee throughout the day. The rooms at this popular, convenient and friendly losmen each have a small verandah and face a central courtyard. They can arrange motorbike rental for about 7500 rp per day.

Also in the centre of town is the Chinese-run *Losmen Pabean* (☎ 21758) at Jalan Pabean 146, also known as Jalan Yos Sudarso. It's better inside than it looks from the outside. Rooms cost 3500/5500/7500 rp for singles/doubles/triples.

Also on Jalan Koperasi, the *Losmen Horas* (☎ 21695), at No 65, is very clean, well-kept and has rooms at 4000/6000 rp with spotlessly clean bathrooms. Virtually next door is the *Latimojong*, at No 64. It's dirt cheap at 1500/2500 rp, but it's extremely basic and definitely a bottom-end place.

Continue further along Jalan Koperasi to *Losmen Wisma Triguna* (☎ 21705) which is operated by the same people as the Horas. It's a little over a km from central Ampenan and the spacious rooms have bathrooms. It's quiet, relaxed and helpful with rooms opening onto a bright verandah or onto the garden for 6000/8000 rp, breakfast included. The people at Horas or Wisma Triguna can help you to organise a climb up Gunung Rinjani, and will rent camping equipment and arrange a guide.

Mataram In Mataram, the *Hotel Kambodja* (☎ 22211) is at Jalan Supratman 10 on the corner with Jalan Arif Rahmat. It's pleasant and has rooms for about 6500/7500 rp.

On the Mataram-Cakra border, there's the *Hotel Pusaka* (☎ 23119) at Jalan Sultan Hasanuddin 23, with doubles starting from

12,500 rp, and up to 35,000 rp with air-con. The cheap rooms are pretty basic but the mid-range rooms are quite good at 17,000 rp a double. Close by, at No 17, is the *Losmen Merpati* with rooms at 3000/4000 rp, 5000/6000 rp and 6000/7000 rp. The cheap rooms are depressingly basic.

At Jalan Pejanggik 40-42 is the *Selaparang Hotel* (☎ 22670) with fan-cooled rooms at about 17,000/20,000 rp. Across the road, at No 105, is the *Mataram Hotel* (☎ 23411) with double rooms from 18,000 rp. Both these mid-range hotels have pleasant little restaurants, and more expensive rooms with air-con, TV, hot water and other mod cons. Also on Jalan Pejanggik, at No 64 just west of Perama, is the *Hotel Hertajoga* (☎ 21775), with fan-cooled rooms at 10,000/13,500 rp. These mid-price places are good value, with comfortable rooms and quiet courtyard gardens.

Just south of the main drag, at Jalan Maktal 15, is the *Hotel & Restaurant Shanti Puri* (☎ 22649) with cheap rooms at 5000/6000 rp and very comfortable rooms up to 10,000/12,000 rp. It's run by a friendly and helpful Balinese family, and they can arrange motorbike and car hire. The *Wisma Chandra* (☎ 23979) at Jalan Caturwarga 55, Mataram, has single/double/triple rooms for 7000/9000/15,000 rp.

The *Hotel Granada* (☎ 22275) is a heavily advertised top-end place on Jalan Bung Karno, a little south of central Mataram. There's a swimming pool and all rooms have air-con. The prices start around 50,000 rp a double and include breakfast. If you want such comfort, the *Puri Indah* (☎ 27633) on Jalan Sriwi Jaya also has a restaurant and a pool; with rooms from 15,000/20,000 rp, or 20,000/30,000 with air-con, it is much better value.

Places to Eat

Ampenan Ampenan has several Indonesian and Chinese restaurants including the very popular *Cirebon* at Jalan Pabean 113, with a standard Indonesian/Chinese menu and most dishes from 1500 to 2500 rp. Next door, at No 111, is the *Pabean* with similar food.

Closer to the Ampenan bemo station is the *Rumah Makan Arafat,* at No 64, with good, cheap Indonesian food. Other alternatives are the *Setia* at Jalan Pabean 129, the *Depot Mina* at Jalan Yos Sudarso 102 and the *Timur Tengah* at Jalan Koperasi 22, right across from the Hotel Zahir.

Mataram There are a couple of interesting restaurants off Jalan Pejanggik in Mataram, several hundred metres down the road from the governor's residence on the same side. The *Garden House Restaurant* is an open-air place with inexpensive nasi campur, nasi goreng and similar standard dishes. They also have a variety of ice creams, including cassata and tutti frutti! Nearby, the *Taliwang* offers local dishes. Continue further along the main road towards Cakra and you come to the more expensive *Rumah Makan Flamboyan,* with seafood and Chinese dishes.

Cakra In Cakra, the *Sekawan Depot Es* has cold drinks downstairs and a seafood and Chinese restaurant upstairs. Round the corner on Jalan Hasanuddin is the *Rumah Makan Madya,* which serves very good, cheap authentic Sasak-style food. A little further north, the *Rumah Makan Akbar* is also worth trying. There are a number of other restaurants in this area, a handful of bakeries and, of course, plenty of cheap and spicy-food opportunities at the Cakra Market.

Things to Buy
One of the last weaving factories still operating in Mataram is Slamet Riady on Jalan Ukirkawi, where women weave delicate gold and silver thread sarongs and exquisite ikats on looms that look like they haven't altered since the Majapahit era.

A bemo will drop you within a few metres of the factory and you're welcome to wander around. The factory is open from 7.30 am. Rinjani Hand Woven, beside the Selaparang Hotel at Jalan Pejanggik 44-46, has a good collection of woven materials.

There are a number of craft and antique shops near the Ampenan cheap hotel area. Try Musdah at Dayan Penen, Jalan Sape 16 – a series of signs leads you down twisting alleys from the Zahir Hotel. Renza Antiques and Rora Antiques, both on Jalan Yos Sudarso, are also good for a browse.

Another good place to look for handicrafts and other local products is the Sweta Market, next to the bemo terminal.

Getting There & Away
See the Lombok Getting There & Away section for details of flights and ferry services to Lombok.

Air There's a Merpati office (☎ 23762) in Ampenan at Jalan Yos Sudarso 6 which also handles bookings and enquiries for Garuda flights. There's a second office (☎ 21037) at Yos Sudarso 22 and another in the Hotel Selaparang at Jalan Pejanggik 40-42 in Mataram.

Bus The Sweta bus terminal at the inland end of the Ampenan-Mataram-Cakra-Sweta development is the main bus/bemo station for the entire island, and the eastern terminal for the local bemos. Fares include Lembar for 1000 rp, Praya 700 rp, Labuhan Lombok 1400 rp and Bayan 1600 rp.

Boat The SP Ferry office at Jalan Pejanggik 49 sells tickets for the KM *Nusa Penida,* one of the ferries to Bali, but it's just as easy to get them at Lembar Harbour.

Hydrofoil The office for the Nawala hydrofoil service (☎ 21655) is at Jalan Langko 11A in Mataram.

Getting Around
To/From the Airport The Selaparang Airport is only a couple of km from Ampenan or Mataram, and about 4500 rp by taxi. Alternatively, walk out of the car park where frequent No 7 bemos come by and run to the Ampenan bemo terminal for 150 rp. You can also travel directly from the airport to Senggigi beach (7500 rp by taxi) or to the Gili Islands (see those sections for details).

Local Transport Bemos shuttle up and down the two main routes between the Ampenan terminal at one end and the Sweta terminal at the other. The fare is a standard 150 rp regardless of distance. You can rent old bicycles for about 2000 rp a day (or 4000 rp for a new one) from the Losmen Horas or Wisma Triguna in Ampenan. For details of car and motorbike rental, see the Lombok Getting Around section.

SENGGIGI BEACH

On a series of sweeping bays, between seven and 12 km north of Ampenan, Senggigi is really a string of beaches which has become the most popular tourist area on Lombok. Promotional work for the big, expensive Senggigi Beach Hotel has focused much more interest on Senggigi and Lombok as a whole.

There are now a few other fancy places in Senggigi, and the Lombok government is encouraging additional four and five-star standard developments. Fortunately, there is still some budget accommodation here.

Senggigi has a fine beach, although it slopes off very steeply. There's some snorkelling off the point and in the sheltered bay around the headland. There are superb views across Lombok Strait to Bali and Gunung Agung – inspiring at sunset. **Batu Bolong**, a few km on the Ampenan side of Senggigi, is a large rock with a hole in it and has a Balinese temple perched on top.

Information

You can change money or travellers' cheques at the Graha Beach Hotel, in the middle of the Senggigi strip; they can also make and confirm bookings with Garuda and Merpati. There's a Perama office further north which runs tours and tourist transport and will also provide information and change money. Other facilities include a Permuntel telephone office and some photo-processing places.

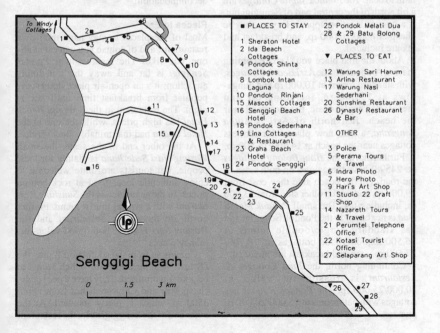

■ PLACES TO STAY	25 Pondok Melati Dua
1 Sheraton Hotel	28 & 29 Batu Bolong Cottages
2 Ida Beach Cottages	▼ PLACES TO EAT
4 Pondok Shinta Cottages	12 Warung Sari Harum
8 Lombok Intan Laguna	13 Arlina Restaurant
10 Pondok Rinjani	17 Warung Nasi Sederhani
15 Mascot Cottages	20 Sunshine Restaurant
16 Senggigi Beach Hotel	26 Dynasty Restaurant & Bar
18 Pondok Sederhana	OTHER
19 Lina Cottages & Restaurant	3 Police
23 Graha Beach Hotel	5 Perama Tours & Travel
24 Pondok Senggigi	6 Indra Photo
	7 Hero Photo
	9 Hari's Art Shop
	11 Studio 22 Craft Shop
	14 Nazareth Tours & Travel
	21 Perumtel Telephone Office
	22 Kotasi Tourist Office
	27 Selaparang Art Shop

Senggigi Beach

Places to Stay

Senggigi is moving up-market. Although there is much mid-range accommodation and an increasing number of expensive places, there's not a great deal for shoestring travellers.

The most popular travellers' place at Senggigi is the *Pondok Senggigi*. It has expanded considerably, but still has a good restaurant and a variety of accommodation including cheap rooms at 6000/8000 rp with mandi and toilet. Newer rooms, with Western-style bathrooms, cost from 15,000/18,000 rp. A 15% tax is added to your food and room bill. The rooms all run off long verandahs which face the tropical garden.

One of the cheapest places to stay is *Pondok Sederhana*, just north of Pondok Senggigi, with rooms staggered up the hillside and sharing a communal mandi and toilet. They're a bit grotty, but the position is good and the prices, from about 5000 rp, are hard to beat. The *Pondok Shinta Cottages* are a bit north of the central part of Senggigi but, if a quieter location appeals to you, they're cheap at 8000/10,000 rp, and breakfast and tax are included.

About the first place you'll strike coming in from Ampenan is the *Asri Beach Cottages*, with standard rooms at 10,000 rp and bungalows at 15,000 rp, including tax and breakfast. They're basic, but clean and near the beach. Just north of Asri is *Atitha Sangraha*, a nice new place with spotless cottages near the beach at 14,500/16,500 rp.

Further north, the *Batu Bolong Cottages* (☎ 24598) have bungalows on both sides of the road. On the beach side they cost from 29,000 rp, and on the other side from 23,000 rp, including tax. The small *Pondok Melati Dua* is next door to the Pondok Senggigi and has standard single/double rooms at 16,500/22,000 rp or cottages at 18,700/27,500 rp – tax and breakfast are included.

Continuing north, the *Lina Cottages & Restaurant* is reasonable value at 20,000/25,000 rp. The *Pondok Rinjani* has cottages with bathrooms at 15,000/20,000 rp plus tax.

Windy Cottages are out by themselves, beyond Senggigi in an area known as Mangset. It's a great location if you want to get away from it all, and the restaurant is good value. They only have eight rooms at 10,000/15,000 rp for singles/doubles.

Lombok's first big 'international standard' hotel, the *Senggigi Beach Hotel* (☎ 23430), is on a side road just north of Pondok Senggigi (US$52/62 up to US$120). At least as classy is the *Lombok Intan Laguna* (☎ 23659). Other pricey places include the *Graha Beach Hotel* (☎ 23782), *Mascot Cottages* (☎ 23865), the *Ida Beach Cottages* (☎ 21013, 21353) and the *Pacific Beach Hotel* at the northern end of Senggigi.

Further north, in Mangset, you'll find the *Bunga Beach Cottages*, another new place with a splendid beach-front position, and comfortable, air-con bungalows at 70,000/80,000 rp. The *Senggigi Palace Hotel* and the *Sheraton* are still being finished, but are unlikely to offer budget accommodation!

Places to Eat

Most of the places to stay have their own restaurants, and of course you can eat at any one you like. The restaurant at *Pondok Senggigi* is far and away the top dining attraction; it's an open-air place deservedly popular from breakfast time until late at night. The restaurant in the *Senggigi Beach Hotel* has high prices, while the one at the *Hotel Graha* had interminably slow service.

At the other end of the scale, the small *Warung Nasi Sederhana* is mainly for local people, but tourists are quite welcome to enjoy authentic local food at rock-bottom prices. In the same area is the *Sunshine Restaurant* with a typical tourist menu. Further north are the *Arlina Restaurant* and the *Warung Sari Harum*, both good-value-for-money places.

Coming in from the south, you'll pass the *Dynasty Restaurant & Bar* which seems to be poorly patronised. They have a pool table, cheap beer and Chinese dishes from about 3500 rp, which is pretty standard. At the other end of the Senggigi strip, the restaurant at *Windy Cottages* serves good food in a delightful seaside setting.

Entertainment

Local rock bands often perform at the *Pondok Senggigi* and the *Hotel Graha*. They're pretty good value, with both visitors and the local young people crowding the dance floor.

Getting There & Away

There's a bemo stop in Ampenan, on the coast road just north of town. A public bemo from there to Senggigi is about 250 rp, more if you are going to the north end of the strip. From the airport, get a bemo to Lendang Bajur, a short distance north. From there, you can catch a bus or bemo to Senggigi – the total fare is about 500 rp.

NARMADA

About 10 km east of Cakra, on the main east-west road crossing Lombok, is this hill and lake laid out as a stylised, miniature replica of the summit of Gunung Rinjani and its crater lake. It was constructed by King Anak Agung Gede Karangasem of Mataram in 1805, when he was no longer able to climb Rinjani to make his offerings to the gods. The temple is still used today and is dedicated to Lord Shiva.

It's a nice place to spend a few hours, but on weekends it's very crowded with locals. A 250 rp admission fee applies and there is another nominal fee to use the swimming pool. People will offer to guide you around the complex. The price is 'up to you' but 500 rp would suffice, if you need a guide at all.

Getting There & Away

There are frequent bemos from Sweta to Narmada for around 200 rp. The gardens are 100 metres south of the main road – take the side road opposite the bemo terminal.

LINGSAR

A few km north-west of Narmada is Lingsar, a large temple complex catering for the Bali-Hindu, Islam and Wektu Telu religions. There are a couple of warungs to the right of the square and just in front of it. You can buy snacks, and also hard-boiled eggs to feed to the holy eels which inhabit the pool in the Wektu Telu Temple. If the temple is locked, ask at one of the warungs for a key.

Getting There & Away

A bemo to Lingsar will cost about 200 rp from either Sweta or Narmada. Ask where to get off because you can't see the temples from the main road. It's a short walk from the bemo stop to the temples.

SURANADI

East of Lingsar is Suranadi, which has one of the holiest temples on Lombok – noted for its ornate Balinese carvings. You can bathe here in cool spring-water baths, and there are also holy eels which you can feed with hard boiled eggs. A little to the west, towards Sesaot, there's a small jungle sanctuary, the **Hutan Wisata Suranadi**, which is a good place for a short walk to observe the jungle flora and fauna.

You can stay in the Dutch-built *Suranadi Hotel*, where rooms cost from around US$12 and cottages US$30. It's no great example of colonial architecture, but there are two good-sized swimming pools, tennis courts, a restaurant and a bar. For 1000 rp, you can use the pools even if you're not staying here.

LEMBAR

Lembar, 22 km south of Ampenan, is one of the main ports of Lombok. The ferries and hydrofoils to and from Bali dock here, and there are regular buses and bemos between Lembar and Sweta during the day. Bus and bemo drivers drop you off almost directly in front of the Lembar ferry office. There's a canteen here where you can buy snacks and drinks while waiting to catch the ferry.

There's only one place to stay in Lembar, the *Serumbum Indah*, with a restaurant and single/double rooms from 12,500/15,000 rp. They're not used to foreign visitors here and it's not very convenient, being about two km north of the harbour on the main road.

SUKARARA

This small village, just 25 km south of Mataram, is one of the traditional weaving centres of Lombok. Nearly every house in Sukarara has an old wooden handloom on which the women weave the complicated and difficult patterns – some so intricate that they take one person three months to finish and involve weaving the hand-dyed threads in four separate directions. The women of this village specialise in highly decorative cloth interwoven with gold or silver threads. There are also coarser, heavier fabrics woven by men for use as blankets.

There are five or six places with looms set up near the street, and you can watch the women weaving, and hear the rhythmic 'clack, clack' of the looms. You'll see the sarongs slung out on display, and most places have a big range inside. You'll have to bargain, but there's such a range of quality and size that it's impossible to give a guide to prices. The best work is magnificent, and well worth paying for.

Places to Stay

If you want to stay the night, check with the *kepala desa* (village headman) or with the woman who runs the warung – she sometimes puts people up for the night.

Getting There & Away

Catch a bemo going from Sweta to Praya, and get off at Puyung, about 5 km before Praya. It should cost about 600 rp. From Puyung, you can hire a dokar for about 200 rp to take you the two km to Sukarara.

REMBITAN & OTHER VILLAGES

From Sengkol down to Kuta Beach is a centre of Sasak culture, and there are many Sasak villages where the people still live in traditional houses and engage in traditional crafts.

Only a couple of km south of Sengkol is Rembitan (or Sade), a traditional, if slightly sanitised, Sasak village with a population of 750. Tourists are welcome to look around – one of the local kids will give you a guided tour for a small (200 to 300 rp) tip. The

Masjid Kuno, an old thatched-roof mosque, tops the hill around which the village houses cluster. Other Sasak villages are dotted around on the nearby hills.

KUTA BEACH

Lombok's Kuta Beach is a magnificent stretch of sand with impressive hills rising around it. It's much less touristed than the better known Kuta Beach in Bali but surfers are finding some good reef breaks accessible from Kuta and there are plans to develop this coast with four and five-star standard hotels. At the annual *nyale* fishing celebration, which usually falls in February-March of each year, people flock to Kuta. Nyale are small worm-like fish, but the celebration is as much to do with courtship as with fishing. Otherwise, it's a very quiet place.

There's a series of beautiful bays and headlands east of Kuta. All of the beach-front land has been bought up by the government for planned tourist resorts. **Segar Beach** is about two km east around the first headland, and you can easily walk there. There's a very good road going five km east to **Tanjung Aan** where there are two superb beaches and the beginnings of the expensive hotels planned for this area.

The road continues another three km to the fishing village of **Gerupak**, where there's a market on Tuesday. From Gerupak, you can get a boat across the bay to Bumgang.

Alternatively, turn north just before Tanjung Aan and go to Serneng. Beyond here, the road deteriorates but you can get to Awang with a motorbike or on foot, then continue into south-east Lombok.

West of Kuta are more fine beaches at **Marwun** and Silung **Blanak**. There are no facilities and there are no direct roads suitable for ordinary vehicles. You'll have to go into Sengkol first, then out again to the coast.

Places to Stay & Eat

The road from the north turns east along the coast, just after the village. Along this beachfront road you'll find most of Kuta's accommodation, which is all of a similar price and quality. After the police station, you pass *Rambitan*, with rooms at 7500 rp, including tea but not breakfast. The *Wisma Segara Anak*, which is next door, has a restaurant, rooms at around 6000/8000 rp and bungalows at around 8000/10,000 rp, including breakfast.

Next along, *Pondok Sekar Kuning*, or 'Yellow Flower Cottage', has double rooms downstairs for 8000 rp; those upstairs have a nice view and cost 10,000 rp. *Anda Cottages*, next door, is the original place at Kuta. It has some trees and shrubs which make it more pleasant, and a good restaurant with Indonesian, Chinese and Western dishes. Rooms here cost from 9000 to 12,500 rp, including breakfast.

A bit further along are the *New Paradise Bungalows* with good food and singles/doubles at 8000/10,000 rp, and the *Rinjani Agung Beach Bungalows* with standard rooms at 8000/10,000 rp and 'suit rooms' at 17,500/20,000 rp, again including breakfast. The old *Mascot Cottages* may be open again when you get there, or continue on to the *Cockatoo Cottages & Restaurant*, the last place along the beach, with a nice restaurant area and rooms for 10,000/15,000 rp, with breakfast.

There are a few cheap, basic homestays in the village, and also the *Losmen Mata Hari*, near the market on the road to Mawan. It has a restaurant and nine small, clean rooms with showers at 8000/10,000, including breakfast.

There's a big, new place at Tanjung Aan, but its opening was apparently delayed by the authorities. It seems to have been acquired by the government's Lombok Tourist Development Corporation, and it's anyone's guess when it will open or what it will charge. There's no doubt about the quality of this location – it's magnificent.

Getting There & Away

To get to Kuta by public transport is difficult. It's no trouble getting a bemo to Praya, but beyond there it's a matter of waiting for another one to Sengkol (500 rp) and then another down to Kuta (300 rp). Market day in Sengkol is Thursday, and there may be more transport then.

AROUND KOTARAJA

The villages of **Kotaraja** and **Loyok** in eastern Lombok are renowned for their handicrafts, particularly their basketware and plaited mats. You may also come across exquisite and intricate metal jewellery, as well as vases, caskets and other decorative objects.

The area is cooler than the lowlands, and a great place to walk through rice fields, jungle and unspoilt villages. **Tetebatu** is a mountain retreat on the southern slopes of Gunung Rinjani, seven km north of Kotaraja. **Lendang Nangka**, a few km east, is an interesting Sasak village and a good base from which to explore the surrounding area. Nearby is **Tojang**, the biggest spring in Lombok. **Pringgasela**, about 10 km east of Kotaraja, is a centre for weaving blankets and sarongs.

Places to Stay & Eat

Wisma Soedjono in Tetebatu has a variety of single/double rooms and bungalows from around 7500/11,000 rp to 25,000/35,000 rp. *Diwi Enjeni*, in the rice fields on the right as you come in from the south, is a new place with rooms at 4000/7000 rp.

At Lendang Nangka, you can stay with Hadji Radiah, the local primary school teacher who speaks good English. He is a mine of information on the area and enthusiastic about having visitors. His operation seems to become more popular with every edition of this book and he now has 12 rooms for guests in the house. It costs 10,000/14,000 rp per day which includes three meals. If his place is full, he can sometimes arrange alternative accommodation for you in a nearby village – they are trying to avoid having too many visitors in the same place.

In Kotaraja, the only place you can stay is with the kepala desa. In Saleh Lenek, near Pringgasela, try *Wisma Longgali Permai*.

Getting There & Away

Kotaraja is 32 km from Sweta. It's easy if you have your own transport, but it can take the best part of a day on public transport. From Sweta, take a bemo to Pomotong for about 800 rp (you may have to go via Narmada). From Pomotong, you can get to Kotaraja by bemo (250 rp) or dokar (horse cart). Bemos are cheaper than dokars, but not as frequent.

To get to Loyok, you can get a bemo from Pomotong to take you as far as the turn-off to the village and then walk the last 300 metres, or get a dokar for about 200 rp per person. Tetebatu and Lendang Nangka are also reached from Pomotong.

LABUHAN LOMBOK

Labuhan Lombok, on Lombok's east coast, is the port for ferries to Sumbawa, the next island. The people are friendly and the harbour looks attractive, but after you've had a look around, there's little to do.

You can climb the hill on the south side of the harbour and watch the boats travelling between here and Sumbawa. North of Labuhan Lombok, there are fishing villages where foreigners are still a curiosity. Look for the thatched houses on stilts on the tidal flats. **Pulo Lampur**, 14 km north, has a black-sand beach and is popular with locals on Sunday and holidays. From **Labuhan Pandan**, you can charter a boat out to explore the uninhabited islands of Gili Sulat and the Gili Petangan group.

Places to Stay

In the village of Labuhan Lombok, you can stay at the basic *Losmen Dian Dutaku*, on the main road coming into town, with rooms at 2600/3600 rp. On Jalan Khayangan, the road round to the ferry port, there's the *Losmen Munawar*, which is simple but quite OK, with rooms at 2500/5000 rp. At Teranset, near Pulo Lampur, you might be able to stay at *Pak Moti's*. He's known locally and has some rooms for rent for about 10,000/15,000 rp with three meals. There are also some tourist bungalows being developed near the sea at Labuhan Pandan.

Places to Eat

There are a couple of basic warungs around the bemo station. You can always buy a fish

at the market and get it cooked at a warung. The *Hidayat Restaurant*, across the road from the bemo station, is a friendly place. Alternatively, there's the fairly clean *Warung Kelayu* right next door.

Getting There & Away

Bus & Bemo There are regular buses between Labuhan Lombok and Sweta. The 69-km trip costs 2000 rp and should take a bit less than two hours. There are other road connections to Masbagik (1000 rp), Pancor (1300 rp), Kopang (1500 rp) and Labuhan Pandan (300 rp). Buses connect to both the ferry port and the terminal in town.

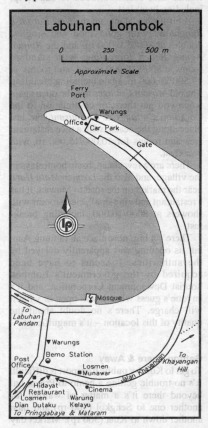

Boat The ferry to Poto Tano on Sumbawa departs from a new port on the north side of the harbour. It's about two or three km from the port to the town of Labuhan Lombok, around the road which skirts the east of the bay. It can be fiercely hot, so don't try to walk. A bemo costs 250 rp. There are several ferries per day and the trip takes about 1½ hours. The ticket office is beside the car park and the fare is around 2500 rp.

There are a couple of food stalls at the port, and one or two warungs serving nasi campur. Guys come on board the boat selling hard-boiled eggs and fried rice wrapped in banana leaves. Take a water bottle with you – it can be an extremely hot ride! The ferries can get very crowded, especially at times such as Ramadan when local people travel.

THE GILI ISLANDS

Off the north-west coast of Lombok are three small coral-fringed islands – Gili Air, Gili Meno and Gili Trawangan – with superb, white sandy beaches, clear water, coral reefs, brilliantly coloured fish and the best snorkelling on Lombok.

Obviously, 'gili' means 'island', so it's a bit silly to call them the Gili Islands, but that is what the thousands of travellers who visit here call them. Development on the islands is being carefully monitored by the local people, to retain and even improve upon the 'islands' environmental quality. Please do what you can to minimise the physical and social impact of your visit.

The islanders are all Muslims, and visitors should respect their sensibilities. In particular, topless (for women) or nude sunbathing is offensive to them, though they won't say so directly. Away from the beach, it is polite for both men and women to cover their shoulders and knees.

Though the attractions of sun, sand and sea are common to all three islands, each one has developed something of an individual character. Unfortunately, it is difficult to go directly from one island to another as there are no regular public boats, so you have to charter one for yourself and as many other people as you can muster. Alternatively, you

have to get a public boat back across to the mainland, then wait for another boat out to the island you wish to visit.

Apart from the hill on Gili Trawangan, all three islands are pancake flat. There are no roads, cars or even motorbikes, so getting around is as easy as walking. Fishing, raising cattle and goats and growing corn, coconuts, tapioca and peanuts are the main economic activities, along with the growing tourist industry.

There are few facilities on these islands although some of the places now have their own electricity generators. There are also small shops with a minimum of supplies. There is no place to change travellers' cheques (but you can change foreign cash on Trawangan), so bring enough cash with you.

Most places to stay come out of a standard mould – you get a plain little bungalow on stilts, with a small verandah out the front. Inside, there will be one or two beds with mosquito nets, the verandah will probably have a table and a couple of chairs. Mandi and toilet facilities are usually shared.

The local tourist authority has set accommodation prices at 10,000/15,000/20,000 rp for singles/doubles/triples with three meals and 6000/9000/13,500 rp for bed & breakfast only. There are a few rooms with private mandis which are more expensive – 12,500/22,500/26,000 rp with three meals, 8000/11,000/16,000 rp for bed & breakfast only. This means that they're charging roughly 4000 rp for lunch and dinner, which is pretty cheap considering the good quality and quantity of food which they usually serve, though you may prefer the freedom to eat wherever you wish.

Getting There & Away

From Ampenan or the airport, you can get to one of the islands and be horizontal on the beach within a couple of hours. Start with a short bemo ride north to Rembiga (about 200 rp). From there, it's 600 rp for a bus to Pemenang, a scenic 1½ hour journey across the Pusuk Pass through lush, green forest. From Pemenang, it's a km or so off the main road to the harbour at Bangsal, 200 rp by

GILI TRAWANGAN

1   Nusa Tiga Homestay
2   Coral Beach Homestay
3   Pasir Putih II
4   Alex Accommodation
5   Excellent Restaurant
6   Good Heart Homestay
7   Homestay Makmur I
8   Pasir Putih I
9   Danau Hijau Bungalows
10 Creative Losmen
11 Melati Losmen
12 Rudy's Cottage Restaurant
13 Dua Sekawan I
14 Pak Majid's Losmen
15 Simple Bungalow
16 Dua Sekawan II
17 Trawangan Beach Cottage & Restaurant
18 Mountain View Cottage & Restaurant, Perama Office
19 Fantasi Bungalows
20 Borobudur Restaurant
21 Holiday Inn Cottages
22 Sandy Beach
23 Paradise Cottages & Restaurant
24 Albatross Diving Adventures
25 Homestay Makmur II
26 Majestic Cottages
27 Rainbow Cottages

GILI MENO

1   Good Heart Restaurant
2   Blue Coral Bungalows
3   Pondok Meno
4   New cottages
5   Janur Indah Cottages
6   Janur Indah Bungalows
7   Matahari Bungalows
8   Malia's Child Bungalows
9   Gazebo Hotel
10 Kontiki Cottage Restaurant

GILI AIR

1   Hink Bungalows
2   Muksin Cottages
3   Hans Bungalows & Restaurant
4   Gusung Indah Bungalows
5   Fantastick Bungalows

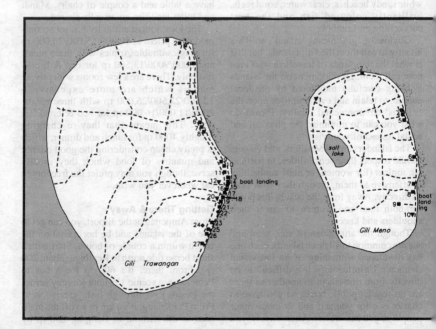

Gili Trawangan

Gili Meno

salt lake

boat landing

boat landing

dokar. Alternatively, you may be able to get a bemo from Sweta direct to Pemenang for about 700 rp.

You can also charter a bemo from Ampenan, which can be quite cheap between a group of people and allows you stops to enjoy the scenery.

6	Gili Air Cottages
7	Gita Gili Sunrise
8	Nusa Tiga Bungalows
9	Gili Beach Inn Bungalows
10	Paradiso Bungalows
11	Sederhana Losmen
12	Bupati's Place Cottages
13	Garden Cottages
14	Village Office
15	Gado Gado Pub
16	Bamboo Cottages
17	Fanta Pub
18	Gili Indah Cottages & Restaurant, Perama Offices
19	Sunset Cottages
20	Salabose Cottages

Perama shuttle buses go from Mataram or Senggigi to Bangsal and the Gili Islands for about 2500 and 5000 rp respectively. It's not as cheap, but it's very convenient.

There's a small information office at Bangsal Harbour where they charge the official fares out to the islands – 700 rp to Gili Air, 900 rp to Gili Meno and 1000 rp to Gili Trawangan. It's a matter of sitting and waiting until there's a full boat load, about 20 people. If you have almost that number waiting, the boat will leave if you can pay the extra fares between you. As soon as you do this, you'll be amazed at how many local people appear from nowhere to fill the boat.

It's a good idea to try to get to Bangsal by 10 am. It's not an unpleasant place to hang around while you're waiting for a boat, and the shaded warungs like the *Parahiangan Coffee House* have good food and coffee.

Boats can be chartered for official prices of 12,500 rp to Gili Air, 15,000 rp to Gili

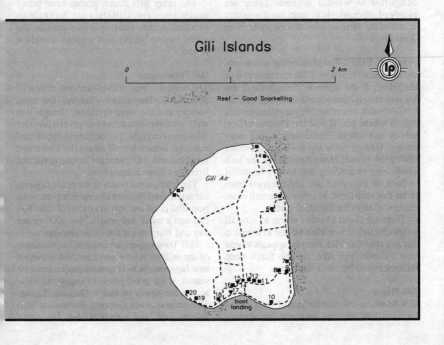

Meno and 17,500 rp to Gili Trawangan. In practice, you can usually beat those prices down a bit. The trip out to Gili Trawangan takes about an hour, less to the other islands. It's quite expensive to charter boats around the islands if you want to try the other beaches, but not too bad if you can get a group together. From Gili Trawangan, it's 12,000 rp to Gili Meno and 15,000 rp to Gili Air. Between Gili Air and Gili Meno, it's 12,500 rp.

Gili Air

Gili Air is the closest island to the mainland. It's also the smallest and the most densely populated, with about 600 people. Beaches run round most of the island and there's a small village at the southern end. Homes and small farms are dotted amongst the palm trees, along with losmen and a couple of 'pubs'.

Because the buildings are so scattered, the island has a pleasant, rural character and it's delightful to wander around. There are plenty of other people to meet but if you stay in one of the more isolated places, socialising is optional.

Places to Stay & Eat Most of the accommodation is scattered round the southern end of the island at the harbour, though there are losmen near the east, north and west coasts.

Gili Indah, one of the bigger places on Gili Air, is where you'll find the Perama office, which has useful information and may change foreign cash. Up north, at the other end of the island, *Hans Bungalows* are well away from everything and have a beautiful outlook on the beach and good reports from those that stay there, but they are much more expensive than the standard prices.

There are about 15 other places to stay, all so similar that it wouldn't be fair to mention any in particular. Pick one that appeals to you in a location you like, or one that's been recommended by other travellers.

Gili Meno

Gili Meno is the middle island in size and location but has the smallest population,

about 300. It is the quietest of the islands, with fewer tourists and tourist facilities. If you want to play Robinson Crusoe, this is the place to do it.

There's a salt lake in the middle of the island which produces salt in the dry season and mosquitoes in the wet season. They're probably no worse than in other places at that time of year, but the usual precautions are called for – mosquito net, repellent, long sleeves and long pants around dusk.

Places to Stay & Eat The accommodation here is mostly on the east beach with a couple places up north. The *Gazebo Hotel* is pretty up-market by Gili standards. They have tastefully furnished and decorated Bali-style bungalows with private bathrooms, air-con and electricity (if it's working). There is also a fancy balcony restaurant. It costs about US$30 for bed & breakfast. Another posh place is being built at the north end of the east coast, with a tennis court no less!

The other half dozen places have pretty much standard Gili Islands bungalows (perhaps a little more spacious than on the other two islands) and charge standard prices.

Gili Trawangan

The largest island, with a local population of about 400, Trawangan also has the most visitors and the most facilities, though it is still undeveloped, even primitive, by Western standards. The accommodation and restaurants/bars are all along the east coast beaches, and this compact layout gives it a friendly village atmosphere.

The white-sand beach is the main daytime attraction, and the snorkelling is superb, with beautiful coral and lots of colourful fish. You can rent a mask and snorkel for 2000 rp per day and flippers for the same amount.

Gili Trawangan also has a hill at the south of the island, where you can find traces of two Japanese WW II gun emplacements. At sunset, it's a good place to enjoy the view across the straits to Bali's Gunung Agung. The sunrise over Gunung Rinjani is also impressive, and one islander described

Trawangan's three main attractions as 'sunrise, sunset, sunburn'! It's certainly hot enough for sunburn, and it can get rather dusty in the dry season.

Places to Stay & Eat The accommodation and prices here are even more standardised than on the other islands. Typical basic bungalows cost 10,000/15,000/20,000 rp for singles/doubles/triples. A couple of places, like *Rainbow Cottages*, have private mandis and cost more. Some others don't provide lunch or dinner, so they're a bit cheaper.

Pick a place you like the look of (some have prettier gardens), or one recommended by a recent visitor, or go with one of the friendly people who will meet you when the boat comes in. The places in the middle of the beach strip may be a bit better for meeting people, while those at the north and south ends of the beach offer more peace and quiet.

Most of the places to stay also serve food, but there's a few convivial restaurants, like the *Excellent* and the *Mountain View*, which are more like bars in the evening. There's usually music and dancing in at least one of them.

GUNUNG RINJANI

At 3726 metres, Gunung Rinjani is the highest mountain in Lombok and the third highest in Indonesia. The mountain is actually an active volcano – the last eruption was in 1901 – and it has a huge half-moon crater with a large green lake and a number of steaming hot springs. Both the Balinese and the local Sasak people revere Gunung Rinjani. To the Balinese, it is equivalent to their own Gunung Agung, a seat of the gods, and many Balinese make a pilgrimage here each year. Full moon is the favourite time for the Sasaks to pay their respects and cure their ailments by bathing in the hot springs. It can get very crowded. You should not attempt the climb during the wet season as the paths are slippery and too dangerous.

There are several routes up Gunung Rinjani, but the easiest one to follow, and the most frequently used, is via the villages of Bayan, Batu Koq and Senaru, on the north-

ern slopes. Bayan is the birthplace of the Wektu Telu religion and traditional Hindu dances are still performed here at certain times. You can stay in Bayan with the kepala desa and there are a couple of warungs, but if you're climbing Rinjani, it's better for you to continue to Batu Koq where there are a few homestays which cost about 5000 rp per person, including breakfast.

You may get a lift on a truck from Batu Koq (500 rp), but otherwise you'll have to walk the four km to Senaru, high up in the foothills of Rinjani. It's a very traditional village, and only recently have they started having regular contact with people in the surrounding area.

From Senaru, it's about six hours to the base camp at Pos III, then about six hours from there up to the rim and down into the crater. After walking around part of the lake's north shore, most people camp near the hot springs and return all the way to Batu Koq the next day. You need three clear days to do it – up and back down again – and probably at least another day to recover. You have to be there early in the morning if you want to see the spectacular view before the clouds roll in.

You can rent equipment from the Wisma Triguna or Losmen Horas in Ampenan and they also organise ascents. The rental for five days is 10,000 rp for a sleeping bag, 12,500 rp for a tent and 2500 rp for stove.

To get to the actual summit of Rinjani takes at least four days from Senaru. The track to the summit branches off about a two-hour walk east of the hot springs. From the junction (about 2400 metres altitude), it's a difficult three or four-hour climb over loose ground to the top (3726 metres). Another option is to traverse the whole mountain by continuing from the hot springs, then descending to Sembalun Lawang and Sembalun Bumbung, two Sasak villages five km apart on the eastern slopes of Rinjani.

Getting There & Away

Several buses a day go to Bayan from Sweta, the first leaving around 9 am. The fare is 1500 rp and it takes about three hours. The last bus back to Sweta departs Bayan around 6 pm. A lift on a motorbike to Batu Koq from Bayan will cost about 700 rp.

On the east side, you have to walk from Sembalun Lawang to Sembalun Bumbung then on to Sapit, where bemo connections with Pringgabaya and Labuhan Lombok are available.

Sumbawa

Amongst the earliest known kingdoms in Nusa Tenggara Barat were the comparatively small kingdoms of the Sasaks in Lombok, the Sumbawans in west Sumbawa and the Bimans and Dompuese in east Sumbawa. These groups of people were animists living in agricultural communities. Today, Sumbawa is a strongly Muslim island. There are also a few traces left of the old sultanates of Sumbawa and Bima which date from the early 18th century.

While there's not a great deal to see in Sumbawa, if you're there at the right time and in the right place – on holidays and festivals – you might see traditional Lombok or Sumbawan fighting. Sumbawan-style is a sort of bare-fist boxing, with the palms bound in symbolic rice stalks – you can possibly see it in east Bali as well. Lombok-style is called Peresehan and is a more violent type of combat involving leather-covered shields and bamboo poles. Most matches seem to end in draws. Water buffalo races take place at one festival, but they are not exactly the Grand National.

Getting There & Away
Air Merpati have flights from Denpasar via Mataram to Sumbawa Besar (76,000 rp from Denpasar) and direct to Bima (116,000 rp). Merpati also connect Bima with Bajawa, Ende, Labuhanbajo, Ruteng (all in Flores) and Tambolaka (Sumba). Flights operate to Kupang via various routes, including Ende and Ruteng.

Boat For details of the daily ferry from

Lombok to Sumbawa, see the preceding Labuhan Lombok section. For details of the regular ferry from Sumbawa to Komodo and Flores, see the following Sape Getting There & Away section. There are irregular ships from Bima to various destinations – Ujung Pandang in Sulawesi and Dilli in east Timor being two possibilities – but it's a case of waiting around the port and seeing what's available.

Pelni's KM *Kelimutu* makes a loop through the islands every two weeks, travelling from Padangbai to Lembar, Ujung Pandang (Sulawesi), Bima, Waingapu, Ende, Kupang and back.

LABUHAN ALAS
Labuhan Alas is the port on the west coast of Sumbawa where you catch the ferry to Lombok. It's not much more than a dock and small village on a pretty little bay. Offshore, there is a Sulawesi fishing village on stilts.

Getting There & Away
There are daily ferries to Labuhan Lombok which depart Labuhan Alas between 7 and 9 am. There are often two or even three boats a day, depending on the season. Buy your ticket from the ticket office at the start of the pier where the buses pull in. There are a couple of stalls here selling snacks and kids selling oranges and fried bananas. When you arrive in Labuhan Lombok, there'll be buses waiting to pick up passengers and take them to various destinations around Lombok.

If you arrive in Labuhan Alas by ferry from Labuhan Lombok, there will be buses waiting at the pier. Direct buses operate to Sumbawa Besar (1500 rp; two hours) and there should be buses to Taliwang (1500 rp; 1½ hours). The road is surfaced the whole length of Sumbawa.

SUMBAWA BESAR
Sumbawa's chief town, Sumbawa Besar, is a ramshackle collection of concrete block houses, thatch-roofed and woven-mat-walled stilt bungalows and shacks which cling to the sides of the hills and have paths leading up to them made of small boulders.

The people here are very friendly and the place has a distinctly 'Asian' feel about it, with numerous dokars rattling down the streets and Muslim men flooding out of the mosques after midday prayer.

The chief attractions are the **Dakam Laka** (Sultan's Palace) and the **Pura Agung Girinatha**. The first is an interesting wooden, barn-like building, set on stilts, with a sloping walkway leading up to the first floor. The other, a Hindu temple near the intersection of Jalan Yos Sudarso and Jalan Setiabudi, contains a few statues and one large, squat *lingam*, a phallic image of the Hindu god Shiva.

There is a large map of Sumbawa on the wall of the restaurant in the Hotel Tambora. It shows the roads (surfaced and unsurfaced), trails, towns and villages, so it's worthwhile checking it out.

Information

Money The Bank Negara Indonesia at Jalan Kartini 10 is open Monday to Saturday from 7.30 to 1 pm. They'll change travellers' cheques from larger companies and will also change cash.

Post The post office is out past the airport, but there are fairly regular bemos there for 200 rp.

Places to Stay

Central Sumbawa Besar is a compact place and there's a cluster of losmen along Jalan Hasanuddin, just a five-minute walk from the bus terminal. Walk down Jalan Kaboja, which is opposite the bus station, to get to Jalan Hasanuddin. All these hotels are within range of the 5 am wake-up call from the mosque – experience indigenous culture at its loudest.

Probably the best of these hotels is the *Hotel Suci* (☎ 21589) with rooms around an attractive courtyard and garden, which keeps out much of the traffic noise. Rooms cost from 5000 to 10,000 rp – they are all clean and have a fan, mandi and toilet.

The *Losmen Dewi* (☎ 21170) has a very friendly manager, and much of the traffic

noise is held at bay. Rooms cost from around 4000 rp with mandi. The rooms are clean but the bathrooms could be cleaner.

The *Losmen Saudara* (☎ 21528) can be horribly noisy. Cheaper rooms without bath start from around 3000 rp. The *Losmen Tunas* (☎ 21212) is a rather nondescript place with rooms from 3500 rp – nothing to rave about. Back up the road, and right next to the bus terminal, is *Losmen Indra* (☎ 21878) which costs 4000 rp and is probably very noisy during the day but, at night, when activity at the bus terminal dies down, it should be fairly quiet.

The best hotel in Sumbawa Besar is the *Hotel Tambora* (☎ 21555), just off Jalan Garuda on Jalan Kebayan II, a 15-minute walk or a short trip in a dokar from the bus terminal. Rooms cost from 6000 rp with mandi to 20,000 rp with TV and air-con.

Places to Eat

The *Rumah Makan Surabaya* is a minute's walk from the bus terminal and serves cheap dishes like nasi campur and nasi goreng. They close very early, around 5.30 pm. On Jalan Wahiddin, the *Rumah Makan Anda* stays open until around 9 pm and has similar prices, standards and food. The *Hotel Tambora* has a pleasant restaurant set in a garden and a rather more varied menu with dishes in the 1500 to 3500 rp range.

There are numerous night-time satay stalls along Jalan Wahiddin, near the junction with Jalan Merdeka.

Getting There & Away

Air Merpati have flights from Denpasar and Ujung Pandang via Mataram to Sumbawa Besar (76,000 rp from Denpasar) and Bima (62,700 rp).

Bus The long-distance bus terminal is on Jalan Diponegoro and fares are posted up on the window of the office. They include: to Empang 2000 rp, Dompu 4000 rp, Bima 5000 rp, Alas 1500 rp and Taliwang 2500 rp. The bus ride to Bima is a six-hour journey (including a half-hour lunch break) and the road is now surfaced the whole way.

Getting Around

Sumbawa Besar is very small – you can walk around much of it with ease (except to more distant places like the post office). The bus terminal is, in essence, the centre of town and there is also a combined bemo and dokar station at the junction of Jalan Setiabudi and Jalan Urip Sumoharjo – it's less than 300 rp by dokar between the two. Bemos seem to operate on a flat rate of 150 rp per person including to the airport, post office or to Labuhan Sumbawa.

BIMA-RABA

This is Sumbawa's main port and the major centre at the eastern end of the island. It's really just a stop on the way through Sumbawa, and there's nothing much to see or do here. Apart from the usual 'hello misters', some of the kids have learnt to say 'I love you'. The only notable attraction of Bima is the large former sultan's palace, now used as a college. The Jalan Flores night market is worth a wander – vendors display posters of Western pop stars side by side with posters of President Suharto.

Information

Money The Bank Negara Indonesia will change major travellers' cheques and foreign currencies.

Post The post office is on Jalan Kampung Salama, which is out in the suburbs, way past the palace – take a dokar. It's open in the mornings from Monday to Saturday.

Places to Stay

Like Sumbawa Besar, Bima is compact and the losmen are all grouped together in the middle of town around the palace.

The best place in Bima is the *Losmen Lila Graha* (☎ 740) on Jalan Belakang Bioskop. It's the one saving grace of the town with its clean rooms from around 4000 to 6000 rp, or better rooms with mandi and toilet from 7000 to 9000 rp. The losmen is a 10-minute walk from the central bus station, or you can take a dokar.

The *Losmen Kartini* on Jalan Sultan Kaharuddin is a large but dingy place with spartan rooms from 5000 to 10,000 rp. You could try bargaining them down. Mosquito-ridden *Wisma Komodo* (☎ 70), on Jalan Sultan Ibrahim and opposite the Sultan's Palace, has large three-bed rooms from around 5000 rp.

Places to Eat

There are quite a few warungs and rumah makan around, but the choice is restricted to nasi ayam or nasi campur. Some places have more extensive menus but they may not have everything that is featured on the menu.

The *Rumah Makan Nirwana*, one of the better places, is on Jalan Belakang Bioskop, near the Losmen Lila Graha. Have them make up a telur dadar udang, or 'shrimp omelette'. It doesn't appear on the menu.

There are a couple of places on Jalan Martadinata including the *Rumah Makan Minang* with good curried chicken. Just down the road and worth trying is the friendly *Rumah Makan Surabaya*. The *Rumah Makan Anda* has a fairly extensive menu. There are various cheap little warungs around the centre of town and the night market has some food stalls serving tasty sweets and snacks.

Getting There & Away

Air The Merpati office (☎ 197, 382) is at Jalan Sukarno Hatta No 30. Merpati connects Bima with Denpasar, Ende, Kupang, Labuhanbajo, Mataram, Ruteng, Tambolaka and Waingapu.

Bus Buses to destinations west of Bima depart from Bima's central bus station, just 10 minutes' walk from the centre of town. See the Sumbawa Besar and Labuhan Alas Getting There & Away sections for details of buses to or from that end of the island.

For buses to the east, you have to go up to Kumbe station in Raba. There are frequent bemos for 150 rp per person from around Jalan Sultan Hasanuddin in Bima – they go through central Bima before heading off to Raba. Minibuses to Pelabuhan Sape – from where you catch the ferry to Flores and

Komodo – depart from Kumbe. The 1½ to two-hour trip costs 1800 rp. Sape only is about 1000 rp.

Boat The Pelni office (☎ 203) is at Jalan Pelabuhan 103. Every two weeks the KM *Kelimutu* calls at Bima on the way to Waingapu, Ende and Kupang. In the reverse direction, it stops in Bima en route to Ujung Pandang, Lombok, Bali and Kalimantan. Ekonomi fares from Bima are: Waingapu 14,700 rp, Ende 11,100 rp, Kupang 18,600 rp, Dilli 23,600 rp, Ujung Pandang 15,800 rp, Padangbai 27,600 rp and Surabaya 40,100 rp.

Getting Around
Bima has plenty of bemos and dokars. Bima's airport is 16 km out of town, bemos are cheap but infrequent and taxis ask the earth but can be bargained down.

SAPE
Sape is a pleasant enough little town. The ferry to Komodo and Flores leaves from Pelabuhan Sape, just down the road from Sape. If you have to wait, then Sape is probably a better place to wait in than Bima.

Places to Stay & Eat
Losmen Give and *Losmen Friendship* are about the only places to stay in Sape – they're basic but OK with single/double rooms at 3000/5000 rp. The Losmen Friendship seems friendlier. Take a dokar there from the bus station.

As for eating, the choice is between bad and worse. The eating here are only memorable for some of the worst variations of nasi campur in all Indonesia! It is much better to stock up on what's available in the market and local shops, or even bring some food with you from Bima.

Getting There & Away
Bus Buses go to Sape from the Kumbe bus station in Bima-Raba. It seems that the earliest buses to Sape depart Kumbe station at around 7.30 am. There may be earlier ones on Monday, Wednesday and Saturday which

connect you with the ferry to Flores Island, but don't count on it.

Ferries to Komodo & Flores Ferries for Komodo and Flores depart from Pelabuhan Sape – take a dokar from Sape from 150 to 250 rp per person. Pelabuhan Sape is nothing more than one street leading down to the dock, lined by stilt houses. The chief hobby here is building anything from a canoe to a galleon beside your house – apparently the people here are from Sulawesi. The ferry schedule is:

Pelabuhan Sape-Komodo-Labuhanbajo – departs Pelabuhan Sape at 8 am every Saturday.
Pelabuhan Sape-Labuhanbajo – departs Pelabuhan Sape at 9 am every Monday and Wednesday.
Labuhanbajo-Komodo-Pelabuhan Sape – departs Labuhanbajo at 8 am every Sunday.
Labuhanbajo-Pelabuhan Sape – departs Labuhanbajo at 9 am every Tuesday and Thursday.

Buy your ticket on the day of departure from the ticket office at the wharf. The fare is 7000 rp from Sape to Komodo and the same from Komodo to Labuhanbajo. It is supposed to take about four hours to Komodo and another three hours from Komodo to Labuhanbajo but count on 12 hours for the whole crossing.

There are additional small charges at the wharf entrance (I have no idea what this is for – probably a harbour tax) and for the boatmen to paddle you out to the ship in a canoe. You can take a motorbike across on the ferry.

Komodo

A hilly, dry, desolate island neatly sandwiched between Flores and Sumbawa. Komodo's big attraction is lizards – four metre, 150-kg lizards, appropriately known as Komodo dragons. From June to September, in the dry season, is the best time to see the dragons as there are more of them out looking for food then. They are carnivores and a goat is the recommended *makan bwaya,* or dragon food. Normally, the dragons eat the deer and wild pig which are found on the island. The only village on the island is **Kampung Komodo**, a fishing village on the eastern coast of the island and worth a look. Also on the coast and a half-hour walk north of the village is **Loh Liang**, the site of the PHPA tourist camp.

Permits

You get your permit for Komodo on the island itself, at the PHPA camp at Loh Liang. Permits cost 1200 rp per person. PHPA is the Indonesian government organisation responsible for managing the country's nature reserves and national parks.

Getting There & Away

You can get to Komodo on the regular ferry that runs between Labuhanbajo in Flores, Komodo and Pelabuhan Sape on Sumbawa. For further details, see Sape Getting There &

Away in the previous Sumbawa section. There are also tours to Komodo from Bali – the usual tour is three days and two nights – look around the travel agents in Kuta. A common method of getting to Komodo is by chartering a motor boat in Labuhanbajo, a port on the west coast of Flores.

DRAGON SPOTTING

The most accessible place to see the dragons has been set up like a little theatre. The PHPA guides will take you to a dried up river bed about a half-hour walk from Loh Liang. A clearing has been made here overlooking the creek. A goat has its throat cut by one of the PHPA people and is then dangled by a rope from a tree that overhangs the river bed. There'll probably be some of the lizards already there since this is now an established feeding spot, but more will come – we saw about seven of the monsters in all, and I mean *monsters!*

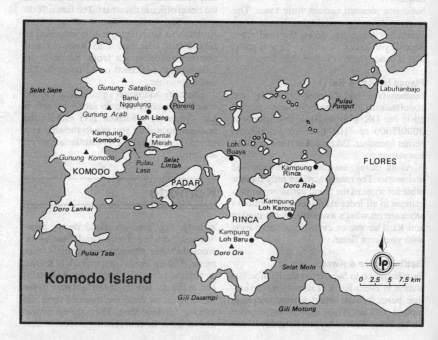

Komodo Island

The PHPA people may insist that you have a goat – saying they won't show you the way to the viewing site without one, though they don't insist that you buy the goat from them. A guide and goat porter will cost you a total of 7500 rp, according to their list of rates. The advantage of having the guide is that you don't have to be the one to kill the goat!

Exactly why you have to have a goat is not clear but the PHPA guys insist that they can't allow the dragons to be fed with anything that might be harmful to them. This is fair enough since it's their job to protect the reptiles. So there's no point buying a large dried fish in the village or in Labuhanbajo as an offering. We bought a small goat from one of the villagers in Kampung Komodo for 20,000 rp and next day, accompanied by a guide and porter, went off to see the dragons.

The guys at PHPA were asking 30,000 rp to get a large goat for us from the village, or 25,000 rp for a small goat. Alternatively, buy a goat in Labuhanbajo (maybe 20,000 rp) and bring it over to Komodo with you.

Recent reports say that the guides are less insistent about bringing a goat. You might want to consult your conscience about whether it's right to kill a goat for the amusement of watching the over-fed dragons tear them apart when children in nearby villages are suffering from malnutrition.

AROUND THE ISLAND

Other things to do on Komodo include climbing up the hills at the rear of Kampung Komodo for a sweeping view across Komodo village and the other islands in the region.

If you go trekking around the island – climbing **Gunung Arab** for example – be warned that this place is very hot! If you really want to trek into the uplands on the island, then make sure you're the sort of person who runs up and down a volcano before breakfast every morning. The PHPA will provide you with a guide. Sights around the island include wild deer and large, poisonous (though not deadly) spiders. I ran into one of their webs stretched right across a

track. It was as tough as plastic thread and harboured an ugly monster.

As for swimming – the PHPA guys say that the sea snakes only come out at night and that you'll only attract sharks if you cut yourself on the coral and bleed. Land snakes are supposed to infest the island – signs are posted around the PHPA camp to warn you to wear trousers and shoes and to watch for snakes.

Wild pigs are commonly seen, often close to the camp – you'll also see them on the beach in front of the tourist camp early in the morning. The Komodo dragons occasionally wander into the PHPA camp, but they avoid the kampung because there are too many people. If you want to go snorkelling bring your own equipment – PHPA *may* have a snorkel and mask for hire.

Places to Stay & Eat

The PHPA has established a large camp at Loh Liang, a half-hour walk from Kampung Komodo. The losmen here is a collection of large, spacious, clean wooden cabins on stilts. The cabins have partitioned compartments, each with a single bed and a curtain which you can draw across for privacy. These cost 4000 rp per person per night and each cabin can accommodate about 10 people.

Each cabin includes a lockable room with two beds costing 8000 rp each. Each hut has two mandis (including toilet) and cleanliness really depends on how recently the huts were last occupied. One cabin is made up entirely of double rooms. Electricity goes on from 6 until 10 pm and is produced by a noisy generator down near the camp office. Once that goes off, there's almost total silence.

Bring your own food! The PHPA restaurant is limited to below-average mee goreng and nasi goreng, plus expensive beverages. You can buy dried fish in Labuhanbajo, as well as biscuits, canned milk, bananas and papayas. Supplies are probably better in Sape or Ruteng, depending on which way you're travelling. For other food, try in Kampung Komodo – you should be able to buy fish and eggs, or perhaps get them to kill and cook a chicken for you (chickens cost around 2500 rp each).

Flores

One of the most beautiful islands in Indonesia, Flores is an astounding string of active and extinct volcanoes. The name is Portuguese for 'flowers', as the Portuguese were the first Europeans to colonise the island. They eventually sold it to the Dutch. The most notable feature of Flores is Catholicism; 95% of the population is Catholic. The church dominates every tiny village and only in the ports will you find any number of Muslims.

Getting There & Away

Air Although Ende is the major town in Flores, it is not the major airport. Only smaller aircraft can fly into Ende and flights are not so frequent as to other centres.

Bouraq connect Maumere in Flores with Denpasar in Bali (157,000 rp) and Kupang in Timor (59,000 rp). Merpati also connect Maumere with Bima in Sumbawa, Ujung Pandang in Sulawesi as well as Kupang in Timor. They connect Bajawa, Labuhanbajo and Ruteng with Bima in Sumbawa and Ende with Kupang in Timor. From these centres, there are flights on to other parts of Indonesia.

Boat Pelni's KM *Kelimutu* makes a regular two-weekly sweep through Nusa Tenggara's islands from Padangbai (Bali) to Lembar, Ujung Pandang (Sulawesi), Bima, Waingapu, Ende, Kupang and return.

Occasionally, there are boats from Ende across to Waingapu in Sumba as well as the usual visits by cargo ships to the main Flores ports of Labuhanbajo, Reo, Maumere, Larantuka, Ende and Mborong. There are also regular passenger ships from Larantuka, the main port on the eastern side of Flores, to Kupang in Timor and regular passenger ships from Larantuka to the islands immediately to the east of Flores. For details on the regular service from Labuhanbajo over to Sumbawa via Komodo, see Sape Getting There & Away in the previous Sumbawa section.

Getting Around

Air Merpati has flights connecting Ende with Bajawa, Labuhanbajo and Ruteng.

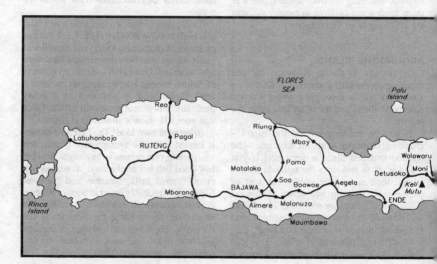

Road The land transport situation in Flores has improved greatly over the last few years. Some stretches of road are being surfaced and there are daily buses or trucks between the main centres (at least during the dry season). The time not to go to Flores is during the wet season when the unsealed roads become impassable! Vehicles get bogged, and a trip that might take hours in the dry season can take days.

In some cases, you can avoid this problem by taking boats around the coast – such as the irregular boats that ply the water from Labuhanbajo to Reo – and from there take a truck up the rather better road to Ruteng. Some spectacular stretches of terrain, such as Ruteng to Bajawa and Bajawa to Ende, really have to be seen from the road.

LABUHANBAJO

This fishing village at the extreme western end of Flores is a jumping-off point for Komodo. If you've got a few days to while away, then Labuhanbajo is a pleasant enough village to do it in. It's a pretty place with a harbour sheltered by several small islands.

There is good snorkelling around the port and nearby islands.

Information

The Bank Rakyat Indonesia branch in Labuhanbajo changes travellers' cheques but the rate is poor. The harbourmaster's office is near the ferry dock. The PHPA office is a two-minute walk from the Losmen Mutiara but they have only a very limited amount of information. The Waicicu tourist information office, 100 metres from the harbour, can be helpful.

Places to Stay & Eat

The *Losmen Bajo Beach,* which has very clean rooms with mandi and toilet, is probably the best place in town. The price depends on what you look like, whether the competition across the road is full up and the relative position of the sun and the moon. Count on something between 5000 and 12,000 rp. Meals are usually around 2500 to 3500 rp each.

Across the road, the *Losmen Mutiara* has been around for years and is a decent little place with rooms from around 3000 rp per person. Three meals per day will cost an additional 4000 rp or you can pay for meals separately – the food is quite good.

The relaxed *Waecicu Beach Losmen,* a 20-minute boat ride from Labuhanbajo, is a string of basic bungalows with mosquito nets and mandis. Accommodation costs 6000 rp per person and includes three good meals – probably the best food on Flores.

A handful of small rumah makan at the southern end of Labuhanbajo serve cheap Indonesian fare. The quality is variable, but the *Banywangi* and *Ujung Pandang* have fair reputations among travellers.

Getting There & Away

Air The Merpati office is on the airport road, south of the town. You'll first see the Kios Berkatusaka on the left and then the Merpati office a little further on the right. It's a further half-hour walk along the stony road to the airport but you might be able to hitch a ride in a jeep. Merpati has flights from

Labuhanbajo to Bima with onward connections to Mataram and Denpasar, and to Ende with onward connections to Kupang.

To/From Komodo & Sumbawa See Sape Getting There & Away in the previous Sumbawa section for details of the Flores-Komodo-Sumbawa ferry, which docks at Labuhanbajo.

Apart from the regular ferry, you can also charter small boats to Komodo. How much you pay depends on who you approach. To go over there, spend a night and return the following day (which is enough time to see the dragons), you would probably be looking at about 25,000 rp for a round-trip charter – if you go straight to a boatman. If you ask the harbourmaster to find you a boat he'll add a 25% commission to the price. Sailing times will probably depend on the time of year and the tides. One group wrote that they had done it as a day trip, departing Labuhanbajo at 3 am! The crossing takes four or five hours.

Negotiations will be required if you want to stay more than one night on the island. Agree upon the price for the boat, regardless of how many people are making the trip – then, if extra people turn up you can spread the cost. Otherwise, agree that the cost is for a particular number of people and that each extra person will be charged a fixed amount. To avoid arguments, it's necessary to make things very clear. People who pay 50,000 to 70,000 rp to charter a boat for five people from Labuhanbajo to Komodo and back have been done!

From Around Flores There are irregular trucks and jeeps along the track between Labuhanbajo and Ruteng and the fare is 4000 rp. Don't try this in the wet as you will definitely get bogged and could end up taking two days to make it to Ruteng. Get a seat in front of the rear axle or you risk wrecking your spine. An alternative to the struggle up the road to Ruteng is the irregular but frequent boats to Reo on the northern coast of Flores. Buses and trucks use a rather better road between Reo and Ruteng.

The boat fare from Labuhanbajo to Reo is about 2500 to 3000 rp. Occasionally, there are boats between Labuhanbajo and Maumere, and Labuhanbajo and Ende.

REO
On an estuary, a little distance up from the sea, is the oversized village of Reo. The large Catholic mission in the middle of the town is Reo's focal point.

Places to Stay & Eat
The *Losmen Telukbayur* (☎ 17) at Jalan Mesjit 8 is a reasonable little two-storey place with rooms for 3500 rp per person. The toilets and mandis could be cleaner but the rooms themselves are OK. The top floor rooms are probably best if you want to avoid the herds of staring kids. The losmen has its own warung.

Getting There & Away
Daily trucks and occasional buses operate between Reo and Ruteng – it takes four hours and costs 1250 to 1500 rp and will get better as more of the road is surfaced. If you're coming in on the boat from Labuhanbajo, there may be a bus or truck waiting at the dock to take people up to Ruteng. There's also a bus run by Toko Garuda Mas in Reo.

Look around the river for small boats going to Labuhanbajo – these seem to be fairly regular and cost 2500 to 3000 rp per person. For boats to Maumere, or further afield, you may have to go to the port of Kedindi which is five km from Reo.

RUTENG
Ruteng is basically just another stop on the way through Flores. For spectacular views of the rice paddies and terraced slopes of the hills and valleys to the north, climb the hill to the north of Ruteng early in the morning. Take the Reo road, and about 10 minutes from Wisma Agung, you will come to a small bridge across a stream. Turn right and head up the track immediately after the bridge.

Information
The Bank Rakyat Indonesia will change foreign cash (like US$ and A$) and major

travellers' cheques. The post office is at Jalan Baruk 6.

Places to Stay

The *Wisma Agung I* (☎ 80) at Jalan Wae Cos 10 is the best place to stay with rooms from 5000 rp. The *Wisma Agung II*, behind Toko Agung on Jalan Motang Rua, is more central but darker, shabbier and more expensive with rooms from 8000 rp. The *Losmen Karya* is a decent little place but it always seems to be 'full' – they don't really want foreigners. Rooms cost from 5000 rp, if you can get in (it seems to help if you're Dutch).

The *Wisma Sindha* on Jalan Yos Sudarso is of similar standard to the Agung, but more expensive with rooms from 7500 rp. The *Wisma Dahlia* is newer, has a restaurant and costs about the same as the Sindha.

Places to Eat

The *Rumah Makan Agung*, run by Wisma Agung, is a pleasant place at the back of Toko Agung in the middle of town. You can get food sent from the restaurant to the hotel. For Chinese, try the *Rumah Makan Dunia Baru* or, for nasi padang, the *Rumah Makan Beringin*.

The *Rumah Makan Indonesia* at the bus station is cheaper and does decent, filling food, although the menu is rather limited. There's a string of little warungs by the adjacent market.

Getting There & Away

Air Merpati (☎ 147) is on Jalan Pertiwi 15 – they have a bus which will take you to the airport for 2000 rp per person. Merpati connects Ruteng with Bima and Ende, and there are onward connections from those centres.

Road Buses and trucks depart from the station next to the market and do the usual pick-up round about town. You can buy tickets from agents like Toko Orion, who charge 500 rp on top of the fare, or front up at the bus station at 7 am.

To Reo, there are trucks for around 1250 rp, or occasional buses for about 1500 rp. It only takes four hours to Reo and trucks even

depart in the early afternoon. You can get to Labuhanbajo either directly by road (but avoid this route in the wet season) or by road to Reo and boat from there.

Bajawa takes about 6½ to seven hours and costs 4000 rp. Ende takes about 12 hours and costs 6500 rp. Buses for both destinations depart around 8 to 9 am. The road from Ruteng to Bajawa makes the strip of bitumen from Sumbawa Besar to Bima look like an eight-lane freeway. In parts, you'd think they built this track by pushing a truck through the jungle which left two tyre marks for others to follow.

It's only when you get to the coast and start climbing into the hills that hug the southern coastline do you start getting views of the string of active and extinct volcanoes that run along the coastline – these are at their most spectacular when you enter into Bajawa at dusk.

BAJAWA

Bajawa is a little town nestled in the hills. Coming in on the road from Ruteng, you'll get a view of the great volcanic **Gunung Inerie** – a spectacular sight in the setting sun. Nearby is **Gunung Wolobobor**, which is an extinct volcano that has had the top half shaved off.

Apart from the spectacular scenery on the way into Bajawa, the main attractions of the area are the traditional houses and odd *ngadhu*. You can see a ngadhu in Bajawa at the end of Jalan Satsuitubu – it's basically a carved pole supporting a conical thatched roof, rather like a large umbrella. In a village a short distance out of Bajawa, on the road to Ende, there are four ngadhu lined up in a row.

Ngadhu are a male symbol which appear to play some sort of role in ancestor worship. They are kept to guard against sickness descending upon the village and also to play a role in preserving fertility – both human and agricultural. They're a sort of all-round 'tree of life' for the Ngada people of the Bajawa plateau area. The female counterpart is the *bhaga*, a structure that looks something like a miniature thatched-roof house.

The Ngada is one of the most traditional, or least 'modernised', of the ethnic groups on Flores. You can take a day trip to the village of **Soa** to visit the Sunday afternoon market, where many Ngada come to trade.

Places to Stay & Eat

Wisma Johny on Jalan Achmad Yani has a friendly manager and rooms from around 3500 rp or from 5000 rp with mandi and toilet. Other places include the *Losmen Dani* on Jalan Gereja near the church, and *Wisma Mawah* at Jalan Berhagia 139. Bus drivers often drop travellers off at the *Losmen Kambera* on Jalan Slamet Riyadi – probably in return for commissions on the not-so-special rooms from 4000 rp. The food here has a good reputation, however, and the family that run the place are forthcoming with information about the area.

The friendly *Rumah Makan Kasih Berhagia,* near the market on Jalan Achmad Yani, has cold beer and inexpensive Indonesian food. Also economical is the *Rumah Makan Komodo Jaya* on Jalan K H Dewentara, near the Losmen Kambera. The *Rumah Makan Beringin* on Jalan Basuki Rachmat has a fair, if limited, range of Padang food. You can stock up on fruit at the market.

Getting There & Away

Air Merpati flies from Bajawa to Bima and Ende, with onward connections. For tickets and reservations, check with the agent on the 2nd floor of Toko Suka Damai, a shop diagonally across from the bus station and next to the Bajawa Market.

Bus Many buses operate between Bajawa and Ende – the fare is 4000 rp, the road is fairly good and the trip takes six hours. Do the trip during the day, as you pass by the spectacular volcanic Gunung Alaboba and travel through a region of deep valleys and rolling hills. In the other direction, getting to Ruteng presents the same problem as leaving Ruteng, as trucks and buses tend to leave early. Fares are listed on a large sign at the Bajawa bus terminal.

ENDE

The capital of Flores is a dull and dusty town – it's easy to see why the Dutch exiled Sukarno here in the 1930s. You can visit the house he lived in but there's nothing much to see. The revolting beach improves as you walk west from the town centre. Whilst the town isn't much, it may be worth coming here to check out the weaving. Ende has it's own distinctive style, and examples of Jopu, Nggela and Wolonjita weaving can also be found in the main street market near the waterfront.

The village of **Wolotopo**, a centre for ikat weaving, is only eight km from Ende and has traditional houses on terraces in the valley side. To get there, take a bemo to Wolowona, cross the bridge and turn right following the path to the black-sand beach of Nanga Nesa. From here, a footpath follows the coast to Wolotopo.

Orientation & Information

Gunung Meja's perfect cone provides a useful landmark to the south-west of the airport. The town straddles a narrow peninsula with the port and airport on the east side, the town on the west. The Bank Rakyat Indonesia is on Jalan Sudirman and will change various types of foreign cash and major travellers' cheques.

Places to Stay

There are places to stay in the town centre, near the airport and dotted in between. Starting from the town side, the *Wisma Dwi Putra* (**☎** 223) on Jalan K H Dewentara is a good place with bright, clean single/double rooms at 8500/14,000 rp, or 27,000 rp with air-con.

Wisma Amica (**☎** 283) at Jalan Garuda 15 is on the airport side of the town centre but it's very popular at 5000 rp per person. Also, a little out from the centre, the curiously named *Nirwana Beaming Inn* (**☎** 199) at Jalan Pahlawan 29 has well-kept, large rooms at 10,000/15,000 rp and other rooms down to 5000/7000 rp. Just round the corner is the *Losmen Solafide* at Jalan One Kore 2, with not so special rooms from 3500 to 7000 rp.

Next door is the *Hotel Merlin* (☎ 465) with rooms from 5000 to 10,000 rp.

Near the airport is the friendly and very well-run *Losmen Ikhlas* at Jalan Achmad Yani. There are a whole variety of rooms costing from 2500 rp for the simplest singles up to 7500 rp for the fanciest doubles with fan and bathroom. Next door is the clean and well-kept *Losmen Safari* (☎ 499) at Jalan Achmad Yani 3, where rooms, all with mandis, cost 6600/11,000 rp.

Between the airport and the town centre, on Jalan Achmad Yani close to the harbour turn-off, is the rock-bottom *Losmen Makmur* at 2500 rp per person. It's strategically situated right next to a mosque.

Places to Eat

Many warungs set up in the evening around the market, serving satay, rice and boiled vegetables. Apart from that, the eating places of Ende are just bare rooms with bright lights – though they do have pretty good food. The *Rumah Makan Terminal* is central and right next to the bus and bemo terminal.

At Jalan Sudirman 6, *Depot Ende* is a bit dreary but the food is OK and the friendly manager is good for local information. Near the airport, across from the Ikhlas and Safari losmen, is the neat and tidy little *Rumah Makan Merlyn*.

Getting There & Away

Air Merpati (☎ 355) is on Jalan Nangka, a 15-minute walk from the airstrip. Ende's short airstrip limits flights to Twin Otters, so there aren't many seats available to or from Ende.

Bus Buses go from Ende to Moni for 1500 rp, to Maumere or Bajawa for 3500 rp and to Wolowaru for 1500 rp. Except on Tuesday, market day in Moni, departures are in the morning or around 12 noon. Maumere departures are in the early morning or late afternoon. The bus takes around seven to eight hours and costs 4000 rp. It's an often spectacular trip with deep gorges and high waterfalls, particularly on the first stretch out of Ende.

Boat Pelni's KM *Kelimutu* stops in Ende every two weeks as it comes in from Waingapu (Sumba) and continues on to Kupang (Timor). It then reverses direction and heads back along the same route. From Kupang, it's a comfortable 11-hour overnight trip which costs about 15,000 rp in Ekonomi class.

Other possibilities from Ende include boats to Labuhanbajo and to Waingapu on Sumba – ask around the harbour.

Getting Around

Bemo fares around town are a flat 200 rp. This includes to the airport, to Wolowona bus station and, quite often, to Pelabuhan Ipi, the main port about 2½ km from the town. If they don't go all the way to the port you may have to walk the last 15 minutes from the junction near the airport.

Wolowona, from where buses run to Moni, Maumere and other points east, is about four km east of the town centre but bemos run there for the same 200 rp.

KELI MUTU

This extinct volcano is the most fantastic sight in Nusa Tenggara if not all of Indonesia. The crater has three lakes – the largest is bright turquoise and next to it there is a deep olive green lake and a bit further away a black lake. Chemicals in the soil account for this weird colour scheme and it changes with time (the green lake was a deep maroon/brown in the mid-70s).

The best time to see Keli Mutu is in the early morning as clouds usually settle down later on and you need strong sunlight to bring out the colours of the lakes. If you get a really bad day – or if you get to the top too late in the day – the clouds will have rolled in covering the lakes and you won't be able to see anything at all!

Getting There & Away

Most visitors base themselves in Moni, the village at the foot of the volcano, and make their way up to the top in the morning. You can set out at 2 am and walk the 11 km to the top in three to four hours, arriving in time for the sunrise. Or, you can hire a horse but it will probably be slower than walking. Easiest of all is to take one of the 2500 rp minibuses which depart for the summit at 4 am. Tickets are sold around Moni the night before. You can take the minibus back down again, soon after dawn, for another 2500 rp, or walk down.

There's a park entry post halfway up the road where you pay a 200 rp entry fee. It probably won't be open on your way up so you pay on your way down. Coming down, there's a shortcut from just beside the entry post which comes out by the hot springs and waterfall. It's fine going down but would be difficult to find, in the dark, on your way up.

See the following Moni section for information on transport to the base of the mountain. You can charter a bemo to take you from Ende up to the top and back again but you might be looking at paying up to 50,000 rp for the round trip. You'd need to depart well before dawn to get there for sunrise. Bemos can be found around the Ende bus station.

MONI (Mone)

Moni is a little village and mission on the Ende to Maumere road at the base of Keli Mutu. About one km before Moni, on the Ende side, is the turn-off road leading to the top of Keli Mutu (a sign hangs over the start of the road – you can't miss it). It's a 15-minute walk from Moni to the start of this road. Moni's Tuesday market is a major local event and attracts a large and colourful crowd.

Places to Stay

Moni is becoming increasingly popular and there's quite a collection of small homestays along the road through town. The *Amina Moe Homestay* and *Friendly Homestay* are popular with nightly costs of 2500 to 3000 rp per person. Both put on excellent evening 'smorgasbords', real all-you-can-eat affairs, costing 2000 rp.

Other homestays along the road are the *Nusa Bunga*, *Daniel's* and *John's*. No doubt more will be popping up. The church run *Wisma Kelimutu* is next to Moni's large church, behind the market field. It's clean, quite comfortable and, since it's back from the road, it's quiet. Rooms are good value at 3500 rp per person.

Just by the Keli Mutu turn-off, a km out of town on the Ende side, *Sao Ria Wisata* has pleasant little bungalows with mandi at 11,000 rp for two.

Places to Eat

Most travellers eat in their homestays, or visit friends at another homestay, but there are also a couple of restaurants. On the Ende side of town, just before the Sao Ria Wisata bungalows, there's the pleasant *Restaurant Kelimut*, perched up above the road. On the other side of town, several hundred metres on towards Maumere, the *Restaurant Wisata* is also a good place for a meal and has a menu featuring the usual Indonesian dishes.

Getting There & Away

Moni is 52 km north-east from Ende and 96 km west from Maumere. From Ende, buses cost 1500 rp and take two to 2½ hours. They tend to leave early in the morning or around 12 noon, although there may be some Maumere bound buses departing in the late afternoon.

From Maumere, buses cost 2500 rp and take four to five hours. They leave Maumere early in the morning and stop for lunch at Wolowaru just 13 km before Moni.

Leaving Moni, you can catch one of the buses from Ende when it returns to the coast or one of the buses from Maumere when they pass through in the early afternoon. Heading to Maumere, the early departures from Ende pass through in the late morning and then there's nothing else until late afternoon or early evening. Moni to Wolowaru takes about half an hour and costs 300 rp.

WOLOWARU

Wolowaru is an oversized village 12 km from Moni on the road to Maumere. From Wolowaru, a road leads off to the villages of Jopu, Wolonjita and Nggela. As you come into Wolowaru from Ende, note the complex of five traditional houses, or rumah adat, distinguished by their high sloping roofs.

Places to Stay & Eat

Losmen Kelimutu, next to the Rumah Makan Jawa Timur (where most buses into town stop), has decent rooms for 3000/4000 rp per person with shared/private mandi. Rates include breakfast. *Losmen Setia,* next to the market, is older but quite OK with rooms at 3000 rp per person, including breakfast.

A third possibility is the *Losmen Hidaya,* behind the Rumah Makan Selara Kita, for only 4000 rp per double. There are three cheap rumah makan: the *Jawa Timur,* the *Bethania* and the *Selara Kita,* each with varied menus of noodle and rice dishes.

Getting There & Away

There are a couple of buses based in Wolowaru that run to Maumere and Ende. Some of the shops in the vicinity of the losmen act as agents and it's often advisable to book departing transport in advance. Fares and approximate travel time are Ende 1500 rp (three hours), Maumere 2500 rp (four hours) and Moni 300 rp.

Otherwise, hang around the Ende to Maumere road and wait for a bus coming through in the direction you want to go. You should be able to get one either to Maumere or to Ende around midday, but don't expect anything in the late afternoon or evening.

NGGELA, WOLONJITA & JOPU

Beautiful and intricately woven sarongs and shawls can be found in these and other small villages. The villages are an interesting and pleasant walk from Wolowaru, so long as you avoid the heat of the day. The volcano-studded skyline is beautiful and near Nggela, which is perched on a clifftop, there are fine views of the ocean.

Nggela has a number of traditional houses but the town's chief attraction is the stunning weaving – all done by hand and using natural dyes. You'll have to bargain hard. For a large and high quality sarong, the starting price might be 100,000 rp but you should be able to knock it down to half that amount. A shawl

can be picked up for around 20,000 to 25,000 rp. Nggela sarongs are also sold in the market at Ende. Wolonjita, about 3½ km inland from Nggela, has similar sarongs to Nggela but doesn't have Nggela's fine views.

At Jopu, a further four km inland, weaving has taken a plunge in the last few years. They no longer use natural dyes and the designs are not as intricate as they used to be. Once, you used to get soft pastel oranges and yellows, but now the yellows are as bright as egg yolk and the cloth is splotched with garish red borders. Jopu sarongs are sold in the market at Wolowaru but there seems to be lots of junk around.

Getting There & Away

There is a rough road leading all the way from Ende to Nggela via Wolowaru, Jopu and Wolonjita. There are irregular vehicles from Ende to Nggela and you may also be able to hitch a ride on a truck, otherwise walk from Wolowaru. At Wolowaru, there is a dirt road which leads off to Jopu four km away, and to Wolonjita which is a further four km. From Wolonjita, there is also a dirt track leading downhill and across the paddy fields to Nggela – about an hour's walk. You can easily get from Wolowaru to Nggela and back in a day, even if you have to walk both stretches.

There is at least one daily boat from Pelabuhan Ipi in Ende which leaves for Nggela very early in the morning. The trip takes about 3½ hours and costs from 750 to 1000 rp.

MAUMERE

Maumere is a medium-size port on the north-east coast and a stopover on the route between Ende and Larantuka. This is still an important mission centre and the Maumere area also has strong ikat-weaving traditions.

Information

Money The Bank Rakyat Indonesia on Jalan Soekarno Hatta will change travellers' cheques but rates are low for anything other than US$ travellers' cheques.

Post & Telecommunications The post office, next to the soccer field on Jalan Pos, is open from Monday to Saturday at the usual hours. There's a telephone and telegraph office on Jalan Soekarno Hatta.

Things to See

In Town The walls of the **cathedral** near the Losmen Bogor are adorned with an unusual series of pictures illustrating the crucifixion of a very Indonesian-looking Jesus. Behind the church is an interesting old cemetery. **Maumere Market**, in the middle of town, is worth some photographs. Ask the old women about the heavy Maumere blankets which are for sale. On Jalan Pasar Baru, beside the market, the Harapan Jaya Art shop has an excellent selection of ikat cloth.

Out of Town The village of **Sikka** has its own distinctive style of weaving and can be reached in an hour by bus from Maumere. **Ladalero**, about 24 km from Maumere, is a major Catholic seminary from where many Florinese priests are ordained. Father Piet Petu's museum is the village's chief attraction and has been going for around 20 years. Recently, Piet Petu has built up a collection of ikat weaving from Sikka, Jopu and other parts of Flores. You'll see examples of design and natural dyes that are now either rare or extinct.

The museum also has an interesting collection of artefacts from all over Indonesia, including ceremonial swords from Kalimantan, statues from Irian Jaya and Chinese and Western imported porcelain. Buses run regularly to Ladalero from Maumere.

Places to Stay

Losmen Wini Rai (☎ 388) is a bit of a walk south of the centre along Jalan Gajah Mada towards the bus station. Single/double rooms in this quiet and very well-kept place are 4000/8000 rp or 7500/12,000 with mandi and fan. A mediocre breakfast is included.

Also quiet, and a little out of the town centre, is *Hotel Gardena* on Jalan Pattirangga, three blocks east from the

market. It's cheap and friendly with rooms with mandi for 5000/10,000 rp, including breakfast.

Possibilities around the centre include *Losmen Bogor II* (☎ 271) next to the Pelni office at Jalan Slamet Riyadi 1-4 near the waterfront. Rooms are comfortable and cost 4000, 6000 and 8000 rp. Right across the road, *Losmen Bogor I* is a bit of a dive but it's certainly cheap at 2500/5000 rp.

On Jalan Pasar Baru, across from the market, *Losmen Beng Goan I* (☎ 247) is quiet and clean with rooms at 4500/8000 rp, or 7000/12,500 rp with mandi. Naturally, there's a *Losmen Beng Goan II* and that's on the other side of the market on Jalan Pasar Baru Barat. It's entered through a shop and is similarly priced, although rather airless. There's a *Losmen Beng Goan III* too, south of the centre on Jalan K S Tubun. It's more expensive and rather dull.

Other possibilities include *Wisma Flora Jaya,* which is centrally located at Jalan Raja Don Thomas, with singles from 5000 to 8000 rp and doubles from 15,000 to 18,000 rp.

Places to Eat

There are a number of small rumah makan around the edge of the market and some night food stalls. *Rumah Makan Santy* is a big, open place with a long, predominantly Chinese menu. It's on Jalan Mangga, north of the market towards the waterfront. For an escape from Indonesia in air-con comfort, try *Losmen Maiwali's* comfortable restaurant where you can get spaghetti, burgers and a truly knockout *es sirsak*. It's on Jalan Raja Don Thomas, across from the Wisma Flora Jaya.

Getting There & Away

Air Bouraq and Merpati fly to Maumere and both connect with Kupang and on to Bali. Merpati fly via Bima (Sumbawa) en route to Bali and also have a direct flight to Ujung Pandang. Bouraq's office (☎ 467) is on Jalan Pasar Baru Timur, across from the market. The Merpati office (☎ 147, 242) is at Jalan Raja Don Thomas 18.

Bus The main bus station is a km or so from the centre on the road to Moni and Ende. Buses between Maumere and Larantuka cost 4000 rp and take about five hours. Buses to Moni are 2500 rp, and 3500 rp to Ende. Trucks occasionally do the trip from Maumere direct to Wolonjita. Buses and bemos leave from around the perimeter of the market.

Boat There are no regular passenger boats out of Maumere, but ships sail between Maumere, Ujung Pandang and Surabaya from time to time. Sometimes, boats go to other parts of Flores, like Reo and Labuhanbajo. Try around the harbour area due north of the Losmen Beng Goan. PT Ujung Tana on Jalan Masjid may be able to arrange passage on boats to Ujung Pandang.

There is a Pelni office on Jalan Slamet Riyadi, next to Losmen Bogor II, where you can get information on regular sailings to and from other Nusa Tenggara ports.

Getting Around
The airport is three km from the town centre, off the Maumere to Larantuku road. Count on around 3000 rp for a taxi or chartered bemo to the airport. The standard bemo fare around town is 200 rp.

WAIARA BEACH
Just off the Larantuka road, 13 km east of Maumere, Waiara is becoming increasingly popular for the scuba diving around offshore islands. There are diving schools associated with the two places to stay at Waiara Beach. *Sao Wisata* has doubles at 30,000 rp while *Waiara Cottages* (also known as *Sea World Club*) has rooms from US$7.50/10 to US$12.50/20.

LARANTUKA
This little port nestles at the base of a high hill at the eastern end of Flores. From here, you can see the islands of Solor and Adonara across the narrow strait. There's not a great deal to see in town, although outside the Holy Mary Church you will find an old

Portuguese cannon and a bell – both painted a ghastly silver.

Information
There's a bank in town but it doesn't offer a foreign exchange service. The post office is several km north of town past the main market.

Places to Stay
Penginapan Rulies Inn must be one of the friendliest and most convivial places in Indonesia; it has rooms at 5000 rp per person. Although it's clean and relatively new, *Hotel Tresna* looks better from the outside than it actually is. Its basic rooms are similarly priced.

Losmen Kartika is a rather seedy looking place but if the Tresna or the Rulies are full, or you want something cheaper, then it's OK, although it can be noisy from the street. Rooms are 3500 rp per person.

Places to Eat
Apart from *Depot Nirwana* on the main street, there's a cluster of anonymous warungs near the wharf.

Getting There & Away
Air The Merpati office is diagonally opposite the large church on the street running parallel to Jalan Niaga. They provide a taxi which will take you the 10 km to the airport for 2500 rp per person. Flights out of Larantuka go to Lewoleba and Kupang only.

Bus Buses between Maumere and Larantuka cost 4000 rp and take five or six hours. If you're coming in on the boat from Lembata or one of the other islands, there'll probably be buses waiting to take passengers to Maumere.

Boat Boats leave from the wharf near the harbourmaster's office – he has information on services out of Larantuka. Also ask around the pier and at the Pelni office on Jalan Niaga. Passenger boats depart almost every day from Larantuka to the islands of Lembata, Adonara and Solor and there are boats twice a week between Kupang in Timor and Larantuka. Boats leave Kupang the day after the Merpati flight from Darwin, and the fare is 10,000 rp.

Lembata

The terrain of Lembata Island is strongly reminiscent of Australia – the palm trees of the coast giving way to gum trees in the hills. Fine ikat comes from villages on the slopes of Ili Api, a smoking volcano near Lewoleba.

LEWOLEBA
Lewoleba is the island's chief settlement and is a relaxed, easy-going place despite the proximity of Ili Api. Between the pier and town is a Bugis stilt village. Some of the inhabitants are pearl divers.

Places to Stay & Eat
Wisma Rejeki, opposite the market in the centre of town, is a pleasant place to stay and has rooms for 4500/9000 rp. Meals here can be excellent. For an extra charge, you can get three meals a day with rice, fish, meat, squid vegetables and egg. There's a large map of Lembata on the wall in the front of the losmen and the manager will fix you up with a guide if you want one to go hiking. You can safely leave excess baggage here.

The only other public accommodation is at the very basic *Penginapan Rachmat*, on the end of Jalan Aulolon and at the back of the market. Rooms here are 3000 rp per person but there's no food service. A row of warungs nearby offer basic sustenance.

Getting There & Away
Air Merpati flies from Larantuka to Lewoleba twice a week, and the flight takes 30 minutes.

Boat Boats to Lewoleba depart daily from Larantuka at 8 am. The 4½-hour trip, which costs 2500 rp, includes a 45-minute stop to load and unload passengers at Waiwerang.

LAMALERA
On the south coast, Lamalera is a whaling village where the villagers still hunt whales. They use small row boats and hand-thrown harpoons. If you want to stay, you can try the missionary or ask the kepala desa.

Getting There & Away
Boat There's a regular boat each Monday from Lewoleba to Lamalera.

Walking There are two roads – the long one and the short one. For the short one, you head out of Lewoleba and ask directions for the nearby village of Namaweke. If you simply ask for the road to Lamalera, you could end up being directed along the main road which follows a wide circular route around the island. Even by the short route, the walk takes about six or seven hours.

Timor

The Portuguese were the first Europeans to land in Timor, in the early 16th century. The Dutch occupied Kupang in the middle of the 17th century and after a lengthy conflict, the Portuguese finally withdrew to the eastern half of the island in the middle of the 18th century. When Indonesia became independent in 1949, the Dutch half of Timor became part of the new republic but the Portuguese still retained the eastern half.

On 25 April 1974, there was a military coup in Portugal and the new government set about discarding the Portuguese colonial empire. Within a few weeks of the coup, three major political parties had been formed in East Timor. After the UDT attempted to seize power in August 1975, a brief civil war between the rival parties, Fretilin and UDT, saw Fretilin come out on top.

However, a number of top generals in the Indonesian army opposed the formation of an independent East Timor and, on 7 December 1975, Indonesia launched a full-scale invasion of the former colony. It can hardly be a coincidence that this happened just one day after US Secretary of State Henry Kissinger had cleared out of Indonesia after a brief visit – presumably having put the US seal of approval on the invasion.

By all accounts, the Indonesian invasion was brutal. Fretilin fought a guerrilla war with marked success in the first two or three years but after that began to weaken considerably. The cost to the Timorese people was horrific, many dying through starvation or disease due to disruption of food and medical supplies. Today, Indonesia seems to have things firmly under control, although there is still a large military presence.

There may be a few Fretilin guerrillas still hiding away in remote corners of this wild and often inaccessible island but, since 1989, East Timor (or Timor Timur) has once again been opened up to visitors. See page 432 for a Stop Press on recent developments in East Timor.

Getting There & Away
Air Kupang, the capital of Timor, is well-connected by air with other parts of Indonesia – Merpati and Bouraq both fly there with connections to a number of other islands in Nusa Tenggara and other parts of the country. A good way to explore Nusa Tenggara is to fly directly from Denpasar (Bali) to Kupang for 174,000 rp and then island hop back.

Merpati have a twice weekly service (currently Wednesday and Saturday) between Darwin in Australia's Northern Territory and Kupang. See the Indonesia Getting There & Away section for more details. This is a terrific way of getting to Indonesia; the flight is popular but usually not too heavily booked.

Kupang is on the no-visa-required entry list. Usually they do not even require that you have an onward ticket when entering via this route, so long as you have at least US$1000 in travellers' cheques.

Boat Pelni's KM *Kelimutu* operates a service down through the Nusa Tenggara islands to Kupang and back every two weeks. The route starts in Semarang (Java) and proceeds through Banjarmasin (Kalimantan), Surabaya (Java), Padangbai (Bali), Lembar (Lombok), Ujung Pandang (Sulawesi), Bima (Sumbawa), Waingapu (Sumba) and Ende (Flores) to Kupang. Straightforward Ekonomi fares to or from Kupang are approximately: Ende 15,000 rp, Waingapu 20,000 rp, Bima 32,000 rp, Ujung Pandang 37,000 rp and Padangbai 50,000 rp.

There are also twice-weekly ferries between Larantuka in Flores and Kupang. The 14-hour trip costs 10,000 rp and tickets are handled by the Perum ASPP ferry office (☎ 21140) at Jalan Cak Doko 20. These ships go from Larantuka to Kupang to Waiwerang to Larantuka. Boats depart from Kupang to Larantuka the day after the Darwin flight arrives.

The mission ship, *Ratu Rosario*, is still plying the water on it's three-week run from Kupang to Surabaya via Larantuka and other islands in Nusa Tenggara. You may be able to get a passage on board this ship if you're in the right port at the right time.

Getting Around
Prior to the Indonesian takeover, the roads in Timor were really rotten. It was debatable whether the Portuguese half was more or less neglected than the Indonesian half. The road from Kupang to Atambua via Soe and Kefamenanu is now well-surfaced. In eastern Timor, some stretches of road are sealed (mostly around Dilli) while some are still pretty rough.

KUPANG
Kupang is the biggest town on the island and capital of the southern province of Nusa Tenggara. If you've been on the other islands of Nusa Tenggara for any length of time, then Kupang comes as something of a shock. Compared to the sedate little towns of Flores or Sumbawa, this is a booming metropolis. It's not a bad place to hang around – Captain Bligh did, after his *Bounty* misadventures.

Past the airport, about 18 km from town, **Baumata** has a swimming pool and caves with stalactites and stalagmites. You need a torch, or a kerosene lamp can be hired from one of the villagers. Bemos run here for 300 rp. The beaches around town are dirty and unappealing but **Pantai Lasiana**, nine km from town, is a beautiful sandy beach and virtually empty. It's a km off the main road and, as an alternative to taking a bemo back, you can walk along the coast.

Information
Tourist Office The Kupang tourist office is on Jalan Soekarno near the bus terminal. There's usually someone around who speaks English and they have some printed information on Timor as well as other parts of eastern Nusa Tenggara.

Money The Bank Dagang Indonesia, down near the waterfront on Jalan Soekarno, will change cash and travellers' cheques. Bank Negara Indonesia on Jalan Sumatera, next to Wisma Maliana, also has a good foreign exchange service. The currency exchange office at Kupang Airport is open when flights arrive from Darwin.

1 Bemo & Bus Terminal	7 Hotel Flobamor II
2 Tourist Information	8 Merpati
3 Toko Dharma Bakti	9 Main Post Office
4 Taman Ria Beach Inn	10 Perum ASPP Ferry
5 Bank Indonesia	Office
6 Bouraq	11 International Backpackers

12 Eden's Guest House
13 Wisma Cendana
14 Pasar Inpres
15 Government Building
16 Korem

See Central Kupang Map

Jl Pahlawan
Jl Siliwangi
Jl Sumatera
Jl Alor
Jl Tim Tim

To Losmen Fangidae & Tenau (port)

Jl Jen Achmad Yani
Jl Soekarno
Jl Tompello
Jl Fatuleu
Jl Sumba
Jl Nanako
Jl Moh Hatta
Jl Prof Yohanes
Jl Car Doko
Jl Sudirman
Jl Lalamentik
Jl Banteng
Jl Palapa
Jl Suprapto
Jl Satsui Tubun
Jl Batako
Jl Kancil
Jl Harimau
El Tori
Jl Raya
Jl Suharto

Jl = Jalan

0   0.5   1 km

Kupang

To Hotel Sasando, Museum NTT, Oehobo Bus Terminal, Hotel King Stone, Rumah Makan Pondok Bambu, Airport, Lasiana Beach & Soe

To Museum, NTT

Jl Perintis Kemerdekaan (joins Jl Tim Tim)

To Bakunase
To Oepura Bemo Terminal & Baun

Post & Telecommunications Poste restante mail goes to the central post office, Kantor Pos Besar, at Jalan Palapa 1. A branch post office is on Jalan Soekarno, diagonally across from the Bank Rakyat Indonesia. The telephone & telegraph office is on Jalan Urip Sumohardjo near the bemo terminal.

Permits If permits should become necessary again for travel outside Kupang, you'd have

to go to Korem (Komando Resor Militer) about 2½ km beyond the main post office on Jalan Lalamentik.

Places to Stay

Kupang's frenetic but easily understood bemo system makes it simple to get to the somewhat scattered accommodation possibilities. Take a three-lamp bemo four km out of town to the backpackers' centre at Jalan

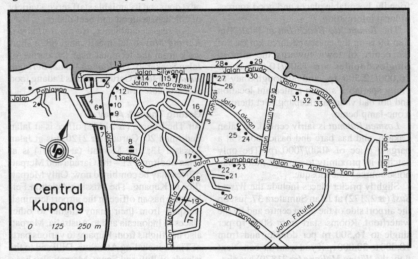

1	Dutch Graveyard	18	Departemen Pendidikan
2	Pelni		& Kebudayaan
3	Teddy's Bar	19	Bank Indonesia
4	Pantai Laut Restaurant	20	Kupang Indah Inn
5	Toko Sinar Baru	21	Kupang Hotel
6	Bank Dagang Indonesia	22	Bemo Interchange
7	Night Warungs	23	Telephone & Telegraph Office
8	Sub Post Office	24	Losmen Rahmat
9	Tourist Office	25	Mosque
10	Restaurant Lima Jaya Raya	26	Merpati
11	Bemo & Bus Terminal	27	Cinema
12	Toko Columbia	28	Beach Market
13	Restaurant Karang Mas	29	Night Warungs
14	Pitoby Travel	30	Rumah Makan Beringin
15	Paris Indah Bus Agent		Jaya
16	Futoby Lodge	31	Wisma Susi
17	Church	32	Wisma Maliana
		33	Bank Negara Indonesia

Kancil. There's *Eden's Guest House* (☎ 21921), just off Jalan Kancil, and *International Backpackers*, a few steps further down the road at Jalan Kancil 37B.

Just off the road is a big, crystal clear spring fed pool. Both the hostels use the spring water for their own small swimming pools. The nightly cost in either hostel is 3000 rp per person in small rooms or dorms. Conditions are pretty basic but they're friendly, hospitable places and good sources of local information.

The *Taman Ria Beach Inn* at Jalan Tim Tim 69 is on the coast and three km east of the centre of town towards the airport. Singles/doubles are 7500/10,000 rp or 10,000/12,500 rp, and although they're pretty spartan it's quite a pleasant location and not bad value for Kupang. Get there on a one-lamp bemo.

Losmen Rahmat is fairly central, on Jalan Lakaan, and has bare and basic rooms at a bargain price of 4000/7000 rp. The only catch is its proximity to a prime Indonesian noise source – the mosque.

Slightly pricier places include the *Wisma Susi* (☎ 22172) at Jalan Sumatera 37, just on the airport side of the town centre and by the waterfront. Rooms start from 8000 rp per single to 16,500 rp per double, and from 18,000 to 30,000 rp if you want air-con. Next door the *Wisma Maliana* (☎ 21879) has similarly priced air-con rooms.

Teddy's Bar (☎ 21142) at Jalan Ikan Tongkol near the bemo terminal has some cheap rooms from around 10,000 rp. Near the church and telephone office and off Jalan Urip Sumohardjo, the *Laguna Inn* (☎ 21559) on Jalan Kelimutu has rooms from around 6000 to 15,000 rp. On the same street, the *Kupang Indah Inn* (☎ 22 6382) is in a similar price bracket. There are a number of pricier places around but *Wisma Cendana* is good value even though its some distance from the centre.

Places to Eat

There are no gourmet delights in Kupang but there are some good night food stalls which set-up across from the tourist office along Jalan Soekarno. One of the best places in town is the *Restaurant Lima Jaya Raya* at Jalan Soekarno 15, near the terminal. The Chinese-Indonesian menu is extensive and reasonably priced.

Visiting Darwinites like to hang out at *Teddy's Bar*, Jalan Ikan Tongkol 1-3. The food is good but a bit pricier than elsewhere in town. The menu includes Western dishes and seafood. The *Pantai Laut Restaurant* is next door and its amiable staff serve a variety of chicken, seafood and beef dishes.

For seaside ambience, try the *Restaurant Karang Mas* at Jalan Siliwangi 88, a short walk from the terminal near the corner of Jalan Soekarno. The *Rumah Makan Beringin Jaya* is on Jalan Garuda and has Padang food at reasonable prices.

Getting There & Away

Air The Bouraq (☎ 21421) office is at Jalan Sudirman 20; Garuda (☎ 21205) is at Jalan Kosasih 13; and Merpati (☎ 21961) is at Jalan Sudirman 21 – the Garuda and Merpati offices may be combined now. Only Merpati flies to Kupang. The Mission Aviation Fellowship has an office in the airport terminal.

Apart from their many flights to other places in Indonesia and to Australia, Merpati also has flights from Kupang to various parts of Timor including Atambua, Dilli and to the islands of Roti and Sawu. Merpati also has a Darwin (Australia) to Kupang flight twice a week.

Bus Buses out of Kupang depart from the Kupang bus station (known simply as the 'terminal') near the waterfront where Jalan Soekarno meets Jalan Siliwangi. They operate to various destinations around west Timor, including Atambua near the old border. Shops near the station act as agents for a number of the bus companies.

It takes about seven to nine hours to Atambua and costs from 5000 to 7500 rp depending on the time of year (more in the wet season) and time of day (night buses cost more than day ones). After departing the station but before actually heading out into the country, buses tend to do a tedious 1½ to two hour picking-up round known as *keliling*, or driving round in circles! Kupang to Soe is 2500 rp.

Boat Pelni is at Jalan Pahlawan 3. The harbourmaster's office is at the harbour at Jalan Yos Sudarso 23. The Pelni service on the KM *Kelimutu*, to and from Ende in Flores and beyond, passes through every two weeks and costs 15,000 rp in Ekonomi class and includes food for the 11-hour trip. Pelni has a few ferries that offer a regional service – the *Elang* loops around Timor and the small islands to the north and there is the *Baruna Eka* and/or *Baruna Fajar* which service Sawu, Ende and Waingapu.

Perum ASPP ferries depart from Kupang Harbour at least every second day for the Termanu Oelaba at Bau on Roti Island. The fare is around 7000 rp and you buy your ticket on the boat on the day of departure – go down and ask when the boat will leave. There's a twice weekly service to Larantuka on Flores, departing the day after the Merpati flight from Darwin arrives. It costs 10,000 rp and operates overnight. Ferries from Kupang also go to Kalabahi (Alor) and Sawu.

Getting Around

To/From the Airport Kupang's El Tari Airport is 15 km east of the centre. Taxis cost a fixed 6500 rp. You might get a bemo from just outside the airport gates, a 200-metre walk, but it's a good half km to the main road where bemos pass by regularly. From there, it's just 250 rp into town. Note that Bouraq flights go from the quite separate Terminal B, some distance from Merpati's Terminal A. There's an excellent branch of the *Pantai Laut* restaurant at the airport – you get both good food and decent-sized servings.

Local Transport Kupang's chief bus and bemo terminal is at the waterfront, on the corner of Jalan Soekarno and Jalan Siliwangi. Kupang Harbour is about seven km from the bus terminal. A bemo from the bus terminal will take you straight to the harbour for 250 rp, and drop you off right at the harbourmaster's office.

Around town, bemos cost a standard 200 rp and are identified by the number of lamps on the roof – you take a one lamp bemo, a two lamp bemo or whatever. The bemos are fast, efficient, brightly painted and incredibly noisy – they like the bass turned up high and a multi-speaker stereo system is *de rigueur*.

SOE

Soe is a dull sprawl of wooden and corrugated-iron-roofed houses. Despite its appearance it would be worth taking a day trip up here to get a look at the western Timorese countryside. There are frequent bemos and buses between Kupang and Soe, leaving from around 7 or 7.30 am. The trip takes anything from 2½ to four hours, depending on the driver and the amount of *keliling* involved.

You can stay in *Wisma Bahagia* on Jalan Diponegoro, where rooms cost from 10,000 rp. *Losmen Anda*, around the corner on Jalan Kartini, is friendly but run-down with rooms from just 3500 rp.

KEFAMENANU

Kefamenanu is a forgettable (and forgotten) place – just a through town on the way to east Timor. If you stop here, the *Losmen Ariesta* has rooms from around 4000 rp and up; the *Losmen Setangkai* is a bit more expensive.

ATAMBUA & ATAPUPA

Atambua is the major town and Atapupa the major port at the eastern end of the originally Indonesian half of the island. Nearby Atapupa is a good place for finding boats to other islands. Either make a good stopping point on a Kupang to Dilli journey.

Places to Stay & Eat

There are a couple of places to stay in Atambua, including at least one that dates back as far as the 1975 edition of *South-East Asia on a shoestring*. The long-running *Wisma Sahabat* is at Jalan Merdeka 7 and offers very basic accommodation from around 4500 rp per person. Better value is the more expensive *Losmen Nusantara* from around 7000 rp per person with breakfast.

Eat at the *Rumah Makan Sinar Kasih*, a five-minute walk from the Wisma Sahabat. They have quite a long menu and decent-sized helpings at reasonable prices. There are also a couple of warungs in the vicinity of the Wisma Sahabat.

DILLI

The old capital of the Portuguese half of the island was a pleasant, lazy place in the days before the invasion. Today, it's relatively prosperous, with lots of new public build-ings, although it's still slow-moving com-pared to frenetic Kupang in west Timor. Check the **Integration Monument** near the waterfront which has a Timorese rapturously breaking his chains of colonial bondage. It looks like a relic from Sukarno's Jakarta statuary collection. A gigantic **cathedral** is another post-Indonesian addition.

Pantai Pasir (White Beach), a couple of km east of the town, is nothing marvellous.

Information

There's a tourist office on Jalan Kaikoli near the university. The Indonesian influence

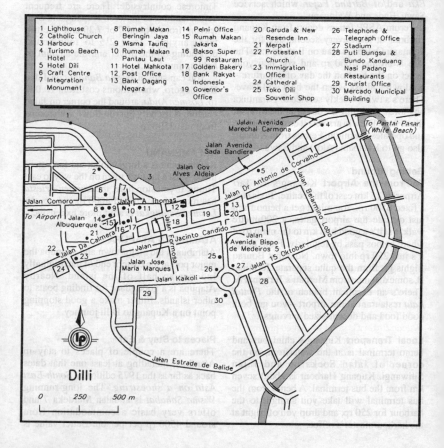

1 Lighthouse	8 Rumah Makan Beringin Jaya	14 Pelni Office	20 Garuda & New Resende Inn	26 Telephone & Telegraph Office
2 Catholic Church	9 Wisma Taufiq	15 Rumah Makan Jakarta	21 Merpati	27 Stadium
3 Harbour	10 Rumah Makan Pantau Laut	16 Bakso Super 99 Restaurant	22 Protestant Church	28 Puti Bungsu & Bundo Kanduang Nasi Padang Restaurants
4 Turismo Beach Hotel	11 Hotel Mahkota	17 Golden Bakery	23 Immigration Office	
5 Hotel Dili	12 Post Office	18 Bank Rakyat Indonesia	24 Cathedral	29 Tourist Office
6 Craft Centre	13 Bank Dagang Negara	19 Governor's Office	25 Toko Dili Souvenir Shop	30 Mercado Municipal Building
7 Integration Monument				

Jalan Avenida Marechal Carmona

To Pantai Pasar (White Beach)

Jalan Avenida Sada Bandiera

Jalan Gov Alves Aldeia

Jalan Dr Antonio de Corvalho

Jalan Belarmino Lobo

Jalan A Thomas

Jalan Comoro

To Airport

Jalan Albuquerque

Jalan Da Calmera

Jalan Formosa

Jalan Jacinto Candido

Jalan Avenida Bispo de Medeiros 5

Jalan 15 Oktober

Jalan Jose Maria Marques

Jalan Kaikoli

Jalan Estrade de Balide

Dilli

0   250   500 m

appears to have been simply overlaid on the old Portuguese colony. Some streets and avenues, *rua* or *avenida* in Portuguese, have simply been renamed Jalan Rua whatever or Jalan Avenida something or other! Toko Dili is a souvenir shop beside the telephone office and across from the stadium. There's also a craft centre near the waterfront.

Places to Stay

There are no accommodation bargains in Dili. *Wisma Taufiq*, on Jalan Comoro and close to the centre, is about the cheapest around with basic but habitable rooms at 7000/10,000 rp. The *Losmen Basmery Indah* (☎ 2731), on Jalan Estrade de Balide near the university, isn't value at 13,500/16,500 rp.

The *Turismo Beach Hotel* (☎ 22029), on Jalan Avenida Marechal Carmona by the waterfront, is somewhat decrepit and neglected but has a certain charm. Rooms start at 9000/15,000 rp, then 19,000/23,000 rp with balcony and bathroom or 25,000/29,000 rp with air-con. All except the cheapest rooms include a decent breakfast. You may have difficulty getting water out of the taps but the bathrooms do have bidets!

On the same road, a bit closer to the town centre, the *Hotel Dili* has rooms at 18,000 rp but is quiet and as dull as a morgue. More expensive places include the *New Resdende Inn*, on Jalan Avenida Bispo de Medeiros 5, and the *Hotel Mahkota*, on Jalan Gov Alves Aldeia – both with rooms from 35,000 rp.

Places to Eat

Many warungs, some with fresh seafood, set up at night in the east end of town. The garden restaurant at the *Turismo Beach Hotel* has good food at reasonable prices. On Jalan Jose Maria Marques in the town centre, the *Golden Bakery* is good for baked produce or try the *Bakso Super 99* for noodles or good ice juice. *Rumah Makan Jakarta* is just around the corner. There are a number of nasi padang places near the telephone office and stadium.

Remarkably, you can still get Portuguese Mateus Rosé wine in Dili! A bottle costs 20,000 rp in the Hotel Turismo.

Getting There & Away

Air There are daily flights between Dilli and Kupang and some connections to other places in Timor. The Merpati office in Dilli (☎ 2477) is at Jalan Da Calmera 8.

Bus Bus ticket prices seem to climb during the wet season, when travel is more arduous. A through ticket from Kupang to Dilli costs from around 15,000 to 20,000 rp but it's a long, gruelling trip.

Most people stay overnight in Atambua. The fare to there can be as low as 7500 rp or as high as 13,500 rp. The trip can take up to 18 hours, or even more during the wet season when the bridge over the River Loes, about 20 km east of Atapupu, is flooded. Buses also run east from Dili to Baukau.

There are three bus stations around town and most buses go from the roundabout by the telephone office, stadium and old Mercado Municipal.

Boat Enquire at the harbour about boat departures. The Pelni office is just behind Rumah Makan Jakarta on Jalan Sebastian da Costa.

Getting Around

Dilli's Comoro Airport is five km west of the town; the standard taxi fare is 4000 rp. Taxis generally cost a flat 600 rp around town.

AROUND DILLI

From Dilli, you can take a sidetrip to **Maubisse** and **Same**, a spectacular trip south. **Ermera** is a coffee growing centre on the road towards the Indonesian half. On the coast beyond Dilli, there's an old Dutch fort in the town of **Maubara**.

Apart from in Dilli and Baukau, the only accommodation in east Timor is at the odd remaining Portuguese guest house, or 'pousada'. There's one in Maubisse where you can stay for 5000 rp. Ermera and Maliana have cheap hotels. A few travellers have reported being allowed to stay at police stations.

BAUKAU

The second largest town in the Portuguese half, Baukau is a charmingly run-down old colonial town. In pre-invasion times, it was the site of the international airport (now a military airbase, although there is talk of reopening it for commercial flights). The altitude makes it pleasantly cool and the beaches, five km sharply downhill from the town, are breathtakingly beautiful.

The old *Hotel Flamboyant*, a hangover from Portuguese days, is still in operation but seems to have had zero maintenance since the Portuguese left – doubles are 10,000 rp. Buses from Dilli to Baukau take about four hours and cost 3000 rp.

BEYOND BAUKAU

An interesting sidetrip from Baukau is to **Tutuala** on the eastern tip of the island. This village has interesting houses built on stilts, plus spectacular views out to sea. There are plans to convert the police station at Tutuala into a losmen. Meanwhile, bring your own food and supplies. Just before Tutuala is **Los Palos** where the old raja's house now has accommodation for 6000 rp.

There is an old Portuguese fort at **Laga**, a town on the coast en route to Tutuala. Another sidetrip is down to **Vikeke** (Viequeque), close to the south coast. On the way you pass Venilale with Japanese WW II bunkers outside the town. There have been rumours of Fretilin activity in the Vikeke area, so it may be closed to foreigners.

Sumba

This dry island, one of the most interesting in the Nusa Tenggara group, is noted for the large decorated stone tombs, found in the graveyards. Sumba is also famous for its ikat blankets with their interesting motifs – including skulls hanging from trees, horse riders, crocodiles, dragons, lions, chickens, monkeys and deer.

Sumba Blankets

Most blankets are blue, red and white – the pastel oranges and browns are only occasionally seen. There's a band of almost incredibly persistent middlemen working the streets of Waingapu with sacks full of blankets. They lay siege to your hotel, hanging around all day and half the night. Every blanket is the 'Number One' blanket but artificial dyes are used to make instant 'antique' blankets and asking prices are exorbitant, although you can bargain. If you want a good blanket then *wait* – they'll eventually bring out the better stuff.

Getting There & Away

Air Flights operate from Bali, Flores, Timor and Sumbawa to the main centres of Tambolaka (the airport for Waikabubak) and Waingapu. Merpati operate a Denpasar-Bima-Tambolaka-Waingapu-Kupang route while Bouraq fly Denpasar-Waingapu-Kupang.

Boat Pelni's KM *Kelimutu* operates through Nusa Tenggara every two weeks and sails from Padangbai (Bali) to Lembar, Ujung Pandang (Sulawesi), Bima, Waingapu (Sumba), Ende (Flores), Kupang (Timor) and return. There are occasionally other ships plying between Waingapu and Ende.

WAINGAPU

There's nothing much to do in Waingapu, but it has some reasonable hotels and restaurants and is a good place for day-tripping to the interesting villages in the surrounding area, where the blankets are made and where the stone tombs can be found.

Orientation & Information

The town has two centres, one around the harbour and one around on the bus station about a km to the south-east. The Bank Rakyat Indonesia on Jalan Achmad Yani, will change major travellers' cheques and cash.

Places to Stay

Hotel Lima Saudara (☎ 83) is in the northern part of town at Jalan Wanggameti 2. The small, somewhat tatty dorm is 3500 rp per person while doubles are just a bit more.

Other accommodation is in the southern part of town. *Hotel Surabaya* (☎ 125) at Jalan Eltari 2 is too near the mosque for comfort. Rooms cost from 4000 to 6000 rp for singles and from 6500 to 10,000 rp for doubles but some bargaining is usually necessary.

Hotel Sandle Wood (☎ 117) at Jalan Panjaitan 23 is a good place. The owner speaks some English and although the better rooms are in the 12,000 to 30,000 rp range (and worth the money), there are some cheaper ones at 7500/12,000 rp. *Hotel Elim* (☎ 180) at Jalan Achmad Yani 55 is run by a Chinese man and his charming wife, who speaks some English. Rooms start from 5000/7000 rp and go up to 12,000/17,000 rp for the better rooms with fan, mosquito nets and mandi.

Places to Eat
For cheap food, try the night warungs around the corner of Jalan Soekarno-Hatta and Jalan Sudirman. A few more set up in the bus station area and there are some basic rumah makan along Jalan Yos Sudarso near the harbour.

Otherwise, eat at the hotels – the best and most expensive food is found at the *Hotel Sandle Wood*. The *Hotel Surabaya* is cheaper and even offers Chinese takeaways. *Hotel Elim* also provides evening meals.

Getting There & Away
Air Merpati (☎ 180) is at Jalan Achmad Yani 73, and Bouraq (☎ 363) is at Jalan Yos Sudarso 57. There are flights between Waingapu and Bima, Denpasar, Kupang and Tambolaka (Waikabubak).

Bus There are generally a couple of buses per day between Waingapu and Waikabubak. The trip takes about 6½ hours, which includes a half-hour meal stop, and costs 3000 rp. Try to book a day or two in advance. The hotels will usually book you a ticket or go to one of the bus agents.

Boat Pelni is located at the port of Waingapu – a bemo for the port costs 250 rp and goes straight past the office. The KM *Kelimutu* calls every two weeks at a special dock at the other end of the harbour – a bemo to this pier is 250 rp per person.

Getting Around
Bemos from the town centre to the airport, six km out, cost 300 rp while a chartered bemo will be about 3000 rp. From the town centre to the port is 250 rp by bemo. There are regular bemos to villages around Waingapu.

AROUND WAINGAPU
Rende
Rende village has several traditional-style buffalo-horn adorned Sumba houses and a number of massive carved stone graves. You may be charged 500 or 1000 rp as a sort of 'admission fee' to the village. Take a bus at around 7 am from Waingapu or, if you miss the bus, a colt to Melolo for 1500 rp (two hours) and then walk from Melolo to Rende. It's a seven km and 1½-hour walk, so take a water bottle!

Umabara
Umabara has several traditional Sumba houses and tombs. A few minutes' walk down the track from Umabara is the village of **Pau**, which also has traditional houses.

Umabara is a half-hour walk from the village of Melolo, which is split by a river. The road to Umabara leads off from the Waingapu side. Have the colt driver drop you off at the start of this road.

Kaliuda
Kaliuda is one of the ikat weaving centres of the area, though the place where most of the weaving is done is just before the village. To get to Kaliuda, take a bus at around 7 am from Waingapu. You can then spend about two hours looking around Kaliuda before catching the same bus as it returns through Kaliuda. It will probably be packed by the time it arrives there, so you may have to insist on being picked up.

WAIKABUBAK

Waikabubak is a neat little town with many traditional houses and old graves carved with buffalo-horn motifs. One of the attractions of western Sumba is the *Pasola*, or mock battle ritual, held near Waikabubak each year. It's a kind of jousting match on horseback and is rather dangerous.

At the village of **Lamboya**, traditional Sumba horseback mock battles are held every year during February – this village is 20 km from Waikabubak. At **Wanokaka**, the battles are held in March. At **Rua Beach**, 30 km south of Waikabubak, the festival is also held in March.

Places to Stay & Eat

Losmen Pelita (☎ 104) on Jalan Achmad Yani is basic but clean with rooms at 3500 rp per person. Meals are served at an additional cost.

The *Hotel Rakuta* on Jalan Veteran is a somewhat musty place with large rooms, big double beds, mandis and toilet from around 8000 to 15,000 rp. The manager speaks some English and is good for information. Another good source of information is the *Losmen Mona Lisa* (☎ 24), which has a variety of comfortable rooms from around 6000 to 15,000 rp. The Chinese owner can arrange transport and accommodation in some of the out-of-the-way villages.

Getting There & Away

The Merpati agent is in the centre of town, on Jalan Achmad Yani.

Getting Around

The only reliable way of getting to the airstrip at Tambolaka, 42 km from Waikabubak, is in the Merpati taxi for 2000 rp per person. There are regular bemos to villages around Waikabubak.

The Losmen Mona Lisa rents motorbikes for around 8000 rp per day and can arrange jeep trips around western Sumba for up to five people from 50,000 to 75,000 rp per day (depending on how well you bargain).

AROUND WAIKABUBAK

Anakalang

Twenty km from Waikabubak is the village of Anakalang with its large graveyard. Anakalang is also the site of the Purung Takadonga – a mass marriage festival held once every two years. The date is determined by the full moon and is different each time. There are regular bemos from Waikabubak to Anakalang and the trip takes about one hour and costs 600 rp.

Galubakul

Almost opposite the Anakalang graveyard is the road leading to the village of Galubakul (formerly Prai Bokul), an hour's walk away. In this village, you'll find the **Umbu Sawola Tomb**, a structure carved out of a single piece of rock and then mounted on supports. The slab cost four million rp, weighs 70 tonnes and took three years to carve. The base of the stone is about five metres long, four metres wide and a bit less than a metre thick.

Kalimantan

The southern two-thirds of the island of Borneo, Kalimantan is a vast, jungle-covered, undeveloped wilderness. Apart from the area around Pontianak and the region from Samarinda to Banjarmasin there are few roads. The boats and ferries of the numerous rivers and waterways are the chief form of long-distance transport, although there are also plenty of flight connections.

Some of the coastal cities have their own

remarkable attractions – the canals of Banjarmasin and the fiery orange sunsets over Pontianak, for example. On the whole, however, apart from its being a diversion between Sulawesi and Java, it is the native Dayak tribes of the inland areas that are the main reason for coming to Kalimantan.

Getting There & Away

Air Bouraq, Merpati and Garuda all fly into Kalimantan and there are lots of flights from other parts of Indonesia. Garuda fares include: Jakarta to Banjarmasin for 186,000

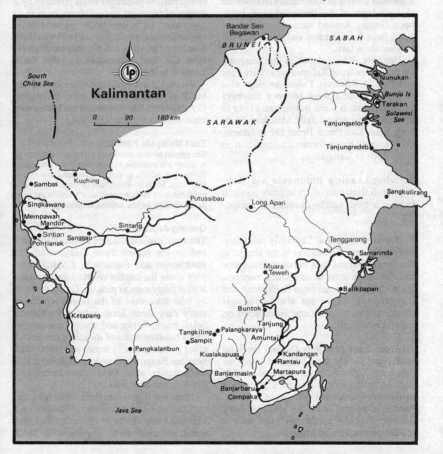

rp, Jakarta to Pontianak 152,000 rp and Jakarta to Balikpapan 238,000 rp. There are some other interesting flight connections available. Garuda will fly you from Kupang in Timor to Tarakan, on the east coast of Kalimantan, in the same day. Bouraq will fly you from Ternate in Maluku to Balikpapan in the same day.

Boat There are shipping connections to Java and to Sulawesi, both with Pelni and other shipping companies. Pelni's KM *Lawit*, KM *Kelimutu*, KM *Tidar*, KM *Kerinci* and KM *Kambuna* all stop at Kalimantan somewhere along their routes. See the introductory Indonesia Getting Around section for details of Pelni fares from Jakarta and the routes the various ships take.

There are also regular ships from the ports on the east coast of Kalimantan to Pare Pare and Palu in Sulawesi. Passenger ships also sail about twice a week between Surabaya and Banjarmasin – see Banjarmasin later in this section for more details. Mahakam Shipping, Jalan Kali Besar Timur 111 in Jakarta, may be worth trying for more information on other ships to Kalimantan.

Arriving/Leaving Indonesia via Kalimantan Kalimantan offers an entry port into Indonesia from nearby destinations including:

To/From Singapore The only visa-free entry point into Kalimantan is the airport at Pontianak. Garuda flies between Singapore and Pontianak three times a week, connecting with flights to and from Balikpapan and Banjarmasin. There are also occasional charter flights to and from Balikpapan on Union Oil aircraft.

To/From East Malaysia Despite the long land border with the Malaysian states of Sabah and Sarawak, crossing here is not that easy. Merpati operates only one flight a week between Pontianak and Kuching in Sarawak. Pontianak Airport is on the visa-free entry list but, if going north, you must have a special permit for east Malaysia.

The only legal land crossing is by road between Kuching and Pontianak. Buses run daily between the two cities for around M$45. However, you must have your Indonesian visa before arrival at the Kalimantan border or risk being turned back. Indonesian visas can be easily obtained at the consulates in Kuching or in Kota Kinabalu. In the opposite direction, an east Malaysia permit is necessary.

At the other side of the island, Bouraq flies three times a week between Tarakan and Tawau in Sabah. There are daily longboats (long, narrow passenger boats powered by a couple of outboard motors) from Tarakan to Nunukan (12 hours; 9000 rp), and from Nunukan there are daily boats to Tawau (four hours; 16,000 rp or M$25). Purchase tickets from CV Tam Bersaudara on Jalan Pasar Lingkas in Tarakan.

Tarakan is not on the 'no visa required' list but it is a legal entry point to Indonesia. Coming from Sabah, you can get Indonesian visas at Kota Kinabalu or Tawau.

East Malaysia Permits

The special permits necessary for entry into Sarawak or Sabah are available in Indonesia at the Malaysian Embassy in Jakarta or at the Malaysian Consulate in Pontianak. Some travellers have had problems obtaining them from these sources, so it's best to get your papers in order before arriving in Indonesia.

Getting Around

There are roads in the area around Pontianak and in the region from Banjarmasin to Balikpapan and Samarinda. Coastal shipping along the eastern coast of the province is also fairly easy to pick up. Going up river by boat into some of the Dayak regions is fairly easy from Samarinda or Pontianak. Small boats, ferries and speedboats use the rivers between some of the major towns and cities – there are daily ferries and speedboats between Banjarmasin and Palangkaraya, and longboats between Tarakan and Berau, and Tarakan and Nunukan.

There are flights into the interior with the regular airline companies (Bouraq and Merpati carry the bulk of the traffic) and there are also many flights with DAS

(Dirgantara Air Service). Other possibilities include the planes run by the oil companies and the missions – if you're lucky and ask the right person, you may be able to pick up a ride.

PONTIANAK

Pontianak, an interesting river city, is only 10 km from the equator, on the confluence of the Landak and Kapuas Kecil rivers. It's a surprisingly large city, with a giant indoor sports stadium and a couple of big girder bridges spanning the river. Like Banjarmasin, it really needs to be seen from the canals, which crisscross the whole city. Or, walk over the bridge from Jalan Gajah Mada for a sweeping view of the river and the houses, and brilliant orange sunsets that make Bali sunsets look ordinary!

This is also the starting point for trips up the Kapuas Kecil River, Indonesia's longest waterway.

Orientation & Information

The main part of the city is on the southern side of the Kapuas River, in the region around the Kapuas bemo terminal. In this vicinity, you'll find markets, a few hotels, airline offices, the Pelni office, banks, etc.

Things to See

Mesjid Abdurrakhman This 18th-century royal mosque was built by Syarif Adbul Rahman, who was Sultan of Pontianak from 1771 until his death in 1808. Built in the Malay style, it's an impressive structure with a high, square-tiered roof. It's a short canoe trip (750 rp for a charter or 150 rp per person in a shared canoe) across the Landak River from the Pinisi Harbour.

Behind the royal mosque is the sultan's former palace, **Istana Kadriyah**. Now a museum, it displays a collection of the royal family's personal effects.

Musium Negeri Pontianak Located near Tanjungpura University, this national museum contains a very good collection of *tempayan,* or South-East Asian water containers, from Thailand, China and Borneo.

There are also Dayak exhibits that illustrate the tribal cultures of west Kalimantan.

Pasir Panjang From Pontianak, take a trip north along the coast to Pasir Panjang, a lovely stretch of beach with clean white sand and calm water, just back from the Pontianak to Singkawang road. Take a Singkawang-bound colt from Pontianak's Sintian terminal – you hurtle there along a nicely surfaced road for 2½ terrifying hours for 3000 rp.

Places to Stay

Accommodation in Pontianak is expensive – it always has been, but the situation has worsened over the last few years as the cheaper places have disappeared.

Backing onto the river, opposite the Kapuas terminal, is the *Hotel Wijaya Kusuma* (☎ 2547) at Jalan Musi 51-53. It's a good, clean hotel with fairly large rooms with fans and sweeping views across the river for 15,000 rp. Try and pick your room, so you avoid those facing the noisy street and get as far away as possible from the booming TV set. There's a Chinese nightclub below which plays woefully soppy Chinese and Indonesian pop songs until midnight.

Close by is the *Wisma Fatimah* (☎ 2250) at Jalan Fatimah 5. It's a pleasant but quite basic place with rooms with a small mandi and toilet at 15,000/20,000 rp. Take a Gajah Mada bemo to get here.

At Jalan Diponegoro 151, the *Hotel Khatulistiwa* is the most atmospheric hotel in Pontianak. It's a rambling wooden building in the centre of town. Clean rooms in the old wing cost from 12,500 to 15,000 rp with fan and mandi. The more expensive air-con rooms are nothing special.

Places to Eat

The best places to eat are the warungs – of which there are untold numbers in this city. Good ones at the Kapuas Indah ferry terminal area offer meals for around 2500 to 3500 rp. Try the night warungs on Jalan Pasar Sudirman for satay kambing (goat satay), steaming plates of rice noodles, kepiting (crab), udang, ikan and vegetables fried in a

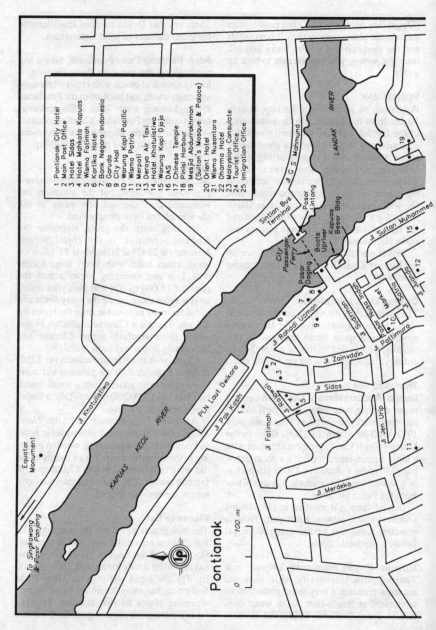

Pontianak

0   100 m

KEY

1 Pontianak City Hotel
2 Main Post Office
3 Hotel Sidas
4 Hotel Mohkota Kapuas
5 Wisma Fatimah
6 Kartika Hotel
7 Bank Negara Indonesia
8 Garuda
9 City Hall
10 Warung Kopi Pacific
11 Wisma Patria
12 Merpati
13 Deroya Air Taxi
14 Hotel Khatulistiwa
15 Warung Kopi Djojo
16 DAS
17 Chinese Temple
18 Pintisi Harbour
19 Mesjid Abdurrakhman
   (Sultan's Mosque & Palace)
20 Orient Hotel
21 Wisma Nusantara
22 Dharma Hotel
23 Malaysian Consulate
24 Tourist Office
25 Imigration Office

LANDAK RIVER

Jl G S Mahmund

Pasar Lintang

Kapuas Besar Bldg

Sintian Bus Terminal

City Passenger Ferry

Boats Upriver

Jl Sultan Muhammed

Pasar Daging

Jl Rahadi Usman

Jl Nusa Indah

Market

Jl Sukarno

Jl Pattimura

Jl Zainuddin

Jl Sidos

Jl Merdeka

Jl Jen Urip

Jl Pak Kasih

PLN Laut Dwikora

KAPUAS KECIL RIVER

Jl Khatulistiwa

Equator Monument

To Singkawang & Pasir Panjang

Jl Fatimah

Jl Rawali

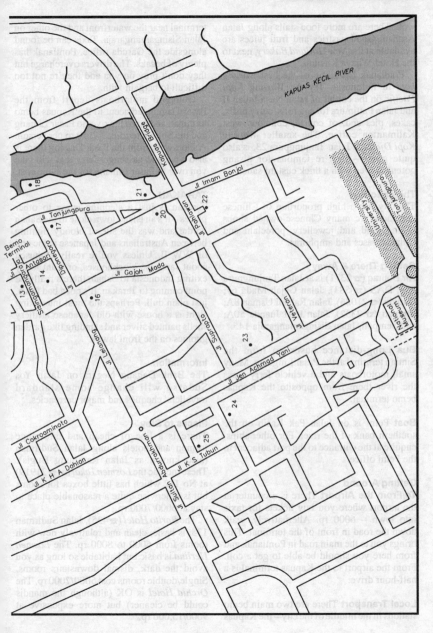

wok. There are more food stalls along Jalan Asahan. Good pastries and fruit juices are available at the *New Holland Bakery*, next to the Hotel Wijaya Kusuma.

Pontianak has some of the best *warung kopi* in Indonesia. Try the *Warung Kopi Pacific* on the corner of Jalan Nusa Indah II and Jalan Pattimura for egg rolls, curry puffs, cakes, pies and, of course, delicious west Kalimantan coffee. The smaller *Warung Kopi Djaja*, at Jalan Tanjungpura 23, is also quite good – they're famous for pisang goreng served with a thick custard sauce.

Things to Buy
The city has a high proportion of Chinese and there are many Chinese-owned shops selling gold and jewellery, porcelain and Chinese vases and amphoras.

Getting There & Away
Air Bouraq (☎ 2371) is at Jalan Tanjungpura 253; DAS (☎ 583), Jalan Gajah Mada 67; Garuda (☎ 21026), Jalan Rahadi Usman 8A; Merpati (☎ 2332), Jalan Ir H Juanda 50A; and Sempati, Jalan Sisingamangaraja 145.

Bus Long-distance buses go from the Sintian terminal at the Pasar Lingtang. Many small motorboats and a vehicle ferry cross the river there from opposite the Kapuas bemo terminal.

Boat Pelni is on Jalan Pak Kasih on the southern bank of the river. For other ships, enquire at the entrance to the port adjacent to the Pelni office.

Getting Around
To/From the Airport There is a counter at the airport where you buy tickets for taxis into town – 6000 rp. Alternatively, walk down the road in front of the terminal. This brings you to the main road in Pontianak and from here you should be able to get a colt. From the airport to the Kapuas terminal is a half-hour drive.

Local Transport There are two main bemo stations in the middle of the city – the Kapuas

terminal near the waterfront and the other on Jalan Sisingamangaraja. Taxis can be found alongside the Garuda office. Pontianak has plenty of becaks. The drivers overcharge but they don't prey on you and they're not too difficult to bargain with.

Outboard motorboats depart from the Pasar Daging, adjacent to the Kapuas bemo terminal, and cross the river to Pasar Lintang and the Sintian terminal – 150 rp per person. A short walk from the Pasar Dagang there is also a car and passenger ferry that will take you over to Pasar Lintang for the same cost.

TARAKAN
Tarakan is just a stepping stone to other places – it's an island town close to the Sabah border and was the site of bloody fighting between Australians and Japanese at the end of WW II. Unless you're really enthused about Japanese blockhouses, or want to try exiting Indonesia to Sabah, there's really no point coming to Tarakan. It's not a bad town, just plain dull. Perhaps the most interesting sight is a house with old Japanese artillery shells painted silver and standing like garden gnomes on the front lawns.

Information
The Bank Dagang Negara on Jalan Yos Sudarso will change some standard travellers' cheques and major currencies.

Places to Stay
There is a line of cheap and mid-range losmen and hotels along Jalan Sudirman (also known as Jalan Kampung Bugis). These include the *Losmen Jakarta* (☎ 21919) at No 112 which has little boxes for rooms but is otherwise quite a reasonable place to stay at 6000/7000 rp.

The *Barito Hotel* (☎ 435), Jalan Sudirman 133, is basic, clean and relatively new with rooms from 6000 to 8000 rp. The *Losmen Herlina* is basic but habitable so long as you avoid the dark, dismal downstairs rooms. Single/double rooms cost 5000/7000 rp. The *Orchid Hotel* is OK (although the mandis could be cleaner) but more expensive at 9000/15,000 rp.

Further along, *Wisata Hotel* (☎ 21245), on Jalan Sudirman near the junction with Jalan Mulawarman, is a basic but pleasant place. Single/double rooms cost from 9500/15,000 rp and the ones at the rear are very quiet.

Places to Eat

There are various places to choose from on Jalan Sudirman and Jalan Yos Sudarso including cheap warungs at the junction of the two streets. Stalls here sell imported apples and oranges! The *Rumah Makan Cahaya*, on Jalan Sudirman (across from the Losmen Jakarta), is memorable for the picture of the Mitsubishi Zero fighter plane on the wall and for their cheap, delicious cumi cumi (squid) and cap cai (fried vegetables). *Depot Theola*, a few doors down on the same street, serves local specialty *nasi lalap*, batter-fried chicken with rice and soup.

Getting There & Away

Air Merpati (☎ 21911) at Jalan Yos Sudarso 10 and Bouraq (☎ 21248, 21987) at Jalan Yos Sudarso 9B have flights to/from Balikpapan and Samarinda. Bouraq also flies between Tarakan and Tawau (Sabah) three times a week.

Bali Air, an offshoot of Bouraq, flies to Berau and Samarinda. Tickets can be booked through the Bouraq office.

Boat The Pelni office is at the port – take a colt from the city centre almost to the end of Jalan Yos Sudarso. The KM *Kerinci* calls into Tarakan on its route around Sulawesi and Kalimantan.

See the Kalimantan Getting There & Away section for details on water transport between Tarakan and Tawau.

Getting Around

To/From the Airport From the airport, buy tickets for taxis at the taxi counter in the airport terminal – it's 4000 rp to the city. Or, walk down the airport turn-off road to the main road and wait for a bemo. You should be able to get one going to the city (300 rp; 10-minute drive). If you've an early flight to catch, expect to have to charter a bemo.

Local Transport Transport around town is by colt and a 200 rp flat rate gets you just about anywhere.

SAMARINDA

Samarinda is another old trading port on one of Kalimantan's mighty rivers. Balikpapan is the place for oil and Samarinda is the place for timber so, in both, there are large and suitably insulated communities of foreign workers and management. If you want to get a look at a timber mill, there's a giant one on the road to Tenggarong, not far out from Samarinda.

Samarinda is also the most commonly used jumping-off point for trips up the river to the inland Dayak areas.

Orientation & Information

The main part of Samarinda is laid out along the northern bank of the Mahakam River. The centre of town is the enormous **mosque** on the riverfront. Running east along the riverfront is Jalan Yos Sudarso and to the west is Jalan Gajah Mada. Most of the offices and hotels are in these two streets or in the streets behind them.

Money The Bank Negara Indonesia is on the corner of Jalan Sebatik and Jalan Batur; it handles only a limited variety of foreign cash or travellers' cheques.

Places to Stay

The *Hotel Hidayah* on Jalan K H Khalid is central with clean, spartan rooms for 6000/8500 rp. The upstairs rooms are quieter than those downstairs.

Further north, along the same road, is the similar *Hotel Rahayu* where rooms range from 7000 to 15,000 rp and include breakfast.

The *Hotel Andhika* (☎ 22358, 23507) at Jalan Haji Agus Salim 37 has clean, quiet (as always, ask for a room away from the foyer) economy rooms from 9000 to 15,000 rp.

Cosier are the two inns on Jalan Pirus, just off busy Jalan Sudirman – the *Wisma Pirus* (☎ 21873) and *Hotel Hayani* (☎ 2265). Wisma Pirus has rooms with shared mandi for 7500 to 10,000 rp and rooms with private mandi in the 15,000 rp range. Hayani, on the other side, has similar rooms with mandi.

Places to Eat

Samarinda is fruit city and people sit outside along Jalan Mas Tenggarong carving giant nangka into manageable segments. Zurzats are cheap and there are also pineapples, bananas and salaks in abundance. The other gastronomic wonder is *udang galah* – giant river prawns which you'll find in the local warungs.

Many warungs open in the evening along Jalan Niaga Selatan and in the vicinity of Losmen Hidayah. Try the *Citra Niaga* hawkers' centre, off Jalan Niaga, for good value and variety. The *Sweet Home Bakery* at Jalan Sudirman 8 has the usual pastries. *Depot AC*, behind the Wella Beauty Salon off Jalan Mulawarman, serves delicious and cheap Chinese breakfasts (bubur ayam – porridge of rice or bean with chicken) and rice dishes (nasi bebek, nasi ayam and nasi tahu) in the early morning. For nasi soto or nasi sop, try the *Warung Aida* at the intersection of Jalan Panglima Batur and Jalan Kalimantan.

Getting There & Away

Air Merpati flies to Balikpapan and connects with Garuda flights elsewhere; the office is at Jalan Imam Bonjol 4. Bouraq (☎ 21105) flies to/from Tarakan, Berau (via Bali Air), Banjarmasin, Surabaya and Jakarta; the office is at Jalan Mulawarman 24.

Bus The long-distance bus station is at Seberang, on the south side of the Mahakam River from the main part of town. To get there, take a longboat from the pier at Pasar Pagi on Jalan Gajah Mada for 350 rp. It only takes a few minutes to make the crossing and they also have boats that take motorbikes across. The bus station is immediately behind the boat dock on the other side. From Seberang station, there are many buses to Tenggarong (1500 rp) and Balikpapan (2500 rp, two hours).

Boat For ships out of Samarinda, try Pelni at Jalan Yos Sudarso 40/56, although the Pelni ships KM *Kerinci* and KM *Kambuna* operate through Balikpapan and Tarakan, not Samarinda. Other places to enquire at close by include Terminal Penumpang Kapal Laut Samarinda, Direktorat Jenderal Perhubungan Laut (both on Jalan Yos Sudarso) and at the various shipping offices along the same street.

Riverboats Boats up the Mahakam River leave from the Sungai Kunjang ferry terminal, south-west of the town centre. Take the green 'taksi A' minibus for 400 rp to the dock. See the following Up the Mahakam River section for further information.

Getting Around

To/From the Airport The airport is in the northern suburbs. There is a taxi counter in the airport building and a taxi costs 6000 rp into the centre of town. Alternatively, you can just walk out of the terminal down Jalan Pipit to Jalan Serindit and catch a public colt for 750 rp into the city.

Getting out to the airport is the main problem. You should be able to catch a colt heading this way from the corner of Jalan Khalid and Jalan Panglima Batur – but beware of getting into empty colts unless you want to charter (or end up chartering) it.

UP THE MAHAKAM RIVER

Samarinda is probably the best jumping-off point for visits to the East Kalimantan Dayak tribes. Some of these are easily reached on the regular longboats that ply the Mahakam River from Samarinda. A good source of information about the Dayak areas is the Kutai guide Jailani, who can be reached through the Rahayu Hotel. He speaks English well and is very friendly and helpful. One traveller's account of a trip upriver follows:

We caught boats from Samarinda to Long Apari up the Mahakam River. We took a taxi boat at 9 am for 7500 rp per person, along with 200 other people, chickens and dogs. With only a few stops for food, we arrived in Long Irian two days later at 7 am. The locals said that this part of the Mahakam River is always busy with tourists and is not worthwhile for meeting members of the Dayak tribes.

Cheap taxis run to Long Bagun, but they are very slow, so we decided to take a longboat instead for 70,000 rp (divided amongst three people). We spent the night in Rukun Damai where there is a longhouse over 150 metres in length. The Dayaks living here are fairly modernised – they all have videos! Nearby is a Punan village – more 'primitive' and interesting. Here, they hunt with blow guns.

When we arrived in Long Bagun, the police stopped us and asked us for a permit from Tenggarong – we didn't have one. No way would he discuss the matter (or be bribed), we were told to go back the following day. We agreed and walked through the jungle to the next village.

Later, we enquired about permits and discovered that when travelling upriver, you should report to the police stations as you go, for your own safety. Permits have not been required since 1986, but communication among police officers is slow.

In Long Bagun, we saw our first Dayaks with long earlobes and tattoos. At night, we saw a medicine man go into a trance in order to cure some members of the village. It went on for a whole night, but was a worthwhile experience.

A couple of days later, we hired a longboat and three Dayaks to go to Long Tuyuk. This cost us a total of 350,000 rp. This part of the Mahakam River has several rapids and, at times, the boat had to be pulled along with ropes tied around trees. We spent the night in a small hut. We continued down the river the next day, reaching Long Tuyuk in the afternoon. At Long Tuyuk, we spent some time hunting for wild pigs with a man named Mr Hibau. He charged us 17,000 rp. From Long Tuyuk, we went by boat to Long Lunuk and from there to Long Apari.

The Dayaks in Long Apari are really wild. Old people still tell you about the days of head-hunting and cannibalism but they are very pleasant and hospitable. Everyone has tattoos and most people carry machetes.

Further up the river, we came across Dayaks who had never seen foreign people. From this point, you can proceed to Sarawak and visit the Iban Dayaks, but you need a guide and a police permit.

You can fly from Long Lunuk to Samarinda with Merpati.

Claudio Stabon, Italy

TENGGARONG

Situated 39 km west of Samarinda, this little riverside town is noted for its **Sultan's Palace**, built by the Dutch in 1936 and now used as a museum. Constructed in the Lego block-style of the period, it's an unusual building with some interesting exhibits. The palace is open at various times from Tuesday to Sunday, and there is a small admission charge.

Places to Stay & Eat

There are two places to stay at which are beside the waterfront and right on the boat dock. The *Penginapan Zaranah I* (☎ 148) has rooms for 4000 rp per person. The *Warung & Penginapan Anda* (☎ 78) is slightly more expensive at 5000/9000 rp. There are a couple of rumah makans and warungs around the market and the boat dock, but nothing memorable.

Getting There & Away

Colts to Tenggarong leave from Samarinda's Seberang bus station, across the river from the main part of Samarinda. The trip takes an hour, costs 2000 rp and the colt pulls into the Petugas terminal just outside Tenggarong.

Getting Around

From the long-distance bus station, you have to get a 'taxi kota', which is another colt, into the centre of Tenggarong for 300 rp. Guys with motorbikes will also take you in for 500 rp. The city taxis run between 7 am and 6 pm. It takes about 10 minutes to get from Petugas terminal to Pasar Tepian Pandan, where you get off for the boat dock, palace and tourist office. Alternatively, take a boat from Samarinda to Tenggarong from the pier in front of the mosque.

BALIKPAPAN

Apart from the clean, comfortable and highly insulated Pertamina, Union Oil and Total residential areas, Balikpapan consists of grubby backstreets and ravaged footpaths, both overrun by rampaging Hondas and Yamahas. The area north of the oil refinery, bounded by Jalan Randan Utara and Jalan Pandanwanyi, is completely built on stilts over the muddy isthmus, and is connected by uneven lurching wooden walkways between the houses. The huge oil refinery dominates the city, and when you fly into the place you'll see stray tankers and offshore oil rigs.

Orientation & Information

A good landmark is the enormous Hotel Benakutai on Jalan Antasari near the waterfront, which is roughly the centre of town. Heading east from Jalan Antasari along the waterfront is the airport road. Heading west along the waterfront is Kelandasan which runs into Jalan Achmad Yani. Heading north, Jalan Antasari merges into Jalan Sutuyo, Jalan Parman and Jalan Panjaitan, at the end of which is the Rapak bus terminal. Most of the hotels and offices can be found on these two streets.

Money The Bank Negara Indonesia on Jalan Antasari will change major travellers' cheques and cash currencies. The branch office in the terminal of Seppingan Airport will also change money and travellers' cheques.

Post There is a post office on Jalan Achmad Yani and also at the airport.

Immigration The immigration office is on the corner of Jalan Achmad Yani and Jalan Sudirman.

Places to Stay

There's not much cheap accommodation in Balikpapan and what is available is usually taken over by resident Indonesians. Best bet is probably the *Penginapan Royal*, nicely located not far from the Pasar Baru, at the beginning of the road to the airport and near the junction with Jalan Antasari. The rooms cost 5000 rp per person and are basic but clean. Rooms at the back should be quiet, but avoid those in the front facing the main street.

There's a string of places on Jalan Panjaitan including *Hotel Aida* (☎ 21006) which is clean and has rooms from 9000/15,000 rp. Close by, the *Hotel Murni* is similarly priced but get a room at the back away from the main street. On the same street, the *Penginapan Mama* is cheap with rooms from 6000 rp and it looks OK but always seems to be full.

Other available accommodation is mid-range or up-market. On Jalan Panjaitan you'll find the fairly basic *Hotel Tirta Plaza* (☎ 22324/132) which has rooms with fan and bath for 18,500 to 22,000 rp. The *Hotel Gajah Mada* (☎ 21046) at Jalan Gajah Mada 108 looks pretty up-market with big beds and bathroom, and prices in the 20,000 to 30,000 rp range. *Hotel Sederhana* on Kelandasan Ulu seems to be OK and has rooms from around 10,000 to 25,000 rp.

The *Hotel Kal Tim* on Jalan Monginisidi is not bad at 20,000 rp. It's in the north-west of the city, opposite the dock from where longboats and speedboats depart for Balikpapan's bus terminal across the water. Colts from the Rapak terminal will take you straight to the hotel.

Places to Eat

One thing that Balikpapan has got to recommend it is good seafood masakan Padang places, although they tend to be expensive. Try *Restaurant Masakan Padang Simpang Raya* next to the Hotel Murni. The *Restaurant Salero Minang* at Jalan Gajah Mada 12B is similarly priced, as is the marginally better *Restaurant Sinar Minang* on Jalan Antasari which also serves up udang galah.

More unusual (for decor) is the *Restaurant Roda Baru* near the Penginapan Royal. You eat amidst a rockery featuring a kitsch collection of plaster storks and lit by a chandelier. The cheapest eats can be found, during the evening, at the numerous warungs and food trolleys along Jalan Dondong near the Hotel Benakutai.

Getting There & Away

Air Merpati (☎ 22380, 24452) is at Jalan Achmad Yani 29, near the Pasar Baru on the road leading out to the airport; it is open Monday to Thursday from 8 am to 3 pm, and Friday to Sunday from 8 am to 12 noon. Bouraq (☎ 21107/087) has an office in the enormous Hotel Benakutai at Jalan Antasari. Garuda (☎ 22300/1, 21768) is diagonally opposite the Hotel Benakutai at Jalan Antasari 21.

Bus Buses to Samarinda (3000 rp) depart

from the Rapak terminal. Buses to Banjarmasin (15,000 rp) depart from the terminal on the opposite side of the harbour to the city. To get to this terminal take a colt from the Rapak bus station to the pier on Jalan Monginisidi. From here, take a speedboat to the other side. The cost is 1500 rp per person or around 6000 rp to charter, and it takes 10 minutes.

Alternatively, a motorised longboat crosses in half an hour and costs 900 rp. The bus terminal is immediately behind where the boats land.

Boat Pelni (☎ 22187) is on Jalan Yos Sudarso. Pelni's KM *Kerinci* and KM *Kambuna* pass through Balikpapan. For other ships to Surabaya, try PT Ling Jaya Shipping (☎ 21577) at Jalan Yos Sudarso 40 and PT Sudi Jaya Agung (☎ 21956) at Jalan Pelabuhan 39.

For ships across to Pare Pare in Sulawesi, go to PT Nurlina. Their office is on the pier where you catch speedboats or longboats to the bus terminal on the other side of the harbour. Departures for the 28-hour trip to Pare Pare go just about every day and cost 30,000 rp.

Getting Around

To/From the Airport Seppingan Airport is a fast 15-minute drive from Pasar Baru along a surfaced road. A taxi from the airport to town is around 7000 rp. In town, you may be able to charter a jeep taxi for less – perhaps from the Pasar Baru at the start of the airport road for about 4500 rp. A taxi seems to be the only way of getting out to the airport as it's right off the normal jeep-taxi runs.

Local Transport Jeep taxis – they look a bit like colts – cost 350 to 600 rp to get you anywhere around town. The chief station for buses and bemos is the Rapak terminal at the end of Jalan Panjaitan. The jeep taxis do a circular route around the main streets. Guys also hang around the Rapak terminal with their motorbikes and will take you as a pillion to anywhere you wish to go.

BANJARMASIN

Banjarmasin is one of the most stunning cities in Indonesia. It is criss-crossed by canals lined with stilt houses and buildings tacked on top of bundles of lashed, floating logs.

Orientation & Information

Although Banjarmasin is quite a big place, almost everything you'll need is packed into a very small area in the region of the Pasar Baru. Several of the cheaper hotels are found along Jalan Achmad Yani, on the opposite side of the river.

Tourist Office The South Kalimantan tourist office at Jalan Panjaitan 3, near the Grand Mosque, can be very helpful and generous with information. The staff can also arrange guides for trekking in the province.

Money The Bank Ekspor Impor and other banks on Jalan Lambung Mangkurat will change only a limited variety of cash or travellers' cheques.

Things to See & Do

In the middle of Banjarmasin is the **Mesjid Raya Sabilal Muhtadin**, a giant mosque with a copper-coloured flying saucer-shaped dome and minarets with lids and spires. The interior is striking. Visitors must pay a small fee to enter.

Canoe Trips The town should really be seen from water level, otherwise it can appear to be like any other Indonesian city. Hire someone to paddle you round in a canoe (a *klotok*) for 3000 rp per hour or two which should be more than enough. Ask around the wharf near the junction of Jalan Lambung Mangkurat and Jalan Pasar Baru. Besides the ordinary canal scenery, there's the floating village of **Muara Mantuil** and several *pasar terapung*, or floating markets.

It's worth taking a boat trip to the river islands of **Pulau Kaget** and **Pulau Kembang**. It takes four to five hours to visit the island of Pulau Kaget, 12 km from town, where you can see the famous proboscis, or

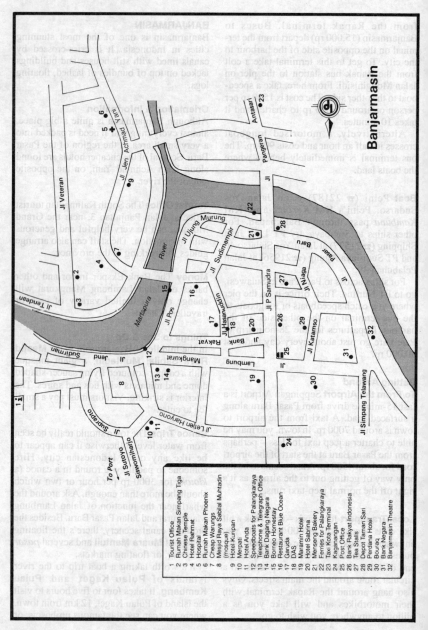

Banjarmasin

1 Tourist Office
2 Rumah Makan Simpang Tiga
3 Chinese Temple
4 Hotel Rahmat
5 Hospital
6 Rumah Makan Phoenix
7 Cheap Warungs
8 Mesjid Raya Sabilal Muhtadin
   (mosque)
9 Hotel Kuripan
10 Merpati
11 Hotel Anda
12 Speedboats for Palangkaraya
13 Telephone & Telegraph Office
14 Bank Dagang Negara
15 Borneo Homestay
16 Restaurant Blue Ocean
17 Garuda
18 DAS
19 Maramin Hotel
20 Hotel Sabrina
21 Menseng Bakery
22 Ferries for Palangkaraya
23 Taxi Kota Terminal
24 Kaganangan
25 Post Office
26 Bank Rakyat Indonesia
27 Tea Stalls
28 Depot Taman Sari
29 Perdana Hotel
30 Borcq
31 Bank Negara
32 Banjarmasin Theatre

long-nosed, monkeys. The much closer Pulau Kembang has an old Chinese temple that's home to hundreds of long-tailed macaques. For these islands, you'd best forget the klotoks and hire a speedboat from the pier at the end of Jalan Pos.

Places to Stay

Some of the cheapies won't take foreigners, which kind of leaves you out in the cold.

The *Borneo Homestay* at Jalan Pos 123 is very cheap at 3000/5000 and centrally located. The young couple who run it are very friendly and speak English.

Otherwise, you're left with medium-priced hotels – all pretty much alike. The rambling *Hotel Rahmat* (☎ 4429) on Jalan Achmad Yani is friendly and clean enough with rooms for 10,000 to 12,500 rp, cheaper without mandi. The nearby *Hotel Kuripan* at No 114 has rooms for about the same rates. The *Hotel Sabrina* (☎ 4442, 4721) at Jalan Bank Rakyat 21 is a bit more up-market with rooms from 14,000 rp or from 20,000 rp with TV and air-con. The *Banua Hotel* at Jalan Katsamo 8 and the *Perdana Hotel* at Jalan Katsamo 3 offer similar standards but at slightly higher charges.

Places to Eat

Cheap warungs and rumah makans can be found along Jalan Veteran. Try places like the *Rumah Makan Sari Wangi* at No 70 the *Es Campur Flamingo*, across the road, the *Rumah Makan Simpang Tiga* at No 22 and lots of others the whole way along. At night, there are many warungs along Jalan Pasar Baru and Jalan Niaga in the area south of Jalan Samudra.

Banjarmasin is famous for its tea cakes, called *wadai*, and the best bakery in town is the *Utarid* at Jalan Pasar Baru 22-28, near the Jalan Antasari bridge. Next to the bridge is a pleasant rooftop cafe, *Depot Taman Sari*, where you can get standard Indonesian and Chinese dishes.

Getting There & Away

Air The Garuda (☎ 4203, 3885) office is at Jalan Hasanuddin 31; Merpati (☎ 4433, 4307) is at Jalan M T Haryono 4; Bouraq (☎ 2445, 3285) is at Jalan Lambung Mangkurat 40D; and DAS (☎ 2902) is opposite Garuda at Jalan Hasanuddin 6, Blok 4.

Bus Buses and colts depart frequently from the Km 6 terminal for Martapura and Banjarbaru, and there are daily buses to Balikpapan (12,000 rp).

Boat There are regular ships (usually two per week) from Banjarmasin to Surabaya which leave from Pelabuhan Trisakti. To get there, take a bemo from Pasar Baru for 300 rp, which will take you straight past the harbourmaster's office. Agents for the ships are opposite the harbourmaster's office and tickets are around 30,000 to 35,000 rp depending on which agent you go to. Agents for ships to Surabaya can also be found on Jalan Lambung Mangkurat, near the junction with Jalan Pasar Baru.

Pelni's KM *Kelimutu* operates a regular Semarang-Banjarmasin-Surabaya service. The fare from Banjarmasin starts at around 30,000 rp for Ekonomi class.

River Ferries *Bis air* (river ferries) go from the new Banjar Raya ferry harbour and cost 9000 rp for the 18-hour trip to Palangkaraya. To get to the harbour, take a bemo from the central station on Jalan Pangeran Antasari for 200 rp. Speedboats take only six or seven hours to Palangkaraya, cost 18,000 rp and depart from the end of Jalan Pos.

Getting Around

To/From the Airport The airport is 26 km out of town on the road to Banjarbaru. To get there, take a bemo from Jalan Pasar Baru to the Km 6 terminal, and then catch a Martapura-bound colt. Get off at the branch road leading to the airport and walk the short distance to the airport terminal.

Alternatively, a taxi all the way to the airport will cost you around 8000 rp – get one of these from the group that hangs out near the Garuda office. If you're travelling light, the guys offering motorbike pillion rides from the Km 6 terminal are a good way to get out to the airport.

For the trip from the airport to the city, buy a taxi ticket at the counter in the airport terminal. Alternatively, walk out the airport building, through the car park, past the post office and the MIG aircraft, turn left and walk down to the Banjarmasin to Martapura highway. From here, you can pick up one of the Banjarmasin to Martapura colts into Banjarmasin.

Local Transport The central bemo station is at the Pasar Baru on Jalan Pasar Baru and from here you get bemos to various destinations around town including the Km 6 terminal for long-distance buses. The bemo fare from Pasar Baru to Km 6 is 300 rp.

Banjarmasin becak drivers are'nt predatory but they do ask hefty prices and are hard to bargain with – the bajaj drivers work in much the same way. Guys with motorbikes, who hang around Pasar Baru and Km 6, will take you wherever you want to go.

MARTAPURA

Drop down to Martapura for a look at the market. It's a photographer's paradise on a good day, with lots of colourfully dressed Banjarmasin women. The market is behind the Martapura bus station.

A few minutes' walk diagonally across the nearby playing field, is a diamond-polishing factory and shop. Ask for the Penggosokan Intan Tradisional Kayu Tangi. You can get colts to Martapura from the Km 6 terminal in Banjarmasin for 700 rp. The trip takes about 45 minutes along a good surfaced road.

BANJARBARU

This town, on the road from Banjarmasin to Martapura, has an interesting **museum** with a collection of Banjar and Dayak artefacts along with statues excavated from ancient Hindu temples in Kalimantan. The museum is officially open on weekends only but there's usually someone around to let you in on other days. To get there take a Martapura colt from Banjarmasin.

CEMPAKA

Cempaka is 43 km south from Banjarmasin. There's a creek here where the people are up to their necks in water panning for gold. Bemos from Martapura are infrequent – enquire at the Km 6 terminal in Banjarmasin if there are any colts going direct to Cempaka. Or, charter a bemo from Martapura bus station for 4000 rp for the round trip which allows a brief stop at the creek.

Sulawesi

Sulawesi's big attraction is the interesting Tanatoraja area in the south-western leg of this strangely-shaped island. Few visitors to Sulawesi get further than the southern area. Travel to the other areas is difficult or time-consuming, although it's getting easier with improvements in the roads and additional air transport.

The Minahasa area of the northern limb of the island is interesting and there are some stunning coral reefs off the coast of Manado, the chief city of the region. But for most people, Sulawesi is simply an Ujung Pandang and Tanatoraja loop.

Getting There & Away

Air There are air connections to a number of Sulawesi cities, chiefly to the capital of Ujung Pandang. Garuda, Merpati, Mandala and Bouraq all fly to Sulawesi. Most visitors either make Ujung Pandang a stepping stone between Java and Bali or Maluku and Irian Jaya. Alternatively, you can make an out and back trip from Java or Bali – you will save a little cash if you're travelling from Bali to Java and visiting Sulawesi as well by flying Denpasar-Ujung Pandang-Surabaya.

Because of its central location, there are all sorts of possibilities available with flights from Ujung Pandang to other parts of Sulawesi and to the other provinces of Indonesia. Flying Garuda, fares to Ujung Pandang include Denpasar 121,000 rp, Surabaya 160,000 rp, Jakarta 253,000 rp, Ambon 175,000 rp, Biak 311,000 rp and Jayapura 418,000 rp. Bouraq has flights from Ujung Pandang to central and northern Sulawesi and to Kalimantan and Maluku, including Balikpapan 143,000 rp, Gorontalo 152,000 rp, Manado 185,000 rp, Palu 108,000 rp, Samarinda 197,000 rp, Tarakan 271,000 rp and Ternate 257,000 rp.

Boat There are Pelni ships to Ujung Pandang and other Sulawesi ports from eastern and western Indonesia. In fact, five of the six regular two weekly Pelni routes take in Ujung Pandang so you can travel to or from Ujung Pandang and most other major centres in the archipelago. See the Indonesia Getting There & Away section for route details.

From Surabaya, the main port of Java with connections to Ujung Pandang, it takes less than 24 hours, a couple of days more around to Bitung (the port for Manado), with several stops in between. Because road transport in Sulawesi is still poor, the coastal ferries tend to be crowded.

It's also possible to get across from Kalimantan to Sulawesi. Two of the Pelni services operate between Ujung Pandang and Balikpapan and then back to Sulawesi. There are other regular passenger ships from various east Kalimantan ports to Pare Pare, Donggala and Palu. Heading east, Pelni connects to ports in Maluku and Irian Jaya.

When looking for ships in any of the ports, check with the Pelni office first and then check around other shipping agents and ask around the port. A really interesting trip would be by Makassar schooner – ask at Paotere Harbour in Ujung Pandang or in Java at Surabaya or Jakarta. Travellers occasionally find schooners going to Nusa Tenggara. Fares are totally dependent on negotiation, of course.

SOUTH-WESTERN PENINSULA
Ujung Pandang

The capital of Sulawesi province is also its largest and liveliest city. The Muslim Bugis are now the dominant group in Ujung Pandang (UP) and the city is best known as the home of their magnificent perahus that still trade extensively through the Indonesian archipelago. In the Dutch era it was known as Makassar.

Orientation The city can be divided into the busy business district along the northern waterfront, the leisure-oriented southern waterfront and a sprawling mixed residential and business area spreading eastward from the Karebosi, a large public square. During Dutch colonial times, the Karebosi was

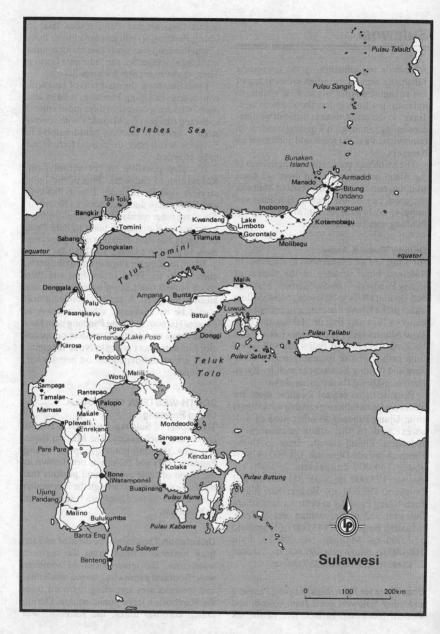

Sulawesi

called the Konigsplein and it was the centre of a very fashionable residential area.

Information The tourist office (☎ 21142) is a long way out of town, on Jalan A Pangerang Petta Rani, a street heading south off the airport road. Despite it's isolation the office is helpful and informative so it's worth making the trip. A double-decker bus No 2 (150 rp) runs straight past this office. Or take a Sentral-Ikip bemo for 250 rp.

The Bank Rakyat Indonesia is on Jalan Achmad Yani and the post office is on the corner of Jalan Supratman and Jalan Slamet Riyadi, south-east of the fort.

Things to See Places of interest in Ujung Padang include:

Perahus You can see Bugis schooners at three perahu ports in and around UP, including the Paotere Harbour, a short becak ride north from the city centre. Though they are nowhere near as impressive as the awesome lineup at the Pasar Ikan in Jakarta, if you've never seen them it's worth a look. Elsewhere along the waterfront, you may see *balolang*, large outriggers with sails, or *lepa-lepa*, smaller outrigger canoes.

Tomb of Sultan Hasanuddin On the outskirts of Ujung Padang is the tomb of Sultan Hasanuddin, leader of the southern Sulawesi kingdom of Gowa in the middle of the 17th century. Conflicts between Gowa and the Dutch had continued almost incessantly since the early part of that century. This only came to an end in 1660 when a Dutch East Indies fleet attacked Gowa and forced Hasanuddin to accept a peace treaty.

To get to the tomb, take a double-decker bus No 2 (150 rp) from the central bus station. The bus goes past the street which leads to the graves, so ask the driver to stop there (the street is marked by a large sign). You can then walk or take a becak the half km or so to the graves. About a 15-minute walk from the grave is the site of Ujung Padang's oldest mosque – notable for its

cemetery with large crypts, each of which contain several graves.

Museum Ballalompoa In an interesting old wooden palace on stilts, this museum has similar exhibits to those in Fort Rotterdam. It's at Sungguminasa, a half-hour, 300 rp trip from the central bemo station. It opens at various times from Monday to Saturday, or on request.

Clara Bundt Orchid Garden & Shell Collection This house is at Jalan Mochtar Lufti 15 (☎ 22572), and its compound contains a large collection of seashells, including dozens of giant clams. Behind the house are several blocks of orchids in pots and trays. These are world famous amongst orchid specialists.

Fort Rotterdam Now known as Benteng Ujung Pandang, this fort was originally built in 1634 then rebuilt in typical Dutch style after their takeover in 1667. The buildings gradually fell into disrepair but a major restoration project has renovated the whole complex, apart from a wall or two. The entire fort is shaped like a turtle facing the sea, a symbol of the Makassarese.

The fort contains two museums. The larger one is more interesting and the smaller one has a rather sad and scruffy collection. There are separate admission charges to both museums and they open daily from 8 am to 4 pm.

Diponegoro Monument The Yogya Prince Diponegoro was exiled to Makassar after the Dutch double-crossed him. His grave is in a small cemetery on Jalan Diponegoro.

Around Town Other interesting Ujung Pandang peculiarities include the brilliantly ornate **Chinese temples** found along Jalan Sulawesi in the middle of town. Check out **Jalan Sombu Opu** – it has a great collection of jewellery shops. Toko Kerajinam, at No 20, is good for touristy souvenirs and there are lots of people around the streets here selling old coins.

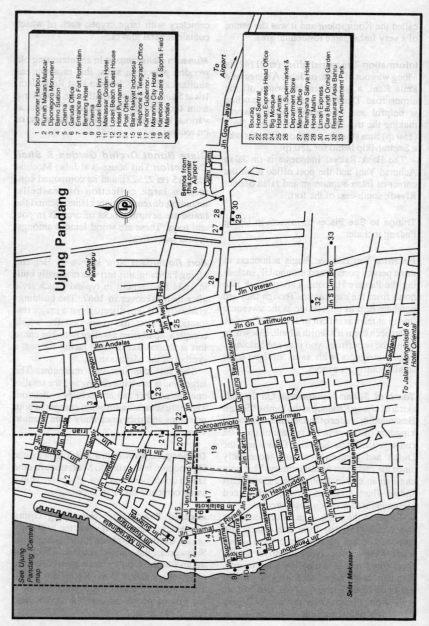

1 Schooner Harbour
2 Rumah Makan Malabar
3 Diponegoro Monument
4 Bemo Station
5 Cinema
6 Garuda Office
7 Entrance to Fort Rotterdam
8 Benteng Hotel
9 Cinema
10 Losari Beach Inn
11 Makassar Golden Hotel
12 Losari Beach Guest House
13 Hotel Purnama
14 Post Office
15 Bank Rakyat Indonesia
16 Telephone & Telegraph Office
17 Kantor Gubernour
18 Marannu City Hotel
19 Karebosi Square & Sports Field
20 Mandala

21 Bouraq
22 Hotel Sentral
23 Liman Express Head Office
24 Big Mosque
25 Hotel Aman
26 Harapan Supermarket & Department Store
27 Merpati Office
28 Ramayana Satrya Hotel
29 Hotel Marlin
30 Liman Express
31 Clara Bundt Orchid Garden
32 Restaurant Asia Bahru
33 THR Amusement Park

Ujung Pandang

Ujung Pandang (Centre)

1	House Nusantara
2	Hotel Murah
3	Rumah Makan Malabar
4	Rumah Makan Empang
5	Schooner Dock
6	Fruit Market
7	Chinese Temple
8	Pelni Office
9	Chinese Temple
10	Chinese Temple
11	Chinese Temple
12	Cinema (Theatre DKM)

Bantimurung This reserve, 41 km from Ujung Pandang, is noted for its waterfall and eroded and overgrown rocky pinnacles and cliffs. There's also a cave with some carvings – scramble along the rocks past the waterfall to the track leading to the cave, a 15-minute walk, and bring a torch. It makes a pleasant day's retreat from Ujung Pandang and is noted for the numerous beautiful butterflies. There is a small admission charge.

To get to Bantimurung, take a bemo from the central bemo station to the town of Maros (600 rp; 30 minutes from Ujung Pandang) and then take another bemo from there (250 rp; 30 minutes). You may end up having to charter a bemo on a weekday. There might be direct bemos from Ujung Pandang on Sunday but the place will probably be crowded then.

Wisma Bantimurung is a very spartan little hotel at Bantimurung. There are lots of little shops around here selling soft drinks.

Places to Stay One of the best places to stay in Ujung Pandang, if you don't want to be near the town centre, is the *Ramayana Satrya Hotel* (☎ 22165, 24153) on Jalan Gunung Bawakaraeng. Rooms cost from 10,000 rp, meals from 2000 to 4000 rp. To get there,

take a bemo from the town centre for 150 rp. Bemos from the airport also pass in front of the Ramayana Satrya.

Also centrally located is the *Hotel Purnama* (☎ 3830) at Jalan Pattimura 3-3A, has basic but clean rooms (the upstairs ones are better) from 11,000 to 17,000 rp. Further out, the *Hotel Oriental* on Jalan Monginisidi has rooms with mandi and toilet for 7500 and 10,000 rp. There's free tea available but recent reports have not been too glowing. There are some good warungs in a street nearby, just ask at the hotel for directions.

The *Hotel Nusantara* has a good central location at Jalan Sarappo 103 and the rooms are only 4000 to 7000 rp but they're sweat boxes – partitioned off from each other by masonite walls with the top enclosed by wire mesh. Not only is it hot and noisy, the mandis are grubby too. This is a one-night-stand job at the most. Diagonally across the road is the similar *Hotel Murah*. The *Benteng Hotel* on Jalan Supratman is a grubby place with rooms at 10,000 rp and plenty of painted ladies.

Dolly Home Stay (☎ 31 8936) at Jalan G Lompohattang 121 has plain single/double rooms at 7000/9000 rp including breakfast and lots of travellers info. The *Mandar Inn* (☎ 82349) at Jalan Annang 11 is a popular new place.

Hotel Sentral at Jalan Bulusaraung 7 is basic, noisy but clean and also often seems to be 'full'. Rooms are around 7000/9000 rp for singles/doubles.

Up-market but very good value is the

Losari Beach Guest House (☎ 23609) at Jalan Penghibur 3 overlooks the waterfront and costs 48,000 rp for large rooms with air-con and hot showers, and breakfast is included. Don't confuse it with the more expensive but grubby Losari Beach Inn, a bit north on the same street.

The small islands of Pulau Keyangan and Pulau Lae Lae, opposite the city, offer accommodation in fishing houses from around 15,000 to 20,000 rp per day, including three meals. Ferries leave in the morning from the pier near Fort Rotterdam for 2000 rp one way.

Places to Eat There are a lots of good seafood restaurants along Ujung Pandang's waterfront serving ikan bakar (barbecued fish) and cumi cumi bakar (barbecued squid) and other dishes. *Astira* on Jalan Penghibur has a pleasant atmosphere and reasonable prices. For lower prices, look for small foodshops called 'Kios'.

Also worth trying are the dozens of night-time food trolleys that stretch along the waterfront, south of the big Makassar Golden Hotel on Jalan Penghibur.

Jalan Sulawesi is a good hunting ground for restaurants – notable places include the little Chinese warung at Jalan Sulawesi 185, which shares space with a sewing shop. The *Rumah Makan Malabar*, at No 290, advertises itself as a specialist in Indian food and a simple Indian curry, roti and rice does make a slight change from Indonesian food. They're famous for their martabak.

The *Asia Bahru Restaurant*, near the corner of Jalan Latimojong and Jalan G Sala, is a pleasant place to eat and when you order a big fish you get a *big* fish! It's a bit pricey but the quality is high. Also try the *Rumah Makan Empang*, at Jalan Siau 7 down by the harbour. Check out the warungs around the THR Amusement Park for a slab of ikan bakar with cucumber, peanut sauce and rice.

Getting There & Away Transport to/from Ujung Pandang includes:

Air Ujung Pandang is the major arrival and departure point for Sulawesi whether it's by air or sea. Surabaya is the main connecting city on Java and you can fly from Surabaya to Ujung Pandang for around 160,000 rp. It's cheaper to fly Denpasar to Ujung Pandang for 121,000 rp. Jakarta to Ujung Pandang costs 252,000 rp with Garuda. Merpati also have connections between Ujung Pandang and Bima in Sumbawa or Maumere in Flores.

Bouraq (☎ 22253) is at Jalan H O S Cokroaminoto 7C. Garuda (☎ 22573) is at Jalan Slamet Riyadi 6. Mandala (☎ 21289) is at Jalan Dr W Sudirohusada 14. Merpati (☎ 24114/118/155) is at Jalan Gunung Bawakaraeng 109.

Bus For most people, the next stop after Ujung Pandang is Tanatoraja. The road to Rantepao, the main town of Tanatoraja, is now surfaced and there are many companies running daily colts and buses there. The best of these is usually reckoned to be Liman Express (☎ 5851) whose office is on Jalan Laiya. The Hotel Marlin on Jalan Gunung Bawakaraeng (opposite the Ramayana Satrya Hotel) is an agent for this bus.

Bus fares from Ujung Pandang to Rantepao are 8000 rp. Try and get your ticket a day in advance. The trip goes via Pare Pare and takes about nine hours, including one or two brief stops at warungs.

Boat See the Indonesia and Sulawesi Getting There & Away sections for more information on sea travel. Pelni (☎ 7962/4) is in an unmarked, orange building at Jalan Martadinata 38, down on the waterfront. At the harbour between Hatta and Sukarno, off Jalan Martadinata, it is sometimes possible to book passage on a perahu to central Sulawesi, Kalimantan or Java.

Getting Around Transport around Ujung Pandang includes:

To/From the Airport Bemos to Ujung Pandang's Hasanuddin Airport (22 km out of town) go from the bemo station to the large intersection a few minutes' walk east of the

Hotel Ramayana Satrya and then to the airport. The airport terminal is off the main road and the bemos will sometimes detour right to the terminal, but you might have to make the short walk from the main road. The fare from the city is 500 rp.

A taxi from the airport to the town centre (buy your ticket at the taxi counter in the terminal) is 9000 rp but if you wander outside you might find jeeps for 7000 rp or so. Alternatively, you can easily walk out to the main road and catch a bemo to the city. It's a short walk, so don't pay a becak rider more than a few hundred rp.

There are several good cheap rumah makans out front and to the side of the airport terminal.

Buses Double-decker buses run from in front of the main bemo station, down Jalan Cokroaminoto and Jalan Sudirman, along Jalan Gunung Bawakaraeng and past the Ramayana Satrya Hotel. They then turn along the airport road and down Jalan A Pangerang Petta Rani. This is the road for the tourist office and the jumping-off point for the tomb of Sultan Hasanuddin. There are bus stops in the city, but further out you just wave the bus down.

Taxis Bosowa Taxi (☎ 31 8689) offers a metered service around town for 800 rp at flagfall and 400 rp per half-km thereafter.

Bemos The main bemo station is at the northern end of Jalan Cokroaminoto, and from here you can get bemos to various destinations around Ujung Pandang.

Becaks For short trips there are becaks – you really need them since Ujung Pandang is too big a place to do much walking. From the Hotel Ramayana Satrya to the waterfront, pay about 700 rp, and from the bemo station to Fort Rotterdam 500 rp. Becak drivers tend to ask ridiculous fares, like 2000 rp for a simple 500 rp trip but they bring the price down fast when you walk away. They're fearless drivers, unafraid to put your life on the line. Getting into the traffic or cutting across streets during peak hour is a truly terrifying experience!

Pare Pare

Pare Pare is a bustling seaport – a mini Ujung Pandang – but without the obnoxious traffic. For the most part, however, it's just a place to hang around in as you await a boat to Kalimantan or northern Sulawesi.

Things to See One sight of note is the small **Museum of Ethnology** on the right side of the highway as you enter Pare Pare from Ujung Pandang. On display are wedding ornaments, brassware, ceramics, musical instruments and various other cultural items traditionally used in north-west Sulawesi.

At the perahu pier, or *pelabuhan perahu*, off Jalan Pinggir Laut, you can check out the local boat scene.

Places to Stay The *Hotel Gandaria (Mess Gandaria)* (☎ 98) at Jalan Bau Massepe 171 has rooms with toilet and shower from 13,000 rp. It's excellent value and only a five-minute walk from the bus station. A large detailed street map of Pare Pare hangs on the wall in the foyer of this hotel and photostat maps of Pare Pare can be bought just down the road at the Toko ABC at Jalan Bau Massepe 183. The owner of the hotel has a collection of ritual ornaments for use in weddings – he's glad to show them to interested parties.

The *Tanty Hotel* on Jalan Hasanuddin is OK – basic and clean. The only problem is the blaring television set in the foyer! Rooms are 13,000 rp but if you're prepared to pay that much you may as well go to the Gandaria and get your money's worth.

A 15 to 20-minute walk from the bus station, the *Hotel Siswa* (☎ 21374) at Jalan Baso Daeng Patompo 30 is a great rambling run-down place. Rooms cost 3500 rp per person and are thinly partitioned but should be OK for a night or two although the toilets and mandis could be cleaner!

A few doors from the Gandaria, the *Losmen Murni* at Jalan Bau Massepe 175 is a warehouse with boxes. Rooms cost 4000 rp per person but they probably won't take you. *Penginapan Palanro* and *Penginapan AM* (☎ 21801) are in the same building on Jalan Bau Massepe. They're similar in price and standard to the Losmen Murni.

Places to Eat The *Restaurant Sempurna* on Jalan Bau Massepe is a nice, clean place and good value with its extensive menu featuring lots of seafood. *Bukit Indah* on Jalan Sudirman is similar. The *Warung Sedap* is an ikan bakar specialist on Jalan Baso Daeng Patompo. There are various little warungs in the vicinity of the Hotel Siswa, along Jalan Bau Massepe, and a night market along the waterfront.

For snacks with a bay view, try the *Anging Mammiri* at Jalan Pinggir Laut 1, right on the waterfront.

Getting There & Away Transport to/from Pare Pare includes:

Bus Regular buses from Ujung Pandang to Rantepao in Tanatoraja pass through Pare Pare. Best of these is Liman Express (☎ 5851) which has an office on Jalan Laiya in Ujung Pandang. The Hotel Marlin on Jalan Gunung Bawakaraeng (oppsite the Ramayana Satrya Hotel) is an agent for this bus. The fare from Ujung Pandang to Pare Pare is 4000 rp.

In Pare Pare, the bus companies have their ticket offices at the bus station. Bus fares to or from Pare Pare are Rantepao 4000 rp, Palopo 4500 rp and Bone via Sengkang 2000 rp.

Boat The main reason to come to Pare Pare is to catch a boat to the east coast of Kalimantan (daily boats go to one port or another) or to Donggala and Toli Toli in Sulawesi. There are ships around three times a week from Pare Pare to Donggala (32,000 rp and a two-day trip) and Toli Toli (40,000 rp and a three-day trip) in northern Sulawesi. For tickets and information, try PT Bukit Harapanjaya (☎ 21975) at Jalan Usahawan 51.

Pelni (☎ 21017) is at Jalan Andicammi

130. The harbourmaster's office is on the waterfront on Jalan Andicammi, and several shipping companies have their offices here. Fares from Pare Pare to Kalimantan ports include Nunukan from 50,000 to 60,000 rp, Tarakan 60,000 rp, Samarinda from 35,000 to 45,000 rp and Balikpapan from 35,000 to 45,000 rp.

There are plenty of other agents and they're easy enough to find – look around the bus station, at the harbour and along the main streets near the waterfront.

TANATORAJA

The Toraja Land (also known as Tanatoraja or Tator) is about 320 km north of Ujung Pandang, a high mountainous area with beautiful scenery and a fascinating culture. The Torajas are now Christianised but they still retain strong animist traditions with traditional and complicated death rituals.

The first thing that strikes you in Toraja are the traditional houses, shaped like buffalo horns (an animal of great mythic and economic importance to the Torajas) with the roof rearing up at front and rear. The houses are remarkably similar to the Batak houses of Lake Toba in Sumatra and are always aligned north-south with small rice barns facing them.

There are a number of villages in the region which are still composed entirely of these traditional houses but most have corrugated iron roofs, and some have been built in strategic locations purely for the benefit of foreign tourists. The beams and supports of the Torajan houses are cut so that they all slot together neatly and the whole house is painted (and carved on the older houses) with chicken and buffalo motifs – often buffalo skulls are used as decoration.

The burial customs of the Torajas are unique. Like the Balinese they generally have two funerals – one immediately after the death and then an elaborate second funeral after sufficient time has elapsed to make the complex preparations and raise the necessary cash. Because they believe you can take it with you, the dead generally go well equipped to their graves. Since this led

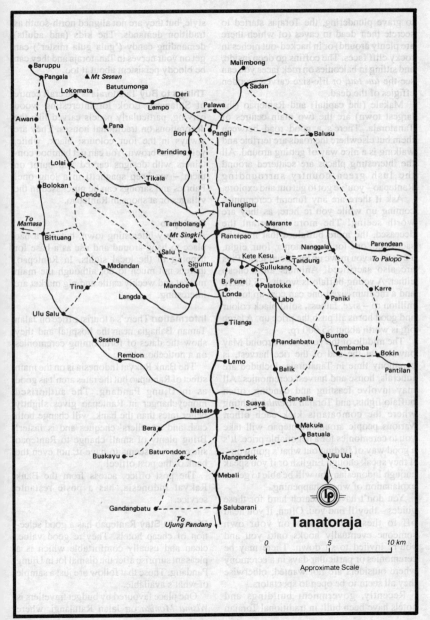

Tanatoraja

0   5   10 km

Approximate Scale

to grave plundering, the Torajas started to secrete their dead in caves (of which there are plenty around) or in hacked-out niches in rocky cliff faces. The coffins go deep inside, and sitting in balconies on rock faces you can see the *tau tau*, or life-size carved wooden effigies of the dead.

Makale (the capital) and Rantepao (the largest town) are the two main centres of Tanatoraja. There's a good road between them but elsewhere the roads are terrible and walking is a nice way of getting around. All the interesting places are scattered around the lush green country surrounding Rantepao – you've got to get out and explore.

Ask if there are any funeral ceremonies coming up while you're here, as they are worth seeing! The more important the deceased, the more buffaloes that must be sacrificed: one for a commoner, four, eight, 12 or 24 as you move up the social scale. Pigs are also sacrificed. Animals ain't cheap either. A young buffalo is worth 175,000 rp and a medium-sized one can cost up to two million rp – size, fatness, solid black colour and good horns all push the price up. A large pig is worth about 85,000 rp.

The middle of the year, from around May onwards at the end of the rice harvest, is ceremony time in Tanatoraja. Included are funerals, house and harvest ceremonies. All may involve feasting and dancing, often buffalo fights, and Torajan *sisemba* fighting where the combatants kick each other. Various people around Rantepao will take you to ceremonies for a negotiable price. It's a good way of finding out what's going on – if they speak enough English or if you speak enough Indonesian you will be able to get an explanation of what's happening.

You don't have to search hard for these guides – they'll find you. Often, if you head off to these ceremonies on your own someone eventually hooks onto you and you're invited to sit down. There may be ceremonies or particular days in a ceremony where outsiders are not wanted, otherwise they all seem to be open to spectators.

Recently, government buildings and hotels have been built in traditional Torajan style, but they are not aligned north-south as tradition demands. The kids (and adults) demanding candy ('gula gula mister') can get on your nerves in Tanatoraja and they can be bloody persistent about it too.

Things to Buy Tanatoraja is the craft centre of Sulawesi. Look for interesting wood carving, particularly panels carved like the decorations on traditional houses. They are always in the four colours: black, white, yellow and brown. You can get bamboo containers with designs carved and burnt on them – we keep spaghetti in a long one! Fabrics and sarongs can be purchased in the villages or at shops in Rantepao.

Rantepao

A not very interesting town, but not a bad place to hang around and use as a base for tripping to the local sights. In Rantepao, there's not much to do, although the main market and weekly cattle and pig market are interesting.

Information There's a tourist office on Jalan Taman Bahagia near the hospital and they show the dates of forthcoming ceremonies on a noticeboard.

The Bank Rakyat Indonesia is on the main street of Rantepao but the rates aren't as good as in Ujung Pandang. The authorised moneychanger in Rantepao gives slightly better rates than the bank, will change both cash and travellers' cheques and is faster! Bring plenty of small change to Rantepao since no one seems to have it, not even the bank or the post office!

The post office, across from the Bank Rakyat Indonesia, has a poste restante service.

Places to Stay Rantepao has a good selection of cheap hotels. They're good value, clean and usually comfortable which is a pleasant surprise after the dismal lot in Ujung Pandang. Those that follow are just a sample of what's available.

One place favoured by budget travellers is *Wisma Monika* on Jalan Ratulangi, where single/double rooms with mandi and toilet are 3000/5000 rp. It's an older, slightly tatty place but it's run by friendly people and is quiet as it's off the main street.

Losmen Flora (☎ 28) at Jalan Sesean 25 is friendly, clean and cheap. A disadvantage is the early morning wake-up calls from the mosque across the road. Whatever you do, don't take a front room because the street below is really noisy. Rooms are 3500 rp per person.

There are several other hotels on the road running off from the Jalan Sesean and Jalan Pahlawan intersection, like the *Hotel Marlin*. Highly recommended is the *Wisma Rosa* which costs 4000/6000 rp for rooms with mandi. It's next to the paddies, just a 10-minute walk from the town centre, and should be quiet at night.

Other places around Rantepao include the *Hotel Indra* (☎ 97) at Jalan Pasar 63. This rather nice place is done out in a sort of traditional Tanatoraja style and has rooms at 7500/10,000 rp.

The *Hotel Barita* at Jalan Pasar 55 is a bunker-style concrete block but it has good rooms with carpet and bathrooms with real bathtubs! They cost 7500/10,000 rp for singles/doubles. Around the corner, at Jalan Ratulangi, is the Toraja-style *Wisma Maria 1* (☎ 30) with a pleasant garden and a collection of Torajan artefacts in the foyer. Rooms cost from 5000/8000 rp, and it's quite popular.

The similar *Wisma Nanggala* (☎ 91) at Jalan Taman Bahagia 81 has rooms with bath for 5000/8000 rp and is also a good choice. The *Hotel Victoria*, at the corner of Jalan Sesean and Jalan Pahlawan, is good value with rooms with bath at 3500 rp per person.

Places to Eat Check out the market in the middle of Rantepao for local food, including bamboo tubes full of *tuak* (palm wine). At night, try tuak in the warungs beside the market place. Tuak is tapped in the morning, carried into town in long bamboo containers (frothing at the top), left to ferment all day and drunk at night. It comes in a variety of strengths, from the colour of lemonade to the stronger orange or red.

If you tire of the kids asking for candy (kascis gula gula), indulge your own sweet tooth around the Rantepao Market. Try wadi bandung, a sweet rice and grated coconut confection wrapped in paper. Or kajang goreng, an almost oversweet concoction of peanuts and treacle (hard) wrapped in a dry palm leaf. Or try a *baje*, a sticky rice and molasses mixture rolled in a dry palm leaf like a Christmas cracker. Going out to the ceremonies is a good chance to try black rice with pig and buffalo meat roasted in bamboo tubes over an open fire.

There are various restaurants, rumah makan and warungs around Rantepao. The nasi campur at *Kios Gembira*, Jalan Pembangunan 44, is good value. There are a couple of places in Rantepao with the 'Dodeng' title, but the original one is the *Chez Dodeng*, just near the corner of Jalan Sesean and Jalan Pahlawan. It's run by a friendly guy named Bitty who speaks some English. He serves excellent food and drink, including a sort of ginger punch called *sarraba* which has almost the same effect as being hit on the head with a buffalo. Recent letters, however, claim that *Dodeng II* is now the better of the two.

There are some cheap warungs and coffee/tuak places around the back of the market. *Warung Makan Rima* at Jalan Pahlawan 115 has a trendy atmosphere and pseudo-Western food, but it's inexpensive and quite good. The *Rumah Makan Satria Desa* at Jalan Diponegoro 15 is a good, cheap place for simple Indonesian food.

Getting There & Away Transport to/from Rantepao includes:

To/From Ujung Pandang There are various agents whose buses and colts run to Ujung Pandang, via Pare Pare, and to Bone. Liman Express has its main office in the Hotel Marlin and has daily departures to Ujung Pandang for 8000 rp. The trip takes about nine to 10 hours, depending on how long you have to endure the picking-up round. Buses to Pare Pare are 4000 rp. See the Ujung Pandang Getting There & Away section for more details of transport to Rantepao.

To/From Poso & Palu There are buses heading north from Rantepao through central Sulawesi to Poso and Palu. Ticket agents for these buses are at the main intersection of Jalan Pasar and Jalan Taman Bahagia opposite the market. Colts to Poso cost 33,000 rp and to Palu are 45,000 rp. For more information on the trip see the following section on central Sulawesi.

Getting Around Central Rantepao is very small and easy to walk around. A number of becaks congregate around the major intersection, but you probably won't have much use for them. Colts and bemos go to various destinations in the surrounding region. Try to have the correct money since small change is scarce.

Jeep Hire A jeep and driver can be chartered from the touristy Restaurant Rachmat in Rantepao for around 25,000 rp a day. For small groups, this is one of the less expensive ways to get around Tanatoraja, hiking aside.

Motorbike & Bicycle Hire Motorbikes can be hired at Ajui's or Studio Foto Hibar for around 10,000 rp a day (bargaining is necessary to get this rate). You can hire bicycles at Toko Abadi.

Road Conditions The roads to Makale, Palopo and Kete Kesu are alright, but the rest are awful. Some are constructed out of nothing more than compacted boulders – you don't get stuck but your joints are shaken to pieces. Other roads, particularly in the wet, are a real horror! The Rantepao to Sadan road, for example, is only 13 km but takes an hour in the wet and that's if you don't get bogged.

Walking is easily the most comfortable means of travel although somewhat slow. On hired motorbikes, you may have to allow two days' recovery after one day's riding!

Bemos run almost continuously from

Rantepao to Makale. and you can get off at the signs for Londa or Lemo and walk. There are also frequent bemos heading out towards Palopo for the sights in that direction. Bemos on the roads north of Rantepao aren't so frequent except on market days.

Makale

There's really nothing to Makale, though some people stay here just to be away from slightly larger and heavily-touristed Rantepao. On Sunday, the town echoes with the singing from local churches which seem to be on every nearby hilltop.

Places to Stay There are a couple of places to choose from and they're all pretty similar but generally clean and basic. *Penginapan Indra* (☎ 43) at Jalan Merdeka 7 (also known as Jalan Sudirman) has rooms for 5000/7500 rp. *Losmen Merry* on Jalan Pahlawan costs 3500 rp per person.

Losmen Martha on Jalan Pongtiku has friendly people and rooms with mandi for 3500 rp per person. *Losmen Litha* on Jalan Nusantara has paper-thin walls with only a framework partition at the top, and costs the same as the Martha.

Places to Eat There's not much choice in places to eat. Try the *Warung Maspul*, the *Kios Ermita* and the *Kios Asra* – none of them are terribly exciting, but the food is cheap.

Getting There & Away Frequent colts run from Rantepao and the trip takes about 30 to 45 minutes, depending on the number of stops for passengers and the fare is 500 rp. You can catch buses and colts directly from Makale to various destinations in Sulawesi. Ask the agents in the shops around central Makale. Liman Express is at Jalan Ichwan 6.

Around Rantepao

The following places (distance in km from Rantepao) are all within fairly easy reach on day trips. If you want to, you can make longer trips and stay overnight in villages as you go. If you do this, don't exploit the

Torajan hospitality – make sure you pay your share. Guides aren't necessary but if you want one they're easy to find. The going rate seems to be about 5000 rp per day, and more for extended trips (ask around first to get the current price).

Many travellers easily find their way around without a guide – the Torajans are friendly and used to tourists, so they rarely bother you and it's great to escape on your own in the beautiful countryside around Rantepao.

Karasbik (one km) On the outskirts of Rantepao, just off the road leading to Makale, the traditional-style houses here are arranged in a square. Apparently the complex was erected some years ago for a single funeral.

Singki (one km) You can climb this small hill just outside Rantepao for a panoramic view over the surrounding area.

Kete Kesu (six km) Just off the main road, south of Rantepao, this is a traditional village with a reputation for wood carving. On the cliff face behind the village are some cave graves. There are some very old hanging graves here and rotting coffins are suspended from an overhang. The houses at Kete Kesu are decorated with more tourist souvenirs than you've probably ever seen.

Sullukang (seven km) Just past Kete Kesu, and off to the side of the main road in this village, there's a derelict shack on a rocky outcrop which contain several derelict *tau tau* (life-sized carved wooden effigies of the dead) almost buried under the foliage. There's also *rante* here – large stone slabs planted in the ground – one of them about four metres high.

Londa (six km) Two km off the Rantepao to Makale road, this is a very extensive burial cave, with a number of coffins containing bones and skulls. Kids hang around outside renting their oil lamps for 1500 rp (you could try bargaining but they're not very amenable

to it) to guide you around. Unless you've got a strong torch, you really do need a guide with a lamp.

Tilanga (nine km) There are several cold and hot springs in the Toraja area, and this natural cold water pool is very pretty. It's an attractive walk along the muddy trails and through the rice paddies from Lemo to Tilanga – keep asking directions along the way.

Lemo (11 km) This is probably the most interesting burial area in Tanatoraja. The sheer rock face has a whole series of balconies carved out for tau tau. The biggest balcony has a dozen figures – like spectators at a sports event. One tall tau tau stands on a slightly depressed section of floor so he can fit in. There would be even more if they weren't in such demand by unscrupulous antique dealers.

It's a good idea to go early in the morning so you get the sun on the rows of figures – by 9 am their heads are in the shadows. A bemo from Rantepao will drop you off at the road leading up to Lemo, from where it's a 15-minute walk.

Siguntu (seven km) Siguntu, a traditional village situated on a slight rise off to the west of the main road, is a pleasant walk from Rantepao. You get there via Singki to Siguntu and then on to the main road at Alang Alang near the Londa burial site.

Marante (six km) This very fine traditional village is only a few metres off the road to Palopo.

Nanggala (16 km) In the same direction (and rather further off the Palopo road) is this traditional village with a particularly grandiose traditional house with a whole fleet – 14 in all – of rice barns. Bemos from Rantepao take you straight there for 500 rp, or they might just drop you off on the main road, and then it's a 1½ km walk.

Palawa (nine km) A traditional village to the north of Rantepao.

Sadan (13 km) A weaving centre further to the north. Bemos go there from Rantepao along a shocking road. The women here have established a tourist market where they sell their weaving.

Batutumonga (23 km) Batutumonga has a good viewpoint from where you can see a large part of Tanatoraja. Bemos go up here occasionally. *Betania Homestay* is a Torajan house with valley views.

Lokomata (26 km) There are more cave graves and beautiful scenery at Lokomata, just a few km past Batutumonga.

Others Pangli (seven km) – house graves; Bori – funeral ceremony site; Pangala (35 km) – traditional village; and Mt Sesean (25 km) – the highest point in Tanatoraja.

CENTRAL SULAWESI

A road bears eastwards from Rantepao to Soroako on the shores of Lake Matana in central Sulawesi. Midway along this road is the village of Wotu and, just after Wotu, another road cuts its way due north to Pendolo on the southern bank of Lake Poso.

The original track from Wotu was cut during WW II by the Japanese using Indonesian labour – there is a monument to the Indonesians at the top of the mountain pass at Perbatasan. Further roadwork has turned the track into a road of sorts and it is now possible to go all the way from Rantepao to Pendolo by colt.

Most of the road from Wotu to Pendolo is literally cut through thick jungle and it's absolutely impassable two paces off to the side. The road is abominable. It is constructed of rocks, gravel, mud, holes and more mud. Often, colts have to be pushed out of metre-deep trenches. It took my vehicle 27 hours to get from Rantepao as far as Pendolo – bogged five times; three stops for food (two at warungs on the Rantepao to Wotu road and the other on the Wotu to Pendolo road); three stops to register with the police; one stop to sleep; and two stops to repair the colt. Count on about 25,000 rp for a colt from Rantepao to Pendolo.

You cross Lake Poso on outriggers powered by an outboard motor. You can transport motorbikes on the Pendolo to Tentena boats – lashed to the side. As a consolation for the Rantepao to Pendolo trip, the road from Tentena (on the northern side of the lake) to Poso is well surfaced.

Some people actually walk from Wotu to Pendolo. 'Don't let anyone talk you into it,' wrote one traveller, 'unless you're crazy or run up and down a volcano every day before breakfast.' If you do walk it, then get good, solid, high walking boots that give plenty of support to the ankles – running shoes are a mistake. Carry a light pack as the road becomes a river after a shower. There's one warung about midway from Wotu to Pendolo and another about 30 km out of Pendolo. The colts pull into these for rest stops. The sun is blistering hot and the air humid and steamy. When it rains it really rains.

At night, you sleep with 15 cm spiders that run away after you've stood on them and plenty of 10-cm-long cockroaches. The jungle comes alive at night and the noise is indescribable – whatever things are out there are in great numbers! You can try sleeping in-between flicking away the creepy-crawlies.

Two guys I met in Manado tried hitching from Mangkutana (north of Wotu) to Pendolo, unaware of how bad the road was. It took them two days, including a 25-km walking stretch. And it pissed down with rain! One compensation for the hard work are the butterflies in this region. Some are as big as your hand and they'll flutter down and land on your finger.

Pendolo

Pendolo is an overgrown village on the southern shores of Lake Poso. Outriggers will ferry you across the lake to Tentena on the northern side for 2500 rp.

Places to Stay & Eat There are three places to stay in Pendolo, all close to the waterfront on Jalan Pelabuhan. *Penginapan Sederhana* has rooms for 2500 rp per person and is pleasant, clean and friendly. *Penginapan Danau Poso* is diagonally across from the Sederhana and similar in standard and price. The *Rumah Makan Cahaya Bone* has beds to crash on. As for eating, there's that and a few warungs along Jalan Pelabuhan.

Tentena

On the other side of the lake, Tentena is similar to Pendolo. Having crossed the lake there are regular buses between Tentena and Poso.

Places to Stay The *Penginapan Wisata Remaja* and the *Hotel & Restaurant Puse Lemba* are both near the waterfront. Further away is the *Wisma Tiberias*.

Poso

Although it's the main town on the northern coast of central Sulawesi there's not much to be said about this town. It's a fairly dull, but pleasant enough place.

Places to Stay *Hotel Nels* on Jalan Yos Sudarso is a good place with rooms at 4000 rp per person. On Jalan Haji Agus Salim, the *Hotel Kalimantan* is also reasonable and with rooms at 4000/5000 rp, it's cheaper.

A few minutes' walk up the road, at the corner of Jalan Haji Agus Salim and Jalan Imam Bonjol, is the *Penginapan Sulawesi* which has rooms from just 2500 rp. They're very basic little cubicles, but the place is clean and the people friendly.

Other hotels to check out are *Penginapan Delie* and *Penginapan Sederhana*, both on Jalan Haji Agus Salim.

Getting There & Away Merpati fly to Poso and their office (☎ 368) is at Jalan Yos Sudarso 9. If travelling by land, Poso is the northern end of the tough route through central Sulawesi. Continuing towards northern Sulawesi there are road connections west to Palu or passenger boats direct from Poso to northern Sulawesi.

Poso to Palu There are regular colts and minibuses to Palu. Try the Merennu Express office at the Penginapan Sulawesi – it's 10,000 rp to Palu. Other bus companies have their offices at the bus terminal or around the large Pasar Sentral across the river. The road

from Poso to Palu isn't bad but the streams that the bus has to ford are rivers in the wet season. A straight through trip takes about seven to nine hours and you pass by transmigrated Balinese villages complete with gamelan orchestras and stone temples.

Poso to Rantepao There are regular buses from Poso to Tentena for 2500 rp, followed by an outrigger trip across Lake Poso to Pendolo for 2500 rp. The boats depart from Tentena around 9 am. In Pendolo, on the other side of the lake, wait for a colt going through to Rantepao in Tanatoraja – it should cost around 25,000 rp. Alternatively, you can ask around in Poso for bus companies making the trip straight through.

To Northern Sulawesi There are ships departing for Gorontalo from Poso two or three mornings a week – the fare is 30,000 rp in deck class. Buy your ticket from Pos Keamanan Pelabuhan at the port. The ships usually stop off at various ports along the coast. The harbourmaster's office (☎ 444/6) is at Jalan Pattimura 3, by the harbour. Pelni is nearby on the same street.

Palu

On the western seaboard of Sulawesi, this seaport is rather larger but just as dull as Poso.

Places to Stay The *Hotel Pattimura* (☎ 22 2311) on Jalan Pattimura is habitable although the bathrooms could do with a clean and traffic noise from the street below penetrates the front rooms. Rooms with bath cost from around 7500 to 12,000 rp. *Hotel Taurus* (☎ 21567) on Jalan Hasanuddin has small rooms, and the mandis and toilets could do with a clean but otherwise it's good value at 6000/10,000 rp.

The *Hotel Pasifik* at Jalan Gajah Mada 130 has rooms from 4000 rp per person. Despite its rough-looking front, this place is quite good inside. *Penginapan Arafah*, near the Hotel Pasifik, is on a street running off Jalan Gajah Mada near the bridge. The rooms are just thinly partitioned little cells but it's clean and at 3000/6000 rp it's cheap.

Places to Eat Head north along Jalan Wahidin and on the left is a string of rumah makans and warungs. The *Kios Bambuden* at Jalan Wahidin 6 is quite good but on the expensive side. The *Depot Dunia Baru*, a big place on Jalan Danau Linau, has reasonable prices.

There are other little warungs and rumah makans scattered about such as the *Rumah Makan Phoenix* at Jalan S Aljufrie 4. In the early evening, there are martabak trolleys set up on Jalan Hasanuddin near the bridge.

Getting There & Away From Palu (or the nearby ports of Pantoloan or Donggala), you can take a ship across to Kalimantan, to northern Sulawesi, or to Pare Pare in southern Sulawesi. Palu is connected by road to Poso in central Sulawesi and to Gorontalo in northern Sulawesi.

Garuda, Merpati and Bouraq all fly to Palu but it's Bouraq who have the best service with direct connections to Ujung Pandang, Manado and Gorontalo (the latter two in northern Sulawesi) or to Samarinda and Balikpapan in Kalimantan. Merpati (☎ 21295) is at Jalan Hasanuddin 33, while Garuda (☎ 21095) is at Jalan S Aljufrie. Bouraq (☎ 21195, 22995) is at Jalan Mawar 5.

Palu to Gorontalo There is a scungy sort of road all the way from Palu to Gorontalo. Try PO Popula on Jalan Sudirman, near the corner with Jalan Hasanuddin, for buses. Palu to Manado is around 45,000 rp but if the road through central Sulawesi is any indication, then you're probably better off flying with Bouraq – Palu to Gorontalo is 72,000 rp and to Manado 123,000 rp.

Palu to Poso & Tanatoraja For colts to Tanatoraja, try CV Alpit Jaya (☎ 21168) at Jalan Gajah Mada 130. Palu to Rantepao is around 35,000 to 45,000 rp. There are various agents for colts to Poso like PO Saba

Jaya on Jalan Gajah Mada 69 or Marrennu Express (☎ 21868) at Jalan Hasanuddin 46.

Palu to Pare Pare Boats to Pare Pare leave either from Wani, Pantoloan (the port for Palu) or from Donggala. Enquire at the shipping offices down at the waterfront in Wani, and at the harbourmaster's office at Donggala and in Pantoloan.

Getting Around Transport around Palu includes:

To/From the Airport The airport is 10 km out of town and probably the best way to get there is to charter a bemo or bajaj. A bajaj will cost about 2500 rp and taxis from the airport to the centre cost 5000 rp.

Local Transport There are colts to Pantoloan and Wani from the junction of Jalan Imam Bonjol and Jalan Gajah Mada in the centre of town. Colts to Pantoloan cost 1000 rp and take 30 minutes. Wani is 2½ km past Pantoloan and costs about 400 rp.

DONGGALA

Donggala can be an amazingly boring place although it's definitely preferable to Palu. There are some pretty stretches of coastline in the surrounding regions so it's really not a bad town to hang around in. From here you can catch a ship to northern or southern Sulawesi.

Places to Stay & Eat
Run by a Chinese family, *Wisma Bakti* is quite pleasant and has rooms at 6000/8000 rp. *Wisma Makmur* is similar. You can eat at the *Rumah Makan Gembira* or the *Rumah Makan Dinda*.

Getting There & Away
There are taxis (1250 rp per person) and bemos departing frequently for Donggala from the vicinity of the Bioskop Istana at the junction of Jalan Imam Bonjol and Jalan Gajah Mada in Palu. It takes half an hour by taxi to cover the 34 km along a well-surfaced road.

NORTHERN SULAWESI (MINAHASA)

On the northern peninsula of Sulawesi, Minahasa is a strong Christian region and was often referred to as the '12th province of the Netherlands' because of the closeness of its ties to Holland during the colonial days.

Manado

Manado is the capital of the province of northern Sulawesi. Unlike Ujung Pandang, it's a tidy, more prosperous-looking city, even though the canals are clogged and filthy. Yet only a half-hour motorboat ride away is the crystal-clear water off Bunaken Island with its brilliant coral reefs. Manado is an interesting place, although the 'sights' are to be found in the surrounding areas.

Information The tourist office (Dinas Pariwisata Sulawesi Utara), off Jalan Eddy Gogola, is open daily, except Sunday, from about 8 am. Take an 'E Gogola' bemo (150 rp) from Pasar 45, get off at the Kantor Imigrasi (immigration office), walk up the little road diagonally opposite Kantor Imigrasi, and this will take you round (veer right) to the tourist office – a 10-minute walk.

The tourist office has an excellent map of the Minahasa region called the *Handy Tourist Map North Sulawesi Indonesia* and a useful booklet (despite the title) called *Visit Indonesia Guide to North Sulawesi as a New Destination*.

The Bank Ekspor Impor Indonesia, on Jalan Yos Sudarso near the corner with Jalan Sutono, changes foreign cash and travellers cheques.

The post office is on Jalan Ratulangi. International phone calls can be made from the Perumtel office on Jalan Ratulangi (near the Hotel Kawanua). There's an international telephone and telegraph office at Jalan Supratman.

Places to Stay There's not a great deal of accommodation at the lower end of the price range in Manado. At the bottom of the barrel, both in terms of price and standards, is the *Penginapan Keluarga* on Jalan Jembatan

Singkil near the bridge. It is a large shed with a floor of thinly-partitioned little boxes at 3000 rp per person. On the credit side, it's centrally located and the people here are quite friendly.

Losmen Kotamobagu is a door or two down from Penginapan Keluarga and has rooms for 4000 rp per person. It always seems to be 'full' but give it a try as it's much better than the Keluarga.

After that, there are a few places in the 7500 to 20,000 rp bracket and all of them are fairly similar. You could try the *Hotel Kota* on Jalan Yos Sudarso, which is a clean and decent place. The *Wisma Mustika* (**☎** 51801) at Jalan Hasanuddin 107 is another pleasant place with a good location and the rooms have fans.

The *Ahlan City Hotel* on Jalan Yos Sudarso is basic but clean, although it's more expensive with rooms in the 10,000 to 20,000 rp range. *Hotel Minahasa* (**☎** 2059, 2559) on Jalan Ratulangi is probably the best of the upper mid-range hotels with rooms from 15,000 to 30,000 rp.

The *Hotel Mini Cakalele* (**☎** 52942) is on a street running off Jalan Ratulangi, immediately past the post office. The rooms are rather overpriced at 20,000 rp and up but they are clean and have a fan and mandi.

Places to Eat The eating houses all the way along Jalan Ratulangi are good and relatively cheap. Try the *Rumah Makan Surya* at No 16, or for a hamburger try the *Sweetsteak* at No 176. You get all the components of a hamburger laid out on a plate with chips and toast – an excellent cheap meal.

Some of the cheaper eats can be found in the small rumah makan in the laneway alongside the Manado cinema. There are more cheap nasi goreng and nasi campur places around the northern boundary of Pasar 45. A group of somewhat up-market places, all of much the same standard, can be found along Jalan Yos Sudarso.

Getting There & Away Transport to/from Manado includes:

Air Bouraq has flights daily to Gorontalo, Palu, Ujung Pandang, Jakarta, Yogyakarta and to the east coast of Kalimantan. Merpati has flights from Manado to Gorontalo, Ternate and Ambon. Mandala flies three times a week to Jakarta and Surabaya. Garuda has flights to Ujung Pandang (185,000 rp), Denpasar (286,000 rp) and Jakarta (415,000 rp).

Bouraq (☎ 2757, 2675) is at Jalan Sarapung 27B; Garuda (☎ 4535, 2247) is at Jalan Sudirman 2; Merpati (☎ 4027/8) is at Jalan Ratulangi 138; and Mandala (☎ 51324) is at Jalan Sarapung 17.

Bus There's a road between Manado and Gorontalo, the main towns of Minahasa. The trip by colt normally takes about 12 hours and costs 13,000 rp. The vehicles, however, have to ford two rivers, so if they're surging monstrously you'll probably end up being stuck until the water recedes. There are also buses all the way through from Manado and Gorontalo to Palu in central Sulawesi. One company running these buses has an office at the terminal in Manado for Gorontalo buses. Fares from Manado to Palu are around 35,000 rp.

Boat Various ships travel the coastal route between Manado (or its port of Bitung), Toli Toli, Kwandang (the port north of Gorontalo) and Donggala (near Palu). There are regular ships between Poso and Gorontalo, usually two or three per week which cost around 17,500 rp to 25,000 for deck class. There are fairly regular ships between Manado or Bitung and Ternate in Maluku. There are many shipping offices for boat tickets near Manado Harbour.

Pelni's KM *Kambuna* ends its loop down from Medan (Sumatra) at Manado. You can use it to travel around the western side of Sulawesi and across to Balikpapan. The Pelni ship KM *Umsini* comes round the eastern side of Sulawesi from Ujung Pandang and continues on to Maluku and Irian Jaya. Pelni (☎ 2844) is at Jalan Ratulangi 3.

Getting Around Transport around Manado is mainly by Suzuki bemo. Pasar 45 is the central bemo station and fares around Manado are a flat 200 rp. Destinations are shown on a card in the front windscreen and *not* on the side of the van. There are various bus stations around town for destinations outside of Manado. Some important places are:

Calaca Bemo Station – just north of Pasar 45. Take a Lapangan bemo from here to the airport. It costs 250 rp and takes 20 minutes.
Gorontalo Bus Station – for buses to Gorontalo. Take a Sario bemo from Pasar 45 (and tell the driver that you want to go to the bus station because the bemo has to make a detour to do this).
Pasar Paal 2 – for colts to Bitung and Airmadidi. To Pasar Paal 2 take a Paal 2 bemo from Pasar 45. Paal 2 is sometimes written as PAL 2.
Pasar Karombasan – for colts to Tondano and Kawangkoan. To Pasar Karombasan take a Wanea bemo from Pasar 45.

The Wanea and Sario bemos from Pasar 45 will take you straight down Jalan Ratulangi which is useful for Merpati, PT Pola Pelita and the restaurants along this road. There are no becaks in Manado. There are *bendis* but they're not much good as long-distance transport.

Around Manado

Bunaken Island The first and foremost attraction of Manado is the stunning coral reefs off Bunaken Island which lies close to Manado. To get a boat to Bunaken, go to Toko Samudera Jaya in the Kuala Jengki (the large market near the bridge across which Jalan Sisingamangaraja extends). Motorboats depart through the day from the Toko Samudera (the shop backs on the river and there are steps leading down to the water where the boats dock). It's 750 rp to Bunaken and you go over in outrigger longboats powered by an outboard motor.

Once on Bunaken Island, you could ask around for a boat to go to the reefs. Or, walk from the village to the long pier close by and climb down the steps into the water. This lands you right on top of the reef.

To see the reef to best advantage, you really need your own boat. It's probably easiest to charter a boat at Toko Samudera. You'll be looking at about 30,000 rp for them to take you out to the reef in the morning, paddle around for a few hours and take you back to Manado in the afternoon. There is a village but no losmen or penginapan on Bunaken.

Alternatively, the travel agency PT Polita Express (☎ 52231, 52768) at Jalan Ratulangi 74 organises expensive scuba diving and glass-bottom boat tours to Bunaken Island. Snorkels and masks (and perhaps fins) can be bought from Toko Akbar Ali in Pasar 45, and possibly from other shops in Manado.

Airmadidi At Airmadidi, or 'Boiling Water', you'll find the *warugas*, odd little tombs built before the Minahasa region was Christianised. They look like small Chinese temples, and the corpses were buried inside in a squatting position with gold, porcelain and household articles – most have been plundered by now. There's a whole group of these tombs at Airmadidi Bawah, a 15-minute walk from Airmadidi bemo station. Colts to Airmadidi, from Pasar Paal 2 in Manado, cost 400 rp.

Kawangkoan During the Japanese occupation of Indonesia in WW II, caves were cut into the hills surrounding Manado to act as air-raid shelters, quarters and storage space for supplies. One group of caves is three km out of Kawangkoan on the road to Kiawa. There are colts to Kawangkoan from Pasar Karombasan (Wanea terminal) in Manado. A bemo from Kawangkoan to the caves costs 200 rp.

Tondano Some of the more impressive Japanese caves are just outside Tondano on the road to Airmadidi. A bus from Airmadidi to Tondano will get you to the caves in 45 minutes. From the caves, you can hitch or walk (takes about an hour) to Tondano bemo station and get a colt back to Pasar Karombasan in Manado.

Batu Pinabetengan This stone, with the vague outline of human figures scratched

into it, is said to be the place where the chiefs of the Minahasan tribes would hold their meetings. The stone is close to Desa Pinabetengan. Take a bemo to Kawangkoan from Manado's Wanea terminal (1200 rp; about 1¼ hours). Then take a bendi from Kawangkoan to Desa Pinabetengan (300 rp; half an hour). The bendi will take you as far as the turn-off road that leads to Batu Pinabetengan and then you have to walk for the last half-hour.

Bitung

Bitung is the port of Manado and you may have to come here to catch a ship. There are many bemos to Bitung from Pasar Paal 2; the trip is 1200 rp and takes an hour along a very good road. Pelni (☎ 152, 226) is on Jalan Jakarta, inside Bitung Harbour compound.

Places to Stay & Eat *Penginapan Beringin* (☎ 240) at Jalan Yos Sudarso 19 has rooms for 7500 rp. The *Penginapan Samudra Jaya* (☎ 114) is OK, basic and clean – rooms with fan, mandi and toilet are 12,500 rp. Least expensive is the *Penginapan Minang* around the corner where rooms are 7000 rp.

There are cheap places to eat in the market area near the Penginapan Beringin.

Gorontalo

This quiet town has streets full of Dutch-built villas; fine examples are the **Rumah Sakit Umum** (Public Hospital) and the **Saronde Hotel**. Near Gorontalo is the port of **Kwandang**, two hours away to the north by bus, where there are the ruins of some interesting European-built fortresses (in Bahasa Indonesia, 'benteng' means fort).

Things to See Places of interest around Gorontalo include:

Benteng Otanaha On a hill at Dembe, overlooking Lake Limbot, are the three towers of this probably Portuguese-built fortress. Take a bendi (600 rp) to the pathway that leads up the hill from Jalan Belibis. Or take a bemo (300 rp), though these are infrequent on this road. There's a sign at the foot of the pathway pointing the way to the fort.

Fortresses at Kwandang On the outskirts of Kwandang are the remains of two interesting fortresses, possibly Portuguese built. Whilst the town itself is nothing (just a Pelni office and a few warungs), the fortresses are well worth visiting. The two fortresses are a short walk off the road leading into Kwandang from Gorontalo.

Places to Stay The *Penginapan Teluk Kau* (☎ 21785) at Jalan S Parman 42 used to be one of the most pleasant places to stay in Indonesia but is now rather run-down. Rooms are 5000 to 8000 rp per person. Just down the road, at No 35, is the *Penginapan Shinta* (☎ 20461), which is OK and similarly priced.

More expensive, but comfortable rooms are available for 10,000/14,000 rp (more with air-con) in the *Hotel Wisata* at Jalan 23 Januari 19. The *Wisma Kartini* on Jalan Kartini is value with rooms for 15,000 rp.

The *Hotel Saronde* (☎ 21735) at Jalan Walanda Maramis 17 is comfortable though not luxurious. It's a Dutch-built villa converted into a hotel and has fan-cooled rooms from 10,000 rp. Slightly cheaper, better doubles are available at the *Hotel Indah Ria* (☎ 20435) on Jalan Achmad Yani from 15,000 rp.

Places to Eat The *Rumah Makan Padang* is a good place with a friendly owner. The *Rumah Makan Dirgahayu* serves goat satay dipped in peanut sauce (tersida sate kambing spesial). There's a string of cheap places serving nasi campur and several quite good nasi padang places up the road which leads

to the cinema in the middle of town. There are also some very cheap warungs in the large Pasar Sentral at the north end of town.

Getting There & Away Transport to/from Gorontalo includes:

Air Bouraq (☎ 21070/870) at Jalan Achmad Yani 34 and Merpati (☎ 21736/7) in the Hotel Wisata at Jalan 23 Januari 19 both fly from Gorontalo to Manado, Ujung Pandang and Palu.

Bus It's a 12-hour, 15,000 rp trip to Manado, the other main town of Minahasa. You can also travel by bus all the way around to Palu but it's a tough trip.

Boat There are a couple of places to try for ships out of Gorontalo and Kwandang. Pelni (☎ 20419) is at Jalan 23 Januari 31 and has another office at the port in Kwandang. Gapsu (☎ 88173) has an office at Jalan Pertiwi 55 in central Gorontalo, and also at Gorontalo Harbour on Jalan Mayor Dullah. Other agents to try include Toko Ujung Pandang on Jalan Suprapto and Toko Sumber Tahnik at Jalan S Parman 94.

Getting Around Transport around Gorontalo includes:

To/From the Airport A Merpati-Bouraq bus shuttles between the town and airport (32 km away) for 3500 rp per person.

Local Transport Bendis or pony carts cost around 400 rp a trip to anywhere in town. Bemos to Gorontalo Harbour are 200 rp.

Maluku (Moluccas)

The islands of Maluku are the fabled spice islands of Indonesia and it was mainly for the spices that grew here and nowhere else that foreign traders, including Europeans, came to Indonesia. Maluku Province consists of a scattered series of islands which lie between Sulawesi and Irian Jaya. The largest islands are Halmahera in the north, looking a little like a small scale version of Sulawesi, and Seram in the south.

Visitors to Maluku usually go to Ambon (a small island near Seram), the Banda Islands to the south-east of Ambon, or

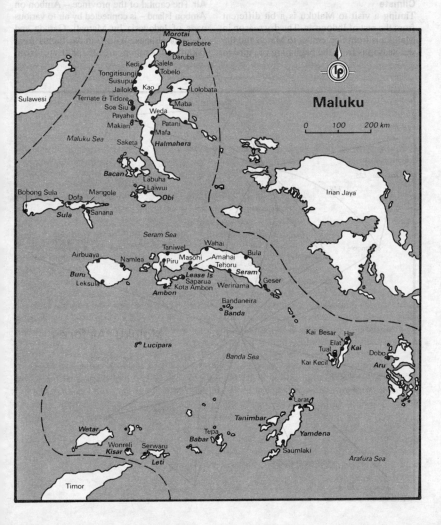

Ternate and Tidore (two adjacent small islands just off Halmahera). These days Maluku is noted for fine tropical scenery and for some interesting relics of early-European contact. Increasing numbers of foreign visitors are making their way to these interesting islands.

Climate

Timing a visit to Maluku is a bit different from the rest of Indonesia. The dry season in Maluku is from September to March and the wet season is from the beginning of April to the end of August. There's not much point in visiting the region in the wet season as the rain pounds down endlessly. This means the islands are nowhere near their best, and since the seas are rough there's less inter-island sea transport.

Getting There & Away

Air The capital of the province – Ambon on Ambon Island – is connected by air to various parts of Indonesia by Merpati, Garuda and Mandala airlines. With Garuda, flights from Jakarta to Ambon are 357,000 rp, from

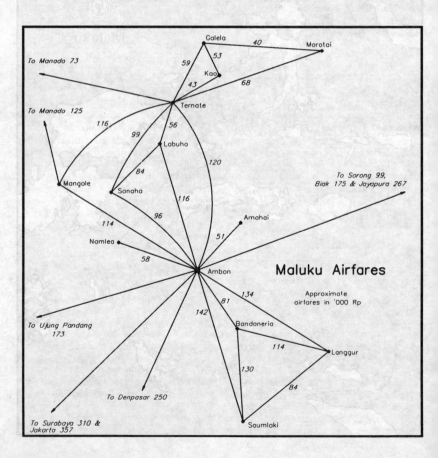

Maluku Airfares

Approximate airfares in '000 Rp

Denpasar 250,000 rp or from Ujung Pandang 173,000 rp.

There are flights to Ternate, the second main town, from other parts of Indonesia – often with Garuda flying you one leg and Merpati flying the last leg.

Bouraq connects Ternate to Kalimantan via Manado in Sulawesi.

Boat Occasionally, there are ships between Ternate and Manado (or its port of Bitung), and Ternate and Sorong. Pelni's KM *Rinjani* connects Java and Sulawesi with Ambon in Maluku while the KM *Umsini* goes to Ternate. The KM *Tidar* sails from Ternate to Ambon and then onto Sulawesi and Kalimantan.

Getting Around
Air If you're planning to do a lot of travel in Maluku, then you need either time or money – preferably both! Money will pay for air tickets if you haven't got time and patience.

Merpati has a number of flights out of Ambon and Ternate to destinations around Maluku. Included are Ambon to Ternate and Ambon to the islands of southern Maluku such as Langgur and Saumlaki. Flights from Ambon to central Maluku include those to Amahai on Seram Island and to Namlea on Buru. There are flights from Ternate to the islands of central and northern Maluku, including Morotai, Galela and Kao.

Boat Transport by sea between adjacent islands is fairly easy. There are regular passenger ferries between Ambon, Saparua and Seram, and frequent motorboats every day make the short hop between Ternate and Tidore. Additionally, there are regular passenger ships from Ternate to various destinations on Halmahera.

Long-distance sea transport around the islands becomes more of a problem. Pelni's KM *Niaga X* makes a regular loop out of Ambon around the southern Maluku islands, including Banda, Tual, Saumlaki and various other ports – the whole loop from Ambon and back takes three weeks. It gives you some chance to hop out and look around

the ports. Another Pelni ship, the KM *Baruna Bhakti*, does a three-week trip to Ambon and back, stopping off at various ports in northern and central Maluku. The fare from Ternate to Ambon is about 15,000 rp in deck class.

AMBON
Ambon, the main town on the island of Ambon and the capital of Maluku province, is a big, dirty, noisy city and expensive when compared to Bali or Java. The island is pretty and has some interesting attractions, which include ruins of European fortifications.

Information
The friendly and helpful tourist office is on the ground floor of Kantor Gubernor, the governor's office . The post office is on Jalan Pattimura. On the same street is the Bank Ekspor Impor which will change major brands of travellers' cheques.

The Kantor Imigrasi (immigration office) (☎ 42128) is at Jalan Batu Capeo 57/5. It's way out in the south-east end of Ambon. There's also an immigration office at the airport where your arrival will probably be registered. You're supposed to register at the immigration office in the city also, though your losmen will probably do this for you. You're also supposed to register once again at the city office before you leave but it doesn't matter if you don't. Bemos from the city centre will take you straight to the office.

Things to See
War Cemetery This WW II cemetery is in the suburb of Tantui, about two km from the centre of Ambon. The cemetery, with its row upon row of marker stones and plaques, is for Australian, Dutch and British servicemen killed in Sulawesi and Maluku. A bemo from the terminal on Jalan Pattimura takes you straight to the cemetery.

Victoria Fortress This old Portuguese fortress on Jalan Slamet Riyadi dates back to 1575. The sea walls are still standing but other parts have decayed and have been replaced by new military buildings.

Siwalima Museum This interesting museum is definitely worth a visit. The fine collection includes 'magic' skulls from a cave in northern Buru which were once worshipped by the local people. There are also model boats made of tortoise shell, sago palm and cloves, and ancestor statues of south-east Maluku. The museum is in the Taman Makmur Hills, just off the road from Ambon to the the village of Amahusu.

To get to the museum, take a bemo from the terminal and get off at the Transmigrasi office – the road leading up to the museum is immediately after the office, and it's a 10-minute walk up to the museum. The museum is open from Tuesday to Sunday.

Places to Stay
Accommodation in Ambon city is really expensive, with nothing at the bottom end of the scale and little of even moderate price. *Penginapan Beta* (☎ 3463) at Jalan Wem Reawaru 114 is a reasonable place in the quieter part of town. It has rooms from around 10,000 rp. Next door at No 115 the *Hotel Transit/Rezfanny* (☎ 41692) is similarly priced and is clean but nothing special.

Nearby, the *Hotel Silalou* (☎ 3197) at Jalan Sedap Malam 41 is good value with rooms from 9000/18,000 rp and is in a convenient central location. Not far around the corner, on Jalan Anthoni Rhebok, *Hotel Sela* (☎ 2422) is a little more expensive.

More expensive places include the *Hotel Amboina* (☎ 41725) at Jalan Kapitan Ulu Paha 5A. It offers several storeys of comfortable air-con rooms costing from around 25,000 rp. The *Hotel Elenoor* (☎ 2834) at Jalan Anthoni Rhebok 30 has rooms for 15,000 rp and is a pleasant enough place but really quite basic for what you're paying.

Places to Eat
Restaurants tend to be expensive and serve Indonesian and Chinese food. *Halim's* on Jalan Sultan Hairun is a Chinese place with good food. Next door, the *Tip Top Restaurant* is cheaper. Try the restaurant in the *Hotel Mutiara* at Jalan Pattimura 90 for a good continental breakfast. Less tourist-oriented

places include the *Pondok Asri* on Jalan Achmad Yani and the *Ice Creamery* on Jalan Sultan Hairun.

Things to Buy
Look for the model boats made entirely of cloves – several shops in the city stock them, try along Jalan Patty and Jalan Pattimura. They also sell flower arrangements made out of mother of pearl.

Getting There & Away
See the Maluku Getting There & Away section for details on flights to Ambon. Garuda (☎ 2481) is on Jalan Achmad Yani. Merpati (☎ 3480), who have the best network of flights in the region, is at Jalan Anthoni Rhebok 28. Mandala (☎ 2444) is at Jalan Patty.

The Maluku Getting There & Away section also covers sea transport, and the Pelni office is at the harbour.

For road transport around the island, colts depart from along Jalan Yos Sudarso or you can charter a taxi from the stand at the corner of Jalan Pala and Jalan Slamet Riyadi.

Getting Around
To/From the Airport Ambon Airport is 48 km out of the city. There is a taxi counter at the airport which changes 15,000 rp, or public bemos cost 1000 rp. Beware of rip-offs at the airport – taxi and bemo drivers will ask the earth. As for getting out to the airport, if you take a public colt from Jalan Yos Sudarso allow lots of time. It's about an hour's drive from Ambon to the airport but take into account the usual Indonesian procrastinations. Alternatively, take a taxi or even charter a bemo.

Local Transport There are becaks around town or you can catch local bemos from the station on Jalan Pattimura – after you've argued your way out of chartering one!

There is a vehicle and passenger ferry from just past Galala village (north of Kota Ambon) to the other side of the harbour – thus cutting short the circuitous road route. Bemos and taxis sometimes use it as a short cut to the airport. The cost is 150 rp per person, 1000 rp for a bemo and the ferry operates every day.

AROUND AMBON
Hila

Hila, a village 42 km from Ambon, is noted for its ruined Portuguese-built fortress and an old Christian church. The fortress was originally built of wooden palisades by the Portuguese at the end of the 16th century and was later rebuilt by the Dutch and renamed **Fort Amsterdam**. The main tower and fragments of the wall remain (the cannons have gone) and the interior of the tower has been taken over by enormous tree roots which, like something out of Tolkien, have wrapped themselves all over the walls from top to bottom.

The **church** is just a few minutes' walk from the fort. Dating from 1780, it is the oldest building in Ambon – it has, however, virtually been rebuilt from the stumps up over the years. There's a Dutch-inscribed plaque on the outside wall. **Wapauwe** is an old mosque near Hila – the original mosque dated back to the early 15th century.

To get to Hila, take a colt from Jalan Yos Sudarso in Ambon (1250 rp) and allow 1½ to two hours for the ride.

Pulau Pombo

Pombo is a tiny, attractive island off the north-east coast of Ambon which has a coral garden where you can go snorkelling. To get there, take a colt from the stand on Jalan Yos Sudarso to the village of Tulehu (one hour, 750 rp). The colt will drop you off at the wharf and from there you can hire a speedboat to go out to Pulau Pombo, a 20-minute ride.

There's a good little beach on Pulau Pombo which is sheltered by the reef. You could get the boat to drop you off in the morning and pick you up in the afternoon and it makes a nice escape. Bring your own food and water – there's a small derelict shelter on the island.

Other Attractions

At **Waai**, 31 km north of Ambon, is a pool which contains a very large 'holy eel'.

Natsepa, 14 km from Ambon, is a reasonable beach but avoid Sunday when the place gets really crowded. Colts go there from Jalan Yos Sudarso (45 minutes, 500 rp).

Leitimor is the southern peninsula of the island and **Ema** and **Naku** are interesting villages to walk to along the south coast.

The coastline at **Latuhalat** and **Namalatu** is supposed to have good scuba diving and snorkelling on the offshore coral reefs. To get there take a colt from Jalan Yos Sudarso, it takes about 45 minutes – Latuhalat is not far past Namalatu. Namalatu is a sort of beach littered with concrete tables and chairs, but if you're going there just for the beach don't bother. On your way down to these places, note the old **Japanese blockhouses** dotted along the coast, particularly between Amahusu and Eri. There's supposed to be another good coral reef off **Amahusu**, which overlooks Ambon Bay.

BANDA ISLANDS

The Bandas consist of a group of seven islands to the south-east of Ambon. If you're looking for somewhere quiet then this is it – there's just a handful of motor vehicles, a fistful of motorbikes and zero televisions. The residents are friendly, the scenery is beautiful and the place is unspoilt by tourism. Apart from the scenery, there are several old forts here to scramble around and some coral gardens where you can go snorkelling and diving.

Information

Buy a copy of Willard Hamilton's *Indonesia Banda* from the museum or the Hotel Raguna in Bandaneira. It gives you a blow-by-blow description of the history of the Banda Islands over the last several hundred years.

BANDANEIRA

Bandaneira, the chief centre of the islands, was a former Dutch settlement. Today it is a rambling collection of interesting but deteriorating Dutch mansions. Notable buildings include the Dutch church on Jalan Greja. Buried beneath the floor of the church is a procession of people. Nutmeg is processed at the government factory and shipped off to Ambon and then exported to other parts of Indonesia as well as overseas.

Things to See
Museum – Rumah Badya The museum is housed in an old Dutch villa which also doubles as a hotel. It includes a small collection of cannon, old coins and modern paintings. One painting depicts the massacre of Bandanese by the Dutch in 1621. It also contains some traditional feathered headdresses and Portuguese helmets.

Fort Belgica Built by the Dutch East Indies Company in 1611, this fort stands above Bandaneira. The towers of the fort seem to be held together by a copious quantity of graffiti.

Fort Nassau Built by the Dutch in 1609 (on the stone foundations laid by but eventually abandoned by the Portuguese), Fort Nassau is below Fort Belgica. It's very overgrown – only three walls and a gateway remain and an old cannon lies rusting on the ground.

Fort Hollandia This fort on Lontar Island was enormous when it was originally constructed by the Dutch in 1621. It was wrecked by an an earthquake in 1743 and there's not much left and what's there is derelict and overgrown. A long flight of steps leads up to it. Get to Lontar Island by motorboat from Bandaneira Pasar.

Gunung Api This volcano juts out of the sea, directly in front of Bandaneira. The island has some good coral in the shallows approximately opposite Taman Laut and diagonally opposite Bandaneira. It's only a short paddle across to Gunung Api from 'Neira in a canoe.

Pulau Karaka (Pulau Sareer) This island lies off Gunung Api and has some fine coral reefs. Karaka is close enough to paddle

across from Bandaneira in a dugout canoe in about an hour. There is also a sea garden between 'Neira and Lontar Island – you can take a canoe out there and snorkel around but the coral is nowhere near as attractive as Pulau Karaka. The hotel complex rents out snorkelling and scuba equipment.

Places to Stay
Bandaneira has several horrendously expensive hotels specifically intended for tourists. The cheaper places may not take foreigners.

The *Penginapan Selecta, Penginapan Delfika* and *Museum Hotel* all cost from around 18,000 rp with meals. The Selecta serves good food although the accommodation is a bit dingy. The Delfika is an old Dutch mansion painted green, white and purple and has big, basic but clean rooms.

More expensive places include the *Laguna Inn* on the waterfront with rooms from 35,000 rp, and the pricey *Maulana Inn*.

Places to Eat
There are a couple of little rumah makans around, like the very cheap *Rumah Makan Nusantara*. You can improve your diet with fried skewered fish or fruit from the market but you'll generally get a wider variety of food in port.

Getting There & Away
Air Merpati flies between Ambon and Bandaneira and their office is on Jalan Kampung Cina.

Boat Various semi-regular boats, about every five days, make the overnight trip from Ambon to Banda. Deck class is 6000 rp.

Getting Around
The town of Bandaneira is very small and easy to walk around. There are few roads and only one on 'Neira leads to the airport. Trails connect to other places on the island and there are some nice walks.

Take motorboats from the pasar to Lontar Island. There are lots of dugout canoes for rent. If you hire one to go out and snorkel, it's easy enough to get out of the canoe and into the water, but virtually impossible to get back in without capsizing it! Locals insist that there are no sharks around.

TERNATE
This island was one of the first places the Portuguese and Dutch established in Maluku and the island is littered with the ruins of old European fortifications. It's a rather slow and placid town, quite a contrast to Ambon. The peace is occasionally broken by intermittent rumblings of the huge volcano to which the town clings.

Information
The Bank Ekspor Impor, on the waterfront on Jalan Pahlawan Revolusi, and the Bank Negara Indonesia, on the same street, will both change US$ travellers' cheques. The post office is also on Jalan Pahlawan Revolusi, near the Bank Negara Indonesia.

Things to See
Kedaton (Palace) of the Sultan of Ternate
This interesting piece of architecture looks more like a European country mansion than a palace and lies just back from Jalan Baballuh, the road leading to the airport. It's now a museum containing a few Portuguese cannon, Dutch helmets and armour. There's not much to see, though the ill-kept building is worth having a look at. To get to the museum, take a bemo from the bemo station on Jalan Pahlawan Revolusi.

Benteng Toloko This small fort is in better condition than others. To get there, take the road from Ternate out towards the airport. Beyond the Sultan's palace but before the airport, a path leads off this road to Dufa Dufa and the Benteng Toloko, which is on a rocky hill above the beach.

Fort Orange (Benteng Oranye) This fort dates from 1637 and is a Dutch construction. It's right in the middle of Ternate, opposite the bemo station. There are forlorn looking cannons, overgrown and sadly crumbling walls and buildings. You can get an idea of its importance, however, from its great size. It's an interesting building to walk around.

Benteng Kayuh Merah At the southern end of Ternate is Pelabuhan Bastion from where you can catch motorboats to Tidore. A km down the road past Pelabuhan Bastion, and just before you get to Desa Kayuh Merah, is Benteng Kayuh Merah. It's a small fort located right on the beach and the waves splash on its walls.

Benteng Kastella Continuing around the island in a clockwise direction from Benteng Kayuh Merah you come to Benteng Kastella – you'd hardly know it was there. The ring road around Ternate cuts straight through what's left of the fort and it's covered in moss and undergrowth, and grazed by goats. The roots of trees have wrapped themselves around the ruins of the main tower

Batu Angus – the Burnt Corner North of Ternate, the 'Burnt Corner' is a volcanic lava flow from the 1737 eruption of Gunung Api Gamalama. What is left today is a massive river of jagged volcanic rocks looking like a landscape from another planet. Take a bemo just past Tarau village to see this. On the subject of volcanic eruptions, there's a display of photos in the airport restaurant of the eruption of the 1721-metre Gunung Api Gamalama in September 1980.

Danau Tolire This large volcanic crater, on the northern side of the island, is now filled with deep green water. The lake is just off the road in the vicinity of Takome but bemos don't seem to go up there very often.

Places to Stay
One of the best places to stay in is the *Wisma Alhilal* (**☎** 21404) at Jalan Monunutu 2/32. It's quite plain but run by a friendly family and is in a good location. Rooms cost from 6000 rp per person and have a fan, mandi and a toilet. Meals here are excellent – mainly barbecued fish or fried chicken with noodles and rice and a liberal dose of chilli.

The *Wisma Sejahtera* on Jalan Lawa Mena

is a very pleasant place with rooms at 7000 rp per person – more with meals. On Jalan Pahlawan Revolusi, opposite the harbour entrance, the basic *Penginapan Yamin* has rooms from 5000 rp per person. Further up the same road, the *Penginapan Sentosa* and *Penginapan Rachmat* are also cheap.

Pricier places include the *Wisma Chrysant* (☎ 21580) at Jalan Achmad Yani 131 and the *Hotel Indah* (☎ 21334) at Jalan Bosoiri 3. The *Hotel Nirwana* (☎ 21787), at Jalan Pahlawan Revolusi 58 near the harbour, is a decent place with rooms from 6000 rp per person without meals. Almost next door is the *Hotel El Shinta* which is much more expensive at 25,000/35,000 rp, meals included.

The *Hotel Merdeka* on Jalan Monunutu costs from 15,000 rp per person and includes meals. It looks like it must have been built by the Dutch.

Places to Eat

Restaurant Siola is a 10-minute walk west of the town centre and probably has the best food (certainly the best surroundings) in town. In the town centre, the best place is the *Restoran Garuda* on Jalan Pahlawan Revolusi. Across the road, the *Kafetaria Garuda* is not so good but the *Gamalama Restaurant* on Jalan Pahlawan Revolusi is a good cheap place.

Further down Jalan Pahlawan Revolusi, the *Rumah Makan Roda Baru* is fairly cheap as Padang food places go. There are more cheap eats at the *Rumah Makan Anugerah* on Jalan Bosoiri, across from the bemo station.

Getting There & Away

Merpati have a wide variety of connections to Ternate from elsewhere in Maluku and further afield. Their office (☎ 314, 648/9) is at PT Eterna Raya, Jalan Bosoiri 81. Bouraq connect Ternate with northern Sulawesi. Bouraq (☎ 21487) is at Jalan Pahlawan Revolusi 58. The harbourmaster's office (☎ 21129/206/214) is at Jalan Achmad Yani 1. Pelni is on Jalan Achmad Yani, by the harbour.

Getting Around

To/From the Airport The airport is at Tarau, close to Ternate township, and you can get there by chartering a bemo from 3000 rp. Or, walk down to the main road from the airport terminal and pick up a bemo for 200 rp.

Local Transport Transport around town and around the island is by Suzuki bemo – there are no becaks here. Bemos cost 150 rp rate to anywhere around town. One way of seeing all the sights quickly in one go would be to charter a bemo – a surfaced road runs in a ring around the island linking Ternate township with Batu Angus, Lake Tolire (less than a 10-minute walk off the main road), Benteng Kastella, Benteng Kayuh Merah and back to Ternate township. It takes a bit less than two hours to circle the island in a bemo, short breaks included.

TIDORE

This is the island adjacent to Ternate. There's a fort above the road as you enter Soa Siu but you need a local to show you the ill-defined track up to it and there's not much to see. The jungle has just about taken over from the fort and you'd really have to be an enthusiast to get worked up about this place. Apparently, there is another fort near Rum.

Getting There & Away

To get to Tidore, take a bemo from Ternate township to Pelabuhan Bastion. Boats powered by outboard motors depart frequently from the Pasar Impris at Pelabuhan Bastion for Rum on Tidore. It takes about half an hour and costs 600 rp. From Rum, take a bemo to the main town of Soa Siu (a 45-minute ride).

Irian Jaya

Irian Jaya is the Indonesian side of the island of New Guinea, and it was only acquired from the Dutch in 1963. Since it had no racial or historical connection with the other Indonesian islands, some interesting arm bending had to be conducted to get the Dutch to hand it over. It was agreed that an 'act of free choice' would later determine if the inhabitants wished to join Indonesia permanently and by choosing a 'representative' selection of voters, a unanimous decision to remain was arrived at! The Indonesians have since moved lots of settlers in from Java or Sulawesi.

The Indonesian occupation has not gone unopposed by the Papuans and since 1963 the Indonesians have had to put down with military force several uprisings of rebellious tribes. Meanwhile, the independence movement known as the Free Papua Organisation (the OPM) continues a guerrilla war against the Indonesians.

The Indonesian settlements are still largely a fringe thing but this could change dramatically in the next decade or so. West Irian has a total population of some 800,000 Papuans and 250,000 Indonesians – 114,000 of the latter having come to the province under the Indonesian government's transmigration schemes. The government has plans to move in many more settlers.

At present, the interior of the province is still inhabited by tribes who, until a few decades ago, had little or no contact with the outside world. They are the only reason to visit Irian Jaya unless you're simply using the island as a transit point to somewhere else.

Irian Jaya also has the highest mountain east of the Himalaya and west of the Andes. Gunung Jayakusema, or Carstenz Pyramid, is a glaciated peak of 5030 metres.

Permits

At present, you are required to have a transit permit to visit Irian Jaya. This requirement seems to come and go every year. Furthermore, if you are going inland – to the Balim Valley for example – you must have another permit, a *surat jalan*, from the police. This is easily obtained at the head police station in Jayapura (on Jalan Achmad Yani). Four photographs is all it takes, and the permit is issued on the spot. There appears to be no limit as to how long you can stay in the interior, so long as you don't exceed the expiry date of your visa or tourist pass.

Certain parts of the interior are off limits to foreign tourists and you won't get a permit for them. However, the situation is changeable so you should check out what's open and what's closed to foreigners when you get to Jayapura. The main police station will tell you where you can and can't go. It may also be possible to get permits for the interior in Biak, but don't count on it.

Visas

Check the Indonesia Facts for the Visitor section about Indonesian visas – Biak is one of the 'no visa required' entry or exit points to Indonesia but Jayapura isn't. If you are arriving from PNG, you must have a visa for entry to Indonesia. If you are exiting from Jayapura to PNG, you must also have a visa for PNG. There is no PNG diplomatic office in Irian Jaya, as the only PNG representation in Indonesia is in Jakarta.

The Indonesian authorities are very touchy about Irian Jaya and its sensitive border with PNG. With these regulations, it's fairly easy to exclude foreigners, or make it so difficult for them they decide not to visit. Australians are the most likely people to find the Indonesians touchy about issuing visas to enter or exit Indonesia through Irian Jaya.

Money

You can change travellers' cheques or foreign currency at the Bank Ekspor Impor in Jayapura or Biak but there are few other places to change money in Irian Jaya. Make sure you change plenty of money before heading into the interior and stock up on small notes and change.

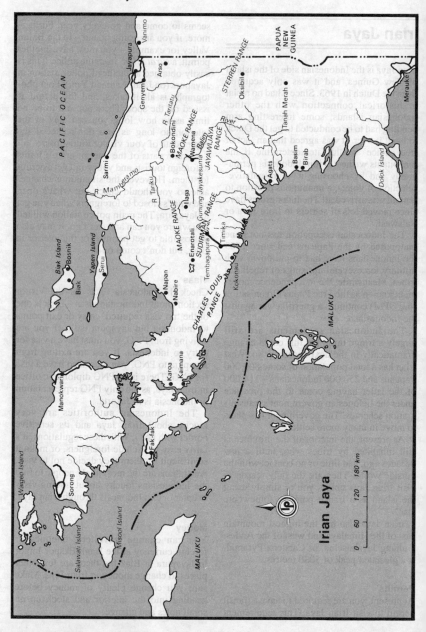

Getting There & Away

Air From PNG, the only way of getting to Irian Jaya is the once-weekly flight on Wednesday between Vanimo and Jayapura with Douglas Airways. This connects with an Air Niugini flight between Vanimo and Wewak. Fares are Wewak to Vanimo US$108 and Vanimo to Jayapura US$51. They're worried about guerrilla activity in the border area, so strolling across the border is definitely not on.

From other Indonesian islands, you can get to Irian Jaya by air with Merpati or Garuda or by sea with Pelni. Garuda is generally more expensive and many flights operate via Biak, the island off the north coast of Irian Jaya. Approximate fares are: 127,000 rp from Jayapura to Biak, 265,000 rp from Jayapura to Sorong, 328,000 rp from Jayapura to Ambon, 418,000 rp from Jayapura to Ujung Pandang and 562,000 rp from Jayapura to Jakarta.

For most travellers, the usual route by air out of Irian Jaya is Jayapura-Biak-Ujung Pandang. Then, after some time in Sulawesi, either across to Kalimantan, Java or (cheapest of all) Denpasar. If you've got no yen to see Jayapura, you can fly in from Wewak in the morning and probably be able to fly out the same day. Increasingly, visitors are also slotting the Maluku Islands between Irian Jaya and Sulawesi.

Irian Jaya can also make a very interesting stepping stone between the rest of Indonesia or PNG and the US. Garuda have a Biak-Honolulu-Los Angeles flight which costs around US$900 return.

Boat Pelni's KM *Umsini* arrives at Jayapura every two weeks at the end of its long voyage from Jakarta via Sulawesi and Maluku. From Jakarta, fares vary from 178,000 rp Ekonomi class to 509,000 rp in 1st class. The KM *Rinjani* plies a fortnightly route between Belawan (in north Sumatra) and Sorong, stopping in Jakarta, Surabaya, Ujung Pandang, Baubau and Ambon.

There are also the odd freighters which ply the Irian Jaya coast and call in at the main ports. Occasionally, there are ships between Sorong and Ternate in Maluku but, as usual, it's just a case of hanging around and seeing what comes by.

Getting Around

Unless you're into mounting big expeditions and are adept at hacking your way through tropical jungle with a machete, then flying is really the only way to get around Irian Jaya. There are roads in the immediate vicinity of the urban areas, and a good paved one extending westwards along the coast from Jayapura. Apart from these, there's nothing. If you want to go inland, you have to fly. Garuda operates some routes, but Merpati carries the bulk of the traffic with many connections from the major centres to other parts of the coast and the interior.

Merpati have flights from Jayapura to Batom, Biak, Karubaga, Lereh, Manokwari, Merauke, Nabire, Oksibil, Sarmi, Senggeh, Serui, Sorong, Tanah Merah and as many as half a dozen flights a day to Wamena. There are also numerous flights fanning out from Merauke on the south coast and Nabire on the north coast. Flights from Biak operate to places in the western sector of the province and the 'bird's head'.

Various mission groups are strongly represented in Irian Jaya, and maintain a communication network of airstrips, light aircraft and, occasionally, helicopters. They *will* accept passengers and charters, subject always to their own immediate needs. The air transport organisations of the missions are known by their initials – the MAF (Mission Aviation Fellowship) and the AMA (Associated Missions Aviation). They have set rates for carrying passengers, and both have their offices at Sentani Airport, Jayapura.

It's your own responsibility to get permits for the places you're visiting in the interior, otherwise you'll be flown straight back to Jayapura at your own expense. Try and book flights on mission planes as far ahead as possible – in fact, you'll probably find the missions very booked up, so be prepared to go back to Jayapura or Biak and then fly out to another inland destination with Merpati.

There are also aircraft operated by various mining companies. Both mission and mining company planes occasionally fly down to Australia – you never know, you may be able to get a ride.

JAYAPURA

Since the end of its Dutch days as Hollandia, Jayapura, or 'Victorious City', has really gone through the name changes. First it was Kota Bahru then Sukarnapura (there's one of his Jakarta-style statues in the town square) before its current name was adopted. The hills of Jayapura slope right down to the sea and the town is squeezed onto all available bits of semilevel land. It's a pretty sight from the air at night with the lights of fishing boats twinkling out on the bay.

This is the usual entry point for Irian Jaya from PNG, and it is the capital of the province but of no particular interest other than that. It's quite a dull place, and apart from the

hills and the Irianese, it looks like any other sizeable Indonesian town. So, there's no real reason to come here unless you're heading inland.

Orientation & Information

Though Jayapura spreads itself up onto the hills and out around the bay, just about everything you'll want – most of the hotels, the shops, police headquarters, airline offices, the large IMBI cinema – are all confined to a very small area in the centre of town down near the waterfront. The two main streets are Jalan Achmad Yani and, running parallel to it, Jalan Percetakan.

Money The Bank Ekspor Impor on Jalan Achmad Yani will change travellers' cheques and cash. Hotel Dafonsoro will also exchange but only for their guests.

Immigration & Permits Kantor Imigrasi

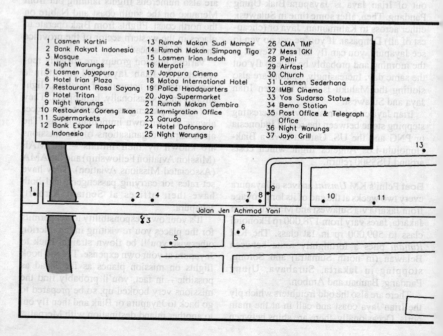

1 Losmen Kartini	13 Rumah Makan Sudi Mampir
2 Bank Rakyat Indonesia	14 Rumah Makan Simpang Tiga
3 Mosque	15 Losmen Irian Indah
4 Night Warungs	16 Merpati
5 Losmen Jayapura	17 Jayapura Cinema
6 Hotel Irian Plaza	18 Matoa International Hotel
7 Restaurant Rosa Sayang	19 Police Headquarters
8 Hotel Triton	20 Jaya Supermarket
9 Night Warungs	21 Rumah Makan Gembira
10 Restaurant Goreng Ikan	22 Immigration Office
11 Supermarkets	23 Garuda
12 Bank Expor Impor Indonesia	24 Hotel Dafonsoro
	25 Night Warungs
26 CMA TMF	
27 Mess GKI	
28 Pelni	
29 Airfast	
30 Church	
31 Losmen Sederhana	
32 IMBI Cinema	
33 Yos Sudarso Statue	
34 Bemo Station	
35 Post Office & Telegraph Office	
36 Night Warungs	
37 Jaya Grill	

Jalan Jen Achmad Yani

(immigration office) is on Jalan Percetakan. The head police station, from which you obtain permits for the interior, is on Jalan Achmad Yani. You can stock up on film at the Variant Color Photo Studio in the IMBI cinema in the town centre.

Things to See

There's not a great deal to see, although a trip to the suburb of **Hamadi**, a 10 to 15-minute drive by colt from Jayapura, is worthwhile. Apart from its interesting market (the Pasar Sentral), stocked with innumerable varieties of fish, a nearby beach was the site of an American amphibious landing on 22 April 1944.

Barges and a Sherman tank rust away on the beach near a small monument to the landing. Further down the beach is a group of rather more intact landing barges (one being used for more peaceful purposes as a toilet and a pig pen) and a Sherman tank with its tracks embedded in the sand. To get to these, you have to walk through a navy base. They'll let you in but you have to leave your passport at the entrance and collect it upon leaving.

Apparently, there are some sunken vessels in the water directly in front of the beach. Colts to Hamadi zoom up and down Jalan Achmad Yani. They can also be caught from the little street near the Bank Ekspor Impor, and the fare is 300 rp.

If you want to while away a few hours then try **Base G**, near the site of an American WW II military base. The beach is pretty dull and the surf can be strong – real dumpers. There are colts to Base G from the terminal at the end of Jalan Percetakan near the IMBI cinema. It drops you off about a 15-minute walk from the beach and the fare is 350 rp.

There's also a **university museum** at Abepura on the road in from the airport. It is supposed to be quite good with a lot of

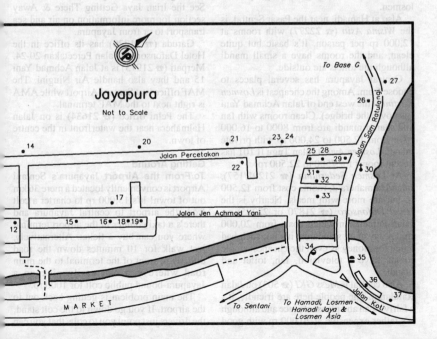

interesting but neglected artefacts and photographs.

Places to Stay

Hotel prices in Jayapura are very high. Cheapest is the *Losmen Hamadi Jaya* in Hamadi, where rooms are from 10,000 rp per person. They're basic but fairly clean, although the mandis and toilets are pretty grotty. This losmen can be rather noisy at night but it's cheap for Jayapura. They bring around a nice breakfast at 5.30 am and pots of tea are readily supplied in the evening.

A colt from the airport will cost you 1500 rp and probably drop you off at the junction of the road leading to the airport and the one leading to Jayapura. From there, it's only a 10-minute walk to the losmen. From Jayapura, there are colts all the time to Hamadi – just hang out on Jalan Koti and wave one down, the fare is 350 rp. The ride from Jayapura to Hamadi only takes about 15 minutes and the colt goes straight past the losmen.

Also at Hamadi, near the Pasar Sentral, is the *Wisma Asia* (☎ 22277) with rooms at 12,000 rp per person. It's basic but quite clean, and the rooms have a small mandi although the toilets are outside.

Central Jayapura has several places to choose from. Among the cheapest is *Losmen Kartini* at the west end of Jalan Achmad Yani (just over the bridge). Clean rooms with fan and shared mandi are from 8000 to 16,000 rp or from 12,500 to 24,000 rp with private mandi. *Losmen Ayu* at Jalan Tugu II 101 has decent rooms for 7500 to 22,500 rp.

At *Losmen Sederhana* (☎ 21291/157), Jalan Halmahera 2, rooms cost from 12,500 rp but are more with meals. Nearby is the *Hotel Dafonsoro* (☎ 21870 or 22285) on Jalan Percetakan which costs from 20,000 rp. By Jayapura standards, it's not such bad value for money as even the cheapest single rooms have a television, fan, toilet and mandi.

Also central is *Mess GKI* (☎ 503) on Jalan Ratulangi. The people here are friendly, it's a fairly clean and pleasant place and although it's rather expensive at 20,000 rp with good meals included. If you're just passing through Jayapura you can stay at the airport at *Losmen Mansapur Roni* on Jalan Yaboso. It's only 100 metres from the terminal and has rooms from 8000 rp.

Places to Eat

The best places to eat in Jayapura are the warungs. Night food stalls in front of the Pelni office serve up gado gado, lontong, tahu, bakso sapi, kikil lontong, bubur and other simple dishes. There are also many warungs around the mosque on Jalan Achmad Yani, serving nasi goreng, nasi campur, soto ayam, mee goreng, mee bakso, mee kuah and nasi telur bakso.

There are several expensive restaurants along Jalan Percetakan, such as the *Rumah Makan Sudi Mampir* (Indonesian and Chinese) and the *Rumah Makan Simpang Tigo* (Padang).

Getting There & Away

See the Irian Jaya Getting There & Away section for more information on air and sea transport to or from Jayapura.

Garuda (☎ 21220) has its office in the Hotel Dafonsoro at Jalan Percetakan 20-24. Merpati (☎ 21913) is at Jalan Achmad Yani 15 and they also handle Air Niugini. The MAF office is at Sentani Airport while AMA is right next to the MAF terminal.

The Pelni office (☎ 21634) is on Jalan Halmahera near the waterfront in the centre of town.

Getting Around

To/From the Airport Jayapura's Sentani Airport is conveniently located a mere 36 km out of town! It's 15,000 rp to charter a colt from the airport to central Jayapura and there's a taxi counter in the airport terminal where you can buy a ticket. Alternatively, just walk for 10 minutes down the road directly in front of the terminal to the main road where you can easily pick up a Jayapura-bound public colt for 1000 rp.

The main problem is getting back out to the airport. If you go down to the colt stand, the drivers just point you to colts that you can charter. There never seems to be one heading to Sentani when you want it – they even tell you to charter vehicles that are already half full. The best way to avoid all this is to walk out of town a little distance up the road for the airport and wait for a colt but allow plenty of time. The straight through trip to the airport takes 45 minutes to an hour.

Local Transport Colts to destinations around Jayapura depart from the stand on Jalan Percetakan near the waterfront, or from near the Bank Ekspor Impor on Jalan Achmad Yani. There are good paved roads in the vicinity of Jayapura. Jayapura to Abepura is 500 rp, Sentani Airport to Abepura 600 rp, and Jayapura to Hamadi 300 rp.

BIAK

On the island of the same name, off the north coast of Irian Jaya, Biak is not much of a town. It's just somewhere on the way to somewhere else. If you've got to spend a few hours here, the most interesting place is the central **Pasar Panir** where they sometimes sell lorikeets and cockatoos. When a Pelni ship goes through, half the crew seem to buy one to sell later in Java. At the end of a flight from Biak to Jakarta, there's the odd sight of birds crammed into cages and boxes being trundled out on the baggage conveyer belts.

Orientation & Information

Like Jayapura, Biak is a fairly compact town. Jalan Prof M Yamin runs from the airport and connects with Jalan Achmad Yani which is Biak's main street and along which you will find many of the town's hotels, restaurants, banks and offices. The other main street, Jalan Imam Bonjol, intersects at right angles with Jalan Achmad Yani.

Money The Bank Ekspor Impor, at the corner of Jalan Achmad Yani and Jalan Imam Bonjol, will change a number of foreign currencies and travellers' cheques. There is also an exchange kiosk in the airport that's open when international flights arrive.

Post The post office is on the road coming in from the airport.

Police & Immigration The head police station is on Jalan Selat Makassar opposite the Pasar Panir – it *might* be possible to get permits for the interior in Biak but don't count on it. The immigration office is at the corner of Jalan Achmad Yani and Jalan Imam Bonjol.

Places to Stay

The *Losmen Maju* (☎ 21218) on Jalan Imam Bonjol costs 10,000 rp per person and is basic but clean. The rooms have a fan and a mandi/toilet. The signless *Losmen Solo* at Jalan Monginisidi 4, just south of the junction of Jalan Imam Bonjol and Jalan Achmad Yani, has clean rooms for 7000 rp per person.

The *Hotel Irian* is straight across the road from the airport. It is also basic but it does have a pretty seaside garden and rooms with mandi/toilet. Rooms are 25,000/40,000 rp.

The *Hotel Mapia* on Jalan Achmad Yani is definitely the nicest of the up-market hotels in Biak. It has cool rooms with large baths and toilets – quite a pleasant place to stay. Rooms (with fan) start from 20,000/30,000 rp.

The *Losmen Atmelia* (☎ 21415), off Jalan Prof M Yamin only 15 minutes from the airport, used to be a cheapie open to the public. Of late, it has been for the use of telecommunications workers only, but it might be worth checking.

Places to Eat

Biak has several places to eat, but not a great many of note. Probably the best are the evening food stalls in front of the Hotel Mapia, or there are some cheap places along Jalan Achmad Yani like the *Rumah Makan Anda*, the *Restaurant Megaria* and the *Restaurant Himalaya*.

Getting There & Away

Garuda and Merpati both fly through Biak. Garuda have a twice weekly Los Angeles-Honolulu-Biak-Denpasar service, a very interesting way of getting to Indonesia from the USA. Garuda (☎ 21416) is on Jalan Achmad Yani. Merpati (☎ 21213/386) is at Jalan Prof M Yamin 1, near the airport.

If you're chasing ships, Pelni is also on Jalan Achmad Yani, but further down the road in a north-westerly direction from the Merpati office and away from the airport. The entrance to the harbour is near the Pelni office and you could try looking here for ships to other parts of the province.

Getting Around

Much of Biak can be covered easily on foot. You can even walk into the city from the airport if you're feeling energetic. From the airport to the centre of town takes about 30 minutes.

A colt from the airport to the town centre is 300 rp and there are regular colts running up and down Jalan Achmad Yani and Jalan Prof M Yamin, so there's no need to charter one to get to the airport.

THE BALIM VALLEY

There are a number of places in the interior worth a visit but top of the list is the Balim Valley where the Dani people were only discovered in 1938. The Danis have adopted many modern conveniences (like steel axes rather than the traditional stone ones) but here you can still see men wearing penis gourds and little else, and some of their other customs have remained intact or have only recently died out.

The Danis maintain their polygamous marriage system – a man may have as many wives as he can afford. Brides have to be paid for in pigs and the man must give five or six pigs to the family of the wife. Women can also change husbands so long as the new husband pays back the former with pigs. Grass skirts usually indicate that a woman is unmarried – although in some parts of the valley, married women also wear them.

One of the more bizarre Dani customs involves the amputation of part of a woman's

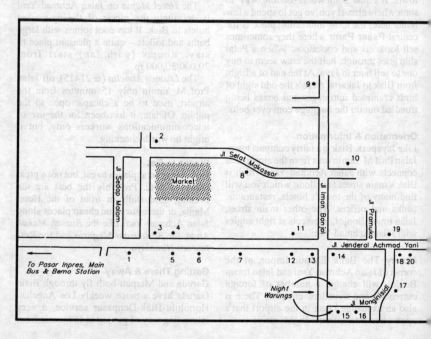

finger when a relative dies, so you'll see many of the older women are missing fingers right up to the second joint – a very common sight. Apparently the practice continued until just a few years ago. The fingers were dried and then buried under a banana tree.

Many Danis wear pig fat in their hair and cover their bodies in soot – intended for health and warmth. The hairstyle looks like a cross between a Beatle's mop-top and a Rastafarian. The Dani women dangle string bags from their heads, carrying fruit and vegetables, firewood, sugar cane and even babies. As the evening closes in, the men, naked except for their penis gourds, stand with their arms folded across their chests to keep warm.

Wamena

The main town of the Balim Valley, Wamena is a neat and rather spread-out place. It makes a good base, although there's not much in the town itself. The market is a focal point and

the villagers come in every day dressed in grass or string skirts and penis gourds. Accommodation in Wamena is expensive. In fact, everything is very expensive compared to the rest of Indonesia but this is understandable as everything has to be flown in. You must report to the police headquarters when you arrive; they're a friendly, helpful bunch.

Information Your permit from Jayapura is taken from you at the airport and you have to collect it on departure from the police headquarters. They may hold your passport. The police station in Wamena cannot give you a permit for other parts of Irian Jaya, apart from Soba and Ninia and places in the Wamena region. Places such as Illaga, Oksibil and Enarotali require permits from Jayapura.

There's a map in the office of the Hotel Balim showing the villages and rivers in the Balim Valley. The Bank Rakyat Indonesia and the post office are both near the airport.

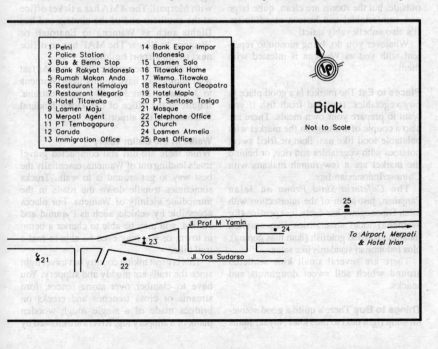

1 Pelni
2 Police Station
3 Bus & Bemo Stop
4 Bank Rakyat Indonesia
5 Rumah Makan Anda
6 Restaurant Himalaya
7 Restaurant Megaria
8 Hotel Titawaka
9 Losmen Maju
10 Merpati Agent
11 PT Tembagapura
12 Garuda
13 Immigration Office
14 Bank Expor Impor Indonesia
15 Losmen Solo
16 Titawaka Home
17 Wisma Titawaka
18 Restaurant Cleopatra
19 Hotel Mapia
20 PT Sentosa Tosiga
21 Mosque
22 Telephone Office
23 Church
24 Losmen Atmelia
25 Post Office

Biak

Not to Scale

Jl Prof M Yamin

Jl Yos Sudarso

To Airport, Merpati & Hotel Irian

Places to Stay The *Hotel Baliem Cottage* on Jalan Thamrin was once Wamena's best hotel but is now a bit shabby. Single/double rooms are 18,000/35,000 rp and this includes breakfast and an afternoon snack. The hotel is made up of grass-roofed, concrete-walled bungalows shaped like Dani huts with a toilet and bathroom in an open-roofed annex.

Better value is *Losmen Anggrek* on Jalan Ambon near the airport. Pleasant single/double rooms downstairs with private mandi are 20,000/32,000 rp; smaller upstairs rooms with shared mandi are 15,000/24,000 rp. *Losmen Syahrial Jaya* (☎ 151) at Jalan Gatot Subroto 51, a five-minute walk from the airport, has clean rooms from 12,000 rp with a small breakfast.

Otherwise, there's the *Nayak Hotel* on Jalan Angkasa, directly opposite the airport terminal. Rooms cost from 20,000/30,000 rp, including breakfast, and other meals are also available. The hotel doesn't look like much more than an army barracks from the outside, but the rooms are clean, quite large and comfortable, and have a mandi/toilet. It's also unbelievably quiet!

Whatever you do, bring mosquito repellent with you as Wamena is infested with them.

Places to Eat The market is a good place to buy vegetables, fruit and fresh fish if you want to prepare your own meals. There are also a couple of warungs in the market with palatable food like nasi ikan or fried sweet potatoes with vegetables and rice, or behind the market are a few rumah makans with Chinese/Indonesian fare.

The *Cafeteria Sinta Prima* on Jalan Panjaitan, just north of the intersection with Jalan Diponegoro, has fairly inexpensive (for Wamena) local specialities like crayfish (udang) and fried goldfish (ikan mas goreng), plus Indonesian standards like satay.

There are several small kios scattered around which sell sweet doughnuts and snacks.

Things to Buy There's quite a good souvenir shop right next to the Hotel Nayak. Items include string bags, intricate bracelets, fibre-coil skirts, necklaces of cowrie shells, penis gourds, stone axes, large black-stone axes and spears. The shop also sells head and arm bands of cowrie shells, feathers and bone, containers made of coconuts, wooden combs and grass skirts.

Some of these things, like the string bags, are cheaper in the market after bargaining. Other things are more expensive. Some of the sellers strike hard bargains so check out prices in both places. The shop is *generally* cheaper than the market.

Getting There & Away Merpati has flights several times a day between Jayapura and Wamena. The MAF and AMA have offices in Wamena and fly to numerous destinations, but again it's a case of waiting around until there's a plane that has space for you and goes to where you want. Be prepared to fly back to Jayapura and back again to some other place in the interior with Merpati. The AMA has a ticket office at the southern end of the airstrip and has flights such as Wamena to Enarotali or Wamena to Illaga. The MAF has an office next to the airport building.

Another airline worth calling on is Airfast who sometimes have flights from Wamena to Jayapura, Port Moresby and Australia. Inquire at the office of Direktorat Jenderal Pelabuhan at the airport.

Walks in the Balim Valley
While there are dirt and compacted gravel roads leading out of Wamena, essentially the best way to get around is to walk. Trucks sometimes trundle down the roads in the immediate vicinity of Wamena. For places accessible by vehicle, such as Pyramid and Akima, you may be able to charter a bemo in town, or you may even be able to rent a trail bike.

This is great hiking country but travel light since the trails are muddy and slippery. You have to clamber over stone fences, ford streams or cross trenches and creeks on bridges made of a single rough wooden plank or a slippery log. Rivers are crossed by dugout canoes, and while you crouch in the canoe and wonder if it's going to tip, the locals go across seven or eight at a time (with their bundles) standing up! If there's no canoe, there might be a raft made of three logs loosely lashed together and pushed along with a pole.

It can also get bloody cold at night up here, so bring warm clothes. It also rains a lot so bring an umbrella and, if you're going to camp out, a waterproof tent. Apart from camping, you can stay with the missionaries, but don't count on it as they've been flooded out with tourists looking for shelter. Staying in the villages should cost you around 5000 rp per person per night.

Local Dani guides, if you can contact them directly, can cost from 6000 rp per day for younger, inexperienced guides (who really act mostly as porters) to 25,000 rp per day for older, more experienced ones. If you can't find a local guide, then the Cafeteria Sinta Prima can arrange them for 25,000 to 30,000 rp per day – try bargaining! You *don't* need a guide for some walks as many places have obvious tracks and roads leading to them. Sometimes you'll be latched on to by a local who'll show you the way. Possible destinations include:

Akima Akima is a nondescript little village, although it is where the 'smoked mummy' is found. The mummy is a weird thing – completely black, decorated with a string mesh cap and cowrie shell beads and a feather. The penis gourd is still there, though the penis has withered away. The body is bunched up in a sitting position, arms wrapped around knees and clawed fingers draped over feet, with the head tucked down. It is said to be 200 years old.

Bargain with the old men who live here (after providing them with a few cigarettes) to show you the mummy. They'll ask for at least 6000 rp per person but you can knock this down to 3000 or 4000 rp.

To get to Akima, walk along the road heading north-west from Wamena Pasar and when you get to the T-intersection turn left. Follow the road past the jail to Hom Hom.

Turn down the road to the river and cross the modern suspension bridge. Then follow the dirt road leading to Akima, it takes about two hours in all from Wamena.

Sinatma Sinatma is a Protestant mission near Wamena, an hour's walk from Wamena airstrip. You walk there past fields of grazing cows near a raging tributary of the Balim River which is crossed by two suspension bridges – frail constructions made of wood and vine and a walkway of thin rough wooden slats.

Pyramid This hill is named after its shape. A motorable road leads from Sinatma all the way to Pyramid via Elegaima but if you walk to Pyramid it's quicker to take this route: Wamena-Hom Hom-Musafak-Miligatmen-Pyramid. There's a dirt road from Wamena to Musafak, negotiable only by motorbike, and from Musafak to Pyramid there is a walking-only track.

Hitigima Near the village of Hitigima there are saltwater wells. Banana stems are beaten dry of fluid and then put in a pool to soak up the brine. The stem is then dried and burned, the ashes collected and used as salt. Salt wells are also found at Jiwika village.

From Wamena, it's an easy 2½ to three hour walk to Hitigima – walk past hills with neat chequerboards of stone fences enclosing cultivated fields. From Wamena, just walk straight down Jalan Achmad Yani, cross the bridge and follow the road. Two hours' walk from the bridge a track branches off the road. There are actually several tracks, so time your walk and ask people along the way. You can see Hitigima from the road but there's no sign and it's not obvious. The salt wells are past Hitigima, about another two hours' walk. There is a trail; it's not easy to follow but you should be able to pick up a guide in Hitigima.

OTHER TOWNS

Visiting other towns in Irian Jaya is hardly worth your time and effort. Perhaps you could fly down to Merauke or Tanah Merah, south of the mountain range, or make your way by air or sea to Fak Fak, Manokwari or Sorong on the 'bird's head', but why bother.

In Sorong, you can stay at *Penginapan* *Indah* on the main road, where rooms cost 9000 rp, or in the similarly priced *Hotel Bangaria*.

East Timor Stop Press

In November 1991 the Indonesian army opened fire on a Timorese protest march in the East Timor city of Dili. The death toll was anywhere from the Indonesian army's figure of 18 to more than 50 according to some independent observers and well over 100 quoted by Timorese sources.

Despite army claims that they were forced to open fire, it is unsure whether the slaughter was either a result of a complete loss of discipline and control or a cold-blooded planned response. A number of foreign visitors witnessed the massacre and one New Zealander was amongst those killed. As this book goes to print it's unclear if the Indonesian authorities will place restrictions on foreign visitors to East Timor. ■

Laos

Laos has been known from antiquity as Lan Xang, or Land of a 'Million Elephants', and by Indochina War-era journalists as the Land of a Million Irrelevants. It is one of the least developed and most enigmatic countries in Asia. With it's small population of less than four million spread over more than 200,000 sq km, Laos is different from its populous neighbours.

Facts about the Country

HISTORY
The country has long been occupied by migrating Thais (an ethno-linguistic family that includes Shans, Siamese, Lao and many smaller tribes) and by Hmong-Mien hill tribes practising slash-and-burn cultivation (as they do to this day). The first Lao *muang*, (principalities), however, were consolidated in the 13th century following the invasion of south-west China by Kublai Khan's Mongol hordes.

In the mid-14th century, a Lao warlord, Fa Ngum, formed his own kingdom, Lan Xang, out of a large coalition of muangs around the town of Luang Prabang. Although the kingdom prospered in the 14th and 15th centuries, it came under increasing pressure from its neighbours and also suffered from internal divisions. In the 17th century, it split up into three warring kingdoms centred around Luang Prabang, Wieng Chan (Vientiane) and Champasak.

By the end of the 18th century, most of Laos came under Thai suzerainty but was also being pressured by the Vietnamese to pay tribute. Unable or unwilling to serve two masters, the country went to war with Siam in the 1820s. After this disastrous challenge, all three kingdoms fell under Thai control. Throughout the 19th century, France was busy establishing a French Indochina in the Vietnamese kingdoms of Tonkin and Annam. By 1893, the French and the Siamese had fashioned a series of treaties that put Lao territories under the protection of the French.

During WW II, the Japanese occupied Indochina and a Lao resistance group, Lao Issara, formed to prevent the return to French rule at war's end. The Franco-Laotian Treaty of 1953 granted full independence to Laos but conflict persisted between royalist, neutralist and Communist factions. The American bombing of the Ho Chi Minh Trail in eastern Laos commenced in 1964 and greatly escalated the conflict between the royalist Vientiane government and the Communist Pathet Lao.

Although the ground war in Laos was far less bloody than in Vietnam or Cambodia, the bombing of the Ho Chi Minh Trail caused many casualties and, eventually, the displacement of most of the population of the eastern provinces, a process that went on until a ceasefire was negotiated in 1973. By this time, Laos had the dubious distinction of being the most bombed country in the history of warfare (the US dropped more bombs on Laos between 1964 and 1973, on a per capita basis, than it did worldwide during WW II).

A coalition government was formed but, with the fall of Saigon in April 1975, it became clear which way the political wind was blowing and most of the rightists left for exile in France. In December 1975, the Lao People's Democratic Republic came into being.

Although the regime has close political ties with Vietnam, Laos has managed, to a large degree, to retain a separate identity. Buddhism is deeply ingrained in the cultural and social fabric of the country and the regime is at pains to explain that Buddhism and Communism are not incompatible. Although many private businesses were closed down after 1975 (and a number of merchants crossed the Mekong to Thailand) there has, since 1979, been a relaxation of the

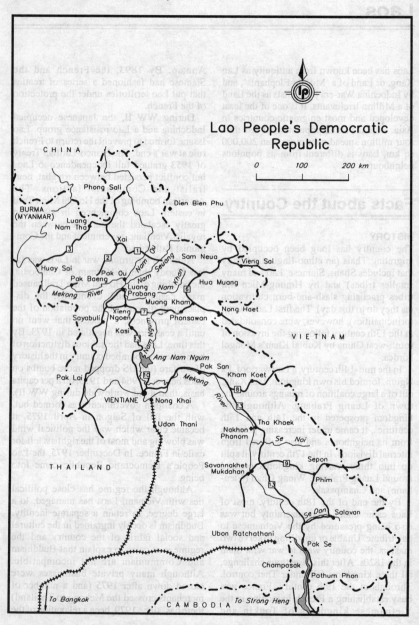

Lao People's Democratic Republic

0   100   200 km

rules and an economic revival with many new shops and restaurants opening.

GEOGRAPHY

Laos covers 235,000 sq km and is bordered by Thailand, Cambodia, Vietnam, China and Burma (Myanmar). Over 70% of the country is mountains and plateaus, and two-thirds is forested.

Most of the population is settled along river valleys. The largest river, the Mekong, or Nam Khong, runs the entire length of the country and provides fertile floodplains for agriculture and the main transportation artery.

The country is divided into 16 provinces *(khwaeng)* plus the prefecture of Vientiane. Below the province is the muang, or district, which is comprised of two or more *tasseng* (sub-districts or cantons), which are in turn divided into *ban* (villages).

CLIMATE

The annual Asian monsoon cycle gives Laos two distinct seasons: May to October is wet and November to April is dry.

Average precipitation varies considerably according to latitude and altitude, with southern Laos getting the most rain overall. The peaks of the Annamite Chain receive the heaviest rainfall, over 300 cm annually.

The provinces of Luang Prabang, Sayabuli and Xieng Khwang, for the most part, receive only 100 to 150 cm a year. Vientiane and Savannakhet get about 150 to 200 cm, as do Phong Sali, Luang Nam Tha and Bokeo.

Temperatures vary according to altitude. In the Mekong River Valley, from Bokeo Province to Champasak Province, as in most of Thailand and Burma, the highest temperatures occur in March and April (these temperatures approach 38°C, or 100°F) and the lowest in December and January (as low as 15°C, or 59°F).

In the mountains of Xieng Khwang, however, December-January temperatures can easily fall to 0°C , or 32°F, at night; in mountainous provinces of lesser elevation, temperatures may be a few degrees higher.

During most of the rainy season, daytime temperatures average around 29°C (84°F) in the lowlands, and around 25°C (77°F) in mountain valleys.

GOVERNMENT

Since 1975, the official name of the country has been the Lao People's Democratic Republic (Sathalanalat Pasathipatai Pasason Lao). Informally, it is acceptable to call the country Laos, which in Lao is *Pathet Lao – pathet* means 'land' or 'country', from the Sanskrit *pradesha*.

The ruling Lao People's Revolutionary Party (LPRP) is modelled on the Vietnamese Communist Party and is directed by the Party Congress, which meets every four or five years to elect party leaders. In practice, the Political Bureau (Politburo), the Central Committee and the Permanent Secretariat are all dominated by Kaysone Phomvihane who is also the Prime Minister of the Council of Government and has enjoyed the full support of the Vietnamese since the 1940s.

Interestingly, the country's constitution, which was only drafted in 1990, contains no reference to socialism in the economy but formalises private trade and fosters foreign investment.

ECONOMY

Although rich in minerals and timber, Laos has not yet exploited these resources. Major exports include hydroelectricity and forestry products. Most goods come via Thailand and the Mekong but a highway to Danang in Vietnam has now been completed

Agriculture, fishing and forestry is carried out by 80% of the population. There is very little manufacturing and foreign aid makes up a large portion of the annual national budget. Much of the domestic trade occurs on the openly tolerated black market. Markets throughout Laos trade freely in untaxed goods smuggled from Thailand (and elsewhere) and the changing of currency (mostly US$ and Thai baht) at free market rates is quite open. Laos is still one of the poorest countries in the world, with an annual per capita income of about US$180.

POPULATION & PEOPLE

The population of Laos is 4.2 million and about half are lowland Lao, most of whom inhabit the Mekong River Valley. Of the remaining half, 10% to 20% are estimated to be tribal Thai (who live in upland river valleys), 20% to 30% are Lao Theung (lower mountain-dwellers mostly of proto-Malay or Mon-Khmer descent) and 10% to 20% are Lao Sung (Hmong or Mien hill tribes who live at higher altitudes).

ARTS

Lao art and architecture can be unique and expressive, although limited in range. Most is religious in nature, including the pervasive image of Buddha and the *wat*, or temple-monastery. Distinctively Lao is the 'Calling for Rain' Buddha, a standing image with a rocket-like shape. Wats in Luang Prabang feature *sim*, or chapels, with steep, low roofs much like the Lanna style in the north of Thailand. The typical Lao *that*, or stupa, is a four-sided, curvilinear, spire-like structure – the best national example is perhaps That Luang in Vientiane. Many other stupas show Thai or Sinhalese influence.

Upland folk crafts include gold and silversmithing, among the Hmong and Mien tribes, and Hmong-Mien weaving. Classical music and dance have been all but lost in Laos. Traditional folk music is still quite popular, however, and usually features the *khaen*, or Lao pan-pipe. Modern Lao pop, derived from the folk traditions, is also quite popular. In the Mekong River Valley, many Lao favour Thai music, which is heard over the radio and imported on cassette tapes.

CULTURE

Historically, traditional culture in Laos has been much influenced by various strains of Khmer, Vietnamese and Thai cultures which entered the territory during periods when Lao principalities were suzerains of these countries. As the lowland Lao and the various Thai tribes are all descended from a common ancestry, the similarities between Lao and Thai culture are strong.

Hence, many of the same standards of conduct which apply for Thailand also apply in Laos. Touching another person's head is taboo and so is the pointing of one's feet at another person or at a Buddha image. Strong displays of emotion are highly discouraged.

When greeting a Lao, the traditional gesture is the *panom* or *wai*, a prayer-like placing together of the palms in front of the face or chest. Nowadays, the handshake is becoming more commonplace, for both men and women.

RELIGION

Most lowland Lao are Theravada Buddhists. Many Lao males choose to ordain as monks temporarily, typically spending anywhere from a week to three months at a wat. Monks are forbidden to promote *phii* (spirit) worship, which has been officially banned in Laos along with *sayasat* (folk magic).

Although the worship of phii is officially forbidden, it remains the dominant non-Buddhist belief system in the country. Even in Vientiane, Lao citizens openly perform the ceremony called *sukwan* or *ba si* in which the 32 guardian spirits known as *khwan* are bound to the guest of honour by white strings tied around the wrists. Each of the 32 khwan are thought to be guardians over different organs in a person's body.

Outside the Mekong River Valley, the phii cult is particularly strong amongst tribal Thai, especially the Black Thai (Thai Dam). Priests *(maw)* who are specially trained in the propitiation and exorcism of spirits preside at important Black Thai festivals and other ceremonies.

The Khamu and Hmong-Mien tribes also practice animism and the latter group combine ancestral worship. During the 1960s some Khamu participated in a 'cargo cult' that believed in the millennial arrival of a messianic figure who would bring them all the trappings of Western civilisation. Some Hmong also follow a Christian version of the cargo cult in which they believe Jesus Christ will arrive in a jeep, dressed in combat fatigues. The Akha, Lisu and other Tibeto-Burman groups mix animism and ancestor cults, except for the Lahu, who worship a supreme deity called Geusha.

LANGUAGE

All dialects of Lao are closely related to languages spoken in Thailand, northern Burma (Myanmar) and pockets of China's Yunnan Province. Standard Lao is close enough to standard Thai (as spoken in central Thailand) that, for native speakers, the two are mutually intelligible. French and English compete for status as the most popular second language, with Russian a distant third. Generally speaking, older Lao will speak some French and younger Lao some English or Russian.

The official language is Lao, as spoken and written in Vientiane. It's spoken with differing accents and with slightly differing vocabularies as you move from one part of the country to the next, especially in a north to south direction, but the Vientiane dialect is most widely understood. Like Thai and Chinese, it's a mostly tonal language with simple grammar. The standard dialect makes use of six separate tones – the word *sao*, for example, can mean 'girl', 'morning', 'pillar' or '20' depending on the tone.

Pronunciation
Consonants

th	t as in English 'tea'.
ph	p as in English 'put' (but never as in 'phone').
kh	k as in English 'kite'.
k	similar to 'g' in English 'good' or k in 'cuckoo' but unaspirated and unvoiced.
t	like English 't' in 'forty' – unaspirated or 'unexploded'; close to 'd' but unvoiced.
p	similar to the 'p' in 'stopper', unvoiced, unaspirated (but not like the 'p' in 'put').
ng	as in English 'sing'; used as an initial consonant in Thai. Practise by saying 'sing' without the 'si'.
ny	similar to the 'ni' in 'onion'; used as an initial consonant in Lao.

All the remaining consonants correspond closely to their English counterparts. Two exceptions are X and V: all instances of 'v' in transcribed Lao words are pronounced as 'w' (eg 'Vang Vieng' should be pronounced Wang Wieng), and all instances of 'x' are pronounced as 's' (eg 'Xieng' should be pronounced Sieng).

Vowels

i	as in English 'it'
ii	as in English 'feet' or 'tea'
ai	as in English 'pipe' or 'I'
aa	long 'a' as in 'father'
a	half as long as 'aa' above
ae	as in English 'bat' or 'tab'
e	as in English 'hen'
eh	like 'a' in English 'hate'
u	as in English 'flute'
uu	as in English 'food'
eu	as in French 'deux'
ao	as in English 'now' or 'cow'
aw	as in English 'jaw'
o	as in English 'phone'
oh	as in English 'toe'

Greetings & Civilities
Greetings
  Sa-bāi-dīi
How are you?
  Sa-bāi-dīi baw
(I'm) fine.
  (Khàwy) sa-bāi-dīi
It doesn't matter
  Baw pēn nyāng (used to mean 'you're welcome', 'no problem', etc)
no (or not)
  baw
thank you
  khàwp jāi

When greeting a Lao, the traditional gesture is the prayer-like *panom* or *wai*.

Getting Around
(I) want to go...
  ...*yàak pǎi*
(I) want a ticket
  Yàak dâi pîi

Where is...?
 ...*yuu sãi* (subject first)
bus
 lot pa-jãm tháang
pedicab
 sãam-lâw
post office
 pãi-sá-nĩi
station
 sá-thãa-nĩi

Food
Do you have ...?
 Mĩi .... baw
(I) don't like it hot & spicy
 Baw mak phét
I only eat vegetarian food
 Khawy kĩn jẽh
market
 talàat
restaurant
 hâan ãahãan

Accomodation
Do you have...?
 Mĩi...baw (subject goes in the middle)
How much?
 thao dãi
bath/shower
 àap nâm
hotel
 hóhng háem
room
 hàwng
toilet
 hàwng nâm (rest room)
 sùam (commode)

Emergencies
(I) need a doctor
 Tâwng-kãan mãw
hospital
 hóhng pha-yáa-bãan
doctor
 mãw

Numbers
1	neung	ໜຶ່ງ
2	sãwng	ສອງ
3	sãam	ສາມ
4	sii	ສີ່
5	hâa	ຫ້າ
6	hók	ຫົກ
7	jèt	ເຈັດ
8	pàet	ແປດ
9	kâo	ເກົ້າ
10	síp	ສິບ
11	síp-ét	ສິບເອັດ
12	síp-sãwng	ສິບສອງ
20	sío	ຊາວ
30	sãm-síp	ສາມສິບ
40	sii-síp	ສີ່ສິບ
50	hâa-síp	ຫ້າສິບ
100	neung hâwy	ໜຶ່ງຮ້ອຍ
200	sãwng hâwy	ສອງຮ້ອຍ
300	sãam hâwy	ສາມຮ້ອຍ
1000	neung phán	ໜຶ່ງພັນ
10,000	neung méun	ໜຶ່ງໝື່ນ ສົບພັນ

Facts for the Visitor

VISAS & TRAVEL RESTRICTIONS
Most travellers to Laos enter on a Tourist Visa which, at last report, is usually issued only to members of package tours. Tours can only be booked through agencies registered with Lao Tourism and the agencies take care of visa arrangements - therefore, no direct involvement with Lao embassies is required.

Lao embassies will occasionally issue Tourist Visas to individuals but the only way to find out is to apply, as their decisions seem to be made on an individual basis (it's never automatic). The embassy in Bangkok is very strict – to get a visa in Bangkok you have to book a minimum two-day tour.

Unless you specifically request to enter Laos from Thailand, via the Nong Khai to Tha Deua ferry, your visa will be stamped 'By Air – Wattay' and you will have to enter via Wattay Airport. Obtaining permission to enter by land is no problem unless you book a package that includes air travel. Once the bridge over the Mekong River, from Nong Khai is finished, entry by bus or train will also be possible.

The Transit Visa is the easiest visa to get but is the most restricted. It is intended for stopovers in Vientiane for air passengers travelling between two other countries. It's common to request this type of visa when travelling between Hanoi and Bangkok (either direction), for example.

The visa is granted upon presentation of a confirmed ticket between the two destinations. The maximum length of stay for the Transit Visa is five days and no extension is allowed. No travel is permitted outside the town of Vientiane on this visa. In Vietnam, the fee for this visa is US\$10.

Once you arrive in Laos, you may have to report to Immigration within three days of your arrival to have your visa validated. This requirement formerly applied to all visa types but recently, however, many visitors on Tourist Visas have been given 14 days upon entry. Check the expiration date written on your visa after passing the immigration checkpoint to see whether you've got your full 14 days.

Travel Passes

Travel passes (*bai anuyaat doen thaang* in Lao, or *laissez passer* in French) are sometimes checked by local police when foreigners show up unexpectedly in Lao towns outside Vientiane – be prepared. They are also sometimes checked when boarding either domestic flights or long-distance river ferries.

Travel passes are issued to tourists (when they purchase a tour package) for only the following provinces outside Vientiane: Luang Prabang, Xieng Khwang, Savannakhet, Salavan and Champasak. Lao Tourism has plans to add Hua Phan, Phong Sali and Luang Nam Tha to the permitted list within the next few years.

Lao Embassies

If you're going to Laos on a package tour, you won't deal directly with any Lao embassy, since tour agencies handle all visa arrangements. To apply for a visa on your own, you can try one of these embassies – Vietnam and Cambodia are the best bets:

Thailand
    Embassy of the Lao People's Democratic Republic, 193 Sathon Tai Rd, Bangkok (☎ 286 0010)

Vietnam
    LPDR Consular Office, 40 Quang Trung St (on 2nd floor of unmarked building across from offices of the Food & Agriculture Organization), Hanoi (☎ 52588)
Cambodia
    LPDR Chancellery, 111 214th St, Phnom Penh (☎ 25 1821)

You can also check with Lao embassies or consulates in other countries which maintain diplomatic relations with Laos, but your chances of getting an individual visa from an embassy or consulate outside Cambodia or Vietnam, except through a tour agency, are somewhat slim.

Visa Extensions

The immigration office of the Ministry of the Interior is on Thanon Talaat Sao near Thanon Lan Xang, opposite the Morning Market, in Vientiane (the only Roman-scripted sign reads 'Ministère d'Interieur'). This is where you get your visa validated or extended. An extension requires the filling out of forms and three passport photos. The application takes about 24 hours to process, and you must leave your passport with Immigration during this time.

The Transit Visa cannot be extended beyond five days. A Tourist Visa can be extended up to a maximum of 14 days. This means that if you arrive in Vientiane on a 'three-day' package (actually two nights and two half-days, for a total of two days in country), you are allowed to apply for an extension and stay on in Vientiane for a combined total of 14 days, without having to buy another package tour. This is by far the most economical way to spend some time in Vientiane. In some cases, it's not necessary to apply for an extension, as you may be given 14 days automatically by airport or pier immigration officials.

The immigration office is open weekdays from 8 to 11 am and from 2 to 5 pm.

Thai Visas

If you're returning to Thailand and plan to stay there beyond 15 days, you'll need a Thai visa. You can apply for one at the Thai

Embassy in Vientiane, which is on Thanon Phon Kheng, a couple of hundred metres north-east of the Pratuxai Monument. A 60-day tourist visa costs 300 baht, payable only in Thai currency. The application process requires three passport photos and takes one to three days to come through (three is normal but one if you can convince them it's urgent).

If you'll be exiting Laos by air or via the river ferry to Nong Khai, and will be in Thailand less than 15 days, you don't need to get a visa in advance. The Thai Embassy in Vientiane may claim it's necessary, but Nong Khai immigration says it isn't. Our experience is that they automatically issue a 15-day transit visa on arrival at the Tha Sadet Pier.

The Thai Embassy is open from 9 am to 12 noon and 2 to 4 pm weekdays.

MONEY
Currency
The official national currency is the *kip*. In reality, the Laotians use three currencies in day-to-day commerce: kip, Thai baht and US$.

Kip notes come in denominations of K1, K5, K10, K20, K50, K100 and K500. Kip coins *(aat)* are available but rarely seen since anything below one kip is virtually worthless. The K20 note is usually the smallest seen.

Exchange Rates
A$1	=	K555
C$1	=	K619
NZ$1	=	K409
US$1	=	K700
UK£1	=	K1240

Changing Money
In early 1989, US$1 bought K470 but, by 1991, you could get K700 per US$1. It seems, however, to be stabilising at that level. Since the dollar figure is more stable, most prices in this chapter are quoted in US$ rather than kip.

Dollars and baht can be exchanged for kip

at the official National Bank rate and the free-market rate, which now seems to be about the same. There's no legal requirement that you change money at the bank – moneychangers operate openly in the outdoor markets of Vientiane and most shop owners will also be glad to give you kip in exchange for cash baht or dollars.

Laos has no currency restrictions on the amount of money you're required to exchange at the official rate (as in Burma) or any 'foreign-exchange certificates' (as in China).

Banking
The only banks that foreigners are allowed to use are La Banque pour le Commerce Exterieur Lao on Thanon Pang Kham near the Lane Xang Hotel and the Joint Development Bank across from the Morning Market, both in Vientiane. They will cash US$ travellers' cheques but require that you take half the cash back in kip at the official rate so you can't simply sign over a travellers' cheque for cash US$. Only the Lane Xang Hotel will take travellers' cheques at this writing but Lao Tourism will accept them in payment for their services.

Cash, therefore, is better than travellers' cheques in Laos but Thai baht are just as good as US$. Other currencies are not accepted in Laos. Security is not generally a problem but a money belt is advisable.

Costs
If it weren't for the current tour requirement, Laos would be a very inexpensive country. The Lao Tourism tours, to provinces out of Vientiane, are actually pretty decent value when you add up everything that's included – though you could do it much more cheaply on your own, especially if you use ground transport rather than air.

In general, food is cheap, hotels are not. The average meal in a Lao restaurant costs less than US$1 per person. A cup of coffee is about US$0.13, and draught beer is only US$0.35 a litre! On the other hand, the Lane Xang Hotel in Vientiane costs US$40 a night for a room that in Thailand would cost half that. The cheapest hotels in Vientiane cost US$8.

Estimating a daily cost is difficult since it depends on how much you try to see, which means how many Lao Tourism packages you purchase at approximately US$100 a day, all-inclusive. In Vientiane, you can get by for about US$10 a day, not counting the cost of the initial package into Vientiane. Towns in southern Laos, like Pak Se or Savannakhet, cost about the same, perhaps a bit lower. Luang Prabang is a little costlier due to the high rates at the two hotels there.

In places where you're not permitted to go costs are much lower, since the average guest lodging only costs around US$2 and food is also cheaper.

Tipping is not customary even in the tourist hotels.

TOURIST OFFICES

So far, the state-run Lao Tourism (Thawng Thio Lao) (☎ 3627) has only one office, which has changed Vientiane locations three times in three years. It's presently at the corner of Thanon Setthathirat and Thanon Pang Kham, near the Fountain Square. Opening hours are from 8.30 am to 4 am Monday to Friday and from 8.30 am to 12 noon on Saturday.

The primary function of Lao Tourism is to sell tour packages rather than to supply travel information. Lao Tourism has yet to open an overseas office and there are rumours that the organisation will be dissolved within the next couple of years. Presently, several travel agencies abroad are authorised to represent Lao Tourism. These agencies, in turn, have smaller unofficial representatives which continue to proliferate.

Try the Khao San Rd area of Bangkok for these agencies. There are representatives in Nong Khai (Thailand) as well, although they are sometimes temporarily closed when Lao Tourism attempts to enforce its official authorisation powers.

BUSINESS HOURS

Government offices are generally open from 8 to 11 am and from 2 to 5 pm. Shops and private businesses open and close a bit later and either stay open during lunch or close for just an hour.

POST & TELECOMMUNICATIONS
Mail

Outgoing mail from Vientiane is fairly dependable and inexpensive but incoming mail is unreliable. Forget about mailing things from upcountry Laos. Local residents, and expats who work outside Vientiane, save their mail and pass it on to acquaintances who are going to Vientiane or Thailand.

Telephones

The domestic phone service is inefficient, with phones often unserviceable and lines down, especially in the rainy season.

International calls can be made only from Vientiane. No IDD is available, but a newly introduced Australian satellite station permits quick overseas connections via Sydney.

TIME

Laos, like Thailand, is 7 hours ahead of GMT. So, when it is 12 noon in Vientiane, it is 1 am in New York, 3 pm in Sydney and 5 am in London.

BOOKS & MAPS

Lonely Planet's *Vietnam, Laos & Cambodia – a travel survival kit* has more detailed information on Laos. Some accounts of the country's recent history include *Contemporary Laos: Studies in the Politics & Society of the Lao People's Democratic Republic* edited by Martin Stuart-Fox and, by the same author, *Laos: Politics, Economics & Society* which provides a better overview.

The State Geographic Service (SGS) has produced a few adequate maps of Laos and the major provincial capitals. The LPDR tourist map of Vientiane and the administrative map of the whole country (labelled in French only as 'Laos – RDPL Carte Administrative') are available in Vientiane at the Lane Xang Hotel and in some souvenir shops along Thanon Samsenthai and Thanon Pang Kham.

The most detailed maps of Laos available are those that were developed by the US Defence Mapping Agency in the '60s and early '70s. These topographic maps, labelled in English and French, are often seen on the walls of government offices. Since little road travel (there are very few roads!) is permitted in Laos, the more general SGS maps are really sufficient for most travel purposes.

The Women's International Group, a local expat association, publishes the informative *Vientiane Guide*, which can be purchased at the Australian Embassy for US$8 or at the Lane Xang Hotel gift shop for US$10.

The Australian Embassy also publishes *A Guide to the Wats of Vientiane*. It's available at the embassy for US$10 or at the Lane Xang Hotel for US$12.

FILM & PHOTOGRAPHY

Colour print film is readily available in larger towns like Vientiane, Savannakhet and Luang Prabang. Ektachrome slide film is available at reasonable prices at a few photo shops along Samsenthai Rd in Vientiane. Outside of Vientiane slide film of any kind is rare. For black & white film or other types of slide film bring your own supply. You can get same day developing and printing done in Vientiane, at Polaroid on Samsenthai Rd, opposite the Vieng Vilay Hotel.

Military installations, soldiers or airports are not to be photographed. Some hill tribes have strong taboos against having their photos taken, so always ask first.

HEALTH

Opisthorchiasis

Apart from health warnings given in the Facts about the Region chapter, travellers in Laos should also be on guard against liver flukes (opisthorchiasis). These are tiny worms that are occasionally present in freshwater fish in Laos. The main risk comes from eating raw or undercooked fish – particularly avoid eating *paa daek* which is a fermented fish used as an accompaniment to rice.

A much less common way to contract liver flukes is by swimming in rivers – the only known area where this may happen is the Mekong River around Khong Island in southern Laos.

Symptoms depend very much on how many of the flukes get into your body. They can range from no symptoms at all to fatigue, a low-grade fever and a swollen or tender liver (or general abdominal pains) along with worms or worm eggs in the faeces.

People suspected of having liver flukes should have a stool sample analysed by a competent doctor or clinic in Vientiane or Bangkok. The usual medication is 750 mg of praziquantel (often sold as Biltricide) taken three times daily and for a week.

DANGERS & ANNOYANCES

Laos seems to be remarkably free of petty theft, at least in relation to visitors. Ordinary precautions, such as locking your hotel room door and keeping your valuables in a secured place, should of course be followed.

About the only known trouble spot is the area around Kasi on the Vientiane to Luang Prabang road. Anti-government rebels have been known to attack vehicles along this road with small arms, grenades & rocket-launchers. In 1989, at least 15 people died in road ambushes, and trucks that ply this route are usually heavily armed.

A safer overland route to Luang Prabang is via Mekong riverboats. Bokeo, Luang Nam Tha and Udomsai provinces in northwestern Laos are areas of semiclandestine heroin production and opium smuggling and are thus areas to avoid – they're officially off limits to visitors anyway.

ACCOMMODATION

Laos has very few hotels – approximately 20 in Vientiane, four or five in Savannakhet, two in Luang Prabang, and one each in Xieng Khwang, Champasak, Salavan and Pak Se. Facilities vary from comfortable rooms with air-con and hot water in Vientiane to guest houses (government-run) without running water in the provinces.

In Vientiane and Luang Prabang, the top tourist destinations, it's difficult to find rooms for under US$10 a night but in other provinces prices drop to as low as US$2, *if* you get there on your own. Lao Tourism would prefer that you pay US$100 a day for a US$2 room, three meals and the services of a guide.

Most hotels, especially those in Vientiane, Luang Prabang and Savannakhet, will require that you fill out a police report (fiche de police) when checking in so that your passport and visa numbers will be on file.

FOOD & DRINK

Lao cuisine is very similar to Thai in many ways. Like Thai food, almost all dishes are cooked with fresh ingredients, including vegetables (phak), fish (paa), chicken (kai), duck (pet), pork (muu) and beef (sin wua) or water buffalo (sin khwai). In Luang Prabang, dried water-buffalo skin (nang khwai haeng) is a popular ingredient in local dishes.

Food is salted with nam paa, a thin sauce of fermented anchovies (usually imported from Thailand) and paa daek, a coarser Lao preparation which has fermented freshwater fish, rice husks and rice 'dust' as its main ingredients. Common seasonings include the galingale root (khaa), ground peanuts (more often a condiment), hot chillies (maak phet), tamarind juice (nam maak khaam), ginger (khing) and coconut milk (nam maak phao). Chillis are sometimes served on the side in hot pepper sauces called jaew.

All meals are taken with rice or noodles. Glutinous rice (khao nio) is the preferred variety although ordinary white rice (khao jao) is also common. Sticky rice is eaten with the hands – the general practice is to grab a small fistful from the woven container that sits on the table, then roll it into a ball which is used to dip into the various dishes. Khao jao is eaten with a fork and spoon. Noodles may be eaten with fork and spoon or chopsticks. The most common noodles in Laos are foe (flat rice noodles) and khao pun (thin white wheat noodles).

The closest thing to a national dish is laap, a spicy beef, duck fish or chicken salad made with fresh lime juice, mint leaves, onions and lots of hot chillies. It can be hot or mild depending on the cook.

In Vientiane, Luang Prabang and Savannakhet, French bread is a popular breakfast food. Sometimes it's eaten plain with kafae nom hawn (hot milked coffee), sometimes it's eaten with eggs (khai) or in a baguette sandwich that contains Lao-style paté and vegetables. When they're fresh, Lao baguettes are superb. Excellent croissants are also available, especially in the bakeries of Vientiane.

Bread (khào jii)
baguette sandwich
   khào jii pa-te
croissants
   khwaa-song
plain bread (usually French-style)
   khào jii

Eggs (khai)
hard-boiled egg
   khai tôm
fried egg
   khai dāo
plain omelette
   khai jīaw
omelette stuffed with vegetables & pork
   khai yat sai

Fish (pāa)
crisp-fried fish
   pāa jēun
grilled fish
   pāa jii
steamed fish
   pāa nèung
grilled prawns
   kûng pîng
giant Mekong catfish
   pāa béuk

Noodles (fõe/mii)
rice noodle soup with vegetables & meat
   fõe nâm
same noodles served on plate with gravy
   lâat naa
fried noodles with soy sauce
   phát siyu
yellow wheat noodles in broth, with
   vegetables & meat
   mii nam

same as mii nam but without broth
mii hàeng

white flour noodles, served with fish curry
sauce
khào pùn

Soups *(kāeng)*

mild soup with vegetables & pork
kāeng jèut

same as above, with bean curd
kāeng jèut tâo-hûu

fish & lemon grass soup with mushrooms
tôm yám pāa

rice soup with fish/chicken
khào tôm pāa/kai

Miscellaneous

spicy beef salad
lâap sîn

roast chicken
kai pîng

chicken fried with chillies
kai phát màak phét

spicy chicken salad
lâap kai

roast duck
pét pîng

rice
khào

fried rice
khào phát

spicy green papaya salad
tam-sòm or *sòm màak-hung*

cellophane noodle salad
yám khào pùn jíin

stir-fried vegetables
phát phák

Beverages *(kheuang deum)*

drinking water
nâm deum

weak Chinese tea
nâm sáa

hot Lao tea with sugar
sáa dām hâwn

hot Lao tea with milk & sugar
sáa hâwn

iced Lao tea with milk & sugar
sáa yén

no sugar (command)
baw sai nâm-tāan

hot Lao coffee with milk & sugar
kāa-fáe nóm hâwn

hot Lao coffee with sugar, no milk
kāa-fáe dām

beer
bīa

orange soda
nâm mák kang

plain milk
nóm jèut

rice whiskey
lâo láo

yoghurt
nóm sôm

THINGS TO BUY

Laos is not a big country for shopping. Many of the handicrafts and arts available in Laos are easily obtainable in Thailand. Hill-tribe crafts can be less expensive in Laos but only if you bargain. Like elsewhere in South-East Asia, bargaining is a local tradition, first introduced by Arab and Indian traders. Most shops now have fixed prices but you can still bargain for fabrics, carvings, antiques and jewellery.

Getting There & Away

AIR

Vientiane's Wattay Airport is the only legal arrival or departure point for all foreign airline passengers. There is a US$5 departure tax.

To/From Bangkok

Bangkok to Vientiane flights operate daily, except Wednesday. On Monday, Tuesday and Saturday, flights are on Lao Aviation's Soviet-built Antonov-24 turboprops; the trip take about one hour and 20 minutes.

On Thursday, Friday and Sunday, Thai International Boeing 737s take about 50 minutes. In each case the fare is US$82 one way.

Thai International is the agent for Lao

Aviation in Thailand, so handle ticketing for both carriers. The fare is never discounted – in fact, those smaller agencies which usually discount international tickets in fact charge more (up to US$40) than the standard fare.

To/From Hanoi
Vietnam Airlines flies the Hanoi-Vientiane-Hanoi route every Thursday for around US$80 each way. Lao Aviation flies on Tuesday for the same fare. Aeroflot's Thursday Hanoi to Moscow flight stops in Vientiane en route.

To/From Ho Chi Minh City
Lao Aviation connects Vientiane with Ho Chi Minh City (Saigon) via Pak Se in southern Laos every Thursday for US$155 each way.

To/From Phnom Penh
Lao Aviation flies from Phnom Penh and Vientiane, Wednesday and Friday, via Pak Se. The flight (as always on an Antonov-24) takes about 3½ hours and costs US$120.

To/From London, Moscow & Rangoon
Aeroflot flies a Tupolev-154 to Vientiane from Moscow via Bombay and Rangoon (Yangon) every Wednesday with connections from London. The fare all the way from London is only US$400.

General Agents for Lao Aviation
Agents for Lao Aviation in the region include:

Thailand
    Thai Airways International, 89 Vibhavadi Rangsit Rd, Bangkok (☎ 233 3810)
Vietnam
    Vietnam Airlines, 25 Trang Thi St, Hanoi (☎ 53842)
Cambodia
    Kampuchea Airlines, 62 Tou Samouth St, Phnom Penh (☎ 2.5887)

Airport Arrival
The government bank has a foreign exchange counter in the terminal, but you're better off changing money on the free market

in town. Since Thai baht and US$ are just as acceptable as kip in Vientiane, there's no need to rush out and change money.

LAND
To/From Thailand
A Lao-Australian plan to construct a bridge over the Mekong River from the Nong Khai railway head (Thailand) to Tha Na Leng (19 km from Vientiane) is soon to commence construction and is expected to be completed by 1993. Once the bridge is up, buses and taxis will go straight into Vientiane from Nong Khai. The next step in the plan is to build a parallel rail bridge in order to extend the Bangkok to Nong Khai railway as far as Vientiane.

To/From Other Countries
Laos shares its land borders with Burma (Myanmar), China, Cambodia and Vietnam but, at present, no overland crossing points are open for foreigners. There is talk, however, of a Bangkok-Vientiane-Danang (Vietnam) bus service commencing and a Bangkok-based company claims to have the agreement of both the Lao and Vietnamese governments for this operation.

RIVER
Nong Khai-Tha Deua-Vientiane
The only place where it is legal for non-Thai foreigners to cross by river into Laos from Thailand is at Nong Khai, in the north-east of Thailand. You must have 'By land' stamped on your visa to be allowed to cross the river – the stamp must be requested in advance from the agency that delivers your visa.

The ferries leave from Nong Khai's Tha Sadet Pier every five minutes or so, from 8 to 11.30 am and from 2 to 4.30 pm daily (except Sunday when the border is closed). The fare is 30B in either direction and must be paid in baht – kip or US$ aren't accepted.

On the other side of the river is the Lao pier, called Tha Deua. At Tha Deua, you pass through immigration (pay a 50B 'entry fee' and 20B 'registration fee') and enter a rustic restaurant area where there's an exchange booth and a duty-free shop. As with airport arrival, there's no reason to change money here when it can be done easily in town.

You have several choices of transport from Tha Deua into Vientiane. Motorbike or car taxis charge a standard 100B per vehicle, reasonable considering that Vientiane is over 20 km away. Alternatively, you can catch a bus for 8B (or a couple hundred kip) that terminates at Vientiane's Morning Market (*Talaat Sao*).

Other Crossings

At this time, foreigners (non-Thais) aren't allowed to cross the Mekong River to Savannakhet from Mukdahan on the Thai side. It's highly likely that at some point in the near future this entry will be opened.

Getting Around

The road system in Laos is undeveloped. Roads around the periphery of Vientiane Prefecture as far as the Nam Ngum Lake are surfaced and adequate for just about any type of vehicle. Elsewhere in the country, rough unsurfaced roads are the rule. Since Laos is 70% mountains, even relatively short road trips take a long time – the 200-km trip from Vientiane to Luang Prabang takes about 18 hours.

The Lao often travel long road distances by arranging rides with trucks carrying cargo from one province to another. Of course, if they can afford it (or the government is paying), they avoid road travel altogether by flying (their fares are often subsidised by the government). The other alternative is river travel which, in many ways, is the most convenient form of transport in Laos.

AIR

You are allowed to book your own flights only if you possess a valid travel pass issued by the Department of Commerce. This usually means booking a tour through Lao Tourism. The result is that most shoestringers won't be flying around Laos.

Vientiane is connected by air with Luang Prabang (US$33; daily), Savannakhet (US$52; daily), Luang Nam Tha (US$54; via Luang Prabang on Wednesday and Sunday), Xieng Khwang (US$27; daily except Tuesday and Sunday), Pak Se (US$85; daily), Sayabuli (US$25; Tuesday and Friday), Sam Neua (US$48; via Xieng Khwang Wednesday and Saturday) and Salavan (US$74; via Savannakhet Thursday only). Most flights are on Antonov-24 turboprop planes but a few use Soviet-built ME-8 helicopters. Two new French ATR-42s have been added to the fleet but it isn't yet certain which routes they'll fly.

All departure and arrival times given throughout this chapter are *scheduled* flight times. In practise, flights are often delayed an hour or two due to weather conditions in the mountains (all destinations with the exception of Vientiane, Savannakhet and Pak Se).

The departure tax for domestic flights is about US$1.

BUS

Because of road conditions, bus services are usually limited to the areas around provincial capitals while long-distance bus services between towns are rare.

Around Vientiane, buses are mostly crowded, dilapidated affairs but very cheap (less than US$1 per 50 km). Where the roads are surfaced, they're a very acceptable way to get from one point to another.

TRUCKS

Outside of Vientiane Province, there are many Russian, Vietnamese or Japanese trucks converted into passenger carriers by adding two long benches in the back. These passenger trucks are called *thaek-sii* (taxi) – or in some areas *sawng-thaew*, which means 'two rows' in reference to the benches in the back.

If you're waiting by the side of the road for a ride, it helps to know whether approaching vehicles are likely to take on passengers, since one truck, from a distance, looks like the next.

You can identify proprietorship by the colour of the licence tags: black tags indicate that the vehicle is licensed to carry paying passengers; yellow means it's a privately-owned vehicle (not very common outside of towns); red is army-owned (not likely to pick up passengers); blue is civil service; and white belongs to embassies or international organisations (who will sometimes pick up foreign passengers).

Trucks may occasionally be stopped and inspected by the Lao army or police. Often, foreigners on a stopped vehicle may be asked to produce travel passes which have been validated for their destination, as it is illegal to board interprovincial transport without a pass.

MOTORBIKE

According to the Ministry of Foreign Affairs, it's illegal for foreigners to drive a motorbike in Laos unless it's a necessary component of their government-approved work.

BICYCLE

In Vientiane, it is possible to rent bicycles, usually in relatively poor condition, for getting around town. Bicycle rentals in other Lao towns are as yet unknown, however. If you manage to bring your own bicycle into the country, cycling would be an excellent way to see the Mekong River Valley area from Vientiane south, which is mostly flat. For the rest of the country you'd need a sturdy mountain bicycle. You should be able to register it with Lao customs upon entry.

BOAT

Rivers are the true highways and byways of Laos, the main thoroughfares being the Mekong, Nam Ou, Nam Khan, Nam Tha, Nam Ngum and Se Don. The Mekong River is the longest and most important water route and is navigable year-round between Luang Prabang in the north and Savannakhet in the south.

River Ferries

For long distances, large diesel-engine river ferries with overnight accommodation are used. Some of these boats have two decks with sleeping areas and on-board food stalls. Others have one deck and stop occasionally for food. On overnight trips check if food is available and, if necessary, bring your own.

River ferry facilities are quite basic and passengers sit, eat and sleep on wooden decks. The toilet is an enclosed hole in the deck. The fare for a typical 24-hour river ferry trip is US$2.50 to US$3. A three-day trip (say upriver from Vientiane to Luang Prabang) is about US$7. As with interprovincial travel by air or road, valid travel passes are required for foreign passengers.

River Taxis

For shorter river trips, such as Luang Prabang to the Pak Ou Caves (US$20), it's usually best to hire a river taxi since the large river ferries only ply their routes a couple of times a week. The long-tail boats (heua hang yao) with engines gimbal-mounted on the stern are the most typical, though for a really short trip, eg crossing a river, a rowboat (heua phai) can be hired. The heua hang yao are not as inexpensive to hire as you might think – figure on around US$4 an hour for a boat with an eight to 10 person capacity.

LOCAL TRANSPORT
Taxis

Each of the three largest towns – Vientiane, Luang Prabang and Savannakhet – has a handful of car taxis that are used by foreign businesspeople and the occasional tourist. The only place you'll find these are at the airports (arrival times only) and in front of the larger hotels. The cars are usually of Eastern European or Soviet origin, eg Volgas and Ladas but, occasionally, you'll run across an older American or new Japanese cars. These taxis can be hired by the trip, by the hour or by the day. Typical all-day rental costs from US$7 to US$12. By the trip, you shouldn't pay more than US$0.50 per km.

Three-wheeled motorbike taxis are also common in the larger towns as well as in some smaller ones. This type of vehicle can be called taxi *(thaek-sii)* or samlor *(saam-law)*, meaning 'three-wheels'. The larger ones made in Thailand are called jumbos *(jamboh)* and can hold four to six passengers. Fares are about US$0.25 per km per vehicle but you must bargain to get the correct rate. They can go any place a regular taxi can, but they aren't usually hired for distances greater than 20 km.

Pedicabs The bicycle samlor is the mainstay of local transport throughout urban Laos. Samlor fares cost about the same as motorbike taxis but are generally used only for distances less than two km. Bargaining is sometimes necessary to get the correct fare, though pedicab drivers seem to be more honest than the motorbike taxi drivers.

TOURS

All tours in Laos are handled by Lao Tourism which has set packages ranging from two nights in Vientiane to 14 days in Vientiane, Luang Prabang, the Plain of Jars, Savannakhet, Pak Se and Champasak. In each destination, Lao Tourism arranges all accommodation, meals, domestic transport and provides a tour guide.

When you book a tour outside of Laos, you must deal with an authorised agent of Lao Tourism (eg Indoswiss, Suite 1102B, 11th Floor, Dusit Thani Building, 946 Rama IV Rd, Bangkok, and Orbitours, GPO Box 3309, Sydney, etc). Lao Tourism sets base fees that they charge all tour agencies and the agencies in turn mark up the price to include their expenses and profit. The costs can vary widely from agency to agency. Deithelm Travel in Bangkok charges an exorbitant US$590 (based on a seven-person minimum) for their three-day Vientiane package. Other agencies can arrange visa-and-accommodation-only packages for as little as US$120.

Therefore the least expensive way to tour Laos is to take the cheapest, shortest Vientiane tour you can find, then extend your Tourist Visa (if necessary) and either travel on your own or book further tours directly

through Lao Tourism. The average cost for one of Lao Tourism's three-day tours outside of Vientiane is a steep US$200 to US$400, depending on the province (the south is the most expensive). The packages includes domestic flights, all meals, accommodation and a guide. You could do four different tours within Laos for less then the cost of one six-day, two-city tour through Deithelm. Or strike out on your own, as many travellers do in spite of regulations.

The least expensive tour company in Bangkok at the moment is MK Ways (☎ 254 5583), 57/11 Wireless Rd or 18/4 Soi Saint Louis 3, Sathon Tai Rd, where a 14-day visa/two-day package can be arranged for US$128. Tourist Visas can also be arranged in Nong Khai at similar costs. To find out more enquire at guest houses like the Mut-Mee, Niyana or the Mekong.

Many Vientiane tours require that you fly into Laos via Vientiane's Wattay Airport. Departure from Laos by ferry (to Thailand) is allowed. If you want to enter by ferry, be sure to request permission in advance through your travel agency.

Vientiane

Originally one of the early Lao river-valley fiefdoms (muang) that were consolidated around the time Europe was emerging from the Dark Ages, Vientiane sits on a bend in the Mekong River amidst fertile alluvial plains. At times controlled by the Burmese, Siamese, Vietnamese and Khmers, it was made a capital city by the French in the late 19th century. Throughout the Indochina War years, royalists, neutralists and leftists vied for control over the city and, thereby, the country. Following the Communist takeover of 1975, it continued to serve as the seat of government.

It's one of the three classic Indochinese cities (including Saigon, or Ho Chi Minh City, and Phnom Penh) that conjure up images of exotic Eurasian settings and has remained amazingly laid-back. Vientiane is actually pronounced Wieng Chan.

Orientation

The city curves along a bend in the Mekong River with the central business district at the middle of the bend. Most of the government offices, hotels, restaurants and historic temples are in this district near the river.

Street signs are mostly written in Lao script only, although signs at major street intersections are also written in French. The French designations for street names vary (eg 'route', 'rue' and 'avenue') but the Lao script always reads *thanon* and it's always best just to avoid possible confusion and use the Lao word.

The main streets in the downtown district are Thanon Samsenthai, which is the main shopping area; Thanon Setthathirat, where several of the most famous temples are located; and Thanon Fa Ngum, which runs along the river. Branching off northward is Thanon Lan Xang, Vientiane's widest street.

The main portion of Thanon Lan Xang is a divided boulevard that leads past the Morning Market to the Pratuxai, or Victory Gate. After the Pratuxai, it splits into two roads, Thanon Phon Kheng and Thanon That Luang. Thanon Phon Kheng leads to the Unknown Soldiers Memorial and the Lao People's Army Museum as well as the Thai Embassy. Thanon That Luang leads to Pha That Luang.

To the north-east of central Vientiane are Pha That Luang and several embassies. To the south-east is the mostly local residential district of Sisattanak and to the west is the similarly residential Sikhottabong.

Information

Tourist Office The Lao Tourism office is on the corner of Thanon Setthathirat and Thanon Pang Kham, opposite Nam Phou Square. This office is marked incorrectly on the government's tourist map of Vientiane, so don't waste your time looking for offices on or off Thanon Samsenthai as indicated. The immigration office has a good wall map showing how to get there.

The only reason to visit Lao Tourism is if you want to book a Lao Tourism package to another province in Laos. For information on what to see and do in and around Vientiane, you're better off relying on this guide or on material available from the Australian Embassy and various souvenir shops.

There is also a separate Vientiane Tourism office, but they always refer people to the main Lao Tourism office and none of the staff speaks serviceable English or French.

Money The Lao Exterior Commerce Bank (La Banque pour le Commerce Exterieur Lao) at 1 Thanon Pang Kham (near Lao Aviation and the Lane Xang Hotel) and the Joint Development Bank at 31-33 Thanon Lan Xang (opposite the Morning Market) are the only banks with the facilities to deal with foreigners.

Banking hours are from 8.30 am to 4 pm Monday to Friday. Lao Exterior Commerce Bank is open from 8.30 am to 12 noon on Saturday.

You can change US$ and Thai baht cash at the free-market rate in the large sheds at the Morning Market.

Post The Post, Telephone and Telegraph (PTT) office is on the corner of Thanon Lan Xang and Thanon Khu Vieng, across from the Morning Market. Business hours are from 8 am to 5 pm Monday to Saturday and from 8 am to 12 noon on Sunday.

Telephone The PTT office is only for calls within Laos. Overseas calls can be arranged at the International Telephone Office (Cabines Telecommuniques Internationales) on Thanon Setthathirat. It's open 24 hours a day but lines are sometimes down during heavy rains.

Bookshops Bring your own reading matter if you can't read Lao or Russian.

The gift shop at the Lane Xang Hotel has a few books in English and rather expensive maps of Vientiane and Laos. If you really want something to read, check with The Library Club at the Australian Residence.

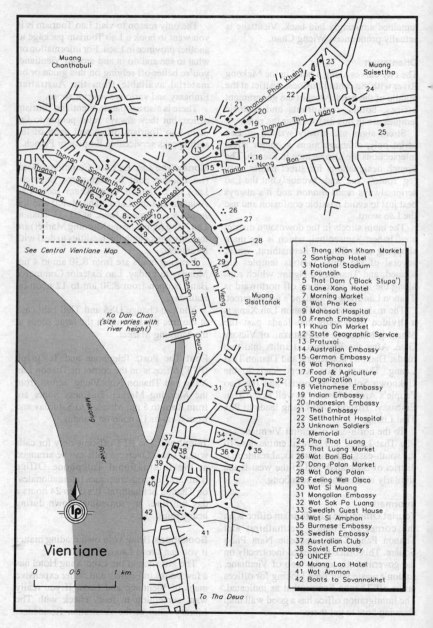

Vientiane

0   0.5   1 km

To Tha Deua

1 Thong Khan Kham Market
2 Santiphap Hotel
3 National Stadium
4 Fountain
5 That Dam ('Black Stupa')
6 Lane Xang Hotel
7 Morning Market
8 Wat Pha Keo
9 Mahosot Hospital
10 French Embassy
11 Khua Din Market
12 State Geographic Service
13 Pratuxai
14 Australian Embassy
15 German Embassy
16 Wat Phonxai
17 Food & Agriculture
   Organization
18 Vietnamese Embassy
19 Indian Embassy
20 Indonesian Embassy
21 Thai Embassy
22 Setthathirat Hospital
23 Unknown Soldiers
   Memorial
24 Pha That Luang
25 That Luang Market
26 Wat Bon Bai
27 Dong Palan Market
28 Wat Dong Palan
29 Feeling Well Disco
30 Wat Si Muang
31 Mongolian Embassy
32 Wat Sok Pa Luang
33 Swedish Guest House
34 Wat Si Amphon
35 Burmese Embassy
36 Swedish Embassy
37 Australian Club
38 Soviet Embassy
39 UNICEF
40 Muang Lao Hotel
41 Wat Ammon
42 Boats to Savannakhet

See the following Vientiane Entertainment section for more information.

Police In an emergency, contact the police kiosk on Thanon Setthathirat.

Medical Care Medical facilities in Vientiane are quite limited. The two state hospitals, Setthathirat and Mahasot, operate on levels of skill and hygiene below that available in neighbouring Thailand. Mahasot Hospital operates a Diplomatic Clinic 'especially for foreigners' that is open 24 hours. In reality, few foreigners use this clinic.

The Australian and Swedish embassies in Vientiane maintain clinics that can treat minor problems. Both clinics are behind the Australian Embassy, off Thanon Phonxai Noi. The Swedish Clinic (☎ 4641) is open daily from 8 to 11 am. The Australian Embassy Clinic (☎ 2477/4691, after hours 2183) is open Monday to Friday from 8.30 am to 12 noon and from 2 to 5 pm (except Wednesday when it closes at 12 noon and stays closed the rest of the day). It is on call 24 hours.

These clinics are staffed by registered nurses but aren't equipped to handle major medical emergencies. Both charge small treatment fees.

Things to See

Topping the list of things to see in Vientiane are the historic *wat* (temples) and *that* (stupas or pagodas), most notably Pha That Luang and Wat Si Saket, as well as the museum at Wat Pha Kaew.

Walking Tour This walk takes you through the central area and past some of the lesser known wats in a leisurely two to 2½ hours. Start at the Lao Tourism office (or near the fountain off Thanon Setthathirat if Lao Tourism has moved again) and walk west on Setthathirat approximately 250 metres to **Wat Mixai** on your left. The *sim* (chapel) is built in the Bangkok style, with a verandah that goes all the way round. The heavy gates, flanked by two *nyak*, or guardian giants, are also in Bangkok style.

Another 80 metres or so, and in the same direction and on the right-hand side of the street, is **Wat Hai Sok** with its impressive five-tiered roof (nine if you count the lower terrace roofs). Opposite, and just a bit farther on, is **Wat Ong Teu** (see the following description for more details), and past Thanon Chao Anou on the next block west and on the left again is **Wat In Paeng**. The sim of this latter wat is nicely decorated with stucco reliefs depicting various mythical characters from the Hindu *Ramayana* and *Mahabharata* epics, as coopted by Buddhism. Over the front verandah gable is an impressive wood and mosaic facade.

Reverse direction, go back to Thanon Chao Anou, turn right (south) and walk until you meet Thanon Fa Ngum along the Mekong River. Just around the corner to the left is **Wat Chan**, a typically Lao temple with skilfully carved wooden panels on the rebuilt sim. Inside is a large bronze seated Buddha from the original temple on this site. In the courtyard are the remains of a stupa with a Buddha image in the 'Calling for Rain' pose.

Continue east on Thanon Fa Ngum until you pass the Lane Xang Hotel on your left. Beyond the hotel a bit, turn left on Thanon Chantha Kumman and walk straight (north) about half a km (passing the Hotel Ekkalat Metropole on the your left) and you'll run into **That Dam**, the 'Black Stupa'. Local mythology says the stupa is the abode of a dormant seven-headed dragon that came to life during the 1828 Siamese-Lao War and protected local citizens.

Pha That Luang The 'Great Sacred Stupa' is the most important national monument in Laos, a symbol of both the Buddhist religion and Lao sovereignty. Construction of the current monument began in 1566 and, in succeeding years, four wats were built around the stupa. Only two remain, Wat That Luang Tai to the south and Wat That Luang Neua to the north. The latter is the monastic residence of the Supreme Patriarch (Pha Sangkharat) of Lao Buddhism.

A high-walled cloister with tiny windows surrounds the 45-metre stupa. The base of the stupa is designed to be mounted by the faithful, with walkways around each level and connecting stairways.

Each level of the monument has different architectural features in which aspects of Buddhist doctrine are encoded – devout Buddhists are supposed to contemplate the meaning of these features as they circumambulate. The tall central stupa, which has a brick core that has been stuccoed over, is supported here by a bowl-shaped base which is reminiscent of India's first Buddhist stupa at Sanchi.

The cloister measures 85 metres on each side and contains various Buddha images. A display of historic sculpture, including not only classic Lao sculpture but also Khmer figures, is on either side of the front entrance (inside). Especially during the That Luang Festival in November, worshippers stick balls of rice to the walls to pay respect to the spirit of King Setthathirat.

The grounds are open to visitors from 8 to 11.30 am and from 2 to 4.30 pm Tuesday to Sunday. Admission is US$0.25 per person. Pha That Luang is about four km north-east of the city centre at the end of Thanon That Luang.

In front of the entrance to the compound is a statue of King Setthathirat. Any bus going north of Thanon Lan Xang will pass within a short walk from the compound.

If you happen to be in Vientiane in mid-November, don't miss the That Luang Festival (Bun That Luang), the city's biggest annual event.

Wat Pha Kaew About 100 metres down Thanon Setthathirat, from Wat Si Saket, is a former royal temple of the Lao monarchy. It has been converted into a museum and is no longer a place of worship.

According to the Lao, the temple was originally built in 1565 by command of King Setthathirat, heir to the Lan Xang throne, in order to house the so-called Emerald Buddha. In Laos the name Pha Kaew means 'jewel Buddha image' although the image is actually made of a type of jade. The image was originally from northern Thailand's Lanna Kingdom but following a skirmish with the Lao in 1779, the Siamese recovered the Emerald Buddha and installed it in Bangkok's royal temple. Later during the Siamese-Lao War of 1828, Wat Pha Kaew was razed.

The temple was rebuilt between 1936 and 1942 in a rather Bangkok-style rococo. Today, the verandah shelters some of the best examples of Buddhist sculpture in Laos. Included are a 6th to 9th century Dvaravati-style stone Buddha, several bronze standing and sitting Lao-style Buddhas and a collection of inscribed Lao and Mon steles. Various royal requisites are also on display inside, along with some Khmer steles, various wooden carvings (door panels, candlestands, lintels) and palm-leaf manuscripts.

Hours and admission for Wat Pha Kaew are the same as for Pha That Luang and Wat Si Saket.

Wat Si Saket This temple is located near the Presidential Palace and is at the north-east corner of Thanon Lan Xang and Thanon Setthathirat. Built in 1818, by King Anouvong (Chao Anou), it is the oldest temple in Vientiane – all others were either built after Wat Si Saket or were rebuilt after destruction by the Siamese in 1828.

In spite of an overall Siamese architectural influence, Wat Si Saket has several unique features. The interior walls of the cloister are riddled with small niches that contain silver and ceramic Buddha images – over 2000 of them. Over 300 seated and standing Buddhas of varying sizes and materials (wood, stone and bronze) rest on long shelves below the niches, and most are sculpted or cast in the characteristic Lao style. Most of the images are from 16th to 19th-century Vientiane but a few hail from 15th to 16th-century Luang Prabang. A Khmer-style Naga Buddha, brought from a Khmer site at nearby Hat Sai Fong, is also on display.

The hours and admission fee are the same as for Pha That Luang and Wat Pha Kaew. A Lao guide who speaks French and English is usually on hand to describe the temple and answer questions – for free.

Wat Sok Pa Luang The full name for this forest temple *(wat pa)* in south Vientiane's Sisattanak district is Mahaphutthawongsa Pa Luang Pa Yai Wat. It's famous for its rustic herbal saunas, which are administered by eight-precept nuns who reside at the temple. After the relaxing sauna (US$2), you can take tea while cooling off. A massage (US$3) is also available.

Wat Sok Pa Luang is also known for its course of instruction in *vipassana*, a type of Buddhist meditation that involves careful mind and body analysis. The abbot and teacher is Ajaan Sali Kantasilo who was born in 1932 in Yasothon, Thailand. He accepts foreign students but only speaks Lao and Thai, so interested persons will have to arrange for an interpreter if they speak neither of these languages.

Taxi, jumbo and samlor drivers all know how to get to Wat Sok Pa Luang. The temple buildings are set back in the woods so all that is visible from the road is the tall ornamental gate.

Wat Xieng Khwan (Buddha Park) The 'Spirit City Temple', 24 km south of the town centre off the road to Tha Deua, is not a true wat as there are no monks in residence and there never have been. Nor is there any traditional Buddhist architecture. Locals often call it 'Buddha Park', a more apt description of its collection of Buddhist and Hindu sculpture in a meadow by the side of the Mekong River.

Pratuxai (Victory Monument) This large monument, very reminiscent of the Arc de Triomphe in Paris, is known by a variety of names. Ironically, it was built in 1969 with US-purchased cement that was supposed to have been used for the construction of a new airport. Since it was to commemorate the Lao who had died in prerevolutionary wars, current Lao maps typically label it 'Old Monument' (Ancien Monument in French, or *Anusawali Kao* in Lao) in order to draw attention to the newer Unknown Soldiers Memorial, erected since the Revolution.

The bas-relief on the sides and the temple-like ornamentation along the top and cornices are typically Lao. Beneath the arch is a small outdoor cafe with snacks and cheap draught beer. A stairway leads to the top of the monument, where you can look out over the city (there's a small entry fee to climb the stairs).

Morning Market The Morning Market *(Talaat Sao)* is on the north-east corner of the intersection of Thanon Lan Xang and Thanon Khu Vieng. It actually runs all day, from about 6 am to 6 pm. The sprawling collection of stalls offer fabric, ready-made clothes, hardware, jewellery, tobacco and other smoking material, electronic goods and just about anything else imaginable. Since the loosening of economic restrictions in 1987, the Morning Market has been expanding.

From about 6 to 8 am, vendors along Khu Vieng in front of the Morning Market sell French bread and the Lao breakfast sandwich *(khao jii pa-te)* – split baguettes filled with a Lao version of paté, a few vegetables and a fish sauce dressing. A few vendors also sell fresh vegetables and fruit during these hours. For the rest of the day you don't see a lot of fresh produce except for the occasional street vendor who may wheel a cart through the market.

Other Markets

East of the Morning Market, just across Thanon Mahasot (or Thanon Nong Bon, as it's labelled on some maps) is the **Khua Din Market** *(Talaat Khua Din)* which offers fresh produce and fresh meats, as well as flowers and assorted other goods.

A bigger fresh market is **Thong Khan Kham Market** *(Talaat Thong Khan Kham)* which is sometimes called the Evening Market since it was originally established to replace the old Evening Market in Ban Nong Duang (which burned down in 1987). Like the Morning Market, it's open all day, but is best in the morning. It's the biggest market in Vientiane and has virtually everything. You'll find it north of the town centre in Ban Thong Khan Kham ('Gold Bowl Fields

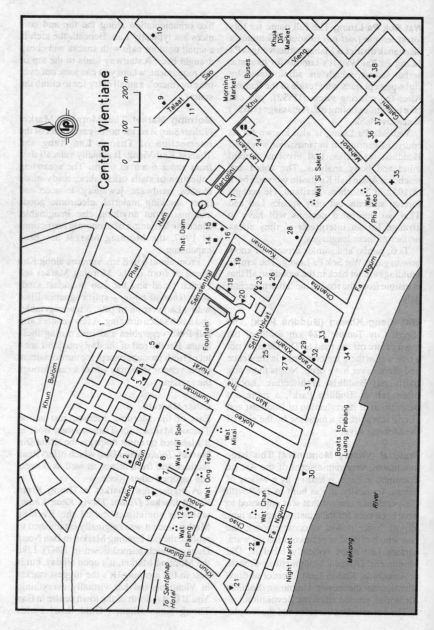

Central Vientiane

0   100   200 m

Village'), at the intersection of Thanon Khan Kham and Thanon Dong Miang.

The **That Luang Market** is just a little south-east of Pha That Luang on Thanon Talaat That Luang. The specialty here is exotic foods like bear paws and snakes that are favoured by the Vietnamese and Chinese.

Festivals

The **That Luang Festival** takes place at Pha That Luang, on the full moon in November. Hundreds of monks assemble to receive alms and floral votives early in the morning on the first day of the festival.

There is also a colourful procession between Pha That Luang and Wat Si Muang. The celebration lasts a week and includes fireworks, music and other entertainment, culminating in a candlelit circumambulation *(wien thien)* of That Luang.

Vietnamese Tet & Chinese New Year (usually centred on a full moon in February) is celebrated with some fervour in Vientiane with parties, fireworks and visits to Vietnamese and Chinese temples. Chinese and Vietnamese-run businesses usually close for three days.

Places to Stay

Vientiane has a choice of about 20 hotels and guest houses, most costing over US$20 per night. Foreigners are allowed to stay at any of them, although if you arrive in Vientiane on a Tourist Visa you'll already have paid for two nights or more at a preassigned place. If you plan to extend your stay, you can then seek out a room at your leisure.

The *Vieng Vilay Hotel* (☎ 3287) on Thanon Samsenthai was once the best value in town at only US$5 to US$10 for clean, spacious rooms with private bath. In 1990-1, it was closed for upgrading and when reopened (in late '91 or early '92) it will probably cost around US$20 a night for the addition of a lift, a fancier lobby and new furniture.

Lao Chaleune (☎ 2408), on Thanon Chao Anou at the corner of Thanon Fa Ngum and near the river, has singles/doubles with air-con at US$10/12. Formerly the Inter Hotel, it's well-located, clean, not so friendly and often full – the restaurant, however, gets high marks.

Opened in 1990, the *Lani Guest House I* (☎ 4175, 2615) at 281 Thanon Setthathirat is a clean and quiet two-storey gem off the street near Wat Hai Sok and Wat Ong Teu. Rooms without bath cost US$8, more expensive air-con rooms are available and there's a discount for stays of a week or more. If it's full, enquire about the *Lani Guest House II*.

Anou Hotel (☎ 3571), on Thanon Heng Boun at the corner of Thanon Chao Anou, reopened after renovations in 1990 with rooms in the US$15 to US$25 range. The new Anou is clean and a favourite for visiting Asian businesspeople.

The *Santiphap Hotel* (also *Santiphab* or *Santipharb*) (☎ 2489, 3305) at 69A Thanon Luang Prabang was formerly the Apollo Hotel. The business-like atmosphere is similar to many other 1970s-vintage Chinese hotels throughout urban South-East Asia. Air-con rooms cost US$16/18, and two-room suites with refrigerators are US$25. All rooms have hot water.

Mekong Guest House (☎ 5975) is at Thanon Tha Deua, Km 4, about 700 metres north-west of the big Mekong Restaurant and about halfway between the city and the Tha Deua ferry crossing. Although it's a bit far from downtown Vientiane, rooms in this recently constructed guest house are only 100B per person.

Muang Lao Hotel (☎ 2278), also at Thanon Tha Deua, Km 4, is a bit out of town on the way to the Tha Deua ferry. It's on the Mekong River, near the Australian Club, and has large, clean and air-con rooms from US$16 to US$20. There's a cafe downstairs so if everything else in town is full it's a good bet.

Places to Eat

Vientiane is good for eating possibilities, with a wide variety of cafes, street vendors, beer halls and restaurants offering everything from rice noodles to filet mignon. Nearly all fit well into a shoestring budget – in fact, it's rather difficult to find anything approaching an expensive restaurant.

Breakfast Most of the hotels in Vientiane offer set 'American' breakfasts (two eggs, toast and ham or bacon) from US$1.50 (Villa That Luang, near Pha That Luang) to US$2.30 (Lane Xang Hotel). Or you could get out on the streets and eat where the locals do. A popular breakfast is khao jii pa-te, a split French baguette stuffed with Lao-style paté (which is more like English or American luncheon meat than French paté) and various dressings.

Vendors who sell breakfast sandwiches also sell plain baguettes (khao jii) – there are several regular bread vendors on Thanon Heng Boun and also in front of the Morning Market. The fresh baguettes are usually gone by 8.30 am at the latest and what's left will be starting to harden.

At the corner of Thanon Samsenthai and Thanon Chantha Kumman is a little open-air cafe that's only open for breakfast and lunch. The family that run it prepare a nice khai ka-ta, eggs fried and served in a small metal pan with French bread on the side. You can also order Chinese doughnuts (pa-thong-ko) or plain bread with cafe au lait (kaa-fae nom hawn).

Two side-by-side cafes on Thanon Chao Anou, *Vinh Loi Bakery House* and *Sweet Home Bakery*, sell excellent croissants in the morning. At Vinh Loi, two croissants, a cup of cafe au lait and a glass of nam saa (weak Chinese tea, served as a chaser) costs about US$0.50 total. The Sweet Home has a menu on the wall in Lao, English and Russian. Other pastries and cakes, as well as ice cream, are for sale at both cafes.

Noodles Noodles of all kinds are very popular in Vientiane, especially along Thanon Heng Boun, the unofficial Chinatown. Basically, you can choose between foe, a rice noodle that's popular throughout mainland South-East Asia (known as kway teow in Thailand, Malaysia and Singapore), and mee, the traditional Chinese wheat noodle.

French Several commendable French and French-Lao restaurants can be found in Vientiane. Most are costly by local standards (from US$5 to US$7 per meal) but they are definitely better value than Vientiane hotels.

One that is particularly good, as well as

inexpensive, is *Santisouk* (once a famous tea-house called La Pagode) on Thanon Nokeo Kumman, near the Lao Revolutionary Museum. The cuisine is of the 'French grill' type and is quite tasty. A filling plate of filet mignon with roast potatoes and vegetables, for example, costs around US$1.10 using free-market kip. A similar plate with filleted fish in a mushroom sauce is US$1.25. It's no wonder Santisouk is one of the most popular restaurants in town.

Of the half dozen or so more expensive French and French-Lao restaurants, only two are worth noting. *Nam Phou* (Fountain) is on the Fountain Circle off Thanon Pang Kham and is frequented by diplomats and UN types because it has probably the best European food and service in Vientiane. Further down Thanon Pang Kham near Lao Aviation is *Le Souriya*, a well-appointed, somewhat pricey place that's owned by a Lao princess.

Lao For real Lao meals, try the Dong Palan Night Market, off Thanon Ban Fai (marked Thanon Dong Palan on some maps) and behind the Nong Chan ponds near the Lan Thong cinema. Vendors sell all the Lao standards, including laap (spicey salad) and ping kai (roast chicken).

The *Haan Kheuang Deum Mixai*, or 'Mixai Drink Shop', is in a wooden building that's open on three sides and overlooks the Mekong River near the intersection of Thanon Fa Ngum and Thanon Nokeo Kumman. The menu is not very extensive, but the laap kai (chicken laap) is very tasty and they have cold draught beer for US$0.35 a litre. This is a great spot to watch the sun set over the Mekong River, with the Thai town of Si Chiengmai as the backdrop. The Mixai is a favourite hang-out for Czechs, Poles and Bulgarians working in Laos. Sometimes when the place is full, the beer runs out by sunset.

The restaurant with the best reputation for Lao food among locals is *Nang Bang* (it may also be called *Nam Kham Bang)*, which is on Thanon Khun Bulom (Khoun Boulom), not far from the Thanon Fa Ngum intersection. It's on the right as you walk north on Khun Bulom. The laap is perhaps their most famous dish.

Thai With an increasing number of Thais visiting Vientiane for business and pleasure these days, it is no wonder that there are more Thai restaurants. On Thanon Samsenthai, just past the Lao Revolutionary Museum, is the *Thai Food* restaurant, which has all the Thai standards, including tom yam kung (shrimp and lemon grass soup) and kai phat bai kaphrao (chicken fried in holy basil). Curries are good here – something you don't see much of in Lao cuisine.

The *Food Garden (Suan Aahaan* in Lao and Thai) is on Thanon Luang Prabang, just before it forks into Thanon Setthathirat and Thanon Samsenthai. In the typical Thai 'food garden' style, tables are set up in the open air and seafood is the house specialty.

Other Out on Thanon Tha Deua at Km 14, next to the Lao Government Brewery, is a thatched-roof restaurant where you can drink Lao beer *(bia sot)* and eat authentic Lao dishes. Bia sot is literally 'fresh beer', and it doesn't get any fresher than this).

Near the immigration office on Thanon Talaat Sao, where you go to get your visa validated, is a grungy house with a sign out front that says 'Indian Food'. If you can rouse the old man sleeping in back, he'll serve you a north Indian-style meal for less than US$1. Better, more expensive Indian food (southern and northern) is available at *Noorjahan* at 370 Thanon Samsenthai. It's open daily 9.30 am to 10 pm.

Entertainment
Dancing Vientiane has a curfew from midnight to 6 am despite which there are at least six discos. Popular places include the *Vienglaty Mai* on Thanon Lan Xang, a bit north of the Morning Market (and on the same side of the street) and the *Feeling Well* on Thanon Ban Fai (or Thanon Dong Palan, depending on the map you follow), a couple of hundred metres beyond the Dong Palan Night Market.

Hotel Clubs The *Lane Xang* and *Santiphap* hotels each have live bands on weekend nights. The *Anou Hotel's* disco may have started up again now that renovations are complete. The *Saysana Hotel's* nightly disco is best on weekends. The *Muang Lao Hotel* frequently has live bands.

Cinema Lao cinemas generally show, in descending order of frequency, Thai, Chinese, Indian, Bulgarian and Russian films. Prints are often in lousy condition but you can hardly argue with the admission charges – less than US$0.15 for the best seats in the house.

The US Embassy screens American movies (with popcorn and beverages for sale) every Wednesday at 7 pm for US$2. The theatre is across the street from the main embassy entrance on Thanon Bartolini.

Le Club France shows French films four times a week at the French Embassy, off Thanon Setthathirat. Check with the embassy for schedules – the club issues a monthly bulletin.

Cultural Clubs The Library Club is in the garden of the Australian Residence in a building called 'the Stockade', which is off Thanon Nehru near the Australian Embassy. It's open to members only on Tuesday and Thursday from 4 to 6.30 pm and also on Saturday from 9 am to 12 noon. An annual membership is US$10 (plus a refundable US$10 deposit).

Le Club France is in the French Embassy compound and features a French library with over 20,000 books and records. They offer French language lessons here and have a bar that's open from 5 am to 5 pm.

Things to Buy
Just about anything made in Laos is available for purchase in Vientiane, including hilltribe crafts, jewellery, traditional fabrics and carvings. The main shopping areas are the Morning Market (including shops along Thanon Talaat Sao), along west Thanon Samsenthai (near the Hotel Ekkalat Metropole) and on Thanon Pang Kham.

Getting There & Away
Vientiane is the only legal port of entry into Laos for foreigners. Hence, the information in the earlier Laos Getting There & Away section applies to Vientiane.

Air Departures from Vientiane are very straightforward. Upstairs in the airport is a restaurant-lounge area with decent enough food. Departure tax is US$5.

Boat Many visitors to Laos, no matter what kind of visa they hold, are required to fly into Vientiane. However, the Lao government doesn't seem to object if you take the river ferry back to Thailand when you are departing.

Lao Immigration officials in town may tell you (if you ask) that you need a letter from them to depart by ferry (which they only issue if for some reason you can't make the flight out). In practice, however, the officials at Tha Deua let anyone through. Check the Thai visa regulations if you plan to stay more than 15 days in Thailand.

Ferries depart from the tiny ferry station at Tha Deua, approximately 20 km southeast of Vientiane. Boats leave about every five minutes, from 8 to 11.30 am and from 2 to 4.30 pm daily (except on Sunday when they don't run at all). The boat ticket is 30B one way. On Saturday afternoon, Thai Immigration charges a 280B 'overtime' fee for stamping your passport on the other side.

Car or motorbike taxis from Vientiane to Tha Deua charge a standard 100B for the trip. You can also ride a bus (it departs roughly every half hour) from the Morning Market out to Tha Deua for the kip equivalent of 8B.

Getting Around
Central Vientiane is entirely accessible on foot. For trips to neighbouring districts, however, you'll need vehicular support.

To/From the Airport Taxis wait in front of the airport for passengers going into town. The going rate for foreigners seems to be 100B, which is overpriced considering it's only a 10 or 15-minute ride to the town centre. If you can catch a motorbike taxi (jumbo), the fare is only 25B or about US$1, but motorbike taxis aren't always available. There are no public buses direct from the airport, but if you walk 100 metres south of the terminal to Thanon Luang Prabang, you can catch a bus into town (turn left) for around 8B.

Going out to the airport, you can catch a Phon Hong bus from the Morning Market.

Bus There is a city bus system but it's not oriented toward central Chanthabuli where most of the hotels, restaurants, sightseeing and shopping are located. Rather, it's for transport to outlying districts to the north, east and west of Chanthabuli. Fares for any distance within Vientiane Prefecture are low – about US$0.25 for a 20-km ride.

Car Taxi Only a handful of car taxis operate in Vientiane, and these are stationed in front of the Lane Xang and Santiphap hotels, at the Morning Market (best rates) as well as at the airport during flight arrival times. For most short trips within town, a pedicab or motorbike is more economical, since car taxis are usually reserved for longer trips (to Wattay Airport or to the Thailand ferry pier in Tha Deua) and for hourly or daily hire. A car and driver for the day costs from US$10 to US$12 if you bargain well. At the Lane Xang Hotel, it's a standard US$20 a day.

Motorbike Taxi The standard size holds two or three passengers. The larger 'jumbos' have two short benches in back and can hold four, five or even six passengers if they're not too large. Hire charges are about the same as for pedicabs but, of course, they're much speedier. A jumbo driver will be glad to take passengers on journeys as short as half a km or, for US$4-5 one way, as far as 20 km.

Bicycle At the moment, there is only one place that rents bicycles on a regular basis. This is the bicycle shop across from the immigration office near the Morning Market, on the south-west corner of Thanon

Lan Xang and Thanon Talaat Sao. Hire charges depend on the condition of the bicycle but usually cost around US$2 a day. Some hotels will occasionally hire bicycles belonging to the staff.

Pedicabs Bicycle samlors in Vientiane charge around US$0.25 per km.

AROUND VIENTIANE
Ang Nam Ngum (Nam Ngum Reservoir)
Approximately 90 km north from Vientiane, Ang Nam Ngum is a huge artificial lake that was created by damming the Nam Ngum River. A hydroelectric plant here generates most of the power used in the Vientiane Valley as well as the power sold to Thailand via high-power wires over the Mekong River.

The lake is dotted with picturesque islands and a cruise is well worth arranging (US$3 per person is the going rate).

Places to Stay Ang Nam Ngum can be visited on a day trip from Vientiane. Lao Tourism has bungalows near the dam and Vientiane Tourism has some on one of the islands, but for these you would probably have to book a tour from Vientiane. Ask around about private accommodation, usually around US$2 a night.

Getting There & Away You don't need a travel pass to go to Ang Nam Ngum from Vientiane. From the Morning Market, you can catch the 7 am bus all the way to Kheuan Nam Ngum (Nam Ngum Dam) for US$0.50. This trip takes three hours and proceeds along Route 13 through Ban Thalat. Taxis in Vientiane charge US$30 return to the lake. If you hire one, ask the driver to take the more scenic Route 10 through Ban Koen, which is about the same distance as via Ban Thalat. Or make a circle route to see both areas.

Northern Laos

LUANG PRABANG

The Luang Prabang area was the site of early Thai-Lao muangs that were established in the high river valleys along the Mekong River and its major tributaries, the Nam Khan, the Nam Ou and the Nam Seuang (Xeuang). The first Lao Kingdom, Lan Xang, was consolidated here in 1353 by the Khmer-supported conqueror Fa Ngum. Luang Prabang remained the capital of Lan Xang until King Phothisarat moved the seat of administration to Vientiane in 1545.

Even after the Lan Xang period, Luang Prabang was considered the main source of monarchical power. When Lan Xang broke up following the death of King Suliya Vongsa in 1694, one of Suliya's grandsons established an independent kingdom in Luang Prabang that competed with the other kingdoms in Vientiane and Champasak. From then on, the Luang Prabang monarchy was so weak that it was forced to pay tribute at various times to the Siamese and the Vietnamese, and, finally, in the early 20th century, to the French when Laos became a French protectorate.

The French allowed Laos to retain the Luang Prabang monarchy, however, as did the fledgling independent governments that followed, and it wasn't until the Vietnamese-backed Pathet Lao took over in 1975 that the monarchy was finally dissolved.

Today, Luang Prabang is a sleepy town of 20,000 inhabitants and it has a handful of historic temples and old French mansions in a beautiful mountain setting.

Orientation

The town sits at the confluence of the Mekong River and the Nam Khan. A large hill called Phu Si (sometimes spelt Phousy) dominates the town skyline at the upper end of a peninsula formed by the junction of the two rivers. Most of the historic temples are between Phu Si and the Mekong. The whole town can easily be covered, on foot, in a day or two.

Information

The Lao Tourism office, in the Mittaphab Hotel on the south-east edge of town, is geared toward guiding package tours around Luang Prabang. Unless you're part of a tour they're not likely to offer much in the way of assistance. If you aren't part of a tour, you'd best avoid them.

Lao Tourism's standard two-day itinerary takes visitors to Wat Chom Si and Wat Xieng Thong on the first day (sometimes other wats if there is time – Luang Prabang flights are often late arriving), then the Palace Museum, the Pak Ou Caves and a couple of nearby villages on the second. If the group is smaller than four people, Lao Tourism will omit the Pak Ou excursion or ask for a surcharge of US$36.

An excellent French guidebook to the town, if you can find it, is *Louang Prabang* by Thao Boun Souk (pen name for Pierre-Marie Gagneaux), which was published in 1974 by the now-defunct Bulletin des Amis du Royaume Lao. The Lao Tourism guides rely heavily on this little book.

Money It is best to bring enough kip from Vientiane for your stay in Luang Prabang. The Mittaphab Hotel can exchange US$ for kip at the official rate. Other than this, there are no moneychanging facilities in town, nor does the black market seem especially active.

Post & Telecommunications The post office (opposite the Phousy Hotel on Thanon Phothisarat) is notoriously unreliable. Calls to Vientiane can be made from the Mittaphab Hotel. As for international calls, wait until you're back in Vientiane.

Things to See

National Museum (Royal Palace) This is a good place to start a tour of Luang Prabang since the displays convey some sense of local history. The palace was originally constructed beside the Mekong River in 1904 as

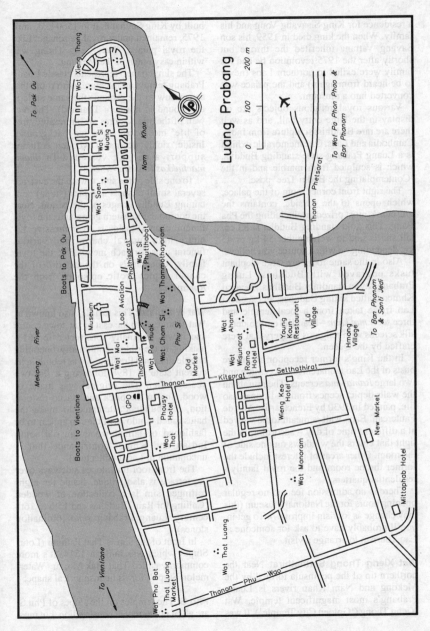

Luang Prabang

a residence for King Sisavang Vong and his family. When the king died in 1959, his son Savang Vattana inherited the throne but shortly after the 1975 revolution he and his family were exiled to northern Laos (never to be heard from again) and the palace was converted into a museum.

Various royal religious objects are on display in the large entry hall, and as well there are rare Buddhist sculpture from India, Cambodia and Laos. One memorable exhibit is a Luang Prabang-style standing Buddha, which is sculpted from marble and in the 'Contemplating the Bodhi Tree' pose.

The right front corner room of the palace, which opens to the outside, contains the museum's most prized art, including the Pha Bang. This gold standing Buddha is 83 cm tall and is said to weigh either 54 kg or 43 kg, depending on which source you believe.

Also in the same room are large elephant tusks engraved with Buddhas, Luang Prabang-style standing Buddhas, several Khmer-crafted sitting Buddhas, an excellent Lao frieze taken from a local temple and three *saew mai khan* – beautiful embroidered silk screens with religious imagery that were crafted by the Queen.

In the King's former reception room are busts of the Lao monarchical succession and two large *Ramayana* screens. The murals on the walls depict scenes from traditional Lao life, painted in 1930 by French artist Alix de Fautereau. Each wall is meant to be viewed at a different time of day – according to the light that enters the windows on one side of the room. Other areas of interest include the former throne room and the royal family's residential quarters.

There is no admission fee and no regular opening hours for the National Museum (this may change as tourism improves). To get in, you'll probably have to ask for someone at Lao Tourism to arrange a visit.

Wat Xieng Thong Setthathirat Near the northern tip of the peninsula formed by the Mekong and Nam Khan rivers is Luang Prabang's most magnificent temple, Wat Xieng Thong ('Golden City Temple'). It was built by King Setthathirat in 1560 and, until 1975, remained under royal patronage. Like the royal palace, Wat Xieng Thong was within easy reach of the Mekong.

The sim (chapel) represents classic Luang Prabang temple architecture, with roofs that sweep low to the ground (the same style is also found in northern Thailand). The rear wall of the sim features an impressive 'tree of life' mosaic set in a red background. Inside, richly decorated wooden columns support a ceiling vested with *dhammachakkas* (dharma-wheels).

To one side of the sim, toward the east, are several small chapels and *that* (stupa) containing Buddha images of the period. Near the compound's eastern gate stands the royal funeral chapel. Inside is an impressive 12-metre high funeral chariot and various funeral urns for each member of the royal family. Gilt panels on the exterior of the chapel depict erotic episodes from the *Ramayana*.

Wat Wisunarat This temple, also known as Wat Visoun, is to the east of the town centre and it was originally constructed in 1513, making it the oldest continually operating temple in Luang Prabang. It was rebuilt in its current state in 1898 following a fire two years earlier. The original was made of wood, and in the brick and stucco restoration, the builders attempted to make the balustraded windows of the sim appear to be fashioned of lathed wood (an old south Indian and Khmer contrivance that is uncommon in Lao architecture).

The front roof that slopes sideways over the terrace is also unique. Inside the high-ceilinged sim is a collection of wooden 'Calling for Rain' Buddhas and 15th to 16th century Luang Prabang *sima* (ordination stones).

In front of the sim is That Pathum (Lotus Stupa) which was built in 1514. It's more commonly called That Mak Mo, or 'Watermelon Stupa', for its hemispherical shape.

Phu Si The temples on the slopes of Phu Si are all of rather recent construction, but most likely there were other temples previously located at this important hill site. None of the temples are that memorable but the top of the hill affords an excellent view of the town.

On the lower slopes of the hill are **Wat Pa Huak** and **Wat Pa Thip**. At the summit is **Wat Chom Si**, the starting point for a colourful Lao New Year procession held in mid-April. Behind this temple is a small cave shrine called **Wat Thammothayaram**, or **Wat Tham Phu Si**. On a nearby crest is an old Russian anti-aircraft cannon that children use as a makeshift merry-go-round. Below Wat Chom Si is **Wat Si Phutthabat**, a temple that boasts a Buddha footprint shrine.

Other Temples Close to the Phousy Hotel and the GPO is **Wat Mai**, or 'New Temple', built in 1796 and at one time a residence of the Sangkharat or Supreme Patriarch of the Lao Sangha. The front verandah is remarkable for its decorated columns and for the sumptuous gold relief panels on the doors that recount the legend of Vessantara (Pha Wet), the Buddha's penultimate incarnation, as well as scenes from the *Ramayana* and local village life. The Pha Bang, which is usually housed in Luang Prabang's National Museum, is put on public display at Wat Mai during the Lao New Year celebrations.

Across the Mekong River from central Luang Prabang are several temples that aren't remarkable except for the pleasant rural settings. **Wat Tham** is in a limestone cave almost directly across the river from Wat Xieng Thong. Many Buddha images from temples that have burned down or fallen into decay are kept here. Nearby Wat Tham are several other caves that are easily found and explored – bring along a torch (flashlight).

Wat Long Khun is a little to the east of Wat Tham and features a nicely decorated portico of 1937 vintage, plus older sections from the 18th century. When the coronation of a Luang Prabang king was pending, it was customary for him to spend three days in retreat at Wat Long Khun before ascending the throne.

At the top of a hill above the previous two

wats is peaceful **Wat Chom Phet**, where one can obtain an undisturbed view of the river.

A few km to the east of town is the recently constructed **Santi Jedi**, or Peace Pagoda. This large yellow stupa contains three levels inside plus an outside terrace near the top with a view of the surrounding plains. The interior walls are painted with all manner of Buddhists stories and moral admonitions.

Wat Pa Phon Phao is a forest meditation wat about three km east of the airport. The teacher, Ajaan Sai Samut, is well-known and respected for his teaching of vipassana, or insight meditation. If travellers would like to meet with Ajaan Sai, they should bring along a Lao interpreter.

Behind the That Luang market in town is a modern Vietnamese-Lao Buddhist temple, **Wat Pha Bat**.

Markets The main fresh produce market, **Talaat That Luang**, is at the intersection of Thanon Phothisarat and Thanon Phu Wao near the river, behind Wat That Luang. A big market for dry goods is held daily off Thanon Setthathirat, the town's broadest avenue. This market will be moving to a new location on the eastern edge of town within the next couple of years. There is a morning fruit and vegetable market where Thanon Setthathirat terminates at the Mekong River.

Places to Stay
The *Phousy (Phu Si) Hotel* is well-located at the corner of Thanon Setthathirat and Thanon Phothisarat (at the site of the former French Commissary), and is within walking distance of both markets. Large rooms with fan and bath are US$20/25 – a bit expensive but there's not much to choose from in Luang Prabang. The Phousy Hotel has an interior restaurant as well as a garden restaurant out front.

The *Mittaphab*, or 'Friendship', Hotel (previously known as the Luang Prabang Hotel) sits on Phu Wao, or 'Kite Hill', on the eastern edge of town. Modern rooms with air-con are US$25/35 and there's also a pool, bar and large restaurant.

The city plans to add two new hotels near

Wat Wisunarat, the *Rama* and the *Wieng Keo*. Both will cater to visiting businesspeople rather than to tourists but they'll be open to foreigners – rates are expected to be around US$10 a night.

Places to Eat

The restaurants in the two tourist hotels are pretty fair. The *Mittaphab Hotel* restaurant is also a bit of a nightspot – the poolside tables are a popular gathering place on weeknights, and on weekends there is usually a live band.

There are numerous small restaurants and cafes along Thanon Phothisarat near the Phousy Hotel, some of which specialise in laap. The *Young Koun Restaurant*, across the street from Wat Wisunarat, has Lao and Chinese food at fairly reasonable prices.

Getting There & Away

Air Lao Aviation has daily flights from Vientiane to Luang Prabang. The flight is only 40 minutes and the fare is about US$33.

As with all travel outside of Vientiane, passengers are supposed to be in possession of a valid travel pass before boarding flights to Vientiane.

Boat Several times a week ferries leave Vientiane's north jetty on the Mekong River for Luang Prabang. The length of the voyage depends on the river height but is typically three nights up and two nights down. The fare is about US$7 per person and on many boats you must bring your own food.

AROUND LUANG PRABANG

Pak Ou Caves

About 30 km by boat from Luang Prabang along the Mekong River, at the mouth of the Nam Ou, are the famous Pak Ou Caves (Pak Ou means 'Mouth of the Ou'). The two caves in the lower part of a limestone cliff are crammed with a variety of Buddha images, most of them are classic Luang Prabang standing Buddhas. The lower cave, called Tham Thing, is entered from the river by a series of steps and can easily be seen in daylight. Stairs to the left of Tham Thing lead around to the upper cave, Tham Phum,

which is deeper and thus requires artificial light for viewing – be sure to bring a torch (flashlight) if you want to see both caves.

On the way to Pak Ou, you can have the boatman stop at small villages on the banks of the Mekong, including one that specialises in the production of *lao lao*, distilled rice liquor.

Getting There & Away You can hire boats from the pier behind the National Palace Museum. A long-tail boat should cost about US$20 for the day, including petrol. The trip takes one to 1½ hours each way, depending on the speed of the boat. If you stop at villages along the way, it will naturally take longer.

Ban Phanom

This Lü village, a few km past the airport (east of Luang Prabang), is well known for cotton and silk hand-weaving. On weekends, a small market is set up in the village for the trading of hand-woven cloth, but you can turn up any time and the villagers will bring out cloth for inspection and purchase. Even if you don't wish to buy, it's worth a visit to see the villagers weaving the cloth on their handlooms.

Buses from Luang Prabang to Ban Phanom leave from Thanon Setthathirat several times a day and cost a few hundred kip.

XIENG KHWANG PROVINCE

Along with Hua Phan, Xieng Khwang is one of the northern provinces that was devastated by the war. Virtually every town and village in the province was bombed between 1964 and 1973. Flying into the province, one is struck at first by the awesome beauty of high green mountains, rugged karst formations and verdant valleys. But as the helicopter or plane begins to descend, you notice how much of the province is pock-marked with bomb craters in which little or no vegetation grows.

The province's population of 120,000 is comprised of lowland Lao, Thai Dam, Hmong and Phuan. The original capital city,

Xieng Khwang, was almost totally bombed out, so the capital was moved to nearby Phonsawan (often spelt Phonsavanh) after the 1975 change of government. Not far from Phonsawan is the mysterious Plain of Jars (Thong Hai Hin).

The moderate altitude in central Xieng Khwang, including Phonsawan and the Plain of Jars, means an excellent year-round climate – not too hot in the hot season, not too cold in the cool season and not overly wet in the rainy season.

Phonsawan

There's not much to the new provincial capital – an airfield, a semipaved main street lined with tin-roofed shops, a market and a few government buildings. Local villagers bring war junk, found in their fields or in the forests, to scrap metal warehouses in town. The warehouses buy the scrap (eg bomb shards, parts of Chinese, Russian and American planes) for US$0.55 a kg, then sell it to larger warehouses in Vientiane, who in turn sell it to the Thais.

Take care when walking in the fields around Phonsawan, as undetonated live bombs are not uncommon. The locals use bomb casings as pillars for new structures and as fenceposts. Muddy areas are sometimes dotted with pineapple bombs or bomblets – fist-sized explosives that are left over from cluster bombs dropped in the 1970s.

Places to Stay & Eat The government guest house, which is on a hill overlooking the town, has 15 rooms with mosquito nets, towels, soap and a shared cold-water shower that is sometimes without water. Rooms are US$2 per person per night. Meals are served at the guest house but must be arranged in advance. The small Plain of Jars Hotel has recently opened in Phonsawan and should cost around US$10 a night.

Along the road that leads from the airfield are several noodle shops. At night, one of the noodle shops has live music. You can also buy food, including fresh produce, in the market in the centre of town.

Getting There & Away Until late 1990, the only way to get to Xieng Khwang from Vientiane was by Lao Aviation helicopter – quite an experience. A slightly upgraded airfield now handles small planes as well. Flights are scheduled to leave Vientiane at 8 am every day, except Tuesday and Sunday, arriving in Phonsawan an hour later. On the return trip, flights are scheduled to leave at 10 am. Delays are common due to mountain fog. The fare is US$27 one way.

Getting Around Buses (actually trucks with benches in back) go from Phonsawan to Muang Kham for US$0.50 or all the way to Nong Haet for US$0.70.

Plain of Jars

About 12 km from Phonsawan is an area of rolling fields where huge jars of unknown origin are scattered about. The jars weigh an average of 600 kg to one tonne each, though the biggest of them weigh as much as six tonnes. They appear to have been fashioned from solid stone, but there is disagreement on this point.

Various theories have been advanced as to the functions of the stone jars – that they were used as sarcophagi, as wine fermenters or for rice storage. No conclusive evidence, confirming one theory or another, has yet been substantiated.

The nearby limestone cave, which has smokeholes in the top, is said to have been a kiln for firing the jars – assuming they're not made of solid stone. Many of the smaller jars have been taken away by collectors, but there are still several hundred or so on the plain.

Tham Piu

In this cave, near the former village of Ban Nameun, nearly 400 villagers, many of them women and children, were killed by a single rocket (most likely from an American aircraft) in 1969. The cave itself is not much to see – just a large cave in the side of a limestone cliff. It's the journey to Tham Piu that is the real attraction, since it passes several Hmong and Thai Dam villages along the way and involves a bit of hiking in the forest.

The cave is a few km beyond the small town of Muang Kham, which is 30 km east of Phonsawan on Route 6. Also in this area is a hot mineral springs *(baw nam hawn)* that feeds into a stream a few hundred metres off the road. You can sit in the stream right where the hot water combines with the cool stream water and 'adjust' the temperature by moving around.

Further east along the same road, 120 km from Phonsawan, is the market town of Nong Haet, only about 25 km short of the Vietnam border.

Getting There & Away To get to Tham Piu, you'd have to take a Nong Haet bus from Phonsawan and ask to be let out at the turn-off for Tham Piu. From the turn-off, start walking towards the limestone cliff north of the road until you're within a km of the cliff.

At this point you have to plunge into the woods and make your way along a honey-comb of trails to the bottom of the cliff and then mount a steep, narrow trail that leads up to the mouth of the cave. It is best to ask for directions from villagers along the way or you're liable to get lost. Better yet, find someone in Phonsawan who knows the way and invite them along for an afternoon hike.

You might be able to hire a jeep and driver in town for around US$20 a day.

Southern Laos

Only three provinces in the south of Laos were open to tourists in 1991: Savannakhet, Salavan and Champasak. The Mekong River Valley, including the towns of Savannakhet (also known as Muang Khanthabuli), Salavan and Pak Se, is mostly inhabited by lowland Lao. The central highlands are populated by a mixture of Phu Thai, Saek (Sek) and Lao peoples.

Although Lao Tourism has tour itineraries for the south, very few people have booked them as yet as the initial interest has been in Vientiane and Luang Prabang.

SAVANNAKHET PROVINCE

Savannakhet is the country's most populous province (312,000) and is a very active trade junction between Thailand and Vietnam. The rural villages of Savannakhet are among the most typically Lao, especially those near the Vietnam border.

The provincial capital is **Savannakhet**, a busy town of 45,000 just across the Mekong River from Mukdahan, Thailand.

Places to Stay

Lao Tourism has restored four government villas for use by tour groups. The *Santiphap Hotel* on Thanon Tha Dan is frequented by businesspeople and it has reasonably-priced rooms.

Getting There & Away

Air Lao Aviation flies Antonov-24 turbo-props to Savannakhet, daily, at 7 am and returns at 9.05 am. Flights take an hour and 10 minutes one way and cost US$52.

Boat A large river ferry leaves Vientiane's south jetty (Tha Heua Lak Si) every Friday morning at 6 am, arriving in Savannakhet on Saturday evening. The fare is around US$3 per person and food is usually available on board. Coming back to Vientiane, boats leave Tuesday morning and arrive Thursday.

SALAVAN PROVINCE

The big attraction in Salavan is the **Boloven Plateau**, which is actually on the border between Salavan and Champasak. On the Se Set (Xet) River (a tributary of the Se Don) are several waterfalls and traditional Lao villages. Lao Tourism has built bungalows at one of the falls for use by their tours. Like the Plain of Jars in Xieng Khwang Province, the Boloven Plateau has an excellent climate.

Near the Vietnamese border, on the former Ho Chi Minh Trail, are a few traditional Boloven (Phu Thai) villages. A Boloven village features houses that are arranged in a circle. Once a year, water buffalo sacrifices are held in the middle of the circle.

The provincial capital of Salavan was all but destroyed in the war. The rebuilt town is a collection of brick and wood buildings with a population of around 40,000.

Getting There & Away

Lao Aviation has a Thursday flight to Salavan via Savannakhet. The flight leaves Vientiane at 7 am, then leaves Savannakhet at 9.05 am, arriving in Salavan at 9.40. In the reverse direction, the flight leaves Salavan at 10.40 am. The fare is US$74 one way from Vientiane or US$22 from Savannakhet.

You can also get to Salavan by bus or truck from Pak Se in Champasak Province.

CHAMPASAK PROVINCE

The Champasak area has a long history that began with the Thai muangs 1000 years ago. Between the 10th to 13th centuries it was part of the Cambodian Angkor Empire. Between the 15th and late 17th centuries, it was an important Lan Xang outpost but it later became an independent Lao Kingdom when the Lan Xang Empire disintegrated at the beginning of 18th century.

Champasak Province has a population of around 160,000 that includes lowland Lao, Khmers and Phu Thai. The province is well known for *mat-mii*, silks and cottons that are hand-woven of tie-dyed threads.

Pak Se

Pak Se is a relatively new town at the confluence of the Mekong and the Se Don that was founded, in 1905, by the French as an administrative outpost. It is now the capital of Champasak Province (formerly three separate provinces – Champasak, Xedon and Sithandon) but has little of interest except the lively market. Lao Tourism accommodation here is in a 30-room restored French colonial villa, outside of town and towards the Boloven Plateau.

Pak Se is also the gateway for trips to the former royal capital of Champasak and the Angkor temple ruins of Wat Phu.

Getting There & Away Pak Se can be reached by road from Salavan or by air from Vientiane. Lao Aviation flies to Pak Se every day at 7 am. On Monday, Wednesday and Saturday they fly via Savan, arriving in Pak Se at 9.45 am. On all other days, the flight is direct and arrives at 8.30 am. The return flights leave an hour after arrival at Pak Se. The fare is US$85 one way.

Friday flights to Pak Se continue on to Phnom Penh at 9.30 am. The one-way fare between Pak Se and Phnom Penh is US$35.

Wat Phu

This Angkor-period (10th to 13th centuries) Khmer temple site is on the lower slopes of Phu Pasak, about eight km from the town of Champasak (population 24,000). The Lao government supposedly has plans to restore the site, with international aid, and establish a national museum in Champasak. It's badly in need of restoration or it will soon be nothing but scrambled chunks of rock.

The site is divided into lower and upper parts joined by a stairway. The lower part consists of two ruined palace buildings at the edge of a pond used for ritual ablutions.

The upper section is the temple sanctuary itself, which once enclosed a large Shiva phallus. Some time later it was converted into a Buddhist temple but the original Hindu sculpture remains in the lintels, which feature various forms of Vishnu and Shiva as well as Kala, the Hindu god of time and death. The *naga* (dragon) stairway leading to the sanctuary is lined with plumeria *(dok jampa)* which is the Lao national tree. The upper platform affords a good view of the valley below.

Festivals Near Wat Phu is a large crocodile stone that may have been the site of the purported Chen La sacrifices. Each year, in June, the locals perform a ritual water buffalo sacrifice to the ruling earth spirit for Champasak, Chao Tengkham. The blood of the buffalo is offered to a local shaman who serves as a trance medium for the appearance of Chao Tengkham.

Another important local festival is Bun Wat Phu, when pilgrims from throughout southern Laos come to worship at Wat Phu in its Buddhist incarnation. The festival lasts three days and features Thai boxing matches, cockfights, music and dancing. It's held as part of Magha Puja (*Makkha Bu-saa*) at the full moon in February.

Getting There & Away Wat Phu is 46 km south from Pak Se but only eight km from Champasak. When hiring a taxi from Champasak, ask for Muang Kao (old city). Champasak can be reached by road or ferry boat (along the Mekong River) from Pak Se.

Um Muang
Um Muang is a Khmer temple ruin of the same period (10th to 13th centuries) as Wat Phu. It's about 45 km south of Pak Se, off Route 13, on a small tributary of the Mekong. What's left of the temple includes an esplanade bordered by *lingas* (sacred Shiva phalli), a large vestibule and lintel remains sculpted with Vaishnavaite motifs.

Macau

Sixty km west of Hong Kong, on the other side of the Pearl River's mouth, is the oldest European settlement in the East – the tiny Portuguese territory of Macau. The lure of Macau's casino gaming tables has been so actively promoted that its other attractions are almost forgotten.

It's actually one of the most fascinating places in Asia – steeped in history and, with a little effort, cheap and comfortable. If you're in Hong Kong, don't miss Macau.

Facts about the Country

HISTORY

Macau has a far longer history than its younger and brasher sister Hong Kong – and it certainly shows. Portuguese galleons were dropping by here in the early 1500s, and in 1557, as a reward for clearing out a few pirates, China ceded the tiny enclave to the Portuguese.

For centuries, it was the principal meeting point for trade with China – a look around the intriguing old Protestant Cemetery will show just how international this trade was. In the 19th century, European and American traders could operate in Canton, up the Pearl River, only during the trading season. They would then retreat to Macau during the off season.

When the Opium Wars erupted between the Chinese and the aggressive (and somewhat unprincipled) British, the Portuguese stood diplomatically to one side and Macau soon found itself the poor relation of the more dynamic city of Hong Kong.

More recently, Macau's existence has depended on the Chinese gambling urge that every weekend sends hordes of Hong Kong's more affluent citizens shuttling off to the casinos. Today, however, Macau does very well as an overflow valve for booming Hong Kong with many thriving industries and an important role as a doorway to the People's Republic of China.

During the Cultural Revolution, Macau suffered more than Hong Kong and virtually capitulated to Chinese management. Later, while the heavy negotiations went on over Hong Kong, the Macau situation was very much on the back burner. With Hong Kong sorted out, the Chinese soon turned their attention to Macau, which will be handed back in 1999, two years after Hong Kong. It's said the Portuguese wanted to last out 500 years, which would have taken them well into the next century. They finally settled for any date which put them one up on Hong Kong!

GEOGRAPHY

Macau's 16 sq km consists of the city itself, which is part of the Chinese mainland, and the islands of Taipa and Coloane, which are joined together by a causeway and linked to Macau city by a bridge.

CLIMATE

The weather is almost identical to that of Hong Kong, with short, occasionally chilly winters, and long, hot and humid summers. November is usually the best month, with mild temperatures and dry weather. Typhoons are most common from June to October.

GOVERNMENT

Officially, Macau is not considered a colony. Instead, the Portuguese government regards Macau as a piece of Chinese territory under Portuguese administration. The colony/Chinese territory has a governor who is appointed by the Portugal's president, but in theory the main governing body is the 23-member Legislative Assembly of which eight members are elected by direct vote, while the remainder are appointed by the Governor and 'economic interest groups'.

ECONOMY

The spin of the wheel and the toss of the dice still play an important part in Macau's economy, but there's also a variety of local industries including textiles and toys. Macau is currently building an airport and deep-water port which are expected to give the economy a major boost.

POPULATION & PEOPLE

Macau has about half a million people. About 95% are Chinese, 3% are Portuguese and there is a sprinkling of other Western nationalities. Nearly 1% of the population is from Thailand, mostly female and employed in what is loosely called the 'entertainment industry'.

CULTURE

The Chinese population is indistinguishable culturally from that of Hong Kong. See the Hong Kong chapter of this book for details.

Of course, the Portuguese minority has a vastly different culture, which they have kept largely intact. Although mixed marriages are not uncommon in Macau, there has been little cultural assimilation between the two ethnic groups – most Portuguese cannot speak Chinese and vice versa.

RELIGION

For the Chinese majority, Buddhism and Taoism are the dominant religions. However, nearly 500 years of Portuguese influence have definitely left an imprint, and Catholicism is very strong in Macau. Many Chinese have been converted and you are likely to see Chinese nuns.

LANGUAGE

Portuguese may be the official language but Cantonese is the real one. However, you will have little trouble communicating with English, especially in hotels. Mandarin Chinese – putonghua – is also very common. See the Hong Kong chapter for a few Cantonese phrases. Here are a few Portuguese words and phrases:

Useful Words & Phrases

How much does this cost?
  quanto custa isso?
Leave me alone!
  me deixa em paz!
The bill please
  a conta por favo
Too expensive
  *caro demai*s guest house
  hospedaria or *vila*
hotel
  pousada
market
  mercado
pier
  ponte-cais
post office
  correios
street
  rua

Facts for the Visitor

VISAS & EMBASSIES

For most visitors, all that's needed to enter Macau is a passport. Everyone gets a 20-day stay on arrival. Visas are not required for nationals of these countries: Australia, Austria, Belgium, Brazil, Canada, Denmark, France, Germany, Greece, Hong Kong, Ireland, Italy, Japan, Luxembourg, Malaysia, Netherlands, New Zealand, Norway, Philippines, Singapore, South Korea, Spain, Sweden, Switzerland, Taiwan, Thailand, UK and USA.

All other nationalities must have a visa, which can be obtained on arrival in Macau. Visas cost 145 patacas for individuals, 290 patacas for married couples and families, 72 patacas for children under 12, and 72 patacas per person in a bona fide group of at least 10 persons. People holding passports from countries which do not have diplomatic relations with Portugal must obtain visas from an overseas Portuguese consulate before entering Macau. The Portuguese Consulate (☎ 522 5488) in Hong Kong is on the 10th

Floor, Tower Two, Exchange Square, Central.

MONEY
Currency
The pataca is divided into 100 avos and is worth about 4% less than the HK$. HK$ are accepted everywhere, which is just as well because there's nowhere to change currency on arrival. So make sure you have some HK$ or you'll have difficulty getting from the Jetfoil Pier into town!

Although Hong Kong coins are quite acceptable in Macau, you'll need pataca coins to make calls at public telephones. Get rid of your patacas before departing Macau – they are hard to get rid of in Hong Kong, though you can change them at the Hang Seng Bank.

Exchange Rates
A$1	=	6.34 patacas
C$1	=	7.07 patacas
HK$1	=	1.04 patacas
NZ$1	=	4.68 patacas
UK£1	=	13.76 patacas
US$1	=	8.00 patacas

Costs
As long as you don't go crazy at the roulette wheel or slot machines, Macau is cheaper than Hong Kong. To help keep costs down, avoid weekends.

Tipping
Classy hotels and restaurants automatically hit you with a 10% service charge, which is supposedly a mandatory tip. Just how much of this money actually goes to the employees is a matter for speculation.

You can follow your own conscience, but tipping is not customary among the Chinese. Of course, porters at expensive hotels have become accustomed to hand-outs from well-heeled tourists.

Bargaining
Most stores have fixed prices, but if you buy clothing, trinkets and other tourist junk from the street markets, there is some scope for bargaining. On the other hand, if you buy from the pawnshops, bargain ruthlessly. Pawnbrokers are more than happy to charge Western tourists five times the going price for second-hand cameras and other goods.

TOURIST OFFICES
Local Tourist Offices
The Macau Government tourist office (☎ 31 5566) is at Largo do Senado, Edificio Ritz No 9, next to the Leal Senado building in the square in the centre of Macau.

Overseas Tourist Offices
On Hong Kong Island, there's an excellent Macau Government tourist office (☎ 540 8180) at Room 305, Shun Tak Centre, 200 Connaught Rd, next to the Macau Ferry Pier.

BUSINESS HOURS & HOLIDAYS
The operating hours for most government offices in Macau are weekdays from 8.40 am to 1 pm and from 3 to 5 pm, and Saturday from 8.40 am to 1 pm. Private businesses keep longer hours and some casinos are open 24 hours a day.

Banks are normally open on weekdays from 9 am to 4 pm, and on Saturday from 9 am until 12 noon.

The Chinese in Macau celebrate the same religious festivals as their counterparts in Hong Kong but there are also a number of Catholic festivals and some Portuguese national holidays. Most important is the Feast of Our Lady of Fatima when the Fatima image is removed from Sao Domingos (St Dominic's) Church and taken in procession around the city.

Macau's main festival time is November when the Grand Prix is held – it's not a good time to go unless you're a racing fan as the place is packed and prices skyrocket. As in Monte Carlo and Adelaide (Australia), the actual streets of the town make up the raceway. There are in fact two races, one for cars and one for motorbikes, plus various support races. The six-km circuit attracts contestants from all over the world.

CULTURAL EVENTS

Find out about cultural events, concerts, art exhibitions and other such activities from the tourist newspaper *Macau Travel Talk*. Free copies are available from the tourist office.

The Dragon Boat Festival is a Chinese holiday well known for its exciting dragon boat races. Similar races are held in Hong Kong and Taiwan. The Dragon Boat Festival, scheduled according to the lunar calendar, usually takes place during June.

The International Music Festival is held during the third week of October.

POST & TELECOMMUNICATIONS
Postal Rates

Domestic letters cost 80 avos for up to 20 grams. As for international mail, Macau divides the world into zones. Zone 1 is east Asia, including Korea, Taiwan, etc; Zone 2 is everywhere else. There are special rates for China and Portugal.

The GPO on Largo do Senado is open from 9 am to 8 pm Monday to Saturday. It has an efficient poste-restante service and English-speaking postal clerks. Large hotels like the Lisboa also sell stamps.

Telephones

Companhia de Telecomunicacoes (CTM) runs the Macau telephone system, and for the most part the service is good. However, public pay phones can be hard to find, being mostly concentrated around the Leal Senado. Most large hotels have one in the lobby, but this is often insufficient and you may have to stand in line to use one.

Local calls are free from a private or hotel telephone. At a public pay phone, local calls cost 1 pataca for five minutes. All pay phones permit international direct dialling (IDD). The procedure for dialling to Hong Kong is totally different to all other countries. You first dial 01 and then the number you want to call – you must *not* dial the country code.

The international access code for every country *except* Hong Kong is 00. To call into Macau from abroad, the country code is 853.

Telephone cards from CTM are sold in denominations of 50, 100 and 200 patacas.

A lot of phones which accept these cards are found around Leal Senado, the Jetfoil Pier and at a few large hotels. You can also make a call from the telephone office at Largo do Senado, next to the GPO. Leave a deposit with a clerk and they will dial the number for you. When your call is completed, the clerk deducts the cost from the deposit and refunds the balance. The clerks speak English and the office is open 24 hours.

TIME

Like Hong Kong, Macau is eight hours ahead of GMT and does not observe daylight-saving time.

When it is 12 noon in Macau, it is also 12 noon in Singapore, Hong Kong and Perth; 2 pm in Sydney; 8 pm the previous day in Los Angeles; 11 pm the previous day in New York; and 4 am in London.

BOOKS & MAPS

Lonely Planet's *Hong Kong, Macau & Canton – a travel survival kit* has a section on Macau with much more information. There are various books on Macau which are available in Hong Kong (try Wanderlust Books, 30 Hollywood Rd, Central) or the Macau Government tourist office on Largo do Senado in Macau. The tourist office also publishes the useful little *Macau Guide Book*.

Books about Portugal has a good selection of books in English as well as Portuguese. You'll find it on Rua Nolasco da Silva near the Cathedral.

MEDIA
Newspapers & Magazines

Other than the monthly tourist newspaper *Macau Travel Talk*, there is no English-language newspaper published in Macau. However, both the *South China Morning Post* and *Hong Kong Standard* are readily available from big hotels and some book-shops. It's also easy to buy foreign news magazines.

Radio & TV

Macau has three radio stations, two of which broadcast in Cantonese and one in Portuguese.

There are no local English-language radio stations, but you should be able to pick up Hong Kong stations.

Teledifusao de Macau (TdM) is a government-run station which broadcasts on two channels. The shows are mainly in English and Portuguese, but with some Cantonese programmes. It's easy to pick up Hong Kong stations in Macau (but not vice versa) and you can also receive stations from China. Hong Kong newspapers list Macau TV programmes.

FILM & PHOTOGRAPHY

You can find most types of film, cameras and accessories in Macau, and photoprocessing is of a high standard. The best store in town for all photographic services is Foto Princesa (☎ 55 5959), 55-59 Avenida Infante D'Henrique, one block east of Rua da Praia Grande. This is also the best place to get quickie visa photos.

HEALTH

The water, purified and chlorinated, is OK to drink. Nevertheless, the Chinese always boil it (more out of custom than necessity). Hotel rooms are always supplied with a thermos filled with hot water.

EMERGENCY

The emergency telephone number for fire, police and ambulance is 999. Medical treatment is available at the government-run Centro Hospital (☎ 51 4499, 31 3731) on Estrada Sao Francisco.

DANGERS & ANNOYANCES

In terms of violent crime, Macau is pretty safe, but residential burglaries and pickpocketing are problems. Most hotels are well guarded, and if you take reasonable care with your valuables you should avoid trouble.

Traffic is heavy and quite a few tourists have been hit while jaywalking. Macau police have been cracking down on this, and though they go easy with foreigners, you can still get fined. Be especially careful at rush hour when the traffic (and the police) come out in force.

Cheating at gambling is a serious criminal offence, so don't even think about it.

ACTIVITIES

Windsurfing is possible at Hac Sa Beach on Coloane Island, and rental equipment is readily available. Two good swimming beaches can be found on Coloane – Hac Sa and Cheoc Van. Cheoc Van Beach also has a yacht club.

Bicycles are available for hire on the two islands of Taipa and Coloane.

Getting There & Away

LAND

Macau is an important gateway into China. You simply take a bus to the border and walk across. Bus No 3 runs between the Jetfoil Pier and the Barrier Gate at the Macau-China border. You can also catch a bus directly from Macau to Canton. Tickets are sold at Kee Kwan Motors, across the street from the Floating Casino.

SEA

To/From Hong Kong

Although Macau is separated from Hong Kong by 65 km of water, the journey can be made in as little as one hour. There are frequent departures from both places throughout the day from 7 am to 9.30 pm.

You have a wide selection of boats to choose from. There are jetfoils, hoverferries, jetcats (jet-powered catamarans), jumbocats (large jetcats) and high-speed ferries. There are still two old hydrofoils plying this route, but they are to be retired soon and will most likely be out of service by the time you read this.

Most of the boats depart from the huge Macau Ferry Terminal next to Shun Tak Centre at 200 Connaught Rd, Sheung Wan, Hong Kong Island. This is easily reached by MTR to the Sheung Wan station.

Hoverferries depart from the China Hong Kong City Ferry Terminal in Tsimshatsui. However, these are far less numerous than jetfoils, so if you can't get a seat, go to Shun Tak Centre on Hong Kong Island.

If you have to return to Hong Kong the same day as departure, you'd be wise to book your return ticket in advance because the boats are sometimes full, especially on weekends and holidays. Even Monday morning can be difficult for getting seats back to Hong Kong. If you can't get on the jetfoil, you might have a chance with the high-speed ferries which have a lot more room.

Jetfoil tickets can be purchased up to 28 days in advance in Hong Kong at the pier and at Ticketmate offices in some MTR stations, or booked by phone (☎ 859 5696) if you have a credit card. Jumbocat bookings (☎ 523 2136) can be made 35 days in advance by telephone if you pay with plastic.

If you buy a ticket at any other place than the pier, be certain you understand which pier the boat departs from. Arrive at the pier at least 15 minutes before departure, but it would be wise to allow 30 minutes because of occasional long queues at the immigration checkpoint.

There are different classes on the jetfoils and high-speed ferries. All other boats have only one class. The Hong Kong Government charges HK$20 departure tax which is included in the price of your ticket. There is no such tax when leaving Macau. The prices in the following table do not include the tax.

In Hong Kong, tickets can be bought at the pier and at Ticketmate kiosks in the Tsimshatsui and Jordan Rd MTR stations.

In Macau, you can book tickets on all boats at the Jetfoil Pier. You can also book

tickets on the jetfoil and high-speed ferry right in the lobby of the Hotel Lisboa. A couple of blocks west of the Hotel Central is a window for booking tickets on the jumbocats. Tickets for the hoverferry can only be booked at the Jetfoil Pier.

To/From China

The daily Macau-Canton ferry leaves Canton from Zhoutouzui Pier, south of the White Swan Hotel. From Macau, it departs from the terminus next to the Floating Casino at 8 pm and arrives in Canton at 7.15 am the next day.

Fares range from 69 patacas in 2nd class, for rooms with six to 22 beds, to 100 patacas in 1st class for a bed in a room with four beds, a shower and TV. Finally, there's also special class, which costs 147 patacas for a cabin with just two beds, as well as a TV and shower.

To/From Taiwan

A ferry runs between Macau and the port of Kaohsiung in Taiwan. The name of the ship is the *Macmosa*.

From Taiwan, one-way 1st-class tickets cost NT$3700, and 2nd class is NT$3000. From Macau, a one-way 1st-class fare is 1060 patacas; 2nd class is 860 patacas. Round-trip fares are exactly double.

There is one boat per week during the winter, but at least two per week during the summer months. The journey takes 24 hours. In winter, the ship leaves Kaohsiung at 4 pm on Wednesday. Departures from Macau are at 2 am on Tuesday. Check departure times – they can change.

In Taiwan, you can buy tickets at the pier

Boats To/From Hong Kong				
Vessel	*Travel Time*	*Weekday*	*Weekend*	*Night*
High-Speed Ferry	90 minutes	HK$48/62	HK$60/74	
Hoverferry	80 minutes	HK$60	HK$73	HK$86
Hydrofoil	75 minutes	HK$68	HK$75	
Jetcat	75 minutes	HK$68	HK$75	
Jetfoil	60 minutes	HK$72/82	HK$78/88	HK$95/108
Jumbocat	60 minutes	HK$78	HK$85	

in Kaohsiung or from Kwanghwa Tour & Travel Service in both Taipei and Kaohsiung. The Taipei office (☎ 02-531 0000) is on the 7th Floor, 72 Sungchiang Rd. The Kaohsiung ticket office (☎ 07-282 1166) is on the 6th Floor, 79 Chunghua 3rd Rd. In Kaohsiung, the boat departs from Pier 1 on Penglai Rd – take bus No 1 or a taxi to get there.

In Macau, the best place to purchase tickets is at the Jetfoil Pier. In Hong Kong, you can buy tickets at Kwanghwa Tour & Travel Service (☎ 545 7071), Room 803, Kai Tak Commercial Building, 317-321 Des Voeux Rd, Central, Hong Kong Island. Taiwan charges a departure tax of NT$200. Macau has no departure tax.

Getting Around

Macau is fairly compact and it's relatively easy to walk almost everywhere, but you'll definitely need motorised transport to visit the islands of Taipa and Coloane. The pedicabs are essentially for touristy sightseeing. They have to be bargained for and it's hardly worth the effort – if there are two of you make sure the fare covers both.

BUS

There are minibuses and large buses, and both offer air-con and frequent service. They operate from 7 am until midnight.

You'll find it easier to deal with the bus system if you buy a good map of Macau showing all the routes. For most tourists, bus No 3A is the most important since it connects the Jetfoil Pier to the central area (Leal Senado) and the Floating Casino, then turns south and terminates at Praca Ponta e Horta. The fare is 1.50 patacas.

Another very useful bus is No 3 which starts at the Jetfoil Pier, goes into the city centre past Leal Senado, then turns north at the Floating Casino and heads north, terminating at the China border. If you're going to or coming from China, this is the bus to take. The fare is 1.50 patacas.

The buses to the Macau islands are as follows:

No 11 – Praca Ponte e Horta, Floating Casino, Avenida Almeida Ribeiro, GPO, Hotel Lisboa, Hotel Hyatt Regency (Taipa), Taipa Village, Macau Jockey Club. Fare: 1.60 patacas

No 21 – Praca Ponte e Horta, Floating Casino, Avenida Almeida Ribeiro, GPO, Hotel Lisboa, Hotel Hyatt Regency (Taipa), Restaurante 1999 (Coloane), Coloane Village. Fare: 2.30 patacas

No 21A – Praca Ponte e Horta, Floating Casino, Avenida Almeida Ribeiro, GPO, Hotel Lisboa, Hotel Hyatt Regency (Taipa), Taipa Village, Restaurante 1999 (Coloane), Coloane Village, Cheoc Van Beach, Hac Sa Beach. Fare: 3 patacas

No 28A – Jetfoil Pier, Hotel Lisboa, Hotel Hyatt Regency (Taipa), Macau University, Taipa Village, Macau Jockey Club. Fare: 2 patacas

No 33 – Fai Chi Kei, Lin Fong Miu (Lotus Temple), Avenida Almeida Ribeiro, Hotel Lisboa, Hotel Hyatt Regency (Taipa), Macau University, Taipa Village, Macau Jockey Club. Fare: 2 patacas

No 38 – Special bus running from the city centre to the Macau Jockey Club one hour before the races. Fare: 3 patacas

TAXI

Macau taxis are black with cream roofs. They all have meters and drivers are required to use them. Flagfall is 5.50 patacas for the first 1½ km, thereafter it's 70 avos every 250 metres. There is a 5 patacas surcharge to go to Taipa, and 10 patacas to go to Coloane, but there is no surcharge if you're heading the other way back to Macau. There is also an additional 1 pataca service charge for each piece of luggage carried in the boot (trunk). Not many taxi drivers speak English, so it would be helpful to have a map with both Chinese and English or Portuguese.

CAR

The mere thought of renting a car in Hong Kong is ridiculous but between a group it might make sense for exploring on Taipa and Coloane. On Macau Peninsula, horrendous traffic and the lack of parking space makes driving more of a burden than a pleasure.

As in Hong Kong, driving is on the left-hand side of the road. Another local driving rule is that motor vehicles must always stop for pedestrians at a crosswalk if there is no traffic light. It's illegal to beep the horn.

Macau Mokes (☎ 37 8851) is Macau's rent-a-car pioneer. They are on Avenida Marciano Baptist, just across from the Jetfoil Pier in Macau. There is a Hong Kong office (☎ 543 4190) at 806 Kai Tak Commercial Building, 317-321 Des Voeux Rd, Sheung Wan, near Macau Ferry Terminal on Hong Kong Island. A moke costs 280 patacas on weekdays and 320 patacas on weekends and holidays.

BICYCLE

You can hire bicycles out on the islands of Taipa and Coloane. On the peninsula, there are no places to hire bikes, and it wouldn't be pleasant riding anyway with the insane traffic.

TOURS

A typical city tour (booked in Macau) of the peninsula takes three to four hours and costs about 70 patacas per person, often including lunch. Bus tours out to the islands run from about 20 patacas per person. You can also book a one-day bus tour across the border into Zhuhai in China, which usually includes a trip to the former home of Dr Sun Yat-sen in Zhongshan County. There are large numbers of tour operators.

Around the Country

THINGS TO SEE
Mainland Macau

There's far more of historical interest to be seen in Macau than Hong Kong. Simply wandering around is a delight – the streets are winding and always full of interest. Old hands say it's now getting speedy like Hong Kong but it has a way to go.

The **ruins of Sao Paulo** (St Paul's) are the symbol of Macau – the facade and majestic stairway are all that remain of this old church, considered by many to be one of the greatest monuments to Christianity in the East. It was designed by an Italian Jesuit and

built in 1602 by Japanese refugees who had fled anti-Christian persecution in Nagasaki. In 1853 the church was totally burned down during a catastrophic typhoon – the light from the burning church on its hilltop site lit the way for people escaping from the typhoon floods. *Macau Guide Book* has a description of the stone carvings on the facade.

The **Fortaleza do Monte** overlooks Sao Paulo and almost all of Macau from its high and central position. It was built by the Jesuits at about the same time as Sao Paulo, but the governor of Macau took it over by the neat trick of coming to dinner and at the close of the meal announcing he was going to stay and his hosts could depart. In 1622, a cannonball fired from the fort conveniently landed in a Dutch gunpowder carrier during an attempted Dutch invasion, demolishing most of their fleet.

The most historic and interesting temple in the city, the **Temple of Kun Iam**, has a whole host of interesting things to search out. In the temple study are 18 wise men in a glass case – the one with the big nose is said to be Marco Polo. It was here in 1844 that China and the USA signed a treaty of 'undying friendship'. The 400-year-old temple complex is dedicated to Kun Iam, the queen of heaven and goddess of mercy.

The **Old Protestant Cemetery** is a fascinating place to wander around (if the door is closed, just knock on it). Lord Churchill (one of Winston's ancestors) and the English artist George Chinnery are buried here, but far more interesting are the varied graves of missionaries and their families, traders, seamen and the often detailed accounts of their lives and deaths. One US ship seems to have had half its crew 'fall from aloft' while in port.

On the Praca Luis de Camoes, the fine little **Luis de Camoes Museum** has items from China and a particularly fine collection of paintings, prints and engravings showing Macau in the last two centuries. It's right next door to the cemetery.

The **Portas do Cerco** (Barrier Gate) used to be of interest because you could stand 100 metres from it and claim that you'd seen into China. You might have seen a bus arriving from China or leaving Macau. Now you can be on the bus yourself so the Barrier Gate is of little interest.

The **Leal Senado** (Loyal Senate) looks out over the main town square and is the main administrative body for municipal affairs. At one time it was offered (and turned down) a total monopoly on all Chinese trade! The building also houses the **National Library**.

The highest point in Macau is the **Guía Fortress** overlooking the Jetfoil Pier, with a 17th-century chapel and lighthouse built on it. The lighthouse is the oldest on the China coast, first lit up in 1865.

One of the most beautiful churches in Macau is the **Sao Domingos Church**, a 17th-century building which has an impressive tiered altar. There is a small museum at the back, full of church regalia, images and paintings.

The beautiful and peaceful **Lou Lim Ieoc Gardens** and the ornate mansion with its columns and arches (now the Pui Ching School) once belonged to the wealthy Lou family. The gardens are a mixture of Chinese and European influences with huge shady trees, lotus ponds, pavilions, bamboo groves, grottoes and odd-shaped doorways.

Macau means the 'City of God' and takes its name from A-Ma-Gau, the Bay of A-Ma. The **A-Ma Temple** (Ma Kok Miu), which dates from the Ming Dynasty, stands at the base of Penha Hill on Barra Point. According to legend, A-Ma, goddess of seafarers, was supposed to have been a beautiful young woman whose presence on a Canton-bound ship saved it from disaster. All the other ships of the fleet, whose rich owners had refused to give her passage, were destroyed in a storm. The boat people of Macau come here on a pilgrimage each year in April or May.

A restored colonial-style building beside the A-Ma Temple houses **Macau Maritime Museum**. These quarters are temporary; it should have its own building by the time you read this. Across the road at the waterfront there are a number of boats including a tug,

a dragon boat and a *lorcha*, a type of sailing cargo-vessel used on the Pearl River.

The Islands

Directly south of the mainland peninsula are the islands of Taipa and Coloane. In the past, these islands were most notable for their pirates, the last raid being as recent as 1910. A bridge connects Taipa Island to the mainland, and a causeway connects Taipa and Coloane.

Taipa This island seems to have become one big construction site with the Hyatt Hotel and Macau University just the first of a number of projects. Taipa village is pleasant and relaxed and there are some fine little restaurants to sample. You can rent a bicycle to explore the village and further afield. There's an **old church**, a couple of **Chinese temples** and the interesting **Taipa House Museum**.

Coloane This island also has a pretty village where you can see junks under construction. Bicycles can also be rented there. Situated in a muddy river mouth, Macau is hardly likely to be blessed with wonderful beaches but Coloane has a couple that are really not bad. **Hac Sa Beach** is a long but not particularly inspiring stretch of sand but tiny **Cheoc Van Beach** is really quite pretty.

PLACES TO STAY

Weekends are a bad time to visit Macau; try to make your trip on a weekday. During the quieter midweek time, it's worth bargaining a little.

Places to Stay – bottom end

The cheapest hotels in Macau are mostly clustered near the Floating Casino. There are also several cheap and cheapish hotels between the Hotel Lisboa and Rua da Praia Grande, a somewhat nicer part of town. Finding them is easy as all the hotels have signs. Cheap hotels usually call themselves *vila*, but often they are called *hospedaria* or *pensao*.

The key to finding a good, cheap room is

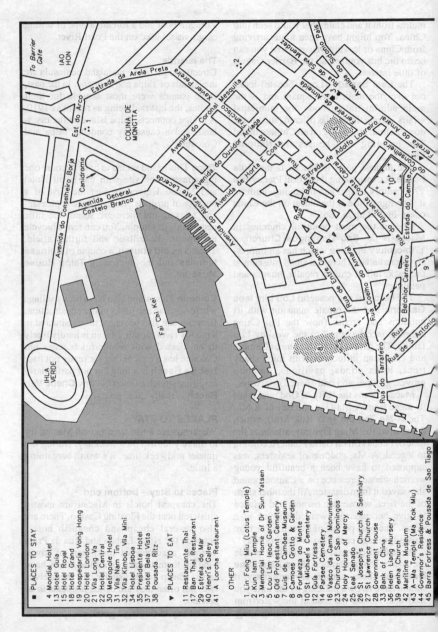

PLACES TO STAY

4   Mondial Hotel
14 Hotel Guia
15 Hotel Royal
18 Hotel Grand
19 Hospedaria Vong Hong
20 Hotel London
21 Vila Long Va
22 Hotel Central
30 Metropole Hotel
31 Vila Nam Tin
32 Vila Kimbo, Vila Mini
34 Hotel Lisboa
35 Presidente Hotel
37 Hotel Bela Vista
38 Pousada Ritz

▼ PLACES TO EAT

11 Restaurante Thai
17 Ban Thai Restaurant
29 Estrela do Mar
40 Henri's Galley
41 A Lorcha Restaurant

OTHER

1   Lin Fong Miu (Lotus Temple)
2   Kun Iam Temple
3   Memorial Home of Dr Sun Yatsen
5   Lou Lim Ieoc Garden
6   Old Protestant Cemetery
7   Luis de Camões Museum
8   Camoes Grotto & Garden
9   Fortaleza do Monte
10 St Michael's Cemetery
12 Guia Fortress
14 Parsee Cemetery
16 Vasco da Gama Monument
23 Church of San Domingos
24 Holy House of Mercy
25 Leal Senado
26 St Joseph's Church & Seminary
27 St Lawrence Church
28 Government House
33 Bank of China
36 Helen Liang Nursery
39 Penha Church
42 Maritime Museum
43 A-Ma Temple (Ma Kok Miu)
44 Governor's Residence
45 Barra Fortress & Pousada de Sao Tiago

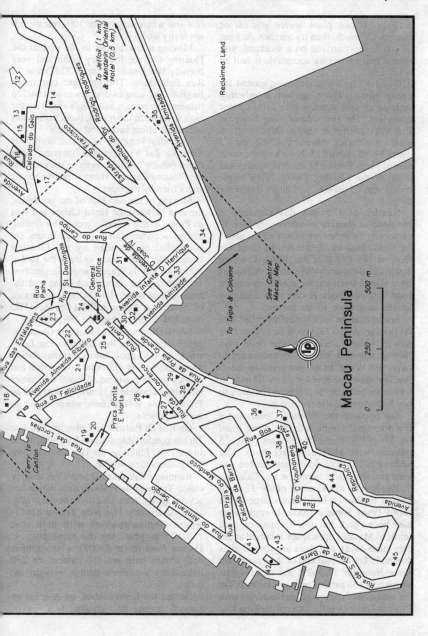

Macau Peninsula

patience. If one place waves you off or charges too much, then try another. As long as you haven't arrived on a weekend, you should find something acceptable in half an hour or so.

Rua das Lorchas is a hunting ground for cheap hotels. There are two numbering systems on this street, which causes some confusion. The *Hospedaria Vong Hong* on Rua das Lorchas is cheap. Depending on which numbering scheme you believe, it's either No 45 or No 253, but it's on the north side of Praca Ponte e Horta (the square) and south of the Floating Casino. Tiny single rooms cost 25 patacas, and larger rooms are 50 patacas.

Nearby, at 175 Rua das Lorchas, is *Hospedaria Namkio* where singles cost 37 patacas. It's a rather run-down sort of place, but it has character. Next to it is the *Hotel San Hou*, at No 159 Rua das Lorchas, where singles/doubles are 64/88 patacas. All rooms have shared bath, but the double rooms are huge with twin beds. Rooms with a balcony are the same price, so ask for one.

Just around the back is an alley called Rua do Bocage. At No 17, you'll find *Hotel Ung Ieong*, though a sign on the door says 'Restaurante Ung Ieong'. The rooms are so huge you could fit an army inside them! Auditorium-sized doubles go for 67 patacas with bath, but look the place over before you pay because it's quite run-down.

Just opposite the Floating Casino and a few doors to the north is the *Hoi Keng Hotel* (☎ 57 2033) where doubles are 130/138 patacas with shared/private bath. The address is 153 Rua do Guimaraes but you enter just around the corner on Rua Caldeira.

Two blocks to the south of the Floating Casino, on Rua das Lorchas, is a large square called Praca Ponte e Horta. It might once have been a park, but now it's just a car park (most of Macau's open space is buried under cars these days), and there are several vilas around it. On the east end of the square *Vila Kuan Heng* (☎ 57 3629) has clean rooms which cost 150 patacas with private bath. On the west side of the square, on the corner with Rua das Lorchas, is the tattered-looking *Vila Hoi Von* where singles are 100 patacas, but not really worth it.

Moving a few blocks to the east of the Floating Casino, the very clean and very friendly *Vila Universal* (☎ 57 3247) is at 73 Rua Felicidade. The manager can speak English and singles/doubles cost 184/276 patacas. The price is amazingly cheap for the high standard of the rooms, but it's often full because it offers such good value.

The *Vila Veng Va* is at the corner of Travessa das Virtudes and Travessa Auto Novo (which is a few doors to the south of the Floating Casino). It has attractive rooms and a friendly manager.

Moving to the east side of the peninsula, the area between the Hotel Lisboa and Rua da Praia Grande is fertile ground for finding budget accommodation, though prices are somewhat higher than by the Floating Casino. One good place to try is the *Va Lai Vila* at 44 Rua da Praia Grande. Singles cost 180 patacas, the rooms look clean and the management is friendly. On the opposite side of the street at 93 Rua da Praia Grande is *Vila Nam Kok* where singles are 188 patacas.

Intersecting with Rua da Praia Grande is a small street called Rua Dr Pedro Jose Lobo where there's a good line of accommodation houses, including *Vila Nam Loon* which has singles for 150 patacas. Around the corner on Avenida Infante D'Henrique, near Rua da Praia Grande, is *Vila Kimbo* where singles go for 130 patacas.

On Rua Dr Pedro Jose Lobo, the *Vila Loc Tin* has comfortable doubles for 180 patacas. In the same building, the *Vila San Sui* costs 150 patacas for a double.

Running off Avenida D Joao IV is an alley called Travessa da Praia Grande which has several good places. One of the best is bright, airy and friendly *Vila Nam Tin* (☎ 81513) where singles/doubles with bath cost 150/175 patacas. On the same alley is *Pensao Nam In* (☎ 81002), where singles with shared bath are 110 patacas, or 230 patacas for a pleasant double with private bath.

Behind the Hotel Lisboa, on Avenida de Lopo Sarmento de Carvalho, is a row of vilas. The *Vila San Vu* is friendly and has nice rooms for 160 patacas.

Places to Stay – mid-range

The *Hotel London* (☎ 83388) on Praca Ponte e Horta has singles/doubles for 200/240 patacas.

True to its name, the *Hotel Central* (☎ 37 3888) is in the centre of town, at 28-26 Avenida Almeida Ribeiro, west of the GPO. Rather dumpy-looking double rooms with baths cost from 220 patacas.

Just on the north side of the Floating Casino, on Rua das Lorchas, is the *Peninsula Hotel* (☎ 31 8899). Singles/twins are 250/300 patacas. This is a new hotel that is clean and well air-conditioned.

On your left as you enter Travessa das Virtudes (just south of the Floating Casino) is the *Hotel Hou Kong* which has singles/doubles for 230/322 patacas.

Just a block to the north of the Floating Casino, at 146 Avenida Almeida Ribeiro, is the *Hotel Grand* (☎ 57 9922) where singles/doubles cost 228/288 patacas.

One block to the east of the Floating Casino is a street called Travessa Caldeira where you'll find the *Hotel Man Va* with doubles at 287 patacas. Nearby, at 71 Rua Felicidade, close to Travessa Auto Novo, is *Hotel Ko Wah* (☎ 75599) which has doubles for 195 patacas.

Another place to consider is the area north of the Hotel Lisboa, on a street called Estrada Sao Francisco. You have to climb a steep hill to get up this street, but the advantage is that the hotels have good sea views. Just past the expensive Matsuya Hotel you'll find the *Vila Tak Lei* at 2A Estrada Sao Francisco, where doubles go for 350 patacas. However, bargaining is entirely possible.

PLACES TO EAT

A long, lazy Portuguese meal with a carafe of red to wash it down with is one of the most pleasant parts of a Macau visit. The menus are often in Portuguese, so a few useful words are cozido (stew), cabrito (kid), cordeiro (lamb), carreiro (mutton), galinha (chicken), caraguejos (crabs), carne de vaca (beef) and peixe (fish). Apart from carafe wine you can also get Mateus Rosé, that best known of Portuguese wines.

Another Macau pleasure is to sit back in one of the many little cake shops *(pastelarias)* with a glass of cha de limao (lemon tea) and a plate of cakes – very genteel! These places are good for a cheap breakfast too. People eat early in Macau – you can find the chairs being put away and that the chef has gone home around 9 pm.

Henri's Galley (☎ 55 6251) is right on the waterfront at 4 Avenida da Republica, on the south end of the Macau Peninsula. Also known as Maxims (not the Hong Kong fast-food chain), Henri's Galley is known for its African chicken, spicy prawns and prawn fondue. They also serve Chinese food.

Right next door is *Cafe Marisol*, where food is both cheap and excellent. They set up outdoor tables so you can take in the view across to the islands.

Also adjacent to Henri's Galley is the *Ali Curry House*, which also has outdoor tables and a wide menu of curry dishes (25 to 35 patacas) and steaks (30 to 40 patacas) with a Portuguese flavour.

For Portuguese and Macanese food which is both good and cheap, the *Estrela do Mar* (☎ 81270) at 11 Travessa do Paiva, off the Rua da Praia Grande, is the place to go. So is the *Solmar* (☎ 74391), at 11 Rua da Praia Grande. Both places are famous for their African chicken and seafood.

Fat Siu Lau (☎ 73580), or 'House of the Smiling Buddha', serves Portuguese and Chinese food. It's at 64 Rua Felicidade, once the old red-light Street of Happiness. Turn left opposite the Central Hotel in Avenida Almeida Ribeiro. It's supposed to be the oldest restaurant in Macau or at least the oldest Macanese restaurant in the colony, dating back to 1903. The speciality is roast pigeon.

Another place known for good Portuguese food is *Portugués* (☎ 75445) at 16 Rua do Campo, and one place known for its good food and fine Spanish decor is *Algarve Sol* (☎ 89007) at 41-43 Rua Comandante Mata e Oliveira, two blocks west of the Hotel Lisboa

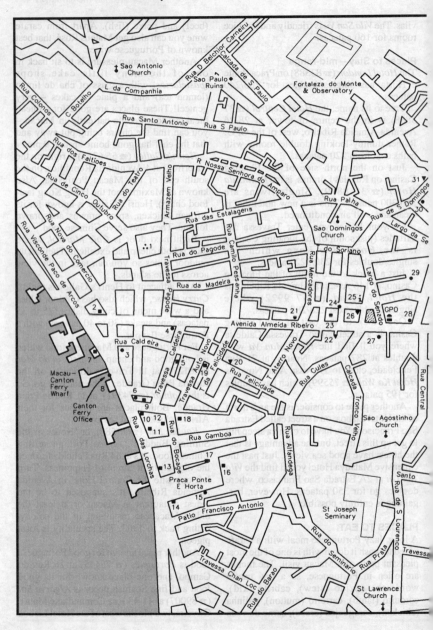

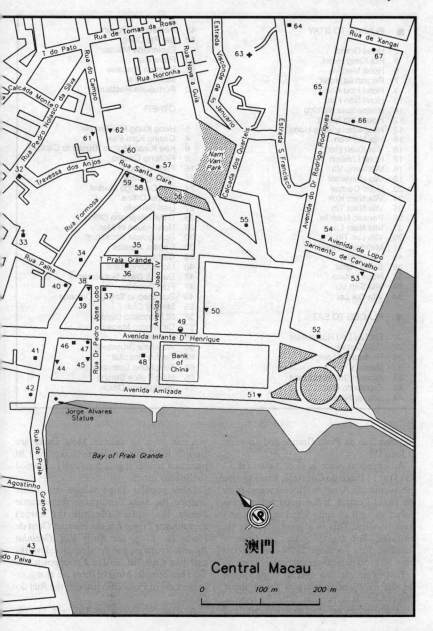

澳門

Central Macau

0   100 m   200 m

■ PLACES TO STAY

2	Hotel Grand
3	Hoi Keng Hotel
5	Hotel Man Va
7	Peninsula Hotel
9	Hotel Hou Kong
10	Hotel San Hou
11	Hospedaria Namkio
12	Hotel Ung Ieong
13	Hospedaria Vong Hong
14	Vila Hoi Von
16	Vila Kuan Heng
17	Hotel London
18	Vila Veng Va
19	Vila Universal
23	Hotel Central
34	Vila Nam Kok
35	Vila Nam Tin
36	Pensao Nam In
37	Vila Nam Loon
39	Vila Loc Tin
41	Metropole Hotel
46	Vila Kimbo
48	Sintra Hotel
52	Hotel Lisboa
54	Vila San Vu
64	Vila Tak Lei

▼ PLACES TO EAT

20	Fat Siu Lau Restaurant
22	Café Safari
26	Restaurant Long Kei
31	Maxim's
38	Algarve Sol Restaurant
43	Estrela do Mar
44	Solmar Restaurant
45	Restaurant Ocean
50	Dai Pai Dong
51	Esplanade Macau
53	Pizza Hut
59	Pizzeria Toscana
61	McDonald's
62	Portugués Restaurant

OTHER

1	Hong Kung Miu Temple
4	Casino Kam Pek
6	Kee Kwan Motors (Buses to Canton)
8	Floating Casino
15	Park 'n Shop
21	Taifung Bank
24	Sao Domingo Market
25	Tourist Office
27	Leal Senado
28	CTM Telephone Office
29	Holy House of Mercy
30	Portuguese Bookshop
32	Capitol Theatre
33	Cathedral
40	Hong Kong Bank
42	Days & Days Supermarket
47	Foto Princesa
49	Bus Stop to Taipa & Coloane
55	Military Club
56	St Francisco Garden
57	Cineteatro Macau
58	Bookstore
60	Watson's Drugstore
63	Centro Hospital
65	Telephone Company
66	Main Police Station
67	Immigration Office

between Rua da Praia Grande and Avenida D Joao IV.

An excellent place is *Café Safari* (☎ 57 4313) at 14 Pateo do Cotovelo, a tiny square off Avenida de Almeida Ribeiro across from the Hotel Central. It has good coffee-shop dishes as well as spicy chicken, steak and fried noodles. This is a good place to eat breakfast. For a good pizza, try *Pizzeria Toscana*, Rua Formosa 28B – pizzas cost from 30 to 50 patacas and the coffee is great.

Lots of people hop over to Taipa village for the excellent restaurants found there. *Pinocchio's* is a popular little Portuguese place where they serve up superb prawns and you can often sit outside. Most dishes are from 20 to 30 patacas, and wine is around 30 patacas a bottle. It gets frantically crowded for Sunday lunch.

Other popular Taipa village restaurants include the very Portuguese *Restaurante Panda*, the Italian (despite the name) *Restaurante Leong Un*, the cheaper *Casa de Pasto Tai Tung*, the *Kung Kai*, *Cozinha Ricardo's Kitchen* and the pleasant sidewalk-café-like *Cafe Tai Lei Lai Kei* opposite the Tin Hau Temple. Most of them are along, or in the case of Pinocchio just off, the Rua do Cunha.

At Hac Sa Beach on Coloane Island,

Fernando's deserves honourable mention for some of the best food in Macau. The atmosphere is also pleasant, and it can get crowded in the evening. There are two main problems with this place. The first is that there is no sign above the door and it's quite easy to wander around for a while looking for it. The restaurant is at the far end of the car park, close to the bus stop. The other problem is that the menu is in Portuguese and Chinese only. Fernando himself (the manager) will gladly translate for you, and he recommends the clams.

Budget travellers should head for the *Esplanade Macau* which sits on the traffic island on Avenida Amizade in front of the Hotel Lisboa and is adjacent to the Bank of China. It's in an outdoor pavilion and opens only in the evening. They serve very good Cantonese dishes like fried noodles for 7 patacas and drinks are also very cheap. Not much English is spoken, but they have an English menu.

One of the most conveniently located street markets is Rua da Escola Commercial, a tiny lane one block west of the Hotel Lisboa, just next to a sports field.

For economy-minded wine lovers, Macau is the one of the best bargains in this book. At one of the cheaper Portuguese restaurants like the Estrela do Mar you can get a bottle of wine for 30 to 40 patacas (Mateus Rosé is 36 patacas). The more expensive Solmar has bottles for around 55 patacas. You can bring a litre of wine or spirits back to Hong Kong, where it's more expensive. Beer in Macau is typically 10 patacas in restaurants.

ENTERTAINMENT
Gambling
Even if gambling holds no interest for you, it's fun to wander the casinos at night. There are three main arenas for losing money. Largest is the *Hotel Lisboa* with all the usual games, a special private room for the really high rollers and row upon row of 'hungry tigers' – slot machines. It's gambling

Chinese-style though, none of the dinner jacket swank of Monte Carlo or the neon gloss of Vegas – at Macau you put your money down, take your chances and to hell with the surroundings.

At the other end of the main street is *Macau Palace*, usually referred to as the 'Floating Casino', and midway between is the Chinese casino where they play games like Dai-Siu (big and small). You can also bet on the games at the Jai-Alai Palace on the waterfront near the ferry terminal.

For 120 patacas, you can watch about 10 graduates of the Crazy Horse in Paris cavort around the stage of Hotel Lisboa attired in outfits ranging from very little to nothing at all. It's called the Crazy Paris Show.

There's also horse racing on Taipa Island and dog racing at the 'Canidrome' (yes, they really call it that).

Discos
The most popular with the locals is the *Mondial Disco* at the Hotel Mondial, Rua da Antonio Basto. There is no cover charge, but you are obligated to buy two drinks for 70 patacas.

Hotel Presidente is home to the *Skylight Disco*. There is no cover charge here, but you must buy one drink for 80 patacas.

THINGS TO BUY
Pawnshops are ubiquitous in Macau, and it is possible to get good deals on cameras, but you must be prepared to bargain without mercy.

The Macau Government tourist office has T-shirts for sale at the bargain price of 25 patacas. They also sell a set of poster-size 'antique maps of Macau' (150 patacas), a set of postcards (5 patacas), umbrellas (30 patacas) and raincoats (35 patacas).

The Sao Domingo Market is in the alley just behind the Hotel Central and next to the Macau Government tourist office. It's a good place to pick up cheap clothing.

Malaysia

Malaysia is a country known more for its beautiful scenery than its points of historical or cultural interest. Travel is easy and comfortable, and the people are exceptionally friendly. Apart from its superb beaches, mountains and national parks, it is one of the most developed and prosperous countries in the region.

Malaysia's fascinating mixture of people range from Peninsular Malays and the commercially-minded Chinese to the diverse tribespeople of Sabah and Sarawak in East Malaysia.

Facts about the Country

HISTORY

Little is known about prehistoric Malaysia, but around 10,000 years ago the aboriginal Malays – the Orang Asli – began to move down the peninsula from a probable starting point in south-west China.

In the early centuries of the Christian era, Malaya was known as far away as Europe. Ptolemy showed it on his early map with the label 'Golden Chersonese'. It spelt gold not only to the Romans but to others as well, for it wasn't long before Indian and Chinese traders also arrived in search of that most valuable metal and Hindu ministates sprung up along the great Malay rivers.

The Malay people were ethnically similar to the people of Sumatra, Java and even the Philippines and from time to time various South-East Asian empires exerted control over all or parts of the Malay Peninsula.

In 1405, the Chinese Admiral Cheng Ho arrived in Melaka with greetings from the 'Son of Heaven' and, more importantly, the promise of protection from the encroaching Siamese to the north. With this support from China, the power of Melaka extended to include most of the Malay Peninsula.

At about the same time, Islam arrived in Melaka and soon spread through Malaya. Melaka's wealth and prosperity soon attracted European interest, and it was the Portuguese who first took over in 1511, followed by the Dutch in 1641 and, finally, the British in 1795.

For years, the British were only interested in Malaya for its seaports and to protect their trade routes, but the discovery of tin prompted them to move inland and take over the whole peninsula. Meanwhile, Charles Brooke, the White Rajah, and the North Borneo Company made similar British takeovers of Sarawak and Sabah, respectively. The British, as was their custom, also brought in Chinese and Indians, an action which radically changed the country's racial mix.

Malaya achieved *merdeka* (independence) in 1957 but there followed a period of instability due to an internal Communist uprising and the external 'confrontation' with neighbouring Indonesia. In 1963, the north Borneo states of Sabah and Sarawak, along with Singapore, joined Malaya to create Malaysia.

Relations with Singapore soured almost immediately and, only two years later, Singapore withdrew from the Malaysian confederation. Sukarno's demise ended the disputes with Indonesia and the Communist threat has simply withered away to become a total anachronism in modern Malaysia.

In 1969, violent intercommunal riots broke out, particularly in Kuala Lumpur (KL), and hundreds of people were killed. The government moved to dissipate the tensions, which existed mainly between the Malays and the Chinese. Moves to give Malays a larger share of the economic pie have led to some resentment amongst the other racial groups but, overall, present-day Malaysian society is relatively peaceful and cooperative.

Elections in 1974 resulted in an overwhelming majority for the *Barisan*, or

National Front, of which the UMNO (United Malays National Organisation) is the key party. All elections since then have seen power remain with the UMNO, although in the most recent elections (in 1990) the opposition presented a real threat to the government for the first time. Despite this, Prime Minister Dr Mahathir Mohammed was returned with a comfortable, if reduced, majority.

Internationally, the country has a very high standing as one of the most rapidly advancing countries of Asia, although it has come under intense pressure to stop exporting tropical timber from its rapidly diminishing rainforests – an issue it has chosen to ignore up until now. Regionally, it is an important member of the Association of South-East Asian Nations (ASEAN) and has a defence agreement with Australia, New Zealand, Singapore and the UK.

GEOGRAPHY

Malaysia consists of two distinct parts. Peninsular Malaysia is the long finger of land extending down from Asia, as if pointing towards Indonesia and Australia, and it accounts for about 40% of the country's area. Although most of the forests have been cleared over the years to make way for plantations of rubber trees and oil palms, there are still stands of virgin forest remaining, largely in the national park of Taman Negara.

The balance of the land area is made up of the states of Sabah and Sarawak which occupy the northern segment of the island of Borneo. Here too, the forests have been cleared for agriculture and timber exports and the tracts of virgin rainforest are still rapidly diminishing. Mt Kinabalu in Sabah is the highest peak in South-East Asia.

CLIMATE

Malaysia has a typically tropical climate – it's hot and humid year round. The temperature rarely drops below 20°C (68°F) even at night and usually climbs to 30°C (86°F) or more during the day.

The west coast of Peninsular Malaysia gets heavier rainfall from September to December. On the east coast, and also in Sarawak and Sabah, October to February is the wet season. Throughout the region the humidity tends to hover around the 90% mark, but on the peninsula you can escape from the heat and humidity by retreating to the delightfully cool hill stations.

GOVERNMENT

Malaysia is a confederation of 13 states and the capital district of Kuala Lumpur. Nine of the peninsular states have sultans and every five years an election is held to determine which one will become the *Yang di-Pertuan Agong*, or 'King' of Malaysia.

The states of Sabah and Sarawak in East Malaysia are rather different from those of Peninsular Malaysia since they were separate colonies, not parts of Malaya, prior to independence. They still retain a greater degree of local administrative autonomy than the peninsular states.

ECONOMY

Malaysia is a prosperous and progressive country and one of the world's major suppliers of tin, natural rubber and palm oil. Indeed, rubber plantations, interspersed with oil palm plantations, seem to cover a large part of the peninsula. In East Malaysia the economy is based on timber and, in Sarawak, oil and pepper are major exports. A great deal of effort is being made to industrialise Malaysia and jump on the hi-tech bandwagon which has proven to be so successful for other regional states.

POPULATION & PEOPLE

Malaysia's population is currently around 17.5 million. The people of Malaysia come from a number of different ethnic groups – Malays, Chinese, Indians, the indigenous Orang Asli of the peninsula and the various tribes of Sarawak and Sabah.

It's reasonable to say that the Malays control the government while the Chinese have their fingers on the economic pulse. Approximately 85% of the population lives in Peninsular Malaysia and the remaining

15% in the much more lightly populated states of Sabah and Sarawak.

There are still small scattered groups of Orang Asli, or 'original people', in Peninsular Malaysia. Although most have given up their nomadic or shifting-agriculture techniques and have been absorbed into modern Malay society, a few groups of Orang Asli still live in the forests.

Dayak is the term used for the non-Muslim people of Borneo. These people migrated to Borneo at times, and along routes, which are not clearly defined. It is estimated that there are more than 200 Dayak tribes in Borneo, the most important being the Iban and Bidayuh. Other smaller groups include the Kenyah, Kayan and Punan, whose lifestyle and habitat is under siege due to the logging activities in Sarawak.

ARTS

It's along the east coast, the predominantly Malay part of Malaysia, that you'll find Malay crafts, culture and games at their liveliest and most widely practised.

Top spinning, or *main gasing*, and kite flying are two popular activities, while *sepak raga*, the national ball game, is played with a lightweight ball woven from strips of rotan. *Silat*, a traditional martial art, is today a highly refined and stylised activity. The wayang kulit is similar to the shadow puppet performances of other South-East Asian countries, in particular Java in Indonesia, and retells the tales from the Hindu epic, the *Ramayana*.

As in other parts of the region, Malay music is principally percussion based.

Crafts

Although originally an Indonesian craft, batik has made itself equally at home in Malaysia. You'll find it in Penang on the west coast although Kelantan is its true home.

Kain songket is a handwoven fabric from Kelantan, the main feature of which is the silver and gold thread. Kelantan is also famed for its silversmiths who work in a variety of ways and specialise in filigree and repousse work. In Kuala Terengganu, brasswork is an equally traditional skill.

CULTURE

As many Muslim countries have in the last decade, Malaysia has been going through a period of increasing concentration on religion and religious activity. It's certainly a world away from the sort of fundamentalism found in other parts of the world, but you still need to be aware of local sensibilities so as not to offend.

It's wise to be appropriately discreet in dress and behaviour, particularly on the stricter Muslim east coast of the peninsula. For women, topless bathing is definitely not acceptable and away from the beaches you should cover up as much as possible. For men, shorts are not offensive, but bare torsos are not considered acceptable in the villages and towns.

RELIGION

The variety of religions found in Malaysia is a direct reflection of the diversity of races

Basket Seller

living there. Although Islam is the state religion of Malaysia, freedom of religion is guaranteed. The Malays are almost all Muslims and there are also some Indian Muslims. The Chinese are predominantly followers of Taoism and Buddhism, though some are Christians. The majority of the region's Indian population come from the south of India and are Hindu.

Although Christianity has made no great inroads into Peninsular Malaysia, it has had a much greater impact upon East Malaysia where many of the indigenous people have converted to Christianity, although others still follow their animist traditions.

LANGUAGE

The official language is Bahasa Malaysia, or Bahasa. You can get along quite happily with English throughout Malaysia and, although it is not the official language, it is often still the linking language between the various ethnic groups, especially the middle class.

Other everyday languages include the Chinese dialects like Hakka or Hokkien. The majority of the region's Indians speak Tamil, although there are also groups who speak Malayalam, Hindi or other Indian languages.

Bahasa is virtually the same as Indonesian but there are a number of different words. Many of the differences are in the loan words – English-based for Malaysian and Dutch-based for Indonesian. See Lonely Planet's *Indonesia Phrasebook* for an introduction to the language, and the Language section in the Indonesia chapter.

Local additions to the English language are always fascinating and a number of Malaysian terms have crept into everyday English in Malaysia. By far the most evident is *bumiputra* and you may read of jobs which are reserved for 'bumiputras'. Literally, it means 'son of the soil' but, in reality, it means a Malay rather than a Chinese or Indian.

Facts for the Visitor

VISAS & EMBASSIES

Commonwealth citizens, citizens of the Republic of Ireland, Switzerland, the Netherlands and Liechtenstein do not require a visa to visit Malaysia. Citizens of the USA, Germany, France, Italy, Norway, Sweden, Denmark, Belgium, Finland, Luxembourg and Iceland do not require a visa for a visit not exceeding three months. Seven-day visas are granted to citizens of Czechoslovakia, Hungary, Poland, USSR, Yugoslavia, Rumania and Bulgaria.

Normally you get a 30-day or 60-day stay permit on arrival, depending on your expected length of stay. This is extendible for up to three months. Note that Sabah and Sarawak are treated in some ways like separate countries. Your passport will be checked again on arrival in each state and a new stay permit issued.

Malaysian Embassies

Visas can be obtained at overseas Malaysian diplomatic missions including:

Brunei
    Lot 12, 6th Floor, Darussalam Complex, Bandar Seri Begawan (☎ 02-28401)
Burma (Myanmar)
    82 Diplomatic Quarters, Pyidaundsu Yeikhta Rd, Rangoon (☎ 20248)
Hong Kong
    24th Floor, Malaysia Building, 50 Gloucester Rd, Wanchai (☎ 5-27 0921)
India
    50M Satya Marg, Chanakyapuri, New Delhi 110021 (☎ 60 1291)
    287 TTK Rd, Madras 600018 (☎ 45 3580)
Indonesia
    17 Jalan Imam Bonjol, Jakarta (☎ 33 6438)
    11 Jalan Diponegoro, Medan, Sumatra (☎ 25315)
    42 Jalan A Yani, Pontianak, Kalimantan (☎ 2986)
Singapore
    301 Jervois Rd, Singapore 1024 (☎ 235 0111)
Thailand
    35 South Sathorn Rd, Bangkok 10500 (☎ 286 1390)
    4 Sukhum Rd, Songkhla (☎ 31 1062)

Visas for Other Countries

Thailand You can get Thai visas from the embassy in KL or the consulates in Penang or Kota Bharu. The consulates are quick and convenient. Thailand consulates in Malaysia include:

Kuala Lumpur
    29 Jalan Yap Kwan Seng (☎ 03-242 3094)
    206 Jalan Ampang (☎ 03-248 8222)
Penang
    1 Jalan Ayer Rajah (☎ 04-23352)

Indonesia For most Western nationalities, a visa is not required on arrival in Indonesia as long as you have a ticket out (not always rigidly enforced) and do not intend to stay for more than two months. The Indonesian consulates in Malaysia include:

Kuala Lumpur
    233 Jalan Tun Razak (☎ 03-984 2011)
Penang
    467 Jalan Burma (☎ 04-25162)
Sarawak
    5A Pisang Rd, Kuching
Sabah
    Jalan Karamunsing, Kota Kinabalu (☎ 088-54100)
    Jalan Kuharsa, Tawau

MONEY
Currency

The Malaysian dollar is known as the *ringgit* and is divided into 100 *sen*. Although it used to be on a par, and was interchangeable, with the Singapore dollar, the mighty Singapore dollar is now worth over 50% more.

Credit cards are widely accepted at major hotels, restaurants and craft shops. Banks are efficient and, in the main centres, there are also plenty of moneychangers.

Exchange Rates
A$1	=	M$2.18
C$1	=	M$2.43
NZ$1	=	M$1.60
UK£1	=	M$4.76
US$1	=	M$2.75

Costs

Malaysia is more expensive than other South-East Asian nations, although less so than Singapore. You get pretty much what you pay for – there are lots of hotels where a couple can get a quite decent room for around US$5, food is refreshingly cheap and the transport is also reasonable and efficient.

TOURIST OFFICES

Malaysia has an efficient national tourist body, the Malaysian Tourist Development Corporation (MTDC). It produces a huge variety of glossy brochures and other literature, most of it fairly useful. There are also a number of local tourist promotion organisations, such as the Penang Tourist Association, who back up the MTDC's activities.

Tourist Offices

The MTDC maintains the following offices in Malaysia:

Johore Bahru
    Ground Floor, KOMTAR Building
    (☎ 07 22 3590)
Kota Kinabalu
    Ground Floor, Wing Onn Life Building, Jalan Sagunting (☎ 088-21 1698)
Kuala Lumpur
    Level 2, Putra World Trade Centre, Jalan Tun Ismail (☎ 03-274 6063)
    KL Visitors Centre, 3 Jalan Sultan Hishamuddin (☎ 03-230 1369)
    Malaysia Tourism Information Centre, Jalan Ampang (☎ 03-243 4929)
Kuala Terengganu
    2243 Ground Floor, Wisma MCIS, Jalan Sultan Zainal Abidin (☎ 09-62 1893)
Kuching
    2nd Floor, AIA Building, Jalan Song Thian Cheok (☎ 082-24 6575)
Penang
    10 Jalan Tun Syed Sheh Barakbah, Georgetown (☎ 04-62 0066)

BUSINESS HOURS

Government offices are usually open Monday to Friday from around 8.30 am to 12.15 pm and from 1 to 5 pm. On Friday the lunch break usually lasts from 11.15 am to 2.15 pm. On Saturday morning, the offices are open from 8.30 am to 1 pm.

Shop hours are also somewhat variable

although Monday to Saturday from 9 am to 6 pm is a good rule of thumb.

FESTIVALS & HOLIDAYS

With so many cultures and religions there is quite an amazing number of occasions to celebrate in Malaysia. Although some of them have a fixed date each year, the Hindus, Muslims and Chinese all follow a lunar calendar which means the dates for many events vary each year.

The major Muslim annual events are connected with Ramadan, the 30 days during which Muslims cannot eat or drink from sunrise to sunset. Hari Raya Puasa marks the end of the month-long fast with three days of joyful celebration. This is the major holiday of the Muslim calendar and it can be difficult to obtain accommodation in all of Malaysia, particularly on the east coast.

Other major festivals include:

14 January
    Thai Pongal – A Hindu harvest festival marking the beginning of the Hindu month of Thai.
January to February
    Chinese New Year – Dragon dances and pedestrian parades mark the start of the new year. Families hold open house, unmarried relatives (especially children) receive *ang pows*, or money in red packets, businesses traditionally clear their debts and everybody wishes you a Kong Hee Fatt Choy (a happy & prosperous new year).
    Thaipusam – This is one of the most dramatic Hindu festivals in which devotees honour Lord Subramaniam with acts of amazing masochism.
March to April
    Easter – On Palm Sunday, a candlelight procession is held at St Peter's in Melaka.
    Panguni Uttiram – On the full moon day of the Tamil month of Panguni, the marriage of Shiva to Parvati and of Lord Subramaniam to Theivani is celebrated.
    Cheng Beng – On Cheng Beng (All Soul's Day) Chinese traditionally visit the tombs of their ancestors to clean and repair them and make offerings.
    Birthday of the Monkey God – The birthday of T'se Tien Tai Seng Yeh is celebrated twice a year. Mediums pierce their cheeks and tongues with skewers and go into a trance during which they write special charms in blood.

April to May
    Songkran Festival – A traditional Thai Buddhist New Year in which Buddha images are bathed.
    Chithirai Vishu – The start of the Hindu New Year.
    Wesak Day – Buddha's birth, enlightenment and death are celebrated by various events including the release of caged birds to symbolise the setting free of captive souls.
1 to 2 June
    Gawai Dayak – Annual Sarawak festival of the Dayaks to mark the end of the rice season. War dances, cockfights and blowpipe events all take place.
4 June
    Birthday of the Yang di-Pertuan Agong – This is the celebration of the official birthday of Malaysia's Supreme Head of State.
29 June
    Festa de San Pedro – A Christian celebration in honour of the patron saint of fishers which is celebrated mainly by the Eurasian-Portuguese community of Melaka.
June to August
    Dragon Boat Festival – Commemorating the death of a Chinese saint who drowned himself. In an attempt to save him, local fishers paddled out to sea, beating drums to scare away any fish that might attack him. To mark the anniversary today, this festival is celebrated with boat races in Penang.
July to August
    Sri Krishna Jayanti – A 10-day Hindu festival celebrating popular events in Krishna's life is highlighted on day eight by celebrations of his birthday. The Laxmi Narayan Temple in KL is a particular focus.
31 August
    National Day – Hari Kebangsaan Malaysia celebrates Malaysia's independence with events all over the country, but particularly in KL where there are parades and a variety of performances in the Lake Gardens.
September
    Moon Cake Festival – The overthrow of the Mongol warlords in ancient China is celebrated by eating moon cakes and lighting colourful paper lanterns. Moon cakes are made with bean paste, lotus seeds and sometimes a duck egg.
    Prophet Mohammed's Birthday – Muslims pray and religious leaders recite verses from the Koran.
September to October
    Festival of the Nine Emperor Gods – Nine days of Chinese operas, processions and other events honour the nine emperor gods. In KL and Penang, fire walking ceremonies are held on the evening of the ninth day.

October to November

    Deepavali – In the Hindu month of Aipasi, Rama's victory over the demon King Rawana is celebrated with the 'Festival of Lights', where tiny oil lamps are lit outside Hindu homes.

22 November

    Guru Nanak's Birthday – The birthday of Guru Nanak, founder of the Sikh religion, is celebrated on this day.

December

    Pesta Pulau Penang – Month-long carnival on Penang Island featuring many water events; dragon-boat races are held towards the end of the festival.

25 December

    Christmas Day

POST & TELECOMMUNICATIONS
Post

Malaysia has an efficient postal system with a reliable poste restante service at the major post offices. Post offices are open from 8 am to 5 pm Monday to Friday and from 8 am to 12 noon Saturday.

Aerogrammes and postcards cost 40 sen to any destination.

Telephone

There are good telephone communications throughout the country. You can direct dial long-distance calls between all major towns in Malaysia. Local calls cost 10 sen for unlimited time.

Convenient card phones, *Kadfon*, are found all over the country and take plastic cards. International calls can be direct dialled from KL, Penang and Kota Kinabalu. The service is fast, efficient and reasonably priced. Calls to Singapore are STD rather than international calls.

TIME

Malaysian time is eight hours ahead of GMT (UTC). When it is 12 noon in Malaysia, it is 2 pm in Sydney, 4 am in London, 11 pm in New York and 8 pm the previous day in Los Angeles.

BOOKS & MAPS

There are a wide variety of books available in Malaysia and a number of good book-shops in which to find them. The main chains are MPH and Berita.

Books

Kampong Boy and the more recently published *Town Boy* by Malaysian cartoonist Lat (Straits Times Publishing) provide a delightful introduction to Malay life. *Culture Shock* by JoAnn Craig attempts to explain the customs, cultures and lifestyles of Malaysia and Singapore's polyglot population to expats working there.

For more detail on the history of Malaysia, a good source is *A Short History of Malaysia, Singapore & Brunei* by C Mary Turnbull (Cassell, Australia, 1980). The 'White Rajahs' in North Borneo have also been well documented and *Nineteenth Century Borneo – A Study in Diplomatic Rivalry* by Graham Irwin (Donald Moore Books, Singapore) is the best book on the fascinating history of Sarawak, Sabah and Brunei.

Vanishing World, the Ibans of Borneo by Leigh Wright (Weatherhill, 1972) has some beautiful colour photographs. Redmond O'Hanlon's *Into the Heart of Borneo* is a wonderfully funny tale of a jaunt through the jungles of north Borneo.

Malaysia has provided a fertile setting for novelists and Joseph Conrad's *The Shadow Line* and *Lord Jim* both use the region as a setting. Somerset Maugham also set many of his classic short stories in Malaya – look for the *Borneo Stories*.

More recent books include Paul Theroux's *The Consul's File* which is based in the small town of Ayer Hitam. Another excellent read is *Turtle Beach* by Blanche d'Alpuget, which gives an insight into the Vietnamese boat people and the impact of their arrival in Malaysia.

Maps

You can get good road maps from petrol stations. Probably the best map is that produced by Shell which has a larger scale as it is two-sided. On the other hand the Mobil map also shows relief.

The Nelles Verlag *Malaysia* map is excellent for the peninsula and East Malaysia. It also has a number of city maps. It has a scale of 1:1.5 million and is widely available in Malaysia.

MEDIA
Newspapers & Magazines
Malaysia has newspapers in English, Malay, Chinese and Tamil. The *New Straits Times* is the main offering in English. In Bahasa Malaysia, the main paper, and the one with highest circulation of any paper, is the *Berita Harian*.

Asian and Western magazines are readily available throughout the region.

Radio & TV
Radio and TV are equally cosmopolitan in their languages and programming, with broadcasts in Bahasa Malaysia and English.

FILM & PHOTOGRAPHY
Malaysia is, of course, a delightful area to photograph. There's a lot of natural colour and activity, and the people have no antipathy to being photographed. There is usually no objection to taking photographs in Chinese temples.

Colour film can be developed quickly, cheaply and competently. Film is cheap and readily available in Malaysia, though slide film is not so cheap and the range is often limited. Processing is also reasonably priced.

HEALTH
Malaysia enjoys good standards of health and cleanliness. The usual rules for healthy living in a tropical environment apply. The main problem to look out for is malaria in East Malaysia, so take those tablets or carry a net, or both.

DRUGS
In Malaysia, the answer is simple – don't. Drug trafficking carries a mandatory death penalty and the list of Malaysian drug executions is a long one and includes Westerners. In almost every village in Malaysia, you will see anti-'dadah' (drugs) signs portraying a skull and crossbones and

a noose. No one can say they haven't been warned!

ACCOMMODATION
For the budget traveller, the best places to track down are traditional Chinese hotels, which are found in great numbers all over Malaysia. They're the mainstay of budget travellers and backpackers, and in Malaysia you can generally find a good room from M$10 to M$16. Chinese hotels are generally fairly spartan – bare floors and just a bed, a couple of chairs, a table, a wardrobe and a sink. A gently swishing ceiling fan completes the picture.

There are a couple of points to remember: couples can sometimes economise by asking for a single since in Chinese hotel language single means one double bed, double means two beds. Don't think this is being tight, as in Chinese hotels you can pack as many into one room as you wish.

The main catch with these hotels is that they can sometimes be terribly noisy. Part of the noise comes from the street, as they're often on main roads, but the traditional dawn chorus of coughing, hacking and spitting has to be experienced to be believed. It's worst in the oldest hotels where the walls don't quite reach the ceiling but are meshed in at the top for ventilation.

Malaysia also has a variety of cheap local accommodation, usually at beach centres. These may be huts on the beach or guest houses – private homes or rented houses divided by partition walls into a number of rooms. A dorm bed costs from M$5 to M$8 and rooms range from M$8 to M$20.

FOOD
While travel in some parts of Asia can be as good as a session with weight watchers, Malaysia is quite the opposite. The food is simply terrific, the variety unbeatable and the costs pleasantly low. Whether you're looking for Chinese, Malay, Indian or Indonesian food, or even a Big Mac, you'll find happiness!

Chinese Food

You'll find the full range of Chinese cuisine in Malaysia. If you're kicking round the backwoods of Sabah or Sarawak, however, Chinese food is likely to consist of little more than rice and vegetables.

Indian Food

Indian food is one of the region's greatest delights. Indeed, it's easier to find good Indian food in Malaysia than in India! You can roughly divide Indian food into southern, Muslim and northern – food from southern India tends to be hotter with the emphasis on vegetarian dishes, while Muslim food tends to be more subtle in its spicing and uses more meat.

A favourite Indian Muslim dish which is cheap, easy to find and of excellent standard

is biryani. Served with a chicken or mutton curry the dish takes its name from the saffron-coloured rice it is served with.

Malay, Indonesian & Nonya Food

Surprisingly, Malay food is not as easily found in Malaysia as Chinese or Indian food, although many Malay dishes, like satay, are everywhere.

Nonya cooking is a local variation on Chinese and Malay food. It uses Chinese ingredients, but employs local spices like chillies and coconut cream. Nonya cooking is essentially a home skill, rather than a restaurant one – there are few places where you can find Nonya food. Laksa, a spicy coconut-based soup, is a classic Nonya dish that has been adopted by all Malaysians.

Other Cuisine

Western fast-food addicts will find that Ronald McDonald, the Colonel from Kentucky and A&W have all made inroads into the regional eating scene.

Tropical Fruit

Once you've tried rambutans, mangosteens, jackfruit and durians how can you ever go back to boring old apples and oranges? Refer to the Food section in the Facts about the Region chapter for all the info on these delights.

DRINKS

Life can be thirsty in Malaysia, so you'll be relieved to hear that drinks are excellent, economical and readily available. For a start, water can be drunk straight from the taps in most larger Malaysian cities. Secondly, there is a wide variety of soft drinks including Coca Cola, Pepsi, 7-Up, Fanta and a variety of F & N flavours including sarsaparilla (for root beer fans). Soft drinks generally cost around M$1.

Fruit juices are popular and very good. With the aid of a blender and crushed ice, delicious concoctions like watermelon juice can be whipped up in seconds. Old-fashioned sugar cane crushers, which look like grandma's old washing mangle, can still be seen in operation.

Halfway between a drink and a dessert are *cendol* and *es kacang*. An es, or ais (ice), kacang is rather like an old-fashioned sno-cone but the shaved ice is topped with syrups and condensed milk and it's all piled on top of a foundation of beans and jellies. It sounds gross and looks lurid but tastes terrific! Cendol consists of coconut milk with brown sugar syrup and greenish noodle-like things topped with shaved ice.

Other oddities? Well, the milky white drink in clear plastic bins sold by street drink sellers is soybean milk which is also sold in a yoghurty form. Soybean milk is also available in soft drink bottles. Medicinal teas are a big deal with the health-minded Chinese.

Beer drinkers will probably find Anchor Beer or Tiger Beer to their taste although the minimum price for a bottle of beer is at least M$2.50. Locally brewed Carlsberg and Guinness are also popular.

Getting There & Away

AIR
To/From Europe, Australia & North America
See the Introductory Getting There & Away chapter for details on airfares to Malaysia from far afield. The usual gateway to Malaysia is KL, although Penang also has international connections. Singapore is also a handy arrival point as it's just a short trip across the causeway from Johore Bahru.

From London, you're looking at UK£270 to UK£300 one way, from the Australian east coast about A$550, and about US$550 one way from the US west coast.

To/From Thailand
You can fly from KL to Bangkok for about M$220, from Penang to Hat Yai for M$80 or to Phuket for slightly more. Add on a Phuket to Bangkok flight and it works out no more expensive than flying to Bangkok directly. Flying from Penang to Hat Yai or Phuket can

save a lot of time wasted in crossing a land border.

To/From Indonesia
There are several interesting variations from Indonesia to Malaysia. The short hop from Medan in Sumatra to Penang costs around US$80. There are also weekly flights between Kuching in Sarawak and Pontianak in Kalimantan (the Indonesian part of the island of Borneo) for M$160. Similarly, at the eastern end of Borneo, there is also a weekly connection between Tawau in Sabah and Tarakan in Kalimantan.

To/From India & Other Places in Asia
Although Indonesia and Thailand are the two 'normal' places to travel to or from Malaysia, there are plenty of other possibilities including Sri Lanka, India, Burma (Myanmar), Hong Kong or the Philippines.

Leaving Malaysia
Departure Tax Malaysia levies airport taxes on all its flights. It's M$3 on the domestic flights, M$5 to Singapore or Brunei and M$15 on other international flights. If you buy your tickets in Malaysia, the departure tax is included in the price.

LAND
To/From Thailand
You can cross the border by land at Padang Besar (rail or road) or Changlun-Sadao (road) in the west, Keroh-Betong (road) in the centre or at Rantau Panjang-Sungai Golok (road) in the east.

Train The rail route into Thailand is on the Butterworth-Alor Setar-Hat Yai route which crosses into Thailand at Padang Besar. You can take the International Express from Butterworth all the way to Bangkok with connections from Singapore and KL. Once in Hat Yai, there are frequent train and bus connections to other parts of Thailand.

Fares from Butterworth to Hat Yai are M$24.20 in 1st class and M$11.20 in 2nd class. To Bangkok, the fares are M$83.30 and M$38.70 respectively. Additional cost for berths ranges from around M$6 to M$25 depending on whether you want a 2nd-class upper, 2nd-class lower, 1st-class ordinary or 1st-class air-con.

Road It is possible to cross the border into Thailand from the west and east coast of Peninsular Malaysia.

West Coast Although there are border points at Padang Besar and Keroh, the majority of travellers cross by road between Penang and Hat Yai. There's a long stretch of no-man's land between these two points, so although you can easily get a bus or taxi up to Changlun on the Malaysian side and on from Sadao to Hat Yai on the Thai side, the actual border crossing is difficult.

There are two easy alternatives – one is a Thai taxi from Georgetown (Penang) for around M$25 to Hat Yai. The other is to cross at Padang Besar, where the railway also crosses and where the border is an easy walk across. Note that the Sadao-Changlun border is only open to 6 pm. From Hat Yai, there are plenty of buses and trains to Phuket, Bangkok or other places.

East Coast From Kota Bharu, you can take a bus No 29 to Rantau Panjang – the 45-km trip takes 1½ hours and costs about M$2. Once there, you've got a half-km walk to the Thai train station at Sungai Golok. An express train departs Sungai Golok for Bangkok every day at 10.55 am and arrives in Bangkok at 7.05 am the next day. There's also a 'rapid' train everyday at 10.05 am which arrives at 6.35 am, the following day. These trains go through Hat Yai.

To/From Indonesia
Road It is possible, although difficult, to cross the land border between Pontianak in Kalimantan (Indonesia) and Kuching in Sarawak (Malaysia). The Malaysian and Indonesian governments have agreed to upgrade this border crossing and build new roads so it will eventually get easier.

From Pontianak, you catch a bus to the Indonesian border town of Entikong (5500

rp). The trip takes eight to nine hours, is very dusty and there are four buses daily. The border closes at 5 pm, so if you arrive too late to cross, you may have to catch a bus 15 km back to the town of Balikarangan (500 rp), where there is accommodation for 3000 rp a single).

From Entikong to the border is six km, so take a motorbike for 500 rp. The border opens at 8 am Indonesian time or 9 am Malaysian time. You can change money at the border or in the town of Batas on the Malaysian side. From the border, catch a bus into Batas and from there another bus to Serian, and another to Kuching.

SEA
To/From Thailand
West Coast There are several yachts operating between Penang and Phuket in Thailand. Typical trips sail the Penang-Langkawi-Ko Phi Phi-Krabi-Phuket route and cost US$180 per person for a four to five-day trip. Look for advertisements in the cheap hotels and restaurants in Georgetown.

Cheaper and more frequent are the small boats that skip across the border from Kuala Perlis in the north-west corner of Malaysia to Setul in Thailand. There are customs and immigration posts here so you can cross quite legally although it's an unusual and rarely used entry or exit point. The fare for the short trip is around M$4 and from Setul you can take a bus to Hat Yai. Make sure you get your passport stamped on entry.

To/From Indonesia
There are three regular services between Malaysia and Indonesia – Penang to Medan and Melaka to Dumai connecting Peninsular Malaysia with Sumatra, and Tawau to Tarakan connecting Sabah with Kalimantan in Borneo.

The Penang to Medan ferry currently operates twice a week using a high-speed catamaran which zips across in a few hours at a cost of M$100 one way (M$180 return) in 1st class and M$90 (M$160) in economy. The Melaka to Dumai ferry costs M$80 one way but you need an Indonesian visa to enter or leave the country via Dumai.

In Borneo, the MV *Sasaran Muhibbah Express* operates between Tawau in Sabah and Nunukan and Tarakan in Kalimantan a few times per week. If travelling to Nunukan or Tarakan from Tawau, it's worth noting that visas cannot be issued on arrival. You must get one before crossing into Indonesia. There are consulates in Sabah at Tawau and Kota Kinabalu.

To/From India

After several years without shipping services, there is once again talk of a regular ship operating between Penang and Madras in India. However, it is unclear when this will happen.

Getting Around

AIR

Malaysian Airlines Systems (MAS) is the country's main domestic operator. The table details some of the main regional routes and their fares in M$ from KL. MAS have many other regional routes in Sarawak and Sabah. They also have a number of special night flights and advance purchase fares, as well as group and family fares.

Destination	Frequency	Fare M$
Alor Setar	four daily	94*
Ipoh	seven daily	55
Johore Bahru	six daily	77
Kota Bharu	four daily	86*
Kota Kinabalu	five daily	380*
Kuala Terengganu	three daily	123
Kuantan	five daily	61
Kuching	five daily	231*
Labuan	three weekly	380
Langkawi	daily	112
Miri	three daily	367
Penang	10 daily	86*
Singapore	eight daily	130

*Cheaper night fares and advanced purchase fares are applicable on some flights on these routes.

Note that fares to Singapore from Malaysia are much cheaper than from Singapore to Malaysia. The Singapore-Penang fare is S$155 but the Penang-Singapore fare is only M$155, substantially less. Unfortunately, if you buy a Singapore-Penang ticket in Malaysia and pay in Malaysian ringgit, the fare is marked up to the Singapore level.

It's also much cheaper to fly to other places in Malaysia from Johore Bahru (JB), just across the causeway from Singapore, than directly from Singapore. MAS operate an airport bus service from central Singapore direct to Johore Bahru Airport.

To/From Sarawak

The regular MAS fare between KL and Kuching is M$231. From Singapore to Kuching, the fare is S$170, but in the opposite direction it's only M$170. Skipping over to JB from Singapore drops the fare to M$147.

To/From Sabah

The cheapest way of getting from Peninsular Malaysia to Sabah is by purchasing an advance-purchase ticket (M$256) from Johore Bahru to Kota Kinabalu (KK); the regular fare is M$301. There are also economy night flights from KL for M$266; the regular fare is M$380. Advance purchase tickets must be paid for 14 days in advance while the night fares only apply to certain flights.

The KK-Singapore fare is M$346 (S$346 from Singapore to KK); it is far cheaper to take the flights to or from Johore Bahru and cross the causeway on the MAS bus which takes you right into Singapore for M$10.

BUS

Malaysia has an excellent bus system. There are public buses on local runs and a variety of privately operated buses on the longer trips as well as the big fleet of Expres Nasional express buses. In larger towns, there may be a number of bus stops – one or two main stations plus those where private companies operate directly from their offices.

Buses are fast, economical, reasonably comfortable and seats can be reserved. On many routes, there are also air-con buses which usually cost just a few ringgit more than the regular buses. They make midday travel a sweat-free activity, but beware because, as one traveller put it, 'Malaysian air-conditioned buses are really meat lockers on wheels with just two settings: cold and suspended animation'.

TRAIN

Malaysia has a modern, comfortable and economical rail service although there are basically only two rail lines. One runs from Singapore to KL, Butterworth and on into Thailand. The other branches off from this line at Gemas and runs through Kuala Lipis up to the north-east corner of the country near Kota Bharu.

KTM (Malaysian Railways) offers concessions to rail travellers including a Rail Pass entitling the holder to unlimited travel for 30 days for M$175 or 10 days for M$85.

Malaysia has two types of rail services. There are the conventional 1st, 2nd and 3rd-class trains with both express and slower ordinary services. On these trains, you can reserve seats on 1st and 2nd class up to 90 days in advance and there are day and overnight trains. On the overnight trains sleeping berths are available in 1st and 2nd class.

The other trains are known as the Ekspres Rakyat (People's Express) and the Ekspres Sinaran. These trains only have carriages with and without air-con, and only stop at main stations. Consequently, they are faster than the regular express trains. In fact, in most respects, these services are definitely the ones to take.

Fares on the Ekspres Rakyat and Ekspres Sinaran are very reasonable, not much more than 3rd class for the carriages without air-con, and not much more than 2nd class for air-con. Ekspres Rakyat and Ekspres Sinaran services only operate between Singapore and KL or KL and Butterworth. Travel time is about six hours between Butterworth and KL, 6½ to seven hours between KL and Singapore.

Fares from Butterworth to KL on the two Ekspres classes are M$25, or M$28 with air-con. On the regular services, the fare varies from M$47.40 (1st class) to M$13.20 (3rd class). Supplementary charges for sleeping berths vary from M$6 to M$20.

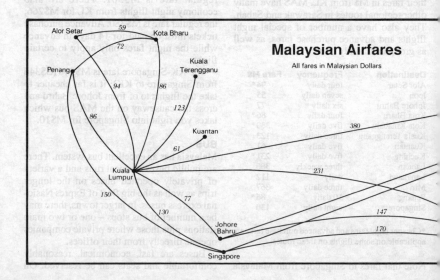

Malaysian Airfares

All fares in Malaysian Dollars

Timetables for the main services are available from railway stations and tourist offices.

In Sabah, there's also a small narrow-gauge line which can take you through the Pegas River gorge from Tenom to Beaufort. It's a great trip and one well worth doing.

LONG-DISTANCE TAXI

Malaysia's real travel bargain is the long-distance taxis. They make Malaysian travel, already easy and convenient even by the best Asian standards, a real breeze. A long-distance taxi is usually a diesel Mercedes, Peugeot or, more recently, a Japanese car.

In almost every town there will be a 'teksi' stand where the cars are lined up and ready to go to their various destinations. As soon as there is a full complement of four passengers, off you go. Between major towns the wait will rarely be long.

Taxi fares generally work out at about twice the comparable bus fares. Thus from KL to Butterworth it's M$30 and KL to Melaka is M$13.

Of course, there has to be a drawback to all this and that is the frightening driving which the taxi drivers often indulge in. They

don't have as many head-on collisions as you might expect, but closing your eyes at times of high stress certainly helps.

CAR

The Automobile Association of Malaysia (☎ 41 7137) is at Lot 20/24 Hotel Equatorial, Jalan Sultan Ismail, KL. They will let you join their organisation if you have a letter of introduction from your own automobile association.

Car Rental

Rent-a-car operations are well established in Malaysia. Major rental operators include Avis, Budget, Hertz, National and Thrifty, although there are others. Unlimited distance rates are typically around M$800 per week including insurance and collision damage waiver. Prices are about the same as in Singapore but there is a hefty surcharge if you take a car from Singapore into Malaysia

HITCHING

Malaysia has long had a reputation for being an excellent place for hitchhiking and it's generally still true. You'll get picked up both

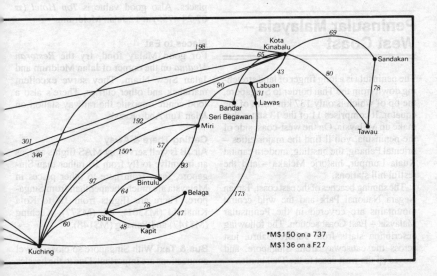

*M$150 on a 737
M$136 on a F27

by expats and by Malaysians and Singaporeans, but it's strictly an activity for foreigners – a hitchhiking Malaysian would probably just get left by the roadside!

BOAT

There are no services connecting the peninsula with north Borneo. On a local level, there are boats between the peninsula and offshore islands and along the rivers of Sabah and Sarawak – see these sections for full details.

LOCAL TRANSPORT

Local transport varies widely from place to place. Almost everywhere there are taxis and in most cases they are metered. In major cities there are buses – in KL the government buses are backed up by private operators.

In many towns there are also bicycle rickshaws. While they are dying out in KL and have become principally a tourist gimmick in many Malaysian cities, they are still a viable form of transport. Indeed in places like Georgetown, with its convoluted and narrow streets, a bicycle rickshaw is the best way of getting around.

Peninsular Malaysia – West Coast

The peninsula is a long finger of land stretching down from the Thai border to Singapore, the tip of which is only 137 km north of the equator. It comprises 11 of the 13 states that make up Malaysia. On the west-coast side of the peninsula, you'll find the major cities – oriental Penang, the bustling, modern capital Kuala Lumpur, historic Melaka – and the restful hill stations.

The shining beaches of the east coast, Taman Negara National Park and the wild central mountains are covered in the Peninsular Malaysia – East Coast section. The following description starts from Johore Bahru, just across the causeway from Singapore, and moves up the west coast to the Thai border.

JOHORE BAHRU

The state of Johore comprises the entire southern tip of the peninsula. It's capital is Johore Bahru (JB), the southern gateway to Peninsular Malaysia as it is connected to Singapore by a 1038-metre-long causeway.

Johore Bahru's history goes back to the mid-19th century when Melaka fell to the Portuguese and the sultans fled and then re-established their capital in this area.

Few people stop for long in JB as both Singapore and Melaka offer better prospects. However, if you do stop, it's worth exploring the **Istana Besar**, the former palace of the Johore royal family and now an impressive museum.

Places to Stay

The *Hotel Chean Seng* is a very basic Chinese hotel with typical partitioned rooms with mesh around the top, fan and bath. It costs M$15 for a room with one large bed and is as basic as you'd expect for that price.

Up the scale a bit is the *Hotel JB* (☎ 07-22 4788) at 80A Jalan Wong Ah Fook. Singles/doubles are M$29/30 with fan and common bath. The rooms here are fairly clean and not as box-like as some other places. Also good value is *Top Hotel* (☎ 07-24 4755) at 12 Jalan Meldrum.

Places to Eat

For good Malay food, try the *Restoran Medina* on the corner of Jalan Meldrum and Jalan Siew Niam. They serve excellent martabak and other curries. There's also a food centre opposite the railway station on Jalan Tun Abdu Razak.

Getting There & Away

Air JB is well served by MAS flights and, as an incentive to fly from JB rather than Singapore, fares from here to other places in Malaysia are much cheaper than from Singapore. There are flights from JB to Kota Kinabalu (M$301), KL (M$77), Kuching (M$147) and Penang (M$148).

Bus & Taxi With Singapore so close, travel connections are important. Due to the hassles

Peninsular Malaysia

0   50   100 km

of crossing the causeway – customs, immigration and so on – there's a much wider selection of buses and long-distance taxis to other towns in Peninsular Malaysia from JB than there are in Singapore.

There are regular buses from JB to Melaka (M$10), KL (M$15), Ipoh (M$26) and Butterworth (M$30). To the east coast there are departures to Kota Tinggi, Kuantan (M$15) and Mersing. From the JB taxi station, there are regular taxis to Kuantan (M$10), Kota Tinggi (M$3.30), Melaka (M$17.40) and KL (M$32.35) – add M$2 for air-con.

Train There are daily trains from JB to KL and Butterworth, and these can be used to get to most places on the west coast. There are also connections to Singapore, although a bus or taxi is quicker.

To/From Singapore The regular bus No 170 operates every 15 minutes between JB and Queen St in Singapore, and it costs 90 sen. The Johore Bahru Express costs M$1 and its Singapore terminal is at Rochor Rd, only a stone's throw from the No 170 bus terminal.

MELAKA

Melaka (Malacca), Malaysia's most historically interesting city, has been the site of some dramatic events over the years. The complete series of European incursions into Malaysia – Portuguese, Dutch and English – occurred here. Yet this was an important trading port long before the first Portuguese adventurers set foot in the city.

In 1405, Admiral Cheng Ho, the 'three-jewelled eunuch prince', arrived in Melaka bearing gifts from the Ming Emperor, the promise of protection from arch-enemies (the Siamese) and, surprisingly, the Muslim religion. Despite internal squabbles and intrigues, Melaka grew to be a powerful trading state and successfully repulsed Siamese attacks.

In 1511, Alfonso d'Albuquerque took the city for the Portuguese and the fortress of A'Famosa was constructed. Finally, the Dutch attacked the city and in 1641 it passed

■ **PLACES TO STAY**

4	Plaza Inn
5	May Chiang Hotel
7	Majestic Hotel
8	City Bayview Hotel
9	Hong Kong Hotel
10	Ng Fook Hotel
11	Ramada Renaissance Hotel
12	Wisma Hotel
13	Paradise Hostel
18	Chong Hoe Hotel
20	Valiant Hotel
21	Central Hotel
24	Palace Hotel
27	Kane's Tours & Hostel
42	Kancil Guest House

▼ **PLACES TO EAT**

19	Kedai Kek New Tai Tee Bakery
22	Tai Chong Hygienic Ice Cafe
23	Sri Lakshmi Vilas Restaurant
29	Jonkers Melaka Restoran
32	Restoran Veni
33	UE Tea House

OTHER

1	Local Bus Stand
2	Taxi Station
3	Express Bus Terminal
6	Church of St Peter
14	Kampung Hulu Mosque
15	Buddhist Temple
16	Cheng Hoon Teng Temple
17	Kampung Kling Mosque, Sri Pogyatha Vinoyagar Temple
25	Bukit China
26	Hang Li Poh Well, Po San Teng
28	Baba-Nonya Heritage Museum
30	Christ Church
31	Church of St Francis
34	Tourist Office
35	Stadthuys
36	St Paul's Church
37	Dumai Ferry Office
38	Porta de Santiago
39	Cultural Museum (Muzium Budaya)
40	Sound & Light Show
41	Proclamation of Independence Museum

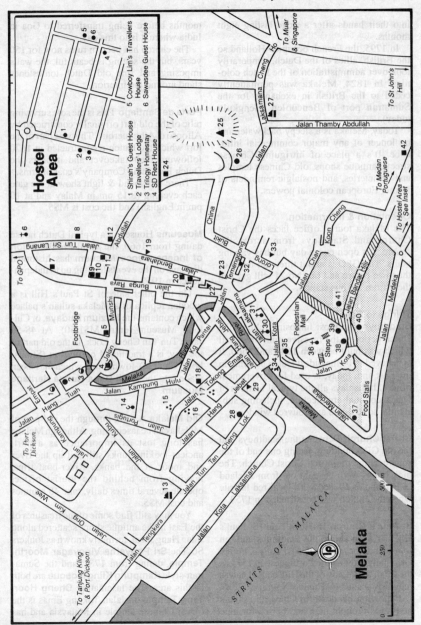

Hostel Area

1 Shiran's Guest House
2 Travellers' Lodge
3 Trilogy Homestay
4 SD Rest House
5 Cowboy Lim's Travellers House
6 Sawasdee Guest House

To Muar & Singapore

To St John's Hill

Jalan Thamby Abdullah

To Medan Portugese

To Hostel Area See inset

To GPO

Jalan Tun Sri Lanang

Jalan Bendahara

Jalan Bunga Raya

Jalan Munshi

Footbridge

To Port Dickson

Jalan Hang Tuah

Jalan Kampung Hulu

Melaka River

Jalan Kampung Pantai

Jalan Bunga

Jalan Kubu

Jalan Portugis

Jalan Hang Jebat

Jalan Tokong

Jalan Emas

Jalan Hang Lekiu

Jalan Tukang Emas

Jalan Hang Kasturi

Jalan Hang Jebat

Jalan Hang Lekir

Jalan Hang Tuah

Jalan Tun Tan Cheng Lok

Jalan Tengkera

Jalan Kota Laksamana

Jalan Ong Kim Wee

To Tanjung Kling & Port Dickson

Jalan China

Jalan Bukit Cina

Lorong Tengkong

Jalan Laksamana

Jalan Kota

Jalan Kota

Jalan Merdeka

Jalan Merdeka

Jalan Bandar Hilir

Pedestrian Mall

Steps

Food Stalls

Laksamana Cheng Ho

Koon Cheng

Jalan Chan Koon Cheng

Melaka

STRAITS OF MALACCA

500 m
250
0

Melaka

into their hands after a siege lasting eight months.

In 1795, the French occupied Holland so the British, allies of the Dutch, temporarily took over administration of the Dutch colonies. In 1824, Melaka was permanently ceded to the British in exchange for the Sumatran port of Bencoolen (Bengkulu today).

Today, Melaka is a sleepy backwater and no longer of any major commercial influence. It's a place of intriguing Chinese streets, antique shops, old Chinese temples and cemeteries, and nostalgic reminders of former European colonial powers.

Orientation & Information
The Melaka tourist office faces the Christ Church and Stadthuys from across the square. It's open every day but has varying hours. The GPO is about three km north of the town centre and bus No 21 will get you there from the bus station.

Things to See
Stadthuys The most imposing relic of the Dutch period is the massive pink town hall which was built between 1641 and 1660. It is believed to be the oldest Dutch building in the East and, today, is used for government offices. It displays all the typical features of Dutch colonial architecture, including substantial solid doors and louvred windows.

Christ Church Between the Stadthuys and the old GPO building, facing one end of the square, is the bright red Christ Church. The pink bricks were brought out from Zeeland in Holland and faced with local red laterite when the church was constructed in 1753.

St Paul's Church Bukit St Paul (St Paul's Hill) rises up above the Stadthuys and, on top, stand the ruins of St Paul's Church. Originally built by the Portuguese in 1571 as the small 'Our Lady of the Hill' chapel, it was regularly visited by Francis Xavier.

Following his death in China, the saint's body was brought here and buried for nine months before being transferred to Goa in India where it is to this day.

The church has been in ruins now for 150 years, but the setting is beautiful, the walls imposing and fine old Dutch tombstones stand around the interior.

Porta de Santiago This is the sole surviving relic of the old fort originally constructed by Alfonso d'Albuquerque. This was part of the fort which the Dutch reconstructed in 1670 following their takeover and it bears the Dutch East India Company's coat of arms.

There is a sound & light show at the gate each evening (8.15 pm in Malay and at 10 pm in English) and the cost is M$5.

Museums Housed in a typical Dutch house dating from 1660, the small **Proclamation of Independence Museum** has historical displays on the events leading up to independence in 1957.

On the other side of St Paul's Hill is a wooden replica of a Melaka sultan's palace which contains the **Muzium Budaya**, or Cultural Museum (entry M$1.50). At 48-50 Jalan Tun Tan Cheng Lock, in the old part of the city, is a traditional *peranakan* (Straits-born Chinese) townhouse which has been made into the small **Baba-Nonya Heritage Museum**.

Old Melaka A walk through the old part of Melaka can be fascinating. Although Melaka has long lost its importance as a port, ancient-looking junks still sail up the river and moor at the banks. River-boat trips, leaving from behind the tourist office, operate several times daily, take 45 minutes and cost M$5.

You may still find some of the treasures of the East in the antique shops scattered along Jalan Hang Jebat, formerly known as Jonkers St. The **Sri Pogyatha Vinoyagar Moorthi Temple**, dating from 1781, and the Sumatran-style **Kampung Kling Mosque** are both in this area. The fascinating **Cheng Hoon Teng Temple** on Jalan Tokong Emas is the oldest Chinese temple in Malaysia and has an inscription commemorating Cheng Ho's epochal visit to Melaka.

Beaches Melaka's beaches used to attract a steady stream of travellers but they offer little attraction these days. **Tanjung Kling** and, a little further out, **Pantai Kundor**, are the main beaches but the Straits of Melaka have become increasingly polluted over the years and it's worst around Melaka itself. There are occasional plagues of jellyfish.

Places to Stay

Hostels Melaka has a number of traveller-oriented hostels. *Paradise Hostel* (☎ 06-23 0821), at 4 Jalan Tengkera just north of the Jalan Kubu intersection, has dorm beds for M$5 and singles/doubles from M$9/12. South of the town centre, *Kancil Guest House* at 177 Jalan Bandar Hilir is very clean, quiet and secure but it is a bit of a walk from the centre with your pack. Dorm beds are M$5, rooms M$8/10 and they rent bicycles for M$3 per day.

On the main road on the Singapore side of town is *Kane's Youth Hostel* (☎ 06-23 5124) at 136A/1 Jalan Laksamana Cheng Hoe (also called Jalan Panjang). Rates are much the same as the other hostels but it is rather cramped and gloomy.

Most of the new backpacker's places are concentrated in an area of reclaimed land just south of Jalan Bandar Hilir known as Taman Melaka Raya. Bus Nos 17 or 21 will take you there from the bus station for 30 sen or a taxi or trishaw will cost about M$5.

Popular places in this area include the *Trilogy Homestay* (☎ 06-24 5319) at 223B Taman Melaka Raya. It's run by a friendly couple and costs M$5 for dorm beds or there are doubles from M$14 to M$18. They also have mountain bikes to rent for M$5 per day. Nearby at 214B is the *Travellers' Lodge* with dorm beds at M$5, and singles from M$9 to M$12 and doubles from M$14 to M$15.

A block over is the popular *Cowboy Lim's Travellers House* at 269 Taman Melaka Raya. Cowboy Lim is quite a character and has dorm beds at M$7 and rooms from M$9/12, which include breakfast. There are

laundry facilities and bicycles for hire. Right across the road is the comfortable new *SD Rest House*. Nearby is *Robin's Nest* at No 247B, with singles/doubles for M$9/$12 and dorm beds for $5. Other places in the same area include the *Holiday Home Stay* at No 305A, *Shirah's Guest House* at No 229-230B, *Amy Homestay* at No 244B and the *Sawasdee Guest House* at 271B.

Hotels Of the cheap hotels, one of the better ones is the *Ng Fook* (☎ 06-22 8055) at 154 Jalan Bunga Raya just north of Jalan Munshi Abdullah. It's basic but OK with double rooms for M$21 or M$28 with air-con. Almost next door is the very similar *Hong Kong Hotel*.

Cheaper still is the *Central Hotel* (☎ 06-22 2984) in a very good location at 31 Jalan Bendahara. Singles/doubles cost M$12/14 with fan. It's a bit shabby but, at these prices, is hard to beat. A few doors down, the *Valiant Hotel* (☎ 06-22 2799) is a step up the scale and has rooms for M$20/25 with fan or M$30/35 with air-con.

The *Chong Hoe Hotel* on Jalan Tokong Emas is in an interesting location and is very well-kept. Rooms are M$14/17 or M$20/25 with air-con in this pleasant hotel. The rambling old *Majestic Hotel* (☎ 06-22 2367), at 188 Jalan Bunga Raya, is a reasonably good deal although it's also rather run-down. The high ceilings and swishing fans add to the cool lazy atmosphere and there's a bar, restaurant and car park. Rooms cost M$20/25 with fan, or M$38/40 with bath and air-con.

Places to Eat

The main place to eat in Melaka is along Jalan Taman, on what used to be the waterfront. The permanent stalls along here serve all the usual food-centre specialities. Just walk along and see what attracts you, but one very good place is *Bunga Raya Restaurant* at No 40 which has excellent steamed crabs.

The Taman Melaka Raya area, where many of the new backpackers' places have sprung up, also has a variety of restaurants, bars and cafes. It's becoming the new restaurant centre for the town.

At 38 Jalan Laksamana, in the centre of town, *Restaurant Kim Swee Huat* has a menu oriented for travellers with an emphasis on Chinese food. For breakfast, you can get muesli, porridge or toast. Other central restaurants include the south Indian *Sri Lakshmi Vilas* on Jalan Bendahara near the intersection with Jalan Temenggong. Continue along Jalan Temenggong to the *Restoran Veni*, another Indian restaurant and a good place for a breakfast *roti chanai*.

Around the corner at 20 Lorong Bukit China, the *UE Tea House* is a great place for a dim-sum breakfast. The *Tai Chong Hygienic Ice Cafe* at 39/72 Jalan Bunga Raya offers a wide variety of ice cream treats and snacks. Try the *Kedai Kek New Tai Tee* on Jalan Bendahara for bakery goods.

Finally, in the heart of the old town on Jalan Hang Jebat, the *Jonkers Melaka Restoran* is in a traditional Peranakan house and serves both Western and Nonya dishes. The set menu of four Nonya dishes for M$12 is a good deal, but this place is only open from 10 am to 6 pm.

Getting There & Away

Bus & Taxi There are plenty of buses and long-distance taxis to Melaka. To or from KL there are 10 daily Jebat Express air-con buses from the express bus terminal for M$6.50. Melaka to Singapore express buses leave the local bus stand hourly from 8 am to 6 pm, and the fare is M$11.

From the express bus terminal, the Murni Express Company runs daily buses to Lumut for M$17. There are also regular buses to Butterworth (M$21.40) and Kuantan (M$11).

Taxis leave from the taxi station just opposite the local bus station and operate to Port Dickson (M$8), Muar (M$4), Kluang (M$4) and KL (M$13).

Boat Two companies operate ferries to Dumai in Sumatra but you need an Indonesian visa to enter or leave via Dumai. The fare is M$80 one way or M$150 return, plus M$9 port charges. You can book tickets at Atlas Travel Service (☎ 06-22 0777) on Jalan

Hang Jebat or at Tunas Rupat Utama Express (☎ 06-23 2505) at 17A Jalan Merdeka, just beyond the tourist office.

Getting Around

A bicycle rickshaw is the ideal way of getting around compact and slow-moving Melaka. By the hour, they should cost about M$7, or M$2 for any one-way trip within the town, but you'll have to bargain.

You can easily walk around the central sights or rent a bike from one of the hostels from M$3 to M$5 a day.

PORT DICKSON

There's nothing of great interest in Port Dickson (PD) itself although it's a pleasant enough small port town. South of the town, however, there is a stretch of beach extending for 16 km to Cape Rachado, and it's almost clean enough to swim in. There are a number of places to stay along the beach and it's an interesting walk along the coast to the cape.

Places to Stay

The beach stretches south of PD to Cape Rachado, but the best beach starts from around the Km 8 peg. The *Port Dickson Youth Hostel* is above the road at 6½ km. It attracts few visitors although it costs just M$7 per night and has freshly painted dorms.

At Km 13, the Chinese *Kong Ming Hotel* (☎ 06-40 5683) is right by the beach. It's nothing special but is reasonably priced at M$23 for a double. Also here is the *Lido Hotel* (☎ 06-40 5273) which is set in spacious grounds. Rooms cost M$30 for a double, M$38 with air-con, and M$45 for a triple.

Getting There & Away

By bus, it's M$3.30 from Melaka and M$3.70 from KL. A taxi is about M$6.50 from either town.

From PD town, there are buses which will drop you off anywhere along the beach.

SEREMBAN

Seremban, the capital of Negri Sembilan, is

the centre of the Malaysian Minangkabau area – closely related to the Minangkabau area of Sumatra. The small **State Museum**, in the lake area overlooking the town centre, is a good example of the Minangkabau style of architecture.

KUALA LUMPUR

Malaysia's capital city is a curious blend of the old and new. It's a modern and fast moving city although the traffic never takes on the nightmare proportions of Bangkok. It has gleaming high-rise office blocks beside multilane highways, but the old colonial architecture still manages to stand out proudly.

It's also a blend of cultures – the Malay capital with a vibrant Chinatown, an Indian quarter and a playing field in the middle of the city where the crack of cricket bat on ball can still be heard.

KL, as it's almost always called, started in the 1860s when a band of prospectors in search of tin landed at the meeting point of the Kelang and Gombak rivers and named it Kuala Lumpur, or 'Muddy Estuary'.

Orientation

The real heart of KL is Merdeka Square, not far from the confluence of the two muddy rivers from which KL takes its name. Just to the south-east of this square is the modern business centre of KL and the older Chinatown. Across the Kelang River is the railway station and the modern National Mosque.

Heading east from the Merdeka Square area is Jalan Tun Perak, a major trunk road which leads to the transport hub of the country, the Pudu Raya bus and taxi station on the eastern edge of the central district.

Running north from Merdeka Square is Jalan Tuanku Abdul Rahman (henceforth known as Jalan TAR) with a number of KL's popular cheaper hotels and more modern buildings. Jalan Raja Laut runs parallel to Jalan TAR and takes the northbound traffic. Both roads are horrendously noisy.

The GPO is just to the south of central Merdeka Square and a little further on is the State Mosque and the KL railway station.

Beyond them is KL's green belt where you can find the Lake Gardens, the National Museum and Monument, and the Malaysian Parliament.

Information

Tourist Offices KL is perhaps a little over-endowed with tourist offices. The Tourist Development Corporation (TDC) tourist information counter (☎ 03-274 6063) is on the 2nd level of the Putra World Trade Centre on Jalan Tun Ismail in the north-west section of KL – rather a long way from the city centre.

More convenient is the KL Visitor's Centre (☎ 03-230 1369) in Balai Kuala Lumpur at 3 Jalan Sultan Hishamuddin. It's next to the Balai Seni Lukis Negara (National Art Gallery) opposite the railway station.

To complete the picture, there's the Malaysia Tourist Information Centre (TIC) (☎ 03-243 4929), housed in the former mansion of a Malaysian planter and tin miner which later became the British and then the Japanese Army headquarters. It is on Jalan Ampang, north-east of the city centre, and is a very modern set-up.

Money There are plenty of banks throughout the central area of KL. For moneychangers, try Jalan Sultan near the Kelang bus station or Jalan Ampang.

Post & Telecommunications The huge GPO is across the Kelang River from the central district. For international calls in business hours, the best place to head for is the previously mentioned Malaysia TIC. At other times, the Telekom office, on Jalan Gereja in the town centre, is open 24 hours a day.

Travel Agencies MSL (☎ 03-298 4132) is in the South-East Asia Hotel just off the top of Jalan TAR. It usually has some interesting fares on offer and is the STA Travel agent. They also handle student cards. See the Student Travel section in the

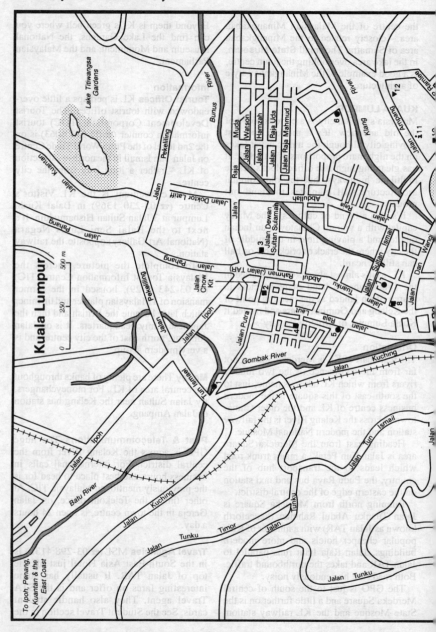

Kuala Lumpur

Lake Titiwangsa Gardens

0   250   500 m

To Ipoh, Penang,
Kuantan & the
East Coast

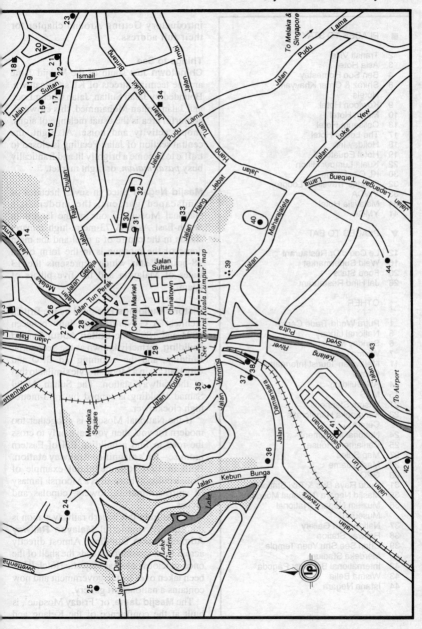

■ PLACES TO STAY

2   Transit Villa
3   Asia Hotel
4   Ben Soo Homestay
8   Shiraz & Omar Khayyam
    Hotels
9   Kowloon Hotel
10 Merlin Hotel
13 Coliseum Hotel
17 The Lodge Hotel
18 Holiday Inn
19 Hotel Equatorial
22 Kuala Lumpur Hilton
30 KL City Lodge
32 Sunrise Travellers Lodge
33 YWCA
34 Malaysia Hotel
41 YMCA

▼ PLACES TO EAT

12 Le Coq d'Or Restaurant
16 Weld Supermarket
20 Food Stalls
26 Jai Hind Restaurant

OTHER

1   Putra World Trade Centre
5   National Library
6   Sunday Market
7   Wisma Loke
11 Malaysian Tourist Information
    Centre
14 AIA Building
15 MAS
21 Wisma Stephens
23 Karyaneka Handicrafts
    Centre
24 National Monument
25 Parliament House
27 Map Sales
28 Masjid Jame
29 GPO
31 Pudu Raya Bus & Taxi Station
35 Masjid Negara (National Mosque)
36 Muzium Negara (National
    Museum)
37 National Art Gallery
38 Railway Station
39 Chan See Shu Yuen Temple
40 Merdeka Stadium
42 International Buddhist Pagoda
43 Wisma Belia
44 Istana Negara

introductory Getting Around chapter for their full address.

Things to See
Chinatown Just south of the Masjid Jame are the teeming streets of KL's Chinatown. Bounded by Jalan Sultan, Jalan Cheng Lock and Jalan Sultan Mohammed, this crowded, colourful area is the usual melange of signs, shops, activity and noise. At night, the central section of Jalan Petaling is closed to traffic to become a brightly lit and frantically busy *pasar malam*, or night market.

Masjid Negara Sited in seven hectares of landscaped gardens, the modernistic National Mosque is one of the largest in South-East Asia. A 73-metre-high minaret stands in the centre of a pool and the main dome of the mosque is in the form of an 18-pointed star which represents the 13 states of Malaysia and the five pillars of Islam.

Historic Buildings Designed by the British architect A C Norman and built between 1894 and 1897, the **Sultan Abdul Samad Building**, formerly known as the Secretariat Building, and the adjoining old **GPO** and **City Hall** are in a Moorish style similar to that of the railway station. The Sultan Abdul Samad Building is topped by a 43-metre-high clocktower.

If the National Mosque is altogether too modern for you, then you have only to cross the road to find a building full of Eastern promise – KL's magnificent **railway station**. Built in 1911, this delightful example of British colonial humour is a Moorish fantasy of spires, minarets, towers, cupolas and arches.

Across from this superb railway station is the equally wonderful **Malayan Railway Administration Building**. Almost directly across from the station stands the shell of the once-gracious colonial Majestic Hotel. It has been taken over by the government and now contains a national art gallery.

The **Masjid Jame**, or 'Friday Mosque', is built at the confluence of the Kelang and

Gombak rivers and overlooks Merdeka Square. This was the place where KL's founders first set foot in the town and where supplies were landed for the tin mines.

Museums & Galleries At the southern end of the Lake Gardens and less than a km along Jalan Damansara from the railway station is the **Muzium Negara** (National Museum). It's full of unusual exhibits, such as the skull of an elephant which derailed a train!

Another strange sight is an 'amok catcher', an ugly barbed device used to catch and hold a man who has run amok. Admission to the museum is free and it is open daily from 9 am to 6 pm except on Friday when it closes between 12 noon and 2.45 pm.

At the **National Art Gallery**, the exhibits change regularly and include art, often modern, from around the world. The art gallery is housed in the former Majestic Hotel, opposite the railway station.

Lake Gardens The 60-hectare gardens form the green belt of KL. You can rent boats on Tasik Perdana for M$4 per hour.

Jalan Ampang Lined with impressive mansions, Jalan Ampang was built up by the early tin millionaires. Today, many of the fine buildings have become embassies and consulates so that the street is KL's 'Ambassador's Row'.

Markets KL has a number of markets which are worth investigating. The **Central Market** in Chinatown was previously the city's produce market but has now been refurbished to become the focus for handicraft and art sales. At night, Jalan Petaling in Chinatown becomes an incredibly busy pasar malam.

The Kampung Bahru area north-east of the city centre is the site each Saturday night for KL's **Sunday Market** (so called, possibly, because it continues into Sunday morning). It's a food and produce market, a handicrafts market and a place to sample a wide variety of Malay foods.

Places to Stay

Hostels KL has a number of good hostels which cater almost exclusively for the budget traveller. Most shoestring travellers find these places ideal. They all offer similar services: dorm beds as well as rooms, cooking and washing facilities, a fridge and a notice board.

A very popular place, right on the edge of Chinatown and only a few minutes' walk from the Pudu Raya bus station, is the *Travellers' Moon Lodge* (☎ 03-230 6601) at 36 Jalan Silang. Run by a very amenable guy named Fred, the hostel is good and offers dorm beds for M$8.50 and a few rooms with fan for M$20 – these prices include breakfast.

Also popular is the *Sunrise Travellers Lodge* (☎ 03-230 8878) at 89-B Jalan Pudu Lama, a small street which loops off Jalan Pudu almost opposite the bus station. Dorm beds cost M$9, or there are rooms for M$23 to M$25 with fan. A light breakfast is also included in the price. If you walk west along Jalan Pudu from the bus station, the street is right beside the petrol station.

Right on Jalan Pudu is the *KL City Lodge* (☎ 03-230 5275), directly opposite the bus station. This is much more a regular hotel but is still popular among travellers. Dorm beds cost M$8.50, or M$10 with air-con, while rooms are M$25 or M$30 with air-con.

Up between Jalan Raja Laut and Jalan TAR is another good place, the *Transit Villa* (☎ 03-441 0443) at 36-2 Jalan Chow Kit, a small road near the 7-Eleven store at the northern end of Jalan Raja Laut. Dorm beds in this friendly place cost M$8.50 or rooms are M$18 to M$26.

A bit closer to the town centre, the *Ben Soo Homestay* (☎ 03-291 8096) is at 61B Jalan Tiong Nam just off Jalan Raja Laut. It's a small family-style homestay with dorm beds at M$8 and rooms at M$20. A minibus No 25 will get you there from the Pudu Raya bus station or a bus No 33 from the railway station.

KL also has a youth hostel. The *Meridian International Youth Hostel* (☎ 03-232 1428) is right in the centre of Chinatown, tucked away at 36 Jalan Hang Kasturi, very close to

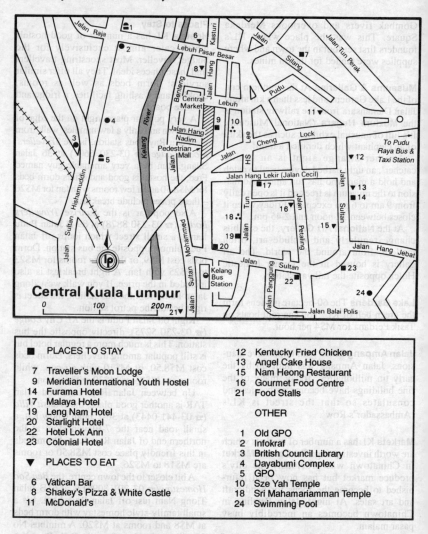

Central Kuala Lumpur

0   100   200 m

■ **PLACES TO STAY**

7   Traveller's Moon Lodge
9   Meridian International Youth Hostel
14 Furama Hotel
17 Malaya Hotel
19 Leng Nam Hotel
20 Starlight Hotel
22 Hotel Lok Ann
23 Colonial Hotel

▼ **PLACES TO EAT**

6   Vatican Bar
8   Shakey's Pizza & White Castle
11 McDonald's

12 Kentucky Fried Chicken
13 Angel Cake House
15 Nam Heong Restaurant
16 Gourmet Food Centre
21 Food Stalls

OTHER

1   Old GPO
2   Infokraf
3   British Council Library
4   Dayabumi Complex
5   GPO
10 Sze Yah Temple
18 Sri Mahamariamman Temple
24 Swimming Pool

Central Market. It is a typical friendly youth hostel with dorm beds at M$6.50 for members and M$7.50 for nonmembers; air-con dorms are M$10.

Finally, there are the Ys. Firstly, the *YMCA* (☎ 03-274 1439) is at 95 Jalan Padang Belia, south of the centre off Jalan Tun

Sambanthan. Its distance from the centre makes it an unattractive option unless you have your own transport. Dorm beds go for M$20, or there are single/double rooms from M$18/25. Take a minibus No 12 and ask for the Lido cinema.

Secondly, the *YWCA* (☎ 03-28 3225),

much more central at 12 Jalan Hang Jebat, has rooms at M$15/25 for women, takes couples for M$35 and has family rooms for M$50 – a good deal.

Hotels – There are many hotels in Kuala Lumpur, including those in the following areas:

Jalan TAR Moving up Jalan TAR from its junction with Jalan Tun Perak, there's the *Coliseum Hotel* (☎ 03-292 6270) at No 100 with its famous old-planter's restaurant. All rooms share common bath facilities and are M$19 for a single with fan and M$26 for a double with air-con. Although in need of renovation, this place is a bargain and, consequently, is often full.

At No 134, the *Tivoli Hotel* (☎ 03-292 4108) is a reasonable Chinese cheapie which charges M$17/21 for rooms with fan and common bath. The *Rex Hotel* at No 134 is similar but not as friendly.

The *Shiraz Hotel* (☎ 03-292 2625) at 1 Jalan Medan Tuanku, on the corner with Jalan TAR, is an unremarkable place at the top of this range and has rooms for M$35/40 with air-con and bath.

At 319-1 Jalan TAR, you'll find *Paradise Bed & Breakfast* (☎ 03-292 2872) but it's not great value, especially as it's quite a long walk from the centre. Dorm beds are M$10 and singles/doubles are M$23/29 or M$29/35 with air-con. A basic breakfast is also included.

Chinatown The cheapest of the Chinese cheapies is *Leng Nam Hotel* (☎ 03-230 1489) at 165 Jalan Tun HS Lee. Basic rooms with fan cost M$17. Another place which seems to attract a steady trickle of travellers is the well-camouflaged *Wan Kow Hotel* at 16 Jalan Sultan. Rooms with fan and common bath cost M$19 for one or two people.

Also good value, and in Chinatown, is the *Colonial Hotel* (☎ 03-238 0336) at 39 Jalan Sultan, where single/double rooms cost M$18/23, or M$26 with air con.

At the top of the range, the comfortable *Hotel Lok Ann* (☎ 03-238 9544) at 113A

Jalan Petaling has air-con doubles for M$54. The *Starlight Hotel* (☎ 03-238 9811) at 90 Jalan Hang Kasturi has doubles with bath and air-con for M$41 and is recommended by many travellers.

Places to Eat

Food Markets KL has some very good night-time eating places. At dusk, Jalan Petaling is closed to traffic between Jalan Cheng Lock and Jalan Sultan and the tables are set up outside the Chinese restaurants, which are on Jalan Hang Lekir between Jalan Petaling and Jalan Sultan. These places are fairly touristy and the prices reflect this, but it's still the best place to eat in the evenings. There are also stalls in this area selling peanut pancakes, sweets, drinks and fruit.

The *Gourmet Food Centre* on Jalan Petaling is a handy little undercover centre offering a variety of food. You can dine outdoors and overlook the river from the front of the Central Market.

Other night markets offering tasty food include the Sunday Market out at Kampung Bahru and a street off Jalan TAR close to the South-East Asia Hotel. Both are good places for Malay food.

Indian Food At 15 Jalan Melayu, near the corner of Jalan TAR and Jalan Tun Perak, there's the *Jai Hind*. It's a good place for Indian snacks and light meals.

Upstairs at 60A Jalan TAR, *Bangles* is an Indian restaurant with a good reputation. Further along, the *Shiraz*, on the corner of Jalan TAR and Jalan Medan Tuanku, is a good Pakistani restaurant. Some prefer the similar *Omar Khayyam* next door.

The *Bilal* restaurants – there are branches at 40 Jalan Ipoh, 33 Jalan Ampang and 37 Jalan TAR – are other good Indian restaurants. They do good roti chanai and martabaks.

For a good selection of south Indian food, head to the Brickfields area where there are four or more daun pisang (banana leaf) restaurants serving rice with vegetarian, fish, chicken and mutton curries. One of the best is *Devi's*.

Chinese Food Chinese restaurants can be found all over the place, but particularly around Chinatown and along Jalan Bukit Bintang, which is off Jalan Pudu past the Pudu Raya bus station. There are excellent lunch-time dim sums at the expensive *Merlin Hotel* and also at the *Overseas* in Central Market.

A local speciality in KL is *bah kut teh*, supposed to have originated in Kelang; it's pork ribs with white rice and Chinese tea, and is a very popular breakfast meal.

Malay Food There are Malay warungs and kedai kopis here and there throughout KL, but especially along Jalan TAR. Several of those in the vicinity of the Coliseum Hotel are excellent and cheap. Look for the *nasi lemak* in the early mornings – coconut rice topped with dried fish, boiled egg, peanuts and curry. The *Restoran Imaf* is a good bet and just down from the Minerva Bookshop. The area around Stadium Merdeka is also renowned for its Malay warungs.

Western Food KL has a surprising variety of Western restaurants including, at the bottom of Jalan TAR, *Kentucky Fried Chicken* and *A&W* takeaways. There are several American-style hamburger joints around the bus station including *Wendy's*, *McDonald's* and *White Castle*.

Not to be missed is the restaurant in the *Coliseum Hotel* on Jalan TAR where they have excellent steaks at around M$20. The place is quite a colonial experience and has hardly changed over the years.

There are lots of restaurants along Jalan Bukit Bintang, including many of the fast-food chains. At No 81, the *Castell Grill* is a more up-market place.

In Chinatown, don't miss the *Angel Cake House* on Jalan Sultan. They offer all kinds of buns and rolls stuffed with chicken curry or cheeses – fresh from the oven. Also available are pizza, macaroni, fruit tarts and chocolate cakes.

And finally, there's *Le Coq d'Or* (☎ 03-242 9732), a restaurant in a fine turn-of-the-century mansion on Jalan Ampang, is expensive but not quite as expensive as the elegant surroundings might indicate. Expect to pay around M$50 for two for a meal which is really just of a reasonable standard.

Entertainment

KL has plenty of discos, bars and the dreaded karaoke lounges. The following nightclubs are all open (and licensed) until 7 am: *Phases 2, Spuds, Betelnut* and *Mirrors* in Wisma Stephens; the *11 LA* in Lorong Ampang; *October Cherry*, 145 Jalan Ampang; *Club Oz* in the Hotel Shangri-La; and the *Tin Mine* in the Hilton.

Karaoke enthusiasts can head for the *Tapagayo* in Jalan Bukit Bintang or *Hearts* in the Ampang Park shopping complex on Jalan Ampang.

For a quiet drink in a bar, the *Coliseum Hotel* at 100 Jalan TAR is a great escape, or the *Vatican* on Lebuh Pasar Besar is a place popular with local expats.

Free dance performances are held in the *Malaysia TIC* (☎ 03-243 4929) at 3.30 pm daily.

Things to Buy

Karyaneka Handicraft Centre, out past the Hilton on Jalan Raja Chulan, displays a wide variety of local craftwork in quasi-traditional settings. Hours are 9 am to 6 pm except for Friday when they close at 6.30 pm.

The night market along Jalan Petaling is a good place to shop for cheap clothes. 'Genuine' Lacoste shirts sell for around M$10, while copy jeans and designer T-shirts are also very cheap and virtually indistinguishable from the real McCoy.

The Central Market complex, housed in a cavernous art-deco building (formerly a wet market) between the GPO and Chinatown, offers an ever-changing selection of Malaysian art, clothes, souvenirs and more.

Getting There & Away

Air KL is well served by many international airlines and there are flights to and from Australia, Singapore, Indonesia, Thailand,

India, Philippines, Hong Kong and various destinations in Europe.

Some of the airline offices in KL include:

Aeroflot
Wisma Tong Ah, 1 Jalan Perak (☎ 03-261 3331)
British Airways
Hotel Merlin, Jalan Sultan Ismail (☎ 03-242 6177)
Cathay Pacific
UBN Tower, 10 Jalan P Ramlee (☎ 03-238 3377)
China Airlines
Amoda Building, 22 Jalan Imbi (☎ 03-242 7344)
Garuda
1st Floor, Angkasa Raya Building, Jalan Ampang (☎ 03-248 3542)
MAS
UMBC Building, Jalan Sulaiman (☎ 03-230 8844)
MAS Building, Jalan Sultan Ismail (☎ 03-261 0555)
For 24-hour reservation call ☎ 03-774 7000
Philippine Airlines
Wisma Stephens, Jalan Raja Chulan (☎ 03-242 9040)
Qantas
UBN Tower, 10 Jalan P Ramlee (☎ 03-238 9133)
Royal Brunei
Blue Moon Travel, Merlin Hotel, Jalan Sultan Ismail (☎ 03-242 6550)
Singapore Airlines
Wisma SIA, Jalan Dang Wangi (☎ 03-298 7033)
Thai International
Kuwasa Building, 5 Jalan Raja Laut (☎ 03-293 7100)

On the domestic network, KL is the hub of MAS services and there are flights to most major towns and cities on the peninsula and in East Malaysia.

Bus There is a wide variety of bus services, the majority of which operate from the busy Pudu Raya bus terminal on Jalan Pudu, just east of Chinatown. There are departures to most places throughout the day, and at night to main towns. Outside the station on Jalan Pudu, there's a dozen other companies, so it's worth checking these as well.

The left-luggage office in the Pudu Raya bus station is open daily from 8 am to 10 pm and the charge is M$1 per item per day. The Kelang bus station also has a M$1 left luggage office.

Typical fares from KL include Singapore M$16, Melaka M$6.25, Johore Bahru M$15, Lumut M$12, Cameron Highlands M$9.25, Ipoh M$8.50 and Butterworth M$14.70.

Train KL is also the hub of the railway system and there are daily departures for Butterworth, Wakaf Bahru (for Kota Bharu), Johore Bahru and Singapore. See the Malaysia Getting Around section for more details.

Taxi While the buses depart from downstairs, the taxis are upstairs in the Pudu Raya terminal although there are also long-distance taxi offices along Pudu Rd near the bus station. There are lots of taxis, and fares include Seremban M$6, Melaka M$13, Johore Bahru M$31, Ipoh M$17, Taiping M$22, Butterworth M$30, Genting Highlands M$8, Kuantan M$22, Kuala Terengganu M$36, Kota Bharu M$40 and Singapore M$36.

Air-con taxis also run on these routes and cost a couple of ringgit more.

Getting Around
To/From the Airport Taxis from the KL International Airport operate on a coupon system. You purchase a coupon from a booth at the airport and use it to pay the driver. Going to the airport is not so simple because the taxi drivers are uncertain about whether they will get a return trip – count on about M$20.

You can also go by bus – No 47 operates every hour or so from the Kelang bus station on Jalan Sultan Mohammed and costs M$1.50. The trip takes 45 minutes but it's a good idea to leave more time since traffic can be bad. The first departure is at 6 am.

Bus There are two bus systems operating in KL. City bus companies include Sri Jaya, Len Seng, Len, Ampang, Kee Hup and Toong Foong. The fares on most of these buses starts from 20 sen for the first km and go up five sen each two km. The faster minibuses operate on a fixed fare of 50 sen anywhere along their route. Whenever possible, have correct change ready when boarding the buses, particularly during rush hours.

Taxi There are plenty of taxis and fares are quite reasonable. Flagfall is M$1 on the aircon taxis. From midnight to 6 am there's an additional 50% supplement on top of the metered fare and extra passengers (more than two) are charged 10 sen each.

KL's taxi drivers are not keen on going to the airport or from the railway station on the meter – in those cases you'll have to bargain your fare. It shouldn't be more than a couple of dollars from the railway station to most places in KL.

Car Rental All the major companies have offices at the airport as well as the following city offices:

Avis
    40 Jalan Sultan Ismail (☎ 03-242 3500)
Budget
    Wisma MCA, 163 Jalan Ampang (☎ 03-261 1122)
Hertz
    214A Kompleks Antarabangsa, Jalan Sultan Ismail (☎ 03-243 3014)
National
    Wisma HLA, Jalan Raja Chulan (☎ 03-248 0522)
Thrifty
    LPPKN Building, Holiday Inn City Centre Annex, 12-B Jalan Raja Laut (☎ 03-293 2388)

AROUND KUALA LUMPUR
Batu Caves
The huge Batu Caves are the best known attraction in the vicinity of KL. They are just 13 km north of the capital, a short distance off the Ipoh road. The caves are in a towering limestone formation and were little known until about 100 years ago. Later, a small Hindu shrine was built in the major cave and it became a pilgrimage centre during the annual Thaipusam Festival.

The major cave, a vast open space known as the **Cathedral Cave**, is reached by a straight flight of 272 steps. Also reached by the same flight of steps is the long and winding **Dark Cave**, but this has been closed for some time because quarrying in the limestone outcrop has made the caves unsafe.

There are a number of other caves in the same formation, including a small cave at the base of the outcrop which has been made into a museum with figures of the various Hindu gods – admission is 50 sen.

To reach the caves, take minibus No 11 (60 sen) from Jalan Pudu or Jalan Semarang, or a Len Seng bus Nos 69 or 70 from Jalan Raja Laut and Jalan Ampang. During the Thaipusam Festival, you can take a train to the caves. Bus No 140 leaves the KL station at 9 am and No 141 leaves Batu Caves at 11.30 am.

National Zoo & Aquarium
East of KL, on the road to Ulu Kelang and about 13 km out, is the 62-hectare site of the National Zoo & Aquarium. Laid out around a central lake, the zoo collection emphasises the wildlife found in Malaysia. There are elephant rides and other amusements for children. The zoo is open daily from 9 am to 6 pm and admission is M$4, plus M$1 if you want to use your camera.

To get there, take Len Seng bus No 177 or a Lenchee bus No 180 from Lebuh Ampang, or you can take minibus Nos 17 or 23 also from Lebuh Ampang.

Orang Asli Museum
About 19 km from KL, on the Genting Highlands road, is this very informative museum which gives some good insights into the life and culture of Peninsular Malaysia's 70,000 indigenous inhabitants. It's well worth a look.

Templer Park
Beside the Ipoh road, 22 km north of KL, Templer Park was established during the colonial period by the British High Commissioner Sir Gerald Templer. The 1200-hectare park is intended to be a tract of jungle, preserved within easy reach of the city. There are a number of marked jungle paths, swimming lagoons and several waterfalls within the park boundaries.

To get there, take bus Nos 66, 72, 78 or 83 from the Pudu Raya terminal.

GENTING HIGHLANDS

The Genting Highlands is a thoroughly modern hill station – casinos are the attraction rather than the jungle walks. Accommodation is relatively expensive, it's about 50 km north from KL and buses and taxis go there from the Pudu Raya bus station.

FRASER'S HILL

Fraser's Hill, set at a cool altitude of 1524 metres, is quiet and relatively undeveloped – possibly because it's not the easiest hill station to get to. As in the Cameron Highlands, there are many beautiful gardens around the town and also many wild flowers carpeting the hills.

The information office (☎ 09-38 2201) is between the golf club and the Merlin Hotel, near the post office. They can supply maps and information brochures and they will also book accommodation in Fraser's Hill.

Places to Stay & Eat

If you're in need of something really reasonably priced, try the *Corona Nursery Youth Hostel* (☎ 09-38 2225), the flower nursery about a 40-minute walk from the information office. Basic rooms are M$7 per person and you can use a gas stove. This place is very isolated at the end of the road and unless you have transport, it is a hassle to get to.

The best place to stay is the relaxed *Gap Rest House* right at The Gap turn-off on the main road, eight km below Fraser's itself. It has spacious rooms for M$21 with bath and these are big enough for three people, with room to spare.

At Fraser's Hill itself, the accommodation is run by the Fraser's Hill Development Corporation (FHDC), a government-contracted bumiputra organisation, and it costs from M$35 upwards.

There's a reasonable selection of places to eat, all near the Puncak Inn. At one end of the inn is the Chinese *Hill View Restaurant*, while at the other end is the friendly Malay *Arzed Restaurant*. Between the two is the Malay *Restoran Puncak*, which serves roti chanai at any time of day.

Getting There & Away

Fraser's Hill is 103 km north of KL and 240 km from Kuantan on the east coast. Fraser's Hill is a little difficult to get to by public transport.

There's a twice-daily bus service from Kuala Kubu Bahru costing M$1.95. The buses depart from Kuala Kubu Bahru at 8 am and 12 noon and from Fraser's Hill at 10 am and 2 pm.

A taxi from Kuala Kubu Bahru is M$30 for the whole taxi. A bus from KL's Pudu Raya bus station to Kuala Kubu Bahru is M$3; a share-taxi M$6.

The last eight km up to Fraser's Hill is on a steep, winding, one-way section. At The Gap, you leave the Kuala Kubu Bahru to Raub road to make this final ascent. Traffic is permitted for 40-minute periods in each direction throughout the day from 7 am to 7 pm. From 7.40 pm to 6 am the road is open both ways and you take your chances! The logic is that you can see the headlights of any vehicle coming the other way.

CAMERON HIGHLANDS

Situated about 60 km north from Tapah, off the KL-Ipoh road, this is the best known and most extensive hill station. The Highlands stand at 1500 metres and the weather is pleasantly cool, not cold. Jungle walks are the thing to do here and, in the shops in Tanah Rata, you can buy somewhat inaccurate maps of the main walks. Most consist of a stroll of an hour or two but some take quite a bit longer and can be tough going.

The only wildlife you are likely to see is the fantastic variety of butterflies, but it was here that the American Thai silk entrepreneur, Jim Thompson, mysteriously disappeared in 1967 – he was never found. The hills around the Highlands are dotted with tea plantations some of which are open for inspection.

Orientation

From the turn-off at Tapah, it's 46 km up to Ringlet, the first village of the Highlands. About 14 km past Ringlet, you reach Tanah Rata, the main town of the Highlands, where

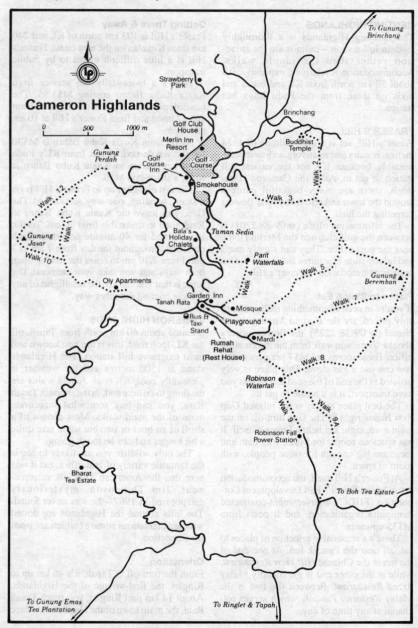

Cameron Highlands

To Gunung Brinchang

Strawberry Park

Brinchang

Golf Club House

Merlin Inn Resort

Buddhist Temple

Golf Course Inn

Walk 2

Golf Course

Smokehouse

Walk 3

Gunung Perdah

Walk 12

Walk 11

Taman Sedia

Bala's Holiday Chalets

Gunung Jasar

Walk 10

Parit Waterfalls

Walk 4

Walk 5

Gunung Bereleman

Oly Apartments

Garden Inn

Tanah Rata

Mosque

Walk 7

Bus & Taxi Stand

Playground

Mardi

Rumah Rehat (Rest House)

Walk 8

Robinson Waterfall

Walk 9

Bharat Tea Estate

Robinson Fall Power Station

Walk 9A

To Boh Tea Estate

To Gunung Emas Tea Plantation

To Ringlet & Tapah

0   500   1000 m

you'll find most of the hotels, as well as the bus and taxi stations. Continue on, and at around the 65 km peg, you reach the other main Highland town, Brinchang, where there are a few more restaurants and cheap hotels.

The road continues up beyond Brinchang to smaller villages and the Blue Valley Tea Estate at 90 km, off to the north-east, or to the top of Gunung Brinchang at 80 km, to the north-west.

Things to See

The **Sam Poh Temple**, just below Brinchang and about one km off the road, is a typically Chinese kaleidoscope of colours with Buddha statues, stone lions and incense burners. **Mardi** is an agricultural research station in Tanah Rata and visits must be arranged in advance.

There are a number of flower nurseries and vegetable and strawberry farms in the Highlands. There is an Orang Asli settlement near Brinchang but there's little reason to visit it.

About 10 km beyond Brinchang is the **Butterfly Garden** where there are over 300 varieties fluttering around. It's worth a visit if you can hitch or if you have your own vehicle.

Places to Stay

The Highlands can be very busy in April, August and December when many families go there for vacations. At these times, it is a good idea to book accommodation. Prices in the cheaper places can vary with demand. Most of the cheap hotels are in Tanah Rata. There are a couple of places in Brinchang but there's little reason to stay there.

The most popular place with travellers is *Bala's Holiday Chalets* (☎ 05-94 1660), about two km from town along the road to Brinchang. Beds in basic share rooms cost M$5, or there's a variety of rooms up to M$50. The views from the lawn are very good and the place is in a quiet area.

Probably the most attractive thing about this place is the fact that Bala runs daily tours at 10 am and 2 pm for M$6 per person. These give you the opportunity to see things that would otherwise be inaccessible. Reasonable meals are available and there's a decent notice board.

Another place which has been recommended is *Father's Guest House*, up a flight of around 100 steps opposite the Oly Apartments, at the Ringlet end of Tanah Rata. Of the regular hotels in Tanah Rata, the best value is the *Seah Meng Hotel* (☎ 05-94 1618) at 39 Main Rd with doubles from M$26. The *Woh Nam Hotel* is also cheap at M$25 but the rooms only have double beds.

Right at the end of the strip is the *Highlands Lodge* (☎ 05-94 1922) at 4 Main Rd. It's a bit seedy but cheap at M$15 for doubles with common bath or there are dorm beds for M$7. The *Federal Hotel* (☎ 05-94 1777) at 44 Main Rd has singles (double bed) with common bath for M$20, or doubles with bath for M$45.

The *Government Rest House (Rumah Rehat)* is a great place to stay, if you can get in. Double rooms, with sitting room and bathroom, cost M$40 but, because it is such a good deal, it is often booked out, especially on weekends and school holidays.

Places to Eat

The cheapest food in Tanah Rata is at the row of Malay food stalls along the main street. One stall, called the *Excellent Food Centre*, has an extensive menu and good food. On Saturday evening it becomes a 'sizzler'-style restaurant and is a cheap place to have a steak. Adjoining this stall is the *Fresh Milk Corner* which, as you may have guessed, sells fresh pasteurised milk, yoghurt and lassis.

On the other side of the road *Restaurant Kumar* and adjacent *Restoran Thanam* both serve good Malay and Indian food including rotis, martabak and biryani.

For something a bit more sophisticated, try the set lunch or dinner at the *Oriental Restaurant*, also in the main street. It's a traditional 'steamboat' meal and is very good value at M$10 per person.

Further along Main Rd is the *Jasmine Restaurant* which has a set four-course

Chinese meal for M$10 – also good value. At the *Roselane Coffee House*, they serve good breakfasts for M$5 and at lunch and dinner have a set meal of soup, main course and ice cream for M$6.30.

If you're staying at *Bala's*, then it's easiest to eat there as well. They have an extensive menu with all the old travellers' favourites and excellent scones, jam and cream. In the evening, they have a set menu banquet which is usually good value, although it gets the thumbs down from a number of travellers.

Getting There & Away

Bus Bus No 153 runs approximately every hour, 8 am to 5 pm, from Tapah to Tanah Rata and the trip takes about two hours. All the bus drivers on this route seem to be frustrated racing drivers and the way they drive can be fairly hair-raising.

Long-distance buses can be booked at Bala's, or at CS Travel & Tours on the main street in Tanah Rata. Destinations include Singapore (M$28), Melaka (M$17.50), Butterworth (M$9), Kuantan (M$22), KL (M$7.50), Kuala Terengganu (M$25), Lumut (M$7.50) and Alor Setar (M$14).

Taxi There are regular taxis from the taxi stand (☎ 05-94 1555) on the main street. Things are much busier in the mornings. The fares are M$6 to Tapah, M$11 to Ipoh and M$20 to KL.

IPOH

The 'city of millionaires' made its fortune from tin mining. There are some interesting cave temples on the outskirts of the town. It's also the best take-off point for Lumut and the island of Pangkor.

The cave temples are both south and north of the town – the most important being the **Perak Tong Temple** about six km north of town and the **Sam Poh Temple** a few km south of town. Both are right on the main road and so easy to get to.

Places to Stay

The *New South Eastern Hotel* (☎ 05-54 8709) at 48 Jalan Lahat is a Chinese cheapie of the most basic variety. The rooms are noisy as it's right on a busy intersection but it is very handy for transport connections. Rooms with fan cost M$13.50.

The main hotel area, however, is around the Jalan Chamberlain area. The *Beauty Hotel* on Jalan Yang Kalsom is reasonably clean and is cheap at M$14 for rooms with fan and common bath. A better bet is the nearby *Cathay Hotel* (☎ 05-51 3322) which charges M$14/19 for singles/doubles with fan or M$18/25 with air-con and bath.

Of a slightly better standard, the *Embassy Hotel* (☎ 05-54 9496) at 35 Jalan Chamberlain has rooms with fan and bath for M$17/21 or M$27 for an air-con double with bath.

A bit better still is the *Win Wah (Winner) Hotel* (☎ 05-51 5177) on Jalan Ali Pitchay, a spotless Chinese hotel with large rooms for M$32 with air-con, bath and hot water – a definite winner.

Places to Eat

Ipoh has plenty of restaurants and the rice noodle dish known as kway teow is reputed to be better in Ipoh than anywhere else in Malaysia. The city's best known place for kway teow is *Kedai Kopi Kong Heng*, on Jalan Leech between Jalan Pasar (Market) and Jalan Station.

Right next door to the Kong Heng, on Jalan Leech, is a new hawkers' centre with plenty of variety – the laksa and popiah are worth trying and the es kacang is excellent. Beer drinkers may not find this place to their liking as alcohol isn't served.

For Malay food, the *Rahman Restaurant* on Jalan Chamberlain is very clean and has a wide range of dishes. They also have an air-con room upstairs but that's closed on Sunday. Finally, for something more familiar there's a *McDonald's* outlet on Jalan Clare near the Central Market.

Getting There & Away

Ipoh is on the main KL to Butterworth road. Lumut buses leave from Jalan Kidd across from the bus station. Destinations and fares include Butterworth (M$6.50), KL

(M$8.20), Lumut (M$3.50), PD (M$13), Alor Setar (M$25), Kuantan (M$19.50), Melaka (M$13) and Singapore (M$25). Tickets should be booked in advance.

Long-distance taxis leave from beside the bus station. Destinations include Taiping (M$6), Butterworth (M$12), Lumut (M$6) and KL (M$17).

PULAU PANGKOR

The island of Pangkor is close to the coast off Lumut and easily accessible via Ipoh. It's a popular resort island known for its fine and, often, quite isolated beaches, many of which can be walked to along an interesting 'around the island' route. A visit to the island is principally a 'laze on the beach' operation, but there are also a number of interesting things to do.

Places to Stay

Almost all of Pangkor's accommodation is grouped at each end of the very pleasant beach at Pasir Bogak, on the opposite side of the island from Pangkor village.

At the far end of the beach is *Khoo's Holiday Resort* (☎ 05-95 1164). This used to be Sam Khoo's Mini Camp and was a popular travellers' hang-out. These days, unfortunately, it has been redeveloped and an ugly concrete building has replaced the attap huts. Dorm beds cost M$7, otherwise rooms start from M$50.

With the demise of Sam Khoo's, the best place to stay at any reasonable price is the *Pangkor Anchor*, a short distance along from Khoo's. Run by the very down-to-earth Mrs Wong, this place is kept spotlessly clean and is well-managed. Small mosquito-proof A-frame huts cost M$12/18, and for this you get a mattress on the floor. It's a good place, although children are not made especially welcome, and there's a bit of the 'lights out' mentality of a strict youth hostel.

A couple of other cheap possibilities operate here but they aren't great.

Places to Eat

Next door to the Pangkor Anchor, the *Fisherman's Place* serves fresh and tasty seafood and Chinese dishes, and they have a good breakfast menu. It's a popular place both with locals and travellers.

In the area of Khoo's, there are a number of hawkers' stalls selling snack food and you also find these in front of the Beach Huts Hotel. Close by are a number of fairly shabby warungs serving cheap and basic meals.

Tucked away along a small dirt road which runs alongside the Pangkor Standard Camp is the *Pangkor Restaurant*, a cheap seafood and Chinese food restaurant which is popular with the locals.

Getting There & Away

The two ferry companies, Min Lian and Feri Expres, run ferries between Lumut and Pangkor village every 20 minutes – from 6.45 am to 7.30 pm from Lumut and from 6.45 am to 6.40 pm from Pangkor.

You can only buy M$2 return tickets but on the return journey you can use the boats of either company, regardless of which one you used to get to the island.

Getting Around

There are buses every half hour or so which run from Pangkor village across the island to the far end of the beach at Pasir Bogak and back again. Pangkor has plenty of taxis. The standard fare is M$3 from Pangkor to Pasir Bogak.

The ideal way to see the island is by bicycle or motorbike. There are a number of places at Pasir Bogak which rent them out and the prices are very reasonable: M$4 per hour or M$25 per day for a motorbike and M$4 per day for a bicycle.

KUALA KANGSAR

The royal town of Perak has the fine **Ubadiah Mosque** with its onion dome and the minarets squeezed up against it as if seen in a distorting mirror. This is the place where rubber trees were first grown in Malaysia.

TAIPING

The 'town of everlasting peace' was once a raucous mining town. It has a beautiful lake and zoo and the oldest museum in the country. Above the town is the little Maxwell Hill station. To get there, you have to take a government Land Rover from the station at the foot of the hill (M$3).

Places to Stay & Eat

Taiping has plenty of cheap Chinese hotels. The *Wah Bee Hotel*, an old wooden place on the main street, has cheap and basic rooms for M$15. Another cheapie is the *Hotel Peace* (☎ 05-82 3379) at 32 Jalan Iskandar which charges around M$12 for a double room with common bath.

Up the scale a notch is the *Hotel Nanyang* (☎ 05-82 4488) at 129 Jalan Pasar, where rooms with fan and bath go for M$18. Better still is the *New Rest House* (Rumah Rehat Baru) (☎ 05-82 2044) in Taman Tasik, which is a curious mixture of Sumatran and classical Roman styles.

Overlooking the Lake Gardens, it's clean, secure and very good value at M$28 for large doubles with fan, or M$39 with air-con. Rooms either have a view out over the prison or the golf course. Unfortunately, minimal maintenance is carried out and there is an air of decay. The restaurant here serves decent meals. It's about a km from the town centre, so you'll need a taxi to get there.

PENANG

The oldest British settlement in Malaysia, predating both Singapore and Melaka, is also one of Malaysia's major tourist attractions. This is hardly surprising as the 285 sq km island of Penang has popular beach resorts and an intriguing and historically interesting town which is also noted for its superb food.

Captain Francis Light sailed up and took over the virtually uninhabited island in 1786. Encouraged by free-trade policies, Georgetown (the city on the island) became a prosperous centre as well as a local Mecca for dreamers, dissidents, intellectuals and artists.

Sun Yat-sen planned the 1911 Canton uprising here, probably in one of the local Hainanese coffee shops. Unmistakably Chinese, it's one of the most likeable cities in South-East Asia. With easy-going

kampungs, sandy beaches, warm water, good food and plenty of things to see, who wouldn't like Penang?

Orientation

Penang's major town, Georgetown, is often referred to as Penang although correctly that is the name of the island (the actual Malay spelling is Pinang and it means betel nut). Georgetown is in the north-east of the island, where the straits between the island and the mainland are at their narrowest.

A vehicle and passenger ferry service operates 24 hours a day across the three-km-wide channel between Georgetown and Butterworth on the mainland. South of the ferry crossing is the Penang Bridge – the longest in South-East Asia – which links the island with Malaysia's north-south highway.

Georgetown is a compact city and most places can easily be reached on foot or by bicycle rickshaw. Two important streets to remember are Lebuh Chulia and Lebuh Campbell. You'll find most of Georgetown's popular cheap hotels along Lebuh Chulia or close to it, while Lebuh Campbell is one of the town's main shopping streets. Jalan Penang is another popular shopping street; in this area you'll find a number of the more expensive hotels including, at the waterfront end of Jalan Penang, the venerable Eastern & Oriental Hotel.

If you follow Jalan Penang south, you'll pass the modern, multistorey blot on the skyline known as the Kompleks Tun Abdul Razak (KOMTAR).

Information

Tourist Office The Penang Tourist Association (☎ 04-36 6665) is on Jalan Tun Syed Sheh Barakbah, close to Fort Cornwallis, in the centre of Georgetown. They are a useful source of information and the office is open from 8 am to 4.15 pm Monday to Friday, and from 8 am to 12.45 pm on Saturday.

The Penang Tourists Guides Association office (☎ 04-61 4461), on the 3rd floor of the KOMTAR, is open daily from 9.30 am to 6.30 pm and is staffed by volunteer guides who really know their stuff.

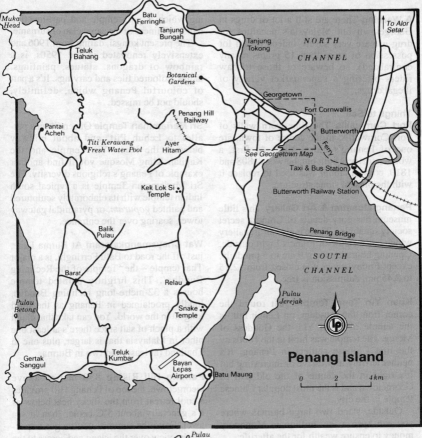

Penang Island

Foreign Embassies Medan, the entry point from Penang to the Indonesian island of Sumatra, is counted as one of the 'usual' entry points where arriving visitors do not need a visa. Which is just as well, because the Indonesian Consulate in Penang has long had a reputation for being unhelpful.

Conversely, the Thai Consulate (☎ 04-23352) at 1 Jalan Ayer Rajah is a good place for obtaining Thai visas. They cost M$31, and numerous places along Lebuh Chulia will provide the forms and obtain the visa for you for an additional M$8.

Travel Agencies Two reliable travel agents are Silver-Econ Travel (☎ 04-62 9882) at 436 Lebuh Chulia and MSL (☎ 04-24748), at 340 Lebuh Chulia (affiliated with Student Travel Australia). Other good, reliable agencies which many travellers deal with are Happy Holidays (☎ 04-62 9222) at 442 Lebuh Chulia, and Best Travels (☎ 04-62 3233), at 440B Lebuh Chulia.

Other The post restante facility at the GPO is efficient and popular, and there's a good bookshop in the E & O Hotel.

A Warning There are still a lot of drugs in Georgetown but Malaysia's penalties for drug use are very severe indeed (death for possession of more than 15 grams of any contraband), so beware of those trishaw riders offering a supermarket variety of illegal drugs.

Things to See

Fort Cornwallis The time-worn walls of Fort Cornwallis, in the centre of town, are one of Penang's oldest sites. At first, a wooden fort was built but, between 1808 and 1810, convict labour was used to replace it with the present stone structure.

Penang Museum & Art Gallery This little museum has gory details of Chinese secret society squabbles. There is also an art gallery which has a statue of Francis Light outside. Opening hours are from 9 am to 5 pm daily, except Friday, when it is closed from 12.15 to 2.45 pm. Admission is free.

Kuan Yin Teng Temple Just round the corner from the museum, on Lebuh Pitt, is the temple of Kuan Yin, the Goddess of Mercy. The temple was built in the 1800s by the first Chinese settlers in Penang. It's neither terribly impressive or interesting but it's right in the centre of the old part of Georgetown and is the most popular Chinese temple in the city.

Outside, stand two large burners where you can burn a few million in Monopoly money to ensure wealth for the afterlife.

Kapitan Kling Mosque At the same time Kuan Yin's temple was being constructed, Penang's first Indian Muslim settlers set to and built this mosque at the junction of Lebuh Pitt and Lebuh Buckingham. In a typically Indian-influenced Islamic style, the yellow mosque has a single minaret. Close by on Lebuh Acheh, the **Malay Mosque** has an unusual Egyptian-style minaret.

Khoo Kongsi The 'Dragon Mountain Hall' is in Cannon Square close to the end of Lebuh Pitt. A *kongsi* is a clan house, a build-ing which is part-temple and part-meeting hall for Chinese of the same clan or surname.

The present kongsi, dating from 1906 and extensively renovated in the 1950s, is a rainbow of dragons, statues, paintings, lamps, coloured tiles and carvings. It's a part of colourful Penang which, definitely, should not be missed.

Sri Mariamman Temple Queen St runs parallel to Lebuh Pitt, and about midway between the Kuan Yin Temple and the Kapitan Kling Mosque you'll find another example of Penang's religious diversity. The Sri Mariamman Temple is a typical south Indian temple with its elaborately sculptured and painted *gopuram*, or pyramidal gateway tower, soaring over the entrance.

Wat Chayamangkalaram At Burma Lane, just off the road to Batu Ferringhi, is a major Thai temple – the 'Temple of the Reclining Buddha'. This brightly painted temple houses a 32-metre-long reclining Buddha, loudly proclaimed in Penang as the third longest in the world. You can take that claim with a pinch of salt since there's at least one other in Malaysia that is larger, plus one in Thailand (at least) and two in Burma.

Penang Hill Rising 830 metres above Georgetown, the top of Penang Hill provides a cool retreat from the sticky heat below as it's generally about 5°C cooler than at sea level. From the summit, you've got a spectacular view over the island and across to the mainland. There are pleasant gardens, a small cafe and a hotel as well as a Hindu temple and a Muslim mosque on the top. Penang Hill is particularly pleasant at dusk as Georgetown, far below, starts to light up.

Take bus No 1 from Pengkalan Weld to Ayer Hitam (every five minutes; 55 sen), then bus No 8 to the funicular station (30 sen). The ascent of the hill costs M$3 for the round trip. There are departures every 30 minutes from 6.30 am to 9.30 pm from the bottom, and to 9.15 pm from the top. There are later departures until midnight on Wednesday and Saturday. The queues here are often horrendous and waits of half an hour and more are not uncommon.

The energetic can get to the top by an interesting eight-km hike which start from the Moon Gate at the Botanical Gardens. The hike takes nearly three hours so be sure to bring along a water bottle.

Kek Lok Si Temple On a hilltop at Ayer Hitam, close to the funicular station for Penang Hill, stands the largest Buddhist temple in Malaysia. The construction commenced in 1890 and took more than 20 years to complete.

The entrance is reached through arcades of souvenir stalls, past a tightly packed turtle pond and murky fish ponds until you reach the Ban Po Thar, or 'Ten Thousand Buddhas' Pagoda.

A 'voluntary' contribution is the price to climb to the top of the seven tier, 30-metre-high tower which is said to be Burmese at the top, Chinese at the bottom and Thai in between.

Around the Island There are a number of other attractions at various points around the island, most of them accessible by public transport.

Beaches Penang's beaches are definitely overrated. They are not as spectacular or as clean as the tourist brochures would have you believe and they suffer from pollution. They are mainly along the north coast, starting with **Tanjung Bungah**, then **Batu Ferringhi** (where the major resorts are) and, lastly, **Teluk Bahang**.

Snake Temple The Snake Temple, at Km 14 on the road to the airport, is reached by bus No 83. Live snakes, suitably doped on the incense smoke, are photogenically draped over you. There's no admission fee but 'donations' are requested. The number of snakes varies throughout the year.

Places to Stay
Hostels Penang has a well-situated but extremely anonymous *Youth Hostel* (Asrama Belia) right next door to the gracious old Eastern & Oriental Hotel on Lebuh Farquhar. It takes in YHA members only and dorm beds cost M$5.

The *YMCA* (☎ 04-36 2211) at 211 Jalan Macalister is close to the Thai Consulate. To get there take bus No 7. Singles/doubles cost M$30/32, or M$35/37 with air-con, and all rooms have showers. There's a M$2 temporary membership charge for nonmembers of the YMCA, but this can be waived if you're a YHA member or have a student card.

Hotels There are a great number of cheap hotels around Georgetown, some of them very pleasant. Stroll down Lebuh Chulia, Lebuh Leith or Love Lane and you'll come across them. Despite their plentitude, Georgetown hotels do seem to fill up, so if you can't find a bed in the more popular places then start looking at the less convenient ones. The hotels that follow are only a selection of the complete range.

One of the most popular is the long-running *New China Hotel* (☎ 04-63 1601) at 22 Lebuh Leith where singles/doubles with fan cost M$18/27. There are also doubles with bath and a somewhat airless dorm. The whole place is very clean, particularly the toilets, but the bar at the back can be noisy at times. There is also a restaurant serving Western food and breakfasts.

Two other popular places, of the same standard as the New China, are the *Swiss Hotel* (☎ 04-62 0133) at 431-F Lebuh Chulia and the *Eng Aun* (☎ 04-61 2333), directly across the road at 380 Lebuh Chulia. The Swiss Hotel has rooms with fan and common bath at M$14/21 for singles/doubles. The Eng Aun charges M$15/19 for large rooms with common facilities. They also have a travel agency downstairs. Both of these spacious hotels attract a steady stream of travellers and have large car parks in front (as does the New China) – which helps to insulate them from street noise.

At 282 Lebuh Chulia, the *Tye Ann Hotel* (☎ 04-61 4875) is very popular, particularly for breakfasts downstairs in their restaurant.

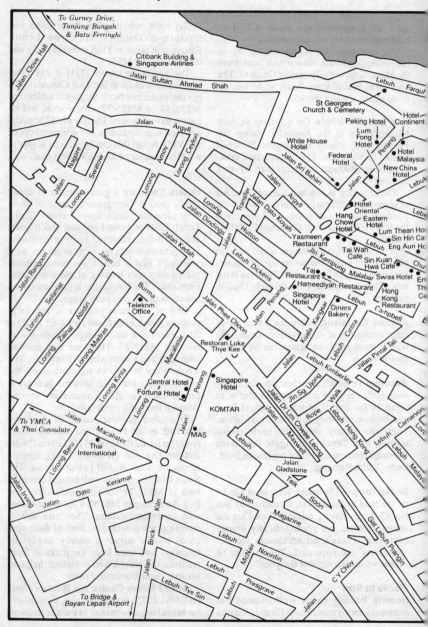

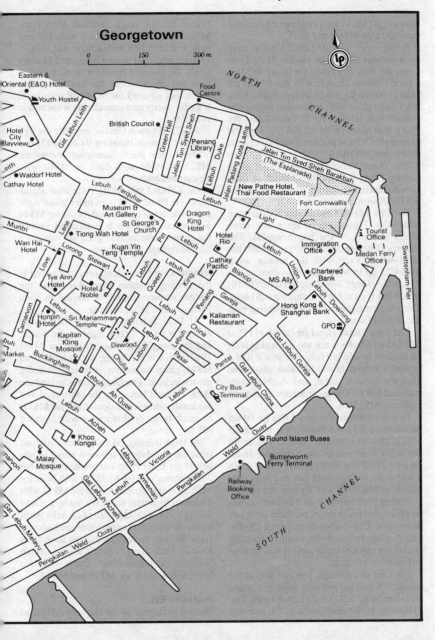

Georgetown

0   150   300 m

Eastern &
Oriental (E&O) Hotel

Youth Hostel

Hotel
City
Bayview

Waldorf Hotel
Cathay Hotel

British Council

Food
Centre

NORTH

CHANNEL

Gat Lebuh Leith

Green Hall

Jalan Tun Syed Sheh

Lebuh Duke

Penang
Library

Jalan Padang Kota Lama

Jalan Tun Syed Sheh Barakbah
(The Esplanade)

Lebuh
Farquhar

Museum &
Art Gallery

St George's
Church

Lebuh

New Pathe Hotel,
Thai Food Restaurant

Fort Cornwallis

Muntri

Lane

Tiong Wah Hotel

Dragon
King
Hotel

Lebuh
Light

Lebuh

Tourist
Office

Wan Hai
Hotel

Lorong Stewart

Kuan Yin
Teng Temple

Pitt

Lebuh
Queen

Lebuh
King

Hotel
Rio

Cathay Pacific

Bishop

Immigration
Office

Kuan

Lebuh
Union

Medan Ferry
Office

Love

Tye Ann
Hotel

Hotel
Noble

Lebuh

Sri Mariamman
Temple

Lebuh

Penang

Gereja

MS Ally

Chartered
Bank

Lebuh Downing

Carnarvon

Honpin
Hotel

Kapitan
Kling
Mosque

Dawood

Lebuh

Lebuh

Lebuh
China

Kaliaman
Restaurant

Hong Kong &
Shanghai Bank

GPO

Market

Buckingham

Chulia

Pasar

Pantai

Gat Lebuh Gereja

Lebuh

Ah Quee

Lebuh
Acheh

City Bus
Terminal

Gat Lebuh China

Khoo
Kongsi

Victoria

Lebuh

Quay

Round Island Buses

Malay
Mosque

Lebuh
Acheh

Armenian

Weld

Butterworth
Ferry Terminal

Gat Lebuh Acheh

Pengkalan

Railway
Booking
Office

SOUTH

CHANNEL

Gat Lebuh Melayu

Pengkalan Weld Quay

Swettenham Pier

Medan Ferry
Office

SOUTH

Rooms cost M$16 for a single or double, and there are also M$6 dorm beds.

In the streets just off Lebuh Chulia, there are a number of popular places. At 35 Love Lane, the *Wan Hai Hotel* (☎ 04-61 6853) is a good Chinese cheapie with dorm beds for M$6 or rooms for M$16 with common bath. It's a quiet place with reasonable rooms and a small roof terrace. At 23 Love Lane, the *Tiong Wah Hotel* (☎ 04-62 2057) is a typical older style Chinese place in a very quiet area; rooms cost M$16/18.

The *Hotel Noble* (☎ 04-61 2372) at 36 Lorong Pasar, just one small block in from Lebuh Chulia, is a quiet place with rooms for M$14/18 with common bath.

Back on Lebuh Chulia, near the junction with Jalan Penang, there are a few more places if none of the above appeal. The *Eastern Hotel* (☎ 04-61 4597) at No 509 has rates which vary with the season, from M$14/22 up to M$16/26. Next door, at No 511, is the *Hang Chow Hotel* (☎ 04-61 0810) which has typical basic rooms for M$14/16. There's a restaurant and moneychanger on the ground floor.

The *Lum Thean Hotel* (☎ 04-61 4117) at 422 Lebuh Chulia is not too promising with its modern facade but behind it you'll find a typical Chinese hotel. It's also about the cheapest air-con place, and doubles with bath cost M$33. Cheaper rooms with fan and bath cost M$17/26.

In a quiet street, the *Hotel Rio* (☎ 04-65 0010) at 64-1 Lebuh Bishop has rooms for M$22/28 with common bath. If you avoid the noisy front rooms, the *Singapore Hotel* (☎ 04-62 0323) at 495H Jalan Penang is not a bad deal. Rooms with fan and bath cost M$19, or M$22/29 with air-con and bath.

During peak travel times it can sometimes be difficult to find a room, but there are many more cheap Chinese hotels on Lebuh Chulia, Lebuh Campbell and the small connecting streets – a quick wander around will turn up any number of them.

For a bit of a splurge, you can stay at the wonderful-looking and very friendly *Cathay Hotel* (☎ 04-62 6271) at 22 Lebuh Leith. The cavernous lobby nearly equals the exterior.

Prices for the huge spotless rooms are M$40/46 for singles/doubles with fan and bath, and M$50/58 with air-con and bath.

Right next door to the Cathay, at 13 Lebuh Leith, the *Waldorf Hotel* (☎ 04-62 6140) is new and characterless but has reasonable rooms (all air-con) for M$41/58 with bath. It's a bit overpriced considering what else is available.

At 273-B Lebuh Chulia, opposite the Tye Ann, the *Honpin Hotel* (☎ 04-62 5243) is a relatively new place. Reasonable rooms are M$25 to M$30 with bath or M$40 with air-con and bath.

On Lebuh Light, there's the *New Pathe Hotel* (☎ 04-62 0195), an older place right by a park. It has good-sized rooms for M$44 with air-con and bath. It's just a pity that all the rooms have frosted glass so you can't take advantage of the view.

Beaches Few travellers seem to stay out at the Penang beaches these days, and the budget accommodation is limited to Batu Ferringhi and Teluk Bahang.

At Batu Ferringhi, there's *Ali's Guest House* (☎ 04-81 1316), right on the beach, and the *Beng Keat Guest House* (☎ 04-81 1987). Ali's is the better, with rooms from M$15, clean bathrooms, a restaurant and a garden in front. The Beng Keat is behind the Batik Fashion House on the main road and has small rooms with a double bed for M$12, or much better double rooms with bath for M$20.

At Teluk Bahang, take the beachward road from the roundabout, follow it round to just before the Balai Polis and on the right at No 365 is *Rama's* (☎ 04-81 1179) with beds for M$5, or single/double rooms for M$12 with discounts for longer stays. It's run by a Hindu family and is well-kept. *Miss Loh* has a guest house off the main road towards the butterfly farm. She can be contacted at the shop at 59 Kwong Tuck Hing. There's a sign saying 'Guesthouse Information'. Dorm beds are M$5, and doubles are M$10 and M$12.

Places to Eat
Penang is another of the region's delightful

food trips with a wide variety of restaurants and many local specialities to tempt you. For a start, there are two types of laksa, or soup, that are particularly associated with Penang. Laksa assam is a fish soup with a sour taste from the tamarind or assam paste and it is served with special white laksa noodles. Originally a Thai dish, laksa lemak has been adopted by Penang. It's basically similar to *laksa assam* with coconut milk being substituted for the tamarind.

Seafood, of course, is very popular in Penang and there are many restaurants that specialise in fresh fish, crabs and prawns – particularly along the northern beach fringe.

Despite its Chinese character, Penang also has a strong Indian presence and there are some popular specialities to savour. Curry kapitan is a Penang chicken curry which supposedly takes its name from a Dutch sea captain asking his Indonesian mess boy what was on that night. The answer was 'curry kapitan' and it's been on the menu ever since.

Martabak, a thin roti chanai pastry stuffed with egg, vegetables and meat, while not actually a Penang speciality, is done with particular flair on the island.

Indian Food Amongst the more popular Indian restaurants is *Dawood* at 63 Queen St, opposite the Sri Mariamman Temple. Curry kapitan for M$5 is just one of the many curry dishes at this reasonably priced restaurant. On Lebuh Campbell, the *Taj* at No 166 and the *Hameediyah* at No 164-A both have good curries and delicious martabak.

The *Yasmeen Restaurant* at 177 Jalan Penang near the corner of Lebuh Chulia, is another place for martabak, but this is also an excellent place for a quick snack of roti chanai with dhal dip – a cheap meal at any time of the day. They also serve excellent chicken and mutton biryani on Friday and Sunday.

Penang has a 'little India' along Jalan Pasar between Lebuh Penang and Lebuh Pitt and along the side streets between. Several small restaurants and stalls in this area offer cheap north (Muslim) and south Indian food.

For something a bit more up-market, try the *Kaliaman Restaurant* on Lebuh Pinang. This air-con place has banana-leaf curries at lunch time for M$3 (or M$4 for nonvegetarian) and does excellent north Indian food in the evenings.

Chinese Food There are so many Chinese restaurants in Penang that specific recommendations are probably redundant.

At 29 Lebuh Cintra, the *Hong Kong Restaurant* is good, cheap and varied, and has a menu in English. At night, this brightly lit restaurant is a real travellers' centre. A number of places around Georgetown provide excellent Hainanese chicken rice. The *Sin Kuan Hiwa Cafe*, on the corner of Lebuh Chulia and Lebuh Cintra, is one that specialises in this.

More good Chinese food can be found at the fancier *Dragon King*, on the corner of Lebuh Bishop and Lebuh Pitt, which specialises in traditional Nonya wedding cuisine and is definitely worth a try. Expect to pay around M$20 for two.

One of the most popular outdoor Chinese places is *Hsiang Yang Cafe*, across the street from the Tye Ann Hotel on Lebuh Chulia. It's really a hawkers' centre with a cheap and good Chinese buffet (rice with three or four side dishes for M$2.50), plus noodle, satay and popiah vendors.

The *Tzechu-lin* at 229-C Burmah Rd is a Buddhist vegetarian restaurant which has excellent food. Expect to spend around M$20 for two.

Breakfasts & Western Food At breakfast time, the popular travellers' hang-out is the *Tye Ann Hotel* on Lebuh Chulia. People visit this friendly little establishment for its excellent porridge, toast & marmalade and other breakfast favourites.

Western breakfasts are also available at the *New China, Eng Aun, Swiss, Cathay* and opposite the Wan Hai Hotel. Another morning hang-out is the tiny *Eng Thai Cafe* at 417B Lebuh Chulia, not far from the Eng Aun and Swiss hotels. There are other small Chinese cafes with Western breakfast menus like the popular little *Sin Hin Cafe* at 402

Lebuh Chulia. The *Tai Wah Coffee Shop* at 487 Lebuh Chulia is a very busy little place, buzzing with activity until late at night.

At the supermarket in the KOMTAR complex you can find all the usual supermarket goodies. The KOMTAR is also a happy hunting ground if you're after fast food. On floors one to three, you'll find *Kentucky Fried Chicken, McDonald's, Shakey's, White Castle, Pizza Hut, A&W* and *Satay Ria*. On the 5th floor there's a pleasant hawkers' centre with all the usual Chinese and local dishes.

For a splurge, the four-course set lunch at the *Eastern & Oriental Hotel* is good value, although you have to sit inside. To eat on the terrace outside you have to order à la carte.

Night Markets Georgetown has a wide selection of street stalls with nightly gatherings at places like Gurney Drive or along the Esplanade. The latter is particularly good for trying local Penang specialities.

The big pasar malam changes venue every two weeks, so check at the tourist office for its current location. It's mainly for clothes and other household goods but there are a few hawkers' stalls. It doesn't really get going until around 8 pm.

Medicated tea is a popular item and one Georgetown tea stall has a sign announcing that it will cure everything from 'headache, stomachache and kidney trouble' to 'malaria, cholera and' (wait for it) 'fartulence'.

Getting There & Away
Air Airline offices in Penang include:

Cathay Pacific
28 Lebuh Penang
MAS
KOMTAR, Penang Rd (☎ 04-62 0011)
Singapore Airlines
Citibank Building, Jalan Sultan Ahmad Shah
(☎ 04-36 3201)
Thai Airways International
Wisma Central, 202 Macalister Rd (☎ 04-36 6233)

The MAS office in the KOMTAR building

is open Monday to Saturday from 8.30 am to 6 pm and Sunday from 8.30 am to 1 pm.

Internationally, MAS fly to Medan in Sumatra (M$124) although, these days, most travellers take the ferry. MAS and SIA have regular flights to Singapore for M$155. MAS and Thai International fly between Penang and Hat Yai, Phuket and Bangkok. Other international connections include direct flights to Hong Kong with Cathay Pacific or to Madras in India with MAS.

Penang is a major centre for cheap airline tickets. These days the better agents are usually OK, but beware of places which ask for big advance payments before they issue you with the tickets. Typical one-way fares being quoted out of Penang include Madras M$680, Hat Yai M$120, Bangkok M$312 and Hong Kong M$720. Other fares may involve flying from KL or even Bangkok.

You can get one-way fares to Sydney (with a free extension to Melbourne) from around M$900 and returns from M$1500; Perth is about the same. For M$1200 you can fly to the US west coast with stopovers in Manila and Honolulu, sometimes in Tokyo as well. Fares to London start from around M$900 with the less popular airlines (Bangladesh Biman and Aeroflot) and from M$1000 with Air Lanka.

Bus The bus terminal is beside the ferry terminal in Butterworth. Some travel agents in Georgetown (several are near the Eng Aun and Swiss hotels for example) offer good bargains on bus tickets. The long-distance buses which these places deal with often leave from somewhere in Georgetown rather than Butterworth.

To Kuala Perlis (for the Langkawi ferry), the bus is M$6 by Ebban Express from the Butterworth terminal. To Lumut (for Pulau Pangkor), it is M$8.50. There are also bus services out of Malaysia to Hat Yai (M$20), Phuket (M$40), Surat Thani (M$40) and Bangkok (M$60) in Thailand.

Typical bus fares from Butterworth to other places include Ipoh M$6.50, KL M$15, Melaka M$26 and Singapore M$30.

Train The railway station is, like the bus and taxi stations, right by the ferry terminal at Butterworth. The Malaysia Getting There & Away and Getting Around sections have details about the Butterworth-KL-Singapore services and the international train services to Hat Yai and Bangkok in Thailand.

You can make reservations at the station (☎ 04-34 7962) or at the railway booking station (☎ 04-61 0290) at the ferry terminal, Weld Quay, Georgetown. There's a good left-luggage facility at the station – the charge is 50 sen per item per day and it's open from 5.30 am to 9 pm daily.

Taxi Yes, the long-distance taxis also operate from a depot beside the Butterworth ferry terminal. It's also possible to book them at some of the hotspot backpacker hotels or directly with drivers. Typical fares include Ipoh for M$13.50, KL for M$31 and Tapah for M$18.

There are Thai taxis operating to Hat Yai – a convenient way of getting across the border. They're usually big old Chevys and you'll find them at the popular cheap hotels in Georgetown – the fare is around M$25.

Car Penang Bridge, completed in 1985, is one of the longest bridges in the world. If you drive across, you'll have to pay a M$7 toll at the toll plaza at Prai on the mainland.

Boat The *Selesa Ekspres* is a high-speed catamaran ferry operating on Tuesday and Friday between Penang and Medan in Sumatra. The fare is M$100 one way (M$180 return) in 1st class and M$90 (M$160) in economy. The service is operated by the Kuala Perlis-Lankawai Ferry Service (☎ 04-62 5630/1) near the tourist office across from Fort Cornwallis.

The same ferry operates regularly between Penang and the Malaysian island of Langkawi to the north. The fare is M$40 (M$70 return) in 1st class, and M$35 (M$60) in economy.

There are several yachts operating between Penang and Phuket in Thailand. Typical trips sail Penang-Langkawi-Ko Phi

Phi-Krabi-Phuket and cost US$180 per person for a four to five-day trip. Check with Maju Travel (☎ 04-61 5170) at 417 Lebuh Chulia.

After a number of years without shipping services, there is once again talk of a regular ship operating between Penang and Madras in India. However, it is unclear when this will happen.

Getting Around
To/From the Airport Penang's Bayan Lepas Airport, with its Minangkabau-style terminal, is 18 km south of Georgetown. A coupon system operates for taxis from the airport. The fare to Georgetown is M$15, or M$18 for an air-con taxi.

You can get a yellow bus No 83 to the airport from Pengkalan Weld Quay for M$1.25 – they operate on this route from 6 am to 10 pm. Taxis take about 30 minutes from the centre of town, the bus an hour.

Bus – Information on buses around Penang includes:

Around the Island Getting around the island by road is easiest with your own transport. The road does not actually run along the coast except on the northern side and you have to leave the main road to get out to the small fishing villages and isolated beaches.

For around M$3 to M$4, depending on where and when you stop, you can make the circuit by public transport. Start with a yellow bus No 66 and hop off at the Snake Temple. Bus No 83 will take you all the way to Balik Pulau from where you have to change to another yellow bus, a No 76, for Teluk Bahang.

There are only half a dozen of these each day and the last one leaves around mid-afternoon so it's wise to leave Georgetown early and check the departure times when you reach Balik Pulau. At Teluk Bahang you're on the northern beach strip and you simply take a blue Hin bus No 93 to Georgetown, via Batu Ferringhi.

Around Georgetown There are three main bus departure points in Georgetown and five types of buses. The city buses (MPPP Buses) all depart from the terminal at Lebuh Victoria which is directly in front of the ferry terminal. Fares range from 25 to 55 sen and the main routes are:

Destination	Frequency	Fare
Ayer Hitam	every 5 min	55 sen
Ayer Hitam from Jelutong	every 20 min	45 sen
Bagan Jermal	every 10 min	45 sen
Bagan Jermal from Jelutong	every 30 min	55 sen
Botanical Gardens	every 30 min	45 sen
Bukit Glogor	every 70 min	55 sen
Jalan Yeap Chor Ee via Jalan Perak	every 10 min	55 sen
Jelutong	every 5 min	45 sen
Green Lane via Caunter Hall Rd	every 16 min	55 sen
Green Lane via Dhoby Ghaut	every 65 min	55 sen
Green Lane via Jalan Patani	every 16 min	55 sen
Kampung Melayu	every 16 min	55 sen
Penang Hill Railway from Ayer Hitam	every 20 min	30 sen

The other main stand is at Pengkalan Weld Quay where you can take green, blue or yellow buses. These are the buses to take if you want to do a circuit of the island or get out to Batu Ferringhi and the other northern beaches. Take a blue Hin bus No 93 to Teluk Bahang or Batu Ferringhi.

The green buses run to Ayer Hitam, like the MPPP bus No 1. Blue buses run to the northern beaches. Yellow buses go to the south and west of the island including the aquarium, Snake Temple, airport and right round to Teluk Bahang.

Taxi Penang's taxis are all metered but getting the drivers to use the meters is nigh on impossible, so it's a matter of negotiating the fare before you set off. Some sample fares from Georgetown are Batu Ferringhi M\$15, Botanical Gardens M\$10, Penang Hill and Kek Lok Si M\$10, Snake Temple M\$15 and the airport M\$15.

Bicycle & Motorbike If you want to pedal yourself you can hire bicycles from various places in Georgetown, including the Eng Aun Hotel which has them for M\$5 per day. There are various places at Batu Ferringhi where you can hire them at more expensive rates.

Motorbikes can also be hired for around M\$25 per day. Most of the places renting motorbikes are in Batu Ferringhi, but on Lebuh Chulia Yasin, a bookstore/-moneychanger next to the Eng Thai Cafe has a few well-maintained 70 to 125 cc bikes for rent, as well as bicycles.

Boat There's a 24-hour ferry service between Georgetown and Butterworth on the mainland. Passenger ferries and ferries for cars and trucks operate from adjacent terminals. Ferries operate every 20 minutes from 6 am to midnight and then every hour after midnight.

The vehicular ferries operate only slightly less frequently, but do not operate at all between 10 pm (10.20 pm from Penang) and 6.30 am, except on Saturday, Sunday and public holidays when they continue until 1.30 am.

Fares are only charged from Butterworth to Penang, and the reverse direction is free. The adult fare is 40 sen and cars with driver cost from M\$4 to M\$6 depending on the engine capacity.

Trishaw Bicycle rickshaws are ideal on Georgetown's relatively uncrowded streets and cost around M\$1 per km, but as with the taxis, agree on the fare before departure.

If you come across from Butterworth on the ferry, grab a trishaw to the Lebuh Chulia cheap hotels area for M\$3. You can, however, walk there in five or 10 minutes. The riders will know plenty of other hotels if your selected one is full. For touring, the rate is around M\$10 an hour.

ALOR SETAR

The capital of Kedah state is on the mainland north of Penang on the main road to the Thai border and it's also the turn-off point for

Kuala Perlis, from where ferries run to Langkawi Island. Few people stay very long in Alor Setar but it does have a few places of interest.

The large open town square has a number of interesting buildings around its perimeter. The **Balai Besar**, or 'Big Hall', was built in 1898 and is still used by the Sultan of Kedah for ceremonial functions. The **Balai Nobat**, an octagonal building topped by an onion-shaped dome, houses the *nobat*, or royal orchestra.

Places to Stay & Eat

There are a number of cheap hotels around the bus and taxi stations in the centre of town. The *Station Hotel* (☎ 04-72 3855) at 74 Jalan Langgar is one of the cheapest in town with rooms from M$16. The *Regent Hotel* (☎ 04-72 1291) at 1536 Jalan Sultan Badlishah is a step up the scale with air-con rooms for M$28. The *Hotel Mahawangsa* (☎ 04-72 1835), at 449 Jalan Raja and diagonally opposite the GPO, has similar rooms at similar rates, although the Regent is slightly better value.

Alor Setar has some surprisingly good and economical restaurants. On Jalan Tunku Ibrahim is the *Restoran Empire*. It's a hawkers' centre in a restored wet market, where there's a good selection of fruit juices, chicken rice, *rojak*, *appam balik* and curry sambal rice. *Mee jawa* is a local speciality – spicy noodles in a sauce of bean curd, squid, potatoes, peanuts, bean sprouts and appam chips – very tasty.

Getting There & Away

Alor Setar is 91 km north of Butterworth. By bus it's M$3.20 to Butterworth, M$12 to Ipoh, M$18 to KL and M$33 to Singapore. A taxi costs M$3 per person to Kuala Perlis and M$7.80 to Butterworth.

There are also buses to Hat Yai in Thailand for M$10 – go to the Tunjang Ekspres office at the bus station. Although you can easily get to Changlun, the Malay border post for Thailand, by bus or taxi, it is then very difficult to cross the long strip of no-man's land to Sadao, the Thai border post, as there

is no regular transport that just goes across the border.

If, however, you go to Padang Besar, where the railway line crosses the border, you can simply walk across and take a bus from there into Hat Yai. Padang Besar can be reached by road, although the main road to Thailand crosses the border at Changlun-Sadao.

KUALA PERLIS

This small port town in the extreme north-west of the peninsula is visited mainly as the departure point for Langkawi. You can also use Kuala Perlis as an unusual gateway into Thailand.

Places to Stay

Kuala Perlis' one and only hotel is the *Soon Hin* opposite the taxi stand where a room will cost you M$12.

Getting There & Away

There are direct buses from Butterworth for M$6. They connect, more or less, with ferry departures. A taxi between Butterworth and Kuala Perlis costs M$10, but departures are infrequent.

From Alor Setar, there are buses at regular intervals for M$2.60 or taxis at M$3 per person (M$12 for an entire taxi). Buses also depart from Kuala Perlis to Padang Besar (for Thailand) for M$1.90 (taxi M$3.30) and to KL for M$20.

See the Malaysia Getting There & Away section for information about the small boats from Kuala Perlis to Setul, just across the border in Thailand.

LANGKAWI

The 99 islands of the Langkawi group are 30 km off the coast from Kuala Perlis, at the northern end of Peninsular Malaysia. They're accessible by boat from Kuala Perlis, Kuala Kedah and Georgetown (Penang) or by air from Penang, 112 km south, and KL.

Langkawi has seen a lot of government-promoted tourist development but it's a long way from being ruined. What it does mean is that you now have a choice of everything from simple, locally-run beach huts to expensive resorts with every conceivable facility.

The infrastructure has also been improved with an immaculate and well-signposted bitumen road right around the island. During school holidays, and at the peak time from November to February, Langkawi gets very crowded but at other times of the year supply far exceeds demand and the prices come down considerably.

It is quite a pleasant place to visit but Langkawi doesn't have the atmosphere (or the beaches) of the islands on the east coast, or even Pangkor further south on the west coast. This is more or less attributable to its relative isolation.

There's not a great deal to see apart from waterfalls (Telaga Tujuh), a rather pathetic hot spring, a legendary tomb and a fresh-water lake on an adjacent island. The best known beaches are Pantai Cenang and Pantai Kok, both on the west coast, on the opposite side of the island from the main town, Kuah.

Kuah's only 'sight' is the picturesque **waterside mosque** with its golden dome and Moorish arches and minarets rising above the palm trees.

Places to Stay

Kuah A short ride by share-taxi will take you from the pier to any of Kuah's accommodation, all of which is strung out along the waterfront around the bay. Kuah is practically a one-street town and that street follows the bay all the way.

The only real budget hotel is about a km past the hospital where the *Malaysia Hotel & Restaurant* (☎ 04-78 8298) is a travellers' favourite run by Mr Vellu and his family. Rooms start at M$12 for a small single with common bath and go up to M$35 for a double with air-con. There's an Indian restaurant downstairs and they also hire taxis, boats, motorbikes and bicycles at lower rates than just about anyone else on the island.

Also on the main street is the *Fairwind Hotel* (☎ 04-78 8287) which has doubles with fan for M$24 and with air-con for

M$35. Right next door is an unofficial hotel, *Langkawi Holidays*, which charges M$35/40 for double rooms with air-con and common bath.

Pantai Cenang Accommodation at Pantai Cenang ranges from basic chalet places to the international standard Pelangi Beach Resort. They are along the two km of beach between the turn-off to Kuah at the northern end and Pantai Tengah to the south. The water tends to be somewhat murky year round so Pantai Kok is a better choice.

At the budget places you pay around M$20 to M$30 for a chalet with bathroom although there are a few cheaper ones with common bath. Lowest costs are at the *Delta Motel* (☎ 04-91 1307), the last place before the headland which separates Pantai Cenang from Pantai Tengah. It's one of the older places and has A-frame chalets for M$30 with bath or M$15 without.

Towards the north is the *Sura* (☎ 04-91 1232) and *Samila*, two basic and cramped places with fairly unattractive chalets for M$25 with bath. Right across the road is the new and racy *Sri Inai* (☎ 04-91 1269) with a restaurant, souvenir shop and cars and motorbikes for hire. The rooms cost M$25.

The *AB Motel* (☎ 04-91 1300) is next, and it is one of the older established places on Pantai Cenang. It is also about the best value here, with big chalets around a lawn for M$20 to M$30, all with bath, and there's a decent restaurant.

Next door to the AB is the *Sandy Beach Motel* (☎ 04-91 1308), probably the most popular place but one which suffers from inept management, overcrowding and a horrendously smelly drain by the road. The A-frame chalets near the beach are quite good but towards the road they are packed a bit too tightly together. They cost M$25 for a double with fan and M$35 with fan and bath. There's also an ugly new block of air-con rooms.

Pantai Kok Pantai Kok, the best beach on the island, has a few places spread out along about 500 metres of beach. The best place is probably the *Last Resort* (☎ 04-74 0545), run by an expatriate Englishman and his Malay wife. There are 20 chalets, some with air-con (M$50), others with fan (M$35) and all have a bath. There is also a restaurant here.

The *Country Beach Motel* (☎ 04-41 1447) next door is in a pleasant spot and the front chalets are well located. Overall, it's good value at M$15 for rooms with common bath, M$20 for double chalets with fan and bath and M$60 with bath and air-con. The restaurant here serves good food and they have motorbikes and bikes for rent.

Places to Eat

In Kuah, Chinese food is available in the restaurants at the *Asia Hotel* and *Langkawi Hotel*. There are a number of other Chinese and Indian restaurants and stalls along the road than runs through Kuah. Fruit stalls line the main road and the main market has an array of fruit and vegetables.

Many of the hotels at Pantai Cenang have restaurants. The one at the *Sandy Beach* is probably the most popular with good food but rather slow service. Next door, the somewhat pricey *Semarak* serves very good food while the *AB* serves cheap seafood.

At Pantai Kok, the *Country Beach* and *The Last Resort* both have restaurants serving seafood and other local dishes.

Getting There & Away

MAS have flights each day between Langkawi and KL (M$112), Penang (M$42) and Singapore (M$180).

The high speed catamaran *Selesa Ekspres* operates five times weekly between Penang and Langkawi. The fare is M$40 (M$70 return) in 1st class and M$35 (M$60) in economy. The service is operated by the Kuala Perlis-Lankawai Ferry Service whose office in Kuah (☎ 04-78 8316) is at 4 Dindong.

Ferries between Kuala Perlis and Langkawi leave hourly in either direction between 8 am and 6 pm, and the trip takes around one hour. Fares depend on demand. If there are plenty of passengers you pay the full fare (M$10 to M$12) but if things are slack they discount it to M$5. There are also regular ferries between Langkawi and the small port town of Kuala Kedah, not far from Alor Setar.

Getting Around

To/From the Airport The only means of transport to or from the airport is taxi. The fares are fixed (and high) and you buy a coupon at the desk before leaving the airport terminal. The charges are M$12 to Pantai Kok, Teluk Ewa, Pantai Rhu or the Langkawi Island Resort, and M$10 to Pantai Cenang or Kuah.

Bus The bus station is opposite the hospital, in the centre of Kuah. The problem with the buses is that services are not that frequent and are limited in scope. The only places served from Kuah are Pantai Cenang and Teluk Ewa.

Motorbike The easiest way to get around is to hire a motorbike (usually Honda 70 stepthrus) for the day. There are many places in Pantai Cenang which rent motorbikes. None seem too fussed about whether you have a licence or not. There are also places in Kuah and Pantai Kok where it's possible to rent them. The charge is usually M$20 to M$30 per day plus fuel.

Bicycle Most of the places with motorbikes also have bicycles for rent. Some mountain bicycles are available and they cost M$12 per day.

Peninsular Malaysia – East Coast

The east coast is lazy, easy-going, relaxing and fun. The people are very hospitable and hitching is relatively easy, although the traffic is light. Beaches and turtles are the main attractions, plus there's a sprinkling of truly delightful tropical islands off the coast.

In contrast to the west coast, with its Chinese dominated cities, the east coast is much more Malay in character.

This section follows the east coast from the south at Johore Bahru, northwards to Kota Bharu.

JOHORE BAHRU TO MERSING
Kota Tinggi

The small town of Kota Tinggi is 42 km from Johore Bahru on the road to Mersing. The town itself is not that interesting but the **waterfalls** at Lumbong, 15 km north-west of the town, are a very popular weekend retreat.

At the falls, you can stay at the *Waterfall Chalet* (☎ 07-24 1957) where rooms cost from M$30 to M$50 per night, complete with cooking facilities and fridges. Weekend bookings are heavy. There is a restaurant on the hillside facing the falls and also a camping area.

If you're desperate for somewhere cheaper to stay, you could try the basic, noisy *Hotel Koko* in town, which has rooms from M$12.

Johore Lama

Following Melaka's fall to the Portuguese, the Malay Kingdom was transferred to Johore Lama, about 30 km down the Johore River from Kota Tinggi. Today, the old fort of Kota Batu, overlooking the river, has been restored. Getting to Johore Lama entails arranging a boat for the downriver trip.

Jason's Bay

A turn-off 13 km north of Kota Tinggi leads down 24 km of rather rough road to the sheltered waters of Jason's Bay. There's 10 km of sandy beach but few facilities at this fairly isolated spot.

Desaru

On a 20-km stretch of beach at Tanjung Penawar, 88 km north-east of Johore Bahru and also reached via Kota Tinggi, this beach resort area is a popular weekend escape for Singaporeans. The beach is quite good but it's not that interesting for foreign visitors to Malaysia.

Accommodation is mostly in top-end resorts, but there is a camping site where you can stay for M$5 per person in tents, or M$26 in chalets. The only place to eat is at the big hotels.

MERSING

Mersing is a small fishing village on the east coast of Peninsular Malaysia. It's the departure point for the boats which travel between the mainland and the beautiful islands lying just off the coast in the South China Sea.

Places to Stay

Sheikh Tourist Agency (☎ 07-79 3767), 1B Jalan Abu Bakar, is the travellers' place with dorm beds for M$5 and the travel agency downstairs provides good information. It's opposite the post office and a few hundred metres before the boat dock.

The *Traveller's Hotel* at the far end of Jalan Ismail is the cheapest and most basic hotel in town with rooms for M$8 if you bargain. Better value is the *East Coast Hotel* (☎ 07-79 1337) at 43A Jalan Abu Bakar, which has clean, large rooms from M$10.

The *Mandarin Hotel*, opposite the local bus and taxi station, is popular with travellers and the Tioman boat touts will take you there. The best thing about this place is the friendly owner and his sharp sense of humour. Unfortunately, his rooms aren't as sparkling as his wit. Basic rooms start at M$12 and most cost from M$15 to M$20.

Much better is the popular *Hotel Embassy* (☎ 07-79 1301) on Jalan Ismail near the roundabout, where clean comfortable rooms with bath and fan cost M$15 to M$25.

The following three hotels have air-con rooms with bath, but the standards are no better than the Embassy. The *Cathay Hotel*, in a small street off Jalan Ismail, has rooms from M$21 while the *Golden City* on Jalan Abu Bakar charges around M$25. The *Mersing Hotel*, on Jalan Dato Mohammed Ali, has carpeted rooms and occasional hot water for M$30.

Places to Eat

For breakfast, Chinese restaurants do the

usual toast, coffee and eggs or the *E&W Bakery* on Jalan Ismail is OK. For a better selection of fresh cakes and bread, try *Sri Mersing Cafe* on Jalan Sulaiman.

For cheap Chinese food, there are lots of cafes on Jalan Sulaiman or Jalan Abu Bakar. For cheap, tasty Indian food, try the *Taj Mahal Restoran* on Jalan Abu Bakar and *Sri Laxmi Restoran* at 30 Jalan Dato Moham-med Ali. For nasi padang food, the restaurant next to the moneychanger on Jalan Abu Bakar is quite good.

Getting There & Away

Mersing is 133 km north of Johore Bahru and 189 km south of Kuantan. The local bus and taxi station is opposite the Mandarin Hotel on Jalan Sulaiman, close to the river. Long-distance buses stop at the Restoran Malaysia opposite the roundabout. You can buy tickets at the restaurant, but as the buses only pass through Mersing on their way to or from Kuantan or Singapore, it can be difficult to get a seat, especially on weekends.

Buses to Kuantan cost M$10, share taxis M$15, while to Johore Bahru it's M$6 by bus or M$11 by taxi.

TIOMAN ISLAND

The largest and most spectacular of the east coast islands, Tioman is 39 km long and 12 km wide. It has beautiful beaches, clear water and coral for snorkelling or diving enthusiasts, but its major attraction has to be the contrasts and diversity it offers – high mountains and dense jungle are only a short walk away from the coast.

As evidence of the island's abundant natural beauty, it's generally quoted that this was the setting for the mythical Bali Hai in the film *South Pacific*.

The popular beaches for foreign back-packers are Air Batang, Salang, Juara and Tekek, while the southern beaches – Genting, Paya and also Tekek – are popular with Malaysian and Singaporean visitors during holidays. It's also possible to walk across the island from Tekek to Juara.

Places to Stay & Eat

Apart from the Tioman Island Resort, which is of international standard, accommodation is mostly in the form of budget huts and longhouse rooms, or more expensive chalets. A lot of the places quote rates of M$4 or M$5 per person, but single travellers will have difficulty finding an individual hut or room for those rates. It's worth bargaining, especially for longer stays.

Rooms are usually in longhouse blocks. Mostly these are cheap plywood construc-tions but can be comfortable motel-style rooms. The cheap rooms aren't as attractive as the huts but often have electricity and sometimes bathrooms. Prices range from M$8 to M$15 and up to M$30 for a good room with bath, fan and mosquito net.

Chalets are wooden bungalows, usually detached with attap roofs, verandahs, baths and electricity. They offer attractive mid-range accommodation for M$25 to M$30.

Kampung Tekek From the boat jetty there are a whole string of anonymous places to the north that provide cheap rooms from M$6 to M$15, depending on the number of people. Just ask for a room at a likely looking place. One of the better places, and one of the few with a sign, is *Rahim's* where older rooms with bath and fan cost from M$10 and newer rooms are M$15.

Further along is *Railey's Villa*. A lot of travellers stay here, mostly because the owner is one of the most persistent touts when the boats arrive. The accommodation is OK, but don't pay any more than M$10 for a hut or M$5 for a dorm bed.

Past Railey's is the well-run *Tioman Enterprise* which has good rooms from M$10. For cheap huts (M$8), ask at the small eating place advertising 'pure island food'.

Towards the northern end of Tekek Bay are a few good places with attractive settings in amongst the greenery. They are quiet, mostly because few people can be bothered walking this far. *Ramli's* has huts for M$10 and chalets for M$25. Next along is *Azura's* with only two chalets for M$25. At the end of the bay is *Mango Grove*, which has a

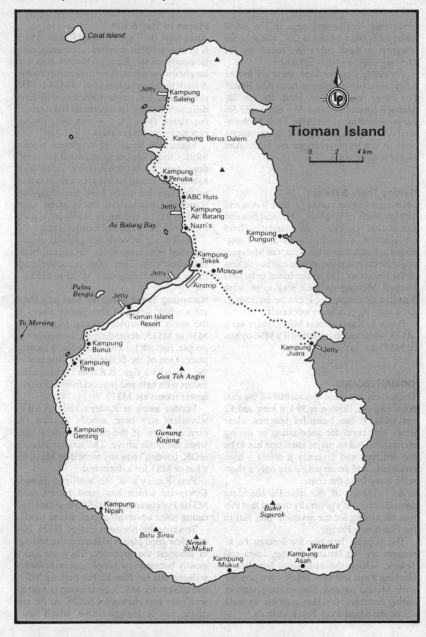

Coral Island

Jetty Kampung
Salang

Kampung Berus Dalem

Tioman Island

0   2   4 km

Kampung
Penuba

ABC Huts

Jetty   Kampung
Air Batang

Nazri's

Air Batang Bay

Kampung
Dungun

Kampung
Tekek

Jetty   Mosque

Airstrip

Pulau   Jetty
Rengis

Kampung

To Mersing

Kampung
Bunut

Kampung
Paya

Kampung
Juara   Jetty

Gua Teh Angin

Kampung
Genting

Gunung
Kajang

Kampung
Nipah

Bukit
Seperok

Batu Sirau

Waterfall

Nenek
SeMukut

Kampung
Mukut

Kampung
Asah

restaurant and a batik shop. Huts cost from M$8 to M$10 per night. It's a good, quiet place but the beach out the front is rocky.

The best stretch of beach and the nicest places to stay are south of the jetty. You can walk along the beach and ford the shallow river, or it's a five-minute walk along the airport road. The first place you come to is *Tekek Inn*, which has rooms and huts for M$15 to M$20 and chalets for M$25. Like all the places on this part of the beach it has its own restaurant.

Next door is the friendly *Sri Tioman* where small huts with mattresses on the floor and mosquito nets cost from M$10 to M$15; chalets cost M$25. The *Coral Reef* is the cheapest place here with basic rooms from M$10 and a few chalets that are usually full. They rent bicycles for M$2 per hour.

Kampung Air Batang This village is north of Tekek. It's the main travellers' centre with a whole host of cheap accommodation and chalets. Huts cost from M$8 to M$10 and most of the places have their own restaurants and serve good, cheap food.

This pretty bay has more greenery than Tekek but, while the beach is good for lazing, most of it is far too rocky for swimming. The exception is the beautiful stretch of beach in front of Nazri's which also has good snorkelling off the point.

ABC is so popular that Air Batang itself is often known as ABC. This is the place to meet other travellers, not to get away from it all. Accommodation ranges from M$10 huts to M$30 chalets. *Nazri's*, at the southern end of the bay, is the other long-established place. It doesn't have ABC's atmosphere, but it does have the best beach. It has a wide variety of huts, rooms and chalets from M$8 to M$30. The restaurant is lively and pumps out the music in the evenings.

If you head north from the jetty, one of the first places you come to is *South Pacific*. A dorm bed is M$4, rooms are from M$8 to M$12 with bath and small chalets on the beach with bath are M$15.

Further along is *Johan's House* with huts, *CT's Cottages* with chalets and then *Tioman*

House with solid wooden huts from M$10. Then there's *Coconut Cafe* with rooms behind and a laundry service next door, followed by *Double Ace. Rinda House*, next to ABC, has some roomy huts with an upstairs sleeping platform for M$12.

Heading south from the jetty is *Zinza's Cafe, Nordin House, Lugam House, Mawar, Warisan Tioman Heritage, Idris, Mahawar Restaurant* and *Seri Bungur* just before Nazri's. These places are spaced out and fairly quiet with huts and rooms for around M$10, but chalets are popping up all over the place.

As for the 'top end', ABC's chalet rooms are reasonable but Nazri's are better. There's a new place right at the jetty with good chalets for M$30. *Warisan Tioman Heritage*, a big place with plenty of chalets crammed together, charges M$25. The nicest place is *CT's Cottages* with just four attractive chalets in a manicured garden setting. Each of them have tiled bathrooms and they cost M$30.

Penuba Bay Over the headland from ABC, the *Penuba Bay Cafe* has a few huts for M$10 and a couple of chalets on the hill. It's certainly peaceful, but accommodation is limited so it's worth checking to see if there's room before lugging your gear over the headland.

Kampung Salang The small bay at Salang is one of the most beautiful on Tioman Island. The only problem is that accommodation is limited and often full. Salang is popular with divers and Ben's Diving Centre, run by a Malay guy who lived in Germany for several years, offers one dive, boat and equipment for M$70 per person or M$80 for two dives.

Indah Salang has a big restaurant and bar but accommodation is still fairly basic. Most rooms, with bath and fan, cost around M$15. The trouble is that they can't cope with the number of people staying here or, as one reader put it, 'are lulled by complacency into near catatonia'.

One of the best buys is the *Salang Damai*

Restaurant. It has good, cheap food and a few rooms for M$10.

Kampung Juara Accommodation is plentiful and slightly cheaper than the other beaches, but because of its isolation, Juara doesn't get as crowded. The beach is excellent, though the sea is very rough in the monsoon season. Two boats a day go from the west of the island, or some of the small boats from Mersing will continue on to Juara for an extra M$15. If enough people want to go direct to Mersing from Juara, a boat costs M$20 per person.

There are at least half a dozen places to stay and many will provide share rooms for M$4 per person. *Happy Cafe,* right by the jetty, is a clean and tidy little establishment where one small room with a double bed and mosquito net costs M$8. *Atan's* has a number of thatched huts for M$8 and chalets for M$14. *Door Ray Me* and *Rainbow Cafe* have huts and rooms for M$8. *Mutiara's* has huts for M$8 and the chalets, with bathrooms and electricity in the evenings, are particularly good value for M$12.

Kampung Paya Paya is a few km south of the Tioman Island Resort. The beach is OK but nothing special. Apart from the expensive *White Sand Beach Resort* (☎ 07-79 2253), there are a few decrepit places to stay. The pick of these is the *Norlida Cafe* with rooms for M$10.

Kampung Genting Genting is the second largest village on the island and more traditional than the other beaches. Very few Westerners ever come here.

There's a whole string of cheap places to stay with rooms for M$8 to M$10. *Shmaimunah House* is on the best part of the beach; huts, rooms and chalets range from M$8 to M$20. *Genting Damai* is the top place with a good restaurant and comfortable chalets for M$25. Next door, the *Genting Village Resort* is good value for groups. It has big four-bed rooms for M$15 and chalets for M$20.

Kampung Nipah This is the place if you really want to get away from it all. The beach is superb with good snorkelling and, apart from a couple of longhouse blocks that are only open during the holiday periods, there's only one place to stay.

Desa Nipah has delightful, traditional-style chalets with bathrooms, but there is no electricity. They range from M$25 to M$70 for a two-storey chalet that sleeps 10 people. Dormitory accommodation is available for M$8 to M$10 and the restaurant is reasonably priced.

Only the boats to and from Mersing stop here, by arrangement, and there are no trails to Nipah. Zamri, the owner, says he can arrange transport to the other beaches if his place is full.

Getting There & Away

Air Tradewinds and Pelangi Air have daily flights to and from Singapore for M$100. Pelangi also flies to KL (M$103) and to Kuantan (M$63).

Boat There are fast, moderate and slow boats from Mersing to Tioman Island. The fast boats, such as the *Pantas Express,* are aircon, take about 1½ hours and cost M$25 one way. They normally only stop at Paya, the resort and Tekek. You can then take the Sea Bus (see the following Getting Around section) to the other beaches.

The Tioman Island Resort's boat, which costs M$30, usually only goes to the resort. It's well worth taking a fast boat during the monsoon season – battling the swells for five hours in a small fishing boat is no fun.

Moderate boats take about three to four hours and cost M$20. The slow fishing boats, which take about four to five hours, cost M$15. These boats will usually drop you off at any of the beaches on the west coast, but check when you buy your ticket. Some will continue to Juara for an extra M$15. The boats go on demand, but there are usually plenty of boats throughout the day.

The Mersing jetty is five-minutes walk from the town centre, and you'll find the offices for boats to all the islands in this area.

The major operator is the Tourist Boats Association (☎ 07-79 2501), 1 Jalan Abu Bakar, which is a cooperative of the Tioman-based boat owners. You can also arrange trips to the other islands.

Getting Around

The excellent Sea Bus service operates regular boats between the resort, Tekek, Air Batang and Salang. They also have two boats per day to Juara. It's also possible to charter boats for M$180 to M$200 per day.

OTHER ISLANDS

Pulau Rawa

This tiny island is 16 km from Mersing. The beach is superb and you can snorkel or dive in the crystal-clear waters, though much of the coral is dead around the island itself.

The *Rawa Safaris Island Resort* (☎ 07-79 1204) is the only place to stay. Simple but comfortable thatched bungalows cost M$50 and rooms cost M$55 to M$80.

Pulau Sibu

Sibu is one of the largest and most popular islands. The beaches are beautiful, the snorkelling is good and there are jungle treks across the island. Windsurfers and canoes can be hired.

O & H Kampung Huts has budget chalets for M$12 to M$15. The restaurant is good and reasonably priced. *Sea Gypsy Village Resort* has traditional-style chalets with bathroom for M$30 and M$35. The more up-market places are the *Sibu Island Resort* (☎ 07-31 6201) and the *Sibu Island Cabanas* (☎ 07-31 7216), where rooms cost from M$50, and deluxe bungalows are M$90.

Pulau Babi Besar

This island is one of the closest to the peninsula. Boats take about an hour to reach the island from Mersing and cost M$18 return. Accommodation is mostly in more expensive chalets. One of the cheapest, *Radhin Chalets* (☎ 07-79 3124), is M$25 for an A-frame chalet.

Pulau Tengah

Near Pulau Babi Besar, Tengah is 16 km off the coast and takes an hour by boat (M$8 one way). *Pirate Bay* (☎ 07-24 1911) is the only resort and chalets cost from M$50/75 for singles/doubles.

Getting There & Away

The Tourist Boats Association will arrange transport out to the islands, see the Tioman section for details.

KUANTAN

About midway up the east coast from Singapore to Kota Bharu, Kuantan is the capital of the state of Pahang and the start of the east-coast beach strip which extends all the way to Kota Bharu.

It is a well-organised, bustling city and is a major stopover point when you are travelling north, south or across the peninsula. The town itself has little to offer the visitor, but there are a number of interesting places nearby.

Teluk Chempedak

Kuantan's major attraction is Teluk Chempedak Beach, about four km from the town. The beach, bounded by rocky headlands at each end, is quite pleasant but there are better beaches on the peninsula. There are a number of walking tracks in the park area on the promontory.

Places to Stay

Kuantan On Jalan Mahkota near the taxi station, the *Min Heng Hotel* (☎ 09-52 4885) is the cheapest place in town at M$10/12 for singles/doubles – it's a classic Chinese cheapie.

The *Tong Nam Ah Hotel* (☎ 09-52 1204) on Jalan Besar near the bus station is a good, cheap hotel with rooms for around M$14. The *Hotel Raya Baru* (☎ 09-52 2344), in between the taxi and bus stations, is better but overpriced at M$26 for a room.

On Jalan Telok Sisek, between Jalan Merdeka and Jalan Bank, are a number of cheap places to stay. The *Hotel New Embassy* (☎ 09-52 4277), 52-54 Jalan Telok

■ PLACES TO STAY

3   Hotel Beserah
5   Hotel Makmur
6   Hotel Pacific
7   Hotel New Meriah
12 Suraya Hotel
13 Hotel New Embassy
16 New Capitol Hotel
19 Min Heng Hotel
20 Samudra River View Hotel
21 Hotel Tong Nam Ah
23 Hotel Raya Baru

▼ PLACES TO EAT

14 Food Stalls
18 Tiki's Restoran

    OTHER

1   Stadium
2   Hindu Temple
4   Local Bus Station
8   MAS
9   Immigration
10 Malayan Banking
11 Post Office
15 Chartered Bank
17 Local Bus Stand
22 Bus Station
24 Tourist Office
25 Taxi Station

Sisek, has good rooms with balcony for M$14 and more expensive rooms with bath and air-con. A few doors along, the *Mei Lai Hotel* is noisy but clean and a good buy at M$12/14 for singles/doubles. On the corner of Jalan Merdeka is the *Hotel Embassy*, which costs M$22 for a room with bath.

For a room with bath, the *New Capitol Hotel* (☎ 09-50 7276), 55 Jalan Bukit Ubi, has spotless rooms for M$20. Near the local bus station are two new Indian-run hotels. They have been cheaply put together by partitioning off the floors above shops, but their newness means they are spotlessly clean and well appointed. The *Hotel Sri Intan* (☎ 09-51 2000), 13-15 Jalan Stadium, has rooms with air-con (that works) and bath from M$25 to M$35. Next door, the *Hotel Makmur* has air-con rooms without bath from M$20 to M$28.

Teluk Chempedak The alternative to staying in Kuantan itself is out at Teluk Chempedak Beach, where there's a wide variety of accommodation. The *Asrama Bendahara* (☎ 09-52 5930) is the lowest priced place to stay with dorm beds at M$7 and rooms from M$15 to M$20. It's a little

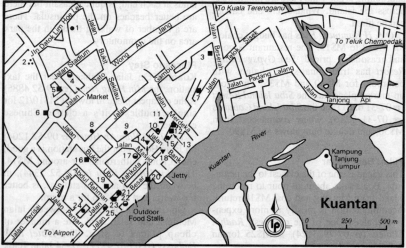

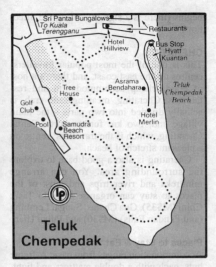

Teluk
Chempedak

overpriced, but has a certain run-down charm. There's a cheap open-air restaurant and it's a friendly place, popular with travellers.

There's a group of 'motels' in the street behind the Hotel Hillview. Some are very seedy and ill-cared-for but the *Sri Pantai Bungalows* (☎ 09-52 4749) at No 19 has good, clean, carpeted rooms with fans for M$22. There are plenty of other places in this street charging from M$18 to M$25 for a room – just ask at a 'room to let' sign.

Near the Bendahara is the *Kuantan Hotel* (☎ 09-52 4755) with good rooms with fan for M$40 and air-con rooms for M$55. Around on the main road, there's the musty *Hotel Hill View* (☎ 09-52 1555) with rooms for M$48.

Places to Eat

Kuantan The food stalls on Jalan Mahkota serve excellent Chinese food and cold beer, as well as satay, Muslim and Indian food. The small Muslim food stalls dotted along the riverbank, behind the long-distance bus station, are a great place to sit and watch the boats pass by. The seafood is particularly good and the prawns are huge.

In the evenings, food stalls set up near the local bus station and there are a few interesting serve-yourself nasi padang places and good Chinese seafood satay – select what you want and cook it in the vats of boiling water.

For breakfast, try *Tiki's Restoran*, up the far end of Jalan Mahkota. It's only open during the day and the two ever-busy brothers who run this place really welcome travellers. There are plenty of good bakeries around, including the one under the Min Heng Hotel, the *Terantum Bakery & Cafe* in the Kompleks Terantum and several along Jalan Bukit Ubi.

Not far from Tiki's Restoran is the popular *Restoran Cheun Kee* which serves good Chinese food for around M$3. There are good Indian restaurants on Jalan Bukit Ubi, past Jalan Gambut.

Teluk Chempedak Food is one of Teluk Chempedak's main attractions. Apart from the food stalls at the end of the beach and the restaurant at the Asrama Bendahara, there's not much in the way of cheap eats. However, the flash restaurants are not as expensive as they look and the food is excellent.

On the foreshore, *Pattaya* and *Restoran Din* are pleasant, open-air places specialising in seafood, though the air-con places on the main road are generally better value. The air-con restaurants serve mostly Chinese seafood and Malay specialities. *Nisha's*, a north Indian restaurant, has good tandoori food and breads.

Getting There & Away

MAS (☎ 09-52 1218) has direct flights from Kuantan to Singapore (M$120) and KL (M$61) and handles bookings for Pelangi Air flights to Kerteh and Tioman.

Buses to KL cost M$11, to Mersing M$11, to Johore Bahru M$15 and to Singapore M$16. To Kuala Terengganu, it's M$8, Kota Bharu (M$15), Melaka M$13 and Penang M$4.50. For Taman Negara there are direct buses to Jerantut (M$7.70).

Taxis cost M$4 to Pekan, M$15 to Mersing and M$5 to Kemaman. To Kuala

Terengganu it's M$17, and M$25 to Kota Bharu. Across the peninsula, it's M$9 to Temerloh, M$13 to Jerantut, M$18 to Raub and M$20 to KL.

Getting Around

Bus No 39 will take you from town to Teluk Chempedak for 50 sen. You can catch it at the local bus station or, more conveniently, at the M3 bus stand on the corner of Jalan Mahkota and Jalan Masjid. For Cherating, take the 'Kemaman' bus No 27 from the main bus station for M$2.20.

AROUND KUANTAN
Beserah

The small, interesting fishing village of Beserah, only 10 km north of Kuantan, is a centre for local handicrafts. **Batu Hitam** is a good beach just north of Beserah.

Places to Stay & Eat The popular shoestring travellers' place in Beserah is known as *Jaafar's Place*. It's a kampung house about half a km off the road on the inland side. It is indicated by a sign, and bus drivers know it. Accommodation costs M$9 a night (including a light breakfast) and other meals are available. The facilities are very basic.

Getting There & Away Buses to Kemaman (No 27), Balok (No 30) or Sungai Karang (No 28) all pass through Beserah. They leave from the main bus station and the fare is 50 sen.

Berkelah Falls

The Berkelah Falls are about 50 km from Kuantan – the final six km to them involves a jungle trek from the main road. The falls come down a hillside in a series of eight cascades. The **Marathandhavar Temple** hosts a major Hindu festival in March or April each year.

Getting There & Away Catch a bus to Maran from the main bus station for M$3.35. At Maran, you'll see a bridge by the river. This is where the three-hour walk to the falls

begins (there is a sign indicating the direction).

CHERATING

This is one of the most popular travellers' centres on the east coast, and there's a host of good, cheap accommodation and restaurants. Cherating, meaning sand crab, is actually divided into two parts – the main village and, two km further north, Pantai Cherating, which is the travellers' centre on a pleasant stretch of beach.

Cherating is also a good base to explore the surrounding area. You can arrange minitreks and river trips and most of the places to stay can organise tours to Tasik Chini (M$35), Gua Charas, Sungai Lembing (and Pandan Falls) (M$30) and Pulau Ular.

Places to Stay & Eat

Accommodation ranges from basic A-frame huts, each with a double mattress and light, but without a fan, to more comfortable 'chalets' with a bathroom. Most of the A-frame huts cost around M$10 and sleep two people whereas the chalets range from M$15 to M$30. Many of the places have their own restaurants and you can easily spend a few days in Cherating and not sample them all.

On the main road are two of the longest running homestays – *Mak Long Teh's* and *Mak De's*. Both places charge M$12 for accommodation, breakfast and dinner, or M$17 including lunch. All-you-can-eat meals at both places are excellent.

Closer to the beach, *Maznah Guest House* is one of the cheapest places at around M$8. *Cherating Indah* has good chalets for M$12 and M$20 with bath. The *Riverside* is popular, with some basic huts for M$8, but most are from M$10 to M$12, or M$18 with bath (worth the extra few ringgit). *Hussaien's Bungalows* has shabby-looking places for M$10, but they are roomy and better than they appear.

Further south is the *Restoran Sayang*, which has a few rooms and huts for M$15, but the best thing here is the Indian set-meals for M$6. The *Coconut Inn* is a friendly, well-kept place with small A-frame huts from M$10, larger ones from M$12 to M$14 and chalets with bath for M$18. Next door is the *Kampung Inn* with a number of chalets from M$15 to M$25 and dorm beds for M$5 per person.

At the other end of the beach is the *Cherating Beach Recreation Centre*, where rooms and huts cost M$10 to M$15 and chalets with bath are M$25. The *Mini Motel* is more up-market than most and has a good restaurant. Air-con rooms cost from M$10 to M$35 and chalets are M$25. Across the road, *Chippy's* has one of the best, and most crowded, restaurants in Cherating.

Getting There & Away
Catch one of the hourly 'Kemaman' buses from the main bus station in Kuantan (M$2.20; one hour). From Cherating to Kuantan, wave down a Kuantan bus from the bus stop outside Mak Long Teh's.

RANTAU ABANG
This is the principal turtle beach and the prime area for spotting the great leatherback turtles during the laying season. The long, sandy beach is good for extended, lonely walks. Swimming is possible but the undertow can be savage.

The Turtle Information Centre, run by the Department of Fisheries, is near the main budget accommodation centre. They have good displays and show films six times a day. The centre is open every day during the turtle-watching season but otherwise it is closed on Friday and public holidays. Note that the nearest bank is at Kuala Dungun, 22 km south.

August is the peak laying season, when you have an excellent chance of seeing turtles, but you may also be lucky in June and July. Full moon and high-tide nights are said to be best. The villagers know the season is about to end when the smaller green turtles come to lay their eggs – a week later the leatherbacks are gone until next year.

Unfortunately, the east coast's primary tourist attraction has resulted in a decline in turtle numbers, but the government is making a concerted effort to preserve the turtles and their egg-laying habitat. The gross behaviour of the past – pulling the turtles' flippers, shining lights into their eyes, taking the eggs and even riding on the turtles' backs – is punishable by heavy fines. Flash photography and shining torches on the turtles is prohibited and you must keep a reasonable distance.

The beach is now divided into three sections during the season – prohibited, semi-public (where you have to buy tickets) and free access – in an attempt to control the 'hey gang, the turtles are up' mentality.

Places to Stay & Eat
Right on the beach and not far from the Turtle Information Centre are two travellers' places. *Awang's* (☎ 09-84 2236) gets most of the travellers. Don't believe their advertised rates of M$3 per person. If you press hard you may be able to get a bed for M$4 but the rooms are mostly M$10 to M$12. They've grown complacent here and the rooms could do with some maintenance, but it has a good restaurant and it is right on the beach.

Ismael's, next door, has similar rooms from M$10 to M$12. It's well-kept, friendly and tends to be less crowded than Awang's. Probably the top budget place, recommended by many travellers, is *Dahimah's*, about one km south towards Dungun. Dorm beds cost M$5 and most rooms cost M$10. They have a good restaurant and arrange trips, including ones to Pulau Tenggol.

Getting There & Away
Rantau Abang is about 58 km south of Kuala Terengganu and 138 km north of Kuantan. Dungun-Kuala Terengganu buses run in both directions every hour and there's a bus stop near the Turtle Information Centre. Rantau Abang to Kuala Terengganu costs M$3 and to Dungun costs M$1. Heading south, you can try to hail down a long-distance bus, or take the bus to Dungun from where hourly buses go to Kuantan. There are also buses to Mersing, Singapore and KL.

MARANG
Marang, a large fishing village at the mouth

of the Marang River, is very picturesque. It's a popular travellers' centre, a beautiful place to relax and the departure point for Pulau Kapas.

Marang is a conservative village, however, especially in the area across the river from the main town, and reserve in dress and behaviour is recommended.

Places to Stay & Eat

The *Marang Inn* (☎ 09-68 1878), on the main street near the bus station, costs M$4 for a dorm and M$10 for a room. It's very popular, good value and has the best food in town.

Most of the guest houses close to town are on the lagoon, a stone's throw from the beach. *Kamal's* is the longest running and one of the best. Dorm beds are M$4, rooms are M$10 and chalets are M$12. The *Island View Resort* (☎ 09-68 2006) is also good, has free bicycles for guests and charges the same as Kamal's. On the hill behind Kamal's is the *Marang Guest House*. It's a notch up from the other guest houses and has its own restaurant, but it's a bit dull. A dorm bed is M$5, and rooms are M$12 and M$15 with bath and mosquito nets.

Apart from the restaurants at the Marang Inn and Marang Guest House, there are good food stalls near the market and some grotty restaurants on the main street.

Two km south of the river, around the 20-km marker, is the *Beach House* (☎ 09-68 2403), which is very welcoming but overpriced at M$25 for a basic chalet. The *Mare Nostrum* (☎ 09-68 1433), around the corner from the Beach House, is also overpriced but better value.

Getting There & Away

Marang is about 45 minutes south of Kuala Terengganu and regular buses run to and from there (M$1) and Dungun.

PULAU KAPAS

Six km offshore from Marang is the beautiful little island of Kapas. There are walks and snorkelling to keep you busy but the island is best avoided during holidays and long weekends when it is overrun by day-trippers.

Places to Stay & Eat

There are three places to stay, each with their own restaurant. The *Kapas Island Beach Resort* (☎ 09-63 2989), *Mak Cik Gemuk Chalets* (09-68 1221) and *Zaki Beach Chalet* (☎ 09-81 1475) all charge M$10 for a single and have chalets or rooms from M$15. It is also possible to camp on the beach to the south, but bring your own food and water.

Getting There & Away

Most boats leave Marang around 9 am and the cost is M$7.50 one way.

KUALA TERENGGANU

Standing on a promontory formed by the South China Sea on one side and the wide Terengganu River on the other side, Kuala Terengganu is the capital of Terengganu state and the seat of the Sultan. Despite a lot of recent oil-based development, the town still has a quiet backwater feel once you get away from the main streets and there's enough to amuse you during a short stay.

Things to See & Do

Most of Kuala Terengganu's colourful atmosphere can be appreciated along Jalan Bandar, Kuala Terengganu's Chinatown. The **Central Market** is colourful and active, and the floor above the fish section has a fabulous collection of batik and songket. Past the market is the **Istana Maziah** and the gleaming new **Zainal Abidin Mosque**.

Pantai Batu Buruk is the city beach and a popular place to stroll in the evening when the food stalls open up. Across the road, the Cultural Centre sometimes stages pencak silat and wayang shows on Fridays between 5 and 6.30 pm.

The jetty behind the taxi station is the place for a 40-sen ferry ride to the boat-building island of **Pulau Duyung**. It's the largest island in the estuary and worth exploring.

Places to Stay

Ping Anchorage (☎ 09-62 0851), upstairs at 77A Jalan Dato Isaac, is the number one travellers' place. Dorm beds are M$5 and rooms range from M$10 to M$12, or M$15

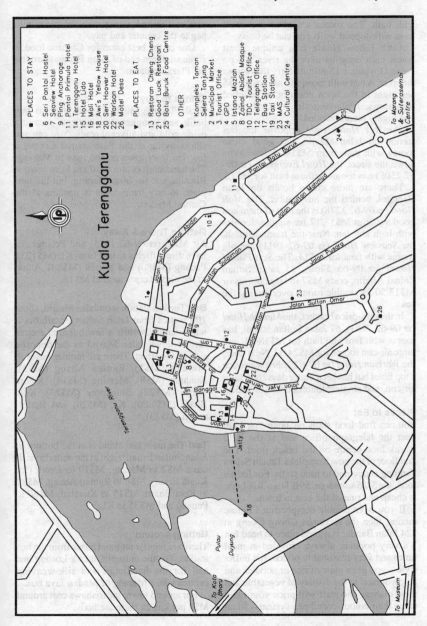

PLACES TO STAY

6 Seri Pantai Hostel
7 Seaview Hotel
9 Ping Anchorage
11 Pantai Primula Hotel
14 Terengganu Hotel
15 Hotel Lido
16 Mali Hotel
18 Awi's Yellow House
20 Seri Hoover Hotel
22 Warisan Hotel
26 Motel Desa

PLACES TO EAT

13 Restoran Cheng Cheng
21 Good Luck Restoran
25 Batu Buruk Food Centre

OTHER

1 Kompleks Taman
2 Selera Tanjung
3 Municipal Market
4 Tourist Office
5 GPO
8 Istana Maziah
10 Zainal Abidin Mosque
12 TDC Tourist Office
17 Telegraph Office
19 Bus Station
23 Taxi Station
24 MAS
24 Cultural Centre

Kuala Terengganu

To Morang
& Suterasemai
Centre

Pantai Batu Buruk

Jalan Sultan Mahmud

Jalan Sultan Zainal Abidin

Jln Sultan Sulaiman

Jalan Pusara

Jalan Sultan Ismail

Jalan Sultan Omar

Jalan Air Jernih

Jln Kota

Jln Masjid

Jln Tok Lam

Jln Banggol

Jalan

Terengganu River

Jetty

Pulau
Duyung

To Kota
Bharu

To Museum

with bath. The rooms are good, but most have wire-topped walls and can be noisy.

Awi's Yellow House is a unique guest house built on stilts over the river. It's on Pulau Duyung, a 15-minute ferry ride across the river. A bed with mosquito net costs M$5 per night in the open dorm or in thatched bungalows. It's a beautiful, relaxed place, and highly recommended.

The *Rex Hotel*, right opposite the bus station on Jalan Masjid, has good clean rooms with bath from M$14. A few doors down the street, the *Hotel Evergreen* (☎ 09-62 2505) has rooms without bath for M$12.

There are more cheap hotels on Jalan Banggol, behind the bus station. The *Mali Hotel* (☎ 09-62 3278) is the best of them and good value at M$13/17 for singles/doubles with bath and fan. Near the Istana Maziah, the *Seaview Hotel* (☎ 09-62 1911) has big rooms with fans for M$14. The *Seri Pantai Hostel* (☎ 09-63 5766), 35 Jalan Sultan Zainal Abidin, costs M$7 in large dorms or M$13.50 for double rooms overlooking the sea.

In the mid-price bracket, the *Meriah Hotel* (☎ 09-62 7983), 67 Jalan Sultan Ismail, has rooms with fans and bath for M$18/24, and large air-con rooms for M$24/32. Next door, the *Warisan Hotel* (☎ 09-62 2688) was once a top hotel but has seen better days. It is fully air-con, and singles/doubles cost M$38/55.

Places to Eat

You can find food stalls on Jalan Tok Lam near the telegraph office and at the Batu Buruk food centre on the beach front. The 2nd floor of the new Kompleks Taman Selera Tanjung is devoted to food stalls. For Indian food, the *Sri Shanmuga*, 59B Jalan Tok Lam, is cheap and one of the best in town.

If you have trouble deciphering Chinese menus, then the *Restoran Cheng Cheng* at 224 Jalan Bandar is a good place to head for. It's very popular, always crowded at meal times and very reasonably priced. It's buffet style – you get a plate of rice or noodles and help yourself to the display of vegetable and meat dishes. The staff will price your meal using their colour-coded peg system – when you've finished eating take the plate with peg to the counter and pay.

One of the best areas for Chinese food is at the southern end of Jalan Banggol around the Plaza Perdana.

Things to Buy

Kuala Terengganu is a good place to buy batik and songket, the intricate weaving using gold and silver threads. You can see silk-weaving at the Suterasemai Centre, a few km from town on the road to Marang. The handicraft centre is 10 km from town at Rhusila, not far from Marang, but the best place to buy handicrafts is upstairs at the Central Market.

Getting There & Away

Air MAS (☎ 09-62 1415) and Pelangi Air have direct flights to and from KL (M$123), Penang (M$80) and Kerteh (M$80). A taxi to the airport costs around M$15.

Bus The bus station is on Jalan Masjid, about 100 metres from Jalan Sultan Ismail, but it will eventually shift a few hundred metres further down Jalan Masjid to the opposite side of the street. There are regular buses to Marang (M$1), Rantau Abang (M$3), Kuantan (M$8), Mersing (M$14), Johore Bahru (M$22), Singapore (M$23), Kota Bharu (M$6.80), KL (M$20) and Butterworth (M$23).

Taxi The main taxi stand is at the bottom of Jalan Sultan Ismail, right at the waterfront. It costs M$2 to Marang, M$10 to Jerteh (for Kuala Besut), M$6 to Rantau Abang, M$12 to Kota Bharu, M$15 to Kuantan, M$60 to Penang and M$35 to KL.

Getting Around

There are regular regional buses from the bus station. For the museum, take a Losong bus and for the handicraft and silk-weaving centres take a Marang or Medan Jaya bus.

For around town, the trishaws cost around M$1 per km, or there are taxis.

MERANG

The sleepy little fishing village of Merang (not to be confused with Marang) is 14 km north of Kuala Terengganu. There's nothing to do here, but the beautiful beach is lined with coconut palms and lapped by clear water. Merang is also the place to get boats to Pulau Redang and other nearby islands.

Places to Stay

For traditional hospitality try *Man's Homestay*, half a km from the T-intersection in the village, on the Penarik road. Facilities are basic and the cost is M$10 per night including all meals. The other place to stay is the *Merang Beach Resort*, overpriced at M$25 but a good place to swim.

Getting There & Away

From Kuala Terengganu, take the Penarik bus and get off at Merang.

KUALA BESUT

Kuala Besut, on the coast south of Kota Bharu, has a reasonably pleasant beach and is an interesting, though grubby, fishing village. A visit to this town is usually just a preliminary to a trip to the Perhentian Islands.

Places to Stay

If you want budget accommodation in Kuala Besut, ask around in the shops on the main street next to the river.

Getting There & Away

From the south, take a bus to Jerteh on the main highway. From there, buses (M$1) go every 40 minutes to Kuala Besut. From Kota Bharu, it's easier to get off at Pasir Puteh and take a bus from there. A share taxi from Jerteh or Pasir Puteh to Kuala Besut costs M$1.50.

PERHENTIAN ISLANDS

A two-hour boat trip from Kuala Besut takes you to the two beautiful islands of Perhentian Besar and Perhentian Kecil, just 21 km off the coast. As far as things to 'see and do' go,

it's a simple case of lazing around watching coconuts fall.

There are beautiful beaches and excellent snorkelling, and if you feel energetic, you can make a 2½ hour crossing of Perhentian Besar on foot along well-marked trails.

Places to Stay & Eat

Perhentian Besar There are two basic choices: the expensive resort or the 'budget-accommodation beach'.

The *Perhentian Island Resort* (☎ 01-33 3910) is 'where reality becomes a fantasy'. The slogan is probably inspired by the superb beach and its beautiful coral, and has nothing to do with drugs! The resort is comfortable and has attractive A-frame chalets for M$32, roomy bungalows for M$52, and a bed in the large, often empty, dorms is M$12. The food is ordinary and expensive for what you get.

The budget-accommodation beach faces the mainland and is just across the strait from the village on Kecil. It's a 20-minute clamber over two headlands from the resort. Accommodation is basic; there is no electricity and washing is done in wells. Food can sometimes be in short supply and snacks, bottled water and cigarettes are expensive so bring your own.

To the left of the beach as you arrive is *Coco Hut*, which has thatched A-frame huts for M$8. Next door is *Hamid's* with rooms for M$10. *Rosli Chalet* caters mostly for divers and a bed in a large tent costs M$3 per person or a dorm bed costs M$5. Rooms are M$15. They also serve breakfast and dinner.

Further along the beach, around the bend, is the *Coral Cave Cafe*, the most popular place to eat. A marvel of architectural simplicity and beauty, it is just a thatched roof strung between the large boulders on the beach with table and chairs beneath. Past the Coral Cave is *Abdul's Chalets*, the quietest and one of the best places to stay. Rooms with big verandahs cost M$10.

Over the headland, next to the rest house, is the *Isabella Coffee Shop* which has good food and great squid. You can also find yourself a quiet place to camp beyond the rest house.

Perhentian Kecil It is possible to rent a room in the village for about M$5 per night, or if you really want to get away from it all, there is a small, basic resort at Pasir Petani with bungalows for M$10. The boats from the mainland will drop you at Pasir Petani, or it's a 30-minute walk from the village.

Getting There & Away
The one-way trip from Kuala Besut to Perhentian costs M$15. Most boats leave Perhentian early in the morning and return late in the morning and throughout the afternoon. The boats will drop you off at any of the beaches. If you stay at the resort or Pasir Petani, it's a good idea to arrange the return journey with the boat captain.

Small boats ply between the two islands for M$1 per person.

KOTA BHARU
In the north-east corner of the peninsula, Kota Bharu is the capital of the state of Kelantan, the termination point of the east coast road and a gateway to Thailand. It's Malaysia at its most Malayan – a centre for Malay culture, crafts and religion. It's also the place to see kite-flying contests, watch batik being made, admire traditional wood-carving, photograph the colourful marketplace and marvel at the skills of songket weavers and silversmiths.

Kota Bharu is a good place to sample traditional Malay culture, but the true Malay spirit is in the villages of Kelantan, and Kota Bharu is a good base to explore the surrounding countryside. If your time is limited you can take a pleasant one or two-hour stroll around the Padang Merdeka area, preferably in the morning when it's cool. The markets and the performances at the Gelanggang Seni shouldn't be missed.

Orientation
In Kota Bharu it can be difficult, initially, to find your way around. Streets change name at random and the numbering system is

■ PLACES TO STAY

6	Ideal Travellers' Guest House
7	City Guest House
8	Hostel Pantai
10	Indah Hotel
14	Temenggong Hotel
17	Thye Ann Hotel
19	Suria Hotel
20	Yee Guest House
21	Kencana Inn
22	Friendly Guest House
23	Town Guest House
24	Mummy's Hitec Hostel
25	Rainbow Inn Guest House
29	Hitect Hostel
30	Hotel Murni
38	Hotel Perdana
39	Rebana Guest House
40	Hotel Irama
41	De 999 Guest House

▼ PLACES TO EAT

1	Food Stalls
9	Restoran Vegetarian
15	Night Market Foodstalls
16	Razak Restoran
35	Foodstalls

OTHER

2	Karyaneka Handicraft Centre
3	State Mosque
4	Royal Museum
5	Istana Balai Besar
11	Bazaar Buluh Kubu
12	Bus stand to PCB
13	Central Market
18	Bus & Taxi Station
26	Royal Thai Consulate
27	Telekom
28	Old Central Market
31	Clocktower
32	MAS
33	State Museum
34	Tourist Information Centre
36	Post Office
37	Cultural Centre (Gelanggang Seni)
42	Silver Smith
43	External (Jalan Hamzah) Bus Station
44	SKMK Langgar Bus Station

chaotic. The centre of town is a bustling area, north of the clocktower, bounded by Jalan Kebun Sultan/Jalan Mahmud, Jalan Pintu Pong, Jalan Temenggong and Jalan Hospital.

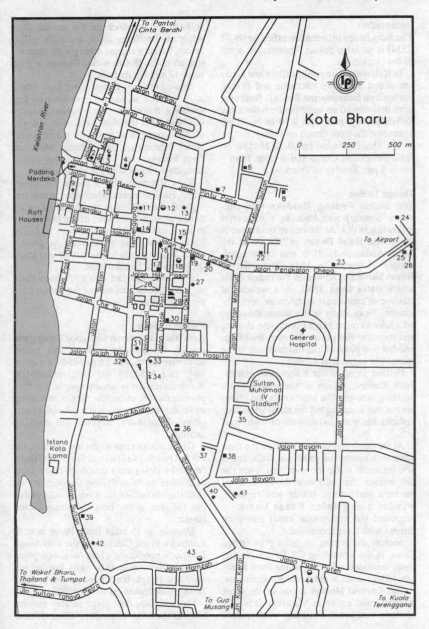

To Pantai
Cinta Berahi

Kota Bharu

0   250   500 m

Kelantan River

Padang
Merdeka

Raft
Houses

Jalan Merbau

Jalan Tok Semian

Jalan Sultan

Jalan Tengku Besar

Jalan Tengku Chik

Jalan Tok Hakim

Jalan Pintu Pong

Jalan Kebun Sultan

Jalan Padang Garong

Jalan Pengkalan Chepa

Jalan Hilir Pasar

Jalan Post Office

Jalan Che Su

Jalan Sultan

Jalan Doktor

Jalan Datuk Pati

Jalan Ismail

Jalan Gajah Mati

Jalan Hospital

General
Hospital

Sultan
Muhamad
IV
Stadium

Jalan Dusun Muda

Jalan Sultan Mahmud

Jalan Zainal Abidin

Jalan Sultan Ibrahim

Jalan Bayam

Jalan Bayam

Istana
Kota
Lama

Jalan Sultan Yahaya Petra

To Wakaf Bharu,
Thailand & Tumpat

Jin Sultan Yahaya Petra

Jalan Hamzah

Jalan Pasir Puteh

Jin Kuala Kerai

Jalan Kuala Kerai

To Airport

To Gua
Musang

To Kuala
Terengganu

Information

The Kota Bharu information office (☎ 09-78 5534) is on Jalan Sultan Ibrahim, just south of the clocktower.

In Kelantan, state public offices and banks are closed Thursday afternoon and Friday, but open on Saturday and Sunday. Banks are open between 10 am and 3 pm from Saturday to Wednesday, and from 9.30 to 11.30 am Thursday; they are closed on Friday.

The Thai Consulate (☎ 09-72 2545) is on Jalan Pengkalan Chepa and is open from 9 am to 4 pm, Sunday to Thursday.

Things to See

The central **Padang Merdeka** (Independence Square) was built as a memorial following WW I. At the end of the square is the **Istana Balai Besar,** or 'Palace of the Large Audience Hall'. It was constructed, mainly of timber, in 1844. The adjacent **Royal Museum,** housed in the Istana Jahar which dates from 1887, is a wonderful mixture of traditional architecture and Victoriana. Next along is the **State Mosque**, which looks more like a Portuguese church, and then the **Religious Council Building,** another fine piece of local architecture in the same vein as the Istana Jahar.

Further along is the **Karyaneka Handicraft Centre,** which is the oldest brick building in town. The handicrafts and prices are not that stunning but the small art gallery upstairs has good exhibitions of traditional arts.

At the other end of the square on the river bank are a number of good food stalls, and if you go south along the river you'll see the raft houses that still exist in defiance of modern amenities. While you're here, wander along **Jalan Pasar Lama,** a neglected but picturesque street that once thrived with river commerce.

Around the corner, in Jalan Post Office Lama, is the interesting CK Lam's antique shop, crammed with everything from hand-carved bird eages to old musical instruments.

The **Central Market** is one of the most colourful and active in Malaysia. It is in a modern octagonal building with traders selling fresh produce on the ground floor while on the floors above are stalls selling spices, basketware and other goods. Near the market is the **Buluh Kubu Bazaar,** a good place to buy handicrafts.

One of the best things about Kota Bharu is the chance to see performances of top-spinning, traditional dance dramas, wayang kulit and other traditional activities. They're at Gelanggang Seni, across the road from the Hotel Perdana on Jalan Sultan Mahmud, from February to October, except during Ramadan. Check with the tourist office.

Kota Bharu is also a centre for Malay crafts. Batik, songket, silverware, woodcarving and kite-making factories and shops are dotted around town. One of the best places to see handicrafts is on the road to Pantai Cinta Berahi. The markets are as good a place as any to buy handicrafts if you know the prices and bargain hard.

For batik, you can also try Wisma Batik on Jalan Che Su just around the corner from the Hotel Murni.

Places to Stay

Kota Bharu is overrun with good cheap guest houses. Competition is fierce and, unless otherwise stated, all charge M$4 for a dorm bed, and M$8/10 for singles/doubles. Accommodation is usually simple, but they provide free tea and coffee, lots of interesting travellers' information and a relaxed atmosphere. Most have bicycles and cooking facilities.

Of the places close to the town centre, the *KB Inn* (☎ 09-74 1786) and *Yee Guest House* (☎ 09-74 1944) are a couple of doors from each other on Jalan Padang Garong, not far from the bus station. Both are friendly places but the Yee is the better accommodation choice.

Upstairs at 35 Jalan Pintu Pong, next to Kentucky Fried Chicken, is the *City Guest House,* a spotlessly clean well-run place which is more quiet than most. Further out on Jalan Pengkalan Chepa is the popular *Town Guest House* (☎ 09-78 5192).

Probably the best place to stay around town is the *Ideal Travellers' Guest House*

(☎ 09-74 42246), in a private house down an alley off Jalan Pintu Pong. It's quiet, central and has a pleasant garden, but is often full. Apart from the standard rates, they have rooms with baths for M$12. They also run the *Friendly Guest House*, a few hundred metres away, just off Jalan Kebun Sultan. It's not as attractive, but is also quiet and has good rooms, most with bath, for M$10/12.

On Jalan Pengkalan Chepa, near the Thai Consulate, is the *Rainbow Inn Guest House*. This house has an agreeable garden and some great artwork on the walls, courtesy of inspired travellers.

Across the road and up an alley is the popular *Mummy's Hitec Hostel* in an old house with a large garden. Mummy is a real character and enjoys a night out with the guests. Extras include free haircuts. A trishaw to the Rainbow Inn or Mummy's Hitec costs about M$1, or take bus Nos 4, 8A or 9, for 40 sen.

The best value in town has to be the *De 999 Guest House* at M$3/6 for good singles/doubles including breakfast and free bicycles. It's not far from the long-distance bus station in the small street directly behind the Hotel Irama, at No 3188-G. The house is hard to find – there's only a tiny sign on the gate.

The *Rebana Guest House*, up an alleyway off Jalan Sultan Zainab, is a long way from the town centre but worth the effort. It's a lovely house, decorated Malay-style, with lots of artwork around. There's a variety of rooms, ranging from the M$4 dorm and pokey M$6 singles, to some beautiful old rooms and chalets in the garden from M$10 to M$15.

Of course, there are also plenty of cheap Chinese hotels. A basic but interesting old hotel is the *Thye Ann Hotel* (☎ 09-78 5907) on Jalan Hilir Pasar opposite the old central market, with huge doubles for M$15. A bit more up-market is the *Suria Hotel* (☎ 09-74 3310), which has large rooms with bath and air-con for M$22/32. It's very good value and they even throw in 'free breakfast for foreigner'.

The *Hotel Tokio Baru* (☎ 09-74 9488), on Jalan Tok Hakim near the Temenggong Hotel, is a better class of cheap hotel with fan rooms from M$26 and air-con rooms from M$32.

Places to Eat

The best and cheapest Malay food in Kota Bharu is found at the night market, opposite the central bus station. The food stalls are set up in the evenings and there's a wide variety of delicious, cheap Malay food. Local specialities include ayam percik (marinated chicken enclosed between bamboo skewers) and nasi kerabu (rice with coconut, fish and spices).

There are more good food stalls next to the river (opposite the Padang Merdeka) and at the stadium. They have a number of stalls selling ABC (air batu kacang – the shaved-ice dessert).

There are plenty of Chinese restaurants around town, including good chicken rice places on Jalan Padang Garong near the Kencana Inn. The *Restoran Vegetarian*, on Jalan Post Office Lama opposite the antique shop, has good Chinese vegetarian food.

The *Razak Restoran*, on the corner of Jalan Datok Pati and Jalan Padang Garong, is cheap and has excellent Indian Muslim food.

Getting There & Away

Air MAS (☎ 09-74 7000) has direct flights to Penang (M$72), Alor Setar (M$59) and KL (M$86).

Bus The state-run SKMK is the largest bus company and runs all the city and regional buses as well as most of the long-distance buses. They operate from the central bus station (city and regional buses) and the Langgar bus station (long-distance buses). All the other long-distance bus companies operate from the Jalan Hamzah external bus station.

SKMK are the easiest to deal with as they have ticket offices at all the bus stations. Long-distance departures are from the Langgar station but, just to make things confusing, a few evening buses also go from the

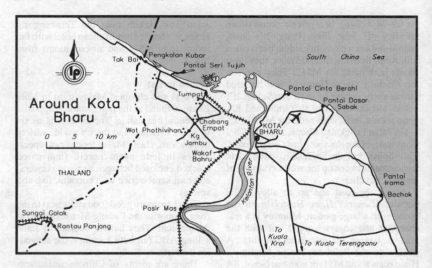

central bus station. Ask which station your bus departs from when you buy your ticket and book as far ahead as possible, especially for the Butterworth (Penang) buses.

There are regular buses to Kuantan (M$16), Kuala Terengganu (M$6.80), Johore Bahru (M$24), Singapore (M$25), KL (M$25), Butterworth (M$18), Jerantut (M$18), Alor Setar, Kuala Lipis, Temerloh, Dungun and Grik.

Train The jungle railway starts at Tumpat and goes through Kuala Krai, Gua Musang, Kuala Lipis, Jerantut (for Taman Negara National Park) and eventually meets the Singapore-KL line at Gemas. Travel is slow but the scenery is certainly worth it. The nearest station to Kota Bharu is at Wakaf Bahru, a 50 sen trip on bus Nos 19 or 27.

Taxi The taxi station is on the southern side of the bus station. Main destinations are Kuala Terengganu (M$12), Kuantan (M$25), KL (M$35), Butterworth (M$30) and Johore Bahru (M$52).

To/From Thailand The Thai border is at Rantau Panjang (Sungai Golok on the Thai side), 1½ hours by bus from Kota Bharu. Bus No 29 from the central bus station costs M$2. From Rantau Panjang, walk across the border and then it's about one km to the station (a trishaw costs M$3). Malaysian money is accepted in Sungai Golok. Share taxis from Kota Bharu to Rantau Panjang cost M$4.

From Sungai Golok, there are daily trains to Surat Thani and Bangkok and buses to Hat Yai.

Getting Around
The airport is eight km from town – take bus No 9 from the old central market. A taxi costs around M$10.

To Pantai Cinta Berahi take bus No 10 for 90 sen.

AROUND KOTA BHARU
There are a number of beaches on the coast around KB. None of them are anything special. **Pantai Cinta Berahi**, the 'Beach of Passionate Love', hardly lives up to its name. It has budget accommodation in the form of the run-down *Long House Beach Motel* and the *HB Village* 1½ km from the village.

The **Pantai Irama**, or 'Beach of Melody',

at Bachok has landscaped gardens along the foreshore and is popular with day-trippers. *Pantai Irama Chalets* (☎ 09-93148), half a km north of the bus station, has good chalets for M$30.

The **Pantai Dasar Sabak**, 13 km from Kota Bharu and three km beyond the airport, was where the Japanese landed in December 1941 during WW II – 1½ hours before they arrived at Pearl Harbor.

Also in the KB vicinity are waterfalls (Pasir Puteh area), a number of Thai temples, including **Wat Phothivihan** at Kampung Jambu with its 40-metre reclining Buddha. There are also a number of interesting river trips you can make. At **Kuala Krai**, 65 km south of KB, there's a small zoo specialising in local wildlife. The *Hotel Kuala Krai* is OK for a night.

Peninsular Malaysia – Coast to Coast

With the completion of the northern East-West Highway, there are now three routes from coast to coast, apart from the crossing in the south between Ayer Hitam and Jemaluang, a little south of Mersing.

EAST-WEST HIGHWAY

The east-west road starts near Kota Bharu and runs roughly parallel to the Thai border, eventually meeting the little-used road north from Kuala Kangsar to Keroh on the Thai border at Grik. The views from the highway are often superb.

The east-west road was a massive undertaking. As well as battling the harsh jungle terrain and monsoon washouts, communist guerrillas also launched regular attacks. The last of the guerrillas gave up a couple of years ago, but the road still has its hazards – travel is restricted at night and there are checkpoints along the road.

Hitching is fairly easy along this stretch if you're on the road early. The road may be subject to closure during the monsoon.

Grik

Grik was once just a logging 'cowboy town' but the East-West Highway and the huge Temengor Dam hydroelectric scheme has really put it on the map. Tasik Temengor is now one of Malaysia's largest lakes. For history buffs, there are many associations here with the exploits of Force 136.

The *Rest House* has ancient but spacious doubles with bath for M$15, and is probably the best place to stay. The much more central *Sin Wah Hotel* has basic but large rooms for M$10.

Getting There & Away There are buses from Ipoh or Kuala Kangsar to Grik every two hours or so. Taxis to or from Kota Bharu cost about M$18.

KOTA BHARU TO KUALA LUMPUR
The Jungle Railway

The central railway line goes largely through aboriginal territory. It's an area of dense jungle and offers magnificent views.

Commencing near Kota Bharu, the line runs to Kuala Krai, Gua Musang, Kuala Lipis, Jerantut (access point for the Taman Negara) and eventually meets the Singapore-KL railway line at Gemas. Unless you have managed to book a sleeping berth right through, you'll probably find yourself sharing a seat with vast quantities of agricultural produce, babies and people moving their entire homes. Expect the train to run at least a couple of hours late (even expresses).

The line's days are probably numbered as roads are rapidly being pushed through. The road now goes all the way from Singapore, through Kuala Lipis to Kota Bharu. The train is a lot slower but definitely more interesting.

Gua Musang

This former logging camp is now rapidly expanding, and planners see it as the centre of a huge new development area carved from the jungle. Logging is still a major industry and the town has a frontier feel to it, but the massive new administrative buildings on the outskirts of town point to its future.

Gua Musang (Musang Cave) owes its name to the caves in the limestone outcrop that tower above the railway station. The superb-looking musang is a native animal that looks like a cross between a large cat and a possum, with long fur and a long curling tail – unfortunately, hunters have killed off these former inhabitants of the caves.

Places to Stay The *Rest House* is a run-down, rambling old place that costs M$16 for a room with shared bathroom. It's friendly and from the verandah you can watch the whole life of swinging Gua Musang – you are, in fact, right opposite the volleyball court.

Getting There & Away Taxis from Kota Bharu to Gua Musang cost M$14, and M$12 from Kuala Krai.

Kuala Lipis

The road from Fraser's Hill through Raub meets the railway line at this town. Kuala Lipis is a well-maintained pretty town with fine rows of colonial shops down the main street. There's not much to do in Kuala Lipis, though it's a pleasant place.

Some visitors make jungle treks from Kuala Lipis, and most people who go on these treks enjoy them. Unfortunately, we have had a number of letters from female travellers making serious complaints about treks organised by Johnny Tan Bok. None of these visitors appear to have raised their concerns with the Malaysian authorities but we strongly recommend that female travellers should not take his treks.

We have had good reports of other treks organised out of Kuala Lipis, but the best advice is to use registered guides such as those at Taman Negara National Park.

Places to Stay Near the railway station are the *Hotel Paris*, *Hotel Central* and *Hotel Tiong Kok*, where you can get a room for around M$14. Johnny Tan Bok has a traveller's place above the Wangli Res-taurant, 100 metres from the bus station, which again female travellers should treat with caution.

Getting There & Away Kuala Lipis is on the railway line. There is a morning express train to Kota Bharu and a night train to Singapore. There are also buses from Kuala Lipis to Kota Bharu, KL and Kuantan.

Jerantut

Jerantut is the gateway to **Taman Negara National Park**. Most visitors to the park spend at least one night here, but the town itself has no real attractions. You can stock up on supplies in Jerantut at the emporium on the main road towards Temerloh.

Places to Stay The dismal *Hotel Tong Heng* has rooms for M$8 while the slightly better *Hotel Wah Hing* has rooms from M$9 to M$14. The *Hotel Jerantut*, with rooms for M$12 to M$17, is definitely worth the extra money.

Right opposite the bus station, the brand new *Hotel Chett Fatt* is a friendly place that welcomes travellers. The rooms are spotlessly clean but a little featureless. It is good value at M$15 for a room with a fan, and M$20 with air-con.

Places to Eat There are food stalls near the bus station and plenty of cheap coffee shops along the main road. The liveliest area at night is on the road to Taman Negara past the emporium, where you can find plenty of Chinese restaurants and a couple of karaoke bars. *Restaurant Liang Fong* has good food and is reasonably priced.

Getting There & Away Jerantut is on the Kota Bharu-Gemas railway line. Buses to Kuantan leave every hour until 4 pm and cost M$6.40 (M$7.70 air-con). A bus to Kota Bahru leaves at 10 am and costs M$18. For buses to KL you have to go via Temerloh – buses to Temerloh leave every half hour and cost M$2.25; taxis cost M$5. Taxis to KL cost M$14.

For Kuala Tembeling and the boats to

Taman Negara, the Jelai Company's blue and white buses leave approximately every two hours from 8 am and cost M$1.10. The buses will drop you at the jetty, 500 metres past the township. A taxi to Kuala Tembeling costs M$3 per person. To catch the 9 am boat to Taman Negara, you have to get the first bus at 8 am.

TAMAN NEGARA

Peninsular Malaysia's great national park covers 4343 sq km and sprawls across the states of Pahang, Kelantan and Terengganu. The part of the park most visited, however, is all in Pahang. Reactions to the park depend totally on the individual's experience. Some people see lots of wildlife and come away happy, others see little more than leeches and find the park hardly worth the effort.

The park headquarters is at Kuala Tahan. There are a number of jungle walks to hides and salt licks where you may see animals. Getting well away from it all requires a few day- long treks and/or expensive trips upriver by boat.

Orientation & Information

Make arrangements for your visit to Taman Negara at the Malaysia TIC (☎ 03-243 4929), 109 Jalan Ampang, KL. You have to make advance bookings for the park boat and the accommodation at Kuala Tahan. A deposit of M$30 is usually requested, but you may be able to make bookings over the phone and pay on arrival. An entry permit costs M$1, a camera licence is M$5 and a fishing licence is M$10.

The park headquarters has a reception centre, a couple of restaurants, a hostel, some chalets and two shops selling a small range of tinned foods, toiletries, batteries, local cakes and snacks. You can rent camping and hiking gear from the shop near reception. Every night at 8.45 pm, there is a free slide show at which a map of Taman Negara and its trails is handed out.

The best time to visit the park is between March and September. It's closed in the rainy season from mid-November to mid-January

and also at Muslim New Year for about one week.

Although everyday clothes are quite suitable around Kuala Tahan, you'll need heavy-duty gear if you're heading further afield. Jungle attire is a good idea both as protection and to make you less conspicuous to the wildlife you want to see. River travel in the early morning hours can be surprisingly cold. Mosquitoes can be annoying but you can buy repellent at the park shop if you're not already prepared.

Leeches are generally not a major problem, although they can be a real nuisance after heavy rain. There are many ways to keep these little blood-suckers at bay – mosquito repellent, tobacco, salt, toothpaste and soap can all be used with varying degrees of success. A liberal coating of Baygon insect spray over shoes and socks works best.

The shop next to the reception centre hires out tents, day packs, water bottles, small cookers, cooking utensils and even light boots (small sizes). Fishing equipment can be borrowed for M$50 deposit which is refunded on return if equipment is intact. Hire of a fishing rod is M$10.

Some of the Orang Asli live close to park headquarters. Locals say that they are supplied with free food to encourage them to settle in the park headquarters area.

If you're overnighting in a hide, you'll need a powerful torch (flashlight). The camp office has a couple for hire, but don't count on there being one available at the time you need it.

Hides & Salt Licks

There are several accessible hides and salt licks in the park. A number of them are close to Kuala Tahan and Kuala Terenggan, but your chances of seeing wildlife will increase if you head for the hides furthest from park headquarters. All hides are built overlooking salt licks and grassy clearings.

If you're staying overnight, you need to take your own sleeping bag, or some sheets from Kuala Tahan (lent free of charge) – you won't need blankets. Each hide costs M$5 per person per night. Even if you're not lucky enough to see any wildlife, the fantastic sounds of the jungle are well worth the time and effort taken to reach the hides. The 'symphony' is at its best at dusk and dawn.

Jenut Tahan is an artificial salt lick less than five-minutes walk from the reception building. It's a clearing which has been planted with pasture grass and there's a nearby waterhole. There's room in the hide for about eight people to sit and watch the salt lick but there are no facilities for sleeping overnight. It is often packed with noisy locals who find this hide a convenient venue for all-night parties – no chance of seeing any animals there!

Jenut Tabing is a natural salt lick, about a one-hour walk from Kuala Tahan. It is equipped with eight beds, a toilet and *mandi* (a large trough or barrel of washing water). Jenut Belau is 1½-hours walk from headquarters and there's no clean water supply at the hide itself.

You can either walk to **Jenut Kumbang** (it takes about five hours from Kuala Tahan) or take the 9 am boat (around M$10) up the Tembeling River to Kuala Terenggan. The hide has six bunk beds, a toilet and basin and a nearby clear stream.

Jenut Cegar Anging is an artificial salt lick established to attract wild cattle and deer. It is 1½-hours walk from Kuala Tahan.

Rivers & Fishing

Anglers will find the park a real paradise. Fish found in the park rivers include the *kelasa*, a superb fighting fish known in India as the mahseer.

Popular fishing rivers include the Sungai Tahan, the Sungai Kenyam (above Kuala Terenggan) and the remote Sungai Sepia. From February to March and from July to August are the best fishing months. A fishing permit costs M$10 and hiring a rod costs M$5 per day.

Several boat trips can be arranged at park headquarters, but they're all expensive. Expect to pay at least M$60 return for the shortest trip in a four seater.

Mountains & Walks

Trails around park headquarters are well-marked, though some of the paths are hard going. Trails are signposted and have approximate walking times marked clearly along the way.

There are two daily walking tours conducted by park officials. They each cost around M$40 per person (minimum of four people), start at 9 am and finish around 3 pm.

Gunung Tahan at 2187 metres is the highest mountain in Peninsular Malaysia; the climb to the summit requires a 2½-day trek from Kuala Tahan to Kuala Teku at the foot of the mountain, and another 2½ days to the summit.

Places to Stay

If you have your own tent, you can camp at park headquarters for M$1 per person per night, otherwise you can hire a tent for M$5. Beyond park headquarters, you can camp anywhere in Taman Negara.

The park hostel, *Asrama*, has comfortable rooms at M$10 per person. There are 12 older chalets that cost M$30 per night and a long block of a dozen or more new chalets that cost M$40.

Further into the park, you'll find *Visitors' Lodges* costing M$8 per person at Kuala Atok, Kuala Terenggan and Kuala Kenyam. At Kuala Perkai and Lata Berkoh, there are two *Fishing Lodges*.

Places to Eat

There are two restaurants at Kuala Tahan with similar menus and prices. The food is ordinary, though they do have Western-style breakfasts for those who can't face pork and fish porridge in the morning.

For tasty local dishes, food stalls are set up at night – you can get delicious mee soup and prices are much less than those at the restaurants. The es kacang is excellent at these stalls. There are two shops in Kuala Tahan where you can buy basic supplies.

Getting There & Away

The entry point into the park is Kuala Tembeling, 18 km from Jerantut. Boats to the park leave the small village of Kuala Tembeling at 9 am and 2 pm from the jetty, 500 metres west of the road. You should book in advance in KL, but travellers have fronted up at the jetty and been lucky enough to get on a boat. The telephone number at the jetty office is 09-26 2284.

The trip to the park headquarters at Kuala Tahan takes three hours (M$30 return). Leaving the park, boats also depart at 9 am and 2 pm and take 2½ hours.

See Jerantut in the previous Kota Bharu to Kuala Lumpur section for details of buses and taxis to Kuala Tembeling. From KL to Jerantut, you have to go via Temerloh if you take the bus. Kuala Tembeling can also be reached by train, though it is less convenient. The station is at Tembeling Halt, 2½ km from the jetty. This is the station between Jerantut and Kuala Lipis and you must make arrangements in advance if you want the train to stop there.

When leaving the park, trains pass Tembeling Halt and Jerantut for Kota Bharu at approximately 6 am, and to Singapore at around 8 pm.

Getting Around

Around Kuala Tahan, there are plenty of jungle tracks and, once you've paid your M$30 for the return boat trip to Taman Negara, you can spend all your time walking and camping in the park, cooking your own food, etc. If you've money to spare, you can hire boats within the park to a number of destinations (starting at around M$60 return).

KUALA LUMPUR TO KUANTAN

This busy road runs 275 km from KL past Bentong and through Temerloh, an important junction town. As an alternative to the direct KL-Kuantan route, you can start north from KL on the Ipoh road and turn off to Fraser's Hill. Continuing from The Gap you reach Raub, a busy gold mining area where the hunt for gold continued right up to 1955, and then, eventually, Kuala Lipis.

You can turn off the road just before Raub and rejoin the main KL-Kuantan road at Bentong or turn off at Benta Seberang for Jerantut, en route to the national park. At Jerantut, you can turn south to Temerloh or continue on to rejoin the KL-Kuantan road midway between Temerloh and Kuantan.

Temerloh

A bustling Chinese town, Temerloh has several cheap hotels and a good rest house. There's also a busy, colourful market there each Saturday afternoon.

The town is on the wide Pahang River and you can sometimes find boats going downriver to Pekan on the coast.

Places to Stay The *San Lin*, near the taxi station, is the best cheapie with big rooms for M$10. The *Rest House*, on a hill overlooking the river, has the best accommodation in town.

Getting There & Away Temerloh is a junction town and buses go to all parts of the peninsula from here.

Tasik Bera

Tasik Bera is the largest lake in Malaysia and around its shores are five Orang Asli kampungs. Around 800 people live at Tasik Bera and it's worth visiting, although you do have to get government permission at the district office in Temerloh.

Once you have the permit, the problem is getting to Tasik Bera. The easiest way is by bus or share-taxi from Temerloh to Triang and then chartered taxi from Triang to Tasik Bera. The most accessible kampung is Kota Iskandar, where there's a government rest house.

Sarawak

Sarawak's history reads much more like Victorian melodrama than hard fact. In 1838, James Brooke, a British adventurer, arrived in Borneo with his armed sloop, *Royalist*, to find the Brunei aristocracy facing rebellion from the dissatisfied inland tribes. He

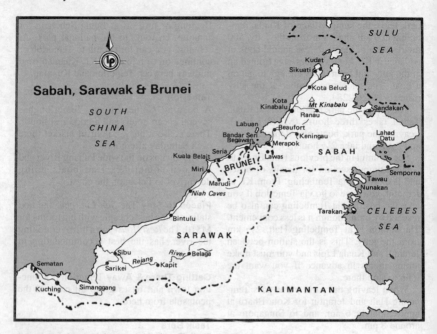

quelled the unrest and in gratitude was given power over part of what is today Sarawak.

Appointing himself 'Rajah Brooke', he successfully cooled down the warring tribes and suppressed head-hunting, eliminated the dreaded Borneo pirates and founded a dynasty that lasted until after WW II. The Brooke family of 'White Rajahs' continued to bring increasing amounts of Borneo under their power until the arrival of the Japanese in WW II.

Today, Sarawak is an economically important part of Malaysia with major oil exports plus timber, pepper, rubber and palm oil production. Although Sarawak suffered even more than Peninsular Malaysia from Communist guerrilla activity, things are peaceful today.

The biggest attractions for the visitor to Sarawak are the longhouses and villages of the diverse Dayak tribes and the amazing rainforests. The pity is that, despite mounting international pressure from all sides, the Malaysian government persists in decimating the forests in order to extract the valuable rainforest hardwoods for export.

It has been estimated that by the end of the century (and maybe earlier if the current rate of logging continues, as now, 24 hours a day under floodlights) there will be no virgin forest left – it will all have been logged over at least once. See it while you can.

Visas & Permits

Even though Sarawak is a part of Malaysia, it has its own immigration controls which are designed, in theory, to protect the indigenous tribal people from being swamped by migrants from the peninsula and elsewhere.

On arrival, you will probably be granted a two-month stay if you ask for it. If you get a shorter permit, it can be extended at immigration offices in Kuching or Miri. The government is touchy about unannounced researchers, journalists, photographers and the like so remember, you're nothing more than a tourist. Travel in the interior is relatively straightforward although permits are required to go almost anywhere away from the coast.

If you plan to visit any of the longhouses above Kapit on the Rejang or Balleh rivers, you'll need a special permit. These are obtainable in Kapit without fuss or fee. Officially, you need an international cholera vaccination certificate for these permits but usually no one checks this.

For travel to Gunung Mulu and elsewhere in the Kelabit Highlands (Bareo and the upper reaches of the Baram River), a permit from the District Officer in Marudi is required. If you are travelling to Gunung Mulu you also need a permit from the National Parks & Wildlife office in Miri.

The National Parks & Wildlife office in Kuching issues permits for the Semenggok Wildlife Rehabilitation Centre and for Bako National Park.

A special permit is also required from the immigration office in Kuching in order to cross the land border between Sarawak and Kalimantan, Indonesia (eg if heading for Pontianak), and it's unlikely you'll get it. An Indonesian visa is also required. Indonesian visas are issued without fuss in Kota Kinabalu but are more problematical at the Kuching and Tawau consulates.

Getting There & Away
Air Routes into Sarawak from neighbouring countries and other parts of Malaysia include:

To/From Singapore & Peninsular Malaysia
See the Malaysia Getting Around section for details on the deals available on these routes.

To/From Indonesia Merpati and MAS both operate weekly flights from Kuching to Pontianak (Kalimantan) and the fare is M$123.

Land From Indonesia, it's possible to get from Pontianak in Kalimantan to Kuching (or vice versa) albeit with some difficulty.

See the Malaysia Getting There & Away section for details.

Getting Around
Air MAS has a comprehensive network of cheap domestic flights served by its fleet of 12-seater Twin Otter aircraft, 737s and Fokker F-50s. Places in Sarawak served by MAS flights are Belaga, Kapit, Long Lellang, Long Seridan, Sibu, Mukah, Kuching, Bintulu, Bareo, Marudi, Miri, Bakelalan, Long Semado, Limbang and Lawas. The new airstrip at Gunung Mulu, commenced in June 1990, may also be open by now.

Flights into the interior are very much subject to the vagaries of the weather, so have some time up your sleeve.

Bus Travel by road in Sarawak is not the endurance test it once was. The trunk road from Kuching to the Brunei border is well on the way to being surfaced all the way.

Between Sibu, Bintulu and Miri there are plenty of buses daily in each direction. There are also buses west from Kuching to Bau, Lundu and Sematan and north to Bako (for the Bako National Park).

Boat Sarawak is the home of incredibly fast passenger launches known by the generic term *expres*. These are long, narrow riverboats which carry around 100 people in aircraft-type seats. All the boats are air-conditioned, fitted with video screens which show nonstop wrestling and kung fu movies, and are powered by turbocharged V12 diesel engines which power them at up to 60 km/h!

The riverboats provide regular services each way from Sibu to Kapit, Bintulu to Tubau and Kuala Baram to Marudi. In the wet season, when there is more water in the rivers, there are also services from Kapit to Belaga, from Marudi to Kuala Apoh and Long Panai, and from Kuala Apoh and Long Panai to Long Terrawan.

KUCHING
Kuching (meaning cat in Malay) is, without doubt, one of the most pleasant and interesting

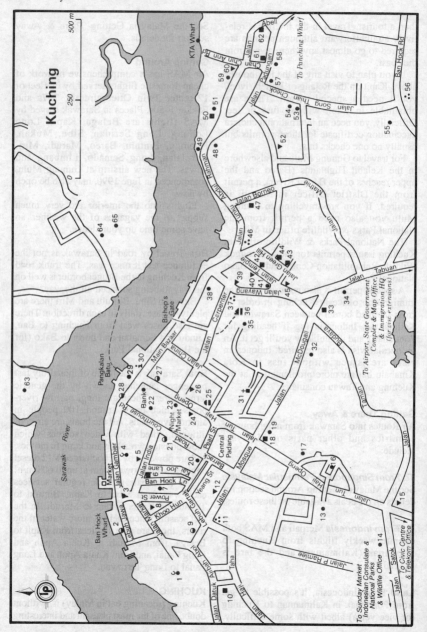

■ PLACES TO STAY	
6	Kiaw Hin Hotel
10	Arif Hotel
18	Aurora Hotel
33	Fata Hotel
36	Anglican Hostel
42	Kuching Hotel, Sin Hwa Travel
43	Green Mountain Lodging House, Orchid Inn, Furama Inn
44	Mandarin Lodging House
47	Hilton Hotel
50	Holiday Inn
61	Kapit Hotel
62	Longhouse Hotel

▼ PLACES TO EAT	
5	Madinah Cafe, Jubilee & Malaya Restaurants
8	Food Centre
12	New Hawkers Centre
15	Food Stalls
24	Fook Hoi Restaurant
26	National Islamic Cafe
39	Food Stalls
40	Food Stalls
45	Hua Jang Cafe
52	Permata Food Centre
60	Pizza Hut

OTHER	
1	Masjid Negara
2	STC Buses
3	Taxis
4	Indian Mosque
7	Electra House
9	Bus Stop
11	Sikh Temple
13	New Museum Building
14	RTM
16	Sarawak Museum
17	Curator's Office
19	Kuching Plaza
20	Police
21	Bus Stop
22	Law Courts
23	Pavilion
25	GPO
27	Bus Stop
28	Bus Stop
29	Square Tower
30	Tourist Office
31	Anglican Cathedral
32	St Thomas' School
34	Cat City Art Shop, Long House Native Art
35	Bishop's House
37	Hong San Temple
38	Yeo Hing Chuan, Sarawak House, Thian Seng Goldsmith
41	Rex Cinema
46	Tua Pek Kong Temple
48	Chartered Bank
49	Singapore Airlines, British Council Library
51	Sarawak Plaza
53	MAS
54	TDC Office
55	Lee Huo Theatre
56	Indian Temple
57	Express Bahagia
58	Tan Brothers
59	Eeze Trading
63	Istana
64	Police Museum
65	Fort Margherita

cities you'll come across in East Malaysia. Although quite a large city, the centre is very compact and seems isolated from the suburbs by the river and parks.

The city contains many beautifully landscaped parks and gardens, historic buildings, an interesting waterfront, colourful markets, one of Asia's best museums, and a collection of Chinese temples, Christian churches and the striking **State Mosque**.

Information

Tourist Offices Of the two tourist offices the better is the Sarawak Tourist Association

(☎ 082-24 2218) on Main Bazaar in the town centre. The office of the federal Tourist Development Corporation (TDC) (☎ 082-24 6575) is on the 2nd floor of the AIA Building on Jalan Song Thian Cheok.

Other Offices For information on the national parks, including permits for the Semenggoh Wildlife Rehabilitation Centre and bookings for the Bako National Park, head for the National Parks & Wildlife office (☎ 082-24 8088) on the 7th floor of the Satok building on Jalan Satok, about a km west of the town centre.

The immigration office (☎ 24 0301) is in the state government offices on Jalan Simpang Tiga, about three km south of the centre on the way to the airport.

For Indonesian visas, take a CCL bus Nos 5A or 6 from near the State Mosque to the Indonesian Consulate at 5A Pisang Rd. You may be lucky and get issued with a tourist visa.

Money For changing travellers' cheques, the best place is the Hongkong & Shanghai Bank on Jalan Tun Haji Openg, near the junction with Main Bazaar.

Post & Telecommunications The GPO is right in the town centre on Jalan Tun Haji Openg. International calls have to be made from the Telekom building on Jalan Batu Lintang. It is about 10 minutes south of the town centre by blue bus Nos 14 or 14A from outside the GPO.

Maps For good maps, the best place is H N Mohd Yahia & Son bookshop in the Holiday Inn on Jalan Tunku Abdul Rahman.

Things to See
Fort Margherita Built by Charles Brooke in the mid-19th century and named after his wife, Margaret, the fort was designed to guard the entrance to Kuching in the days when piracy was commonplace. It is now an interesting police museum (Muzium Polis). To get there take one of the small *tambangs* (ferry boats) which ply back and forth between the landing stage behind the Square Tower and the bus stop below the fort.

Sarawak Museum This is one of the best museums in Asia and should not be missed. It consists of two segments, the old and new, connected by a foot bridge over Jalan Tun Haji Openg. Built in the style of a Normandy town house, the old part was opened in 1891 and was strongly influenced by the anthropologist Sir Alfred Russell Wallace, a contemporary of Darwin, who spent two years there at the invitation of Charles

Brooke. The original section was expanded in 1911.

You can easily spend a few hours there and to top it all, it's free. The museum is open Saturday to Thursday from 9.15 am to 6 pm and closes for lunch between 12 noon and 1 pm. It's closed all day Friday.

Temples, Mosques & Churches The most interesting of these are the Chinese temples and the best of these is perhaps the **Hong San** at the junction of Jalan Carpenter and Jalan Wayang at the back of the Rex cinema. Others include the **Tua Pek Kong** at the junction of Jalan Temple and Jalan Tunku Abdul Rahman, and the **Kwan Yin Temple** on Jalan Tabuan, built in honour of the goddess of mercy.

The **Masjid Negara** (State Mosque), completed in 1968, is visually impressive but otherwise uninteresting. Of the Christian churches perhaps the most interesting is the futuristic, single-roofed **Roman Catholic Cathedral** past the Sarawak Museum on Jalan Tun Haji Openg.

Places to Stay
One of the popular places is the *Anglican Cathedral Hostel* (☎ 082-41 4027) on the hill at the back of St Thomas's church. A 'donation' of M$20/25 for a single/double gets you a large, spotlessly clean room with fan, polished wooden floors, comfortable beds, cane chairs, clean toilets and showers and good views. The hostel is not registered as a hotel, so be a little discreet about using it. The easiest way to get to it is to take the steps at the end of the lane, off Jalan Carpenter and between Nos 68 and 70.

Best of the hotels is the friendly *Kuching Hotel* (☎ 082-41 3985), opposite the Rex cinema on Jalan Temple. Rooms are M$16/20 for singles/doubles and all are equipped with fan and sink. The *Arif Hotel* is a friendly place not far from the State Mosque. It's a good place and pretty good value at $20 for a room with fan.

Up the scale a bit, try the *Green Mountain* (☎ 082-24 6952) at No 1 Jalan Green Hill, which has some rooms with a fan and bath at $25/28. For the cheapest air-con rooms, go to the *Mandarin* (☎ 082-41 8269) at 6 Jalan Green Hill. It has rooms for $30 with bath and TV.

Places to Eat

The best food you'll come across in Sarawak is in Kuching, so make the most of it. For tasty Malay food, head for Jalan India. The *Jubilee, Madinah* and *Malaya* restaurants are next to each other and, although there's little to choose between them, the Jubilee is probably the best. Not far away on Jalan Carpenter, you'll find the *National Islamic Cafe* which also serves tasty, cheap Malay food and has excellent rotis and martabak.

There are a couple of very small hawker centres which seem to operate in front of old Chinese temples. There's one on Jalan Wayang opposite the end of Jalan Carpenter (Rex cinema Hawker Centre) and another on Jalan Carpenter itself, near Jalan China.

Fast-food freaks won't go hungry either – there's a *Pizza Hut* on Jalan Tunku Abdul Rahman out past the Holiday Inn, a *Kentucky Fried Chicken* in the Sarawak Plaza next to the Holiday Inn and a *Sugar Bun* outlet in the Kuching Plaza on Jalan McDougall.

Things to Buy

Kuching is one of the best centres in Sarawak for buying tribal artefacts. Shops selling arts and crafts are scattered around the city but be warned that prices are outrageously high.

The best area is along Main Bazaar at the Jalan Wayang end. Shops along here include Yeo Hing Chuan at No 46, the very flashy and expensive Sarawak House (☎ 082-25 2531) at No 67 and the Thian Seng Goldsmith at No 48.

Borneo pottery is a popular local craft and there are factories near the airport where all sorts of very attractive glazed and unglazed jars, pots and vases are produced.

Getting There & Away

Air The MAS office (☎ 082-24 4144) is near the TDC on Jalan Song Thian Cheok. Singapore Airlines (☎ 082-24 0266) is in the Ang Chang Building on Jalan Tunku Abdul Rahman.

The Indonesian airline Merpati, which has weekly flights to Pontianak (Kalimantan), is handled by the Sin Hwa travel agency on Jalan Temple, opposite the Rex cinema. MAS fly to Sibu, Bintulu, Miri, Labuan and Kota Kinabalu.

Bus Long-distance STC green buses depart from the terminus on Lebuh Jawa, which is a continuation of Jalan Gambier. Destinations include Bau (No 2), Lundu (2B), Serian (3, 3A), Sri Aman (15) and the airport (12A).

Boat Boat services to/from Kuching include the following:

Kuching-Sarikei-Sibu There are several operators running expres boats between Kuching and Sibu. There is little to choose between them, although departure times differ. They all take around four hours, a change of boat (from a sea-going boat to a smaller river boat) is required at Sarikei and, of course, they have violent videos for your entertainment. Expres Bahagia, Expres Pertama and Follow Me all charge M$25, while Concorde Marine charges M$28.

All boats leave from wharfs in the industrial suburb of Pending, about six km east of the city centre. Catch bus Nos 17 or 19 from outside the market on Main Bazaar and tell the driver which boat you are catching. A taxi costs M$8.

Kuching-Sibu-Bintulu-Miri There are a few companies which operate cargo/passenger boats to Sibu and further along the coast. The Siam Company (☎ 082-24 2832) at the back of the shop at 28 Main Bazaar is one of these operators. The Sarawak Tourist Association is quite helpful with information about these boats.

Getting Around

To/From the Airport A taxi between Kuching Airport and the city centre costs M$12, and 50% more after midnight. Bus No 12A operates every 40 minutes between the airport and the centre of town for about 80 sen.

Bus You'll probably only need to take buses to the airport, immigration, the National Parks & Wildlife office or to the wharfs where launches to Sibu depart from. Most local bus fares are under 60 sen. The tourist offices can supply you with exact routings.

Taxi Taxis wait around the market and also at the area where long-distance buses drop passengers. A taxi to the wharf costs M$8.

Boat Small boats and expres boats serve the Sarawak River, connecting the small villages around Kuching. You can also charter boats.

AROUND KUCHING
Semenggok Wildlife Rehabilitation Centre
The Semenggok sanctuary, 32 km south of Kuching, is a rehabilitation centre for orang-utans, monkeys, honey bears and hornbills which have either been orphaned or kept illegally by locals. It's interesting, but the Sepilok sanctuary in Sabah is better.

The centre is reached from the Forest Department Nursery along a plankwalk through the forest – a very agreeable walk. A permit is required in order to visit the sanctuary and these can be arranged, free of charge, at the National Parks & Wildlife office in Kuching. To get there, take an STC Penrissen bus No 6 from Kuching (40 minutes; M$1.20).

Bako National Park
This park is at the mouth of the Bako River, north of Kuching, and contains some 27 sq km of unspoilt tropical rainforest and some beautiful marked walking trails – well worth a visit. A permit is needed to visit the park and this, along with accommodation bookings, must be made in advance at the National Parks & Wildlife office in Kuching.

There are rest houses, hostels and a camp site at the park. Hostel cabins sleep six to a room and a bed costs M$2.10 per person, or there are permanent tents (basically fly sheets) on raised platforms with open fireplaces which cost M$2 each.

The park canteen has a variety of goods for sale (mainly tinned food) but there is also fresh bread and vegetables. There's no need to bring a lot of food with you, although prices are higher at the park than they are elsewhere.

The park is 37 km from Kuching and can be reached by a Kampung Bako bus (No 6) from near the Sikh temple in Kuching town, followed by a boat from Kampung Bako.

UP THE REJANG RIVER
The Rejang is the main 'highway' of central and southern Sarawak, and most of the trade in the interior is carried out along it. It is also the way the logs from the forests in the upper reaches of the Rejang (and its tributaries the Balleh, Belaga and Balui rivers) are brought down to Sibu for processing and export. The number of log-laden barges on the river is astounding but equally depressing.

If you wish to travel up the Rejang, the best time is in late May and early June, as this is the time of the Dayak harvest festival, so there is plenty of movement on the rivers and the longhouses welcome visitors. There's also plenty of celebrations, which usually involve the consumption of copious quantities of *arak* and *tuak* (rice wine).

On the river, there is hotel accommodation only in Song, Kanowit, Kapit and Belaga.

Visiting a Longhouse
If you intend to visit a longhouse then you need plenty of time. The best place to head for is Kapit, a small administrative town upriver, where you should be able to find someone to take you to a longhouse – ask around and make yourself known. Before heading upriver from Kapit, you need to get a permit from the state office. It only takes a few minutes but they're not available on Saturday afternoon or Sunday.

Many travellers head for the stretch of the Rejang River between Kapit and Belaga. This area is easily accessible as there are expres boats operating between the two towns, in the wet season at least. Perhaps a more interesting river is the Balleh River, which branches off to the east a short distance upstream from Kapit.

At Belaga, the Balui and Belaga rivers merge and become the Rejang River. To travel up either of these rivers from Belaga requires permission from the Resident in Belaga, and this is generally not given. The Katibas River joins the Rejang at Song (between Sibu and Kapit) and this is also a good river to explore and no permits are required.

Having found someone to take you, you'll need to stock up on gifts with which to 'pay' for your visit. Alcohol, cigarettes and sweets are the most appreciated.

On arrival at the longhouse, ask for the *tuai rumah* (headman). You'll then probably be offered a place to stay for the night, and you'll be invited to join them for a meal.

What to Take

Apart from gifts, other indispensable items include a torch, mosquito repellent, a medical kit with plenty of aspirin and Panadol (you'll probably be seen by all and sundry as the local healer), and some Lomotil, Imodium or other antidiarrhoeal.

Some Useful Iban Phrases

Good morning
Salamat pagi
Good afternoon
Salamat tengah-hari
Good night
Salamat malam
Goodbye
Salamat tinggal
How are you?
Gerai nuan?
Pleased to meet you
Rindu amat betemu enggau nuan
See you again
Arap ke betemu baru
Thank you
terima kasih
Who is the headman?
Sapa tuai rumah kita ditu?
What is your name?
Sapa nama nuan?
Where do we bathe/wash?
Dini endor kitai mandi?
Can I take a photograph of you?
Tau aku ngambi gambar nuan?

SIBU

Sibu is the main port city on the Rejang River

A Longhouse

and will probably be your first river stopover. There's not a lot to do in Sibu so most travellers only stay overnight and head off up the Rejang the next day. It's worth climbing the tower of the Chinese temple as there are great views over the river.

Places to Stay

By far the best budget place to stay is the Methodist guest house, *Hoover House*, next to the church on Jalan Pulau. It's excellent value at M$10 per person but the only problem is that it's often full.

All over town, you'll see signs saying *bilik untuk sewa* (or variations on that), which means 'rooms for rent', but these places are often brothels. Of the regular hotels, one of the better places is the friendly *Hoover Lodging House* (☎ 084-33 4490), not to be confused with the Methodist guest house. It's at 34 Jalan Tan Sri, in a rather seedy area and just a few minutes walk from the bus station. The rooms are a bit on the small side and many don't have windows, but at M$10/15 for a single/double what do you want?

The *Hotel Malaysia* (☎ 084-33 2298) on Jalan Kampung Nyabor, a friendly place, has rooms with fan and common bath for M$15. Another reasonable place is the *Mandarin Hotel* (☎ 084-33 9177) at 183 Jalan Kampung Nyabor, although you need to get a room at the back as it's on a noisy road. Doubles with fan and bath cost M$16.

The *Miramar Hotel* (☎ 084-33 2433) at 47 Jalan Channel is quite popular with travellers. Fan-cooled rooms with private bathrooms cost M$21. From the windows you get a great view of the night market stalls which are set up in the street below.

A good hotel in the mid-price range is the *New World Hotel* (☎ 084-31 0311) on the corner of Jalan Wong Nai Song and Cross Rd. All rooms have air-con, bath and TV, and cost M$35/40.

Places to Eat

The best cheap food in Sibu is found at the various hawker centres and food stalls. On the ground floor of the New World Hotel is a cafe with a few food stalls selling a variety of foods, and there is an excellent bakery at one end.

For hawker food, there's a small two-storey food centre at the end of Market Rd, at the rear of the Palace cinema. Here you'll find stalls selling Malay curries, roti, laksa, Chinese food and es kacang.

In the late afternoon, stalls set up near the market, mainly outside the Miramar Hotel, and these are great for picking-up snack foods such as pau (steamed dumplings), barbecued chicken wings and all manner of sweets.

The *Sugar Bun*, diagonally opposite the church on the large roundabout, not far from the bus station, is OK for breakfast or Western-style fast-food snacks. For those so inclined, there's a *Kentucky Fried Chicken* outlet on Jalan Wong Nai Song.

Getting There & Away

There are flights from Sibu to Kapit (M$48), Belaga (M$76), Marudi (M$100), Kuching (M$60), Bintulu (M$64), Miri (M$93) and KK (M$156).

Lanang Bus Company has three buses daily to Bintulu (M$14.80; four hours). Syarikat Bus Company has air-con buses to Bintulu and Miri (M$35). See the Kuching section for details about road transport between Kuching and Sibu.

All expres boats to Sarikei and Kuching (change at Sarikei) leave from the Sarikei Wharf in front of the Chinese temple. There are four companies operating to Kuching and the trip takes around four hours and costs M$25 to M$28 depending on the company.

Getting to Kapit is the first leg of the journey up the Rejang River. The newest expres launches which do this trip cover the 130 km or so from Sibu to Kapit in a shade over two hours! The older boats do it in 2½ to three hours for M$15.

KAPIT

This small town on the eastern bank of the Rejang River dates from the days of the White Rajahs and still sports an old wooden fort built by Charles Brooke. If you are looking for a lift and introduction to a longhouse, ask at the Petronas or Shell fuel barges.

For permits for travel beyond Kapit, go to the Pejabat Am office on the 1st floor of the state government complex. It takes about 15 minutes but, remember, the office is not open on weekends.

Places to Stay

The place to head for in Kapit is the *Rejang Hotel* (☎ 084-79 6709) which has cheap (and hot) single rooms on the top floor for M$10, or fan-cooled doubles with bath for M$18 – good value. The *Hiap Chiong* and the *Kapit Longhouse*, the towns two other cheap hotels, are brothels first and hotels second, and are not particularly pleasant places to stay.

There's good mid-range accommodation at the *Ark Hill Hotel* (☎ 084-79 6168) where all rooms have air-con, bath, TV and cost M$35.

Places to Eat

Far and away the best place to eat is the *River View (Ming Hock) Restaurant*, on the top floor of the market building. As well as regular Chinese food, they also have a variety of local foods including venison, frogs' legs and prawns – these are not available every day. There are views of the river from the balcony and it's a pleasant place to sit in the evenings and sip a beer.

The *Ung Tong Bakery*, next to the market, has excellent buns and coffee and is a good bet for breakfast.

Getting There & Away

MAS fly Sibu-Kapit-Belaga and back on Thursdays and Sundays. The fare to Belaga is M$47 and to Sibu M$48.

There are frequent expres launch departures to Sibu from 8 am until around 3 pm for M$15. During the wet season, expres launches leave for Belaga daily from the main jetty. The trip takes up to six hours and costs M$20. During the dry season, when the river is low, the expres boats can't get through the Pelagus Rapids about an hour upstream of Kapit. Small cargo boats still do

the run, however. They are slow and uncomfortable, take around eight hours and charge M$40.

There are also cargo boats heading up the Balleh River on a daily basis as far as Interwau – ask at the fuel barges in Kapit.

BELAGA

Belaga is just a small village and government administration centre on the upper reaches of the Rejang where the river divides into the Belaga and Balui rivers. There is a Kayan longhouse within walking distance from Belaga town and many others further afield.

Permits are required for travel upriver from Belaga, but they are hard to get. There's no need to have a permit to travel on the logging route to Tubau and Bintulu.

Places to Stay

The *Sing Soon Hing Hotel* (☎ 084-46 1257) is a reasonable Chinese cheapie with fan-cooled rooms from M$18 and rooms with air-con at M$27. The *Belaga Hotel* (☎ 084-46 1244) is the cheapest in town with rooms at M$15 with fan, or M$25 with air-con.

Getting There & Away

In the dry season, it's possible to travel from Belaga to Bintulu. The journey is far from easy and can take a couple of days. The first step is to take a boat up the Belaga River about half an hour to the head of the logging road at the Kastima Camp. To hire a longboat for this section costs about M$60.

Once at the road, it's a matter of sitting and waiting for a vehicle. This vehicle takes you to the logging camp (known as Centre Camp), a trip of about two hours along a road through the forest. There is a canteen at the camp where you can buy food and there's also some basic accommodation.

From the logging camp, a Landcruiser leaves at 1 pm daily for the trip to Tubau. From Tubau, there are frequent expres boats to Bintulu (the last leaves at 12 noon) which cost M$14 and take about 3½ hours. If you are stuck in Tubau, there is accommodation for M$10.

BINTULU

Bintulu is a modern, air-conditioned boom town which is best passed through as quickly as possible, unless you want holes burned in every pocket. There's absolutely nothing of interest in the town.

Places to Stay

There are a few mostly nameless *rumah tumpangan* (guest houses) along the waterfront road and not far from the bus station. They just have partitioned rooms with fans and common bathrooms – basic but adequate for a night if you're stuck. The average charge is M$15 per double room.

A better bet is the *Capitol Hotel* (☎ 086-34667), just off Keppel Rd in the town centre. Big scruffy rooms with fan cost M$15, or M$25/35 gets you a room with air-con and bath. This place has certainly seen better days but it is habitable.

The best mid-range place is the *Sunlight Hotel* (☎ 086-32577) on the corner of Jalan Abang Galau and Jalan Pedada. All rooms have air-con and bath, and cost M$48/55 for a large room with shabby bathroom.

Places to Eat

The best place to eat in the evenings is at the stalls by the market on Keppel Rd. By the bus station is the *Seaview Restoran* where you can get standard Chinese tucker and they do good toasted sandwiches and coffee for breakfast.

For good Malay food, there's the *Abidaa Cafe* on Jalan Masjid, near the bus station.

Getting There & Away

MAS has daily flights from Bintulu to Sibu (M$53), Kuching (M$97), Miri (M$57) and Kota Kinabalu (M$110). The airport is smack in the middle of town.

There are two daily buses which go directly to Batu Niah from Bintulu. The trip takes about 2½ hours and the fare is M$10. You can take a Miri bus and get off at the Batu Niah junction, but from there it's an eight-km walk to Batu Niah and another three km to the national park. To Miri, there are five buses daily and the journey takes about four hours. There are five buses daily from Bintulu to Sibu (M$15, M$18 with air-con).

It's sometimes possible to find cargo/passenger boats from Bintulu to either Sibu or Miri. Check with the agents along the waterfront. There are expres launches up the Kemena River as far as Tubau. The journey takes about 3½ hours and costs M$14. They leave from the jetty, just a few minutes walk from the bus station.

NIAH NATIONAL PARK & NIAH CAVES

A visit to the Niah Caves is one of the most memorable experiences in East Malaysia. The Great Cave, one of the largest in the world, is in the centre of the Niah National Park which is dominated by the 394-metre-high limestone massif of Gunung Subis, visible from far away. In the 1950s, a human skull, estimated to be 35,000 old, was found. There was also traces of habitation from that time and up until the caves were deserted in the 15th century.

The caves are a source for that most famous Chinese dish, bird's nest soup. Countless tiny swifts build their nests in crevices in the walls and ceilings of the cave, constructing them out of hardened sticky saliva. Collecting the nests is a dangerous occupation – as you'll see once inside the caves.

Guano (bird and bat excrement) is also collected from the cave floors for use as fertiliser. It's quite a sight each evening as the vast population of swifts flock in from the dayshift while the bats leave on the nightshift.

A permit is needed to visit the Painted Cave but this is issued as a matter of course when you check in at the park headquarters on arrival. The park HQ is four km from the village of Batu Niah and the caves themselves are a further three km along a plankwalk – an interesting one-hour walk. The plankwalk continues inside the caves, so it's impossible to get lost, although a torch (flashlight) is essential.

Places to Stay

The *Visitors' Hostel* at the park headquarters is a great place to stay. Cooking facilities are provided and there's electricity from 6 pm to midnight. A bed costs M$3 per night. Bring food with you. On the opposite side of the river are four two-bedroom *rest houses* which are completely self-contained. The charge is M$30 for a double room or M$60 for the whole rest house.

In the town of Batu Niah, there are a couple of hotels. *Niah Caves Hotel* (☎ 086-73 7726) is clean, reasonably cheap at M$15/26 for singles/doubles and has good basic food in the restaurant downstairs.

Getting There & Away

Whether you come from Bintulu or Miri, you will end up at Batu Niah. From there, the best way to get to the park headquarters is to ask around for a lift. Private cars often double as taxis and the rate is M$4 per person or M$8 for the whole vehicle if you are alone. An alternative is to hire a longboat from behind the market for M$10.

To Batu Niah, there are two direct buses daily from Bintulu (M$10, 2½ hours) and four from Miri (M$9, two hours).

MIRI

Miri is just another boom town based on oil money which has managed to attract a large number of expats, prostitutes and transvestites. Most travellers stay only overnight when heading to Brunei, the Niah Caves, Gunung Mulu or Bareo.

Information

To obtain permits for Gunung Mulu and accommodation bookings, go to the National Parks office (☎ 085-36637) in Jalan Raja which is behind the Majlis Islam Building. The MAS office (☎ 085-41 4144) is on Jalan Yu Seng about 10-minutes walk from the

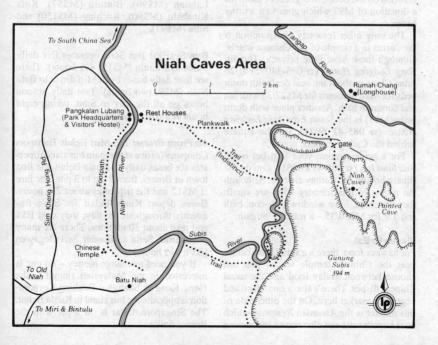

Niah Caves Area

To South China Sea

To Tangap River

Rumah Chang (Longhouse)

Pangkalan Lubang (Park Headquarters & Visitors' Hostel)

Rest Houses

Plankwalk

gate

Niah Caves

Painted Cave

Sim Kheng Hong Rd

Niah River

Footpath

Trail (Indistinct)

Subis River

Trail

Chinese Temple

To Old Niah

Batu Niah

Gunung Subis 394 m

To Miri & Bintulu

0   1   2 km

town centre. The post office and the Telekom office are about 15 minutes walk from the town centre along Jalan Brooke.

If you want to organise a trip to Gunung Mulu or elsewhere in the interior, travel agencies which travellers have used and found to be reliable are Seridan Mulu Tour & Travel Services, Lot 140, 2nd floor on Jalan Bendahara (☎ 085-41 6066) and Malang Sisters Travel Agency, Lot 255, 1st floor, Beautiful Jade Centre, Halaman Kabor (☎ 085-38141).

Places to Stay

Miri is a fairly lively town, not only because of the oil and development, but also because Bruneians in search of a bit of action flock here on weekends.

Finding a cheap room is almost impossible. Everything is air-con – even the brothels – and expensive. The cheapest place is the *Red Crescent Society* where you can get a mattress on the floor of a big breezy room for a donation of M$3 which goes to a worthy cause.

The only other remotely cheap option is the dorms in a couple of the Chinese hotels, although these have little privacy. The *Tai Tong Lodging House* (☎ 085-34072) at 26 Jalan China is about the best deal with dorm beds for M$6 or rooms for M$27/35 with fan and common bath. Another place with dorm beds (M$5) is the *South East Asia Lodging House* (☎ 085-41 6921), on the square behind the Cathay cinema.

For a private room, your best bet is the *Fairland Inn* (☎ 085-413 8981), also on the square behind the Cathay cinema. Although the rooms in this friendly hotel are small, they are clean, have windows, air-con, bath and TV for M$30/35 – a relative bargain.

Places to Eat

For hawker food, there's a small food centre near the Chinese temple where you can choose between Malay food and the usual Chinese dishes. There's also a small fruit and vegetable market here. On the other side of this market is the *Aseanika Restoran* which does superb rotis and also serves Indonesian food. For tasty food, try the *Seaview Cafe* on the corner of Jalan China, near the Chinese temple.

In Wisma Pelita, you'll find a branch of the local *Sugar Bun* fast-food chain.

Entertainment

Miri has a surprisingly good live entertainment scene in the evenings – discos, live bands and the inevitable karaoke lounges. Most places are along Jalan Yu Seng.

The Cottage is a small pub which has some interesting local bands, while across the road the flashier *Pub* has bigger acts from KL and elsewhere. *The Ranch* is a similar place and others include *Strawberry Lounge*, *Rupan Lounge* and the *Q-Ta Steakhouse*.

Getting There & Away

Air MAS has services from Miri to Marudi (M$29), Bareo (M$70), Long Lellang (M$66), Limbang (M$45), Lawas (M$59), Labuan (M$90), Bintulu (M$57), Kota Kinabalu (M$90), Kuching (M$150) and Sibu (M$93).

Bus Syarikat Bas Suria operates five daily buses to Bintulu (M$15, 4½ hours). There are four daily buses from Miri direct to Batu Niah (M$9, two hours). Two daily air-con buses go all the way to Sibu, taking eight hours at a cost of M$35.

To/From Brunei The Miri Belait Transport Company (office at the main bus stand) operates six buses daily to Kuala Belait, the first town in Brunei, from 7 am to 3 pm. The fare is M$12 and the trip takes about 2½ hours. Buses depart Kuala Belait for Seria frequently throughout the day; they cost B$1 and take about 30 minutes. There are many buses from Seria to Bandar Seri Begawan (B$4; 1½ hours).

If you need to change money – no one is interested in the Malaysian ringgit – the Hong Kong & Shanghai Banking Corporation is opposite the bus stand in Kuala Belait. The Singapore dollar is on a par with the Brunei dollar.

LIMBANG

This town is the divisional headquarters of the Limbang District, sandwiched between Brunei and Sabah. There is nothing of interest in the town itself but you may well find yourself coming through on the way to or from Brunei.

Places to Stay & Eat

One of the cheapest places is the *Bunga Raya Hotel* (☎ 085-21181) opposite the wharf. Basic dorm accommodation costs M$10 per night and there are rooms from M$30.

The *Cita Rasa Restoran* in the Limbang Recreation Club has breakfasts for M$7 and meals from M$2 to M$11.

Getting There & Away

MAS has flights to Miri (M$45), Labuan (M$30), Lawas (M$25) and Kota Kinabalu (M$60).

There are several boats daily to Bandar Seri Begawan, the capital of Brunei. The trip takes about 30 minutes and costs M$7 from Limbang and B$7 from Brunei.

There are also boats to Punang, further up the coast, from where it's just a short minibus ride to Lawas.

LAWAS

Like Limbang, there is very little to do in Lawas but, once again, you may find yourself here while en route to or from Brunei, on your way up to the Kelabit Highlands and Bakelalan or, in order to take the short flight to Miri, skipping clean over Brunei.

Places to Stay

The cheapest place is the *Government Rest House* on the airport road – if you can get in. Failing that, there's the *Federal Hotel* (085-85115) which is expensive with rooms from M$40.

Getting There & Away

There are flights from Lawas to Kota Kinabalu (M$47), Miri (M$59), Limbang (M$25), Bakelalan (M$46) and Long Semado (M$40).

You can also take a bus to Merapok which is on the Sarawak-Sabah border (M$3.50; 40 minutes).

THE KELABIT HIGHLANDS

If you're heading out for a long trek into the interior to places such as Bareo, Lio Matoh and Long Lellang, the first step is to get a permit from the Resident in Miri. It's straightforward but does take a day or so. You can also get these permits from the District Officer in Marudi.

From Miri, the first stage of the journey is by road to Kuala Baram on the Baram River and near the Brunei border. The fare is M$2.10 and buses depart Miri hourly (at least) from 6 am to 5.30 pm.

There are regular boats from Marudi to Long Lama. From Long Lama to Long Akah, reckon on about M$25 and one to 1½ days, and from there to Lio Matoh about the same. In the dry season, when the river is low, this trip costs considerably more as you have to hire a boat, driver and frontman.

See the following Gunung Mulu Getting There & Away section for details of the trip from Miri to the national park.

Marudi

Marudi is devoid of attractions but you will probably find yourself coming through here on your way to or from the interior. Unless you fly from Miri to Bareo, you need to get a permit from the District Office here to head further upstream or to Mulu.

Places to Stay & Eat The popular *Grand Hotel* (☎ 085-55712), Marudi Bazaar, is a good place four or five blocks from where the expres launches dock. The cheapest room (single or double) is M$13.50. *Mulu Air-Con Inn* (☎ 085-55905) and the *Hotel Zola*, close by, have both been recommended.

Ah Jong's is a good place for breakfast as they have fresh bread and doughnuts.

Getting There & Away MAS operates flights from Marudi to Miri (M$29), Bareo (M$55), Sibu (M$100) and Long Lellang (M$46). The airstrip at Gunung Mulu may be finished by now, in which case there'll be flights there from Miri and probably Marudi.

The expres boats from Kuala Baram to Marudi operate hourly and cost M$12. If heading upriver, there is an expres boat to Kuala Apoh or Long Terrawan (depending on water level), daily, at 12 noon (M$18, 3½ hours).

Bareo

Bareo sits on a beautiful high valley floor in the Kelabit Highlands, close to the Indonesian border, and it makes an ideal base for treks into the highlands. Bareo has shops where you can stock up on supplies and gifts to take to the longhouses, as does Bakelalan.

There are interesting treks around Bareo to places such as Pa Lungan, Bakelalan, Long Semado and Lio Matoh. You need to be well-prepared and hire local guides.

Places to Stay The *Bareo Lodging House* is M$8 per person but it's nothing special and you may want to head straight out to the longhouses.

Getting There & Away MAS flies Twin Otters from Bareo to Miri (M$70), usually via Marudi (M$55). The flights are very much dependent on the weather, and it's not uncommon for flights to be cancelled, so make sure your schedule is not too tight.

Gunung Mulu National Park

Since Gunung Mulu National Park reopened in late 1985 it has become one of the most popular travel destinations in Sarawak. Unfortunately, it's also one of the most expensive places to visit. Reports from travellers vary and some feel the expense worthwhile whereas others don't.

It is Sarawak's largest national park, covering 529 sq km of peat swamp, sandstone, limestone and montane forests. The two major mountains are **Gunung Mulu** (2377 metres of sandstone) and **Gunung Api** (1750 metres of limestone).

The park is noted for its many underground caves. Cave explorers recently discovered the largest cave chamber in the world, the Sarawak Chamber, and the 51-km-long Clearwater Cave, one of the longest in the world.

Permits & Information Permits for Gunung Mulu National Park must be obtained at the National Parks office (☎ 085-33361) in Miri. A permit for the park is necessary. Visitors must book and, if in a group, pay a deposit of M$20 per group for accommodation.

There are no walking trails around park headquarters and, unfortunately, you cannot go anywhere without taking a guide – this is annoying as you often don't need one. Guides' fees vary between M$20 and M$30 per day.

Places to Stay A bed in one of the park's four six-bed dorms costs M$6. There's also a rest house with a six-bed room for M$60 and deluxe double rooms for M$150. You can cook your own food as there are gas cookers and you can use the cutlery, crockery, pots and pans. There is a small canteen at park headquarters selling basic tinned foods, bread, milk, eggs and margarine.

Getting There & Away The new airstrip at the national park may be open by now, in which case there'll be flights from Miri and probably Marudi.

When coming from Miri by bus and river, take the 6 am bus to Kuala Baram if you want to get there in one day. From Kuala Baram, you can take an expres launch up the Baram River to Marudi (M$12; three hours).

Take the daily midday expres boat from Marudi to Long Terrawan (if the river is high) for M$18, or to Kuala Apoh (if there's less water) for M$10, from where you can get another launch to Long Terrawan for M$7.

From Long Terrawan, a longboat meets the 12 noon boat from Marudi and leaves for Mulu around 3.30 pm, arriving at around 6 pm. The cost is set at M$35 per person if there are more than four people, or M$150 for the whole boat for four or less people.

Sabah

Once part of the great Brunei Empire, Sabah eventually came under the influence of the North Borneo Company after centuries of being avoided due to its unpleasant pirates. At one time, Kota Kinabalu was known as Api Api, 'fire, fire', from the pirates' tiresome habit of repeatedly burning it down. Eventually, in 1888, North Borneo, along with Brunei and the Brooke family's Sarawak, came under British protection.

Today, Sabah is an integral part of Malaysia and its economy is based chiefly on timber, with agriculture making up the balance. The road network is limited to one almost completely surfaced road running from Merapok to Tawau, via the main population centres of Kota Kinabalu and Sandakan. Elsewhere, travel is along terrible roads, by river, or the eccentric little railway which runs from Beaufort to Tenom in the south-west of the state.

The principal attractions for the visitor are in the scenery and the wildlife. Mt Kinabalu is the highest mountain in South-East Asia and is well worth the trek. Other highlights include Sepilok Orang-utan Rehabilitation centre in Sandakan and the Turtle Islands off the coast. Unfortunately, Sabah is quite expensive but with planning it's possible to keep the costs down.

Facts for the Visitor

Visas & Permits Sabah is semiautonomous and, like Sarawak, has its own immigration controls. On arrival, you are likely to be given a month's stay permit and it's rare to be asked to show money or onward tickets.

Permits can be quickly and easily renewed at an immigration office, which can be found at most points of arrival.

General Costs Sabah is an expensive place to travel around. Only at Kinabalu National Park, Poring Hot Springs and Sandakan will you find accommodation that could be classed as 'budget'. Elsewhere, it's the familiar story of at least M$20 per night and often much more.

Getting There & Away

Air Flights to Sabah from other parts of Malaysia and neighbouring countries include:

To/From Peninsular Malaysia & Singapore See the Malaysia Getting Around section for details of these fares.

To/From Hong Kong MAS and Cathay Pacific each have two flights weekly between Kota Kinabalu and Hong Kong. The fare is approximately M$660, but you will probably find cheaper tickets on Philippine Airlines.

To/From the Philippines MAS flies to Manila five times a week. Philippine Airlines also operates on this route – the fare is US$189 and flight time is just under two hours.

From time to time, there have been flights between Kota Kinabalu, or other towns in Sabah, and Zamboanga in the southern Philippines' island of Mindanao. At present they are, once again, out of operation.

To/From Indonesia There are weekly international flights (on Sunday) from Tawau in Sabah to Tarakan in Kalimantan (Indonesia). The Indonesian feeder airline, Bouraq, also flies three times a week between Tawau and Tarakan. The fare is around M$180.

Boat Services to Sabah from other parts of Malaysia and neighbouring countries include:

To/From Peninsular Malaysia There are no longer any boats connecting Peninsular and East Malaysia.

To/From Brunei There are a number of interesting options for travel between Sabah and Brunei. See the Brunei Getting There & Away section for more details.

To/From Indonesia The MV *Sasaran Muhibbah Express* operates three times a week between Tawau and Nunukan (M$25; 15,000 rp) and Tarakan (M$60) in Kalimantan.

If you are travelling to Nunukan or Tarakan, it's worth noting that visas cannot be issued on arrival and you must get one before crossing into Indonesia.

KOTA KINABALU

Known as Jesselton until 1963, Kota Kinabalu (KK) was razed during WW II to prevent the Japanese using it as a base. Now, it's just a modern city with wide avenues and tall buildings without any of the historical charm of Kuching. All the same, KK, as the locals call it, is a pleasant city, well landscaped in parts, and its coastal location gives it an equable climate.

Orientation

The city sprawls for many km along the coast, from the international airport at Tanjung Aru to the new developments at Tanjung Lita. The centre, however, is quite small and most places are within easy walking distance.

Information

Tourist Office The tourist office (☎ 088-21 1732) of the TDC is in the Wing On Life Building on Jalan Segunting at the northern end of the city centre. The Sarawak Tourist Promotion Corporation should by now have moved into its new premises in the old post office on Jalan Gaya, close to the TDC tourist office.

Other Offices The Sabah Parks office (☎ 088-21 1585) is very conveniently situated in Block K of the Sinsuran Kompleks on Jalan Tun Fuad Stephens. Before going to Mt Kinabalu, Tunku Abdul Rahman National Park or Poring Hot Springs, you must go to this office to make reservations for accommodation (and guides, if required).

The Sabah Foundation has its offices in the much-vaunted Sabah Foundation building at Likas, a few km north of the city

■ PLACES TO STAY

6	Hotel Jesselton
7	Ang's Hotel
8	Hotel Capital
11	Hyatt Kinabalu International
22	Travellers Rest Hostel
25	Hotel Rakyat
27	Central Hotel
28	Hotel Nam Tai
29	Pine Bay Hotel
30	Putera Hotel
31	Full On Resthouse
32	Islamic Hotel
34	Ruby Inn
38	Hotel Pertama
39	Hotel Mutiara
40	Hotel Shangrila

▼ PLACES TO EAT

1	XO Steakhouse
5	Kentucky Fried Chicken
23	Kedai Kopi Seng Hing
24	Night Food Stalls
25	New Arafat Restaurant
33	Sri Melaka Restoran
37	Restoran Tioman

OTHER

2	Hong Kong & Shanghai Bank
3	TDC Tourist Office
4	Sarawak Tourist Promotion Corporation
9	Wisma Sabah
10	Wisma Merdeka
12	KK Supermarket
13	Minibuses to Kota Belud, Kudat
14	Minibuses to Beaufort, Keningau, Tenom
15	Minibuses to Mt Kinabalu, Ranau, Sandakan
16	Council Offices & Library
17	City Buses
18	GPO
19	Minibuses to Airport, Penampang, Likas, Beaufort
20	Central Market
21	Sabah Parks
26	Centrepoint
35	Immigration Office
36	Cinemas

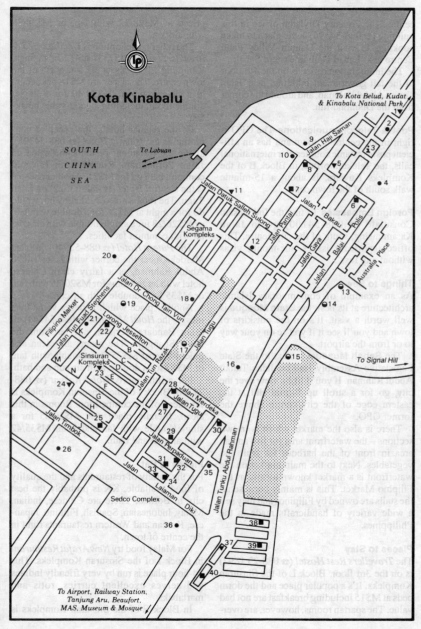

Kota Kinabalu

SOUTH
CHINA
SEA

To Labuan

To Kota Belud, Kudat
& Kinabalu National Park

To Signal Hill

To Airport, Railway Station,
Tanjung Aru, Beaufort,
MAS, Museum & Mosque

Jalan Haji Saman

Jalan Datuk Salleh Sulong

Segama
Kompleks

Jalan Pantai

Jalan Bakau

Jalan Gaya

Jalan Balai

Jalan Polis

Australia Place

Jalan Dr Chong Tain Vun

Filipino Market

Jalan Tun Fuad Stephens

Lorong Jesselton

Jalan Tun Razak

Jalan Tugu

Sinsuran
Kompleks

Jalan Merdeka

Jalan Tugu

Jalan Timbok

Jalan Perpaduan

Jalan Laiaman

Jalan Diki

Jalan Tunku Abdul Rahman

Sedco Complex

centre. The Forestry Division office in this building (☎ 088-34596) is the place to make bookings to visit the Danum Valley Field Centre near Lahad Datu in eastern Sabah.

The immigration office is on the 4th floor of the tall government building, near Jalan Tunku Abdul Rahman, and around the corner from the Diamond Inn.

Post & Telecommunications The GPO is right in the centre of town and has an efficient poste restante counter. For international calls, the Telekom office, in Block B of the Kompleks Kuwara, is about a 15-minute walk south of the town centre.

Foreign Embassies To find the Indonesian Consulate (☎ 088-54100) go to Jalan Karamunsing, south of the city centre. This office reportedly issues one-month visas without any fuss.

Things to See
As an example of contemporary Islamic architecture at its best, the **State Mosque** is well worth a visit. It's on the outskirts of town and you'll see it if you're on your way to or from the airport.

The **Sabah Museum** is next to the State Legislative Assembly Hall on Jalan Tunku Abdul Rahman. If you'd like a view over the city, go for a stroll up **Signal Hill** at the eastern edge of the city centre above the former GPO.

There is also the market which is in two sections − the waterfront area for fish and an area in front of the harbour for fruit and vegetables. Next to the main market on the waterfront is a market known locally as the Filipino Market. This is mainly because all the stalls are owned by Filipinos and they sell a wide variety of handicrafts made in the Philippines.

Places to Stay
The *Travellers Rest Hostel* (☎ 088-23 1892) is on the 3rd floor, Block L of the Sinsuran Kompleks. It's a popular place and the dorm beds at M$15 including breakfast are not bad value. The spartan rooms, however, are over-priced at M$28/32 with fan, or M$34/38 with air-con.

The other hostel option is *Cecilia's Bed & Breakfast* (☎ 088-35733) at 413 Jalan Saga, Kampung Likas, about six km north of the town centre. The prices are M$18 per person in a share room or M$30/40 for a single/double room, including a good-value breakfast.

Of the regular hotels, the cheapest non-brothel is the *Islamic Hotel* (☎ 088-54325), above the restaurant of the same name on Jalan Perpaduan. Rooms with fan and common bath go for M$21. Another cheapie is the *Central Hotel* (☎ 088-53522) on Jalan Tugu. The rooms are very shabby but would do for a night at M$26 for a double with fan, or M$26/28 for a single/double with air-con, all with common facilities.

The *Putera Hotel* (☎ 088-53940) on Jalan Merdeka, near the corner with Jalan Tunku Abdul Rahman, is a fairly clean Chinese hotel with large rooms for M$20/25 with fan, or M$35 for a double with air-con.

Another place which is better value than most is the *Hotel Mutiara* (☎ 088-54544) on Jalan Bandara Berjaya, not far from the Hotel Shangrila. The rooms are clean and quiet and cost M$25 for a double with fan, or M$37 for a double with air-con and bath.

For a little more, *Hotel Rakyat* (☎ 088-21100) Block I of the Sinsuran Kompleks is far ahead of the competition. Rooms in this clean, friendly place cost M$30/35 for a single/double with fan and bath, M$35/42 with air-con and bath.

Places to Eat
For the variety of restaurants and the quality of food available, KK is probably the best city in Borneo. There are Chinese, Indian, Malay, Indonesian, Spanish, Filipino, Japanese, Korean and Western restaurants right in the centre of town.

For Malay food try *New Arafat Restaurant* in Block I of the Sinsuran Kompleks. This 24-hour place is run by very friendly Indians and serves excellent curries, rotis and martabaks.

In Block E of the Sinsuran Kompleks is

the *Kedai Kopi Seng Hing*, an unremarkable Chinese cafe, which serves a truly remarkable prawn mee soup at lunch time – it is recommended.

For hawkers' food, there's a lively night market which sets up in the evenings in the vacant lot at the southern end of the Sinsuran Kompleks. Many of the stalls sell second-hand clothes and are run by Filipinos, but there's a good variety of food stalls; you can even get that Indonesian delicacy *coto makassar*, or buffalo-gut soup, if you're feeling adventurous.

For something a little more up-market there's the *XO Steakhouse* at 54 Jalan Gaya at the northern end of town. It serves excellent (but expensive) 'air chilled' steaks which have been flown in from Australia and the USA.

In the Karamunsing Kompleks, on the opposite side of the roundabout from the Kompleks Kuwasa, there's a nonsmoking *Kentucky Fried Chicken* outlet.

Getting There & Away

Air The MAS office (☎ 088-51455) is on the ground floor of the Karamunsing Kompleks, about a five-minute walk south of the Hotel Shangrila along Jalan Tunku Abdul Rahman.

Philippine Airlines (☎ 088-23 9600) is also in the Karamunsing Kompleks. Cathay Pacific (☎ 088-54733) is in the Kompleks Kuwara, and British Airways (☎ 088-58511) have an office at 19 Jalan Haji Saman. Royal Brunei Airlines (088-24 0131) is handled by an agent in Wisma Sabah.

Around Sabah & Sarawak KK is the hub of the MAS network in Sabah and there are regular flights to Brunei (M$65), Bintulu (M$110), Kuching (M$198), Labuan (M$43), Lahad Datu (M$88), Miri (M$90), Sandakan (M$69), Tawau (M$80), Limbang (M$60) and Lawas (M$47).

Bus The area east of the council offices and right up to Australia Place is the departure point for taxis and minibuses to everywhere north, south and east. The large open plot of land behind the GPO is a very busy minibus

park. Most buses from here are local but some also go to Beaufort and Penampang.

All minibuses leave when full and there are frequent early morning departures. There are fewer departures later in the day and for some destinations, such as Ranau, the last bus departs around lunch time. For long-haul trips, like KK to Sandakan, the last bus may leave as early as 8 am, so unless you're up at the crack of dawn you could find yourself stuck for another night. Some examples of minibus fares from KK are:

Beaufort (90 km) – regular departures up to about 3 pm, two hours on a very good road; M$7.

Kota Belud (77 km) – departures up to 2 pm daily, two hours on a road that is sealed all the way; M$5.

Kudat (122 km) – departures up to about 1 pm, four hours on a road which is partially sealed; M$12.

Sandakan (386 km) – minibus departures in the early morning only, about eight hours; M$35. The road is sealed as far as Ranau but it's a pretty rough ride from there to Telupid and around Batu 32. It's paved in and around Sandakan.

Keningau (128 km) – regular departures up to about 1 pm, about 2½ hours on a road which is surfaced all the way.

Ranau (156 km) – early morning departures, the last bus leaves at 12.30 pm and takes about two hours. All buses pass Kinabalu National Park. The road is very good.

Tenom – regular departures on a good sealed road, M$25 by taxi, M$20 by minibus.

If you're heading for Kinabalu National Park from KK you can get there by taking Ranau or Sandakan minibuses. Get off at the park headquarters, which is right by the side of the road. Ask the driver to drop you off there. The fare to the park headquarters is M$10 and takes about 1½ hours.

Train The railway station is five km south of the city centre at Tanjung Aru, close to the airport. There are daily trains to Beaufort and Tenom at 8 and 11 am and the trip takes four hours to Beaufort, seven hours to Tenom. Minibuses are quicker and easier.

Taxi Besides the minibuses, there are share-taxis to most places. They also go when full and their fares are at least 25% higher than the minibuses. Their big advantage is that they are faster and more comfortable.

Boat There are twice daily boats to Labuan (M$28 in economy; M$33 in 1st class) from the jetty behind the Hyatt Hotel. The *Duta Muhibbah Dua* leaves at 8 am taking 2¾ hours, while the *Labuan Express* leaves KK at 2 pm and takes 2¼ hours

Getting Around

To/From the Airport To get to the airport take a 15-minute taxi ride for M$10, or a red 'Putatan' bus for 65 sen from Jalan Tunku Abdul Rahman and ask to be dropped at the airport.

Taxis operate on a coupon system and prices are listed at the airport desk. It's quite easy to hitch into town from the airport.

Taxi Local taxis are plentiful in the extreme. They are not metered so it's a matter of negotiating the fare before you set off. Taxi stands are all over town, but most can be found in the large area between the council offices and the GPO.

AROUND KOTA KINABALU
Tunku Abdul Rahman National Park

The park has a total area of 4929 hectares and is made up of the offshore islands of Gaya, Mamutik, Manukan, Sapi and Sulug. Only a short boat ride from the city centre, they offer good beaches, crystal-clear waters and a wealth of tropical corals and marine life.

Getting There & Away Coral Island Cruises have boats from behind the Hyatt Hotel to the islands six times daily. To Mamutik, Manukan or Sapi, it's M$12 and to Sulug or Police Beach it's M$18. For more information contact the office on the ground floor of Wisma Sabah.

SOUTH OF KOTA KINABALU
Tambunan

Across the Crocker Range from Penampang, Tambunan is an agricultural service town about 90 km from KK. This was the stamp-

ing ground of Mat Salleh, who rebelled against the British late last century.

The main reason for visiting Tambunan today is to see the Tambunan Village Resort Centre. It is built totally out of bamboo and was constructed by the young people on the Operation Raleigh expedition in 1987.

Places to Stay The *Tambunan Village Resort Centre* charges M$25 for a double room in the longhouse and also has chalets for M$35 and motel rooms for M$30.

Tenom

Tenom is the home of the friendly *Murut* people, most of whom are farmers. It's a very pleasant rural town, and is also the railhead on the line from Tanjung Aru (KK).

Despite the peaceful setting, there's absolutely nothing to do in the town itself. Just outside of town, the **Tenom Agricultural Research Station** makes an interesting diversion, and the train ride to Beaufort is highly recommended.

Places to Stay The cheapest hotel in town is the *Hotel Lam Fong* near the railway station. It's about as basic a place as you'll ever find but it's clean, if shabby, and costs M$10/15 with a bit of bargaining.

If you can't face the Lam Fong, the next best place is the *Hotel Syn Nam Tai* on the main street. It's also a basic Chinese cheapie and has rooms for M$15/20 with common bath.

Probably the best value in town is the *Hotel Kim San* (☎ 087-73 5485) in the new group of shops set back from the main road. The friendly, pipe-sucking Chinese owner, Michael Wong, is a good source of information on things to do in the area. The rooms cost M$25.

Places to Eat The *Yun Lee Restaurant* on the main street is popular with the locals, but it closes very early in the evening, as do most of them. One place that is open in the evening is the *Restaurant Fon Hin*, not far from the Hotel Kim San.

For good Malay food, rotis and martabak

try the *Bismillah Restaurant* in the Sabah Hotel.

Getting There & Away There are plenty of minibuses from Tenom to Keningau and fewer to KK and Tomani. Taxis also make the run to Keningau (M$5) and on to KK (M$25). The 46-km train journey to Beaufort is recommended.

Beaufort

Beaufort is a quiet little provincial town on the Padas River with a fair amount of charm, although there's absolutely nothing to see or do so it's unlikely you'll stay more than one night.

Places to Stay & Eat The cheapest option is the *Hotel Beaufort* (☎ 087-21 1911) where air-con rooms with bath and TV cost M$30/36, although the singles are definitely on the small side. By the cinema, the *New Padas Hotel* has singles/doubles with air-con and bath for M$37/42.

The restaurant on the ground floor of the *Hotel Beaufort* does pretty reasonable Chinese food. Otherwise, there are a number of Chinese coffee shops around town which offer the standard rice or mee dishes.

Getting There & Away There are frequent minibus departures for KK (two hours; M$7) and less frequently to Sipitang. For Menumbok (for Labuan Island), there are plenty of minibuses until early afternoon. The trip, along a reasonable gravel road, takes one hour and costs M$8.

It's a spectacular railway trip between Beaufort and Tenom, where the line follows the Padas River through steamy jungle. At times the dense jungle forms a bridge over the narrow track. On weekdays, the railcar costs M$10, the diesel train M$4 but on Sunday the fares are M$14 and M$6 respectively.

Labuan Island

Off the coast from Menumbok, Labuan is one of the departure points for the trip to Brunei. Labuan is a Federal Territory and is governed directly from KL. The island acts as a duty-free centre and as such attracts many day-tripping Bruneians, as well as Malaysians, for quick shopping sprees.

Places to Stay A good bet is the *Dahlia Hotel* near the bus station, which has rooms for M$26 with fan, and M$32 with air-con. More expensive is *Victoria Hotel* (☎ 087-42411) on Jalan Tun Mustapha, where prices start from M$70.

Getting There & Away There are regular flights to Kota Kinabalu (M$43), KL (M$380), Kuching (M$173), Miri (M$57), Lawas (M$31) and Limbang (M$30).

There are regular boat connections with Brunei – see the Brunei chapter for full details. To the Sabah mainland, there are 12-seater launches which shuttle back and forth between Labuan and Menumbok. The latter is really nothing more than a jetty, a restaurant and a few houses. The crossing takes about 30 minutes and costs M$10.

From Menumbok, there are frequent minibuses to Beaufort (one hour; M$8) and KK (two hours; M$15). The small launches also connect Labuan and Sipitang. They operate throughout the day when full, take about one hour and cost M$20.

There are also two launches connecting Labuan and KK daily.

Sipitang

Sipitang is the closest Sabah town to the Sabah-Sarawak border. There is an immigration office but everything is fairly relaxed.

Places to Stay If you have to stay in Sipitang for the night there's a *Government Rest House*, about a km from the centre on the Merapok road, which costs M$12 per person. A more basic fleapit in the centre of the village costs less than this.

Getting There & Away Minibuses and share-taxis depart for Beaufort every day around 7 to 8 am and cost M$7 per person. To the Sarawak border at Merapok, it's a half-hour trip. There's not much traffic but you shouldn't have to wait too long. The usual cost is M$2.

Small 12-seater launches leave when full for the one hour trip to Labuan.

NORTH OF KOTA KINABALU
Kota Belud

The town is the venue of Sabah's largest and most colourful tamu and as such is a magnet for travellers. The tamu takes place every Sunday – get there as early as possible.

The tamu at Kota Belud attracts all manner of traders from quasi-medical commercial travellers selling herbal remedies and magic pills to water buffalo owners who haggle all morning over the price of a cow or a calf.

Places to Stay & Eat The *Hotel Tai Seng* has 20 rooms from M$20 upwards while the *Hotel Kota Belud* (☎ 088-97 6576) on Jalan Francis has clean air-con rooms from M$28.

The best place to eat is the popular *Indonesia Restoran*, in the gravel car park behind the Kota Belud Hotel. It does simple dishes like nasi goreng and is open until 8 pm.

Getting There & Away There are plenty of minibuses operating between Kota Belud and KK (M$5; 2½ hours). To Kudat, there is one bus daily (M$10; 2½ hours) which departs about 10 am from outside the petrol station.

Kudat

Kudat, near the north-eastern tip of Sabah, has some of the best beaches in Sabah. The beaches are definitely for those who want tranquillity and who expect little in terms of facilities – very few people find their way up to this part of Sabah.

Places to Stay At the bottom of the heap is the *Hasba Hotel* (☎ 088-61959) with basic rooms from M$16 to M$25. The rooms are stuffy, hot and dirty.

The *Hotel Sunrise* (☎ 088-61517) is the largest and best place to stay in town; rooms cost from M$30 up to M$58 with air-con and bathroom. The *Kudat Hotel* (☎ 088-61 6379)

on Little St has air-con rooms from M$30 to M$35.

Getting There & Away Several minibuses a day make the three to four-hour trip from KK for M$10.

MT KINABALU

Sabah's number one attraction is the highest mountain in South-East Asia with views from the top which can stretch all the way to the north coast, Kalimantan in the south and islands of the Philippines in the east. Getting to the top of the 4011-metre peak is not so much a climb as a steep and stiff walk. It's well worth it with fantastic views and some very interesting plant life.

The climb to the top requires an overnight halt on the way, so bring plenty of warm clothes – you can also hire sleeping bags. A M$10 climbing permit is required for Mt Kinabalu; it's M$2 for students and free for children under 13. Hiring a guide (at least from Panar Laban to the summit) is supposedly compulsory although a lot of people get away without one. The guide's fee is a minimum of M$25 per day for one to three people, M$28 for four to six people and M$30 for seven to eight (the maximum).

On the first day, you get to within about 700 metres of the summit and there are numerous huts. In the morning, you leave well before dawn to be at the top before the clouds roll in around mid-morning. The trip back down to the park HQ takes the rest of the day.

The accommodation and catering at the park headquarters is excellent and well organised. It's in a beautiful setting with a magnificent view of Mt Kinabalu when the clouds are not obscuring the slopes and summits.

You should make advance reservations for accommodation both there and at Poring Hot Springs at the Sabah Parks office in KK. At the administration building, a slide and video show is presented from Friday to Monday at 7.30 pm and gives an excellent introduction to the mountain.

It's well worth spending a day exploring

the well-marked trails around park head-quarters. At 11.15 am each day, there is a guided walk which starts from the administration building and lasts for one to two hours. It's well worth taking and follows an easy path.

Places to Stay & Eat

Park Headquarters The cheapest place is the 46-bed *Old Fellowship Hostel* which costs M$10 per person, or M$3 for students with official ID. The 52-bed *New Hostel* is more expensive at M$15 (M$4 for students). Both hostels are clean and comfortable, have cooking facilities and a dining area with an open fireplace. Blankets and pillows are provided free of charge. The rest of the accommodation at park headquarters is very expensive.

The cheaper and more popular of the two restaurants is known as *Kinabalu Dalsam*. It's down below reception and offers Malay, Chinese and Western food at reasonable prices. There's also a small shop which sells a limited range of tinned foods, chocolate, beer, spirits, cigarettes, T-shirts, bread, eggs and margarine.

The other restaurant is in the main administration building, just past the hostels. It's more expensive than the Dalsam though the food is quite good. Both restaurants are open from 7 am to 9 pm.

On the Mountain On your way up to the summit, you will have to stay overnight at one of the 54-bed *Laban Rata Rest House* at Panar Laban, which costs M$25 per person in four-bed rooms. Surprisingly, it has both electricity and a restaurant.

The mountain huts are equipped with wooden bunks and mattresses, gas stoves, cooking facilities and some cooking utensils. You can hire sleeping bags for M$2 so there's no point in lugging your own all the way to the top of the mountain. Take a torch and your own toilet paper. Don't expect a warm Swiss-type chalet with a blazing fire at these huts. They're just tin sheds with the absolute minimum of facilities.

There are three huts at 3300 metres: the 12-bed *Waras* and *Panar Laban* huts and the 44-bed *Guntin Lagadan Hut*. There's also the 10-bed *Sayat-Sayat Hut* at 3750 metres. A bed in any of these huts costs M$4 per person, M$1 for students or, if the huts are full, M$1 for anyone sleeping on the floor.

The huts at 3300 metres are the most popular as it's as far as most people can comfortably get in one day and there's a canteen in the nearby Laban Rata Rest House which is not only open for regular meals but also opens from 2 to 3 am so you can grab some breakfast before attempting the summit. It's *very* cold in the early mornings (around 0°C, or 32°F!), so take warm clothing with you.

Getting There & Away

There are several minibuses daily from KK to Ranau which depart up to about 1 pm. The 85-km trip as far as park headquarters takes about 1½ to two hours and the fare is around M$8. If you're heading back towards KK, minibuses pass the park headquarters between about 8 am and 12 noon to 1 pm daily.

There is a large bus to Sandakan which passes park headquarters around 9 am. There are also other minibuses which pass Kinabalu National Park on their way to Ranau and Sandakan, but the last one goes by before 2 pm.

The 22-km journey to Ranau (M$3) takes about half an hour, while the trip to Sandakan (M$27) takes at least six hours, although it will become quicker as the road is improved.

RANAU

Ranau is just a small provincial town halfway between KK and Sandakan. Nothing much ever happens but it has a friendly population.

Few travellers stay overnight here as the big attraction is Poring Hot Springs, about 19 km north of the town.

Places to Stay & Eat

The *Hotel Ranau* (☎ 088-87 5531), opposite the petrol stations, is the first place you see when entering the town. Rooms start at M$23 for a single without air-con.

Probably the best place to eat is the Chinese restaurant around the corner from the Hotel Ranau, on the top side of the first block. The food is good, the menu varied and prices very reasonable.

Getting There & Away

To KK minibuses and taxis depart daily up to about 2 pm, cost M$10 and take about three hours. Minibuses leave for Sandakan from around 7.30 am, cost M$25 and take at least six hours, although this should decrease as the road is improved.

To Poring Hot Springs, there are share-taxis for M$3 on weekends. On weekdays, you may have to hitch (difficult) or charter a taxi (M$15) as there are few minibuses.

PORING HOT SPRINGS

The Poring Hot Springs are also part of the Kinabalu National Park but are 43 km away from the park headquarters and 19 km north of Ranau.

There are tubs for soaking in, walking trails for a bit of exercise and an excellent jungle canopy walkway for a monkey's-eye view of the forest – all well worth the M$5.

As is the case at Mt Kinabalu, it is important to reserve accommodation in advance at the Sabah Parks office in KK.

Places to Stay & Eat

The 24-bed *Poring Hostel* costs M$8 per person (M$2 for students); blankets and pillows are provided free of charge. There's a camping ground which costs M$2 per night where pillows and blankets can be hired for 50 sen each. There are also more expensive cabins.

There are cooking facilities at Poring but you should take your own food from Ranau as there's only one small, expensive shop outside the park and it has a very limited range.

Getting There & Away

Access is by minibus, taxi or hitching the 19 km along the bitumen road from Ranau – see the Ranau section for details.

SANDAKAN

The former capital city of Sabah, Sandakan is today a major commercial centre where the products of the interior – rattan, timber, rubber, copra, palm oil and even birds' nests from the Gomantong Caves – are brought to be loaded onto boats for export.

The main attractions, however, are well outside the city. At **Sepilok** is one of the world's three orang-utan sanctuaries and it's well worth a visit. There's also the Gomantong Caves across the other side of the bay, where edible birds' nests are collected for that famous Chinese soup. Offshore, there's one of the world's few turtle sanctuaries where giant turtles come to lay their eggs.

Information

The Sabah Parks office (☎ 089-27 3453) is on the 9th floor of Wisma Khoo Siak Chew at the end of Lebuh Tiga. This is where you need to come to make a reservation to visit the Turtle Islands National Park (Taman Pulau Penya).

For a permit for Gomantong Caves, you need to pay a visit to the Urban Forest & Forest Recreation Division of the Forestry Department, housed in a flash new building at Batu 7, about 500 metres past the 11 km peg on the Ranau road.

Places to Stay

Most travellers seem to head straight for *Uncle Tan's* (☎ 089-66 9516) out at Batu 16. Tan is a friendly retired schoolteacher who takes travellers into his house. He charges M$15 for a dorm bed, which includes a huge breakfast. Free tea and coffee is provided throughout the day and evening meals are served, usually of excellent local dishes, for a bargain M$5.

There is room for a dozen or so people and the atmosphere is very friendly. As a sideline Tan runs very low-key (and cheap) trips to both the Turtle Islands and to a jungle camp he has on the lower Kinabatangan River.

One of the better places in town is the *Hotel Hung Wing* (☎ 089-21 8895) on Jalan Tiga. It's a mid-range hotel with some cheaper rooms which are great value.

Generally, the higher the floor, the cheaper the room. If you're willing to climb to the 6th floor, you'll find clean, spacious rooms with bathroom and fan for M$20/30.

Also on Jalan Tiga is *Hotel Paris* (☎ 089-21 8488) which has clean rooms from M$25/30 with fan and bath. The *Mayfair Hotel* (☎ 089-21 9855) at 24 Jalan Pryer only has air-con rooms and these go for M$32/40 with bath.

A good, clean Chinese place is the *Hotel En Khin* (☎ 089-21 7377) at 50 Lebuh Tiga, almost opposite the Hung Wing. All rooms have air-con and bath, and cost M$32/40.

Places to Eat

For good Malay food, try the *Habeeb Restoran* on Jalan Pryer. They do excellent martabak and also have an air-con room upstairs. There are a couple of similar places close by including the *Aysha* and *Buhari*.

For a Western breakfast or snack, there are a few choices. The best is probably *Fairwood Fastfood* on Jalan Tiga, which is open from 7 am and has a good-value set breakfast. Another possibility is the *Apple Fast Food* restaurant on the ground floor of the Hotel Nak on Jalan Edinburgh.

Getting There & Away

Air Sandakan is on the MAS domestic network and there are regular flights to KK (M$69), Lahad Datu (M$40) and Tawau (M$78).

Bus All long-distance minibuses leave from the area next to the footbridge over Jalan Tiga; local minibuses leave from the area next to the old Port Authority building. There are buses to KK which cost M$35 and take eight hours. You can take the same transport to Kinabalu National Park headquarters for M$27.

Minibuses to Ranau cost M$25, and the journey takes up to six hours. The road as far as Batu 32 (where the Lahad Datu road heads

off to the south-east) and on to Telupid should now be surfaced all the way.

There is one bus for Lahad Datu and Tawau daily at 5.30 am, but there are also many minibuses which leave throughout the morning to Lahad Datu, some going on to Tawau. The trip to Lahad Datu takes about three hours and costs M$15.

Getting Around

If you're arriving or leaving by air, the airport is about 11 km from the city. There are minibuses throughout the day connecting the two which leave from the local minibus stand. To get to the airport from the town centre take a Batu 7 airport minibus. A taxi to or from the airport costs M$10.

AROUND SANDAKAN
Sepilok Orang-utan Rehabilitation Centre

Apes are brought to Sepilok to be rehabilitated to forest life, and so far the centre has handled about 80 of them. About 20 still return regularly to be fed but it's unlikely you'll see anywhere near this number at feeding time – three or four is a more likely number.

The apes are fed from two platforms, one in the middle of the forest (platform B) about 30-minutes walk from the centre, and the other close to the headquarters (platform A). The latter platform is for the juvenile orang-utans and they are fed daily at 10 am and 2.30 pm. At platform B, the adolescent apes which have been returned to the forest are fed daily at 11 am. For this feeding, the rangers leave from in front of the Nature Education Centre at 10.30 am daily.

In addition to the orang-utans, there are a couple of Sumatran rhinos at the centre. The visiting hours at the centre are Saturday to Thursday from 9 am to 12 noon and from 2 to 4 pm and on Friday from 9 to 11.30 am and from 2 to 4 pm.

Don't miss this place as it's well worth a visit.

Getting There & Away To get to the centre, take the blue Labuk bus marked 'Sepilok

Batu 14' from the local bus stand next to the Central Market on the waterfront (M$1.20, 45 minutes).

Turtle Islands National Park

The Taman Pulau Penyu comprises three small islands 32 km north of Sandakan. Pulau Selingan, Pulau Bakungan Kecil and Pulau Gulisan are visited by marine turtles which come ashore to lay their eggs, mostly between the months of August and October, each year.

Places to Stay It's not possible to visit the islands on a day trip, so any excursion involves staying overnight. The only accommodation is at a *Sabah Parks Chalet* on Pulau Selingan, which costs M$30 per person per night. Bookings must be made in advance at the Sabah Parks office in Sandakan as facilities are limited.

Getting There & Away There are no regular services, so you'll probably have to charter an expensive boat to take you there. If you can manage to round up a few people who also want to visit the sanctuary, it's well worth chartering a boat.

Uncle Tan in Sandakan organises trips out to the islands, and he's about as cheap as you'll find.

Gomantong Caves

These caves are across the bay from Sandakan and about 20 km inland. They are famous as a source of swiftlets' nests, which are the basis for birds' nest soup.

Permits to visit the caves are required and you need to get these in advance from the Forest Department headquarters in Sandakan.

Getting There & Away The problem with the caves is their inaccessibility. If you still want to visit Gomantong then, again, Uncle Tan in Sandakan is probably the best person to see.

KINABATANGAN RIVER

The Kinabatangan River is one of the main rivers in Sabah and flows generally northeast to enter the sea east of Sandakan. Although logging is widespread along the upper reaches of the river, below the Sandakan to Lahad Datu road the jungle is relatively untouched.

It is an ideal place to observe the wildlife of Borneo and sightings of the native proboscis monkeys are common along the banks in the morning and evening. Orang-utans are also seen from time to time.

This area is virtually inaccessible but Uncle Tan (see the Sandakan section) has a jungle camp about an hour downstream from the Sandakan to Lahad Datu road. While it is extremely basic, it does give the traveller the opportunity to get out of the towns and stay in the jungle.

He charges M$15 per person per day for accommodation and meals. It's not the Hilton but is perfectly adequate. The only other charge is M$130 for transport from Sandakan to the camp and return, so obviously it's better if you have a few days to spare. Many travellers come to the camp with the intention of staying a couple of days, but stay much longer.

LAHAD DATU

Lahad Datu is a busy little plantation and timber service town of 20,000 people. There are very few tourists and probably the only reason for visiting is if you are en route to or from the excellent Danum Valley Field Centre, 80 km west of Lahad Datu (see the following Around Lahad Datu section), run by the Sabah Foundation.

The town is full of Filipino and Indonesian migrants and refugees, and the streets are full of women trying to make a few ringgit selling cigarettes.

Information

The Sabah Foundation office (☎ 089-81092) is on the 2nd floor of the Bangunan Hap Seng on the main street.

Places to Stay

The cheapest place, that isn't a brothel, is the *Rumah Tumpangan Malaysia* (☎ 089-83358), just off the main street and on a side street between the Ocean Hotel and the cinema. It's basic but clean enough; rooms with fan and common bath are M$26/31.

Next up the scale is *Ocean Hotel* (☎ 089-81700) on the main street opposite the Hap Seng Building. It's a very good hotel with good-sized rooms, all with air-con and bath, for M$38/48.

Places to Eat

One of the best places for Muslim Malay food is the *Restoran Kabir* near the mini-Secretariat and the minibuses. They serve excellent curries, rotis and martabak and there is an air-con room upstairs.

In the evenings, the hawkers set up their stalls in the area behind the Hotel Mido and a couple of ringgit will get you a decent feed.

Getting There & Away

MAS operate services between Lahad Datu and KK (M$88), Sandakan (M$40) and Tawau (M$40).

The long-distance minibuses leave from outside the buildings near the mini-Secretariat. There are frequent departures for Sandakan (3½ hours; M$10), Semporna (2½ hours; M$8) and Tawau (2½ hours; M$15).

The Sabah Foundation vehicle to the Danum Valley Field Centre leaves from the Han Seng Building on Monday, Wednesday and Friday at around 3 pm.

AROUND LAHAD DATU
Danum Valley Field Centre

Located on the Segama River, 85 km west of Lahad Datu, this field centre has been set up by the Sabah Foundation and a number of private companies to provide facilities for research, education and recreation in an untouched rainforest area. It's curious that a number of the private companies are involved in logging in Sabah.

It's necessary to get a permit (M$15) and make bookings in advance, preferably with the Sabah Foundation office in KK but, failing that, at the office in Lahad Datu.

A guide is obligatory on your first walk

into the forest from the centre and for this you have to pay M$20 for half a day.

Places to Stay & Eat There are two places to stay – a self-catering, 30-bed *hostel* and a *rest house*. A bed in the hostel costs M$30, while the rest house rooms cost M$45 per person.

Cooking facilities and utensils are provided in the hostel but you need to bring all your own food. Rest house guests, and anyone staying at the hostel, can get good meals at the rest house for M$30 per day.

Getting There & Away A Sabah Foundation vehicle leaves the centre on Monday, Wednesday and Friday at 9 am and returns from Lahad Datu on the same days at around 3 pm – the one-way cost is M$30. If you have to arrange your own transport from Lahad Datu it costs around M$130 to charter a vehicle to take you in.

SEMPORNA

Semporna, between Lahad Datu and Tawau, has a large stilt village and there's a cultured pearl farm off the coast. About the only time you're likely to come through here is if you are on an organised diving trip to Sipadan Island, off the coast to the south-east.

Places to Stay & Eat

The only hotel in Semporna is the very nice, but also expensive, *Dragon Inn Hotel* which charges M$68/78.

The *Floating Restoran & Bar*, halfway along the short causeway which connects the town to the Dragon Inn, has excellent local fish for M$7.

Getting There & Away

There are plenty of minibuses between Semporna and Lahad Datu for M$8 (2½ hours; 160 km) and Tawau for M$4 (1½ hours; 110 km).

TAWAU

A mini-boomtown on the very south-east corner of Sabah close to the Indonesian border, Tawau is a provincial capital and centre for export of the products of the interior – timber, rubber, Manila hemp, cocoa, copra and tobacco.

There's precious little to do or see in Tawau – it's just a town you pass through on the way to or from Tarakan in Kalimantan.

Information

The MAS office (☎ 089-77 2703) is in the Wisma SASCO, close to the centre of town. Bouraq, the Indonesian feeder airline, uses Merdeka Travel at 41 Jalan Dunlop as its agent. The Indonesian Consulate is on Jalan Kuharsa, some distance from the centre of town, but at last report it wasn't issuing visas.

For bookings for the boat to Sipadan and Indonesia, the Sarasan Tinggi Co (☎ 089-77 2455) has its office in the centre of town near the local bus stand.

Places to Stay

The best value is definitely the *Ambassador Hotel* (☎ 089-77 2700) at 1872 Jalan Paya, just out of the town centre. Rooms in this hotel are fairly large, have air-con and bath, and cost M$23 – for one, two or three people.

Hotel Soon Yee (☎ 089-77 2447), next to the market, is clean and friendly and is not bad value at M$20 for a single with fan or M$28/34 for singles/doubles with air-con and bath – the rooms are definitely a bit on the small side.

Places to Eat

For good Malay food, try the *Restoran Sinar Murni* – good chicken curry here.

For hawker food, there are the stalls in the Central Market and the Tawau Food Plaza on the 2nd floor of the otherwise empty multistorey building. At night, the food stalls along the road near the waterfront get going and are definitely the best places to eat.

For a bit of a splurge, the restaurant in the *Hotel Emas* has a steamboat buffet in the evenings, not bad value at M$16 per head. They also serve a Western breakfast for M$8. The coffee shop in the *Marco Polo Hotel* has a breakfast buffet for M$14.

Getting There & Away

MAS has flights between Tawau and KK (M$80), Sandakan (M$61) and Lahad Datu (M$40). There are also international flights to Tarakan in Kalimantan (Indonesia) with MAS and Bouraq.

There are frequent minibuses to Semporna (1½ hours; M$4) and Lahad Datu (2½ hours; M$15). There's also a large bus daily at 5.30 am which goes all the way to Sandakan.

The ferry MV *Sasaran Muhibbah Express* operates three times weekly between Tawau and Nunukan and Tarakan in Kalimantan. It leaves from the customs wharf around the back of the large supermarket.

The same vessel that serves the Tawau-Tarakan run goes to Sipadan Island on Sunday for a day trip.

The Philippines

The Philippines are the forgotten islands of this book. Because they're off the regular overland route they've never attracted the travelling hordes in great numbers. So, if you make the effort to get there, you're in for a pleasant surprise. The food's pretty good, accommodation is easy to find, you've got over 7000 remarkably diverse islands to choose from, and if island-hopping attracts you, the Philippines are the place to go. There are cheap flights and boats go to everywhere – they are very frequent, remarkably cheap and reasonably comfortable, although not all that safe.

Add ease of travel to islands of very friendly people, many of whom speak English, and it's hard not to have a good time. In fact, many travellers reckon the Philippines is their favourite country in the whole region. Despite the continuing post-Marcos instability, most of the Philippines is still a safe and pleasant place to visit.

Facts about the Country

HISTORY

The Philippines is unique among the countries of South-East Asia, both for the variety of its colonisers and for its energetic attempts to cast off the colonial yoke. The Filipinos are a Malay people, closely related to the people of Indonesia and Malaysia. Little is known about their precolonial society, as the Spaniards – who ruled the country for over 300 years – energetically eradicated every trace of what they felt was 'pagan' in the culture.

Ferdinand Magellan, a Portuguese who had switched sides to arch-rival Spain, set off from Europe in 1519, with instructions to sail round the world, claim anything worth claiming for Spain and to bring back some spices (a very valuable commodity in Europe). Finding a way round the southern tip of South America took nearly a year but, finally, the small fleet (two of the original four ships) reached the Philippines in 1521.

At the island of Cebu, Magellan claimed the lot for Spain and managed to make a few Christian conversions to boot. Unfortunately, he then decided to display Spanish military might to his newly converted flock by dealing with an unruly tribe on the nearby island of Mactan. Chief Lapu-Lapu managed to kill Magellan. The Cebuans decided their visitors were not so special after all and the survivors scuttled back to Spain, after collecting a cargo of spices on the way. They arrived in the sole remaining ship in 1522.

The Philippines, named after King Philip II of Spain, was more or less left alone from then until 1565 when Miguel de Legaspi stormed the no-longer-friendly island of Cebu and made the first permanent Spanish settlement. In 1571, Spanish HQ was moved to Manila and from here Spain gradually took control of the entire region – or more correctly converted the region, since Spanish colonial rule was very much tied up with taking the cross to the heathen.

The Spanish were far from alone in the area: other European powers and the Japanese and Chinese also made forays into the Philippines and, throughout the Spanish period, the strongly Muslim regions of Mindanao and the Sulu Archipelago were neither converted nor conquered.

After the defeat of the Spanish Armada by the English in 1588, Spain entered a long period of decline and its control of the region was never fully exploited. The Philippines was generally treated as a subsidiary of Spain's colony in New Spain – Mexico. The colony was a continual drain on the Spanish treasury until the introduction of tobacco in 1782 started to make it profitable.

From 1762, as a result of the Seven Years' War in Europe, the British took control of Manila for over a year, but never extended their rule far into the countryside. Internal

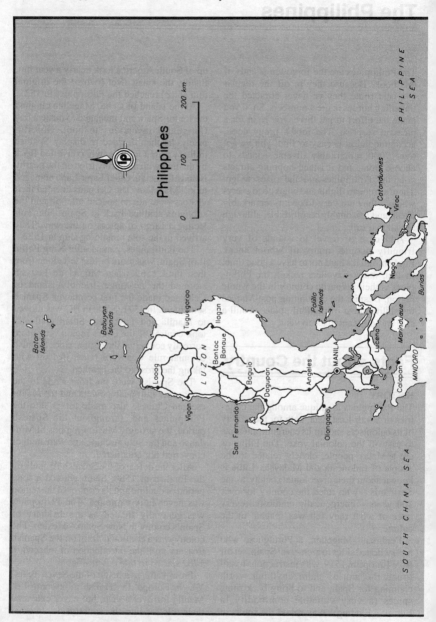

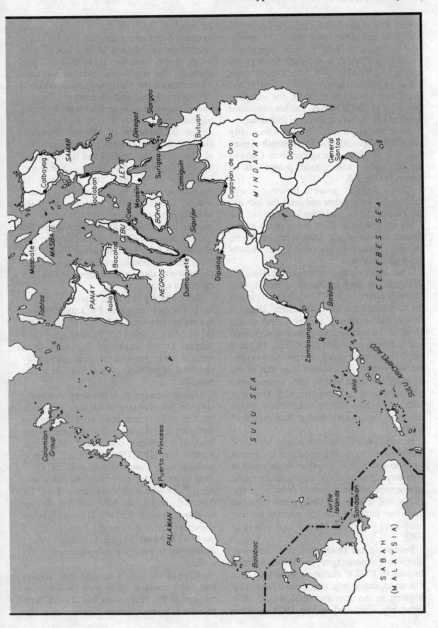

events were more threatening to Spanish rule and it is estimated that over 100 revolts against Spanish power were organised. Finally the Spanish sealed their fate by executing Jose Rizal in 1896, after a mockery of a trial. A brilliant scholar, doctor and writer, Rizal had preferred to work for independence by peaceful means, but his execution sparked off the worst revolt to that time.

Nevertheless, it was the USA who finally pushed the Spanish out. The Spanish-American war of 1898 soon spread from Cuba to the Philippines and Spanish power was no match for the US.

One colonial power, however, was exchanged for another and once the inevitable Filipino revolt had been stamped out, the USA set out to convert the country to the American way of life. They were, no doubt, suitably amazed to discover it had already been Christianised.

The American colonial period, or 'tutelage' as they preferred to call it, was abruptly ended by WW II when the Japanese military occupied the islands until Douglas MacArthur 'returned' in 1944. And, at the close of the war, independence was granted – it had been promised in 1935 for 10 years later. The American colonial period was considerably more enlightened than that of the Spanish, but it left equally deep impressions, particularly on the economy, since American companies had firmly entrenched themselves in the country during their period of control.

In addition, Filipino democracy was to be modelled on the American pattern and events were to prove that a system wide open to vote-buying in its home environment could spawn spectacular abuses in Asia. So in the 1950s and 1960s the Philippines bounced from one party to another, usually similar, party until Ferdinand Marcos took power in 1965.

Following his re-election (this feat was previously unmanaged) in 1970, Marcos decided in 1972 to declare martial law. This was done, ostensibly, to reduce the anarchy reigning in the country which would have inevitably worsened as the 1974 election

approached. Also, no doubt, he liked being in control and under the constitution could not run for a third term. Martial law, as is its wont, soon become total control and although the previously endemic violence was curtailed the Philippines suffered from stifling corruption and the economy became one of the weakest in an otherwise booming region.

The assassination of Marcos' opponent Benigno Aquino, in 1983, pushed opposition to Marcos to new heights and further shook the tottering economy. Marcos called elections for early 1986 and for once the opposition united by supporting Aquino's widow, Corazon 'Cory' Aquino. With the world's press watching closely Marcos and Aquino both claimed to win the election but 'people power' rallied behind Cory Aquino and within days Ferdinand and Imelda had slunk off to Hawaii, leaving a spectacular collection of shoes and a country in less than excellent shape.

Since coming to power, Aquino's position has not been an easy one. For a start many of her supporters were only behind her to get rid of Marcos and once he was gone their support for her weakened. Secondly, there are still many pro-Marcos elements heavily involved in politics, in business and in the military.

Losing the support of the army was probably the decisive step in Marcos' downfall, but the military has been far from consistently loyal to Aquino and there are constant fears of a military coup. And, of course, there's the NPA (New People's Army) pushing for a Communist revolution. Does Aquino soft pedal with them and risk alienating those who want them stamped on? Or does she jump on the NPA and risk stirring up a hornet's nest? And would the army jump if she ordered it to anyway? Finally, there's the MNLF (Moro National Liberation Front) continuing to push for independence in the south.

Worst of all, there's no sign that Aquino has really come to grips with the endemic corruption the Philippines has always been prone to. Some observers even claim the only change is that the hands in the till are now those of the Aquino family and friends rather than Marcos cronies. The Philippines continues to stumble along, while a large proportion of the of the South-East Asian region enjoys the economic boom, and things are far from stable.

GEOGRAPHY
The official statistics state that the Philippines is comprised of over 7000 islands – but what is an island and what is a rock that occasionally appears above water level? Together, they make a land area of about 299,000 sq km, 94% of which is on the 11 largest islands.

The Philippines can be conveniently divided into four areas: (1) the largest island of Luzon (site of the capital, Manila) and the nearby island of Mindoro; (2) the Visayas, the scattered group of seven islands south of Luzon; (3) Mindanao, the Muslim trouble-centre in the south and the second largest island in the country, with the string of islands in the Sulu Archipelago, like stepping stones to Borneo; and (4) the island of Palawan, nearly 400 km long but averaging a width of only 40 km.

CLIMATE
The Philippines is typically tropical – hot and humid year round. Although the actual climate map of the country is fairly complex, it can be roughly divided into a January-June dry and a July-December wet. January, February and March are probably the best months for a visit as it starts to get hotter after March, peaking in May. In some places it seems to rain year round and, in others, it rarely rains at all. From May to November there may be typhoons.

ECONOMY
The economy is principally agricultural. Like several other countries in the region, the Philippines is potentially self-sufficient in rice and other important foods but, due to poor yields and the continued evils of absentee landlordism in a peasant society, it generally ends up having to import rice along with fish and meat. All of these could conceivably be produced locally. Slow or nonexistent progress towards much-needed land reform has been a problem in the Philippines ever since independence.

Copra, sugar and *abaca* (a fibre from a relative of the banana plant) are the principal agricultural exports. Forestry and some gold and silver mining are other important economic activities. There is some industry and it has been growing in recent years. Endemic corruption and inefficiency have meant that the boom conditions of other South-East Asian nations have failed to rub off on the Philippines.

POPULATION & PEOPLE
The population of the Philippines is estimated to be about 60 million and still growing too fast for comfort. The people are mainly of the Malay race although there is the usual Chinese minority and a fair number of *mestizos* – Filipino-Spanish or Filipino-American. There are still some remote pockets of pre-Malay people living in the hills, including the stone-age Tasaday who were discovered in a remote Mindanao valley as recently as 1972.

ARTS & CULTURE
The Philippines has developed a mixed culture from the historic blending of foreign influences with indigenous elements. Today, the Muslims and some of the isolated tribes are the only people whose culture remains unadulterated by Spanish and American influences. The ability of the Filipinos to improvise and copy is very apparent: you need only see how the army jeeps left by the Americans were converted into colourful, shining-chrome taxis through painstaking detailed work before Filipinos began to produce these vehicles themselves.

The ideas of the New Society propagated by Marcos really caught the national consciousness of the Filipinos in the 1970s, just as People Power did in the 1980s. People recollected their cultural heritage and began to care about their traditional arts and crafts.

Consequently, the national language is

strongly used today in theatre, and literature and *kundimans* – romantic and sentimental love songs – are popular again. The good old folk dances, foremost among them the national dance *tinkling*, have become a new tourist attraction.

RELIGION

The Philippines is unique for being the only Christian country in Asia – over 90% of the population claims to be Christian and over 80% Roman Catholic. The Spanish did a thorough job! Largest of the minority religions are the Muslims who live chiefly on the island of Mindanao and in the Sulu Archipelago.

When the Spanish arrived, toting their cross, the Muslims were just establishing toeholds in the region. In the northern islands the toehold was only a small one and easily displaced, but in the south the people had been firmly converted and Christianity was never able to make strong inroads.

LANGUAGE

As in Indonesia there is one nominal national language and a large number of local languages and dialects. It takes 10 languages to cover 90% of the population! English and Spanish are still official languages, although the use of Spanish is now quite rare. English is also not as widespread as in the American days, although the English-speaking visitor will not have any trouble communicating – it remains the language of secondary school education and to say someone 'doesn't even speak English' means they've not gone beyond primary school.

Tagalog, or Pilipino, the local language of Manila and parts of Luzon, is now being pushed as the national language. It sounds remarkably like Indonesian. Listen to them roll their rrrrs. Lonely Planet's *Pilipino Phrasebook* has the full story. The following words are in Pilipino:

Greetings & Civilities
good morning
   magandáng umága

goodbye
   paálam
good evening
   magandáng gabí
hello
   haló
welcome or farewell
   mabúhay

Useful Words & Phrases
How many?
   ilán?
How much?
   magkáno?
That one
   iyón
Too expensive
   mahál
Where is?
   saán ang?
yes
   oó
no
   hindí
good
   mabúti
bad
   masamá
bank
   bangko
boat
   sakayán
cheap hotel
   múrang hotél
price
   halagá
train station
   estasyón ng tren

Food & Drink
beer
   serbésa
coffee
   kapé
food
   pagkaín
milk
   gátas
restaurant
   restorán

sugar
asúkal
water
túbig

Numbers

1	*isá*
2	*dalawá*
3	*tatló*
4	*apát*
5	*limá*
6	*ánim*
7	*pitó*
8	*waló*
9	*siyám*
10	*sampú*

Facts for the Visitor

VISAS

Visa regulations vary with your intended length of stay. The simplest procedure is to simply arrive without a visa, in which case you will be permitted to stay for up to 21 days. If you obtain a visa overseas it will usually allow a 59-day stay and is usually issued free of charge. If you already have a visa on arrival make sure the immigration officers know this or your passport will still be stamped for just 21 days.

To extend the 21-day stay period to 59 days apply with your passport and the relevant documents to the immigration office in Manila, Cebu City or Angeles City. The Manila office is at the Department of Immigration & Deportation, Magallanes Drive, Intramuros, Manila. The extension costs P300 for the Visa Waiver plus P10 for a Legal Research Fee. If you want the four hour Express Service it costs an additional P250. You must be neatly dressed if you apply in person at the office – rubber thongs/flip flops will ensure an instant refusal. A number of travel agencies will handle the extension application for a P100 to P200 fee.

After 59 days it gets really complicated although it's possible to keep on extending for about a year. Further extensions cost P100 per month for the Extension Fee but after you've added in Alien Head Tax (P125), Alien Certificate of Registration (P250), Emigration Clearance Certificate (P250), plus a whole series of Legal Research fees you're soon looking at the wrong side of P1000.

Staying beyond six months also involves a Certificate of Temporary Residence (P400) and after one year there's a travel tax (P1620).

MONEY
Currency
The unit of currency is the peso (P, correctly spelt piso), divided into 100 centavos (c). Throughout this section when it says 'c' it means centavos not cents of another currency. The only foreign currency to have in the Philippines is US dollars – it's no longer true to say that nothing else is considered to exist but the dollar certainly exists more than most.

Furthermore, American Express travellers' cheques are more easily exchanged than other varieties. There are no particular hassles with the peso although you'll need an exchange receipt if you want to convert any back on departure.

The main problem is that changing travellers' cheques can be slow, particularly away from Manila. Of the banks, the Philippines Commercial International Bank is said to offer the best rates for travellers' cheques but Philippine National Bank or American Express are faster. Around Ermita, along Mabini St in particular, there are a great number of moneychangers who are much faster than the banks and give a better rate for cash. The rate varies with the size of the bill – US$100 and US$50 bills are best, US$1 bills are hardly wanted at all.

Rates tend to vary from one changer to another so shop around. Some of the moneychangers will change travellers' cheques as well, but at a worse rate. Even at banks cash tends to get a better rate than cheques, unlike in many other countries.

You are only permitted to take P500 out of the country with you but try not to take any as they're difficult to exchange abroad. You can buy them at a discount in Hong Kong.

There is said to be a small black market but the rate is only minimally better and it's not worth the risk. The risk is real – there are a lot of money rip-off scams in Manila and any offer of a spectacular exchange rate is bound to be a set-up. There is a wide and interesting variety of tricks involving sleight of hand and other subterfuges.

Exchange Rates

A$1	=	P21.2
C$1	=	P23.6
NZ$	=	P15.6
UK£1	=	P45.9
US$	=	P26.7

Costs

Despite high inflation, prices remain lower in the Philippines than in most other countries in the region. Some things seem amazingly cheap and local transport and beer are two good examples. Airfares within the Philippines are also good value but not as comparatively cheap as in past years. The reduced flow of visitors to the Philippines also works in your favour as there's more competition for your custom which keeps prices down.

TOURIST OFFICES

The vast Department of Tourism (DOT) office in Manila could be more aptly called the Temple of Tourism. The smaller regional DOT offices can be quite different – often very knowledgeable, all the facts at their fingertips and, best of all, ready at hand with useful information sheets on their localities. During the Marcos era this entity was known as the Ministry of Tourism (MOT) and some offices (and printed information) may still bear this name.

Philippine Airlines (PAL) may also have some useful information.

BUSINESS HOURS

Businesses open their doors to the public between 8 and 10 am. Offices, banks and public authorities have a five-day week. Some offices are also open on Saturday mornings. Banks open at 9 am and close at 3 pm. Embassies and consulates are open to the public mainly from 9 am to 1 pm.

Offices and public authorities close at 5 pm. Large businesses like department stores and supermarkets continue until 7 pm, and smaller shops often open until 10 pm.

POST & TELECOMMUNICATIONS
Post

The Philippine postal service is generally quite efficient. You can get mail sent to you at poste restantes at the GPO in all the major towns. Opening hours in Philippine post offices are not the same everywhere. Many close at 12 noon, others shut on Saturdays as well. The following hours can usually be relied upon: Monday to Friday from 8 am to 12 noon, and from 1 to 5 pm.

Telephones

You do not find telephones everywhere in the Philippines; in an emergency try the nearest police station, which in many areas will have the only telephone. Telephone numbers are always changing so obtain a local directory before calling.

In contrast to overseas calls, local calls in the Philippines are full of problems. It can take a ridiculously long time to be connected and the lines over long distances are bad. International calls are simple in comparison.

TIME

The Philippines is eight hours ahead of GMT. When it is 12 noon in the Philippines it is 2 pm in Sydney, 4 am in London, 11 pm in New York and 8 pm in Los Angeles.

Remember that most locals operate on 'Philippine time' with its attendant lack of punctuality. Allow flexibility in rendezvous times.

BOOKS & MAPS

If you want a lot more information on travelling in the Philippines, then look for

Lonely Planet's *The Philippines – a travel survival kit.* There has been a spate of books about Cory Aquino and the downfall of Marcos. You'll see them in every bookshop in Manila and, no doubt, more will be along in the next few years. Manila has a good selection of bookshops.

The Nelles Verlag *Philippines* map is an excellent map of the islands at a scale of 1:1,500,000. *The Philippine Motorists' Road Guide* is available in bookshops.

MEDIA

After 20 years of press censorship under Marcos, the change of government brought a flood of new national and local newspapers and magazines indulging in a marvellous journalistic free for all; many are in English.

Radio and TV operate on a commercial basis, and there are 22 TV channels. Five broadcast from Manila, sometimes in English and sometimes in Tagalog.

DANGERS & ANNOYANCES

The Philippines has rip-offs like anywhere else, but in recent years it has had more of them. New tricks pop up every year so it's always wise to be on your toes.

Beware of people who claim to have met you before. 'I was the immigration officer at the airport when you came through' is one often-used line. Manila has lots of fake immigration officers ready to dupe the unwary. There are also fake police officers and a favourite scam is to ask to check your money for counterfeit notes. When they return it the money may well be fake, or some of it may be missing.

Don't accept invitations to parties or meals from people who accost you in the street. Drugged coffee is a favourite with these folk and when you wake up your valuables will be long gone. Baguio is a popular place for unexpected invitations.

Beware of pickpockets in crowded areas of Manila or on tightly packed jeepneys or buses. Favourite places are around Ermita, especially in the crowded PAL office and in Rizal Park. Sleight of hand scams by street moneychangers are another speciality. Invitations to card games are another good way to lose money.

ACCOMMODATION

Finding cheap hotels is no problem. The exception may be Manila, but even there you'll find a wide selection of reasonably priced guest houses and medium-priced hotels. Even the biggest hotels will offer attractive discounts.

There are quite a few youth hostels or YH-associated places around the country, so a YH card (student cards are also generally acceptable) is worth having. Even in Manila you can get dorm-style accommodation for P50 to P80 and away from the big cities rooms often cost P60 or less. In the Mountain Province, and at some of the beach resorts, the places will be pretty basic – no electricity, for example.

Maintenance in many hotels is a little lackadaisical so it's worth checking if the electricity and water are working before you sign in. Places in North Luzon tend to be cheaper than in the southern islands or elsewhere. Beware of fires in cheap hotels – Filipino hotels don't close down, they burn down. Check fire escapes and make sure windows will open. Finally, it's often worth asking for a discount, or bargaining a little on prices as they'll often come down.

FOOD

The Filipinos have taken on US fast foods wholeheartedly, so there are plenty of hamburgers and hot dogs. Chinese food is also widely available and in Chinese restaurants there is actually one of the few reminders of Spain – a lot of the menus are in a mixture of Spanish and English. Local Filipino food, usually called 'native' food, is a bit like Indonesian *nasi padang* in that all the food is laid out on view – and to Western palates it would often taste a lot better if it were hot. It's worth a splurge to try really good authentic Filipino food as it can be really delicious. Some popular dishes include:

Adobo – stewed chicken and pork pieces.

Arroz caldo – boiled rice with chicken, garlic, ginger and onions.

Balut – a popular street-side snack, boiled duck egg containing a partially formed duck embryo – yuck!

Bangus – milkfish, lightly grilled, stuffed and baked.

Crispy pata – crispy fried pig skin, another delicacy or feast dish.

Gulay – vegetable dish simmered in coconut milk, particularly gabi leaves.

Inihaw – grilled fish or meat.

Lechon – a feast dish, roast baby pig with liver sauce.

Lumpia – spring rolls filled with meat or vegetables, Lumpia Shanghai are small fried spring rolls filled with meat.

Mami – noodle soup, like mee soup in Malaysia or Indonesia.

Menudo – stew with vegetables and small liver pieces or chopped pork.

Mongos – chick peas, similar to Lebanese humus.

Pancit – noodle dish, either Pancit Canton (spicy, thick noodles) or Pancit Guisado (less spicy, thin noodles).

Pinangat – Bicol vegetable dish laced with very hot peppers – 'the Bicol express'.

There are also a number of Filipino drinks worth sampling (apart from Coke, which they must consume faster than any country apart from the US):

Halo-Halo – a crushed ice, flavouring and fruit dessert. It means 'all mixed together' and is similar to an *es kacang* in Malaysia.

Iced buko – buko is young coconut.

Kalamansi – the tiny lemons known as kalamansi are served as lemon juice or with black tea. They are thought to have amazing curative effects.

San Mig – San Miguel beer must be the cheapest beer in the world and it's also very good.

Tuba – coconut wine, can be very strong.

THINGS TO BUY

There are a wide variety of handicrafts available in the Philippines and you will find examples of most crafts on sale in Manila. Clothing, cane and basket work, woodcarving and all manner of regional specialities can be found. See the various Manila, Luzon and islands sections for more details.

Getting There & Away

AIR

Apart from occasional boats from Hong Kong or Taiwan and illegal smuggling routes from Sabah through the Sulu Archipelago, the best way to get to the Philippines is to fly. Although Cebu now has an international airport, Manila is virtually the only international gateway, so, for probably 99% of visitors to the Philippines, Manila is their first experience of the country.

Hong Kong is very much the regional gateway to the Philippines and fares are typically available from around US$130. You can also look for cheap fares from Singapore or Bangkok. Manila is not a great bargain centre for flying out of but, if you shop around the travel agents, you could be able to get tickets to Europe for US$550 to US$650 or to the West Coast of the USA for US$500 to US$600.

There are very few alternatives to Manila as an entry point to the Philippines. Once, there were flights to Mindanao from Sabah (Malaysia) and from Kalimantan (Indonesia) but they don't seem to have operated for some time. These days from Borneo you would have to fly all the way from Kota Kinabalu or Bandar Seri Begawan to Manila. There is no interesting air connection between Indonesia and the Philippines.

Getting Around

AIR

Philippine Airlines (PAL) runs a frequent and often economical service to most parts of the country. The only thing that can really be said against it is that there are often flights from Manila to town A, B or C but rarely flights between towns A, B and C. They're pretty security conscious so expect to be thoroughly frisked.

Student-card holders, under 26 years of age, are eligible for a 15% discount on

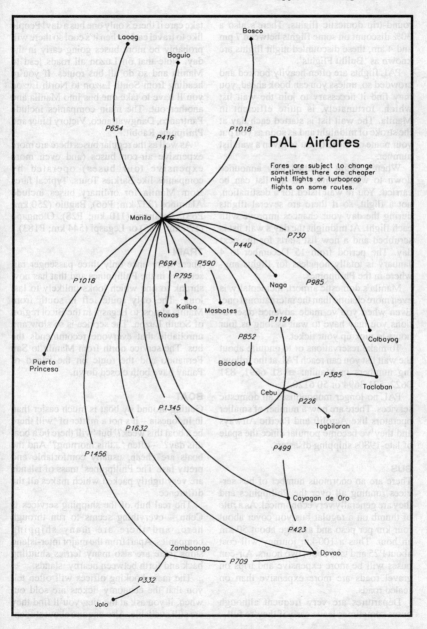

PAL Airfares

Fares are subject to change
sometimes there are cheaper
night flights or turboprop
flights on some routes.

Basco

Laoag

Baguio

P654

P416

P1018

Manila

P730

P440

P694

P590

P795

Naga

P985

Kalibo

Roxas

Masbates

P1018

P1194

P852

Colbayog

Bacolod

Puerto
Princesa

P385

Cebu

Tacloban

P226

P1345

P1632

P1456

Tagbilaran

P499

Zamboanga

P332

Cayagan de Oro

P423

P709

Davao

Jolo

round-trip domestic flights. There's also a 30% discount on some flights between 7 pm and 4 am, these discounted night flights are known as 'Bulilit Flights'.

PAL flights are often heavily booked and crowded so, unless you can book ahead, you may find it necessary to join the wait list which, fortunately, is quite efficient in Manila. The wait list is started each day at the stroke of midnight and as soon as you put your name on the list, you're given a wait list number.

When a flight is called they announce down to what number on the list can be carried. You're wait listed for a destination, not a flight, so if there are several flights during the day your chances improve with each flight. At midnight the day's wait list is scrubbed and a new list starts for the next day. The period from 15 December to 4 January is totally hopeless for flights anywhere in the Philippines.

Manila's domestic airport, incidentally, is even more chaotic than the international one. Even when you've made advance reservations you may have to wait as long as four hours to pick up your ticket.

To make reservations or to enquire about the wait list you can reach PAL at the following numbers in Manila: ☎ 81 6691, 831 0622, 521 3694 or 50 6120.

PAL no longer monopolises all domestic services. There are now a number of smaller operators like Aerolift and Pacific Airways and they've become popular since the spate of late-1980s shipping disasters.

BUS

There are an enormous number of bus services running all over the Philippines and they are generally very economical. As a rule of thumb on a regular bus you cover about four km per peso and average about 50 km an hour. Thus a 100-km journey will cost about P25 and take about two hours. Air-con buses will be more expensive and trips on gravel roads are more expensive than on sealed roads.

Departures are very frequent although buses sometimes leave early if they're full – take care if there's only one bus a day! People like to travel early when it's cool so there will probably be more buses going early in the day. Note that on Luzon all roads lead to Manila and so do all bus routes. If you're heading from South Luzon to North Luzon you'll have to take one bus into Manila and another out. The main companies include Pantranco, Dangwatranco, Victory Liner and Philippine Rabbit.

As well as the regular buses there are more expensive air-con buses (and even more expensive tour buses) operated by companies like Sarkies Tours. Typical fares from Manila for ordinary buses include Alaminos (237 km; P66), Baguio (250 km; P63), Batangas (110 km; P28), Olongapo (126 km; P45) or Legaspi (544 km; P183).

TRAIN

There were once only three passenger rail services in the Philippines and that has now shrunk to one which looks unlikely to last long. The only route left is south from Manila almost to Legaspi in the Bicol region of South Luzon. The service is so slow and unreliable that everyone recommends the bus. The service north from Manila to San Fernando and the route on the island of Panay have both closed down.

BOAT

Getting around by boat is much easier than in Indonesia – it's not a matter of 'will there be a boat this week?' but 'will there be a boat this day?' – often '...this morning?' And the boats are cheap, usually comfortable and pretty fast. The Philippines' mass of islands are very tightly packed which makes all the difference.

The real hub of the shipping services is Cebu – everything seems to run through here, and there are many shipping companies. Apart from the major inter-island ships there are also many ferries shuttling back and forth between nearby islands.

The main booking offices will often tell you that the economy tickets are sold out when, if you ask at the pier, you'll find they are still available. Also enquire about student discounts, some shipping lines give 20% or 30%. Fares differ markedly from company to company but some typical fares by a variety of shipping lines from Manila are shown in the table.

Ship travel has its disadvantages. The first is that standards do vary and some of the boats are dirty, badly kept and overcrowded. A rough voyage with plenty of seasick fellow passengers can be a real trial. The more serious problem is safety. A disastrous collision just before Christmas 1987 where a Sulpicio Line ship went down, with something like 2000 deaths and only 24 survivors, focused international attention on something Filipinos have been all too aware of for some time.

The small local boats are often the worst as they may be grossly overloaded and safety equipment simply nonexistent. Even the very short trips can be risky – there have been some unhappy incidents at Boracay (no deaths but people have lost all their gear), and the Roxas (Mindoro) to Tablas (Romblon) boats are particularly bad.

Drinks are usually available on board but, on longer trips, it's not a bad idea to bring some food supplies. Be prepared for long unscheduled stops at ports along the way. It's important to allow for a flexible schedule if travelling by ship.

LOCAL TRANSPORT
Jeepneys

The true Filipino local transport is the jeepney. The recipe for a jeepney is: take one ex-US-Army jeep, put two benches in the back with enough space for about 12 people, paint it every colour of the rainbow, add tassles, badges, horns, lights, aerials, about a dozen rear-view mirrors, a tape deck with a selection of Filipino rock music, a chrome horse (or better a whole herd of them) and anything else you can think of. Then stuff 20 passengers on those benches for 12, add four more in front and drive like a maniac. But they're cheap and you'll find them in cities and doing shorter runs between centres.

At one time it was thought the jeepney was a threatened species, disappearing to be replaced by the new locally manufactured South-East Asian utility vehicles. But now it seems the Filipinos are simply making brand new ex-US-Army-style jeeps. They're stretched so you can get more passengers in but otherwise they're just like jeepneys have always been.

The usual jeepney fare is P1.50 for up to the first four km and then 50c (sometimes only 25c) a km. You pay on getting out, or anywhere along the way if you prefer and know what it's going to be. To stop a jeepney (when you want to get off) you can rap on the roof, hiss or use the correct term which is *para* or *bayad* which is Tagalog for payment.

For longer journeys in the country, it's wise to find out what the fare should be before you set off. Beware of 'Special Rides' where you charter the whole vehicle. Try not to be the first person to get into an empty jeepney, because if the driver suddenly takes off you may find you've chartered it. Take care also if several men suddenly get in to a jeepney and all try to sit near you. Chances are you're being set up to be pickpocketed – get off and find another vehicle.

Taxis

Taxis are all metered in Manila and they are almost the cheapest in the world. Insist that the meter is used and make sure you have plenty of small change, the driver certainly won't if it's to his advantage. In smaller towns, taxis may not be metered and you will have to negotiate your fare beforehand – tricycles are cheaper. PU-Cabs, found in some larger towns but not in Manila, are small unmetered taxis.

Other Local Transport

The other local transport, mainly found in smaller towns, are tricycles, which are small Japanese motorbikes with a crudely made side-car. Normal passenger load should be two or three but six and seven are not unknown! Fares generally start at P1 – longer distances are by negotiation. You'll also see some bicycle trishaws. *Calesas* are two-wheeled horse carriages found in Manila's Chinatown, in Vigan in North

Luzon and in Cebu City where they are known as *tartanillas*.

Manila

The capital of the Philippines and by far the largest city, Metro Manila has a population of over 10 million. Although it sprawls for a great distance along Manila Bay the main places of interest are fairly central. Manila is not a city of great interest in itself, it's really just an arrival and departure point for the rest of the Philippines. Once you've seen the Spanish remains in Intramuros you've pretty much seen all Manila has to offer in an historic sense.

The other Manila attraction, however, is entertainment – there are countless reasonably priced restaurants, pubs, folk music clubs, girlie bars, pick-up joints and anything else you could ask for. Apart from closing the *jai alai fronton*, Cory Aquino doesn't seem to have altered much of Manila's raunchy nightlife.

Orientation & Information

Manila is quite a sprawling town but the main places of interest and/or importance to the visitor are concentrated just south of the Pasig River. Immediately south of the river is Intramuros, the old Spanish town, where many of Manila's historic buildings are. South of that is the long rectangle of Rizal Park (the Luneta), the lungs of the central area.

Then south again is Ermita, the often raucous area for restaurants, bars, hotels, travel agencies, airlines and Manila's active sex-and-sin side. You'll find not only the big international hotels but many of the medium and low-priced places in Ermita. There's more cheap accommodation across Taft Ave, the road that parallels the coast beside Ermita. Although the Ermita area is the visitor's downtown Manila, the businessman's downtown is Makati – several km away.

Beware of overfriendly Filipinos in Manila. Unwary tourists are often picked up around Luneta or simply pickpocketed while wandering the park. Beware of the Manila slum areas too. It is here that 'a mad scramble to pick your pockets ensues', one visitor commented!

Tourist Office The Department of Tourism's grand office (☎ 59 9031, 50 1928) is in Ermita at the Taft Ave end of Rizal Park. The actual TIC is on the ground floor. The staff are friendly and hand out lots of useful brochures and a good Manila map. There are smaller counters just behind customs at the airport and at the nearby Nayong Pilipino complex.

The DOT also maintains a 24-hour tourist assistance hotline (☎ 50 1660/728) for 'travel information, emergency assistance, lost & found and language problems'.

STA Travel (☎ 832 0680) have their student travel office at 4227 Tomas Claudio St, in Paranaque, beside the Excelsior Hotel.

Post Office The main GPO for poste restante mail is near the river in Intramuros. There's a post office in Ermita on Mabini but the small office at the harbour end of Rizal Park, near the Manila Hotel, is generally not so busy.

Bookshops The Casalinda Bookstore in the Philbank Building on the corner of Ayala Ave and Herrera St, Makati, is a small shop with a good selection of books on the Philippines. The National Bookstore at 701 Rizal Ave in Santa Cruz is the largest bookstore in the Philippines and has a number of other branches in the Metro Manila area. Solidaridad on Padre Faura is particularly good for political books.

For maps go to the Bureau of Coast & Geodetic Survey on Barraca St in San Nicolas.

Other Information There's a laundromat in R Salas St, Ermita, between Mabini and Adriatico Sts. Mayer Photo in Carlos Palanca St, Quiapo, has cheap film. There are more camera shops around the corner in

Hidalgo St. There's a convenient 7-Eleven on the corner of Padre Faura and Adriatico St in Ermita.

Things to See

Intramuros The bitter fighting at the end of WW II did a pretty good job of flattening Manila but there are still some places of interest in Intramuros, the oldest part of the city.

The first Chinese settlement at the site of Manila was destroyed almost immediately by Limahong, an unfriendly Chinese pirate who dropped by in 1574. The Spanish rebuilt this centre as a fort. In 1590 the wooden fort was replaced by stone and it was gradually extended until it became a walled city which they called Intramuros. The walls were three km long, 13 metres thick and six metres high. Seven main gates entered the city, in which there were 15 churches and six monasteries – and lots of Spanish who kept the Filipinos at arm's length.

The walls are just about all that was left after WW II finished off what MacArthur had started. During the 1930s he had his HQ there and 'modernised' the place by knocking down lots of old buildings and widening those nasty narrow streets.

San Agustin The church and monastery of San Agustin is one of the few buildings left from the earliest construction. It was here in 1898 that the last Spanish governor of Manila surrendered to the Filipinos. There is a museum inside which is open daily from 8 am to 12 noon and 1 to 5 pm. Admission is P20 for adults and P15 for children.

Cathedral The Roman Catholic Cathedral is also in Intramuros and has a history that reads like that of a lot of Spanish-built churches in the Philippines. Built 1581, damaged (typhoon) 1582, destroyed (fire) 1583, rebuilt 1592, partially destroyed (earthquake) 1600, rebuilt 1614, destroyed (earthquake) 1645, rebuilt 1654-71, destroyed (earthquake) 1863, rebuilt 1870-79, destroyed (WW II) 1945, rebuilt 1954-58. On that average an earthquake should knock it down again in 2006.

Fort Santiago The ruins of the old Spanish fort, at one time connected to Intramuros, stand just north of the cathedral. They are now used as a pleasant park – you can see the collection of the Presidents' cars (rusting) and climb up top for the view over the Pasig River. The most interesting part of the fort is the **Rizal Shrine Museum** with many items used or made by the Filipino martyr. The room in which he was imprisoned before his execution can be seen. The shrine is open daily from 9 am to 12 noon and 1 to 5 pm and entry is P2.50.

Fort Santiago's darkest days took place during WW II when it was used as a prison by the Japanese. During the closing days of the war, they went on an orgy of killing, and in one small cell the bodies of 600 Filipinos and Americans were discovered.

Fort Santiago is open daily from 8 am to 9 pm and admission is P2.50.

Rizal Park – The Luneta Intramuros is separated from Ermita, the tourist centre, by the Rizal Memorial Park, better known as the Luneta. It's a meeting and entertainment place for all of Manila – particularly on Sunday when it's packed with people, ice cream and balloon sellers and all kinds of activities are conducted. At the bay end of the park is the **Rizal Memorial**. Rizal's execution spot is close by.

A Japanese and a Chinese garden flank the planetarium – favourite meeting spots for young couples. It's a little difficult, however, to hide behind a miniature Japanese tree for a passionate clinch. There's a small admission fee to each of these parks. Further up there are fountains, a roller-skating circuit and a children's amusement park.

At the Taft Ave end there's a gigantic pond with a three-dimensional map of the Philippines. Once you know a little of the geography of the country it's fascinating to wander around it and contemplate just how many islands there are. There's a three-metre-high viewing platform beside it. Also

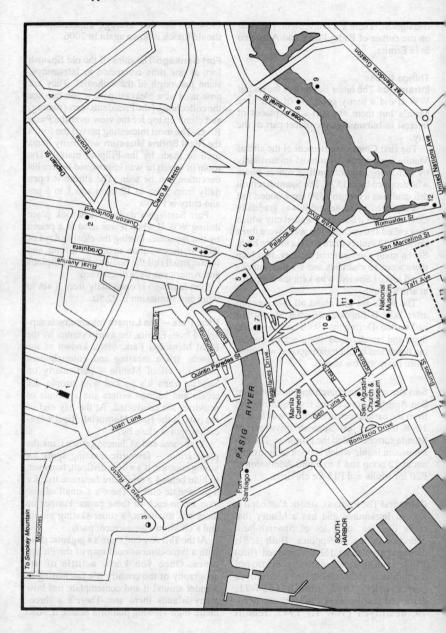

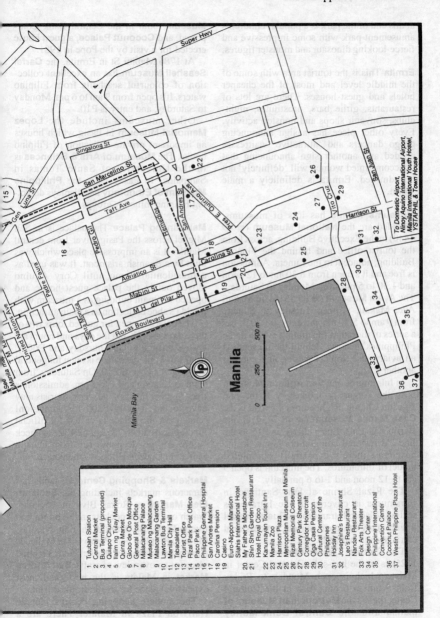

Manila

0   250   500 m

1 Tutuban Station
2 Central Market
3 Bus Terminal (proposed)
4 Quiapo Church
5 Ilaim ng Tulay Market
   Quinta Market
6 Globo de Oro Mosque
7 General Post Office
8 Malacanang Palace
   Museo ng Malacanang
9 Malacanang Garden
10 Lawton Bus Terminal
11 Manila City Hall
12 Tabacalera
13 Tourist Office
14 Rizal Park Post Office
15 Paco Park
16 Philippine General Hospital
17 San Andres Market
18 Carolina Pension
19 Casino
   Euro-Nippon Mansion
20 Silahis International Hotel
   My Father's Moustache
21 Shin Shin Garden Restaurant
   Hotel Royal Coco
22 Kanumayan Tourist Inn
23 Manila Zoo
24 Harrison Plaza
25 Metropolitan Museum of Manila
26 Rizal Memorial Coliseum
27 Century Park Sheraton
28 Corregidor Hovercraft
29 Olga Casa Pension
30 Cultural Center of the
   Philippines
31 Holiday Inn
32 Josephine's Restaurant
   Leo's Restaurant
   Nandau Restaurant
33 Folk Arts Theater
34 Design Center
35 Philippine International
   Convention Center
36 Coconut Palace
37 Westin Philippine Plaza Hotel

at this end of the park is a popular children's amusement park with some impressive and fierce-looking dinosaur and monster figures.

Ermita This is the tourist area with some of the middle level and most of the cheaper hotels and guest houses. There are lots of restaurants, girlie bars, prostitutes, nightclubs, souvenir shops and nonstop activity. Every other place has a sign announcing go-go dancers and 'attractive' waitresses needed and another sign announcing that unaccompanied women will 'definitely' not be admitted. Ermita is definitely a male world.

Museums Manila has lots of museums. Included are the **National Museum** (☎ 49 4440) in the Executive Building, across from the tourist office and behind the Finance Building, adjacent to the Luneta. Admission is free and it's open from 8.30 am to 12 noon and 1.30 to 5 pm from Monday to Saturday. The **Ayala Museum** (☎ 85 5316) on Makati Ave, Makati, is open Tuesday to Sunday from 9 am to 5.30 pm and entry is P20. It has a series of dioramas illustrating events in the Philippines' history. Behind the museum is an aviary and tropical garden and entry is another P22.

In Intramuros, the **San Agustin Museum** is in the Augustine monastery at the San Agustin Church. Right across the road is the **Casa Manila Museum** (☎ 48 7734) in the Barrio San Luis. Entry charge is P15 to the fine old restored colonial-era home. In the basement there's a partially completed model of Intramuros. The museum is open 9 am to 12 noon and 1 to 6 pm daily.

The Rizal Shrine at Fort Santiago in Intramuros is covered in the Intramuros section. Also in Intramuros is **Puerta Isabel II** with many liturgical objects, processional carriages and old bells.

The **Cultural Center Museum** (☎ 832 1125) is in the bay-side Cultural Center in Malate which is open Monday to Friday from 9 am to 6 pm. Also at the Cultural Center there's the **Metropolitan Museum of Manila** and the **Central Bank Money Museum**, both in the Central Bank Compound, and **Coconut Palace**, a guest house erected for a visit by the Pope in 1981.

At 1786 Mabini St in Ermita, the **Carfel Seashell Museum** has an excellent collection of colourful seashells from Filipino waters. It's open from 9 am to 6 pm, Monday to Saturday, and entry is P10.

Other museums include the **Lopez Memorial Museum** in Pasig which houses an important private collection of Filipino books. The **Museum of Arts & Sciences** is in the University of Santo Tomas in Sampaloc. In Pasay City, the **Philippine Museum of Ethnology** has displays depicting Filipino minority groups.

Malacanang Palace The palace is in San Miguel across the Pasig River from central Manila. It is an impressive place which was built by a Spanish aristocrat. It was used as a presidential home until Cory Aquino moved out to the palace guest house and opened the main building as a museum with Imelda's shoe collection as a main attraction.

The palace is open for guided tours two or three days a week, but the days and hours are always changing. On Thursday and Friday, from 1 to 3 pm, the palace is open for general viewing at a cost of P10. On Saturday, from 9 am to 12 noon and 1 to 3 pm, admission is free. At other times of the week, tourists may have to pay a hefty P200 for admission! Sometimes the palace is closed for official functions so call 40 7775 or 62 1321 to check before you go. Jeepneys run from Quiapo Market at Quezon Bridge to the palace.

Markets & Shopping Centres Manila has numerous markets including the **Baclaran Flea Market** on Roxas Blvd in Baclaran. Watch out for pickpockets in the bright and lively **Divisoria Market** in San Nicolas. **Pistang Pilipino** near Pedro Gil in Malate is a fairly lifeless tourist market but it's a good place for an overview of crafts. **San Andres Market** in Malate is the best (and most expensive) place for exotic tropical fruit.

The modern shopping centres include Harrison Plaza in Malate. There are a number of centres like Makati Commercial Center in Makati, Araneta Center in Cubao, SM City in Quezon City and Greenhills shopping centre in San Juan. There are good fast-food places and a cinema complex in these shopping centres.

The Extremes – Forbes Park & Tondo To appreciate the depths of the nation's problems, it's worth visiting Forbes Park and Tondo to find the opposite spectrum of the Philippines 'haves' and 'have nots'. Forbes Park is a cluster of opulent mansions in the southern part of Makati. Take a taxi from the Makati Commercial Center as you're unlikely to get by the guards on foot.

In North Harbour, the slum quarter of Tondo is the other side of the equation and, at Smokey Mountain, you reach the depths of Philippines poverty where about 3000 families live in huts actually on the municipal tip. They comb the garbage for saleable or recyclable refuse.

Other Across the river, **Chinatown** is interesting to wander through, and the luxurious **Chinese Cemetery**, about two km north of Chinatown near the Abad Santos Metrorail terminal, is a bizarre attraction. A tricycle from the station to the south gate will be P5. It's in the north of Santa Cruz, just where Rizal Ave becomes Rizal Ave Extension.

Quiapo, an older and more traditional part of Manila, has the Quiapo Church by Quezon Bridge. The **wooden statue of Christ** known as the 'Black Nazarene' can be seen here.

Nayong Pilipino is the Filipino edition of 'the whole country in miniature'. It's out by the international airport and it has lots of handicraft shops as well as a good little folk museum with some incredible photographs of the forgotten Tasaday tribe. Entry is P80 for tourists and P12 for Filipinos, and it's open 9 am to 6 pm and to 7 pm on Saturday and Sunday.

Places to Stay

There is a wide variety of accommodation possibilities in Manila, many of them close to the central Ermita area. Cheapest are the hostel and Ys but there are also many cheap hotels and pensions.

Hostels & Guest Houses Many of the cheaper guest houses and pensions offer dormitory accommodation. There are numerous small places around Ermita ranging from rock bottom in prices and standards and up. Some of the streets in Ermita can be very noisy so check where the room is if you're going to stay in a guest house on a busy street.

At times a lot of the cheaper places are full. If you've just arrived in Manila, it might be a good idea to check the DOT information desk at the airport, where there's an exhaustive list of just about everything available in the city. Many of the guest houses can be booked through the tourist office desk at the airport – a few phone calls could save you a lot of walking.

The *Youth Hostel Philippines* (☎ 59 2507) at 1572 Leon Guinto St has dorm beds in fan-cooled rooms at P75 – with a YHA card it is P2 less. There are also singles/doubles from P160. If you're heading up country you can store baggage here for P10 a day.

Manila International Youth Hostel (☎ 832 0680) at 4227 Tomas Claudio St, Paranaque, has dorm beds for P75 (YHA members P50). It's a good clean place with a garden and is also the office for YSTAPHIL, the Youth & Student Travel Association of the Philippines. It is next to the Excelsior Hotel, on the corner of Roxas Blvd (asking for the Excelsior will make taxi trips easier).

The *Town House* (☎ 833 1939) at the Villa Carolina Townhouse, 201 Roxas Blvd, Unit 31, Paranaque, has dorm beds with fan for P50, singles with fan for P80, doubles with fan from P140 to P180 and with fan and bath for P220. It is pleasant with a friendly atmosphere created by Bill and Laura, who like travelling themselves. It's in a small side street called Sunset Drive and is only about five-minutes away by taxi (which costs P15) from the Domestic Airport and the Ninoy Aquino International Airport.

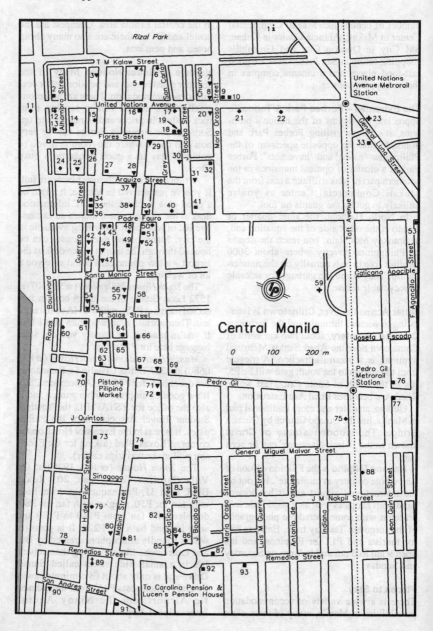

■ PLACES TO STAY

2	The Miramar
5	Mabini Pension & Majestic Apartments
9	Manila Pavilion Hotel
10	Hilton Hotel
14	Swagman Hotel
16	Southern Cross Inn
18	Hotel Soriente
27	Richmond Pension
32	Pension Filipinas
33	Jetset Executive Mansion
34	Diamond Inn
35	Sandico Apartment Hotel
36	Iseya Hotel & Restaurant
41	Luisa & ECA Pension House
49	Tower Hotel
51	Luisa Pension House & Munchen Grill
53	Casa Dalco
58	Sundowner Hotel
61	Sleepy Cheaper Guest House
62	Old Heidelberg & Swiss Bistro
63	White House Tourist Inn
64	La Soledad Pension
65	Ermita Tourist Inn
66	Santos Pension House
67	Mabini House
69	Manila Midtown Hotel
72	Rothman Inn Hotel
73	Pension Natividad
74	Olga Casa Pension
76	Youth Hostel
77	New Olga Casa Pension
82	Malate Pensionne
83	Lucky Pensionne
87	Remedios Pensionne House
91	Casa Dalco (II)
92	Circle Pension
93	Remedios 628

▼ PLACES TO EAT & ENTERTAINMENT

3	Hong Kong Restaurant
7	Kentucky Fried Chicken
8	McDonald's
20	Max's
25	Down the Road
26	Myrna's Restaurant
28	Shakey's Pizza
29	Birdwatchers Swagman

30	Barrio Fiesta
31	Seafood Restaurant
37	Holandia
39	Kamayan & Kashmir Restaurants
42	Lili Marleen
43	Edelweiss
44	Mrs Wong's Tea House
46	Swiss Hut
47	Guernica's Restaurant
52	Mister Donut
54	Australian Club
55	Hula Hut & Rosie's Diner
56	Al-Sham's
57	Kowloon House
61	Fischfang
68	El Comedor Restaurant
71	Zamboanga Restaurant
78	Shakey's Pizza
79	Weinstube
80	Hobbit House
84	Hard Rock Café
85	Café Adriatico
86	Moviola
90	Aristocrat Restaurant

OTHER

1	Tourist Office
4	Pakistan Airlines
6	Singapore Airlines
11	US Embassy
12	JAL, Japan Asia Airlines
13	Korean Airlines
15	Telex Office
17	Alemar's Book Shop
19	International Supermarket
21	American Express
22	Western Police Station
23	Manila Medical Centre
24	Northwest Orient Airlines
38	The Bookmark
40	Solidaridad Book Shop
45	Padre Faura Shopping Centre
48	PT & T Telegrams
50	7-Eleven
59	Philippine General Hospital
60	Philippine Airlines (PAL)
70	Thai Airlines
75	PLDT Long Distance Telephone
81	Carfels Seashell Museum
88	Philippine Airlines (PAL)
89	Church of Malate

Malate Pensionne (☎ 59 3489) at 1771 Adriatico St, Malate, is off the main road and, therefore, quieter. This friendly and helpful place has a small restaurant area downstairs and is probably the most popular travellers' centre in Manila. A dorm bed costs P70 with fan and P90 with air-con. Single rooms cost P210 with fan, P300 with fan and private bathroom and, lastly, P400 with air-con and private bathroom. Prostitutes from the nearby strip are kept at bay.

At 2116 Carolina St, Malate, the *Carolina Pension* (☎ 522 3961) has rooms from around P100 up towards P300 for a room with air-con and bath. *Lucen's Pension House* (☎ 522 2389), not far away at 2158 Carolina St, has a variety of rooms with fan and air-con from around P200.

Santos Pension House (☎ 59 5628) at 1540 Mabini St, Ermita, across from Kowloon House, also has a pleasant atmosphere and used to be something of a Peace Corps hang-out before the US recalled all PC volunteers. The dorm is no more. Doubles with fan are P230, with fan and bathroom P280 and with air-con and bathroom P380. The rooms vary in quality but they're clean and there's a restaurant.

In the central Ermita area, the well-run *White House Tourist Inn* (☎ 522 1535) is at 465 Pedro Gil St, on the corner of M H Del Pilar. A single/double with fan and bath is P240/320, or with air-con and bath P420. There's a restaurant in this quite reasonable place. The *Richmond Pension* (☎ 58 5277) is tucked away at 1165 Grey St, Ermita, and has small rooms with fan for P130/220 and rooms with air-con for P280.

The *Mabini Pension* (☎ 59 4853) at 1337 Mabini St, Ermita, has dorm beds at P80, singles/doubles with fan for P180/220, doubles with fan and bath for P280 or with air-con and bath for P400. Although the rooms vary it's clean and the people there are friendly and helpful.

The *ECA Pension House* (☎ 521 8769, 59 5257) is at 1248 Jorge Bocobo St, Ermita, and has singles with fan from P140 to P180, doubles with fan for P230 and singles/doubles with fan and bath for

P300/330. Doubles with air-con and bath are P480.

Pension Filipinas (☎ 521 1496) is at 542 Arkansas St, Ermita, close to the corner of Maria Y Orosa. It's well kept and pleasant and has all air-con rooms for P300/350.

There are two 'Olga Casas'. *Olga Casa Pension* (☎ 59 6265) at 640 Vito Cruz, Malate, is near the Century Park Sheraton Hotel. In this fine old building, rooms with fan are P200/240 or doubles with fan and bath are P270. With air-con and bath prices range from P320 to P420.

There's also the *New Casa Olga Pension* on Leon Guinto St, Malate, on the corner with Pedro Gil. Here rooms with fan are P160/190 or a double with fan and bath is P240.

There are also a couple of Casa Dalcos, both quite pleasant. The *Casa Dalco* (☎ 50 7558) at 1910 Mabini St, Malate, is just down from Hobbit House. The air-con rooms are small and simple and cost from P380 to P500. The second *Casa Dalco* (☎ 59 8522, 50 8825) is a beautiful old house at 1318 F Agoncillo St, on the corner of Padre Faura and across Taft Ave from Ermita. Rooms here start from P180 with fan, P200 for a double with fan and bath, P300 with air-con or P400 with air-con and private bath.

The *Lucky Pensionne* (☎ 521 4845, 59 7166) is at 1726 Adriatico, Malate, and has a restaurant and very small rooms with fan at P120/160. At the *Diamond Inn* at 1217 M H Del Pilar St, Ermita, a double with air-con and bath is P250 but the street side of the building is noisy. *La Soledad Pension House* (☎ 50 0706) at 1529 Mabini St, Ermita has singles/doubles with fan for P120/170 or doubles with air-con for P280. There's a common room and kitchen facilities in this clean and well-run place.

The *Pension Natividad* (☎ 521 0524) at 1690 M H Del Pilar St, Malate, has dorm beds with fan for P80 or with air-con they are P110. Doubles with fan and bath are P450 and with air-con and bath P600. At 1511 M H Del Pilar St, Ermita, the *Sleepy Cheaper* (☎ 521 9019) has simple but clean rooms with fan for P125/150 or doubles with fan and bath for P250.

There are a couple of more expensive guest houses on Remedios St. *Remedios Pensionne House* (☎ 58 5277) at 609 Remedios St, Ermita, is a simple private guest house with good singles with fan for P150, with fan and bath for P250 or singles/doubles with air-con and bath for P350/400. Another *Remedios* (☎ 572 2985) at 628 Remedios has very basic rooms for P100/130 and up. Nearby is the *Circle Pension* (☎ 522 2920) at 602 Remedios St, Malate, with simple, clean, well-kept single/double rooms with fan for P250/330 or with air-con for P350/430.

The *Midtown Inn* (☎ 58 2882) at 551 Padre Faura St burnt down and its replacement at the same location will cost from P300 for a single room with fan and bath. All rooms facing the street are very noisy.

Hotels & Apartments Manila has a number of middle range hotels, slightly more expensive than the pensions and guest houses. In this same bracket there are numerous apartments, usually with cooking facilities. Although they are usually intended for longer term visitors it is possible to stay at some on a short term basis.

The *Southern Cross Inn* (☎ 58 6883/951) at 476 United Nations Ave, Ermita, has small and pretty basic rooms with TV, fridge, air-con and bathroom for P680. The entrance is on Mabini St. The *Sundowner Hotel* (☎ 521 2751) at 1430 Mabini St, Malate, has an attractive lobby and is a departure point for tour buses to various locations around Manila including Puerto Galera. Air-con rooms with fridge are P930/1234.

The *Swagman Hotel* (☎ 50 5816/28) at 411 A Flores St, Ermita, is a clean and well-kept place with rooms at P645 with fan, P810 with air-con. The air-con rooms also have a fridge and TV. At 1549 Mabini St, the *Ermita Tourist Inn* (☎ 521 8770/3) is also good value with air-con rooms with bath from P425 to P495. They also offer weekly and monthly rates and meals in the restaurant are good value.

The *Sandico Apartment Hotel* (☎ 59 2036) on M H Del Pilar St, Ermita, has rooms with air-con and bath, fridge and TV for P330/530. The *Majestic Apartments* (☎ 50 7606/7) at 1038 Roxas Blvd, Ermita, on the corner of United Nations Ave has rooms with air-con and bath from P450 per single and P480 per double.

The *Kanumayan Tourist Inn* (☎ 57 3660/9) is at 2284 Taft Ave, Malate, and has pleasant air-con rooms at P695/820, and there's also a beautiful swimming pool in the garden. Across Taft Ave, the *Jetset Executive Mansion* (☎ 521 4029/30) is at 1205 General Luna St, Ermita, and has air-con rooms at P540 or one-bedroom apartments at P685.

Other middle bracket places include the central and convenient *Rothman Inn Hotel* (☎ 521 9251/60) at 1633-1635 Adriatico St, Malate, with air-con rooms at a variety of prices from P800 to P950. The more expensive rooms have fridges. Directly above the International Supermarket, the *Hotel Soriente* (☎ 59 9133) is at 595 A Flores St, Ermita, on the corner of Jorge Bocobo St, and has clean air-con rooms at P690.

Places to Eat
Manila is full of places to eat – all types of food and at all types of prices. The tourist ghetto of Ermita is a good hunting ground. Although you'll pay more here than in other parts of the Philippines, you'll still find good, reasonably priced food of all types. Apart from Filipino food and a variety of other Asian cuisines there are also Western fast-food operators and a choice of fixed-price buffets at the best hotels.

The recommendations that follow are essentially in Ermita and Malate because most visitors will be staying there. There are plenty of other restaurants in Makati, Binondo, Intramuros and in other parts of Manila.

Filipino Food On busy M H Del Pilar St, Ermita, *Myrna's* is a popular and often crowded little place appealing essentially to local people rather than the tourist crowds. It's closed on Sunday and a meal typically costs about P80.

Barrio Fiesta at 110 Jorge Bocobo St is a

popular place for real Filipino food and is usually full of people really tucking in. Try crispy pata or kare-kare in this bright, cheerful and busy place. The menu is extensive but the prices are a little more expensive than ordinary restaurants, about P100 to P200 for a meal.

Definitely more expensive but probably worth it is the *Kamayan* on Padre Faura St in Ermita, near the corner with Mabini St. The name means 'bare hands' because that's what you eat with, knives and forks aren't used. The food, however, is not only authentic but it's also delicious – tasty, well prepared and relatively expensive. Across the back of the restaurant is a line of tapped water jars for you to wash your hands before and after eating. A meal costs about P200.

The *Aristocrat*, on the corner of Roxas Blvd and San Andres St, Malate, is good value despite the name. This big Filipino restaurant is the most popular of the six Aristocrats in Manila. Try lapu lapu fish (expensive) or the fish soup here – a meal costs about P100.

Further down Roxas Blvd, in Pasay City, *Josephine's* has superb seafood and live music in the evenings. A meal in this well-known restaurant costs about P125.

Other Asian Restaurants You can try plenty of other regional and Western cuisines in Manila. The *Sea Food Market* at 1190 Jorge Bocobo St, Ermita, right across the road from Barrio Fiesta, positively bounces. You select your fish or other seafood from a display area on one side and it's cooked up by a squad of short order cooks lined up along an open window on the street side.

They're all frantically stirring woks, scooping pots and juggling frying pans while flames leap high. An even larger squad of waiters and waitresses jostle near the counter on the other side. It's wonderful entertainment for passers-by. A meal here will cost about P200 and you can round it off with coffee and cakes in the *Café Alps* next door.

Manila has a great number of Japanese and Chinese restaurants. For simple and economical Chinese food try *Mrs Wong's* *Tea House* on the corner of Padre Faura and M H Del Pilar Sts, Ermita. A meal will cost about P50.

Other good Chinese restaurants include the *Hong Kong Restaurant* on M H Del Pilar St, Ermita, and *Kowloon House* on Mabini St, Malate. There are even more Chinese restaurants across the river in Chinatown and Binondo.

Next to the Kamayan Restaurant on Padre Faura there's good north Indian food at *Kashmir* – about P200 for a meal. *Al-Sham's* on Mabini St, Malate, is slightly cheaper. For Japanese food, the *Iseya Restaurant* on Padre Faura St in Ermita, is good value with a P50 business lunch and regular meals at around P75. There are a number of Thai restaurants in Makati including the *Sukhothai* on Makati Ave where you can eat for about P75. The *Vietnam Food House* on Harrison St, Pasay City, is small but popular and also costs about P75.

Western Restaurants There are plenty of Western restaurants like the very pleasant *Café Adriatico*, at 1790 Adriatico St. This is a good place for a drink or a meal, there are tables outside and others, upstairs, overlook the Rotary Circle street scene. The food ranges from burgers to pasta, it's not cheap but it is a very relaxed, stylish place to dine.

The German and Swiss influence can be felt strongly down M H Del Pilar St, Ermita, where you can eat at *Edelweiss, Fischfang* or the *Swiss Hut* for P75 to P100. At similar prices, try the *München Grill Pub* on Mabini St, Ermita, or *Old Heidelberg* on Soldado St, Ermita, where there is a small beer garden. Just next door is the *Swiss Bistro*, a popular meeting place serving European food and good sandwiches.

On the corner of Adriatico St and Pedro Gil, Ermita, *El Comedor* offers traditional Spanish food at around P250. There's live music in the pleasant and slightly cheaper *Guernica's* on M H Del Pilar St, Ermita.

Other international possibilities include Australian-style food and beer at the *Rooftop Restaurant* on top of the Iseya Hotel at the corner of Padre Faura and M H Del Pilar Sts,

Ermita. There's a good view over the bay and an Aussie barbecue on Sunday. Mexican food can be found at *Aunt Mary's Aunt* in Greenbelt Square, Makati Ave, Makati, or at *Tia Maria* on General Luna St, off Makati Ave. *Max's* on Maria Orosa St, Ermita, is one of 10 branches around the city and offers a variety of chicken dishes at about P100.

Buffets All-you-can-eat breakfast buffets typically cost P100 to P150 at the big hotels in Manila. The *Sundowner Hotel* on Mabini St, Ermita, offers one at P90.

At the big tourist hotels lunch buffets typically cost P120 to P180, plus 25% government tax and service. Dinner at one of these places would be P200 to P300 and is often accompanied by cultural entertainment or a fashion show.

Fast Food & Cheap Eats Manila has lots of fast-food places including a selection of *McDonald's, Kentucky Frieds, Pizza Huts* and *Shakey's Pizzas*. Shakeys are quite a Philippines institution – you'll find one at the corner of Mabini and Arquiza and another on Remedios near Roxas Blvd and they do pretty good pizza. The Harrison Plaza shopping centre, beside the Century Park Sheraton Hotel, has a *Pizza Hut, McDonald's* and *Kentucky Fried* all together. Doughnut specialists are also popular and 7-Elevens are also appearing in the Philippines. *Jollibee* is a local burger chain with numerous branches and there's one on Padre Faura, Ermita.

If you're looking for cheap eats there's street food at any time, the small bakeries are good for a pan de sal breakfast while the residents of the *Malate Pensionne* often seem reluctant to shift from their low-priced restaurant area.

Entertainment
There is plenty to do after hours in Manila. Around Ermita you'll find good folk music, jazz or rock in the bars. All it costs in most places is a beer at a peso or two above normal rates.

Music The folk clubs often have amazing 'replicas' of Dylan, Simon & Garfunkel, James Taylor or other Western pop stars. Try the popular *Hobbit House* at 1801 Mabini St. After 8.30 pm there's a P80 minimum charge and waiters here are indeed all hobbit-sized as it's entirely staffed by dwarfs. There's good food, particularly during the happy hour when there's no cover charge. Further along from Ermita, in Malate, *My Father's Moustache*, at 2144 M H Del Pilar St, also has good folk music.

Jazz can be heard in several of the international hotels but, particularly, in *Birdland* on the corner of Tomas Morato St and Timog Ave, Quezon City. There's a P75 to P120 cover charge.

Bars There are plenty of bars where you can sit quietly with a cold beer. Try *Lili Marleen, Edelweiss, Guernica's, Gordon's* or the *Weinstube*, all on M H Del Pilar St, Ermita. Others include the *Southern Cross* on United Nations Ave, *Holandia* on Arquiza St and the *Boomerang Club* on Mabini St. Every nationality is catered for!

On the other hand there are also several blocks of M H Del Pilar with virtually side-by-side bars and pick-up joints. You'll find that cold beer is on the menu but quiet is definitely not. They range from big, glossy and well-run bars like the *Australian Club, Superstar* or the *Firehouse* to many locally run bars in this red hot red-light district.

There's usually a cheaper happy hour from 12 noon to 8 pm; otherwise, at a typical Ermita bar, drink prices tend to gyrate up and down depending on what's happening behind or on top of the bar. At 'showtime', which usually means whoever is dancing around on the bar takes off what little they had on, prices jump. Gentlemen who decide to purchase what is really on sale here should be aware that every other establishment along this strip of M H Del Pilar seems to be offering quick cures for sexually transmitted diseases.

Bistros & Music Lounges Places for a drink and a snack have become very popular.

The *Café Adriatico* at 1790 Adriatico St, Malate, near the Remedios Circle started the craze and is still a favourite. Next door is the *Hard Rock Café*, with an aeroplane crashing into the roof and rock music videos.

Also on Remedios Circle is *Moviola* with a piano bar and restaurant, while nearby on Remedios St is the lively *Penguin Café*. In Makati the *Bistro RJ* in the Olympia Building, Makati Ave, features live '50s and '60s music with admission costs varying from P50 to P100 (depending on the night).

Discos Manila is very much disco-land with popular places like *Billboard* on Makati Ave, Makati. Entry is P50 on Friday and Saturday nights but it's free on other nights. *Rumours* on South Drive, Makati Commercial Center, is the biggest disco in Manila and entry is P50.

Others include *Stargazer* in the Silahis Hotel, Roxas Blvd, Malate, and *Club Valentino* in the Manila Midtown Hotel, on the corner of Pedro Gil and Adriatico Sts, Ermita. *Lost Horizon* is in the Philippine Plaza Hotel, Cultural Center complex, Malate, while *La Cage* on Roxas Blvd, Pasay City, caters to the same crowd who used to frequent the Coco Banana, once so beloved by gays and transvestites.

Other The jai alai fronton, opposite Rizal Park, was shut down by Aquino's administration for corruption and bet fixing. No sign of when it will reopen. The casinos in the *Silahis Hotel* on Roxas Blvd, Malate, and in the *Manila Pavilion Hotel* on United Nations Ave, Ermita, are in operation again, however. Cockfights are a popular local activity and there are cockpits at various places which operate on Sunday. Films are advertised in the daily press.

Pistang Pilipino on the corner of M H Del Pilar and Pedro Gil Sts, Malate, has afternoon and evening cultural performances which are free. The 11 pm variety show has a P50 cover charge, or P150 when it includes a buffet. *Zamboanga Restaurant* on Adriatico St, Malate, has nightly features of Filipino and Polynesian dancing.

All around the Ermita tourist belt you'll see signs, usually outside Japanese restaurants or bars, saying *karaoke*. This is Japanese-style sing-along where they play the backing music to well-known popular songs and the customers take turns at putting in the words.

Things to Buy
The Philippines is a great handicraft centre and you can find all sorts of interesting things around Manila but, not surprisingly, you'll find them even cheaper out in the country. There are many handicraft shops and centres around Manila – check out the handicrafts bazaar between M H Del Pilar St and Roxas Blvd and the variety of handicraft places at the Nayong Pilipino (demonstrations there on Monday). The Shoemart department store at the Makati Commercial Center is good for souvenirs if you can't get around the country. Prices are fixed and competitive.

In Intramuros, the El Amanecer Building at 744 General Luna St, has Silahis for art and crafts, Chang Rong for antiques and Galeria de las Islas for paintings and sculptures on its three floors. Further up General Luna, opposite San Agustin, is the beautiful Casa Manila complex.

Good buys include canework, carvings, hanging-lamps of shell and clothes. It's hard not to look like a caricature of Marcos in a Barong Tagalog but the short-sleeved version, Barong Polo, is cool and fashionable – authentic ones are made of *pina*, a fabric woven from pineapple fibre.

Bargaining is not done as much in the Philippines as in other South-East Asian countries but you should still haggle a little.

Getting There & Away
Manila is virtually the only entry point to the Philippines. See the Philippines Getting There & Away section for details on flying to the Philippines. Manila is the centre for bus travel to the north and south and for ships from Luzon to the other islands of the Philippines. What little remains of Luzon's railway system also runs from Manila.

Air Manila is the centre for all air services in the Philippines. See the Philippines Getting Around section for details of PAL operations. International departure tax is P250.

Bus The Philippines has a great number of bus companies and they operate from many bus stations. To further complicate matters, some individual companies will have more than one terminal – there might be a south terminal for southbound services and a north one for northbound, for example.

There is no single central long-distance bus station in Manila although the Lawton terminal, just north of Rizal Park and across from the town hall, does have services to a number of popular closer destinations including Batangas (for Puerto Galera) and Santa Cruz (for Pagsanjan). There are continuing rumours about the Lawton terminal being relocated but, so far, it hasn't been. Several terminals including those on E de los Santos Ave (EDSA) in south Manila can be reached by Metrorail.

Coming in to Manila from other centres, buses will generally be signed for their terminal rather than for Manila. The sign may simply announce that the bus is heading for 'Lawton', 'Monumento' or 'Avenida' and it's assumed you know that these are destinations within Manila.

BLTB (Batangas-Laguna-Tayabas Bus Company) (☎ 833 5501) is at EDSA, Pasay City (near Victory and Philtranco lines). Buses operate to Nasugbu, Calamba, Batangas, Santa Cruz (for Pagsanjan) and Lucena.

Lawton Terminal is opposite the city hall. Get a jeepney heading for Monumento from Mabini St or Metrorail to Central terminal. Buses from here run to Batangas, Santa Cruz and Lucena.

Pantranco (☎ 951081) is at 325 Quezon Avenue, Quezon City. Get a jeepney toward Philcoa or Project 8 from Taft Avenue or Mabini St, though these are not frequent. Buses operate to Alaminos and the other beach resorts in Hundred Islands and the north, Cagayan Valley (Tuguegarao, Aparri), Baguio, Bataan, Angeles and Tarlac.

Philippine Rabbit (☎ 711 5819) is at 819 Oroquieta, Santa Cruz (entrance in Rizal Avenue). This station is known as 'Avenida', and if you're coming from the north take a Philippine Rabbit bus marked 'Avenida via Dau'. It takes the Dau Expressway from Angeles and is much faster. Avoid 'Avenida via Caloocan' buses.

The second station is at Rizal Avenue Extension, Caloocan City (Jeepneys toward Monumento from Mabini St or Metrorail go to the R Papa station). Buses operate to various destinations in south-west and central Luzon including Angeles, Baguio, Balanga, Batac, Laoag, Malolos, Mariveles, Olongapo, San Fernando (Pampanga & La Union), Tarlac and Vigan.

Philtranco (☎ 833 5061) is at EDSA, Pasay City. Get a jeepney towards Baclaran from Taft Avenue or MH Del Pilar St or Metrorail to EDSA station. Buses from here run to Daet, Naga, Tabaco, Legaspi, Sorsogon, Leyte and Mindanao.

Victory Liner (☎ 361 1514) is at 713 Rizal Avenue Extension, Caloocan City. Jeepneys toward Monumento from Mabini St or Metrorail go to the North terminal. Buses go to Olongapo and Alaminos from the North terminal.

The south Victory Liner terminal (☎ 833 0293) is at E de los Santos (EDSA) Avenue, Pasay City. Jeepneys and buses heading for Baclaran leave from Taft Ave or M H Del Pilar St – change in Baclaran or before, or take the Metrorail to the EDSA station. Buses from this terminal run to Olongapo, Zambales, Baguio and Dagupan City.

Train The Philippines' shrinking rail operation has contracted to just the one route south from Manila to the Bicol region, and it is much slower and less reliable than the bus services. You are not recommended to use it.

Boat The shipping companies generally advertise departures in the Manila English-language dailies. Cebu, in the Visayas, is the main hub of Filipino shipping, but there are plenty of departures from Manila. Galactica Travels (☎ 521 8770), beside the Ermita Tourist Inn, sells tickets for Aboitiz Lines, Palawan Shipping Corporation and Sweet Lines, saving a trip to the wharves.

Nearly all inter-island departures are made from North Harbour in Manila. If you have trouble finding it ask a coastguard opposite Pier 8. A taxi from Ermita to North Harbour should cost about P30. In the other direction, travelling to Ermita from the harbour after a ship arrival, is likely to be more expensive. Nobody's meter seems to work properly and the fare is likely to be P50 to P100. The jeepney route between the harbour and Ermita is circuitous and slow.

Shipping company offices in Manila are:

Aboitiz Lines
    King's Court Building, Pasong Tamo St, Makati (☎ 88 7451, 816 4875)
    Pier 4, North Harbor, Tondo (☎ 21 7581, 217 3339, 21 8175)
    Destinations: Panay, Romblon
Asuncion Shipping Lines
    3038 Jose Abad Santos St, Tondo (☎ 71 1 0590)
Carlos Gothong Lines
    Pier 10, North Harbor, Tondo (☎ 21 3611, 21 4121)
    Destinations: Cebu, Mindanao, Panay
Negros Navigation Lines
    Negros Navigation Building, 849 Pasay Rd, Makati (☎ 86 4921/5)
    Pier 2, North Harbor, Tondo (☎ 21 7526, 21 9071, 21 7477)
    Destinations: Negros, Panay, Romblon
Palawan Shipping Corporation
    551 Victoria St, Intramuros (☎ 40 5294, 49 1372, 48 3611)
    Pier 10, North Harbor, Tondo
    Destinations: Panay, Cuyo, Palawan
Sulpicio Lines
    415 San Fernando St, San Nicolas (☎ 47 9621, 47 5346)
    Pier 12, North Harbor, Tondo (☎ 20 1781)
    Destinations: Cebu, Leyte, Masbate, Mindanao, Negros, Palawan, Panay, Samar
Sweet Lines
    Pier 6, North Harbor, Tondo (☎ 20 1791, 26 3527)
    Destinations: Cebu, Mindanao
William Lines
    1508 Rizal Ave Extension, Caloocan City (☎ 361 0764)
    Pier 14, North Harbor, Tondo (☎ 21 9821, 40 5458)
    Destinations: Cebu, Leyte, Mindanao, Palawan, Panay, Romblon, Samar

Getting Around

To/From the Airport If Manila is your first stop on a first visit to Asia then hold your breath, it's pure chaos out there. For some reason the Filipinos seem totally unable to make the airport work, a complete contrast to efficient, smooth operations like Hong Kong, Bangkok or Singapore. In fact, when things do work (like the efficient Golden Cabs) they're immediately banned!

Domestic and international flights go from the same airport but the terminals are some distance apart. Manila International Airport (MIA) has officially been renamed Ninoy Aquino International Airport (NAIA).

Bus There are buses from the airport despite any tales the taxi vultures will tell you but pickpockets and bag slashers often ride these buses, looking for tired arriving passengers carrying all their valuables. If you want to try the buses the stop is about 150 metres to the right of the exit. Take a yellow DMTC bus to Ermita. They go down Taft Ave and you can get off at Pedro Gil. Don't take the grey California bus.

There is a new shuttle bus service operated by Sunshine Transportation. Their counter is at the left exit when leaving the arrival lobby. The fare is US$1 or P25 plus P10 for luggage. Buses go to Makati or the Domestic Airport and from there either to the Manila Hotel, Escolta or to Cubao. The bus to Escolta goes through Malate and Ermita passing many hotels and pension houses.

Metrorail Another economic alternative is a P15 taxi trip to the Baclaran Metrorail Terminus from where you can ride the train to Pedro Gil or United Nations Ave station for P4.50. The Baclaran Terminus is only two km from the airport.

Taxi It's only 12 km from the city centre and since taxi fares are very low it should be pretty cheap to get between the airport and the centre. If you can find a taxi with an honest meter and if the always chaotic traffic hasn't fallen into one of its black hole periods, that is. On the meter the fare between the airport and Ermita should be about P50 to P70 but the drivers will try for at least P150 or much more if they can get it.

All Manila's taxis are metered, for what it's worth. The relatively honest Golden Cabs have been replaced by the relatively honest Royal Class taxis (white and blue) or you can tangle with the highly suspect yellow taxis. The latest plan is to allow only 'airport taxis' to service the airport with a flat

P300 charge to Ermita or Makati. Protests are expected.

At the arrival level there's an official taxi despatcher (turn left as you leave the terminal) but even though there's a sign posted showing what the fares should be to various destinations the drivers will try to renegotiate as soon as you're clear of the terminal. Make sure you have change or your ability to negotiate will be severely reduced!

If there aren't any Royal Class taxis at the arrival level, you should be able to find one upstairs on the departure level, usually standing about 50 metres to the left of the exit. Take your bag inside the car with you or ensure it's safely stowed in the trunk and the lid is locked down before you depart.

When going out to the airport you can take any taxi. You will also probably have better luck at getting a properly working meter.

Other Other alternatives include free hotel limousine services, usually provided if you book a room with one of the hotels represented at the accommodation counters near the main exit in the arrivals hall.

Taxis heading into town will usually travel along the coast on Roxas Blvd. If you do find yourself on a local bus you may come into the tourist area along Taft Avenue. Look for the elevated Metrorail line above the road. Ermita will appear to your left with a cluster of high buildings before you pass Rizal Park and the imposing twin buildings of the Department of Tourism and the National Museum.

PAL have a shuttle bus to the domestic terminal, ostensibly only for their own passengers but a polite request will normally get you on board.

The departure tax is P250 for international flights.

City Buses For areas around Manila, buses depart from the Lawton terminal across Taft Ave from the city hall – beside the Intramuros walls. There's a comprehensive bus system around Manila but it's a little difficult to find your way around until you've got some idea of Manila's geography

and can recognise the destination names. There are many different bus companies. Metromanila buses are more modern, blue in colour and easier to get around on. Fares are from P1.50 on regular buses. The air-con Love Buses cost a flat P10.

Buses, like jeepneys, generally display their destinations on a board in front. This might be a large complex like NAIA (Ninoy Aquino International Airport), a street name like Ayala (Ayala Ave, Makati) or a whole suburb like Quiapo. The Escolta-Ayala/Medical Center service is a Love Bus route which runs along M H Del Pilar St through Ermita to Makati (the embassies) and the Makati Commercial Center, then returns along Mabini St to Ermita.

Metrorail The quick and convenient Metrorail or Light Rail Transit trains run on an elevated line which runs right along Taft Ave beside Ermita. It extends as far as the Bonifacio Monument (Monumento) at Caloocan in the north and south to Baclaran (Pasay), quite close to Manila Airport.

It's very convenient for getting to the Philtranco/Victory Liner (EDSA) terminals in the south and the Philippine Rabbit and Victory Liner bus terminals in the north. It is also an alternative way of getting to the airport. When traffic is really clogged up you'd probably get to the airport faster (and cheaper) by taking the Metrorail to the South terminal and then taking a taxi from there. The fare is a flat P4.50.

Taxi There are countless metered taxis (make sure the meter is on) and it's generally held that the Golden Cab taxis (which are actually black) and Royal Class (blue & white) are much better than the more prolific yellow ones. Meters in the these cabs are said to 'work better' and the drivers are less inclined to argue about the fares. Always ensure you have plenty of spare change before starting out. Don't believe phoney fare adjustment cards.

Jeepney Jeepneys are very reasonably priced with fares from P1.50. As with the

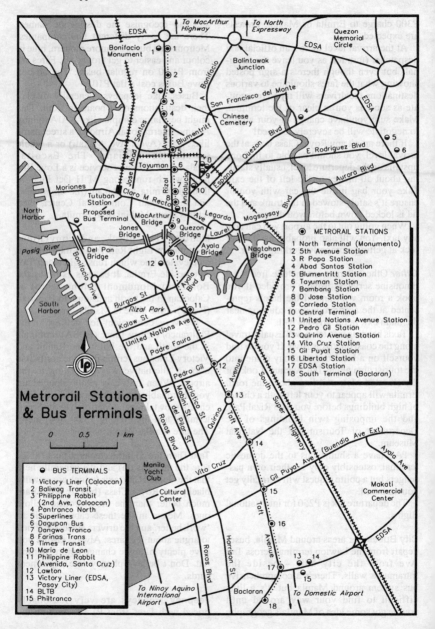

Metrorail Stations & Bus Terminals

0   0.5   1 km

⊙ METRORAIL STATIONS
1 North Terminal (Monumento)
2 5th Avenue Station
3 R Papa Station
4 Abad Santos Station
5 Blumentritt Station
6 Tayuman Station
7 Bambang Station
8 D Jose Station
9 Carriedo Station
10 Central Terminal
11 United Nations Avenue Station
12 Pedro Gil Station
13 Quirino Avenue Station
14 Vito Cruz Station
15 Gil Puyat Station
16 Libertad Station
17 EDSA Station
18 South Terminal (Baclaran)

⊙ BUS TERMINALS
1 Victory Liner (Caloocan)
2 Baliwag Transit
3 Philippine Rabbit
     (2nd Ave, Caloocan)
4 Pantranco North
5 Superlines
6 Dagupan Bus
7 Dangwa Tranco
8 Farinas Trans
9 Times Transit
10 Maria de Leon
11 Philippine Rabbit
     (Avenida, Santa Cruz)
12 Lawton
13 Victory Liner (EDSA,
     Pasay City)
14 BLTB
15 Philtranco

buses, it can be a little difficult to find your way around but they're so cheap it's no great loss to get on the wrong one. Most jeepneys pass by the city hall, north of Rizal Park. Heading north, they usually split there and either head north-west to Tondo, straight north to Monumento and Caloocan or north-east to Quezon City or Cubao or various other destinations in that direction.

Heading south, the routes from north of the river converge at City Hall then split to either go down Taft Ave or M H Del Pilar.

Around Manila

Luzon is the largest island in the Philippines and has a lot to offer apart from Manila itself. The places in this Around Manila section can all be visited as day trips from the capital although a number are worth overnight stops, or can be combined with visits to places further afield. The attractions around Manila include the US bases north of Manila and on the Bataan Peninsula and the WW II battle site of Corregidor at the entrance to Manila Bay. South of Manila, prime attractions include beach resorts, the Pagsanjan rapids and the Taal Lake volcano. These can be visited en route to South Luzon or to the island of Mindoro.

OLONGAPO & SUBIC
North-west of Manila, on the Bataan Peninsula, Olongapo has a US Navy base and its principal activities have been described as 'beer and prostitution'. It's definitely a raunchy, honky-tonk place! There are lots of bars but also some so-so beaches around Subic but San Miguel, slightly north of Subic Bay, is better than any of the beaches between Olongapo and Subic.

There's considerable discussion in the Philippines at present over whether the US should be allowed to retain their bases in the Philippines and, if so, at what cost.

Places to Stay
At 1697 Rizal Ave in Olongapo the *Bayside*

Hotel (☎ 5440) has rooms from P120 to P250. Despite its location in the middle of the red-light district the *MGM Hotel* at 87 Maysaysay Drive is good and clean with rooms from P180. There are other overpriced and nondescript hotels along Rizal Ave.

Along the coast, from Olongapo to Subic and Barrio Barretto, there are several resorts with rooms from P120 or so.

Getting There & Away
It's a two to three-hour bus ride from the Victory Liner station in Manila, quite an adventurous trip up and over the mountains. From Baguio buses depart hourly and the trip takes six hours. It's only 12 km from Olongapo to Subic but watch out for pick-pockets on the jeepneys.

ANGELES CITY
Visitors to the Angeles City area (including Mt Arayat National Park) should expect periodic disruptions to the local travel infrastructure due to continued volcanic activity at Mt Pinatubo.

After slumbering for over 600 years, Mt Pinatubo exploded on 12 June 1991 (ironically during a Philippines Independence Day parade in Angeles City) and over the next three days erupted 26 times, hurling golf-ball-sized fragments of pumice within a 40-km radius. It covered hundreds of square km in South Luzon with grainy volcanic ash. The eruption and resulting volcanic mudflows have so far been responsible for 49 deaths, the abandonment of Clark Air Force Base (one of the largest US military facilities in the world and the evacuation of hundreds of thousands of people from the vicinity.

Although Angeles City authorities claim that it's 'business as usual' in Pinatubo's volcanic aftermath, the local economy has been devastated by Clark's abandonment and seismically sensitive areas are certain to be off-limits. As of September 1991, the Angeles area was still experiencing severe volcanic ash slides, some which washed out bridges and roads. Seismologists estimate that the volcano will remain active for at least a year and possibly longer.

San Fernando, not to be confused with San Fernando La Union north of Baguio, is between Manila and Angeles City and is notorious for its Easter celebrations when at least one local religious fanatic has himself nailed to a cross.

Places to Stay

The *Liberty Inn* (☎ 4588) on MacArthur Highway, Balibago has rooms from P200. Diagonally opposite in a small sidestreet is the *Far Eastern Hotel* (☎ 5014), which is cheaper with rooms with fan and bath from P120. The *Executive Inn* (☎ 3939), on Sampaguita St in Clarkview, has clean rooms for P200 to P280.

Getting There & Away

There are several Philippine Rabbit buses daily from Manila. They take about an hour but make sure the bus is marked 'Expressway/Dau'. Alternatively, there are many bus services operating to North Luzon via Dau, from where you are able to catch a jeepney or tricycle the short distance back to Angeles.

There are several daily air-con buses from Manila. One leaves from the Sundowner Hotel on Mabini St, Ermita, at 10 am and another from the Swagman Hotel, A Flores St, at 1 pm. The so-called Clark Bus or Embassy Bus from the Manila Pavilion Hotel, and various other big hotels, leaves at 10 am or 5 pm.

There are hourly Victory Liner services from Olongapo which take two hours. Victory Liner also have hourly buses from Baguio. They're marked 'Olongapo' and take four hours. Many of the services between Manila and North Luzon go via Dau, a short tricycle ride from Angeles.

Bus services from Manila or Baguio to Olongapo usually go through San Fernando.

CORREGIDOR

This small island, at the mouth of Manila Bay, was the US-Filipino last stand after the Japanese invaded. It certainly wasn't as impregnable as planned but it did hold out for a long time. Now it's a national shrine and you can look around the underground bunkers and inspect the rusty relics of the fortress armaments.

The Philippine army runs the place today and there may be someone who will be happy to show you some of the less accessible places. There's lots of WW II junk lying around, plus the shattered remains of MacArthur's prewar HQ and a museum of the war with a good three-dimensional map. There are stunning views and sunsets from the summit of the highest hill and a soft drink stand which sells Coke and San Miguel beer.

Getting There & Away

Corregidor tours have always been somewhat changeable as new operators pop up and old ones fold up. At present Sun Cruises operates a twice daily, five-hour hydrofoil tour from the landing near the Manila Hotel. The first tour leaves at 7 am and the second at 1 pm sharp. Cost is P950 and includes transport to and from the wharf, a bus tour on the island and lunch on the way back. On Sundays, there's a special discounted tour that only costs P500. Check for the latest tour information with MV Island Cruiser Company (☎ 58 8809, 521 0791/2).

There is a more adventurous, but not much cheaper, alternative to these cruises. First of all, take a Philippine Rabbit bus to Mariveles on the Bataan Peninsula. It's a three-hour trip. Get off just before Mariveles at the covered bus stop (shortly after Cabcaban). From there take a trishaw or tricycle to the former Villa Carmen Beach Resort where the owner will organise a round trip boat to the island for P500. It's about 13 km out and there's a landing fee on the island. Realise, however, that you will probably spend more time and, therefore, more money if you decide to organise it yourself.

Another alternative is to take a bus to Balanga and then a minibus or jeepney to Mariveles down the old National Highway, past the gate of the Villa Carmen. At weekends it is sometimes possible to arrange transport with US Navy personnel from the

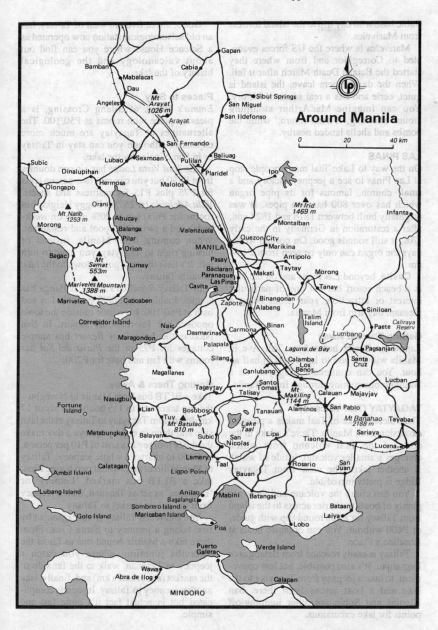

Around Manila

0   20   40 km

Subic base who day trip to the island fortress from Mariveles.

Mariveles is where the US forces evacuated to Corregidor and from where they started the Bataan Death March after it fell. When the day-trippers leave, the island is quiet, eerie and has a real sense of history. You can imagine MacArthur stomping around shouting, 'I shall return,' while the bombs and shells landed nearby.

LAS PINAS

On the way to Lake Taal many people stop at Las Pinas to see a jeepney factory and a small church, famous for its pipe organ which has over 800 bamboo pipes. It was originally built between 1816 and 1824 and, after a restoration in Germany in the early '70s, it still sounds good. On normal weekdays the organ can only be seen from 2 to 4 pm.

Cavite, beyond Las Pinas and on the bay, is a beach resort but not one of particular interest or attraction, apart from being a pleasant day-trip from Manila.

Getting There & Away

Zapote or Cavite buses from Taft Ave in Manila will get you to Las Pinas in half an hour. You can continue to Tagaytay on a Nasugbu bus coming through from Manila.

TAGAYTAY (Taal Volcano)

The volcanic lake of Taal makes a pleasant excursion from Manila. There's a lake in the cone of the Taal volcano from which emerges a smaller volcano, inside of which is another lake. The view from Tagaytay Ridge is pretty incredible.

You can climb the volcano and there are plenty of boats to charter across to the island from Talisay for P500 round trip with guide, or P400 without. You can organise boats at Rosalina's Place.

Talisay is easily reached from Batangas or Pagsanjan. It's also possible, but less convenient, to take a jeepney from Tagaytay to the lake and a boat across from there. San Nicolas and Subic are other jumping-off points for lake excursions.

Buco, about five km west of Talisay, has an old seismological station now operated as a Science House where you can find out about vulcanology and the geological history of the lake.

Places to Stay

Emma's Place, at Silang Crossing, is a pleasant place with rooms at P50/100. The alternatives at Tagaytay are much more expensive although you can stay in Talisay or in San Nicolas by the lake.

The Taal Vista Lodge has air-con doubles from P850 but you can rent two-person tents for P75 plus P15 for mattress and sheets. Villa Adelaida (☎ 267) at Foggy Heights has rooms for P600 (up to 20% more on weekends) and a swimming pool and restaurant. When coming from Manila, instead of turning right to Tagaytay, you have to turn left. It's near the road going down to the lake towards Talisay.

In Talisay Rosalina's Place at Banga has singles/doubles at P50/90 or with fan and bath at P60/100. It's a little outside the town opposite the International Resort. In San Nicolas the Lake View Resort has simple cottages for P75 or the Playa del Sol has rooms with fan and bath for P200.

Getting There & Away

Take a BLTB bus from Manila to Nasugbu – the trip takes one to 1½ hours. It's about 17 km down from Tagaytay to Talisay at the lake side and three to eight jeepneys a day make the dusty journey at a cost of P10 per person, or P200 to charter a whole jeepney. Talisay to Manila direct takes about two hours. First, take a BLTB bus marked 'Lemery' or 'Batangas' as far as Tanauan, then a jeepney from the public market to Talisay.

You can reach Talisay from Pagsanjan by first taking a jeepney to Santa Cruz. From there take a Manila-bound bus as far as the Calamba junction, where you catch a jeepney to Tanauan, walk to the far side of the market (about half a km) and, finally, take another jeepney to Talisay. It sounds complicated but in actual fact it's quite fast and simple.

To get to Tagaytay take a jeepney from the Calamba junction through Binan to Palapala and a bus from there to Tagaytay. Or continue past Calamba to Alabang, get a jeepney from there to Zapote and catch a bus coming from Manila through Zapote to Tagaytay.

The easiest way from Batangas to Talisay is to take a Manila bus as far as Tanauan and a jeepney from there down to Talisay. Total travel time is about two hours.

There's also an interesting back-roads route from Batangas to Lake Taal. Take a jeepney from Batangas to Lemery, a dusty 1½-hour ride. From there, take a jeepney to San Nicolas on the south-western shore of the lake.

NASUGBU & MATABUNGKAY

Matabungkay is the most popular beach in the neighbourhood of Manila and is busy on weekends. Nasugbu has better beaches, including **White Sands**, three or four km north of the town. You can get there by tricycle or outrigger.

Places to Stay & Eat

The *Swiss House Hotel* in Matabungkay has rooms with fan for P250/400 or there's the *Coral Beach Club* at P600 for a double with fan and bath. Nasugbu is more expensive.

Getting There & Away

BLTB buses for Nasugbu take about two hours from Manila and leave almost hourly. For Matabungkay get off the bus at Lian and travel the last few km by jeepney. It takes three or four stages by jeepney between Matabungkay and Batangas.

BATANGAS

Batangas can make a good base for visiting Lake Taal, Los Banos and sites along the coast, but the main reason for coming here is to take the ferry service across to the island of Mindoro. If you don't leave Manila early enough you won't arrive in Batangas in time to get a boat across to Mindoro that day.

Lobo is about 30 km south-east of Batangas and beautiful **Grethel Beach** is a three km tricycle ride from the town. There

are several cottages on the beach but you have to prepare your own food. **Anilao** is another beach resort, in the other direction around the coast from Batangas, but the beach is better, further on, at Lemery.

Places to Stay & Eat

On the outskirts of town *Alpa Hotel* (☎ 2213) has rooms with fan for P75/125, with air-con for P200/230 and with air-con and bath for P250/370. There's also a restaurant and a swimming pool.

JC's Pension House on Del Pilar St has singles/doubles at P60/120 with fan or doubles with air-con and bath for P250. The *Guesthaus* (☎ 1609) at 224 Diego Silang St, on the corner of Del Pilar St, has rooms with fan for P70 and with fan and bath for P100. On Rizal Ave Extension you'll find *Mascor Hotel* (☎ 3063) which has singles/doubles with fan and bath for P150/250 or with air-con and bath for P200/300.

The *New Grand Plaza Restaurant* on Evangelist is very clean and pleasant.

Getting There & Away

Batangas buses go from the Lawton terminal in Manila. Always ask for Batangas City to avoid confusion with the general Batangas area, and try to get a Batangas Pier bus, otherwise you'll have to take a jeepney for the final stretch. The 2½-hour trip costs about P30. BLTB has air-con buses which are only a few pesos more expensive but not all of them go to the pier.

Try to get to Batangas reasonably early if you want to get the Puerto Galera boats at 12.30 pm. Beware of pickpockets on these buses. They often operate in groups of three. Be prepared for the onslaught of Puerto Galera accommodation touts when you arrive at the pier.

The Sundowner Hotel in Mabini St, Ermita, has a daily air-con bus and ship service which departs Manila at 9 am.

To get to Batangas from Pagsanjan, take a jeepney to Santa Cruz, a Manila-bound bus from there to the Calamba junction and, from there, either a jeepney direct to Batangas or a jeepney to Tanauan. In Tanauan wait for a

Batangas-bound bus coming through from Manila and take that.

LOS BANOS & CALAMBA

The **Los Banos Botanical Gardens** has a big swimming pool and the town is noted for its **hot springs** (which can also be found in nearby Pansol). Los Banos is also the location of the **International Rice Research Institute** where the rice varieties that prompted the Asian 'green revolution' were developed.

Just before Los Banos is Calamba, where national hero Jose Rizal was born. **Rizal House** is now a memorial and museum. Coming from Calamba, the junction of a path leading to **Rainbow Falls** is about one km before Los Banos.

Getting There & Away

Buses from Manila for Los Banos or Santa Cruz will get you to both towns. Calamba is the junction town if you're travelling down to Batangas or to Lake Taal.

SAN PABLO & ALAMINOS

There are a wide variety of hikes around San Pablo. There's an easy hour's stroll around **Sampaloc Lake** in an extinct volcanic cone. Alternatively, make the longer half-day trip to the twin lakes of **Pandin** and **Yambo**.

Near here at Alaminos, **Hidden Valley** is a private park with lush vegetation, natural springs, a swimming pool and a hefty admission charge of P500 or, on Sunday and holidays, P600.

The 1144-metre-high **Mt Makiling** is best reached from Alaminos or Los Banos, while from San Pablo you can climb 2188-metre-high **Mt Banahao**.

Places to Stay

The *Sampaloc Lake Youth Hostel* (☎ 4448) has dorm beds for P70. A tricycle from the church or plaza in San Pablo will only cost a few pesos. The very simple *City Inn Agahan* at 126 Colago Ave has rooms for P30/60.

More expensive San Pablo possibilities include the *San Rafael Swimming Pool*

Resort with singles/doubles at P250/400 (and two swimming pools).

At Alaminos you can stay at *Hidden Valley Springs* for P700 to P800 which includes the resort entry charge. Reservations are made in Manila (☎ 50 9903).

Getting There & Away

Buses going from Manila to Lucena, Daet, Naga and Legaspi in South Luzon, or San Pablo direct buses, all run via Alaminos en route to San Pablo (about two hours). It's about five km from Alaminos to Hidden Springs and tricycles will firmly demand P50 for this short trip.

From Pagsanjan take a jeepney to Santa Cruz and another from there to San Pablo.

PAGSANJAN

Situated 70 km south-east of Manila in the Laguna province, this is where you can shoot the rapids by canoe. The standard charge for a canoe is P300 for one or two people, P450 for three, including the entry fee. You are paddled upriver to the falls (good place for a swim) by two *banqueros* and then come rushing down the rapids – getting kind of wet on the way. At the last major waterfall you can ride on a bamboo raft for an extra P20.

You'll probably get hassled for extra money since plenty of rich tourists come here and toss pesos around. It's reported that if you're unwilling to give in to demands for increased payment, you will not enjoy the rest of the trip. Some boatman aggressively demand P500 or even P1000 as a tip. So you have been warned! Banqueros organised by the Youth Hostel, Pagsanjan Falls Lodge or the Willy Flores Lodge are reported to be more reasonable, but you're certainly expected to at least tip the boatmen.

The final scenes of *Apocalypse Now* were shot along the river but, despite all the tourist hype, this is no nail-biting white-water maelström, more a gentle downriver cruise most of the time. The water level is highest, and the rapids are at their best, in August and September. The best time to go is early in the morning before the tourist hordes arrive, so spend the night in Pagsanjan. The various hotels are all willing to arrange boats for you, no doubt taking a cut on the proceeds. On weekends it's terribly crowded.

Places to Stay

Avoid the accommodation 'guides' at Pagsanjan as their commission will cost you extra. There is plenty of accommodation, particularly along Garcia St, the road which runs along the river, doubling back from beside the post office. On the main road into town the clean and neat *Camino Real Hotel* (☎ 2086) at 39 Rizal St has rooms from P200 to P450, depending on whether they have fan, air-con and/or bathroom.

Along Garcia St, the *Pagsanjan Village Hotel* (☎ 2116) at No 803 has singles for P100, singles/doubles with fan at P150/200 or doubles with air-con at P250 and with air-con and private bathroom for P350. The *Willy Flores Lodge* at 821 Garcia St has rooms for P45 per person. It's a simple, clean place with a homely atmosphere and they'll help you organise boat trips. Miss Estella y Umale's *Riverside Bungalow* (☎ 2465) is nearby at 792 Garcia St. There are two bungalows at P150 with fan and P300 with air-con. Miss Estella is a good cook.

Continue over a km out of town, in this direction, and you reach the *Pagsanjan Falls Lodge* (☎ 1251) which has a great site by the riverside but is extremely worn down, musty, tatty and desperately needs major renovations. Worse still, it has become notorious as a pick-up joint for Western pederasts. Rooms with fan are P350 and with air-con and bath are P450/500.

Places to Eat

There are plenty of good eating places in Pagsanjan. Right on the plaza in town is the pleasant *D'Plaza* which serves great sauteed chicharo with cauliflower. Turn left from the square and you soon come to the *Dura-Fe Restaurant* on General Jaina St. Or turn right, cross the river, and you'll find the very pleasant *Maulawin Bistro* with excellent food. Finally, just before the Pagsanjan Falls Lodge, and thus some distance out of town, there's the *D&C Luncheonette*.

Getting There & Away

Laguna Co buses, from the Lawton terminal in Manila, can be hailed as they go down Taft Ave – they take two to three hours to Santa Cruz. In the mornings, these buses can be quite crowded, so for an early morning departure you'd best go direct to the Lawton terminal. BLTB buses also operate to Santa Cruz from where jeepneys run the last few km to Pagsanjan. Some Laguna buses go all the way there.

See the Batangas and Tagaytay sections for transport details from Pagsanjan. Several changes of jeepney or bus are required en route but the process sounds more complex than it actually is.

As an alternative route back to Manila from Pagsanjan, you can follow the lesser-used route on the north side of Laguna de Bay back to Manila. It's more scenic, the roads are paved and buses and jeepneys operate on this route – it's only slightly further.

From Santa Cruz, you can continue south through Lucena to the Bicol region in the south or take the ferry from Lucena to the island of Marinduque. Lucban, en route to Lucena, is an interesting little town which looks much like it must have under Spanish rule.

North Luzon

After a spell on the beaches at Hundred Islands, most travellers continue north to the famed rice terraces in the Mountain Province. The *Igorot* and *Ifugao* villages around Banaue and their superb rice terraces have been dubbed the 'eighth wonder of the world'. North Luzon also has the popular summer capital of Baguio and the interesting old town of Vigan with its many reminders of the Spanish period.

Things to Buy

In North Luzon look for wood carvings by the Ifugao tribespeople and also for interesting hand-woven fabrics. The cottons are produced in such limited quantities that they rarely even reach Manila. They're much cheaper in Bontoc or Banaue than in Baguio. The baskets and wooden salad bowls are remarkably cheap, but a little bulky to carry home.

ZAMBALES COAST

The Zambales coast stretches north from Olongapo to Hundred Islands but, although there are some good stretches of beach, few travellers come this way. **San Antonio**, about an hour north of Olongapo, is a pleasant little town with a market. From nearby Pundaquit, you can arrange trips out to **Camera** and **Capones** islands. Further north at Botolan, you can venture inland to the country of the *Ayta Negritos* in the Zambales mountains.

Iba is the capital of the province and has several beach resorts, most of them rather run-down. **Masinloc**, further north towards Santa Cruz, also has some places to stay and diving possibilities. Buses run up the Zambales coast from Manila via Olongapo.

HUNDRED ISLANDS, LUCAP & ALAMINOS

The most popular of the west-coast resort areas is Hundred Islands, with the nearby towns of Lucap and Alaminos. Actually there are more than 100 islands and if swimming or just lazing around and sunbathing are your thing then this is a good place.

Unfortunately, the snorkelling and diving isn't as good as it once was due to long term use of dynamite for fishing, and because the water is less than crystal clear. Lucap, just three km from Alaminos, is the main accommodation centre for the islands and, from here, you can hire boats to get out to them. There are no beaches on the coast and only a few of the islands have beaches. There are, however, plenty of hidden coves, caves and coral reefs.

There is a tourist office on the Lucap Pier which has a map of the islands and arranges boats. A day trip costs about P150 for up to six people and gives you about six hours on the islands – quite enough. **Quezon**, the largest island, is being developed as a tourist resort. Other popular islands for snorkelling include **Cathedral**, **Parde** and **Panaca**. Lucap has a marine biological museum and a fishery research centre.

Hundred Islands is still remarkably untouristed so be prepared to fend for yourself. November and May are the best beach months. If you haven't got snorkelling equipment you can rent it at Lucap or, more cheaply, rent or buy it in Manila.

Places to Stay

Prices vary considerably with the season, jumping up at Easter week and April and May weekends. Most of the accommodation is in Lucap.

The *Kilometre One Tourist Lodge* has rooms with fan at P65/110 and is clean, simple, has a restaurant and also functions as a youth hostel. It's a km from town, as the name indicates. *Gloria's Cottages* have rooms with fan and bath for P100. Opposite is the *Ocean View Lodge & Restaurant* which is clean and has a good restaurant. Rooms start from P110/135 with fan, P120/150 with fan and bath and P380/450 with air-con and bath.

The *Lucap Hotel* has dorm beds at P60, rooms with fan at P100/180, with fan and bath for P120/200, with air-con for P180/250 and with air-con and bath for P200/300. *Maxime by the Sea* has a beautiful terrace and rooms from P80/150 with fan and bath or P200/250 with air-con and bath.

In Alaminos, the *Alaminos Hotel* on Quezon Ave has rooms at P60/80, with fan and bath for P100/120 or with air-con and bath for P200/220.

If you want to camp out on the islands, there's a P10 fee on Quezon, Governor's and Children's islands. Quezon has a pavilion for P200, a cottage with rooms for six costs P600 on Governor's while on Children's there are tents to rent from P50 to P150. Bring your own food.

Places to Eat

The wharfside canteens are a good place for cheap eats. The *Ocean View Restaurant* is one of the lodge restaurants with good inexpensive food. The *Last Resort Restaurant* is one of the few places which doesn't close down early in the evening. Lucap is a quiet place at night. If you need a beer, catch a tricycle to nearby Alaminos where the *Plaza Restaurant* usually has a folk singer, or there's the *Imperial Restaurant*.

Getting There & Away
Dagupan and Pantranco North buses run hourly from Manila to Alaminos, taking about five hours. You can also catch these buses at Dau, near Angeles City. Victory Liner have several buses daily for the six-hour trip from Olongapo to Alaminos. A few Pantranco North buses operate to Alaminos from Baguio, taking about four hours.

Getting Around
From Alaminos, it's just a short tricycle ride to Lucap at P6 for up to four passengers (although they'll try for as much as P30).

An outrigger from Lucap to the islands officially costs P200 for up to six people plus P5 entry fee per person. For P50 to P80 you can be dropped off and picked up later. Four or five hours is enough for most people, especially where there is no shade. Quezon is the most popular island and you can get drinks at the kiosk there.

BOLINAO
Bolinao is a small town at the north-west point of Lingayen Gulf with some reasonable beaches nearby. There's a **museum** on the outskirts of town and an **historic fortress church** dating from 1609.

Places to Stay & Eat
The *A&E Garden Inn*, in the centre, has rooms with fan for P60/80, with fan and bath for P100/120 or with air-con and bath for P250/300. By the sea the *Celeste Sea Breeze Resort* is P100/150. *Capitan Cascante* is also by the sea and has rooms or cottages from P50 to P200. All three of these places have restaurants.

Getting There & Away
There are regular buses, minibuses and jeepneys to Bolinao from Alaminos. Manila is six hours away and there are several buses daily.

LINGAYEN, DAGUPAN & SAN FABIAN
Dagupan is mainly a transport hub but there are also some beaches in the vicinity, none of them particularly memorable. Between Lingayen and Dagupan you can try **Lingayen Beach** (15 km from Dagupan), **Blue Beach** (three km away at Bonuan) while **White Beach** is 15 km north-east at San Fabian. White Beach is really brownish-grey.

Places to Stay & Eat
Lingayen The *Viscount Hotel* (☎ 137) on Maramba Blvd has rooms at P100 with fan and bath or P200 with air-con and bath. On Lingayen Beach, the *Lion's Den* costs P180 and *Letty & Betty Cottages* P100.

Dagupan The *Villa Milagrosa Youth Hostel* (☎ 4658), in the Maramba Building at 26 Zamora St, has singles/doubles with fan and bath for P75/125.

Other possibilities include the *Lucky Lodge & Restaurant* (☎ 3452) on M H Del Pilar St, with rooms with fan at P40/60 and with fan and bath at P60/80. The *Vicar Hotel* (☎ 2616, 3253) on A B Fernandez Ave has rooms with fan at P30/42, with fan and bath at P70/100 or doubles with air-con and bath at P120.

The *Victoria Hotel* (☎ 2081), also on A B Fernandez Ave, is rather more expensive with rooms with fan and bath at P205/225 or with air-con and bath from P245/280. On Blue Beach at Bonuan, which is about three km out of Dagupan, the *Tondaligan Cottages* (☎ 2593/5) has air-con rooms with bath for P280/360.

San Fabian Near the market in nearby San Fabian the *Residenz Patty Mejia* has rooms at P30/60. It's a fine big private house with garden and a kitchen, which you can use for a small charge. The *Holiday Village & Beach*

Resort is not very clean but it does have a restaurant. There are singles/doubles with fan for P60/75, doubles with air-con and bath for P200 and cottages for P100.

Breman's Rest House has rooms with fan for P100. The *Center Beach Resort* has cottages for P150/200, or rooms with fan and bath for P200/250 but it is rather run down. The *Lazy A Resort* has rooms with fan and bath for P150 and with air-con and bath for P280.

Getting There & Away

Frequent Pantranco North and Dagupan Bus services operate from Manila and take about two hours. There are a few Pantranco North buses between Baguio and Dagupan each day, also taking about two hours. Buses from Baguio go via San Fabian to Dagupan. Between the two towns, you can take a Baguio bus or a local minibus service.

AGOO & ARINGAY

Between San Fabian and Bauang is Agoo with a **basilica** rebuilt after an 1892 earthquake; it was partly damaged by the 1990 earthquake. Aringay has the small **Don Lorenzo Museum** which was also badly hit by the 1990 earthquake.

BAUANG

Further north on the coast, Bauang has a long stretch of beach with many resort hotels. There are better beaches in the Philippines, but Bauang is only an hour or two's travel from Baguio in the hills and this probably accounts for its popularity. San Fernando (La Union) is just six km north of Bauang and the beach area is between the two – about two km north of Bauang and four km south of San Fernando. Lots of jeepneys shuttle back and forth.

Places to Stay

Bauang's hotels are mainly along the long grey sand beach between Baccuit and Paringao, which in turn are between Bauang and San Fernando. Prices at these places are often negotiable.

The *Jac Corpuz Cottages*, between the

Leo Mar and Lourdes resorts at Baccuit, have basic rooms from P80. The *Lourdes Beach Homes* have large cottages with fan and bath for P100/120 but they've definitely seen better days. At the *Leo Mar Beach Resort* simple but well-kept rooms with fan and bath cost from P250. At this southern end of the beach you'll also find the *Hide Away Beach Resort*, a large house with rooms from P250 to P300.

The *Mark Teresa Apartel* (☎ 3022) is on the highway at Paringao and has apartments with two bedrooms for P300. Next to it is the *Château Inn* with clean rooms with fan for P150. Also in Paringao is the *China Sea Beach Resort* (☎ 41 4821) with cottages at P550/650, a restaurant and a swimming pool. Similar in price, and in Paringao, are *Coconut Grove Resort, Bali Hai Resort* and *Cabana Beach Resort*. These hotels offer boat rentals, wind surfing as well as other entertainment possibilities.

Places to Eat

Food in the resort hotels tends to be expensive so, for cheaper meals, go into Bauang or San Fernando. The *Anchorage, Fisherman's Wharf* and *Bali Hai* are all pretty good. The *Ihaw-Ihaw Restaurant*, next to the Tobacco Roll Disco on the highway serves grills or you can eat well and cheaply at the pleasant little *Jasmin Restaurant* on the same side of the road towards San Fernando.

Getting There & Away

The many buses from Manila to Bauang take over five hours and some continue north to Vigan and Laoag. It takes over an hour from Baguio on Philippine Rabbit or Marcitas Liner and slightly less by jeepney. It's a nice trip down the winding road to the coast but try to sit on the left side for the best views. Jeepneys take about 30 minutes to get to San Fernando.

SAN FERNANDO (LA UNION)

The 'city of the seven hills' is the capital of the La Union Province and the **Museo de La Union** next to the Provincial Capitol gives a cultural overview of the region.

Places to Stay

On Rizal St, the *Casa Blanca Hotel* (☎ 3132) has rooms at P60/70 with fan, P80/100 with fan and bath or P130/160 with air-con and bath. It's a beautiful, large house with simple rooms.

The *Plaza Hotel* (☎ 2996) on Quezon Ave (which becomes the main highway) has rooms with fan and bath from P175/210 and with air-con and bath from P265/290.

There are several resorts three km south-west along the beach at Poro. The *Ocean Deep Resort* (☎ 41 4440) has rooms with fan and bath for P175/250. In Urbiztondo, about five km north near San Juan, the *Hacienda Beach Resort* has rooms and cottages for P150/200 or the *Mona Liza Cottages* (☎ 41 4892) are P100/150.

Places to Eat

The *Mandarin Restaurant* has reasonably priced food and there are lots of cheap snack places around, a number of which offer complete fixed-price meals. Places to try include the *New Society Restaurant*, opposite the market in Burgos St, the *Crown Restaurant* and the *Garden Food Center*. The special daily menus at the *Midway Restaurant* in the Plaza Hotel are good value.

Getting There & Away

There are numerous daily buses from Manila which take six hours. See Bauang for other transport information.

BAGUIO

At an altitude of about 1500 metres, Baguio is much cooler than Manila and for this reason it once served as a summer capital. It's still popular as an escape from the lowland heat. It's a laid-back place with plenty of parks and an interesting market. It's also good for buying handicrafts (although you have to bargain aggressively in order to get a good price).

Baguio is also famed for its 'faith healers' to whom many people flock each year. To most travellers, however, the town's main role is as a gateway to the Mountain Province and the amazing rice terraces.

On 16 July 1990, Baguio was struck by a disastrous earthquake which caused a great deal of damage. Repairs and rebuilding will continue for some time.

Things to See

The **City Market** has local produce and crafts including basketware, textiles, woodcarvings and jewellery. There's a small **Mountain Province Museum** next to the tourist office. **Burnham Park** is in the town and the **Baguio Botanical Gardens** are a km out. There are scenic views over the surrounding countryside from the **Statue of Our Lady of Lourdes**.

In **La Trinidad**, the provincial capital just to the north of the city, visit the governor's offices and see the Kabayan mummies. These remarkably well-preserved mummified bodies were brought from burial caves in the north.

Places to Stay

Many of the places mentioned in the previous edition of this book were destroyed or damaged beyond repair by the earthquake, including the Emerald Inn, the Happiness Lodge and the Traveller's Lodge.

The *Highland Lodge* (☎ 7086) at 48 General Luna Rd has friendly staff and rather small rooms at P70/110 or with bath at P150/180. The dank *Diamond Inn* (☎ 2339) at 16 East Jacinto St has dorm beds for P40, singles/doubles for P60/80 or with bath for P100/130. The simple but well-kept *Baguio Goodwill Lodge* (☎ 6634) at 58 Session Rd has rooms for P120/200 or P250/300 with bath. For P90 you can get a bed in the clean dorm at the *Baden Powell International Hostel* (☎ 442 5836) on Governor Pack Rd. Quiet, ultra-clean rooms go for P300.

The *Baguio Village Inn* (☎ 3901, 4649) is a clean and quiet place just out of town at 355 Magsaysay Ave, and has rooms at P85/170 or with bath for up to P200/350. Near the Philippine Rabbit bus station on Lapu Lapu St, the *Baguio Garden Inn* (☎ 6398) has rooms for P120 or P225 with bath.

The *Mido Hotel* (☎ 2575) on Session Rd has rooms at P100/150 or P200/250 with

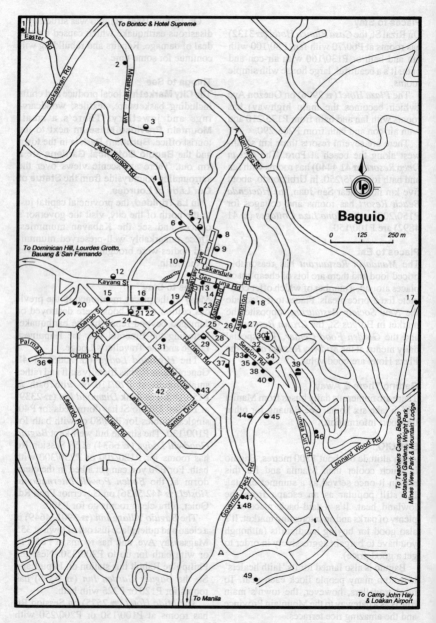

1	Easter School of Weaving
2	Baguio Village Inn
3	Times Transit Bus Terminal
4	Leisure Lodge
5	Honeymoon Disco
6	Dream World Disco
7	Jeepneys to Bell Church
	Philippine Rabbit Bus Terminal
8	Baguio Garden Inn
	Country Music World
9	Dangwa Tranco Bus Terminal
	Skyland Express Bus Terminal
10	Silver Lodge
11	Market
12	Jeepneys to Dominican Hill, Lourdes Grotto & Asin Hot Springs
13	Diamond Inn
	Folkden
14	Highland Lodge
15	Swagman Attic Hotel
16	Pier 66
17	Brent School
18	St Louis Filigree Shop
19	Maharlika Livelihood Center
20	Town Hall
21	Cypress Inn
22	168 Folkhouse
	Orange County
23	Mido Hotel
	Sunshine Restaurant
24	Marcitas Liner Bus Terminal
25	Philippine National Bank
26	New Plaza Hotel
27	Fire Place
28	456 Restaurant
	Baguio Goodwill Lodge
29	Jeepneys to Mines View Park
30	Cathedral
31	Ganza Steak & Chicken House
32	Bread of Life
33	Sizzling Plate
34	Patria de Baguio
	Songs Music Lounge
35	Philippine Airlines
36	Mount Crest Hotel
37	Burnham Hotel
38	Mario's Restaurant
39	Post Office
40	Amapola Café
41	Benguet Pine Pensione
42	Burnham Park
43	The Solibao
44	Pantranco North Bus Terminal
45	Victory Liner Bus Terminal
46	Casa Vallejo
47	Mountain Province Museum
48	Tourist Office
49	Convention Centre

bath. *Casa Vallejo* (☎ 3045, 4601) at 111 Session Rd Extension costs P180/260 or P280/380 with bath. It's a fine and well-kept house with a pleasant atmosphere. *Benguet Pine Pensione* (☎ 7325), at 82 Chanum St on the corner of Otek St, is also a beautiful old house. In this clean and quiet place dorm beds cost P80, doubles P170 or with bath P250.

Places to Eat
The *Dangwatranco bus terminal* has some good and cheap restaurants. The Chinese *Kayang Restaurant* on Magsaysay Ave changes its menu daily but shuts at 9 pm. At both the *Ganza Steak & Chicken House* and The *Solibao* in Burnham Park you can eat outside.

There are various other restaurants along Session Rd, Baguio's main street, like the small and cheap *Taste of Thai* or the *Barrio Fiesta*. Also on Session Rd the *Sizzling Plate* is a good place for a proper breakfast. The *456 Restaurant* is rather expensive and not that special.

Pier 66 on Abanao St is a popular beer garden with fast food. At the *Bread of Life* coffee shop you can get good cheese and European sausages as well as coffee and bread. Finally, the *Star Café* serves a hearty Ifugao breakfast.

Entertainment
There are a number of good folk music places in town. On Assumption Rd try the *Fire Place* or there's the *Folkden* in the street by the Diamond Inn.

On Abanao St, the *168 Folkhouse* stays open around the clock. A few doors away *Orange Country* has country & western and rock & roll music. The entrance to *Country Music World* is at the back of the Baguio Garden Inn and you can sometimes hear really good Igorot songs. At Patria de Baguio on Session Rd jazz is played at *Songs*.

Around the Philippine Rabbit bus terminal there are some go-go bars and discos such as *Dream World Disco* or the *Honeymoon Disco*. Slightly better clubs like *Chapparal* are on Marcos Highway.

Getting There & Away

Air PAL has 50-minute flights from Manila to Baguio five times a week. Jeepneys to the airport leave from Mabini Rd, between Session and Harrison Rds.

Bus Philippine Rabbit, Pantranco North, Victory Liner, Dangwatranco and Dagupan Bus all operate from Manila to Baguio daily and take about six hours (Victory Liner has the most extensive schedule and comfortable buses). Fares are P120 for ordinary buses and P150 for air-con. It takes about half an hour less from Baguio to Manila since it's downhill at first. You can catch these buses from Dau, near Angeles City.

There are hourly Victory Liner buses from Olongapo to Baguio (six hours), several Pantranco North buses from Dagupan (two hours) and several Philippine Rabbit and Marcitas Liner buses from San Fernando (two hours).

Dangwatranco have two or three daily bus services to Banaue, which depart early in the morning and take nine hours. Dangwatranco departures to Bontoc are also in the morning and take eight hours. Dangwatranco is also the operator to Sagada, a daily early morning bus, which takes about seven hours.

MOUNTAIN PROVINCE

Mountain Province starts 100 km north-east of Baguio and is famed for interesting tribes and spectacular rice terraces. If you've spent much time in South-East Asia, deliberately going to a place just to see more rice terraces seems a little weird, but these are definitely special.

Some 2000 to 3000 years ago the Ifugao tribespeople carved terraces out of the mountain sides around Banaue which are as perfect today as they were then. They run like stepping stones to the sky – up to 1500 metres high – and if stretched end to end would extend over 20,000 km. The Ifugao people are still, in the more remote areas, quite primitive, although head-hunting is no longer practised.

Getting There & Away

You can approach Mountain Province from two directions. The more spectacular route is by the rough, winding mountain road that climbs up from Baguio to Bontoc, the main town in the region. The trip takes seven or eight hours and from there you can make a variety of side trips to places like Sagada or continue on to Banaue, the main town for rice terraces and another three or four-hour trip.

The faster alternative route is direct from Manila via the Nueva Viscaya Province – on good roads the bus trip only takes seven to eight hours. The Baguio-Bontoc-Banaue road is often cut during the wet season, but it's far more interesting so you should try to make the trip in at least one direction by this route.

July to August is the wettest period. The road reaches a height of 2000 metres and is the highest road in the Philippines. Dangwatranco is the main operator for bus services north of Baguio.

BONTOC

Bontoc is the first major town you come to from Baguio and the main town of the area. It's possible to walk from here to the villages of the Igorot people – they build their rice terraces with stone dykes, unlike the earth terraces of Banaue. Take food and water for yourself and dried fish or other gifts for the villagers.

The village of **Malegcong** is a two or three-hour walk into the mountains. You have to follow a narrow creek for about 200 metres before you reach the footpath leading to the village. It's not a bad idea to take a guide with you. Always ask permission before taking photographs of the people here.

The excellent **Bontoc Museum** is run by the local Catholic mission and includes a typical village of native huts – Bontoc as it was prior to the American period – plus many head-hunting relics and Chinese vases, and a P10 donation is all it costs. Bontoc is a good place to buy locally woven materials, woodcarvings and other handicrafts of Mountain Province.

Places to Stay & Eat

Bontoc seems to have suffered even more than most from the traditional Filipino hotel fate – fire. The *Mountain Hotel* (☎ 3018) is now a concrete (fireproof?) building and has singles for P25 and doubles for P40 to P50. Near the bus stop, the simple but well-kept *Bontoc Hotel* has rooms for P35 per person and has good food.

The *Chico Terrace* (☎ 3099) has rooms with bath, also at P35 per person. The popular *Happy Home Inn*, opposite the bus stop, has good accommodation at P40/70 for singles/doubles plus larger rooms with attached bathroom for P150.

The *Pines Kitchenette & Inn* is slightly more expensive with rooms from P45/90 or P160 for a double with bath. It's about five minutes' walk from the bus stop and there's also a good, although pricey, restaurant.

Food is pretty good in Bontoc – try the great cinnamon rolls in the local bakery. Bontoc is also a centre for the Filipino passion for dog meat – about which there has been much controversy in the West of late. 'Cheap and not bad,' reported one obvious dog-loving traveller.

Getting There & Away

There are five Dangwatranco buses daily between Baguio and Bontoc, generally departing in the early morning. Some start from La Trinidad, a couple of km north of Baguio, and it's worth going there by jeepney as they're pretty full by the time they get into Baguio.

The 150-km trip takes seven or eight hours. On from Bontoc to Banaue there is usually a daily jeepney at 6.30 to 7.30 am and a daily (except Sunday) bus at 10 to 11 am. The bus takes over two hours, the jeepney is as much as an hour faster. As elsewhere in Mountain Province transport is somewhat unreliable. If you can't find regular transport you can charter a jeepney.

You can cross over from the coast to Bontoc or Sagada by taking a jeepney from near Tagudin, north of San Fernando, to Cervantes and another jeepney or bus from there towards Baguio. Get off at Abatan and catch a Baguio to Bontoc bus. This is a lengthy, time-consuming and rough trip.

SAGADA

Only 18 km from Bontoc, the village of Sagada is famed for its **burial caves**. The people are friendly and it's a good place to buy local weaving. The cliff-face burial caves here are somewhat similar to those of the Toraja people of Sulawesi in Indonesia. You'll probably need a local guide and some sort of light to explore the more extensive caves.

Near Sagada is the **Bokong Waterfall** with a natural swimming pool. A little further toward Bontoc is the **Eduardo Masferré Studio** with photographs of life in Mountain Province in the '30s to the '50s.

Places to Stay & Eat

The places to stay in this popular little town all seem to follow a standard charging policy of around P40 per person.

Julia's Guest House is very popular – 'quaint, charming, cosy and rustic', was how one traveller described it and many others have given similar reports. There's great vegetarian food, as much tea or coffee as you want and flowers on the tables!

Other places include the *San Joseph's Rest House*, across from the hospital where the bus stops. It's also friendly and well-kept and the food is superb value. The *Mapiyaaw Sagada Pension*, about a km up the hill from Sagada itself, is clean and has hot water. Or there's the *Sagada Guest House* which once again is a pleasant place and does good meals, particularly breakfasts.

You can also eat at the convent, close to the church. The *Shamrock Cafe* and the *Moonhouse Cafe* are other good places. The food at the latter is very good and the bar is the 'in' place to spend the evening. Banana cake is a Sagada speciality and is served in all of the places.

Getting There & Away

There are daily Dangwatranco, Skyland Express and Lizardo Trans buses from Baguio in the early morning. The trip takes eight hours. The Dangwatranco buses start from La Trinidad, a few km north of Baguio. It's wise to take a jeepney to the La Trinidad bus terminal well before departure to ensure a seat.

A jeepney from Bontoc to Sagada only takes an hour but there are only two or three a day, usually early in the morning or in the afternoon.

BANAUE

From Bontoc the road turns south and runs through incredibly spectacular countryside to Banaue, the heart of the terrace scenery. It's a narrow, rough road and travel is slow – but what a view. Take the right side of the bus to appreciate it best.

There are many hiking trails in the vicinity of Banaue – obtain details from the youth hostel. **Batad** is one of the best viewpoints and takes two hours to walk to after an 11-km jeepney ride from the town. There are a number of small places to stay in Batad. Near Batad, there's a delightful waterfall with good swimming. The **Ifugao villages** and the **handicraft centres** in Banaue are also worth visiting.

Information

There is no bank in Banaue but, if you're really stuck, you can probably change money at the Banaue Hotel (at a bad rate). The information office has a good P2 map of Banaue's surroundings.

Places to Stay

Banaue There are plenty of small places to stay here, mainly at around P35 to P50 per person. The town also appears to suffer from hotel fires, so there are often changes in the line-up. The *Jericho Guest House* is simple, clean and has rooms at P35/50, or try the *Travellers Inn* at P35/70.

The popular *Wonder Lodge* (☎ 4017) also has singles/doubles at P35/70, as does the *Brookside Inn*.

The orderly and well-kept *Half Way Lodge* (☎ 4082) has singles at P35, doubles at P60 to P75 or rooms with bath at P200/250. There's also a restaurant. Just a few steps away the very pleasant *Stairway Lodge* is a good, clean place with a restaurant and rooms with balconies. Singles are P40, doubles P60 to P75 and doubles with bath P200. The *J&L Lodge* (☎ 4035) has rooms at P50/100 but it's slightly out of Banaue on the way to the Banaue Hotel.

Green View Lodge (☎ 4022) has dorm beds for P50, singles for P250 and doubles for P315 to P350. At the *Terrace Ville Inn* singles with bath are P150, doubles P300 to P350. *Sanafe Lodge* (☎ 2110) has dorm beds for P55 to P100 or rooms with bath for P350/470.

Finally, the expensive Banaue Hotel administers the *Banaue Youth Hostel* where dorm beds are P110. You can use the hotel swimming pool.

Batad Places in Batad are spartan but the atmosphere is friendly and it's worth staying here, rather than just day-tripping from Banaue. The *Hillside Inn, Mountain View Inn, Romeo's Inn, Foreigner's Inn* or *Simon's Inn* cost around P20 per person.

In Cambulo, *Lydia Domanlig* offers overnight accommodation for P10 per person.

Places to Eat

Most hotels have small restaurants or offer meals – the *Stairway, Half Way* and *Las Vegas* restaurants are all good and cheap.

Meals at the *Youth Hostel* are not such good value as the portions are small. The *Banaue Hotel*, on the other hand, has good food and, if there are enough guests, Ifugao dances are held at night. Entry is P10. The *Patina Bar Folkden* also has live music and you can get a beer or snacks until late.

Getting There & Away

You can reach Banaue from either direction but, while the Bayombong route is faster, the Bontoc route is much more interesting.

From Baguio, there are two daily Dangwatranco buses via Bayombong. They leave early in the morning and take about nine hours. At busy times these buses will leave an hour early if they're full.

Also from Baguio, via Bontoc, you have to overnight in Bontoc en route. From Bontoc it takes about three hours on the bus which departs daily (except Sunday) early in the morning. Arrive very early for a good seat. There's also a faster daily jeepney.

From Manila, the daily Dangwatranco bus leaves early in the morning and takes 10 hours up but only seven hours back to Manila. If you miss the direct bus take a Pantranco North bus to Solano, just before the Banaue turn-off. From there, jeepneys run to Lagawe and then, to Banaue, and take another two or three hours.

Getting Around

You can get transport 12 km of the way to Batad from Banaue but the rest of the way you have to walk. A chartered jeepney for that first stretch will cost P250 to P350 and carry up to 14. The driver will either wait at the turn-off or come back for you the next day at a prearranged time. It takes about two hours along the signposted path from between Dalican and Bangaan. Beware of self-appointed, but expensive, 'guides'. Walking all the way would take about five hours.

VIGAN

North of San Fernando, this interesting old town was second only to Manila during the Spanish era and today is the best preserved Spanish town in the country. If you're interested in old Spanish architecture and ancient-looking churches this region of Ilocos is prime hunting ground.

It's fascinating just wandering around the town, taking in the narrow streets, listening to the clip-clop of horse-drawn calesas. 'Vigan', according to one traveller, 'is the only town in the Philippines with a population of 10,000 or more without a single disco. Local teenagers sit around the cathedral and discuss theology.' Just out of Vigan, **Puerto Beach** is a pleasant fishing village.

Things to See

The house where Jose Burgos, executed by the Spanish in 1872, was born now houses the **Ayala Museum**. It's behind the capitol building, has lots of old antiques, paintings and photographs and the curator is delighted to tell tourists of the history of the area. The **Sequirino Museum** on Quirino St is the old house of former President Quirino. Ferdinand Marcos was also from this region and the **National Museum** on Liberation Blvd is partly used as a showcase for the Marcos era. It also gives a good idea of life during the Spanish rule. The **Cathedral of St Paul** dates from 1641 and is one of the oldest and largest churches in the country.

Places to Stay

At 1 Bonifacio St, *Grandpa's Inn* is a nice place run by friendly people. Single rooms are P40; rooms with fan and bath are P90 or with air-con and bath P180. The *Cordillera Inn* (☎ 2526), at 29 Mena Crisologo St on the corner of General Luna St, has rooms with fan at P50/100 or with air-con and bath at P340/380.

The *Vigan Hotel* on Burgos St has rooms with fan and bath for P115/160 or with air-con and bath for P200/275. The cheaper but clean and fairly good *Venus Inn,* on Quezon Ave, has rooms with fan for P50/80 and with air-con and bath for P180/250. Finally, the spartan *Luzon Hotel,* on General Luna St, has rooms at P35/70 or with fan for P45/90.

Places to Eat

There's great ice cream and good sandwiches at the *Vigan Plaza Restaurant* in Florentino St. The *Tower Café,* on Burgos St (corner of the main plaza, opposite the cathedral), and the *Unique Café,* also on Burgos St, offer barbecues and beer.

The *Venus Restaurant,* in the Venus Inn on Quezon Ave, offers Chinese and Filipino food while the *Victoria Restaurant,* also on Quezon Ave, offers different menus each day. The *Cool Spot Restaurant* is a lovely open-air place, behind the Vigan Hotel and on Quirino Blvd, and is known for its good steaks.

Most places close by 9 pm but *Marius Place* on Quezon Ave is a good folk pub open until midnight or even later. *Cafe Franziska*, next to the Times Transit terminal, is also open late, or try the *PNB Snack* beer garden near the Philippine National Bank.

Getting There & Away

From Manila, the trip takes six to eight hours with Philippine Rabbit, Times Transit, Farina Trans or Maria de Leon. Some buses continuing north to Laoag bypass the town in which case you will have to take a tricycle from the highway. Buses also connect from San Fernando, Aparri and Laoag. You can reach Vigan from Baguio via San Fernando or by the coast from Hundred Islands and Dagupan, again via San Fernando.

It's about two hours beyond Vigan to Laoag and you can continue right around the north of Luzon to Claveria, Aparri, Tuguegarao and back down to Manila.

LAOAG

There are many old Spanish churches in the Ilocos Norte Province and Laoag, the capital of the province, has **St William's Cathedral**, built between 1650 and 1700. Near Laoag, in **Bacarra**, the town's church has a massive and earthquake-damaged belltower. Salt is produced at Seksi Beach, four km from Pasuquin which, in turn, is 10 km from Laoag.

South-east of the town is **Sarrat**, birthplace of the former president, Ferdinand Marcos. His home is now the **Marcos Museum**, open daily. More Marcos memorabilia can be found at the so-called **Malacanang del Norte** in Batac. A few km south-west of Batac is the fortress-like **Paoay Church** in a style referred to as 'earthquake baroque'.

Places to Stay & Eat

At the popular *City Lodging House* on General Antonio Luna St, rooms with fan are P50/100 and there's a restaurant. The *Modern Hotel*, on Nolasco St, has rooms with fan for P40/80 and with fan and bath for P170. The *Texicano Hotel* (☎ 22 0606/290)

on Rizal St has rooms in the old building with fan for P60/70, with fan and bath for P80/105 and with air-con and bath for P200/230. In the new building air-con rooms are P270/320.

Hotel Casa Llanes (☎ 22 1125) on Primo Lazaro Ave has rooms with fan and bath for P120 and with air-con and bath for P200. The *Pichay Lodging House* (☎ 22 1267), in Primo Lazaro Ave, has singles with fan and bath for P100, doubles for P120 to P140 or with air-con and bath for P180. This may be the best place in town.

The *City Lunch & Snack*, on the corner of General Antonio Luna and Nolasco Sts, has good cheap Chinese and Filipino dishes and reasonably priced breakfasts. The *Magic Bunny* and the *Dohan Food & Bake Shop* on Rizal St are also worth trying. *Peppermint Bakeshop* on F R Castro Ave on the corner of Hernando Ave is good although meals are more expensive.

McBurgee, as the name suggests is a fast-food place, and *Colonial Fast Food* is an air-con restaurant which serves tasty Filipino food; both are on F R Castro Ave.

Getting There & Away

There are twice-weekly flights between Manila and Laoag. Buses from Manila take 10 hours and from Vigan three hours. Less frequent buses travel around the north coast to Claveria (four hours) and Aparri (eight hours).

LAOAG TO APARRI

At **Pagudpud**, 60 km north of Laoag, there is one of the best beaches in North Luzon. Claveria's beach resort was badly hit by a typhoon in 1987. There are Ita tribespeople living south of Claveria and you can also make trips from here to the **Babuyan Islands**. Aparri's only real interest is for deep-sea fishing.

Places to Stay & Eat

In Pagudpud, the *Villa del Mar* has basic rooms from P50 to P150 and cottages with two rooms and a kitchen for about P500.

The *Victoria Hotel* on De Riviera St,

Aparri, has rooms for P30/60. The *Pipo Hotel* at 37 Macanaya District has rooms with fan for P40/80 or with fan and bath for P60/100.

The *Dreamland Hotel* has rooms with fan for P40/60, with fan and bath for P60/100 or with air-con and bath for P100/150. The Dreamland also has a restaurant, otherwise the only decent place to eat is the *Magnolia Restaurant* near the river.

Getting There & Away

It takes two hours from Laoag to Pagudpud, two more hours to Claveria and another four from there to Aparri. There are regular buses between Manila and Aparri, running up the eastern side of Luzon and taking about 11 hours.

TUGUEGARAO

The **Callao Caves** are near Penablanca, about 25 km west of Tuguegarao. There are some good walks in the **Sierra Madre**.

Places to Stay

The *LB Lodging House* on Luna St has rooms at P30 per person or there's the *Olympia Hotel* (☎ 1805) on Washington St where rooms with fan and bath are P35/79 or with air-con and bath P75/100.

Georgie's Inn (☎ 1434) in Aguinaldo St has rooms with fan and bath for P60/90 or with air-con and bath for P150/180. The *Pensione Abraham* (☎ 1793) on Bonifacio St is slightly cheaper but not so good.

On Gonzaga St, *Hotel Delfino* (☎ 1952/3) has singles with air-con and bath for P109 and doubles for P145 to P175. This is the best hotel in town and also has a restaurant and disco. At Penablanca you can stay in the *Callao Caves Resort* where rooms cost P50 to P150 or there are cottages for P300 to P420.

Places to Eat

Opposite Pensione Abraham, the *Pampanguena Restaurant* changes its menu daily and has a surprisingly large choice of cakes. Other possibilities include the *Olympia Hotel* and the restaurants at *LB Lodging*

House and *Georgie's Inn*. *Apollo Restaurant* is an Ihaw-Ihaw restaurant near the Pantranco bus terminal.

Getting There & Away

PAL flies between Manila and Tuguegarao daily. Pantranco North buses from Manila take nine hours and depart hourly. There's a daily bus to Bontoc, via Banaue, taking 10 hours.

BALER & EAST LUZON

Much of *Apocalypse Now* was shot near Baler on the wild east coast of North Luzon. The town itself is not very interesting but you can visit the surrounding country and the coast.

Places to Stay & Eat

The *Amihan Hotel* on Bitong St has rooms with fan for P40/75 or doubles with fan and bath for P90. There are various places along the beach in Sabang like *Maharlika Beach Rest House* where rooms are P100, *Ocean View Lodge* with rooms at P100 to P150 or *MIA Surf & Sports Resort* with rooms with fan at P70/100.

Getting There & Away

It takes 2½ hours to get from Manila to Cabanatuan and another four hours from there to Baler. If coming south from Tuguegarao you also change buses at Cabanatuan.

South Luzon

The South Luzon Bicol region is composed of four provinces and two islands (Catanduanes and Masbate). Plenty of buses (and the odd train) run here from Manila or you can fly there. The major attraction of the Bicol region is the majestic Mayon volcano, claimed to be the most perfectly symmetrical volcano cone in the world.

Getting There & Away

You can get south to the Bicol region from

Manila by bus or rail. Buses to Legaspi all pass through Naga. Philtranco buses depart from the terminal on EDSA Ave in Pasay City and the trip takes nine to 11 hours. There are also air-con buses at night, which leave at 7 and 8 pm. The fare to Legaspi ranges from P190, depending on the bus. The train service south is no longer worth considering.

Things to Buy

In South Luzon, abaca products are the main craft. Abaca is a fibre produced from a relative of the banana tree. It's best known end-product was the rope known as Manila hemp (as opposed to Indian hemp, produced from fibre of the marijuana plant!) but today it's made into all manner of woven products including bags or place mats. *Pili* nuts are a popular favourite of the Bicol region.

Around Daraga you can find oddities like marble eggs from Romblon or whole suites of furniture made from used car tyres! Some interesting pottery can be found in Tiwi.

LUCENA CITY

The capital of Quezon Province, Lucena City is a departure point for boats to Marinduque & Romblon. They leave from the river harbour of Cotta Port, just outside the town. About six km out of the city is the not very pleasant Dalahican Beach. Take along water and food if you intend to go hiking in the **Quezon National Park**, one of the largest wildlife reserves in Luzon.

Places to Stay & Eat

Cheap hotels are mainly in the Barrio Ayam area – get there on a jeepney or tricycle. They include the *Tourist Hotel* (☎ 71 4456) with a restaurant and singles at P40, singles/doubles with fan and bath for P60/80 or with air-con and bath at P90/110.

The *Lucena Fresh Air Resort* (☎ 71 2424, 71 3031) is in the Isabang district at the edge of town as you enter from Manila. Rooms with fan cost P78, with fan and bath P155 or with air-con and bath P275. There's also a restaurant and pool.

The *Casa Arias Garden Restaurant*, in the centre near the BLTB bus station, is good.

Getting There & Away

Philtranco, Superlines and BLTB buses operate to Lucena City from Manila, taking about 2½ hours. Some services continue south to Daet, Naga, Legaspi or Matnog.

Supreme Lines buses from Santa Cruz/Pagsanjan to Lucena City take three hours but it may be faster to take a jeepney from Santa Cruz to Lucban and another from there to Lucena City.

SAN MIGUEL BAY

San Miguel Bay, with its beaches and islands, is an interesting detour on the route south. **Daet** is a good overnight stop en route to the bay. **Mercedes**, a small coastal village about 10 km north-east of Daet, has a 6 to 8 am fish market and from here you can reach **Apuao Grande Island** in San Miguel Bay with its white sand beach. You can cross the bay to Bagacay and continue from there to Naga.

Places to Stay & Eat

In Daet, the *Hotel Alegre* on Justo Lukban St has rooms with fan and bath for P50/80. Singles with air-con and bath are P100 to P120 and doubles P120 to P150. There's a loud disco downstairs. On the outskirts on Vinzons Ave the *Mines Hotel* (☎ 2483) has rooms with fan and bath for P110/155 or with air-con and bath for P270/320.

The centrally located and cheap *Karilagan Hotel* (☎ 2265) has rooms with fan and bath for P120/160 or with air-con and bath for P230/280.

A few streets away from the Karilagan Hotel, the *Golden Horse* has good food.

Getting There & Away

PAL have flights to Daet from Manila three times a week.

Buses from Manila take about seven hours to Daet, some continuing to centres further south. It's about three hours further south to Legaspi, via Naga. Jeepneys go to Mercedes, the jumping-off point for the San Miguel Bay islands.

NAGA

This otherwise uninteresting town has the **Penafrancia Festival** (late-September) which includes a huge and colourful procession.

Places to Stay

The *Naga City Guest House* (☎ 2503) on Burgos St has some singles with fan for P65, doubles with fan and bath are P95 and air-con rooms with bath are P150/180. It's a good place as is the *Fiesta Hotel* (☎ 2760) on Padian St, which has a restaurant and disco on the roof. Rooms are P55/75 with fan, P105/130 with fan and bath and P185/220 with air-con and bath.

The *Crown Hotel* (☎ 2585) on Burgos St is in the town centre on Plaza Martinez overlooking the Martyrs' Square, the San Francisco Church and the Pantranco bus terminal. There are singles at P56, with fan at P90 or with fan and bath at P125. Singles with air-con and bath are P280 to P380 whereas doubles are P360 to P505.

The *Lindez Hotel* (☎ 2414), also on Burgos St, has rooms with fan at P55/95, with fan and bath at P100/130 or with air-con and bath from P155/200. The *Midtown Traveller's Pension* (☎ 2474) at 38 General Luna St is a good, clean place with dorm beds at P88, rooms with fan and bath at P155/200 or with air-con and bath at P150/285.

The *Aristocrat Hotel* (☎ 5230/71) on Elias Angeles St is probably the best hotel in town with very clean rooms at P86/135. Singles with fan and bath are P148 to P186, doubles P186 to P221. Singles with air-con and bath are P185 to P292 and doubles P228 to P381.

Places to Eat

The *Crown Restaurant* under the Crown Hotel offers air-con comfort. The *Aristocrat Hotel Restaurant* is also recommended. and there are daily specials at the *New China Restaurant* on General Luna St.

Getting There & Away

PAL has a daily flight from Manila which takes one hour. Philtranco buses take 8½ hours from Manila and there are also buses from Daet (1½ hours) and Legaspi (two hours).

IRIGA & LAKE BUHI

About midway between Naga and Legaspi, Iraga is the jumping-off point for visits to **Lake Buhi** where the smallest food-fish in the world are netted (with tiny mesh nets!). You can see the fish in the aquarium in the Municipal Building. Boat trips from the market building are expensive but there's a much cheaper ferry which crosses the lake.

Places to Stay & Eat

Just as you come into town from Naga, the *Lemar Lodge* (☎ 594) on San Nicolas St has singles/doubles with fan for P50/70, with fan and bath for P80/100 or doubles with air-con and bath for P150.

Bayanihan Hotel (☎ 556/8), on Governor Felix Alfelor St and close to the railway line, has singles at P45 or rooms with air-con and bath at P120/165.

The *Ibalon Hotel* (☎ 352/3) on San Francisco St and below the grotto on the hill, is small and elegant and has rooms at P280/360. This is probably the finest hotel in South Luzon.

Getting There & Away

Jeepneys to Lake Buhi leave from outside the Bayanihan Hotel.

LEGASPI

The main city of the Bicol region hugs the waterfront in the shadow of the Mayon volcano. The 'headless monument' on the waterfront to those who died at the hands of the Japanese in WW II is sadly neglected. In the **St Raphael Church**, on Aguinaldo St and across from the Rex Hotel, the altar is a 10-tonne volcanic rock from Mayon.

Legaspi is actually divided into two parts. Inland from the port area is the Albay area of the town. Here you will find the tourist office beside Penaranda Park, near the cathedral. The two areas are linked by Rizal Ave.

Places to Stay

There are plenty of cheap hotels around Legaspi but none of them will win any prizes for high accommodation standards.

On Magallanes St, close to the centre of

town, the basic *Peking Lodge* (☎ 3198) has rooms with fan for P45/65, with fan and bath for P80/90, and with air-con P130/150.

There is quite a choice along Penaranda St, parallel to the waterfront. *Catalina's Boarding House* (☎ 3593) is a timber building with large rooms with fan at P40/60. On the same street the *Ritz Inn* (☎ 2670) is only reasonably clean and the rooms facing the street are noisy. Singles/doubles are P40/50, with fan P60/70, with fan and bath P80/90 and with air-con and bath P140/170.

Still on Penaranda St, the *Shirman Lodge* (☎ 3031) has singles with fan and bath for P55 to P65 or doubles for P60 to P75. Rooms with air-con and bath, in this simple but good hotel, are P200/220. *Hotel Xandra* (☎ 2688) is also on Penaranda St and has rooms with fan for P50/70, with fan and bath for P100/140 or with air-con and bath for P180/250.

Across the road from the Rex Theatre, but on E Aguinaldo St, the rather run-down *Rex Hotel* (☎ 2743) has rooms with fan and bath for P80/105 or with air-con and bath for P140/190.

Tanchuling International House (☎ 2788, 3494) on Jasmin St has clean and spacious rooms and is only a few minutes' walk from the town centre. There's a fan-cooled dorm at P50 or it's P75 if you want air-con. Rooms with fan are P90/112, with fan and bath P137/182 or with air-con and bath are P225/270.

More expensive places include the *Legaspi Plaza Hotel* (☎ 3344) with rooms with fan and bath for P180/298 or with air-con and bath for P276/342.

Places to Eat
Legaspi offers a wide choice of places to eat – like the *Peking House Restaurant* a couple of doors down from the Rex Theatre and the *New Legaspi*, across Penaranda St. All are clean-looking places offering all-inclusive meals. The food is basically Chinese with some Filipino dishes. Try the New Legaspi's pineapple pie for a special treat.

Shangrila Restaurant is also on Penaranda St. Otherwise, there's the *Four Seasons Restaurant* on Rizal St and the very economical *Oakroom Restaurant* near the Xandra Hotel.

The *Waway Restaurant* on Penaranda St has a local reputation for Filipino food. Watch out for the 'Bicol express' here – dishes with red-hot peppers that get you running for relief at express speed.

The *Hongkong Dimsum & Tea House* on Penaranda St has a combo in the evenings and there's also live music nightly at the *Aura Music Lounge & Restaurant* in the Legaspi Plaza Hotel. The *Legaspi Ice Cream House* makes wonderful ice cream.

Getting There & Away
Air PAL have daily fights from Manila which take 45 minutes.

Bus It's 10 to 12 hours by bus from Manila to Legaspi. Buses to Tabaco take about an hour. Direct buses to Matnog generally come through from Manila and may well be full. It's probably easier to take local services to Sorsogon or Irosin and change there.

AROUND LEGASPI
Santo Domingo
This long, black sand beach is 15 km northeast of Legaspi and sometimes has quite high surf. Jeepneys run from Legaspi to Santo Domingo and tricycles from there to the resorts along the beach.

Daraga & Cagsawa
The 1814 eruption of Mayon totally destroyed the villages of Camalig, Cagsawa and Budiao on the southern side of Mayon. The **Cagsawa Church** was rebuilt in an ornate baroque style at nearby Daraga. It's just a short jeepney ride from Legaspi. The **Cagsawa ruins** are a short distance west of Daraga. There are also some ruins at **Budiao**, about two km from Cagsawa, but they are not so interesting.

Camalig
The interesting **Hoyohoyopan Caves** are about 10 km from Camalig – hire a tricycle there and back or take a jeepney. In Camalig, the church has artefacts that were excavated from the caves in 1972 but, unfortunately, the small museum is no longer open due to the dangerous state of the building. Camalig

is about 14 km from Legaspi and is reached by jeepneys and buses. Tricycles operate from Camalig to the caves.

MAYON

Derived from the word 'beautiful' in the local dialect, Mayon is claimed to be the world's most perfect volcanic cone. You can best appreciate it from the ruins of Cagsawa church. In 1814, Mayon erupted violently, killing 1200 people including those who took shelter in the church. To get to Cagsawa, take a jeepney bound for Camalig and alight at the Cagsawa sign, from where it's a few minutes' walk.

Mayon is said to erupt every 10 years and recently it's been doing even better than that. The spectacular eruption in 1968 was followed by another in 1978 and then another in late 1984. Thousands of people were evacuated from the area during the 1984 eruption.

If you want to appreciate Mayon from closer up, you can climb it in a couple of days – the tourist office in Legaspi will fix you up. Usual cost for two people includes a guide, porter and tent for US$50. Provisions are extra. Count on P120 for two people plus P60 for a second porter if you don't want to carry your own food and gear.

You take a jeepney to Buyuhan (extra cost) and then climb 2½ hours to Camp 1 (Camp Amporo) at about 800 metres. If you start late you spend the night in the simple hut there. Another four hours takes you to Camp 2 (Camp Pepito), at about 1800 metres. Here you have to use a tent as there is no hut. The night can be fairly cold and from here it's a four-hour climb to the summit.

The last 250 metres is a scramble over loose stones and steep rocks; it's advisable to be roped. Going down takes three hours from the crater to Camp 2, two hours to Camp 1 and two hours to the road.

Take warm clothing, a sleeping bag and provisions for two days. You can try hiring a guide and porter in Buyuhan for about P250 a day. You may try the Santa Misericordia Volcano Observatory near Santo Domingo where an experienced guide can be arranged for P600 to P700 for parties of up to four. To try the ascent without a guide is reckless and

irresponsible as many of the harmless looking canyons turn out to be dead ends with sheer drops.

The *Mayon Rest House* is a good viewpoint, 800 metres up the 2450-metre volcano, but it is semi-derelict and you must bring your own bedding and food if you intend to stay. To get there, take a Ligao-bound jeepney from Tabaco to the turn-off from where it's an eight-km walk (or hitch) to the rest house. Alternatively, hire a jeepney from Tabaco or, more economically, persuade the regular Ligao jeepney, for a consideration, to make the detour to the rest house. Above the rest house is the Mayon Volcano Observatory, only 700 metres below the summit. Water is available at the the observatory but bring supplies. You can reach the top and descend in a day.

TABACO

Tabaco is just a departure point for the Catanduanes ferry.

Places to Stay

Tony's Hotel on Riosa St near the market has rooms with fan and bath for P50/70 or with air-con and bath for P110/140. The *EF-Palace Restaurant* is in the same building or try the very clean *Royal Crown Canteen* opposite the Municipal Hall.

Getting There & Away

Buses go direct to Tabaco from Manila or it's just 45 minutes from Legaspi and another half hour on to Tiwi.

TIWI

The hot springs at Tiwi are a real disappointment. They've been commercialised in very bad taste and the development of geothermal power plants in the area has pretty well dried them up. The hostel is still a pleasant place to stay while you explore the area. There are beaches, bubbling pools of hot mud, steam issuing from the ground, the geothermal plant and some interesting old church ruins in the town of Tiwi.

Places to Stay

About three km beyond the town of Tiwi

you'll find the *Bano Youth Hostel* at the hot springs. There's a swimming pool outside and thermal baths in the basement. Rooms are P45/95 with fan and bath or P170/200 with air-con and bath.

The *Tiwi Hot Springs Resort*, next to the youth hostel, has rooms with fan for P100/150 or doubles with air-con and bath for P200.

Getting There & Away

Jeepneys from Penaranda St in Legaspi run directly to Tiwi or you can go via Tabaco. It's a three-km tricycle ride from Tiwi to the hot springs. There are two daily Philtranco buses from Manila to Tiwi.

CATANDUANES

This island, east of Legaspi, can be reached by ferry from Tabaco or by air from Legaspi. There are some excellent beaches, good snorkelling and pleasant waterfalls, but few tourists come here. The main town and accommodation centre is **Virac**. **Puraran**, 30 km north-east, has a wonderful long white beach.

Places to Stay

In the main town of Catanduanes Island you can stay at the cheap *Cherry Don* (☎ 516), right on the central town square, where singles/doubles are P30/60 or P35/75 with fan.

The *Stars & Stripes Lodge* (☎ 635) on Rizal Ave has rooms at P75/100 or P85/110 with fan. The more expensive *Catanduanes Hotel* (☎ 280) on San Jose St has rooms with fan and bath for P100/200.

Getting There & Away

PAL fly daily to Virac from Legaspi. The ferry to Virac, on Catanduanes, departs Tabaco daily and takes three or more hours.

SORSOGON, GUBAT & BULAN

Sorsogon, the capital of the southernmost province of Luzon, is really just a transit region to the Visayas. The unexciting **Rizal Beach** is at nearby Gubat. Ferries cross to Masbate from Bulan.

Places to Stay

The *Dalisay Hotel* (☎ 6926), 182 V L Peralta St,

Sorsogon, is simple and clean with rooms at P30/50, P60 for a double with fan or P80/100 for singles/doubles with fan and bath.

At the *Rizal Beach Resort Hotel*, at Gubat, rooms are P140/240 with fan and bath or P280 for an air-con double with bath.

Mari-El's Lodging House (☎ 721) by the pier in Bulan is dirt cheap at P20/40 for singles/doubles, P25/50 with fan.

Getting There & Away

Buses to Sorsogon, from Legaspi, leave every half hour and take 1½ hours. It's 3½ hours from Legaspi to Bulan.

BULUSAN & IROSIN

Mt Bulusan is the 1560-metre volcano at the centre of the Juban-Bulusan-Irosin triangle. Nearby, is a small crater lake of the same name, a pleasant six-km walk from Bulusan.

Places to Stay

The *Bulusan Lodging House* behind the town hall has clean rooms at P50/100 or P60/120 with fan. At the *Mateo Hot & Cold Springs Resort* in Irosin rooms are P40/80.

Getting There & Away

Buses from Legaspi go to Irosin or to Bulan via Irosin in about 2½ hours.

MATNOG

Right at the southern tip of Luzon, this is the departure point for boats to Allen on Samar.

Places to Stay

Mely's Snack House costs P25 per person. It's a simple place and the only one left in Matnog. If they miss the last ferry, most Filipinos prefer to sleep in the big waiting room at the pier.

Getting There & Away

Buses run to Irosin from Legaspi, from where you continue by jeepney. You can do the trip with all connections in 3½ hours. There are also direct Philtranco buses, but the bus comes straight through from Manila and it can be difficult to get a seat. Coming from Allen there are usually jeepneys waiting to meet the ferry.

Other Islands

Although Luzon is the main island and offers a lot of things to see and do, it is only the start – there are still nearly 7000 islands left to explore. The majority of these 'other islands' are in the group known as the Visayas. This tightly packed scattering of islands lies between Luzon to the north and Mindanao to the south. The main Visayan islands are Samar, Leyte, Bohol, Cebu, Negros, Panay and Romblon. It is in these islands that you can really come to grips with Filipino island-hopping. With so many islands, so many ferries and boats and such relatively short distances to travel between them, the possibilities are immense.

Cebu, the central Visayan island, is the travel centre of the group, and its capital, Cebu City, is one of the most historic and interesting cities in the Philippines, as well as being third in size to Manila and Davao. It was here that Magellan landed on his epic circumnavigation of the world and here that the Spanish first claimed the Philippines.

At the extreme south of the Philippines is the large island of Mindanao. This is the second largest of the Philippine islands and the centre for much of the unrest in the country. The predominantly Muslim Mindanaoans have campaigned long and hard for separation from the rest of the country. There is also Palawan, the long, narrow island that almost looks like a bridge from Luzon to the Malaysian state of Sabah. It has been described as the last frontier of the Philippines.

Very close to Luzon and easily reached from that island, Mindoro has become a very popular escape due to its beautiful beaches and relaxing accommodation possibilities. Finally, sandwiched between Mindoro and Luzon, is the smaller island of Marinduque. Of course, big islands have little islands and two of the most popular beach escapes are of this nature – Boracay Island off Panay and Camiguin off Mindanao.

Things to Buy

In Cebu you'll find lots of shell jewellery and guitars. Making guitars is a big business on Mactan Island near Cebu City. They vary widely in price and quality. In Cebu City, guitar alley is Lincoln St, where you also find cheaper ukeleles.

Iloilo is also known for its shellcraft and for fabrics, particularly the *pina* fabric used to make *barong* shirts. This is also a good town in which to look for 'santos', antique statues of the saints. Other Visayan buys include baskets in Bohol, ceramics in Bacolod and marble items from Romblon.

In Mindanao the barter trade market in Zamboanga is somewhat overrated. Because the smuggling instinct was so ingrained the government gave up fighting and legalised it for this one market only. There you will find everything from Indonesian batiks to Japanese radios. But if you've recently been to Yogya in Indonesia (for the batiks) or Hong Kong (for the radios), you'll be unimpressed. For local crafts go to the neighbouring Central Market as some interesting stalls can be found in amongst the vegetables, meat and produce. The Rocan shell shop is worth a look if you like shells. *Badjao* sea gypsies bob up and down in their outriggers beside the Lantaka Hotel. They sell shells, coral and ship models.

In Davao, once you've checked out the brassware, jewellery and handicrafts, devote your time to sampling the amazing variety of fruits – durians are the Davao speciality. Cagayan de Oro and Marawi are centres for Muslim arts and crafts.

Island Hopping

In the Visayas, possibilities for island-hopping in the Philippines are at their best. A possible island-hopping circuit of the Visayas could take you to most of the places of interest with minimal backtracking. Starting from Manila you could travel down to the Bicol region, and from Matnog at the southern tip of the island there are ferries every day across to Allen at the northern end of Samar.

The new road, down the west coast of

Samar, means it is now a quick and relatively easy trip through Calbayog and Catbalogan then across the bridge to Tacloban on the island of Leyte. This was where MacArthur 'returned' towards the end of WW II. From Tacloban or Ormoc there are regular ships to Cebu City or, less regularly, from Maasin to Bohol.

Cebu was where Magellan arrived in the Philippines and there are a number of reminders of the Spanish period. From Cebu there are daily ferries to the neighbouring island of Bohol, famed for its 'Chocolate Hills'. Ferries also cross daily between Cebu and Negros, either in the south of the island to Dumaguete or closer to Cebu City from Toledo to San Carlos. You can then continue by bus to Bacolod from where ferries cross to Iloilo on Panay.

From Iloilo, in the south of Panay, you can travel to Caticlan at the north-west tip and make the short crossing by outrigger to the beautiful, relaxing island of Boracay. After a spell of lazing on the beach you can find another outrigger to cross to Tablas Island in the Romblon group, usually to Looc in the south. Take a jeepney to Odiongan and a boat from there to Roxas in Mindoro. Another bus ride will take you to Puerto Galera, a popular travellers' beach centre.

Finally, there are daily ferries to Batangas, only a few hours by bus from Manila. All things considered, that makes an interesting and adventurous loop taking in most of the islands of the Visayas.

Bohol

It's a short ferry trip from Cebu City to the island of Bohol. Its 'Chocolate Hills' are strangely rounded and look rather like chocolate drops when the vegetation turns brown in the dry season. They are about 60 km from Tagbilaran, the main town. Bohol is an easy-going, quiet sort of place with some fine beaches, relatively untouched forests and interesting old churches.

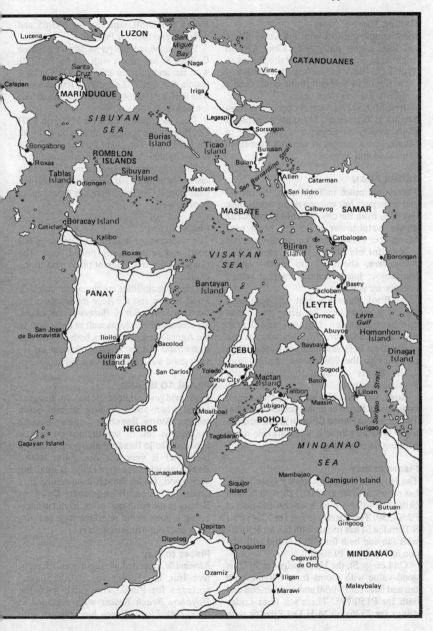

Getting There & Away

Most people get to Bohol via Cebu. There are PAL flights daily from Cebu City to Tagbilaran plus a couple of daily ferries to Tagbilaran (three to four hours), a number of daily ferries to Tubigon (three hours) and a couple to Talibon (four hours).

Aerolift and PAL both fly every day from Manila to Tagbilaran. There are a couple of ships weekly to Leyte, a weekly ship to Manila and a number of services to ports in Mindanao and Negros.

TAGBILARAN

There's not much in Tagbilaran, the capital and main port, but you can make worthwhile day trips from the city. The old **Punta Cruz pirate watchtower** is 15 km north near Maribojoc. Loon, a few km north-west, has a beautiful old church dating from 1753. **Antequera**, about 10 km north-east of Maribojoc, has a Sunday market where basketware is sold.

At **Bool**, three km east of Tagbilaran, there's a monument recalling the blood compact between Legaspi and Rajah Sikatuna. **Baclayon**, four km east, is the oldest town in Bohol with one of the oldest churches in the Philippines, dating from 1595. Boats go from there to nearby Pamilacan Island.

Loay has an old church and outrigger boats go up the river to the **Tontonan Falls**. The large **San Pedro Church** in Loboc dates from 1602 and there is a remarkable naive painting on its ceiling.

Places to Stay

The *Traveller's Inn*, on Carlos P Garcia Ave, has rooms with fan at P100/120, with fan and bath at P140/160 or with air-con and bath at P250/350. The *Executive Inn* (☎ 3254) on J S Torralba St has rooms with fan for P50/70, with fan and bath for P80/100 and with air-con and bath for P150/200.

On Lesage St, the *Vista Lodge* (☎ 3072) is good value with rooms from P40/60, with fan and bath for P70/90 and with air-con and bath for P150/175. There's a *Vista Lodge Annex* (☎ 2326) on M H Del Pilar St with

rooms at P35/50, with fan for P45/65 and with fan and bath for P60/80.

The *Dagohoy Hotel* (☎ 3479) on Cellestino Gallares St has rooms with fan for P60/120, with fan and bath for P80/160. On Carlos P Garcia Ave, the *LTS Lodge* (☎ 3310) has rooms with fan for P110/190 and with air-con and bath for P280/380.

The *Gie Garden Hotel* (☎ 3182) on M H Del Pilar St has rooms with air-con and bath for P250/380. The *Hotel La Roca* (☎ 3179) is on Graham Ave, on the northern edge of town towards the airport and has rooms with fan and bath for P170/230 or with air-con and bath from P330/380. There's is a swimming pool as well.

Places to Eat

The restaurant at the *Gie Garden Hotel* has good and economically priced food. The *Garden Café* is a pleasant place next to the church.

Other possibilities are the reasonable *JJ's Food Stream* and the *Rose Restaurant*. The *Leoning Snack Bar & Bakery* serves cakes, ice cream and snacks as well as breakfast. In the Agora Market complex both the *Harvest Restaurant* and the *Horizon Restaurant* are very good but a bit more expensive.

PANGLAO ISLAND

Two bridges connect Bohol to Panglao Island where there are now several beach resorts. **Alona Beach** is popular but the seagrass is full of sea urchins so care is required. **Doljo Beach** is also good although the water is very shallow. **Palm Island Beach**, about a km east of Doljo, is small but very good. **Bikini Beach** disappeared in a recent typhoon. **Hinagdanan Cave** at Bingag in the north-east of the island is interesting to look at but resist the urge to swim in its cool but diseased waters.

Places to Stay

Alonaville, operated by Tagbilaran's Executive Inn, has rooms for P100/150 and cottages for P200. They also own the *Hoyohoy Beach Resort* with cottages at P300/400. *Playa Blanca* has cottages with bath for P210. There's a restaurant and they will arrange excursions by boat and jeep.

Alona Kew White Beach has double rooms for P250, cottages for P400 and a fine, big restaurant. They also arrange excursions. The *Bohol Divers Lodge* has cottages at P300 to P400.

The other places are all expensive – there's the *Bohol Beach Club* barely two km east of Alona Beach, the *Panorama Lodge* at Dauis and the *Momo Beach Resort* at Momo Beach.

At Palm Island Beach the *Palm Island Beach Resort* has rooms for P150/250 and a good cheap restaurant.

Getting There & Away

Minibuses go from the Agora Market in Tagbilaran to the island. Those marked 'Panglao' go right across the island to Panglao town near Doljo Beach. Those marked 'Panglao-Tauala' go along the southern coast and detour to Alona Beach. It takes two hours to Panglao town or Alona Beach and costs P6. By tricycle it costs P80 and takes an hour but they'll ask P100.

OTHER ISLANDS

There's some superb diving around Bohol. **Balicasag Island**, just 10 km south-west of Panglao Island, is surrounded by a coral reef. **Pamilacan** is a beautiful little island, 20 km south-east but it gets very few visitors. **Cabilao Island**, 30 km north-west of Tagbilaran, has excellent diving and snorkelling.

CHOCOLATE HILLS

Legends relate that the Chocolate Hills are either the teardrops of a heartbroken giant or the debris from a battle between two giants, but the scientific explanations for these curious, similarly shaped hills are more mundane. Some scientists think the hills are the result of volcanic eruptions at the time when this area was submerged. Others think that this is nonsense, believing that the hills are the result of special weathering of a marine limestone formation over impermeable claystone.

The hills (there are more than 1000 of

them) are around 30 metres high, and hiking in the area is best in the December to May dry season. At this time they are also most 'chocolate-like' since the vegetation has turned brown.

Places to Stay

The *Chocolate Hills Complex* is right in amongst the hills, about 53 km from Tagbilaran. It's a km off the main road on the top of the highest hill. Cottages (doubles) are P150 and the hostel dorm is P50. There's also a swimming pool and a good restaurant.

Getting There & Away

Carmen, the town for the Chocolate Hills, is 58 km from Tagbilaran – everybody on the bus will assume you're going there so there is no chance of missing the place where you get off. There is a bus every 30 to 60 minutes. It's about two hours by bus between the Chocolate Hills and Tubigon.

OTHER PLACES

Tubigon is a small town from where ships operate to and from Cebu. **Talibon** also has shipping services to Cebu and is the jumping off point for nearby Jao Island. From **Ubay**, on the east coast, boats run to Leyte.

Places to Stay

The *Alexandra Reserva Lodging House* is near the wharf and bus terminal in Tubigon and has rooms with fan for P40/60. The *Lapyahan Lodge* in Talibon has rooms at P30/60 or with fan and bath for P50/100. In Ubay, you can stay in the *Royal Orchid Pension House* where rooms are P50/100 or P60/120 with fan.

Getting There & Away

From Tubigon, buses to Carmen take two hours, and to Tagbilaran, 1½ hours. Buses from Tagbilaran to Talibon take four hours and go via Carmen and the Chocolate Hills at the midpoint of the trip. Tagbilaran to Ubay buses also go via Carmen.

Camiguin

Off the north coast of Mindanao, this is an idyllic, small, get-away-from-it-all sort of place. The name is pronounced like 'come again'! The tiny island actually has seven volcanoes, best known of which is Hibok-Hibok which last erupted in 1951. The beaches are nothing special, but the people are great.

Getting There & Away

There may be occasional ships from other islands, but the usual route is from Balingoan in Mindanao to Binone on Camiguin. A ferry crosses three or more times daily and the trip takes an hour or more.

If you leave Cebu in the evening you can reach Cagayan de Oro in 10 hours, make the 1½-hour bus trip to Balingoan and then ferry across to Camiguin, arriving by mid-afternoon. The faster trip is directly from Cebu City to Mambajao, the capital of Camiguin Province, by ship (MV *Luzille*, Georgia Shipping Lines) on Wednesday or Friday. The trip takes eight hours.

Several times a week, though irregularly, there are ships from Jagna, on Bohol, to Agoho, on Camiguin.

Getting Around

The 65-km circuit of the island takes about three hours actual travel time and it's best to go clockwise and start early for the best connections. Mambajao to Binone is made by jeepney as is Binone to Catarman. Take a tricycle from Catarman to Bonbon, then its a four-km walk and a short tricycle ride from Yumbing to Mambajao. There's only one jeepney a day between Catarman and Mambajao, although there are several connections Mambajao-Binone-Catarman. Motorbikes can be rented for about P200 a day in Mambajao.

MAMBAJAO

This, the capital and main town on Camiguin, is where you'll find most of the accommodation, tourist information in the Provincial Capitol building and a bank where you can change travellers' cheques.

Places to Stay

The *Tia's Pension House*, near the Municipal Hall, has rooms for P50/100. There are also *Tia's Beach Cottages*, just a few minutes from the centre in Tapon, with cottages for P200. The very basic *Camiguin Travellers' Lodge* has singles/doubles for P70/80.

Just a five-minute walk from the town proper, at Cabua-an Beach, there is *Gue's Cottage* which is clean, quiet and costs P70 to P80 for two. Between Agoho and Bugong there are beach bungalows, and some have kitchens.

AROUND THE ISLAND

Starting from Mambajao, and travelling anti-clockwise, at **Kuguita** there's a beach and some coral where you can snorkel. Another four km takes you to **Agoho** where the *Caves Resort* is a beautiful place near the beach with rooms from P50 to more than P150. The food here is also good value. Some other possibilities are the *Camiguin Seaside Lodge* and the *Morning Glory Cottages*, both with dorm beds, rooms and cottages.

Continuing beyond Yumbing, you can walk from Naasag to the **Tangub Hot Springs. Bonbon** has some interesting church ruins and a cemetery which is submerged in the sea and only visible at low tide. Near Catarman, a track leads to the **Tuwasan Falls.** Down at the southern end of the island, there's a 300-year-old **Moro watchtower** at Guinsiliban.

Binone is near the artificial Tanguine Lagoon where the *Travel Lodge Lagoon* has rooms from P40 per person and more expensive cottages. The rather run-down *Mychellin Beach Resort* is opposite Mantigue (Magsaysay) Island in Mahinog and has rooms from P120/180 and cottages from P140. Finally, **Magting** has a pebble beach but you can snorkel offshore from outriggers. *Padilla's Beach Cottages* are P35 per person and, again, there are cottages as well.

Hibok-Hibok Volcano

The 1800-metre Hibok-Hibok volcano can be climbed in the dry season – enquire at the tourist department in the Provincial Capitol building, Mambajao. A guide is useful as the weather on the mountain is changeable and you can easily get lost. The volcano erupted disastrously in 1951 and it's now monitored from the Comvol station. You can have a look around, and this is also a good place to stay on the way up or down.

Katibawasan Waterfall

The waterfall, with good swimming, is three km from Pandan, which in turn is only two km from Mambajao. Near here is the Ardent Hot Spring.

White Island

Three km off Agoho, this small island is just a sand spar. There is no shade but there is great diving. Count on P100 to P150 to rent a boat for the round trip but arrange a definite time to be picked up.

Cebu

The most visited of the Visayan islands, Cebu is also the shipping hub of the Philippines. The number of shipping companies and agents in Cebu City and the number of ships at the dock is quite incredible. This is also the place where Magellan first landed in the Philippines so it also has the longest history of European contact.

Getting There & Away

Shipping company addresses in Cebu City include:

Aboitiz Lines
  Osmena Blvd (☎ 75440, 93075)
George & Peter Lines
  Jakosalem St (☎ 75508, 74098)
Carlos Gothong Lines
  Reclamation Area (☎ 73107, 95545)
Sulpicio Lines
  Reclamation Area (☎ 73839, 79956)

Sweet Lines
  Arellano Blvd (☎ 97415, 77431)
William Lines
  Reclamation Area (☎ 92471, 73 6619)

To/From Bohol There are several departures daily between Cebu City and Tagbilaran and Tubigon on Bohol. The crossing takes 2½ hours to Tubigon (P50) and four hours to Tagbilaran (P40 to P75 depending on class). PAL also flies Cebu City to Tagbilaran. There is plenty of transport from Tagbilaran or Tubigon to the Chocolate Hills so there's no reason to prefer one route over the other.

To/From Camiguin The usual route is Cebu to Cagayan de Oro or Butuan in Mindanao by air, then a bus to Balingoan from where ferries run across to Binone three times daily.

To/From Leyte A variety of ships operate between Cebu City and Baybay, Maasin, Ormoc, Tacloban and other ports on Leyte. There are flights with PAL or Pacific Airways between Cebu City and Ormoc, Tacloban and Maasin.

To/From Luzon You can fly between Cebu City and Manila or Legaspi. Lots of ships operate between Cebu and Manila and the trip takes about 20 to 24 hours.

To/From Mindanao There are an enormous number of ships operating between Cebu and Mindanao. It takes 10 to 12 hours between Cebu City and Butuan, Cagayan de Oro, Dipolog, Iligan, Ozamiz or Surigao. Zamboanga is about 16 hours away and Davao about 24 hours. There are an equally wide variety of flights between Cebu City and major towns on Mindanao.

To/From Negros There are two departures daily (one on Sunday) between Toledo on Cebu and San Carlos on Negros and the trip takes two hours. There are connecting buses between San Carlos and Bacolod. Other less regular routes between these narrowly separated islands include Bato to Tampi, Talisay to San Jose and Liloan to Sibuyan in the far

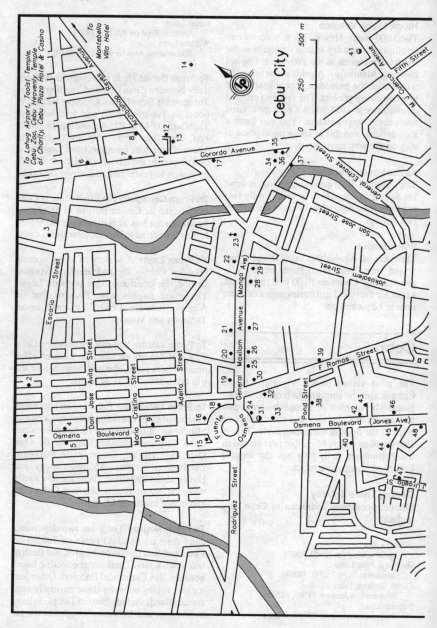

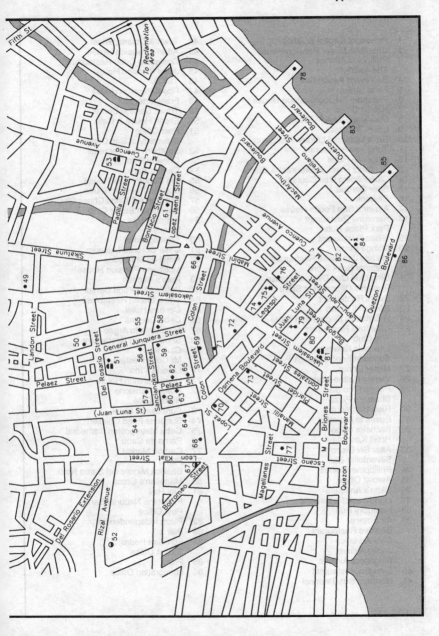

1 Provincial Capitol Building	42 Town & Country Hotel
2 Cebu Mayflower Pension House	43 Arbel's Pension House
3 Philippine Airlines	44 Cosina sa Cebu Restaurant
The Apartelle	45 Jovel Pension House
4 Boulevard Restaurant	46 YMCA
5 Food Street	47 Royal Pension House
6 Pistahan Filipino Seafood House	48 Frankfurter Hof
7 Hotrod Diner	49 Travel Service Center
8 Maanyag Pension House	50 Elicon House & Cafe
9 Love City Disco	51 Post Office
10 Rizal Memorial Library & Museum	University of San Carlos
11 Tung Yan Restaurant	52 Southern Bus Terminal
12 Magellan Hotel	53 General Post Office
13 St Moritz Hotel, Restaurant & Disco	54 Central Bank
14 Club Filipino Golf Course	55 Big Country Folk House
15 Beer Garden	56 Surigao Pension House
16 Citibank	57 Our Place & Cebu Chess Club
17 Alavar's Sea Foods House	58 Bayanihan Super Club
18 Kurofune Restaurant	59 Bottoms Up
Park Place Hotel	Manny's
19 Ginza Restaurant	60 Tagalog Hotel
20 Mango Plaza	61 Casa Gorordo Museum
Mikado Japanese Restaurant	62 Hotel de Mercedes
National Book Store	McSherry Pension House
21 Ding Qua Qua Dimsum House	63 Pete's Kitchen
Rustan's Department Store	Pete's Mini Food Center
22 Swiss Restaurant	64 Snow Sheen Restaurant
23 Iglesia Ni Cristo	65 Century Hotel
24 Robinson's Department Store	66 Cebu Queens
25 Little Italy Restaurant	67 Minibuses to Argao
The Club	68 Snow Sheen Restaurant
26 Lawiswis Kawayan	69 Club 99
Sunburst Fried Chicken	Mr Cook Restaurant
27 Mister Donut	70 Lovena's Inn
28 Vienna Kaffee-Haus	71 Hope Pension House
29 Puerto Rico Bar	72 Ruftan Pensione
Shakey's Pizza	Ruftan Café
30 Ric's Barbecue	73 Sundowner Hotel
31 Buses to Airport	74 Sunburst Fried Chicken
32 Bachelor's Too	75 Cebu Metropolitan Cathedral
Hotel Kan-Irag	76 Patria de Cebu
33 After Six Disco	77 Carbon Market
Silverdollar Bar	78 Pier 3
34 Philippine Airlines	79 Basilica Minore del Santo Nino
35 Aerolift Office	80 Magellan's Cross
36 Likha's Antiques	81 City Hall
37 Lighthouse Restaurant	Philippine National Bank
38 Kentucky Pub	Post Office
39 Air France	82 Plaza Independencia
Beehive Restaurant	83 Pier 2
Café Adriatico	84 Fort San Pedro
Japan Airlines	Tourist Office
Singapore Airlines	85 Pier 1
40 Sinugba Restaurant	86 Immigration Office
41 Northern Bus Terminal	

south; from Guihulngan to Tangil in the centre; and from Cadiz via Bantayan Island to Hagnaya in the north. Ships also operate between Dumaguete and Cebu City.

To/From Other Places There are also connections between Cebu and Palawan, Panay, Samar and Siquijor.

Getting Around
Buses run from Cebu City's Southern bus terminal to Toledo and the other west coast departure points from Cebu to the neighbouring island of Negros.

CEBU CITY
Cebu City is the capital and main city on the island of Cebu and Colon St is claimed to be the oldest street in the Philippines. The city is currently undergoing considerable redevelopment and modernisation. It's an easy-going city with plenty of places to stay and eat.

Orientation & Information
Colon St is the main street in the town and where you will find most of the restaurants, hotels and travel agencies. There are virtually no street signs in Cebu, so if you're looking for a particular street you'll have to ask. There has also been some recent street renaming.

The tourist office is inside Fort San Pedro. Explain that you're going into the office and you shouldn't have to pay the fort admission charge. Citibank or Interbank, both on Osmena Blvd, are good places to change money.

If you are arriving or leaving by ship take great care with your valuables – pickpockets are notorious around the Cebu dock area and it's easy to lose things in the crush. They also work the Colon St and Osmena Blvd area, particularly in the late afternoon and evening.

Things to See
Fort San Pedro This is the oldest Spanish fort in the country. It was originally built in 1565 by Legaspi to keep out the marauding

pirates with whom the Spanish were having more than a little trouble. Today, it is gradually being restored and the main entrance is very impressive. Entry is P5.

Cross of Magellan A small circular building, opposite the town hall, houses a cross which is said to contain fragments of the actual cross brought here by Magellan and used in the first conversions.

Basilica of San Agustin Opposite the Magellan kiosk is the only basilica in the Far East. The *Santo Nino*, an image of Jesus as a child, was said to have been given to Queen Juana by Magellan on the queen's baptism in 1521. It's the oldest religious relic in the country.

Other There's an interesting **small museum** in the University of San Carlos. Overlooking the town, in the ritzy Beverley Hills residential area, is a gaudy **Taoist temple**. To get to the temple take a Lahug jeepney and ask to stop at Beverley Hills – you've then got a 1½-km walk uphill. Alternatively, take a taxi for about P20.

Colon St in Cebu is said to be the oldest street in the Philippines but you'd never know it. The interesting **Carbon Market** sells produce and handicrafts, and is at the end of M C Briones St. In the downtown Parian district, the **Casa Gorordo Museum** is a restored and period-furnished home dating from the turn of the century.

Places to Stay
At 61 Osmena Blvd, about halfway from Fuenta Osmenta (the airport bus stops here) to the city centre, the *YMCA* (☎ 72125) has good dormitory accommodation at P80 through to rooms with fan for P120. Couples are accepted and there's a charge for short-term membership.

Only about 100 metres away, the *Town & Country* (☎ 78190) is also on Osmena Blvd and is reasonably plush and modern. Sometimes known as the Town House, it has rooms with fan for P75, with fan and private bath for P168 and with air-con P268.

654 The Philippines – Cebu

Opposite the YMCA at 24 K Uytengsu Rd (off Osmena Blvd) is the clean, quiet *Jovel Pension House* (☎ 92990) with singles/doubles for P200/250 or P310/350 with air-con.

In the same area, down a side street between these two places, is the popular little *Arbel's Pension Hotel* (☎ 62393) at 57E Osmena Blvd with singles/doubles at P90/120. Some of the rooms don't have windows. At 165 J Urgello St, about a half km from the Town & Country, the *Royal Pension House* (☎ 93890) is clean, pleasant and rooms are from P100.

The *Ruftan Pensione & Cafe* (☎ 79138) near the corner of Legaspi and Manalili Sts, much closer to the centre, is related to Arbel's. It's a good, clean place and has simple rooms at P130/180, rooms with private bath, coffee and toiletries for P250/350. *Hope Pension House* (☎ 93371) is only 100 metres away on Manalili St and is reasonably good with rooms from P150/170, more with air-con.

In the centre, on P Burgos St opposite the Cebu Cathedral, is the *Patria de Cebu* with rooms from P70 but it's grubby. The peaceful *Cebu Mayflower Pension Hotel* (☎ 72948) is near the Capitol and has rooms with fan for P70/95, and P180/225 with air-con. *Lovena's Inn* (☎ 99212) on Osmena Blvd is nicely central and has rooms from P120 with fan, more with air-con but all have bathrooms.

Elicon House (☎ 21 0367), on the corner of P del Rosario and General Junquera Sts, has fan rooms for P100, with and air-con and bath for P200. It's a good, clean place and the Elicon Cafe is right downstairs. The *Tagalog Hotel* (☎ 72531) on Sanciangko St has rooms from P200 or from P250 with bathroom and air-con.

Right at the bottom of the low-price range is the *Cebu Queens* at 5 Colon St. Rooms cost from P55 but it's a bit of a dive. Finally, if you have an early flight, the *Silangan Hotel* near the airport is reasonable value at P300 with air-con and bath. At the better quality places in Cebu, it's worth asking if they've got rooms without air-con, if you're looking for cheaper accommodation. They'll always try to steer you towards air-con first of all.

Places to Eat

There are lots of places to eat at in Cebu, many of them along Colon St – you can, of course, eat much more cheaply off this beaten track. The *Snow Sheen Restaurant* is near the corner of Osmena Blvd and Colon St and has very good and low-priced Chinese and Filipino food. There is another *Snow Sheen* around the corner in Colon St. *Pete's Kitchen*, on Pelaez St, also has keenly priced Chinese and Filipino food. Nearby is *Pete's Mini Food Center*, a big, partly open-air restaurant.

Near the Royal Pension House on Ascension St is the *Cosina sa Cebu*, a favourite student hang-out. The *Tung Yan Restaurant* on Gorordo Ave is expensive but it's probably the best Chinese restaurant in town. The *Ruftan Cafe*, on Legaspi St, is good for breakfast, as is the cheap *YMCA Restaurant* on Osmena Blvd.

General Maxilom Ave (it used to be Mango Ave) has lots of places to eat including a *Shakey's Pizza*, the airy *Farm*, *Kalilili Chicken* and the *Lighthouse* for Filipino food. The *Swiss Restaurant*, on this same street, has excellent European food.

Gardenia's, at Cebu Capitol Commercial complex on North Escario St, has good food at reasonable prices and a stunning setting. At the *Farmhouse*, at 406 Gorordo Ave, you cook your own food. For fresh seafood, try the *Pistahan Filipino Seafood Restaurant* at 329 Gorordo.

If you're looking for something open in the wee hours, there's the 24-hour *Maynila: A Native Restaurant*, opposite the Casino Filipino in Lahug, Nivel Hills.

Entertainment

Cebu City is nearly as active as Manila when it comes to entertainment. Try *Our Place* for cheap beer and good food. There are plenty of discos, nightclubs and go-go joints or there's the *Casino Filipino*, in Lahug, if you really feel like throwing money around.

Getting There & Away

Cebu is the major travel hub in the southern islands of the Philippines with flights and shipping services radiating out in all directions. There are frequent flights and ships between Manila and Cebu City, in particular.

There are several buses daily from the Southern bus terminal for the 1½-hour trip from Cebu City to Toledo on the other coast. You also find buses at the Southern bus terminal for Santander and Moalboal, other departure points for Negros.

Getting Around

To/From the Airport There's a shuttle bus to the city which costs P12.50. The PAL office is on General Maxilom Ave in the north part of the city, inconvenient for most other places in Cebu City. Alternatively, you can take a taxi for about P65 or take a tricycle from near the terminal to the Mactan Bridge (P3) and a jeepney into the city (P3) from there.

Local Transport Jeepneys around Cebu City cost about P2. There are also lots of PU-Cabs, the local taxi-trucks, which have a flat charge. The boat piers are not far from the centre and you can take a PU-Cab into the city. The Southern bus terminal in Cebu City is on Rizal Ave and the Northern bus terminal is on MacArthur Blvd.

AROUND CEBU
Mactan Island

The island where Magellan met Lapu-Lapu (and lost) is now the site for Cebu's airport and is joined to Cebu by a bridge. On the island there is a monument to Lapu-Lapu, and this is the place where guitars, one of the big industries in Cebu, are manufactured. Magellan also rates a monument. Around the island there are now a number of beach resorts.

At Maribago Beach, you can stay at the *Club Kon-Tiki Resort* (☎ 81 5191) where there are rooms at US$23/25 or a dormitory bed for US$5. Maribago also has a number of more expensive hotels.

Bantayan Island

Off the north-west coast of Cebu, on the south coast of Bantayan Island, there are some good beaches. The island can also be used as a stepping stone to Negros.

Places to Stay The *Santa Fe Beach Resort* in Talisay, just north of Santa Fe, has rooms from P140. Just south is the more expensive *Kota Beach Resort* while the *Saint Josef Lodge* and the *Admiral Lodging House* are cheaper places in Bantayan.

Getting There & Away Buses run from Cebu City's Northern bus terminal to San Remigio and Hagnaya, taking about three hours. There are boats twice daily from Hagnaya to Santa Fe, taking two hours. A daily boat connects Bantayan with Cadiz on Negros.

Toledo

Toledo is the jumping-off point for boats to San Carlos on Negros Island. It is about 1½ hours by bus from Cebu City.

Places to Stay If you have to stay here enquire about the *Lodging House* at the *Vizcayno Restaurant*.

Moalboal

There's good reasonably priced scuba diving at **Pescador Island**, near Moalboal, and a number of beach resorts near the town.

Places to Stay & Eat You can stay in town but it's better to rent a cottage on the beach for P80 to P250 depending on the facilities. Try *Pacita's Nipa Hut, Eve's Kiosk, Norma's Travellers' Rest House, Pacifico's Cottages* and *Cora's Palm Court*. They are all at the lower end of the price scale.

The beach discos can be very loud, so try for a place as far from them as possible if you want some peace and quiet. There's good food at most of these places or slightly more expensive, but delicious, dishes at *Hannah's Place*.

Getting There & Away Numerous buses make the daily 90-km, two-hour trip from

Cebu City for P25. A friendly bus driver may even take you right down to the beach so it's worth asking. Otherwise take a tricycle from Moalboal for about P15.

Transport between Moalboal and Toledo is tricky and may require several changes. Buses run regularly to San Sebastian, at the southern of the island, from where ships make the short crossing to Negros.

Leyte

As is the case with Samar, few Westerners get to Leyte, so you can expect to be stared at a lot. Although there are some outstanding national parks and an impressive mountain region there is little tourist development on Leyte. It's notable for being the island where MacArthur fulfilled his promise to return to the Philippines. Towards the end of WW II Allied forces landed here and started to push the Japanese out.

Getting There & Away

Between Leyte and Cebu you can fly daily, from Tacloban to Cebu City, with PAL. There are also flights from Cebu City to Maasin and Ormoc. Ships operate between Cebu City and a variety of ports around Leyte. It takes about six hours from Ormoc (five days a week), five hours from Bato (three days a week) or Baybay (three days a week). Outriggers take about four hours between Carmen on Cebu and Isabel on Leyte and operate daily.

There are also daily outriggers connecting Ubay on Bohol with Bato and Maasin. The trip takes about four hours to either port. To Mindanao, buses run from Tacloban to Liloan in the south of the island, from where a ferry takes you across to Lipata, 15 km north of Surigao, and from there buses continue to Cagayan de Oro or Davao. The ferry crossing takes three hours. There are also daily ships from Maasin to Surigao.

The San Juanico Bridge connects Leyte with neighbouring Samar. There are daily buses from Tacloban via Catbalogan and Calbayog in Samar and right on through Luzon to Manila, a 25-hour trip in total. PAL has daily flights between Tacloban and Manila.

Getting Around

Buses go hourly between Tacloban and Ormoc – the trip takes four to five hours. Ormoc to Baybay and Tacloban-Baybay-Maasin also have regular bus services.

TACLOBAN

The small port of Tacloban is the capital of Leyte and home town of the great shoe collector, Mrs Marcos. There are a variety of shops along Justice Romualdez St which sell local handicrafts. Seven km out of town, **Red Beach** (it isn't red, as that was just a WW II codename) is the exact place where Douglas MacArthur fulfilled his famous 'I shall return' pledge in October 1944. There's a memorial statue showing MacArthur wading ashore. Take a jeepney there but return by getting another jeepney in the same direction; it loops back via Palo.

For a short period Tacloban served as the capital of the Philippines until Manila was liberated.

Information

There are great views over the town and its busy port from the base of the Christ statue, reached from the market along Torres St.

Places to Stay

Tacloban offers a wide variety of places to stay but it can get pretty hot in this town so air-con can be worth having. Running water is a consideration as the city's water supply is somewhat erratic. *San Juanico Travel Lodge* at 104 Justice Romualdez St has singles/doubles at P60/100 or with bath at P100/150. It's hard to find (no sign) and gets mixed reports – 'clean and friendly' report some travellers, 'a dump', say others.

Manabó Lodge (☎ 3727) on Zamora St has rooms from P120/160. The *Allee Lodge*, on the corner of Burgos and M H Del Pilar Sts, is cheap but not very special with rooms from P50, with bathroom from P70 and even more with air-con.

Cecilia's Lodging House at 178 Paterno St is spartan but reasonably good value from around P80 but more expensive with bathroom or air-con. *LSC House* (☎ 3175) on Paterno St, is also known as the Leyte State College Mini Hotel, and it's pricier with rooms from around P175 to P300.

More expensive places include the *Primerose Hotel* (☎ 2248) on the corner of Zamora and Salazar Sts – air-con rooms range from P200 to P500 but it's musty and not value. The *Tacloban Village Inn* (☎ 2926) on Imelda Ave has air-con rooms from P200/320. *Tacloban Plaza Hotel* (☎ 2444) on Justice Romualdez St and the *Manhattan Inn* (☎ 4170) on Rixal Ave are good clean places with similarly priced rooms.

Places to Eat
You can start the day at the *Good Morning Restaurant* with its adjoining bakery on Zamora St. *Sunburst Fried Chicken* on Burgos St has good chicken and Filipino dishes. The *Asiatic Restaurant* and the *Savory Steak House*, both on Zamora St, have good Chinese and Filipino food.

Still on Zamora St, the *Rovic Restaurant* offers international cuisine, as does the *Veranda Café* in the expensive Leyte Park Hotel. The *Lapyahan House of Seafood* is an eat-with-your-fingers place on Real St.

Entertainment
There's live music at night in the open-air *Sinugba Fiesta* on M H del Pilar St. Plus there's a variety of discos around town.

ORMOC
Ormoc is just the jumping-off point for boats to Cebu. Near Ormoc is the start of the 50-km **Leyte Nature Trail**, which crosses right over the island from Lake Danao to Lake Mahagnao. Unfortunately, NPA activity makes the Leyte National Park an unsafe area to visit.

Places to Stay & Eat
Eddie's Inn (☎ 2499) is on Rizal St, on the corner with Lopez Jeana St. It's 250 metres from the bus terminal and has simple doubles from P60. On the corner of Bonifacio and Cataag Sts, the *Shalom Pensione* (☎ 2208) has simple but clean rooms from P40/80.

The *Hotel Don Felipe* (☎ 2460) on Bonifacio St, has rooms from P100/150. The more expensive rooms with air-con are the best you'll find in Ormoc. On the same street the *Pongos Hotel* (☎ 2482) has very similar prices.

The Don Felipe has a good restaurant or try the *Magnolia Sizzler*, on the corner of Bonifacio and Lopez Jeana Sts.

OTHER PLACES
From Barauen (take a bus there from Tacloban), you can visit the magnificent **Mahagnao Volcano National Park** which has a number of walking trails. You can camp near the **Lake Danao National Park** where there is a very deep and large crater lake – get there from Ormoc. There are some good diving possibilities around Leyte but they have not been developed as yet. You can soak in the **Tungonan Hot Springs**, just north of Ormoc, but the area has been desecrated by a geothermal project.

Biliran Island can be reached by taking a bus from Tacloban to Naval. At Naval, you can stay at the *LM Lodge* on Vicillento St. This area is undeveloped and has great snorkelling. A few km north of Almeria is the pleasant little *Agta Beach Resort* on a pretty bay with cottages for P45/90. There are cheap rooms in the *Lodging House* at Caibiran.

Marinduque

The small island of Marinduque is sandwiched between Mindoro and Luzon. It's noted for its Easter Moriones festivals, in particular at Boac, but also at Mogpog and Gasan. On Good Friday, the *antipos*, or self-flagellants) engage in a little religious masochism as they flog themselves with bamboo sticks.

Getting There & Away

There are usually one or two boats daily from Lucena City in Luzon to Balanacan. The crossing takes four hours and jeepneys meet the boats and go to Boac. Crossings are also made between Lucena City and Buyabod, the harbour for Santa Cruz.

There's a daily service from Gasan, between Boac and Buenavista, to Pinamalayan on Mindoro. The crossing takes three hours or more.

BOAC

On Easter Sunday at Boac, one of the most colourful religious ceremonies in the Philippines takes place. Dressed as Roman centurions wearing large carved masks, the participants capture Longinus, the centurion who was converted after he had stabbed Christ in the side with his spear. The festival ends with a *pugutan* (mock beheading) of the hapless Longinus.

Places to Stay

Cely's Lodging House (☎ 1519) on 10 de Octobre St has rooms with fan at P60/120. On Nepomuceno St, the *Boac Hotel* has simple singles with fan for P60 or rooms with fan and bath for P90/140.

On the beach at Caganhao, between Boac and Cawit, is the *Pyramid Beach Resort* with rooms at P60. The pebbly beach also has the *Aussie Pom Guest House* with simple rooms at P100. A short way out of Boac, towards Mogpog, is *Swing Beach Resort* (☎ 1252) on Deogratias St. Rooms here are P150 per person.

The *Sunraft Beach Hotel* in Cawit, eight km from Boac, has rooms from P100 or there's the *Seaview Hotel* where rooms with fan and bath are P185/245.

SANTA CRUZ

Boac is the capital but Santa Cruz is the largest town and has an impressive church dating from 1714. Diving trips can be made from Santa Cruz.

Places to Stay & Eat

The *Park View Lodge* near the town hall has simple rooms at P50/100. On the corner of Palomares and Pag-asa Sts the *Tita Amie Restaurant* is the best place to eat.

OTHER PLACES

From Buenavista, on the south coast, you can climb **Mt Malindig**, a 1157-metre dormant volcano. The weekend **Buenavista Market** is worth seeing. The **Tres Reyes Islands** are 30 minutes by outrigger from Buenavista – **Gaspar Island** has a small village and a nice coral beach. **White Beach**, near Torrijos, is probably the best beach on Marinduque. The town of **Gasan** is also heavily involved in the Easter passion play.

Masbate

The small island of Masbate is between Luzon and the main Visayan group. It's noted for its large cattle herds but very few travellers come here.

Getting There & Away

There are a couple of ships a week from Cebu (45 hours) and a daily boat making the four-hour trip from Bulan in South Luzon. Boats go from Mandaon on Masbate to Sibuyan Island in Romblon Province. There are flights and boats between Masbate and Manila, and between Masbate and Legaspi.

MASBATE

Masbate is also the main town on the island. **Bitu-on Beach**, a few km south-east, has some cottages which make a good alternative to staying in town.

Places to Stay & Eat

The *Crown Hotel* in Zurbilo St has simple rooms with fan at P50/100 for singles/doubles. The *St Anthony Hotel* is more expensive at P120/180 or P250/280 with air-con.

Try *Peking House,* in the port area, for good food or the *Petit Restaurant* opposite the St Anthony Hotel in Quezon St.

Mindanao

The island of Mindanao, second largest in the country, is the Philippines' biggest trouble spot. Mindanao has a large Muslim population and they have long chafed at Christian rule. Armed at one time by Libya's fervent (and oil-rich) Gaddafi, the Mindanao guerrilla force (the Moro National Liberation Front) has staged a long-running battle with the government forces. It is wise to enquire carefully and think twice before travelling through troubled areas.

Mindanao certainly isn't a new trouble spot. This was the one area of the Philippines where the Muslim religion had gained a toehold by the time the Spanish arrived, and throughout the Spanish era, the situation varied from outright rebellion to uneasy truce.

Getting There & Away

You can fly to Mindanao from Cebu or Manila. There are flights to a number of major cities in Mindanao including Zamboanga, Davao, Cagayan de Oro and Surigao. There are several ships weekly from Cebu to various Mindanao ports and also from Leyte, Negros and Panay. From Manila there are a couple of ships each week to Zamboanga, taking about 36 hours.

There are also regular weekly ships to neighbouring Bohol while Leyte is connected by the Liloan to Lipata (just north of Surigao) ferry service with through buses to and from Tacloban. Balingoan on Mindanao is the jumping-off point for visit to Camiguin Island.

Getting Around

It is wise to be careful when travelling by bus in Mindanao – guerrilla shoot-ups do occur and bus travel is none too safe in any case. The tourist office will advise you on which routes are safe and which ones to forget.

From Zamboanga, there are buses to Pagadian and Dipolog. From Pagadian, you can continue to Iligan from where another bus ride will take you to Cagayan de Oro. Buses continue from Cagayan de Oro to Surigao from where you cross to Leyte. If you're feeling adventurous, you can head south from Cagayan de Oro to Marawi. Davao can be reached from Cagayan de Oro or Iligan. There are also shipping services around the coast.

SURIGAO

From Surigao, you can travel by bus, taking the ferry across to Leyte, and on through Leyte, Samar and right through Luzon to Manila. There are a number of beautiful small islands around Surigao on the northeast tip of Mindanao. They can be reached from General Luna on the island of Siargao. The five to six-hour trip out to the island from Surigao passes through beautiful scenery with many small islands. You can stay in Dapa or General Luna if you ask around.

Places to Stay

The *Flourish Lodge* on Borromeo St, Port Area, has simple but reasonably good rooms from P60/70. At 100 Borromeo St the *Litang Hotel* (☎ 667) has rooms from P40 for a bare single to around P200 for a double with bath and air-con.

At 311 San Nicolas St, the *Garcia Hotel* (☎ 658) is a good place with a variety of rooms from P80/120. Back on Borromeo St, the *Tavern Hotel* (☎ 293) starts at P60/120 for the simplest fan-cooled rooms and goes up to around P300 for an air-con double with bath. It's a pleasant place with a seaside restaurant.

Places to Eat

The *Tavern Hotel* has a pleasant open-air restaurant, or *Cherry Blossom Restaurant*, on the corner of San Nicolas and Vasques Sts, is worth trying for good food and live music.

Getting There & Away

It's about six hours to Cagayan de Oro by bus and eight hours to Davao.

Getting Around

A tricycle between the airport and town is about P10. Most boats use the wharf south of town but the ferries to and from Leyte operate from the Lipata wharf, about 15 km north-west. A regular tricycle trip should be less than P5 per person (P50 for a 'special ride') but there are also buses.

BUTUAN

Butuan is just a junction town three hours south of Surigao by bus but it's thought that this might be the oldest settlement in the Philippines.

Places to Stay

Near the bus terminal on Langihan Rd, the *A&Z Lowcost Lodging House I* is very cheap with rooms from P30/60, more with fan. There's another *A&Z (No II)* on the corner of Burgos and San Francisco Sts.

The simple and straightforward *Elite Hotel* (☎ 3133), on the corner of San Jose and Concepcion Sts, costs from P50/70 with prices stepping up as you add fan, air-con or a bathroom. The *Imperial Hotel* (☎ 2199) on San Francisco St has rooms from P50/80, again with more expensive rooms with fan and bath or air-con and bath.

The pricier *Century Hotel* (☎ 2547) on Villanueva St has rooms with bath at P120/190 with fan and P260/300 with air-con.

Getting There & Away

Butuan is about two hours by bus from Surigao with onward connections to Davao (four hours), Cagayan de Oro (three hours plus) and Iligan.

BALINGOAN

Midway between Butuan and Cagayan de Oro, this is the port for ferries to nearby Camiguin Island. You can stay in *Ligaya's Restaurant & Cold Spot* for just P25/40 or there's a similar place opposite.

CAGAYAN DE ORO

On the north coast, Cagayan de Oro is an industrial town and the centre of the Philippines' pineapple industry. The **Xavier University Folk Museum** is worth a visit but, otherwise, there's not much to see here.

Places to Stay

The *Casa Filipina Lodge* (☎ 3383) on Borja St has fairly basic rooms from P50/100 plus more expensive rooms with bathroom. The annexe rooms are nice and quiet. The friendly and well-run *Mabini Lodge* (☎ 3539), at 113 Mabini St on the corner of Don A Velez St, is fairly new, and has clean rooms from P60/120 and has a restaurant.

The *City Pension* (☎ 2843), on the corner of Capistrano and Yacapin Sts, has reasonable air-con rooms for P140. The *New Golden Star Inn* (☎ 4079) at 129 Borja St is another straightforward, but good, hotel. Rooms cost from P90/130 with fan.

The *Oro United Inn* (☎ 4884) on Gomez St is more expensive with rooms with bath at P120/160 or P170/220 with air-con. The *Bonair Inn* (☎ 5431) on Don Sergio Osmena St is similarly priced. At the top end of the price bracket is *Hotel Tropicana* (☎ 3494) on Don A Velez with air-con rooms with bathroom at P340/375.

Places to Eat

The *Spoon Restaurant* on Capistrano St has good meals and the menu changes daily. Opposite, is the *Ice Cream Palace* which does a tasty, although rather expensive, chop suey. On the same street is *Thrive's Chicken House*.

On Don A Velez St, you can get big, cheap meals at the *Bagong Lipunan Restaurant*. The *Patio Restaurant* in the VIP Hotel is pretty good value and is open 24 hours. A little further north is the air-con *Caprice Steak House* and the small *Salt & Pepper Restaurant* which has cheap beer. Cagayan de Oro has plenty of discos and bars.

Getting There & Away

There are almost hourly buses to Butuan via Balingoan, taking three hours plus. Davao is eight to 10 hours away and Iligan only an hour. Zamboanga is a 16-hour bus trip and these depart when full.

Getting Around
The airport is 10 km from town and P50 by PU-Cab if you bargain hard. The main bus terminal is on the edge of town beside the Agora Market and jeepneys run between there and the town centre. Lookout for a Divisoria jeepney from the station or a Gusa/Cugman jeepney from the town. The wharf is five km out. Beware of pickpockets on local transport.

ILIGAN
Iligan is a major industrial city but there is not much of interest here apart from the **Maria Christina Falls**, nine km from the city. Iligan is the jumping-off point for visits to Marawi and the Lake Lanao area, 33 km south. This is a centre of guerrilla activity so make enquiries first before setting out. The route through from there to Cotabato is in a trouble zone.

The **Aga Khan Museum** in Marawi is noted for its exhibits of the Mindanao Muslim culture. You can find some local handicrafts here too.

Places to Stay
The *Maxim Inn* (☎ 20601) on Quezon Ave has rooms from P60/70 – those facing the road are noisy. *Jade Tourist Inn* (☎ 21158) is on Tibanga Ave on Baslayan Creek, some distance out from the centre. Rooms start at P80/150.

The *Maria Christina Hotel* (☎ 20645), on the corner of Aguinaldo and Mabini Sts, is the best central hotel with rooms from P250/330.

At Marawi you can stay in the expensive *Marawi Resort Hotel* or you can try the Mindanao State University (MSU) guest house, although it no longer accommodates tourists.

Places to Eat
Iligan has a surprising variety of restaurants, but they tend to close early. The *Canton Restaurant* does Chinese food, while mid-price range places with Filipino dishes include the *Iceberg Café & Restaurant* and the *Bahayan Restaurant*. The *Bar-B-Q Inn*, on the plaza, is good for an evening meal or try the open-air *Terrace Garden Restaurant* at the Iligan Village Hotel, out of town.

Getting There & Away
Iligan is only about an hour from Cagayan de Oro and there are jeepneys and minibuses as well as regular buses. Buses to Zamboanga usually start in Cagayan de Oro and come via Iligan. Jeepneys and shared taxis operate between Iligan and Marawi.

DIPOLOG & DAPITAN
Close to the city of Dipolog, Dapitan is the site of Jose Rizal's period of exile from 1892 to 1896. The city waterworks and a grass-covered relief map of Mindanao, in the town square, were made by Rizal. A few km away from the city is the place he stayed in which has a dam he built to create a swimming pool. Other attractions include a fruit-bat roosting place and some good swimming and diving areas.

Places to Stay
Ranillo's Pension House (☎ 3030) on Bonifacio St in Dipolog has rooms from P60/80 but is more with bathroom or air-con. On Magsaysay St, the *Ramos Hotel* (☎ 3299) costs from P75/95 for the simplest rooms with fan.

More expensive places include the *Hotel Arocha* (☎ 3397) on Quezon Ave with rooms from P140/160 up to around P400 for an air-con double with bath.

Getting There & Away
PAL fly between Dipolog and Zamboanga. Buses take about 13 hours via Pagadian where you may have to change buses.

ZAMBOANGA
The most visited city in Mindanao is Zamboanga which acts as the gateway to the Sulu Archipelago.

Information
The tourist office is in the Lantaka Hotel, east of the town centre towards Fort Pilar and Rio Hondo.

Things to See

Fort Pilar & Rio Hondo Fort Pilar is a rather run-down old Spanish fort on the waterfront south of the city. Some restoration is going on and there's now a **Marine Life Museum**. From the fort battlements, you get a good view to Rio Hondo, the Muslim village on stilts a little further down the coast.

Markets & Shops

The **Barter Trade Market**, with hints of the town's former smuggling-capital status, is near the Lantaka Hotel. The colourful **Fish Market** at the docks is busy in the late afternoon.

Parks

The **Pasonanca Park** is a large park in the hills, a little beyond the airport – the main attraction here is the famous tree house. Nearby is **Climaco Freedom Park**, named after a murdered mayor of Zamboanga.

Islands

Ten minutes across the bay by *banca* (outrigger) is the island of **Santa Cruz**, with good swimming, snorkelling and a beautiful beach. It costs around P200 to rent a boat for the round trip. You can rent snorkelling equipment at the waterfront Lantaka Hotel. The island of **Basilan**, about a two-hour boat ride away, is the centre for the colourful Yakan tribespeople.

Places to Stay

The *Unique Hotel* (☎ 3598), on Corcuera St near the wharf, is straightforward but well-kept, with rooms from P70/120. Centrally located on Governor Lim Ave, *Josefina's Pension House* (☎ 4142) is also a spartan, straightforward place and has rooms from P60.

The *New Pasonanca Hotel* (☎ 4579), on the corner of Almonte and Tomas Claudio Sts, has clean but small rooms from P120 with fan and bathroom. *Atilano's Pension House* (☎ 4225) on Mayor Jaldon St is similar in price with big, comfortable rooms and good food.

The *Mag-V Royal Hotel* (☎ 4614), on the corner of San Jose Rd and Don Basilio Navarro St, is a bit out of town but it's clean, well-kept and the rooms are spacious

1	Santa Cruz Market (New Market)
2	Bus Terminal
3	Airport
4	Alta Mall Building
5	Lutong Pinoy
6	Village Zamboanga
7	Atilano's Pension House
8	Hospital
9	GM's Super Disco
10	Zamboanga Hermosa Hotel
11	New Astoria Hotel & Seafood Restaurant
12	New Pasonanca Hotel
13	King's Palace Disco
14	Paradise Pensionhouse
15	Mag-V Royal Hotel
16	Food Paradise / Hotel Paradise
17	Sulpicio Lines
18	Athletic Field
19	SKT Shipping Lines
20	George & Peter Lines / Immigration Office
21	Sunflower Luncheonette
22	Buses to San Ramon
23	Josefina's Pension House
24	Barter Trade Market
25	Philippine National Bank
26	Town Hall
27	Basilan Shipping Lines / Sweet Lines
28	Philippine Airlines
29	Lantaka Hotel / Tourist Office
30	Boulevard Restaurant by the Sea
31	Market
32	Jeepneys to Pasonanca Park & Taluksangay
33	Unique Hotel
34	Post Office
35	Fish Market
36	Alavar's House of Seafoods
37	Casa de Oro
38	Wharf

although not all of them have windows. Prices vary from around P80 to P300.

The *New Astoria Hotel* (☎ 2075/7) on Mayor Jaldon St has reasonable rooms with fan and bath for P180 and with air-con for P300. The centrally located and well-kept *Hotel Paradise* (☎ 2936) on R Reyes St has air-con rooms with bathroom for P240/280. *Paradise Pensionhouse* (☎ 3005/8) is a little more expensive and is also centrally located

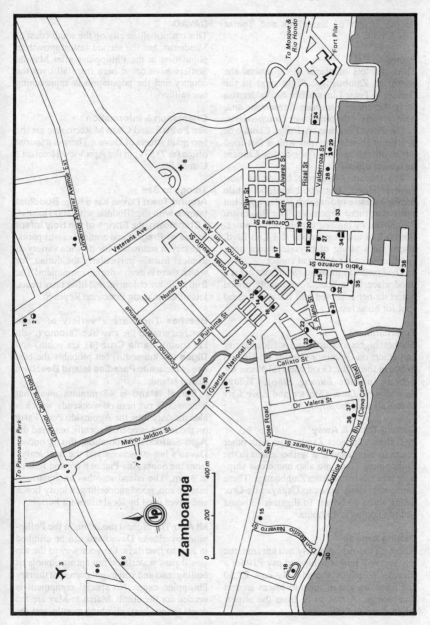

on the corner of Barcelona and Tomas Claudio Sts.

Places to Eat

There are lots of places to eat around the centre of Zamboanga. Right next to the George & Peter Lines office on Valderroza St is the cheap *Flavorite Restaurant* and, nearby, there's the *Sunflower Luncheonette*.

The *Food Paradise* on Tomas Claudio St is a popular meeting spot with a fast-food outlet on the ground floor and a Chinese restaurant upstairs.

The *Abalone Restaurant*, beside the New Astoria Hotel, has good seafood while *Alavar's House of Seafoods* is also good but somewhat more expensive. The *Boulevard Restaurant by the Sea* is right on the waterfront out of town on Justice R T Lim Blvd. There are a string of bayside places here, good for open-air dining at sunset.

The *Lantaka's* pleasant waterfront bar is a good place for a beer, a reasonably priced buffet dinner is served and it's also a good spot for breakfast.

Entertainment

The best nightspots are found outside the city and others on Governor Camins Rd kick on to late in the night. Good cheerful places for a beer include *Lutong Pinoy*, *Village Zamboanga*, *Latin Quarter* and *Love City Disco*, all near the airport.

Getting There & Away

PAL flights connect Zamboanga with other towns in Mindanao and further afield in the Philippines. There are also numerous shipping services to and from Zamboanga. There are several daily buses to Cagayan de Oro, taking about 15 hours. To Iligan is 13 hours and to Dipolog is 15 hours.

Getting Around

Although the airport is only two km from the city you will probably have to pay P10 for a tricycle. Jeepneys should only cost P1.50 and there are lots of them to places around Zamboanga. A taxi to or from the airport might demand P60.

DAVAO

This cosmopolitan city on the south coast of Mindanao, has the second fastest growth in population in the Philippines after Manila. Settlers have come here from all over the country and the population is approaching one million.

Orientation & Information

San Pedro St and Claro M Recto Ave are the two main streets of Davao. There is a tourist office (☎ 71534) in the Apo View Hotel on J Camus St.

Things to See

Around Town Davao has a large **Buddhist temple** with the 'Buddha with 1000 hands', a **Chinatown**, the **Shrine of the Holy Infant Jesus of Prague** and some pleasant parks. The city is renowned for its wide variety of tropical fruits – particularly the durian, for which there is even a durian monument! The fruit stalls are colourful and offer tasty treats, lots of them along Ponciono Reyes St.

Beaches There are a variety of black beaches around the city like **Talomo** (eight km south), **Santa Cruz** (41 km south) and **Digos** (59 km south) but probably the best one is the white **Paradise Island Beach** on Samal Island.

Samal Island is 45 minutes away but bancas only run here on weekends, which is also the only time the Aguinaldo Pearl Farm on the island is open. Recently renamed the Agro-Seafoods Corporation, this is one of Davao's big attractions and the boat leaves from the Santa Ana Pier at 8 am and returns at 3 pm. The island also has an aquarium, marine zoo, good snorkelling, a lousy beach and caves used by local tribes for burials.

Mt Apo The highest mountain in the Philippines overlooks Davao and can be climbed in four to five days. On your way to the top you'll pass waterfalls, hot springs, pools of boiling mud and you might even spot the rare Philippine eagle. No special equipment is needed for the climb. March to May are the driest (hence best) climbing months and the tourist office can offer advice and arrange guides.

Places to Stay

The *Tourist Lodge* (☎ 78760), on the edge of town at 55 MacArthur Highway, has singles/doubles with fan for P90/110 plus more expensive rooms with bathroom and with air-con. It has a restaurant but it's some distance out and standards leave something to be desired.

The *El Gusto Family Lodge* (☎ 63832) at 51 A Pichon St (Magallanes St) has rooms from P60/100 up to around P200 for an air-con room with bath. *Le Mirage Family Lodge* (☎ 63811) on San Pedro St is a good place with very similar prices. The *Fortune Inn* (☎ 76688) on Magsaysay Ave has singles with fan for P80, with fan and bath for P100 or rooms with air-con and bath for P150/270.

Men Seng Hotel (☎ 75185) on San Pedro St is fairly good value. The rooms, which vary in standard and cleanliness, have big beds and cost from P120/150 or more with air-con. *Pension Felisa* (☎ 79937) on Monteverde St has singles with fan for P180 and air-con rooms with bath at P240/300. *Royale House* (☎ 73630) at 34 Claro M Recto Ave starts at P95/150 with fan and goes up to P270 to P350 for air-con doubles.

More expensive places include the *Hotel Maguindanao* (☎ 78401) at 80 Claro M Recto Ave, opposite the cathedral. Rooms with air-con and bath are P400 to P500.

Places to Eat

Dencia's Kitchenette on Pelaya St, the *Shanghai Restaurant* on Magsaysay Ave and the *Men Seng Restaurant*, in the Men Seng Hotel on San Pedro St, all have good cheap Chinese food.

San Pedro St also has the *Kusina Dabaw* for Chinese and Filipino dishes and the *Merco Restaurant* where the ice cream is excellent. Try the *Sunburst Fried Chicken* on Anda St for fried chicken. On Torres St, the *Harana II Restaurant* and the *Sarung Banggi II Restaurant* are both good for barbecues while at the Muslim fishing village

near Magsaysay Park anything that swims is likely to end up on the grill.

Davao's fruit stalls are famous and they are interesting places so don't forget to sample a durian if they're in season. PAL ban durians from their aircraft.

Entertainment

Davao has the usual Filipino assortment of bars and discos.

Getting There & Away

PAL fly from Cagayan de Oro, Zamboanga and further afield. There's at least one weekly ship between Zamboanga and Davao. Buses take about six hours from Butuan, 10 from Cagayan de Oro, four from General Santos City and more than eight from Surigao.

Getting Around

The airport is 12 km north-east of the centre, say P50 by taxi or P1 by a tricycle to the main road, from where you can get a jeepney for P2.50. To town, take the jeepney 'San Pedro', from town to the airport junction take the 'Sasa' jeepney.

Davao's jeepneys are not as organised as in other towns. They don't ply specific routes but just shunt around at random. Call out where you want to go and, if it interests the drivers, they may stop. Or take the mini-car taxis which cost a flat fare to anywhere in town.

GENERAL SANTOS CITY (DADIANGAS)

There's not a great deal of interest in this city in the south-west of Mindanao. It's in a major fruit-producing area.

Places to Stay

The unpretentious *Concrete Lodge* (☎ 4876) on Pioneer Ave has rooms with fan and bath for P80/120. The *South Sea Lodge I* (☎ 5146) on Pioneer Ave is very similarly priced. There's also a *South Sea Lodge II* on Salazar St, on the corner of Magsaysay Ave.

The *Pioneer Hotel* (☎ 2422) on Pioneer Ave has rooms from P110 (single with fan and bath) up to P220 (double with air-con and bath). On P Acharon Blvd, the clean and well-kept *Matutum Hotel* (☎ 4901) costs from P150/240 and has a good restaurant.

Getting There & Away

Buses take four hours to Davao or an hour to Koronadel (Marbel).

Mindoro

The relatively undeveloped island of Mindoro is the nearest 'last frontier' to Manila – the Philippines have quite a few last frontiers. Because you can get there very easily from Manila many travellers make the trip to try the beautiful beaches.

Puerto Galera vies with Boracay as the best place in the Philippines for simply lazing on the beach, although it's well on its way to becoming a victim of its own popularity. Mindoro's population is concentrated along the coastal strip and the inland is mainly dense jungle and mountains.

Getting There & Away

To/From Luzon The usual route to Mindoro is from the Luzon port of Batangas City to Calapan or Puerto Galera. You can get buses directly to Batangas City from the Lawton and BLTB bus terminals in Manila for P45 (regular) to P65 (air-con) but beware of pickpockets who work overtime on this route. You have to leave Manila as early as possible in the morning in order to get to Puerto Galera the same day. The earliest bus leaves about 5 am.

The ferry crossing takes two to three hours and there are two Batangas to Calapan services and three Batangas to Puerto Galera services. The services to Puerto Galera are at 6, 9 am, 12 noon and sometimes at 3 pm (depending on time of year and weather conditions). The fare is P48. The services to Calapan are at 5 or 6 pm, so you would then have to stay overnight in Calapan before continuing to Puerto Galera.

From the Sundowner Hotel on Mabini St, Ermita, a daily Sunshine Run air-con bus departs at 9 am to connect with the company's 12 noon Si-kat ferry from Batangas which arrives at Puerto Galera at 2.30 pm. The through trip costs P220.

To/From Other Islands From Pinamayalan on Mindoro you can continue on to Marinduque, Boracay (Panay) or Romblon. It's becoming quite a popular route from Mindoro to Boracay, thus combining the two very popular beach destinations of Puerto Galera and Boracay. You can either go there via Tablas Island in the Romblon group of islands, by way of Bongabong or Roxas, or direct to Boracay from Roxas. Be careful, some of the boats on this route are leaky buckets often dangerously overloaded.

There's a big outrigger from Roxas to Boracay on Monday and Thursday which takes seven hours. If it has to go via Looc in Romblon it takes at least 10 hours. The fare is about P150. There's a big outrigger from Bongabong to Carmen on Tablas on Wednesday, Friday and Sunday for P78. It takes about six hours and continues from Carmen to the town of Romblon on Romblon. Another big outrigger operates from Roxas to Looc, on Tablas, on Sunday and Friday, and takes four hours.

PUERTO GALERA

The fine beaches and excellent snorkelling around Puerto Galera have been attracting travellers for some time. There are lots of little coves and bays, some which require a boat to get to, so get a group of travellers together and split the cost. There are also some pleasant walks but the whole area is starting to become very popular, especially with German travellers who have just about turned it into a German colony.

There are many places to stay at the various beaches which include **La Laguna**, **White Beach** at San Isidro (seven km out of town), **Sabang Beach**, **Balete Beach**, **Long Beach**, **Mountain Beach** and **Santo Nino**. Sabang and La Laguna are both really overdeveloped these days. The beach is dirty and there are far too many shoddy huts, restaurants and bars. You really have to go further afield to find pleasant places.

Information
The Rural Bank in Puerto Galera changes cash and may also change travellers' cheques. The Margarita shopping centre changes both.

Places to Stay
In Town Rooms in Puerto Galera generally cost from around P100 in low season to P200 in high season, although there are still a few cheaper places. *Christine's Place* is on the edge of town, at quiet Balete Beach, and has rooms for P75, as does friendly *Malou's Hilltop Inn*.

The simple *Melxa's Greenhill Nipa Hut* has rooms with fan for P120. *Bahay Pilipino* is cheaper with rooms with fan for P70/100 or there's *Jelliz* at P60/100.

The *Fishermen's Cove Beach House* is on a quiet bay about a km out of town towards White Beach, and has rooms at P50 or, with bath, they are P100. *Cathy's Travellers Inn* is the same price and also has cottages with bath for P150. It's about two km out of town towards Halige and Boquete Beaches.

Near the wharf, the *El Canonero Marivelis Hotel* has rooms with fan and bath for P100 and there is a restaurant. The *Villa Margarita Bamboo House* has rooms with fan and bath for P100 or there's the *Villa Margarita White House* with singles with fan and bath for P100 to P125 and doubles for P150. Villa Margarita also runs the *Holiday Garden Apartelle* where doubles with fan and bath are P250 and apartments are P400.

The *Hundora Beach Resort* on Hundora Beach on the southern edge of town has rooms with fan and bath for P180 and a restaurant. About 1½ km out of town, towards Sabang, the *Encenada Beach Resort* has rooms or cottages with fan and bath for P500.

At the Beaches You're liable to be hassled by touts for the beach cottages all the way from Batangas. Some even start on you on the bus from Manila. Out at the beach there are lots of cottages from around P100 to as high as P250 a day. When one bay or beach is built out they simply move along to the next one. The places that follow are just a small selection of the numerous possibilities.

The beaches include Sabang Beach, Big and Small La Laguna beaches, White Beach (San Isidro) and Mountain Beach. An outrigger from Puerto Galera to Sabang takes about half an hour from the pier (for P150; four passengers per boat) or you can take the track by the Koala Club and walk it in about 1½ hours.

Sabang Beach suffers from severe over-development. The discos overpower the beach and you should measure how far your accommodation is from these sources of noise. *Travellers' Station* has good cottages from P100 to P175. Cottages at *Seashore Lodge* are P150 to P250 while at *John's Place* they are P200. The *Terraces Garden Resort* has good rooms on a slope above the beach at P250.

You can walk around the coast from here to the La Laguna beaches which are better for sunning and snorkelling. Small La Laguna is quieter than the main La Laguna Beach. At Small La Laguna, *China Moon* has cottages at P80 or there's *Nick & Sonia's Cottages* and *Full Moon* both at P100. The *El Galleon Beach Resort* has rooms at P150 to P200. On the slopes *Carlo's Inn* has rooms for P150 to P250 and apartments at P250 to P450.

At Big La Laguna, there's *Marina's Inn* with cottages at P120 to P150 or *Rosita's* at P150 to P250.

Further afield, at White Beach, *Lodger's Nook* has cottages for P80 or with fan and bath for P100 to P150. At *Crystal Garden Beach Resort* cottages are P120 with fan and bath. The *White Beach Nipa Hut* has simple cottages with fan and bath for P120 to P150. *Summer Connection* is on the slope at the western end of White Beach and has cottages for P150. Or try *Cherry's Inn* or *White Beach Lodge*, both with cottages at P150.

At Tamaraw Beach, next along from White Beach, the *Tamaraw Beach Resort* has cottages at P120 or better ones with bath for

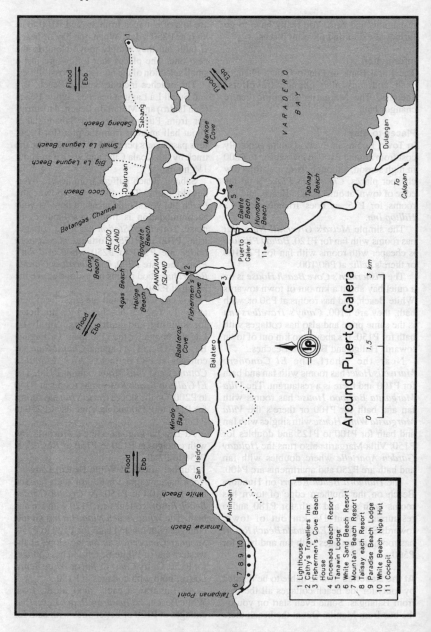

Around Puerto Galera

1 Lighthouse
2 Cathy's Travellers Inn
3 Fishermen's Cove Beach House
4 Encenada Beach Resort
5 Tanawin Lodge
6 White Sand Beach Resort
7 Mountain Beach Resort
8 Talisay each Resort
9 Paradise Beach Lodge
10 White Beach Nipa Hut
11 Cockpit

VARADERO BAY

To Calapan

Dulangan

Tabinay Beach

Hundora Beach

Balete Beach

Puerto Galera

Markoe Cove

Sabang

Sabang Beach

Small La Laguna Beach

Big La Laguna Beach

Coco Beach

Daluruan

Batangas Channel

MEDIO ISLAND

Long Beach

Agas Beach

Halige Beach

Boquete Beach

PANIQUIAN ISLAND

Fishermen's Cove

Balateros Cove

Balatero

Minolo Bay

San Isidro

White Beach

Aninoan

Tamaraw Beach

Talipanan Point

Flood Ebb

Ebb Flood

Flood Ebb

0   1.5   3 km

P180 to P200. Continue to Talipanan Beach to find the more expensive *Talisay Beach Resort*. The *Mountain Beach Resort* has pricier cottages at P250 to P300 or there's the *White Sand Beach Resort* at P75 to P100.

Mountain Beach, a half-km jeepney ride beyond White Beach, is fairly quiet. You can walk to Santo Nino Bay from the pier and it's only a km from town towards White Beach.

Places to Eat
Restaurants around the docks in the town include *El Canonero*, *Rendezvous* and *Typhoon*. The *Pier Pub* serves pizza. Most of the beach cottages have restaurants.

Getting There & Away
There are several jeepneys daily between Calapan and Puerto Galera, a two-hour trip. The road does not continue westward from Puerto Galera to Wawa and you have to take a boat (P15 but they'll try for P50) and you can then continue from Wawa to Abra de Ilog and on to Mamburao by road.

Southward to San Jose from Puerto Galera requires several stages – two hours to Calapan, four hours to Roxas, one hour to Bulalacao and another four hours on a rough road to San Jose.

Getting Around
From Puerto Galera, jeepneys and bancas run to the various beaches. A jeepney to Sabang is P10 but the unsealed road can be impassable after heavy rain.

A jeepney to White Beach, at San Isidro, also costs P10 and some go on to White Sand Beach at Talipanan Point for P15. It takes about 45 minutes to walk from White Beach to White Sand Beach.

CALAPAN
Calapan is just a jumping-off point for Luzon.

Places to Stay
The *Travellers' Inn* (☎ 1926) on Leuterio St has singles/doubles at P50/70 or air-con doubles at P250. *Riceland Inn I* on Rizal St has rooms from P50 to P75 with fan, P95 to P120 with fan and bath or P215 to P225 with air-con and bath.

Getting There & Away
Puerto Galera is two hours away by jeepney and Roxas is four hours away.

BONGABONG, ROXAS & MANSALAY
You can get boats for Romblon from Bongabong or Roxas and, for Boracay, from Roxas. From Mansalay, further south from Roxas, you can walk to the villages of the Mangyan tribes.

Places to Stay
In Bongabong, the *Mabuhay Lodging House* is cheap at P40/70. Roxas has the *Santo Nino Restaurant & Lodging House* with hard beds at P40 per person and a good restaurant. The *Catalina Beach Resort* in Roxas is good value at P35 a night and the copious meals are cheap. An alternative to staying in Roxas is to stay at the *Melco Beach Inn*, along the beach a little way at Dangay. The beach is nothing special but it's OK as a place to wait for a boat and has cottages at P40/70.

Getting There & Away
See the introductory Getting There & Away section for the Mindoro section for boat information. From Calapan buses take three hours to Bongabong and four hours to Roxas.

SAN JOSE
From San Jose, it may be possible to visit the Mangyan tribes or you can rent a boat to **Ambulong** or **Ilin Island** for swimming and snorkelling. **Apo Reef**, a popular diving spot well offshore, can be reached from San Jose or Sablayan.

Places to Stay & Eat
The *Jolo Hotel* (☎ 618) on Rizal St, the *Midtown Pension House* on Raja Soliman St and the *Sikatuna Hotel* (☎ 697) on Sikatuna St all have cheap rooms from around P40/60 for the simplest rooms. Rooms with fan and bath cost up to P75/100.

San Jose has good places to eat including

the *Shanghai Restaurant* on Rizal St and *Coras Restaurant* on the corner of Liboro and Bonifacio Sts.

Getting There & Away

It usually takes several stages to round the southern end of Mindoro between Roxas and San Jose and the road is often none too good. On to Mamburao, via Sablayan, is tough going and takes eight hours by jeepney, that is if the road is passable at all. Take an outrigger (about 11 hours) if the road is out.

MAMBURAO & SABLAYAN

Few travellers get this far up the west coast of Mindoro.

Places to Stay

The *Traveller's Lodge* in Mamburao has rooms at P50/100 or with fan and bath for P75/120. In Sablayan, the *Emely Hotel* costs P35/70.

Getting There & Away

There are flights between Mamburao and Manila. See the Puerto Galera section for travel between Mamburao and the west coast.

Negros

Sandwiched in between Cebu and Panay, and well connected by ferry services in both directions, is the sugar island of the Philippines. The oppressive conditions under which the sugar plantation workers have laboured, and the cruel methods by which some of the plantation owners have kept their power, has made this another of the Philippines' major trouble spots.

Getting There & Away

There are two ferry departures daily, except Sunday (when there is only one), between Toledo in Cebu and San Carlos in Negros. The crossing takes two hours. Other regular services across the comparatively narrow waters between the two islands are from Tampi to Bato, San Jose to Talisay and Sibuyan to Liloan in the far south; Tangil to Guihulngan in the centre; and Hagnaya via Bantayan Island to Cadiz in the north. Ships also operate between Cebu City and Dumaguete.

The next island north is Panay and the popular route from Negros to Panay is the Bacolod to Iloilo boat service but you can also go via Guimaras Island. The Bacolod to Iloilo boat operates two or three times daily and takes two hours. Allow an hour to get from Bacolod to the Banago wharf. Other Negros to Panay connections include the daily ships from Victorias to Culasi and Malayu-an, both near Ajuy, on the east coast of Panay.

There are less frequent shipping connections between Negros and other islands including Bohol, Luzon (a 24 to 30-hour trip) and Mindanao. PAL flies to Bacolod and Dumaguete from Cebu City and from Manila, Pacific Airways flies from Iloilo to Bacolod.

Getting Around

It's 313 km between Bacolod and Dumaguete which are at opposite ends of the island. The trip takes 7½ hours and it's wise to take an express bus as it avoids the many small village stops. Bacolod to San Carlos takes two or three hours.

BACOLOD

Bacolod is a typical Filipino city of no great interest. You can visit the huge **Victoria Milling Company Central**, one of the world's largest sugar refineries, 35 km north of the city. Bacolod is also one of the major ceramics centres of the Philippines.

Places to Stay

On Burgos St, the *YMCA* (☎ 26919) is a basic and fairly clean place with rooms with fan at P90/110. The run-down *Halili Inn* (☎ 81548) on Locsin St has rooms from P60/80 for narrow-bedded rooms with fan. Expect to pay up to P170/220 for the better air-con rooms with bathroom.

The more expensive *Best Inn* (☎ 23312)

on Bonifacio St also has a wide price range, starting at P80/110 for the basic rooms with fan. This is no hotel for late-risers – it's noisy in the morning.

Although it's some distance out of town, the *Family Pension House* (☎ 81211) at 123 Locsin St Extension is reasonably clean and comfortable and has a quiet city edge location. Rooms with bathroom cost P130 with fan and P200 with air-con.

Las Rocas Inn (☎ 27011) at 13 Gatuslao St starts at P100 for fan-cooled singles and moves up through P170/240 for rooms with bathroom to P320/380 for the better air-con rooms. The *Bascon Hotel* (☎ 23141) on Gonzaga St is neat and clean and has air-con rooms at P300/360 and a restaurant. Finally, the *Sea Breeze Hotel* (☎ 24571/5) on San Juan St is one of the best places in town with rooms at P500/550.

Places to Eat
Reming's & Sons Restaurant in the city plaza serves good Filipino fast food as does the air-con *Gaisano Food Plaza* on Luzuriaga St. On Gatuslao St, *Ihaw-Ihaw Restaurant* in the Las Rocas Hotel serves cheap Filipino dishes.

Next door to the Best Inn on Bonifacio St the *Kong Kee Diners & Bakery* does economically-priced Chinese and Filipino dishes. The *Ang Sinugba Restaurant* on San Sebastian St is clean, well-kept and does good native food while *Mira's Café* on Locsin St serves native coffee. Try the *Cactus Room Restaurant* in the Family Pension House for a good choice of steaks. Nearby, is *Alavar's Sea Foods House* with excellent Zamboanga-style dishes.

There are many fast-food restaurants and all-night places in the Reclamation Area but transport back to the city can be difficult.

Getting There & Away
There are a number of Ceres Liner buses daily between Bacolod and Dumaguete – a nine-hour trip. It's about four hours, again by Ceres Liner, between San Carlos and Bacolod. Jeepneys run to Mambucal, Ma-ao, Silay and Victorias.

Getting Around
A PU-Cab from the airport to the centre shouldn't cost more than P20 or you can stop a passing jeepney, as they all go to the city plaza. Banago Wharf is about seven km north, say P7 by jeepney or P25 by PU-Cab. The Northern bus terminal is a P1.50 trip on a jeepney labelled 'Libertad' or 'Shopping'.

DUMAGUETE
Dumaguete is a very pleasant little town, centred around the large Silliman University campus. There's a small **anthropological museum** here and a cheap cafeteria. There are many good beaches around Dumaguete including **Kawayan** to the south and **El Oriente** and **Wuthering Heights** (!) to the north. **Silliman Beach**, close to the town, is not very good. **Camp Lookout**, 14 km west of the city, provides fine views over Dumaguete and across to Cebu and Bohol.

Places to Stay
The comfortable *Opena's Hotel* (☎ 3462) on Katada St has singles with fan at P70 and rooms with bath at P140/180 or P210/240 with air-con. The owners also operate *Summerland Resort* on black sand Amlan beach, 23 km to the north-west.

On the corner of Rizal Ave and San Juan St, the *Al Mar Hotel* (☎ 3453) is a homely place with rooms ranging from fan-cooled singles at P80 to air-con doubles with bathroom at P240. On Real St, the pleasant *Hotel El Oriente* (☎ 3486) starts at P110 and follows the same upward path to P295/345 for the better rooms with air-con and bathroom. *El Orient Beach Resort* in Mangnao, south of Dumaguete, is clean, comfortable and similarly priced.

The *Panorama Hotel* is an attractive, large house at Cangmating Beach, Sibulan, about six km to the north. Rooms here are good value at P110/220 with fan or P300 for a double with bathroom. On Silliman Ave, the *Insular Hotel* (☎ 3495) is a good place near the university, but is more expensive, with rooms from around P280 to P400.

Places to Eat

You can eat well and cheaply at *Opena's Restaurant* in Opena's Hotel, or at *Ree's Restaurant* on the corner of Alfonso and Legaspi Sts. The *Orient Garden Restaurant* is on the corner of Alfonso and San Juan Sts.

There's excellent food at the Chinese *Chin Long Restaurant* on Rizal Blvd. *Jo's Cake House & Restaurant* is a student hang-out with fruit juices, cakes and chicken inato, a popular speciality. *Kamagong Restaurant,* on the corner of Locsin and Ma Cristina Sts, is also popular with students.

Try the *Kamay Kainan Seafood House,* on the corner of San Juan and Santa Catalina Sts, for folk music. The barbecue stands along Rizal Blvd, near the Aquino Freedom Park, are popular after dark.

Getting There & Away

Ceres Liner buses from Bacolod, via San Carlos, take nine hours and from San Carlos five hours. There are less frequent Bacolod to Dumaguete buses round the southern end of the island via Hinobaan. This longer and rougher trip takes 12 hours.

OTHER PLACES

Mambucal

Mambucal, a pleasant resort town with hot springs, is just an hour from Bacolod. It takes three or four days to climb the **Kanlaon volcano** from here. A local guide plus equipment (tent and cooker) will cost about P700.

You can stay in the simple *Pagoda Inn* for P60 or in the *Mambucal Health Resort* for even less. Mambucal is just a one-hour jeepney ride from Libertad (Hernaez) St in Bacolod. The morning trip back can be much longer because of frequent stops.

Sugar Plantations

Old steam locomotives used on the sugar cane fields, until recently, can be seen at the **MSC** (Ma-ao Sugar Central). Ma-ao is an hour by jeepney from Bacolod. The **Hawaiian-Philippine Sugar Company** in Silay has a 180-km rail network and some excellent steam engines. Silay is only half an hour from Bacolod.

Guided tours of the **Vicmico** (Victorias Milling Company) plant are operated daily from the porter's lodge. Again, there are some fine old steam locomotives but Victorias also has the St Joseph the Worker Chapel with its famous mural of the 'Angry Christ'. Victorias is an hour by bus or jeepney from Bacolod and it's a further 15 minutes to the Vicmico sugar mill.

San Carlos

San Carlos, jumping-off point for Cebu, is nothing special but little speedboats cross to nearby Sipaway Island for only a few pesos. It's a pleasant and quiet place with some good beaches but bring your own food and water.

Cheap places to stay include *Van's Lodging House* near the pier (P35/70), the *Papal Lodge* on V Gustilo St (P45/90) or the more expensive *Coco Grove Hotel* on Ylagan St (P70 to P450).

Maluay (Malatapay) & Zamboanguita

Right at the south of the island, this is the best area near Dumaguete for beaches and snorkelling. You can charter a boat from here to get to popular offshore Apo Island. A day trip will cost about P300 but costs more from Maluay (Malatapay) than Zamboanguita.

Two km beyond Zamboanguita, if coming from Dumaguete, is the friendly and well-maintained *Salawaki Beach Resort* with dorm beds for P45 and cottages for P160 to P270.

Hinobaan

Most visitors take the shorter route round the north coast of the island but you can also take the much longer and rougher southern route via Hinobaan, site of a gold rush in 1982. The *Gloria Mata Lodging House* and *Mesajon Lodging House* are both simple and very cheap. Bacolod to Dumaguete, via Hinobaan, takes about 12 hours.

Palawan

Off to the west of the Visayas, Palawan is the long thin island stretching down to the Malaysian north Borneo state of Sabah. Things to do and see here are mainly natural – islands, scuba diving and caves with underground rivers and wildlife.

Getting There & Away

There are a variety of shipping services which ply a variety of routes between Manila and ports on Palawan. Alternatively, there are daily PAL flights between Manila and Puerto Princesa, plus services with Aerolift and Pacific Airways from Manila to other centres on the island. You can also reach Palawan from Cebu, Panay, Romblon and other islands.

Getting Around

Puerto Princesa, the capital, is roughly halfway down the island. Buses and jeepneys run up and down the island, as far as Brooke's Point (seven to nine hours' drive south) or to El Nido and Port Barton to the north.

PUERTO PRINCESA

The capital of the island is a relatively small town with a population of about 60,000. It's simply a place to use as a base for excursions to elsewhere on the island. Palawan is popular for scuba diving and there are several diving outfits in town.

Information

There's a tourist office at the airport but it's usually deserted. The hostels probably have the most reliable and up-to-date information.

Places to Stay

Mrs Abordo (☎ 2206) at 36 Sand Oval St rents out rooms with fans to students and travellers for P40/80. The pleasant *Duchess Pension House* (☎ 2873) on Valencia St has clean fan-cooled rooms for P45/90 and more expensive doubles with bathrooms.

Abelardo's Pension (☎ 2068), 62 Manga St, has reasonably good rooms with fan for P60/120 or with fan and bath for P80/160. The *Garcellano Tourist Inn* (☎ 2314) at 257 Rizal Ave has a large, quiet courtyard. Rooms starts at P70 for a single with fan or P90/130 for rooms with fan and bath. *Civens Lodge* has a quiet location on Mendoza St and its basic rooms cost P70/80.

Yayen's Pension (☎ 2261) on Manalo St Extension is a pleasantly run place with a coffee shop and a garden. Rooms start at P50/90 and P110/140 with bathroom. *Sonne Gasthaus*, a quiet place at 366 Manalo St Extension, has rooms at P120/160 or ther are cottages at P250.

More expensive places include the *Circon Lodge* (☎ 2738) on Valencia St. Rooms with fan and bath are P210 or with air-con P300. It's clean and has a restaurant. On Rizal Ave near the airport, the *Badjao Inn* (☎ 2761) is a clean, well-kept place with higher prices.

Places to Eat

There's a cosmopolitan selection of restaurants along Rizal Ave. Try the attractive *Café Puerto* for French food or the *Roadside Pizza Inn* for Italian. The *Pink Lace* prepares everything from Filipino, Chinese, Indian and Mexican to Vietnamese! At the *Kamayan Folkhouse & Restaurant*, you can try Filipino dishes and you get the choice of sitting on the terrace or in a treehouse.

Head to *Zum Kleinen Anker* for a cold beer or to the *Tipanan Restaurant* and *El Burrito* for seafood and more Mexican dishes. At the entrance to the Vietnamese refugee camp, two km out of town behind the airport, the *Pho Dac Biet Restaurant* has cheap Vietnamese food and French-style bread.

Entertainment

Café Nostalgia offers golden oldies while the *Kamayan Folkhouse & Restaurant* has folk singers. There are also several discos around town.

Getting Around

There are plenty of tricycles for getting

around town and they will take you out to the airport for a few pesos.

CENTRAL PALAWAN

There are various places within day-trip distance of Puerto Princesa, such as **Santa Lucia** with its hot spring, reached by boat from Puerto Princesa's harbour.

Sabang is famed for the St Paul's National Park with its long underground river. To get there, take a jeepney between 8 and 10 am from Puerto Princesa. From Sabang, you can either take a boat for P300 or walk to the mouth of the river – it takes about three hours. There are even a few cottages in Sabang where you can stay for P50.

There's good diving in **Honda Bay**, off Tagburos, only 10 km from Puerto Princesa. There are many small islands in the bay. **Nagtabon Beach** is another interesting swimming spot, but like the underground river getting there is time-consuming.

SOUTH PALAWAN

At **Quezon**, halfway from Puerto Princesa to the southern end of the island, is the jumping-off point for the **Tabon Caves**. There's a small **National Museum** in Quezon and the caves have yielded some interesting stone-age finds. It takes five hours to reach Quezon and from there half an hour by boat to the caves. You can stay at the *Dias Boarding House,* right by the wharf, or rooms are nearly as cheap at the *Paganiban Lodge. Tabon Village Resort* at Tabon Beach has rooms at P60/80 or cottages at P100/130.

Brooke's Point, further south, is the jumping-off point for **Ursula Island** but the island's interest to bird-watchers has been drastically reduced by a plague of rats.

NORTH PALAWAN

From **San Rafael**, you can visit the villages of the Bataks. You can stay two km east of San Rafael at the basic, but habitable, *Duchess Beachside Cottage* on Tanabag Beach.

There's good diving off **Roxas**, three to four hours further north from San Rafael. On the opposite coast, **Port Barton** on Pagdanan Bay is something of a travellers' hang-out. There are a number of fine islands in the bay, some good beaches and excellent snorkelling. Two popular spots are **Exotica Island** and the aquarium at **Albagin Island**. You can stay at *Elsa's Beach House* in rooms (P45/90) or cottages (P160/220) or at the similarly priced *Swissippini Lodge. El Busero Inn* is a little more expensive and the owner organises diving trips. The *Paradiso Beach Resort* has dorm beds as well as rooms and cottages.

Right up in the north-west of Palawan, there's more fine diving in the islands of the **Bacuit Archipelago**. El Nido, on the mainland, can be reached by road during the dry season when there is at least one jeepney daily from Taytay.

Panay

The large, triangular Visayan island of Panay has a number of decaying forts and watchtowers – relics from the days of the Moro pirates – plus some interesting Spanish churches. The south coast, which stretches from Iloilo, around the southern promontory at Anini-y, to San Jose de Buenavista has many beaches and resorts. The Ati-Atihan Festival in January, in Kalibo, is one of the most popular in the Philippines. Last, but far from least, off the north-west tip of the island is the delightful little island of Boracay, one of the Philippines' major travellers' centre.

Getting There & Away

There are a variety of flights and shipping services to Panay from Manila, Cebu City and other major centres. PAL fly from Manila to Iloilo, Kalibo and Roxas City while Aerolift and Pacific Airways fly to Caticlan. Travellers bound for Boracay head for Kalibo or Caticlan but the Kalibo flights are often heavily booked.

You can reach Panay by boat from Cebu, Leyte, Luzon, Mindanao, Mindoro, Negros, Palawan and Romblon. The shortest crossing is the two to 2½-hour trip from Bacolod in Negros to Iloilo. There are several boats daily.

It's possible (with some difficulty) to travel from Mindoro to Boracay via Tablas in Romblon Province but this can be a dangerous trip as the outrigger boats are often not a match for severe conditions in the Tablas Strait.

ILOILO

The capital city of Panay, Iloilo, is a large and interesting town which was very important during the Spanish era. There's the small but interesting **'Window on the Past' museum** in the city plus the coral **Molo Church**. Iloilo is noted for its *jusi* (raw silk) and *pina* (pineapple fibre) weaving. Today, Sinamay Dealer on Osmena St has the only remaining loom.

Places to Stay

New Iloilo International House (☎ 72865) on J M Basa St has singles/doubles with fan for P80/100, with fan and bath for P100/120 and with air-con and bath for P170/190. *D'House Pensione* (☎ 72805) at 127 Quezon St is a homely place with a restaurant and rooms at P80/150.

The *Iloilo Lodging House* (☎ 72384) on Aldeguer St has rooms with fan P80/140, with fan and bath for P120/160 and with air-con and bath for P140/200. The rooms are small and bathrooms are shared between two rooms. The *Eros Travellers Pensionne* (☎ 76183) on General Luna St has rooms with fan and bath for P100 and with air-con and bath for P150/180. The similar *Family Pension House* (☎ 72047, 79208), also on General Luna St, has rooms with fan and bath for P90/130 or air-con doubles for P190.

The *New River Queen Hotel* (☎ 79997, 76443) on Bonifacio Drive has rooms with fan and bath for P170/200 and with air-con and bath for P260/300. Other middle bracket places include *Madia-as Hotel* (☎ 72756), hidden away in a lane off Aldeguer St.

Rooms with fan and bath are P170/185 or with air-con and bath are P250/260. It's clean and comfortable and has a restaurant.

Centrally situated, in a lane between J M Basa and Iznart Sts, *Centercon Hotel* (☎ 73431/3) has rooms with fan for P150 and with air-con and bath for P225/285.

Places to Eat

You can get good Chinese and Filipino meals, or a proper Western breakfast, upstairs in either *Mansion House Restaurant* or in the *Summer House*, both on J M Basa St. *Angelina* on Iznart St is recommended.

Batchoy is a speciality of the western Visayas and consists of beef, pork and liver in noodle soup, and the *Oak Barrel* on Valeria St is one of the best of the batchoy restaurants. *The Tavern Pub*, on the corner of Quezon and Delgado Sts, is air-con, well-kept and cosy although prices are slightly higher than the usual. You can eat Filipino food with your fingers at *Nena's Manokan* restaurants in Bonifacio Drive and General Luna St.

The airy *Tree House Restaurant*, of the Family Pension House, has a pleasant atmosphere while the *Golden Salakot*, in the Hotel Del Rio, serves fairly cheap buffet lunches and dinners. The *King Ramen Restaurant*, also touted as the 'House of the Japanese Noodles', and the *Aldous Snack Bar* keep long hours. In good weather, the open-air *Fort San Pedro Drive Inn* is popular for beer and barbecues.

If you have a sweet tooth, don't miss the *S'Table Restaurant & Snack Bar* in J M Basa St, which probably has the best selection of cakes in Iloilo. For snacks and ice cream, try the *Magnolia Ice Cream & Pancake House* in Iznart St.

Getting There & Away

Buses from Iloilo to Kalibo and Caticlan leave from Rizal St. You can also reach Caticlan, from where boats run to Boracay, via Kalibo. There are a variety of flights to Iloilo.

Getting Around

The airport is about seven km out and a PU-Cab there costs P40.

GUIMARAS ISLAND

Guimaras Island, between Panay and Negros, makes a pleasant day-trip from nearby Iloilo. There is a fairly good swimming beach about a 45-minute walk from Nueva Valencia. The Isla Naburot beach resort, south-west of San Miguel, is beautiful and the walk to the Daliran Cave from Buenavista is pleasant, although the cave is not that memorable.

Places to Stay

The *Guimaras Hotel & Beach Resort* has rooms with fan and bath for P120 or cottages for P80/160 but there's no swimming beach here although there is a pool. The *Isla Naburot Resort* is lovely but, at P1100 per person, it's also expensive as are other resorts on the island.

Getting There & Away

Small ferries cross from Iloilo to the island almost hourly and take less than half an hour.

THE SOUTH COAST

The south coast, from Iloilo to Anini-y on the southern tip of Panay and around to San Jose de Buenavista on the opposite coast, is full of interest. At **Guimbal**, 28 km west of Iloilo, is an old Spanish watchtower – from this cone-shaped, now moss-covered, building smoke signals were once sent up to warn of pirate attacks.

The 1787 **Miagao Church** is 11 km further on. It was originally built as a fort, as well as a religious centre, hence the two sturdy sandstone towers. Look for the relief sculpture of St Christopher surrounded by coconut and papaya trees.

The **Church of San Joaquin**, 15 km further again, was built of white coral in 1869 and its facade is carved as a sculpture of the Spanish victory at the battle of Tetuan in Morocco, 10 years earlier.

All along the coast, between Arevalo and San Joaquin, there are beach resorts with

cottages available to rent but the beaches are unexceptional. It's a very attractive coastal road and, at Anini-y and San Jose de Buenavista, there are good sites for diving.

Getting There & Away

Buses depart every two hours from Iloilo to San Jose de Buenavista – a two-hour trip barring breakdowns. Only one bus a day makes the excursion down the peninsula, at the south-west end of the island, to Anini-y.

SAN JOSE DE BUENAVISTA

This town is known to Filipinos as San Jose Antique, since it's the capital of Antique Province. Ships operate from here to Palawan.

Places to Stay

The *G&G Lodge* (☎ 446), on J C Zaldivar St in the market, has rooms at P45/90 and a restaurant. The *Binirayan Hotel* (☎ 226) is P95/140.

Getting There & Away

Although there are regular buses from Iloilo, transport further north is difficult. It takes four hours on a bad road to Culasi and another three to Pandan. From Culasi you can visit Mararison Island.

ROXAS

Roxas City is nothing special, just a stop on the way to or from Manila, Romblon or Boracay. The **Halaran Festival** takes place in October.

Places to Stay

The *Beehive Inn* (☎ 418) on Roxas Ave has rooms with fan for P40/60, with fan and bath for P70/90 and with air-con and bath for P145. The *River Inn* (☎ 809) on Lapu Lapu St has rooms with fan for P55/70 or with air-con for P160 but the doors close at 9 pm.

The pleasant *Halaran House* (☎ 675) on Roxas Ave has singles with fan for P75, singles/doubles with fan and bath for P100/135 or with air-con and bath for P135/175. *Halaran Plaza,* (☎ 649) on Rizal St and opposite the city hall, is also quite good with rooms with fan and bath for P120/145 or with air-con and bath for P145/175.

Well located on Baybay Beach, between the airport and the harbour, is *Marc's Beach Resort* (☎ 103) with cottages for P60, rooms with fan and bath for P160 or with air-con and bath for P200. Another good place in Baybay is *Villa Patria Cottages* (☎ 180) with rooms with fan and bath for P220/240-260 or with air-con and bath for P300/400.

Places to Eat

Of the few restaurants in Roxas City, *John's Fast Foods* on Roxas Ave, opposite Halaran House, is remarkably cheap and has a large selection of Filipino and Chinese dishes. *Halaran House Restaurant* serves *comida*, or well-priced meals of the day, but not beer.

Getting There & Away

R&K Transit or air-con Nandwani's Tourist Transport buses operate several times daily from Iloilo to Roxas City and take over four hours. Several buses a day go from Roxas City to Kalibo, departing between 5 am and 12 noon and taking over three hours.

KALIBO

The only real item of interest here is the annual **Ati-Atihan Festival** in January, the Mardi Gras of the Philippines. Similar festivals are held elsewhere in the country but this one is the most popular.

Places to Stay

Gervy's Lodge (☎ 3081) on R Pastrada St has simple rooms for P40/80. In the same street the *RB Lodge* (☎ 2604) has rooms with fan for P40/80 or doubles with air-con and bath for P190.

Comfortable *Apartel Marietta* (☎ 3302) on Roxas Ave has rooms with fan for P60/110. The *Green Mansions* (☎ 2244) on M Laserna St has dorm beds with fan for P60, rooms with fan for P70/130 and with fan and bath for P110/220.

There are several hotels on S Martelino St. The *Glowmoon Hotel* has pleasant rooms with fan for P60/90, doubles with fan and bath for P160 and rooms with air-con and bath for P200/270. The *Hotel Casa Felicidad* (☎ 3146) has dorm beds with fan for P60, rooms with fan and bath for P160/220 and with air-con and bath for P220/320. *Casa Alba Hotel* (☎ 3146) has dorm beds with fan for P80 and rooms for P80/110, with fan for P160/220 and with air-con and bath for P270/370.

The *LM Plaza Lodge*, on Martyrs St, has rooms with fan for P60/90, with fan and bath for P80/100 and with air-con and bath for P260/280. A little outside of town is the pleasant *Bayani Resort Hotel*, in Old Busuang, with singles with air-con and bath for P160 and doubles for P200 to P220.

During the Ati-Atihan Festival, prices in Kalibo may triple and it can be almost impossible to find a hotel room.

Places to Eat

The *Peking House Restaurant*, on Martyrs St, and the *Bistro* next to the *Casa Alba Hotel*, on S Martelino St, have good Chinese food. The *Cafe au Lait* on Martyrs St is also good while *Glowmoon Hotel* has a restaurant with excellent, if not that cheap, food.

Getting There & Away

PAL flights between Manila and Kalibo are very heavily booked so make reservations well ahead of time and reconfirm as early as possible. PAL also flies between Cebu City and Kalibo.

Ceres Liner buses operate Iloilo to Kalibo daily and take five hours. From Kalibo the buses leave from the service station on the south-eastern edge of town.

Buses from C Laserna St in Kalibo to Roxas City take over three hours and there are also minibuses.

From Kalibo to Caticlan, where boats cross to Boracay, takes about two hours by bus from Roxas Ave. If you arrive by plane from Manila in the early afternoon you might be able to get to Boracay the same day if you take a tricycle straight from the airport. There are sometimes jeepneys or minibuses directly from the airport.

IBAJAY

Between Kalibo and Caticlan, this small village claims to have the original Ati-Atihan Festival. You can stay in the *Western Horizon Hotel* opposite the service station for P60/110.

CATICLAN

Outrigger boats cross from Caticlan to Boracay and there's also a small airport for the increasingly popular flights from Manila. Sunday, market day, merits a trip from Boracay.

Places to Stay

The *Twin Pagoda Inn*, near the pier, has rooms for P70/130.

Getting There & Away

Jeepneys from Kalibo take two or more hours and leave several times daily. There are direct buses from Iloilo to Caticlan but it takes seven hours – five to Kalibo and two more to Caticlan. Big passenger boats from Manila or Puerto Princesa dock at Malay, five km south-west of Caticlan. Tricycles form Caticlan cost P20 to the airport and P20 to P30 to Malay.

BORACAY

This superb little island, off the north-west tip of Panay, has beautiful clear water and splendid beaches. It is seven km long, only a km wide and you can walk across it in just 15 minutes.

Despite rapid growth, it doesn't suffer from the comprehensive and thoughtless overdevelopment which has plagued Puerto Galera. Beach and water activities, general lazing and watching the sunset are daily attractions at Boracay. Electricity will soon arrive at Boracay but bring along a torch (flashlight).

Information

DOT's Boracay Field Office, in a bungalow on White Beach, has loads of information about the island, including boat lists and maps.

Several places at the beaches will change

dollars or travellers' cheques but at a poor exchange rate.

Things to See

Besides the snorkelling spots and wonderful sunsets, there are two minor attractions at the north end of the island: the **Museum of Shells & Native Costumes** at Ilig Iligan and a **cave** inhabited by fruit bats between Ilig Iligan and Yapak.

Places to Stay

There are three little villages connected by walking tracks – Yapak at the north, Balabag in the middle and Manoc Manoc in the south. Accommodation is in comfortable little cottages for two with a verandah and, usually, with a bathroom. There are now a handful of much more flashy places, some of them at the more remote beaches.

Most of the cottages are along White Beach, between Balabag and Angol. There are so many of them and they are so alike that it's probably easiest to simply be dropped off in the middle of the beach and to wander around until you find a suitable place. Take care of your valuables, there have been some thefts.

Good cheap places in Angol include *Pacing's Nipa Hut* at P90 to P160, *Moreno's Place* at P90 to P130 and *Deling's Cottages* at P110. Moving up the beach to Mangayad, there's *Lea Homes* and *Trafalgar Lodge* at P110 to P160 and *Magic Palm* at P110.

Balabag also has several places at around P110. The *6C Place* has cottages at P90 to P160, *Sunshine Cottages* at P110 to P130, *Bans Beach House* at P110 to P160 and *Seabreeze Cottages* at P160.

There are many places that charge around P220 (up to P400 in high season from November to February). One of these is *Roy's Rendezvous* in Angol at P160 to P220. Mangayad offers the greatest choice in this range with *La Isla Bonita Cottages* at P160, *Treasure Island* at P220, *Holiday Homes* at P220 to P270, *Shangrila Oasis Cottages* at P160 to P270, *Family Cottages* at P180 and *Aqua Blue Cottages* at P160. In Balabag, *Galaxy Cottages* has cottages for P160 to

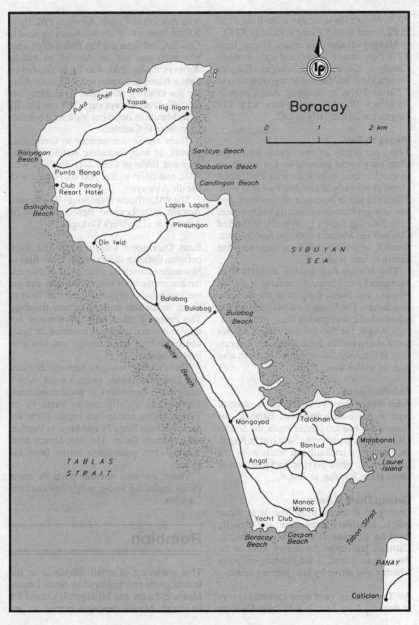

Boracay

0   1   2 km

Puka Shell Beach
Yapak
Ilig Iligan

Banyogan
Beach
Punta Bonga
Club Panoly
Resort Hotel
Balinghai
Beach

Santoyo Beach
Sanbaloron Beach
Candingon Beach

Lapus Lapus

Pinaungon

Din Iwid

SIBUYAN
SEA

Balabog
Bulabog
Bulabog
Beach

White Beach

TABLAS
STRAIT

Mangayad
Angol

Talobhan
Bantud
Malobonot

Laurel
Island

Manoc
Manoc

Yacht Club
Boracay
Beach

Cacpan
Beach

Tabon Strait

PANAY

Caticlan

P270, *Nena's Paradise Inn* costs from P160 to P270 and *Willy's Place* is P220 to P270.

Mangayad also has many places from P270 (low season prices) and up – *Bamboo Cottages, Casa Pilar Cottages, Tonglen Homes, Vista del Mar* and *Mango Ray* all cost P270 to P370. In Balabag *Red Coconut, Jackson's Place, Jony's Place* and *VIP Lingau* are all similarly priced.

Places to Eat

There are plenty of restaurants which are often busy in the evening so you may have to wait for up to an hour for your food. Book ahead or eat early if you don't want to wait. Thanks to gas or kerosene refrigerators, you can now get cold drinks nearly everywhere.

In Balabag, there's great paella at the *Red Coconut* and Mexican dishes at *Jony's Place. Jonah's*, opposite the Beachcomber, has excellent fruit juices.

The *Mango Ray* garden restaurant in Mangayad has a beautiful setting or there's Filipino and Swiss delights at the *Bamboo Restaurant*. The *Green Yard* has good wiener schnitzel and veal cordon bleu.

In Angol, the *Starfire* and *Happy Homes* serve cheap meals. Fruit salads are a speciality at the *Jolly Sailor*, where you can also pick up useful travel hints.

Entertainment

After dinner, there's dancing, good music or pool at the *Beachcomber* at Balabag, the *Bazura Bar* one km further south, the *Sharks Disco* in Mangayad or the *Sulu Bar* in Angol. Or else, sip a cocktail and while away the balmy night while playing backgammon or chess at the *Sun Bar* in Angol.

Getting There & Away

Getting to Boracay from Manila is either quick, relatively expensive and heavily booked or else it's time-consuming. Caticlan, just across the narrow strait on the Panay main island, is the jumping-off point whether you arrive by bus, jeepney or air.

Air The quickest (and most expensive) way to Boracay from Manila is to fly to Caticlan with Aerolift or Pacific Airways. PAL fly to Kalibo from where it's two hours by road to Caticlan, and fares are less than half of what you must pay for the Aerolift or Pacific Airways flights. PAL also fly to Tugdan on Tablas Island in the province of Romblon but the sea crossing from there to Boracay via Santa Fe is not always easy. You can also fly from Manila to Iloilo but it's a long bus ride from there to Caticlan.

There are air connections to some other islands, as well, including Kalibo to Cebu City and Iloilo to Cebu City on Cebu with PAL, and Iloilo to Bacolod on Negros with Pacific Airways.

The PAL office is at the South Seas Resort, Aerolift is at Lorenzo Resort and Pacific Airways is at Dublin's Cottages.

Boat Outriggers shuttle back and forth between Caticlan and Boracay. From June to November, during the south-west monsoons, the sea on the west side of Boracay can get too rough for outriggers. They then have to tie up on the east coast, at or near Bulabog. The crossing takes only 15 minutes but they're inclined to grossly overload the boats and more than one traveller has lost gear from a capsize.

There's a big outrigger between Boracay and Looc, on Tablas, twice a week, which takes about two hours in good conditions. There's also a daily one to Santa Fe on Tablas, taking one to two hours. There are jeepneys from Santa Fe and Looc to Tugdan, the airport on Tablas. The boat departs from Tablas when passengers arrive from the airport.

There are also several ports in north Panay, including Malay, only a few km from Caticlan.

Romblon

This scattering of small islands is in the middle of the area bordered by South Luzon, Masbate, Panay and Mindoro. It's noted for its marble. Marble carving is carried out and an extensive range of souvenirs is produced. There are some good beaches and the town of Romblon has a notable cathedral. The three main islands of the group are Romblon and the two larger islands, Sibuyan and Tablas.

Romblon is useful as a stepping stone from the beach resort of Puerto Galera on Mindoro to the resort island of Boracay, just off Panay and directly south of Tablas.

Getting There & Away

PAL flies daily, except Sunday, between Manila and Tugdan on Tablas Island.

Regular boats operate between Lucena on Luzon and Magdiwang on Sibuyan Island and between Lucena and Romblon town on Romblon Island. There are also services between Manila and various Romblon ports. Other boats, some of them large outriggers, operate between Romblon ports and Masbate, Mindoro, Palawan and Panay.

See the Mindoro and Boracay sections for details of Mindoro to Tablas and Tablas to Boracay travel, used by some intrepid travellers as a route between the two popular beach centres of Puerto Galera and Boracay.

ROMBLON ISLAND

The small port of **Romblon** on Romblon Island is the capital of the province. **San Andres** and **Santiago Hill forts** were built by the Spanish in 1640, while the **San Joseph Cathedral** dates from 1726 and houses a collection of antiques. There are good views from the **Sabang** and **Apunan lighthouses**. **Lugbon Island** shelters the bay and has a beautiful white beach.

Places to Stay & Eat

The *Sea Side Lodge*, by the harbour, has rooms for P60. The well-kept *Marble Hotel* is slightly more at P75/100. Also by the harbour is the *Kawilihan Food House* but the *Tica Inn* is probably the best restaurant in town.

You can stay in the *Selangga Tree House*, at Agnay and six km from Romblon town, for P50 per person.

Getting There & Away

Boats go about four times weekly between Romblon town and Sibuyan Island in two hours. There are daily outriggers to San Agustin on Tablas Island taking 45 minutes.

TABLAS ISLAND

Tablas is the largest island in the Romblon group. The main towns are San Agustin, Odiongan, Looc and Santa Fe.

Places to Stay

The *S&L Lodge* in San Agustin is cheap at P30/50. In Odiongan, the *Shellborne Hotel* costs P50/90 or P50/100 with fan and bath. In Looc, the *Plaza Inn* is P40/70 or P50/90 with fan and bath. The *Tablas Pension House* is P50/90. Tugdan has the *Gutierrez Cool Spot* at P30/60 or the *Airport Pension House* at P60/110.

Getting There & Away

Flights to Tugdan from Manila are almost always heavily booked. Jeepneys meet the plane and go to San Agustin (one hour), Santa Fe (one hour) and Looc (45 minutes).

San Agustin is the port for boats to Romblon town. Odiongan's small harbour is just outside the town and, from here, boats go to Manila and to the islands of Palawan and Mindoro. Looc is the port for boats to Boracay. They cost P50 per person (although they ask P80) and there's a connecting jeepney service from the airport in Tugdan. There's also a daily boat from Santa Fe to Carabao (the island between Tablas and Boracay), Boracay and Caticlan on Panay. The two-hour trip to Boracay costs P70.

SIBUYAN ISLAND

Sibuyan is more mountainous and less developed than the other islands. There are several **waterfalls** and the 2050-metre **Mt Guiting-Guiting**.

Samar

The large Visayan island of Samar acts as a stepping stone from Luzon to Leyte. There is a regular ferry service from Matnog, at the southern end of Luzon, to Allen and San Isidro at the northern end of Samar. From there, the Pan-Philippine Highway runs along the coast and a bridge connects Samar with Leyte.

This recently constructed road has made transport through Samar much easier but elsewhere the island is fairly undeveloped so finding transport can be hard going. Samar also experiences guerrilla activity so check the situation before venturing there. The northern part of Samar and the west coast are usually OK. The Sohoton National Park, near Basey in southern Samar, is the island's outstanding attraction.

Getting There & Away

There are a number of ferries daily between Matnog and Allen, and between Matnog and San Isidro. The crossing takes one to two hours. Buses between Catbalogan and Tacloban, in Leyte, take two hours.

ALLEN

This is simply a port town for the ferry service to Luzon.

Places to Stay

There are a number of cheap hotels at around P40 per person. They include *La Suerta Lodging House*, *Bicolana Lodging House* and *El Canto Lodging House*.

Getting There & Away

Several buses daily operate between Allen and Catbalogan via Calbayog, taking over three hours all the way.

CATARMAN

As a provincial capital, Catarman is a busy trade centre in northern Samar with **Tamburosan Beach** only four km away.

Places to Stay

The *Sanitary Lodging House* (great name!) is on Bonifacio St and costs P30 per person. On Jacinto St, the *Rendezvous Lodging House* is also P30 per person. Others include

the more expensive *Island Hotel* on Rizal St where rooms cost P40 per person.

CALBAYOG

Calbayog is just another 'through' town although the road from Allen runs along the coast almost the entire way. The views are especially fine around **Viriato**, between Allen and Calbayog. The **Blanca Aurora Falls** are about 50 km south-east of Calbayog. They're reached by riverboat to Buenavista (one hour) from near the village of Gandara. Check first to find out if the NPA is active in the area.

Places to Stay

The *Wayside Lodging House* has good spartan rooms with fan for P25/50. At the *Calbayog Hotel* rooms with fan are P40/80 and there's a restaurant. The *San Joaquin Inn* (☎ 386/7) on Nijaga St costs P45/90 for rooms with fan, P80/160 with fan and bath and P270 for a double with air-con and bath.

The best hotel in Calbayog is the *Seaside Drive Inn* (☎ 234), in Rawis, with rooms at P50/100, with fan and bath for P120 or with air-con and bath for P240.

Getting There & Away

There are a couple of daily Golden Eagle buses and several jeepneys between Catarman and Calbayog, via Allen. Several buses a day go from Catbalogan to Calbayog (two hours). There are some slower jeepneys.

CATBALOGAN

There are beaches around Catbalogan, but it's really just a stepping stone to Tacloban on Leyte. Buses go across to the east coast from here.

Places to Stay & Eat

The *Town Hotel* on San Bartolome St has simple rooms at P25/50 or with fan for P30/60. *Amparo's Hotel* on Allen St costs P25/50 and has a restaurant.

Kikay's Hotel (☎ 664) on Curry Ave has rooms for P30/60, or doubles with air-con for P160 and with air-con and bath for P180. The *Fortune Hotel* (☎ 680) on Del Rosario St has rooms with fan for P70/110, with fan and bath for P140 and with air-con and bath for P220. On the same street, *Tony's Hotel* has rooms with fan and bath for P70/130.

You can get good meals in the *Fortune Restaurant* in the hotel of the same name. *Tony's Kitchen* is another cheap restaurant where you can eat well.

Getting There & Away

Several buses and jeepneys run daily from Catarman to Catbalogan, via Allen and Calbayog. Going to Catbalogan, the trip takes five hours from Catarman, four hours from Allen and two hours from Calbayog.

Sulu Archipelago

The string of islands that dribble from Zamboanga to Sabah in north Borneo are home for some of the most fervently Muslim people in the country. The Spanish and Americans never dominated them and, even now things still aren't under total control.

Jolo is the main town and island, and the old walled city, with its gate and watch-towers, is worth seeing. The people of the archipelago are great seafarers – many, particularly the Badjao, or 'sea gypsies', live on houseboats or in houses built on stilts over the water. Smuggling and piracy occur in the area and some of the practitioners are reputed to be very well equipped and armed.

Singapore

Singapore is a small island at the tip of the Malay Peninsula. It thrives on trade and, through a combination of hard work and efficient if at times repressive government, has become the most affluent country in Asia after Japan. It's a crossroads for travellers but also offers a wide variety of places to visit, things to buy and some of the best food in Asia.

Singapore, with its preoccupation with cleanliness and orderliness, can be a pleasant break from the more hectic travelling you find elsewhere in the region. It's also tending to become more and more antiseptic and dull – just another big city with numerous huge hotels and air-conditioned shopping centres.

Facts about the Country

HISTORY

Singapore's improbable name, it means 'Lion City', came from a Sumatran prince who thought he saw a lion when he landed on the island – it was much more likely a tiger. Singapore would have drifted on as a quiet fishing village if Sir Stamford Raffles had not decided, in 1819, that it was just the port he needed. Under the British it became a great trading city and a military and naval base, but that didn't save it from the Japanese in 1942.

In 1959, Singapore became internally self-governing, in 1963 it joined Malaysia and, in 1965, changed its mind and pulled out of this federation. The reason behind this was a basic conflict of interests between 'Malaysia for the Malays' and Singapore's predominantly Chinese population. Under Prime Minister Lee Kuan Yew, Singapore made the best of its independence. Trade, tourism and industrialisation soon made up for the loss of British military bases.

Mr Lee's somewhat iron-fisted government also turned Singapore into a green, tidy garden city where no one dares to litter the streets, or even carelessly drop cigarette ash. The economy is dynamic, the water from the taps is drinkable, smoking in public places is forbidden, big cars are taxed more heavily than small ones and all drivers are heavily discouraged from venturing into the city centre during rush hour.

Singapore's progressive attitudes have another side: criticism of the government is not a recommended activity, the press is tightly controlled and the minuscule elected opposition has always had a hard time. It has even been loudly mooted as to whether the country actually needs any opposition to the People's Action Party! Lee Kuan Yew finally stepped down from the leadership in 1990 but it is more than likely that he will continue to pull the strings from the background.

Complaints about the Communist threat have a somewhat hollow ring in Singapore these days. One commentator noted that anybody planning a Marxist revolution would have to ensure they provided plenty of parking spaces for the downtrodden masses' BMWs, Mercedes and late-model Japanese cars.

GEOGRAPHY

The population squeezes itself into a low-lying 616 sq km island at the tip of the Malay Peninsula, not much more than 100 km north of the equator. A 1000-metre long causeway connects Singapore with Johore Bahru in Malaysia. A second link to Malaysia is on the drawing board.

CLIMATE

Singapore is hot and humid all year round as it is situated so close to the equator. It does get better at night, however, and the weather never seems to be quite as sticky as Bangkok, 1500 km to the north. November to January tend to be the wettest months, and it can rain every afternoon for weeks on end.

ECONOMY

The economy is based on trade, shipping, banking, tourism and light industry (often hi-tech). Ship building and maintenance is also an important industry. Along with Hong Kong, Taiwan and South Korea, Singapore is one of East Asia's economically booming 'Mini-dragons'.

POPULATION & PEOPLE

Singapore's polyglot population of 2.5 million is made up of 77% Chinese, 15% Malay, 6% Indian and the remaining 2% of any and every nationality you can imagine. Curiously, after years of promoting birth control, the government has decided they've been too successful and you will now see many posters promoting the joys of the three child family! Of course, it has a Singapore twist to it – there are extra incentives to having children if the parents have university degrees.

RELIGION

Tha variety of religions found in Singapore is a direct reflection of the diversity of races living there. The Chinese are predominantly followers of Taoism and Buddhism, though some of them are Christians. Malays are overwhelmingly Muslim, and most of the region's Indians are Hindus from the south of India.

LANGUAGE

English is widely spoken, as is Malay, Tamil and a number of Chinese dialects. After a spell in Singapore, you may come to the conclusion that Chinese is not a language to be whispered or even spoken. It is a language to be howled, yowled, shrieked and screamed. In any Chinese restaurant, you will witness how. The 'official' Chinese dialect is Mandarin – you may see public signs urging Chinese citizens to 'Speak Mandarin, Not Dialect!'.

Facts for the Visitor

VISAS

Most Western nationalities do not require visas, and you are granted an initial two weeks on entry. A two-week extension should not be difficult but beyond a month it becomes increasingly hard. The government obviously feels that a month is long enough for anybody to do their shopping. Enquire at the Immigration Department, South Bridge Centre, 595 South Bridge Rd.

Singapore used to have a strict attitude towards 'hippies', and long hair or scruffy clothes could cause you all sorts of problems. Furthermore, evidence of your financial soundness or possession of a ticket to faraway places was required before you could enter the country. However, although laws still insist that people with long hair be given a hard time, in actual fact Singapore is fairly relaxed and few travellers report any real hassles these days.

Singapore is generally a good place to get visas. It's the best place in the region for Indonesian visas (☎ 737 7422), although visas are only now required if you're going to enter by some really odd route. The Thai Embassy (☎ 737 2644) is also reasonably fast and efficient. Burmese (Myanmar) visas are now issued only in conjunction with an organised tour.

The Indian High Commission has a pretty poor reputation, but then so do plenty of other Indian consular offices.

MONEY

The Singapore dollar is divided into 100 cents and is worth over 50% more than the Malaysian dollar. Once, the two currencies were directly interchangeable but now even the coins are different. The Brunei dollar, however, is still on par with the Singapore dollar.

There are no pitfalls in changing money in Singapore but if you're watching every cent it is worth shopping around the banks a bit – exchange rates tend to vary and many banks

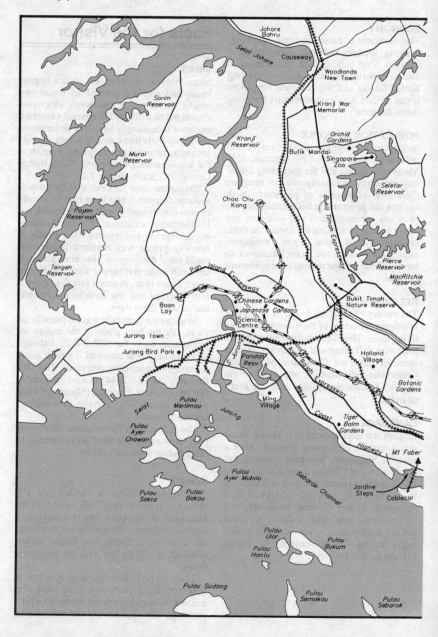

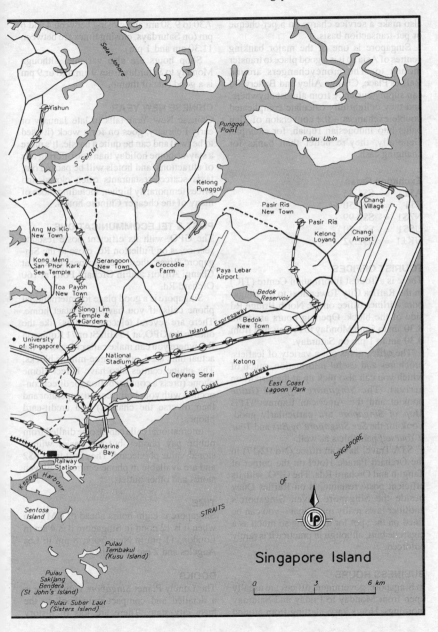

Singapore Island

0   3   6 km

also make a service charge on a per-cheque or per-transaction basis.

Singapore is one of the major banking centres of Asia so it is a good place to transfer money to. The moneychangers around Raffles Place, Change Alley and Battery Rd can supply currency from almost anywhere, and they delightfully calculate complicated double exchanges – the conversion of Thai bahts into Indonesian rupiah, for example. Generally, they're better than banks for changing cash.

Exchange Rates

A$1	=	S$1.35
C$1	=	S$1.50
NZ$1	=	S$0.99
US$1	=	S$1.70
UK£1	=	S$2.92

TOURIST OFFICES

There is a Tourist Information Centre (TIC) in the Raffles City Tower next to the Singapore Airlines office on the North Bridge Rd side of the block. Opening hours are from 8.30 am to 5 pm Monday to Friday, and from 8.30 am to 1 pm on Saturday.

The office gives out a variety of leaflets, brochures and useful information, much of which you can also pick up at the airport on arrival. The *Singapore Official Guide* booklet and the American Express/STPB *Map of Singapore* are particularly good. Look for the *See Singapore by Bus* and *Tour it Yourself* pamphlets as well.

STA Travel have an office (No 02-17) in the Orchard Parade Hotel on the corner of Tanglin and Orchard Rds. The GPO, with its efficient poste restante, is on Raffles Quay beside the Singapore River. Singapore's antilitter laws really mean that – you can be fined on the spot for dropping so much as a cigarette butt, although in practice it is rarely enforced.

BUSINESS HOURS

In Singapore, government offices are usually open from Monday to Friday and Saturday mornings. Hours vary, starting from around 7.30 to 9.30 am and closing between 4 and 6 pm (on Saturdays, closing times are between 11.30 am and 1 pm).

Shop hours are also variable, although Monday to Saturday from 9 am to 8 or 9 pm is a good rule of thumb.

CHINESE NEW YEAR

Chinese New Year falls in late January or early February, goes on for a week (it used to be two) and can be quite a hassle. It's more a stay-at-home holiday than one offering lots of attractions, and hotels will be packed out, taxis scarce, restaurants often closed and prices temporarily higher, including those of many of the cheaper Chinese hotels.

POST & TELECOMMUNICATIONS

The GPO, with its efficient poste restante service, is on Fullerton Rd, close to the Singapore River; there are also post offices at Changi Airport and in Orchard Point at 160 Orchard Rd.

Singapore is a good place for international phone calls, if you have to contact home. There are several telecom centres, like the ones in the GPO, at 15 Hill St or 71 Robinson Rd, where you can make calls charged by the actual time used, not in three-minute blocks. The phone centres also have Direct Home phone (press a country button for direct connection with your home country operator and then reverse the charges) and credit-card phones.

International calls can also be dialled from public pay phones but it's easier with a stored-value phonecard. They cost from S$2 and are available in phone centres, 7-Eleven stores and other outlets.

TIME

Singapore is eight hours ahead of GMT. So when it is 12 noon in Singapore it is 4 am in London, 11 pm in New York, 8 pm in Los Angeles and 2 pm in Sydney.

BOOKS

The Lonely Planet *Singapore City Guide* is a detailed and compact guidebook to the busy city state. There are lots of history books and a number of novels about Singapore to read. Try *The Singapore Grip* by J G Farrell for an enthralling novel based on the fall of Singapore in WW II.

Singapore probably has the best bookshops in South-East Asia. The main MPH shop on Stamford Rd is excellent, but there are numerous other good bookshops around the city including other MPH branches, Times Bookshops, Kinokuniya Bookshops and Book Stops. The Centrepoint shopping complex on Orchard Rd has branches of Times and MPH.

MEDIA

Singapore three Chinese daily newspapers have a combined circulation of over 350,000. There are three English-language newspapers (the establishment *Straits Times*, the *Business Times* and the *New Paper*) and there is also a Malay and an Indian daily.

There are seven radio stations transmitting in four languages – Malay, Mandarin, Tamil and English – on the AM, FM and short-wave bands. Singapore also has three TV stations: 5 and 8 which transmit in all the four languages, and Channel 12 which transmits mostly in English.

HEALTH

Health worries are not so much of a problem in Singapore. It possesses the best medical facilities in the region and many people come here from neighbouring countries if they need medical attention. If you need to renew vaccinations, try the Vaccination Centre (☎ 222 7711), Block 1, Level 5, 226 Outram Rd, on the corner of Chin Swee Rd. It is open from 8 am to 1 pm and from 2 to 4.30 pm weekdays, and on Saturday from 8 am to 12.30 pm. It is closed on Sunday and public holidays.

Many of the shopping centres have a floor dedicated to medical services. Try the 3rd floor of the Peace Centre on Selegie Rd, near the Bencoolen St area. There are several doctor's surgeries where you can get vaccinations, and the 3rd-floor pharmacy has antimalarials, cholera vaccine and gamma-globulin.

A visit to a doctor costs from S$20 to S$40. A consultation with a senior nurse costs S$30 at the Singapore General Hospital on Outram Rd, near the Chinatown and Outram Park MRT stations.

FOOD

The food in Singapore is simply terrific; the variety is unbelievable and the costs are pleasantly low. For information on the types of food available, see the Singapore Places to Eat section.

THINGS TO BUY

Shopping is a big attraction in Singapore. There are plenty of bargains to be had although a few ground rules should be followed if you want to get your money's worth. First of all, don't buy anything unless you really want it and, secondly, don't buy anything unless you know the savings are worth the hassles of carting it back home.

There are lots of discount houses in the West whose prices for many items may be competitive with those of Singapore.

Prices & Bargaining

When buying, except for in big department stores, you have to bargain, and to do so with a measure of success you need some idea of the value of what you want. The prices in big department stores will provide a good guide or check the *Shopping & Eating* booklet available at Changi Airport.

After all, it's no feat to knock $160 down to $140 if a fixed-price place has it for $120 all along. Maintain a lack of interest when bargaining (there are plenty of other shops) but remember, when you've made an offer, you're committed.

Guarantees & Compatibility

Make sure a guarantee is an international one. It's no good having to bring something back to Singapore for repair. Check that electronic goods are compatible with your home country – voltages vary, and TVs and VCRs made for Japan and the USA operate on a different system to most other countries.

Where to Shop

Almost anywhere is one answer, but some good places include People's Park, a huge non-touristy shopping centre where you'll find clothes, watches, electronic gear, cameras and so on. There's also a Chinese emporium here. There are many ultra-modern centres, particularly down Orchard Rd and its periphery. For modern consumer goods, the fixed price shops at Changi Airport offer surprisingly competitive rates to the shops in town.

For oddities, try Arab St and the nearby Thieves Market, Serangoon Rd or Chinatown. For luxury goods, it's Orchard Rd again.

What to Buy

Almost anything – Levis or other brand-name jeans at cheap prices, cameras and film (cheaper by the dozen although Singapore is no longer a real bargain basement for film), tape recorders, pre-recorded tapes, radios, typewriters, calculators, watches (cheap ones for Indonesia, expensive ones for India if you're planning to resell them) and even Persian carpets.

Chinese emporiums and some night markets have good money belts. All sorts of Chinese crafts can be found at emporiums. Funan Centre on North Bridge Rd near the Peninsula Hotel has several floors of shops which offer inexpensive computer peripherals. Note, however, that cheap pirated software is no longer available in Singapore.

Getting There & Away

AIR

Singapore is a major travel hub and flights operate in and out of Changi Airport at all hours. Singapore International Airlines (SIA) and Malaysian Airlines System (MAS) have flights between Singapore and Kuala Lumpur, Penang, Kuching and Kota Kinabalu in Malaysia.

There are also frequent flights between Singapore and Bangkok in Thailand, Jakarta in Indonesia and Hong Kong. Also see the following Sea section about travelling to Indonesia by ferry via the Riau Archipelago.

Singapore is a very good place for looking for cheap airline tickets although Penang, Bangkok and Hong Kong are other equally competitive centres. Agents like Airmaster Travel and Airpower Travel, in the same building at 36 Selegie Rd, just off Bras Basah Rd, are worth trying. STA Travel (☎ 734 5681) in the Orchard Parade Hotel, on the corner of Orchard and Tanglin Rds, is also worth trying. Others advertise in the travel section of the *Straits Times* classified columns.

Fares vary according to when you want to fly and who you want to fly with. The cheapest fares are likely to be with the least loved airlines and at the least popular times. Various Eastern European and Middle Eastern airlines, Aero-flot, Bangladesh Biman, Air Lanka and others are all cheaper than the big European operators, Qantas, Thai, SIA and the like. Flights departing only on every second Wednesday at 3 am are also likely to be cheaper than flights offering regular departures at civilised hours!

Some typical cheap one-way fares being quoted from Singapore include South-East Asian destinations like Bangkok (S$190 to S$220), Denpasar (S$420 one way or S$550 excursion return), Jakarta (S$180 one way or S$300 return) and Hong Kong (S$550 one way or S$750 return). To the subcontinent, you can fly to Madras or Bombay for S$550 or to Kathmandu for S$600.

Fares to Australia or New Zealand include Sydney or Melbourne S$750/1250 for one way/return, and Auckland S$900 one way via Indonesia or S$1000 via Australia. London or other European destinations cost from S$750 one way with the less popular carriers, and from S$850 with a more popular one. If a stopover in India or Nepal is included, the fare will probably be around S$1100.

One-way fares to the US west coast are around S$900 direct and stopovers in Manila or Tokyo cost more. You are able to fly via Indonesia for around S$1050, and via Australia or New Zealand for S$1500.

There are always some special multistop deals on offer, eg Singapore-Bangkok-Hong Kong-Taipei-Los Angeles with Air China (CAAC) for S$1000, and you could add Tokyo and Honolulu to that route for a few dollars more.

Warning

If you're flying between Singapore and Malaysia, note that it's much cheaper to fly from Malaysia to Singapore than Singapore to Malaysia. The fares are actually identical in dollar terms although the Malaysian dollar (or ringgit) is over 50% less than the mighty Singapore dollar.

It's also much cheaper to fly to Malaysian destinations from Johore Bahru, just across the causeway from Singapore, than directly from Singapore. MAS operate a connecting bus service from downtown Singapore to Johore Bahru Airport.

Singapore Airport

Changi International Airport is now divided into Changi I and Changi II, connected in less than two minutes by the Changi Skytrain. Singapore's ultramodern Changi Airport is vast, efficient, organised and was built in record time.

At the airport, there are banking and moneychanging facilities, post offices, left-luggage facilities and a variety of shops. There's also a free hotel reservation service open from 8 to 11.30 am, although it does not book rooms in the cheapest hotels. In the transit area there's a day-room facility where you can get a shower for S$5. If you're in transit for a long time you can even take a free two-hour tour of the city and kids are catered for with an imaginative play area.

There are plenty of eating places at the airport (this is Singapore after all, food capital of South-East Asia), including a *Swensen's* ice cream bar upstairs, a Chinese restaurant, a Japanese restaurant, a cafe serving Malay, Nonya and Indian food and the *Transit Buffeteria* and *Wing's Cafeteria*.

If you are one of the many air travellers fed up with overpriced and terrible food at airports, then Changi Airport has the answer to that too – Changi has a *McDonald's* and a *Noodle Restaurant* with food at normal, not inflated, prices.

Even better, take the elevator beside McDonald's on the arrival level of the Changi I terminal and press the button for the basement 1 'Food Centre'. There you'll find a complete Singapore hawkers' centre with Chinese and Malay food! It's essentially the airport staff cafeteria but the public are quite welcome. There's also a supermarket in the basement.

Departure Tax

Airport departure tax from Singapore is S$5 to Malaysia and Brunei and S$12 further afield.

LAND
Bus

Although there are plenty of buses operating from Singapore into Malaysia, the choice is much greater in Johore Bahru where there is also a wide variety of taxi services. To get to Johore Bahru, you can take bus No 170 from the Ban San terminal, at the corner of Queen and Arab Sts, for 80c.

You can also catch the bus on Rochor Rd, Rochor Canal Rd or Bukit Timah Rd. For S$1.50, you can take the direct express bus operated by Singapore-Johore Express which departs from the Ban San terminal every 10 minutes. The Ban San terminal is very convenient for the Bencoolen St backpackers' places.

Don't be worried if the bus departs while you're clearing immigration and customs for Malaysia as you can just hop on the next one that comes along. There are plenty of moneychangers at Johore Bahru or you can change money before leaving Singapore.

Most long-distance buses for Singapore leave from the Malaysia bus terminal at the corner of Lavender St and Kallang Bahru. It is to the north-east of Bencoolen St, near the top end of Jalan Besar. You can get there on bus Nos 122, 133, 145 or 147 from Victoria St or take the MRT to Lavender station and board one of those buses from the Kallang Rd bus stop. It's a hot half a km walk to the

Malaysia bus terminal station from the MRT station. There is a moneychanging facility at the terminal.

Masmara (☎ 732 6555) is the main agent for buses to Malaysia and has an office at the station (☎ 294 7034) and at 05-53 Far East Plaza, 14 Scotts Rd. Ekoba-Hasry-Hosni Express (☎ 296 3164) has Kuala Lumpur and Penang buses from the Lavender station. The trip to KL takes about eight hours, mainly because the road is very busy in both directions. Parts of it are now divided and have toll booths.

Melacca-Singapore Express (☎ 293 5915) has Melaka buses at 8, 9, 10, 11 am, and 1, 2, 3 and 4 pm. The six-hour trip costs M$11. Butterworth (Penang) has one departure daily for S$31, Kuantan has three at S$16, and Kota Bharu one at S$30. Kuala Lumpur-Singapore Express (☎ 292 8254) also has departures for KL from the Ban San terminal at 9 am, 1 and 10 pm for S$16.10.

Many of the air-con buses are really flashy – new and immaculate with radio, TV and toilet.

Train

Singapore is the southern termination point for the Malaysian railway system, although Singapore has no real system of its own. When you leave Singapore you clear immigration and customs at the station so there is no further delay at the causeway when crossing into Malaysia. See the Transport section in the Malaysia chapter for full details on the rail system from Singapore, right through Malaysia and into Thailand. Phone the Singapore railway station (☎ 222 5165) for schedule and fare information.

Taxi

Taxis also run into Malaysia from the Ban San terminal. The fare to Johore Bahru is S$4 per person or S$16 for the whole taxi. If you're not Singaporean or Malaysian, you may have to pay more as you will take longer at the border. At busy times and weekends, the bus will probably be faster than a taxi since they can use the special bus lanes.

The Malaysia Taxi Service (☎ 298 3831) at 290 Jalan Besar or the Kuala Lumpur Taxi Service (☎ 223 1889) at 191 New Bridge Rd have services from Singapore directly to Malaysian destinations.

Hitching

If you want to hitchhike through Malaysia, cross the border to Johore Bahru first.

SEA

There used to be lots of shipping services out of Singapore, but very few still operate – it's almost all airlines today.

To/From Indonesia

Curiously, there are no direct shipping services between any of the major towns of Indonesia and its near neighbour, Singapore. You can, however, travel by sea between the two countries via the Riau Archipelago, the Indonesian islands to the south of Singapore.

Batam and Bintan, the two major islands closest to Singapore, are undergoing extensive Singapore-financed development and there are numerous high-speed ferry services shuttling across. It takes less than half an hour to reach Batam Island at a cost of S$16 one way.

A smaller number of services also operate to Tanjung Pinang on neighbouring Bintan Island at a cost of around S$45 one way.

You don't require a visa to enter Indonesia via Batam or Bintan. From Batam, you can fly to Jakarta or to other centres in Indonesia, or you can continue on to Bintan by boat from where you can again fly or take a boat to Sumatra or Java. For full details of this interesting and economical entry route into Indonesia see the Riau Archipelago section in the Indonesia chapter.

To/From Malaysia

The overwhelming majority of travellers to or from Malaysia will either be coming through Changi Airport or crossing the causeway by road or rail. Take bus Nos 1 or 2 from central Singapore out to Changi village, near Changi Airport, and for S$4 you can take a ferry across to Pengerang in

Malaysia. This interesting back-door route into Malaysia operates from 7 am to 4 pm.

Getting Around

TO/FROM THE AIRPORT
Singapore's Changi International Airport is at the extreme eastern end of the island, about 20 km from the city. An expressway runs on reclaimed land to the city and with fast bus services, it is no problem getting into town.

You've got a choice of taxis or convenient public buses. For the public buses follow the signs in the airport terminal to the basement bus stop. The air-con bus No 390 runs to the Bencoolen St-Beach Rd-Middle Rd cheap accommodation enclave and on to Orchard Rd where many of the expensive hotels are located. The fare is a flat S$1.20 and you are supposed to have the correct change so get some when you change money on arrival. The bus operates every 10 to 12 minutes from 6 am to midnight, and takes about half an hour.

As the bus approaches the city, it comes off the flyover into Raffles Blvd and then Stamford Rd. For Beach Rd, get off beside the towering, round Raffles City complex on your right, just past the open playing field of the Padang on your left. Half a km along, the National Museum is the place to get off for Bencoolen St. The bus then continues up Penang and Somerset Rds and Orchard Blvd (parallel to Orchard Rd) and then returns along Tanglin and Orchard Rds.

If you are going to the airport, catch the bus on Orchard or Bras Basah Rds.

Taxis from the airport are subject to a S$3 supplementary charge on top of the metered fare, which will probably be from S$10 to S$15 to most places. This only applies from the airport and not from the city.

BUS
Singapore has a comprehensive bus network with frequent buses. You rarely have to wait more than a few minutes for a bus and they will get you almost anywhere you want to go. If you intend to do a lot of travelling by bus in Singapore, a copy of the *Bus Guide* is an essential investment. Buses go along the same route into and out of the city. The free *See Singapore by Bus* pamphlet also gives a good introduction to Singapore bus travel.

Fares start from 50c and go up in 10c increments to a maximum of 80c. There are also an increasing number of air-con bus routes which start at 60c and go up to S$1.20. Most buses are OMO (one-man operated) buses which either charge a flat fare or a stepped flat fare depending on where you board. Either way you are supposed to have the exact fare as change is not given.

If you plan to see a lot of Singapore by bus, a bus pass is a wise investment. Many hotels and all the YMCAs sell *The Singapore Explorer*, a pass good for unlimited bus travel throughout the island on both the SBS (Singapore Bus Service, red & white buses) and TIBS (Trans-Island Bus Service, orange & yellow buses) lines. The two options are a one-day pass costing S$5 or a three-day pass for S$12.

MRT
Singapore's ultramodern Mass Rapid Transit (MRT) system is now completely operative and is the easiest, fastest and most comfortable way of getting around the city. The Somerset, Orchard and Newton MRT stations are all close to Orchard Rd. Dhoby Ghaut station is closest to Bencoolen St. Bugis St and City Hall stations straddle Beach Rd.

Fares vary from 50c to S$1.40. You check the fare from a fare map, press the appropriate button on the ticket vending machine for the fare you want, and insert money. The machine gives you your ticket and change, and you then use the ticket to enter and exit at the stations. You can also buy stored value tickets for S$10; the exit machine electronically deducts fares from the encoded card and returns the card to you until its full value has been utilised.

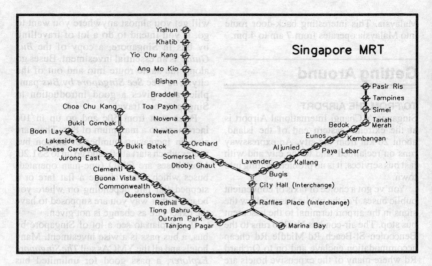

Singapore MRT

Yishun
Khatib
Yio Chu Kang
Ang Mo Kio
Bishan
Braddell
Toa Payoh
Novena
Newton
Orchard
Somerset
Dhoby Ghaut
Choa Chu Kang
Bukit Gombak
Boon Lay
Lakeside
Chinese Garden
Jurong East
Bukit Batok
Clementi
Buona Vista
Commonwealth
Queenstown
Redhill
Tiong Bahru
Outram Park
Tanjong Pagar
Lavender
Bugis
City Hall (Interchange)
Raffles Place (Interchange)
Marina Bay
Aljunied
Paya Lebar
Kallang
Eunos
Kembangan
Bedok
Tanah Merah
Simei
Tampines
Pasir Ris
Kallang
Pasir Ris
Tampines
Simei
Tanah Merah
Bedok
Kembangan
Eunos
Paya Lebar
Aljunied

Trains run from around 6 am to midnight and operate every four to eight minutes.

TAXI

Singapore has plenty of taxis, all air-con, metered, neat and clean with drivers who know their way round and have been taught to be polite, believe it or not!

Flag fall is S$2.20 for the first 1½ km then 10c per 275 metres for the first 10 km and 10c per 250 metres beyond 10 km. From midnight to 6 am, there is a 50% surcharge over the metered fare. Radio bookings cost an extra S$2 but only S$1 if you book 30 minutes in advance. A small surcharge is levied for a third and fourth passenger and for baggage in the boot. NTUC (☎ 452 5555) is one of the biggest companies. Don't forget that there is a surcharge from (but not to) the airport.

Singapore's Central Business District (CBD) regulations prohibit cars from entering the centre between 7.30 and 10.15 am, unless they have four people on board or pay for a special CBD licence. This also applies to taxis so, unless you're willing to pay for the day licence, you'll find, during that time, that taxis into the centre are scarce. The cost is S$3 and there's a S$1 surcharge for trips which are leaving the CBD between 4 and 7 pm on weekdays, and 12 noon to 3 pm on Saturday.

OTHER

Bicycle rickshaws or trishaws are having something of a revival as a night-time tourist attraction. Always agree on the fare beforehand if you try one. You still see a few genuine ones in Chinatown and in the other older sections of town.

You can easily rent cars in Singapore, although it is rather pointless when you consider parking costs, CBD licences and the excellent public transport which is available. It is more expensive to take a car which has been registered in Singapore into Malaysia than to rent one there. Cars with Singapore registration which cross the causeway into Malaysia must have the tank three quarters full of fuel! It's to stop would be tax evaders filling up with the cheaper Malaysian stuff.

Check the following Things to See section for details on the ferries out to various islands. Walking is hot work but no hassle in Singapore but just watch out for those open storm drains.

Bicycling in Singapore may not have too much appeal but if you want a bicycle to ride further afield, then Singapore could be a good place to buy it. Check the yellow pages of the phone directory.

Around the Country

THINGS TO SEE
Singapore offers an accessible selection of varied Asian flavours in a small package. There's a modern central business district, a nearby but fast disappearing old Chinatown, relics of a British colonial past as well as a colourful Little India.

River & Central Business District
The river, which has been cleaned up, is no longer the city-state's commercial artery but it's still in the heart of Singapore, flanked by the business district, Chinatown and colonial Singapore.

Start at Raffles Place, the trading centre of a city that thrives on trade. The banks, offices and shipping companies are clustered around here. You'll also find the remains of **Change Alley**, now just a shopping arcade, although there are still moneychangers here. From **Clifford Pier**, you can get a good view over the teeming harbour or take a boat tour on the river and harbour. From there, walk along what used to be the waterfront to **Merlion Park**, where the Singapore's Merlion symbol spouts water over the Singapore River.

Singapore River was comprehensively cleaned up in the '80s and the picturesque view of the crowded bumboats, backed by towering office blocks, is another part of Singapore consigned to the history books. At the southern end of the business district, the old **Telok Ayer Centre**, a fine old cast-iron Victorian market place, was dismantled during the MRT construction but is now set to reopen as a food centre with shops.

Colonial Singapore
The centre of colonial Singapore is north of the river. Here you'll find **Empress Place** with Raffles' statue overlooking the river near where he first set foot on the island. The Empress Place building is now a museum (see the Museum section later in this chapter). Nearby is the **Victoria Concert Hall & Theatre**, home of the Singapore Symphony Orchestra. **Parliament House** has had a varied history as mansion, court house, colonial government centre and, now, the seat of independent Singapore's parliament.

North of Empress Place, cricket matches still take place on the open expanse of the **Padang**, overlooked by the **Supreme Court** and **City Hall**. On Beach Rd, north of the Padang, **Raffles Hotel** is another symbol of colonial Singapore; it reopened in 1991 after an extensive restoration. It continues to ooze tradition, and a Singapore Sling in the Long Bar (the drink was concocted there in 1915) or tea on the lawn is a part of the Singapore experience.

Singapore has a number of colonial era churches and other Christian edifices including the Catholic **Cathedral of the Good Shepherd**, **St Joseph's Institution**, the Anglican **St Andrew's Cathedral** and the **Convent of the Holy Infant Jesus**. The Armenian **Church of St Gregory the Illuminator** is the oldest church in Singapore but it is no longer used for services. These buildings are all near Bras Basah Rd and the Bencoolen St travellers' accommodation centre.

Continue up Coleman St past the Armenian Church to **Fort Canning Hill** where there's a good view over the city, some minor remains of the old fort and poignant gravestones from the Christian cemetery, set into walls at the foot of the hill.

Chinatown
It seems strange to have a Chinatown in a Chinese town, but the area north of the city centre as far as New Bridge Rd is just that. It's a maze of streets, shops and stalls with overhanging windows from which poke flagpoles of laundry.

Much of this area, some of the most picturesque in Singapore, was ploughed under

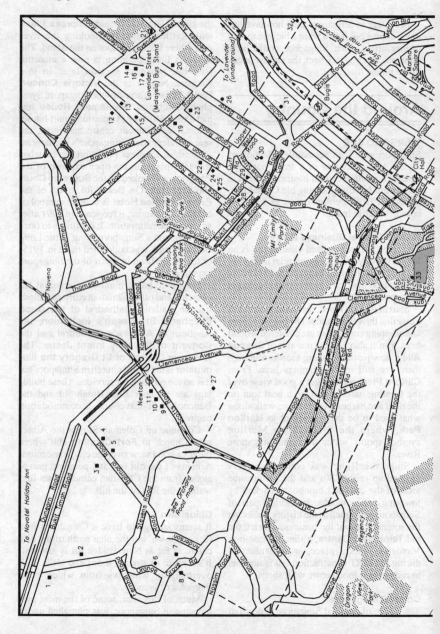

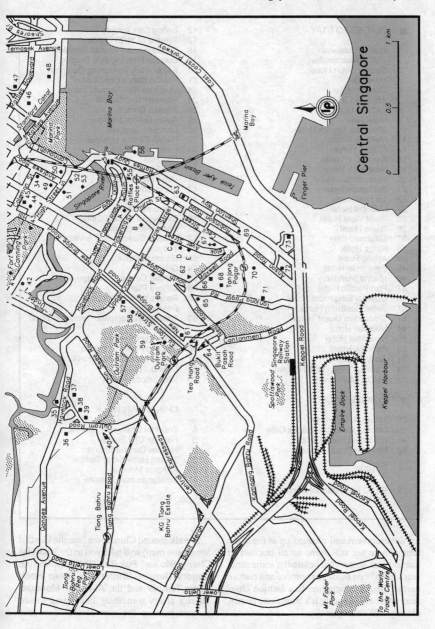

Central Singapore

■ PLACES TO STAY

1	Hotel Equatorial
2	YMCA Metropolitan
3	Sloane Court Hotel
4	Hotel VIP
5	Garden Hotel
7	Shangri-La Hotel
8	Ladyhill Hotel
9	Hotel Asia
10	Sheraton Towers Hotel
11	Melia at Scotts
14	Palace Hotel
16	Kam Leng Hotel
19	New Park Hotel
20	International Hotel
22	Broadway Hotel
23	Tai Hoe Hotel
27	Cairnhill Hotel
35	River View Hotel
36	Glass Hotel
37	Miramar Hotel
38	Kings Hotel
39	Apollo Hotel
45	Peninsula Hotel
46	Marina Mandarin
47	Pan Pacific Hotel
48	Oriental Singapore Hotel
57	Great Southern Hotel
61	Chinatown Guest House
64	Majestic Hotel
66	New Asia Hotel
68	Air View Hotel
71	Amara Hotel
72	Harbour View Dai-Ichi Hotel
73	YMCA Chinatown

▼ PLACES TO EAT

25	Indian Restaurants
29	Madras New Woodlands Cafe
43	Hill Street Food Centre
62	Maxwell Food Centre

OTHER

6	RELC International Centre

12	Leong San Temple
13	Temple of 1000 Lights
15	Sri Srinivasa Perumal Temple
17	Sunday Morning Bird Singing
18	Farrer Park Swimming Complex
21	Kalang Bahru Bus Station
24	Veerama Kali Amman Temple
26	Berseh Food Centre
28	Zhujiao Centre
30	Abdul Gafoor Mosque
31	Ban San Terminal
32	Hajjah Fatima Mosque
33	National Theatre
34	City Hall
40	Bird Singing
41	Van Kleef Aquarium
42	Liang Court
44	Funan Centre
49	Supreme Court
50	Singapore Cricket Club
51	Parliament House
52	Victoria Concert Hall & Victoria Theatre
53	Empress Place
54	GPO
55	Clifford Centre & Change Alley
56	Clifford Pier
58	People's Park Complex
59	Pearl's Centre
60	Chinatown Complex - Market & Food Place
63	Telok Ayer Centre
65	Tanjong Pagar Complex
67	Chinese Methodist Church
69	DBS Building
70	International Plaza

CHINATOWN WALK

A	Wak Hai Cheng Bio Temple
B	Fuk Tak Ch'i Temple
C	Nagore Durgha Shrine
D	Thiang Hock Keng Temple
E	Al-Abrar Mosque
F	Sri Mariamman Temple

for development and cleaned up at the same time. There are still some small pockets of interest and, somewhat belatedly, some measures have been made to preserve and restore part of the old Singapore. In a fashion characteristic of Singapore, it's been done neatly, cleanly and antiseptically.

A walk around Chinatown (see the Central Singapore map) will take you to the **Wak Hai Cheng Bio** and **Fuk Tak Ch'i** temples, the **Nagore Durgha Shrine**, the **Thian Hock Keng Temple** and the **Al-Abrar Mosque**. There's alway something interesting to see as you wander the convoluted 'five-foot ways'. **Tanjong Pagar**, wedged between Neil and Tanjong Pagar Rds, is the showpiece of restored Chinatown. Also in this intriguing area is the Sri Mariamman Temple, see the following Temples & Mosques section.

Little India

Although Singapore is predominantly Chinese, there's a colourful Indian district around Serangoon Rd. The smell of spices and curries wafting through the area is as much a part of the district's flavour as the colours and noises.

Attractions in Little India include the **Zhujiao Centre** market, the backstreets from Serangoon Rd with their exotic little shops and the temples including the **Veerama Kali Amman** and **Sri Srinivasa Perumal** temples. The Temple of 1000 Lights is on the northern edge of Little India and is covered in the later Temples & Mosques section.

East of Little India is Jalan Besar where you can find bird singing meets, (see the following Parks & Gardens section) on Sunday morning around Petain Rd, and an active red-light district (see the Singapore Entertainment section) any night of the week.

Arab St

Arab St is the Muslim centre, especially along North Bridge Rd. Here you'll find markets with Malaysian and Indonesian goods, the **Sultan Mosque** and the **Istana Kampong Glam**. The *istana*, or palace, was the centre for Malay royalty which predated Raffles' arrival.

Other Areas

The **Orchard Rd** area is a corridor of big hotels and busy shopping centres. Beyond Orchard Rd are the fine old colonial homes where the wealthy elite of Singapore still live. Holland Village is an expat enclave out on the westwards continuation of Orchard Rd.

Peranakan Place, at Orchard and Emerald Hill Rds, is one old fashioned exception to the glass and chrome gloss of Orchard Rd. In recent times, there has been a resurgence of interest in Peranakan culture in Singapore. *Peranakan* is the term for Straits-born Chinese, also called *Nonyas* (women) and *Babas* (men). Traditionally, the Straits-born Chinese have spoken a Malay dialect and practised their own customs, a hybrid of Chinese and Malay. This is probably the nearest Singapore comes to having a cultural identity.

Peranakan Place is a lane of restored shophouses, one of which is a small museum (entry S$4), and from time to time various Peranakan cultural events such as weddings, dramatic performances and food festivals take place here.

If you want to find the Malay influence within Singapore head for **Geylang Serai**, a Malay residential area, or the **Katong** district. There are still some *kampungs* (Malay villages) in remote corners of the island or on the smaller islands to the north-east like Pulau Ubin and Pulau Tekong.

In early '91, an illegal immigrant, in the form of a wild elephant, swam across to one of these islands from nearby Malaysia and it terrified local residents until it was rounded up, tranquillised and shipped back home!

At the far eastern end of the island is **Changi**, the village from which the airport takes its name, which makes an interesting excursion. There's a reasonable beach and at Changi Prison there's a fascinating little museum about the prisoner of war camp operated by the Japanese during WW II. It's open from 8.30 am to 12.30 pm and from 2 to 4.45 pm Monday to Friday plus Saturday morning.

See the Singapore Getting There & Away section for information on getting from Changi to Malaysia by ferry. Bus Nos 1 and 2 run to Changi from the Bencoolen St and Raffles City area. At the other end of the island, **Jurong** has interesting attractions which are covered in later sections.

Temples & Mosques

There's a whole dictionary of religions in Singapore, so you'll find a lot of temples. On

Telok Ayer St in Chinatown, the **Thian Hock Keng Temple** dates from 1840 and is one of the most colourful in Singapore.

On South Bridge Rd, right in the heart of Chinatown, the **Sri Mariamman Temple** is a technicolour Hindu shrine with brilliant statuary on the tower over the entrance. It was originally built in 1827 but its present form dates from 1862. Several times a year there are fire-walking ceremonies inside – the firewalkers start at a slow ceremonial pace but soon break into a sprint!

The **Temple of 1000 Lights** on Race Course Rd near Little India has a fine 15-metre-high seated Buddha, illuminated, for a small fee, by the promised 1000 lights. There is also a mother-of-pearl replica of the Buddha's footprint. The temple's official name is the Sakaya Muni Buddha Gaya Temple. The **Sultan Mosque** on North Bridge Rd is the biggest mosque in Singapore. It was originally built in 1825 but totally replaced a century later.

The large **Siong Lim Temple** is a km east of the Tao Payoh MRT station, near Paya Lebar Airport. The recently rebuilt **Chettiar Hindu Temple** is on Tank Rd near the intersection of Clemenceau Ave and River Valley Rd. There are a number of temples and mosques in Chinatown.

Museums

On Stamford Rd the **National Museum** traces Singapore's ancestry back to Sir Stamford Raffles himself and includes many items related to the island's early history. There is also an art gallery and the Haw Par jade collection. It's open from 9 am to 4.30 pm daily, and admission is S$1.

Empress Place Museum has exhibits designed to make Singaporeans more aware of their Chinese heritage. It's open from 9.30 am to 9.30 pm daily, and entry is S$6.

The **Singapore Science Centre** on Science Centre Rd in Jurong, has handles to crank, buttons to push and levers to pull – all in the interest of making science come alive. It's open from 10 am to 6 pm Tuesday to Sunday, and admission is S$2. The 3D Omni-theatre costs an extra S$6. To get there

take the MRT to Jurong East and walk a half km or take a bus No 355. Alternatively, take a bus to Jurong interchange and bus Nos 157 or 178 from there.

Parks & Gardens

There are numerous parks and gardens in Singapore including the fine **Botanic Gardens** on Cluny and Holland Rds, not far from Tanglin Rd. Or, you can climb **Mt Faber**, or **Bukit Timah**, about as high as you can get in Singapore. **East Coast Park**, out towards the airport, has swimming, windsurfing and bicycle rental.

Tiger Balm Gardens, originally built with the fortune amassed from the Haw Par brother's miracle medicament, has recently had a major overhaul. Much of the gory and crazy charm of the old gardens has disappeared and it's now much more of a tame fun park. Entry is an overpriced S$16 – skip it.

Out at Jurong, there's the adjoining **Chinese & Japanese Gardens**, right by the Chinese Garden MRT station. The **Jurong Bird Park** is interesting, even if you're not a feathered-friend freak. There's even a two-hectare walk-in aviary which alone contains 3000 birds. The bird park is open from 9 am to 6 pm daily, and admission is S$5. Get there on bus Nos 250, 252 or 253 from the Jurong bus interchange.

Sunday morning bird-singing sessions are one of Singapore's real pleasures. Bird lovers get together to let their caged birds have a communal sing-song while they have a cup of coffee. The main centre is at the junction of Tiong Bahru and Seng Poh Rds, near the Havelock Rd hotel enclave. It's a half km walk from the Tiong Bahru MRT station or a number of buses run there. Another bird-singing session takes place just off Jalan Besar, near the Palace Hotel. It's all very organised – tall pointy birds go in tall pointy cages and little fat ones in little fat cages.

The **Zoological Gardens** is at 80 Mandai Lake Rd in the north of the island. The orang-utan colony and the Komodo dragons are major attractions. The zoo is open from 8.30 am to 6 pm daily, and entry is S$5. Take bus No 171 from Stamford and Orchard Rds to the zoo or the Zoo Express shuttle buses from major hotels. The Mandai Orchard Gardens are beside the zoo.

Orchids are not the only thing cultivated for cash in Singapore. Crocodiles are cultivated to become handbags at the **Singapore Crocodile Farm** or exploited in other ways at the **Jurong Crocodile Paradise** and the **Singapore Crocodilarium**. The **Van Kleef Aquarium** on River Valley Rd in Fort Canning Park has crocodiles and turtles as well as thousands of fish. It's open from 10 am to 6 pm daily, and entry is S$1.

Islands, Beaches & Water Sports

Singapore's sprinkling of islands to the south have undergone a lot of development over the past few years. **Sentosa** has been the most developed – it's rather plastic, although very popular as a local weekend escape. Entry to the island is S$3.50 which includes return ferry transport from the World Trade Centre.

Most attractions on the island cost extra but monorail and bus transport on the island is included in the entry cost. Alternatively, you can take the cable car to the island from Mt Faber or the World Trade Centre. Return cost on the cable car is S$6 and the views are the best part of a Sentosa visit.

Attractions here include the Surrender Chamber with waxworks figures showing the formal surrender of Japanese forces in 1945. Then there's Butterfly Park, the Mystery Maze, the Rare Stone Museum, the Pioneers of Singapore exhibit and much more of a similar nature – you get the picture.

There are also sports facilities, beaches and a huge aquarium under construction. You might even bump into Singapore's longest serving political prisoner, who is now under 'island arrest'. Where else but in Singapore would a suspected Communist be confined to a fun park?

Other islands are not as developed as Sentosa. There are ferry trips several times a day (much more frequently on weekends) to **St John's** and **Kusu** islands. Tiny Kusu has a Chinese temple and a Malay shrine, and both are good places for a quiet swim. The round trip ferry ticket costs S$5. The islands are crowded on weekends.

There are other islands both to the north and south – boats to the other islands of the southern group can be arranged from Jardine Steps, or you can hire bumboats from there or Clifford Pier. To go to the northern islands, boats can be hired from Sembawang or from Punggol Boatel at Punggol Point. **Pulau Ubin** and **Pulau Tekong** can be easily reached from Changi village. These islands have some quiet beaches and popular seafood restaurants.

Further south still are the islands of the Indonesian Riau Archipelago. See the earlier Indonesia chapter for information on how to use these islands as a fascinating stepping stone between Singapore and Indonesia.

Of course, you don't have to leave the main island of Singapore to find watersports. There's the huge **East Coast Lagoon** on the East Coast Parkway to the airport and the **CN West Leisure Park** at Jurong. You'll find pools, waterslides and other attractions at **Big Splash** on the East Coast Parkway.

The **Farrer Park Swimming Complex** is the nearest public swimming pool to the Bencoolen St area. Head to the **East Coast Sailing Centre** for windsurfing or sailing. Scuba diving trips are made to the islands south of Singapore.

PLACES TO STAY

Singapore's ongoing redevelopment has split budget accommodation into two neatly divided categories – a steadily decreasing number of the traditional old Chinese hotels and a continually increasing number of backpackers' hostels or crash pads.

Most of the small, old family-run Chinese hotels are in areas destined for redevelopment and, every year, another once-popular cheap hotel disappears – to be replaced by even more air-con shopping centres. You can be certain that no new hotels are planned that do not have air-con, bars, restaurants, high-speed lifts, swimming pools and all the other necessities of modern tourism.

Meanwhile, the Singapore answer for

backpackers – the hostels or crash pads – have sprung up like wildfire. Bencoolen St, off Bras Basah Rd, once the centre for cheap hotels, is now the main hostel centre although a number of a cheap hotels still survive here.

The Singapore hotel surplus, which continued through most of the '80s, has finally dried up and terrific bargains at big hotels are no longer so easily found. In fact, there's a yawning chasm between the remaining Chinese cheapies and the bottom rung of the 'international standard' hotels – Singapore has a severe shortage of middle-range accommodation.

The airport hotel desk doesn't handle the cheapest places – the Majestic Hotel in Chinatown (doubles at S$45) is about the cheapest they go. Nevertheless, if your budget will stretch to their standards, they often offer much better deals than you would get yourself if you simply turned up at the front desk of larger hotels.

During Chinese New Year, it can be very difficult to find a room in Singapore and some places are prone to sudden price increases. Larger hotels add a 3% government tax and 10% service charge to your bill while smaller hotels usually include the 3% tax in their room rate and don't add a service charge.

Singapore's cheap accommodation is mainly concentrated in Bencoolen St and other streets that run off Bras Basah Rd to the north-east. See To/From the Airport in the Singapore Getting Around section for where to get off the No 390 airport bus for this enclave. From the railway station, take bus Nos 10, 97, 100, 125 or 850 to this area. Dhoby Ghaut is the nearest MRT station. From the Lavender St bus station, most buses on Jalan Besar go down Bencoolen St.

The Bencoolen St area is nothing special but it's within walking distance of the city centre, Orchard Rd and Little India. Nearby streets with cheap accommodation include Prinsep St, Middle Rd, Victoria St and Selegie Rd, further towards Little India.

Another cheap accommodation enclave is found on Beach Rd near the Raffles Hotel.

It's a few blocks from Bencoolen St towards the ever-receding waterfront; if you aspire to the Raffles, but can't afford the prices, at least you can stay nearby! Somehow, the several blocks north-east along Beach Rd from the Raffles have managed to remain a little enclave of old Singapore, unaffected by all the demolition around them. You can get there on the airport bus No 390, or the area is between the City Hall and Bugis MRT stations.

Further north on Jalan Besar, there are several older hotels. Jalan Besar is the continuation of Bencoolen St but, apart from being close to Little India and Arab St, it's neither central nor convenient.

Chinatown is one of the most interesting areas in which to stay and has a few cheaper hotels, most within walking distance of the railway station and the Outram Park and Tanjong Pagar MRT stations.

Camping

You can camp out at Sentosa Island where there are pre-erected four-person tents for S$12 per night. There's also the good *East Coast Campsite* on East Coast Parkway at the five-km marker. Unfortunately, there are no buses stopping on this expressway. You have to get off at the bus stop in Upper East Coast Rd and then walk for 15 minutes and, from the end of Bedok Rd, a walking track leads under the expressway right to the camp.

The site has a clean, well-lit reading and TV room, and there are a few shops and a hawkers' centre nearby. The site is deserted during the week but very busy on weekends and school holidays.

Hostels

Singapore's hostels are all mildly illegal since they're just residential flats which have been broken up into dormitories and cubicle-like rooms. But then this is Singapore and free enterprise is what counts! The trouble with them is that the jam-packed crowds tend to overstretch the limited facilities and the rooms are often small.

In addition, everybody there will be a

traveller, just like yourself. On the other hand, they're good sources of information, good places to meet people and you won't find cheaper accommodation in Singapore.

Bencoolen St Almost down at the Bras Basah end of Bencoolen St, you'll find *Peony Mansions*, the longest running of these places. It's at 46-52 Bencoolen St, on top of a furniture showroom (at last count, it's also been a Mazda, BMW and Holden car dealership). There's no sign at all – go around back and take the lift to the 5th floor and knock on the door at 50E.

Like all these places, it's rather anonymous.

Inside you can stay for S$6 a night in simple dormitory-style accommodation that has seen better days. Some private rooms are also available for S$20. There are other flats in the block, like *Latin House* (☎ 339 6308), on the 3rd floor at No 46.

Across the road, *Bencoolen House* (☎ 338 1206) is on the 7th floor of 27 Bencoolen St between the Strand and Bencoolen hotels. It's pretty good value at S$6 for dorm beds, and from S$25 to S$45 for rooms; there's also a kitchen you can use.

Down the road towards Albert St, at 173-175 Bencoolen St, is another centre for hostels in the new Hong Guan Building.

■ PLACES TO STAY		50 Westin Plaza Hotel
		52 YMCA
5	Plaza Hotel	53 YWCA
6	Golden Landmark Hotel	54 Westin Stamford Hotel
8	Sim Lim Lodging House	55 New Mayfair Hotel
10	South Seas Hotel	
12	Backpack Guest House	▼ PLACES TO EAT
14	Why Not Homestay (Rainbow Building)	
		3 Zam Zam Restaurant
17	New 7th Storey Hotel	7 Komala Vilas
18	Hawaii Guesthouse & Goh's Homestay	15 Wing Siong Fatty's Restaurant
		20 Sahib Restaurant
19	South-East Asia Hotel	33 Swee Kee Restaurant
21	Why Not Homestay (Bencoolen Street)	47 Rendezvouz Restaurant
		57 Satay Club
23	Sun Sun Hotel	
24	Ah Chew Hotel	OTHER
25	Das Travellers' Inn	
26	Lido Hotel	1 Kali Ammam Temple
27	Soon Seng Long Hotel	2 Ban San Bus Terminal (for Johore Bahru)
28	Tai Loke Hotel	
32	Kian Hua Hotel	4 Sultan Mosque
34	Shang Onn Hotel	9 Sim Lim Tower
35	Metropole Hotel	11 Mosque
37	Allson's Hotel	13 Selegie Centre
38	Victoria Hotel	16 Fu Lou Shou Complex
39	Hotel Bencoolen	22 Selegie Complex
40	Peony Mansions & Latin House	29 Peace Mansion
41	Airmaster Travel Centre & Airpower Travellers' Club	30 Peace Centre
		31 Parklane Shopping Mall
42	San Wah Hotel	36 Bras Basah Complex
43	Bencoolen House	49 Cathedral of the Good Shepherd
44	Tiong Hoa Hotel	51 Singapore Tourist Promotions Board
45	Strand Hotel	56 MPH Bookshop
46	Bayview Inn	58 US Embassy
48	Carlton Hotel	59 Church of St Gregory the Illuminator

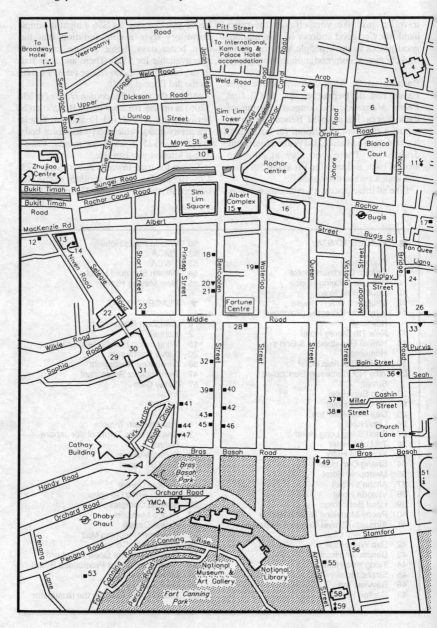

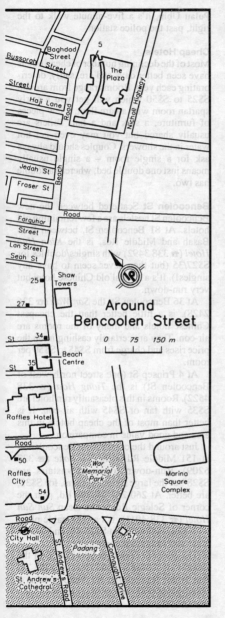

Around Bencoolen Street

There are no outside signs here either so, again, go around to the back and up the elevator by the parking lot. On the 2nd floor is the *Hawaii Guest House* (☎ 338 4817) where the dorm is S$7 and spartan rooms range from S$20 to S$30. Kitchen, laundry and storage facilities are available.

One of the longest running and most popular hostels, *Goh's Homestay* (☎ 339 6561) has a reception desk on the 6th floor, but also has rooms on the 5th. The cost of accommodation is S$7 or S$9 in the smaller four-bed dorms and there are a few rooms for S$25. There's a good notice board and an eating and meeting area where you can get drinks, snacks and breakfast.

The slickly run and very popular *Why Not Homestay* (☎ 338 0162/6095) has one branch at 127 Bencoolen St (next to the Sahib Restaurant) and another in the Rainbow Building at 189 Selegie Rd, near Little India. The Bencoolen St branch has a popular bar-cum-travellers' meeting place downstairs; dorm beds are S$8 to S$10 with rooms around S$20. Breakfast is available. At the Rainbow Building branch, there are more, and better, rooms at S$25 to S$40.

Just around the corner from the Rainbow Building on Selegie Rd is the *Backpack Guest House* at 15 MacKenzie Rd. It's friendly, more quiet than most hostels and a dorm bed costs from S$5 or S$7 in the smaller dorms; rooms are S$25 to S$30.

Back towards Bras Basah Rd, *Airmaster Travel Centre* (☎ 338 3942) at 36B Prinsep St, a block north-west from Bencoolen St, is another popular hostel. Dorm beds are S$6 and rooms cost from S$20. On the 3rd floor is the *Airpower Travellers' Club* (☎ 284 3700, 337 1392) with dorm beds for S$6, or S$7 with air-con, and rooms range from S$15 to S$30.

Both these places provide excellent information and are popular travel agents for cheap tickets to almost anywhere. They are of a similar, basic standard but Airpower gets the most travellers' recommendations.

Beach Rd The *Das Travellers' Inn* (☎ 294 9740) on the 2nd floor (room 4) at 87 Beach

Rd is a long-running place that has had more moves than the Israelites. A bed in a cramped dorm costs S$6, or it is S$8 in a seven-bed dorm. There are some private rooms for S$15, and despite the apparent squalor it's very popular.

Chinatown The only cheap place in Chinatown is the *Chinatown Guest House* (☎ 220 0671), 5th Floor, 325D New Bridge Rd, opposite Pearl's Centre. When it fills up, it's more reminiscent of a Calcutta slum than Chinatown, with wall-to-wall dorm beds for S$7 per person and inadequate bathroom facilities.

Other Areas One of the most expensive, but best, hostels is the *Sky-Scraper* (☎ 737 4600) on the 3rd Floor, Skyvilla, 376 Clemenceau Ave. It's near the heart of Orchard Rd and is a 10-minute walk to the Newton Circus Hawker Centre. The dorms are closed-off balconies with two beds, cost S$10 per person and include a cooked breakfast and free coffee and tea throughout the day. There is also a wide variety of private rooms ranging from S$25 for small partitioned rooms to S$50 for air-con rooms with bath.

The *Friendly Rest House* (☎ 294 0847) is at 357A Serangoon Rd, just past Kitchener Rd, but the door is actually around the corner from Serangoon Rd on Perumal Rd. It's inconvenient and unpopular with travellers but the rooms are better than average and good value at S$14 and S$20.

Sandy's Place, (☎ 252 6711) on the 4th floor of the Goodwill Mansion, at 355 Balestier Rd, has mattresses on the floor for S$6 and beds for S$8. Rooms are available from S$20 to S$25. The building is clean and the management is friendly.

If you really want to get away from it all, the *Nature Traveller House* (☎ 542 6124) is on Pulau Ubin, an island off the north-east coast of Singapore. It can be reached by ferry from Changi village. There are a number of dorm beds from S$5 to S$7 and double rooms from S$12 to S$30 in this quiet retreat by the sea. From where the ferry docks at Pulau Ubin, it's a five-minute walk to the right, past the police station.

Cheap Hotels
Most of the declining number of cheap hotels have seen better days and are, sadly, deteriorating each year. Rooms range from around S$25 to S$50 which will get you a fairly spartan room with a bare floor, a few pieces of furniture, a sink and a fan. Toilets are usually shared but you may even get hot water in the showers. Couples should always ask for a single room – a single usually means just one double bed, whereas a double has two.

Bencoolen St Scattered between the new Bencoolen St hostels are a few remaining old hotels. At 81 Bencoolen St, between Bras Basah and Middle Rds, is the *Kian Hua Hotel* (☎ 338 3492) with singles/doubles for S$27/35 (but they never seem to have any singles!). It's a typical old Chinese hotel but very run-down.

At 36 Bencoolen St, the *San Wah* (☎ 336 2428), is a little better than the cheapest Chinese hotels and many of the rooms are air-con. They are certainly cashing in on the price rises and charge from S$45 to S$50 per room.

At 4 Prinsep St (one street north-west of Bencoolen St) is the *Tiong Hoa* (☎ 338 4522). Rooms in this pleasantly run hotel are S$35 with fan or S$45 with air-con. It is better than most of the cheap hotels in this area and good value in comparison.

Just around the corner from Bencoolen St at 151 Middle Rd is the *Tai Loke* (☎ 337 6209). Run-down rooms downstairs are S$28 but the large rooms upstairs, for S$32, are better. At 260-262 Middle Rd, near the corner of Selegie Rd, is the clean *Sun Sun Hotel* (☎ 338 4911). It's a reasonable place with singles/doubles at S$25/40, and there's a bar and restaurant downstairs.

The *Victoria Hotel* (☎ 338 2381), in the shadow of Allson's Hotel (formerly the Tai Pan Hotel Ramada) at 87 Victoria St is a faded place with air-con doubles with bath from S$40.

The *South-East Asia Hotel* (☎ 338 2394) at 190 Waterloo St (which runs parallel to Bencoolen St) is a bit more costly, but it has air-con and is quiet and fairly new; singles/doubles are S$50/55. This is the hotel for the lazy sightseer – within 200 metres of the hotel you'll find a Buddhist temple, a Hindu temple, a market, food stalls and a shopping centre. The street also comes alive with flower sellers and fortune tellers during the day.

Beach Rd The hotels here are generally better kept and cheaper than those around Bencoolen St.

The clean and friendly *Shang Onn* (☎ 338 4153), at 37 Beach Rd on the corner of Purvis St, has rooms for S$26/30. On Middle Rd, just off Beach Rd, are a couple more cheapies. The good but rather inconspicuous *Soon Seng Long* (☎ 337 6318) at 26 Middle Rd has large and clean rooms from S$20 to S$30. Further along Middle Rd at No 54 is the *Lido* (☎ 337 1872) with rooms for S$25/30.

At the corner of Liang Seah St and North Bridge Rd is the *Ah Chew Hotel* (☎ 336 3563), a very traditional old Chinese Hotel. 'It's nothing to sneeze at', reported a guest, but this is strictly a last resort.

Jalan Besar Another batch of cheap hotels can be found on and around Jalan Besar. It is not as convenient as the other areas, but it is close to the Lavender St bus station if you arrive by long-distance bus from Malaysia.

Only a few steps from Rochor Canal Rd, on the corner of Mayo St and Jalan Besar, is the *South Seas Hotel* with air-con singles/doubles for S$35/S$40. The rooms are quite good but they get a lot of noise from Rochor Canal Rd. Across Mayo St is the *Sim Lim Lodging House* with clean rooms for S$30, but it is usually full with long-term residents.

The *International* (☎ 293 9238) is at 290 Jalan Besar, on the corner of Allenby Rd, with single/double rooms for S$25/35. It's an architecturally interesting old hotel and has a large restaurant downstairs. Further north at 383 Jalan Besar, right opposite

Bugis Square Food Centre, is the *Kam Leng* (☎ 298 2289). It's a classic old hotel with wire-topped walls and old furniture. It has good, clean rooms at S$24 for a room with a fan and S$30 for air-con.

At the northern end of Jalan Besar at 407A-B, near Lavender St, is the spotlessly clean *Palace Hotel* (☎ 298 3108) with singles/doubles at S$20/24. It's good for the price and is close to the Lavender St bus station.

I stayed at the Palace back in 1972 and spent three months there in 1975 while I wrote the very first edition of this book.

Tony Wheeler

Another good, cheap hotel is the *Tai Hoe Hotel*, right near the New Park Hotel on the corner of Verdun and Kitchener Rds. Rooms with fan cost S$20; air-con rooms are S$30.

Chinatown Oddly, there are few hotels in Chinatown and nearly all are in the areas already mentioned north-east of Bras Basah Rd.

The *Great Southern* (☎ 533 3223) at the corner of Eu Tong Sen and Upper Cross Sts is opposite the People's Park complex. It's nothing special and gets a lot of traffic noise, but it is right in the heart of Chinatown. Rooms with fan cost S$30 and air-con rooms are S$42.

One of the best cheap hotels in Singapore is the *Majestic Hotel* (☎ 222 3377) at 31 Bukit Pasoh Rd on the south-western edge of Chinatown. Bukit Pasoh Rd runs between New Bridge and Neil Rds. It's a quiet street lined with traditional houses and buildings, but all are well maintained, in good condition and brightly painted. There's a pleasant park nearby where, in the morning and evening, people do tai chi and Taekwondo exercises. The hotel is immaculate and rooms are pleasant – many have a balcony. Singles/doubles are S$37/45, and S$47/59 with bath.

Not far away on Peck Seah St are a couple of carpeted, air-con hotels, more pretentious than the Majestic, but not nearly as good. The

New Asia (☎ 221 1861) is on Maxwell Rd at the corner of Peck Seah St. The rooms are pokey and overpriced at S$50/60. A couple of doors down at 10 Peck Seah St, the *Air View Hotel* (☎ 225 7788) is slightly better than the New Asia and costs $36/55, or S$40/60 with TV.

Other Areas The *New Mayfair Hotel* (☎ 337 4542) is at 40-44 Armenian St near Orchard Rd, behind the National Museum. It's in one of Singapore's oldest streets and within walking distance of many attractions. Rooms with air-con and bath cost from S$45.

The *Mitre Hotel* (☎ 737 3811), 145 Killeney Rd, is the cheapest hotel anywhere near Orchard Rd (half a km to the north). It's run-down but cheap with rooms for S$34 with air-con and bath.

The Ys

Singapore has a number of YMCAs and YWCAs. All of the YMCAs in Singapore take men, women and couples.

The *YMCA International House* (☎ 337 3444) is at 1 Orchard Rd. It is more like a top mid-range hotel and has rooms for S$55 single, S$65 double, S$75 family and S$90 superior, plus a 10% service charge. All rooms have air-con, TV and telephone, and are very good value for what you get, so bookings are essential. A bed in the large dorm costs S$20, which isn't such good value.

The facilities at this YMCA are exceptionally good with a fitness centre, swimming pool (on the roof), squash and badminton courts and a billiards room. There's also a restaurant which offers a cheap daily set meal and a McDonald's in the YMCA building which actually offers room service! You can phone down to have a Big Mac delivered to your room.

The *Metropolitan YMCA* (☎ 737 7755) at 60 Stevens Rd has good rooms but is less conveniently located and lacks the facilities of the Orchard Rd YMCA. Singles/doubles with bathroom, TV and air-con cost S$62/72.50.

The *Metropolitan YMCA International*

Centre (☎ 222 4666), also called the Chinese YMCA, is at 70 Palmer Rd, near the railway station. If you want to be near Chinatown or the waterfront, this is your place. They have singles with air-con but common shower for S$25, doubles with air-con and shower are S$37.

The *YWCA Hostel* (☎ 336 1212) at 6-8 Fort Canning Rd is behind Supreme House, quite close to the Orchard Rd YMCA. A double room with air-con and shower costs S$45. Nice dorm rooms are available for S$15. They only take women or couples, and this place has been recommended by solo women travellers as a safe and secure place.

Mid-Range Hotels

At the end of the 1980s, Singapore suddenly went from having a surplus of hotels to having a shortage of them, and any hotel with the slightest pretensions immediately shoved their prices up. The result is a severe shortage of mid-range hotels, or at least of hotels charging mid-range prices. Lots of distinctly lower class hotels try to charge higher class prices.

The recession may make a bit of difference but many middle-range places are simply second stringers or a bit run-down. See the Orchard Rd YMCA International House, under the previous Ys section, for what is probably the best mid-range bargain in Singapore. Other cheaper hotels like the Majestic in Chinatown or the South-East Asia Hotel on Waterloo St could scrape into the mid-range category.

Add 13% for government tax and service to the prices quoted below. Some good middle range possibilities include:

Hotel Bencoolen (☎ 336 0822) at 47 Bencoolen St has
    singles/doubles at S$85-110/S$90-125. It's a
    smaller modern hotel with air-con and bath-
    rooms, situated amongst the rock-bottom
    Chinese hotels, but it's cheaply put together and
    no bargain.
Broadway Hotel (☎ 292 4661), 195 Serangoon Rd,
    has singles/doubles at S$80-90/S$90-100. It is
    one of the few hotels in Little India, and, although
    the rooms need a little maintenance, they have
    TV and are comfortable. There's a good, cheap

Indian restaurant downstairs and all-in-all it's good value in this price range.

Lloyd's Inn (☎ 737 7309), 2 Lloyd Rd (off Killiney Rd), is a pleasant, small but modern hotel that is less than a 10-minute walk from Orchard Rd. The location is quiet and the rooms are competitively priced at S$70/80.

Metropole Hotel (☎ 336 3611), 41 Seah St, has singles/doubles at S$70-95/S$80-95. It's a fairly new, eight-storey hotel, behind the Raffles, and is one of the better mid-range places.

New 7th Storey Hotel (☎ 337 0251), 229 Rochor Rd, has rooms from S$59 to S$75 and is an up-market cheapie – Rochor Rd runs from Beach Rd to Bencoolen St, parallel to Middle Rd.

Station Hotel (☎ 222 1551) at Singapore railway station on Keppel Rd has singles/doubles at S$45/50. It has seen better days and is a little inconveniently located for most things in modern Singapore. However, it may be ideal if you've just arrived after a long train trip and can't face heading straight into the city.

Strand Hotel (☎ 338 1866), 25 Bencoolen St, costs S$110/120 and although it's better than the Bencoolen, practically next door, it's very pricey.

PLACES TO EAT

In Singapore, you find every kind of Asian and Western food. For its combination of wide variety, high quality and low prices Singapore has to be the food capital of Asia. Best of all it's accessible and there are no problems with understanding menus, searching out places or getting what you want.

Hawkers' Food

Hawkers run the mobile food stalls – food is sold, right on the street, from pushcarts and tables and stools are set up around them. This is the base line for Singapore food, the place where it all starts, where the prices are lowest and the eating, quite possibly, is the most interesting.

Real, mobile, on-the-street hawkers have almost totally disappeared, but they've been replaced by hawkers' centres where a large number of nonmobile hawkers can all be found under the one roof. Scattered amongst them are tables and stools, and you can sit and eat at any one you choose – none of them belongs to a specific stall. Indeed, a group of you can sit at one table, all eat from different stalls and, at the same time, have drinks from another.

One of the wonders of food-centre eating is the way in which various operators keep track of their plates and utensils – and manage to chase you up with the bill. The real joy of the food centres is the sheer variety. While you're having Chinese food your companion can be eating a biryani and across the table somebody else can be trying the satay. As a rough guide, most one-dish meals cost from S$1.50 to S$3, increasing for more elaborate dishes.

Hawkers' centres exist all over Singapore and more spring up as areas are redeveloped and the hawkers are moved off the streets. There's even a pretty good food centre in the basement of Changi Airport! All centres are licensed by the government and subject to health department regulations, so all should be perfectly safe and healthy.

The Hawkers' Variety Some typical hawkers' food you may find includes carrot cake, or chye tow kway, (S$1.50 to S$3) – also known as radish cake. It's a vegetable and egg dish, tasting a bit like potato omelette, and totally unlike the Western health-food idea of carrot cake.

Indian biryanis cost from S$2 to S$4 or you can have a martabak for around S$2. Naturally, chicken rice and char siew, or roast pork, will always be available in food centres (S$1.80 to S$3). All the usual Cantonese dishes like fried rice (S$1.50 to S$3), fried vegetables (S$3), beef & vegetables (S$5), and sweet & sour pork (S$3 to S$5) are available, plus other dishes like fish heads with black beans & chilli from S$3 to S$5.

There will often be Malay or Indonesian stalls with satay from 25c to 35c a stick, mee rebus from S$1 to S$1.20 and gado gado or mee soto at similar prices. Won ton mee, a substantial soup dish with shredded chicken or braised beef, costs from S$2 to S$3.

You could try a chee chong fun, a type of stuffed noodle dish, which costs from S$1.50, depending on whether you want the noodles with prawns, mushrooms, chicken or pork. Hokkien fried prawn mee costs from S$1.50 to S$3, prawn mee soup from S$1 to S$2, popiah (spring rolls) $1 and laksa from S$1.50 to S$2. There's also a whole variety of other dishes and soups.

Or you can opt for Western food like sausage, egg & chips for S$3.40, burgers for S$3 or fish & chips for S$3. Drinks include beer for S$3, soft drinks from 60c, ice kacang for 80c or sugar-cane juice from 50c to 80c, depending on the size. Fruit juices such as melon, papaya, pineapple, apple, orange or starfruit range from 80c to S$1.50. To finish up, you might try a fruit salad for S$2 or a pisang goreng (fried banana) for 50c.

City Centre In the business centre, *Empress Place*, beside the Singapore River, and *Boat Quay*, directly across from it on the other bank, are pleasant places to sit beside the river and have a meal. They are both very busy at lunch time. Boat Quay closes in the evening.

On the waterfront is *Telok Ayer Market* on Robinson Rd at the corner of Boon Tat St. The building itself is a wonderful example of intricate Victorian cast-iron architecture in the railway-station style. It was dismantled during the building of the MRT but is now back on the original site and lovingly restored. It will reopen in late 1991 and is destined to house tourist shops as well as food stalls.

North of the river on Hill St, the *Hill St Food Centre* is popular and across the road the *Funan Centre* has a more up-market air-con food-stall area on the 7th floor.

The famous *Satay Club*, by the waterfront at the foot of Stamford Rd near Raffles City and the Padang, is a colourful place to dine. The satay here is the best in Singapore but make sure you specify how many sticks (30c a time) you want, or they'll assume your appetite is much larger than you will. It's only open in the evening, when the waterfront is also a popular strolling area. There are Chinese food stalls in the circular building next to the Satay Club, and this is a good place for steamboat.

Orchard Rd *Newton Circus Hawker Centre* is at the top (north-eastern) end of Scotts Rd, near the Newton MRT station. It is very popular with tourists and, therefore, tends to

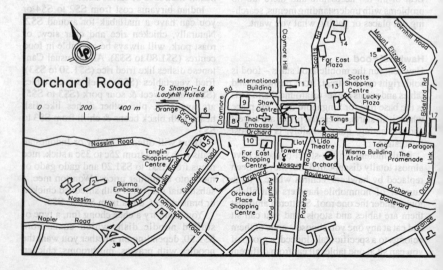

be a little more expensive, but it is lively and open until the early hours of the morning. For a minor extravagance, try the huge prawns.

South-east of here, down Orchard Rd, another popular food centre is upstairs in the *Cuppage Centre*. The downstairs section is a vegetable and produce market with a great selection of fruit. It is mainly a daytime centre and closes around 8 pm. The open court from the centre to Orchard Rd is very popular for an evening beer or an outdoor meal.

The *Scotts Picnic Food Court* in the Scotts shopping centre on Scotts Rd, just off Orchard Rd by the Hyatt Hotel, is quite a different sort of food centre. It's glossier and more restaurant-like than the general run of food centres, and the stalls around the dining area are international. As well as a variety of Chinese possibilities, Indian, Western and vegetarian food is available. Also in the same vein are the food stalls downstairs in *Orchard Towers* on the corner of Orchard and Claymore Rds.

	HOTELS		
		14	Goodward Park Hotel
		15	York Hotel
1	Hotel Premier	16	Mandarin Singapore
2	Century Park Sheraton	17	Crown Prince Hotel
3	Marco Polo Hotel	18	Phoenix Hotel Singapore
4	Regent Hotel	19	Holiday Inn Park View
5	Ming Court Hotel	20	Mitre Hotel
6	Orchard Hotel	21	Grand Central Hotel
7	Boulevard Hotel	22	Supreme Hotel
8	Orchard Towers	23	Meridien Singapore Hotel
9	Negara Hotel	24	Cockpit Hotel International
10	Singapore Hilton	25	Lloyd's Inn
11	Royal Holiday Inn Singapore	26	Imperial Hotel
12	Dynasty Hotel	27	Bay View Inn
13	Hyatt Regency Singapore	28	New Mayfair Hotel

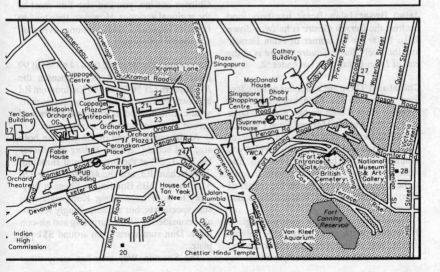

Bencoolen St In the Bencoolen St area, there are a number of good food centres near Rochor Canal Rd. The *Albert Centre* on Albert St, between Waterloo and Queen Sts, is an extremely good, busy and very popular centre which has all types of food at low prices.

The *Albert St Complex* on the corner of Bencoolen and Albert Sts now contains the famous Fatty's Chinese restaurant. *Wing Siong Fatty's Restaurant* is at No 01-33 of the complex, and a number of food stalls are around the corner. Across the street in the basement of the Sim Lim Square complex is the *Tenco Food Centre*, a relatively new and very clean establishment. One of the stalls is called *Excellent Duck*.

The *Fortune Centre*, at the corner of Middle Rd and Bencoolen St, also has a few food stalls on the 1st floor which are in an air-con setting. The *ABC Eating House* is a cheap cafeteria-style restaurant presenting a number of hawkers' dishes.

On the corner of Bukit Timah and Serangoon Rds, at the start of Little India, the large *Zhujiao Centre* is a market with a number of food stalls upstairs. As you would expect, Indian food dominates.

Jalan Besar Jalan Besar has two food centres: the *Berseh Centre* is halfway down Jalan Besar on the corner of Jalan Berseh, and the lively *Bugis Square Centre* is at the end of Jalan Besar near Lavender St.

Chinatown There are a number of excellent food centres in the Chinatown area. The *People's Park Complex* has a good, large food centre, and the *Maxwell Food Centre* is an old-fashioned centre on the corner of South Bridge and Maxwell Rds. While you wander around Chinatown you can find some of the best Chinese food stalls in town at the *Chinatown Complex* on the corner of Sago and Trengganu Sts, where there is also a market.

There's also a hawkers' centre alongside the *Tanjong Market*, not far from the railway station, and at the *Amoy St Food Centre*, where Amoy St meets Telok Ayer St.

Other The *Rasa Singapura Food Court* has shifted from Tanglin Rd to the Bukit Turf Club on Turf Club Rd. During the week, it's open for lunch and dinner until 11 pm. On weekends, it's open all day until midnight but you have to pay entry to the races until 6 pm. The *Taman Serasi Food Centre* has one of the best settings – it is next to the Botanical Gardens north-west of the city centre on Cluny Rd, just off Napier Rd.

For Malay food during the day, go to the *Geylang Serai Market* on Changi Rd in Katong. This is the predominately Malay area in Singapore, and it's worth a visit just to see the market, which is more traditional than in the new complexes. To get there, take the MRT to Paya Lebar station and walk east along Sims Ave to Geylang Serai.

Chinese Food

Singapore has plenty of restaurants serving everything from a south Indian rice plate to an all-American hamburger, but naturally it's Chinese restaurants that predominate. They range from streetside hawkers' stalls to fancy five-star hotel restaurants and a whole gamut of possibilities in between. Although Cantonese is the most readily available Chinese cuisine, you can also find most of the regional varieties. However, they tend to be more expensive than common, everyday Cantonese restaurants.

Cantonese The *Manhill* (☎ 474 6635) at 99 Pasir Panjang Rd and its companion the *Hillman* (☎ 221 5073) at 159 Cantonment Rd are two traditional Cantonese restaurants with excellent food at moderate prices and served in straightforward surroundings.

At the opposite end of the scale, in both size and setting, are the *Peking Mayflower* (☎ 737 1224) at the International Building, 360 Orchard Rd, and the *Mayflower* (☎ 220 3133) at the DBS Building on Shenton Way. They're both huge Hong Kong-style dim sum specialists, but are surprisingly reasonable considering all the carpeting and air-con there. Dim sum starts from around S$1 per plate.

The Shenton Way area has many other

good Chinese eating places. Remember that dim sum is a lunch time or Sunday breakfast dish and that in the evening these restaurants revert to other menus.

The *Majestic* (☎ 223 5111) on Bukit Pasoh Rd near Chinatown is a pleasantly old fashioned Cantonese restaurant. The moderately priced and very good *Xiang Man Lou* (☎ 338 7651) has good food in a glittering, gaudy setting. It is on the 1st floor of the Bras Basah complex on the corner of Bain St and North Bridge Rd near the Raffles Hotel.

Wing Siong Fatty's Restaurant (☎ 338 1087), at 01-33 Albert complex on Albert St near the corner of Bencoolen St, is one of the cheapest and most popular places to eat in town. Fatty's used to be further up Albert St near Serangoon Rd and has been a Singapore institution for decades.

Beijing If you've got a yen to try Peking duck, then the *Eastern Palace* (☎ 337 8224) on the 5th floor of Supreme House, 9 Penang Rd, is one of the best Beijing restaurants. The *Imperial Herbal Restaurant* (☎ 337 0491), in the Metropole Hotel, 41 Seah St, near Raffles Hotel, has an extensive range of good Beijing-style food and you can order dishes recommended by the resident herbalist. Lu Bian, or 'the whip', provides extra potency for men.

Szechuan Szechuan, or Sichuan, restaurants are common as this spicy food is popular with Singaporeans. Restaurants include the reasonably priced *Omei* (☎ 737 2735) in the Grand Central Hotel, at the cheaper end of the scale, and the expensive *Golden Phoenix* (☎ 732 0431), in the Hotel Equatorial, at the other. *Long Jiang* (☎ 732 1111) in the Crown Prince Hotel, at 270 Orchard Rd, is moderately priced and comes recommended.

Hokkien Hokkien food is not all that popular despite the large number of Hokkiens in Singapore, but *Beng Hiang* (☎ 221 6684) at Food Alley, 20 Murray St, is renowned for its Hokkien food. In fact, Food Alley is a great place to try all of Singapore's various

cuisines. It features around 10 mid-range restaurants representing most Chinese and Indian cuisines.

Beng Thin Hoon Kee (☎ 553 7708), on the 5th floor of the OCBC Centre on Chulia St, is a short walk from Raffles Place MRT station and it offers moderately priced Hokkien seafood. *Prince Room Restaurant* (☎ 337 7021), on the 3rd floor of the Selegie complex, 285 Selegie Rd, has good steamboats for S$10 per person.

Teochew Teochew (also called Chiu Chao or Chao Zhou) food, from the area around Swatow in China, is widely available. You can sample it at the traditional *Chui Wah Lin* (☎ 221 3305) at 49 Mosque St, or at the Ellenborough St Market which is noted for its Teochew food stalls.

In the DBS Building on Shenton Way is the *Swatow Teochow* (☎ 221 7936) where you can try the roast goose or shark's fin soup. There is also a branch at Centrepoint on Orchard Rd.

Hainanese Originally from Hainan in China, chicken rice is a dish of elegant simplicity and in Singapore they do it better than anywhere. *Swee Kee* (☎ 337 0314) at 51 Middle Rd, close to the Raffles Hotel, is a long-running Hainanese specialist with a very good reputation. Chicken and rice served with chilli, ginger and thick soya sauce is S$3.30. They also do steamboats – a S$20 version has a stock enriched by various Chinese herbs and Mao Tai, a spirit made from sorghum.

A stone's throw from Swee Kee, you'll find *Yet Con* (☎ 337 6819) at 25 Purvis St which some claim is the best of all Singapore's chicken-rice places. This area, north-west of Beach Rd is something of a Hainanese stronghold. You will also find chicken rice at most food centres.

Vegetarian Chinatown has some good-value vegetarian restaurants, including the *Happy Realm* (☎ 222 6141) on the 3rd floor of Pearl's Centre on Eu Tong Sen St and also the *Kingsland Vegetarian Restaurant*

(☎ 534 1846) on the 3rd floor of the People's Park complex.

Near Bencoolen St, *Kwan Yim* (☎ 338 2394) is another traditional and long-running vegetarian restaurant. It's at 190 Waterloo St in the South-East Asia Hotel.

At 143 and 153 Kitchener Rd, between Jalan Besar and Serangoon Rd, the *Fut Sai Kai*, which translates as 'monk's world', is another spartan old coffee shop where the speciality is vegetarian cooking. Prices are not cheap but it offers a good chance to sample a slightly unusual variation of Chinese cuisine.

Seafood Singapore has another local variation on Chinese food which is worth making the effort to try. Seafood in Singapore is simply superb, whether it's prawns or abalone, fish-head curry or chilli crabs. Most of the better seafood specialists are some distance out from the city centre but the trip is worthwhile.

The *UDMC Seafood Centre* at the beach on East Coast Parkway is very popular in the evenings. It's a collection of restaurants rather than a hawkers' centre but the prices are moderate for seafood. Here you will find the *Chin Wah Heng* with the usual glass tanks containing crabs, eels, prawns and fish all ready for the wok. The *Red House Seafood Restaurant* is good value and the *Bedok Sea View* is also very popular.

At 610 Bedok Rd, the *Long Beach Seafood Restaurant* (☎ 344 7722), one of Singapore's best known seafood places, is famous for its black pepper crabs and 'live drunken prawns' (soaked in brandy). It is casual and you can dine outside or in the air-con section.

Other seafood restaurants include the *Choon Seng* (☎ 288 3472), at 892 Ponggol Rd, Ponggol Point, at the north end of the island and, also, *Jurong Seafood Restaurant* (☎ 265 3525), at 35 Jurong Pier Rd on the south-west coast near the Jurong Bird Park. The trip out to Ponggol Point, on bus Nos 82 or 83, is quite an experience in itself as you pass miles of cemeteries and then chicken and pig farms. It is surprisingly rural for Singapore.

Indian Food

Three types of Indian food are found in Singapore: south Indian, Indian Muslim and north Indian.

South Indian food is mostly vegetarian and Little India is the main centre for it. You can get a thali, an all-you-can-eat rice plate with a selection of vegetable curries, for less than S$5.

Indian Muslim food is something of a hybrid. It is the simpler south Indian version of what is, basically, north Indian food. Typical dishes are biryani, served with chicken or mutton curry, roti and martabak. It can be found all over Singapore but the main centre is in North Bridge Rd opposite the Sultan Mosque. Indian Muslim food is also well represented in the hawkers' centres and you can have a superb chicken biryani from just S$2.50 to S$3.50.

For the rich north Indian tandoori food and curries, you have to go to more expensive restaurants. They can be found all around Singapore, but once again Little India has a concentrated selection.

To sample eat-with-your-fingers south Indian vegetarian food, the place to go is the Little India district off Serangoon Rd. The famous and extremely popular *Komala Vilas* (☎ 293 6980) at 76 Serangoon Rd was established soon after the war and has an open downstairs area where you can have masala dosa (S$1.50) and other snacks.

The upstairs section has air-con and you can have their all-you-can-eat rice meal for S$4. Remember to wash your hands before you start, use your right hand and ask for eating utensils only if you really have to! On your way out, try an Indian sweet from the showcase at the back of the downstairs section.

Two other rice-plate specialists are *Sri Krishna Vilas* at 229 Selegie Rd and *Ananda Bhavan* at 219-221 Selegie Rd. There are several other Indian eateries on and off Serangoon Rd and a main contender in the local competition for the best south Indian food is *Madras New Woodlands Cafe* (☎ 297 1594) at 14 Upper Dickson Rd off Serangoon Rd, around the corner from Komala Vilas. A branch of the well-known Woodlands chain in India, New Woodlands serves freshly prepared vegetarian food in very clean air-con rooms. The yoghurt is particularly good. Prices are about the same as at Komala Vilas.

Race Course Rd, a block north-west from Serangoon Rd, is also a good area for curry. Try the *Banana Leaf Apolo* (☎ 293 8682) at 56 Race Course Rd for superb nonvegetarian Indian food, including Singapore's classic fish-head curry for around S$4. The very popular *Muthu's Curry Restaurant* (☎ 293 7029), also on Race Course Rd at No 78, specialises in fish-head curry and other seafood dishes.

In between these two are a couple of good north Indian restaurants with typically dark decor. The *Delhi Restaurant* (☎ 296 4582) at 60 Race Course Rd has Mughlai and Kashmiri food, with curries from S$6 to S$10. Expect to pay around S$20 per person with bread, side dishes and drinks. *Nur Jehan* (☎ 292 8033) at 66 Race Course Rd is slightly cheaper and also has tandoori and other north Indian food.

For cheap north Indian food in Little India, the small *Bombay Coffee House*, in the Broadway Hotel at 195 Serangoon Rd, has good curries and kormas from S$3 to S$6 and breads such as naan for S$1. The *Ranu Mahal*, 13 Upper Dickson Rd opposite the New Woodlands, also has cheap north Indian food as well as south Indian dishes.

For Indian Muslim food (chicken biryani for S$3.50, as well as martabak and fish-head curry), there are a string of venerable establishments on North Bridge Rd, near the corner of Arab St, opposite the Sultan Mosque. Each of them has the year of founding proudly displayed on their signs out front, and they are great places for biryani and other reasonably priced Indian dishes.

The *Victory* (established 1910) is at 701 North Bridge Rd, the *Zam Zam* (established 1908) is at 699 and the *Singapore* (established 1911) is at 697 North Bridge Rd.

Further along is the *Jubilee* at 771 North Bridge Rd, and, at 791-797, the *Islamic* is very similar.

There's a small, basic Indian Muslim place called the *Sahib Restaurant* at 129 Bencoolen St, near Middle Rd and across from the Fortune Centre. They have very good food and specialise in fish dishes, including fish-head curry, but have chicken and vegetable items too. Meals are around S$4 and they are open 24 hours.

The *Moti Mahal Restaurant* (☎ 221 4338), another up-market north Indian place, proudly proclaims it is 'one of the best Indian restaurants anywhere (Far Eastern Economic Review)' on the sign out front. It doesn't quite live up to the review but the food is good and costs around S$20 per person. It's in Food Alley at 18 Murray Terrace, near the corner of Maxwell and Neil Rds.

Malay & Nonya Food

You can find Malay and Nonya food in the central business and Orchard Rd districts of Singapore, and there is the occasional stall or two at some of the food centres. *Bibi's Restoran*, on the 2nd floor of Peranakan Place at 180 Orchard Rd, has a selection of Nonya snacks. Nearby, at 36 Emerald Hill Rd, is the excellent *Azizas Restaurant* (☎ 235 1130), which serves authentic Malay meals for around S$20 per person.

Bintang Timur (☎ 235 3539) also has good Malay food and is similarly priced. It is on the 2nd floor of the Far East Plaza, 14 Scotts Rd, and there is a branch in the UIC Building at 5 Shenton Way in the city centre. *Satay Anika* has satay and other dishes served in sanitised surroundings on Orchard Rd. There are two restaurants – in the Scotts Picnic Food Court in the Scotts shopping centre and on the 1st floor of Centrepoint at 176 Orchard Rd.

Reasonably priced Nonya food can be found at *Nonya & Baba Restaurant* (☎ 734 1382), 262-264 River Valley Rd, not far from the corner of Tank Rd. There are Nonya buffets at the King's and Apollo hotels in Havelock Rd, and the Bayview Inn in Bencoolen St has a good lunch-time buffet for S$12 on Wednesday, Saturday and Sunday. In Holland Village, the *Baba Cafe* (☎ 468 9859) at 25B Lorong Liput has good-value food served in an attractive setting.

One of the best places to go for Malay and Nonya food is east of the city in the Geylang Serai and Katong districts. Along (and just off) Joo Chiat Rd between East Coast and Geylang Rds, in particular, are good hunting grounds for all kinds of Asian foods – Indian, Malay, Nonya, nasi padang, various kinds of Chinese, Thai and Middle Eastern. This area probably has the liveliest local night scene in the city.

There is a place on East Coast Rd just past Siglap Rd called *East Peranakan Inn* that has good Nonya and Malay food. Another branch is the *Peranakan Inn* (☎ 440 6194) at 210 East Coast Rd. Slightly pricier Nonya food (S$4 to S$10 per dish) is served in an air-con room at *Guan Hoe Soon* (☎ 440 5650), 214 Joo Chiat Rd. It is open from 11 am to 10 pm.

Other Asian Food

If you like the fiery food of north Sumatra, there are a number of nasi padang specialists, one of the best known being *Rendezvouz* at 4-5 Bras Basah Rd, on the junction with Prinsep St. It's open only at lunch time from 11 am to 3 pm and is closed on Wednesday. They also have a second branch at 02-19 in

the Raffles City shopping centre on Bras Basah Rd which is open daily until 9.15 pm, but closed on Wednesday. *Salero Bagindo* is a nasi padang chain with restaurants in the Tanglin shopping centre, 19 Tanglin Rd, and the Far East Plaza, 14 Scotts Rd.

There are several Thai restaurants along Joo Chiat Rd in the Katong district – *Chiangmai* at 328 Joo Chiat Rd, *Pattaya Eating House* at 402 Joo Chiat Rd, and *Haadyai Beefball Restaurant* at 467 Joo Chiat Rd. Closer to town, the *Parkway Thai* (☎ 737 8080) in Centrepoint, 176 Orchard Rd, has an extensive menu and is moderately priced. *Paregu* (☎ 733 4211) in Orchard Plaza, 150 Orchard Rd, has excellent food and also features Vietnamese dishes.

There is no shortage of good Japanese restaurants in Singapore where this food is, of course, expensive. Try the elegant *Ginga* (☎ 732 9922) in the River View Hotel, or *Nadaman* (☎ 737 3644), a branch of the Japanese chain, in the Shangri-La Hotel in Orange Grove Rd.

Finally, there's Taiwanese food and for this, try the *May Garden* in Orchard Towers or the reasonably priced *Goldleaf* at 160 Orchard Rd.

Western Food

Fast Food Yes, you can get Western fast food in Singapore too – there's even a couple

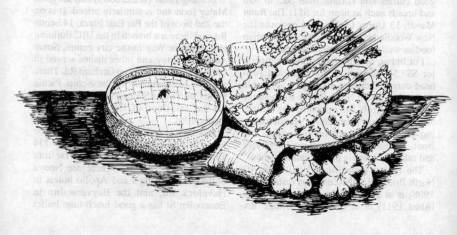

of dozen *McDonald's*. You'll find them along Orchard Rd near Scotts Rd, round the corner on Scotts Rd itself, in front of the Plaza Singapura and at the Orchard Rd YMCA. There are lots more all over town including one at People's Park and Changi Airport.

There are also *A&W Root Beer, Kentucky Fried Chicken* (nearly 40 of them), *Burger King, Dunkin' Donuts, Dennys, Pizza Hut, Baskin Robbins* and *Swensen's Ice Cream* outlets, so there's no shortage of Western fast food.

Italian If you want to sample good Italian food in Singapore, steer clear of the chain stores which are run by youths suffering from corporate brainwashing and serving soggy pizza and pasta with insipid sauces.

Pete's Place (☎ 733 1188) in the Hyatt Regency Singapore is the best value for good Italian food. It is presented in a rustic setting and there's a good salad bar. *Pasta* (☎ 467 0917), 23 Lorong Mambong, Holland Village, has home-made pasta for reasonable prices.

Grand Italia (☎ 733 0188) in the Glass Hotel is more up-market but is also good value considering the quality and variety of the dishes. *Prego Ristorante Italiano* (☎ 338 8585) in the Westin Stamford Hotel and *Ristorante Bologna* (☎ 338 3388) in the Pan Pacific Hotel are the two top Italian places to eat at in town.

Other Cheaper Western-style restaurants can be found at places like the *Ponderosa* (☎ 336 0139) in the Plaza Singapura, where you can get a steak and can serve yourself from the salad bar.

For up-market Western food at bargain prices, the Singapore Hotel Association's Training & Educational Centre (☎ 235 9533) at 24 Nassim Hill has two restaurants, *Bouganville* and *Rosette*. Now open to the public, the place is really a training centre for the preparation and presentation of hotel dining room food. They offer, in their fairly elegant setting, set five-course meals at lunch and dinner as well as an à la carte menu

with items such as escargot, Scottish salmon and duck à l'orange. Lunch is S$13.20 and dinner is S$16.50.

El Felipes Cantina (☎ 733 3551), B1-01 Orchard Towers at the corner of Orchard and Claymore Rds, is the best place for Mexican food. It has huge serves and moderate prices. Many other non-Asian food possibilities can be found around town but they're often decidedly expensive.

Breakfast
The big international hotels have their large international breakfast buffets (around S$18 to S$20) but there are also lots of little places for breakfast around the Bencoolen St cheap-hotel area. Most of them will rustle you up toast and jam without too much difficulty. Try the coffee bar right next to Airmaster Travel on Prinsep St.

There are a number of small Indian coffee shops which do cheap Chinese and Indian breakfasts. Take your pick of dosa and curry, or *you-tiao* and hot soy milk. Roti chanai with a mild curry dip is a delicious and economical breakfast available at *Meng Tong* at 74 Bencoolen St or *Tong Hoe* at 84 Bencoolen St – two places that look ripe for redevelopment, so they may not be there for long.

There are many places which do a fixed-price breakfast – continental or American. Try the *Silver Spoon Coffee House* in Supreme House on Penang Rd, off Orchard Rd, for a S$4.50 breakfast. Another good breakfast location is *Mr Cucumber* in the Clifford Centre off Raffles Place – here, a continental breakfast is S$2.90.

McDonalds and *A&W* do fast-food breakfasts and you can have a McDonald's 'big breakfast' for S$3.50 or hotcakes and syrup for S$1.50.

Odds & Ends
Naturally, Singapore has many places to eat which fit into an obscure odds & ends category. If you want a light snack at any time of the day, there are quite a few Chinese coffee bars selling interesting cakes which go nicely with a cup of coffee or tea.

For Western-style pastries, head for the *Café d'Orient de Delifrance* at Peranakan Place on Orchard Rd – the croissants and coffee are hard to beat for breakfast. Other branches are in Shenton House, 3 Shenton Way; 02-19 Clifford Centre, 24 Raffles Place; 02-136 Marine Centre and in the Dynasty Hotel, 320 Orchard Rd.

The small *L E Cafe* at 264 Middle Rd, under the Sun Sun Hotel almost at Selegie Rd, is an interesting place with European and oriental cakes and pastries. It is a good place for breakfast or a snack. Or, try cakes, cookies, yoghurt and muesli in *Steeple's Deli* at 02-25 Tanglin shopping centre on Tanglin Rd. They also do great deli-style sandwiches from S$6 to S$8.

Long John Silver is a fish & chip food chain that does good seafood meals, including fish, chips and corn on the cob for S$5.50. There's one near Scotts Picnic Food Court and one next to Centrepoint shopping complex on Orchard Rd.

In Singapore, there are plenty of supermarkets stocked with everything from French wine and Australian beer to yoghurt, muesli, cheese and ice cream. A pot of tea on the lawn at the Raffles Hotel is a fine investment and a chance to relive the Singapore of an earlier era. You can get a beer (S$3 to S$3.50) at almost any coffee shop but there are also plenty of bars as well as the big hotels.

ENTERTAINMENT

At night, eating out is one of the favourite Singaporean occupations and it takes place at the hundreds of restaurants and countless food-centre stalls. *Pasar malams*, or night markets, sell everything imaginable. They're at different venues each night – the tourist office can advise you. Chinese street-operas still take place around the city – fantastic costumes and (to Western ears) a horrible noise. There are a number of 'instant Asia' style cultural shows put on in and around Singapore, including Instant Asia, ASEAN Night, Malam Singapura and the Lion City Revue.

Modern live music is an import with Western or Filipino musicians working the Orchard Rd hotels and nightspots. Check the Thursday *Straits Times* for what's on and where. Cover charges are typically S$15 to S$25. Try *Brannigans* in the Hyatt Regency, *Anywhere* on the 4th floor of the Tanglin shopping centre or *Bibi's* at Peranakan Place. There are lots of discos like *The Warehouse* at 332 Havelock Rd or the expensive *Hard Rock Cafe* at Orchard Place, Cuscaden Rd.

Risque nightlife is not on in Singapore. The famous Bugis St, once a colourful hangout for transvestites, disappeared with the construction of the MRT but is about to reappear, no doubt in in a totally plastic reconstruction.

Singapore does have a highly active red-light district, stretching from Jalan Besar to Serangoon Rd and parallel to Desker Rd, but Singaporeans in search of sex and sin usually head across the border to Johore Bahru in Malaysia or to nearby Batam Island in the Riau Archipelago of Indonesia.

Thailand

There is probably more visible historical evidence of past cultures in Thailand than in any other South-East Asian country. If you've got the slightest interest in ruins, deserted cities and Buddhas, Thailand is the place to go. It's a remarkably fertile country, a major agricultural exporter and very much one big city and a lot of countryside – Chiang Mai, the second largest city, is a village compared to Bangkok.

Easy travel, excellent and economic accommodation, some fine beach centres and an interesting (but very hot!) cuisine make Thailand a very good country to visit. Thailand's economic boom of the last few years has been accompanied by an equally spectacular tourist boom; it's a very popular country.

Facts About the Country

HISTORY

Thailand's history often seems very complex – so many different peoples, kings, kingdoms and cultures have had a hand in it. The earliest civilisation in Thailand was probably that of the Mons who brought a Buddhist culture from the Indian subcontinent. The rise of the Davaravati kingdoms in central Thailand was ended by the westward movement of the energetic Khmers whose influence can be seen in Thailand at Phimai and Lopburi. At the same time, the Sumatran-based Srivijaya Empire extended up through Malaya and into southern Thailand.

Kublai Khan's expansionist movements in China speeded up the southern migration of the Thai people and, in 1220, Thai princes took over Sukhothai, their first Siamese capital. Other Thai peoples migrated to Laos and the Shan states of Burma. Another Thai kingdom called Lanna Thai (Million Thai Rice-Fields), under King Mengrai, formed in Chiang Rai in northern Thailand and later

moved to Chiang Mai. In 1350, the Prince of U Thong founded still another Thai capital in Ayuthaya which eventually over-shadowed Sukhothai. For two centuries, Ayuthaya was unsurpassed, pushing the Khmers right out of Siam and the Khmer capital of Angkor was abandoned to the jungles, which hid it almost to this century.

In the 16th century, the Burmese – archrivals of the Thais – who had become disunited after Kublai Khan's sacking of Pagan, regrouped and wrought havoc in Thailand. Chiang Mai, which Ayuthaya had never absorbed, was captured by the Burmese in 1556, and in 1569 Ayuthaya also fell to them. Their success, however, was short lived and, in 1595, the Thais recaptured Chiang Mai. During the next century, European influences first appeared in Thailand, but the execution of the Greek, Constantine Phaulkon, emissary of the French, ended that little episode.

In the 18th century, the Burmese attacked again and in 1767, after a prolonged siege, took and utterly destroyed Ayuthaya. The Siamese soon regrouped and expelled the Burmese, but Ayuthaya was never reconstructed. In 1782, the new capital at Thonburi was moved across the river to its present site at Bangkok, and the still-ruling Chakri Dynasty was founded under King Rama I. In the 19th century, while all the rest of South-East Asia was being colonised by the French, Dutch and British, Siam managed to remain independent. By deftly playing off one European power against another, King Mongkut (Rama IV) and Chulalongkorn (Rama V) also managed to obtain many of the material benefits of colonialism.

In 1932, a peaceful coup converted the country into a constitutional monarchy and, in 1939, the name was changed from Siam to Thailand. During WW II, the Phibul government complied with the Japanese and allowed them into the Gulf of

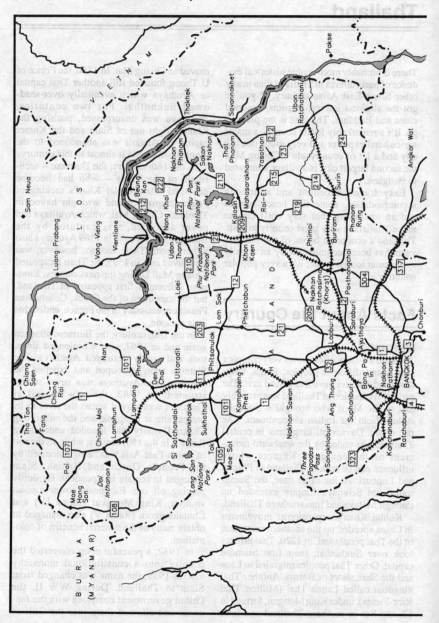

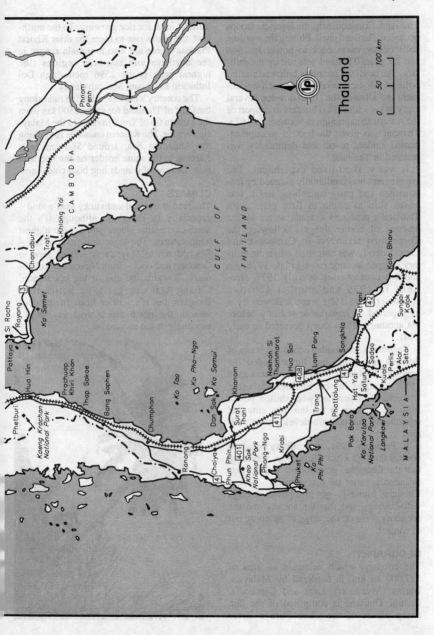

Thailand. Consequently, the Japanese troops occupied Thailand itself. Phibul, the wartime collaborator, came back to power in 1948 and for years Thailand was run by the military. The next two premiers followed similar policies of dictatorial power, self-enrichment and allowed the US to develop several army bases within Thai borders in support of the American campaign in Vietnam. In 1973, Thanom was given the boot in an unprecedented student revolt and democracy was restored in Thailand.

It was a short-lived experiment. The government was continually plagued by factionalism and party squabbles, and it was never able to come to firm grips with Thailand's problems – made worse by the upsurge of border dangers following the Communist takeovers in Cambodia and Laos. Nobody was surprised when the military stepped in once more in late 1976. An abortive counter-coup in early 1977, elections in 1979 and another abortive counter-coup in 1981 were followed by a long period of remarkable stability before yet another military coup occurred in early 1991.

Thailand's remarkable economic boom of the last few years has further aided the country's prospects. Democratic elections in 1988 brought in the business-oriented Chatichai Choonvahan who shifted power from the military to the business elite and relentlessly pursued pro-development policies.

In February 1991, the military regained control through a bloodless coup, reasoning that the Chatichai government was corrupt (allegedly most of his cronies – if not Chatichai himself – got into power through vote-buying), and that the society and the economy were on the verge of spinning out of control.

GEOGRAPHY

The country, which occupies an area of 517,000 sq km, is bordered by Malaysia, Burma (Myanmar), Laos and Cambodia. Central Thailand is composed of the flat, damp plains of the Chao Phraya River

estuary, ideal for rice growing. To the north-east, the plains rise to meet the drier Khorat Plateau. There are also mountain ranges in the northern and southern regions (the highest peak is the 2596 metre-high Doi Inthanon in Chiang Mai province).

The country's eastern coastline runs along the Gulf of Thailand for some 1500 km from the eastern tip of Trat Province to the Malaysian border. The western coastline runs along the Andaman Sea, around 560 km from Ranong to the same border on the opposite side. Dozens of islands hug both coastlines.

CLIMATE

Thailand is tropical and sticky year-round – especially in Bangkok, although it's the north-east plains where you get the highest temperatures. The three seasons are: hot – from March to May; rainy – from June to October; and cool – from November to February. Towards the end of the hot season, Chiang Mai can get even hotter than Bangkok but it's a drier heat. In the cool season, the north can almost get 'cold', especially in the mountains.

The rainy season rarely brings things to a complete halt and it's not a reason to put off visiting Thailand. Towards the end of the season, when the ground is completely saturated, Bangkok is often flooded. This is in large part due to poor planning – more and more canals are being filled in and wells are drilled indiscriminately, thus lowering the water table, and the whole place is sinking anyway!

ECONOMY

Rice is the mainstay of the Thai economy and is widely exported to surrounding countries. Other major export products are tapioca, maize, sugar, rubber, tin, cement, pineapple, tuna and textiles. Some people would say sex and sin is a very marketable Thai commodity, particularly in Bangkok.

Many economists are painting a bright economic future for Thailand, saying that it will join the ranks of the NICs (Newly Industrialised Countries) like Korea and Taiwan within five to 10 years. Others say that the infrastructure is far from ready to handle the current rate of growth (about 10% per annum) and change. Average annual per capita income is about US$1418 but there is a wide gap between affluent Bangkok and the much less affluent countryside.

POPULATION & PEOPLE

Thailand's population is about 54 million. Although basically homogeneous, there are many hill tribes in the northern area and some Malays in the south, as well as numbers of Mon, Khmer, Phuan and other common South-East Asian ethnic groups. About 10% of the population is Chinese, but they're so well assimilated that almost no one bothers to note the difference. There are also a large number of refugees from Burma (Myanmar), Laos and Cambodia in festering camps in the border areas, and Thailand has also been affected by the Vietnamese refugee problem.

CULTURE
Conduct

Monarchy and religion are the two sacred cows in Thailand. Thais are tolerant of most kinds of behaviour as long as it doesn't insult one of these.

Monarchy The monarchy is held in considerable respect in Thailand and visitors should be respectful too – avoid disparaging remarks about the king, queen or anyone in the royal family. One of Thailand's leading intellectuals, Sulak Sivarak, was arrested in the early '80s because of a passing reference to the king's fondness for sailing when he called him 'the skipper'.

While it's OK to criticise the Thai government and even Thai culture openly, it's considered a grave insult to Thai nationhood as well as to the monarchy not to stand when you hear the national anthem (composed by the king, incidentally).

Religion Correct behaviour in temples entails several guidelines, the most important of which is to dress neatly (no shorts or tank tops) and to take your shoes off when you enter any building that contains a Buddha image. Buddha images are sacred objects, so don't pose in front of them for pictures and definitely do not clamber upon them.

Monks are not supposed to touch or be touched by women. If a woman wants to hand something to a monk, the object should be placed within reach of the monk and not handed directly to him.

When sitting in a religious edifice, keep your feet pointed away from any Buddha images. The usual way to do this is to sit in the 'mermaid' pose in which your legs are folded to the side, with the feet pointing backwards.

Social Gestures

Traditionally, Thais greet each other not with a hand shake but with a prayer-like palms-together gesture known as a *wai*. If someone wais you, you should wai back (unless waied by a child).

The feet are the lowest part of the body (spiritually as well as physically) so don't point your feet at people or point at things with your feet. In the same context, the head is regarded as the highest part of the body, so don't touch Thais on the head.

Thais are often addressed by their first name with the honorific *Khun* or a title preceding it. Friends often use nicknames or kinship terms like *phii* (elder sibling) or *nong* (younger sibling).

Dress & Attitude

Beach attire is not considered appropriate for trips into town and is especially counter-productive if worn to government offices (eg when applying for a visa extension). As in most parts of Asia, anger and emotions are rarely displayed and generally get you nowhere. In any argument or dispute, remember the paramount rule is to keep your cool.

RELIGION

Buddhism is the dominant religion for about 95% of the population. Orange-robed monks and Buddhas sitting, standing, reclining and made of gold, marble, stone or whatever are common sights. The prevalent form of Buddhism practised is the Theravada (Council of the Elders) school. Also known as Hinayana, it is the same as that found in Sri Lanka, Burma (Myanmar), Laos and Cambodia. Theravada Buddhism emphasises the potential of the individual to attain Nibbana (nirvana) without the aid of saints or gurus.

In Thailand's four southernmost provinces – Yala, Narathiwat, Pattani and Satun – there's a large Muslim minority.

LANGUAGE

Although Thai is a rather complicated language with its own unique alphabet, it's fun to try at least a few words. The *Thai Phrasebook* by Lonely Planet gives a handy basic introduction to the language. The main complication with Thai is that it is tonal; the same word could be pronounced with a rising, falling, high, low or level tone and could, therefore, theoretically have five meanings!

The 'ph' in a Thai word is always pronounced like an English 'p', not as an 'f'.

Greetings & Civilities

hello
 sawàt dii
How are you?
 pen yangai?
I'm fine
 sabàay dii
excuse me
 khăw thôht
please
 karuna or *proht*
thank you
 khàwp khun

Time & Dates

when?
 mêu-arai?
today
 wan níi
tomorrow
 phrûng níi
yesterday
 mêua waan

Getting Around

Where is the ...?
 ...yùu thîi năi?
bus
 rót meh
train
 rót fai
hotel
 rohng raem
post office
 praisanii
station
 sathăanii

Useful Words & Phrases

yes (female)
 khâ
yes (male)
 khráp
no
 mâi
How much?
 thâo rai?
too expensive
 phaeng pai

It doesn't matter (or never mind)
mâi pen rai
I do not understand
mâi khâo jai
What is this in Thai?
nîí phaasǎa thai riâk wâa arai?
toilet
hâwng sûam

Numbers

1	*nèung*
2	*song*
3	*sǎam*
4	*sìi*
5	*hâa*
6	*hòk*
7	*jèt*
8	*pàet*
9	*kâo*
10	*sìp*
11	*sìp èt*
20	*yîi sìp*
21	*yîi sìp èt*
30	*sǎam sìp*
100	*nèung roi*
200	*song roi*
1000	*nèung phan*

There are several different words that can be used to mean 'I' but the safest are *phóm* for men and *dǐichán* for women. You can also omit the pronoun altogether and say, for example *mâi khâo jai*, 'do not understand'.

Mâi pen rai is a very useful phrase although it actually has far more meanings than simply 'it doesn't matter'. It can mean 'don't bother', 'forget it', 'leave it alone', 'take no notice', or even 'that's enough'.

Facts for the Visitor

VISAS

You've got a variety of choices in the visa game for Thailand. First of all, you can enter Thailand without any visa and be granted a 15-day stay permit. Officially, you must have an outward ticket but in practice this does not always seem to be rigidly enforced.

On my last visit to Thailand, my passport was checked at Changi Airport (Singapore) and since there was no Thai visa I was asked if I had an onward ticket, which I did. There was no check on arrival in Bangkok but the lack of both a visa *and* a ticket could have caused problems in Singapore. The major catch with the 15-day permit is that no extension is possible – 15 days is your lot.

The one-month transit visas costs around US$5 and (like the 15-day permit) cannot be extended. From the traveller's point of view, the best deal is a two-month tourist visa which costs approximately US$10; in Penang, they're M$31. They are issued quickly and without fuss. Singapore, Penang, Kota Bharu and Kathmandu are all good places to get Thai visas. New Zealanders take note: you can travel in Thailand for up to 90 days without a visa.

A one-month extension to your tourist visa is possible but costs 500B. You'll need two photos and photocopies of the photo and visa pages of your passport.

If you are leaving Thailand and then returning (for example – going to Burma (Myanmar) for a week), you can get a re-entry visa, but this is double the cost of a single-entry visa so there's no savings. The immigration office in Bangkok for these visas is on Soi Suan Phlu. If you can provide a good reason for getting one (business for example), nonimmigrant visas are also available – these cost US$15 and are valid for 90 days.

Other Visas

Bangkok is a popular place for getting visas for onward travel, particularly for people heading on to West Asia.

Following the upheavals in the Punjab, visas are now required for most nationalities visiting India. The Indian Embassy (☎ 258 0300) in Bangkok is at 46 Soi Prasanmit (Soi 23), off Sukhumvit Rd. This embassy can be slow in issuing visas. In Chiang Mai, however, there is an efficient Indian Consulate and visas are no problem at all.

Visas are not required in advance for Nepal. They can be obtained on arrival at the airport or at the land borders. This 'on arrival' visa is only valid for seven days, however, and extending it is such a time-consuming hassle that it's well worthwhile obtaining a visa in advance if you have the time. The Nepalese Embassy (☎ 391 7240) is at 189 Soi Phuengsuk (Soi 71), a long-way down Sukhumvit Rd.

All nationalities require visas for entry into Burma (Myanmar), Laos, Vietnam and Cambodia. They are only issued to tourists through approved travel agencies. A number of agencies in the Khao San Rd area can make these arrangements. Typically, the cost is around 2000B for a Vietnam visa which takes five days to issue. Visas for Laos are similarly priced.

Most travellers doing the Indochina circuit start by flying to Saigon (Ho Chi Minh City) in Vietnam. There they apply for their Cambodian visa and make a Saigon-Cambodia-Saigon sidetrip. They can then travel up to Hanoi where they apply for a Laotian visa and travel Hanoi-Vientiane-Bangkok. Numerous agents around Bangkok handle visas for Vietnam – try MK Ways (☎ 254 5583) at 57/11 Wireless Rd, or 18/4 Soi Saint Louis 3, Sathon Tai Rd.

Visas for Bangladesh are required for some nationalities, and the embassy (☎ 391-8070) is at 8 Soi Charoenmit (Soi 63), Sukhumvit Rd. Travellers heading for China usually get their visas in Hong Kong but they can be obtained in Bangkok from around 500 or 600B, again the Khao San Rd agents will have the news.

MONEY
Currency

The *baht* (B) is divided into 100 *satang*, although 25 and 50 satang are the smallest coins you'll see. Coins come in 1B (three sizes), 5B (two sizes) and new 10B denominations. Notes are in 10B (brown), 20B (green), 50B (blue), 100B (red) and 500B (purple) denominations of varying shades and sizes. Changing a note larger than 100B can be difficult in small towns and villages.

In upcountry markets, you may hear prices referred to in *saleng* – a saleng is equal to 25 satang.

Exchange Rates

A$1	=	20B
C$1	=	23B
NZ$	=	15B
US$1	=	26B
UK£1	=	48B

The baht is aligned with the US$, and the US$-baht rate fluctuates only slightly from day to day. Baht rates against other currencies will, of course, fluctuate relative to the US$.

Changing Money Banks give the best exchange rates and are generally open from 8.30 am to 3.30 pm Monday to Friday. Avoid hotels, which give the worst rates. In the larger towns and tourist destinations, there are also foreign exchange kiosks that are open longer hours, usually from around 8 am to 8 pm. All banks deduct an 8B service charge per cheque – thus you can save money by using larger denomination travellers' cheques (eg cashing a US$100 cheque will cost you 8B while cashing five US$20 cheques will cost 40B).

There is no black market for US$ but Bangkok is a good centre for buying Asian currencies, particularly those of neighbouring countries where black-market money changing flourishes (eg Laos and Burma) – try the moneychangers on New (Charoen Krung) Rd for these.

Credit cards are becoming widely accepted at hotels, restaurants and other business establishments. Visa and Mastercard are the most commonly accepted, followed by American Express and Diners Club. Cash advances are available on Visa and Mastercard at many branches of the Thai Farmers Bank.

Costs

Thailand is an economical country to visit and it offers excellent value for your money. Transport is reasonably priced, comfortable and reliable. Finding a place to stay is rarely difficult, although the tourist boom has created some problems in the high seasons (from December to January and from July to August). Costs are low and you get good value for your money. So long as you can stand a little spice, the food is also very good and cheap.

Bangkok is, of course, more expensive than elsewhere in the country. In part, that's because there are lots of luxuries available in Bangkok which you simply won't be tempted with upcountry. So many cheap guest houses have sprung up in the Banglamphu area of the city that accommodation needn't necessarily be any more expensive in Bangkok than elsewhere in the country. Of course, the Bangkok hassles – noise and pollution being the main ones – also drive you to look for extra comfort, and air-conditioning can be very nice.

One good way to save money is to travel in the off seasons, which in Thailand means from April to June or from September to October. During these periods, tourist destinations are less crowded and prices for accommodation are generally lower. In the remainder of the year, hotels and guest houses often raise their prices to whatever the traffic will bear.

Tipping

Tipping is not customary except in the big tourist hotels of Bangkok, Pattaya, Phuket and Chiang Mai. Even here, if a service charge is added to the bill, tipping isn't necessary.

Bargaining

Bargaining is mandatory in almost all situations. Arab and Indian traders brought bargaining to Thailand early in the millennium and the Thais have developed it into an art. Nowhere in South-East Asia is it more necessary not to accept the first price, whether dealing with Bangkok taxi drivers or village weavers. While bargaining, it helps to stay relaxed and friendly – gritting your teeth and raising your voice is almost always counterproductive.

TOURIST OFFICES

The Tourist Authority of Thailand (TAT) has an office at the airport, another in central Bangkok and quite a few in regional centres around the country (see the regional sections for addresses). They have a lot of useful brochures, booklets and maps and will probably have an information sheet on almost any Thai subject that interests you. The TAT is probably the best tourist office in South-East Asia for the production of useful information sheets rather than (often useless) pretty colour brochures.

Each regional office also puts out accommodation guides that include cheap places to stay. In Bangkok, they sell the invaluable bus map which lists all the Bangkok bus routes. The flip side of the bus map has a pretty good map of Thailand with Thai script as well. Make sure any map you get has names on it in Thai as well as English.

BUSINESS HOURS

Most businesses are open from Monday to Friday. Many retail establishments and travel agencies are also open on Saturday. Government offices are open from 8.30 am to 4.30 pm and some close, from 12 noon to 1 pm, for lunch.

HOLIDAYS & EVENTS
National

There's always a festival somewhere in Thailand. Many are keyed to Buddhist or Brahmanic rituals and follow a lunar calendar. Thus they fall on different dates (by the Western solar calendar) each year, depending on the phases of the moon.

Such festivals are usually centred around the wats and include: Makkha Bucha (full moon in February – commemorating the gathering, without prior summons, of 500 monks to hear the Buddha speak); Wisakha Bucha (full moon in May – commemorating the birth, enlightenment and death of the Buddha); Asanha Bucha (full moon in July – commemorating the Buddha's first public discourse); and Khao Phansaa (full moon in July – celebrating the beginning of the Buddhist Rains Retreat).

For other holidays, the Thai government

has assigned official dates that don't vary from year to year, as follows:

1 January
  New Year's Day
6 April
  Chakri Memorial Day
12-14 April
  Songkran Festival (Thai New Year)
1 May
  National Labour Day
5 May
  Coronation Day
12 August
  Queen's Birthday
23 October
  Chulalongkorn Day
5 December
  King's Birthday
10 December
  Constitution Day
31 December
  New Year's Eve

On the above dates, government offices and banks will be closed. Some businesses will also choose to close on these days. As in any country, the days before and after a national holiday are marked by heavy air and road traffic as well as full hotels.

Local & Regional

Many provinces hold annual festivals or fairs to promote their specialties, eg Chiang Mai's Flower Festival, Kamphaeng Phet's Banana Festival, Yala's Barred Ground Dove Festival and so on. A complete, up-to-date schedule of events around the country is available from TAT offices in each province or from the central Bangkok TAT office.

POST & TELECOMMUNICATIONS

The Thai postal system is relatively efficient and few travellers complain about undelivered mail or lost parcels. Poste restante mail can be received at any town in the country that has a post office. In addition, most hotels and guest houses will be glad to hold mail for guests as long as the envelopes are so marked.

The telephone system is also fairly modern and efficient – larger amphoe muang (provincial capitals) are connected with the IDD system. The central post office in any amphoe muang will house or be located next to the international telephone office. There is usually someone at this office who speaks English. In any case, the forms are always bilingual.

TIME

Thailand has one time zone, which is seven hours ahead of GMT. This means that when it's 12 noon in Bangkok, it's 5 am in London, 1 am in New York, 10 pm in Los Angeles and 3 pm in Sydney.

BOOKS & MAPS

Bangkok has some of the best bookshops in South-East Asia. See the Bangkok Bookshops section for details.

Travel Guides

Lonely Planet's Thailand – a travel survival kit provides much more detail on the country than can be squeezed into this chapter. Discovering Thailand (Oxford University Press) by Clarac & Smithies is good for architectural and archaeological points of interest, even if it's dated. The Insight Guide Thailand, another Apa coffee-table guidebook, is rich in photos and background information.

Arts

Several books on Thai arts have appeared over the years. Perhaps the easiest to find (but not necessarily the most accurate) is Arts of Thailand (hardback) by Bangkok's dynamic duo, writer Steve Van Beek and photographer Luca Invernizzi Tettoni. William Warren and Tettoni have authored a worthy book on Thai design called Thai Style (hardback).

Culture

Denis Segaller's Thai Ways and More Thai Ways (both paperbacks) are readable collections of cultural vignettes relating to Thai culture and folklore. Mai Pen Rai by Carol Hollinger (paperback) is often suggested as an introduction to Thai culture but is more a cultural snapshot of Thailand in the 1960s.

More useful as a cultural primer is Robert & Nanthapa Cooper's *Culture Shock! Thailand & How to Survive It*, part of a series that attempts to educate tourists and business travellers in local customs.

Hill Tribes

The Hill Tribes of Northern Thailand by Gordon Young (Monograph No l, The Siam Society, paperback) covers 16 tribes, including descriptions, photographs, tables and maps. Young was born among Lahu tribespeople of third-generation Christian missionaries, speaks several tribal dialects and is an honorary Lahu chieftain. *From the Hands of the Hills* by Margaret Campbell (hardback) has beautiful pictures of hill tribe handicrafts. *Peoples of the Golden Triangle* by Elaine & Paul Lewis (hardback) is also good, very photo-oriented and expensive.

History & Politics

The Indianized States of South-East Asia (paperback) by George Coedes, *The Thai Peoples* by Erik Seidenfaden (hardback, out of print), *Siam in Crisis* (paperback) by Sulak Sivarak and *Political Conflict in Thailand: Reform, Reaction, Revolution* (hardback) by David Morrell & Chai-anan Samudavanija are all worth reading.

Maps

Bangkok Thailand Tour'n Guide Map has the most up-to-date bus map of Bangkok on one side and a fair map of Thailand on the other – it is usually priced around 40B. The bus side is quite necessary if you plan to spend time in Bangkok and want to use the very economical bus system. It is available at most bookstores in Bangkok which carry English-language materials. A better map of the country is published by Nelles Verlag. It costs around US$7 and is also available at many Bangkok bookstores, as well as overseas.

Even better is a 48-page bilingual road atlas called *Thailand Highway Map*, published by the Roads Association of Thailand, that includes detailed highway department maps, dozens of city maps, driving distances, and lots of travel and sightseeing information. The cost is around 120B, a bargain for anyone planning to do extensive road travel.

There are also Nancy Chandler's very useful city maps of Bangkok and Chiang Mai. These heavily annotated sketch maps serve as up-to-date and informative guides as well, highlighting local sights, noting local markets and their wares, outlining local transport and recommending restaurants.

MEDIA

Newspapers

Two English-language newspapers, the *Bangkok Post* (morning) and the *Nation* (afternoon), are published daily in Thailand and distributed to most provincial capitals throughout the country. The *Post*, the better of the two, is regarded by many journalists as the best English-language daily in South-East Asia.

The Singapore edition of the *International Herald Tribune* is widely available in Bangkok, Chiang Mai and heavily-touristed areas like Pattaya and Phuket.

Radio & TV

Bangkok's national public radio station, Radio Thailand, broadcasts English-language programmes over FM frequency 97 mHz from 6 am to 11 pm. FM 107 is another public radio station and is affiliated with Radio Thailand and Channel 9 on Thai public television. They feature some surprisingly good music programmes with British, Thai and American disc jockeys. The Voice of America, BBC World Service, Radio Canada and Radio Australia all have English and Thai-language broadcasts over short wave radio.

A schedule of the evening's programmes and frequencies can be found in the *Nation* and *Bangkok Post* newspapers.

There are four television networks in Bangkok. Upcountry TV stations will generally receive only two networks, channel 9 and a local private network with restricted hours.

FILM & PHOTOGRAPHY

Print film is inexpensive and widely available throughout Thailand. Slide film is also inexpensive but it can be hard to find outside of Bangkok and Chiang Mai – be sure to stock up before heading upcountry. Film processing is generally quite good in the Thailand's larger cities and also quite inexpensive. Kodachrome must be sent out of the country for processing which can take up to two weeks.

Pack some silica gel with your camera equipment to prevent mould growing on the inside of your lenses. Keep an eye on your camera – they're very expensive in Thailand and are thus tempt to thieves.

Hill tribespeople in some of the more visited areas expect money if you photograph them, while certain Karen and Akha flee a pointed camera. Use discretion when photographing villagers anywhere in Thailand as a camera can be a very intimidating instrument. You may feel better leaving your camera behind when visiting certain areas.

HEALTH

Refer to the Health section of the Facts about the Region chapter for general health information relevant to South-East Asia. Further specifics on Thailand include:

Malaria

Malaria is mostly restricted to a few rural areas in Thailand, most notably the islands of the eastern seaboard (Chonburi to Trat), and the provinces (but not the capitals) of Chaiyaphum, Phetchabun, Mae Hong Son and Tak. Virtually all strains of malaria in Thailand are resistant to chloroquine and thus it's advisable to take an alternative.

Thailand's Malaria Control Centre recommends avoiding contact with mosquitoes from dusk to dawn (when they bite) by making liberal use of repellents, mosquito nets and proper clothing (long-sleeved shirts and long pants). The less you're bitten, the less chance you have of contracting the disease.

Japanese Encephalitis

A few years ago, this viral disease was practically unheard of. Although long endemic to tropical Asia (as well as China, Korea, Japan and eastern USSR), there have been recent rainy season epidemics in north Thailand and Vietnam which increase the risk for travellers. A night-biting mosquito is the carrier for JE and the risk is said to be greatest in rural zones near areas where pigs are raised or rice is grown, since pigs and certain wild birds, whose habitat may include rice fields, serve as reservoirs for the virus.

People who may be at risk of contracting Japanese encephalitis (JE) in Thailand are those who will be spending long periods of time in rural areas during the rainy season (July to October). If you belong to this group, you may want to get a JE vaccination. Check with the government health service in your home country to see if it's available at home before you leave. If not, arrange to be vaccinated in Bangkok, Hong Kong or Singapore, where the vaccine is easy to find.

Timing is important in taking the vaccine, however; you must receive at least two doses, seven to 10 days apart. The USA Center for Disease Control recommends a third dose 21 to 30 days after the first for improved immunity. Immunity lasts about a year at which point it's necessary to get a booster shot, then it's every four years after that.

The symptoms of Japanese encephalitis are sudden fever, chills and headache, followed by vomiting and delirium, a strong aversion to bright light, and sore joints and muscles. Advanced cases may result in convulsions and coma. Estimates of the fatality rate for JE range from 5% to 60%.

As with other mosquito-borne diseases, the best way to prevent JE (apart from vaccination) is to avoid mosquito bites.

AIDS

As of November 1990, the Ministry of Health had recorded 23,548 known cases of HIV-positive individuals, including 69 cases of full-blown AIDS. In spite of rumours to the contrary, the Thai government keeps all

AIDS-related records open to public scrutiny and is trying to educate the general public about AIDS prevention.

In Thailand, the disease is most commonly associated with intravenous heroin use but is also known to be transmitted through sexual contact, both heterosexual and homosexual. If you're going to have sex in Thailand, use condoms.

DANGERS & ANNOYANCES

There's always a lot of talk about safety in Thailand – guerrilla forces along three international borders, muggings, robberies and who-knows-what get wide publicity. Communist insurgency in the north and north-east was wiped out in the early 1980s, and in the south it came to an official end in 1989. The remaining danger areas are along the Burmese (drug-smuggling and ethnic insurgents) and Cambodian (Khmer Rouge) border areas. Take extra care when travelling in these areas and avoid travelling at night.

Robberies and hold-ups, despite their publicity, are relatively infrequent. If there is a rule of thumb, however, it's that the hold-up gangs seem to concentrate more on tour buses than on the ordinary buses or the trains, probably assuming that the pickings will be richer.

Precautions

Theft in Thailand is still usually a matter of stealth rather than strength. You're more likely to be pickpocketed than mugged. Take care of your valuables, don't carry too much cash around with you, and watch out for razor artists (they slit bags open in crowded quarters) and the snatch-and-run experts in Bangkok. Don't trust hotel rooms, particularly in the beach-hut places like Ko Samui and Ko Pha-Ngan. Try not to have your bag on the roof of buses or in the underfloor luggage compartments.

Also, take caution when leaving valuables in hotel safes. Many travellers have reported unpleasant experiences after having left valuables in Chiang Mai guest houses. On their return home, they received huge credit card bills for purchases (usually jewellery)

charged to their cards in Bangkok. The cards had, supposedly, been secure in the hotel or guest house safe while the guests were out trekking! Women in particular, but men also, should ensure their rooms are securely locked and bolted at night. Inspect cheap rooms with thin walls for strategic peep-holes.

Thais are a friendly lot and their friendliness is usually genuine. Nevertheless, on trains and buses, particularly in the south, beware of strangers offering cigarettes, drinks or chocolates. Several travellers have reported waking up with a headache sometime later to find their valuables have disappeared. Travellers have also encountered drugged food or drink from friendly strangers in bars and from prostitutes in their own hotel rooms.

Keep zippered luggage secured with small locks, especially while travelling on buses and trains. This will not only keep out most sneak thieves, but prevent con artists posing as police from planting contraband drugs in your luggage. That may sound paranoid, but it happens.

Armed robbery appears to be on the increase in remote areas of Thailand but the risk of armed robbery should still be considered fairly low. The safest practice in remote areas, however, is not to go out alone at night and, if trekking in north Thailand, always walk in groups.

Jii-Khoh

Small upcountry restaurants are sometimes hang-outs for drunken *jii-khoh*, an all-purpose Thai term that refers to the teenage playboy-hoodlum-cowboy who gets his kicks by violating Thai socio-cultural norms. These oafs sometimes bother foreign women (and men) who are trying to have a quiet meal ('Are you married?' and 'I love you' are common conversation openers). It's best to ignore them rather than trying to make snappy comebacks – they won't understand them and will most likely take these responses as encouragement.

If the jii-khohs persist, find another restaurant. Unfortunately, restaurant proprietors will rarely do anything about such disturbances.

Scams

Over the years, LP has received dozens of letters from victims who've been cheated out of large sums of money by con men posing as 'friendly Thais'. All of the reports have come from Bangkok and Chiang Mai, and they always describe invitations to buy gems at a special price or participate in a card game. The usual practice is for the con artists to strike up an easy friendship on the street (often near Wat Phra Kaew), then invite the foreigner along to observe a gem purchase or card game in which the friendly stranger will participate. After explaining how easy it is to make heaps of money in the gem or card scheme, the foreigner is invited to invest. It may seem hard to believe, but lots of visitor fall for these schemes, which always end in huge financial losses.

If you become involved in one of these scams, the police (including the tourist police) are usually of little help. It's not illegal for gem stores to sell gems at outrageously high prices. In the case of the card game, everyone's usually gone by the time you come back with the police. Some gem outlets to treat with caution include H Thai Gems Centre, Pinklao Gems, Vimarn Gems, Ploy and Phayathai Gem Centre.

Remember gems and card games are this year's scam so, no doubt, some totally new and highly original scheme will pop up next year. The contact men are usually young, friendly, personable, smooth talking 'students'. They prey on younger travellers – if you're in your 20s you're a prime target. We've even heard of combining the old drugging games with the new selling ones – 'I never thought of buying gems until I drank that soft drink they gave me'.

ACCOMMODATION

For consistently good value, the cheap Thai hotels are amongst the best in the region. Almost anywhere in Thailand, even Bangkok, you can get a double for 100B or less. In fact, Bangkok has had such a proliferation of small guest houses that it's actually become easier to find rooms in the rock-bottom price category.

There can often be an amazing variance in prices in the same hotel. You'll find fancy air-con rooms at over 300B and straightforward fan-cooled rooms at a third of that price. Even the smallest towns will have a choice of hotels, although 'hotel' will often be the only word on them in Roman script. Finding a specific place in some smaller towns can be a problem if you don't speak Thai.

A typical Thai 100B room is plain and spartan but will include a toilet, a shower and a ceiling fan. Rooms with a common toilet can cost from 60 to 80B. The Banglamphu places in Bangkok are likely to be a little more basic and not have bathrooms. At the less touristed beach centres of southern Thailand, you'll find pleasant individual beach cottages for 80B and less.

As in Malaysia, many of the hotels are Chinese-run and couples can often save money by asking for a single – a single means one double bed, a double means two.

FOOD & DRINKS

Thai food is like Chinese with a sting – it can be fiery. The problem with eating Thai style is knowing what to get, how to get it and, finally, how to get it for a reasonable price. Outside of the tourist areas, few places have a menu in English and as for having prices on a menu... To make matters worse, your mangled attempts at asking for something in Thai are unlikely to be understood. Make the effort for there are some delicious foods to be tried. *Eating in Thailand*, a useful leaflet available from the tourist office, has English descriptions and the equivalent Thai script.

Many Thai restaurants are actually Chinese serving a few of the main Thai dishes amongst the Chinese or some Thai-influenced Chinese ones. In the south, look for delicious seafood, and in the north and north-east there are various local specialities centred around 'sticky' rice.

Soft drinks are cheaper than almost anywhere in South-East Asia, which is just as well since the Thais brew tea and coffee in a very non-Western way. Some say they taste like the two have been mixed together and left to stew for a month. Others grow to like them strong, milky and sweet. Thais also have a penchant for putting salt in fruit drinks. More dairy products are available in Thailand than anywhere else in Asia – including very good yoghurt.

Beer is good but fairly expensive. Singha is the most popular brand – 25 to 30B for a small bottle and 45 to 55B for a large. There are a variety of local firewaters including the famous Mekong whisky which is about half the strength of Scotch and drunk in enormous quantities.

Examples of Thai food and drink include:

Food
fried rice
  khâo phàt
  with chicken
    khâo phàt kài
  with pork
    khâo phàt mǔu
  with prawns
    khâo phàt kûng
pork, chicken or prawn soup
  kaeng jèut
spicy lemon soup
  tôm yam
Indian-style curry
  kaeng kari
Thai curry
  kaeng phèt
curried chicken
  kaeng kari kài
thin rice noodles with tofu, vegetables & egg
  phàt thai
stir fried vegetables
  phàt phàk lǎi yàng
beef in oyster sauce
  néua phàt nám-man hǎwy
chicken with vegetables & peanut sauce
  phrá raam long sǒng kài
fried prawns
  kûng tâwt
grilled fish
  plaa phǎo

clear fine noodle salad
  yam wún sên
fried eggs
  khài dao
scrambled eggs
  khài kuan
omelette
  khài jii oh

Drinks
black coffee
  kafae dam ron
white coffee
  kafae ron
black tea
  cha dam ron
white tea
  cha ron

Khâo phàt is the daily national dish – a close cousin to Chinese fried rice or Indonesian nasi goreng. It usually comes with sliced cucumber, a fried egg on top and some super hot peppers to catch the unwary. When you don't know what else to order, this will almost always be available. Beef in oyster sauce, a popular Chinese dish, is another Thai favourite.

A Thai dish I developed a real liking for is sour hot beef, *yam néua*, a very spicy and hot concoction of shredded beef with salad. *Phàt thai* is fried noodles, beansprouts, peanuts, eggs, chillies and often prawns – good value at any street stall.

Getting There & Away

Except for people coming from Malaysia, almost all visitors arrive by air. There are plenty of land crossing-points between Thailand and Burma (Myanmar), Laos or Cambodia, but very few border crossings are made. Officially, at least! By air, however, Bangkok is a major arrival point for flights from all over the world.

AIR
See the introductory Getting There & Away

chapter for the prices of fares to Bangkok from Europe, Australia and North America. You can also fly to Bangkok from various other Asian cities such as Hong Kong, Manila, Singapore, Kuala Lumpur, Penang, Colombo, Rangoon, Dhaka, Calcutta and Kathmandu. Bangkok is a major access point for Burma (Myanmar) and Nepal. Although Bangkok is the main entry point for Thailand, you can also fly into Chiang Mai from Hong Kong or to Hat Yai from Penang (Malaysia).

Bangkok is a popular place for buying airline tickets, although it's no longer the number-one bargain centre of the region. Some typical one-way fares available from Bangkok include Colombo US$198, Hong Kong US$160, Manila US$240, Penang US$104, Singapore US$140, Taipei US$240, Rangoon (Yangon) US$100 and Vientiane US$80. European destinations cost from around US$300 to US$400, and flights to Los Angeles or San Francisco cost from US$400 to US$500. Interesting routes include Tokyo via Manila for US$395, New York via Bombay and Paris for US$650, Denpasar via Singapore US$250, Bangkok-Rangoon-Dhaka for US$200 or Bangkok-Rangoon-Kathmandu for US$220.

Over the years, we have had a lot of letters complaining about various travel agencies in Bangkok – and a few saying what a good deal they got. Remember nothing is free, so if you get quoted a price way below other agencies be suspicious. In smaller agencies, insist on getting the ticket before handing over your cash. Don't sign anything either.

A favourite game has been getting clients to sign a disclaimer saying that they will not request a refund under any circumstances. Then, when they pick their ticket up, they find it is only valid for one week or something similar – not very good when you're not planning to leave for a month or two yet. Alternatively, the ticket may only be valid within certain dates, or other limitations may be placed upon it.

Another catch is you may be told that the ticket is confirmed (OK) only to find on closer inspection that it is only on request

(RQ) or merely open. Or even worse, the ticket actually has OK on it when in actual fact no reservation has been made at all. So read everything carefully and remember – *caveat emptor*, buyer beware. STA Travel (☎ 281 5314/5), the Student Travel Australia outlet, is friendly, knowledgeable and reliable. They're at the Thai Hotel, 78 Prachatipatai Rd, quite close to the Khao San Rd travellers' enclave.

Reconfirmation

Flights in and out of Thailand are often overbooked these days so it's imperative that you reconfirm any return or ongoing flights you have as soon as you arrive in Thailand. If you don't, there's a very good chance you'll be bumped from your flight at the airport. It never hurts to reconfirm more than once.

TO/FROM MALAYSIA

There are a variety of ways to cross the Thai-Malaysian borders. You can fly or go by bus, train or taxi. There are border crossings at several places on the east and west coast. There's even one place where you can cross the border by boat.

Air

The simplest and fastest way is to fly between Penang and Hat Yai – the fare is around M$113 or 1050B. On flights that continue on to Phuket, you can leave the beach at Penang in the morning and be on the beach in Phuket in the afternoon. You can also, of course, fly straight through from Penang or Kuala Lumpur to Bangkok. The fare is virtually identical via Hat Yai or Phuket, if you prefer to stop off. Of course, from Penang to Bangkok is a route where you can usually find discounted tickets – expect to pay around M$300 in Penang.

Train

The International Express will take you from Butterworth (Penang) to Hat Yai and Bangkok without a change of trains. There are also connecting services to or from Singapore and Kuala Lumpur. The train, which only has 1st and 2nd-class tickets, now operates every day and, it appears, without the border delays which used to be a problem on the train services.

The International Express departs Bangkok at 3.15 pm daily, arrives in Hat Yai at 7.04 am the next day and in Butterworth at 12.25 pm that afternoon. From Malaysia, it leaves Butterworth at 1.40 pm, arrives in Hat Yai at 4.38 pm and in Bangkok at 8.35 am the next day. Fares from Butterworth to Hat Yai are M$12.70 for 2nd class and M$28.40 for 1st. From Butterworth to Bangkok is M$46.50 and M$100 respectively. From Bangkok, the fares to Butterworth are 431B in 2nd class and 927B in 1st.

There is an additional express surcharge on the International Express of M$3.20 or 30B. Berth charges on the International Express are M$10.80 or 100B for a 2nd-class upper berth, M$16.20 or 150B for a 2nd-class lower berth and M$27 or 250B for 1st class. You can travel between Bangkok and Hat Yai on other trains in 3rd class but the only service across the border between Hat Yai and Butterworth is the International Express.

Land

West Coast The basic land route between Penang and Hat Yai is by taxi. It is fast, convenient and, for around M$25 or 220B, not expensive. The taxis that operate this route are generally big old Chevrolets, all Thai-registered. From Penang, you'll find the taxis at the various travellers' hotels around Georgetown. In Hat Yai, they'll be at the railway station or along Niphat Uthit 2. Magic Tour, downstairs from the Cathay Guest House in Hat Yai, has buses for only 200B which leave twice daily and take five hours. This is the fastest way of travelling by land between the two countries and you cross the border with the minimum of fuss.

On the map, it looks pretty easy to travel between Malaysia and Thailand by local transport, but in actual fact the long stretch of no-man's land between Changlun, the Malaysian border post, and Sadao, the Thai

equivalent, makes crossing the border rather difficult. It's quite easy to get to either side by local bus or taxi but finding a ride across the actual border is not easy at all. There is no bus or taxi service across the border. I've hitched across on three occasions, once getting a ride on a Thai fish truck and arriving at the other end smelling a little odd! However, there is not exactly a steady flow of vehicles across the border and they're unwilling to pick up hitchhikers.

If, however, you go a few km west to Padang Besar, where the railway line crosses the border, you can easily just walk across the border. Buses run there from either side, and there's also a train from Butterworth to the border.

East Coast From Kota Bharu, you can take a share taxi to Rantau Panjang – 45 km for about M$4.50. It's then just half a km (maybe nearer a km) stroll across the border to the town of Sungai Kolok. From here, trains run to Hat Yai and Bangkok. The actual border used to be very inconspicuous and it was easy to miss the immigration authorities as you entered Malaysia, which caused lots of problems when you came to extend your stay or to depart. It's now much more visible but is still only open from 6 am to 6 pm.

Unusual Routes

There are also some unusual routes between Malaysia and Thailand. One of the oddest is to go to Kuala Perlis (the jumping-off point for Langkawi Island) and take a long-tail boat for about M$4 to Satun (or Satul), just across the border in Thailand. These are legal entry and exit points with immigration and custom posts. On arrival in Satun, it costs about 10B for the three km ride from the docks to immigration. You can then bus into Hat Yai. Again, make sure you get your passport properly stamped.

You may also be able to get a boat to Satun via Pulau Langkawi, a large Malaysian island on the Thai-Malaysian marine border. When they're running, boats to Langkawi leave Satun about every one or 1½ hours and cost from M$8 to M$10. Though it's cheaper to go straight to Satun from Kuala Perlis,

Langkawi is worth a stop if you have the time.

Another possibility is to take a yacht between Penang and Phuket. From time to time, there have been people running yachts back and forth on a regular basis.

Getting Around

AIR

Thai International has merged with Thai Airways so that international and domestic routes are now operated by the same company. They have a useful flight network around Thailand – the Airfares in Thailand chart shows the main routes and fares. It's not much used by budget travellers because ground level transport is generally so good. Domestic flights use turboprop, Boeing 737 and Airbus aircraft.

The internal fares are generally firmly fixed but it's quite possible that you'll be able to find cheaper tickets for the international sectors such as Bangkok to Penang. On some sectors, there are operations by propjet and jet aircraft. In these cases, fares will be lower on the prop aircraft than the jets. The fares shown on the airfares chart are all for jet travel.

In 1989, a new company called Bangkok Airways began flying selected routes – Bangkok-Ko Samui-Phuket and from Bangkok to Ranong. The company is trying to get rights to fly to other destinations in Thailand not served by Thai International, including several cities in the south and north-east. A company with amphibious aircraft, Yellowbirds, is trying to get permission to fly between various beach and island destinations.

BUS

The Thai bus service is widespread and phenomenally fast – terrifyingly so much of the time. Nothing would get me to sit in the front seats of a Thai bus as some drivers have a definite kamikaze streak. There are usually air-con buses as well as the normal ones, and on major routes there are also private, air-con tour buses. The air-con buses are so cold that blankets are handed out as a matter of routine and the service is so good it's embarrassing. You often get free drinks, pillows, free meals and even 'in-flight movies' on some routes! There are often a number of bus stations in a town – usually public and private stations.

TRAIN

The government-operated trains in Thailand are comfortable, frequent, punctual, moderately priced and rather slow. On comparable

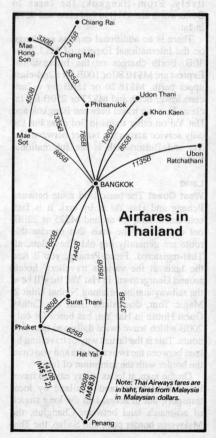

Airfares in Thailand

Chiang Rai
Mae Hong Son
Chiang Mai — 330B
375B
Udon Thani
535B
Phitsanulok
450B
Khon Kaen
1335B
Mae Sot
765B
10800B
855B
885B
Ubon Ratchathani
1135B
BANGKOK
1620B
1445B
1850B
3775B
385B
Surat Thani
Phuket
625B
Hat Yai
1410B (M$112)
1050B (M$83)
Penang

Note: Thai Airways fares are in baht, fares from Malaysia in Malaysian dollars.

routes, the buses can often be twice as fast, but the relatively low speed means you can often leave at a convenient hour in the evening and arrive at your destination at a pleasant hour in the morning.

Train fares plus sleeping-berth charges make train travel appear a bit more expensive than bus travel. However, with a sleeping berth you may save over the cost of the bus fare plus one night's hotel costs. The trains have a further advantage over the buses in that they're far safer and the food on board is really very good. All in all, Thailand's railways are a fine way to travel.

There are four main railway lines plus a few minor side routes. The main ones are: the northern line to Chiang Mai; the southern line to Hat Yai (where the line splits up to enter Malaysia on the west coast via Padang Besar and to terminate near the east coast at Sungai Kolok); the eastern line to Ubon Ratchathani; and the north-eastern line to Nong Khai.

Very useful condensed railway timetables are available in English at the Hualamphong railway station in Bangkok. These contain schedules and fares for all rapid and express trains as well as a few ordinary trains.

In mid-1991, the State Railway of Thailand (SRT) announced that it would start a new express service. It is hoped that travel between Chiang Mai and Bangkok will now take 10 hours as opposed to the 13 hours it took previously. The new trains will operate on the Bangkok to Ubon Ratchathani, Bangkok to Udon Thani and Bangkok-Surat Thani-Hat Yai routes.

Bookings

Unfortunately, the trains are often heavily booked, so it's wise to book ahead. At the Hualamphong station in Bangkok, you can book trains on any route in Thailand. The advance booking office is open from 8.30 am to 6 pm, Monday to Friday, and from 8.30 am to 12 noon, on Saturday, Sunday and holidays. Seats, berths or cabins may be booked up to 90 days in advance.

Charges

There is a 30B surcharge for express trains and a 20B surcharge for rapid trains – the greater speed is mainly through fewer stops. Some 2nd and 3rd-class services are air-con in which case there is a 50B surcharge. Sleeping berths also cost extra. In 2nd class, upper berths are 70B, lower berths are 100B or both an extra 100B if the sleeping berths are air-con. The lower berths are cooler since they have a window whereas upper do not. In 1st class, the berths cost 250B per person in two berth cabins and 350B in single berth cabins. Sleepers are only available in 1st and 2nd class, but that apart, 3rd class is not too bad.

Fares are roughly double for 2nd class over 3rd and double again for 1st class over 2nd. Count on around 180B for a 500-km trip in 2nd class. You can break a trip for two days for each 200 km travelled but the ticket must be endorsed by the stationmaster, which costs 1B.

Rail Passes

The SRT issues a 'Visit Thailand Rail Pass' that's good for 20-days unlimited travel anywhere on the rail system. The Blue Pass includes unlimited 2nd and 3rd-class passage but doesn't include supplementary charges for rapid or express service, air-con or sleeping berths. The cost is 1500B for adults and 750B for children under 12. The Red Pass also covers unlimited 2nd and 3rd-class travel but includes all supplementary charges – it costs 3000B for adults and 1500B for children under 12.

The passes can be purchased at Hualamphong station's advance booking office. On busy lines (eg from Bangkok to Chiang Mai or from Bangkok to Surat Thani), however, you'll still need to make advance reservations.

HITCHING

Although hitching is not the relatively easy proposition it is in Malaysia, it is possible to hitch through Thailand. In places, traffic will be relatively light and the wait for a ride can be quite long. It is certainly done though. A traveller reports:

Hitching in Thailand is *great!* Very easy. Truck drivers usually give rides and hand out cigarettes but only speak Thai. The truck drivers are all speed freaks but very cool. I hitched all the way from Bangkok to Hat Yai (with stops at many places) and never waited more than five or 10 minutes for a ride.

I would hate to see it get abused though. The police at road checks in the south often found me rides when it was dark. People are always willing to throw you in the back of pick-ups and I even got two rides in old Fords. Great! Truck drivers stop at little truck pitstops to change tyres and you meet really neat people. Songthaews sometimes pick you up just for fun. Some of the best times are had just walking along in the sunset and talking to the farmers. Besides, who needs the bus schedules, I'm on vacation.

BOAT

There are lots of opportunities to travel by river or sea in Thailand. You can take boats out to many offshore islands and there are many riverboats operating on Thailand's large number of waterways. The traditional Thai runabout for these river trips is the long-tail boat, so called because the engine operates the propeller via a long open tailshaft. The engines are often regular car engines with the whole thing mounted on gimbals – the engine is swivelled to steer the boat.

LOCAL TRANSPORT

There is a wide variety of local transport available in Thailand. In the big cities, you'll find taxis, which are never metered. Always negotiate your fare before departure. Then there are *samlors*, Thai for three-wheels. There are regular bicycle samlors (cycle rickshaws) and also motorised samlors which are usually known as *tuk-tuks* from the nasty put-put noise their woefully silenced two-stroke engines make. You'll find bicycle samlors in all the smaller towns throughout Thailand. Tuk-tuks will be found in all the larger towns as well as in Bangkok. Both of these systems of transport require bargaining and agreement on a fare before departure, but in many towns there is a more or less fixed fare anywhere in town.

Songthaew literally means 'two-rows' and these small pick-ups with a row of seats down each side also serve a purpose rather like tuk-tuks or minibuses. In some cities, certain routes are run on a regular basis by songthaews or minibuses.

Finally, there are regular bus services in certain big cities. Usually in Thailand, fares are fixed for any route up to a certain length – in Bangkok up to 10 km. Of course, there are all sorts of unusual means of getting around – horse-drawn carriages in some smaller towns, and ferries and riverboats in many places. In some of the more touristed centres, you can also rent motorbikes or bicycles at very economical rates.

Bangkok

Thailand's coronary-inducing capital is surprisingly full of quiet escapes if you make your way out of the busy streets. Before you get out, you will have to put up with some of the worst traffic jams in Asia, noise, pollution, annual floods and sticky weather. It's hardly surprising that many people develop an instant dislike for the place, but beneath the surface Bangkok has plenty to offer. There are lots of sights, cheap accommodation and some excellent food.

Bangkok, or Krung Thep as it is known to the Thais, became the capital of Thailand after the Burmese sacked Ayuthaya in 1767. At first, the Siamese capital was shifted to Thonburi, across the river from Bangkok, but in 1782 it was moved to its present site.

Orientation

The Chao Phraya River divides Bangkok from Thonburi. Almost the only reason to cross to Thonburi (apart from the Southern bus terminals or the Bangkok Noi railway station) is to see the Temple of the Dawn.

The main Bangkok railway line virtually cuts off a loop of the river and within that loop is the older part of the city, including most of the interesting temples and the

Chinatown area. The popular Banglamphu travellers' centre is also in this area.

East of the railway line is the new area of the city where most of the modern hotels are located. One of the most important roads is Rama IV Rd which runs right in front of the Hualamphong railway station and eventually gets you to the Malaysia Hotel area. A little to the north, and approximately parallel to Rama IV, is Rama I which eventually becomes Sukhumvit Rd with many popular hotels, restaurants and entertainment spots.

Information

Tourist Offices There are tourist offices at the airport and in Bangkok – the Thai tourist office is very good for detailed leaflets and information sheets. You'll find the city office of the Tourist Authority of Thailand (TAT) at 4 Ratchadamnoen Nok (☎ 282 1143/7). It's open from 8.30 am to 4.30 pm every day.

One thing to buy from them (or elsewhere) as quickly as possible is a Bangkok bus map (40B). It's very easy to follow and an absolute necessity for coping with Bangkok's frenetic bus system. *Nancy Chandler's Map of Bangkok* is a colourful map of Bangkok's unusual attractions. It has all the Chao Phraya Express river-taxi stops in Thai script and costs 70B.

Money Thai banks have currency exchange kiosks in many areas of Bangkok, heavily concentrated in the Sukhumvit Rd, Khao San Rd, Siam Square and Silom Rd areas. Hours vary from location to location but they tend to be open from 8 am to 8 pm daily.

Close to the GPO are a number of moneychangers along New (Charoen Krung) Rd, good if you want to buy other Asian currency such as Burmese kyats.

Post & Telecommunications The GPO is on New (Charoen Krung) Rd and has a very efficient poste restante service open from 8 am to 8 pm on weekdays and from 9 am to 1 pm on weekends and holidays. Every single letter is recorded in a large book and you're charged 1B for each one. They also have a

packing service here if you want to send parcels home.

After the GPO is shut, you can send letters from the adjacent central telegraph office which is open 24 hours. This is also a place where you can make international telephone calls at any time of the day or night. Hotels and guest houses usually make service charges on every call, whether they are collect or not.

Travel Agents Bangkok is packed with travel agents of every manner and description but if you're looking for cheap airline tickets it's wise to be cautious. Ask other travellers for advice about agents. The really bad ones change their names frequently so saying this week that J Travel, for example, is not to be recommended is useless when they're called something else next week. Wherever possible, try to see the tickets before you hand over the money.

The STA Travel agent in Bangkok is Tour Center (☎ 281 5314) at the Thai Hotel, 78 Prachatipatai Rd. They sell discount air tickets and seem reliable. We have yet to receive a negative report about them.

Three agents that are permitted to do Thai railway bookings at regular SRT fares are Airland (☎ 251 9495), 866 Ploenchit Rd; Songserm Travel Center (☎ 250 0768, 252 5190), 121/7 Soi Chalermnit, Phayathai Rd; and Viang Travel (☎ 280 1385), Viengtai Hotel, Tanee Rd. Other agencies can arrange rail bookings but will slap on a surcharge of 50B or more per ticket. The TAT Head Office has the addresses of all the different sales agencies.

Bookshops Bangkok has some of the best bookshops in South-East Asia. Asia Books at Soi 15-17, Sukhumvit Rd, has an excellent selection of English-language books. There are also branches in the Landmark Hotel on Sukhumvit Rd, opposite Soi 5, and in the Peninsula Plaza. DK (Duang Kamol) Books, with branches in Siam Square, the Mahboonkrong Center, Patpong Rd and Soi 8, Sukhumvit Rd, also has a wide selection.

On Patpong Rd, The Bookseller, is

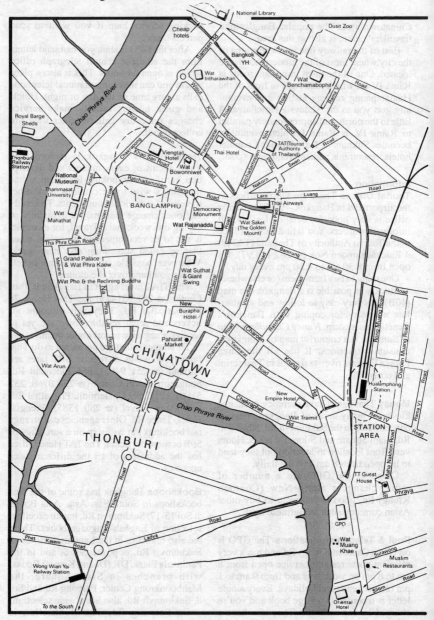

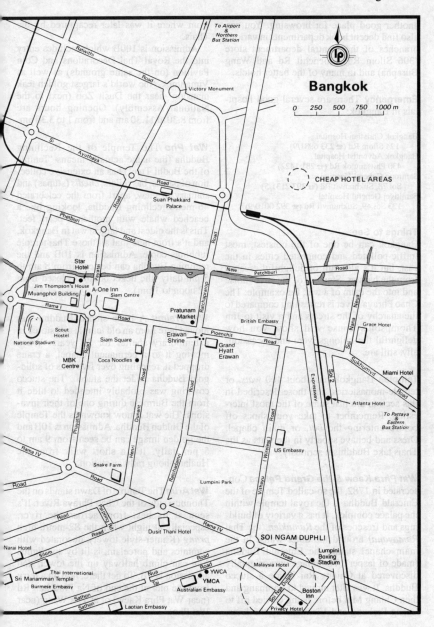

Bangkok

0   250   500   750   1000 m

CHEAP HOTEL AREAS

Victory Monument

Ratwithi Road

Si Ayuthaya Road

Phetburi Road

Suan Phakkard Palace

New Petchburi Road

Star Hotel

Jim Thompson's House
Muangphol Building

A-One Inn
Siam Centre

Rama I Road

Scout Hostel

National Stadium

Pratunam Market

Erawan Shrine

Grand Hyatt Erawan

British Embassy

Ploenchit Road

Sukhumvit

Grace Hotel

Nana

Soi 2

Miami Hotel

Atlanta Hotel

To Pattaya & Eastern Bus Station

Siam Square

MBK Centre

Coca Noodles

Phyathai Road

Rama IV Road

Dunant Road

Henri Dunant Road

Ratchadamri Road

Snake Farm

US Embassy

Vithayu (Wireless) Road

Lumpini Park

Dusit Thani Hotel

Rama IV Road

SOI NGAM DUPHLI

Narai Hotel

Silom Road

Thai International

Sri Mariamman Temple

Burmese Embassy

Surasak Road

Nua Road

Tai Road

YWCA

YMCA

Australian Embassy

Sathon Road

Laotian Embassy

Lumpini Boxing Stadium

Malaysia Hotel

Sri Ngam Duphli

Boston Inn

Privacy Hotel

To Airport & Northern Bus Station

another good place for browsing. You can also find decent book departments in various branches of the Central department store (306 Silom Rd, Ploenchit Rd and Wang Burapha) and in many of the better hotels.

Emergency There are several good hospitals in Bangkok:

Bangkok Christian Hospital
    124 Silom Rd (☎ 233 6981/9)
Bangkok Adventist Hospital
    430 Phitsanulok Rd (☎ 281 1422)
Samrong General Hospital
    Soi 78, Sukhumvit Rd (☎ 393 2131/5)
Samitivej General Hospital
    133 Soi 49, Sukhumvit Rd (☎ 392 0010/9)

Things to See

Bangkok can be one of the noisiest, most traffic-polluted and congested cities in the east, but it's also full of delightful escapes from the hassles. Step out of the street noise and into the calm of a wat, for example. The Chao Phraya River is refreshing compared to the anarchy of the streets and a visit to Jim Thompson's house will show you how delightful the khlongs were and, occasionally, still are.

Temples Bangkok has about 400 *wats*, or temple-monasteries, and those described in this section are just some of the most interesting. Remember to take your shoes off before entering the *bot*, or main chapel. Dress and behave soberly in the wats as the Thais take Buddhism seriously.

Wat Phra Kaew & the Grand Palace Consecrated in 1782, the so-called Temple of the Emerald Buddha is the royal temple within the palace complex. It has a variety of buildings and frescoes of the *Ramakien* (the Thai *Ramayana*) around the outer walls. In the main chapel stands the Emerald Buddha (made of jasper). The image was originally discovered at Chiang Rai inside a stucco Buddha. It was later moved to Lampang and then Chiang Mai before being carried off to Luang Prabang and Vientiane by the Laos,

from where it was later recaptured by the Thais.

Admission is 100B which includes entry into the Royal Thai Decorations and Coin Pavilion (on the same grounds) as well as Vimanmek, 'the world's largest golden teak mansion' near the Dusit Zoo (next to the National Assembly). Opening hours are from 8.30 to 11.30 am and from 1 to 3.30 pm.

Wat Pho The Temple of the Reclining Buddha (the name actually means 'Temple of the Bodhi Tree') has an extensive collection of panels, bas reliefs, *chedis* (stupas) and statuary to view, apart from the celebrated 46-metre reclining Buddha, looking like a beached whale with mother-of-pearl feet. This is the oldest and largest wat in Bangkok, and it's from here that all those Thai temple rubbings come. Admission is 10B and the reclining Buddha can be seen from 8 am to 5 pm daily (the ticket booth is closed from 12 noon to 1 pm).

Wat Traimit A large stucco Buddha was moved here from an old temple and stored in a temporary shelter for 20 years. When moving it to a permanent chapel, a crane dropped it, revealing over five tons of solid-gold Buddha under the stucco. The stucco covering was probably intended to hide it from the Burmese during one of their invasions. The wat is now known as the Temple of the Golden Buddha. Admission is 10B and the golden image can be seen from 9 am to 5 pm daily. It's a short walk from the Hualamphong railway station.

Wat Arun The Temple of Dawn stands on the Thonburi side of the Chao Phraya River. It's seen at its best from across the river, especially at night when the 82-metre-high *prang* (Khmer-style tower), decorated with ceramics and porcelain, is lit by spotlights. You can climb halfway up the tower, and admission is 5B. To get there, hop on a ferry from the pier at the end of Na Phra Lan Rd (near Wat Phra Kaew) or at Tha Wang (near Wat Pho).

Wat Benchamabophit The Marble Temple is relatively new (built by Rama V in 1899) and has a huge collection of Buddha images from all periods of Thai Buddhist art. There is a pond full of turtles beside the temple – admission is 10B.

Wat Saket The Golden Mount is a most ugly lump of masonry atop an artificial hill. As Bangkok is pancake flat, it provides a fine view from the top. Admission is free, but it costs 5B to the top terrace.

Other Temples Across Mahachai Rd from Wat Saket is **Wat Rajanadda**, the site of a popular market selling Buddha images, amulets and charms. **Wat Bowonniwet** on Phra Sumen Rd is the headquarters for a minority Thammayut monastic sect. **Wat Intharawihan**, just north of Banglamphu on Wisut Kasat Rd (near the junction with Samsen Rd), has an enormous standing Buddha image. The 'giant swing', **Sao Ching Cha**, used to be the centre for a spectacular festival which is no longer held.

A small Hindu temple, **Sri Mariamman**, sits on the corner of Pan and Silom Rds. The three main deities contained therein are Khanthakumara, Ganesh and Uma Devi, although a whole pantheon of Hindu and Buddhist statuary lines one wall.

National Museum Supposedly the largest museum in South-East Asia, this is a good place for an overview of Thai art and culture before you start exploring the former Thai capitals. All the periods and styles of Thai history and art are shown here. The museum on Na Phrathat Rd is open from 9 am to 12 noon and from 1 to 4 pm, but is closed on Monday and Tuesday – admission is 30B. There are free tours of the museum, conducted in English, on Tuesday (Thai culture), Wednesday (Buddhism) and Thursday (Thai art) – all begin at 9.30 am.

Jim Thompson's House On Soi Kasem San 2, Rama I Rd, this is the beautiful house of the American Thai silk entrepreneur Jim Thompson, who disappeared without trace

back in 1967 in the Cameron Highlands in Malaysia. His house, built from parts of a number of traditional wooden Thai houses and furnished with a superb collection of Thai art and furnishings, is simply delightful. Pleasantly sited on a small *khlong* (canal), the house is open daily from 8 am to 5 pm. Admission is 40B for anyone under 25 and 100B for everyone else.

Floating Market The Thonburi floating market is really a tourist trap – although there are still plenty of produce boats, there are often even more tourist boats. It's picturesque but with all the tourist shops, snake farms and the like it all looks a bit artificial. Tours cost around 120B and generally depart from the Oriental Hotel's pier, where a group can also hire their own boat. The various travel agencies around Banglamphu or the Malaysia Hotel book these tours and they're generally OK.

An alternative and far less touristed floating market can be seen at Khlong Damnoen Saduak, 104 km west from Bangkok, beyond Nakhon Pathom. If you want to go there, you'll probably have to stay in Nakhon Pathom and take an early morning bus to Samut Songkhram, getting off at Damnoen Saduak. The market reaches its peak around 8 am.

Thai Classical Dance The National Theatre hosts classical Thai dance performances periodically – call 224 1342 weekdays between 8.30 am and 4.30 pm for the current schedule. Special exhibition performances by the Chulalongkorn University Dance Club are offered the last Friday of every month at 5.30 pm.

To see some Thai classical dance for free, hang out at the Lak Muang Shrine near Sanam Luang or the Erawan Shrine. Another good venue is the Center for Traditional Performing Arts on the 4th floor of the Bangkok Bank, just off Ratchadamnoen Rd in Bangkok. Free public performances are given every Friday at 5 pm – arrive at least an hour early for a seat.

Several Bangkok restaurants sponsor

dinner performances that feature a mix of dance and martial arts, all very touristy (the food is usually nothing special), for around 250 to 500B. At 11 am on Thursday and Sunday, there's a dance and martial arts performance (the Kodak Siam show) at the historic Oriental Hotel for 80B.

Other An interesting **river tour** in Bangkok can be made by taking a Chao Phraya River taxi from Soi Klongsung (lots of buses go there) as far north as Nonthaburi. This is a three-hour, 10B trip with plenty to see along the way. The Klong Bangkok Noi canal taxi route from Tha Phra Chan, next to Thammasat University, only costs a few baht and takes you along a colourful route, seemingly far from Bangkok.

All sorts of oddities can be found at the enormous **Weekend Market** which takes place opposite the Northern bus terminal. Take an air-con bus No 2, 3, 9, 10 or 13. It's open all day on Saturday and Sunday, and you can find almost anything there from opium pipes to unusual posters. It also has lots of other activities to watch. There are a number of other interesting markets around Bangkok.

At the **Pasteur Institute (Snake Farm)** on Rama IV Rd, snakes are milked of their venom every day at 11 am and 2 pm (11 am only on weekends and holidays) – admission is 80B. Bangkok has a **Chinatown** with a thieves' market and an Indian district on its periphery.

Thai boxing, where they kick as well as punch, is quite a scene. There are stadiums at Lumpini (Rama IV Rd) and Ratchadamnoen Nok Rd (by the TAT office). Admission prices start from around 180B and go up to 800B for ringside seats. The out-of-the-ring activity is sometimes even more frenzied and entertaining than that within the ring.

The **Oriental Hotel** is an attraction in its own right. It's the Raffles of Bangkok and is consistently voted the best hotel in Asia. Somerset Maugham and Joseph Conrad are among the Oriental's historic guests (commemorated in the hotel's Authors Wing). Be

sure to dress nicely or you may be barred from entering the lobby. Some Patpong Rd bars are good places for whiling away an afternoon watching video movies.

Oddities At the shrine outside the Erawan Hotel, people come to seek help for some wish they want granted – like their girlfriend to marry them. The person promises that if the grant is made they will pay for something to be done – a favourite promise is to pay for 20 minutes dancing by the Thai dancers who are always ready and waiting for such commissions.

In the British Embassy grounds (access difficult), a statue of Queen Victoria is prayed to by women without children since the good Queen is reputed to be very helpful with pregnancies. At the Southern and Northern bus terminals, there are amazing family-planning supermarkets run by the enterprising Mr Mechai who revolutionised and popularised family planning and contraception in Thailand.

Outside Bangkok The **Ancient City** (Muang Boran in Thai) is an artificial tourist attraction 33 km out of Bangkok which spreads over 80 hectares. Admission is a steep 270B and you can get there on a bus No 25 from Sukhumvit Rd to Pak Nam and then on a small local bus.

There is also a **Crocodile Farm** in the same area and the **Rose Garden Country Resort** south of Bangkok. About 15 km out of the city, there's an excellent swimming pool complex at **Siam Park.** Bus No 27 gets you there, although not every No 27 goes to Siam Park. Entry is 60B, which ensures it is not very crowded.

Places to Stay
There are all sorts of places to stay in Bangkok with a wide range of prices but they are mainly concentrated in certain distinct areas.

Banglamphu is the number one travellers' centre with a simply amazing number of budget-priced guest houses, together with restaurants, snack bars, travel agents and all the other back-up facilities. A big advantage of Banglamphu is that it's very central for many of Bangkok's major tourist attractions.

Soi Ngam Duphli, at one time the main travellers' centre, is quieter and slightly more expensive but still attracts many visitors. Then there's the Sukhumvit Rd area with some travellers' hotels amongst the more expensive places. Much more central are the noisy Hualamphong station, Chinatown and Siam Square areas.

Competition in the Banglamphu area is so fierce that you can still get a room in Bangkok for scarcely more than it was 10 years ago. The cheapest rooms start from around 70B for a single or 100B for a double

1	Phra Athit Pier (for Chao Phraya Express)	15	Chana Songkhram Police Station
2	UNICEF	16	Viengtai Hotel
3	Beer & Peachy Guest House	17	Post Office
4	New Siam Guest House	18	Wat Bowonniwet
5	Ngam Pit & Apple Guest House	19	National Museum
6	Rose Garden & Golf Guest House	20	Royal Hotel
7	Wang Ngar Restaurant	21	Bovorn-Nivet Youth Hostel
8	Merry V Guest House	22	Nice Guest House
9	Mango Guest House	23	Central Guest House
10	Siam Commercial Bank	24	New Privacy Guest House
11	Chusri Guest House	25	Post Office
12	Tum I/Haircut Guest House	26	Sweety Guest House
13	Apple Guest House	27	Democracy Guest House
14	Wat Chana Songkhram	28	Vijit Restaurant
		29	Prasuri Guest House

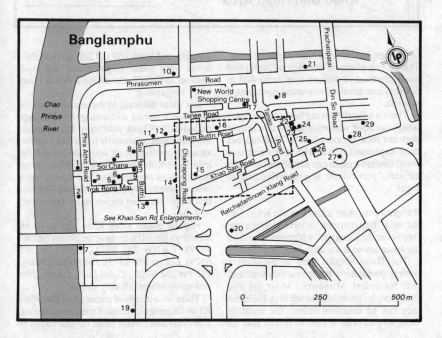

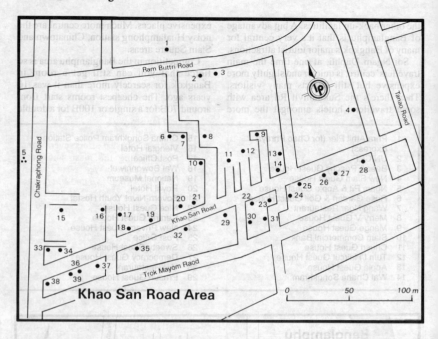

Khao San Road Area

in the Banglamphu and Hualamphong areas. The air-con places in Soi Ngam Duphli and along Sukhumvit Rd are now from 400 to 500B. Some hotels give student discounts if you ask.

There's a hotel booking desk at the airport which can book you into many of the cheaper (but not rock-bottom) hotels. Thailand has been experiencing a tourist boom and as a result finding a room can sometimes be quite difficult, particularly if you arrive late at night.

Banglamphu Also known as the Khao San Rd area, Banglamphu is over towards the river, near the Democracy Monument and on the route towards the airport.

The Banglamphu area is pleasantly central, particularly for the various wats and the National Museum. Most of the Banglamphu guest houses are very basic but they can be excellent value. The standard Banglamphu price is around 70B or 80B for

a single, and from 100 to 120B for a double. Some very basic guest houses are even cheaper in the off seasons, so it doesn't hurt to try bargaining.

It's quite difficult to recommend any of them since names and management change periodically. Check your room first because, in some cases, a 'room' is just a tiny cubicle, virtually partitioned off with cardboard. Like losmen at Kuta Beach on Bali, there are so many places around Khao San Rd it's just a case of wandering about until you find one that suits. The map shows many, but not all of them.

Popular places along Khao San Rd or on the alleys just off it include the *Bonny* (☎ 281 9877), *Top* (☎ 281 9954), *Hello* (☎ 281 8579), *Lek* (☎ 281 2775), *160 (Marco Polo)*, *VIP* (☎ 282 5090), *Good Luck, Chada, Nat* and many others, all very similar.

There are a couple of places along Khao San Rd which are not in the usual guest house mould. The *Khao San Palace Hotel* (☎ 282 0578) at

1	Viengtai Hotel
2	Roy's Snacks
3	ST Guest House
4	Harn & VS Guest House
5	Wat Chana Songkhram
6	Student Guest House & several others
7	Cafe Charlie
8	Dolls Guest House & several others
9	Charoendee Hotel
10	Buddy Beer Restaurant
11	Khao San Palace Hotel
12	Nit Jaroen Suke Hotel
13	Best Guest House
14	GTA & Nat Guest House
15	Chuanpis, Chakrapong & J Guest House
16	Wally Guest House
17	Chart Guest House, No Name Bar & Royal India Restaurant
18	Hello Guest House & Restaurant
19	Mama's Guest House
20	Lek Guest House
21	Buddy Guest House
22	Dior Guest House
23	Marco Polo/160 Guest House
24	VIP Guest House
25	Rit's Cafe & Ice Guest House
26	Grand Guest House
27	CH Guest House
28	Chada Guest House
29	Popular Cafes
30	Bonny & Top Guest House
31	Good Luck Guest House
32	PB Guest House
33	Chana Songkhram Police Station
34	Siam Guest House
35	Chart Guest House
36	PR Guest House
37	Hello Restaurant
38	Ploy Guest House
39	NS Guest House

139 Khao San Rd is Chinese-owned and costs from 200B for a room with a fan and a bath. Next door is the popular *Nit Jaroen Suke* (or Nith Charoen Suke) (☎ 281 9872) which has similar rooms and rates but slightly better service. The *Charoendee Hotel*, at No 189, is a funky old hotel that is run-down but a change from the usual Khao San Rd guest houses – rooms cost around 120B. The *Viengtai Hotel* on Ram Buttri Rd

is a big jump above the regular Khao San Rd places with single/double rooms at 900/1200B.

A new, as yet unnamed soi has been constructed parallel and just south of Khao San Rd, which connects with Chakraphong Rd via Trok Mayom. Here you'll find the *Joe, 7-Holder* and, by now, probably several other guest houses.

There's a small soi east off Tanao Rd (at the end of Khao San) that offers several more cheapies, including the plain and basic *Central* (☎ 282 0667), *Nice, New Privacy, Sweety* (☎ 281 6756), *C H II* and *Nat II* guest houses, all at the usual Khao San rates. This network of alleys is fairly quiet since it's back off the main road.

Another relatively quiet area is the network of sois and alleys between Chakraphong Rd and Phra Athit Rd to the west of Khao San Rd, including Soi Rambuttri, Soi Chana and Trok Rong Mai. Good choices include the *New Siam* (Soi Chana, ☎ 282 4554), *Merry V* (Soi Rambuttri), *Mango* (Soi Rambuttri), *Tum 1* (Rambuttri Rd), *Apple* (Soi Rambuttri), *Rose Garden* (Trok Rong Mai; ☎ 281 8366) and the *Golf* (Trok Rong Mai). On Phra Athit Rd, near the river, are the *Beer* and *Peachy* (☎ 281 6471) guest houses, which are slightly up-market for Banglamphu with rates from 100 to 300B.

The guest houses along Chakrapong Rd tend to be a bit noisy as it's a fairly major thoroughfare. North of Khao San Rd, off Phra Sumen Rd, are a couple of newer guest houses. The *Apple II* on Trok Kai Chae is a find with a 40B dorm and 100B doubles.

Khao San Rd is an amazingly cosmopolitan place these days. Back in the old Asia overland days of the early 1970s, there were the three Ks – travellers' 'bottlenecks' where you were bound to meet up with anybody travelling trans-Asia. These days you could substitute Khao San for Kabul to make it three with Kuta and Kathmandu.

All along the road are the little signs indicating it's a travellers' hang-out – countless small guest houses and restaurants with fruit salad and muesli on the menu. At night, they spill out first across the sidewalk and then right into the street. Loud rock music booms out from the cassette sellers; clothes are sold from shops and sidewalk stalls; books are bought and traded; travel agents offer cheap tickets and fake student cards; and there are places to store your baggage or wash your clothes.

Buses and taxis seem to come and go constantly, disgorging one band of backpackers and picking up another who are patiently waiting with their packs by the roadside. This one block of intense activity is definitely the travellers' centre of Bangkok.

Around Banglamphu More guest houses have started to pop up around the Banglamphu area. Go up Chakrapong Rd and then Samsen Rd (it changes names) north from Banglamphu and after about a km, just before the National Library, Phitsanulok Rd dead-ends on Samsen Rd and Si Ayuthaya Rd crosses it. At 71 Si Ayuthaya Rd, on the river side of Samsen Rd, is the very popular *Sawatdee* (☎ 281 0757). It's very basic but clean and well-kept and the family who run it are friendly and helpful. It's reasonably quiet (except in the rooms right at the front) and conveniently close to a terrific market as well as a Chao Phraya Express stop on the river. Rooms are 60B, 80B and 100B.

Beside Sawatdee, and purportedly owned by a member of the same family, is the *Shanti Lodge* (☎ 281 2497) where rooms are 60/120B. At 57 Si Ayuthaya Rd, is another family branch, the similarly priced *Paradise* (☎ 282 4094) which has dorm beds for 50B. Keep an eye on your bill at the Paradise as some travellers have reported overcharging. There's a lot of friendly family competition between these places. One alley back, at No 83, the *Tavee Guest House* (☎ 280 1447) costs 110B for doubles and has a 50B dorm. This is becoming another little travellers' enclave.

Close by here is the *Bangkok International Youth Hostel* (☎ 282 0950) at 25/2 Phitsanulok Rd. It has a 40B dorm and singles/doubles with toilet and shower at 150/200B if you have a youth hostel card (10B more without).

Back from here towards Khao San Rd, the *Noi Guest House* (☎ 282 2898) of Chiang Mai fame has recently opened a branch in Banglamphu on Soi Pantom between Phra Sumen and Wisut Kasat Rds. It's on the 4th floor of an apartment building and gets a good breeze most of the time. Rooms are 60B per person and there's a 50B dorm.

Off by itself, near the Northern bus terminal and the Weekend Market, is the *KT (Kam Thorn) Guest House*, at Inthamana 44, off Sutthisaan Rd. Rooms in this beautiful old family-run house are 80/160B. You can get there on bus Nos 54, 74 or 204.

Soi Ngam Duphli Just off Rama IV Rd, this was for many years the travellers' centre of Bangkok but the places are no longer the best value to be found. Get there on an ordinary bus No 4, 13, 14, 22, 27, 46, 47 or 74, or a No 7 air-con bus, getting off just after the roundabout on Rama IV Rd.

Once, the prime attraction here was the *Malaysia Hotel* – back in the Vietnam War days this was one of the hotels quickly thrown together for the R&R trade. It is multistorey and has air-con, a swimming pool and all that sort of thing. When the war ended they decided to cut prices to the bone and fill it with the travellers who were invading the region at that time. Of course, in the intervening years, the prices have crept higher and were prevented from going through the roof simply because no maintenance was done on the building at all. The Malaysia was a sort of working test on how long a building could hang together with much abuse and no care.

Now the Malaysia has been cleaned up and is just another mid-range hotel. A backpack these days looks quite out of place in the lobby (now filled with video machines) and, although the famous noticeboard has made a small-scale reappearance, it's really just a memory. The Malaysia (☎ 286 3582) is at 54 Soi Ngam Duphli. There are 120 rooms, all with air-con and bathroom from 414 to 650B a single, and from 486 to 700B for a twin.

Right across the road is the *Tungmahamek*, or *Privacy Hotel* (☎ 286 8811), which acts as an overflow centre for the Malaysia Hotel. It's probably a bit quieter, and the rooms, all air-con, are 300B for a double. The third largest

Soi Ngam Duphli place is the *Boston Inn*, just off Soi Ngam Duphli on Soi Si Bamphen. Rooms here start at 170B but they are extremely run-down and represent perhaps the worst value in Bangkok.

Today, there are also many smaller guest houses around Soi Ngam Duphli – in that respect, it's becoming a quieter, slightly up-market version of Khao San Rd. They include the *Anna Guest House* at 21/30 Soi Ngam Duphli or the *Lee Guest House* at 21/38, each with rooms starting at 80B. The *Sweet House Complex* (☎ 286 5774) at 5/24 Soi Ngam Duphli has single/double/triple rooms at 60/70/100B, rooms with bath for 140B and better air-con rooms from 200 to 250B.

There are three *Freddy Guest Houses* in the area with rooms from 80 to 100B. *Freddy's II* (☎ 286 7826) seems to be popular. Other places to stay include *My Place*, *Sabai House*, *Kit's*, *Welcome*, *Madam*, *Sala Thai Daily Mansion* (☎ 287 1436), *Lee 3* and the *RSC*. Apart from the hotels there are also lots of travel agencies, restaurants, bars and all manner of 'services' in the area.

The *YWCA* (☎ 286 1936) is close to the Soi Ngam Duphli area at 13 Sathon Tai Rd. Rooms have air-con, baths and cost from around 300B. There's also a 100B dormitory. This Y takes only women guests and has a restaurant, swimming pool and other facilities. At 27 Sathon Tai is the more expensive *YMCA* (☎ 286 5134), where rooms start at 600B – both men and women can stay here.

Sukhumvit Rd North of Rama IV Rd and running out from the centre, much like Rama IV, this is a major tourist centre. Take an ordinary bus No 2, 25, 40, 48 or an air-con No 1, 8, 11 or 13. The hotels here are not Bangkok's top-notch places, although most of them are out of the budget traveller's price range. There are a few worthwhile places scattered in amongst them, however. All the small lanes running off Sukhumvit Rd are called Soi, and then a number – so the bigger the number the further up (east) Sukhumvit

Rd it is. All even numbers are to the south and odd to the north.

Starting at the Rama I end (Rama I changes into Sukhumvit Rd), you'll find the *Atlanta Hotel* at 78 Soi 2. At one time, (before the Malaysia rose to the top) this was the number one travellers' hotel, but then for a while there were so many dope raids nobody could get any sleep and its popularity plummeted. Now it's reasonably popular once again and has rooms from 150/200B with fan but shared bath and up to 250/300/350B with air-con. Facilities include a restaurant and swimming pool.

Further up at Soi 13, the *Miami Hotel* (☎ 253 5611/3) is one of the cheaper tourist hotels. Rooms with fan are 180B, or around 500B with air-con. The Miami was once comfortable, clean and well kept but recent reports says it's a dive – ask to see a room first and get a reduction if it's not up to par.

The *Crown* (☎ 258 0318) at Soi 29 was once a mid-range R&R joint in the same class as the old Miami but standards here have also been slipping. Rooms start at around 220B and all have air-con. The *Golden Palace Hotel* at 15 Soi 1 is better and costs from around 300B. There are many other hotels tucked here and there along Sukhumvit sois.

Guest houses are also beginning to appear on Sukhumvit Rd, just like everywhere else in Bangkok. Try the *Disra House* (☎ 258 5102) between Soi 33 and Soi 33/1 (off the access street to the Villa cinema). Clean, comfortable rooms range from 80 to 120B. Of similar standard is the *SV Guest House* (☎ 253 0606) at 19/35-36 Sukhumvit Rd, Soi 19.

Chinatown-Hualamphong Station This is one of the cheapest areas in Bangkok but also one of the noisiest. The traffic along Rama IV Rd has to be heard to be believed. There are several hotels right alongside the station but these station-area cheapies are no bargain compared to the even cheaper places over in Banglamphu, and it's nowhere near as pleasant a place to stay.

The *Sri Hualamphong Hotel* (☎ 214 2610)

at 445 Rong Muang Rd is one of the better ones with rooms at around 100B with fan. The *Sahakit (Shakij) Hotel* is a few doors down towards Rama IV Rd, while between the two is the rather basic *Jeep Seng* (☎ 214 2808) and the equally forgettable *Toonkee*. There are numerous good cheap eating places right around the station but take care here – some of Bangkok's best pickpockets and razor artists work the station area.

Across Rama IV near Wat Traimit, the *New Empire Hotel* (☎ 234 6990) at 572 Yaowarat Rd has doubles from 190B up to 300B with air-con. It is kind of noisy but in a good Chinatown location near the intersection of Yaowarat and New (Charoen Krung) Rds. The *Burapha* (☎ 221 3545/9), at the intersection of Chakraphet and New (Charoen Krung) Rds and on the edge of Chinatown, is similar. There are a number of other Chinatown hotels around, but most don't have signs in English.

There is, however, one place in this area which is very popular with travellers and that is the *TT Guest House* (☎ 235 8006), about a 10-minute walk south from the station at 138 Soi Wat Maha Phuttharam, Maha Nakhon Rd. It's just off Si Phaya Rd and a short walk from the GPO and river. From the station, turn left and walk a block along Rama IV Rd then turn right (south) down Maha Nakhon Rd. There will be signs close to Si Phaya Rd. It's worth the effort to find this comparatively large, well-kept and popular place. Dorm beds are 50B, single/double rooms 60/100B and there's a spacious open-air sitting and restaurant area downstairs.

Siam Square Near the National Stadium, on Rama I Rd, there are more places including the *National Scout Hostel* (Sala Vajiravut) which is one of the cheapest places in Bangkok. You'll find it on the 4th floor of the National Scout Executive Committee Building near the National Stadium. There are five dorms, each with 12 beds at 30B each. Women can stay (there's no need to be a Boy Scout but the dorms are gender-segregated) and it's not a bad place, although the

traffic is a little noisy. Bring a padlock for your cupboard. Bus Nos 15, 25, 40, 48, 54, 73 or 204 will get you there. The No 29 airport bus goes near this area, stopping at the Rama I and Phayathai Rds intersection.

Nearby Soi Kasem San 1, off Rama I opposite the National Stadium, has a couple of places which are good value – like the *Star Hotel* (☎ 215 0020/1). Rooms are air-con and cost 350B, or 500B with TV. Right on the corner of this Soi and Rama I Rd is the *Muangphol Building* (☎ 215 3056/0033) which offers very good rooms for 450B and a restaurant downstairs. The *Pranee Building* next door has 400B rooms but no restaurant.

More home-like are the family-run *A-One Inn* (☎ 215 3029) and the *Bed & Breakfast Inn* (☎ 215 3004), both of which are at the end of Soi Kasem San 1 and cost 400/500B for air-con rooms. Both have small dining areas on the ground floor. Rates at the Bed & Breakfast Inn include breakfast but rooms are a bit larger at the A-One.

Places to Eat
Banglamphu & Around There are lots of cheap eating places around Banglamphu including several on the ground floors of Khao San Rd guest houses. For the most part, these places serve Western and Thai food prepared for Western palates. Popular places include the two *Hello Restaurants* and the recently opened *Buddy Beer Restaurant*. For more authentic fare, try the many Thai places along Ram Buttri Rd, just north of Khao San Rd. Of outstanding value and selection is the 8th floor food mall in the *New World Shopping Centre*, three blocks north of Khao San Rd.

The *Yok Yor* on Samphraya Pier has good seafood, a menu in English and main dishes costing from around 40B.

Phra Athit Rd, over towards the river where you find the Trok Rong Mai guest houses, has some inexpensive restaurants and food stalls. Under the Phra Pinklao Bridge, the *Wang Ngar Restaurant* has a great position looking out over the river, and there are also a number of food stalls there.

The *Vijit Restaurant*, on the circle surrounding the Democracy Monument in Banglamphu, has an extensive Thai menu and is a popular lunch spot for Thai office workers.

Soi Ngam Duphli There are several travellers' centre restaurants in Soi Ngam Duphi, none of them outstanding. Cheaper food can be found at the open air restaurants on Soi Si Bamphen, near the Boston Inn. *My Place* and *Sabai* are popular. The curry shops out on Rama IV Rd are good value or there's a collection of street vendors across Rama IV Rd next to the Lumpini Boxing Stadium.

Hualamphong Lots of good cheap restaurants, mostly Chinese, can be found along Rong Muang Rd by the station. On the soi leading to the TT Guest House, *Pan* is a neat little restaurant.

Siam Square The Siam Square sois have plenty of good places in varying price ranges. Try the big noodle restaurant *Coca* on Henri Dunant Rd, close to Rama I Rd. At 93/3 Soi Lang Suan, Ploenchit Rd, is the *Whole Earth Restaurant* which does good Thai and Indian vegetarian food.

Directly opposite the Siam Center on Rama I Rd, there's a *Kentucky Fried Chicken*, a *Pizza Hut*, a *Dunkin' Donuts* and a string of other American-style fast-food eateries. *Uncle Ray's* has some of the best ice cream in Bangkok.

The 6th floor of the *MBK*, or *Mahboonkrong Center* (on the south-west corner of Rama I and Phayathai Rds), has a magnificent Singapore-style food centre with everything from steak and salad to Thai vegetarian fare. It's open from 10 am to 9 pm daily. On the 4th floor of the same building are a number of other food vendors as well as several slightly up-market restaurants serving Western or Japanese food. At street level there are a host of fast-food places.

At the intersection of Soi Kasem San I and Rama I Rd is the excellent, inexpensive *Thai Sa-Nguan* restaurant, where curry and rice is 10 to 15B a plate. Good kway teow (rice

noodles) and khao man kai (chicken rice) are also available here.

Sukhumvit Rd The *Yong Lee Restaurant* at 211 Sukhumvit Rd near Soi 15 and Asia Books, does standard Thai and Chinese food. *Laikhram*, down Soi 49 with several twists and turns, has superb Thai food at not too outrageous prices. It's so far down Soi 49 you may want to take a tuk-tuk from Sukhumvit Rd. A second branch has opened on Soi 33 and there's also one at Thaniya Plaza, Silom Rd.

On Soi 12, *Cabbages & Condoms*, famous for its name alone, is run by Thai's hyperactive family planning association. By Soi 17, there's the fancy *Robinson's Department Store* with a branch of *McDonald's* at street level and a basement supermarket and food centre, featuring everything from *Dunkin' Donuts* to frozen yoghurt, ice cream, noodles and a variety of Thai food stands.

Patpong & Silom Rds At 30/37 Patpong 2, the *Thai Room* has reasonable Thai-Chinese-Mexican food. Try the *Bobby's Arms* on Patpong Rd for a good Aussie-Brit pub. Halfway down Silom Rd, across from the Narai Hotel, you can get good Indian snacks near the Tamil temple. The nearby *Deen Muslim Restaurant* has a wide variety of Thai and other food and lots of different ice creams. Near the Patpong Rd end of Silom Rd, there's an *A&W Hamburger Restaurant*, a *Kentucky Fried Chicken* and a *Mister Donut*. At the other end of Patpong Rd, there's a *Pizza Hut*.

Right across from the end of Silom Rd, at 1354-1356 New (Charoen Krung) Rd, is the *Muslim Restaurant*. There's a second *Muslim Restaurant* further along at 1221 New (Charoen Krung) Rd, near the post office. These places are travellers' standbys with good north Indian curries. The *Royal India* at 392/1 Chakraphet Rd in Pahurat is probably better. The *ATM Shopping Centre*, on Chakraphet Rd and opposite the Royal India, has an Indian food centre on the top floor. The alley alongside the centre features cheap Indian food stalls as well. For south

Indian food, try the *Simla Cafe* at 382-384 Soi 34 off Silom, which serves idlis, dosas and a few other south Indian snacks along with a wide selection of north Indian dishes.

There are several other interesting possibilities along Silom Rd like the *Maria Bakery* at 1170-72. At 1272 New (Charoen Krung) Rd, the *Jimmy Bakery* also does Thai, Chinese and Western food and ice cream. *Chalie One* at 1472 New (Charoen Krung) Rd has light meals and snacks and Foremost ice cream. The *Silom Village* shopping complex has a couple of good Thai restaurants. On Soi Pramoun, down towards the river end of Silom Rd, the *Thanying Restaurant* has excellent Thai food – count on around 200B for a complete meal, including a beer and dessert.

Entertainment

Bangkok is, of course, the Oriental sin-city extraordinaire and hordes of (male) package tourists descend upon the city simply to sample its free-wheeling delights. Patpong Rd, just off Silom Rd, is the centre for the city's spectator sports, while massage parlours are found at many hotels and in the tourist ghettos like Sukhumvit Rd or, of course, on Patpong Rd.

In Thailand, a 'body massage' means the masseuse's not yours. As one traveller told it in Burma (Myanmar) : '...and then she took all her clothes off, and then she took all my clothes off, and then I missed my flight to Burma'. Or, there are the coffee bar pick-up joints like the infamous Grace Hotel at Soi 3, Sukhumvit Rd. Other go-go bar ghettos are the Nana Plaza group on Soi 4, Sukhumvit Rd, and the alley known as Soi Cowboy, parallel to Sukhumvit Rd between Sois 21 and 23. Alongside the railway tracks, opposite Soi 1, there's a collection of very rustic open-air bars.

Last – but far from least – many Bangkok visitors find that indulgence in the pleasures of sin-city can easily lead to social diseases. Careless males should be aware, if they are travelling on to India or Nepal, that getting plugged full of penicillin is much easier to arrange in Bangkok than anywhere further

west. Thailand also has a serious AIDS problem (see Health in the Thailand Facts for the Visitor section), so the use of condoms really is imperative. Less physical problems also occasionally befall Bangkok revellers – wallets have disappeared while people's pants were down.

Of course, Bangkok also has plenty of straightforward nightspots. Not every bar is a pick-up joint and even in the ones that are you can have just a drink, if that's all you want.

Things to Buy

Anything you can buy out in the country you can also get in Bangkok – sometimes the prices may even be lower. Silom Rd and New (Charoen Krung) Rd are two good shopping areas that cater to tourists.

Better deals are available in Bangkok's large open-air markets at Chatuchak Park (Weekend Market), Yaowarat (Chinatown), Pratunam and Pahurat. Things to look for include:

Cotton & Silk Lengths of cotton and the beautifully coloured and textured Thai silk can be made into clothes or household articles. There are some good shops along Silom Rd but the fabric stalls in the Indian district of Pahurat are cheaper.

Temple Rubbings Charcoal on rice paper or coloured on cotton, these rubbings are made from temple bas reliefs – or they were once. Today, they're made from moulds taken from the temple reliefs. Wat Pho is a favourite place with a very wide choice, but check prices at shops in town before buying at Wat Pho as they often ask too much.

Clothes The Thais are very fashion conscious and you can get stylish clothes ready made or made to measure at attractive prices. You'll find trendy tailor shops in all the small towns too, and they are often cheaper than in Bangkok.

Gems Buyer beware. Unless you know stones, Bangkok is no place to seek out 'the big score'. *Never* accept an invitation from a tout or friendly stranger to visit a gem store, as the visit will soon turn into a confidence game in which you're the pigeon. See Dangers & Annoyances in the Thailand Facts for the Visitor section for more details on gem scams.

If you want to learn about gemstones before having a look around (a very sensible idea), visit the Asian Institute of Gemological Sciences (☎ 513 2112; fax 236 7803) at 484 Rachadaphisek Rd in the Huay Kwang district. The institute offers reputable, reasonably priced gemology courses of varying lengths. The staff can also assess the authenticity and quality of stones (but not their value) that are brought to them.

Other Silver, bronze and nielloware (silver inlaid with black enamel) items include a variety of jewellery, plates, bowls and ornaments. Antiques are widely available but you'd better know what you're looking for. Temple bells and carved wooden cow bells are nice souvenirs. There is a string of art galleries along New (Charoen Krung) Rd from the GPO where you will find those attractive little leaf paintings – nicely framed and small enough to make handy little presents.

The Weekend Market near the Northern bus terminal is, of course, a great place to look for almost any oddity. Behind the Chalerm Thai Theatre at Wat Rajanadda, there's an amulet market where you can buy an amulet to protect you against almost anything. Bangkok is a great place to buy student cards (100B) – some fine fakes are produced here, but make sure you give them a good university name or you'll end up with something like 'University of Australia'.

Getting There & Away

Bangkok is the central travel focus in Thailand. Unless you enter by crossing the border in the south from Malaysia, this is the place where you're most likely to arrive in Thailand. It's also the centre from where travel routes fan out across the country.

Air Bangkok is a major centre for international ticket discounting. Check the Thailand Getting There & Away section for various warnings about discounted tickets. It's also the centre for Thai International's domestic flight schedules.

Bangkok International Airport Bangkok Airport's glossy new international terminal is fine and has a good value restaurant/snackbar on the 4th floor. The post and telephone office in the departure hall is open 24 hours. The domestic terminal is smaller and quite separate.

Right across the road from the terminal (take the Airport Hotel pedestrian bridge), there's the Don Muang town area with lots of little shops, a market, many small restaurants and food stalls and even a wat. If you have to stay near the airport, there's the expensive *Airport Hotel* or the rather dismal *Bamboo Guest House*, several hundred metres north of the terminal on the Don Muang side.

Departure Tax The departure tax on international flights is 200B. You're exempted from paying it if you're only in transit and have not left the transit area. Domestic departure tax is 20B.

Bus The Bangkok bus terminals are:

North
  Northern Route Terminal, Phahonyothin Rd (☎ 279 4484)
East
  Eastern Route Terminal, Soi 40 (Ekamai), Sukhumvit Rd (☎ 392 3310)
South
  Southern Route Terminal (air-con buses), Charan Sanitwong Rd, Thonburi (☎ 411 4978/9)
  New Southern Route Terminal (ordinary buses), Highway 338 and Phra Pinklao Rd (☎ 434 5557)

The Northern terminal is on the road out to the airport. Go there for buses to Ayuthaya, Sukhothai, Chiang Mai and Chiang Rai plus the towns in the north-east. The Southern terminals, where you will get buses for Nakhon Pathom, Kanchanaburi, Hua Hin,

Surat Thani, Phuket and Hat Yai, are across the river. The Eastern terminal out along Sukhumvit Rd has buses for Pattaya and Ancient City. All terminals have good left-luggage facilities.

Train There are two main railway stations. The big Hualamphong station on Rama IV Rd handles services to the north, north-east and some of the services to the south. The Thonburi, or Bangkok Noi, station handles some services to the south. If you're heading south ascertain from which station your train departs.

Getting Around

To/From the Airport The Bangkok Airport is 25 km north of the city centre, and there are a variety of ways of getting from there to your hotel on arrival.

City Buses from the Airport There's a highway straight into the city just a few steps outside the airport. Walk out there and you can get an air-con public bus No 4 into the city for just 15B. It's less if you get off in north Bangkok but you've got to sort this out before you pay. Bus No 4 goes down Vibhavadi Rangsit Rd to Ratchaprarop/Ratchadamri Rd, crosses Phetburi, Rama I, Ploenchit and Rama IV Rds, then goes down Silom Rd, turns left on New (Charoen Krung) Rd and continues across the river to Thonburi.

Alternatively, bus No 13 from the airport goes down Phahonyothin Rd, turns left at the Victory Monument to Ratchaprarop Rd then travels south to Ploenchit Rd and east on Sukhumvit Rd all the way to Bang Na. Air-con bus No 10 also goes by the airport. Bus No 4 stops running at 7 pm and Nos 10 and 13 at 8 pm.

If money is all-important, you can take a regular bus No 29 which follows a similar route to the No 13 but continues beyond Sukhumvit Rd to Rama IV Rd (get off there for the Soi Ngam Duphli hotels) and then turns right to the Hualamphong station area. The No 59 bus goes straight to the Democracy Monument area which is handy if you're going to Banglamphu/Khao San Rd. Fares for these are just 3B and they run until 10 pm (No 29) and 9.30 pm (No 59).

Train The railway into Bangkok also runs right by the airport. You can get a train straight to Hualamphong station for 8B. Walk over the pedestrian bridge from the international terminal to the Airport Hotel. The railway station is right in front of the hotel. The departure times aren't always that convenient, however. It's timed for commuters to or from work, not for passengers to or from the airport.

Taxis & Shuttles Greedy Thai International touts try to steer all arriving passengers toward one of their expensive limousine services, but just ignore them and head straight for the city taxi counter. Regular taxis from the airport are 180B, or 200B if you buy a ticket at the city taxi counter tucked away at the far end of the arrival hall. Between three or more people, it's as cheap as the airport bus and rather more convenient. If you're taking a taxi to the airport from Bangkok, the usual fare is 150B.

You can also flag down taxis on the highway just outside the airport, and they will be a bit cheaper. Thai International's airport limousine is just a glorified air-con taxi service costing a flat 300B – a definite rip-off.

Thai International also has an airport shuttle bus for 60B that drops off passengers at the Asia Hotel city terminal, near Siam Square (within walking distance of the Muangphol Building, A-One Inn, etc). There is also a Thai International minibus which goes to most major hotels (and some minor ones, if the driver's in the mood) for 100B per person. It seems to depart erratically – they'd prefer to put you in the 300B limousine. There are air-con buses direct to Pattaya from the airport each morning and afternoon for around 200B.

Regular minibuses operate to the airport from the Khao San Rd accommodation enclave. They charge 50B.

Choosing If you really want to save money, the public bus or the train is fine – except you may have real trouble getting your gear on board the bus. The air-con buses are great, usually not crowded at all and no great financial burden. You just have to know where you're going and when to get off. So overall, if it's your first time in Bangkok, I'd suggest the 180B taxi fare. Particularly if there are several of you to split the cost.

Bus The Bangkok bus service is frequent and frantic – a bus map is an absolute necessity. Get one from the tourist office or from bookshops and newsstands for 40B. The buses are all numbered and the bus map is remarkably easy to follow. Don't expect it to be 100% correct though – routes change regularly. For any journey under 10 km, the fare is 2B, and over 10 km it jumps to 3B – out to the airport for example. The No 17 bus does a useful circuit of the city attractions and terminates near the National Museum and Emerald Buddha.

There are also a number of public air-con buses with numbers that may cause confusion with the regular buses. They start at 5B but jump to 15B on the long trips. Take care when hopping on a bus that it's not the air-con one if you're economising. Apart from the cool comfort, the air-con buses are uncrowded, especially in comparison to the mayhem on the regular buses. In the last few years, new flat-fare, no-conductor buses have been introduced on a few lines. They cost 3B.

At peak hours, an unofficial and mildly illegal shadow service of private bus-trucks operates on the same routes and with the same numbers as the public buses. They're necessary, which is why no attempt is made to control them.

Taxi & Samlor You must fix fares in advance for other taxis or the hideously noisy little three-wheeled samlors. The samlors must be one of the prime causes of Bangkok's pollution. Samlors (also known as tuk-tuks) are really only useful for shorter trips. When the distances get longer they often become more expensive than regular taxis. Often, you need real endurance to withstand a long samlor trip and, half the time, the drivers don't know their way around Bangkok anyway.

Around central Bangkok, taxi fares should generally be from 50 to 70B – fares jump 10 or 15B late at night or with heavy traffic. You have to bargain, but since there are plenty of taxis it doesn't require much effort.

Bicycle Cycling in Bangkok sounds like a recipe for disaster but, out in the country, bicycling in Thailand can be fine. Larnluang Trading, at 355 Luang Rd between Worachak and Suapa Rds in Chinatown, has been recommended for bicycles. There are also other bicycle shops along this road.

Boat River travel through and around Bangkok is not only much more interesting and peaceful than fighting your way through town in a bus or taxi, it is also much faster. There are a number of regular services along the Chao Phraya River through Bangkok and on the associated khlongs (canals). Boats also buzz back and forth across the river from numerous points on one side to the other.

Easiest to use and understand is the Chao Phraya Express that runs up and down the river although it only stops at certain landing stages, like the Oriental Hotel. This river-bus service costs 3B, 5B or 7B depending on the distance you travel. You buy your ticket on the boat. The Chao Phraya Express is a big, long boat with a number on the roof.

Bangkok still has quite a few khlongs but it's no longer the 'Venice of the East'. More and more of the canals are being filled in to become roads for Bangkok's ever-growing traffic jams. Periodic floodings in the city are in part due to the loss of drainage the canals used to provide.

Places you can still go to include the khlong behind Sukhumvit Rd, along which long-tailed boats run. Pratunam Market is a good place to eat and even has a unique floating red-light district – the name means 'watergate'! In Thonburi, the floating market is now thoroughly spoilt but there are others

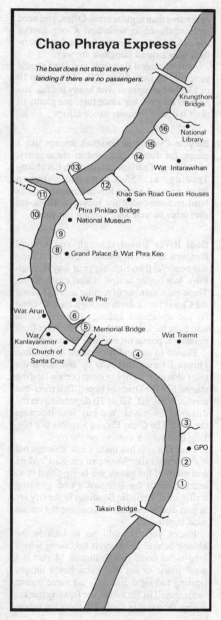

Chao Phraya Express

The boat does not stop at every landing if there are no passengers.

Krungthon Bridge

16 National Library

15

14

13

12 Wat Intarawihan

11 Khao San Road Guest Houses

Phra Pinklao Bridge

10 National Museum

9

8 Grand Palace & Wat Phra Keo

7

Wat Arun 6 Wat Pho

Wat Kanlayanimitr 5 Memorial Bridge

Church of Santa Cruz

4 Wat Traimit

3

GPO

2

1

Taksin Bridge

MAIN STOPS OF THE CHAO PHRAYA EXPRESS

1. Oriental Hotel
2. Wat Muang Khae
3. Si Phraya
4. Ratchawong - for Chinatown
5. Saphan Phut, Memorial Bridge
6. Rachini
7. Tha Tien - for Wat Pho
8. Tha Chang - for Grand Palace
9. Maharat - for Thammasat University
10. Phrannok
11. Rot Fai - Bangkok Noi Railway Station
12. Phra Athit - for Khao San Rd Guest Houses
13. Wat Daowadung
14. Wat Samphraya
15. Wisut Kasat - for Wat Intarawihan
16. Thewet - for National Library & Sawatdee Guest House

– and other interesting river trips elsewhere in Thailand.

Skytrain The much ballyhooed Skytrain project was finally approved in 1986. The aerial train, financed by the government (25%) and Japanese and European banks (75%), is expected to reach the end of its first phase by the mid-1990s. Initially, there will be two lines – an east-west artery, from Phrakhanong to Bang Seu (23 km), and a north-south one, from Lat Phrao to Sathon Rd (11 km).

Around Bangkok

There are a number of interesting places within day-trip distance of Bangkok – some also make interesting stepping stones on your way north, east or south. You can stop at Ayuthaya on your way north, for example, or Nakhon Pathom on your way south.

AYUTHAYA

Until its destruction by the Burmese in 1767, this was the capital of Thailand. It is 86 km north of Bangkok. Built at the junction of three rivers, an artificial channel has converted the town into an island. To find your way around, get a copy of the excellent guidebook and map available from the museum either here or in Bangkok.

During the 10 days leading to the Songkran Festival in mid-April, there is a sound and light show with fireworks over the ruins. This is a great time to visit Ayuthaya, but you might want to take refuge in a smaller town during the final water-throwing days of Songkran itself – unless you fancy staying wet for the day!

Things to See

Places to see are either 'on the island' or 'off the island'. There's a 10 to 20B admission charge to some of the ruins between 8 am and 4.30 pm. The best way to see the ruins is by bicycle. These can be rented at the guest houses. Tuk-tuk tours cost from 200 to 300B for a day's sightseeing.

Museums The **Chao Sam Phraya National Museum** is open from 9 am to 12 noon and from 1 to 4 pm, Wednesday to Sunday. Admission is 20B on weekdays and it's free on weekends. There's a second national museum at the **Chan Kasem Palace**, and the opening hours are the same.

For a historical overview of the Ayuthaya period, check out the new **Ayuthaya Historical Study Centre** near Wat Yai Chai Mongkon. Japanese funded, this ambitious new facility houses hi-tech displays that cover not only art and archaeology but also the social and political history of the period.

On the Island The **Wat Phra Si Sanphet** is the old royal temple with its three restored chedis. Adjoining it is **Wihan Phra Mongkon Bopit**, housing a huge bronze seated-Buddha. **Wat Thammik Rat** is particularly appealing for its overgrown, deserted feeling and the stone lions which guard a toppling chedi.

Wat Suwan Dararam was built towards the close of the Ayuthaya period and has been completely and very colourfully restored. **Wat Ratburana** and **Wat Phra Maha That** are both extensively ruined but majestic. **Wat Lokaya Sutha** has a huge reclining Buddha image. Queen Suriyothai lost her life protecting her husband during an elephant-back duel; her **memorial pagoda** stands by the river.

Off the Island The **Wat Phanan Choeng** was a favourite of Chinese traders and has a big seated Buddha. **Wat Chai Wattanaram** used to be one of Ayuthaya's most overgrown, evocative-of-a-lost-city type of ruin with stately lines of disintegrating Buddhas. Today, some hard restoration work (and the wonders of modern cement) has produced a row of lookalike brand new Buddhas! It's still a lovely wat with nice gardens.

The **Golden Mount** to the north of the city has a wide view over the flat country. Also to the north is the **elephant kraal** – the last of its kind in Thailand. **Wat Yai Chai Mongkon** to the south-east has a massive ruined chedi which contrasts with surrounding contemporary Buddha statues.

Places to Stay

Guest Houses The *Pai Thong Guest House* (☎ 24 1830) is on the river within walking distance of the railway station. Rooms in need of a clean are 70B with fan and shared bath. Food is served but watch that you don't get more dishes than you ordered as you'll be charged for it. To get there from the train station, cross the river and turn left at the road at the other end of the bridge, then walk about 75 metres till you see a sign on your left.

The family-run *BJ Guest House* (☎ 25 1512) is down a soi off Naresuan Rd near the bus terminal and the Si Samai Hotel. Rates are 50B per single and 80B per double. There's a small restaurant downstairs.

Hotels At 13/1 Naresuan Rd, the *Thai Thai* (☎ 25 1505) has comfortable rooms with bath from 120B up to 200B with air-con. The *U Thong Hotel* (☎ 24 2618), on U Thong Rd near the boat landing and the Chan Kasem Palace, is noisy but otherwise tolerable with rooms for 100B with fan or

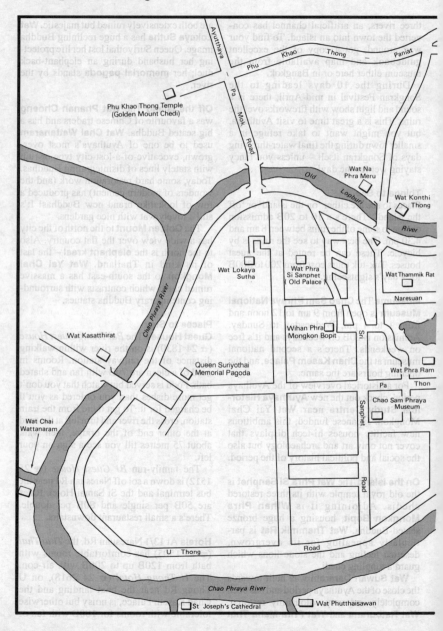

Phu Khao Thong Temple
(Golden Mount Chedi)

Wat Na
Phra Meru

Wat Konthi
Thong

Old Lopburi River

Wat Lokaya
Sutha

Wat Phra
Si Sanpet
(Old Palace)

Wat Thammik Rat

Naresuan

Wat Kasatthirat

Wihan Phra
Mongkon Bopit

Sri Sanpet

Wat Phra Ram

Queen Suriyothai
Memorial Pagoda

Pa Thon

Chao Sam Phraya
Museum

Chao Praya River

Wat Chai
Wattanaram

U Thong

Chao Phraya River

St Joseph's Cathedral

Wat Phutthaisawan

Ayutthaya

Phu Pa Mok Road

Khao Thong Paniat

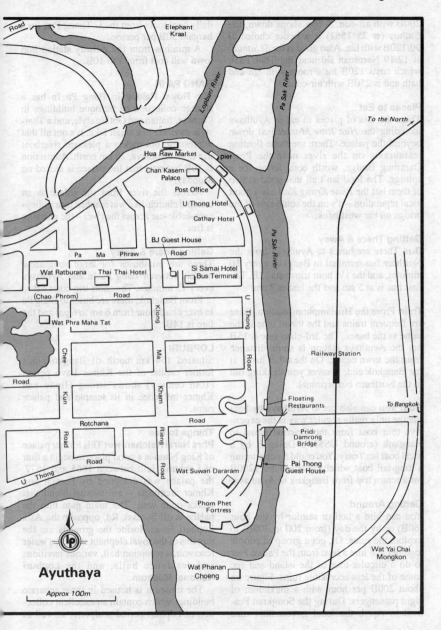

Ayuthaya

Approx 100m

200B with air-con. A few shops down, the *Cathay* (☎ 25 1562) is a better choice at 90/120B with fan. Also good is the *Si Samai*, at 12/19 Naresuan Rd near the Thai Thai, which costs 120B for a room with fan and bath and is 250B with air-con.

Places to Eat

There are lots of places to eat in Ayuthaya including the *Hua Raw Market* just down beyond the palace. There are three floating restaurants on the river near the Pridi Damrong Bridge, worth considering for a splurge. The food isn't all that good at two of them but the *Phae Krung Kao* has a good local reputation – it's on the south side of the bridge on the west bank.

Getting There & Away

Bus There are buses to Ayuthaya from the Northern bus terminal in Bangkok every 10 minutes, and the 1½ hour trip costs 17B. The first bus is at 5 am and the last at 7 pm.

Train From the Hualamphong station, there are frequent trains and the travel time is the same as the buses. The 3rd-class fare is 15B but the Ayuthaya station is some distance from the town centre. On the other hand, at the Bangkok end, it saves you trekking out to the Northern bus terminal.

Boat You can also get to Ayuthaya by boat but the only really regular way is the expensive tour boat from the Oriental Hotel in Bangkok (around US$30). Doing it by a local boat isn't easy. You could try chartering a long-tail boat which costs around 1200B for a return trip from Bangkok to Ayuthaya.

Getting Around

You can hire a taxi or samlor by the hour (60B) or by the day (from 200 to 300B) to explore the ruins. Or, get a group of people together and hire a boat from the Palace Pier to do a circular tour of the island and see some of the less accessible ruins. Figure on about 200B per hour with a maximum of eight passengers. During the Songkran Festival in April, the local government runs

daily boat tours from the U Thong Pier for a bargain 50B per person.

A minibus from the railway station into town will cost from 5 to 10B.

BANG PA IN

The **Royal Palace** in Bang Pa In has a strange collection of baroque buildings in Chinese, Italian and Gothic style, and a Thai-style pavilion in a small lake. It's not all that interesting, but makes a pleasant riverboat trip from Ayuthaya, 20 km north. Admission is 10B but note that the palace is closed on Monday.

Across the river from the palace is an unusual church-like wat reached by a trolley-cum-cable-car across the river – the crossing is free.

Getting There & Away

There are minibuses (or large songthaew trucks) between Bang Pa In and Ayuthaya every 15 minutes. The short trip costs 6B.

From Bangkok, there are buses to Bang Pa In every half-hour from 6 am to 6 pm and the fare is 14B.

LOPBURI

Situated 154 km north of Bangkok, this former capital of the Khmer Lavo period (10th century) shows strong Hindu and Khmer influence in its temple and palace ruins.

Things to See

Phra Narai Ratchaniwet This former palace of King Narai is a good place to begin a tour of Lopburi. Built between 1665 and 1677, the palace was designed by French and Khmer architects – an unusual blend that works quite well. The main gate into the palace is off Sorasak Rd, opposite the Asia Lopburi Hotel. Inside the grounds are the remains of the royal elephant stables, a water reservoir, a reception hall, various pavilions and residence halls, and the **Lopburi National Museum**.

The museum is housed in three separate buildings which contain an excellent collection of Lopburi period sculpture, as well as an assortment of Khmer, Dvaravati, U Thong and Ayuthaya art, traditional farm implements and dioramas of farm life. It's open Wednesday to Sunday from 9 am to 12 noon and from 1 to 4 pm. Admission into the grounds is free and museum entry is 10B.

Other Ruins Most important is the **Prang Sam Yot**, or 'sacred three spires', which was originally built as a Hindu shrine and is reckoned to be the finest Khmer structure in the region. **Prang Khaek** and **Wat Phra Si Ratana Mahathat** are also notable.

Phaulkon's House, the home of the Greek adviser to Ayuthaya during its heyday, is also in Lopburi. Phaulkon was beheaded by the king's ministers when he began courting French influence in the area. You can get a good map of Lopburi from the tourist office.

Places to Stay & Eat

You can do a day trip to Lopburi from Ayuthaya but if you want to stay, the *Thai Sawat* on Na Kala Rd, close to the railway station, is about the cheapest around at 50B. Also on Na Kala Rd, opposite Wat Nakhon Kosa, the *Indra* costs 70B for passable rooms with fan and bath. On the same road, but closer to the railway station, is the *Julathip* which doesn't have an English sign. Rooms with fan and bath are 60B, but ask to see them first.

Still on Na Kala Rd, the *Suparaphong* is not far from Wat Phra Sri Ratana Mahathat and the railway station. It's similar in price and standard to the Julathip and the Indra. Overlooking King Narai's palace, the *Asia Lopburi* (☎ 41 1892) is on the corner of Sorasak and Phra Yam Jamkat Rds. It's clean and comfortable and has two Chinese restaurants downstairs. Rooms with fan and bath are 120B. *Muang Thong* (☎ 41 1036), across from Prang Sam Yot, has noisy but adequate rooms for 100B with fan and bath plus some cheaper rooms without bath for 60B.

There are several Chinese restaurants along Na Kala Rd, parallel to the railway line, but they tend to be a bit pricey. The places on the side streets of Ratchadamnoen and Phra Yam Jamkat Rds are better value.

Getting There & Away

Bus Buses leave about every 10 minutes from Ayuthaya or every 20 minutes from Bangkok – the three-hour trip costs 32B. From Kanchanaburi, you can get to Lopburi via Suphanburi and Singhburi on a series of public buses or share taxis.

Train You can reach Lopburi from Bangkok by train for 28B in 3rd class, and 57B in 2nd.

One way of visiting Lopburi on the way north is to take the train from Ayuthaya (or Bangkok) early in the morning, leave your gear at the station for the day while you look around and then continue north on the night train.

Getting Around

Samlors go anywhere in Lopburi for 5 to 10B.

SARABURI

There's nothing of interest in Saraburi itself, but between here and Lopburi you can turn off to the **Phra Phutthabat**. This small and delicately beautiful shrine houses a revered Buddha footprint. Like all genuine Buddha footprints, it is massive and identified by its 108 auspicious distinguishing marks. In February and March, there are pilgrimage festivals at the shrine.

Places to Stay

Try the *Thanin* or *Suk San* at Amphoe Phra Phutthabat – both cost 100B. In town, the *Kiaw An* (☎ 21 1656) on Phahonyothin Rd also has rooms from 100B. Other hotels include the slightly cheaper *Saraburi* (☎ 21 1646, 21 1500) opposite the bus stand.

ANG THONG

Ang Thong is between Lopburi and Suphanburi. Outside this small town, **Wat Pa Mok** has a 22-metre-long reclining Buddha.

Places to Stay

Rooms cost from 80B in the *Bua Luang* (☎ 61 1116) on Ayuthaya Rd.

SUPHANBURI

This very old Thai city has some noteworthy Ayuthaya-period chedis and one Khmer prang. **Wat Phra Si Ratana Mahathat** (is there a more popular name for a wat in Thailand?) is set back off Malimaen Rd close to the city centre. A staircase inside its Lopburi-style Khmer prang leads to the top.

West of Suphan town (about seven km) is **Don Chedi**, a pagoda that commemorates the 16th-century mounted elephant duel between Thailand's King Naresuan and the Prince of Burma. Naresuan won, thus freeing Ayuthaya from Pegu rule. During the week of 25 January, there's an annual **Don Chedi Monument Fair** in which the elephant battle is re-enacted in full costume.

Places to Stay

The *King Pho Sai* (☎ 51 1412) at 678 Nane Kaew Rd has rooms from 100B. The *KAT* (☎ 51 1619/39) at 433 Phra Phanwasa and the *Suk San* (☎ 51 1668) at 1145 Nang Pim Rd are similarly priced.

NAKHON PATHOM

At 127 metres, the gigantic orange-tiled **Phra Pathom Chedi** is the tallest Buddhist monument in the world. It was begun in 1853 to cover the original chedi of the same name. Nakhon Pathom is regarded as the oldest city in Thailand – it was conquered by Angkor in the early 11th century and in 1057 was sacked by Anawrahta of Pagan in Burma. There is a museum near the chedi and outside the town is the pleasant park of **Sanam Chan** – the grounds of the palace of Rama VI. In November, there's a **Phra Pathom Chedi Fair** that packs in everyone from fruit vendors to fortune tellers.

From Nakhon Pathom, you can make an excursion to the **floating market** at Klong Damnoen Saduak. This has become a popular, less-touristed alternative to the over-commercial Bangkok floating market. All you have to do to get there is to hop on a bus bound for Samut Songkhram to the south and ask to be let off in Damnoen Saduak or *talaat nam* (floating market).

Places to Stay & Eat

On Lungphra Rd, near the railway station, the *Mitsamphan Hotel* (☎ 24 2422) has rooms from 80B with fan and bath, and more with air-con. The *Mittaowan*, on the right as you walk towards the chedi from the train station, has rooms at 90B with fan and bath.

The *Mitphaisan* (its English sign says 'Mitfaisal') is further down the alley to the right from the Mittaowan and has rooms from 100B. All three 'Mit' hotels are owned by the same family. The Mittaowan is probably the best.

There's an excellent fruit market along the road between the train station and the Phra Pathom Chedi. The excellent *Ha Seng* Chinese restaurant is on the south side of the road which intersects the road from the train station to the chedi. Turn right if walking from the chedi and walk about 20 metres.

Getting There & Away

Nakhon Pathom is 56 km west of Bangkok. Every weekend, there's a special rail trip to Nakhon Pathom and on to Kanchanaburi. Otherwise, you can get there by bus from the Southern bus terminal in Bangkok or by rail. Buses leave every 10 minutes and cost 13B for the one-hour trip. The rail fare is 14B in 3rd class.

KANCHANABURI

During WW II, the infamous bridge over the River Kwai was built here, 130 km west of Bangkok. The bridge that stands today is not the one constructed during the war – that was destroyed by Allied air raids – though the curved portions of the structure are original. The graves of thousands of Allied soldiers can be seen in Kanchanaburi or you can take a train across the bridge and continue further west where there are caves, waterfalls and a neolithic burial site.

The town was originally founded by Rama I as protection against Burmese invasion over the Three Pagodas Pass, which is still a major smuggling route into Burma (Myanmar).

Information

There's a good TAT office near the bus station. Kanchanaburi (pronounced Kan-cha-NA-buri) is often referred to as 'Kan'.

Things to See

Death Railway Bridge The bridge made famous by the film *Bridge Over the River Kwai* spans the Khwae Yai River, a tributary of the Mae Klong River, a couple of km north of town. The bridge was only a small but strategic part of the Death Railway to Burma and was in use for 20 months before the Allies bombed it in 1945.

Every year, during the first week of December, there's a nightly light and sound show at the bridge. It's a pretty impressive scene with the sounds of bombers and explosions, and fantastic bursts of light. The town gets a lot of tourists during this week, so book early if you want to attend.

Get to the bridge from town by catching a songthaew (2B) along Pak Praek Rd (parallel to Saengchuto Rd towards the river) heading north.

JEATH War Museum This interesting little outdoor museum is run by monks. It's set up just like a POW camp on the actual spot in Kawchow where there was a camp during the war. Entry is 20B and it's worth seeing. It's estimated that 16,000 Western POWs died in the construction of the 'Death Railway' to Burma but the figures for labourers, many forcibly conscripted from Thailand, Burma (Myanmar), Indonesia and Malaysia, was even worse. As many as 100,000 to 150,000 may have died in this area during WW II.

Other There are two Allied **war cemeteries** near Kanchanaburi, one just north of town off Saengchuto Rd near the railway station, and the other across the river west of town, a few km down the Khwae Noi tributary. The town also has an interesting **Lak Muang**, or

city pillar shrine, two blocks north-east of the tourist office on Lak Muang Rd.

Wat Tham Mongkon Thong is well known for its famous 'Floating Nun' who meditates while floating in a pool of water. This cave temple is some distance west of town.

Places to Stay

Guest Houses The *Nita Guest House* (☎ 51 1300), at Visutrangsi Rd on the way to the JEATH War Museum, is a friendly place with a 35B dorm and rooms from 50B. The *UT Guest House* is in a beautiful old house and charges a flat 50B per person for rooms or dorm beds. It's on Pak Praek Rd near the bridge.

A bit more expensive but good value is the *VL Guest House*, across the street from the River Kwai hotels. Clean, spacious rooms with fan and bath are 100B for singles or doubles. Larger rooms which hold four to eight persons cost 50B per person. The VL has a small dining area downstairs and they rent bicycles and motorbikes.

Over the last few years, a host of budget places have opened up along the river in town, near the floating restaurants. The *PG Guest House* at 277/303 Pak Praek Rd has comfortable rooms for 40B per person. Also on Pak Praek Rd, near the Aree Bakery, is the cut-above-the-rest *VS Guest House* with single/double rooms at 50/80B.

If you want to stay out near the bridge, the *Bamboo Guest House* (☎ 51 2532) at 3-5 Soi Vietnam, on the river about a km before the Japanese War Memorial, has rooms for 50B per person.

You can also stay on the river in a raft house (or over the river in the case of bungalows built on piers) from 25 to 40B per person depending on the raft. Two popular places of this sort are the *River* and *VN* guest houses where small, basic rooms are 40/70B. Both are on the river not far from the railway station.

The *Nitaya Raft House*, further south along the river near Wat Neua, is cheaper at 25B per person. *Jolly Frog Backpackers* is a recent addition in the floating restaurant area

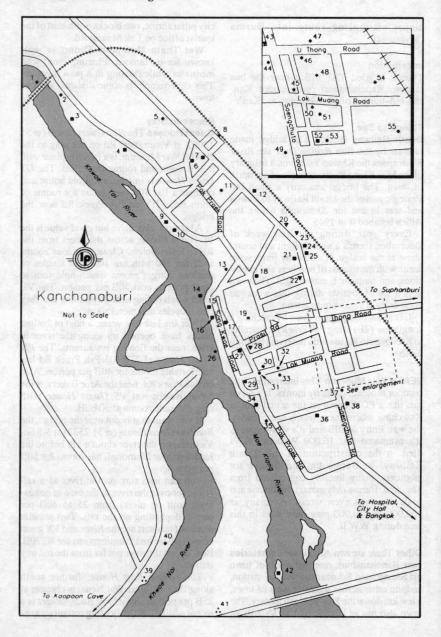

Kanchanaburi

Not to Scale

Khwae Yai River

Khwae Noi River

Mae Klang River

Pak Praek Road

Saengchuto Road

U Thong Road

Lak Muang Road

Prasit Rd

Song Kwai Road

To Suphonburi

To Hospital,
City Hall
& Bangkok

To Kaopoon Cave

See enlargement

U Thong Road

Lak Muang Road

Saengchuto Road

■	PLACES TO STAY		OTHER
3	Bamboo Guest House	1	Bridge on the River Kwai
4	UT Guest House	2	Japanese War Memorial
6	Si Muangkan Hotel	5	Petrol Stations
7	Rung Rung Bungalows	8	Railway Station
9	VN Guest House	11	Kanchanaburi War Cemetery
10	River Guest House	13	Songthaews to bridge
12	Luxury Hotel	19	Markets
14	Nitaya Raft House	29	Ferry Pier
15	Sam's Place	30	Post Office
16	Supakornchai Raft	31	Town Gate of Kanchanaburi
17	PG Guest House	32	City Pillar Shrine (Lak Muang)
18	Ni-Dar Guest House	33	Municipal Office
21	Prasopsuk Bungalow	35	JEATH War Museum
24	River Kwai Hotel #1	37	Tourist Authority of Thailand (TAT)
25	River Kwai Hotel #2	39	Wat Tham Kao Pun
27	VS Guest House	40	Chung Kai Allied War Cemetery
34	Nita Raft House	41	Wat Tham Mangkon Thong
36	Nita Guest House	44	Taxi Stand
38	Thai Seree Hotel	45	Thai Military Bank
42	Kasem Island Resort	46	Bangkok Bank
52	BT Guest House	47	Telephone Centre
		48	Market
▼	PLACES TO EAT	49	Police Station
		50	Thai Farmers Bank
20	Sabai-Jit Restaurant	51	Market
22	Issan Restaurant	53	Bus Station
23	Sunya Rux Restaurant	54	Movie Theatre
26	Floating Restaurants	55	Movie Theatre
28	Aree Bakery		
43	Chinese Restaurant		

– it costs 70B for a double with verandah, mossie screens and shared bath. Other places come and go but they're all pretty similar. Slightly up-market is *Sam's Place*, where rooms with shared bath are 70B.

Hotels The *River Kwai Hotel* (☎ 51 1269) at 284/4-6 Saengchuto Rd has rooms with fan and bath from 90B – don't confuse it with the expensive Rama of River Kwai next door Across the road, at No 277, the *Prasopsuk Bungalows* has good 90B bungalows – it's a better deal than the River Kwai if you don't mind the horizontal mirrors next to the beds.

About midway between the River Kwai Hotel and the tourist office at 60/3 Saengchuto Rd, the *Wang Thong* (☎ 51 1046) has rooms with fan and bath from 90B. Not as centrally located, but still good value,

the *Luxury Hotel* (☎ 51 1168) is a couple of blocks north of the River Kwai Hotel and offers clean rooms from 70B.

Places to Eat

There are plenty of places to eat along the northern end of Saengchuto Rd near the River Kwai Hotel. The quality generally relates to the crowds! Good, inexpensive eating can also be found in the markets along Prasit Rd and between U Thong and Lak Muang Rds east of Saengchuto Rd.

The *Sunya Rux*, near the River Kwai hotels, serves traveller-oriented dishes but the quality here seems to have slipped and they won't serve Thais. The *Sabai-jit* restaurant, just north of the River Kwai Hotel, has an English menu and consistently good food. A restaurant called *Art & Beer*, across from the railway station, also features unusual dishes like beer-marinated beef and phat thai (fried rice noodles with tofu, vegetables, egg and peanuts) without the noodles. Beer prices are low.

Down on the river, there are several large floating restaurants where the quality of the food varies but it's hard not to enjoy the atmosphere. Across from the floating restaurants along the road are several smaller, cheaper food stalls which open in the evenings.

The *Aree Bakery* has excellent baked goods, ice cream and, reported one visitor, 'a breakfast I thought only Mom could make'.

Getting There & Away

Bus Regular buses leave Bangkok every 20 minutes daily for Kanchanaburi from the Southern bus terminal in Thonburi. The trip takes about three hours and costs 28B. Aircon buses are less frequent and cost 53B. The last bus back to Bangkok leaves Kan around 6.30 pm.

Train The regular train costs 28B for 3rd class. There are only two a day and they both leave from the Bangkok Noi station in Thonburi, not from Hualamphong.

A special diesel railcar trip departs Thonburi on weekends and holidays at 6.15 am and returns at 7.30 pm. You stop in Nakhon Pathom for a short tour, and continue across the Kwai bridge to Nam Tok from where you can take a minibus to the Khao Pang Falls. The fare is 60B and you have to book a week or two in advance – there are usually no-shows, so it's worth turning up on spec.

Getting Around

You can hire motorbikes from the Honda dealer, two blocks north of the TAT office, and from the VL Guest House. The cost is 150B per day and they are a good way of getting to the rather scattered attractions around Kanchanaburi.

Samlors within the city are 5 to 10B a trip. Regular songthaews in town are 3B but be careful you don't 'charter' one or it'll be a lot more.

AROUND KANCHANABURI

There are numerous interesting excursions to be made from Kanchanaburi.

Waterfalls

The **Erawan Falls** are an interesting 1½ to two hour bus trip beyond Kanchanaburi. Take an early morning bus from the bus station. It costs 17B to the end of the line from where you have to walk a couple of km to the start of the waterfall trail.

For the lazy or those with the money, minibuses cruise by the river guest houses around 9 am daily and take passengers right into Erawan Park for 60B per person – they return around 3.30 pm. There's a 5B admission charge to the two-km footpath which goes along the river and past seven waterfalls. There are plenty of good plunge pools so take along your swimming gear but make an early start since the last bus back is at 4 pm.

Other waterfalls are generally too far from Kanchanaburi for a day trip. For overnighters, the **Sai Yok** and **Huay Khamin** falls are the most interesting. Overnight raft trips head down the Khwae Noi River from the Sai Yok Falls.

Three Pagodas Pass

These days it's relatively easy to travel up to the pass (Chedi Sam Ong in Thai) and have a peek into Burma (Myanmar). Getting there requires an overnight pause in Sangkhlaburi, 223 km north from Kan. The village on the Burma (Myanmar) side of the pass has been the scene of firefights between the Mon and Karen insurgents – both armies want to control the collection of 'taxes' levied on border smuggling.

In March 1990, the Burmese government regained control of the area, rebuilt the bamboo village in wood and concrete and renamed it Payathonzu. A row of tourist shops have been built and there are plans to allow tourists over the border for day trips (crossing has never been a problem and still isn't). There is even talk of reopening the road all the way to Moulmein.

On the Thai side of the border is the headquarters of the All Burma Students Democratic Front (ABSDF), where self-exiled Rangoon students have set up an opposition movement with the intention of ousting the Ne Win government from Burma. The three pagodas themselves are rather inconspicuous, small and white-washed monuments.

Other

There are a few places of interest along the road to Sangkhlaburi. From Kanchanaburi, take the Nam Tok Sai Yok road. A few km past the river you can visit the **Phu Phra Cave**; it costs 30B to have the lights turned on. Another pause can be made at the **Prasat Muang Sing Temple**, a western outpost of the Khmer Empire. At Km 60, you pass the **Sai Yok Noi Falls** and another 44 km takes you past the **Sai Yok Yai National Park**. Just past Km 107, there's the **Hin Dat Hot Springs**. Remember to dress discreetly if you decide to try them out.

Places to Stay

At Thong Pha Phum, the last town before Sangkhlaburi, there are several places to stay for around 80B a night.

In Sangkhlaburi, the *Sri Daeng Hotel* is on the first street to the left when you enter town and has rooms for 100B. Two km east of the bus station, near the lake, is the *P Guest House* with rooms from 60 to 80B. There's a resort with bungalows for 300B at the Three Pagodas Pass.

Getting There & Away

You can get to Sangkhlaburi by public bus or on a rented motorbike from Kan. This is not a road for the inexperienced motorcyclist – lots of dangerous curves, steep grades and long stretches without available assistance. If you go by motorbike, refuel in Thong Pha Phum, 150 km north of Kan – there isn't another fuel stop before Sangkhlaburi, another 70 km away. From Sangkhlaburi, there are songthaews to the pass.

KO SI CHANG & SI RACHA

Off the town of Si Racha, 105 km south of Bangkok, Ko Si Chang, a scenic and very untouristed island, is popular as a monastic retreat and also has some fair beaches. The monks stay in caves in the limestone ridge in the centre of the island. There's an abandoned palace from the reign of King Chulalongkorn on the western side of the island and a Chinese temple on the east.

Places to Stay & Eat

The hotels on piers over the waterfront in Si Racha are the best places to stay. The *Siriwattana, Sam Chai* and *Siwichai* all have rooms from 100B. Diagonally across from the Thai Panich Bank, on Si Racha's main street, is the *Chao Ban* restaurant with good food. Ditto for the Chinese-owned seafood-specialist *Chu-A Lee*, although the latter can be rather pricey. The cheapest food is in the day & night market near the clocktower at the southern end of town.

There are three hotels on Ko Si Chang now, including the *Tiewpai Guest House* which has rooms from 120B and dorm beds from 40B. The other two places cost about 100B per room.

Getting There & Away

There are buses to Si Racha about every half-hour from the Eastern bus terminal in Bangkok. The fare is 28B and the trip takes 1½ hours. A boat shuttles out to Ko Si Chang several times daily from a pier in Si Racha, off Soi 14. The fare is 20B each way and the trip takes about 40 minutes.

PATTAYA

Thailand's biggest and most popular beach resort is a long way from being its nicest. Situated 154 km south of Bangkok, a fourth 'S' (for sex) can be added to Sun, Sea & Sand in this gaudy and raucous resort. Pattaya is designed mainly to appeal to European package tourists, and there are plenty of snack bars along the beach strip proclaiming that 'bratwurst mit brot' is more readily available than khao phat.

Pattaya consists of a long beach strip of

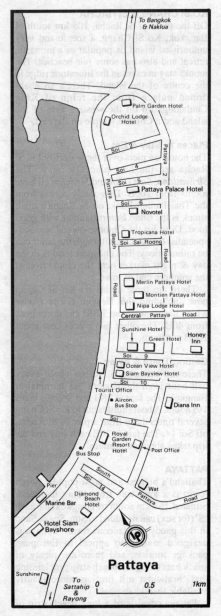

Pattaya

```
                    ↑ To Bangkok
                      & Naklua
```

Palm Garden Hotel
Orchid Lodge Hotel
Soi 2
Soi 4
Soi 5
Pattaya Palace Hotel
Soi 6
Novotel
Tropicana Hotel
Soi Sai Roong
Merlin Pattaya Hotel
Montien Pattaya Hotel
Nipa Lodge Hotel
Central   Pattaya   Road
Sunshine Hotel
Green Hotel
Honey Inn
Soi 9
Ocean View Hotel
Siam Bayview Hotel
Soi 10
Tourist Office
● Aircon.
  Bus Stop
Soi 13
Diana Inn
Royal Garden Resort Hotel
Post Office
Bus Stop
South
Soi 14
Pier
Diamond Beach Hotel
Wat
Pattaya   Road
Marine Bar
Hotel Siam Bayshore
Sunshine
```
          To
        Sattahip
          &
        Rayong
```
0   0.5   1km

---

mainly expensive hotels. The beach is drab and dismal and if you venture into Pattaya's equally uninviting water you run the risk of being mowed down by a ski-boat lunatic, an out-of-control jet-ski or simply dropped on from above by a para-sailor. Pattaya is *not* my idea of fun. Its one real attraction is the rather beautiful offshore islands where the snorkelling is good.

Places to Stay & Eat

Although Pattaya is basically a package-tourist, big-hotel deal, there are a handful of cheaper places squeezed in the small sois, back off the main beach road. Cheap in Pattaya would be expensive just about anywhere else in Thailand. This is true even when compared to Ko Samui or Phuket.

Most of the less expensive places are concentrated along sois 10, 11 and 12. The *Siam*, *Wang Thong* and *Sea Horse* guest houses all have rooms for around 150B. One of the best accommodation values in Pattaya is the *Diana Inn* (☎ 42 9675) on Pattaya 2 Rd, which has super-clean rooms, hot water and a swimming pool for 175B.

The *Pattaya Youth Hostel* has large, clean rooms at 40/60B (including breakfast) plus better rooms from 150B. It's on North Pattaya Rd about 300 metres behind the Montien Pattaya Hotel.

Most food in Pattaya is expensive – cheap eating here means *Pizza Hut* or *Mister Donut*! Shops along the back street on Pattaya 2 Rd have good Thai food. Look for cheap rooms back here, too.

Getting There & Away

There are departures every half-hour from the Eastern bus terminal in Bangkok for the 2½ hour, 29B trip to Pattaya. Air-con buses are 53B. There are also all sorts of air-con tour buses to Pattaya from a number of tour companies. At 11 am and 9 pm, there are buses direct from Don Muang Airport for 180B one way.

Getting Around

Songthaews cruise Pattaya Beach and Pattaya 2 Rds for 5B per person. Don't ask the fare first or drivers will think you want a charter.

RAYONG

Most of Thailand's *nam plaa* (fish sauce) comes from Rayong. There are a few pleasant beaches here at this 'real' Thai resort beyond Pattaya. Prices aren't much lower than in Pattaya (for beach places) though they are better value. For most travellers, Rayong is just a quick bus change on the way to Ko Samet.

Places to Stay & Eat

The *Rayong Hotel* at 65/3 Sukhumvit Rd and the *Otani* at No 169 have rooms from 100B. There are good cheap eats at the market near the Thetsabanteung cinemas, and beside the river there's a very good open-air restaurant belonging to the Fishermen's Association.

If you get stuck in Ban Phe, the port town for Ko Samet, you can stay at the *Nuan Napa* or *Queen* hotels for 80 to 100B.

KO SAMET

Further east beyond Rayong town, this small island is off the coast from Ban Phe. It used to be a very quiet and untouristed place but is now packed almost year round. Though no competitor to Ko Samui for natural attractions, the beaches are superb. An advantage of Ko Samet is that the weather is usually good here when Ko Samui is getting its worst rain. The downside is all the bungalow development and rubbish that's accumulating in places. Also, water is rationed at some bungalows – a reasonable policy given the scarcity of water on the island.

There are rumours that the National Park Service may step in soon and order most of the bungalows to close down to preserve the environment. This could make Ko Samet a far more pleasant place to visit.

Places to Stay

Beach accommodation costs from 50 to 250B and is mainly concentrated along the north-east coast. *Naga Bungalows*, between Ao Tubtim and Hat Sai Kaew near the concrete mermaid, is recommended, as are

Odd's Little Hut and *Tubtim*. There are plenty of others to choose from, even a couple of places on Coconut Bay (Ao Phrao) on the western side of the island. Avoid Ao Wong Deuan on the central east coast – it's crowded and overpriced. Another warning: during Thai national holidays all of Ko Samet can get quite crowded.

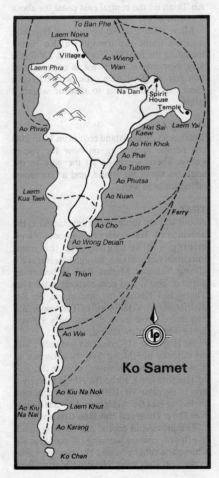

Getting There & Away

It's a three hour, 69B bus ride from the Eastern bus terminal in Bangkok to Rayong, then a 10B bus to Ban Phe (the touts will find you). For just 1B more, however, you can get a direct bus from Bangkok to Ban Phe, so why bother with Rayong? A round-trip ticket is 120B. From Ban Phe, a fishing boat will take you out to Na Dan on the north end of Ko Samet for around 25B or, at most, 30B tops. Other boats go to Ao Wong Deuan or Ao Thian on the central east coast for about 5 to 10B more.

Many Khao San Rd agencies in Bangkok organise round-trip transport to Ko Samet including the boat fare for around 220B one way. Not only is this twice as expensive as doing it on your own, you won't have a choice of which boat to take or where it stops.

Getting Around

Taxi trucks on the island cost from 10 to 20B per person depending on how far you're going. There are trails all the way to the southern tip of the island, and a few cross-island trails as well.

TRAT

About 400 km south-east from Bangkok, the province of Trat borders Cambodia. Gem-mining and smuggling are the most important occupations, though tourism at Ko Chang National Marine Park is becoming popular. You'll find gem markets at the Hua Thung and Khlong Yo markets in Bo Rai district, about 40 km north of Trat town. You can make good buys if (and only if) you know what you're buying.

As Highway 318 goes east and then south on the way to Khlong Yai, the province of Trat thins to a narrow sliver between the Gulf of Thailand and Cambodia. Along this sliver are a number of little-known beaches, including **Hat Sai Si Ngoen**, **Hat Sai Kaew**, **Hat Thap Thim** and **Hat Ban Cheun**.

The provincial capital has nothing much to offer except as a jumping-off point for Ko Chang and other islands. You can get information on Ko Chang National Marine Park in **Laem Ngop**, a small town 20 km south-west of Trat. This is also where you get boats to Ko Chang.

Places to Stay

Town The *Tang Nguan Seng 2* (☎ 51 1028) at 66-71 Sukhumvit Rd and *Thai Roong Roj* (*Rung Rot*) (☎ 51 1141) at 196 Sukhumvit Rd have rooms from 80 to 180B. The *Max & Tick Guest House*, at 58-60 Sukhumvit Rd, next to the municipal market and bus terminal, is new, clean and costs 50B per person or 40B per person in a triple.

Laem Ngop There's really no reason to stay here since most boats to the island leave in the afternoon and it's only 20 km from Trat. The cosy *Laem Ngop Guest House* has rooms and bungalows from 70B. The *Sukjai, Paradise* and *Wang Mai Ngam* all have fan-cooled rooms for 150B.

Places to Eat

The municipal market in the centre of town will satisfy your nutritional needs cheaply, day or night. On the Trat River, north-east of town, is a smaller night market with seafood.

Getting There & Away

Regular buses from Bangkok's Ekamai terminal to Trat cost 70B and take seven to eight hours. By air-con bus, it's 128B and takes about five hours.

Getting Around

Samlors around town cost from 5 to 10B per person, Mazda taxi trucks and motorbike taxis are 5B. A door-to-door minibus from Trat to Bo Rai is 30B.

KO CHANG NATIONAL MARINE PARK

Ko Chang is the second largest island in Thailand after Phuket; the park actually covers 47 of the islands off Trat's coastline. The main island has a few small villages supported by coconuts, fishing and smuggling but increasing numbers of tourists are attracted to the small bays and beaches, especially along the eastern side of the island. In the interior are a series of scenic waterfalls called **Than Mayom (or Thara Mayom) Falls.**

Nearby islands with bungalow accommodation include **Ko Kut, Ko Lao-Ya** and **Ko Mak.**

Places to Stay

Ko Chang Starting at the northern tip of the island at Ao Khlong Son, the *Manop*, the *Malee* and the *Manee* all have basic huts from 50 to 60B a night, bath outside. A bit further down at Hat Sai Khao are the similarly priced *Sabai*, *Sunsai*, *Cookie* and *Kaeo*.

On Ao Khlong Phrao, you'll find huts at the *Chaichet Resort, Magic, Nang Nuan, Tantawan, Kaibae* and several others.

Down along the south coast at Ao Bang Bao is the *Bang Bao Beach Resort* (☎ 51 1597/604) at 50 to 100B for average bungalows. You may also be able to rent rooms cheaply in nearby Ban Bang Bao. At Than Mayom National Park, on the east coast, there are a few park bungalows at the usual national park rates. A couple of private places, *Thanmayom* and *Maeo*, also rent huts from 60 to 100B a night.

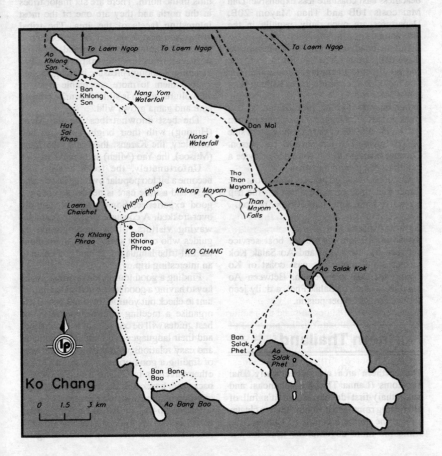

Ko Chang

To Laem Ngop

To Laem Ngop

To Laem Ngop

Ao Khlong Son

Ban Khlong Son

Nang Yom Waterfall

Dan Mai

Hat Sai Khao

Nonsi Waterfall

Khlong Phrao

Tha Than Mayom

Khlong Mayom

Than Mayom Falls

Laem Chaichet

Ao Khlong Phrao

Ban Khlong Phrao

KO CHANG

Ao Salak Kok

Ban Salak Phet

Ban Bang Bao

Ao Salak Phet

Ao Bang Bao

0   1.5   3 km

Ko Kut At Hat Taphao on the west coast, the *First* has basic huts for 50B with bath outside. If this one is closed, try village homes in nearby Ban Hin Dam.

Getting There & Away
Ko Chang Take a songthaew (7B) or share taxi (10B) from Trat south-west to Laem Ngop on the coast, then a ferry to Ko Chang. Ferry fares differ according to the beach destination: 30B to Ao Khlong Son, 60B to White Sand (Hat Sai Khao), 70B to Ao Khlong Phrao and so on. Ferries to the beachless east coast are less expensive: Dan Mai costs 10B and Than Mayom 20B. Departures are once daily, usually in the afternoon.

For the unadventurous, air-con minibuses leave daily from Khao San Rd in Bangkok and go direct to Laem Ngop for 200B. The fare includes a ferry ride to Ao Khlong Son.

Other Islands Two or three fishing boats a week go to Ko Kut from the Tha Chaloemphon Pier on the Trat River towards the eastern side of Trat town. The fare is 50B per person. Coconut boats go to Ko Kut once or twice a month from a pier on the canal.

Coconut boats go to Ko Mak from the Canal Pier once or twice a week – the trip takes five hours and costs 50B per person.

Getting Around
Ko Chang There is a daily boat service between Than Mayom and Ao Salak Kok further south along the east coast of Ko Chang for 20B per person. Between Ao Salak Kok and Ao Salak Phet, a daily jeep service costs 10B per person.

Northern Thailand

The northern area was where early Thai kingdoms (Lanna Thai, Hariphunchai and Sukhothai) first developed, so it's full of interesting ruins. Most visitors tend to cluster around the northern capital of Chiang Mai, while the more adventurous head for the somewhat more remote provinces of Chiang Rai, Mae Hong Son, Nan and Phrae. From here, you can make treks through the area inhabited by Thailand's many colourful hill tribes. This too is the region of the infamous Golden Triangle where Thailand, Laos and Burma (Myanmar) meet and from where much of the world's opium comes.

Hill Tribe Treks
One of the most popular activities from Chiang Mai, Chiang Rai or Mae Hong Son is to take a trek through the tribal areas in the hills in the north. There are six major tribes in the north and they are one of the most interesting facets of the area. The tribal groups are also found across the border in Burma (Myanmar) and Laos and, to them, political lines on the maps have little meaning. Although pressure is being applied to turn them to more acceptable types of agriculture, opium is still a favourite crop up here and ganja grows wild.

The best known tribes are the Meos (Hmong) with their bright costumes and jewellery, the Karens, the Lisus, the Lahu (Musoe), the Yao (Mien) and the Akha.

Unfortunately, the treks have really become a bit too popular over the last decade or so and a little care is needed to ensure a good experience. Some areas are simply over-trekked. A constant stream of camera-waving visitors, often accompanied by guides who cannot speak English let alone the hill-tribe languages, is hardly a ticket to an interesting trip.

Finding a good tour guide is probably the key to having a good trek, but it's also important to check out your fellow trekkers. Try to organise a meeting before departure. The best guides will be conversant with the tribes and their languages and have good contacts and easy relations with them. The best way of finding a good operator is simply to ask other travellers in Chiang Mai. People just back from a trek will be able to give you the low-down on how their trek went.

For an up-to-date list of trekking operators, visit the TAT office. Making a recommendation here would be meaningless since guides often change companies and operators open and close with alarming frequency.

Treks normally last four days and three nights, and the usual cost is around 800B, although longer treks are also available. Bring a water bottle, medicines and money for lunch on the first and last day and for odd purchases. Don't bring too much money or other valuables with you – it seems that every year some parties get 'held up' by local bandits. You can leave your gear behind in Chiang Mai with your hotel or the trek operator. A useful check list of questions to ask would be:

1. How many people in the group? 'Six is a good maximum,' reported one traveller, although others have said that 10 is equally OK.
2. Can they guarantee no other tourists will visit the same village on the same day, especially overnight?
3. Can the guide speak the language of each village to be visited? Can he speak English too?
4. Exactly when does the tour begin and end? The three-day treks of some companies turn out to be less than 48 hours.
5. Do they provide transport before and after the trek or is it just by public bus – often with long waits?

You can also just head off on your own or hire a guide or porter by yourself, but the treks are not that expensive and there are some areas where it is unwise to go. If you've got to bring gifts for the villagers, make it Band-aids and disinfectant rather than cigarettes and candy. It may be more for show but it doesn't do any harm. 'Toothpaste and soap,' suggested another clean-minded traveller.

Most people who go on these treks have a thoroughly good time and reckon they're great value. Comments included 'the best experience of my life...I hope we left the villages as we found them', and 'the area we covered was only recently opened for trekking and the guides were some of the nicest people I have ever met'.

Note, however, that there have been a number of incidents of hold-ups and robbery over the years. This area of Thailand is relatively unpoliced, with a 'wild west' feel. Enquire around that everything is OK before setting blithely off into the wilds. People who run into trouble often discover afterwards that their guide didn't really know where they were going, or went into areas they should have known were not safe.

Hill Tribe Directory

The term hill tribe refers to ethnic minorities living in the mountainous regions of north and west Thailand. The Thais refer to them as *chao khao*, literally meaning mountain people. Each hill tribe has its own language, customs, mode of dress and spiritual beliefs.

Most are of seminomadic origins, having migrated to Thailand from Tibet, Burma, China and Laos during the past 200 years or so, although some groups may have been in Thailand much longer.

The Tribal Research Institute in Chiang Mai recognises 10 different hill tribes but there may be up to 20 in Thailand. The institute's 1986 estimate of the total hill tribe population was 550,000.

The following descriptions cover the largest tribes which are also the groups most likely to be encountered on treks. Linguistically, the tribes can be divided into three main groups: the Tibeto-Burman (Lisu, Lahu, Akha); the Karenic (Karen, Kayah); and the Austro-Thai (Hmong, Mien). Comments on ethnic dress refer mostly to the female members of each group as hill tribe men tend to dress like rural Thais. Population figures are 1986 estimates.

The Shan (*Thai Yai*) are not included as they are not a hill tribe group per se as they live in permanent locations, practice Theravada Buddhism and speak a language very similar to Thai.

Lonely Planet's *Thai Hill Tribes Phrasebook* gives a handy, basic introduction to the culture and languages of a number of the tribes.

Akha (Thai: *I-kaw*)

Population: 33,600
Origin: Tibet
Present locations: Thailand, Laos, Burma (Myanmar), Yunnan
Economy: rice, corn, opium
Belief system: animism, with an emphasis on ancestor worship.
Distinctive characteristics: head dresses of beads, feathers and dangling silver ornaments. Villages are along mountain ridges or on steep slopes from 1000 to 1400 metres in altitude. The Akha are amongst the poorest of Thailand's ethnic minorities and tend to resist assimilation into the Thai mainstream. Like the Lahu, they often cultivate opium for their own consumption.

Hmong (Thai: *Meo* or *Maew*)

Population: 80,000
Origin: south China
Present locations: south China, Thailand, Laos, Vietnam
Economy: rice, corn, opium
Belief system: animism
Distinctive characteristics: simple black jackets and indigo trousers with striped borders or indigo skirts, and silver jewellery. Most women wear their hair in a large bun. They usually live on mountain peaks or plateaus. Kinship is patrilineal and polygamy is permitted. They are Thailand's second largest hill tribe group and are especially numerous in Chiang Mai Province.

Karen (Thai: *Yang* or *Kariang*)

Population: 265,600
Origin: Burma
Present locations: Thailand, Burma (Myanmar)
Economy: rice, vegetables, livestock

Belief system: animism, Buddhism, Christianity – depending on the group.
Distinctive characteristics: thickly woven V-neck tunics of various colours (unmarried women wear white). Kinship is matrilineal and marriage is endogamous. They tend to live in lowland valleys and practice crop rotation rather than swidden (slash and burn) agriculture. There are four distinct Karen groups – the White Karen (Skaw Karen), Pwo Karen, Black Karen (Pa-o) and Kayah. These groups combined are the largest hill tribe in Thailand, numbering a quarter of a million people or about half of all hill tribe people. Many Karen continue to migrate into Thailand from Burma (Myanmar), fleeing Burmese Government persecution.

Lahu (Thai: *Musoe*)

Population: 58,700
Origin: Tibet
Present locations: south China, Thailand, Burma (Myanmar)
Economy: rice, corn, opium
Belief system: theistic animism (supreme deity is *Geusha*) and some groups are Christian.
Distinctive characteristics: black and red jackets with narrow skirts for women. They live in mountainous areas at about 1000 metres. Their intricately woven shoulder bags (*yaam*) are prized by collectors. There are four main groups – Red Lahu, Black Lahu, Yellow Lahu and Lahu Sheleh.

Lisu (Thai: *Lisaw*)

Population: 24,000
Origin: Tibet
Present locations: Thailand, Yunnan
Economy: rice, opium, corn, livestock
Belief system: animism with ancestor worship and spirit possession.
Distinctive characteristics: the women wear long multi-coloured tunics over trousers and sometimes black turbans with tassels. Men wear baggy green or blue pants pegged in at the ankles. They wear lots of bright colours. Premarital sex is said to be common, along with freedom in choosing marital partners. Patrilineal clans have pan-tribal jurisdiction, which makes the Lisu unique among hill tribe groups (most tribes have power centred at the village level with either the shaman or a village headman). Their villages are usually in the mountains at about 1000 metres.

Mien (Thai: *Yao*)

Population: 35,500
Origin: central China
Present locations: Thailand, south China, Laos, Burma (Myanmar), Vietnam
Economy: rice, corn, opium
Belief system: animism with ancestor worship and Taoism.

Distinctive characteristics: women wear black jackets and trousers decorated with intricately embroidered patches and red fur-like collars, along with large dark blue or black turbans. They have been heavily influenced by Chinese traditions and use Chinese characters to write the Mien language. They tend to settle near mountain springs at between 1000 and 1200 metres. Kinship is patrilineal and marriage is polygamous.

Getting There & Away

The straightforward way of getting to the north is simply to head directly from Bangkok to Chiang Mai either by bus, train or air. Fortunately, there are also some more unusual routes, although the old 'Laotian Loop' – which took you from Bangkok to Vientiane, Luang Prabang and Ban Houei Sai, then back into Thailand to Chiang Rai and eventually Chiang Mai – is no longer possible. You can still, however, make an interesting northern loop from Bangkok to Chiang Mai and back through north-east Thailand.

From Bangkok, you can visit the ancient capitals of Ayuthaya, Lopburi and Sukhothai on your way to Chiang Mai. If you visit these ancient cities southbound rather than northbound, you'll hit them in chronological order. Or, you could take a longer and less 'off-the-beaten-track' route by first heading west to Nakhon Pathom and Kanchanaburi and then back-tracking and travelling north-east by bus to Suphanburi and Ang Thong en route to Ayuthaya.

From Chiang Mai, you can head north to Fang and take the daily riverboat down the Kok River (a tributary of the Mekong) to Chiang Rai. From there, you can head back towards Chiang Mai, get off at Lampang and either catch a bus via Tak to Sukhothai or take the train to Phitsanulok. From Phitsanulok, you can bus it to Lom Sak and then Loei and Udon Thani. There is also a road between Lom Sak and Khon Kaen. Udon Thani and Khon Kaen are both on the rail and bus routes back to Bangkok but there are a number of other places worth exploring in the north-east before heading back to the capital.

CHIANG MAI

Thailand's second largest city is a bit of a tourist trap – full of noisy motorbikes and souvenir shops – but it offers interesting contrasts with the rest of the country and there is plenty to see. It's also a useful base for trips further afield.

At one time, Chiang Mai was part of the independent Lanna Thai (Million Thai Rice-Fields) Kingdom, much given to warring with kingdoms in Burma and Laos, as well as Sukhothai to the south. You can still see the moat that encircled the city at that time, but the remaining fragments of the city wall are mainly reconstructions. Originally founded in 1296, Chiang Mai fell to the Burmese in 1556, but was recaptured in 1775.

Orientation

The old city of Chiang Mai is a neat square bounded by moats. Moon Muang Rd, along the east moat, is one of the main centres for cheap accommodation and places to eat. Tha Phae Rd runs east from the middle of this side and crosses the Ping River where it changes name to Charoen Muang Rd. The railway station and the GPO are both further down Charoen Muang Rd, a fair distance from the centre.

Information

Tourist Office The TAT (☎ 22 2022) have recently moved into a new office (not shown on most Chiang Mai maps) on Chiang Mai-Lamphun Rd, a couple of hundred metres south of the Nawarat Bridge. They have piles of useful hand-outs on everything from guest house accommodation to trekking.

Post & Telecommunications The main post office in Chiang Mai is on Charoen Muang Rd near the railway station. It is open Monday to Friday from 8.30 am to 4.30 pm. Overseas calls, telexes, faxes and telegrams can be arranged here 24 hours a day.

In 1990, the Chiang Mai telephone system was in the midst of renumbering, so many of the local publications list numbers that are no longer correct. Eventually, all numbers in

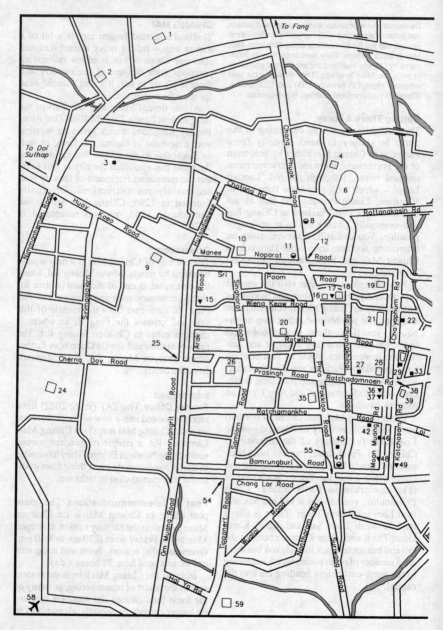

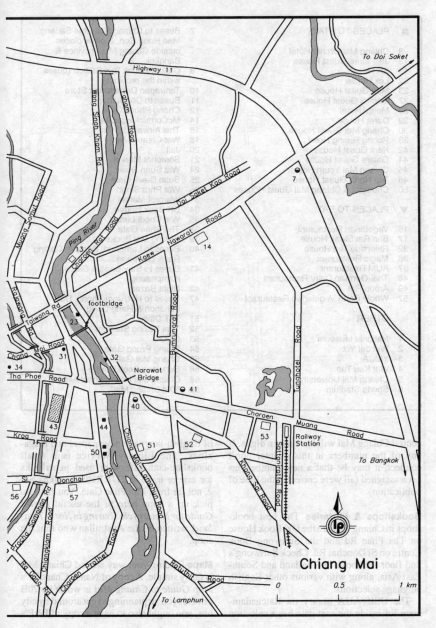

■ PLACES TO STAY

9 Chiang Mai Orchid Hotel
13 Je T'aime Guest House
19 SK House
22 Lek House
23 Mee Guest House
27 Gemini Guest House
28 Montri Hotel
29 Daret House
30 Chang Moi Guest House
33 Roong Ruang Hotel
42 Kent Guest House
44 Galare Guest House
45 Chiang Mai Youth Hostel
46 Top North Guest House
50 Chumpol & Chiang Mai Guest Houses

▼ PLACES TO EAT

15 Vegetarian Restaurant
17 Ban Rai Steak House
32 Riverside Tea House
36 Magic Restaurant
37 AUM Restaurant
48 Thai-German Dairy Restaurant
49 Aroon Rai
57 Whole Earth Vegetarian Restaurant

OTHER

1 National Museum
2 Wat Jet Yot
3 YMCA
4 Wat Kuu Tao
5 Chiang Mai University
6 Sports Stadium

7 Buses to Chiang Rai, Mae Sarieng, Mae Hong Son, & other places outside Chiang Mai Province & Bangkok
8 Chiang Phuak Bus Station (buses within the province)
10 Tantrapan Department Store
11 Buses to Doi Suthap
12 Chang Phuak Gate
14 McCormick Hospital
16 Thai Airways
18 Wat Chiang Man
20 Jail
21 Somphet Market
24 Wat Suan Dawk
25 Suan Dawk Gate
26 Wat Phra Singh
31 Warorot Market
34 DK Book House
35 Wat Chedi Luang
38 Tha Phae Gate
39 Chiang Mai Books
40 Buses to Lamphun, Pasang, Chiang Rai & Lampang
41 Buses to Baw Sang & San Kamphaeng
43 Night Bazaar
47 Buses to Hot, Jom Thong, Doi Inthanon & Hang Dong
51 TAT Office
52 Thai Boxing Stadium
53 GPO
54 Suang Prung Gate
55 Chang Mai Gate
56 Suriwong Book Centre
58 Chiang Mai International Airport
59 "Old Chiang Mai"

central Chiang Mai will have seven digits. If any of the numbers in this chapter don't connect, it may be that a new number has been assigned (all were correct at the time of publication).

Bookshops & Libraries The best bookshops in Chiang Mai are the DK Book House on Tha Phae Rd and the Suriwong Book Centre on Si Donchai Rd. Check Suriwong's 2nd floor for books on Thailand and South-East Asia, along with various other English language selections.

The USIS/AUA library on Ratchadamnoen Rd inside the east gate has a selection of English-language newspapers and magazines. The Library Service is a small bookshop-cum-cafe with used paperbacks for sale or trade at 21/1 Ratchamankha Soi 2, not far from Tha Phae Gate. You can also pick up a copy here of the useful *Pocket Guide for Motorcycle Touring in North Thailand*, written by the Australian who runs the shop.

Maps Finding your way around Chiang Mai is fairly simple. A copy of Nancy Chandler's *Map Guide to Chiang Mai* is worth its 70B price. If you're planning to get around by city bus, you ought also to have a copy of P&P's

Tourist Map of Chiang Mai: Rose of the North which has a good bus map on one side and a very detailed highway map of northern Thailand on the other.

Police The Tourist Police can be reached in Chiang Mai by dialling 24 8974 from 6 am to midnight or 22 2977 after hours. Their office is attached to the TAT office on Chiang Mai-Lamphun Rd.

Warning Beware of drug busts in Chiang Mai. Some guest houses and samlor drivers have been known to supply you with dope and then turn you in. Also take care with valuables stored at guest houses while out trekking. A few years ago, Thailand was swept by a range of credit-card scams and a favourite method was borrowing credit cards from trekkers' baggage while they were away. Months later, back in their home country, they would discover enormous bills run up during the period they were trekking.

We still get a steady trickle of complaints about valuables going missing while guest houses were looking after them and credit cards still seem to be a favourite target. Removing the odd travellers' cheque is another trick. Over the last five years, we've probably had more reports of thefts from Chiang Mai guest houses than anywhere else in Asia – it rivals the similar stream of letters we used to get about thefts from small hotels in Lahore, Pakistan.

Hospitals The McCormick Hospital (☎ 24 1107) on Kaew Nawarat Rd is the travellers' best bet. A consultation and treatment for something simple costs about 250B. Suandok Hospital has a malaria centre.

Things to See

Wat Chiang Man This is the oldest wat within the city walls and was erected by King Mengrai, Chiang Mai's founder, in 1296. Two famous Buddha images are kept here in the smaller *wihan* (chapel) to the right of the main bot. One is the Crystal Buddha which, like Bangkok's Emerald Buddha, was once

shuttled back and forth between Siam and Laos.

Wat Phra Singh In the centre of town, this well-kept wat was founded in 1345. There are a number of interesting buildings here but the supposedly 1500-year-old Phra Singh Buddha image is a subject of some controversy and its exact history is unknown.

Wat Chedi Luang Originally constructed in 1411, this wat contains the ruins of a huge chedi which collapsed in a 1545 earthquake. It has been planned to restore it for several years now and it looks like they're finally getting around to it.

Other Wats The **Wat Jet Yot** has seven (jet) spires (yot) and was damaged by the Burmese in 1566. It's near the Chiang Mai Museum and is modelled (imperfectly) after the Mahabodhi Temple in Bodh Gaya, India, where the Buddha attained enlightenment. **Wat Kuu Tao** has a peculiar chedi like a pile of diminishing spheres.

The **Wat Suan Dawk** was originally built in 1383 and contains a 500-year-old bronze Buddha image and colourful Jataka murals showing scenes from the Buddha's lives. **Wat U Mong**, a forest temple outside the city, also dates from Mengrai's rule and has a fine image of the fasting Buddha. On Sundays, a German monk teaches meditation classes at U Mong.

National Museum The National Museum has a good display of Buddha images and northern Thai handicrafts. It is open from 9 am to 4 pm, Wednesday to Sunday, and admission is 10B.

Other The **Tribal Research Centre** at Chiang Mai University has a good small museum of hill-tribe artefacts. Head out west from the city centre towards Wat Suan Dawk – it's two blocks north once you get to the university. **Old Chiang Mai** is a touristy 'instant hill tribes' centre. There are Thai and hill-tribe dance performances here every night.

The annual dry-season **Songkran** (Water Festival) takes place, with particular fervour, in mid-April in Chiang Mai. The late December to early-January **Winter Fair** is also a great scene with all sorts of activities and lots of colourful visitors from the hills. The biggest festival of them all is the **Flower Festival**, held during the first week of February. This festival features parades in which the various amphoes, or districts, throughout Chiang Mai Province compete for the best flower-bedecked float and enter their most beautiful young women in the Queen of the Flower Festival contest.

You'll often see local hill tribespeople in Chiang Mai – check the night bazaar just off Tha Phae Rd. There are lots of handicrafts on sale in Chiang Mai. In the centre of town, Chiang Mai's jail has a large, resident foreigner population, most of them from drug busts.

Places to Stay

Guest Houses In Chiang Mai, travellers' accommodation is usually in guest houses. There are plenty of them with prices mainly in the 50 to 100B bracket. The guest house definition is a rather loose one, some cheap hotels have changed their name in English to 'guest house' while retaining the word 'hotel' in Thai. It's simply a convenient buzz word. Many of the guest houses are along Moon Muang Rd on either side of the east moat. Others can be found along Charoen Rat Rd, on the east side of the Ping River, or on Charoen Prathet Rd, on the west side of the river. The latter streets are some distance from the city centre, but convenient for the railway station and Chiang Rai buses.

TAT lists over 100 guest houses at last count – so if you don't like one, move. During peak periods (from December to March and from July to August), it may be best to go to the TAT office first, pick up a free copy of the guest house list, and make a few calls to find out where rooms are available. All guest houses have phones these days.

Costs are typically 70 to 80B for a double room. Popular ones include the *Lek House* at 22 Chaiyaphum Rd, near the Chang Moi Rd intersection. It's quiet and has a nice garden. Single/double rooms with fan and bath are 80/100B downstairs and 100/120B upstairs (larger, newer rooms). There's a good restaurant and breakfast is 15B. Nearby, the *Pao Come Guest House* has similar facilities and cheaper rooms (50/70B), should you find Lek House full.

The *Chang Moi Guest House* (☎ 25 1839) at 29 Chang Moi Rd is behind the New Chiang Mai Hotel and has rooms for 50/60/70B plus a triple for 100B. Avoid the two small annexed rooms in front which can be noisy. Nearby is the popular *Happy House* at 11 Chang Moi Rd, with big, clean rooms for 100B/180B. Also on Chang Moi Rd is the comfortable *Eagle House* (☎ 23 5387) at 70/80B, or 60B with shared bath. The long-standing *VK Guest House*, down an alley off Chang Moi Rd near Tha Phae Rd, is quiet and friendly – it costs 50/70B for basic but clean rooms; a triple with bath costs 35B per person.

On Chaiyaphum Rd, in the same area, is the extremely popular *Daret House* at 70/100B but it's almost always full – simply because it's so visible. Also near the east moat, the *PK Guest House* is another long-term survivor at 109 Moon Muang Rd (Soi 7) and costs the standard 60/80B for rooms with fan and bath. Similar is the *SK House* at 30 Moon Muang Rd, Soi 9.

Also inside the moat is the *Peter Guest House* at 46/3 Moon Muang Rd. Rooms with fan and bath cost from 60 to 80B. The *Top North Guest House* at 15 Soi 2, Moon Muang Rd, is an efficiently-run place for 150B single and 200B double. All rooms have a fan and bath. Up from the original Youth Hostel at 7 Soi 6, Phra Pokklao Rd, is the *Nat Guest House*, a comfortable place with rooms from 80B.

The *Chiang Mai Youth Hostel* (☎ 21 2863) at 31 Phra Pokklao Rd (Soi 3) has a dorm at 40B per person, singles from 50B and doubles from 60B with a student or YHA card, 10B more without. There is another branch on Changklam Rd with more mid-range rates – 250B for a room with fan and bath and 300B with air-con.

Chumpol Guest House (☎ 23 4526), 89 Charoen Prathet Rd, has rooms from 70 to 120B. Next door is the popular *Chiang Mai Guest House* (☎ 23 6501) at No 91 with rooms from 100 to 200B.

The *Gemini Guest House* at 22 Ratchad-amnoen Rd is an old teak house with dorm beds at 20B or rooms from 50 to 80B. The *Je T'aime Guest House* (☎ 23 4912) at 247 Charoen Rat Rd is a long-running favourite in a peaceful and relaxed garden-like setting. It's rather far from the city centre, but that doesn't seem to bother people. The rooms all have a fan and shower, and cost from 50/60B for singles/doubles. They'll arrange to pick you up from the bus or train station if you phone.

Isra Guest House at 109/24 Huay Kaew Rd, Suthep (near the Rincon Hotel), is modern and clean with prices from 30B. Although it's a long way out, it's on a bus route and they lend out bicycles for free.

Two pleasant places along Charoen Rat Rd next to the Ping River are the *Gold Riverside* at 282/3 and the *Mee Guest House* at 193/1. Both have rooms in the 60 to 80B range. There are lots of others tucked away throughout Chiang Mai.

Hotels Apart from the guest houses, there are also plenty of hotels, in all price ranges. About the least expensive is the *Thai Charoen* (☎ 23 6640) at 164-6 Tha Phae Rd, between the moat and the TAT office – Summit Trekking is out front. Rooms with fan and bath cost from 60B. The *Roong Ruang Hotel* (☎ 23 6746) at 398 Tha Phae Rd, near the east side of the moat, has a good location and clean rooms at 180/200B.

The *YMCA* (☎ 287 2727/1900) is at 2/4 Mengrai-Rasni Rd, above the north-west corner of the moat. After recent renovations, it's gone up-market – 90/100B for all air-con rooms. *Sri Rajawong* (☎ 23 5864) is at 103 Rajawong Rd, between the east moat and the river, and costs from 70B for a fan-cooled room with bath. The

Muang Thong (☎ 23 6438) at 5 Ratchamankha Rd is similarly priced, and the *Nakhorn Ping* (☎ 23 6024), 43 Taiwang Rd near the Prince Hotel, costs 90B.

Moon Muang Golden Court (☎ 21 2779), off the street at 95/1 Moon Muang, is good value for 100/150B with fan and private bath. Hot water showers are also available.

Places to Eat

Western-Thai Along either side of the east moat near Tha Phae Gate are a number of places that pack in the travellers attracted to Western food and fruit drinks. The long-running *Daret* has moved operations across the moat to Chaiyaphum Rd. They do some great drinks and Westernised Thai food but service can be slow when it's crowded. *Magic* has taken over Daret's old digs on Moon Muang Rd and offers a similar menu. Along a little bit, the *Thai-German Dairy Restaurant* is another long-running travellers' centre.

The *JJ Bakery* under the Montri Hotel has a good menu of Thai, Chinese, and Western food at very reasonable prices, especially considering how clean the place is and the fact that it has air-con. The *Pizza Peacock* at 138 Tha Phae Rd is open from 10 am until 12 midnight.

The popular *Ban Rai Steak House* is next to Wat Chiang Man, behind the Thai Airways office. It's just the place for people in dire need of an infusion of steak and potatoes or a shish-kebab with potatoes and vegetables. It's the 'nearest thing to home in Asia', reported one happy traveller. Back on Moon Muang Rd, the *Orchid Pub & Steakhouse* serves up similar Western-style food.

The *Riverside Tea House* at 9-11 Charoen Rat Rd, on the banks of the Ping River, features 'home-style cooking' and country/ folk music. On weekend nights it's quite the scene. Another popular night-time hang-out for food (inexpensive, large portions), drinks and music (mostly blues and jazz) is *Moo's Blues*, at 608 Loi Kroa Rd.

Thai South of Tha Prae Rd, on the moat, is the big open air *Aroon Rai* which specialises in northern Thai food and is a great place to try sticky rice and other northern specialities. Get a group together in order to try the maximum number of dishes – some of them are *very* hot and spicy. Nearby, between the New Chiang Mai Hotel and Tha Phae Gate, the *Thanam Restaurant* is smaller but even better for local food. It's very clean and no alcohol is served.

Along Kotchasam Rd, just south of the Loi Kroa Rd intersection, are several restaurants serving cheap and tasty north-eastern food including grilled chicken and sticky rice.

Chiang Mai is famed for its fine noodles. *Koliang*, on the corner of Moon Muang and Ratchamankha Rds, does great 'boat noodles'. *Khao soi*, a concoction of spicy curried chicken with flat wheat noodles, is the true Chiang Mai speciality. *New Lamduon Fahharm Kao Soi* (formerly Khao Soi Lam Duang) on Charoen Rat Rd and not far from the Je T'aime Guest House, is particularly good and their noodles cost just 8B a bowl. Even the king has tried them! More towards the centre of town is a noodle shop opposite Tha Phae Gate, on Chaiyaphum Rd (near the entrance to the Times Square Guest House), where khao soi is also the specialty.

Vegetarian Chiang Mai has several vegetarian places such as the very cheap *Sala Mangsawirat* (the English sign reads 'Vegetarian Food') on Arak Rd at the west moat, near the Wieng Kaew Rd intersection. It's closed on Friday and Saturday. Or, try *Whole Earth*, which is run by the local Trancendental Meditation (TM) folk and is a little more expensive. It's on Si Donchai Rd, past the Changklam Rd intersection, and has Thai and Indian vegetarian fare. There's also a traveller-oriented vegetarian place, right by the Magic on Moon Muang Rd, called *AUM Vegetarian Restaurant*. Reports are mixed on this one – we liked it but some people think the food's not so great.

Behind the mosque, on Charoen Rat Rd (Soi 1), are several inexpensive Thai-Muslim restaurants which serve a few vegetarian dishes.

Markets There is a very large night bazaar just west of Chiang Mai Gate on Bamrungburi Rd, a great place to make an evening of eating and drinking. The Warorot Market, at the intersection of Chang Moi and Changklam Rds, is open from 6 am to 5 pm daily. Upstairs, inside the market, are vendors who serve excellent and very cheap Chinese rice and noodle dishes.

Things to Buy

There are a lot of things to attract your money in the northern capital of Chiang Mai, but basically the city is a very commercial and touristy place and a lot of junk is churned out for the undiscerning – so buy carefully. The night bazaar in Chiang Mai, near the expensive hotels, is a good place to look for almost anything, but you have to bargain hard.

Very attractive lengths of cotton and silk can be made into all sorts of things. Go to Pasang, south of Lamphun, for cotton. For Thai silk, with its lush colours and pleasantly rough texture, try San Kamphaeng, east of Chiang Mai. Although very touristy these days, the fabric is cheaper here than in Bangkok.

For ceramics, Thai Celadon, about six km north of Chiang Mai, turns out ceramic-ware modelled on the Sawankhalok pottery that used to be made at Sukhothai and exported all over the region hundreds of years ago. Other ceramics can be seen close to Old Chiang Mai.

All sorts of wood carvings and laquerware are available, and you'll see lots of antiques around, including opium weights – the little animal-shaped weights used to measure out opium in the Golden Triangle.

There are a number of silverwork shops close to the South Moat Gate. The hill tribe jewellery – heavy chunky stuff – is very nice. Plain and embroidered clothes are available at low prices but check the quality carefully.

You can also take a bus out to Baw Sang (east of Chiang Mai), the umbrella village, where beautiful paper umbrellas are hand painted. A huge garden one is around 500B, but postage and packing can add a fair bit more. Attractive leaf paintings – framed – are also made here.

Getting There & Away

Air You can fly to Chiang Mai three or four times daily from Bangkok. The flight takes an hour and the normal fare is 1300B – a special night fare is less. There are also flights between Chiang Mai and other towns in the north including Chiang Rai. You can enter Thailand at Chiang Mai since there is a regular Thai International connection with Hong Kong.

Bus Regular buses from Bangkok take nine or 10 hours to reach Chiang Mai and cost from 133 to 150B; air-con buses cost from 240 to 280B and take about eight hours. There are lots of buses from the Northern bus terminal in Bangkok, starting at 5.30 am and finishing at around 9 pm. The fare depends on the routing. A variety of more expensive tour buses also make the trip from Bangkok to Chiang Mai – a 'VIP' bus with only 30 reclining seats is 370B.

Several travel agencies on Bangkok's Khao San Rd offer air-con bus tickets from 180 to 200B which include a free night's accommodation in Chiang Mai. Some of these trips work out OK. Others are rip-offs in which the Chiang Mai guest house charges bathroom and electricity fees in lieu of a room charge. The only real advantage to these trips is that they depart from Khao San Rd, saving you a trip to the Northern bus terminal. But the entire bus will be loaded with foreigners – not a very cultural experience.

If you're intending to hop from town to town on your way north, Chiang Mai buses operate via Phitsanulok, Sukhothai, Uttaradit and Lampang.

Train The trains to Chiang Mai from Bangkok are rather slower, although this is no problem on the overnight service since it gives you a night's sleep if you have a sleeper. There are express trains at 6 and 7.40 pm, which arrive at 7.30 and 8.05 am respectively, plus a rapid train at 3 pm which arrives

at 5.15 am. On the express, you can get 2nd-class tickets for 285B plus the sleeper cost. Third-class tickets are only available on the rapid trains and cost 141B. Whether travelling by bus or train, you should book in advance if possible.

Getting Around

To/From the Airport A taxi from the airport costs 60B, door-to-door minibuses are 40B and a songthaew will be 5 to 10B. The airport is only two or three km from the city centre.

Local Transport You can rent bicycles (from 20 to 25B a day) or motorbikes (from 150 to 250B) to explore around Chiang Mai – check with your guest house or the 65 Motorcycle Rental Service, on Moon Muang Rd near the Tha Phae Gate. There are plenty of songthaews around the city with standard fares of 5B, and city buses cost 2B.

Hordes of songthaew jockeys meet incoming buses and trains at Chiang Mai – they wave signs for the various guest houses and if the one you want pops up you can have ride free to there.

AROUND CHIANG MAI
Doi Suthep

From the hill-top temple of **Wat Phra That**, there are superb views over Chiang Mai. Choose a clear day to make the 16 km, hairpinned ascent to the temple. A long flight of steps, lined by ceramic-tailed *nagas* (dragons) leads up to the temple from the car park.

The **Phu Ping Palace** is five km beyond the temple – you can wander the gardens on Friday, Saturday and Sunday. Just before the palace car park, a turn to the left will lead you to a **Meo village**, four km away. It's very touristed since it's so near to Chiang Mai, but the opium 'museum' is worth a visit if you're in the vicinity.

Getting There & Away Minibuses to Doi Suthep leave from the Elephant Gate and cost around 35B – downhill it's 25B. For another 5B, you can take a bicycle up with you and zoom back downhill.

Baw Sang & San Kamphaeng

The 'umbrella village' of Baw Sang is nine km east of Chiang Mai. It's a picturesque though touristy spot where the townspeople engage in just about every type of northern Thai handicraft. Four or five km further down highway 1006 is San Kamphaeng which specialises in cotton and silk weaving. Pasang, however, is probably better for cotton.

Getting There & Away Buses to Baw Sang (sometimes spelled Bo Sang or Bor Sang) leave from the north side of Charoen Muang Rd in Chiang Mai, between the river and the GPO, every 15 minutes. The fare is 4B to Baw Sang and 5B to San Kamphaeng.

Elephants

A daily 'elephants at work' show takes place near the Km 58 marker on the Fang road north of Chiang Mai. Arrive around 9 am or earlier to see bath-time in the river. It's really just a tourist trap, but probably worth the admission price. Once the spectators have gone, the logs are all put back in place for tomorrow's show!

It's a good idea to have a picture of an elephant to show the bus conductor, or 'elephant' may be interpreted as 'Fang', the town further north. There's a northern Thailand elephant meeting in November each year – hotel and food prices go up at that time.

Another place to see elephants is the **Elephant Training School** (really) on the Chiang Rai to Lampang road. From Lampang, it's about 14B on a bumpy old bus. A big sign on the roadside in Thai and English (on the other side) indicates the location. You have to walk a couple of km up and down hills to get to the well-hidden school – you might be able to find an elephant to follow!

The place is set up for tourists and has seats and even toilets, but nobody seems to know about it. When the trainer feels like it, sometime between 8 am and 12 noon, the show begins and you'll see them put through their paces. The elephants appreciate a few pieces of fruit – 'it feels like feeding a vacuum cleaner with a wet nozzle,' reported one visitor. Any bus on the main road will take you on to Lampang or Chiang Rai.

Lamphun

This town, only 26 km south of Chiang Mai, has two interesting wats. **Wat Phra That Haripunchai** has a small museum and a very old chedi, variously dated at 897 or 1157 AD. There are some other fine buildings in the compound. **Wat Chama Thevi**, popularly known as Wat Kukut, has an unusual chedi with 60 Buddha images set in niches. Another Haripunchai-era wat in the town, **Wat Mahawan**, is a source of highly reputable Buddhist amulets.

Places to Stay

Si Lamphun (☎ 511 1760) on the town's main street, Inthayongyot Rd, has rooms for around 100B. *Suan Kaew Bungalows*, at Km 6 on the highway from Lamphun to Lampang, has rooms from 80B.

Getting There & Away Buses depart Chiang Mai regularly from the south side of Nawarat Bridge on Lamphun Rd. The fare is 6B, or 8B by minibus. A minibus straight through to Pasang will cost 10B.

Pasang

Only a short songthaew ride south of Lamphun, Pasang is a centre for cotton-weaving. The Nantha Khwang shop has good locally made cotton goods.

NAKHON SAWAN

At this fairly large town on the way north, there are good views from the hilltop **Wat Chom Kiri Nak Phrot** and interesting boat trips can be made from the jetty.

Places to Stay

If you stay here, the *Arak* at 45-47 Arak Rd and the *Sala Thai* (☎ 22 2938) at 217-225 Matulee Rd have 100B rooms with fan and bath. Or, there's the *Asia* (☎ 21 3752) at 956 Phahonyothin Rd (the highway through town from Bangkok) with rooms from 80B.

The *Wang Mai*, at the market on the waterfront, is a good place with doubles at 90B with bath, and it has a good restaurant downstairs.

KAMPHAENG PHET

This town is only a couple of km off the road from Bangkok to Chiang Mai. There are a number of relics within the old city and very fine remains of the long city wall. Outside the wall is **Wat Phra Si Ariyabot** with the shattered remains of standing, sitting, walking and reclining Buddha images. **Wat Chang Rop**, or 'temple surrounded by elephants', is just that – a temple with an elephant-buttressed wall.

Places to Stay

It can be a little difficult to find places here since few signs are in English script. *Nitaya Prapha* (☎ 71 1381) at 49 Thesa Rd is a little squalid and has rooms from 60B. It's on the main road leading to the river bridge. There are food stalls opposite at night and the main ruins are around the corner beyond the food stalls – further down the road away from the bridge towards Sukhothai.

At 114 Ratchadamnoen Rd, the *Ratchadamnoen*, in the newer part of the city, has rooms for 80B as well as more expensive air-con ones. One of the friendlier places is the *Gor Choke Chai (Kaw Chokchai) Hotel* (☎ 71 1247) at 7-31 Ratchadamnoen Rd (Soi 6) – the rooms start at 80B.

Getting There & Away

The bus fare from Bangkok is 69B, or 126B with air-con. Most visitors come here from Sukhothai (20B), Phitsanulok (27B) or Tak (14B).

PHITSANULOK

There's not a great deal of interest in this town, which is mainly used as a stepping stone to other places. It's on the rail line between Bangkok and Chiang Mai, and it's here you get off for Sukhothai. **Wat Phra Si Ratana Mahathat** (known locally as Wat Yai) is an interesting old wat, however, and

it contains one of the most revered Buddha images in Thailand.

Places to Stay & Eat

If you come straight out of the railway station and turn left by the expensive *Amarin Nakhon Hotel* on the corner of the first and second right turns, you'll find some cheaper hotels. The rather grubby *Haw Fah* at 73 Phyalithai Rd and the *Unachak* both have rooms from 90B. The *Phitsanulok* is similar.

For a more relaxed atmosphere, consider the *Phitsanulok Youth Hostel* (☎ 24 2060) at 38 Sanam Bin Rd (take bus No 3 from the railway station). Large double rooms are 120B (100B for IYH cardholders) and the dorm is 50B per person (40B for cardholders). The hostel has a modest restaurant and there are several cheap eateries in the vicinity.

At any of the 'flying vegetable' restaurants in town, cooks fling fried morning glory vine through the air from wok to plate, held by a waiter who has climbed onto the shoulders of two colleagues (or onto a truck in the night market)! Floating restaurants along the river are also popular.

Getting There & Away

Buses for Sukhothai go from the town centre, but the stations for buses to the east or north are on the other (east) side of the railway tracks, on the outskirts of town. From Chiang Mai or Bangkok, you can reach Phitsanulok by bus or rail. Buses from Bangkok cost 72B, or 130B with air-con. You can also fly there from Bangkok.

Getting Around

Grey buses run between the town centre and the airport or bus station for 2B. The big hotels also run free buses to and from the airport, or a songthaew costs 5B.

SUKHOTHAI

Sukhothai was Thailand's first capital but its period of glory was short. From its foundation as a capital in 1257, it only lasted a little over 100 years to 1379 before being superseded by Ayuthaya. Nevertheless, its achievements in art, literature, language and law, apart from the more visible evidence of great buildings, were enormous. In many ways, the ruins visible today at Sukhothai and the other cities of the kingdom, like Kamphaeng Phet and Si Satchanalai, are more appealing than Ayuthaya because they are less commercial and more off the beaten track.

Orientation & Information

Old Sukhothai, known as Muang Kao, is spread over quite an area but bicycles can be hired. New Sukhothai has a good market but otherwise it's an uninteresting place, 12 km from the old town. Sukhothai is 55 km east of the Bangkok to Chiang Mai road from Tak. A guidebook and map, available at the old town entrance, is essential for exploring the scattered ruins. The ruins are divided into five zones and there is a 20B admission fee into each zone.

Things to See

Ramkhamhaeng National Museum

This museum offers an introductory look at Sukhothai history and culture, and is a good place to begin your explorations. They also sell guides to the ruins here. It's open daily from 9 am to 4 pm and admission is 20B.

Wat Mahathat

This vast assemblage, the largest in the city, once contained 198 chedis – apart from various chapels and sanctuaries. Some of the original Buddha images still remain, including a big one amongst the broken columns. The large ornamented pond provides fine reflections.

Wat Si Chum

A massive seated Buddha figure is tightly squeezed into this open, walled building. A narrow tunnel inside the wall leads to views over the Buddha's shoulders and on to the top. Candle-clutching kids used to guide you up and point out the 'Buddha foot' on the way but in recent years the tunnel has been closed to visitors.

Other

The Wat Si Sawai, with three prangs and a moat, was originally intended to be a Hindu temple. It's just south of Wat Mahathat. Wat Sa Si is a classically-simple Sukhothai-style wat set on an island. Wat Trapang Thong, next to the museum, is reached by a footbridge crossing the large lotus-filled pond which surrounds it. It is still in use. Somewhat isolated to the north of the city, Wat Phra Pai Luang is similar in style to Wat Si Sawai. Wat Chang Lom is to the east and the chedi is surrounded by 36 elephants. Wat Saphan Hin is a couple of km west of the old city walls on a hillside and features a large standing Buddha looking back to Sukhothai.

Places to Stay

New Sukhothai is a clinical and dull town, although there are some good hotels and restaurants.

Guest Houses Guest houses are popping up like mushrooms and include the *No 4 Guest House* (☎ 61 1315) in a large house at 234/6 Charot Withithong Rd, Soi Panitsan, near the Rajthanee Hotel. Dorm beds are 30B and single/double rooms cost 60/80B. They also have a second branch at 170 Thani Rd. *Sky House*, next to the bus terminal, has rooms for 80B with shared bath. The nearby *Somprasong Guest House* is similar.

Yupa House (☎ 61 2578) is near the west bank of the Yom River at 44/10 Prawet Nakhon Rd, Soi Mekhapatthana. The family that run Yupa are friendly and often invite guests to share family meals. They have a 30B dorm, plus rooms of various sizes from 60 to 100B. Other guest houses include the *O-2* at 26/4 Rajuthit Rd.

Hotels Near the town centre, the *Sukhothai Hotel* (☎ 61 1133) at 5/5 Singhawat Rd has a sign in English, Thai and Chinese. The rooms are in the 80 to 100B range (more expensive with air-con) and it's run by pleasant people. 'Too friendly,' said a solo female traveller about unwelcome advances.

Other places include the *Sawastipong* (☎ 61 1567) at 56/2 Singhawat Rd which has rooms from 100B and isn't bad. The *Chinnawat Hotel* at 1-3 Nikhorn Kasem Rd

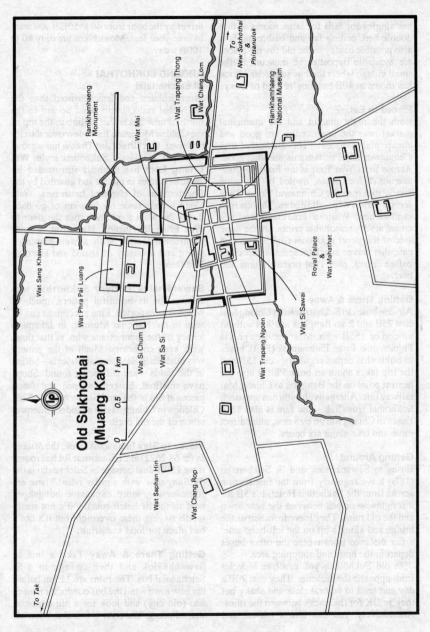

Old Sukhothai (Muang Kao)

To New Sukhothai & Phitsanulok

Ramkhamhaeng Monument
Ramkhamhaeng National Museum
Wat Mai
Wat Trapang Thong
Wat Chang Lom
Wat Sang Khawat
Wat Phra Pai Luang
Wat Si Chum
Wat Sa Si
Wat Trapang Ngoen
Royal Palace & Wat Mahathat
Wat Si Sawai
Wat Saphan Hin
Wat Chang Rop

To Tak

0   0.5   1 km

has singles for 80B for large rooms with a double bed, ceiling fan and bathroom. It is also possible to stay in the old town – places are available opposite the museum in the small village where the bus stops. *Mr Vitoon* has rooms at 40B but they're kind of noisy.

Places to Eat

Both the night market and the municipal market near the town centre are good and cheap places to eat. The *Sukhothai* and *Chinnawat* hotel restaurants are also good. Across from Win Tour is the *Rainbow Restaurant & Ice Cream*, owned by the same family that runs the Chinnawat Hotel. They serve a variety of noodle dishes, Thai curries, sandwiches, Western breakfasts and ice cream at very reasonable prices. On the same side of the street is *Dream Cafe*, an air-con cafe that serves snacks, espresso and other coffee drinks, plus Thai herbal liquors and beer.

Getting There & Away

Air-con buses to Sukhothai from Chiang Mai cost 75B and from Bangkok are 90B without air-con or 155B with. Most services go via Phitsanulok. From Phitsanulok (Phit), buses to Sukhothai depart regularly, cost 15B and the trip takes about an hour. Phit is also the nearest point on the Bangkok to Chiang Mai railway line. Alternatively, you can approach Sukhothai from Tak – the fare is also 15B. Buses to Chiang Rai go by a new, more direct route and take about six hours.

Getting Around

Buses to Sawankhalok and Si Satchanalai (18B) leave regularly from the intersection across from the Sukhothai Hotel. It's 5B for a songthaew or bus between the new town and the old ruins. They leave from across the bridge and along a bit on the left-hand side, a fair distance from where the other buses depart in the hotel and shopping area.

In old Sukhothai, you can hire bicycles from opposite the museum. They cost 20B a day and tend to be brakeless and shaky but they're OK for the tracks between the ruins. Alternatively, you can hire a tuk-tuk and

driver by the hour from 40 to 50B if you want to save your feet. Motorbikes are only 80 to 100B a day.

AROUND SUKHOTHAI
Si Satchanalai

More isolated and less touristed than the Sukhothai ruins, these stand 56 km to the north of new Sukhothai. Climb to the top of the Golden Mountain for a view over the city and river. **Wat Chedi Jet Thaew** has a group of stupas in classic Sukhothai style. **Wat Chang Lom** has a chedi surrounded by Buddha statues in niches and guarded by the fine remains of elephant buttresses. Walk along the riverside for two km or go back down the main road and cross the river to **Wat Phra Si Ratana Mahathat**, a very impressive temple with a well-preserved prang and a variety of seated and standing Buddhas.

Sawankhalok Pottery Sukhothai was famous for its beautiful pottery, much of which was exported. Fine specimens can be seen in the National Museum in Jakarta, a legacy of the Indonesians who, at that time, were keen collectors. Much of the pottery was made in Si Satchanalai. Rejects – buried in the fields – are still being found. Shops have misfired, broken, warped and fused pieces at Sukhothai and Si Satchanalai. Thai Celadon in Chiang Mai is a modern interpretation of the old craft.

Places to Stay In Sawankhalok, the *Muang In* (☎ 64 2622) at 21 Kasemrat Rd has rooms from 150B. Just outside Si Satchanalai is the *59 Bungalow* with similar rates. There are some newer, more expensive bungalows next to the Si Satch ruins – it's not really worth staying there overnight but it's not a bad place for food and drink.

Getting There & Away Take a bus to Sawankhalok and then change to a Si Satchanalai bus. The ruins are 11 km before the new town – tell the bus conductor *muang kao* (old city) and look for a big corn-cob shaped prang. The river is less than a km off the road and there is now a suspension bridge across it. The last bus back leaves around 4 pm.

TAK

This is just a junction town from Sukhothai on the way north to Chiang Mai. It's pronounced 'Tahk' not 'Tack'. From here, you can visit the Lang San National Park and you have to pass through Tak to get to Mae Sot.

Places to Stay & Eat

If you have to stay here, then try the *Tak* (☎ 51 1234) at 18/10 Mahadtai Bamrung Rd or the *Thavisak* at No 561, on the same road; rooms at either start at 100B. The *Sa-nguan Thai* (☎ 51 1265) at 619 Taksin Rd has rooms from 100B, or from 150B with air-con. A traveller who made a lengthy pause here, and liked the place, recommended the *Mae Ping* (☎ 51 1807) opposite the food market on Mahadtai Bamrung Rd, the main street. Rooms here are 80B and there is a good coffee bar downstairs.

MAE SOT

This wild town sits on Thailand's border facing the Burmese town of Myawaddy and, as such, is a big centre for smuggling between the two countries. The area used to be a hotbed of Communist guerrilla activity in the 1960s and 1970s, but is now merely a relay point for the highly profitable trade in guns, narcotics, teak and gems. The local population is an interesting mixture of Thais, Chinese, Indians, Burmese and Karen tribespeople.

Songthaews can take you right to the Moci River border from Mae Sot for 5B. If the border is open you may be permitted to cross the footbridge to Myawaddy for the day. The Pan-Asian Highway (Asia Route 1) continues on from here all the way to Istanbul, if only you were allowed to follow it.

Highway 1085 runs north from Mae Sot to Mae Hong Son province and makes an interesting trip.

Places to Stay & Eat

The *Mae Moei Hotel*, on the main street near

the post and police offices, has rooms from 40 to 50B. On the next street over is the *Siam Hotel* (☎ 53 1376) with rooms for 100B. At the west end of town towards the river, the *Mae Sot Guest House* at 736 Intharakhiri Rd has dorm beds for 30B and single/double rooms for 60/80B. They also hand out helpful area maps.

There is a good chicken-rice stall and a tea shop next door to the Siam Hotel. The market also has good takeaway food.

Getting There & Away

Air Thai flies between Phitsanulok and Mae Sot via Tak four days a week. The fare is 370B.

Bus Air-con minibuses (25B) and share taxis (50B) to Mae Sot leave hourly, 6 am until 6 pm, from the Tak bus station. The trip takes 1½ hours. There is a daily air-con bus to Mae Sot from Bangkok's Northern air-con bus terminal that leaves at 10.15 pm for 179B.

LAMPANG

South-east of Chiang Mai, this town was another former home for the Emerald Buddha. The old town's fine wats include **Wat Phra Saeng** and **Wat Phra Kaew** on the banks of the Wang River to the north of the town. In the village of Koh Kha, 20 km south-west of Lampang, **Wat Lampang Luang** was originally constructed in the Haripunchai period and restored in the 16th century. It's an amazing temple with walls like a huge medieval castle. Getting there is a little difficult, so start out early in the day.

Places to Stay & Eat

At 213-215 Boonyawat Rd, the friendly *Si Sa-Nga* (☎ 21 7070) has large rooms with fan and bathroom for 80B. There are a number of other hotels along Boonyawat Rd, most with rooms starting at 100B.

Good Thai food is available in the place next to the large ice-cream parlour on Ropwiang Rd, or there are several good food stalls near the railway station.

Getting There & Away

There are regular buses between Lampang and Chiang Mai, Chiang Rai, Phitsanulok or Bangkok. The bus station in Lampang is some way out of town. It's a few baht by samlor, more if you arrive late at night. You can also get air-con buses to Bangkok or Chiang Mai from Lampang. An air-con bus can be taken from town and then you don't have to go out to the bus station.

DOI INTHANON

Thailand's highest peak, Doi Inthanon (2595 metres), can be visited as a day trip from Chiang Mai. There are some impressive waterfalls and pleasant picnic spots here. Between Chiang Mai and Doi Inthanon, the small town of Chom Thong has a fine Burmese-style temple, **Wat Phra That Si Chom Thong**.

Getting There & Away

Buses run regularly from Chiang Mai to Chom Thong for 12B. From there, you take a songthaew the few km to Mae Klang for about 10B and another to Doi Inthanon for 30B.

MAE HONG SON

North-west of Chiang Mai – 368 km away by road and close to the Burmese border – this is a crossroads for Burmese visitors, opium traders and local hill tribes. There are several Shan-built wats in the area and a fine view from the hill by the town. It's a peaceful little place that's fast becoming a travellers' centre.

Places to Stay

All the hotels are on the two main streets, Khunlum Praphat and Singhanat Bamrung Rds. *Siam* (☎ 61 1148) and *Methi (Mae Tee)* (☎ 61 1121), both on Khunlum Praphat Rd, are pretty good at 100B for a room with fan and bath. On Singhanat Bamrung Rd, the *Sa-Nguan Sin* and *Suk Somchai* are cheaper but not so good.

There is also a plethora of inexpensive guest houses scattered around Mae Hong Son (MHS). About a km north-west of town is the new location of the long-running *Mae Hong Son Guest House*, along with the motel-like *SR House* and the secluded *Sang Tong Huts* with its panoramic views. Rates are typical of all guest houses in MHS, from 50 to 70B for basic accommodations. As tourism develops, look for new bungalow operations to be built in this neighbourhood since there's plenty of space.

Also on Khunlum Praphat Rd is the *Garden House*, set back off the road a bit – rustic single/double rooms are 50/80B. On the same road is *Khun Tu Guest House* with rooms from 80B. North of MHS, they have another guest house called *Khun Tu Tarzan's House Resort* with similar rates.

Don Guest House is near the south end of Khunlum Praphat Rd next to the Khai Muk Restaurant. Very basic rooms cost 30B for a single and from 40 to 50B for a double. The friendly *Lanna Lodge* is down an alley opposite the Thai Farmer's Bank on Khunlum Praphat – rooms in the old house are 50B and bungalows are 100B.

In the area of Jong Kham Lake are several very pleasant guest houses including *Jong Kham*, *Holiday House* and *Rim Nong*. All are friendly little places with rates starting at 50 to 80B.

Places to Eat

Many guest houses cook Western-style meals and, as well, offer northern Thai food. *Khai Muk* and *Fai Khum* are good restaurants on Khunlum Praphat Rd. A little more expensive, but also very good, is *Ban Buatong*, across from the Siam Hotel.

In Mae Sariang (south of MHS), the *Inthira* restaurant, on the outskirts on the Chiang Mai side, is said to prepare some of the best chicken in holy basil in Thailand. They also do batter-fried frogs!

Getting There & Away

Air Mae Hong Son must be getting more popular – there are now daily flights from Chiang Mai. There are also daily flights between MHS and Chiang Mai for 330B.

By bus, it's nine hours from Chiang Mai to MHS via Mae Sariang. There are about five departures a day, and the trip costs 97B, or 175B in an air-con bus. Coming back, you can take the shorter route through Pai and Mae Taeng on Route 1095. Although this route is slow and windy, recent road improvements mean the trip can take as little as seven hours (don't count on it to be on time, however). The scenery is quite spectacular in parts and you can break the trip by staying overnight in Pai, which is an interesting, somewhat remote kind of place.

PAI

This little two-street town between Chiang Mai and Mae Hong Son, a good base for exploring the surrounding country, is becoming increasingly popular for trekking. For a view of the town, climb the hill to nearby **Wat Phra That Mae Yen**.

Places to Stay

Guest houses line the two main streets in Pai. Across from the bus terminal is the *Duang Guest House* where clean rooms with hot showers cost 30B per person. At the far western end of this road, past the hospital, is the *Kim Guest House*. It's a bit isolated but quiet, and rooms cost from 30 to 40B per person.

The *Pai Guest House*, the town's first, is back towards Chiang Mai on the main road through town – rates are 30B per person. Across the street, behind the Pai Guest House in the Sky Cafe, is the *Pai in the Sky Guest House* with none-too-special rooms for 30B per person. Others on this street, all similar, include *Charlie's, Tao* and *Nunya's*, with rooms from 50 to 80B with fan. Charlie's provides complimentary tea and fruit for guests.

Spacious rooms are available at the *Wiang Pai Hotel*, a traditional wooden hotel with rooms from 50 to 100B. On the south edge of town, off the road a bit, is the *Shan Guest House*, run by a Shan who tries hard to please. Bungalows with bath are 40/50B and there are also single/double rooms in the main building for 30/50B. Further still, on the other side of the road, is the *New Pai in*

the *Sky Guest House* with clean but characterless rooms for 60/80B.

There are several bungalow operations along the Pai River east of town, including the *Riverside, Pai River Lodge* and *Pai Resort*, all with accommodation in the 40 to 80B range.

Places to Eat

Most of the eating places in Pai are along the main north-south and east-west roads. The *Homesick Restaurant, Vegetarian Cafe* and *Pai in the Sky Cafe* all serve Western and modified Thai food at moderate prices, thus cornering most of the traveller business. The Homesick has good wholemeal bread and mat seating.

For authentic local food, try the *Muslim Restaurant* for noodle and rice dishes, or the *Khun Nu* which has a variety of Thai dishes. The *Nong Beer* restaurant is also quite good. All of the guest houses in Pai serve food as well.

Getting There & Away

The Chiang Mai to Pai road is now completely paved. It takes just four hours to travel between the towns – the bus fare is 50B.

FANG

North of Chiang Mai, this town was also founded by Mengrai in 1268 but there is little of interest today apart from the earth ramparts of his old city. Fang is, however, a good base for hill tribe visits or for the downriver ride to Chiang Rai. It's 152 km north of Chiang Mai and there are some points of interest along the way apart from the elephant camp mentioned in the previous Around Chiang Mai section. The **Chiang Dao Caves** are five km off the road and 72 km north of Chiang Mai. The **Mae Sa Cascades** are seven km off the road at Mae Rim, a further 13 km north.

Places to Stay

If you must stay in Fang, then the *Fang Hotel* has rooms from 80B. Alternatives are the cheaper *Si Sukit* or the *Metta*.

It's probably better not to stay in Fang itself but at Tha Ton, from where the boats run downriver to Chiang Rai. You can stay at the *Karen Coffee Shop* (Phanga's House) whose manager is also good for information on visiting the local hill tribes for around 40B per person. 'Great rat stew and fried cicadas there,' reported one travelling gourmet. Rundown, filthy and deserted said another.

Thip's Travellers Guest House seems to get better reports and costs 50/60B for singles/doubles. The *Siam Kok Guest House*, in the opposite direction from the bridge, has similar rates and a pleasant cafe downstairs. Further on the road nearest the pier is the *Chan Kasem Guest House* with rooms from 40B.

Getting There & Away

It takes three hours from Chiang Mai to Fang. The fare is 35B by regular bus and 40B by minibus – the buses go from the new bus station north of White Elephant (Chang Phuak) Gate. It's 7B from Fang to Tha Ton.

AROUND FANG

Trekking in the immediate vicinity of Fang isn't all that interesting as most of the villages are either Shan or Chinese (not hill tribe at all) or Lahu, and in this area the Lahu no longer wear their traditional costume.

Further north, towards the Burmese border, there are some interesting trekking areas with fewer tourists where you will find Karen, Lisu and Akha villages. Across the river from Tha Ton, you can get taxis east to the villages. Go at least to **Ban Mai**, a quiet, neat, untouristed Shan village on the river. Another four or five km takes you to **Muang Ngarm**, a Karen village. Accommodation may be available in Sulithai, a Kuomintang Chinese village to the east, and in Laota, a Lisu village.

RIVER TRIP TO CHIANG RAI

The downriver trip from Fang to Chiang Rai is a bit of a tourist trap these days – the villages along the way sell Coke and there are lots of TV aerials. But it's still fun. The open, long-tail boat departs Tha Ton at around 11.30 am to 12.30 pm. To catch it straight from Chiang Mai, you have to leave at 7 or 7.30 am at the latest and make no stops on the way. In this case, the 6 am bus is the best bet. The fare on the boat is an expensive 160B and the trip takes about three to five hours. The length of time depends on the height of the river.

You get an armed guard on the boat, but he seems to spend most of the time asleep with his machine gun in a plastic sack. The trip finishes just in time to catch a bus back to Chiang Mai so it can really be a day trip from Chiang Mai. It's better to stay in Fang, however, then travel on through Chiang Rai or Chiang Saen. You may sometimes have to get off and walk. It's also possible to make the trip (much more slowly) upriver, despite the rapids.

These days, some travellers are getting off the boat in Mae Salak, a large Lahu village about a third of the way to Chiang Rai from Fang. From here, it is possible to trek to dozens of tribal villages to the south in the Wawi area. The fare as far as Mae Salak is 40B.

CHIANG RAI

Although this town was once the home of the Emerald Buddha, it's of no real interest – just a stepping stone for other places like Fang, Chiang Saen and Mae Sai. It is, however, an alternative starting point for hill tribe treks. Chiang Rai is 105 km north from Chiang Mai.

Places to Stay

The original *Chiang Rai Guest House* has just moved to 77 Pratu Chiang Mai Rd. We haven't seen it yet but hope it's cleaner than the old location. Safer choices are the *Pon House* at 503 Ratanaket Rd and the *Chat Guest House* near the Kok River Pier. These have rooms from 30 to 70B a bed, hot water and good music.

Also near the Kok River boat pier (for boats from Tha Ton), at 445 Singhakai Rd, is the *Mae Kok Villa* which has dorm accommodation for 30B and single/double rooms with fan and hot water for 140/160B. Near

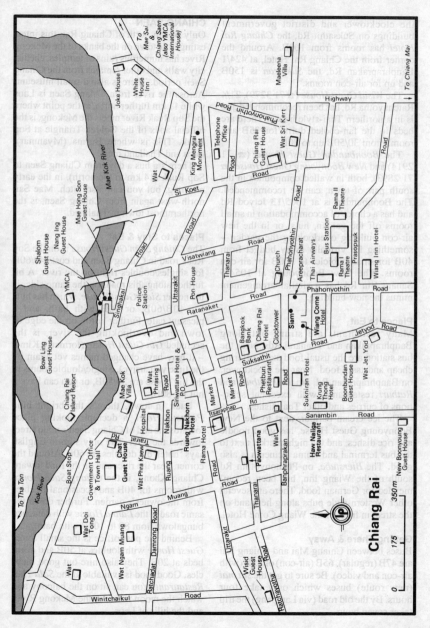

the clocktower and district government buildings on Suksathit Rd, the *Chiang Rai Hotel* has rooms from 100B. Around the corner from the Chiang Rai Hotel, at 424/1 Banphraprakan Rd, the *Sukniran* is 150B and up for air-con rooms.

The *Wisid Guest House* (☎ 71 3279), 21/4 Ratchayotha Rd, has been recommended and is in a northern Thai-style house. There are beds in the fan-cooled dorm for 25B and rooms from 30/50B up to 80B

The *Boonbundan Guest House* (☎ 71 2914) and *New Boonyoung Guest House* (☎ 71 2893), both in walled compounds in the south part of town, can be recommended. The Boonbundan is at 1005/13 Jetyod Rd and has a choice of accommodation in small rooms off the garden, huts, or in the new air-con building overlooking the garden – something for virtually every budget from 40B for small cubicles to 300B for air-con rooms. The New Boonyoung at 1054/5 Sanam Bin Rd has a similar arrangement minus the new building.

Places to Eat

Many restaurants are strung out along Banphraprakan and Thanarai Rds. Near the bus station are the usual food stalls offering cheap and tasty food. Near the clocktower, on Banphraprakan Rd, are the *Phetburi* and *Ratburi* restaurants, with excellent selections of curries and other Thai dishes.

The ice cream parlour, next to the New Boonyoung Guest House, has good noodle and rice dishes, and the night market next to the bus terminal and Rama I cinema is also good. The *Bierstube*, on Phahonyothin Rd south of the Wiang Inn, has been recommended for German food. There are several other Western-style pubs along here and on the street in front of the Wiang Come Hotel.

Getting There & Away

Buses between Chiang Mai and Chiang Rai are 47B (regular), 65B (air-con) or 85B (with air-con and video). Be sure to get the *sai mai* (new route) buses which only take four hours. By the old road (via Lampang) the trip takes seven hours.

CHIANG SAEN

Only 61 km north of Chiang Rai, this interesting little town on the banks of the Mekong River has numerous ruins of temples, chedis, city walls and other remains from the Chiang Saen period. There is also a small museum. Across the river from Chiang Saen is Laos while 11 km further north, at the point where the Sop Ruak River meets the Mekong, is the official apex of the Golden Triangle at Sop Ruak. This is where Burma (Myanmar), Laos and Thailand meet.

There's a bus a day from Chiang Saen to Sop Ruak (14 km to the north), in the early morning, but you can also hitch. Mae Sai, north-west again from Chiang Saen, is the northernmost town in Thailand.

Places to Stay & Eat

The *Chiang Saen Guest House* is on the Sop Ruak road in Chiang Saen and costs 40/60B for singles/doubles right on the river. A bit further along this road, on the same side, is the newer *Siam Guest House*, which has huts for 40B/60B, or 70B with bath, and a pleasant cafe. Further north, on the edge of town and overlooking the river, is the secluded *Gin Guest House* (formerly Kim's – it may have changed names yet again by the time you arrive). Single/double rooms in the big house are 30/50B, or you can have a hut for 80B.

Back in town, there's the bright blue *Poonsuk Hotel*, a decrepit looking place towards the end of Chiang Saen's main street towards the river. The only sign in English says 'hotel' but doubles are 60B. Around the corner, near the river and on the road toward Chiang Khong, is the *Chiang Saen House* with rooms for 40B and occasional freebies from the owner's garden. Further down the same road is the *Lanna House* with detached bungalows from 80 to 100B with bath.

Behind the post office is the small *Suree Guest House* with doubles at 50B and dorm beds at 20B. They also hire out good bicycles. Good food is available at the *Sala Thai Restaurant*. You can sit on the balcony and watch the moon rise over the Mekong River and the hills of Laos.

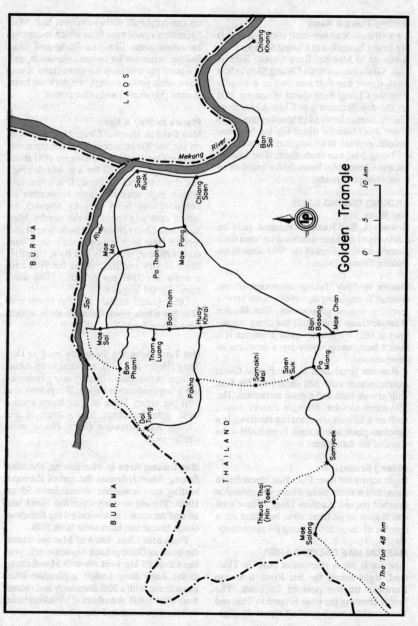

Golden Triangle

LAOS

BURMA

THAILAND

Chiang Khong

Ban Sai

Mekong River

Sop Ruak

Chiang Saen

Mae Ma

Sai River

Maw Pang

Pa Thon

Maw Thon

Ban Thom

Huay Khrai

Ban Basang

Mae Chan

Mae Sai

Ban Phami

Thom Luang

Pakha

Doi Tung

Samokhi Mai

Seen Suk

Pa Miang

Samyaek

Theuat Thai (Hin Taek)

Mae Salong

To Tha Ton 48 km

0   5   10 km

Getting There & Away

It's a 40 minute to two-hour (very variable!) trip from Chiang Rai to Chiang Saen for 15B. A bus up to Mae Sai from Chiang Saen is 15B. Take a tuk-tuk from Chiang Saen to Sop Ruak if you can find one or hire a bicycle from the Chiang Saen Guest House for 25B for the day. Returning to Chiang Mai from Chiang Saen is faster (4½ hours versus nine) if you don't take the direct Chiang Mai bus. Instead, go back to Chiang Rai first and take a Chiang Mai bus from there. The Chiang Saen to Chiang Mai buses take a roundabout route over poor roads.

AROUND CHIANG SAEN

Sop Ruak

Nowadays, Sop Ruak is besieged daily by bus loads of package tourists who want their pictures taken in front of the 'Welcome to the Golden Triangle' sign.

Places to Stay Taking advantage of the Golden Triangle myth, development here is reaching absurd proportions. The *Golden Triangle Guest House* still has clean bungalows at 60B with bath – quite a bargain if it hasn't been swept away by a new tourist development.

Another good deal is the *Poppy Guest House*, which only has three huts for 80B with private bath and a good restaurant. The 150-room *Golden Triangle Resort Hotel*, built on a hillside overlooking the river, is a 1st-class place with rooms from 500B – the wave of the future here.

Chiang Khong

Right across the river from Ban Houei Sai in Laos, this was the place where you started or finished the old 'Laotian Loop'. There's no real reason to go there now, but there are a number of cheap hotels along the main street.

MAE SAI-MAE SALONG AREA

Mae Sai is the northernmost point in Thailand, right across the Sai River from the Burmese trading post of Tachilek. The bridge crossing the river is open to Thai and Burmese citizens, but at last reports foreigners can only walk halfway across. Still, Mae Sai makes a good base from which to explore mountain areas like Doi Tung and Mae Salong, infamous for opium cultivation, and is a good place to shop for gems (only if you know what you're doing), lacquerware from Burma (Myanmar) and other crafts.

Places to Stay & Eat

Mae Sai The *Mae Sai Guest House* is right on the Sai River, a couple of km from the bridge. Comfortable bungalows cost from 40B a single to 120B for a newer double, and the restaurant is good. It is often full during high seasons (from November to February and from July to August), in which case you could try the nearby *Mae Sai Plaza Guest House*, an imitation of the former. Near the town entrance is the *Chad Guest House*, which is run by a friendly Shan family and has rooms for 70B and a dorm for 30B per person. They also have a good kitchen.

Other places include the *Top North* and *Mae Sai* hotels along the main street which have rooms from 70 to 100B.

Doi Tung Area On the twisty road to Doi Tung (Highway 1149), adjacent to an Akha village, is the *Akha Guest House* overlooking a large mountain valley. Bungalows are 50B per night. Three or four hours southwest, near Samakhee Mai village, is the *Chiang Rai Mountain Guest House* with similar rates.

Mae Salong Area In Mae Salong, the *Mae Salong Guest House* at the end of the road leading into town has rooms from 50 to 100B. The old wooden Chin Sae Hotel just around the corner is now called the *Rainbow Guest House* and has rooms from 50B.

From Mae Chan, south of Mae Sai where the road to Chiang Saen branches off, you can travel 13 km west towards Mae Salong to the *Laen Tong Lodge*, a pleasant little guest house with a 30B dormitory and rooms from 80 to 100B. A number of travellers have written to recommend this place.

Being so close to Burma, I was anxious to try some authentic Burmese cuisine. I was told there was none available in Mae Sai but a friendly Burmese-Indian shop assistant at one of the shops selling Burmese lacquerware said he could arrange something. He sent his mate off on a motorcycle across the bridge into Burma. He reappeared about 10 minutes later with a veritable feast of quite acceptable curry-type fare plus rice, all contained in transparent plastic bags. I was given a table and chair at the back of the shop and tucked in. It cost 20B.

Andrew Stables, Hong Kong

Getting There & Away

Buses to Mae Sai leave frequently from Chiang Rai for 15B and take 1½ hours. From Chiang Saen, it's 14B and from Chiang Mai, a bus costs 60B, or 104B with air-con.

To get to Doi Tung, you take a 7B bus from Mae Sai to Ban Huai Khrai and then a songthaew up the mountain for 30B going, and 20B returning. If you get off at the Akha Guest House, the fare should only be 10B.

To get to Mae Salong, get a bus from either Chiang Rai or Mae Sai to Ban Basang, the turn-off for Mae Salong. This bus is 10B. Then it's 40B up and 30B down for the hour-long trip to Mae Salong. The modern name for this town is Santikhiri.

PHRAE

Along with Nan, Phrae has been neglected by tourists and travellers alike because of its seeming remoteness from Chiang Mai, but from Den Chai (a town on the Bangkok to Chiang Mai rail line) it's easily reached by bus along Highway 101.

Phrae is probably most famous for the distinctive indigo-dyed cotton farmer's shirt seen all over Thailand. Temple architecture in Phrae is a bit unusual since you'll find both Burmese and Lao styles – see **Wat Chom Sawan** for Burmese-style, and **Wat Phra Non** and **Wat Phong Sunan** for Lao-style.

The **Muang Phi**, or 'Ghost land', is a strange geological phenomenon about 18 km north of Phrae where erosion has created bizarre pillars of soil and rock. Phrae is also the last habitat of the Mrabri hill tribe, whom the Thais call *phii thong leuang*, or 'spirits of the yellow leaves'.

Places to Stay

Several cheaper hotels can be found along Charoen Muang Rd, including *Kanchana*, *Siriwattana* and *Thep Wiman*, all of which have rooms starting at 60 to 70B.

Getting There & Away

From Chiang Mai's Arcade bus station, buses leave at 8 and 11 am, and 3 and 5 pm. The fare is 49B and the trip takes four hours. An air-con bus leaves from the same station at 10 am and 10 pm for 68B.

Trains to Den Chai from Bangkok are 188B in 2nd class or 90B in 3rd class, plus supplementary charges as they apply. Buses and *songthaews* leave Den Chai frequently for Phrae and cost around 20B.

NAN

Nan has opened up recently, since the Thai government brought this formerly bandit-infested region under control. **Wat Phumin** and **Wat Phra That Chae Haeng** are two important temples in Nan. In October and November, boat races on the river feature 30-metre wooden boats with crews of up to 50 rowers.

Places to Stay & Eat

The *Amorn Si* at 97 Mahayot Rd or the *Nan Fah* at 438-440 Sumonthewarat Rd both have rooms at around 80B. The *Sukkasem* (☎ 71 0141) at 29/31 Ananworaritdet Rd is more expensive from 100 to 160B. The *Kiwi Guest House*, Nan's first guest house, has accommodation for 50B per person if you can find it – it has changed location a couple of times.

Getting There & Away

Buses run to Nan from Chiang Mai (71B, and 100B for air-con) and Sukhothai (60B). You can also fly there from Chiang Mai, Chiang Rai and Phitsanulok. The most direct way to Nan is from Den Chai via Phrae.

North-East Thailand

The north-east is the least visited region of Thailand, although in many ways it is the most 'Thai'. There are a number of places here of interest. In part, the lack of tourists can be accounted for by the region's proximity to Laos and Cambodia and tales of hold-ups and Communist guerrilla actions. In fact, travel is generally OK in most areas and, if anything, is better now than it was a few years ago.

Among north-easterners, this part of Thailand is known as Isaan, from the Sanskrit name for the Mon-Khmer Isana Kingdom— a pre-Angkor culture that flourished in the area of (what is now) north-eastern Thailand and Cambodia. A mixture of Lao and Khmer influence is a mark of Isaan culture and language. Points of major interest in the north-east include the scenic Mekong River and the many Khmer temple ruins, especially those from the Angkor period.

Getting There & Away

There are railway lines operating from Bangkok to Udon Thani and Nong Khai on the Laotian border in the north-east or to Ubon Ratchathani, near the Cambodian

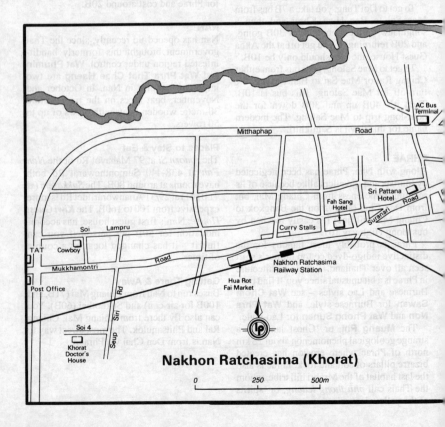

Nakhon Ratchasima (Khorat)

0   250   500m

border, in the east. You can make an interesting loop through the north-east by travelling first north to Chiang Mai and the other centres in the north and then to Phitsanulok, Khon Kaen, Loei and Udon Thani. Several north-east cities are also accessible by air from Bangkok.

NAKHON RATCHASIMA (KHORAT)

Although Khorat is mainly thought of as a place from which to visit the Khmer ruins of Phimai and Phanom Rung, it has a number of attractions in its own right. They include the **Mahawirong Museum** in the grounds of Wat Sutchinda with a fine collection of

Khmer art objects. It's open from 9 am to 12 noon and from 1 to 4 pm Wednesday to Sunday. The **Thao Suranari Shrine** is a popular shrine to Khun Ying Mo, a heroine who led the local inhabitants against Laotian invaders during the reign of Rama III.

The TAT office in Khorat will supply you with a map of the city and a list of hotels, restaurants and other useful information. The office is on Mitthaphap Rd at the western edge of town, beyond the railway station.

Places to Stay

At 68-70 Mukkhamontri Rd, near the railway station, the *Fah Sang* is clean and

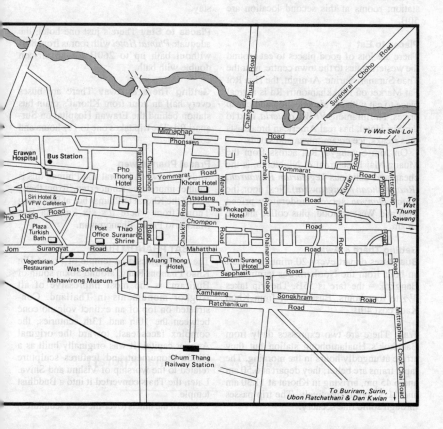

friendly with rooms from 75 to 150B. *Pho Thong* at 179 Pho Klang Rd, in the 80 to 120B bracket, is noisy but liveable. A couple of blocks west, the *Siri Hotel* is central and friendly. Rooms start from 70B. The *Tokyo Hotel* on Sureerathani Rd has good big singles with bath for 100B.

The *Thai Phokaphan* at 104-6 Atsadang Rd is inside the city moats and costs 90/150B for singles/doubles, more for air-con. The *Khorat Doctor's House* (☎ 25 5846) at 78 Suep Siri Rd Soi 4, near Silver Lake Park, is quiet and comfortable and has four large rooms for 50/80B. The owner has opened another branch nearer the town centre, close to the Hua Rot Fai Market and the railway station; rooms at this second location are 50B.

Places to Eat

There are lots of good places to eat around the western gates to the town centre, near the Thao Suranari Shrine. At night, the Hua Rot Fai Market on Mukkhamontri Rd is a great place to eat with a wide selection and cheap prices. The infamous *VFW Cafeteria*, next to the Siri Hotel, has real American breakfasts plus steaks, ice cream, pizza and salads.

On Jom Surangyat Rd, across from the Muang Mai Restaurant & Nightclub, is the cheap and delicious *Vegetarian Restaurant* (*Raan Aahaan Mangsawirat*). Next door, the *Black Canyon* serves moderately-priced Thai and Western food, plus coffee and ice cream.

Getting There & Away

Bus Buses depart every 20 minutes to half an hour from the Northern bus terminal in Bangkok – the fare is 55B. The trip takes 3½ to four hours. Buses to or from Khon Kaen cost 40B.

Train There are two expresses daily from Bangkok's Hualamphong station but they arrive at ungodly hours in the morning. The rapid trains are better; they depart at 6.50 am and 6.45 pm, arriving in Khorat at 11.30 am and 11.35 pm respectively. The trip passes through some fine scenery.

AROUND KHORAT
Pakthongchai

This silk-weaving centre is 28 km south of Khorat. Buses go there every half an hour for 10B.

Phimai

This 12th-century Khmer shrine was constructed in the style of Cambodia's Angkor Wat and was once directly connected by road with Angkor. The main shrine has been restored and is a beautiful and impressive piece of work. There is also a ruined palace and an open-air museum. Admission to the complex is 20B. Phimai itself is nothing special but it's a pleasant enough place to stay.

Places to Stay There's just one hotel, the adequate *Phimai Hotel* with rooms from 80B without bath up to 260B for an air-con double with bath.

Getting There & Away There are buses every half an hour from Khorat's main bus station behind the Erawan Hospital on Suranari Rd. The trip takes one to 1½ hours and costs 14B.

Prasat Phanomwan

Midway between Khorat and Phimai, this is another impressive Khmer ruin. To get there, get off the Khorat to Phimai bus at Ban Long Thong from where it's six km, via Ban Makha, to Prasat Phanomwan.

PRASAT PHANOM RUNG

The recently restored temple of Prasat Hin Khao Phanom Rung, around 50km south of Buriram, is the most impressive of all Angkor monuments in Thailand. Constructed on top of an extinct volcano cone between the 10th and 13th centuries, the complex faces east, toward the original Angkor capital. It was originally built as a Hindu monument and features sculpture related to the worship of Vishnu and Shiva. Later, the Thais converted it into a Buddhist temple.

One of the lintels (over-the-door sculptures)

mysteriously disappeared from the temple between 1961 and 1965. When it was later discovered on display at the Art Institute of Chicago, the Thai government and several private foundations began a long campaign to get the art returned to its rightful place. In December 1988, it was finally returned.

An informative guide, *The Sanctuary Phanomrung*, is sold near the entrance to the complex for 20B (they'll ask 50B but don't pay it).

Places to Stay & Eat

Several inexpensive hotels are available in Buriram. Right in front of the Buriram railway station is the *Chai Jaroen* (☎ 60 1559) with fairly comfortable rooms from 60B. The *Grand Hotel* (☎ 61 1089), up Niwat Rd and west of the station, has fair rooms with fan and bath starting at 90B, and 200B with air-con. Further south-east from the railway station is the *Prachasamakhi*, a Chinese hotel with a restaurant downstairs on Sunthonthep Rd. Adequate rooms here are 50B, or 70B with bath.

In the evenings, in front of the railway station, a small night market with good, inexpensive food is held. At the Samattakan and Thani Rds intersection is a larger night market that has mostly Chinese and a few Isaan vendors. The *Maitrichit* restaurant, on Sunthonthep Rd near the Prachasamakhi Hotel, has a large selection of Thai and Chinese standards from morning till night.

There is one, cheap, friendly and noisy hotel in Nang Rong, on the way to Phanom Rung from Khorat.

Getting There & Away

Prasat Phanom Rung can be approached from Khorat, Buriram or Surin. From Khorat, take a Surin-bound bus and get out at Ban Ta-Ko, which is just a few km past Nang Rong. The fare is about 20B. From the Ta-Ko intersection, occasional songthaews go as far as the foot of Khao Phanom Rung (15B) or catch any one going south to Lahan Sai. Songthaews at the foot of Khao Phanom make the final leg for 5B.

If you take a Lahan Sai truck, get off at the

Ban Don Nong Nae intersection (there are signs here pointing to Phanom Rung) – this leg is 3B. From Don Nong Nae, you can get another songthaew to the foot of the hill for 10B, charter a pick-up for 40B one way or hitch. A motorbike taxi all the way from Ta-Ko to Phanom Rung costs 60 to 70B.

From Surin, you take a Khorat-bound bus and get off at the same place on Highway 24, Ban Ta-Ko, then follow the directions above.

Buses from Khorat to Buriram leave every half an hour during the day, take about 2½ hours and the fare is 33B.

KHON KAEN

The midpoint between Khorat and Udon Thani, Khon Kaen is also the gateway to the north-east from Phitsanulok. The branch of the **National Museum** here has an excellent Thai sculpture collection. Khon Kaen also happens to be the centre for the production of Buddha sticks.

Kalasin, which is between Khon Kaen and Sakon Nakhon, is a pleasant town and a good base for a visit to the **Phu Pan National Park**.

Places to Stay & Eat

There are plenty of hotels in Khon Kaen but not all of them have their names up in Roman script. *Thani Bungalow* (☎ 22 1470), on Reun Rom Rd near the railway station and the market, is good value at 80 to 120B with fan and bath. The *Roma Hotel* (☎ 23 6276), at 50/2 Klang Muang Rd, has rooms from 100B. Cheaper is the *Saen Samran* at 55-59 Klang Muang Rd, where rooms cost from 60 to 100B.

Next to the Roma Hotel is *Kai Yang Thiparot*, a good place for kài yâng (roast chicken) and other Isaan food. Khon Kaen has a lively night market with plenty of good food stalls next to the air-con bus terminal.

In Kalasin, 80 km east of Khon Kaen, you can stay at the old wooden *Kalasin Hotel* from 50B, or at the slightly more expensive but very comfortable *Saengtawng Hotel*.

Getting There & Away

From Khorat, it's 2½ hours to Khon Kaen

by bus and the fare is 40B. You can also do the trip by rail since Khon Kaen is on the Bangkok-Khorat-Udon Thani rail line.

UDON THANI

This was one of the biggest US Air Force bases in Thailand during the Vietnam era – one of those places from where they flew out to drop thousands of tons of bombs into the jungle in the hope that somebody might be standing under one of the trees. It's got nothing much to offer apart from massage parlours and ice-cream parlours. Ban Chiang, 50 km east, has some interesting archaeological digs – the excavations at **Wat Pho Si Nai** are open to the public, and there's a recently constructed museum.

Places to Stay

The *Queen Hotel* at 6-8 Udon-Dutsadi Rd has rooms with fan and bath from 80B. In the centre of town, the *Tokyo* at 147 Prachak Rd has rooms of similar standard and price, and more expensive rooms with air-con. At 123 Prachak Rd, the *Si Sawat* has cheaper rooms in the old building from 60B.

The *Saiwong* at 39 Adunyadet Rd, off Udon-Dutsadi Rd near the Chinese temple, is a small wooden Chinese hotel with clean rooms for 50B. Along Prachak Rd, you'll find several other small, inexpensive hotels, including the *Mit Sahai* and the *Malasi Saengden*, both with rooms for 60B.

Places to Eat

Udon Thani has plenty of restaurants – many with Western food – but you can also find places that specialise in the ahaan isaan food of the north-east region. Try the *Rung Thong* at the west side of the clocktower. On Prachak Rd, *Rama Pastry* has good pastries, coffee and air-con.

Six km north of Udon, *Suan Kaset Rang San* has good and inexpensive northern-style seafood. Udon also has some interesting nightspots including the Charoen Hotel's dark cafe and the Tibet Club. Try the north-east's own Thai beer, Khun Phaen, in Udon.

Getting There & Away

There's a daily express train from Bangkok which costs 200B in 2nd class, 95B in 3rd class and takes 11 hours overnight. Take a sleeper – it's worthwhile on this long trip. Buses from Bangkok depart frequently and cost 110B – the trip also takes 11 to 12 hours. There are also regular flights to Udon Thani.

A bus from Khorat to Udon Thani is 60B and takes four to five hours. There are regular buses between Udon and Ban Chiang to the east throughout the day for 20B.

NONG KHAI

Right on the Mekong River, this is the major crossing point to get to Vientiane in Laos. It's 624 km from Bangkok and only 55 km north of Udon Thani. The city is developing fast as it gears up for trade with Laos and a road and railway bridge will soon join the two countries. Visas for Laos are sometimes available from travel agencies here. These depend on the on-again, off-again policies of Lao Tourism. If you manage to get a visa, you can take the ferry across to Tha Deua, from where taxis run into Vientiane.

Things to See

Most of the interesting sights are out of town. **Wat Phra That Bang Phuan**, 12 km to the south-east, is one of the most sacred temple sites in the north-east because of a 2000 year-old Indian-style stupa originally found here (it was replaced or built over by a Lao-style chedi in the 16th century). **Wat Hin Maak Peng**, 60 km north-west, is a quiet and peaceful place on the banks of the Mekong.

Nearer to town, **Phutthamamakasamak-hom** (thank God it's normally referred to as Wat Khaek) is a strange Hindu-Buddhist sculpture garden. It's four or five km east of town.

Places to Stay

Guest Houses *Mutmee (Mat-mii)* is on the river off Meechai Rd and has rooms from 50 to 90B. They have a pleasant garden restaurant overlooking the river. Also on Meechai Rd is the newer *Sawadee* with small but clean rooms for 80B and the *Mekong* with rooms overlooking the river for 50B/80B.

Several blocks further east on Meechai Rd is *Niyana* at No 239 – dorm beds are 30B and rooms cost from 40 to 70B. They also rent bicycles and motorbikes and arrange river trips. By now, they may have a branch on the river as well. Other guest houses are opening up in Nong Khai as more people are visiting Vientiane.

Hotels The *Prajak Bungalows* (☎ 41 1116) at 1178 Prajak Rd has rooms with fans from 80B. There are more expensive rooms with air-con and a cheap restaurant in front. The *Phunsap Hotel* (the English sign says 'Pool Sub'!) is on Meechai Rd and has reasonable rooms with fan and bath for 80B. 'Clean as a hospital room,' reported one visitor.

The *Sukhaphan Hotel* on Banthoengjit Rd is a nicely renovated old Chinese hotel with single/double rooms for 60/70B. *Pongwichit*, at 723 Banthoengjit Rd and right across the street, has clean 90B rooms with fan and bath.

Places to Eat
Overlooking the Laos ferry pier, *Udom Rot* has good food and a pleasant atmosphere. *Thiparot*, next to the 'Pool Sub', serves excellent Thai, Chinese and Laotian food, including the giant Mekong catfish (the largest fish in the Mekong River). The French influence in Laos has crept over the border and into the local pastry shops.

Getting There & Away
Nong Khai is the end of the rail line which runs from Bangkok through Khorat, Khon Kaen and Udon Thani. The basic fare is 215B in 2nd class and 103B in 3rd class, not including supplementary charges.

By bus, it's 120B, or 204B with air-con, from Bangkok and takes nine or 10 hours. From Khorat, it takes four hours and costs 75B. Udon is only 1¼ hours away, and the fare is 20B.

NONG KHAI TO LOEI
Following the Mekong River from Nong Khai into Loei province, you'll pass through the towns of Si Chiangmai, Sangkhom, Pak Chom and Chiang Khan. Each of these small towns has a couple of guest houses with accommodation from 50 to 70B. Although there are no major attractions along this route, it's a nice area to take a break from the road. Relaxing walks along the Mekong River are just the thing for frazzled nerves.

LOEI
From here, you can climb the 1500-metre **Phu Kradung** mountain, about 50 km south-east of Loei. The mountain is in a national park with trails and cabins available if you want to stay. The climb takes about four hours if you're reasonably fit.

Places to Stay
Guest Houses The *Pin Can Saw Guest House* at 35/10 Soi Saeng Sawang has small but tidy single/double rooms for 50/70B. If you go up one more street from Soi Saeng Sawang and make a left turn, you'll come to the *Muang Loei Guest House* on the right. Rates are similar to the Pin Can Saw and the English-speaking management distributes travel information.

Hotels The *Sarai Thong* on Ruamjit Rd has rooms from 60 to 120B, all with fan and bath. It's off the street, quiet and clean. The *Sri Sawat*, nearby on Ruamjit Rd, is similar in price and facilities. The *Phu Luang Hotel* (☎ 81 1532/570) at 55 Charoen Rat Rd near the market costs from 120B.

Places to Eat
The market at the intersection of Ruamjai and Charoen Rat Rds has cheap eats including some local specialities. Near the Bangkok Bank on Charoen Rat Rd, the *Chuan Lee* and the *Sawita* are two pastry/coffee shops that also sell a range of Thai and Western food. There's good, cheap food at the *Nawng Neung* on the west side of Ruamjai Rd, around the corner from the bus station.

Getting There & Away

Buses run directly from Bangkok to Loei, or you can get there from Udon for 31B or from Phitsanulok via Lom Sak for around 80 to 90B, depending on the bus. Buses to Phu Kradung, 75 km to the south, leave the Loei bus station in the morning. Direct buses to Chiang Mai cost 110B.

LOM SAK

It's an interesting trip from Phitsanulok to this colourful, small town on the way to Loei and Udon Thani. It's also a pleasant trip from here to Khon Kaen. There are several places to stay near the bus stop, including the *Sawang Hotel* which also has good Chinese food.

BEUNG KAN

This small dusty town on the Mekong River, 185 km east of Nong Khai, has a Vietnamese influence. Nearby is **Wat Phu Thawk**, a remote forest wat built on a sandstone outcrop.

NAKHON PHANOM

There's a great view of the Mekong River from this otherwise dull city with a large Lao and Vietnamese presence. **Renu Nakhon**, a village south of Nakhon Phanom (on the way to That Phanom), is renowned for its big Wednesday handicraft market.

Places to Stay

Pong, on the corner of Pon Keo and Bamrung Muang Rds, has rooms at 60B but it's run-down and not very clean. *Charoensuk* at 692/45 Bamrung Muang Rd is adequate at 80B for a room with fan and bath. The *Si Thep Hotel* (☎ 51 1036) at 708/11 Si Thep Rd costs from 60B up to around 200B for fancier air-con rooms.

The *First Hotel* at 370 Si Thep Rd is a good place with clean rooms from 90B with fan and bath. The *Windsor Hotel* at 692/19 Bamrung Muang Rd has very nice rooms at similar prices to the First, but it's not so quiet. Behind the Windsor, on the corner of Si Thep and Ruamjit Rds, is the *Grand* with similar rooms for 70B.

Places to Eat

Along Bamrung Muang Rd near the Windsor Hotel, there are several good and inexpensive restaurants. Try the *Tatiya Club* on the corner of Fuang Nakhon and Bamrung Muang Rds for a glittery Thai night out.

Getting There & Away

There are regular buses from Nong Khai to Nakhon Phanom via Sakon Nakhon for 50B. Direct buses are 70B.

THAT PHANOM

This remote north-east town, on the banks of the Mekong River, has the famous **Wat That Phanom** which is similar in style to Wat That Luang in Vientiane, Laos. There's also some interesting French-Chinese architecture around the town, again showing the Laotian influence. A Lao market convenes by the river every morning.

Places to Stay & Eat

Sang Thong is just off Phanom Panarak Rd, near the Lao-style arch of victory, in the old town. Adequate rooms cost 70B in this colourful place. The *Chai Von (Wan)* is similar in style and price and on the opposite side of Phanom Panarak Rd.

In the mornings, you can buy fresh-baked French baguettes and strong coffee from French-speaking vendors by the pier. Along the road between the pier and the wat are several noodle shops.

Getting There & Away

Songthaews from Nakhon Phanom to That Phanom cost 12B and take about 1½ hours. Stay on until you see the chedi on the right. Sakon Nakhon is two to three hours north-west by bus at a cost of 17B.

YASOTHON

Although it's a bit out of the way if you're doing the Mekong circuit, the two-hour bus trip from Ubon Ratchathani is worth making to witness the annual **Rocket Festival** (from 8-10 May). This popular north-east rain-and-fertility festival is celebrated with particular fervour in Yasothon.

Places to Stay

The *Udomporn* at 169 Uthairamrit Rd has rooms from 70 to 80B. Or try the air-con *Surawet Wattana* at 128/1 Changsanit Rd with rooms from 80 to 125B. The *Yothnakhon* (☎ 71 1122) at 169 Uthairamrit Rd costs from 100 to 150B, again with air-con.

Getting There & Away

A bus to Yasothon from Ubon costs 25B.

UBON (UBOL) RATCHATHANI

This was another major US Air Force base during Vietnam days. The **Wat Pa Nanachat** monastery at nearby Warin Chamrap has a large foreign contingent studying there. Ask for 'wat farang'! **Wat Thung Si Muang** in the centre of town and **Wat Phra That Nong Bua** on the outskirts are also interesting. The latter has a good copy of the Mahabodhi stupa in Bodh Gaya, India.

Places to Stay

Several of the cheaper hotels are along Suriyat Rd. The *Suriyat Hotel* at No 47/1-4 has basic rooms with fan for 80B, and rooms with air-con for 160B. The *Dollar* at No 39/5 Suriyat Rd is similar. The *Homsa-ad (Hawm Sa-at)* at No 80/10 Suriyat Rd is only 60 to 80B.

The *Racha Hotel* at 149/21 Chayangkun Rd, north of the city centre, starts at 90B for clean rooms with fan and bath. At 224/5 Chayangkun Rd, north of the Racha Hotel and municipal market and next to the flashy Pathumrat Hotel, is the *99 Hotel (Ubon Rat)*. All rooms have air-con and bath, and cost 160B – ask for a discount. The *Tokyo* is at 178 Uparat Rd, near the city centre. It's very nice, well-kept and single/double rooms with fan and bath cost 85B/120B, or 140B/160B with air-con.

At 220/6 Ratchabut Rd, in this same part of town, is the cheaper *Si Isan*, where rooms start at 60B/80B with fan and bath.

Places to Eat

The *Loet Rot* at 147/13 Chayangkun Rd, near the Racha Hotel, has excellent noodle dishes.

Or, there's the *Raan Khao Tom Hong Thong*, a Chinese-Thai restaurant on Kheuan Thani Rd (not far from the Ratchathani Hotel on the same side of the street) that has a large selection of dishes on display.

The family-run *Sakhon* restaurant, on Pha Daeng Rd near the provincial offices, has the best Isaan food in Ubon. Try the knockout *laap pet* (spicy duck salad).

There are two cheap but excellent vegetarian restaurants in Ubon. At 108/4 Phalo Chai Rd, near the Central Memorial Hospital and the Bodin Hotel, is *Sala Mangsawirat* (look for the Thai numbers as there is no English sign). The other vegetarian place, across from Sapsit Prasong Hospital on Sapsit Rd, has similar Thai vegetarian cuisine for about the same prices.

For breakfast, the *Chiokee* on Kheuan Thani Rd is very popular among local office workers. It's cheap and offers Thai, Chinese and Western-style breakfasts.

Getting There & Away

There is an express and two rapid trains daily from Bangkok with fares of 95B in 3rd class and 200B in 2nd class. By bus, there are frequent departures daily from the Northern bus station in Bangkok with fares of 130B in the regular buses. Buses from Nakhon Phanom take six to seven hours and cost 60B. There are also more expensive and faster tour buses.

SURIN

There's no reason to visit Surin any time of year except in late November when the elephant roundup is held here. There are elephant races, fights, tug-of-wars and anything else you can think of to do with a couple of hundred elephants. If you've ever had an urge to see a lot of elephants at one time, this is a chance to get it out of your system! There are a lot of day or overnight trips from Bangkok during this time.

Places to Stay

Hotel prices soar during roundup time but normally the *Krung Si* (☎ 51 1037) on Krung Si Rd has rooms from 80 to 100B. The *New*

Hotel (☎ 51 1341/22) at 22 Tanasarn Rd costs from 100 to 180B and has some more expensive air-con rooms. Cheaper are the three hotels near the railway station, the *Nimit Thong*, *Hom Sa-at* and *Saeng Charoen* – all small places with 80B rooms.

Getting There & Away

Regular buses from the Northern bus terminal in Bangkok cost 90B. There are many special tour buses at roundup time. You can also get there on the Ubon Ratchathani express and rapid trains for 70B in 3rd class and 153B in 2nd class. Book seats well in advance in November.

Southern Thailand

The south of Thailand offers some of the most spectacular scenery in the country plus beautiful beaches, good snorkelling, fine seafood and a good selection of things to see. There are roads along the east and west coasts; the east-coast road runs close to the railway line.

The south is very different from the rest of Thailand in both its scenery and people. Here, the rice paddies of the central area give way to the rubber and palm-oil plantations which you also see right down through Malaysia. Many of the people are also related to the Malays in both culture and religion. This 'difference' has long promoted secessionist rumblings and the Thai government still has to grapple with occasional outbreaks of violence in the south.

The two main attractions of the south are the beautiful islands of Phuket and Ko Samui. Both offer a wide range of accommodation (Phuket less so than to Ko Samui) and some superb beaches. In fact, either island makes Pattaya look like a bad dream.

Other attractions of the south include the awesome limestone outcrops which erupt from the green jungle and the sea between Phang-Nga and Krabi, beyond Phuket. Chaiya has some archaeologically interesting remains while deep in the south is Hat

Yai, a rapidly growing modern city with a colourful reputation as a weekend getaway from Malaysia.

Getting There & Away

You can travel south from Bangkok by air, bus or rail. The road south runs down the east coast as far as Chumphon where you have a choice of climbing over the narrow mountain range and continuing down the west coast (for Phuket) or continuing south on the east coast (for Ko Samui). If you take the road on the west coast, there's a small shrine at the top of the mountain pass near Chumphon. Truckies beep their horns as they pass it.

The railway line also follows the east-coast route and the two routes, east and west, meet again at the southern town of Hat Yai. From Hat Yai, you can continue on the western side into Malaysia to Alor Setar and then Penang. Or, you can head off to the eastern coast and cross the border from Sungai Kolok to Kota Bharu.

RATCHABURI

This unexciting town is on the way south from Nakhon Pathom, well before you get to the coast and Hua Hin. The *Zin Zin Hotel* on Railway Rd is cheap.

PHETBURI (Phetchaburi)

Phetburi, 160 km south of Bangkok, has a number of interesting old temples. You can make a walking tour of six or seven of them in two or three hours. They include the old Khmer site of **Wat Kamphaeng Laeng**, the early Rattanakosin-era **Wat Yai Suwannaram** and others.

On the outskirts of town next to the Phetkasem highways is **Khao Wang**, a hill topped by a restored King Mongkut palace. You can walk up the hill to the historical park or take a cable car for 5B. Entry to the park is 20B.

Further afield is **Kaeng Krachan National Park**, Thailand's largest. There is public transport from Phetburi as far as Tha Yang on Highway 4. From there, you must hitch or charter a truck to the park entrance.

Places to Stay & Eat

The *Chom Klao* is on the east side of Chomrut Bridge and has rooms for 60 and 80B. The *Nam Chai*, a block further east, is similarly priced but not such good value. The *Phetburi* is on the next street north of Chomrut Bridge and behind the Chom Klao; it has rooms at 80B with fan and bath. For a meal, try the *Khao Wang Restaurant* in front of the *Khao Wang Hotel* (☎ 42 5167), one of the best hotels in town. The Khao Wang Hotel has rooms from 90B but standards have dropped recently.

Getting There & Away

Buses leave regularly from the Southern bus terminal in Thonburi for 35B, or 54B with air-con. The bus takes about 2½ hours.

Buses to Phetburi from Hua Hin are 10 and 15B.

HUA HIN

This town, 230 km south of Bangkok, is the oldest Thai seaside resort. Hua Hin is still a popular weekend getaway, although it's a quiet, conservative and dignified place compared with raucous Pattaya, and the beach is not all that good. Hua Hin has an interesting market, and the pier area, where the local fishing fleet lands its catch, is always colourful and full of activity. Rama VII had a summer residence here and the royal family still uses it.

The Hotel Sofitel Central Hua Hin is fronted by trees and shrubs trimmed into such shapes as roosters, ducks, women opening umbrellas, giraffes and snakes.

Places to Stay

Accommodation in Hua Hin tends to be a bit on the expensive side since it's so close to Bangkok. Rates are usually higher on weekends and holidays, so go during the week for the best deals.

Cheaper places include the pleasant *Hua Hin Ralug (Raluk)* (☎ 51 1940) at 16 Damnoen Kasem Rd, which has rooms with fan and bath from 100B – and terrible food according to one visitor! Around Phetkasem Rd, there's the *Chaat Chai*, at No 59/1, with

rooms from 90B, or the *Damrong*, at No 46, with similar prices. The *Suphamit*, just off Phetkasem Rd and behind the bank, has very clean rooms for 170B.

In the area of the Raluk Hotel are several guest houses in the 100B range. Opposite the Raluk, the *Gee Cuisine* restaurant has a few basic rooms in the back from 80 to 130B. Back across the street again, next to the more expensive Sirin Hotel, is the *Thai Tae (Thae) Guest House* which has basic rooms with fan and bath for 150B, and larger rooms for 200B.

If you turn left at Thai Tae Guest House, when coming from the railway station, you'll enter Naretdamri Rd, a hot spot for small hotels and guest houses. A few doors down from the corner is *Dang's House*, where there are small rooms for 60B and larger rooms for 120B and 150B (these are weekday rates). A bit beyond Dang's, look for a 'Rooms for Rent' sign and you'll find other basic rooms for 100B.

If you can afford it, the *Hotel Sofitel Central Hua Hin* (☎ 51 2021/40) is a fine experience. Formerly the Railway Hotel, this delightfully old-fashioned place was built by German railway engineers. It's just off the beach on Damnoen Kasem Rd. The rooms are big, the ceilings are high and the service is polished. Rooms have been expensive (900B and up) by shoestring standards since a French conglomerate took over the hotel in 1986. Movie buffs may recognise the place as the Hotel Le Phnom from the film *Killing Fields*.

Places to Eat

Hua Hin is noted for its seafood – available near the piers or at the night market (always settle the price before ordering). Along Naretdamri Rd are a number of touristy restaurants with touristy prices, such as the *Beergarden*, *Headrock Cafe* and *La Villa*.

Getting There & Away

Buses run from the Southern bus terminal in Bangkok. There are frequent departures for the four-hour trip and the cost is 41B, or 74B with air-con. Trains en route to Hat Yai in the south also stop in Hua Hin. The trip takes around 4½ hours and costs 44B in 3rd class and 92B in 2nd class. The supplement on the three daily rapid trains is 20B, and 30B for the express. Buses from Phetburi are 15B.

Getting Around
Samlor fares in Hua Hin have been set by the municipal authorities so there shouldn't be any haggling. As posted they are: from the railway station to the beach – 10B; from the bus terminal to Sofitel Central – 15B; and from Chatchai Market to the fishing pier – 5B.

PRACHUAP KHIRI KHAN
This provincial capital is sleepy compared to Hua Hin but, unfortunately, there's no swimming beach. Some fine seafood can be found here, however. South of Ao Prachuap, around a small headland, is the small but scenic Manao Bay, ringed by limestone mountains and small islands. The beach is off limits to foreigners because of the Thai Air Force base there.

A few kms north of town is another bay, Ao Noi, and a small fishing village with a few rooms to let. Again, there's no beach to speak of.

Places to Stay
The centrally located *Yutichai* (☎ 61 1055) at 35 Kong Kiat Rd has fair rooms with fans and baths from 80 to 120B. Around the corner on Phitak Chat Rd is the cheaper *Inthira Hotel* with rooms in the 60 to 80B range but it's noisier and has peepholes. The *King Hotel* (☎ 61 1170), further south on the same street, has rooms from 60 to 120B.

Facing Ao Manao is the *Suksan*, which has rooms with a fan from 80 to 140B, but it's very much one big brothel in the evenings. A better bayside choice is the plain but well-kept *Mirror Mountain Bungalows*, which is owned by the city. A one-room bungalow (which sleeps two) is 150B a night with fan and bath; a two-room bungalow (which sleeps four) is 350B.

Getting There & Away
From Bangkok, buses are 63B, and 105B with air-con. From Hua Hin, buses are 21B and they leave from the bus station on Sasong Rd every 20 minutes from 7 am to 3 pm.

It's also possible to catch a train from Hua Hin to Prachuap for 19B in 3rd class.

THAP SAKAE & BANG SAPHAN
South of Prachuap Khiri Khan, near the border with Chumphon Province, are these two districts. Both have minor beach areas that are fairly undeveloped. The town of Thap Sakae is set back from the coast and isn't much – north and south of town, however, are the beaches of **Hat Wanakon** and **Hat Laem Kum**. There are a couple of guest houses around and you can ask permission to camp at Wat Laem Kum, 3½ km from Thap Sakae. You can buy food at the fishing village of Ban Don Sai, nearby and to the north.

Bang Saphan isn't much either, but the long beaches here are beginning to attract some development. You can seek out the beaches of **Hat Sai Kaew, Hat Ban Krut, Hat Ban Nong Mongkon, Hat (Ao) Baw Thawng Lang, Hat Pha Daeng** and **Hat Bang Boet**. Getting around can be a problem since there isn't much public transport between these beaches. The manager at the Talay Inn in Thap Sakae can sometimes arrange transport to nearby beaches.

Places to Stay & Eat
Thap Sakae Near the seaside, in a small fishing village about 2½ km east of town, is the *Talay Inn* (☎ 67 1417). It's in a cluster of bamboo huts on a lake fed by a waterfall. It costs 50B per person and good food is available.

Bang Saphan Along the bay of Ao Bang Saphan, the *Hat Somboon Sea View, Sarika Villa, Sung Haeng Hotel, Sai Kaew Beach Resort* and *Wanwina Bungalows* are tourist bungalows in the 150 to 250B range. The *Krua Klang Ao* restaurant is a good place for seafood.

Getting There & Away

Buses from Prachuap to Thap Sakae are 6B and from Thap Sakae to Bang Saphan cost 8B. If you're coming from further south, buses from Chumphon to Bang Saphan are 25B.

You can also get 3rd-class trains between Prachuap, Thap Sakae and Bang Saphan for a few baht on each leg.

RANONG

Ranong is 600 km south of Bangkok and 300 km north of Phuket. Only the Chan River separates Thailand from Kawthaung (Victoria Point) in Burma (Myanmar) at this point. There's a busy trade back and forth, supplying Burmese needs – the focus of the sea trade is the Saphaan Plaa Pier which is eight km south-west of town (5B on a No 2 songthaew).

Much of the town centre is Hokkien Chinese in flavour. Just outside of town is the 42°C (107°F) **Ranong Mineral Hot Springs** at Wat Tapotaram. At the southern end of Ranong Province is **Laem Son National Park**, a wildlife and forest preserve along the coast consisting of mangrove swamps, sandy beaches and uninhabited islands.

Places to Stay & Eat

Along Ruangrat Rd in Ranong are a number of cheaper places including the *Rattanasin* and the *Suriyanon* with single/double rooms for 60/70B. The *Asia* (☎ 81 1113) and *Sin Tavee* (☎ 81 1213) on the same road are in the 100 to 150B range.

The somewhat expensive *Jansom Thara Hotel*, up on the main road, is the place to stay for mineral bathing since all the hotel's water is piped in from the hot springs. Rooms start at 1000B.

For inexpensive Thai and Burmese breakfasts, try the morning market on Ruangrat Rd. Also along Ruangrat Rd are several traditional Hokkien coffee shops with marble-topped tables. The *Sombun*, across from the Rattanasin Hotel, has great seafood and standard Thai-Chinese dishes.

Getting There & Away

Buses from Chumphon are 27B, or 45B from Surat. Buses from Takua Pa are 32B, or 60B from Phuket. The bus terminal in Ranong is outside of town near the Jansom Thara Hotel.

Air-con minivans run between Phuket (opposite the Imperial Hotel) and the Jansom Thara Hotel in Ranong for 180B.

CHAIYA

Just north of Surat Thani and 640 km south of Bangkok, this is one of the oldest cities in Thailand and has intriguing remains from the Sumatran-based Srivijaya Empire. Indeed, one local scholar believes this was the real centre of the empire, not Palembang – the name is a Thai abbreviation of 'Siwichaiya', or Srivijaya. The restored **Borom That Chaiya** stupa is very similar in design to the candis (shrines) of central Java.

Outside of town, **Wat Suanmok** is a complete contrast, a modern centre established by Thailand's most famous Buddhist monk, Ajaan Phutthathat (Buddhadasa).

Places to Stay & Eat

There are guest quarters in *Wat Suanmok* ('with vast numbers of mosquitoes,' reported a visitor) but most visitors make Chaiya a day trip from nearby Surat Thani. Too many travellers treat Suanmok and other forest wats as open zoos – visit it only if you are genuinely interested in Buddhism or meditation. Chaiya also has a nice old Chinese hotel just off the main road and close to the railway station. Rooms with a fan are 60B.

About 10 minutes from town, on the coast, there's a long pier with two seafood restaurants.

Getting There & Away

Chaiya is on the railway line only 20 km north of Surat Thani, so you can get there by rail, bus or even taxi. Wat Suanmok is about seven km out of Chaiya. Buses run there directly from Surat Thani bus station so it isn't necessary to go right into Chaiya – you can get to the wat from the Chaiya railway station by motorbike for 15B.

SURAT THANI

This busy port is of interest for most travellers only as a jumping-off point for the island of Ko Samui, 30 km off the coast.

Places to Stay

A lot of Surat Thani's hotels are transient specialists, so you're quite likely to sleep better on the night ferry, without all the nocturnal disturbances as customers come and go. With the rail, bus and boat combination tickets, there's no reason to stay in Surat at all.

There are quite a few places along Na Muang Rd, not far from Ban Don. At No 428, the *Muang Thong* (☎ 27 2560) is clean and comfortable although somewhat expensive – a double room with fan and bath costs 120B. Nearby, off Na Muang Rd on Chon Kasem Rd, the *Surat* (☎ 27 2243) is OK, although rather dirty, at 80 to 100B.

Other cheaper places along Na Muang Rd include the *Ban Don* (enter through the Chinese restaurant) which has rooms with fan and bath at 70B – it's one of the best bargains in Surat Thani. The *Surasor* has big, comfortable doubles with bath for 80B. The *Lipa Guest House* is a newer place by the bus station with rooms for 80B.

In Phun Phin near the railway station, the *Tai Fah* and the *Kaew Fah* hotels have rooms for around 70B.

Places to Eat

The market near the bus station has good, cheap food or, in Ban Don, try the places on the waterfront. The 3rd-floor restaurant in the Muang Thong has good breakfast food or, for a minor splurge, try the *Pailin Restaurant* in the Tapee Hotel where the seafood is excellent.

Getting There & Away

Surat Thani is on the main railway and bus route from Bangkok to Hat Yai. The fare from Bangkok to Surat Thani is 125B in 3rd class and 244B in 2nd class. The Surat Thani train station is, however, 14 km out of town at Phun Phin. If you're heading south to Hat Yai, you may decide it is easier to take a bus rather than go to the station only to find there are no seats left.

From the Southern bus terminal in Bangkok, the trip to Surat Thani takes 11 hours and costs 135B, or 225B for an air-con bus. Private tour buses cost from 200B. Departures are usually in the early morning or in the evening. From Surat Thani, buses run to Songkhla, Hat Yai and Phuket.

Getting Around

From the railway station to the pier for Ko Samui ferries, buses leave every five minutes and cost 5B. The buses that meet the night express are free, but if you arrive at a time when the buses aren't running, a taxi to Ban Don costs about 60 to 80B.

KO SAMUI

This beautiful island, off the east coast, is very much a travellers' centre well on its way to becoming a fully fledged tourist resort. An airport was finally completed here in 1987 and car ferries have been landing for several years, so it's hardly as 'untouched' as it once was, but at least you can't drive there over a bridge (as you can to Phuket). For now, there's still accommodation at nearly every budget level.

Ko Samui is the largest island on the east coast and the third largest in Thailand. It's about 25 km long, 21 km wide and is surrounded by 80 other islands, all except six of them uninhabited. The main town is Na Thon, and most of the population is concentrated there or at a handful of other towns scattered around the coast. Coconut plantations are still a primary source of income, and visitors go relatively unnoticed outside of the beach areas.

The beaches are beautiful and, naturally, are the main attraction. But Ko Samui also has a number of scenic waterfalls – particularly **Hin Lat**, three km east of Na Thon, and **Na Muang**, 10 km south-east of Na Thon in the centre of the island. Although Hin Lat is closer to Na Thon, Na Muang is the more scenic.

Near the village of Bang Kao, there's an interesting old chedi at **Wat Laem Saw** while the **Wat Phra Yai** (Big Buddha Temple), with its 12-metre-high Buddha image, is at the north-eastern end of the island, on a small rocky islet joined to the main island by a causeway. The monks are pleased to have visitors but proper attire (no shorts) should be worn on the temple premises.

Information
The best time to visit Ko Samui is from February to late June. July to late October is very wet and from then until January it can be very windy. During the high season, from December to February and from July to August, accommodation can get a little tight. The water is not as clear on the west coast of the island as the east.

Be cautious with local agents for train and bus bookings back on the mainland – these don't always get made, or are not for the class you paid for. Several travellers have written to complain of rip-offs here. Mail can be sent to poste restante at the GPO, Na Thon.

Places to Stay & Eat
There are literally hundreds of places to stay at the beaches, ranging in cost from 40B a night to 1000B and over. Hat Chaweng and Hat Lamai are the two most popular and both have beautiful sand and clear, sparkling water. Lamai has a good coral reef, while Chaweng is the largest beach with probably the best water and a small island opposite.

Bo Phut and Big Buddha beaches are both

Ko Samui

on the bay which encloses Ko Faan, the Big Buddha island, and these are rather quieter. Thong Yang is also very quiet as are the little coves and tidal flats along the south shore. You can get further away from it all on the neighbouring islands of Ko Pha-Ngan and Ko Tao.

Na Thon If you want to stay in the town, there are a number of hotels to choose from. The *Chao Ko Bungalow* is the most expensive with rooms from 300B, and the *Jinta Hotel* costs from 100B. Nearer the pier and waterfront shops is the *Palace Hotel* with large rooms from 120B. The *Samui Bungalow*, near the post office, has small rooms for 120B.

Several restaurants face Na Thon's harbour and offer a combination of Western food and Thai seafood. One of the oldest and best is the *Chao Koh*. *Pha-Ngan* and *Si Samui* are also good for seafood. On the next street back from the waterfront are a couple of American-style delis, a pizza joint, a good curry shop, *Samui Air*, and a Hokkien coffee shop that has somehow managed to hold out in the tourist onslaught.

Chaweng There are about a dozen bungalow 'villages' strung along here, the island's longest beach, and they are constantly upgrading themselves to drive room rates higher. The cheaper ones are all much the same and cost from 80B a night for a small bungalow – knock it down a bit for a longer stay or during the off-season when some will go as low as 40B. In North Chaweng, you'll find *Matlang Resort, Blue Lagoon, Samui Island Resort, Marine, Moon, Family, Poppy Inn* and *K John Resort*.

Towards the centre of the beach, prices rise a bit. For example: *Chaweng Villa* with rooms from 80 to 200B; *Lucky Mother* from 50 to 120B; *Coconut Grove* from 60 to 200B; and *Chaweng Garden* from 150 to 200B. At the south end of the beach around a headland is Chaweng Noi, where the more expensive resorts like the *Imperial* and the *Tropicana*, both in the 1500B plus range, are taking hold. Surviving backpacker standbys

include the *Sunshine, Maew, Thawee* and *Sak*, all with bungalows from 50 to 100B. Hurry, they probably won't last long!

Lamai Samui's second most popular beach has managed to hold off the bigger tourist developments but is, nonetheless, feeling the price squeeze. Cheaper huts at the north-east end of the beach are at *Comfort, No Name, Suan Thong Kaid, Blue Lagoon, Silver Cliff* and, back from the beach, *My Friend* – all with huts starting at around 50 to 150B. More expensive and newer places include the *Island Resort, Rose Garden* and *Spanish Eyes*, in the 100 to 200B range.

Lamai's central section begins with a string of 100 to 400B places: *Mui, Fantasy Villa, Magic, Coconut Villa* and the *Weekender*. The Weekender has a wide variety of bungalows and activities to choose from, including a bit of nightlife. The *Coconut Beach* is a find at the bay's centre – it still only charges from 50 to 80B. The *Lamai Inn* is also reasonable at 80 to 150B.

Next comes *Marina Villa, Sawatdi, Mira Mare, Sea Breeze* and *Aloha*, 100 to 250B places with elaborate outdoor dining areas. At the southern end of central Lamai Beach is a mixture of 50 to 200B places, including the long-standing *White Sand, Palm, Nice Resort* and *Sun Rise*. The Sun Rise is the cheapest with acceptable 40 to 80B huts.

Beyond a headland, between Lamai Bay and Bang Nam Cheut, are some of Ko Samui's cheapest digs, including *Rock, Anika, Noi, Best Wishes* and *Rocky's*, all with huts from 30 to 50B.

Big Buddha *Family Village* gets good reviews and costs from 50 to 150B. *Big Buddha Bungalows*, from 50 to 150B, is still OK. *Ocean View* is about the cheapest place left at 50 to 80B for simple huts. *Sunset* is similarly priced and also good. The rest are in the 100 to 200B range.

Bo Phut There are about 15 places to stay here, in spite of which the area manages to stay fairly quiet. *Sunny, Bophut Guest House* and *Sala Thai* all cost from 40 to 100B. The long-running *Peace* has huts from 40 to 200B. *Calm* bungalows are old-style Samui and charge 50 to 60B. *World* has moved up-market with new bungalows from 60 to 400B.

Toward the village is *Boon Bungalows*, a small operation with 40 to 60B huts, and the up-market *New Boon Privacy* owned by the same family – the restaurants at both of these places are good. West of Boon's is *Ziggy Stardust*, a clean place with huts from 150 to 250B. Cheaper in this area are *Smile House*, *Miami* and *Oasis*, all with huts in the 30 to 100B range.

The village has a couple of cheap local-style restaurants as well as a couple of farang places with French names.

Others At Hat Mae Nam, 14 km north-east of Na Thon, the *Friendly, La Paz Villa, Silent Holiday, Golden Hut* and *Shangri-La* are all economical beach places with huts in the 40 to 80B range. While the scene at Mae Nam is not quite as picturesque as at Chaweng or Lamai, the swimming and sand are quite OK.

Along the southern end of the island, you'll find bungalows tucked away into smaller bays and coves. If the development along Chaweng and Lamai is too much for you, this area might be just the ticket – all you need is a motorbike and a Ko Samui map. As at Lamai, the places along the southern end are pretty rocky which means good snorkelling but not so good swimming.

Try Ao Na Khai and Laem Set, areas just beyond the village of Ban Hua Thanon, for the best southern beaches. Other possibilities include Ao Thong Krut and Ao Bang Kao. Bungalows here start at 50B, or 100B with bath.

At Thong Yang Bay and other seaside areas along Samui's west coast, bungalows are springing up everywhere as the car ferry from Don Sak docks on this side. None of them are anything special nor are they cheap, and the beaches tend to become mud flats during low tide.

Getting There & Away

You can fly directly to Ko Samui from Bangkok with Bangkok Airways or there are two ferry companies. Altogether there are four ferry piers on the Surat coast (Ban Don, Tha Thong, Khanom and Don Sak – only three are in use at one time) and two piers on Ko Samui (Na Thon and Thong Yang). This can make things a bit confusing at times but if you just follow the flow of travellers everything will work out.

Express Boats from Tha Thong From November to May, three daily express boats go to Samui's Na Thon Pier from Tha Thong in Surat and take two to 2½ hours to reach the island. Departure times are usually 7.30 am, 12 noon and 2.30 pm – these are subject to change according to weather conditions. From June to October, there are only two express boats a day at 7.30 am and 12.30 pm – the seas are usually too high in the late afternoon for a third sailing in this direction. Passage is 80B one way and 150B return.

From Na Thon back to Surat, there are departures at 7.15 am, 12 noon and 3 pm from November to May or at 7.30 am and 3 pm from June to October. The morning boat includes a bus ride to the train station in Phun Phin. The afternoon boats include a bus to the train and bus station.

Night Ferry There is also a slow boat for Ko Samui that leaves the Ban Don Pier each night at 11 pm, reaching Na Thon around 5 am. This one costs 60B for the upper deck (with pillows and mattresses) and 30B down below (straw mats only). The night ferry back to Ko Samui leaves Na Thon at 9 pm and arrives at 3 am.

Car Ferry From Talaat Mai Rd in Surat, you can get bus and ferry combination tickets straight through to Na Thon. These cost 50B, or 80B for an air-con bus. Pedestrians, cars and motorbikes can also take the ferry directly from Don Sak. It leaves at 9 am, 2 and 5.30 pm and takes one hour to reach the Thong Yang Pier on Ko Samui. The fares are: pedestrians 40B; motorbikes and driver 70B; and a car and driver 180B.

Don Sak, in Surat Thani Province, is about

60 km from Surat Thani. A bus from the Surat bus station is 10B and takes 45 minutes to an hour to arrive at the Don Sak ferry. If you're coming north from Nakhon Si Thammarat, this might be the ferry to take, although from Surat, the Tha Thong ferry is definitely more convenient.

Tour buses run directly from Bangkok to Ko Samui, via the car ferry from Don Sak for around 250B. From Ko Samui, air-con buses to Bangkok leave from near the pier in Na Thon twice daily, arriving in Bangkok in the early morning (there's a dinner stop in Surat the evening before). Or, for 50B, you can take a minibus from the ferry which gets you to the Surat Thani train station in time to catch the 6.30 pm express to Bangkok (you'd better book the train ticket in advance). Through buses are also available from Ko Samui to Hat Yai and other points south. Check with the several travel agencies in Na Thon for the latest routes.

Combination Tickets The State Railway of Thailand does rail, bus and ferry tickets straight through to Ko Samui from Bangkok or the reverse (eg 650B for a 2nd class, air-con berth). You end up paying about 50B more this way than if you book all the segments yourself.

Getting Around

It's about 19 km from Na Thon to Bo Phut on the north coast, and 23 km to Chaweng on the east. Minibuses and songthaews operate all day. Official fares from Na Thon are 10B to Lamai, Mae Nam or Bo Phut; and 15B to Big Buddha or Chaweng.

Often you'll be met in Na Thon (even on the ferry at Ban Don) and offered free transport if you stay at the place doing the offering.

You can rent motorbikes on Ko Samui – these are better value at Na Thon than at the beaches. Smaller 80 cc bikes cost 150B a day and larger ones are 200B – ask for discounts for multiday rentals.

KO PHA-NGAN

North of Ko Samui is the island of Ko Pha-Ngan, which is nearly as big, but generally more quiet and tranquil than Ko Samui. It also has beautiful beaches, some fine snorkelling and the **Than Sadet Falls**.

The Songserm ferry boats from Surat and Ko Samui (Na Thon) dock at Thong Sala on Pha-Ngan's west coast, although there are also smaller boats from Mae Nam and Bo Phut on Ko Samui to Hat Rin on the island's southern end. Travellers are already searching for even more isolated islands beyond Ko Pha-Ngan.

Places to Stay

Near Thong Sala The beaches here are not among the island's best, but since they're close to Thong Sala, people waiting for an early boat back to Surat Thani or on to Ko Tao sometimes stay here. On Ao Bang Charu, the *Sea Surf, Phangan Villa, Moonlight, Sun Dance, Half Moon, Coco Club* and *Chokkhana Beach* are all in the 40 to 100B range. Further south-east of here, towards Ban Tai, are a few other places from 30 to 40B, including the *Windward, Boon* and *P Park*.

Just north of Thong Sala are the *F-One, Chan* and *Vantana* at 30B and up. *Siripun* and *Phangan* also have huts with baths from 80B. Further north of Thong Sala, at the southern end of Ao Wok Tum, are the basic *Tuk, Kiat, OK* and *Darin* from 30 to 50B. A little farther down around the cape of Hin Nok are *Porn Sawan, Cookies* and *Beach*, with the same rates and facilities.

Ban Tai to Ban Khai Between the villages of Ban Tai and Ban Khai is a series of sandy beaches with well-spaced collections of bungalows, all in the 30 to 50B range. They include *Pink, Liberty, Jup, No Name, Windy Huts, Green Peace, Laem Thong, Thong Yang, Booms Cafe* and *Silvery Moon*.

Laem Hat Rin This long cape has beaches along both its westward and eastward sides. They're getting very crowded these days, especially on the eastward side (which has the best beach) – according to recent reports it has become a sort of tropical Manchester

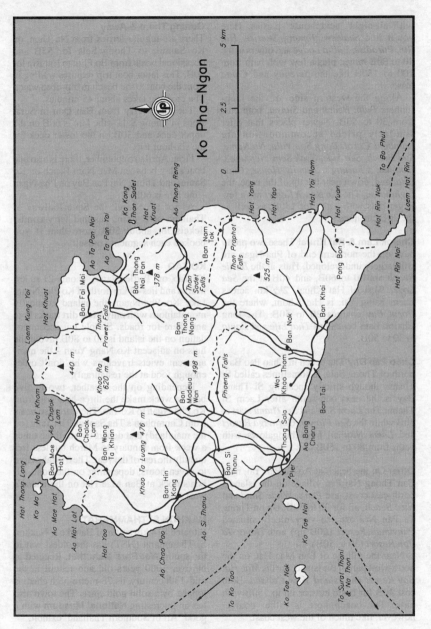

with all-night 'acid house' parties. Here you'll find *Seaview, Tommy, Sunrise, Hat Rin, Paradise, Palita Lodge* and others in the 40 to 80B range, plus a few with bath from 100 to 150B like the *Serenity* and *China Rose*.

Along the western side are the long-runners *Palm Beach* and *Sunset*, both cost from 30 to 50B. Newer places that offer similarly priced accommodation are *Rainbow, Coral, Bang Son Villa, No Name, Sun Beach, Sea Side, Sook Som, Neptune's, Dolphin, Charung's, Family House, Chok Chai* and, down near the tip of the cape, the *Lighthouse*. The *Rin Beach Resort* has a few larger huts with baths for 150B, as well as the 30B cheapies.

Chalok Lam & Hat Khuat These two pretty bays on the northern end of Pha-Ngan are still largely undeveloped. Huts at the *Bottle Beach* are 30 to 60B, and 40B at the *Sea Love*. West of Hat Khuat, 2½ km across Laem Kung Yai, is Hat Khom, where the *Coral Bay* charges 30 to 50B. The long Chalok Lam beach has *Thai Life* and *Fanta* at 30 to 50B.

Chao Pao Bay The beach in Chao Pao Bay, north of Thong Sala, is sometimes called Si Thanu, though strictly speaking Si Thanu Bay is the next one south after Laem Si Thanu. The *Laem Son* and *Sri Thanu* start at 30B while the *Sea Flower, Gornviga Resort* and *Laem Niat* all have bungalows with baths from 80 to 150B.

Other On the beach at Ao Ta Pan Yai, near Ban Thong Nai Pan village on the island's north-east coast, are *Pen's, White Sand* and *Nice Beach*, all for 30 to 50B. Up on Thong Ta Pan Noi are the very nicely situated *Panviman Resort* (60B up) and *Thong Ta Pan Resort* (30 to 50B).

Near the village of Ban Mae Hat, on the north-west part of the island, are the *Mae Hat Bay Resort* and *Island View Cabana*. Both cost 40B for basic huts or up to 150B with bath. The beach here is rather coarse, however, like much of the west coast.

Getting There & Away
There are regular ferries from Na Thon, on Ko Samui, to Thong Sala for 55B and occasional boats from Bo Phut to Hat Rin for 50B. This latter boat trip requires wading in from the boat to the beach in hip-deep water. The crossing takes about 45 minutes.

The night ferry from Ban Don in Surat stops in Thong Sala – the fare is 60B on the upper deck and 30B on the lower deck for the six-hour trip.

From April to September, there is also one boat a day between Mae Nam Beach on Ko Samui and Thong Nai Pan Bay on Pha-Ngan – the fare is 60B.

As for Ko Samui, the State Railway of Thailand sells train, bus and ferry combo tickets for about 50B more than if you booked each segment yourself.

KO TAO
Ko Tao, or 'Turtle Island', is only 21 sq km in area and lies 44 km north of Ko Pha-Ngan. Like Ko Pha-Ngan, the island is mostly mountainous with only a few dirt tracks here and there for roads. Simple hut accommodation on the island is 30 to 80B (avoid the huts on adjacent Ko Nang Yuan – the management evicts travellers who don't order enough food at the restaurant).

Depending on the weather, two to five boats a week make the three-hour trip from Ko Pha-Ngan to Ko Tao. There are also boats from Chumphon's Tha Saphan Tha Yang (on the mainland) that depart two to three times a week from January to March but less frequently the rest of the year. The trip takes five to seven hours, depending on the boat. All boats dock at Ban Mae Hat on the island's west side.

NAKHON SI THAMMARAT
Situated 814 km south of Bangkok, Nakhon Si Thammarat (NST) has the oldest wat in the south, **Wat Phra Mahathat**. Reputed to be over 1000 years old and rebuilt in the mid-13th century, its 78-metre-high chedi is topped by a solid gold spire. The town also has an interesting **National Museum** with a good 'Art of Southern Thailand' exhibit.

NST is also noted for its neilloware (a silver and black alloy-enamel jewellery technique) and for the making of leather shadow puppets and dance masks. The town is also supposed to produce the 'best' gangsters in Thailand!

Places to Stay

Most hotels are near the train and bus stations. On Yomarat Rd, across from the railway station, is the *Si Thong* with adequate rooms for 70B with fan and bath. Alternatively, try the *Nakhon* at 1477/5 Yomarat Rd or the *Yaowarat*, both similarly priced.

On Jamroenwithi Rd (walk straight down Nerámit Rd opposite the station for two blocks and turn right), the *Siam*, at No 1407/17, is a large hotel with rooms from 80B with fan and bath. Across the street is the *Muang Thong*, at No 1459/7, with rooms from 100B. Near the Siam, on the same side of the street, is the *Thai Fa* which is good value as the rooms are equally good and 20B cheaper.

Places to Eat

Two very good and inexpensive Chinese restaurants, located between the Neramit and Thai Fa hotels on Jamroenwithi Rd, are the *Bo Seng* and the *Yong Seng* – neither have English signs.

Getting There & Away

From the Southern bus terminal in Bangkok, it takes 12 hours to Nakhon Si Thammarat and the fare is around 150B, or 270B by air-con bus. Daily buses from Surat Thani cost about 65B. You can also get buses to or from Songkhla or Hat Yai.

By train, you usually have to get off at Khao Chum Thong, about 30 km to the west, since NST is not on the main southern trunk line. From there, you can continue by bus or taxi. The daily Nos 47 (rapid) and 15 (express) trains, however, make the trip all the way to NST via a small branch line. Either way, the fare is 133B in 3rd class and 279B in 2nd class.

PHATTALUNG

The major rice-growing centre in the south, Phattalung is also noted for its shadow puppets. The town has a couple of interesting wats, and **Lam Pang** is a pleasant spot for eating and relaxing beside the inland sea, on which Phattalung is situated. The **Thale Noi Waterbird Sanctuary** is 32 km north-east of Phattalung, and the cave **Tham Malai** is just outside the town.

Places to Stay

Most of Phattalung's hotels are along Ramet Rd, the main drag. The dingy *Phattalung 1* at 43 Ramet Rd costs 70B with fan and bath. The *Phattalung 2* at 34/1 Ramet Rd is slightly better for 100B. The *Thai Sakon* (the English sign reads 'Universal Hotel') is a little west and has adequate rooms at 80B. Across from the Grant cinema on the corner of Charoentham Rd, the *King Fah* is similar to the Universal. The *Thai Hotel* on Disara-Nakarin Rd is the best place in town at 150B per double, more for air-con.

Places to Eat

The market off Poh-Saat Rd is a good place for cheap takeaway food. Other good eating places are along Pracha Bamrung Rd, just past the Thai Hotel.

Getting There & Away

Buses from Phattalung to Nakhon Si Thammarat or Hat Yai take 1½ hours and cost 30B.

SONGKHLA

This unexciting beach resort is about 30 km from Hat Yai – plenty of buses and share-taxis operate between the two towns. Songkhla is on a peninsula between Thale Sap Songhla, the inland sea, and the South China Sea.

Things to See

Offshore are two islands known as 'cat' and 'mouse'. Although the beach is not very interesting, Songkhla has an active waterfront with brightly painted fishing boats, an interesting **National Museum** (admission

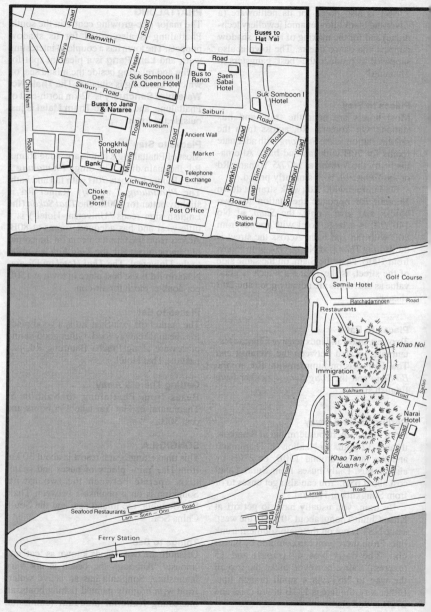

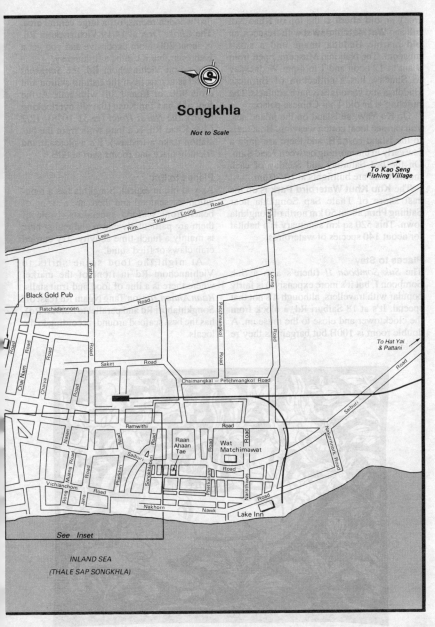

Songkhla

Not to Scale

To Kao Seng
Fishing Village

Rim Talay Loung Road

Leon Talay Road

Pratha Road

Black Gold Pub

Ratchadamnoen

Chai Nam Road

Chaiya Road

Petchmangkol Road

Loung Road

To Hat Yai
& Pattani

Saket Road

Chaimangkal – Petchmangkol Road

Nakornork Road

Saihuri Road

Ramwithi Road

Road

Nasan Road

Saiburi Road

Songkhlaburn Road

Road

Raan
Ahaan
Tae

Wat
Matchimawat

Road

Road

Narathiwes Road

Muang Road

Phetkung Road

Road

Phetkung Road

Vichianchom Road

Rong Road

Jana Road

Nakhorn Road

Nawk

Lake Inn

See Inset

INLAND SEA

(THALE SAP SONGKHLA)

free), an **old chedi** at the top of Khao Noi hill and **Wat Matchimawat** with frescoes, an old marble Buddha image and a small museum. The National Museum, open from 9 am to 12 noon and 1 to 4 pm Wednesday to Sunday, has a collection of Burmese Buddhas and various Srivijaya artefacts. The building is an old Thai-Chinese palace.

On **Ko Yaw**, an island on the inland sea, you can see local cotton weaving. Boat taxis to the island cost 5B, and there are quite a few early in the morning between 7 and 8 am. On the last Saturday and Sunday of each month there are bullfights at 10.30 am.

The **Khu Khut Waterbird Park** is on the east shore of Thale Sap Songkhla near Sathing Phra, about 50 km north of Songkhla town. This 520 sq km sanctuary is a habitat for about 140 species of waterbirds.

Places to Stay

The *Suk Somboon II* (there's also a Suk Somboon I, but it's more expensive) is fairly popular with travellers, although it's not that special. It's at 18 Saiburi Rd, a block from the clocktower and close to the museum. A double room is 100B but bargain as they're just wooden rooms, off a large central area. The *Choke Dee*, at 14/19 Vichianchom Rd, is about 20B more expensive and you get a bathroom, but it can be a little noisy.

Also on Vichianchom Rd, the *Songkhla Hotel* is across from the fishing station and costs 90B, or from 120B with bath. At the foot of Khao Tan Kuan (the hill overlooking town), the *Narai Hotel* (☎ 31 1078), 12/2 Chai Khao Rd, is a long walk from the bus station (take a trishaw). It's a pleasant and friendly place and rooms start at 80B.

Places to Eat

As you might expect, Songkhla has a reputation for seafood and there are a string of beach-front seafood specialists. None of them are particularly cheap and eating here is mainly a lunch-time activity. Try curried crab claws or fried squid.

At night, the food scene shifts to Vichianchom Rd in front of the market where there is a line of food and fruit stalls. *Raan Ahaan Tae*, on Tang Ngam Rd (east off Songkhlaburi Rd and parallel to Saiburi Rd), has the best seafood around, according to the locals.

The *Black Gold Pub* on Sadao Rd, towards Samila Beach, is the local evening hang-out for expats who work for oil companies in Songkhla. The *Kao Noi Sukiyaki*, which is between the Songkhla Hotel and the Choke Dee Hotel but across the road, has good food, reasonable prices, an English menu and air-con.

Getting There & Away
Buses from Surat Thani to Songkhla cost 150B. Air-con buses from Bangkok take 19 hours and cost 319B. Regular buses are 185B but add a few baht more to Hat Yai. By train, you have to go to Hat Yai first. There are buses and share-taxis from Hat Yai to Songkhla – 7B by bus and 12B by taxi.

Although the usual route north from Songkhla is to backtrack to Hat Yai and then take the road to Phattalung and Trang, you can also take an interesting back-road route. There's a bus trip to Ranot, 63 km north at the end of the Thale Sap lagoon, and further buses connect to Hua Sai (32 km) and then Nakhon Si Thammarat (56 km).

Getting Around
Samlors around Songkhla cost 3B (4B at night) and songthaews are 3B for anywhere on their routes.

HAT YAI
A busy crossroads town, Hat Yai is 1298 km south of Bangkok where the east and west coast roads and the railway line all meet. Apart from being the commercial centre of the south, Hat Yai is also a popular 'sin centre' for Malaysians who pop across the border on weekends to partake of Thailand's freewheeling delights.

Orientation & Information
The three main streets – Niphat Uthit 1, 2 and 3 – all run parallel to the railway line. The TAT office is at 1/1 Soi 2 Niphat Uthit 3 Rd. Four of Hat Yai's cinemas have English-language sound rooms. Hat Yai is often spelt Haadyai.

Things to See
A few km out of town, towards the airport and just off Phetkasem Rd, **Wat Hat Yai Nai** has a large reclining Buddha image – get a samlor heading in that direction and hop off after the U Thapao Bridge. On the first and second Saturday of each month, bullfights (bull versus bull) are held at Hat Yai. It's always a heavy betting game for the Thai spectators.

The **Southern Cultural Village Show & Mini Zoo** (what a name) puts on an afternoon show several days a week for about 150B. It includes music, dances, ceremonies, sword and long-pole fighting and other entertainment. To get there, take a tuk-tuk down Phetkasem Rd towards Songkhla.

The **Ton Nga Chang Waterfall**, 24 km west of the city, features seven-tiered cascades in the shape of a pair of elephant tusks – October to December is the best time to visit.

Places to Stay
There are a lot of places to stay in Hat Yai but most of them are there to cater for the Malaysian dirty-weekend trade – it's not a traveller's dream town. You can look for places in two categories – the remaining traditional places and the cheaper modern hotels. The old-style Thai hotels with their wood-partitioned rooms are gradually being torn down as Hat Yai develops.

Currently very popular with travellers is the *Cathay Guest House*, on the corner of Niphat Uthit 2 and Thamnoonvithi Rds. Rooms here start at 80B and there is also a 50B dorm. The management is quite helpful with information on local travel and travel to Malaysia or further north in Thailand. The *Angel Guest House*, 127 Thamnoonvithi Rd, has basically the same rates as the Cathay except that for 50B you can get a closet-like room instead of a dorm bed.

The *Savoy* is 3½ blocks from the station on Niphat Uthit 2 Rd. It has adequate 80B rooms although most rooms are 120B or more. The *Thai Hotel* on That Uthit Rd has rooms with fan for 120B, and cheaper rooms on the top floor for 90B.

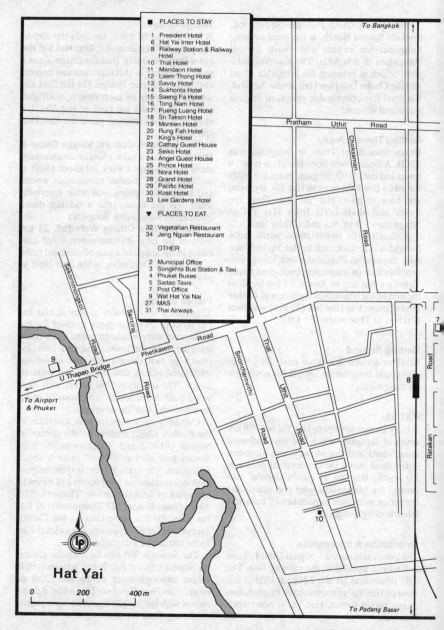

■ PLACES TO STAY

1 President Hotel
6 Hat Yai Inter Hotel
8 Railway Station & Railway Hotel
10 Thai Hotel
11 Mandarin Hotel
12 Laem Thong Hotel
13 Savoy Hotel
14 Sukhonta Hotel
15 Saeng Fa Hotel
16 Tong Nam Hotel
17 Pueng Luang Hotel
18 Sri Taksin Hotel
19 Montien Hotel
20 Rung Fah Hotel
21 King's Hotel
22 Cathay Guest House
23 Seiko Hotel
24 Angel Guest House
25 Prince Hotel
26 Nora Hotel
28 Grand Hotel
29 Pacific Hotel
30 Kosit Hotel
33 Lee Gardens Hotel

▼ PLACES TO EAT

32 Vegetarian Restaurant
34 Jeng Nguan Restaurant

OTHER

2 Municipal Office
3 Songkhla Bus Station & Taxi
4 Phuket Buses
5 Sadao Taxis
7 Post Office
9 Wat Hat Yai Nai
27 MAS
31 Thai Airways

Hat Yai

0   200   400 m

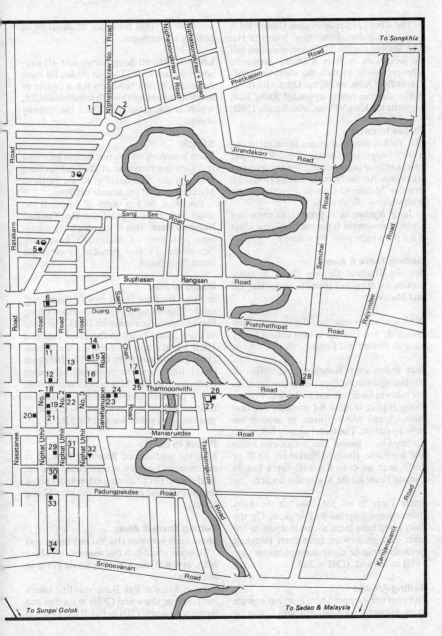

The *King's Hotel* on Niphat Uthit 1 Rd is one of the older of the 'new' hotels in Hat Yai. Rooms start at 120B and are often full on weekends as it is a Malay favourite. Cheaper hotels include the short-time specialist *Tong Nam*, on Niphat Uthit 3 Rd (from 80B), and the newly upgraded *Rung Fah*, opposite the King's Hotel, which costs 150B.

Places to Eat

Hat Yai has plenty of places to eat including a lot of appetising-looking restaurants and places selling cakes, confectionery, fruit and ice cream. Across from the King's Hotel, the popular *Muslim-O-Cha* is a particular with visiting Malaysians.

Jeng Nguan is a good, inexpensive Chinese restaurant at the end of Niphat Uthit 1 Rd (turn right from the station).

Getting There & Away

See the Thailand Getting There & Away section for details of travel between Hat Yai and Malaysia.

Air There are at least two flights daily from Bangkok, and Hat Yai is also connected by air with Phuket and Penang.

Bus Buses from Bangkok cost 190B, or 339B with air-con. There are many agencies for buses to Bangkok and for taxis to Penang along Niphat Uthit 2 Rd towards the Thai Airways and MAS offices, or around the railway station. The travel agency below the Cathay Guest House also books tour buses and is reliable. Buses to Phuket are 100B, or 160B with air-con. It's 15B for a bus to Padang Besar on the Malaysian border.

Train There is no 3rd class on the daily International Express to Bangkok. On the daily rapid train there are no sleepers in 3rd class. Straightforward fares from Bangkok (without rapid or express supplements) are 149B in 3rd and 313B in 2nd.

Getting Around

To/From the Airport There is no bus service to the airport, 11 km out of town. Count on about 60 to 100B for a taxi or about 50 or 60B for a songthaew.

Local Transport Songthaews cost 4B anywhere around town. The bus station for most departures is on Phetkasem Rd, a couple of hundred metres north of Thamnoonvithi Rd, which is the main road from the railway station.

SATUN

There's nothing of interest in this province in the south-west corner of Thailand but from here you can take boats to Kuala Perlis in Malaysia or visit the islands offshore.

Pak Bara, 60 km north of Satun, is the usual jumping-off point for **Ko Tarutao National Park**. This is the area's big attraction, just north of Malaysia's Langkawi. Nowadays, it's also possible to get boats direct from Satun.

Places to Stay

In Satun, the *Rian Thong Hotel* ('Rain Tong' on the English sign) is near the Rian Thong Pier and has large rooms for 100B. The more modern *Satun Thani* in the town centre is 100B but it's noisy, or there's the not-so-clean *Thai Niyom* from 60B. The *Udomsuk* (☎ 71 1006) near the municipal offices on Hatthakam Seuksa Rd is better value at 80B.

It's possible to stay on Ko Tarutao in national park bungalows from 50 to 60B, or you can pitch your own tent for 5B.

Places to Eat

Near the gold-domed Bambang Mosque in the centre of town are several cheap Muslim food shops. For Chinese food, wander about the little Chinese district near the Rian Thong Hotel.

Getting There & Away

Share-taxis between Hat Yai and Satun cost 35B, buses about half that amount. It's about M$4, say 40B, for a boat to Kuala Perlis in Malaysia.

From Satun to Pak Bara, you first take a bus (10B) or share-taxi (20B) to La-ngu and then a songthaew (7B) to Pak Bara. Boats to

Tarutao cost 120B per person, or you can charter a boat large enough for eight to 10 people for 500B. They run between November and April – the park is closed for the remainder of the year.

PHUKET

Phuket is barely an island, since it's joined to the mainland by a bridge -- yet conversely, it's more than just an island since it's surrounded by countless other smaller islands, some of them just swimming distance from the shore.

Phuket has been a major tin-mining centre, but these days it's the rapidly expanding resort role that is most important. The town of Phuket is pleasant but it's the beautiful beaches and the offshore islands which are the main attraction, and there are plenty of them.

Virtually all transport radiates from Phuket and the popular beaches are scattered all over the island. Phuket Island is very hilly, and often the hills drop right into the sea except where there are beaches. Beach accommodation in Phuket is becoming downright high-class these days – there is now a Club Med on Kata Beach and the even more lavish Phuket Yacht Club on Nai Han.

Phuket's main drawback is that a lot of the development seems to be carried out with total disregard for aesthetics or planning. The beach bungalows at Ao Karon for instance are comfortable, cheap and ugly. More and more of them are being scattered haphazardly up the slopes among the palm trees. Already, the local cowboys are zooming up and down the beach on their motorbikes.

As usual, the problems of water supply – and more importantly water pollution – have not been thought of. A lot of places in Phuket have all the makings of an instant tourist slum. There's also the usual nude bathing problems, although those who feel like flaunting the royal decree banning it have only to stroll down the beach a little way in most places to get right away from it all.

Information

The TAT office, on Phuket Rd, has a list of standard songthaew charges to the various beaches. The Thai Airways office is on Ranong Rd and the post office is on Montri Rd.

In earlier days, Phuket was known for periodic thefts and muggings, but now it seems to be as safe or safer than most other places in Thailand. If there is a theft, the TAT is your best bet in catching the culprits. Be cautious in the water as there have been a number of drownings at Phuket beaches.

Phuket Beaches

Patong Development in Phuket has been rapid and relatively recent – the first time I came here in the early '70s Ao Patong (Ao means beach, Ko means island) had just one little restaurant where you could lay your sleeping bag on the floor. Now there are at least 50 hotels and guest houses, and innumerable restaurants.

Ao Patong is still very pleasant and has more of a variety of accommodation than most of the other beaches, although food is a little more expensive than at Ao Kata or Ao Karon. There's also more going on at night here than at the other beaches. The beach itself is long, white, clean and lapped by the proper picture-postcard clear waters. Ao Patong is 15 km west of Phuket town.

Karon & Kata Only a little south of Ao Patong is Ao Karon, 20 km from Phuket. This is really a triple beach: there's the long golden sweep of Ao Karon, then a smaller headland separates it from the smaller but equally beautiful Ao Kata, or more correctly Ao Kata Yai. Another small headland divides it from Ao Kata Noi where you'll find good snorkelling. Offshore, there's the small island of **Ko Pu**.

Most of the development is centred around the two Kata beaches and the southern end of Karon Beach. Development is creeping north and, no doubt, there will eventually be a strip of hotels and guest houses like Ao Patong. Ao Karon and the two

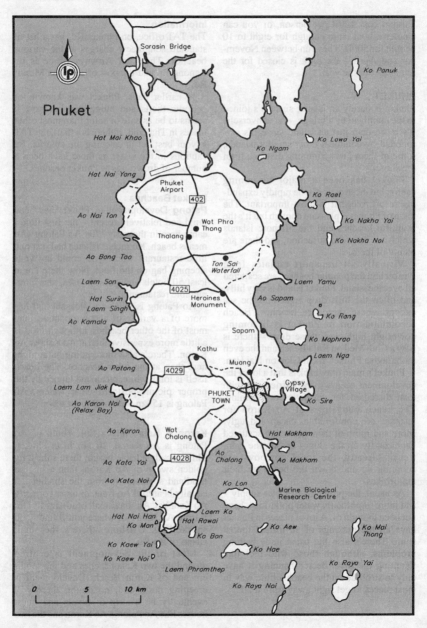

Phuket

Sarasin Bridge

Ko Panuk

Hat Mai Khao

Ko Lawa Yai

Ko Ngam

Hat Nai Yang

Phuket Airport

402

Ko Raet

Ao Nai Ton

Wat Phra Thong

Ko Nakha Yai

Thalang

Ko Nakha Noi

Ao Bang Tao

Ton Sai Waterfall

Laem Son

4025

Laem Yamu

Hat Surin

Heroines Monument

Ao Sapam

Laem Singh

Ao Kamala

Ko Rang

Sapam

Ko Maphrao

Kathu

4029

Muang

Laem Nga

Ao Patong

Gypsy Village

Laem Lam Jiak

PHUKET TOWN

Ko Sire

Ao Karon Noi (Relax Bay)

Ao Karon

Wat Chalong

Hat Makham

4028

Ao Chalong

Ao Makham

Ao Kata Yai

Ao Kata Noi

Ko Lon

Marine Biological Research Centre

Laem Ka

Hat Nai Han

Hat Rawai

Ko Man

Ko Aew

Ko Mai Thong

Ko Kaew Yai

Ko Ban

Ko Hae

Ko Kaew Noi

Laem Phromthep

Ko Raya Yai

Ko Raya Noi

0   5   10 km

Ao Katas are beautiful beaches with that delightful, squeaky-feeling sand.

Nai Han South again from Ao Kata is Hat Nai Han, a pleasant small beach which was one of the last hold-outs for cheap bungalows until the Phuket Yacht Club moved in. Now it's more of a scene but still pleasant.

You can walk along a coastal track from Ao Karon to Hat Nai Han in about two hours. In fact, you could probably walk right around the island on coastal tracks. The roads radiate out from Phuket town and you have to backtrack into town and out again to get from one beach to another by road – even though they are just a couple of km apart along the coast. **Ao Sane** is a pleasant little place between Kata and Nai Han.

Rawai If you turn round the southern end of the island from Hat Nai Han you'll come to Hat Rawai, another tourist development. Again these are mostly more expensive places and the beach is not so special. At low tide, there's a long expanse of mud exposed before you get to the sea. People staying at Rawai often travel out to other beaches to swim. Rawai is a good place to get boats out to the islands scattered south of Phuket. There is good snorkelling at **Ko Hae**.

Other Beaches Between Rawai and Phuket town, there are more places to stay dotted along the nicely beached south-east stretch of coast. These are generally more expensive places, however. **Ao Chalong**, close to the Ao Kata road turn-off from the Rawai road, has a few places. There are also other places to stay, or just to laze in, dotted round the island.

A little north of Ao Patong is **Hat Surin**, a long beach which is less sheltered and has a little rougher water than the normal Phuket calm. **Ao Kamala** has a wide calm bay but not so good a beach. It is just a km or so south of Hat Surin. Between the two there's an absurdly beautiful little beach, **Laem Singh** – the very image of a tropical paradise.

Other Attractions
If the attraction of beaches starts to pall, Phuket also has a number of waterfalls and other novelties. The **Thai-Danish Marine Biological Research Centre** has an interesting fish collection. It's open from 8 am to 12 noon and from 2 to 4 pm – take a songthaew to Ao Makham. There is good snorkelling at many points around Phuket. **Ko Hae** is said to be particularly good and you can get boats out to the island for around 100B from the Rawai Seaside Hotel.

At **Mai Khao** (Airport Beach), turtles come ashore to lay their eggs from late October to February. They can be elusive, though. Mai Khao is an hour's walk from Nai Yang.

Places to Stay & Eat – Phuket Town
Most people head straight out to the beaches but should you want to stay in town – on arrival or departure night for example – there are some pleasant places. The *Sin Tawee* (☎ 21 2153) at 81 Phang-Nga Rd is a vast, rambling, rabbit warren of a place, but quite pleasant. They have rooms from 100B and rather better ones with bathrooms at higher prices. There is a good, although slightly expensive, restaurant next door.

The *Charoensuk* at 136 Thalang Rd has rooms from 60B. It's the cheapest place in town and an interesting place to stay. At 19 Phang-Nga Rd, the *On On* has rooms from around 80B and a lot of character.

Other places include the *Ko Sawan* at 19/8 Poonpol Rd, near the waterfront, with rooms from 80B. The *Thara* on Thep Kasatri Rd has rooms with fan and bath for 70B. About 100 metres south of the Thara, the *Suk Sabai Hotel* is good value with clean, well-kept rooms for 80B.

The big eating centre in town is the *Mae Porn* restaurant, on the corner of Phang-Nga Rd and Soi Pradit, near the Sin Tawee and On On hotels. They have a vast selection of fresh Thai, Chinese and Western food at good prices. Even cheaper is the *Raan Jee Nguat*, around the corner on Yaowarat Rd across from the closed Siam cinema – fine

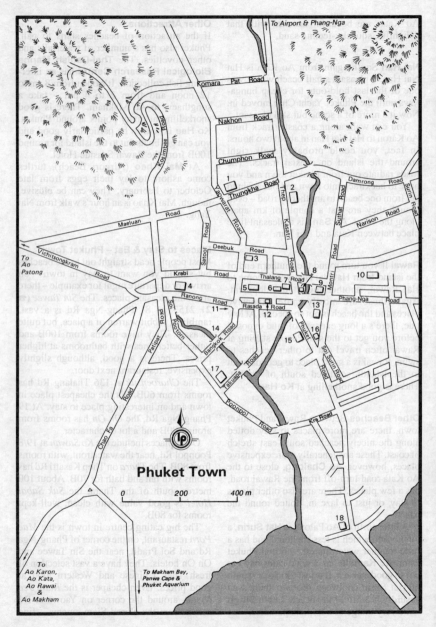

To Airport & Phang-Nga

Komara Pat Road

Nakhon Road

Chumphon Road

Thungkha Road

Maeluan Road

Deebuk Road

Krabi Road

Ranong Road

Rasada Road

Bangkok Road

Takuapa Road

Poonpol Road

Kra Road

Damrong Road

Surin Road

Narison Road

Thalang Road

Phang-Nga Road

Vichitsongkram Road

Kotaimbee Road

Satool Road

Kasatri Road

Suthat Road

Montri Road

Phuket Road

Soi Surin Road

Patipat Road

Chao Fa Road

Pootorn Road

Thep Road

To Ao Patong

Phuket Town

0   200   400 m

To Karon,
Ao Kata,
Ao Rawai
&
Ao Makham

To Makham Bay,
Panwa Cape &
Phuket Aquarium

1	Phuket Merlin Hotel
2	Thara Hotel
3	Jee Nguat Restaurant
4	Thai Airways
5	On On Hotel
6	Sin Tawee Hotel
7	Charoensuk Hotel
8	Siam Hotel
9	Post Office
10	Bus Station
11	Songthaews
12	Mae Porn Restaurant
13	Pearl Hotel
14	Day Market
15	Night Market
16	TAT
17	Ko Sawan Hotel
18	Immigration Office

Phuket-style noodles with curry are 5B. The night market on Phuket Rd is also good.

Places to Stay & Eat – Phuket Beaches

The two main centres for travellers are Ao Patong and Ao Kata-Karon. Ao Patong is more developed and more expensive, Ao Kata-Karon is a bit more laid-back in spite of the Club Med. It's initially a little confusing since the Kata name seems to encompass places at both the Kata beaches and the south end of Karon. There are numerous other beaches of course, some of them very quiet and peaceful. Nai Han still has the cheapest beach accommodation.

Ao Patong This was the original beach development and now encompasses a whole beach full of hotels, restaurants, snack bars, motorbike-hire places, windsurfing shops and all manner of things to do. If you want a little more night-time activity, then Ao Patong may appeal to you more than the other, sleepier places. Although the accent here is on the more expensive places, there are also a number of cheapies, but the costs are a bit higher than elsewhere.

The *Bangla*, with bungalows from 100B, is among the cheaper places. The *Seven Seas* has various standard rooms starting at 150B. Others in the 200 to 300B range include the

Happy Heart, Paradise, Royal Palm and the *Sala Thai*. During the low season from May to October, you should request a discount of 30% to 40%. Food also is a little more expensive here. You pay a few baht more for anything from a Coke or fruit drink to a complete meal.

Ao Kata & Karon Although bungalow rates have soared (up to 3000B a night at the Club Med), there are still a few places in the 80 to 100B range. They're all fairly similar – pleasant little wooden bungalows with your own toilet, shower and a verandah. Popular places include the *Tropicana Beach Bungalows* or, right next to it, the *Kata Villa* (☎ 21 1014) – very similar or even a little nicer – from 100B. They're both right at the south end of Karon along with *Kata Noi Bay Inn, Kata Noi Beach Inn* and *Coolbreeze*.

Along Karon, there are a number of places with prices from 200B, but *Dream Hut, Happy Hut, Kata Tropicana, My Friend* and *Karon Bungalow* have managed to keep their rates around 100B.

The accommodation area is backed up with a whole collection of very similar beach restaurants featuring the usual traveller's dishes from porridge or pancakes to fruit drinks and banana fritters. Prices for accommodation and food go hand in hand at Phuket – Kata is cheaper than Patong for accommodation and the same applies for food prices.

Nai Han South of Kata and north of Rawai, this used to be a get-away-from-it-all beach that was a bit more remote. Now development has placed bungalows on every bit of available space and the Phuket Yacht Club has added a new class of traveller. In spite of this, however, it remains Phuket's least expensive beach. The *Sunset, Ao Sane* and *Jongdee* have bungalows from 80 to 100B, while *Nai Han Ya Nui* and *Nai Han* are 150B.

Rawai This beach is, like Patong, more expensive. Cheapest places are the *Pornmae Bungalows* from 100 to 200B, and *Salaloi* for 100 to 250B. There are a number of restaurants dotted along the beach.

Other Beaches Not all the beaches have accommodation but if you do want to get away from it all, you can certainly find other, more remote places. Nai Yang, close to the airport and a good 30 km from Phuket, has a pleasant national-park complex with bungalows at 80B.

Getting There & Away

Air You can fly to Phuket from Bangkok or Hat Yai – there are several flights every day. There are also daily flights between Phuket and Surat Thani. You can shift from the beach in Phuket to the beach in Ko Samui in just seven hours reported one traveller. You can also fly from Phuket to Penang if you want to get on to Malaysia quickly.

Bus From Hat Yai to Phuket, it's eight hours by bus for about 100B. Buses from the Southern bus terminal in Bangkok take 13 or 14 hours and cost 170B, or 300B with air-con. Buses from Bangkok usually go overnight, which probably helps reduce the scare quotient. Other buses from Phuket include Phang-Nga in 1¾ hours for 25B; Krabi in 3½ hours for 40B; Surat Thani in six to 7½ hours for 65B; Nakhon Si Thammarat in eight hours for 80B; and Trang in six hours for 65B.

Boat Phuket has become a popular yachting centre. It's sometimes possible to get yacht rides from here to Penang, Sri Lanka or further afield.

Getting Around

To/From the Airport The airport is 11 km out of town and getting there can be a little problematical. Songthaews are infrequent but should cost around 15B; a taxi could run into the hundreds of baht. Thai Airways has a limousine into town for 50B per person.

Local Transport When you first arrive in Phuket, beware of the local rip-off artists who will be on hand to tell you the tourist office is five km away, that the only way to get to the beaches is to take a taxi or that a songthaew from the bus station to the town centre will cost you a small fortune.

Actually, songthaews run all over the island from a central area. The tourist office (which is also in the town centre) puts out a list of the standard charges to all the beaches and other popular destinations plus the recommended charter costs for a complete vehicle. Around town, the standard fare is 5B. Out of town, the standard fares to all the beaches vary from around 10B (Kata, Karon, Patong and Rawai) to 15B (Nai Yang and Nai Han).

You can also hire motorbikes (usually 100 cc Japanese bikes) from various places at the beaches or in Phuket town from around 150 to 250B a day.

Tours There are many tours from Phuket. One of the most popular and (according to some people) good value is the 'James Bond' Tour to Phang-Nga. You're looking at around 250B for the all-day tour including lunch, the bus trip both ways, the boat trip and a stop to see an interesting reclining Buddha on the way back. The Ko Phi Phi trip, around 400B, is also interesting. If you want to book a straight passage to Ko Phi Phi, without a tour, the fare is 250B one way. There are also a variety of scuba-diving trips and local island visits.

PHANG-NGA

Situated 94 km from Phuket town on the route to Hat Yai, Phang-Nga makes a good day trip from Phuket by motorbike. On the way to the town, turn off just five km past the small town of Takua Thung and visit the cave **Tham Suwan Kuha** which is full of Buddha images. Tha Don (with the Phang-Nga customs pier), between here and Phang-Nga, is the place where you hire boats to visit Phang-Nga Bay with its Muslim fishing villages on stilts, strangely shaped limestone outcrops soaring out of the sea and the water-filled caves. Yes, these are the James Bond islands from the film *Man with the Golden Gun*.

Places to Stay & Eat

There are a number of fairly nondescript

hotels with rooms in the 40 to 80B range. Along Phetkasem Rd, Phang-Nga's main street, you'll find the *Rak Phang-Nga* and the *Lak Muang* (☎ 41 1125/288), two typical places with 80 to 100B rooms. The hotel with the most character and facilities is *Thawisuk*, the place with the blue facade in the middle of town with clean rooms for 80B. There are other similarly priced places like the *Padoong* or the *Tan Prasert* on the western side of the town toward the customs pier.

You can buy good seafood at the stalls across from the movie theatre in Phang-Nga's main market.

KRABI

This small town offers similar offshore excursions to Phang-Nga but there are good local beaches to check out as well: **Noppharat Thara**, **Ao Nang** and **Phra Nang** are currently popular (see the following Places to Stay – Beaches section for the latest developments). The longest beach is along Ao Nang, a lovely spot easily reached from Krabi. Phra Nang Bay is perhaps the most beautiful of all the beaches in this area.

A Bangkok conglomerate has recently purchased most of Cape Phra Nang and is building resort villas on Phra Nang Beach. For the next two years or so, while the development is being constructed, the beach may be closed to visitors.

Than Bokkharani Botanical Gardens, a 10B songthaew ride from town near Ao Luk, make an interesting excursion.

Places to Stay & Eat – Town

Guest Houses New guest houses are popping up all over town. Most offer little cubicles over shophouses for 60 to 80B. *B&B*, *Pee Pee* and *Su* are typical with rooms from 60 to 80B. On Prachacheun Rd, *Fairly Tour* has clean rooms from 70 to 80B, or 40B for a dorm bed. There are others such as *Krabi* on Preusa Uthit Rd and *Jungle Book* across from the floating restaurant on Uttarakit Rd. Each charge 60B for rooms, or 80 to 100B if bath is included.

Guest houses just south-west of town are quieter. Out on Jao Fa Rd is the rather plain *Fawlty Tower Guest House* for 30B per person and the *Chao Fa Valley* from 80 to 300B (it has a restaurant out front). On Soi Ruam Jit, parallel to Jao Fa Rd, are the *Ruamjid* and *Lek* guest houses, both with fair rooms for 70 to 80B. Others are tucked away along streets leading out of town – all similar.

Hotels The *New Hotel* (☎ 61 1318) on Phattana Rd has adequate rooms for 120B with fan and bath. The *Thai* on Itsara Rd is overpriced so give it a miss. The *Vieng Thong* (☎ 61 1188/288) at 155 Uttarakit Rd has rooms from 250B.

Both the *Vieng Thong* and the *Thai* hotels have rather expensive coffee shops. At night, food vendors set up along the waterfront and there is a good morning market in the centre of town.

Places to Stay – Beaches

Ao Nang This has been a centre for budget accommodation, though rates are gradually increasing with demand. Near the turn-off for the pricey Krabi Resort are *Ao Nang Ban Leh* with 70B huts and the *Ao Nang Hill* from 40 to 60B. Going south along the beach, the *Ao Nang Beach* costs 50B for simple huts or 150B for larger huts with bath.

Further along the beach, you'll come to a turn to the left which leads to the *Princess Garden* with 50B huts or it's 120B with bath. Back on the beach road is *Phra-Nang Inn* (☎ 61 2173/4) with roomy bungalows with fan and bath from 150 to 250B. They also have a good restaurant. Next door, the *Ao Nang Villa* has a few bungalows for 60B, or from 150B with bath.

Further up the road is the *Krabi Seaview Resort* – 80B for simple huts and up to 450B for larger huts with air-con and bath.

Rai Leh Beach (West) Accessible by boat only. *Railay Village*, *Railae Bay* and *Sunset Beach* have bungalows in the 200 to 300B range.

Phra Nang Beach Accessible by boat only. Staying here used to give access to three beaches: Phra Nang, West Rai Leh and East Rai Leh (or Nam Mao).

Now it seems that all bungalows on this beach are being moved out by the Dusit Thani Group, who will be constructing a 'world-class villa resort' here over the next two years. This will most likely mean that no accommodation will be available here in the interim. Ask in town to confirm this.

Rai Leh Beach (East) There are three smaller bungalow operations with rates from 50 to 150B. This beach tends toward mud flats during low tide.

Getting There & Away

Buses from Phuket to Krabi are 38B and leave twice a day from the terminal on Phang-Nga Rd. There are several buses a day from Phang-Nga to Krabi for 22B. From Surat Thani, it's 50B and the trip takes four hours. A bus and boat combo ticket to Ko Samui is an outrageous 230B.

Buses to and from Krabi arrive and depart at Taalat Kao, just outside Krabi proper – a songthaew into town is 2B.

Getting Around

Boats to the various beaches at Rai Leh and Phra Nang leave from the Jao Fa Pier on the Krabi waterfront and cost 30B per person. Noppharat Thara Beach and Ao Nang can be reached by songthaew for 15B.

KO PHI PHI

Ko Phi Phi, four hours south of Krabi by boat, has white beaches, good diving and a huge cavern where the nests for bird's nest soup are collected. There are actually two islands: Phi Phi Don is inhabited and has a small fishing village and a couple of groups of bungalows. Phi Phi Le is uninhabited and is the site for licensed swallow's nest collecting – one of the nest caverns has some curious paintings.

Unfortunately, runaway growth has almost completely spoiled the atmosphere on Phi Phi Don, in spite of the fact that the island is part of a designated national marine park. Phi Phi Le remains protected not because it's part of the park (it isn't) but because the swallow's nest collectors make sure no one interferes with the ecology. Because all the accommodation is on Phi Phi Don, it can only be recommended these days if you're quite keen on snorkelling at nearby reefs. Otherwise, give it a miss.

Places to Stay & Eat

During high season, all accommodation on Phi Phi Don tends to be booked solid. At Ton Sai, the *Pee Pee Islands Cabana* has bungalows from 100 to 500B but it is even more for a big nine-person bungalow. There's also a 70B dorm. The cheaper bungalows at Pee Pee Cabana are probably worth the extra cost over the other island bungalow places. The *Ma-Yah Kitchen* here is rather expensive. The Pee Pee Cabana has its own boats to bring fresh food from the mainland – vegetable supplies on the island are limited.

Other places at Ton Sai include the *Phi Phi Resort* which has small bungalows for 100B, and 150B for large. Over on Lo Dalam, the north side of the isthmus, are *Gift 2* with simple huts from 50 to 70B, *Vally* at 100B for huts with baths and *Phi Phi Krabi Resort* with nice bungalows for 300B up with baths. Also on this beach, the *Charlie Beach Resort* has large huts with bath and beach views from 150 to 350B.

East of Ton Sai, the *Laem Hin Bungalows* are on a rocky peninsula. The huts are 60/70B and a bit close together. On the other side of the peninsula is *Long Beach Bungalow* with simple 80B huts, or 150B with bath. The snorkelling is good here.

Getting There & Away

There is at least one boat a day, sometimes two or three, from Krabi's Jao Fa Pier. They only run regularly from November to May but during the monsoon it depends on the weather – the return fare is 200B. Today, commercialism is starting to catch up with Ko Phi Phi and there are frequent tours from Phuket. Although the distance is about the same from Phuket or Krabi they're much cheaper from Krabi. There is now, however, a ferry service from Phuket with the *Sea King* which takes about 1½ hours and costs 150B.

There are also daily boats to Ko Phi Phi from Ao Nang, west of Krabi, from October/November to April/May for 100B per person.

TRANG

The town of Trang is a bustling little place between Krabi and Hat Yai with a history that goes back to the 1st century AD when it was an important centre for seagoing trade. Trang probably reached its peak during the 7th to 12th centuries at the height of the Srivijaya Empire.

The geography of the surrounding province is similar to that of Krabi and Phang-Nga but it's much less frequented by tourists. The **Vegetarian Festival** is celebrated fervently in September/October. Trang's coastline has several sandy beaches and coves, especially in the Sikao and Kantang districts. From the road between Trang and Kantang is a turn-off west onto an unpaved road that leads down to the coast. At the coast, a road south leads to Hat Yao, Hat Yong Ling and Hat Jao Mai. The road north leads to Hat Chang Lang and Hat Pak Meng. There are also several small islands just off the coast, including Ko Muk, Ko Kradan, Ko Hai and Ko Sukon.

Places to Stay & Eat

There are a number of places on the main street running down from the clocktower. The *Ko Teng* (☎ 21 8622) has rooms from 110B and a good restaurant downstairs. The *Wattana* (☎ 21 8184) is on the same stretch and is a little more expensive. Over on Ratchadamnoen Rd is the inexpensive *Petch (Phet) Hotel* (☎ 21 8002) with adequate rooms with fan and bath for 70B. They also have a restaurant downstairs. Moving up market, the *Queen's Hotel* (☎ 21 8522) is great value at 140B for a big room with fan and a shower with hot water!

Adjacent to the Queen's Hotel, the *Phloen Restaurant* has a very broad selection of rice

and noodle dishes, plus a few vegetarian specials. Trang is known for its coffee shops, which serve local Khao Chong coffee. Try the funky *Kafae Khao Chong* food stall on Phattalung Rd or the *Sinjew* on Kantang Rd, which is open all night.

Getting There & Away

Buses from Satun, Hat Yai or Krabi to Trang are 35B. A share taxi from the same cities is around 50B. From Phattalung, it's 15B by bus and 20B by share taxi.

KHAO SOK NATIONAL PARK

About midway between Phuket and Surat Thani, this national park has wonderful jungle and some crystal-clear rivers. You can stay at the *Tree Tops Guest House* in tree-house bungalows for around 250B, or you can camp for 50B. To get there, take a Phuket-Surat Thani bus via Takua Pa and look for the Tree Tops sign at the Km 108 marker.

SUNGAI KOLOK

This small town in the south-east is a jumping-off point for the east coast of Malaysia – its function is much like Hat Yai's for the busier west coast. Recently, another border crossing has been added 32 km east in Ban Taba, a shorter and quicker route to Kota Bharu, Malaysia. Eventually, this crossing is supposed to replace Sungai Kolok's but, for the time being, both are functioning.

Information

There's a bank in the town centre, or Malaysian dollars can be changed at the bus station or in shops. It's easier to bring baht with you from Malaysia and you can change money at the border. Just around the corner from the bus station, there's a tourist police post where they speak some English.

Places to Stay

There are few English signs in this border town to the Malaysian east coast. In the centre of town, however, there are a number of places to stay although they are a bit grotty. The town is just a 10B trishaw ride from the border or a five-minute walk straight ahead from the railway station.

Cheapies include the *Savoy Hotel* and, next door, the *Thailieng Hotel* with rooms from 80 to 160B. Over on the corner of Arifmankha and Waman Amnoey Rds is the pleasant *Valentine* at 170B with fan, and 260B with air-con. There's a coffee shop downstairs and free fruit and coffee is provided to guests.

Places to Eat

There are lots of cheap restaurants – for a cheap and delicious breakfast early in the morning, try coffee and doughnuts at the station buffet.

Getting There & Away

When you cross the border from Malaysia, the railway station is about a km straight ahead on the right-hand side. The bus station is a further km beyond the railway station, down a turning to the left.

Bus & Share Taxi
Share taxis from Yala are 60B and the bus is 25B. From Narathiwat, the share taxi is 30B; the bus is 20B. There are no buses direct to Hat Yai from Sungai Kolok. Buses north go through Songkhla on their way to Bangkok.

Train
From Hat Yai, the 3rd-class rail fare is about 35B. From Bangkok, fares are 180B in 3rd class and 378B in 2nd class, before the rapid, express or sleeper supplements.

Vietnam

In the decades following WW II, the name 'Vietnam' came to signify to many Westerners both a brutal jungle war and a spectacular failure of American power. When people talked about 'Vietnam', they really meant the American war in Indochina, not Vietnam the country.

The real Vietnam, with its unique and rich civilisation, highly cultured people, hauntingly beautiful mountains, ancient rainforest, cool highlands, intensively cultivated Mekong and Red River deltas, pristine palm-fringed beaches and bustling cities, was almost entirely ignored.

This is now changing. For the first time since the reunification of the country in 1975, Vietnam is welcoming travellers from the West. Travel to Vietnam requires a bit more creativity and perseverance than visiting other countries in the region, but, finally, it is possible.

Facts about the Country

HISTORY

A 1000 years of Chinese rule over the Red River Delta (all of Vietnam at the time), marked by tenacious Vietnamese resistance and repeated rebellions, ended in 938 AD when Ngo Quyen vanquished the Chinese armies at the Bach Dang River.

During the next few centuries, Vietnam's emperors reorganised the administrative system, founded the nation's first university (the Temple of Literature in Hanoi), promoted agriculture and built the first embankments for flood control along the Red River. Vietnam repulsed repeated invasions by China and expanded in a southward direction along the coast at the expense of the kingdom of Champa, which was wiped out in 1471.

The first contact between Vietnam and the West took place in Roman times. Recent

European contact with Vietnam began in the 16th century, when European merchants and missionaries arrived. Despite restrictions and periods of persecution, the Catholic Church eventually had a greater impact on Vietnam than on any country in Asia except for the Philippines.

In 1858, a joint military force from France and the Spanish colony of the Philippines stormed Danang after the killing of several missionaries. Early the next year, they seized Saigon. A few years later, Vietnamese Emperor Tu Duc signed a treaty that gave the French part of the Mekong Delta region and promised missionaries the freedom to proselytise everywhere in the country. In 1883, the French imposed a Treaty of Protectorate on Vietnam.

Throughout the colonial period, opposition to French rule was expressed in a variety of ways, ranging from the publishing of political tracts to an attempt to poison the French garrison at Hanoi. The response of the colonial authorities to all such activities was often brutal. Ultimately, the most successful anticolonialists proved to be the Communists. The first Marxist group in Indochina, the Vietnam Revolutionary Youth League, was founded by Ho Chi Minh in Canton, China, in 1925.

During WW II, the only group that did anything significant to resist the Japanese occupation was the Communist-dominated Viet Minh (which from 1944 received funding and arms from the American Office of Strategic Services (OSS), predecessor of the CIA). During the last months of WW II, a horrific famine caused the deaths of two million of northern Vietnam's 10 million people.

When WW II ended, Ho Chi Minh – whose Viet Minh forces already controlled large parts of the country – declared Vietnam independent. French efforts to reassert control soon led to violent confrontations and full-scale war. In May 1954, Viet Minh forces, led by General Vo Nguyen Giap, captured the French garrison at Dien Bien Phu. This stunning and catastrophic defeat shattered public support in France for the war.

The Geneva Accords of mid-1954 provided for a temporary division of the country into two zones at the Ben Hai River (near the 17th Parallel). When the leader of the southern zone, an anti-Communist Catholic named Ngo Dinh Diem, refused to hold elections scheduled for 1956 (he was convinced that the Communists would win, as was the USA), the Ben Hai line became the de facto border between the Democratic Republic of Vietnam, with its capital at Hanoi, and the Republic of Vietnam, ruled from Saigon.

In about 1960, the Hanoi government changed its policy of opposition to the Diem regime from one of 'political struggle' to one of 'armed struggle'. The National Liberation Front (NLF), a Communist guerrilla group better known as the Viet Cong (VC), was founded to fight against Diem.

From the first, the Diem government had difficulty retaining control of its territory in the face of Viet Cong activities. After Hanoi ordered regular North Vietnamese Army units to infiltrate into the South in 1964, the situation for the Saigon regime became desperate. In 1965, the USA – which saw preventing the fall of South Vietnam as an important part of the worldwide struggle to contain Communism – committed its first combat troops. They were soon joined by soldiers from South Korea, Australia, Thailand and New Zealand. By December 1965, there were 184,300 US military personnel in Vietnam; in the spring of 1969 there were 543,000.

The Tet Offensive of early 1968 marked a crucial turning point in the war. As the country celebrated Tet, the Vietnamese New Year, the Viet Cong launched a stunning offensive in over 100 cities and towns. As the TV cameras rolled, a VC commando team temporarily took over the courtyard of the US Embassy building in the centre of Saigon. Many ordinary Americans, who had been hearing for years that the US was winning, stopped believing what they were being told by their government.

The Paris Agreements, signed in 1973, provided for a cease-fire, the total withdrawal of US combat forces and the release by Hanoi of American prisoners of war. The agreement made no mention of approximately 200,000 North Vietnamese troops then in South Vietnam.

By this time, nearly 58,000 Americans were listed as killed or missing-in-action. Almost a quarter of a million South Vietnamese soldiers had been killed, and North Vietnamese and Viet Cong casualties were in the hundreds of thousands. About four million civilians, 10% of the country's population, had been killed or injured. Huge areas of forest land had been defoliated with Agent Orange.

A massive North Vietnamese ground attack across the 17th Parallel in January 1975 – a blatant violation of the Paris Agreements – panicked the South Vietnamese military and government. A tactical withdrawal to more defensible positions deteriorated into a chaotic rout as soldiers deserted in order to try to save their families. Whole brigades disintegrated and fled southward. On 30 April 1975, Saigon surrendered to the North Vietnamese Army.

The takeover of the South by the North was accompanied by large-scale political repression. Despite repeated promises to the contrary, hundreds of thousands of people, many of whom had opposed the previous regime, were rounded up and imprisoned without trial in forced-labour camps euphemistically known as 're-education camps'. Hundreds of thousands of southerners fled their homeland by sea and overland through Cambodia.

After repeated attacks on Vietnamese border villages, Vietnam invaded Cambodia at the end of 1978, driving the murderous Khmer Rouge from power and setting up a pro-Hanoi regime in Phnom Penh. The Vietnamese say that the last of their forces left Cambodia in September 1989.

In early 1979, China invaded northern Vietnam following a campaign of repression

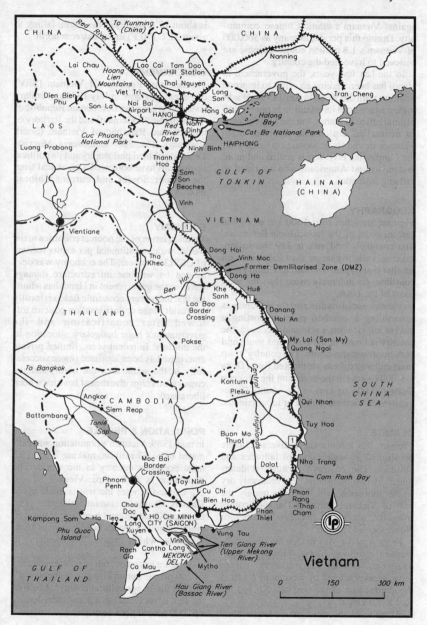

Vietnam

against Vietnam's ethnic-Chinese community. During this period, as many as 500,000 of Vietnam's 1.8 million ethnic-Chinese are believed to have fled the country

In the last few years, the government in Hanoi has been making an effort to improve relations with the West. In April 1991, Washington announced its intention to open up an official office in Hanoi, but the USA refuses to normalise diplomatic relations with Vietnam or end its economic embargo until the Cambodian civil war is settled and more is done to find Americans who are listed as missing in action.

GEOGRAPHY
Vietnam stretches over 1600 km along the eastern coast of the Indochinese Peninsula. The country's land area is 329,566 sq km, making it slightly larger than Italy and a bit smaller than Japan. Vietnam has 3260 km of coastline, considerably more than the west coast of the USA.

Vietnamese often describe their country as resembling a bamboo pole supporting a basket of rice on each end because the country is broad in the north and south and very narrow in the centre. The country's two main cultivated areas are the Red River Delta (15,000 sq km) in the north and the Mekong Delta (60,000 sq km) in the south. Three-quarters of Vietnam is hilly or mountainous.

CLIMATE
Vietnam has a remarkably diverse climate because of its wide range of latitudes and altitudes. The country's weather is determined by two monsoons. The relatively dry winter monsoon, which affects mainly the part of Vietnam north of Danang, comes from the north-east between October or November and March.

From April or May to October, the south-western monsoon blows, bringing warm, damp weather to the whole country – except those areas sheltered by mountains (such as the central part of the coastal strip and the Red River Delta.

At sea level, the mean annual temperature is about 27°C (81°F) in the south, falling to about 21°C (70°F) in the extreme north

GOVERNMENT
The Socialist Republic of Vietnam (SRV) came into existence in July 1976 as a unitary state comprising the Democratic Republic of Vietnam (North Vietnam) and the territory of the defeated Republic of Vietnam (South Vietnam). The SRV espouses a Marxist-Leninist political philosophy and its political institutions have borrowed a great deal from the former Soviet and current Chinese models.

ECONOMY
Vietnam is one of the poorest countries in the world, with an estimated per capita income of US$130 per year. The economy was devastated by wartime infrastructure damage but even the government in Hanoi has admitted that the present economic fiasco is mostly the result of the collectivisation policies followed after reunification and the government's huge budgetary allocation to the military. In recent years, limited private enterprise has been legalised (more successfully in the south than the north) and the country's foreign investment laws have been liberalised.

POPULATION & PEOPLE
In mid-1989, Vietnam's population was estimated to be 67 million, making it the 12th most populous country in the world. The population is 84% ethnic-Vietnamese and 2% ethnic-Chinese; the rest is made up of Khmers, Chams (a remnant of the once-great Champa Kingdom) and members of some 60 ethno-linguistic groups (also known as Montagnards, which means 'highlanders' in French).

Vietnam has an overall population density of 200 people per sq km, one of the world's highest for an agricultural country. Much of the Red River Delta has a population density of 1000 people per sq km.

ARTS & CULTURE
Conduct
When dealing with local people, it is important to be extremely sensitive to indications that they are worried that contact with you may get them into trouble with the police. Vietnamese are much less afraid of being seen with Westerners than they were a few years ago. There are still reports, however, of conversations with Westerners resulting in police questioning and harassment.

Shoes must be removed inside Buddhist pagodas. In Chinese pagodas, on the other hand, shoes can usually be left on. Be sure not to let the bottoms of your feet point towards other people or anything sacred, especially figures of Buddhas.

Ao Dais
The graceful Vietnamese national dress – these days worn almost exclusively by women – is known as the *ao dai* (pronounced 'ow-zai' in the north and 'ow-yai' in the south). It consists of a close-fitting blouse with long panels in the front and back that is worn over loose black or white trousers.

Water Puppetry
Water puppetry *(roi nuoc)*, a uniquely Vietnamese art form, is thought to have developed when determined puppeteers in the Red River Delta managed to carry on with the show despite flooding. Water puppetry draws its plots from the same legendary and historical sources as other forms of traditional theatre. Water puppetry can be seen at the Saigon Zoo, in Hanoi and at Thay Pagoda, near Hanoi.

RELIGION
Four great philosophies and religions have shaped the spiritual life of the Vietnamese people: Confucianism, Taoism, Buddhism and Christianity.

Popular Religion
Over the centuries, Confucianism, Taoism and Buddhism have fused with popular Chinese beliefs and ancient Vietnamese animism to form what is known collectively as the 'Triple Religion' *(Tam Giao)*, which is sometimes referred to as Vietnamese Buddhism. The religious life of the Vietnamese is also profoundly influenced by ancestor worship, which dates from long before the arrival of Confucianism or Buddhism.

Islam
Muslims, mostly ethnic-Khmers and Chams, constitute about 0.5% of the population.

Christianity
Catholicism was introduced into Vietnam in the 16th century by missionaries from Portugal, Spain and France. Pope Alexander VII assigned the first bishops to Vietnam in 1659, and the first Vietnamese priests were ordained nine years later. Foreign missionaries and their Vietnamese followers were ruthlessly persecuted during the 17th and 18th centuries.

Today, Vietnam has the highest percentage of Catholics (8% to 10% of the population) in Asia outside of the Philippines. Since 1954, in the North, and 1975, in the South, Catholics have faced restrictions on their religious activities.

Caodaism
Caodaism is an indigenous Vietnamese sect that was founded with the intention of creating the ideal religion by fusing the secular and religious philosophies of both East and West. It was established in the early 1920s based on messages revealed in seances to Ngo Minh Chieu, the group's founder. The sect's colourful headquarters is in Tay Ninh, 96 km north-west of Saigon. There are currently about two million followers of Caodaism in Vietnam.

LANGUAGE
Perhaps the trickiest aspect of Vietnamese for Westerners trying to pick up a bit of the language is learning to differentiate between the six tones, each of which is represented by a different diacritical mark. Thus, every syllable in Vietnamese can be pronounced six different ways. Depending on the tones, the word *ma* can be read to mean phantom,

mother, rice seedling, tomb or horse. *Ga* can mean railroad station and chicken as well several other things.The Latin-based *quoc ngu* script, in wide use since WW I, was developed in the 17th century by Alexandre de Rhodes, a brilliant French Jesuit scholar who first arrived in Vietnam in 1627.

Pronunciation & Tones

Most of the names of the letters of the quoc ngu alphabet are the same as the names of the letters in French. Dictionaries are alphabetised as in English except that each vowel/tone combination is treated as a different letter. The consonants of the Romanised Vietnamese alphabet are pronounced more-or-less as they are in English with a few exceptions.

c	Like a 'K' but with no aspiration.
đ	With a crossbar; like a hard 'D'.
d	Without a crossbar; like a 'Z' in the north and a 'Y' in the south.
gi	Like a 'Z' in the north and a 'Y' in the south.
kh	Like '-ch' in the German *buch*.
ng	Like the '-ng a-' in 'long ago'.
nh	Like the Spanish 'Ñ' (as in *mañana*)
ph	Like an 'F'.
r	Like 'Z' in the north and 'R' in the south.
s	Like an 'S' in the north and 'Sh' in the south.
tr	Like 'Ch-' in the north and 'Tr-' in the south.
th	Like a strongly aspirated 'T'.
x	Like an 'S'.
-ch	Like a 'K'.
-ng	Like '-ng' in 'long' but with the lips closed.
-nh	Like '-ng' in 'sing'.

Pronouns

he
  câu ấy or *anh ấy*
I
  tôi
she
  cô ấy

they
  họ
we
  chúng tôi
you (to an older man/men)
  (các) ông
you (to an older woman/women)
  (các) bà
you (to a man/men) of your own age
  (các) anh
you (to a woman (women) of your own age)
  (các) cô

Greetings & Civilities

Can you speak...?
  (Insert appropriate form of you) *có nói tiếng...được không?*
Don't worry, it doesn't matter.
  Không sao đâo,đừng.
I am not a Russian.
  Tôi không phải là người Liên Xô. **or**
  Không phải Liên Xô.
I can't.
  Tôi không thể.
I can speak a little Vietnamese.
  Tôi có thể nói một ít tiếng Việt.
I come from...
  Tôi đến từ...
My name is...
  Tên tôi là...
Thank you very much.
  Cám ón rất nhiều.

Some Useful Words & Phrases

Do you understand?
  (Insert appropriate form of you) *có hiêú không?*
I like...
  Tôi thích...
I don't like...
  Tôi không thích...
I don't understand.
  Tôi không hiêú.
I want (+ verb or noun)...
  Tôi muốn ...
I don't want...
  Tôi không muốn....
I need (+ verb or noun)...
  Tôi cần ...

boulevard				
đại lộ (precedes the name)				

change money
   đổi tiền
come
   tới
fast
   nhanh (in the north), *mau* (in the south)
give
   cho
hotel
   khách sạn
man
   nằm
office
   văn phòng
Overseas Vietnamese
   Việt Kiều
post office
   bưu điện
restaurant
   nhà hàng
slow
   chậm
street
   đường, phố (precedes the name)
telephone
   điện thoại (abbreviated *DT*)
tourism
   du lịch (pronounced 'zoo lick'/'you lick')
understand
   hiểu
water
   nước
woman
   nữ

Numbers

first	*nhất*
second	*nhỉ*
1	*một*
2	*hai*
3	*ba*
4	*bốn*
5	*năm*
6	*sáu*
7	*bảy*
8	*tám*
9	*chín*
10	*mười* or *chục*

11	*mười một*
19	*mười chín*
20	*hai mươi*
21	*hai mươi mốt*
30	*ba mươi*
90	*chín mươi*
100	*một trăm*
200	*hai trăm*
900	*chín trăm*
1000	*một nghìn*
10,000	*mười nghìn*
100,000	*trăm nghìn*
1 million	*một triệu*

From three upwards, the cardinal and ordinal numbers are the same.

Facts for the Visitor

VISAS & EMBASSIES

Whilst more perseverance is needed to travel to Vietnam than to nonsocialist countries in the region, arranging the necessary paperwork is not all that daunting. By far the best place to get Vietnamese visas is Bangkok, although for a while the Vietnamese Embassy in Vientiane was giving out tourist visas with no hassles.

Vietnamese visas specify where you are permitted to enter and leave the country – usually Ho Chi Minh City's Tan Son Nhut or Hanoi's Noi Bai airports. Make sure the officials issuing your visa know what you need. If you later decide to exit from a place not listed on your visa, go to the Saigon or Hanoi office of the Foreign Ministry and ask them to make the necessary amendments to your visa.

It is no longer necessary to book a tour in order to get a visa but visas are still more readily available through travel agencies than from Vietnamese diplomatic offices. There is no such thing as a standard price for a Vietnamese visa yet, so you have to shop around.

In Bangkok, visas typically cost around 2000B (about US$80). Many agencies offer good deals for visas plus the necessary flights to and from Vietnam. There are numerous agencies around Khao San Rd in Bangkok that specialise in procuring Vietnamese visas. Vista Travel at 24/4 Khao San Rd seems to be particularly knowledgeable. Other agencies worth trying include:

Air People Tour & Travel
    183 Rajdamri Rd (☎ 254 3921/2/3/4/5)
Exotissimo Travel
    21/17 Sukhumvit Soi 4 (☎ 253 5240/1, 255 2747)
MK Ways
    57/11 Wireless Rd (☎ 254 5583)
Red Carpet Service & Tour
    459 New Rama 6 Rd (☎ 215 9951, 215 3331)

It takes five to 10 days to issue the visa in Bangkok.

Visas for Vietnam are also readily available in Hong Kong, although there are not yet direct flights between Hong Kong and Vietnam. Phoenix Services (☎ 722 7378), Room B, 6th Floor, Milton Mansions, 96 Nathan Rd, Kowloon, is a good source and charges HK$1200 (US$150) for a visa which takes about 10 days to issue. An express three-day service costs HK$1400. They also offer a Hong Kong-Bangkok-Saigon and return ticket plus visa package for HK$4890.

Visas can also be obtained in Australia through STA Travel for around A$90 or from other travel agencies at both higher and lower costs. They take about two weeks to issue.

Vietnamese Embassies
Vietnam's more useful embassies in the region include:

Cambodia
    The consular section is opposite 749 Achar Mean Blvd, Phnom Penh (☎ 2.3142). It is open from 7.30 to 11 am and from 2 to 5 pm (except Saturday afternoon, Sunday and public holidays). Visas usually take two days.
Laos
    Thanon That Luang (☎ 5578)
Malaysia
    4 Pesiaran Stonor, Kuala Lumpur (☎ (03) 248 4036
Thailand
    83/1 Wireless Rd, Bangkok (☎ 02-251 7201/2/3, 251 5836). The visa section is open weekdays from 8.30 to 11.30 am and from 1 to 4 pm.

Visa Extensions
Like everything else in Vietnam these days, visa regulations are in a state of flux and may change overnight. To find out the latest information, ask other travellers before you go – Khao San Rd in Bangkok is a good place to look for recent visitors to Vietnam.

Vietnam Tourism representatives will tell you that visa extensions are given only to people who book another tour with them. Officials of the Immigration Police will say that they need a letter of recommendation from Vietnam Tourism in order to issue a visa extension. Back at Vietnam Tourism, the officials will tell you that they cannot write such a letter for you if you do not book a tour – Catch 22.

The golden rule in Vietnam, however, is if you don't like the answer you get from one office, try another. In Saigon, there are now many people who seem to be able to wheedle the necessary pieces of paperwork out of the appropriate authorities.

Registration
All foreigners must register with the Immigration Police within two days of their arrival in Vietnam. Whereas visas (issued by the Foreign Ministry) get you into Vietnam, registration means that you have the permission of the Immigration Police (an arm of the powerful Interior Ministry) to stay wherever you are. If you're on a tour, this will be taken care of automatically but if not, contact the office address given to you by whoever issued your visa – Vietnam Tourism, TOSERCO (if you're in Hanoi) or, as a last resort, the nearest Immigration Police office.

If at all possible, do not hand your original papers (passport, visa, internal travel permits, etc) over to the police – you may have difficulty getting them back, especially if you've been accused of breaking Interior Ministry rules. Give them photocopies instead. If the police cause you any serious problems, tell them you intend to contact your ambassador. If they try to fine you, haggle!

Internal Travel Permits

Foreigners must also have internal travel permits *(giay phep di lai)*, issued by the Interior Ministry, to go anywhere outside the port-of-entry in which they registered with the Immigration Police. In general, permits are not required for day trips but are necessary if you want to spend the night somewhere.

The Interior Ministry keeps changing its policies on issuing travel permits to individual travellers, but they seem to prefer to try out more liberal guidelines in Hanoi, where they can keep an eye on things. Internal travel permits are issued by TOSERCO in Hanoi and the Immigration Police in Saigon and Hanoi for travel to certain destinations during a specific period of time.

All individual travellers, including those bearing internal travel permits, are required to register with the local police when they arrive at any place where their intended stay is more than 48 hours. Because hotels are required to register guests with the police – that's why they collect tourists' passports and locals' identity papers – this will probably be taken care of for you.

While Maureen and I were in Vietnam we met one group of travellers who had set out from Saigon with dodgy travel permits (the issuing office wasn't really eligible to issue them). They were arrested and fined in Mytho and sent back. The men in the group were fined US$50 (one American pleaded poverty and was excused!), the women paid US$20.

We also met three cyclists who were being followed by a guide on a motorbike for US$15 a day. First prize went to a group we met in Danang – their permits were declared suspect in Dalat but the helpful police there issued them with new permits allowing them to go all the way to Hanoi by bus or train and without having to have a guide!

Tony Wheeler

MONEY
Currency

The dong is the currency of Vietnam (it is abbreviated by a 'd' following the amount). Banknotes in denominations of 20d, 50d, 100d, 200d, 500d, 1000d, 2000d and 5000d are presently in circulation but you rarely see notes under 100d.

The foreign currency of choice in Vietnam is the US$ which virtually acts as a second local currency. Other major currencies are not readily accepted. Travellers' cheques in US$ dollars can be exchanged for dong at certain banks. Lost or stolen travellers' cheques cannot be replaced in Vietnam.

Needless to say, the black market, which is illegal, is interested only in US$ cash and large-denomination bills are preferred. An ample supply of US$1, US$5 and US$10 notes is indispensable for tips, small expenses and for change in dollar-denominated transactions (such as hotel bills) – although there are so many US$ floating around in Vietnam that you will find change can usually be given in dollars!

Be sure to bring enough US$ cash for your whole visit and to keep them safe, preferably in a money belt. Unless you borrow from a Westerner or have someone carry it into the country for you, it is almost impossible to get money into Vietnam quickly.

Exchange Rates

A$1	=	7500d
C$1	=	8362d
NZ$1	=	5526d
UK£1	=	16,254d
US$1	=	9450d

Banks and major hotel exchange desks all seem to offer the same bank rate these days but the commission can vary, typically from 1% to 2.5%. Vietnam Airlines charge a 5% commission if you want to pay for domestic airfares with travellers' cheques rather than US$ cash.

Apart from banks, there are also authorised exchange bureaus, especially in Saigon. Make sure you get a receipt for exchange transactions – customs officials sometimes do check your currency declaration when you leave the country.

There is a relatively open black market in Vietnam, typically offering 5% to 10% over the bank rate. Avoid changing money on the street. You're much better off completing transactions in a shop; US$100 will get you hundreds of the 2000d notes, so checking takes time!

At present, the only credit cards acceptable in Vietnam are Visa, and only if they are issued by a non-US bank and the user is not an American. This will change as soon as the US stops its economic embargo of Vietnam.

Costs

Vietnam is one of the best travel bargains in the world, with decent hotels, excellent food and serviceable transport all available at good prices. The only exception is where special 'foreigners only' prices are charged and, unfortunately, this is happening more often.

A cheap hotel might cost 25,000d (US$3) for Vietnamese (and Russians) but other nationalities, including overseas Vietnamese, will be charged US$10 or US$15. Similar pricing policies apply to airline tickets (Saigon to Danang is US$30 for Vietnamese and US$81 for foreigners) and railways.

If these foreigner's prices can be avoided, ascetics can get by on less than US$10 a day. For US$15, a backpacker can live fairly well. Buses are the cheapest form of transport (and if you can get the dong prices, most trains are cheaper still). Dong prices are rising very rapidly but at the same time the dong is being devalued against the US$ – for this reason, most prices are quoted in US dollars.

Tipping

Tipping is not expected but it's enormously appreciated. For someone making US$10 per month, 5% or 10% of the cost of your meal can easily equal a day's wages. Government-run hotels and restaurants that cater to tourists usually have an automatic 10% service charge.

People you have worked with greatly appreciate small gifts such as a pack of cigarettes.

WHEN TO GO

There are no especially good or bad seasons for visiting Vietnam. When one region is wet, cold or steaming hot, there is always somewhere else that is sunny and pleasantly warm.

Visitors should take into account that around Tet, the colourful Vietnamese New Year celebration which falls in late January or early February, flights into, out of and around the country are likely to be booked solid, and accommodation can be almost impossible to find.

WHAT TO BRING

Helpful items are a pocket short-wave radio (the only way to get hard news outside Saigon), US$ bills in small denominations, Western cigarettes (to give as tips), tampons, contraceptives and an umbrella (during the monsoon seasons).

TOURIST OFFICES

Vietnam Tourism (Du Lich Viet Nam) and Ho Chi Minh City's Saigon Tourist are state-run organisations that are responsible for all aspects of a tourist's stay in Vietnam – everything from visas to accommodation and transport. These bodies have neither the inclination nor the staff to keep tabs on individual travellers (though the police often seem to have both), but you may have to work through them to get visa extensions and internal travel permits.

It is often possible to bypass Vietnam Tourism by working directly with provincial tourism authorities who, like every organisation in Vietnam from the Foreign Ministry on down to the smallest industrial concern, crave US$.

BUSINESS HOURS & HOLIDAYS

Offices, museums, etc are usually open from 7 or 8 am to 11 or 11.30 am and from 1 or 2 pm to 4 or 5 pm. Most museums are closed on Monday.

Tet (Tet Nguyen Dan), the Vietnamese New Year, is the most important annual festival. Marking the new lunar year as well as the advent of spring, this week-long holiday falls in late January or in early February.

The date on which Saigon surrendered to Hanoi-backed forces in 1975, 30 April, is commemorated nationwide as Liberation Day.

POST & TELECOMMUNICATIONS

International post from Vietnam is slow and expensive: a 10 gram letter, which may take six weeks to arrive, will set you back about US$1. Tariffs for international telephone calls are also pricey – for the first three minutes, it is US$18 to the USA, US$15 to Western Europe and US$12 to Australia.

TIME

Vietnam, like Thailand, Cambodia and Laos, is seven hours ahead of GMT. When it is 12 noon in Vietnam, it is 5 am in London, 1 am in New York, 10 pm in Los Angeles and 3 pm in Sydney.

BOOKS & MAPS

Lonely Planet's *Vietnam, Laos & Cambodia – a travel survival kit* has the full story on the three recently reopened countries of Indochina. The two classic books from the French colonial period are Graham Greene's novel *The Quiet American*, and Norman Lewis' account of travels in the regions in the early 1950s, *A Dragon Apparent*. Amongst the many books on the war, Jonathan Schell's *The Real War* and *Dispatches* by Michael Herr are among the best.

Maps of Vietnam are readily available in Saigon, or get the Nelles Verlag *Vietnam, Laos & Kampuchea* map which, unfortunately, seems to omit many important minor place names.

MEDIA

The English-language *Vietnam Weekly* is published in Hanoi.

The *Voice of Vietnam* broadcasts in 11 foreign languages including English, French, Spanish and Japanese. In Hanoi, the daily English broadcast can be picked up from 6 to 6.30 pm on 1010 kHz on the medium-band (AM).

Foreign radio services such as the BBC World Service, Radio Australia and Voice of America can be picked up on short-wave frequencies.

FILM & PHOTOGRAPHY

Vietnamese airports are equipped with ancient X-ray machines that will severely damage or destroy *any* film, whether it is exposed or unexposed and no matter how low the ASA or Din rating is. Do *not* let customs X-ray your film as you leave the country. Remember, also, that baggage is X-rayed when it arrives in Vietnam (to check for contraband electronic equipment). Do not put your film in your checked luggage! Your best bet, even on domestic flights, is to keep all film on your person.

HEALTH

Agent Orange Vietnamese health professionals, faced with an abnormally high incidence of diseases known to be caused by dioxin and other chemicals found in the defoliant Agent Orange, believe that there is a link between US defoliation during the war and spontaneous abortions, stillbirths, birth defects and other human health problems.

The risks of short-term exposure are probably minimal, but because the effects are potentially devastating, women – especially those in the early months of pregnancy – may want to consider either postponing their visit or travelling only in the undefoliated north, where dioxin levels in the soil are very low.

Malaria Chloroquine resistance has been reported in Vietnam.

DANGERS & ANNOYANCES

Since 1975, many thousands of Vietnamese have been maimed or killed by rockets, artillery shells, mortars, mines and other ordnance left over from the war. While cities, cultivated areas and well-travelled rural roads and paths are safe for travel, straying away from these areas could land you in the middle of a minefield which, though known to the locals, may be completely unmarked. *Never* touch any relics of the war you may come across – such objects can remain lethal for decades. Don't become a statistic!

Beware of pickpockets and drive-by thieves, especially in Saigon. Travellers on the trains report that on slow sections (which in Vietnam are extremely slow), gear can be snatched straight through the windows. If you're fast, reported one visitor, you can jump off the train, run the would-be-thief down and even reboard.

ACCOMMODATION

Until 1989, 'capitalist' tourists were allowed to stay in only a few large tourist-class hotels that required payment in US$. These days, all sorts of options are available, ranging from almost international-standard hotels in Saigon to district-level official guest houses without electricity.

Vietnam Tourism may tell you that you can only stay in their dollar-priced hotels – don't listen to them. Smaller hotels (most run by the various echelons of provincial and municipal government, large state companies and central government ministries) are becoming aware of the benefits of admitting foreign guests. Unless there is a serious crackdown on individual travel, very few are likely to refuse a request for a room.

In hotels for domestic travellers, Westerners are often steered toward the most expensive room available. If you prefer something simpler, quickly look around for a posted price list and point good-naturedly to the prices.

FOOD

One of the delights of visiting Vietnam is the amazing cuisine – there are said to be nearly 500 traditional Vietnamese dishes – which is, in general, superbly prepared and very cheap. The Vietnamese bake the best bread in South-East Asia – a French style *petit pain* loaf of bread costs just US$0.05. Buy some jam (ask for *confiture*) to make a cheap breakfast.

Condiments

Nuoc mam (pronounced something like 'nuke mom') is a type of fermented fish sauce, identifiable by its distinctive smell, which is found with all Vietnamese meals.

Soups

Pho is the Vietnamese name for the noodle soup that is eaten at all hours of the day, but especially for breakfast. It is prepared by quickly boiling noodles and placing them into a bowl along with greens (shallots, parsley) and shredded beef, chicken or pork. A broth made with boiled bones, prawns, ginger and nuoc mam is then poured into the bowl. Some people take their pho with chilli sauce or lemon.

Vegetarian Food

Because Buddhist monks of the Mahayana tradition are strict vegetarians, Vietnamese vegetarian cooking (*an chay*) has a long history and is an integral part of Vietnamese cuisine. In general, the focus of vegetarian cuisine in Vietnam has been on reproducing traditional dishes prepared with meat, chicken, seafood or egg without including these ingredients. Instead, tofu, mushrooms and raw, dried, cooked and fermented vegetables are used. Because it does not include many expensive ingredients, vegetarian food is unbelievably cheap.

On days when there is a full or sliver moon (the beginning and middle days of the lunar month), many Vietnamese and Chinese do not eat meat, chicken, seafood or eggs – or even nuoc mam. On such days, some food stalls, especially in the marketplaces, serve vegetarian meals. To find out when the next sliver or full moon will be, consult any Vietnamese calendar.

How to Read a Menu

On menus, dishes are usually listed according to their main ingredient. For instance, all the chicken dishes appear together, as do all the beef dishes, and so on. Usual headings for menu categories are:

beef	*bo*
fish	*ca*
crab	*cua*
frog	*ech*
chicken	*ga*
eel	*uon*
oyster	*so*
shrimp	*tom*

Getting There & Away

AIR

The only practicable way into or out of Vietnam for Western travellers (except those coming from Cambodia) is by air. Bangkok, only 80-minutes flying time from Ho Chi Minh City, has emerged as the most convenient port of embarkation for air travel to Ho Chi Minh City (US$290 return) and Hanoi (US$347 return), in part because the Vietnamese Embassy in Bangkok is the easiest place to get visas. There are also flights from most South-East Asian capitals and Australia (Sydney and Melbourne). It is extremely important that you reconfirm your flight out of the country.

LAND & RIVER

For information on bus travel between Saigon and Phnom Penh and passenger ferry services between the Mekong Delta and Phnom Penh, see the Cambodia Getting There & Away.

When the politics are sorted out and the Vietnamese relax their restrictions, it should be possible to go overland from Thailand to Vietnam via Laos and Cambodia. Reportedly, a Bangkok company is currently negotiating to start a Bangkok-Vientiane (Laos)-Danang (Vietnam) bus service. Vietnam's land borders with China have been closed since the 1979 Chinese invasion but it is rumoured that this border may reopen.

Getting Around

AIR

All air travel within Vietnam is handled by Vietnam Airlines (Hang Khong Viet Nam), the national carrier. Flights fill up fast (some are literally standing room only) so reservations should be made at least several days before departure. Make sure you reconfirm all flights. Many provincial destinations can be included as a stopover on flights between Hanoi and Saigon: there are daily Ho Chi Minh City-Danang-Hanoi and return flights. From Ho Chi Minh City to Danang, it costs US$81 for foreigners; Danang to Hanoi is US$80.

Reservations and ticketing for internal flights are handled by Vietnam Airlines' domestic booking offices. In a given city, reservations can only be made for travel originating in that city. The baggage weight limit on domestic flights is 20 kg. 'Capitalist tourists' must pay for air tickets in US$ cash at a higher fare than locals pay. Travellers' cheques can be exchanged at a bank for a special voucher whose value must equal or exceed the ticket price.

BUS

Vietnam's extensive bus network reaches virtually every corner of the country. Many cities have several bus stations between which responsibilities are divided according to the location of the destination (whether it is north or south of the city) and the type of service being offered (local, express, etc).

Almost all Vietnamese buses suffer from frequent breakdowns, tiny seats or benches, almost no legroom and chronic overcrowding. Most intercity buses depart very early in the morning.

TRAIN

The 2600 km Vietnamese railway system runs along the coast between Saigon and Hanoi and links the capital with Haiphong and points north. Odd-numbered trains travel southward; even-numbered trains go northward. The Reunification (Thong Nhat) trains link Saigon and Hanoi. The fastest Reunification trains, STN3 and STN5 going south and STN4 and STN6 going north, take 52 hours to get from Saigon to Hanoi (and vice versa). Recently, a special twice-weekly tourist train, labelled TN8 northbound, has started operation.

There are two classes of train travel in Vietnam: hard sitter and hard sleeper. Reservations for all trips, especially for sleepers, should be made at least one day in advance.

In any given city, reservations can be made only for travel originating in that city.

The main disadvantage of rail travel is that officially, foreigners and overseas Vietnamese are supposed to pay a surcharge of between 375% and 480% over and above what Vietnamese pay! Local prices for train tickets are a great deal – a bit cheaper than buses, even. But the foreigners' surcharge makes long-haul rail travel by sleeping berth almost as expensive as flying. Some foreigners have managed to pay local dong prices but many have left Vietnam's train stations disappointed.

CAR

Cars with drivers can be hired from a variety of sources, including Vietnam Tourism, provincial and municipal tourism authorities, bus companies, government ministries and even a few private companies. Vietnam Tourism charges US$0.35 per km travelled.

Our Citröen

Maureen and I went to Vietnam in 1991 with the intention of travelling between Saigon and Hanoi by bus, train and air. That initial plan was ditched when we discovered we would have to be accompanied by a guide (US$15 to US$20 per day), so we then went in search of a car to rent. A trip from Saigon via Dalat, Nha Trang, Quy Nhon and Danang to Hué is about 1400 km, which at US$0.35 a km came to about US$500. Even half price on the return trip brought the total cost to US$750.

Asking around, however, we found Easiway Travel (☎ 31337), 34 Pham Ngoc Thach, Quan 3, Ho Chi Minh City, who charged less than half the Vietnam Tourism price for a seven-day trip in a fine old Citröen DS. A group of Frenchmen who had travelled in the same car prior to us paid US$560 for a 16-day trip all the way to Hanoi. Between four people, this worked out to be a very reasonable daily cost. Easiway also did all the chasing around for travel permits for us.

Until issuing travel permits is simplified, and you can travel by bus or train without having to be accompanied by a guide, car travel may well be the best way to explore Vietnam. It also makes a lot of sense if your time is limited since even short trips by bus or train can take a very long time.

Tony Wheeler

BICYCLE

You can ride through Vietnam on your own bicycle, although you may be required to pay a guide to follow you by motorbike! It is possible to bring bicycles in by air.

By far the best way to get around Vietnam's towns and cities is to do as the locals do: ride a bicycle. In a few places it is possible to rent bicycles from US$0.50 to US$1 per day. Some travellers buy a cheap bicycle, use it during their visit, and at the end either sell it or give it to a Vietnamese friend. Locally produced bicycles are available from about US$25, but they are of truly inferior quality. Basic cycling safety equipment isn't often available in Vietnam.

The major cities have bicycle parking lots, usually just a roped-off section of sidewalk, which charge a few hundred dong to guard your bike (bicycle theft is a major problem).

HITCHING

Westerners have reported great success at hitching. In fact, the whole system of passenger transport in Vietnam is premised on people standing along the highways and flagging down buses or trucks. To get a bus, truck or other vehicle to stop, stretch out your arm and gesture towards the ground with your whole hand. Drivers will expect to be paid for picking you up.

LOCAL TRANSPORT
Cyclo

When travelling by cyclo (pedicab or samlor) agree on a price *before* setting off. In the south, many of the cyclo drivers are former South Vietnamese Army soldiers. The drivers who wait where there are lots of tourists expect to be paid more than the going rate.

Honda Ong

A Honda ong is an ordinary motorbike on which you ride seated behind the driver. To find one, ask the locals if they know someone with a motorbike who'd like to make a bit of money – or try flagging down a motorbike driven by a young male. For longer distances, the price should be about the same as a cyclo. Agree on the fare before driving off.

Saigon & Cholon

Ho Chi Minh City (population 3.5 million) covers an area of 2056 sq km and stretches from the South China Sea to near the Cambodian border. The downtown section (District 1) is Saigon, a name still used by most people to refer to the whole city. The huge Chinese district (District 5), known for its many Chinese pagodas, is called Cholon.

The huge numbers of people and their obvious industriousness give Saigon, capital of South Vietnam for nearly 20 years from 1956 to 1975, a bustling, dynamic and vital atmosphere. The economic changes sweeping Vietnam – and their social implications – are more evident in Saigon and Cholon than elsewhere in Vietnam.

Orientation
Downtown Saigon is centred around Nguyen Hue and Le Loi Blvds. The Rex Hotel (Ben Thanh Hotel), which is at the intersection of these two streets, is a convenient landmark. Ben Thanh Market fronts a traffic roundabout at the southern end of Le Loi Blvd. Dong Khoi St (known as Tu Do St before 1975 and as Rue Catinat under the French) stretches 1.1 km from the waterfront to Notre Dame Cathedral.

The centre of Cholon, about five km to the west, is around Hung Vuong and Chau Van Liem Blvds.

Information
Tourist Office The main southern office of the state tourism authority, Vietnam Tourism (☎ 92442, 90775), is at 69-71 Nguyen Hue Blvd in downtown Saigon. It is open from 7.30 to 11.30 am and from 1 to 4.30 pm, Monday to Saturday. The staff of Vietnam Tourism are friendly but have only a limited interest in individual travellers. They are a good source of information, however, about visa extensions and their assistance may be crucial in extending your stay.

Saigon Tourist, another government-run travel agency, has its main office (☎ 24987, 98914) at 49 Le Thanh Ton St (corner Dong Khoi St). It is rumoured to be possible for individual foreigners to book tours here.

For internal travel permits, you can try Fimexco Tourist Service, which is above the antique shop at 71C Dong Khoi St.

Immigration Police The Immigration Police office (☎ 99398, 97107) at 161 Nguyen Du St (on the corner of Cach Mang Thang Tam Blvd) is open from 8 to 11 am and from 1 to 4 pm. If you're going from Ho Chi Minh City to Cambodia, and then returning to Vietnam, a re-entry visa costs US$10.

Money At Tan Son Nhut Airport, US$ can be changed at the bank rate (the highest legal rate) at the exchange window to the right as you exit the customs hall.

At 29 Ben Chuong Duong St (on the corner of Nguyen Thi Minh Khoi St), two blocks south of Ham Nghi Blvd, is the Bank for Foreign Trade of Vietnam (Ngan Hang Ngoai Thuong Viet Nam; ☎ 94223). It is open from 7 to 11.30 am and from 1.30 to 3.30 pm daily (except Saturday afternoons and the last day of the month). The foreign exchange section is upstairs. This is one of the few places where currencies other than the US$ can be exchanged.

There are a number of Vietcombank exchange offices around. Other places that change money include the jewellery shops at 71C Dong Khoi St (☎ 91522) and 112 Nguyen Hue Blvd (☎ 25693), where there are legal exchange windows.

Also try the Cosevina offices (☎ 92391) at 102 Nguyen Hue Blvd and on the 2nd floor of the Saigon Intershop, which is at 101 Nam Ky Khoi Nghia St (just off Le Loi Blvd). All the major tourist hotels change money. The Continental Hotel's exchange counter gives the bank rate and only takes 1% commission.

To find a shopkeeper willing to trade dong for US$ on the black market, ask around discreetly. The men who come up to you on the street offering great rates are con artists.

Post & Telecommunications Saigon's French-style General Post Office (Buu Dien

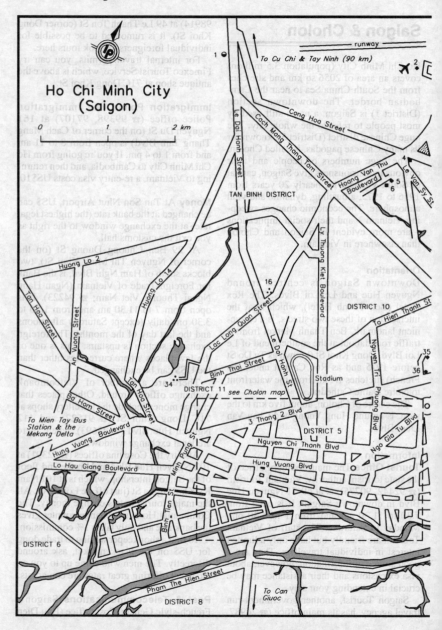

Ho Chi Minh City
(Saigon)

0   1   2 km

To Cu Chi & Tay Ninh (90 km)

Cong Hoa Street

Le Dai Hanh Street

Cach Mang Thang Tam Street

Hoang Van Thu Boulevard

Le Van Sy St

TAN BINH DISTRICT

Huong Lo 2

Huong Lo 14

Ly Thuong Kiet Boulevard

DISTRICT 10

To Hien Thanh St

Tan Hoa Street

An Vuong Street

Lac Long Quan Street

Le Dai Hanh St

Nguyen Tri Phuong Blvd

Ba Hom Street

Binh Thai Street

Stadium

34

DISTRICT 11   see Cholon map

To Mien Tay Bus
Station & the
Mekong Delta

Hung Vuong Boulevard

Lo Hau Giang Boulevard

3 Thang 2 Blvd

DISTRICT 5

Nguyen Chi Thanh Blvd

Ngo Gia Tu Blvd

Minh Phung St

Hung Vuong Blvd

Binh Tien St

DISTRICT 6

Pham The Hien Street

To Can
Giuoc

DISTRICT 8

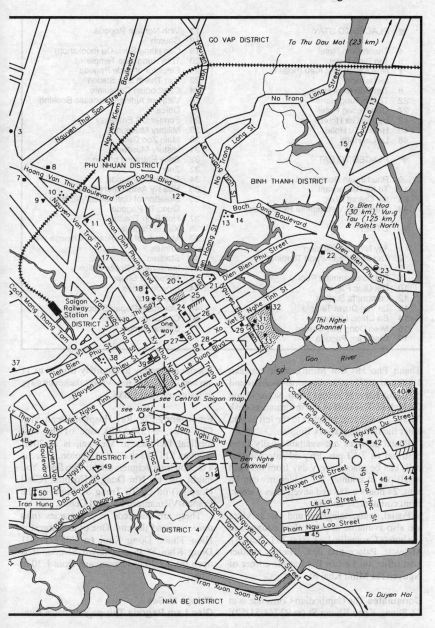

■ **PLACES TO STAY**	17 Vinh Nghiem Pagoda
	18 Church
4 Thanh Binh Hotel	19 Cua Hang Sach Cu (bookshop)
6 Tan Binh Hotel	20 Tran Hung Dao Temple
7 Nha Khach Viet Kieu (hotel &	21 Emperor of Jade Pagoda
restaurant)	23 Van Thanh Bus Station
8 Tan Son Nhat Hotel	24 Cambodian Consulate
22 Thanh Tung Hotel	26 Vietnam Airlines Domestic Booking
27 Que Huong Hotel	Office
42 Hoang Gia Hotel	28 Former US Embassy
45 Hoang Tu Hotel	29 Military Museum
46 Le Lai Hotel	30 Main Zoo Gate
	31 History Museum
▼ **PLACES TO EAT**	32 Back Entrance of Zoo
	33 Zoo
9 Phu Nhuan Restaurant	34 Giac Vien Pagoda
11 Tri Ky Restaurant	35 Hoa Ky Amusement Park
25 Ice Cream Shop	36 Skeleton of Unfinished Viet Nam
49 Traditional Vietnamese Restaurants	Quoc Tu Pagoda
	37 Hoa Binh Theatre
OTHER	38 Xa Loi Pagoda
	39 Museum of American & Chinese War
1 Tay Ninh Bus Station	Crimes
2 Tan Son Nhut Airport Terminal	40 Stadium
3 Airport Gate	41 Immigration Police Office
5 Public Swimming Pool	43 Motorbike Shops
10 Dai Giac Pagoda	44 Bicycle Shops
12 Lambretta Station	47 Bus Depot
13 Le Van Duyet Temple	48 Motorbike Repair Shops
14 Ba Chieu Market	50 Cho Quan Church
15 Mien Dong Bus Station	51 Bicycle Shops
16 Giac Lam Pagoda	

Thanh Pho Ho Chi Minh), built between 1886 and 1891, is at the north-western end of Dong Khoi St across from Notre Dame Cathedral. The staff at the information desk (☎ 96555, 99615), which is to the left as you enter the building, speak English.

Postal services are available daily from 6.30 am to 7.30 pm. Prepaid international calls can be placed every day from 6.30 am to 10 pm at counter 27. Telegrams can be sent, 24 hours a day and seven days a week, from counters 31 and 32.

Postal, telex, telegraph and fax services are also available at post office counters in the hotels Caravelle, Le Lai (at 76 Le Lai St), Majestic, Palace and Rex. There's another post office on Le Loi Blvd at the corner of NguyenThi Minh Khai St.

Consulates The Cambodian Consulate is at 41 Phung Khac Khoan St (☎ 92744/51/52).

It's open Monday to Saturday from 8 to 11 am and from 2 to 5 pm. Visas take seven days to issue and cost US$8.

Emergency Cho Ray Hospital (Benh Vien Cho Ray; ☎ 55137/8), one of the best medical facilities in Vietnam, is at 201B Nguyen Chi Thanh Blvd in Cholon. There is a section for foreigners on the 10th floor. You might also try Nhi Dong 2 Hospital (Grall Hospital) on Ly Tu Trong St, opposite the Franco-Vietnamese Cultural Centre.

There are hundreds of pharmacies (*nha thuoc*) around the city. One of the largest is Hieu Thuoc Dong Khoi (☎ 90577), 201 Dong Khoi St in downtown Saigon. It is open from 7.30 to 12 noon and from 1.30 to 5 pm.

Things to See
Giac Lam Pagoda This pagoda dates from

1744 and is believed to be the oldest in the city. The architecture and style of ornamentation have not changed since the 19th century. It is well worth the trip from central Saigon.

The best way to get there is to take Nguyen Chi Thanh Blvd or 3 Thang 2 Blvd to Le Dai Hanh St. Go north-west on Le Dai Hanh St and turn right onto Lac Long Quan St. Walk 100 metres and the pagoda gate will be on your left. It is open to visitors from 6 am to 9 pm.

Giac Vien Pagoda Giac Vien Pagoda is similar architecturally to Giac Lam. Both pagodas share a similar atmosphere of scholarly serenity, though Giac Vien, which is right next to Dam Sen Lake in District 11, is in a more rural setting. Giac Vien was founded by Hai Tinh Giac Vien about 200 years ago. It is said that the Emporer Gia Long, who died in 1819, used to worship at Giac Vien. Today, 10 monks live here.

Because of the impossibly confusing numbering on Lac Long Quan St, the best way to get to Giac Vien Pagoda is to take Nguyen Chi Thanh Blvd or 3 Thang 2 Blvd to Le Dai Han St. Turn left (south-west) off Le Dai Han St on to Binh Thoi St and turn right (north) at Lac Long Quan St. The gate leading to the pagoda is at 247 Lac Long Quan St (but if you are asking for directions show someone the following cryptic address: 161/35/20 Lac Long Quan St).

Pass through the gate and go several hundred metres down a dirt road, turning left at the 'tee' and right at the fork. The pagoda is open from 7 am to 7 pm but come before dark as the electricity is often out.

Emperor of Jade Pagoda This pagoda, known in Vietnamese as Phuoc Hai Tu and Chua Ngoc Hoang, was built in 1909 by the Canton congregation, and is a gem of a Chinese temple. Filled with colourful statues of phantasmal divinities and grotesque heroes, it is one of the most spectacular pagodas in the city.

The statues, which represent characters from both the Buddhist and Taoist traditions, are made of reinforced papier mâché. It is at 73 Mai Thi Luu St in a part of Saigon known as Da Kao (or Da Cao). To get there, go to 20 Dien Bien Phu St and walk half a block north-westward (to the left as you head out of Saigon towards Thi Nghe Channel).

Notre Dame Cathedral The Notre Dame Cathedral, built between 1877 and 1883, is in the heart of Saigon's government quarter. Its neo-Romanesque form and two 40-metre-high square towers, tipped with iron spires, dominate the skyline. If the front gates (at the north-western terminus of Dong Khoi St) are locked, try at the door on the side of the building that faces Reunification Hall.

Mariamman Hindu Temple Mariamman Hindu Temple, the only Hindu temple still in use in the city, is a little piece of southern India in central Saigon. There are only 50 to 60 Hindus here, all Tamils, but the temple (referred to in Vietnamese as Chua Ba Mariamman), is also considered sacred by many ethnic Vietnamese and Chinese. The temple, which is only three blocks from Ben Thanh Market at 45 Truong Dinh St, was built at the end of the 19th century and dedicated to the Hindu goddess Mariamman. It is open daily from 7 am to 7 pm.

Saigon Central Mosque Built by south Indian Muslims in 1935 on the site of an earlier mosque, the Saigon Central Mosque is an immaculately clean and well-kept island of calm in the middle of bustling central Saigon. In front of the sparkling white and blue structure at 66 Dong Du St, with its four nonfunctional minarets, is a pool for ritual ablutions before prayers. As with any mosque, take off your shoes before entering the sanctuary.

Tam Son Hoi Quan Pagoda This pagoda, known to the Vietnamese as Chua Ba Chua, was built by the Fukien Chinese congregation in the 19th century; it retains in unmodified form much of its original rich ornamentation. The pagoda is dedicated to

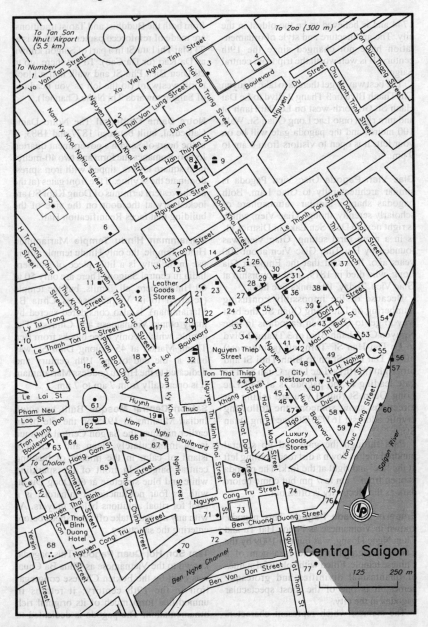

To Tan Son
Nhut Airport
(5.5 km)

To Number

To Zoo (300 m)

Central Saigon

0   125   250 m

■ PLACES TO STAY

11 Ben Nghe Hotel
19 Hai Van Hotel
21 Huong Duong Hotel
24 Rex Hotel (Ben Thanh Hotel)
30 Continental Hotel
34 Kim Do Hotel
36 Caravelle Hotel (Doc Lap Hotel) & Air
   France Reservations Office
38 Khach San 69 Hai Ba Trung (hotel)
41 Palace Hotel (Huu Nghi Hotel)
43 Saigon Hotel
48 Bong Sen Hotel
49 Huong Sen Hotel
52 Dong Khoi Hotel
56 Saigon Floating Hotel
59 Majestic Hotel (Cuu Long Hotel)
64 Van Canh Hotel
66 Vinh Loi Hotel

▼ PLACES TO EAT

7 Madame Dai's Restaurant
15 Food Stalls/Fruit & Vegetable Market
18 Kim Son Restaurant
20 Kem Bach Dang (ice cream parlour)
22 Kem Bach Dang (ice cream parlour)
29 Givral Pâtisserie & Café
37 Ham-bu-go Ca-li-pho-nia
40 Brodard Café
42 Nha Hang 95 Dong Khoi (cafe)
44 My Canh 2 Restaurant
46 Nha Hang 51 Nguyen Hue
   (restaurant)
50 Nha Hang 32 Ngo Duc Ke (restaurant)
51 Pho Hien Hanoi (soup shop)
53 Nha Hang 5 Me Linh (restaurant)
58 Maxim's Restaurant
63 Tin Nghia Vegetarian Restaurant
67 Thang Loi Restaurant

OTHER

1 Museum of American & Chinese War
  Crimes
2 Orderly Departure Program (ODP)
  Office

3 French Consulate Compound
4 Former United States Embassy
5 Reunification Hall
6 Visitors' Entrance to Reunification
  Hall
8 Notre Dame Cathedral
9 GPO
10 Mariamman Hindu Temple
12 Municipal Library
13 Museum of the Revolution
14 Hotel de Ville (Town Hall)
16 Ben Thanh Market
17 Saigon Intershop & Minimart
23 Phnom Penh Bus Garage
25 Vietnam Airlines International
   Booking Office
26 Saigon Tourist 'Tourist Guide Office'
27 Aeroflot Reservations Office
28 Philippine Airlines Reservations
   Office
31 Municipal Theatre
32 District 1 Post Office
33 Cua Hang Bach Hoa (department
   store)
35 Cosevina
39 Central Saigon Mosque
45 Vietnam Tourism
47 Microbus Office (Cong Ty Dich Vu Du
   Lich Quan 1)
54 Ton Duc Thang Museum
55 Me Linh Square & Tran Hung Dao
   Statue
57 Small Motorised Boats for Rent
60 Dining Cruise
61 Tran Nguyen Hai Statue
62 Ben Thanh Bus Station
65 Art Museum
68 Phung Son Tu Pagoda
69 Vietnam Bank
70 An Duong Vuong Statue
71 Foreign Exchange Bank
72 Marriage Taxis
73 National Bank Building
74 Pre-1967 US Embassy
75 Terminal for Ferries to the Mekong
   Delta
76 Boats across the Saigon River
77 Ho Chi Minh Museum

Me Sanh, the Goddess of Fertility. Both men and women – but more of the latter – come here to pray for children. The pagoda is at 118 Trieu Quang Phuc St, Cholon, very near 370 Tran Hung Dao B Blvd.

Nghia An Hoi Quan Pagoda This pagoda, built by the Trieu Chau Chinese congregation, is noteworthy for its gilded woodwork. It is at 678 Nguyen Trai St, Cholon, and is open from 4 am to 6 pm.

Quan Am Pagoda At 12 Lao Tu St, Cholon, one block off Chau Van Liem Blvd, this pagoda was founded in 1816 by the Fukien Chinese congregation. The roof is decorated with fantastic scenes, rendered in ceramic, from traditional Chinese plays and stories. The tableaus include ships, houses, people and several ferocious dragons. The front doors are decorated with very old gold and lacquer panels.

Phuoc An Hoi Quan Pagoda Built in 1902 by the Fukien Chinese congregation, this pagoda is one of the most beautifully ornamented in the city. Of special interest are the many small porcelain figures, the elaborate brass ritual objects, and the fine wood carvings on the altars, walls, columns and hanging lanterns.

From outside the building, you can see the ceramic scenes, each made up of innumerable small figurines, which decorate the roof. It is at 184 Hung Vuong Blvd, Cholon (near the intersection of Chau Van Liem St).

Cha Tam Church This church, built around the turn of the century, is an attractive white and pastel-yellow structure at the south-western terminus of Tran Hung Dao B Blvd at 25 Hoc Lac St, Cholon.

Phung Son Pagoda This is a Vietnamese Buddhist pagoda (also known as Phung Son Tu and Chua Go) which is extremely rich in statuary made of hammered copper, bronze, wood and ceramic. It is in District 11 at 1408 3 Thang 2 Blvd, Cholon, which is a block from Hung Vuong Blvd. The side entrance (to the left as you approach the building) is open from 5 am to 7 pm.

History Museum The History Museum, built in 1929 by the Société des Études Indochinoises and once the National Museum of the Republic of Vietnam, displays artefacts from 3300 years of human activity in what is now Vietnam. Just inside the main entrance to the Zoo (on Nguyen Binh Khiem St at Le Duan Blvd), it is open

from 8 to 11.30 am and from 1 to 4 pm daily except Monday.

Museum of American & Chinese War Crimes This museum, housed in the former US Information Service building, is on the corner of Le Qui Don and Vo Van Tan Sts near central Saigon.

Museum of the Revolution Housed in a white neoclassical structure built in 1886 and once known as Gia Long Palace, the Museum of the Revolution (☎ 99741) is at 27 Ly Tu Trong St. Deep underneath the building is a network of reinforced concrete bunkers used in the '50s and early '60s by South Vietnamese President Diem. The museum is open from 8 to 11.30 am and from 2 to 4.30 pm, Tuesday to Sunday.

Reunification Hall The Reunification Hall (☎ 90629), built in 1966 to serve as South Vietnam's Presidential Palace, has been left just as it looked when Saigon surrendered to North Vietnamese forces in 1975. The striking architecture alone makes a visit well worth the effort. The visitors' entrance is at 106 Nguyen Du St. The entrance fee is US$0.50 per person (minimum five people).

Former US Embassy The fortified former US Embassy building, completed in 1968, is on the corner of Le Duan Blvd and Mac Dinh Chi St. The compound, which may be closed to the public, is now used by the government-owned Oil Exploration Corporation.

Zoo & Botanical Garden The Zoo and its surrounding gardens, founded by the French in 1864, are a delightful place for a relaxing stroll under giant tropical trees, which thrive amidst lakes, lawns and carefully tended flower beds. There are sometimes water puppet shows here. The History Museum is just inside the main gate, which is on Nguyen Binh Khiem St at the intersection of Le Duan Blvd.

Markets The **Ben Thanh Market**, the city's largest, is 700 metres south-west of the Rex

Hotel at the intersection of Le Loi, Ham Nghi and Tran Hung Dao Blvds and Le Lai St. It was built in 1914, and the main entrance, with its belfry and clock, has become a symbol of Saigon. Cholon's main marketplace, **Binh Tay Market**, is on Hau Giang Blvd, about one km south-west of Chau Van Liem Blvd.

Places to Stay

Most visitors prefer to stay in central Saigon or a few minutes walk from the centre around the market area where the city's currently most popular budget hotel is located.

Alternatively, there are places around the bus and train stations, near the airport and in the Chinatown area of Cholon. The more expensive hotels are in central Saigon.

Central Saigon – bottom end The *Kim Do Hotel* (☎ 93811) at 133 Nguyen Hue Blvd affords all of the advantages of the Rex Hotel (a mere 100 metres away) at a fraction of the cost. There are huge rooms (overlooking Nguyen Hue Blvd) with bath and ceiling fan (and perhaps a few bats) at US$7/10 for singles/doubles. An air-con room in the newer section at the back costs US$17/20.

The *69 Hai Ba Trung Hotel* (☎ 91513) is, as its name suggests, at 69 Hai Ba Trung St. Singles or doubles with ceiling fans cost US$7 for foreigners. The *Palace*, or Dong Khoi Hotel (☎ 92178), is a grand old French-era building at 8 Dong Khoi St (on the corner of Ngo Duc Ke St). For foreigners and overseas Vietnamese, spacious air-con rooms cost around US$15.

The seedy *Saigon Hotel* (☎ 99734) is at 47 Dong Du St, across from the Saigon Central Mosque. Doubles with ceiling fan, in this sleazy but conveniently located dive, range from US$10 to US$22.

Central Saigon – middle & top end The classiest hotel in Saigon is the venerable *Hotel Continental* (☎ 94456) at 132-134 Dong Khoi St – rooms range from US$50 to US$100 plus. Another preferred hotel is the similarly priced *Rex Hotel* (☎ 92185/6), also known as the Ben Thanh Hotel, at 141

Nguyen Hue Blvd. This place once served as a billet for US military officers. The pricier five-star *Saigon Floating Hotel* (☎ 90783) was towed to its mooring at Me Linh Square from Australia's Great Barrier Reef in 1989, where it had gone spectacularly bankrupt.

Another old favourite is the *Doc Lap Hotel* (☎ 93704), still called the *Caravelle*, at 19-23 Lam Son Square (opposite the Hotel Continental). The *Majestic* (☎ 95515, 91375), also known as the Cuu Long Hotel, was once the city's most elegant hotel. It overlooks the Saigon River at 1 Dong Khoi St. The *Palace*, or Huu Nghi Hotel (☎ 97284, 92860), is at 56-64 Nguyen Hue Blvd. It occupies the second tallest building in the city.

Market Area The *Hoang Tu Hotel* (☎ 22657) at 187 Phan Ngu Lao St is the backpackers' centre in Saigon. It's near the big Le Lai Hotel, just beyond Ben Thanh Market. Rooms range from around US$3.50 to US$5, getting progressively cheaper as you have to climb more steps from the street! It's clean, well-kept and the rooms have bathrooms. Downstairs, there's a good restaurant, and rental bicycles are available. At present, foreigners can pay the dong price here; if a more expensive US$ tariff is introduced for foreigners, its popularity may decline.

The *Van Canh Hotel* (☎ 94963) at 184 Calmette St (corner Tran Hung Dao Blvd) has rooms with bath for foreigners from US$10 to US$12. The *Thai Binh Duong Hotel* (☎ 22674) at 92 and 107 Ky Can St is a good middle-priced place with air-con rooms from US$15 to US$20.

Rooms in the *Ben Nghe Hotel* (☎ 91430, 95019) at 35 Nguyen Trung Truc St, not far from Reunification Hall, begin at US$15. The refurbished *Vinh Loi Hotel* (☎ 92672; 30 rooms) occupies the upper floors of a 10-storey building at 129-133 Ham Nghi Blvd; it's in a neighbourhood with a reputation for pickpockets and thieves. For foreigners, single/double rooms cost US$20/28.

Cholon There are plenty of hotels in Cholon but once you have seen the pagodas there's

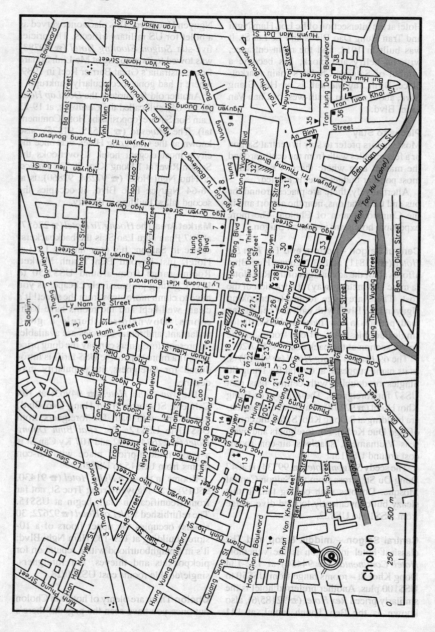

PLACES TO STAY	
3	Phu Tho Hotel & Restaurant
9	Quoc Thai Hotel
10	Dong Khanh 5 Hotel
14	A Chau Hotel
15	Quoc Dan Hotel
16	Thu Do Hotel
17	Truong Thanh Hotel
21	Phenix Hotel (Phuong Huong Hotel)
22	Song Kim Hotel
23	Truong Mai Hotel
29	Arc En Ciel Hotel
30	Bat Dat Hotel
33	Phu Do 1 Hotel
34	Dong Khanh Hotel
36	Hoa Binh Hotel
37	Dong Kinh Hotel
38	Hanh Long Hotel

PLACES TO EAT	
31	Tiem Com Chay Thien Phat Duyen (vegetarian restaurant)

35	Tiem Com Chay Phat Huu Duyen (vegetarian restaurant)

OTHER	
1	Phung Son Pagoda
2	Khanh Van Nam Vien Pagoda
4	An Quang Pagoda
5	Cho Ray Hospital
6	Phuoc An Hoi Quan Pagoda
7	Taxi Stand at Pham Ngoc Thach
8	Nha Sau Church
11	Binh Tay Market
12	Cholon Bus Station
13	Cha Tam Church
18	Quan Am Pagoda
19	Electronics Market
20	Ong Bon Pagoda
24	Thien Hau Pagoda
25	GPO
26	Tam Son Hoi Quan Pagoda
27	Nghia An Hoi Quan Pagoda
28	Cholon Mosque
32	Luxury Goods Market

no real reason for staying here . The *Phenix*, also known as the Phuong Huong Hotel (☎ 51888), is in the centre of Cholon at 411 Tran Hung Dao B Blvd. Foreigners are charged from US$10 to US$15 for rooms with fan or air-con. Just up the street is the *Truong Thanh Hotel* (☎ 56044) at 111-117 Chau Van Liem Blvd, where you may be able to get a room from US$3 if you can pay the dong price.

Half a block away at 125 Chau Van Liem Blvd is the *Thu Do Hotel* (☎ 59102) which is also cheap if you can pay in dong. The *Truong Mai Hotel* (☎ 52101) is at 785 Nguyen Trai St, just off Chau Van Liem Blvd, and has rooms from US$6 to US$8.

The *Bat Dat Hotel* (☎ 51662), 238-244 Tran Hung Dao B Blvd, is near the pricier Arc En Ciel Hotel. For foreigners, doubles with fan are around US$8, and from US$10 to US$20 with air-con. The *Phu Do 1 Hotel* (☎ 56821) is two blocks from Tran Hung Dao B Blvd on Ngo Quyen St. The official street address is 634-640 Ben Ham Tu St. Doubles here cost from US$3 to US$5. Further east is the slightly more expensive

Dong Khanh Hotel (☎ 50678) at 2 Tran Hung Dao B Blvd.

The *Hoa Binh Hotel* (☎ 55133), 1115 Tran Hung Dao Blvd, has rooms from US$3 to US$6. The *Dong Kinh Hotel* (☎ 52505) is two blocks off Tran Hung Dao Blvd at 106-108 Tran Tuan Khai St. Foreigners are charged US$10 to US$20 for air-con doubles. The *Hanh Long Hotel* (☎ 50251) is at 1025-1029 Tran Hung Dao Blvd.

Elsewhere Near the airport, the *Tan Binh Hotel* (☎ 41175/ 67/99) at 201/3 Hoang Viet St has rooms with fans in a building across the street from the main part of the hotel from US$10 to US$20. To get there, turn off Hoang Van Thu Blvd opposite No 312 and go south for one block.

The *Thanh Tung Hotel* (☎ 91817) at 310 Xo Viet Nghe Tinh St (on the corner of Dien Bien Phu St) is only about two km from Mien Dong bus station and a km or so from Van Thanh bus station. Rooms with a fan cost US$2 if you can pay the dong price. The *Mien Tay Bus Station* (☎ 55955) in An Lac has a few rooms for overnight stays behind the ticket counters in the building to the left of the station gate as you enter. The cost is less than US$1 per night. At the *Saigon Railroad Station*, there is dormitory accommodation *(nha tro)* across the parking lot from the station building.

Places to Eat

Food Stalls The cheapest food in Saigon is sold on the streets. In the mornings, pho, a tasty soup made of noodles, bean sprouts, shallots and pork, chicken or beef is on sale at tiny sidewalk stands that disappear by 11 am. A serving costs less than US$0.25. Late at night, food stands appear on the sidewalk of Nguyen Hue Blvd between the Kim Do and the Rex hotels and at other central Saigon locations.

Pho can be found at *Pho Hien Hanoi*, a soup shop in the heart of Saigon at 50 Dong Khoi St. A large bowl of delicious beef pho costs about US$0.50. There is another pho shop at 99 Nguyen Hue Blvd.

Sandwiches with a French look and a very Vietnamese taste are sold by street vendors. Fresh French *petits pains* (rolls) are stuffed with something resembling luncheon meat (don't ask) and cucumbers, and seasoned with soy sauce. A sandwich costs about US$0.15 to US$0.40, depending on what's in it and whether you get overcharged. Sandwiches filled with soft cheese, which is imported, cost a bit more.

Just west of the Central Market, there is a cluster of food stalls. Mobile food stands often set up in the vicinity of Nos 178 and 264 Dien Bien Phu St.

Vietnamese *Nha Hang 51 Nguyen Hue*, 51 Nguyen Hue Blvd, serves superior Vietnamese food at very reasonable prices (about US$1 per person for a meal). It is open from 10.30 am to 2 pm and from 4 to 7 pm. *Nha Hang 32 Ngo Duc Ke*, just off Nguyen Hue Blvd at 32 Ngo Duc Ke St, is almost as good and they have (inferior) beer on tap. It is open from 10.15 am to 2 pm and from 4.15 to 8 pm.

The restaurant on the ground floor of the *Kim Do Hotel* at 133 Nguyen Hue Blvd is

slightly better than Nha Hang 51 Nguyen Hue. This place, which stays open until 10 pm, offers solid, preprepared dishes for reasonable prices (about US$1.50 per person for a meal). The stuffed crab is excellent.

Near the Ben Thanh Market is *Nha Hang Thang Loi* (☎ 98474), also known as Victory Restaurant, at 55 Ham Nghi Blvd (on the corner of Nam Ky Khoi Nghia St). The fare includes European and Vietnamese dishes.

There are a number of restaurants whose specialty is traditional (as opposed to everyday) Vietnamese cuisine along Nguyen Cu Trinh St, which is about 1½ km from Ben Thanh Market towards Cholon. They're an easy walk from the popular Hoang Tu Hotel and can be found at Nos 85, 113, 125 and 131. Chinese-style steamboat (where you cook the food at the table) is popular here and a meal costs about US$1.50.

Restaurants specialising in more exotic fare (such as cobra, python, bat, turtle, pangolin and wild pig) include *Nha Hang 5 Me Linh* (☎ 22623), across Me Linh Square from the Saigon Floating Hotel; *My Canh 2 Restaurant*, just off Nguyen Hue Blvd at 125 Ho Tung Mau St (corner Ton That Thiep St), which is open from 10.30 am to 10 pm; and *Tri Ky Restaurant* (☎ 40968), which is about four km from central Saigon at 82 Tran Huy Lieu St (around the corner from the mosque at 5 Nguyen Van Troi St).

Cafes For light Western-style meals or something to drink, there are a number of cafes in central Saigon. *Nha Hang 95 Dong Khoi* is on the corner of Mac Thi Buoi St at 95 Dong Khoi St; it is open from 5.30 am to 9.30 pm. The *Hotel Continental* has a coffee shop whose large picture windows overlook Lam Son Square.

The government-owned *Givral Pâtisserie & Café* at 169 Dong Khoi St (across the street from the Hotel Continental) has the best selection of cakes and pastries in the city. It is open from 7 am to 11 pm. The house specialty is ice cream served in a baby coconut (kem trai dua). Check your bill here carefully!

Another good source of cakes and the like,

including elephant ears and banana cake, is *Cua Hang Ban Banh & Kem* (☎ 24673) at 11 Nguyen Thiep St (between Nguyen Hue Blvd and Dong Khoi St). It is open from 7 am to 9 pm.

For the best ice cream (kem) in town, try *Kem Bach Dang* and *Kem Bach Dang 2*, which are on Le Loi Blvd on either side of Nguyen Thi Minh Khoi St. Behind the Municipal Theatre, on Hai Ba Trung St, fast food has arrived in Vietnam at *Ham-bu-go Ca-li-pho-nia* for less than US$1 per burger.

Restaurants Without a doubt, the best of the restaurants in Saigon (and probably all of Indochina) is *Maxim's* (☎ 96676, 25554) at 13-17 Dong Khoi St (next to the Majestic Hotel). It is open from 4 to 9.30 pm. The menu of French and Chinese dishes is truly voluminous. There is a live show from 7 pm which may feature anything from Western classical music to rock & roll and a stunning hula hoop artiste!

Numerous enthralled backpackers have reported that this place is absolutely not to be missed. Reservations are necessary for dinners on Saturday and Sunday – count on about US$15 for a very complete meal for two.

The restaurants of the hotels *Rex* (5th floor), *Caravelle* (9th floor) and *Palace* (15th floor) are especially good and reasonable in price. There is also a decent restaurant in the *Majestic Hotel*. Near Maxim's, at 63 Dong Khoi St, is the very trendy and pricey *City Restaurant*.

La Bibliothèque de Madame Dai (Madame Dai's), run by Madame Nguyen Phuoc Dai, a lawyer and former vice-chairperson of the South Vietnamese National Assembly, is an intimate little restaurant consisting of half a dozen small tables set in her old law library. It is in an unmarked building at 84A Nguyen Du St, not far from Notre Dame Cathedral. Reservations should be made at least one day in advance; a complete meal is about US$25 for two.

Vegetarian The ethnic-Vietnamese owners of *Tin Nghia Vegetarian Restaurant* are strict Buddhists. This tiny establishment, which is open daily from 7 am to 8 pm, is about 200 metres from Ben Thanh Market at 9 Tran Hung Dao Blvd. The prices are incredibly cheap.

In Cholon, *Tiem Com Chay Thien Phat Duyen* is a small Chinese vegetarian restaurant at 509 Nguyen Trai St, about one km east of Chau Van Liem Blvd. *Tiem Com Chay Phat Huu Duyen*, also Chinese, is at 952 Tran Hung Dao Blvd (on the corner of An Binh St, where Tran Hung Dao B Blvd begins) – it is open from 7 am to 10 pm. Across An Binh St, at 3 Tran Hung Dao B Blvd, is another Chinese place, *Tiem Com Chay Van Phat Duyen*, which is open from 7 am to 9 pm.

Self-Catering Fruit, vegetables and other basics are sold in the city's marketplaces. The *Dalat Fruit Kiosk* (kiosk no 13), which is outside the Kim Do Hotel on Nguyen Hue Blvd, has a good selection of seasonal fruits, but make sure you do not get short-weighed or overcharged. The best bakery in town is, according to many Saigonese, *Nhu Lan Bakery* at 66 Ham Nghi Blvd. Western products are sold in the *Minimart* (☎ 98189, extension 44) on the 2nd floor of the Saigon Intershop, which is at 101 Nam Ky Khoi Nghia St. It is open from 9 am to 6 pm daily.

Entertainment

Downtown Saigon is *the* place to be on Sunday and holiday nights. The streets are jam-packed with young Saigonese, in couples and groups, cruising the town on bicycles and motorbikes, out to see and be seen. Later, couples retire to parks around the city for more intimate activities!

The *Municipal Theatre* (☎ 91249, 91584) is on Dong Khoi St between the Caravelle and Continental hotels. It was built in 1899 for use as a theatre but later served as the heavily fortified home of the South Vietnamese National Assembly. Each week, the theatre has a different evening programme.

There is disco dancing on most nights at the *Rex, Caravelle, Majestic* and *Saigon Floating* hotels and at other spots around town. Good places for an evening beer include the open-air cafe beside the Municipal Theatre or the rooftop bar of the Rex Hotel. An imported can of San Miguel, Tiger or Heineken costs about US$1 but weak local beers are a bit cheaper. The Rex is a bit more expensive.

Things to Buy

Souvenirs and crafts are both more readily available and of generally higher quality in Saigon than in Hanoi. Typical souvenir handicrafts are sold at innumerable shops in central Saigon, especially along Dong Khoi St. Many of these places also offer overpriced antiques. Lac Long's, a shop at 143 Le Thanh Ton St (two blocks from the Hotel de Ville), sells fine exotic leathers and much more.

Kerbside stalls along Le Loi Blvd, between Dong Khoi St and Nguyen Hue Blvd, and on Nguyen Hue Blvd, between Le Loi Blvd and the Palace Hotel, offer the best selection of maps available in Vietnam. Overall, the most accurate and up-to-date map of Saigon is printed on cheap paper in pastel colours and is dated 9.1988 in the lower right-hand corner.

For real and fake US, Chinese and Russian military surplus, the place to go is Dan Sinh Market at 104 Nguyen Cong Tu St (next to Phung Son Tu Pagoda).

For film and other photographic needs, there are a number of stores along Nguyen Hue Blvd. There is a large photo shop at 118-120 Dong Khoi St (☎ 96614). The latest Japanese-made one-hour colour developing equipment has been installed in stores at 66A Nguyen Hue Blvd, 110-112 Dong Khoi St (☎ 22035) and in the Eden Colour Photo Centre at 4 Le Loi Blvd. If you need passport photos for visa applications, go to 30 Le Loi Blvd.

Getting There & Away

Air The domestic booking office of Vietnam Airlines (☎ 99910/80) is at 27B Nguyen Dinh Chieu St, about two km from the centre of Saigon. It is open from 7 to 10.45 am and from 1 to 3.45 pm daily (except Sunday).

The Vietnam Airlines international booking office (☎ 92118), downtown at 116 Nguyen Hue Blvd, is open Monday to Saturday from 7.30 to 11 am and from 1 to 4 pm. This office acts as the general sales agent for all airlines serving Ho Chi Minh City and is the only place in town where you can purchase international airline tickets.

Flight reservations can be made either here or at Aeroflot (☎ 93489; 4H Le Loi Blvd), Air France (☎ 90981/2; 130 Dong Khoi St) and Philippines Airlines (☎ 25538; 4A Le Loi Blvd). You have to make Thai International reconfirmations at the airport (☎ 46235). Their airport office opens at 9 am from Sunday to Friday.

Bus Buses to points south of Ho Chi Minh City are based at Mien Tay bus station in An Lac. Buses to and from places north of the city use Mien Dong bus station. Tay Ninh bus station serves points north-east of Saigon. Van Thanh bus station serves destinations in Song Be and Dong Nai provinces.

Mien Tay Bus Station Mien Tay bus station (Ben Xe Mien Tay; ☎ 55955) is about 10 km west of Saigon in An Lac, a part of Binh Chanh District (Huyen Binh Chanh) of Greater Ho Chi Minh City.

To get there, take Hau Giang or Hung Vuong Blvds west from Cholon, and then continue past where these thoroughfares merge. As you head out of the city, Mien Tay bus station is on the left, opposite 130 Quoc Lo 4. There are buses from central Saigon to Mien Tay bus station from the Ben Thanh bus station (at the end of Ham Nghi Blvd near Ben Thanh Market).

Express buses depart twice a day at 4.30 am and 3 pm. Express-bus tickets are sold from 3.30 am for the early buses and from 12 noon for the afternoon runs. Express-bus tickets are also on sale at 121 Chau Van Liem Blvd in Cholon; 142 Hung Vuong Blvd west of Cholon; and at 638 Le Hong Phong St in District 10.

Tickets for nonexpress buses are sold from 3.30 am to 4 pm at counters marked according to the province of destination.

Nonexpress buses leave from platforms arranged by province.

To reserve a seat on any bus, ask a Vietnamese-speaker to phone the bus-station office at ☎ 55955.

Mien Dong Bus Station Buses to places north of Ho Chi Minh City depart from the Mien Dong bus station (Ben Xe Mien Dong; ☎ 94056), which is in Binh Thanh District about six km from central Saigon on Quoc Lo 13 (National Highway 13) – Quoc Lo 13 is the continuation of Xo Viet Nghe Tinh St. The station is about two km north of the intersection of Xo Viet Nghe Tinh and Dien Bien Phu Sts.

The station's main gate is opposite 78 Quoc Lo 13 (according to the new numbering) and next to 229 Quoc Lo 13 (according to the old numbering). To get there, you can take a bus from Ben Thanh bus station (at the end of Ham Nghe Blvd near Ben Thanh Market). A cyclo from the city centre should cost about US$1.50.

Almost all the express buses leave daily between 5 and 5.30 am. Express tickets are sold between 4 am and 4 pm in the room marked Quay Ban Ve Xe Toc Hanh (express-bus ticket counter). To make express-bus reservations by telephone, have a Vietnamese-speaker call ☎ 94056.

Many of the nonexpress buses leave around 5.30 am. Tickets for short trips can be bought before departure. For long-distance travel, tickets should be purchased a day in advance. The nonexpress ticket windows are open from 5 am until the last seat on the last bus of the day is sold. Tickets for many buses that leave from the Mien Dong bus station can also be purchased at the Mien Tay bus station in An Lac.

Other Bus Stations To get to Tay Ninh bus station (Ben Xe Tay Ninh), head all the way out west on Cach Mang Thang Tam St. The station is about 1½ km past where Cach Mang Thang Tam and Le Dai Hanh Sts merge.

Van Thanh bus station is in Binh Thanh District at 72 Dien Bien Phu St, about 1½

km east of the intersection of Dien Bien Phu and Xo Viet Nghe Tinh Sts. As you head out of Saigon, go past where the numbers on Dien Bien Phu St surpass the 600s. A cyclo ride from central Saigon should cost less than US$1. The station is open from 6 am to 6 pm.

To Phnom Penh Daily buses to Phnom Penh leave from the garage (☎ 93754) at 155 Nguyen Hue Blvd, across Le Thanh Ton St from the Hotel de Ville (City Hall) and next to the Rex Hotel. A one-way ticket costs about US$3.

Microbuses Cong Ty Dich Vu Du Lich Quan 1 (☎ 90541) at 39 Nguyen Hue Blvd offers the fastest transport in town to Vung Tau, Dalat and Nha Trang. The office is open from 7 am to 7 pm.

Train The Saigon railway station (Ga Sai Gon; ☎ 45585) is in District 3 at 1 Nguyen Thong St. Trains from here serve cities along the coast north of Saigon. The ticket office is open from 7.15 to 11 am and from 1 to 3 pm daily.

Dormitory accommodation is available across the parking lot from the main terminal building. To get to the station, turn off Cach Mang Thang Tam St next to No 132/9. Go down the alley for about 100 metres and then follow the railway tracks to the left.

Car Marriage taxis – huge American cars from the '50s and early '60s – can be hired from Hop Tac Xa Xe Du-Lich (Tourist Car Corporation; ☎ 90600), which is opposite the Foreign Exchange Bank and across the street from 43 Ben Chuong Duong St (corner Nam Ky Khoi Nghia St).

Cars can also be hired from Trung Tam Du Lich Thanh Nien Viet Nam (the Youth Tourism Centre at 44 Ngo Duc Ke St), the microbus company (39 Nguyen Hue Blvd), the Phnom Penh bus garage (155 Nguyen Hue Blvd), Mien Tay bus station and Vietnam Tourism.

Boat Passenger and goods ferries to the

Mekong Delta depart from a dock (☎ 97892) at the river end of Ham Nghi Blvd.

Getting Around

To/From the Airport Ho Chi Minh City's Tan Son Nhut International Airport is seven km from the centre of Saigon. The taxis for hire outside the customs hall will try to grossly overcharge, so bargain hard. A fair price into town is about US$5, and there's an airport taxi desk charging from US$6 to US$10.

Cyclos (pedicabs) can be hailed outside the gate to the airport, which is a few hundred metres from the terminal building. A ride to central Saigon should cost about US$1.50. You can also try to flag down a motorbike (Honda ong) and hitch a ride seated behind the driver – this should be about the same.

Bus There is only limited local public transport. No decent bus map is available and bus stops are mostly unmarked. Ben Thanh bus terminal, which offers transport to other parts of Ho Chi Minh City, is on the other side of the roundabout from Ben Thanh Market.

There is a major depot for local buses on Le Lai St, a few blocks south-west of Nguyen Thai Hoc Blvd. Several bus lines link Saigon and Cholon – the most convenient begins on Nguyen Hue Blvd near the river and ends at Binh Tay Market.

Bicycle The best place in to buy a decent (read 'imported') bicycle is at the shops around 288 Le Thanh Ton St (on the corner of Cach Mang Thang Tam St). For cheap and poorly assembled domestic bicycles and parts, try the ground floor of Cua Hang Bach Hoa, the department store on the corner of Nguyen Hue and Le Loi Blvds. The Viko-trade Company at 35 Le Loi Blvd has locally made components.

For on-the-spot bicycle repairs, look for an upturned army helmet and a hand pump sitting next to the curb. There is a cluster of bicycle repair shops around 23 Phan Dang Luu Blvd.

Rental bicycles are becoming increasingly common in Vietnam. You can hire bicycles from the newsstand opposite the Rex Hotel for around US$1.20 a day or from the Hoang Tu Hotel for about half that much.

Cyclo Cyclos are the best way of getting around town and can be hired by the hour for about US$0.60. Always agree on fares beforehand.

Around Saigon

THE TUNNELS OF CU CHI

The tunnel network of Cu Chi District, now part of Greater Ho Chi Minh City, became legendary during the 1960s for its role in facilitating Viet Cong control of a large rural area only 30 km from Saigon. At its height, the tunnel system stretched from the South Vietnamese capital to the Cambodian border.

In the district of Cu Chi alone, there were over 200 km of tunnels. After ground operations against the tunnels claimed large numbers of casualties and proved ineffective, the Americans turned their artillery and bombers on the area, leaving it defoliated and pockmarked with craters.

Parts of this remarkable tunnel network (enlarged and upgraded versions of the real McCoy) are open to the public at Ben Duoc, about 30 km beyond Cu Chi itself. A short video, followed by a tour of the tunnels, costs US$2 for foreigners. The unadulterated tunnels, though not actually closed to tourists, are hard to get to and are seldom visited.

Getting There & Away

Hiring a taxi, or 'marriage taxi', in Saigon for the trip out to Cu Chi costs about US$15 to US$20 – not all that expensive if the cost is split by a group. If you want to visit the 'real' tunnels rather than those open to the public, make this clear to your driver beforehand.

TAY NINH

Tay Ninh town (population 26,000), capital of Tay Ninh Province, serves as the headquarters of one of Vietnam's most interesting indigenous religions, Caodaism. Built between 1933 and 1955, the **Caodai Great Temple** is a rococo extravaganza combining the architectural idiosyncrasies of a French church, a Chinese pagoda, the Tiger Balm Gardens and Madame Tussaud's Wax Museum.

The Religion of Cao Dai

Caodaism is the product of an attempt to create the ideal religion through the fusion of secular and religious philosophies from both East and West. The result is a colourful and eclectic potpourri that includes bits and pieces of Buddhism, Confucianism, Taoism, Hinduism, native Vietnamese spiritism, Christianity and Islam. Among Westerners that the Caodai especially revere is Victor Hugo (look for his likeness at the Great Temple).

Caodaism was founded in 1926 after messages were communicated to the group's leaders by spirits. By the mid-1950s, one in eight southern Vietnamese was a Caodai. Today, the sect has about two million followers. All Caodai temples observe four daily ceremonies, which are held at 6 am, 12 noon, 6 pm and midnight.

Places to Stay & Eat

In the town of Tay Ninh, there are a couple of hotels a few hundred metres east and then north of the old triple-arch bridge. *Nha Hang So 1* (Restaurant No 1) is on the western side of the river near the triple-arch concrete bridge.

Getting There & Away

Tay Ninh is 96 km north-west from Ho Chi Minh City on National Highway 22 (Quoc Lo 22). The Caodai Holy See complex is four km east of Tay Ninh, in the village of Long Hoa.

Bus Buses from Ho Chi Minh City to Tay Ninh leave from the Tay Ninh bus station (Ben Xe Tay Ninh) in Tan Binh District and the Mien Tay bus station in An Lac.

Taxi The easiest way to get to Tay Ninh is by taxi, or 'marriage taxi' – perhaps on a day trip that includes a stop in Cu Chi. An all-day round trip by marriage taxi should cost about US$40. No special permits are required as long as you return to Saigon to sleep.

VUNG TAU

Vung Tau, formerly Cap Saint Jacques, is a beach resort on the South China Sea, 128 km south-east of Saigon. Vung Tau's beaches are not Vietnam's nicest but are easily reached from Ho Chi Minh City and have thus been a favourite of the Saigonese since French colonists first began coming here around 1890. Seaside areas near Vung Tau are dotted with the villas of the pre-1975 elite, now converted to guest houses and villas for the post-1975 elite.

In addition to sunning on the seashore and sipping sodas in nearby cafes, visitors to this city of 100,000 can cycle around or climb up the Vung Tau Peninsula's two mountains. There are also a number of interesting religious sites around town, including several pagodas and a huge standing figure of Jesus blessing the South China Sea.

Orientation

The triangular Vung Tau Peninsula juts into the South China Sea near the mouth of the Saigon River. The centre of town is on the south-western side of the triangle in a level area. Large Mountain (or Nui Lon), a 520-metre-high hill north of the city with a radar installation on top, is circumnavigated by Tran Phu St. The hill to the south of town, which is circumnavigated by Ha Long St, is called Small Mountain (or Nui Nho). Back Beach (Bai Sau) stretches along the south-eastern side of the triangle; Thuy Van St runs along Back Beach.

Information

Vung Tau Tourism's main office (☎ 2138, 91961) is at 59 Tran Hung Dao Blvd (on the corner of Ly Tu Trong St). Two other organisations may provide tourist services (eg cars, accommodation): OTAS (☎ 2279), a Czech-Vietnamese joint venture company

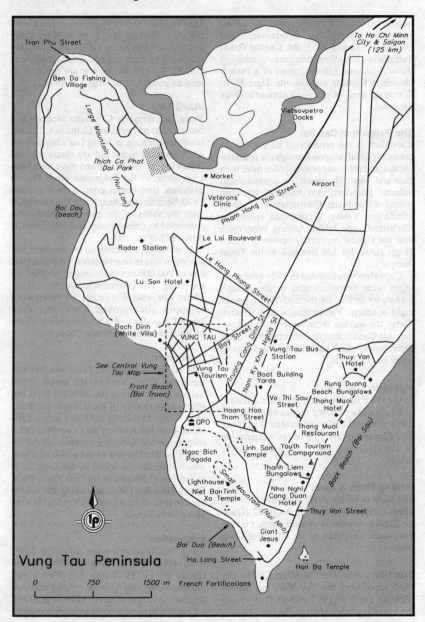

Vung Tau Peninsula

0   750   1500 m

whose offices are in the Pacific Hotel at 4 Le Loi Blvd; and the Oil Service Company (OSC), which is based at 2 Le Loi St.

The GPO (☎ 2377, 2689, 2141) is at 4 Ha Long St, on the southern end of Front Beach. The very active Immigration Police operate out of the police station at 14 Le Loi St

Things to See & Do

Beaches The main bathing area on the peninsula is **Back Beach** (Bai Sau, also known as Thuy Van Beach), an eight km long stretch of sun, sand and Soviets a couple of km west of the town centre. **Front Beach** (Bai Truoc, also called Thuy Duong Beach), which is rather dirty, rocky and eroded, borders the centre of town.

Bai Dau, a quiet coconut palm-lined beach, is probably the most relaxing spot in the Vung Tau area. The beach, which is about three km north of town, stretches around a small bay nestled beneath the verdant western slopes of Large Mountain (Nui Lon). **Bai Dua** (Roches Noires Beach) is a small beach about two km south of the town centre on Ha Long St.

Walks The six km circuit around Small Mountain (Nui Nho), known to the French as *le tour de la Petite Corniche*, begins at the southern end of Front Beach and continues on Ha Long St along the rocky coastline. The 10 km circuit around Large Mountain begins at the northern end of Front Beach.

Other Sights The **Hon Ba Temple** is on a tiny island just south of Back Beach. It can be reached on foot at low tide. **Niet Ban Tinh Xa**, one of the largest Buddhist temples in Vietnam, is on the western side of Small Mountain. Built in 1971, it is famous for its five-tonne bronze bell, a huge reclining Buddha and intricate mosaic work.

An enormous Rio de Janeiro-style figure of **Jesus** (Thanh Gioc) with arms outstretched gazes across the South China Sea from the southern end of Small Mountain. The figure, 30 metres high, was constructed in 1974.

The 360-degree view of the entire penin-sula from the **lighthouse** (*hai dang*; altitude 197 metres), built in 1910, is truly spectacular, especially at sunset. The narrow paved road up Small Mountain to the lighthouse intersects Ha Long St 150 metres south-west of the GPO.

Bach Dinh, the White Villa *(Villa Blanche)*, is a former royal residence set amidst frangipanis and bougainvilleas on a lushly forested hillside overlooking the sea. The main entrance to the park surrounding Bach Dinh is just north of Front Beach at 12 Tran Phu St. It is open from 6 am to 9 pm.

Thich Ca Phat Dai, a must-see site for domestic tourists, is a hillside park of monumental Buddhist statuary built in the early 1960s. Thich Ca Phat Dai, which is open from 6 am to 6 pm, is on the eastern side of Large Mountain at 25 Tran Phu St. To get there from the town centre, take Le Loi Blvd north almost to the end and turn left onto Tran Phu St.

Places to Stay

The *Duyen Hai Hotel* (☎ 2585) is at 23 Tran Hung Dao Blvd. Nearby, at 37 Tran Hung Dao Blvd, is the *Khach San Tran Hung Dao* (☎ 2359). Prices at both these places are very reasonable.

The *Lu Son Hotel* (☎ 2576) is a bit north of town at 27 Le Loi Blvd according to the new numbering system, and at 12 Le Loi Blvd by the old system. The cheaper rooms are popular with domestic tourists but foreigners are charged US$15 for a 1st-class room.

One of the best deals in town is the *International Hotel* (☎ 2571), also known as the Khach San Quoc Te, at 242 Bacu St (on the corner of Le Loi St). For foreigners, singles cost from US$6 to US$18 and doubles are US$8 to US$20. The Czech-run *Pacific Hotel* (☎ 2279/39), also known as the Thai Binh Duong Hotel, is at 4 Le Loi St (on the corner of Ly Tu Trong St); singles/doubles cost US$17/19. The *Ha Long Hotel* (☎ 2175) is on Thong Nhat St across from the church; singles cost US$15.

One of the cheapest (and dirtiest) places in town, *Nha Tro P.04* (☎ 2473/38), which is

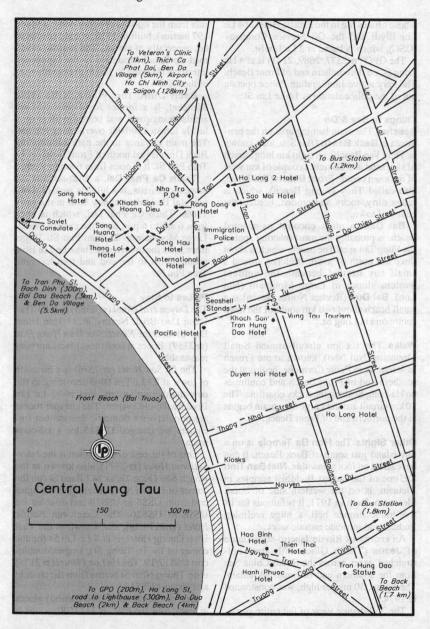

To Veteran's Clinic
(1km), Thich Ca
Phat Dai, Ben Da
Village (5km), Airport,
Ho Chi Minh City
& Saigon (128km)

Khoa Huan
Dieu
Hoang

Thu
Street

Le
Lo

Le
Lo
Street

To Bus Station
(1.2km)

Ha Long 2 Hotel

Song Hong
Hotel

Nha Tro
P.04

Rang Dong
Hotel

Sao Mai Hotel

Tan

Tan

Thuong

Do Chieu Street

Khach San 5
Hoang Dieu

Soviet
Consulate

Song
Huang
Hotel

Duy

Lo

Immigration
Police

Street

Quang

Song Hau
Hotel

Thang Loi
Hotel

Bacu

Trong

Street

International
Hotel

To Tran Phu St,
Bach Dinh (300m),
Bai Dau Beach (3km),
& Ben Da Village
(5.5km)

Trung

Boulevard

Seashell
Stands

Tu

Kiet

Hung

Ly

Vung Tau Tourism

Pacific Hotel

Street

Khach San
Tran Hung
Dao Hotel

Duyen Hai Hotel

Dao

Front Beach (Bai Truoc)

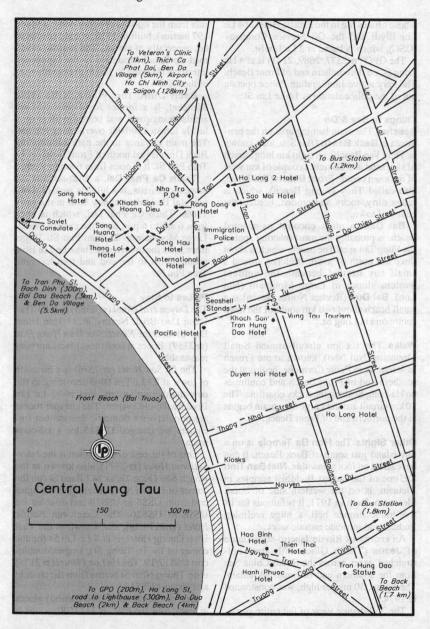

Ha Long Hotel

Thong - Nhat Street

Central Vung Tau

0   150   300 m

Kiosks

Nguyen

Boulevard

Du

Street

To Bus Station
(1.8km)

Hoa Binh
Hotel

Thien Thai
Hotel

Nguyen

Trai

Hanh Phuoc
Hotel

Cong

Dinh

Tran Hung Dao
Statue

To Back
Beach
(1.7 km)

To GPO (200m), Ha Long St,
road to Lighthouse (300m), Bai Dua
Beach (2km) & Back Beach (4km)

Truong

also known as Nha Khach P.04, is at 1 Thu Khoa Huan St (on the corner of Duy Tan St and Le Loi Blvd). A room for four costs US$2.

There are several cheap places to stay along Back Beach. The *Nha Nghi Cong Duan* (☎ 2300), run by the National Bank workers' trade union, is at 15 Hoang Hoa Tham St (corner Thuy Van St). *Nha Nghi* is not far away at 76 Thuy Van St. You might also try *Phong Tro* at 47 Thuy Van St.

The *Thanh Liem Bungalows* at 46A Thuy Van St (on the corner of Hoang Hoa Tham St) offer red, white & blue bungalows with steep thatched roofs. Each bungalow has a double bed and costs US$2 per night. The *Youth Tourism Campground* (Khu Du Lich Thanh Nien; ☎ 2336) at 46A Thuy Van St (next to the Thanh Liem Bungalows) has rooms from US$2.50 to US$4. A four person tent costs US$1.50 to rent.

Bai Dau is lined with inexpensive guest houses, as is Bai Dua.

Places to Eat

For excellent seafood, try the *Huong Bien Restaurant* along Front Beach at 47 Quang Trung St. There are several places nearby and quite a few more along Tran Hung Dao Blvd. The largest restaurant along the Back Beach is *Thang Muoi Restaurant* (☎ 2515), 7-9 Thuy Van St. There are several cafes at the southern end of Back Beach.

At Bai Dau, you might try the seaside restaurant run by An Giang Tourism; it's at 41 Tran Phu St, which is across the street from 114 Tran Phu St. At Bai Dua, there are restaurants at Nos 88 and 126 Ha Long St.

Getting There & Away

Buses to Vung Tau from Ho Chi Minh City leave from the Mien Dong and Van Thanh bus stations. Express microbuses depart from the Cong Ty Dich Vu Du Lich Quan 1 (☎ 90541) at 39 Nguyen Hue Blvd; the 128 km trip takes two hours.

Vung Tau bus station (Ben Xe Khach Vung Tau) is about 1½ km from the city centre at 52 Nam Ky Khoi Nghia St. To get

there from Front Beach, take either Bacu or Truong Cong Dinh Sts to Le Hong Phong St. Turn right and then turn right again onto Nam Ky Khoi Nghia St. Express buses and microbuses to Ho Chi Minh City also depart from the Ha Long (on Thong Nhat St near the church) and Hanh Phuoc (at 11 Nguyen Trai St) hotels.

The Mekong Delta

The Mekong Delta, the southernmost region of Vietnam, is renowned for its richness. It constituted an important part of the Khmer Kingdom until the 18th century and was the last region of modern-day Vietnam to be settled and then annexed by the Vietnamese.

MYTHO

Mytho, the capital of Tien Giang Province, is a quiet city of 90,000 easily reached as a day trip from Saigon, yet very near some of the most beautiful rural areas of the Mekong Delta (such as Ben Tre Province).

Information

Tien Giang Province Tourism (☎ 3591, 3154) has an office on the northern edge of the city at 56 Hung Vuong Blvd. It is open from Monday to Saturday.

Things to See

Island of the Coconut Monk Until his imprisonment by the Communists for anti-government activities and the consequent dispersion of his flock, the Coconut Monk led a small community a few km from Mytho on Phung Island (Con Phung). In its heyday, the island was dominated by a fantastic open air sanctuary that looked like a cross between a cheap copy of Disneyland and Singapore's Tiger Balm Gardens. The best way to get from Mytho to Phung Island is to hire a motorised wooden boat, which should cost US$2.50 per hour.

Mytho Central Market Mytho Central Market, along Trung Trac and Nguyen Hue

Sts, is closed to traffic. The streets are filled with stalls selling everything from fresh food (along Trung Trac St) and bulk tobacco to boat propellers.

Places to Stay

The *Ap Bac Hotel* (☎ 3593), also known as the Grand Hotel, is the largest in town. Foreigners are charged US$10 for a double with air-con, and rooms with fans cost US$3. The *Rach Gam Hotel* at 33 Trung Trac St has doubles with ceiling fans and bath for US$2.

Prices at the *Lac Hong Hotel* (☎ 3918), 85-87 30 Thang 4 St, range from US$1 for a single to US$2 for a large double; toilets are communal. The run-down *My Tho Hotel* at 67 30 Thang 4 St has rooms without fans for around US$1 – a double with a ceiling fan costs US$1.50.

Khach San 43 (☎ 3126) is a clean, modern place at 43 Ngo Quyen St with doubles which start at US$2.

Places to Eat

Thien Thanh Restaurant is at 65 30 Thang 4 St. Across the street, next to the Tan Long Island ferry dock, is *Cuu Long Restaurant*. There are about half-a-dozen good places along Trung Truc St.

Getting There & Away

Bus Mytho is served by nonexpress buses which leave Ho Chi Minh City from Mien Tay bus station in An Lac.

The Mytho bus station (Ben Xe Khach Tien Giang; ☎ 3359) is several km west of town; it is open from from 4 am to about 5 pm. To get there from the city centre, take Ap Bac St westward and continue on to National Highway 1.

Car By car, the drive from Ho Chi Minh City to Mytho on National Highway 1 takes about 90 minutes.

Getting Around

Motorised seven-metre boats can be hired at an unmarked ferry landing on Trung Trac St at the foot of Thien Ho Duong St. Ferry boats to points across the river also dock here.

Wooden rowboats to Tan Long Island leave from the pier at the foot of Le Loi St, next to Cuu Long Restaurant.

CANTHO

Cantho (population 150,000), capital of Hau Giang Province, is the political, economic, cultural and transportation centre of the Mekong Delta.

Information

The office of Hau Giang Province Tourism (☎ 20147, 35275) is at 27 Chau Van Liem St. The GPO is at the intersection of Hoa Binh Blvd and Ngo Quyen St.

Things to See

The ornamentation of the **Munirangsyaram Pagoda** at 36 Hoa Binh Blvd is typical of Khmer Hinayana Buddhist pagodas, lacking the multiple Bodhisattvas and Taoist spirits common in Vietnamese Mahayana pagodas. The **Central Market** is strung out along Hai Ba Trung St.

Places to Stay

Quoc Te Hotel (☎ 35793/5, 20749) is along the Cantho River at 12 Hai Ba Trung St. Foreigners are charged US$10/14 to US$18/22 for singles/doubles. The *Hau Giang Hotel* (☎ 35537/81, 20180) is at 34 Nam Ky Khoi Nghia St; rooms cost from US$13/17 to US$18/22 (plus a 10% service charge). The *Hoa Binh Hotel* (☎ 20537, 35598) is at 5 Hoa Binh St. Here, a double costs US$2. There are a number of cheaper hotels around town.

Places to Eat

The *Ninh Kieu Restaurant* is on a boat across Hai Ba Trung St from the Quoc Te Hotel. There is also a restaurant in the *Quoc Te Hotel*. The *Bong Mai Restaurant* is at 19-23 Phan Dinh Phung St.

There are a number of restaurants that cater to locals along Nam Ky Khoi Nghia St, between Phan Dinh Phung and Dien Bien Phu Sts. Mobile stands selling soup and French-roll sandwiches are often set up on Hoa Binh Blvd near the GPO.

Getting There & Away

By car, the 168 km ride from Ho Chi Minh City to Cantho along National Highway 1 usually takes about four hours. The main bus station in Cantho is several km out of town at the intersection of Nguyen Trai and Tran Phu Sts.

OTHER AREAS

When travel restrictions to the Mekong Delta are relaxed, places to consider visiting include: **Ben Tre** (renowned for its rich agricultural lands and network of waterways); **Tan An; Vinh Long; Long Xuyen** (whose modern Catholic Church is one of the largest in the Delta); **Chau Doc** (there is a well-known mosque across the river in Chau Giang District and a number of pagodas and temples at Sam Mountain); **Rach Gia** (on the Gulf of Thailand); and **Ha Tien** (a coastal town almost on the Cambodian border near which there are a number of grottoes and beaches). **Phu Quoc Island** is a large island 45 km west of Ha Tien.

All these places have cheap accommodation and are served by buses and, in some cases, scheduled ferry services. The government seems to be most sensitive about travel to border provinces.

South-Central Coast

PHAN RANG-THAP CHAM

The twin cities of Phan Rang and Thap Cham (population 38,000), famous for their production of table grapes, are in Thuan Hai Province in a region of semidesert. The area's best known sight is the group of Cham towers known as Po Klong Garai, from which Thap Cham (Cham Tower) derives its name. Thuan Hai Province is home to tens of thousands of descendants of the Cham people, many of whom live in and around Phan Rang-Thap Cham.

Orientation & Information

National Highway 1 is called Thong Nhat St as it runs through Phan Rang. The office of Thuan Hai Tourism (Cong Ty Du Lich Thuan Hai; ☎ 74) is in the Huu Nghi Hotel at 1 Huong Vuong St.

Things to See

Phan Rang-Thap Cham's most famous landmark is **Po Klong Garai**, four brick towers constructed at the end of the 13th century during the reign of Cham monarch, Jaya Simhavarman III. The site is seven km towards Dalat from Phan Rang on a hilltop several hundred metres north of National Highway 20.

Places to Stay

The main tourist hotel in Phan Rang is the *Huu Nghi Hotel* (☎ 74) at 1 Huong Vuong St. Foreigners are charged a hefty US$25 for a double. To get there, turn west (left if you are heading north) off Thong Nhat St between Nos 267 and 269 and go on for 100 metres. The *Phan Rang Hotel* is at 354 Thong Nhat St, which is 150 metres south of the pink pagoda in the market area; a single room costs US$1.

The *Thong Nhat Hotel* (☎ 2049) at 164 Thong Nhat St is a modern, four-storey run-down place with more than its fair share of vermin. Foreigners are asked to pay a lot more than locals.

Places to Eat

A local delicacy is roasted or baked gecko (dong) served with fresh green mango.

Thu Thuy Restaurant is a three-storey eatery at 404 Thong Nhat St. *Nha Hang 426* is across the street from the local bus station. *Nha Hang 404* is at 404 Thong Nhat St. For soup, try *Pho 129* at 231 Thong Nhat St (just south of the Protestant church).

Getting There & Away

The Thap Cham railway station is about six km west of National Highway 1 within sight of the Cham towers. Phan Rang intercity bus station (Ben Xe Phan Rang; ☎ 2031) is on the northern outskirts of town opposite 64 Thong Nhat St. The local bus station (Ben Xe) is at the southern end of town across the street from 426 Thong Nhat St.

NHA TRANG

Nha Trang (population 200,000), the capital of Khanh Hoa Province, has what is probably the nicest municipal beach in all of Vietnam. The turquoise waters around Nha Trang are almost transparent, making for excellent fishing, snorkelling and scuba diving.

Orientation

Tran Phu Blvd runs along Nha Tranh Beach (which is six km long), becoming Tu Do St south of the airport. The centre of Nha Trang is around the Nha Trang Hotel on Thong Nhat St.

Information

Khanh Hoa Province Tourism (Cong Ty Du Lich Khanh Hoa; ☎ 22753) rents out diving equipment. Their office is on the 2nd floor of a building on the grounds of the Hai Yen Hotel, which is at 40 Tran Phu St. The office is open from 7 to 11.30 am and from 1.30 to 5 pm Monday to Saturday.

The Nha Trang Ship Chandler Company, also known as Nha Trang Ship Chanco (Cung Ung Tau Bien; ☎ 21195), at 74 Tran Phu Blvd may also have watersports equipment. Nha Trang Tourism (☎ 21231) has its office at 3 Tran Hung Dao St (on the grounds of the Hung Dao Hotel).

The GPO is at 2 Tran Phu Blvd, which is near the northern end of Nha Trang Beach. It is open daily from 6.30 am to 8.30 pm and handles international telephone calls. The Bank for Foreign Trade (Ngan Hang Ngoai Thuong; ☎ 21054) at 17 Quang Trung St offers the standard bank rate. It is open from 7 to 11.30 am and from 1 to 5 pm Monday to Saturday except Thursday afternoon.

Things to See

Po Nagar Cham Towers The Cham towers of Po Nagar, or 'The Lady of the City', were built between the 7th and 12th centuries on a site used by Hindus for worship as early as the 2nd century AD. Today, both ethnic-Chinese and Vietnamese Buddhists come to Po Nagar to pray and make offerings according to their respective traditions. Shoes

■ **PLACES TO STAY**

3	Nha Nghi 378 Bo Noi Vu (hotel)
8	Thang Loi Hotel
11	Viet Ngu Hotel
13	Nha Trang Hotel
15	Kuong Hai Hotel
17	Nha Khach 25 Phan Chu Trinh (hotel)
23	Railway Station Dormitory (Nha Tro)
26	Thong Nhat Hotel
28	Nha Khach Nha Trang Hotel
30	Hung Dao Hotel
33	Hai Yen Hotel
37	Khach San 58 Tran Phu (hotel)

▼ **PLACES TO EAT**

5	Lac Canh Restaurant
6	Nha Hang 33 Le Loi (restaurant)
12	Pho Hanoi (soup shop)
14	Binh Minh Restaurant
19	Ice Cream Shops
27	Cafes
34	Cafes
39	Cafes

OTHER

1	Short-Haul Bus Station
2	Dam Market Lambretta Station
4	Dam Market
7	GPO
9	Giant Seated Buddha
10	Long Son Pagoda
16	Foreign Trade Bank
18	Pasteur Institute & Yersin Museum
20	Stadium
21	Youth Tourism Express Bus Office
22	Nha Trang Railway Station
24	Nha Trang Cathedral
25	Bien Vien Tinh (hospital)
29	Church
31	Express Bus Station
32	Khanh Hoa Province Tourism
35	War Memorial Obelisk
36	Lien Tinh Bus Station
38	Nha Trang Ship Chandler Company

should be removed before entering the towers.

The towers of Po Nagar stand on a granite knoll two km north of Nha Trang on the left

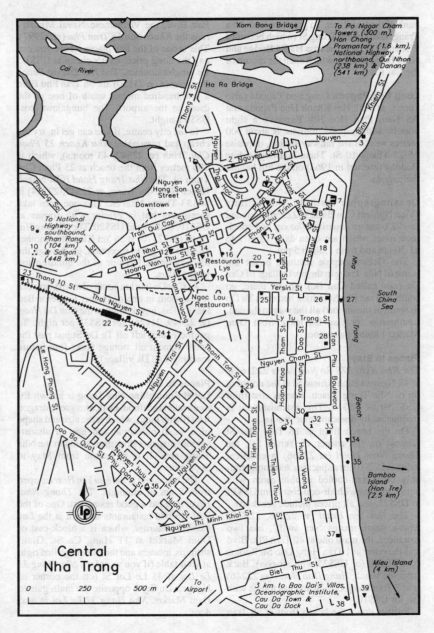

To Po Nagar Cham
Towers (300 m),
Hon Chong
Promontory (1.6 km),
National Highway 1
northbound, Qui Nhon
(238 km) & Danang
(541 km)

Xom Bong Bridge

Cai River

Ha Ra Bridge

Binh Khiem St

Nguyen

2 Thang 4 St

Phuong Sai

Nguyen Cong Tru

Nguyen Hong Son
Street
Downtown

Nguyen Hoc St

Hoang Tu St

Phan Boi Chau St

Dinh Phung St

To National
Highway 1
southbound,
Phan Rang
(104 km)
& Saigon
(448 km)

Quang Trung

Tran Qui Cap St

Yet Kieu St

Thong Nhat St

Phan Chu Trinh

Pasteur St

Hoang Van Thu St

Thanh Phuong St

Restaurant
Lys

Ngoc Lau
Restaurant

Yersin St

Nha Trang

South
China
Sea

23 Thang 10 St

Thai Nguyen St

Ly Tu Trong St

Nguyen Trai St

Le Thanh Ton St

Hoang Hoa Tham St

Dao St

Tran Hung Dao St

Tran Phu Boulevard

Nha Trang Beach

Le Hong Phong St

Cao Ba Quat St

Phu Dong St

Nguyen Huu Huan St

Tran Nguyen Han St

Huynh St

To Hien Thanh St

Nguyen Chanh St

Hung Vuong St

Nguyen Thien Thuat St

Bamboo
Island
(Hon Tre)
(2.5 km)

Nguyen Thi Minh Khai St

Biet Thu St

Mieu Island
(4 km)

Central
Nha Trang

0   250   500 m

To
Airport

3 km to Bao Dai's Villas,
Oceanographic Institute,
Cau Da Town &
Cau Da Dock

bank of the Cai River. To get there from Nha Trang, take Quang Trung St (which becomes 2 Thang 4 St) north across Ha Ra Bridge and Xom Bong Bridge, which span the mouth of the Cai River.

Long Son Pagoda Long Son Pagoda (also known as Tinh Hoi Khanh Hoa Pagoda and An Nam Phat Hoc Hoi Pagoda), a sight popular with domestic tourists, is about 500 metres west of the railway station, opposite 15 23 Thang 10 St. There is a huge white Buddha (erected in 1963) on the hill behind the pagoda.

Oceanographic Institute This institute (Vien Nghiem Cuu Bien; ☎ 22536), founded in 1923, has an aquarium *(ho ca)* and specimen room which are open daily from 7 to 11.30 am and from 1.30 to 5 pm.

The Oceanographic Institute is six km south of Nha Trang in the port village of Cau Da (also called Cau Be). To get there, go south on Tran Phu St (which becomes Tu Do St south of the airport) all the way to the end. Lambrettas for Cau Da leave from Dam Market Lambretta station.

Places to Stay

The *Nha Nghi 378 Bo Noi Vu* (☎ 22216) is at 48 Nguyen Binh Khiem St at the northern tip of Nha Trang Beach. Rooms cost from US$1.50 to US$10. This establishment is frequented by domestic tour groups.

On the beach front at 18 Tran Phu St (almost on the corner of Yersin St), the *Thong Nhat Hotel* (☎ 22966) is excellent value at US$10 for a spacious and commendably clean fan-cooled double room with bath. Doubles with air-con cost from US$17 to US$25, and all prices include breakfast.

The *Hai Yen Hotel* (☎ 22828, 22974), whose name means 'sea swift', has two entrances, the main one at 40 Tran Phu Blvd and the other at 1 Tran Hung Dao St. Rooms cost US$10 (or US$25 with air-con). Back from the beach, *Hung Dao Hotel* (☎ 22246) is at 3 Tran Hung Dao St and has rooms with fan for US$10.

Further down the beach front at 58 Tran

Phu Blvd, the Vietnamese Naval Ministry runs the *Khach San 58 Tran Phu* (☎ 22997). This is one of the few places where you can pay the dong price, so it's cheap at US$3/5 for singles/doubles. The *Hai Duong Beach Bungalows* (☎ 21150) are on Tran Phu Blvd a few hundred metres south of one of the gates to the airport. The bungalows cost US$3 a night.

In the city centre, if you can get in, try the cheap and reasonable *Nha Khach 25 Phan Chu Trinh* (☎ 22897; 43 rooms), which is 500 metres from the beach at 25 Phan Chu Trinh St. The *Nha Trang Hotel* (Chi Nhanh Khach San Nha Trang; ☎ 22347, 22224) is at 133 Thong Nhat St. This one does take foreigners but is pricier with rooms at US$10, US$15 and US$20. The *Khuong Hai Hotel* (☎ 22470) at 36 Yet Kieu St is another cheapie. To get to reception, go through the hallway on the left side of the building and up the stairs.

At Cau Da (six km south of town), you can rent a room in one of former Emperor Bao Dai's villas, now known as the *Cau Da Hotel* (☎ 22449, 21124), for US$35 per night. To get there, turn left off Tu Do St just past the white cement oil storage tanks (but before reaching Cau Da village).

Places to Eat

Local Specialties Nha Trang is known for its excellent seafood. Delicious green dragon fruit (thanh long), which is the size and shape of a small pineapple and has an almost-smooth magenta skin, grows only in the Nha Trang area. It is in season from May to September.

The restaurant at the *Hai Yen Hotel* is open from 5 am to midnight. The *Thong Nhat Hotel* also has a good restaurant. One of the best seafood restaurants in town is the *Lac Canh Restaurant*, which is a block east of Dam Market at 11 Hang Ca St. Giant shrimps, lobsters and the like are grilled right at your table (if you so order). *Nha Hang 33 Le Loi* at 33 Le Loi St (on the corner of Nguyen Du St) is opposite the main gate to Dam Market. *Nha Hang 31 Le Loi* is next door.

In the town centre, you might check out the *Binh Minh Restaurant* at 64 Hoang Van Thu St (on the corner of Yet Kieu St); their Vietnamese dishes are excellent. *Pho Hanoi* at 21 Le Thanh Phuong St is open from 5.30 to 10 am and from 3 to 10 pm. The *Restaurant Lys* at 117A Hoang Van Thu St is a big, bright and energetic place with an English menu. Also centrally located, there's great seafood at the *Ngoc Lau Restaurant* at 37 Le Thanh Phuong St.

There is a vegetarian restaurant, *Quay Hang Com Chay*, in the covered semi-circular food pavilion north-east of the main building of Dam Market. The restaurant is right across from stall No 117. There is a collection of small ice cream cafes at the junction of Yersin and Quang Trung Sts.

Getting There & Away

Air Vietnam Airlines flies from Ho Chi Minh City to Nha Trang at least weekly. The one-way fare is US$39. There are also regular flights to Nha Trang from Danang and Hanoi. Vietnam Airlines' Nha Trang office (☎ 21147) is at 82 Tran Phu St.

Bus The Lien Tinh bus station (Ben Xe Lien Tinh; ☎ 22192) is Nha Trang's main intercity bus terminal. It's opposite 212 Ngo Gia Tu St. There is dormitory accommodation here.

Express buses leave from two different stations. The Youth Tourism Express-Bus office (Du Lich Thanh Nien; ☎ 22010) is just off Yersin St at 6 Hoang Hoa Tham St. Tickets are sold daily from 4 am to 6 pm. The other buses leave from the Express bus station (Tram Xe Toc Hanh; ☎ 22397, 22884) which is about 150 metres from the Hung Dao Hotel at 46 Le Thanh Ton St. The ticket office is open every day from 6 am to 4.30 pm.

Train The Nha Trang railway station (Ga Nha Trang; ☎ 22113), overlooked by the nearby Cathedral, is across the street from 26 Thai Nguyen St. The ticket office is open from 7 am to 2 pm only.

Getting Around

Boat The best place to hire boats for excursions out to the many offshore islands around Nha Trang is the Cau Da fishing boat dock, known as Ben Do Cau Da.

Local Transport Dam Market Lambretta station (Ben Xe Lam Cho Dam) is on Nguyen Hong Son St near the corner of Nguyen Thai Hoc St. It is due north of the main building of Dam Market, which is a round modern structure several stories high.

Lambrettas from Dam Market Lambretta station go to Cau Da (also known as Cau Be and Chut), where the Oceanographic Institute and the fishing-boat dock are located. The Hai Yen Hotel rents bicycles for US$2 a day.

QUI NHON

Qui Nhon (or Quy Nhon; population 188,000) is the capital of Binh Dinh Province and one of Vietnam's more active second-string seaports. The beaches in the immediate vicinity of the city aren't great and the city is a bit dingy. Qui Nhon, however, is a convenient and pleasant place to break the long journey from Nha Trang to Danang.

Orientation

Qui Nhon is on a peninsula shaped like the nose of an anteater. The tip of the nose (the port area) is closed to the public. The main west-east thoroughfares are Tran Hung Dao and Nguyen Hue Sts. The latter runs along the Municipal Beach on the peninsula's southern coast. The streets around Lon Market constitute Qui Nhon's town centre.

Information

Binh Dinh Province Tourism & Ship Chandler Company (Du Lich Cung Ung Tau Bien Binh Dinh; ☎ 2329) is 600 metres east of the centre of town across the street from 78 Tran Hung Dao St. The office is poorly organised.

The Foreign Trade Bank (Ngan Hang Ngoai Thuong) is at 148 Tran Hung Dao St (on the corner of Le Loi St). The GPO is in the south-western part of town on the corner

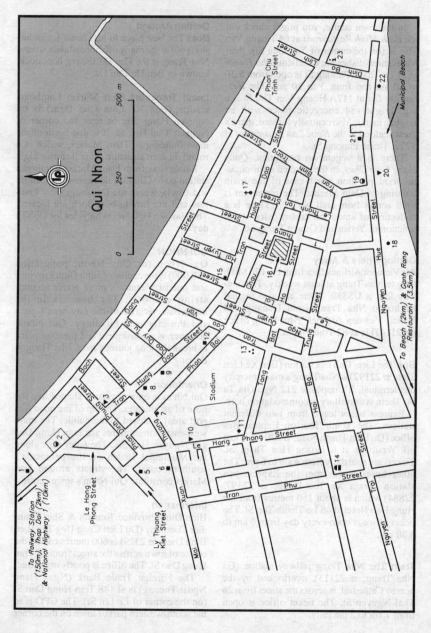

Qui Nhon

of Hai Ba Trung and Tran Phu Sts. It is open daily from 6 am to 8 pm, and international telephone calls can be placed from here.

Beaches

Qui Nhon Municipal Beach, which extends along the southern side of the anteater's nose, consists of a few hundred metres of clean sand shaded by a coconut grove. The nicest section of beach, near which there is a small zoo, is across from the Quy Nhon Tourist Hotel. A longer, quieter bathing beach begins about two km south-west of the Municipal Beach. To get there, follow Nguyen Hue St westward.

Places to Stay

Nha Khach Ngan Hang Dau Tu (☎ 2012) is two blocks from the bus station at 399 Tran Hung Dao St. This place is central (though it's a bit far from the beach), the rooms are clean and quiet, and the management is friendly. Rooms with fans start at US$1.50. To get to the reception desk, go almost to the back of the building and turn up the stairs to the right. The *Qui Nhon Peace Hotel* (Khach San Hoa Binh; ☎ 2900) is half a block away opposite 66 Tran Hung Dao St; doubles cost US$3.

Nha Khach Huu Nghi (☎ 2152) at 210 Phan Boi Chau St is a bit grimy but remains popular with domestic travellers. Doubles with fan cost US$1.50, and most rooms come with bath. *Viet Cuong Hotel* (☎ 2434), a basic but serviceable place midway between the bus and railway stations (about 100 metres from each), is at 460 Tran Hung Dao St. Doubles cost from US$1.50.

The modern *Dong Phuong Hotel* (☎ 2915, 2562) at 39-41 Mai Xuan Thuong St (near the corner of Le Hong Phong St) has doubles starting at US$2. The *Olympic Hotel* (Khach San Lien Doanh; ☎ 2375) is next to the stadium. Doubles range from US$2 to US$4. The entrance is opposite 167 Le Hong Phong St (on the corner of Tang Bat Ho St).

Places to Eat

One of the best eateries in town is the *Vu Hung Restaurant* (☎ 2375, 2908), which is on the roof of the Olympic Hotel. *Huu Nghi Restaurant* is on the ground floor of Nha Khach Huu Nghi. The *Dong Phuong Restaurant* is on the ground floor of the Dong Phuong Hotel – it is open from 6 am to 11 pm. The *Tu Hai Restaurant* (☎ 2582) is on the 3rd floor of Lon Market (on the side overlooking Phan Boi Chau St); it is open from 6.30 am to 10 pm.

For tasty food at rock-bottom prices, try the *Ngoc Lien Restaurant*, a favourite with Qui Nhonians, at 288 Le Hong Phong. There are several other simple restaurants in the immediate vicinity.

There is a line of soup shops along Phan Boi Chau St at Nos 286, 288, 290 and 292. They are open from 6 am to 10 pm. *Pho 350*, also open from 6 am to 10 pm, is a soup restaurant at 350 Tran Hung Dao St. *Cang*

Tin, a restaurant along the Municipal Beach at 14 Nguyen Hue St, sells pho in the morning.

Getting There & Away

Air Weekly flights link Ho Chi Minh City and Hanoi with Phu Cat, an airfield 36 km north of Qui Nhon. Small trucks to Phu Cat depart from the Short-haul transport station. In Qui Nhon, the Vietnam Airlines booking office (☎ 2953) is near the Thanh Binh Hotel in the building next to 30 Nguyen Thai Hoc St.

Bus Qui Nhon bus station (Ben Xe Khach Qui Nhon; ☎ 2246) is opposite 543 Tran Hung Dao St (across from where Le Hong Phong St hits Tran Hung Dao St). The non-express ticket windows are open from 5 am to 4 pm. The express-ticket window (Khach Di Xe Toc Hanh), which is in the fenced-in enclosure next to the nonexpress windows, is open from 4 am to 4 pm. There is another Express bus station (☎ 2172) 100 metres from the Quy Nhon Tourist Hotel at 14 Nguyen Hue St.

Vehicles to places within a 50 km radius of Qui Nhon depart from the Short-haul transport station (Ben Xe 1 Thang 4), which is at the intersection of Phan Boi Chau and Mai Xuan Thuong Sts.

Train The city of Qui Nhon is poorly served by rail. Qui Nhon railway station (Ga Qui Nhon; ☎ 2036) is at the end of a 10-km spur line off the main north-south track. The station is 70 metres from Tran Hung Dao St on Hoang Hoa Tham St, which intersects Tran Hung Dao St between Nos 661 and 663. The nearest the Reunification trains get to Qui Nhon is Dieu Tri, 10 km from the city. Small trucks from Qui Nhon to Dieu Tri leave from the Short-haul transport station.

QUANG NGAI CITY

Quang Ngai City, 15 km from the coast, is something of a backwater. Some of the most bitter fighting of the Vietnam War took place in this area. The infamous My Lai Massacre

of 1968 took place 14 km from here, and a memorial has been erected on the site.

Orientation

National Highway 1 is called Quang Trung St as it passes through Quang Ngai.

Site of the My Lai Massacre

Son My subdistrict was the site of the most horrific war crimes committed by American ground forces during the Vietnam War. The My Lai Massacre consisted of a series of atrocities carried out all over Son My sub-district, which is divided into four hamlets, one of which is named My Lai. The largest mass killing took place at Tu Cung Hamlet in Xom Lang subhamlet (also known as Thuan Yen subhamlet), where the Son My Memorial was later erected.

The site of the My Lai Massacre is 14 km from Quang Ngai. To get there from town, head north on Quang Trung St (National Highway 1) and cross the long bridge over the Tra Khuc River. A few metres from the northern end of the bridge you will come to a triangular concrete stele indicating the way to the Son My Memorial. Turn right (east-ward, parallel to the river) on the dirt road and continue for 12 km.

If you don't have a car, the best way to get to Son My District from Quang Ngai is to flag down a motorbike (Honda ong) from near the bus station or along Quang Trung St and ride out there seated behind the driver.

Places to Stay

Khach San So 1 (Hotel No 1) is 50 metres from the bus station at 42 Nguyen Nghiem St. Rooms cost from US$1 to US$1.50. The sheets aren't changed often. *Khach San So 2* (Hotel No 2) is about 100 metres west of Quang Trung St at 41 Phan Boi Chau St. Rooms are similarly priced. Hotel No 2, about 400 metres from the bus station, is probably a bit nicer than No 1.

The only proper hotel in town is *Nha Khach Uy Ban Thi* (☎ 2109), which is actu-ally a guest house used mostly by government officials. Foreigners are charged US$20 for a double. Nha Khach Uy Ban Thi is approximately 300 metres from Quang Trung St at about 52 Phan Boi Chau St.

Places to Eat

The restaurant at *Nha Khach Uy Ban Thi*, the government guest house, is the only real restaurant in Quang Ngai. The *Tiem An 72 Restaurant* at 72 Nguyen Nghiem St is about 150 metres from the bus station.

There are cafes at 47, 51 and 53 Phan Boi Chau St (near Hotel No 2) but they don't have much to eat. Meat and bean sprout crêpes, fried over open fires, are sold in the evenings on Phan Dinh Phung St between Tran Hung Dao and Nguyen Nghiem Sts. *Pho 79*, on the corner of Quang Trung and Tran Hung Dao Sts, has soup.

Getting There & Away

Bus Quang Ngai City bus station (Ben Xe Khach Quang Ngai) is opposite 32 Nguyen Nghiem St, which is about 100 metres east of Quang Trung St (National Highway 1).

Train The Quang Ngai railway station (Ga Quang Nghia or Ga Quang Ngai) is three km west of the town centre. To get there, take Phan Boi Chau St west from Quang Trung St (National Highway 1) and continue going in the same direction after the street name changes to Nguyen Chanh St. At 389 Nguyen Chanh St (which you'll come to as Nguyen Chanh St curves left), continue straight on down a side street. The railway station is at the end of the street.

Central Highlands

The Central Highlands cover the southern part of the Truong Son Mountain Range and include the provinces of Lam Dong, Dac Lac (Dak Lak) and Gia Lai-Kon Tum (Gia Lai-Con Tum). The region, which is home to many ethno-linguistic minority groups (Montagnards), is renowned for its cool climate, beautiful mountain scenery and innumerable streams, lakes and waterfalls. Except for Lam Dong Province (where Dalat is located), the Central Highlands are at present closed to foreigners.

DALAT

Dalat (elevation 1475 metres), which is situated in a temperate region dotted with lakes and waterfalls and surrounded by evergreen forests, makes a pleasant break from the hot coastal towns. The city's population of 125,000 includes about 5000 members of ethno-linguistic minorities. Dalat was established by the French as a hill station in 1912. It's economy is now based on tourism (300,000 domestic tourists visit every year) and the cultivation of garden vegetables and flowers.

Information

The headquarters of Lam Dong Province Tourism (☎ 2125, 2366, 2021) is at 12 Tran Phu St, across the street from the Dalat Hotel. The Lam Dong Youth Tourism Co (Hiep Hoi Du Lich; ☎ 2136, 2318) runs sightseeing excursions and camping trips in and around Dalat for groups of young Vietnamese. The main office of this private company is on the 2nd floor of the Lang Bian Youth Hostel, which is down Nguyen Thi Minh Khai St from the Central Market.

US dollars can be changed at the usual hotel rate in the Palace Hotel. The GPO is across from Lam Dong Province Tourism at 14 Tran Phu St.

Note As of last reports, Americans are not allowed to visit Dalat.

Things to See

French Governor-General's Residence This former Governor-General's residence (Dinh Toan Quyen, or Dinh 2; ☎ 2093), now used as a guest house and for official receptions, is a dignified building of modernist design built in 1933. It is about two km west from the centre of town up the hill from the intersection of Tran Hung Dao and Khoi Nghia Bac Son Sts. It is open to the public from 7 to 11 am and from 1.30 to 4 pm.

Bao Dai's Summer Palace This palace

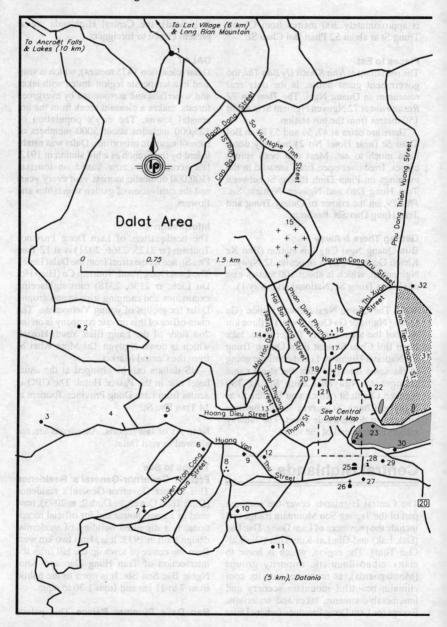

To Lat Village (6 km)
& Lang Bian Mountain

To Ancroët Falls
& Lakes (10 km)

1

Bach Dang Street

TS Cao Ba Quat

So Viet Nghe Tinh Street

Phu Dong Thien Vuong Street

Dalat Area

15

0   0.75   1.5 km

Nguyen Cong Tru Street

32

Bui Thi Xuan Street

Dinh Tien Hoang St.

Hai Ba Trung Street

Phan Dinh Phung Street

14   16

17

Mai Hoc De Street

19   18

Hai Thuong Street   20   21   22   31

3   24   23

2   5   13   Thang St.   30

4   Hoang Dieu Street   See Central
                                          Dalat Map

6   Huong Van

Huyen Tran Cong Chua Street

8   9   12   25   28   29

7   Thu Street   26   27   20

10

11

(5 km), Datania

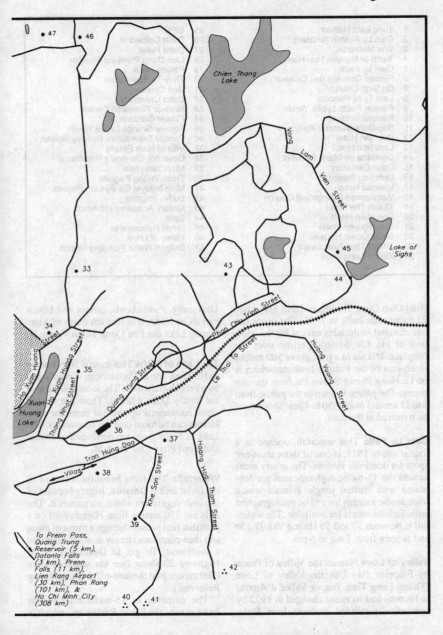

1	Tung Lam Hamlet	25	GPO
2	Cam Ly Airstrip (unused)	26	Dalat Cathedral
3	War Memorial	27	Dalat Hotel
4	Tomb of Nguyen Huu Hao	28	Lam Dong Province Tourism
5	Cam Ly Falls	29	Palace Hotel
6	Former Couvent des Oiseaux	30	Thuy Ta Restaurant
7	Du Sinh Church	31	Golf Course
8	Lam Ty Ni Pagoda	32	Dalat University
9	Former Petite Lycée Yersin	33	Nuclear Research Centre
10	Pasteur Institute	34	Flower Gardens
11	Bao Dai's Summer Palace	35	Former Grande Lyceé Yersin
12	Duy Tan Hotel	36	Former Crémaillére Railway Station
13	Lam Son Hotel	37	Villa of Nam Phung
14	Domaine de Marie Convent	38	Governor-General's Residence
15	Dalat Cemetary	39	Minh Tam Hotel
16	Linh Son Pagoda	40	Thien Vuong Pagoda
17	Mimosa Hotel	41	Minh Nguyet Cu Sy Lam Pagoda
18	Vietnamese Evangelical Church	42	Su Nu Pagoda
19	Thanh The Hotel	43	Military Academy (off-limits)
20	Lien Hiep Hotel	44	Dam
21	Cao Nguyen Hotel	45	Small Restaurants
22	Small Guest Houses	46	Valley of Love
23	Thanh Thuy Restaurant	47	Dragon Water Pumping Station
24	Xuan Huong Dam		

(Biet Dien Quoc Truong, or Dinh 3) is a tan, 25-room villa built in 1933. The decor has not changed in decades except for the addition of Ho Chi Minh's portrait over the fireplace. It is set in a pine grove 500 metres south-east of the Pasteur Institute, which is on Le Hong Phong St two km from the city centre. The palace is open to the public from 7 to 11 am and from 1.30 to 4 pm. Shoes must be removed at the door.

Cam Ly Falls This waterfall, opened as a tourist site in 1911, is one of those must-see spots for domestic visitors. The grassy areas around the 15-metre-high cascades are decorated with stuffed jungle animals which Vietnamese tourists love to be photographed with. Refreshments are available. The waterfall is between 57 and 59 Huong Van Thu St and is open from 7 am to 6 pm.

Valley of Love Named the Valley of Peace by Emperor Bao Dai, the Valley of Love (Thung Lung Tinh Yeu, or Valleé d'Amour in French) had its name changed in 1972 by romantically-minded students from Dalat

University. Paddleboats, canoes and horses can all be hired. It is five km north of Xuan Huong Lake out Phu Dong Thien Vuong St.

The Lake of Sighs This natural lake, known as Ho Than Tho in Vietnamese, was enlarged by a French-built dam. The forests in the area are hardly Dalat's finest. There are several small restaurants up the hill from the dam. Horses can be hired near the restaurants. The Lake of Sighs is six km north-east of central Dalat out Phan Chu Trinh St.

Waterfalls The most beautiful waterfall in the Dalat area is **Datanla**, largely because of the lush vegetation which surrounds it. The falls are 350 metres from Highway 20 on a path that first passes through a forest of pines and then continues steeply down the hill into a rainforest. To get to Datanla, turn off Highway 20 about five km south of town (200 metres past the turn-off to Quang Trung Reservoir).

The entrance to 15-metre-high **Prenn Falls** is near the Prenn Restaurant, which is

13 km from Dalat towards Ho Chi Minh City and Phan Rang.

Lang Bian Mountain

This mountain, known in Vietnamese as Lam Vien, has five volcanic peaks ranging in altitude from 2100 to 2400 metres. The hike up to the top of Lang Bian Mountain – the view is truly spectacular – takes three to four hours from Lat Village. The path begins due north of Lat and is easily recognisable as a red gash in the green mountainside. It is possible to hire young locals as guides.

To get to the Montagnard village of Lat from Dalat, a distance of 12 km, head north on Xo Viet Nghe Tinh St. At Tung Lam Hamlet, there is a fork in the road marked by a shot-up cement street sign. Continue straight on (that is, north-westward) rather than to the left.

Pagodas & Churches

The **Lam Ty Ni Pagoda**, which is about 500 metres north of the Pasteur Institute at 2 Thien My St, has flower beds and gardens constructed over the past 20 years by the one monk who lives there.

Thien Vuong Pagoda, also known simply as Chua Tau (the Chinese pagoda), is popular with domestic tourists, especially ethnic-Chinese. Set on a hilltop amidst pine trees, the pagoda was built by the Trieu Chau Chinese congregation. It is about five km south-west of town, out on Khe Sanh St. **Minh Nguyet Cu Sy Lam Pagoda**, built by the Cantonese in 1962, is across the road.

Dalat Cathedral, on Tran Phu St next to the Dalat Hotel, was built between 1931 and 1942 for use by French residents and vacationers. Inside, the stained glass windows bring a bit of medieval Europe to Dalat. The pink **Domaine de Marie Convent**, once home to 300 nuns, is on a hilltop at 6 Ngo Quyen St, which is also called Mai Hac De St.

Places to Stay

Because of its popularity with domestic travellers, Dalat has an extensive network of cheap, well-run hotels, guest houses and dormitories. Not all of them will accept foreign visitors.

Town Centre & Market Area The *Thuy Tien Hotel* (☎ 2444) is in the heart of the town's old French section on the corner of Duy Tan and Khoi Nghia Nam Ky Sts. Doubles cost US$6. The spacious rooms are equipped with balconies and hot water, but unfortunately, it is often full. The *Phu Hoa Hotel* (Khach San Phu Hoa; ☎ 2482) is a block away at 16 Tang Bat Ho St but they may not accept foreigners. Ditto for *Phuoc Duc Guest House* (Nha Nghi Phuoc Duc; ☎ 2200) which is near Rap 3/4 cinema at 4 Khu Hoa Binh St. *Hotel Vinh Quang 1* is not far away at 11 Nguyen Van Troi St.

There are small guest houses along Nguyen Chi Thanh St at Nos 6, 12, 14, 20, 22, 34, 36, 40 and 80.

The *Thanh Binh Hotel* (☎ 0325) is across the street from the main building of the Central Market at 40-42 Nguyen Thi Minh Khai St. Around the corner is *Nha Khach* ('Guest House'; ☎ 2375) at 27A Nguyen Thi Minh Khai St. Also on the loop of road that goes around the Central Market complex is *Tan Son Dormitory* at 20B Nguyen Thi Minh Khai St – each room has six beds.

Nha Khach 90 (☎ 2468), which is up behind the Central Market area on a hilltop above Xuan Huong Lake, is at 12 Phan Boi Chau St. There are half a dozen small guest houses a few hundred metres down Phan Boi Chau St at 4, 4C, 4F, 1/3 and 1 Bui Thi Xuan St.

If you're unsuccessful at these cheaper hotels around the central area, you may have more luck at the *Anh Dao Hotel* (☎ 2384), up the steps from the Central Market on Nguyen Chi Thanh St. Rooms are US$6, US$9 and US$12. Directly across the roundabout from the market, the big *Hai Son Hotel* (☎ 2379) also readily accepts foreign visitors and has a wide variety of rooms from US$7 right up to US$32 for singles, and from US$10 to US$38 for doubles.

Phan Dinh Phung St There are several hotels along Phan Dinh Phung St, which is

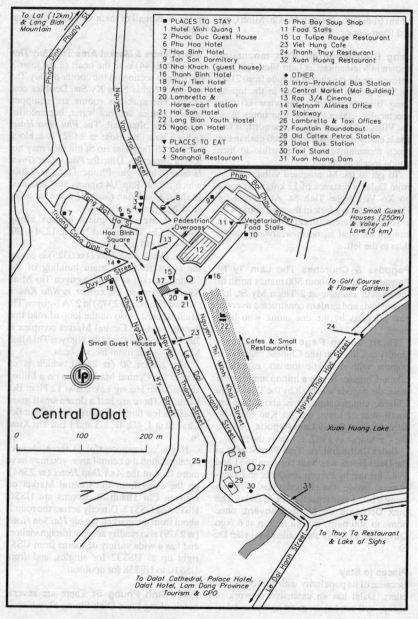

To Lat (12km)
& Lang Bidn
Mountain

■ PLACES TO STAY	
1 Hotel Vinh Quang 1	5 Pho Bay Soup Shop
2 Phuoc Duc Guest House	11 Food Stalls
6 Phu Hoa Hotel	15 La Tulipe Rouge Restaurant
7 Hoa Binh Hotel	23 Viet Hung Cafe
9 Tan Son Dormitory	24 Thanh Thuy Restaurant
10 Nha Khach (guest house)	32 Xuan Huong Restaurant
16 Thanh Binh Hotel	
18 Thuy Tien Hotel	● OTHER
19 Anh Dao Hotel	8 Intra-Provincial Bus Station
20 Lambretta &	12 Central Market (Mai Building)
Horse-cart station	13 Rap 3/4 Cinema
21 Hai Son Hotel	14 Vietnam Airlines Office
22 Lang Bian Youth Hostel	17 Stairway
25 Ngoc Lan Hotel	26 Lambretta & Taxi Offices
	27 Fountain Roundabout
▼ PLACES TO EAT	28 Old Caltex Petrol Station
3 Cafe Tung	29 Dalat Bus Station
4 Shanghai Restaurant	30 Taxi Stand
	31 Xuan Huong Dam

Phan Boi Chau Street

To Small Guest
Houses (250m)
& Valley of
Love (5 km)

Pedestrian
Overpass

Vegetarian
Food Stalls

Hoa Binh
Square

Phan Dinh Phung St

Nguyen Van Troi Street

Long Bot Ho St

Truong Cong Dinh St

Duy Tan Street

Khoi Nghia Nam Ky Street

Le Dai Hanh Street

Nguyen Chi Thanh Street

Nguyen Thi Minh Khai Street

To Golf Course
& Flower Gardens

Small Guest Houses

Central Dalat

0   100   200 m

Cafes & Small
Restaurants

Xuan Huong Lake

Nguyen Thai Hoc Street

To Small Guest Houses

To Thuy Ta Restaurant
& Lake of Sighs

To Dalat Cathedral, Palace Hotel,
Dalat Hotel, Lam Dong Province
Tourism & GPO

Le Dai Hanh Street

north-west down Truong Cong Dinh St from the town centre. The *Hoa Binh Hotel*, opposite 64 Truong Cong Dinh St at 127 Phan Dinh Phung St, has rooms for US$3.

The similarly priced *Cao Nguyen Hotel* is at 90 Phan Dinh Phung St. Across the street is the *Lien Hiep Hotel* (☎ 0319) at 147 Phan Dinh Phung St. *Thanh The Hotel* (☎ 2180) is a modern building at 118 Phan Dinh Phung St, and the *Khach San Van Hue* is next door. The *Mimosa Hotel* (☎ 0320) is at 170 Phan Dinh Phung St, while the *Lan Huong Guest House* (Nha Nghi Lan Huong) is at No 190.

The *Lam Son Hotel* (☎ 2362) is about a km west of the town centre in an old French villa at 5 Hai Thuong St; it is also very cheap. Although the rooms are nothing special, the *Duy Tan Hotel* (☎ 2216) at 82 3 Thang 2 St, near the corner with Hoang Van Thu St, is popular for people with cars as there's a car park. Rooms start from US$7 for doubles – slightly better rooms are US$10.

Top-End Without a doubt, the classiest place to stay in town is the *Palace Hotel* (Khach San Palace; ☎ 2203), a grand old place overlooking Xuan Huong Lake built between 1916 and 1922. Another vintage hostelry is the *Dalat Hotel* (Khach San Da Lat; ☎ 2363), constructed in 1907, which is at 7 Tran Phu St.

Many of Dalat's 2500 chalet-style villas can be rented; so can rooms in the Governor-General's Residence and Bao Dai's Summer Palace. For more information, contact Lam Dong Province Tourism.

Places to Eat

The *Shanghai Restaurant* is at 8 Khu Hoa Binh Quarter, on the other side of Rap 3/4 cinema from the Central Market. It serves Chinese, Vietnamese and French food from 8 am to 9.30 pm. Around the corner at 2 Tang Bat Ho St is *Pho Bay*, which specialises in pho (soup).

Cafe Tung at 6 Khu Hoa Binh St was a famous hang-out for Saigonese intellectuals during the 1950s. Old-timers swear that the place looks just like it did when they were young. As it did back then, Cafe Tung serves

only tea, coffee, hot cocoa, lemon soda and orange soda – to the accompaniment of mellow French music.

La Tulipe Rouge Restaurant (☎ 2394) is across the square from the main building of the Central Market at 1 Nguyen Thi Minh Khai St. It is open from 6 am to 9 pm. The fare includes Chinese, European and Vietnamese dishes.

There are dozens of food stalls in the covered area behind the main Central Market building. A number of cafes and small restaurants are along Nguyen Thi Minh Khai St between the Central Market and Xuan Huong Lake.

There are three vegetarian food stalls, each signposted com chay (vegetarian food), in the area of covered food stalls behind the main building of the Central Market. They are right across the street from 27A Nguyen Thi Minh Khai St.

Thuy Ta Restaurant (☎ 2268) is built on piles over the waters of Xuan Huong Lake. The panoramic view from the verandah encompasses almost the whole of the lake's forested coastline. The restaurant, which is directly below the Palace Hotel, is open from 6 am to 9 pm; it's a great place for breakfast. There are good restaurants in the *Palace Hotel* and the *Duy Tan Hotel*.

Getting There & Away

The road from Phan Rang to Dalat crosses the 980-metre Ngoan Muc Pass, also known as Bellevue Pass.

Air Dalat is served by Lien Khang Airport, which is about 30 km south of the city. At present, there are weekly flights to and from Ho Chi Minh City (US$28 one way) and Hanoi (US$143 one way). The Vietnam Airlines office in Dalat (☎ 0330) is at 5 Truong Cong Dinh St, across the street from Rap 3/4 cinema.

Bus The Dalat bus station (Ben Xe Dalat; ☎ 2077) is 100 metres towards the Central Market from Xuan Huong Dam (next to the old Caltex petrol station). The ticket office is open from 4.30 am to 5.30 pm. The

Intraprovincial bus station (Ben Xe Khach Noi Thanh) is one block north of Rap 3/4 cinema.

Getting Around

Taxi Rentable Peugeot 203s, all of them black with white roofs, park on the Central Market side of Xuan Huong Dam (next to the bus station) and near Rap 3/4 cinema. Lam Dong Tourism also rents out cars.

Hiking & Cycling The best way to enjoy the forests and cultivated countryside around Dalat is on foot, seated on horseback or pedalling a bicycle. Some suggested routes include:

1) Head out 3 Thang 4 St, which becomes National Highway 20, to the pine forests of Prenn Pass and Datanla Waterfall.
2) Go via the Governor-General's Residence onto Khe Sanh Rd and on to Thien Vuong Pagoda.
3) Taking Phu Dong Thien Huong St from Dalat University to the Valley of Love.
4) Go out to Bao Dai's Summer Palace and from there, after stopping at Lam Ty Ni Pagoda, head via Thien My and Huyen Tran Cong Chua Sts to Du Sinh Church.

DANANG

Danang (formerly Tourane), Vietnam's fourth-largest city (population 400,000), has become a leader in implementing economic reforms. Among the Danang-area sites of interest to visitors are the Marble Mountains, China Beach (Bai Non Nuoc), the ancient port town of Hoi An (Faifo), the Cham towers at My Son, Hai Van Pass (Col des Nuages) and Lang Co Beach.

Orientation

The main east-west artery of Danang is known at various points along its length as Hung Vuong St (in the city centre), Ly Thai To St (near the Central Market) and Dien Bien Phu St (out around the Intercity bus station). This thoroughfare is intersected by Bach Dang St, which runs along the Han River; Tran Phu St, one block west of Bach Dang St; and Phan Chu Trinh St (or Phan

■ **PLACES TO STAY**

1	Nha Nghi Du Lich Thanh Binh (hotel)
2	Dong Da Hotel (Khach San Huu Nghi)
3	Danang Hotel
4	Hai Van Hotel
5	Song Han Hotel
6	Railway Hotel
10	Nha Khach (hotel)
13	Khach San 32 (hotel)
20	Dong Kinh Hotel
26	Thu Do Hotel
28	Khach San Yen Minh Hotel & Thanh Thanh Hotel
34	Hai Chau Hotel
35	Pacific Hotel (Thai Binh Duong Hotel)
36	Orient Hotel (Phuong Dong Hotel)

▼ **PLACES TO EAT**

15	Thanh Lich Restaurant
17	Seamen's Club (cafe)
19	Nha Hang 72 (restaurant)
25	Chin Den Restaurant
27	Cafe
30	Thanh Huong Restaurant
33	Ice Cream (Kem) Cafes
37	Tiem An Binh Dan (restaurant)
38	Tu Do & Kim Do Restaurants
39	Quan Chay Vegetarian Restaurant

OTHER

7	Foreign Trade Bank (Vietcombank)
8	People's Committee of Quang Nam-Danang Province
9	Market
11	Cao Dai Temple
12	Ancient Renault Buses
14	Vietnam Airlines Booking Office
16	GPO
18	Danang Tourism & Tourist Shop
21	Former US Consulate
22	Ferries across the Han River
23	Short-Haul Pickup Truck Station
24	Con Market
29	Municipal Theatre
31	Cho Han (market)
32	Danang Cathedral
40	Phap Lam Pagoda (Chua Tinh Hoi)
41	Cham Museum
42	Tam Bao Pagoda
43	Pho Da Pagoda

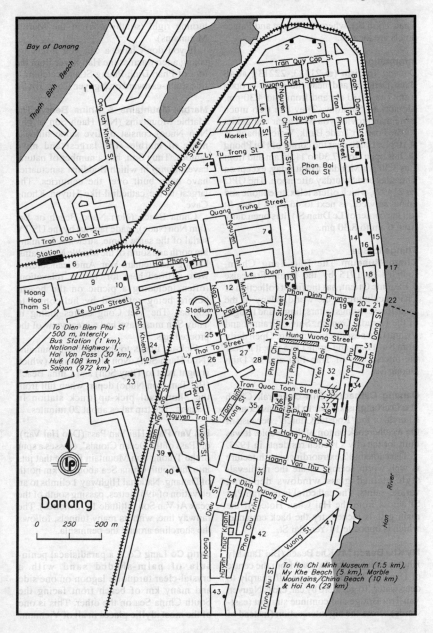

Bay of Danang

Thanh Binh Beach

Market

Station

Hoang Hoa Tham St

To Dien Bien Phu St
500 m, Intercity
Bus Station (1 km),
National Highway 1,
Hai Van Pass (30 km),
Huế (108 km) &
Saigon (972 km)

Tran Quy Cap St

Ly Thuong Kiet Street

Nguyen Du

Le Loi St

Phan Boi Chau St

Ly Tu Trong St

Quang Trung Street

Tran Cao Van St

Hai Phong St

Le Duan Street

Le Duan Street

Stadium

Phan Dinh Phung Street

Hung Vuong Street

Ong Ich Khiem St

Dong Da Street

Pham Ngu Lao St

Ly Thai To Street

Tran Quoc Toan Street

Le Hong Phong St

Hoang Van Thu St

Le Dinh Duong St

Phan Chu Trinh St

Huynh Thuc Khang St

Vuong St

Han River

Danang

0   250   500 m

To Ho Chi Minh Museum (1.5 km),
My Khe Beach (5 km), Marble
Mountains/China Beach (10 km)
& Hoi An (29 km)

Chau Trinh St), where the Orient and Palace hotels are located.

Information

Danang Tourism (☎ 21423, 22213), at 48 Bach Dang St and near the GPO, is open from 7 to 11.30 am and from 1 to 4.30 pm, Monday to Saturday. They can't do much more than provide you with a car and guide.

The Foreign Trade Bank, Vietcombank, is at 108 Le Loi St near the corner of Hai Phong St. It is open from 7.30 to 11.30 am and from 1 to 3.30 pm Monday to Saturday, except on Thursday and Saturday afternoon. The GPO (☎ 21499), which offers telex, telephone and postal services, is next to 46 Bach Dang St (on the corner of Le Duan St). It is open daily from 6 am to 8.30 pm.

Things to See

Cham Museum The Bao Tang Cham, founded in 1915 by the École Française d'Extrême Orient, has the finest collection of Cham sculpture in the world. Many of the sandstone carvings (altars, lingas and images of the Garuda, Ganesh, Shiva, Brahma and Vishnu) are absolutely stunning. Open daily from 8 to 11 am and from 1 to 5 pm; it is near the intersection of Tran Phu and Le Dinh Duong Sts.

Danang Cathedral This cathedral, Chinh Toa Da Nang, is known to locals as Con Ga Church, or the 'Rooster Church', because of the weathercock on top of the steeple. It was built for the city's French residents in 1923.

The cathedral's extraordinary architecture is well worth seeing, as are the medieval-style stained glass windows depicting various saints. The cathedral is on Tran Phu St across from the Hai Chau Hotel. If the main gate is locked, try the back entrance, which is opposite 14 Yen Bai St.

My Khe Beach My Khe Beach (Bai Tam My Khe) is about six km by road from the centre of Danang. The beach drops off sharply to deep water. To get there by car, cross Nguyen Van Troi Bridge and continue straight (east-wards) across the big intersection (instead of turning right (southwards) to the Marble Mountains).

If you don't have a car, you might try taking a ferry across the Han River from the foot of Phan Dinh Phung St and catching a ride south-eastward on Nguyen Cong Tru St.

Marble Mountains & China Beach The Marble Mountains (Ngu Hanh Son or Nui Non Nuoc) consist of five stone hillocks made of marble. The largest and most famous, Thuy Son, has a number of natural caves *(dong)* in which Buddhist sanctuaries have been built over the centuries. The largest is the cathedral-like Huyen Khong Cave.

China Beach (Non Nuoc Beach or Bai Tam Non Nuoc), made famous by the US TV serial of the same name, stretches for many km north and south of the Marble Mountains. During the Vietnam War, American soldiers were airlifted here for 'rest & relaxation' (often including a picnic on the beach) before being returned by helicopter to combat. The Viet Cong cadres hiding in Thuy Son must have had a great view of the proceedings.

Pick-up trucks to the Marble Mountains (Ngu Hanh Son), Non Nuoc Hamlet (which is right next to Thuy Son) and China Beach (Bai Tam Non Nuoc) depart when full from the Short-haul pick-up truck station in Danang. The trip takes about 20 minutes.

Hai Van Pass Hai Van Pass (Deo Hai Van), or 'Pass of the Ocean Clouds', crosses a spur of the Truong Son Mountain Range that juts into the South China Sea about 30 km north of Danang. National Highway 1 climbs to an elevation of 496 metres, passing south of the peak Ai Van Son (altitude 1172 metres). The railway line, with its many tunnels, follows the shoreline around the peninsula.

Lang Co Lang Co is a paradisiacal penin-sula of palm-shaded sand with a crystal-clear turquoise lagoon on one side and many km of beach front facing the South China Sea on the other. This is one of the most idyllic places in all of Vietnam.

There are spectacular views of Lang Co, which is just north of Hai Van Pass, from both National Highway 1 and the train linking Danang and Hué.

Lang Co railway station, served by non-express trains, is almost exactly midway between Danang and Hué. National Highway 1 also passes by Lang Co.

My Son My Son, which is 60 km south-west of Danang, is Vietnam's most important Cham site. During the centuries when nearby Simhapura (Tra Kieu) served as the political capital of Champa, My Son was the site of the most important Cham intellectual and religious centre and may also have served as a burial place for Cham monarchs. My Son is considered to be Champa's counterpart to the grand cities of South-East Asia's other Indian-influenced civilisations: Angkor (Cambodia), Bagan (Burma/Myanmar), Ayuthaya (Thailand) and Borobudur (Java).

You can get a good view of the outlines of Simhapura, the capital of Champa from the 4th to the 8th centuries, from the Mountain Church (Nha Tho Nui), which is on the top of Buu Chau Hill in the town of Tra Kieu.

During the Vietnam War, the My Son area was the sight of very heavy fighting. Beware of mines – do not stray from the paths!

Places to Stay
The *Danang Hotel* (☎ 21179) at 3 Dong Da St is at the northern tip of the peninsula on which Danang is situated. It's about a two km walk from both the town centre and popular restaurants but the rooms, though plain and somewhat run-down, are cheap with doubles at US$5. Even by Vietnamese standards, the electrical wiring looks lethal. Next door at 7 Dong Da St is the *Dong Da Hotel* (☎ 22563), also known as *Khach San Huu Nghi*. Foreigners are charged US$6 to US$12.

A bit closer to the railroad station and town centre is the *Hai Van Hotel* (☎ 21300) at 2 Nguyen Thi Minh Khai St. Foreigners pay US$7 for a double with air-con. The *Song Han Hotel* (☎ 22540) is alongside the Han River at 26 Bach Dang St. Single/double

rooms, some with air-con, cost from US$12/16 to US$25/30 for foreigners.

The *Hai Chau Hotel* (☎ 22722) at 177 Tran Phu St has a great location, but recently, prices for foreigners have taken a mighty upward leap – singles/doubles are now US$12/18 or US$24/26.

Cheaper places in central Danang include the *Thanh Thanh Hotel* (☎ 21230) at 54 Phan Chu Trinh St where rooms are from US$6 to US$12. A couple of doors down is the cheaper *Khach San Yen Minh*.

To the left of the parking lot as you exit the railway station building is the four storey *Khach San Duong Sat 29-3* (☎ 22794). The 200 dorm beds come with mats only and cost less than US$1 a night.

There are a number of places around the Intercity bus station offering extremely basic dormitory accommodation. *Nha Tro Ben Xe* (Bus Station Dormitory) is a yellow building on the east side of the bus station parking lot (across the street from 208 Dien Bien Phu St). There are two establishments simply called *Nha Tro* at 196 and 198 Dien Bien Phu St. *Phong Tro So 1* is at 194 Dien Bien Phu St, and *Phong Tro So 2* is down the block at 214 Dien Bien Phu St. *Nha Khach* is at 186 Dien Bien Phu St.

Out at China Beach, the *Non Nuoc Hotel* (☎ 21470, 22137) has singles/doubles with both air-con and fan for US$22/25 (plus 10% service). The restaurant will change US$. The hotel is often full, so call first if you don't have reservations.

Places to Eat
The best restaurant in Danang (and one of the best in Vietnam) is the *Tu Do Restaurant* (☎ 22039) at 172 Tran Phu St, 100 metres from the Hai Chau Hotel. It is open from 7 am to 9 pm. Some of the prices here are higher than you'd generally expect to pay but you can still eat well at a very reasonable price.

Next door at 174 Tran Phu St is the slightly flashier *Kim Do Restaurant*, where the food is also excellent. A few doors down in the other direction at 166 is *Tiem An Binh Dan Restaurant*, a modest place with reasonable prices. Turn the corner on to Tran Quoc Toan St, and there's a collection of popular ice-cream (*kem*) places.

The *Thanh Huong Restaurant* (☎ 22101) at 40 Hung Vuong St (on the corner of Tran Phu St) is a small, friendly place with a local clientele. It's a good place for morning pho. There are dozens of food stalls behind the main building of Con Market, which is on Ly Thai To St at Ong Ich Khiem St. *An Vong Restaurant* is at 137 Hung Vuong St. Near the GPO at 42 Bach Dang St, the *Thanh Lich Restaurant* has an extensive menu in English, French and Vietnamese.

Quan Chay at 484 Ong Ich Khiem St (162 Ong Ich Khiem by the old numbers) is a vegetarian food stall half a block from Phap Lam Pagoda (Chua Tinh Hoi), and about a km from the city centre; it is open daily from 7 am to 4 pm.

Finally, for a late evening drink, head for the extremely popular *Tuoi Hong Cafe* at 34 Phan Dinh Phung St (on the corner of Phan Chu Trinh St). It's the music which makes this place so popular with local young people.

Things to Buy

Danang seems particularly well-endowed with tailors, many of whom have shops along Hung Vuong St. For a pittance over the cost of the cloth, you can have high-quality shirts, trousers and skirts tailored to measure. Cloth is available either from the tailors' stock or at the cloth stalls near the intersection of Hung Vuong and Yen Bai Sts.

Getting There & Away

Air The Danang office of Vietnam Airlines (☎ 21130) is at 35 Tran Phu St. There are daily flights to and from Ho Chi Minh City and Hanoi.

Bus The Danang Intercity bus station (Ben Xe Khach Da Nang; ☎ 21265) is about three km from the city centre on the thoroughfare known, at various points along its length, as Hung Vuong, Ly Thai To and Dien Bien Phu Sts. The ticket office for express buses is across the street from 200 Dien Bien Phu St.

It is open from 7 to 11 am and from 1 to 5 pm. The nonexpress ticket office is open from 5 am until the late afternoon.

Lambrettas and small passenger trucks to places in the vicinity of Danang (including the Marble Mountains, China Beach and Hoi An) leave from the Short-haul pick-up truck station opposite 80 Hung Vuong St. The station operates from about 5 am to about 5 pm.

Train Danang railway station (Ga Da Nang) is about 1½ km from the city centre on Haiphong St (at the northern end of Hoang Hoa Tham St). The train ride to Hué is one of the nicest in the country (though driving up and over Hai Van Pass is also spectacular).

Boat There's a regular boat service between Danang and Haiphong.

Getting Around

The Danang Hotel at 3 Dong Da St hires out bicycles for less than US$1 per day.

HOI AN (FAIFO)

Hoi An (Faifo) was one of South-East Asia's major international ports during the 17th, 18th and 19th centuries. Today, parts of Hoi An look exactly as they did a century-and-a-half ago. Hoi An was the site of the first Chinese settlement in southern Vietnam.

Information

The Hoi An Tourist Service and Monuments Management Authority (Ban Quan Ly Di Tich; ☎ K72), which can provide a tour guide if contacted before your arrival, is at 100 Tran Phu St.

Things to See

Japanese Covered Bridge This bridge (Cau Nhat Ban, or Lai Vien Kieu) connects 155 Tran Phu St with 1 Nguyen Thi Minh Khai St. The first bridge on this site was constructed in 1593 by the Japanese community of Hoi An to link their neighbourhood with the Chinese quarters across the stream.

Houses The **Tan Ky House** at 101 Nguyen

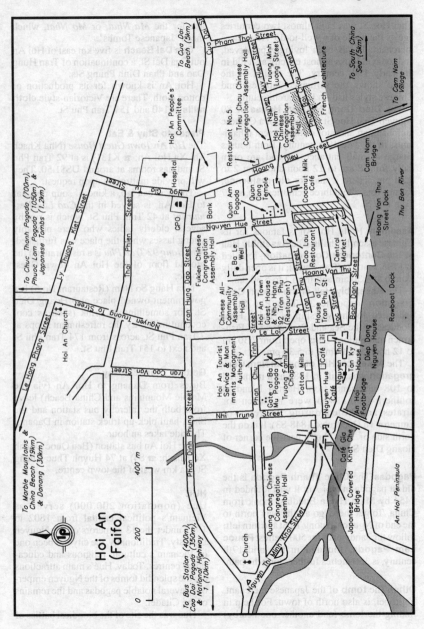

Hoi An
(Faifo)

Thai Hoc St was built almost two centuries ago as the home of a well-to-do Vietnamese merchant. It has been lovingly preserved, and today it looks almost exactly as it did in the early 19th century. The design of the house shows the influence Japanese and Chinese styles had on local architecture.

The **Diep Dong Nguyen House** at 80 Nguyen Thai Hoc St was built for a Chinese merchant, an ancestor of the present inhabitants, in the late 19th century. Both houses charge a small entrance fee and are open daily from 8 am to 12 noon and from 2 to 4.30 pm. There is another **old residence**, dating from about three centuries ago, at 77 Tran Phu St.

Assembly Halls Hoi An is famous for its Chinese assembly halls. The **Assembly Hall of the Cantonese Congregation**, founded in 1786, is at 176 Tran Phu St; it is open daily from 6 to 7.30 am and from 1 to 5.30 pm.

The **Assembly Hall of the Fukien Congregation**, opposite 35 Tran Phu St, is dedicated to the worship of Thien Hau, Goddess of the Sea and Protectress of Fishermen and Sailors – it is open from 7.30 am to 12 noon and from 2 to 5.30 pm.

The **Assembly Hall of the Hai Nam Congregation** was built in 1883 as a memorial to 108 merchants from Hainan Island in southern China who were mistaken for pirates and killed during the reign of Emperor Tu Duc (ruled 1848-83). It is on the north side of Tran Phu St near the corner of Hoang Dieu St.

Pagodas The **Chuc Thanh Pagoda** is the oldest pagoda in Hoi An. It was founded in 1454 by Minh Hai, a Buddhist monk from China. To get there, go all the way north to the end of Nguyen Truong To St and turn left; follow the sandy path for 500 metres. **Phuoc Lam Pagoda**, founded in the mid-17th century, is 350 metres further along the path.

Other The **tomb** of the Japanese merchant, Yajirobei, is also north of town. For help in finding the tomb (and another one nearby) ask for the *Ma Nhat*, or *Mo Nhat*, which mean 'Japanese Tombs'.

Cua Dai Beach is five km east of Hoi An out Cua Dai St, a continuation of Tran Hung Dao and Phan Dinh Phung Sts.

Hoi An is known for its production of cotton cloth. There are Victorian-style **cloth mills** at 140 and 151 Tran Phu St.

Places to Stay & Eat

The *Hoi An Town Guest House* (Nha Khach Thi Xa Hoi An; ☎ K131) is at 92 Tran Phu St and has rooms at around US$1.50. They will provide mattresses upon request.

The best cau lao, a kind of soup peculiar to Hoi An, is served in the *Cao Lau Restaurant* at 42 Tran Phu St, which is run by several elderly ladies who were probably young lasses when the place was furnished. *Nha Hang 92 Tran Phu* is a restaurant on the ground floor of the Hoi An Town Guest House.

Nha Hang So Nam (Restaurant No 5) is a government-owned place at 5 Hoang Dieu St. For something to drink (such as cool coconut milk), try the refreshment shops at 7 Tran Phu St, across from 174 Tran Phu St and next to 151 Tran Phu St.

Getting There & Away

Buses from Danang to Hoi An (via the Marble Mountains and China Beach) leave from both the Intercity bus station and the Short-haul pick-up truck station in Danang. The ride takes an hour.

The Hoi An bus station (Ben Quoc Doanh Xe Khach; ☎ 84) at 74 Huynh Thuc Khang St is a km west of the town centre.

HUÉ

Hué (population 200,000) served as Vietnam's political capital from 1802 to 1945 under the 13 emperors of the Nguyen Dynasty. Traditionally, the city has been one of Vietnam's cultural, religious and educational centres. Today, Hué's main attractions are the splendid tombs of the Nguyen emperors, several notable pagodas and the remains of the Citadel.

Hué was the site of the bloodiest battles of

the 1968 Tet Offensive and was held by the Viet Cong and North Vietnamese for 25 days.

Orientation

Hué is bisected by the Perfume River (Huong Giang, or Song Huong). The Citadel is on the left (northern) bank. Across the Dong Ba Canal from Dong Ba Market are the subdistricts of Phu Cat and Phu Hiep, known for their Chinese pagodas.

On the right (southern) bank of the Perfume River is the New City, once known as the European Quarter. Le Loi St runs along the river. The Royal Tombs are spread out over a large area to the south of the New City.

Information

Tourist Office The offices of Thua Thien-Hué Province Tourism (Cong Ty Du Lich Thua Thien-Hué; ☎ 2369, 2288, 2355) are in the building to the right as you enter the gate of the Huong Giang Hotel, which is at 51 Le Loi St. The office is open from 7 to 11.30 am and from 1.30 to 5 pm. Hué City Tourism (Cong Ty Du Lich Thanh Pho Hué; ☎ 3577) is at 18 Le Loi St (on the corner of Ha Noi St).

Money Hué's only foreign exchange bank is the Industrial & Commercial Bank (Nhan Hang Cong Thuong; ☎ 3275) at 2A Le Quy Don St. It is open Monday to Saturday from 7 to 11.30 am and from 1.30 to 4 pm. The Huong Giang Hotel will also change money.

Post International postal and telephone services are available at the GPO, which is opposite 7 Hoang Hoa Tham St and open from 6.30 am to 9 pm. International postal, telephone and telex services are available at the post office (☎ 3093) on the 2nd floor of the Huong Giang Hotel (☎ 2122) at 51 Le Loi St. The postal windows are supposed to be open from 9 am to 1 pm and from 5 to 9 pm.

Things to See

The Citadel Construction of the moated Citadel (Kinh Thanh), whose perimeter is 10 km, was begun in 1804 by Emperor Gia Long on a site chosen by geomancers. The emperor's official functions were carried out in the **Imperial Enclosure** (Dai Noi, or Hoang Thanh), a citadel-within-the-citadel whose six-metre-high-wall is 2½ km in length. The Imperial Enclosure has four gates, the most famous of which is Ngo Mon Gate.

Within the Imperial Enclosure is the **Forbidden Purple City** (Tu Cam Thanh), which was reserved for the private life of the emperor. Wide areas within the Citadel, especially within the Forbidden Purple City, are devoted to agriculture – a legacy of the destruction of 1968.

The 37-metre-high **Flag Tower**, just south of Ngo Mon Gate, is Vietnam's tallest flagpole. During the VC occupation of Hué in 1968, the Viet Cong flag flew defiantly from the tower for 3½ weeks. Just inside the Citadel ramparts, near the gates and to either side of the Flag Tower, are the **Nine Holy Cannons**, symbolic protectors of the palace and kingdom, which date from 1804.

The principle gate to the Imperial Enclosure is **Ngo Mon Gate** (Noontime Gate), which faces the Flag Tower. It is open from 6.30 am to 5.30 pm. The entrance fee for foreigners is US$1. **Thai Hoa Palace** was used for the emperor's official receptions and other important court ceremonies, such as anniversaries and coronations. The Nine Dynastic Urns, weighing 1900 to 2600 kg each, symbolise the power and stability of the Nguyen throne.

The beautiful hall which houses the **Imperial Museum** was built in 1845. It was restored in 1923 when the museum, which is just outside the Imperial Enclosure on Le Truc St, was founded. It is open from 6.30 am to 5.30 pm.

Royal Tombs The **Tombs of the Nguyen Dynasty** (1802-1945) are seven to 16 km south of Hué. They are open from 6.30 am to 5 pm daily and the entrance fee to each tomb is US$1. The best way to tour the Royal Tombs is by bicycle.

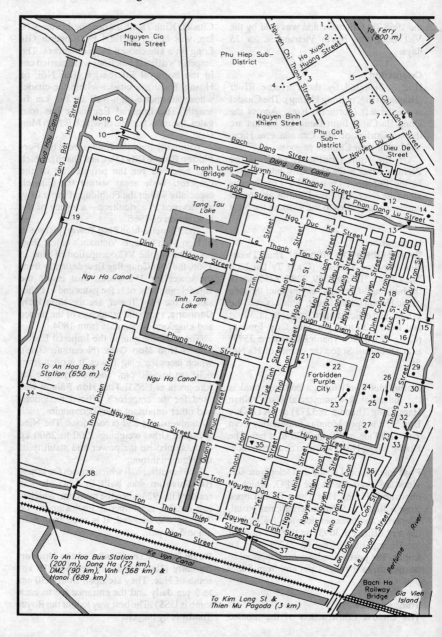

Nguyen Gia Thieu Street

Phu Hiep Sub-District

Nguyen Chi Thanh Street

Ho Xuan Huong Street

To Ferry (800 m)

Chi Lang Street

Chua Ong St

Nguyen Du St

Nguyen Binh Khiem Street

Phu Cat Sub-District

Dieu De Street

Mang Ca

Gia Hoi Canal

Tang Bat Ho Street

Bach Dang Street

Dong Ba Canal

Thanh Long Bridge

Huynh Thuc Khong Street

Phan Dong Lu Street

1968 Street

Tang Tau Lake

Ngo Duc Ke Street

Le Thanh Ton St

Nguyen Dieu Street

Chi Dieu Street

Dinh Cong Trang Street

Tong Duy Tan St

Dinh Tien Hoang Street

Ngu Ha Canal

Tinh Tam Lake

Tinh Tom Street

Nhat Le Street

Ngo Si Lien St

Mai Thuc Loan Street

Dang Thuyen Street

Le Truc St

Phung Hung Street

Duan Thi Diem Street

Ngu Ha Canal

To An Hoa Bus Station (650 m)

Phien Street

Tue Tinh Street

Doan Thoi Phan Street

Forbidden Purple City

Le Huan Street

Thong 8 Street

Nguyen Trai Street

Quang Phuc Street

Thach Han Street

Han Thuyen Street

Ngo Thoi Nhiem Street

Nguyen Thien Thuat St

Dong Tran Con St

Nho Dong Tran Con Street

Le Duan Street

Tran Nguyen Dan St

Yet Kieu Street

Lon Dong Tran Con Street

Ton That Thiep Street

Triew Quang Phuc Street

Nguyen Cu Trinh Street

Ke Von Canal

To An Hoa Bus Station (200 m), Dong Ha (72 km), DMZ (90 km), Vinh (368 km) & Hanoi (689 km)

To Kim Long St & Thien Mu Pagoda (3 km)

Perfume River

Bach Ho Railway Bridge

Gia Vien Island

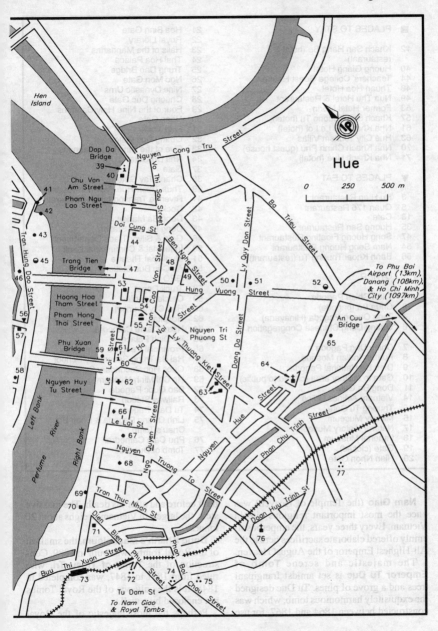

Hue

Hen Island

Dap Da Bridge

39

40

Chu Van Am Street

Phom Ngu Lao Street

41

42

Doi Cung St

43

45

Trang Tien Bridge

44

46

47

48

49

53

Hoang Hoa Tham Street

Phom Hong Thai Street

54

55

Phu Xuan Bridge

56

57

59

58

60

61

Nguyen Huy Tu Street

62

66

Le Lai St

67

68

69

70

71

Dien Bien

Buu Thi Xuan Street

73

72

74

75

76

77

Nguyen Cong Tru Street

Vo Thi Sau Street

Ben Nghe Street

Hung Vuong Street

Ly Quy Don Street

Bà Triệu Street

50

51

52

An Cuu Bridge

64

65

63

Dong Da Street

Nguyen Tri Phuong St

Ly Thuong Kiet Street

Hue Street

Phan Chu Trinh Street

Nguyen Truong To Street

Tran Thuc Nhan St

Doan Huy Trinh St

Phan Boi Chau Street

Chou Street

Tu Dam St

To Nam Giao & Royal Tombs

Perfume River

Left Bank

Right Bank

Le Loi Street

Ha Noi Street

Tran Cao Van Street

0   250   500 m

To Phu Bai Airport (13km), Danang (108km), & Ho Chi Minh City (1097km)

■ PLACES TO STAY

12	Khach San Hang Be (hotel & restaurant)
40	Huong Giang Hotel
44	Teachers' College Guest House
48	Thuan Hoa Hotel
49	Nua Thu Hotel & Restaurant
53	Former Hotel Morin
57	Khach San Thuong Tu (hotel)
61	Nha Khach 18 Le Loi (hotel)
63	Hué City Tourism Villas
70	Nha Khach Chinh Phu (guest house)
71	Nha Khach Hué (hotel)

▼ PLACES TO EAT

3	Hu Hiep Restaurant
5	Quan 176 Restaurant
13	Cafe
35	Huong Sen Restaurant
47	Song Huong Floating Restaurant
54	Nam Song Huong Restaurant
56	Banh Khoai Thuong Tu (restaurant)

OTHER

1	Trieu Chieu Pagoda
2	Chua Ba (pagoda)
4	Tang Quang Pagoda (Hinayana)
6	Quang Dong Chinese Congregation Hall
7	Chieu Ung Pagoda
8	Former Indian Mosque
9	Dieu De National Pagoda
10	Gate to military area (closed to public)
11	Dong Ba Gate
14	Vietnam Airlines Office
15	Thuong Tu Gate
16	Military Museum
17	Natural History Museum
18	Imperial Museum
19	Gate (closed)
20	Hien Nhon Gate

21	Hoa Binh Gate
22	Royal Library
23	Halls of the Mandarins
24	Thai Hoa Palace
25	Trung Dao Bridge
26	Ngo Mon Gate
27	Nine Dynastic Urns
28	Chuong Duc Gate
29	Four of the Nine Holy Cannons
30	Ngan Gate
31	Flag Tower
32	Quang Duc Gate
33	Five of the Nine Holy Cannons
34	Nha Do Gate
37	Gate
38	Chanh Tay Gate
39	Thua Thien-Hué Province Tourism
41	Riverine Transportation Cooperative
42	Dock
43	Dong Ba Market
45	Dong Ba Bus Station
46	Gold & Silver Trade Department
50	Industrial & Commercial Bank
51	Municipal Theatre
52	An Cuu Bus Station
55	GPO
58	Truck Depot
59	Cercle Sportif
60	Hué City Tourism
62	Hospital
64	Notre Dame Cathedral
65	An Dinh Palace
66	Provincial People's Committee
67	Hai Ba Trung Secondary School
68	Quoc Hoc Secondary School
69	Ho Chi Minh Museum
72	Bao Quoc Pagoda
73	Railway Station
74	Tu Dam Pagoda
75	Linh Quang Pagoda & Phan Boi Chau's Tomb
76	Phu Cam Cathedral
77	Tomb of Duc Duc

Nam Giao (the Temple of Heaven) was once the most important religious site in Vietnam. Every three years, the emperor solemnly offered elaborate sacrifices here to the All-Highest Emperor of the August Heaven.

The majestic and serene **Tomb of Emperor Tu Duc** is set amidst frangipani trees and a grove of pines. Tu Duc designed the exquisitely harmonious tomb, which was constructed between 1864 and 1867, for use both before and after his death. The massive stele, the largest in Vietnam, weighs about 20 tonnes.

Dong Khanh's Mausoleum, the smallest of the Royal Tombs, was built in 1889. Construction of the **Tomb of Thieu Tri**, who ruled from 1841 to 1847, was completed in 1848. It is the only one of the Royal Tombs not enclosed by a wall.

Perhaps the most majestic of the Royal

Tombs is the **Tomb of Minh Mang** who ruled from 1820 to 1840. The tomb, which is 12 km from Hué on the left bank of the Perfume River (there's a ferry from a point about 1½ km south-west of Khai Dinh's Tomb), is known for the harmonious blending of its architecture with the natural surroundings.

The gaudy and crumbling **Tomb of Emperor Khai Dinh**, who ruled from 1916 to 1925, is perhaps symptomatic of the decline of Vietnamese culture during the colonial period. Begun in 1920 and completed in 1931, the grandiose reinforced concrete structure makes no pretence of trying to blend in with the countryside.

The architecture, completely unlike that of Hué's other tombs, is an unfortunate synthesis of Vietnamese and European elements. Even the stone faces of the mandarin honour guards are endowed with a blend of Vietnamese and European features.

Pagodas, Temples & Churches The **Thien Mu Pagoda** (also known as Linh Mu Pagoda), built on a hillock overlooking the Perfume River, is one of the most famous structures in all of Vietnam. Its 21-metre-high octagonal tower, the seven-storey Thap Phuoc Duyen, was built by Emperor Thieu Tri in 1844 and has become the unofficial symbol of Hué.

The pagoda, founded in 1601, is on the banks of the Perfume River, four km south-west of the Citadel. To get there from Dong Ba Market, head south-west (parallel to the river) on Tran Hung Dao St, which turns into Le Duan St after Phu Xuan Bridge. Cross the railway tracks and keep going on Kim Long St. Thien Mu Pagoda can also be reached by sampan.

The **Bao Quoc Pagoda** was founded in 1670 by a Buddhist monk from China, Giac Phong. It was given its present name, which means 'pagoda which serves the country', in 1824 by Emperor Minh Mang, who celebrated his 40th birthday here in 1830. In the orchid-lined courtyard behind the sanctuary is the cage of a most extraordinary parrot (*nhong*). To get to the pagoda, head south from Le Loi St on Dien Bien Phu St; turn

right immediately after crossing the railway tracks.

Notre Dame Cathedral (Dong Chua Cuu The) at 80 Nguyen Hue St is an impressive modern building which combines functional aspects of a European cathedral with traditional Vietnamese elements, including an Oriental spire. If you find the gate locked, ring the bell of the yellow building next door.

There are quite a few pagodas and Chinese congregational halls in Phu Cat and Phu Hiep subdistricts, which are across the Dong Ba Canal from Dong Ba Market. The entrance to **Dieu De National Pagoda** (Quoc Tu Dieu De), built under Emperor Thieu Tri (ruled 1841-47), is along Dong Ba Canal at 102 Bach Dang St. During the 1960s, it was a stronghold of Buddhist and student opposition to the South Vietnamese government and the war. Hué's Indian Muslim community constructed the **mosque**, at 120 Chi Lang St, in 1932.

Chieu Ung Pagoda (Chieu Ung Tu) opposite 138 Chi Lang St was founded by the Hai Nam Chinese congregation in the mid-19th century and was rebuilt in 1908.

The **Quang Dong Chinese Congregational Hall** (Chua Quang Dong), founded almost a century ago, is opposite 154 Chi Lang St. **Chua Ba**, a pagoda, across the street from 216 Chi Lang St, was founded by the Hai Nam Chinese congregation almost 100 years ago. It was damaged in the 1968 Tet Offensive and was later reconstructed.

Tang Quang Pagoda (Tang Quang Tu), which is just down the road from 80 Nguyen Chi Thanh St, is the largest of the three Hinayana (Theravada) pagodas in Hué. Built in 1957, it owes its distinctive architecture to Hinayana Buddhism's historical links with Sri Lanka and India (rather than China).

Other Sights The Quoc Hoc Secondary School on the right bank is one of the most famous secondary schools in Vietnam. Many of the school's pupils, including (briefly) Ho Chi Minh, later rose to prominence in both North and South Vietnam.

The Trang Tien Bridge (formerly the Nguyen Hoang Bridge) across the Perfume

River was blown up in 1968 and later repaired. The newer Phu Xuan Bridge was built in 1971.

Thuan An Beach Thuan An Beach (Bai Tam Thuan An), 13 km north-east of Hué, is on a splendid lagoon near the mouth of the Perfume River. Lambrettas and old Renaults from Hué depart for Thuan An from the Dong Ba bus station. You might also try hiring a sampan to make the trip by river. At Thuan An, you can stay at the Tan My Hotel.

Places to Stay

Right Bank *Nha Khach Hué* (☎ 2153) is 200 metres from the railroad station at 2 Le Loi St; there are a variety of rooms from US$6 to US$12. *Nha Khach 18 Le Loi* (☎ 3720) at 18 Le Loi St is run by Hué City Tourism. Doubles cost US$7, or US$10 with air-con.

The *Huong Giang Hotel* (☎ 2122) is at 51 Le Loi St, which is almost directly across the Perfume River from Dong Ba Market. Single/double rooms cost US$20/22 to US$30/35 (plus 10% service).

The most delightful accommodation in Hué are three small villas *(Nha Khach)* along Ly Thuong Kiet St. Run by Hué City Tourism, they each have a homey living room and some of the nicest rooms in town – meals are prepared on request for US$8 per day. Doubles/triples in the villa at 18 Ly Thuong Kiet St (☎ 3889; 5 rooms) cost US$16/20. Next door at No 16 there is a slightly larger villa (☎ 3679). The villa at No 11 (four rooms) charges US$16 for a double, US$18 for a triple and US$20 for a quad.

Another interesting place is *Nha Khach Chinh Phu*, a palatial villa once used as the palace of the Governor of Central Vietnam and later, after reunification, as a guest house for important visitors. It's by the river at 5 Le Loi St, across the road from Nha Khach Hué; an enormous double room with equally spacious bathroom and veranda will cost US$15.

Left Bank *Khach San Thuong Tu* at 1 Dinh Tien Hoang St is not far from the Phu Xuan Bridge. *Khach San Hang Be* (☎ 3752) at 73

Huynh Thuc Khang St fronts Dong Ba Canal several blocks north-west of Dong Ba Market. These places are grubby but cheap – although they may not accept foreigners.

Places to Eat

Left Bank *Banh Khoai Thuong Tu* at 6 Dinh Tien Hoang St is a few blocks from the Flag Tower; it is open from 7 am to 8 pm. This restaurant serves a traditional Hué speciality, banh khoai, which is a crêpe with bean sprouts, shrimp and meat inside. It is eaten with greens, starfruit slices and nuoc leo, a thick brown sauce made with peanuts, sesame seeds and spices. Another Hué speciality, available here, is bun thit nuong, which is noodles, greens, fruit and fried dried meat eaten with nuoc leo.

Delicious sweet soups (che) made with such ingredients as beans and bananas are served either hot or iced in shops at 10 and 12 Dinh Tien Hoang St.

Quan 176 at 176 Chi Lang St is a small place in Phu Cat subdistrict. They serve traditional Hué pastries, including banh nam (a flat cake of rice flour, meat and shrimp fried in a banana leaf), banh loc (a chewy cake made of rice flour and shrimp and baked in a banana leaf) and cha tom (a flat cake made of meat, shrimp and egg).

The *Hang Be Restaurant* (☎ 3752) at 73 Huynh Thuc Khang St is on the ground floor of the Hang Be Hotel. Within the citadel, the *Huong Sen Restaurant* at 42 Nguyen Trai St is a pavilion on pylons in the middle of a lotus pond. It's a great place for a sunset Huda beer (poured over ice) from the Hué brewery.

Right Bank The restaurant on the 4th floor of the Huong Giang Hotel at 51 Le Loi St serves Vietnamese, European and vegetarian dishes. The food is decent and the prices are surprisingly reasonable. The *Song Huong Floating Restaurant*, moored by the river just north of Trang Tien Bridge, also offers fine views and reasonable prices.

The *Nam Song Huong Restaurant* at 7 Hoang Hoa Tham St, whose fare includes delicious soup and egg rolls, is opposite the GPO. It is open from 8.30 am to 9 pm.

Things to Buy

Hué is known for producing the finest conical hats in Vietnam. The city's speciality are 'poem hats' which, when held up to the light, reveal black cut-out scenes sandwiched between the layers of translucent palm leaves.

Dong Ba Market, which is on the left bank of the Perfume River a few hundred metres north of Trang Tien Bridge, is Hué's main market.

Getting There & Away

Air The booking office of Vietnam Airlines (☎ 2249) is a block from Dong Ba Market at 16 Phan Dang Luu St. It is open Monday to Saturday from 7 to 11 am and from 1.30 to 5 pm. Hué is served by Phu Bai Airport, once an important American air base, which is 14 km south of the city centre.

Bus Buses to places north of Hué depart from An Hoa bus station (Ben Xe An Hoa or Ben Xe So 1; ☎ 3014), which is at the western tip of the Citadel across from 499 Le Duan St (on the corner of Tang Bat Ho St). Almost all buses depart at 5 or 5.30 am. Tickets for some buses that leave from here can be purchased at An Cuu bus station.

Buses to points south of Hué leave from An Cuu bus station (☎ 3817), which is opposite 46 Hung Vuong St (on the corner Nguyen Hue St). The ticket windows are open from 5 to 11 am and from 1 to 6 pm.

Vehicles to destinations in the vicinity of Hué depart from Dong Ba bus station (Ben Xe Dong Ba; ☎ 3055), which is on the left bank of the Perfume River between Trang Tien Bridge and Dong Ba Market. There are entrances at 85 and 103 Tran Hung Dao St. Lambrettas go to An Cuu bus station, An Hoa bus station, Phu Bai Airport and Thuan An Beach.

Train Hué railway station (Ga Hué; ☎ 2175) is on the right bank at the south-west end of Le Loi St. The ticket office is open from 6.30 am to 5 pm.

Getting Around

Many sights in the vicinity of Hué, including Thuan An Beach, Thien Mu Pagoda and several of the Royal Tombs, can be reached by river. You might try hiring a boat behind Dong Ba Market or at the Riverine Transportation Cooperative (Van Tai Gioi Duong Song), whose office is right across Dong Ba Canal from Dong Ba Market.

Boats may also be available near Dap Da Bridge, which is a bit east of the Huong Giang Hotel. Hué Tourism and Thua Thien-Hué Province Tourism can arrange outings on the Perfume River.

Bicycles can be hired for US$1 a day from the Nha Khach Hué Hotel.

DMZ & Vicinity

From 1954 to 1975, the Ben Hai River served as the demarcation line between the Republic of Vietnam (South Vietnam) and the Democratic Republic of Vietnam (North Vietnam). The Demilitarised Zone (DMZ) consisted of an area five km to either side of the demarcation line.

Orientation

The old DMZ extends from the coast westward to the Lao border; National Highway 9 (Quoc Lo 9) runs more-or-less parallel to the DMZ. The Ho Chi Minh Trail (Duong Truong Son), actually a series of roads, trails and paths, ran from North Vietnam southward (perpendicular to National Highway 9) through the Truong Son Mountains and western Laos.

To prevent infiltrations and to interdict the flow of troops and materiel via the Ho Chi Minh Trail, the Americans established a line of bases along National Highway 9. A number of them can be visited in a day trip by car from Dong Ha.

Information

The office of Quang Tri Province Tourism (Du Lich Quang Tri; ☎ 239) is at the Dong Truong Son Hotel, which is three km from Dong Ha out Tran Phu St. Cars and guides are said to be available here, but you'll do better to arrange a guided visit to the area through Thua Thien-Hué Tourism in Hué.

Warning

At many of the places listed in this section you may find live mortar rounds, artillery shells and mines strewn about. *Never* touch any leftover ordnance and watch where you step. Even the local scrap collectors have left them there because they are unsafe!

BEN HAI RIVER

Twenty-two km north of Dong Ha, National Highway 1 crosses the Ben Hai River, once the demarcation line between North and South Vietnam, over the decrepit Hien Luong Bridge.

TUNNELS OF VINH MOC

The remarkable tunnels of Vinh Moc are yet another monument to the determination of the North Vietnamese to persevere and triumph, at all costs, in the war against South Vietnam and the USA.

In 1966, the villagers of Vinh Moc, facing incessant US aerial and artillery attacks, began tunnelling by hand into the red clay earth. After 18 months of work, the entire village of 1200 persons was relocated underground. The whole 2.8 km tunnel network, which remains in its original state, can be visited with a guide. Bring a torch (flashlight).

The turn-off to Vinh Moc from National Highway 1 is 6½ km north of the Ben Hai River, in the village of Ho Xa. Vinh Moc is 13 km from National Highway 1.

TRUONG SON NATIONAL CEMETERY

Truong Son National Cemetery (Nghia Trang Liet Si Truong Son) is a memorial to the tens of thousands of North Vietnamese soldiers killed along the Ho Chi Minh Trail. Row after row of white tombstones stretch across the hillsides in a scene eerily reminiscent of the endless lines of crosses and Stars of David in US military cemeteries.

The road to Truong Son National Cemetery intersects National Route 1 13 km north of Dong Ha and nine km south of the Ben Hai River. The distance from the highway to the cemetery is 17 km.

A rocky cart path, passable (but just barely) by car, links Cam Lo (on National Route 9) with Truong Son National Cemetery. The 18 km drive from Cam Lo to the cemetery passes by newly planted rubber plantations and the homes of the Bru (Van Kieu) tribespeople.

CAMP CARROLL

The gargantuan 175 mm cannons at Camp Carroll were used to shell targets as far away as Khe Sanh, over 30 km away. These days, there is not much to see here except a few overgrown trenches and the remains of their timber roofs. Bits of military hardware and lots of rusty shell casings litter the ground.

The turn-off to Camp Carroll is 11 km west of Cam Lo, 24 km east of the Dakrong Bridge and 37 km east of the Khe Sanh bus station. The base is three km from National Highway 9.

KHE SANH TOWN

Set amidst beautiful hills, valleys and fields at an elevation of about 600 metres, the town of Khe Sanh (Huong Hoa) is a pleasant district capital once known for its French-run coffee plantations. Many of the inhabitants are Bru tribespeople who have moved here from the surrounding hills. A popular pastime among the hill-tribe women is the smoking of long-stemmed pipes.

KHE SANH COMBAT BASE

Khe Sanh Combat Base, site of the most famous siege (and one of the most controversial battles) of the Vietnam War, sits silently on a barren plateau surrounded by vegetation-covered hills often obscured by mist and fog. In early 1968, about 500 Americans (the official figure of 205 American dead was arrived at by statistical sleight-of-hand) and uncounted thousands of North Vietnamese and local people died violently here.

To get to Khe Sanh Combat Base, turn north-westward at the triangular intersection 600 metres towards Dong Ha from Khe Sanh bus station. The base is on the right-hand side of the road 2½ km from the intersection.

LAO BAO

Lao Bao, 18 km from Khe Sanh, is right on the Tchepone River (Song Xe Pon), which marks the Vietnam-Laos border. Towering above Lao Bao on the Lao side of the border is Co Roc Mountain, once a North Vietnamese artillery stronghold. Two km towards Khe Sanh from the border crossing (at present it is closed to foreigners) is the lively Lao Bao Market.

Places to Stay

Dong Ha *Nha Khach Dong Ha* (☎ 361) is a pleasant official guest house 300 metres west of the French blockhouse (Lo Khot) on Tran Phu St. Rooms cost US$12 for foreigners. The large *Dong Truong Son Hotel* (Khach San Dong Truong Son; ☎ 239) is three km out Tran Phu St from the old French blockhouse.

The decrepit and filthy *Khach San Dong Ha* (☎ 213) is next to the bus station. Rooms for four, with mats and mosquito nets but without fans, cost US$2. The only good thing about this place is its proximity to the bus station.

Khe Sanh The *guest house* of the District People's Committee (Nha Khach Huyen Huong Hoa; ☎ 27 from the Dong Ha telephone exchange) is 300 metres south (towards Laos) from Khe Sanh bus station.

Places to Eat

Dong Ha There are a number of eateries along National Highway 1 (Le Duan St) between the bus station and Tran Phu St. There are more places to eat on Tran Phu St between the blockhouse and Nha Khach Dong Ha. There is a nice restaurant at the *Dong Truong Son Hotel*.

Getting There & Away

Bus Buses from Hué to Dong Ha depart from An Hoa bus station. Citröen Tractions to Dong Ha leave from Hué's Dong Ba bus station. In Dong Ha, the bus station (Ben Xe Khach Dong Ha; ☎ 211) is at the intersection of national highways 1 and 9.

The bus station in Khe Sanh (Ben Xe Huong Hoa) is on National Highway 9, approximately 600 metres south-west (towards the Lao frontier) from the triangular intersection where the road to Khe Sanh Combat Base branches off. There are buses from here to Hué, Dong Ha and Lao Bao.

Train To get to the Dong Ha railway station from the bus station, head south-east on National Highway 1 for one km. The railway station is 150 metres across a field to the right (south-west) of the highway. There is only a very limited local train service.

North-Central Vietnam

VINH

The port city of Vinh is the capital of Vietnam's most populous and second largest province, Nghe Tinh, which is famous for its revolutionary spirit – both Phan Boi Chau (1867-1940) and Ho Chi Minh (1890-1969) were born here. Now, Nghe Tinh Province is one of the most destitute regions of one of the poorest countries in the world. It is a tragic fact that of the province's children, 72% are malnourished. Mountains cover 80% of Nghe Tinh.

While there is almost nothing of interest in the city, it is a convenient place to stop for the night if you are travelling overland between Hué and Hanoi.

Orientation

As National Highway 1 enters Vinh from the south, it is called Nguyen Du St – it becomes Tran Phu St in town. As National Highway 1 enters Vinh from the north, it becomes Le Loi St and then Quang Trung St. Quang Trung St (which runs north-south) and Tran

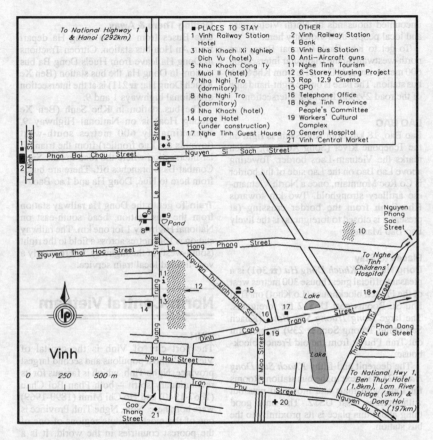

PLACES TO STAY
1 Vinh Railway Station
   Hotel
3 Nha Khach Xi Nghiep
   Dich Vu (hotel)
5 Nha Khach Cong Ty
   Muoi II (hotel)
7 Nha Nghi Tro
   (dormitory)
8 Nha Nghi Tro
   (dormitory)
9 Nha Khach (hotel)
14 Large Hotel
    (under construction)
17 Nghe Tinh Guest House

OTHER
2 Vinh Railway Station
4 Bank
6 Vinh Bus Station
10 Anti–Aircraft guns
11 Nghe Tinh Tourism
12 6–Storey Housing Project
13 Rap 12.9 Cinema
15 GPO
16 Telephone Office
18 Nghe Tinh Province
    People's Committee
19 Workers' Cultural
    Complex
20 General Hospital
21 Vinh Central Market

Phu St intersect one block north of Vinh
Central Market.

Information
The office of Nghe Tinh Tourism (Cong Ty
Du Lich Nghe Tinh; ☎ 4692, 2285) is on the
3rd storey of a six-storey building in the
housing project on Quang Trung St between
Le Hong Phong St and Rap 12/9 cinema. The
office is about 700 metres north of Vinh
Central Market.

The GPO is on Nguyen Thi Minh Khai St
300 metres north-west of Dinh Cong Trang
St. It is open from 6.30 am to 9 pm.

International and domestic telephone calls
can be made from the calling office (Cong
Ty Dien Bao Dien Thoai), which is in a little
building on Dinh Cong Trung St near the
corner of Nguyen Thi Minh Khai St. The
office, which is 100 metres west of the gate
to the Nghe Tinh Guest House, is supposed
to be open from 7 am to 9 pm.

Things to See
The **Kim Lien Village,** where Ho Chi Minh
was born in 1890, is 14 km north-west of
Vinh. The house in which he was born can
be visited, and there is a museum nearby.

Vinh Central Market is at the southern end of Cao Thang St, which is the southern continuation of Quang Trung St.

Places to Stay

Within the precincts of the bus station, cheap dormitory beds are available at *Nha Nghi Tro* (☎ 4127), which is on the southern edge of the bus parking area next to the ticket office. *Nha Khach* is across Le Loi St from the bus station next to the pond – a room costs US$1.50. *Nha Nghi Tro* (☎ 2362) is on Le Loi St 60 metres south (to the right as you exit) of the bus-station gate. A room costs US$1, a bed even less.

As you leave the railway terminal, the *Vinh Railway Station Hotel* (Khach San Duong Sat Ga Vinh; ☎ 24) is to the left – a room costs US$2. *Nha Khach Xi Nghiep Dich Vu* (☎ 4705) is a modern structure just north of the intersection of Le Loi and Phan Boi Chau Sts about a km due east of the railway station. Single/double rooms cost US$3/6.

Nha Khach Cong Ty Muoi II (☎ 2425) is down an alley that intersects Le Loi St 150 metres south of Phan Boi Chau St.

The nicest place to stay in Vinh is the *Nghe Tinh Guest House* (Nha Khach Nghe Tinh; ☎ 3175), which is on Dinh Cong Truong St 200 metres north-east of Le Mao St. Rooms cost US$10 to US$20.

The *Ben Thuy Hotel* (Khach San Ben Thuy; ☎ 4892) is on Nguyen Du St (National Highway 1) 1.8 km towards the bridge over the Lam River from the intersection of Nguyen Du and Truong Thi Sts.

Places to Eat

There is a restaurant on Dinh Cong Trang St next door to the reception building of the Nghe Tinh Guest House. There are a number of small restaurants on Le Ninh St, just outside the gate to the railway station. The food stalls in Vinh Central Market are behind the main building.

Getting There & Away

Bus Vinh bus station (Ben Xe Vinh; ☎ 4127, 4924) is on Le Loi St about one km north of the Central Market. The ticket office is open from 4.30 am to 5 pm daily.

Train Vinh railway station (Ga Vinh; ☎ 4924) is one km west of the intersection of Le Loi and Phan Boi Chau Sts, which is 1½ km north of the Central Market.

Hanoi

Hanoi, the capital of the Socialist Republic of Vietnam, is a drab but pleasant and even charming city. Its charm comes from the city's famous lakes, shaded boulevards and verdant public parks. The city centre is an architectural museum piece, its blocks of ochre buildings retain the air of a French colonial town of the 1930s. The people of Hanoi are known for being more reserved, but more traditionally hospitable, than their southern compatriots.

The city of Hanoi (population 925,000) is a small part of Greater Hanoi, which has a land area of 2139 sq km and a population of 2.8 million. The city is 72 km inland from the Gulf of Tonkin.

Many Westerners, (both backpackers and businesspeople) report being harassed by the police in Hanoi, especially at the airport.

Orientation

Hanoi is situated on the right bank of the Red River (Song Hong). In the centre of Hanoi is Hoan Kiem Lake. To the north of the lake is the Old Quarter. South and south-west of the lake is the modern city centre. The colonial-era buildings in this area house many of Hanoi's hotels, state stores and nonsocialist embassies. Ho Chi Minh's Mausoleum is to the west of the Citadel, which is still used as a military base.

Information

Tourist Office The head office of Vietnam Tourism, where they take little interest in individual travellers, is at 54 Nguyen Du St (☎ 57080, 52986, 55963).

The Hanoi Tourism & Service Company,

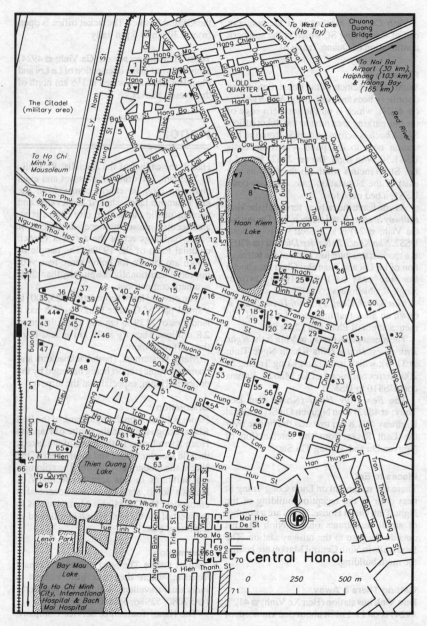

Central Hanoi

■	PLACES TO STAY	14	Aeroflot Office
		15	National Library
5	Phung Hung Hotel	16	Vietnam Airlines International Office
25	Government Guest House	18	Traditional Medicines Pharmacy
27	Thong Nhat Hotel	20	State General Department Store
29	Dan Chu Hotel	22	Foreign Language Bookstore
35	Dong Loi Hotel	23	International Telephone Office
36	Railway Service Company Hotel	24	GPO
43	Khach San Chi Lang	26	Foreign Trade Bank
45	Ministry of Transportation Guest House	28	Thong Nhat Bookstore
		30	Revolutionary Museum
47	Khach San 30-4 (hotel)	31	Municipal Theatre
56	Hoa Binh Hotel	32	History Museum
59	Hoan Kiem Hotel	33	Algerian Embassy
66	Nha Tro (dormitory)	37	West German Embassy
		38	UNDP & UNICEF
▼	PLACES TO EAT	39	Australian Embassy
		40	'Hanoi Hilton' Prison
1	Piano Restaurant	41	19th December Market
2	Cha Ca Restaurant	42	Hanoi Railway Station
3	Chau Thanh Restaurant	44	Egyptian Embassy
4	Restaurant 22	46	Ambassadors' Pagoda
7	Thuy Ta Restaurant	48	Workers' Cultural Palace
9	Restaurant Francais	49	Immigration Police Office
10	Food Stalls	50	Iraqi Embassy
13	Palace Restaurant & Dancing	51	Cambodian Embassy
17	Bo Ho Restaurant	52	Indian Embassy
19	Sophia Hotel & Restaurant	53	Vietcochamber
21	Bodega Café	54	French Embassy
34	Huong Sen Restaurant	57	Indonesian Embassy
55	Small Restaurants	58	Finnish Embassy
69	Restaurant 202	60	Lao Embassy Consular Section
70	Hoa Binh Restaurant	61	FAO Office
		62	Vietnam Tourism Head Office
	OTHER	63	Belgian Embassy
		64	Japanese Embassy
6	Shoe Market	65	Lao Embassy
8	Ngoc Son Temple & Huc Bridge	67	Kim Lien Bus Station
11	Saint Joseph Cathedral	68	TOSERCO
12	Vietnam Airlines Domestic Office	71	Bicycle & Motorbike Shops

much more commonly known by its acronym TOSERCO (☎ 52937, 63541), is at 8 To Hien Thanh St (on the corner of Mai Hac De St). This may still be the best place in Vietnam for individual travellers to get visa extensions and internal travel permits. Ask fellow travellers for the latest on official paperwork.

Immigration Police The Immigration Police office is at 89 Tran Hung Dao St. It is open Monday to Saturday from 8 to 11 am and from 1 to 5 pm.

Money The best place to change money is at the Bank for Foreign Trade (☎ 52831) at 47-49 Ly Thai To St as it offers the best legal rate in town. It is open daily from 8 to 11.30 am and from 1.30 to 3.30 pm except on Saturday afternoon, Sunday and national holidays. All the major tourist hotels can change dollars at the front desk.

Post & Telecommunications The GPO (Buu Dien Trung Vong; ☎ 54413), which occupies a full city block facing Hoan Kiem Lake, is at 75 Dinh Tien Hoang St. Postal, telex and domestic telephone services are available from 6.30 am to 8 pm. Telegrams can be sent 24 hours a day. International telephone calls can be made from the office (☎ 52030) on the corner of Dinh Tien Hoang and Dinh Le Sts, which is open daily from 7.30 am to 9.30 pm.

Foreign Embassies Useful embassies in Hanoi include:

Cambodia
    At 71 Tran Hung Dao St , it is open from 8 to 11 am and from 2 to 4.30 pm daily except Sunday (☎ 53788, 53789).
China
    46 Hoang Dieu St (☎ 53736/7)
Laos
    At 22 Tran Binh Trong St (☎ 54576), the consular section (☎ 52588) is on the 2nd floor of an unmarked yellow building at 40 Quang Trung St, opposite the FAO office. It is theoretically open Monday to Friday from 8 to 11 am and from 2 to 4.30 pm. Three photos and plane tickets are required for a five-day transit visa, which costs US$17 and takes at least 24 hours to issue.
Thailand
    Khu Trung Tu – E1 (☎ 56043/53, 62644)

Emergency The International Hospital (Benh Vien Quoc Te; ☎ 62042), where foreigners are usually referred, is on the western side of Kiem Lien St a little south of the Polytechnic University (Dai Hoc Bach Khoa).

In winter, the hospital's outpatient clinic is open from 8 am to 12.30 pm and from 1 to 4.30 pm. In summer, it is open from 7.30 am to 12 noon and from 1 to 4.30 pm. There is an on-site pharmacy. Westerners must pay in US$.

Things to See
Lakes, Temples & Pagodas Hanoi's famous **One Pillar Pagoda** (Chua Mot Cot) was built by Emperor Ly Thai Tong, who ruled from 1028 to 1054. Tours of Ho Chi Minh's Mausoleum end up here. The entrance to **Dien Huu Pagoda** is a few metres from the staircase of the One Pillar Pagoda.

The **Temple of Literature** (Van Mieu), founded in 1070, is a rare example of well-preserved traditional Vietnamese architecture. Vietnam's first university was established here in 1076 to educate the sons of mandarins.

In 1484, Emperor Le Thanh Tong ordered that steles be erected in the temple premises recording the names, places of birth and achievements of men who received doctorates in each triennial examination, beginning in 1442. The complex is bounded by Nguyen Thai Hoc, Hang Bot, Quoc Tu Giam and Van Mieu Sts. It is open from 8.30 to 11.30 am and from 1.30 to 4.30 pm, Tuesday to Sunday.

Hoan Kiem Lake is an enchanting body of water right in the heart of Hanoi. Legend has it that in the mid-15th century, Heaven gave Emperor Le Thai To (Le Loi) a magical sword which he used to drive the Chinese out of Vietnam. One day after the war, while out boating, he came upon a giant golden tortoise swimming on the surface of the water. The creature grabbed the sword and disappeared into the depths of the lake. Since that time, the lake has been known as Ho Hoan Kiem (Lake of the Restored Sword) because the tortoise restored the sword to its divine owners.

Founded in the 18th century, **Ngoc Son Temple** is on an island in the northern part of Hoan Kiem Lake.

West Lake (Ho Tay), which covers an area of five sq km, was once ringed with magnificent palaces and pavilions. These were destroyed in the course of various feudal wars. **Tran Quoc Pagoda** is on the south-eastern shore of West Lake. **Truc Bach Lake** is separated from West Lake by Thanh Nien St.

The **Ambassadors' Pagoda** (Quan Su; ☎ 52427) is the official centre of Buddhism in Hanoi, attracting quite a crowd (mostly old women) on holidays. During the 17th century, there was a guest house here for the ambassadors of Buddhist countries. The Ambassadors' Pagoda is at 73 Quan Su St (between Ly Thuong Kiet and Tran Hung Dao Sts). It is open to the public every day from 7.30 to 11.30 am and from 1.30 to 5.30 pm.

Ho Chi Minh's Mausoleum In the tradition of Lenin and Stalin before him and Mao after him, the final resting place of Ho Chi Minh is a glass sarcophagus set deep inside a monumental edifice that has become a pilgrimage site.

The mausoleum is open to the public on Tuesday, Wednesday, Thursday and Saturday mornings from 8 to 11 am. On Sunday and on holidays, it is open from 7.30 to 11.30 am. The mausoleum is closed for two months a year (usually from September to early November) while Ho Chi Minh's embalmed corpse is in the USSR for maintenance.

All visitors must register and check their bags and cameras at the reception hall on Chua Mot Cot St, where a you can view a 20-minute video in English and other languages, about Ho Chi Minh's life and accomplishments.

The following rules are strictly applied to all mausoleum visitors:

1) People wearing shorts, tank-tops, etc will not be admitted.
2) Nothing (including day packs and cameras) may be taken into the mausoleum.
3) A respectful demeanour must be maintained at all times.
4) For obvious reasons of decorum, photography is absolutely prohibited inside the mausoleum.
5) It is forbidden to put your hands in your pockets.
6) Hats must be taken off inside the mausoleum building.

To ensure that these directives are carried out, honour guards will accompany you as you march single-file from near reception to the mausoleum entrance.

After exiting from the mausoleum, the tour will pass by the Presidential Palace, constructed in 1906 as the palace of the Governor General of Indochina. Ho Chi Minh's house, built of the finest materials in 1958, is next to a carp-filled pond. Nearby is what was once Hanoi's botanical garden and is now a park. The tour ends up at the One Pillar Pagoda. The new Ho Chi Minh Museum is nearby.

Museums The **History Museum**, once the museum of the École Française d'Extrême Orient, is one block east of the Municipal Theatre at 1 Pham Ngu Lao St. The **Army Museum** is on Dien Bien Phu St; it is open daily except Monday from 7.30 to 11.30 am only. The displays include scale models of various epic battles from Vietnam's long military history, including Dien Bien Phu and the capture of Saigon.

Next to the Army Museum is the hexagonal Flag Tower, which has become one of the symbols of the city. It is part of a Vauban-style citadel constructed by Emperor Gia Long (ruled 1802-19) and is still used by the military.

The huge, new **Ho Chi Minh Museum** is near Ho's mausoleum. It's an amazing place with a highly varied and very modern display absolutely reeking with symbolism. Some of it is rather curious – the art connections to Ho Chi Minh's time in Paris are a little hard to fathom. Others displays are simply superb – the arrival of US influence in Indochina is shown by a '58 Edsel bursting through the wall, an American commercial failure to symbolise the later military failure.

St Joseph Cathedral Stepping inside neo-Gothic St Joseph Cathedral (inaugurated in 1886) is like being instantly transported to medieval Europe. The cathedral is noteworthy for its square towers, elaborate altar and stained-glass windows. The first Catholic mission in Hanoi was founded in 1679.

The main gate to St Joseph Cathedral is open daily from 5 to 7 am and from 5 to 7 pm, the hours when masses are held. At other times of the day, guests are welcome but must enter via the compound of the Diocese of Hanoi, the entrance to which is a block away at 40 Nha Chung St. After walking through the gate, go straight and then turn right. When you reach the side door to the cathedral, ring the small bell high up to the right of the door to call the priest, who will let you in.

Hanoi Hilton The 'Hanoi Hilton' is the nickname given to a prison in which US prisoners-of-war – mostly aircraft crewmen

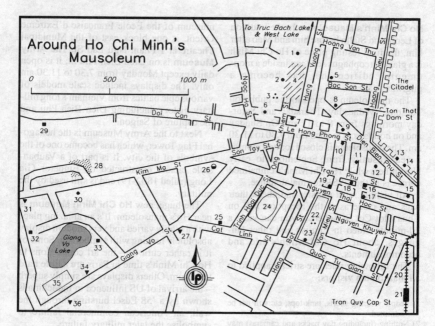

Around Ho Chi Minh's Mausoleum

0   500   1000 m

To Truc Bach Lake & West Lake

The Citadel

Giang Vo Lake

■ PLACES TO STAY

25 Ministry of Foodstuffs Guest House
29 La Thanh Hotel
32 Giang Vo Hotel
33 Thang Long Hotel

▼ PLACES TO EAT

20 Huong Sen Restaurant
27 Phuong Nam Restaurant
31 Restaurant 79
34 Dong Do Restaurant
36 Small Restaurants

OTHER

1   Presidential Palace
2   Ho Chi Minh's Mausoleum
3   One Pillar Pagoda & Dien Huu Pagoda
4   Ba Dinh Square
5   National Assembly Building
6   Ho Chi Minh Museum

7   Reception for Ho Chi Minh's Mausoleum
8   Ministry of Foreign Affairs
9   Albanian & Hungarian Embassies
10 Romanian Embassy
11 Chinese Embassy
12 Lenin Statue
13 Flag Tower
14 Army Museum
15 East German Embassy
16 Mongolian Embassy
17 North Korean Embassy
18 Bulgarian Embassy
19 Fine Arts Museum
20 Huong Sen Restaurant
21 Hanoi Railway Station
22 Temple of Literature
23 Entrance to Temple of Literature
24 Stadium
26 Kim Ma Bus Station
28 Swedish, Burmese & Malaysian Embassies
30 Finish Embasssy
35 Exhibition Hall

– were held during the Vietnam War. The high walls of the forbidding triangular building, officially known as Hoa Lo Prison, are pierced by precious few barred windows. The structure, which was constructed by the French in the early 20th century, is bounded by Hai Ba Trung, Tho Nhuom and Hoa Lo Sts. Photography is forbidden.

Long Bien Bridge The Long Bien Bridge, which crosses the Red River 600 metres north of the new Chuong Duong Bridge, is a fantastic hodge-podge of repairs dating from the Vietnam War. American aircraft repeatedly bombed the strategic river crossing (which at one time was defended by 300 anti-aircraft guns and 84 SAM missiles), yet after each attack the Vietnamese somehow managed to improvise replacement spans and return it to road and rail service.

Places to Stay

Central Hanoi Near the railway station, the old and distinctly decrepit *Dong Loi Hotel* (Khach San Dong Loi; ☎ 55721) is on the corner of Le Duan and Ly Thuong Kiet Sts. In 1991, it was finally getting some long overdue maintenance but at US$8 for singles and US$10 to US$15 for doubles, it is no bargain. It's one of the few cheaper places where foreigners are welcome.

Other rock-bottom possibilities near the railway station, where it *may* be possible to get a room, include the *Khach San Chi Lang* (☎ 57171), right across from the station at 113 Le Duan St. *Khach San 30-4* (☎ 52611) is down the block at 115 Tran Hung Dao St.

Another option is the *Railway Service Company Hotel* (☎ 52842) at 80 Ly Thuong Kiet St; reception is upstairs. The *Phung Hung Hotel* (☎ 52614), a bit over a km north of the railway station, is at Phung Hung St on the corner of Duong Thanh St – foreigners are charged US$5 each.

The *hotel* at 136 Hang Trong St (just west of Hoan Kiem Lake) charges US$5 for a room. *Nha Tro* (☎ 52405), whose name simply means 'dormitory,' is across the street from the Kim Lien bus station. It is one of the many buildings bearing the address 100

Le Duan St (on the corner of Kham Thien St). This place is open 24 hours a day, so if your bus comes in very late at night (when the city's other hotels are closed), it's a good place to crash until morning.

There are several top-end hotels in central Hanoi like the old, but reasonably well-kept, *Dan Chu Hotel* (☎ 53323) at 29 Trang Tien St near the Municipal Theatre. Singles/doubles cost from US$29/34 to US$36/42 plus 10%. The city's most venerable hotel, the Thong Nhat Hotel (formerly the Metropole) at 15 Ngo Quyen St, is being completely renovated.

Swedish Embassy Area The *Giang Vo Hotel* (☎ 53407, 56598) consists of several five-storey apartment blocks. One entrance to the hotel, which is 3½ km west of the city centre, faces Giang Vo Lake; there is another entrance on Ngoc Khanh St. Rooms cost from US$2 to US$4. The *Ministry of Foodstuffs Guest House* (Nha Khach Cong Nghiep Truc Pham; ☎ 55302) is at 40 Cat Linh St.

One of the least expensive of Hanoi's major hotels is *Thang Long Hotel* (☎ 57796, 52270), a 10-storey building which overlooks Giang Vo, a small lake 3½ km west of the city centre. Rooms on the upper floors are offered at reduced rates (US$14 for a double) because the lifts are so often out of order.

Places to Eat

Central Hanoi The *Sophia Restaurant* at 6 Hang Bai St (between Hai Ba Trung St and Hoan Kiem Lake) serves edible food at moderately high prices. Nearby, at 57 Trang Tien St, the *Bodega Café* serves pastries, ice cream and drinks and is particularly popular in the evenings.

A few doors down at 35 Trang Tien St, *Nha Hang Tran Tien* has an enormously popular takeaway ice-cream counter on the street; ice creams (kem) cost from just US$0.03 to US$0.05! Inside, there's a cafe area notable for its state of absolutely filthy squalor and large numbers of staff sitting around doing nothing. Clearly government run!

Kem enthusiasts will also find a number of ice cream places along Hang Trong St by the lakeside where an ice cream is about US$0.12.

There are a number of small eateries on Hang Bai St on the corner of Ly Thuong Kiet St. The *Dan Chu Hotel Restaurant* serves quite good food at very reasonable prices.

Restaurant 202 (Nha Hang 202) is 1½ km south of Hoan Kiem Lake at 202 Pho Hué. One of the best restaurants in the city, it is a favourite of the diplomatic community and has a predominantly French influenced menu. Across the street at 163 Pho Hué is the *Hoa Binh Restaurant*.

Near the railway station, the *Huong Sen Restaurant* (☎ 52805), run by Hanoi Tourism, is at 52 Le Duan St. There are a number of other places to eat in the immediate vicinity of the railway station, including a restaurant next to the lobby of the Dong Loi Hotel. There are quite a few small restaurants around Kim Lien bus station.

Fresh vegetables can be purchased at the *19th of December Market* (Cho 19-12), whose two entrances are opposite 61 Ly Thuong Kiet St and next to 41 Hai Ba Trung St. Dog meat is available from curb-side vendors a few hundred metres north of the History Museum on Le Phung Hieu St near Trang Quang Kha St.

Old Quarter *Restaurant 22* (also known as Quang An Restaurant) is at 22 Hang Can St. The entrance is through a narrow passageway and up the stairs. Another favourite of the expat community is *Cha Ca Restaurant*, which is at 14 Cha Ca St – it specialises in fish (in fact, cha ca means 'fried fish'). Cha Ca St, which is a two-block-long continuation of Luong Van Can St, begins about 500 metres north of Hoan Kiem Lake.

Nha Thinh Restaurant is at 28 Luong Van Can St. Not far away at 50 Hang Vai St is the *Piano Restaurant*. As the name suggests, there is live music every evening. The waitresses all wear 'Piano Restaurant' T-shirts. The *Chau Thanh Restaurant* is just round the corner at 48 Hong Ga St.

There are a number of food stalls in the alley between 202 and 204 Hang Bong St. Nearby at 192 Hang Bong St is a small restaurant. *Bittek Restaurant*, also known as Le Français, is off Hang Gai St at 17 Ly Quoc Su St. Bittek means 'beefsteak'.

Thuy Ta Restaurant at 1 Le Thai To St is on the shore of Hoan Kiem Lake. It is about 200 metres south of the intersection of Le Thai To and Hang Gai Sts.

Swedish Embassy Area *Restaurant 79* is at 79 Kim Ma St, which is a few hundred metres west of the Swedish Embassy. The excellent *Phuong Nam Restaurant* is on Giang Vo St in Block I1, which is near the corner of Cat Linh St. There are several small places to eat across Giang Vo St from the exhibition hall.

Entertainment

The 900-seat Municipal Theatre (☎ 54312), which faces eastward up Trang Tien St, was built in 1911 as an opera house. Performances of various sorts are held here in the evenings.

Dancing, both ballroom and disco, is all the rage with young Hanoi residents who can afford it. The *Palace Restaurant* on Nha Chung St near the lake is a popular locale, and the *Dan Chu Hotel* has 'Soirées Dansantes'.

Invitations to see performances of water puppetry, a wonderful art form unique to Vietnam, can sometimes be procured through Vietnam Tourism, TOSERCO or a foreign embassy. An opportunity to see water puppetry is a treat not to be missed.

The endearingly amateurish State Circus often performs in the evenings in a huge tent near the entrance to Lenin Park (Cong Vien Le Nin).

Things to Buy

Greeting cards with hand-painted silk covers are available around town for US$0.10 or so. Souvenir T-shirts with permanent colours can be purchased or especially ordered at 45

Hang Bong St. Bao Hung is a very popular T-shirt shop at 1 Ly Quoc Su St. There are a number of other T-shirt and hat shops nearby.

Attractive gold-on-scarlet banners, usually given as awards for service to the Party or State, can be ordered to your specifications (with your name or date of visit, for instance) at 13 and 40 Hang Bong St. Hang Gai St and its continuation, Hang Bong St, are a good place to look for embroidered tablecloths and hangings.

There are quite a number of stores around Hanoi offering new and antique Vietnamese handicrafts (lacquerware, mother-of-pearl inlay, ceramics, sandalwood statuettes, etc).

Getting There & Away

Air Hanoi's Noi Bai Airport, as you may see before landing or after taking off, is ringed with the craters of American bombs. Customs and police officials at the airport have a reputation for arbitrariness and unpleasantness.

The Vietnam Airlines domestic booking office at 16 Le Thai To St (on the corner of Hang Trong St) is next to Hoan Kiem Lake. It is open from 7.30 to 11 am and from 1 to 3 pm.

Vietnam Airlines international booking office handles reservations (☎ 55284) and ticketing (☎ 53842) for all airlines serving Hanoi. It is on the corner of Trang Thi and Quang Trung Sts and is open from 8 to 11.30 am and from 1 to 3.30 pm daily except Saturday afternoon and Sunday.

The Aeroflot office (☎ 56184) is diagonally opposite the Vietnam Airlines international booking office. It is open from 8 to 11.30 am and from 3.30 to 6 pm Monday to Saturday.

A departure tax on international flights, of US$5 (payable in US$ or dong) is levied.

Bus Hanoi has several main bus terminals. Kim Lien bus station serves points south of Hanoi. Kim Ma bus station serves destinations that are north-west of the capital. Buses to points north-east of Hanoi leave from Long Bien bus station, which recently moved to the east bank of the Red River.

Kim Lien bus station (Ben Xe Kim Lien; ☎ 55230) at 100 Le Duan St (on the corner of Nguyen Quyen St) is 800 metres south of the railway station. The express bus *(toc hanh)* ticket office, which is open every day from 4.30 am to 5 pm, is across the street from 6B Nguyen Quyen St.

Kim Ma bus station (Ben Xe Kim Ma; ☎ 52846) is opposite 166 Nguyen Thai Hoc St (on the corner of Giang Vo St).

Train The Hanoi railway station (Ga Ha Noi; ☎ 52628) is opposite 115 Le Duan St (at the western end of Tran Hung Dao St). The ticket office is open from 7.30 to 11.30 am and from 1.30 to 3.30 pm only.

Getting Around

To/From the Airport It's 30 km from Hanoi to Noi Bai Airport. Buses depart from the Vietnam Airlines domestic booking office at 16 Le Thai To St (on the corner of Hang Trong St). The schedule both to and from the airport depends on the departure and arrival times of domestic flights, and you can only count on getting out to the airport very early in the morning. The fare is less than US$1.

Taxis are easy to find for US$10 and are less if you bargain hard. Officially, it's US$10 for a Russian taxi and US$15 for a Japanese one! In the city, taxis congregate around the Vietnam Airlines international booking office.

Bus & Tram Service on Hanoi's bus lines is rather infrequent – routes are marked on some city maps. Hanoi's antiquated electric tram system appears to have, finally, ground to a complete halt.

Cyclo & Bicycle Cyclos are the main form of transport around town; they're slightly cheaper than in Saigon. But the best way to get around Hanoi is by bicycle. As of last reports, the only place renting out bicycles is the Thang Long Hotel (☎ 57796) on Giang Vo St; it charges US$0.25 per hour.

There are dozens upon dozens of bicycle (and motorbike) shops along Pho Hué (Hué

St) south of Restaurant 202, which is at 202 Pho Hué.

The North

Stretching from the Hoang Lien Mountains (Tonkinese Alps) eastward across the Red River Delta to the islands of Halong Bay, the northern part of Vietnam (Bac Bo), known to the French as Tonkin, includes some of the country's most spectacular scenery.

The mountainous areas are home to many distinct hill-tribe groups, some of which remain relatively untouched by Vietnamising and Westernising influences.

Unfortunately, most of the north is still off-limits to tourists (at least to individual travellers).

SAM SON BEACHES
The two Sam Son Beaches, among the nicest in the north, are 16 km south-east of Thanh Hoa City. They are a favourite vacation spot of Hanoi residents who can afford such luxuries. Accommodation ranges from basic bungalows to multistorey hotels.

TAM DAO HILL STATION
Tam Dao Hill Station (elevation 930 metres), known to the French as the Cascade d'Argent (Silver Cascade), was founded by the French in 1907 as a place of escape from the heat of the Red River Delta. Today, the grand colonial villas are a bit run-down, but Tam Dao retains its refreshing weather, beautiful hiking areas and superb views.

CUC PHUONG NATIONAL PARK
Cuc Phuong National Park, established in 1962, is one of Vietnam's most important nature preserves. The park, 222 sq km of primary tropical forest, is home to an amazing variety of wildlife.

Places to Stay
The *rest house* at park headquarters charges US$12 per night.

Getting There & Away
Cuc Phuong National Park is 140 km south from Hanoi (via Ninh Binh) but sections of the road are in poor condition. With a car, it is possible to visit the forest as a day trip from Hanoi.

HAIPHONG
Haiphong, Vietnam's third most populous city, is the north's main industrial centre and one of the country's most important seaports. Greater Haiphong covers 1515 sq km and has a population of 1.3 million. Haiphong proper covers 21 sq km and is home to 370,000 inhabitants. In May 1972, President Nixon ordered the mining of Haiphong Harbour to cut the flow of Soviet military supplies to North Vietnam.

Information
Haiphong Tourism (☎ 47486) is at 15 Le Dai Hanh St. The GPO is at 3 Nguyen Tri Phuong St (on the corner of Hoang Van Thu St).

Places to Stay
The French-era *Huu Nghi Hotel* (☎ 47206) is at 62 Dien Bien St. The *Bach Dang Hotel* (☎ 47244) is at 42 Dien Bien St, and the *Duyen Hai Hotel* (☎ 47657) is at 5 Nguyen Tri Phuong St. Other hotels you might try include the *Ben Binh Hotel* on the corner of Dien Bien and Ben Binh Sts; the *Hong Bang Hotel* at 64 Dien Bien St; and the *Cat Bi Hotel* at 29 Tran Phu St.

Getting There & Away
Haiphong is 103 km from Hanoi on National Highway 5. The two cities are also linked by rail.

DO SON BEACH
Palm-shaded Do Son Beach, 21 km south-east of Haiphong, is the most popular seaside resort in the north and a favourite of Hanoi's expat community.

Places to Stay
Places to stay in town include the *Do Son Hotel* (☎ 10 from the Do Son telephone

exchange), the *Van Hoa Hotel*, the *Hoa Phuong Hotel* and the *Hai Au Hotel*.

CAT BA NATIONAL PARK

About half of Cat Ba Island (total area of 354 sq km) and 90 sq km of adjacent inshore waters were declared a national park in 1986 in order to protect the island's diverse eco-systems. These include tropical evergreen forests on the hills, freshwater swamp forests at the base of the hills, coastal mangrove forests, small freshwater lakes, sandy beaches and offshore coral reefs.

Getting There & Away

Cat Ba National Park is 133 km east from Hanoi and 30 km east of Haiphong. A boat to Cat Ba is supposed to depart from Haiphong every day at 6 am; the trip takes about 3½ hours. The park headquarters is at Trung Trang.

HALONG BAY

Magnificent Halong Bay, with its 3000 islands rising from the clear, emerald waters of the Gulf of Tonkin, is one of the natural marvels of Vietnam. The vegetation-covered islands, which are spread out over an area of 1500 sq km, are dotted with innumerable beaches and grottoes created by the wind and the waves.

Information

Quang Ninh Tourism's office (☎ 08 from the Halong telephone exchange) is in the town of Bai Chay, which is across the water from Hong Gai.

Grottoes

Because the islands of Halong Bay are made of soft rock, the area is dotted with thousands of caves of all sizes and shapes. Among the better known are **Hang Dau Go** (Grotto of the Wooden Stakes), known to the French as the Grotte des Merveilles (Cave of Marvels), the **Grotto of Bo Nau** and the two-km long **Hang Hanh Cave**.

Places to Stay

In the town of Bai Chay, the *Ha Long Hotel* (☎ 238) charges Westerners US$35 for a room. The place next door costs only US$4. Other hotels you might try include the *Bach Long Hotel* (☎ 281), the *Hoang Long Hotel* (☎ 264) and the *Son Long Hotel* (☎ 254).

Getting There & Away

The 165-km trip from Hanoi to Halong Bay takes about three hours by car and five hours by public bus. The Bai Chay bus station is about one km from the Ha Long Hotel. Buses from Hanoi to Halong Bay depart from the Long Bien bus station.

Getting Around

It is possible to hire a motorised launch to tour the islands and their grottoes. To find a boat, ask around the quays of Bay Chay or Hong Gai.

DIEN BIEN PHU

Dien Bien Phu was the site of that rarest of military events, a battle that can be called truly decisive. On 6 May 1954, Viet Minh forces overran the beleaguered French garrison at Dien Bien Phu after a 57-day siege, shattering French morale and forcing the French government to abandon its attempts to re-establish colonial control of Indochina. Except for a small museum, there is not all that much to see at Dien Bien Phu these days.

Getting There & Away

A minimum of five days is required for an overland expedition from Hanoi to Dien Bien Phu (420 km each way): two days to get there, a day to visit the area and two days to come back. Visitors report that getting there is half the fun. As the road nears Dien Bien, it winds through beautiful mountains and high plains inhabited by hill tribes (notably the Black Tai and Hmong) who still live as they have for generations.

Index

ABBREVIATIONS

MAPS

TEXT

Map references are in **bold** type

916 Index

Thanks

We greatly appreciate the contributions of travellers who took the time and energy to write to us. Writers (apologies if we've misspelt your name) to whom thanks must go include:

Maria Achour (Sw), Cherry Acklanel (Aus), Ruedi Aeppli (CH), Ulla & Titi Ahlroth (Fin), Julie Ainslie (UK), Ian Alexander (UK), Janet Allen (USA), Steve Annecone (USA), Gil Anspacher (USA), Sophy Ashworth (UK), Debra Atkinson (Aus), John Atwell (USA), Gerry Avenell (UK), Briar Averill (NZ), Jack Bailey (USA), Lindsey Baker (UK), John Barnett (NZ), Mrs Dione Bartels (Aus), Paul Barton, Roger Beach (UK), Dr Gerda Bedet (Nl), Andreas Bengtsson (Sw), Hugh Berke (C), Priscilla Berry, Daniel Bertsch (D), Kees Bikker (Nl), Mikael Billros (Sw), T M Billson (UK), Barry Jon Black (UK), Ruud Blacker (Nl), Katrina Bodewes (Aus), Martin Bohnstedt (A), Patrick Boman (F), Ian & Rachel Bond, Gordon Bonin (Aus), Abby Bortone (I), Pam Bowers (UK), Mary Bradley (UK), Tessa Brock (UK), Ronald Brook (UK), Catherine & Ebe Brunner (US), Hildegard Burkent (Nl), Bev Burns (Aus), Judy Butler (UK), Jennifer Byrne (Aus), Francis Cagney (Ire), Don Cameron (C), Corinne Campbell (Aus), William Carpmael (UK), Elizabeth Carter Shaw (UK), Robert Carty (UK), Landraud Catherine (F), Robin Chakrabarti (UK), Jane Chan (USA), Sarah Chilvers, Jacky Church (UK), Timothy Clarke (UK), Miss L R Cole (UK), Elizabeth Collins (Aus), Michelle Connors (Aus), Tara & Peter Cooper, Randle Cooraa (USA), Monica Costello (USA), John A Courtney Jr (USA), Lucinda Cox, Lindsay Cozens (Aus), Marco Crolla (Aus), Finbar Cullen (UK), Phillip Martin Cummings (USA), Fabrice Curty (F), Martin Damgaard (Dk), John A Dau (USA), Grant James Davies (Aus), Jonothan Davies (UK), Andrew Dembina (Aus), Des & Sandy (Aus), Joe Doherty (Ire), Ilana Doubov (Aus), Jean Dreesen (B), Sophie Dumoulin (F), Jim Dunn, Brian Dyke (UK), Marjorie Eckman (USA), P Edgar (UK), Jenny Edwards (Aus), Lucy Edwards (Aus), Lars Eklund (Sw), Mike Elder (UK), Sam Eldred (UK), Keith Ellis (UK), Edith & Henny van der Elsen (Nl), A J van Engen (Nl), Theresia Erdtmann (USA), Michael Evans, Bryan Everts (Aus), B Whitworth & Mark Eyre (NZ), Simon Farrell, J A de Feijter (Aus), Faerthen Felix (USA), David Ferran (Sp), Eric Filippino (USA), James Fisher (USA), Jane Flintoff, Sandra Frank (Aus), Jill & Nick Franklin (C), Sharen Franklin (Aus), Hamiosh Fraser (NZ), Peter Freeman (Aus), Patricia Gallagher (UK), Liz Gay, Bethany Gladhill, Teik Poh Goh (Sin), Paul Gold (UK), Donna Goldin (Aus), Anna Goldstein (USA), Anna Goller (Dk), Royston Goodridge (UK), Simon P Goulet (C), Adam Grant (UK), Jacquie Gray, Mitch Greenhill (USA), Paul Greening, M

Grimshaw (UK), Ian Guthrie (USA), Diana Hainsworth, Jytte Halborg (Dk), Jack & Denise Hammersley, Maria de Lourdes Hancock (UK), Soren Hansen (Dk), Judy Harland (UK), Deborah Harnett (UK), Caryl Hart (UK), Jim Hart (UK), Roger Hatfield (UK), Cody Hawver (Aus), John Heelas (Aus), Ann-Christine Hellstrom (Sw), Marie Henscher (USA), Steve Henson (UK), Scott Herman-Giddens (USA), Andreis Hessberger (D), James Higgins, Don Hill (Aus), Jane Hinds (NZ), Pierre Hirsch (Can), Andreas Hofer (A), Mette Hoiriis (Dk), Miel Hollander (Nl), Ian Hollingsworth (UK), Axel Homberger (D), Mike Hope (UK), J Bird & L Horsfall (C), Patrick Horton (Aus), Bill Howell (USA), Bryan Howorth (UK), Gill Huggan (A), David & Greeba Hughes (UK), Paul Hunter (Nl), Robyn Hurst (Aus), Brendon Hyde (Aus), Mark Ingledew (UK), Helle Jaeger (Dk), J A M Jaelfaelt (Sw), Daniel Jaffe (UK), Silvia Jager (D), Robert Jenkins (Aus), Joaninha (USA), K Johnston (C), Henrik Josefsson (Sw), Andrew Joyce, Bruno Kahn (F), John Kasteel (Aus), Devender Kaur (M), Beat Keller (Aus), Jean-Yves Kerherve (F), Gunnar Kihlberg (Sw), Thomas Kirchmaier (D), Brian Kliesen (USA), Ed Klock (USA), Alan Knight (Aus), Magnus Koch (Aus), Gary L Koethner (US), Michael Konik (USA), Don Kornelly (USA), Sebastian Krug (D), Ken Kupperman (USA), Elizabeth Lachmayr, Mathieu Lamarre (C), Oliver Lang (A), David Langley (Aus), Steve Langoulant (Aus), Claire Larrivee (Aus), Darren Lawlor, Frances Lee (Tw), Garry & Karen Levido (Aus), Adam Levy (USA), Warren Lewis (USA), Alfred Li (HK), Constance Lim (C), Ake Lindahl (Sw), Peter Lindgren (Sw), Evan Llewellyn (C), H Lohmer, Jose M Lomas (Sp), Penny Lovatt (USA), Nicola Lovell (UK), Andrew Ludasi (C), Birgitta Lyrdal (Sw), Ulf Magnusson (Sw), Anne-Emmanuelle Maire (F), Loliei Manassen (Nl), Geoff Mann, Kevin Manser (Aus), Diego Marconi (I), Suzanne Marshall (USA), Chris Martin (USA), Ajeet N Mathur (I), Tim Matthews, Kate McAndrew (UK), Ian McClelland (UK), Mike McGrath (SA), K McMurray (UK), Andy McNeilly (Aus), Dave Mead (UK), Mark Medley, Michael Menes (USA), Stephen G Meredith (Aus), Tim Meredith (USA), Ton van Meurs (Nl), Donald E Meyer (USA), H Meyer (UK), Sarah & Ray Midgley (UK), Jack & Trudy Moelker (Nl), Lars-Olov Mohlin (Sw), Kelvin Moody (NZ), Samantha A Moore (USA), Mike Morgan (C), John Morrow (NZ), John Mortimer (C), Wade Mullings (Aus), Steve & Lyn Murray (UK), Janet Narres (C), Mike Naylor (NZ), Chuong Nguyen (C), Sarah Norris (UK), John Norwood, Jac Nyskens (Nl), Sean O'Shea, Hank Obermayer (USA), Peter Onderwater (Nl), Susan Ormiston (USA), Elaine Orr (C), Kenneth Orr (Aus), Mary Osborn (HK), Len Outram, Angela Patilla (UK), T J Pawlowski (USA), Harry Pearson (NZ), Mark Pearson (Dk), Chris Perez , Per Persson (Sw), Jeffrey Lee Pierce (USA), Irianto Pongrekum

922

(In), Stephen Porter (UK), Chris Pritchard (Aus), Melanie Pursey (UK), Ken & Elisabeth Rae (Aus), Ms Lalita Ranesh, Mike Raship (USA), Yves Rault (F), Nick Reed (UK), Sian Llewellyn Rees (UK), Frances Reid (Aus), Sam Reid (Aus), Mark Rhomberg (USA), Dan Rickerts (UK), Stuart Roach (UK), Annie Roberts (USA), Richard Roberts (UK), Anthony Rodwell (Aus), Peter Rogers (UK), Beryl Rose, Martin Roughton (UK), Jenny Roxman (Sw), Barbara Sandhu (USA), Gary Sandler (Aus), Jordan H Sankel (USA), Ann Santarelli (F), Indra Saputra (In), Glen Schlueter, Detlef Schultze (Sw), Poul Schwartzenberg (Dk), Karen Searer (Aus), Linda Seaton, Mark Self (USA), Mandy Seymonoff (Aus), Ana Lee Shelton (F), Tina & Kevin Shirley (NZ), Harry Shubart (USA), Roland Sieber (CH), Anthony Skevington (UK), Jan Michael Skorzewski, Andy Smith (UK), Anthony Smith (NZ), Luke Smith (Aus), Michael Smith (US), Patrick Spaull (Aus), Steve Spiegel (CH), Wolfgang Spude (D), Rick & Di Stephens (Aus), Yvonne Stinson (USA), Ian Stirling (UK), Penny Stone (UK), Ruedi Stumpf (CH), Sukhaimi Suja, K Sumner (UK), Mats Svensson (Sw), K J Swinburn (UK), Van Duyse Sylvain (B), Alison Tarrant (UK), Nina Teicholz (USA), Mark A Teitelbaum (USA), Dick Templeton (USA), Martin Thirkettle (UK), Duncan Thompson (Aus), Robert Thompson (USA), Angela Thwaites (UK), F Tischler (C), Alexandra Tomlin (Aus), Marlon Touysserkani (D), Mrs W Trelilles, Denise Tschudin (CH), Henk Tukker (Nl), Boyd Tyerman (C), Elaine Ulph (UK), E Mark Unger (USA), Gerrit de Vaal (Nl), P M & H J Varnes (Aus), Ed van der Veen (Nl), Jenny Visser (NZ), Margaret Wade (USA), Ainda & Hats Wallstrome (Sw), Ian D Walter (Aus), Hilary Waterman (UK), E Welch-Carre (USA), Conrad Wenham (Aus), Eileen S Westgate (USA), Mick White (UK), Kate Wilkinson (USA), Brian Williams, Terry Wilson (C), Dave Winter (Aus), Dieter Wittstock (D), Anne Wobb (USA), Mr S J Woodhull (UK), John & Stella Wray (UK), Heather Wright (UK), James Wright (UK), Mr Yip Yip (HK), John Yoder (USA), Wendy Zaman.

A – Austria, Aus – Australia, B – Belgium, C – Canada, CH – Switzerland, D – Germany, Dk – Denmark, F – France, Fin – Finland, HK – Hong Kong, Ire – Ireland, I – Italy, In – Indonesia, M – Malaysia, Nl – Netherlands, NZ – New Zealand, P – Philippines, SA – South Africa, Sin – Singapore, Sp – Spain, Sw – Sweden, Tw – Taiwan, UK – United Kingdom, USA – United States

Dear traveller

Prices go up, good places go bad, bad places go bankrupt...and every guidebook is inevitably outdated in places. Fortunately, many travellers write to us about their experiences, telling us when things have changed. If we reprint a book between editions, we try to include as much of this information as possible in a Stop Press section. Most of this information has not been verified by our own writers.

We really enjoy hearing from people out on the road, and apart from guaranteeing that others will benefit from your good and bad experiences, we're prepared to bribe you with the offer of a free book for sending us substantial useful information.

Thank you to everyone who has written and, to those who haven't, I hope you do find this book useful – and that you let us know when it isn't.

Tony Wheeler

It is now possible to make the Vietnam-Cambodia-Laos loop by flying from Bangkok to Phnom Penh, then continuing overland to Saigon and Hanoi from where there are flights to Laos. From Vientiane you can continue back to Bangkok by air or land. An alternative for part of the journey is to travel overland from Bangkok to Phnom Penh.

The following information in this Stop Press has been compiled with the help of letters sent to us by these travellers: Greg Alford & Lisa Croker (Aus), M M Adams, John Beales (UK), Mark Elliot, E Dickens (UK), Michael Elmore, Jules Flach (CH), B Graham (UK), Sarah Kydel (UK), L Lustig & L Norwitz (USA), Calum McInnes (AUS), Ingrid Maun (USA), Jens Peters (D), Steve Pottinger (UK), Jeffrey Rubin, Martin Schell, Eva Scherb (USA), Eric Sipco (USA), Johan Sjoberg (S) and Tony Wheeler (Aus).

MYANMAR (BURMA)

Burma had a change of leadership on 23 April 1992 when the ailing General Saw Maung resigned and was replaced by General Than Shwe. Although the new leader stopped the offensive against the Karen rebels and has taken a softer line against dissidents including the Nobel Prize winner Aung San Suu Kyi, changes have really only been cosmetic, rather than hard-line.

Money & Costs

Currently the official exchange rate is US$1 to 6.26 kyats.

Visas & Permits

Burma has re-introduced the 14-day 'foreign independent traveller' visas, which means you no longer have to take a fully catered, expensive package through a travel agent, so long as you arrange your initial accommodation in Yangon and outline your itinerary in advance, with your visa application. The visa should take several days to process.

CAMBODIA

Politically, Cambodia is more stable now due to the United Nations-sponsored peace talks which have resulted in the three warring factions signing a peace treaty and agreeing to free elections being held under the watchful eye of the United Nations and its peace-keeping force. Unfortunately, some groups of the Khmer Rouge are still fighting government troops in Kompong Thom Province.

Visas & Permits

A traveller, recently returned from Cambodia, reported that travel permits are no longer required to travel around the country. This, however, has not been substantiated.

Visas are much easier to obtain now, but Bangkok is still the most popular place to get them and Saigon is still the most popular entry point for shoestringers.

Another traveller has reported that for an overland trip from south-eastern Thailand, via Phnom Penh to Saigon, you will need a Cambodian visa, which can be obtained from the foreign ministry in Phnom Penh. The application can be sent by fax (873) 177 0102, marked to the attention of Sok Ann-fm. If any clarification is required, you can ring them on ☎ (855) 232 6133 or 232 6144. Submit this information to the fax machine along with a copy of your passport. Your visa will be ready to pick up at the border when you enter Cambodia, at which time they will ask you for a US$20 visa fee. They might also ask for five passport-size photos. You should allow 10 days for visa processing.

The next thing required is permission from the Thai Supreme Command to leave the country across the border at Aranyaprathet. The Supreme Command can be found in the Ministry of Foreign Affairs, near the Royal Palace in Bangkok. Once across the border, cars will be there and drivers are willing to take you to Phnom Penh for 1500B.

Cambodian visas can be obtained in Hanoi or Saigon. It takes about four days for a visa to be issued in Saigon for around US$20 – reports suggest that US$150 can get you the visa in 48 hours. In Bangkok, a visa can cost up to US$100 from a travel agent.

It is also possible to obtain a Cambodian visa on arrival at the airport in Phnom Penh for US$20.

Getting Around

Air travel to Cambodia is becoming easier as more airlines commence operations to Phnom Penh. Bangkok Airways, best known for their Bangkok to Ko Samui flights, was the first to start Bangkok to Phnom Penh services – they have now been joined by other airlines including Thai International, who now have a daily flight costing 6990B.

Money & Costs

The current official exchange rate is US$1 to 2000 riels. If you have cash, moneychangers will give you approximately 15% more than the official rate. It is also possible to change Vietnamese dong and even Thai baht.

Banque du Commerce Extérieur du Cambodge will now not only cash US dollar travellers' cheques, but other hard currency travellers' cheques for a 1% commission.

Visa and MasterCard are accepted as long as they are not issued at any US bank. US dollars can be purchased. There is no commission except US$30 for the phone call to Bangkok for approval, no matter how much or how little money you are asking for.

Phnom Penh

New hotels are popping up rapidly in the capital including the five-star *Hotel Cambodiana*. Backpackers usually head for the *Hotel Capital* on 182 St, right across from the O Russei bus station. Rooms here with one bed (single or double) cost US$8; with two beds they are US$12. If it's full, they can usually suggest economical alternatives. A more expensive option is the *Hotel Renakse* (☎ 2-2457) on Lenin Blvd, across from the old Silver Pagoda compound of the Royal Palace. This fine old building has 23 air-conditioned doubles at US$30 to US$50, and more are planned.

New restaurants are also popping up rapidly. The *Restaurant Thmor Dar* is on 128 St, just beyond the corner of 107 St. It's large, bright, new and serves delicious food, although it's wise to check the prices before ordering more exotic dishes. A much smaller establishment with the same name is just on the other side of 107 St.

Both of the lakeside restaurants are named Boeng Kak. The northernmost one is *Restaurant Raksmey Boeng Kak* and turns out delicious food, particularly the traditional duck soup. Phnom Penh's real surprise is the slick *No Problem Cafe*, number-one gathering spot for the expat community, with good food and cold drinks.

Angkor Wat

Angkor Wat has opened up considerably. A number of the more remote temples which were formerly closed to visitors have now been opened, although an armed escort is still provided at some sites. You no longer have to be accompanied by a guide and you can also rent bicycles or motorcycles to conduct your own exploration of the far-flung sites.

In Siem Reap, the small town just south of Angkor Wat, the *Grand Hotel d'Angkor* is being refurbished which means that the room prices will rise, probably dramatically. The nearby *Villa Apsara* has reopened with rooms at US$32 to US$40 and the *Hotel de la Paix* is also being rebuilt. Other hotels will soon follow, but the visitor flow already exceeds capacity and local residents have been renting out rooms in their homes.

The restaurant scene at Siem Reap is also changing quickly and at the *Samapheap Restaurant*, beside the river and just south of Route 6, you can find superb Cambodian food for just US$2 to US$3 per person. In the town centre the *Restaurant Monorom* is another new addition with good Chinese food at similar prices. Children scuttle around the main temple sites selling cold soft drinks and there's a refreshment stand opposite the main entrance to Angkor Wat.

There are rumours that direct flights will soon start from Thailand to Siem Reap and that the road from Thailand will reopen. Meanwhile you still have to fly there from Phnom Penh, but flights now operate at least twice daily.

Preah Vihear

The ancient Khmer site of Preah Vihear in central Cambodia has also reopened to visitors, although it's reached from Thailand rather than through Cambodia. The site is just across the border into Cambodia, about three hours by bus from the Thai city of Ubon Ratchathani. The Thais are actually promoting this Cambodian ruin as a means of attracting visitors to their neglected north-east region. At the border you have to pay 100B to temporarily exit Thailand and another 100B for a temporary visit to Cambodia, but no visas are required. The site has been attracting 500 or more visitors a day since it opened.

INDONESIA

A Garuda ticket purchased overseas usually has the domestic airport departure tax included in it. Sometimes you might be asked to pay the departure tax again, but there is no reason why you should. If they insist that you pay the tax again, you should politely point out that you have paid it, or ask to see the airport manager.

Money & Costs

The current official exchange rate is US$1 to 2068 rp.

Getting There & Away

Shipping a car from Darwin, Australia, to Kupang, Timor, can be arranged through Perkins Shipping (☎ (089) 81 4688), Frances Bay Drive, Darwin, Northern Territory. Their postal address is GPO Box 1019, Darwin, NT 5794. Perkins has one medium-sized ship, the *Coringyle Bay*, which plies a Darwin-Kupang-Singapore-Darwin route. The cost of shipping a car to Kupang is about A$850. To ship the car to Singapore would cost about A$1700.

Permission from both the Australian Customs and the Indonesian authorities is necessary to take a car into Indonesia. Australian Customs is no problem, providing the car and its papers are in order. The ease of approval from the Indonesians varies, so it is best to work through one of their consulates, such as in Darwin.

At the very least, the car owner will need a Carnet de Passage for the car. This can be acquired through various automobile associations and costs about A$60.

Dangers & Annoyances

Motorists beware! The police are enforcing road rules with a vengeance in an effort to decrease the annual road death toll of 10,000.

In a country where annual per capita income is only US$600, running a red light could cost up to US$1000; riding a motorcycle without a helmet US$500; driving with an expired licence up to US$3000, or six months in jail. Although many cars in Indonesia lack safety belts, failing to wear one could set the driver back as much as US$1500. The new fines went into effect September 1992.

Beware of Krishen at *Krishen's Yoghurt House* in Medan, Sumatra. We have received many letters from travellers complaining about his dishonesty – it would appear that Krishen is an unscrupulous character, not to be trusted under any circumstances.

LAOS

The official rate of exchange for US$1 is K720.

Thai baht, US dollars and kip are all acceptable and interchangeable in Vientiane – US dollars for large transactions, Thai baht for medium and kip for small transactions.

Banks will take US travellers' cheques as well as US and Thai currency but none will let you cash money with a Visa card. The best rate in Vientiane is obtained from the gold merchants at the morning market, which, despite its name, is open until 5 pm. This market also has the best shopping.

MALAYSIA

Happy Holidays Travel Bureau, at 442 Lebuh Chulia in Penang, sell the Penang to Medan high-speed ferry tickets for M$73 plus M$6 which includes the bus into Medan. This is cheaper than the M$80 plus M$6 charged in most places which does not necessarily include the bus to Medan.

The official exchange rate for US$1 is M$2.62.

PHILIPPINES

Fidel Ramos narrowly won the presidential elections in June 1992. The ex-general was President Corazon Aquino's selected candidate, as she had chosen not to run for a second term. The new cabinet is now dominated by the country's business elite,

unlike Aquino's cabinet, which had members from a wide range of the political spectrum including left wing lawyers and right wing generals.

Money & Costs

The current official exchange rate is US$1 to P25.

Getting Around

Aerolift has cancelled flights from Manila to Cebu, Dipolog, Iligan, Lubang, Ormoc, Surigao and Tagbilaran.

Philippine Airlines (PAL) has cancelled flights from Cebu to Bislig and Iligan, and flights between Manila and San Fernando La Union are irregular. New connections are: Cebu to Camiguin, Manila to Busuanga, Manila to Dipolog and General Santos City to Iloilo.

North Luzon

In Baguio, the Philippine Airlines office has moved, perhaps only temporarily, to Harrison Rd, behind the Burnham Hotel.

Negros

The new bus terminal at Dumaguete is now about 300 metres south of town.

Panay

On Boracay Island there is a Philippine Airlines office at the South Sea Beach House in Angol. The post office has moved next to the Starfire Restaurant in Angol.

Palawan

Since Philippine Airlines started flying twice a week between Manila and Busuanga, this northern Palawan island of Busuanga has been attracting more and more tourists, particularly divers.

THAILAND

Second-hand bookshops in Bangkok can be a rip off. Used paperbacks are often being sold for the same price as the recommended retail price, and yet bookshops pay very low prices when buying books.

Khao San Rd has several health clinics

that offer inoculations at very high prices. A better and cheaper place is the Christian Hospital.

Money & Costs

The current official exchange rate is US$1 to 25B.

Dangers & Annoyances

One of the more recent ruses for relieving travellers of their money takes place at Bangkok airport. When leaving customs, a young girl greets tourists and escorts them to the 'information and taxi desk'. There, a man who speaks very good English explains that a taxi voucher is required to go to any hotel in Bangkok. He holds up a voucher with his finger over the fare and says this is the only authorised taxi at the airport. The price is 450B. After he is paid, the man folds the voucher and escorts you to a porter who shows you to the taxi. Only when in the taxi does one realise that the correct fare is 350B.

It is still apparently easy to find an unofficial taxi costing 150B.

VIETNAM

Beware of pickpockets in Saigon, especially around the market and waterfront areas. They're not very determined, but if you're careless you will lose things.

Visas & Permits

It is now quite easy, although still fairly expensive, to get a visa for independent travel in Vietnam. In Melbourne, Australia, Vietnam Ventures (☎ (03) 428 0385), 92 Victoria St, Richmond, Victoria, 3121 or Direct Flights in Sydney (☎ (02) 313 6897) will arrange visas for independent travellers to Vietnam, Laos and Cambodia. The Vietnamese visa takes two weeks to obtain, costs A$100 and two forms and photos are required. See a travel agent in your country and they may be able to organise a visa for you. If this option is not available, then try Bangkok as it is a favourite place for obtaining visas and many travel agencies around Khao San Rd will issue them in approximately a week at a cost of about

2000B. Your visa states your arrival and departure points (usually Saigon's Tan Son Nhut airport and Hanoi's Noi Bai airport) so make sure you stipulate where you will arrive and where you will depart. If you get it wrong you can change it fairly readily at the Immigration Office. It costs US$1 to rewrite a departure point from Saigon to Hanoi. Sometimes the visa is issued on a separate form so the issuing office does not need to keep your passport. You can usually get the length of time you ask for, and it can be extended quite easily. It is better to arrive in Saigon and depart from Hanoi, as Saigon is an easier city to enter.

A permit is essential for visiting Tay Ninh province on the Cambodian border, which includes the Cao Dai temple and the Cu Chi tunnels. Day tours run by agents such as *Kim's Cafe* and *Sinh Cafe* in Saigon, frequently fail to mention this small technicality and it means that you could be stopped and fined by the police. In one recent incident, a Sinh Cafe minibus tour was pulled over by the police, which led to the driver and guide taking off into the bush, leaving the tourists to deal with the police. They were eventually allowed to proceed after each tourist had paid a US$5 fine.

A one-month visa to Vietnam purchased in Bangkok costs US$75 and takes four days to process. The same visa in Phnom Penh costs US$20. In Hong Kong, however, the two week visa costs HK$450, takes three to four days to process and is available from some travel agents.

It is advisable to have a few photocopies of your passport, visa and travel permits, as some travellers have reported problems with getting their original copies back from hotels and the police – bribes were asked for in some instances.

Registration is no longer necessary.
Travel permits are still required, and are as easily obtainable in Saigon as in Hanoi. It takes four or five days to obtain a permit officially. The quickest way to get one is to use the black market. One agent to contact in Saigon is Ann Tourist (☎ 23866). Places like

Sinh Cafe can arrange a permit in 24 hours. It's advisable, at this stage, to nominate as many places that you think you may wish to visit. Price varies depending on who you go to – US$15 to US$25. You can't always get places you want on the permit. Many travellers who didn't have a ticket to fly out of Hanoi were only given permits for as far north as Hue, ie, no places in the north were permitted.

One traveller at Hanoi airport was forced to pay US$5 to retain his Vietnamese visa which contained written proof that he'd been to Hanoi. Other independent travellers have reported problems upon arrival at Hanoi airport.

Visits to the coastal provinces and cities are fairly simple to arrange in a few days, with the exception of Cam Ranh Bay which is closed to foreigners. It remains difficult for US citizens to obtain a travel permit in Saigon for Dalat in Lam Dong Province. The Hanoi police, however, are still issuing travel permits to Dalat. The central highlands and interior provinces (including parts of the DMZ) remain out of bounds, but some of the provinces bordering China, like Lao Cai or Lang Son, are open to travellers.

It is also possible to enter China from Vietnam, or exit China to Vietnam.

Money & Costs

The current official exchange rate is US$1 to 10,500d.

It has become much easier to change travellers' cheques and cash in the big cities and currently, the exchange rate is better in the banks than on the street. Any exchange requires an inordinate number of Vietnamese banknotes.

Special US dollar denominated tourist prices apply at most hotels and for air and train travel. Thus, a Vietnamese may pay US$3 (in dong) for a hotel room and the same room could cost a foreigner US$10. A local can fly Saigon to Danang for US$28, but it will cost a foreigner US$81. Apart from these exceptions you can pay for most things at local dong prices, so food and local transport are generally very cheap. You will be lucky

if you find any hotel where you can pay the local dong price – if you do, you're getting excellent value!

It is apparently extremely easy for foreigners to open dollar accounts at the Vietcombank on 29 Ben Chuong Duong, District 1. The minimum deposit is US$200. They even pay interest at fair rates. Many banks throughout the world can wire money to Vietcombank. It's cheaper and easier to do business with them than using a Bangkok bank.

Getting There & Away

There are now flights to Hanoi from Hong Kong.

Some people have problems leaving Hanoi as seats on all flights are usually booked up. It is advisable to book your seat as soon as possible and well in advance of your visa expiring. Waits of up to nine days are not uncommon, but if you are on a waiting list you can get lucky and fly out a bit earlier.

The taxi fare between Hanoi airport and the city is US$30, but between Saigon airport and the city it's somewhat less – US$7 to US$10.

If flying out of Hanoi, it's easy to reserve seats on a bus through Vietnam Airlines International. Their office is on Quang Trung Street and there about six or seven departures a day timed to connect with flights. Tickets cost US$2 to US$3.

In mid-1992 a couple of independent travellers reported problems upon arrival at Hanoi airport. Appparently, if you didn't have a 'sponsor' waiting to pick you up, you would be detained before going through Customs, and wouldn't be able to leave the airport until agreeing to pay US$40 to a travel company that then became your sponsor. The US$40 got you a ride into Hanoi by van, drop-off at a hotel, and all the necessary paper work to stay in Hanoi. The company would then try to hit you for more money to get you a travel permit, usually also demanding that you pay for at least one guided tour outside of Hanoi with them – all while holding your passport for the initial permits. We have not heard of any other reports since.

Getting Around

Most travellers use buses and trains to get around, while others who can afford it hire a car. Four Canadians paid US$75 each for a car from Saigon to Hue! Others took a car from Danang to Hue – 105 km for US$20 which they split between four. It would appear that for getting to easily accessible places, hire-car rates are competitive and therefore good value. For out of the way places, with no other way of getting there, hire car drivers will ask outrageous prices.

Tony & Maureen Wheeler rented a fine old Citroen DS for a week to travel to Saigon, Dalat, Nha Trang, Danang, Hue, Danang, after which the driver went back to Saigon whilst they flew on to Hanoi. They used Easiway Travel, 34 Pham Ngoc Thach St, Ho Chi Minh City.

Dangers & Annoyances

Travellers should beware of the possibility of being hit or having stones thrown at them. Public violence is not uncommon in Vietnam and small foreigners, especially women, often get picked upon.

Also, it is absolutely essential to leave metal shutters on the windows of trains pulled down. Firstly, this will prevent theft at stations and by other passengers; secondly, it will preclude being hit by rocks thrown by youths and young boys.

Saigon

In Saigon/Ho Chi Minh City, the favourite hotel for travellers is the *Hoang Tu Hotel* at 187 Pham Ngu Lao St, near the market and central Saigon. The *Prince Hotel* next door, is similar. You can pay in dong, and rooms are around US$6 to US$12. According to a number of reader' letters, the once excellent *Maxim's Restaurant* is a big disappointment and way overpriced. Ballroom dancing is a big deal throughout Vietnam – even in Hanoi. The Friday, Saturday and Sunday-night cruise, when thousands of people on

bicycles and motorcycles circulate around the centre of Saigon, is another not-to-be-missed sight.

Kim, of *Kim's Cafe* in Saigon (a long time travellers' hangout) is gaining an unpopular name for herself due to her dishonesty. One example being that she apparently promised four people a minibus for US$40, to be shared with others. On the nominated day, the minibus, didn't appear, but she promised it would be ready the next day. The next day, again no minibus – instead she offered them a car for US$75 each! Similarly, a reader's letter talks of being abandoned halfway through a tour by one of Kim's drivers.

Hue

In Hue, prices for the various tombs, museums and Imperial Palace have tripled. As of 3 February 1993, entry to the Imperial Palace is US$3.50 while the tombs charge US$3. There is also a US$12 charge for a video camera at the Imperial City (US$8 at the tombs) and interior photos at the tombs and palace are US$2. Not surprisingly, this exorbitant increase has severely cut down the number of tombs travellers are likely to visit; the best sights are probably the Imperial Palace and the Tu Duc tomb.

Travellers' Tips & Comments

The authorities charged with looking after the beautiful beaches of Danang are quickly becoming more accustomed to the needs of tourists. China beach has uniformed guards and ticket collectors for the parasols and deck chairs which are neatly laid out on the water's edge.

Lan – UK

Many tour guides, hustlers and commission men hang out in the downstairs area of the Vien Dong Hotel, Ho Chi Minh City and tell everybody who has just arrived that it's impossible and illegal to travel independently, and that you need to take a tour. Strictly speaking you must have a guide, but in reality this is ignored. As long as you have a travel permit you can go freely on your own in the areas on your permit.

Steve Hodgkiss – The Netherlands

Lonely Planet Guidebooks

Lonely Planet guidebooks cover every accessible part of Asia as well as Australia, the Pacific, South America, Africa, the Middle East, Europe and parts of North America. There are five series: *travel survival kits*, covering a country for a range of budgets; *shoestring guides* with compact information for low-budget travel in a major region; *walking guides*; *city guides* and *phrasebooks*.

Australia & the Pacific
Australia
Bushwalking in Australia
Islands of Australia's Great Barrier Reef
Fiji
Melbourne city guide
Micronesia
New Caledonia
New Zealand
Tramping in New Zealand
Papua New Guinea
Papua New Guinea phrasebook
Rarotonga & the Cook Islands
Samoa
Solomon Islands
Sydney city guide
Tahiti & French Polynesia
Tonga
Vanuatu

South-East Asia
Bali & Lombok
Bangkok city guide
Myanmar (Burma)
Burmese phrasebook
Cambodia
Indonesia
Indonesia phrasebook
Malaysia, Singapore & Brunei
Philippines
Pilipino phrasebook
Singapore city guide
South-East Asia on a shoestring
Thailand
Thai phrasebook
Vietnam, Laos & Cambodia
Vietnamese phrasebook

North-East Asia
China
Mandarin Chinese phrasebook
Hong Kong, Macau & Canton
Japan
Japanese phrasebook
Korea
Korean phrasebook
Mongolia
North-East Asia on a shoestring
Taiwan
Tibet
Tibet phrasebook
Tokyo city guide

West Asia
Trekking in Turkey
Turkey
Turkish phrasebook
West Asia on a shoestring

Middle East
Arab Gulf States
Egypt & the Sudan
Egyptian Arabic phrasebook
Iran
Israel
Jordan & Syria
Yemen

Indian Ocean
Madagascar & Comoros
Maldives & Islands of the East Indian Ocean
Mauritius, Réunion & Seychelles

Mail Order

Lonely Planet guidebooks are distributed worldwide. They are also available by mail order from Lonely Planet, so if you have difficulty finding a title please write to us. US and Canadian residents should write to Embarcadero West, 155 Filbert St, Suite 251, Oakland CA 94607, USA; European residents should write to Devonshire House, 12 Barley Mow Passage, Chiswick, London W4 4PH; and residents of other countries to PO Box 617, Hawthorn, Victoria 3122, Australia.

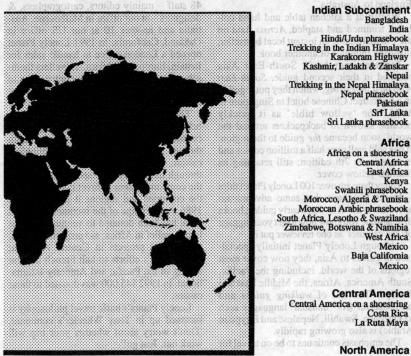

Indian Subcontinent
Bangladesh
India
Hindi/Urdu phrasebook
Trekking in the Indian Himalaya
Karakoram Highway
Kashmir, Ladakh & Zanskar
Nepal
Trekking in the Nepal Himalaya
Nepal phrasebook
Pakistan
Srī Lanka
Sri Lanka phrasebook

Africa
Africa on a shoestring
Central Africa
East Africa
Kenya
Swahili phrasebook
Morocco, Algeria & Tunisia
Moroccan Arabic phrasebook
South Africa, Lesotho & Swaziland
Zimbabwe, Botswana & Namibia
West Africa
Mexico
Baja California
Mexico

Central America
Central America on a shoestring
Costa Rica
La Ruta Maya

North America
Alaska
Canada
Hawaii

South America
Argentina, Uruguay & Paraguay
Bolivia
Brazil
Brazilian phrasebook
Chile & Easter Island
Colombia
Ecuador & the Galápagos Islands
Latin American Spanish phrasebook
Peru
Quechua phrasebook
South America on a shoestring
Trekking in the Patagonian Andes

Europe
Eastern Europe on a shoestring
Eastern Europe phrasebook
Finland
Iceland, Greenland & the Faroe Islands
Mediterranean Europe on a shoestring
Mediterranean Europe phrasebook
Poland
Scandinavian & Baltic Europe on a shoestring
Scandinavian Europe phrasebook
Trekking in Spain
Trekking in Greece
USSR
Russian phrasebook
Western Europe on a shoestring
Western Europe phrasebook

The Lonely Planet Story

Lonely Planet published its first book in 1973 in response to the numerous 'How did you do it?' questions Maureen and Tony Wheeler were asked after driving, bussing, hitching, sailing and railing their way from England to Australia.

Written at a kitchen table and hand collated, trimmed and stapled, *Across Asia on the Cheap* became an instant local bestseller, inspiring thoughts of another book.

Eighteen months in South-East Asia resulted in their second guide, *South-East Asia on a shoestring*, which they put together in a backstreet Chinese hotel in Singapore in 1975. The 'yellow bible' as it quickly became known to backpackers around the world, soon became *the* guide to the region. It has sold well over half a million copies and is now in its 7th edition, still retaining its familiar yellow cover.

Today there are over 100 Lonely Planet titles – books that have that same adventurous approach to travel as those early guides; books that 'assume you know how to get your luggage off the carousel' as one reviewer put it.

Although Lonely Planet initially specialised in guides to Asia, they now cover most regions of the world, including the Pacific, South America, Africa, the Middle East and Europe. The list of *walking guides* and *phrasebooks* (for 'unusual' languages such as Quechua, Swahili, Nepalese and Egyptian Arabic) is also growing rapidly.

The emphasis continues to be on travel for independent travellers. Tony and Maureen still travel for several months of each year and play an active part in the writing, updating and quality control of Lonely Planet's guides.

They have been joined by over 50 authors, 48 staff – mainly editors, cartographers, & designers – at our office in Melbourne, Australia and another 10 at our US office in Oakland, California. In 1991 Lonely Planet opened a London office to handle sales for Britain, Europe and Africa. Travellers themselves also make a valuable contribution to the guides through the feedback we receive in thousands of letters each year.

The people at Lonely Planet strongly believe that travellers can make a positive contribution to the countries they visit, both through their appreciation of the countries' culture, wildlife and natural features, and through the money they spend. In addition, the company makes a direct contribution to the countries and regions it covers. Since 1986 a percentage of the income from each book has been donated to ventures such as famine relief in Africa; aid projects in India; agricultural projects in Central America; Greenpeace's efforts to halt French nuclear testing in the Pacific and Amnesty International. In 1992 $45,000 was donated to these causes.

Lonely Planet's basic travel philosophy is summed up in Tony Wheeler's comment, 'Don't worry about whether your trip will work out. Just go!'